# On the Rails
# around Europe

## THOMAS COOK

On 5 July 1841 Thomas Cook, a 32-year-old printer from Market Harborough, in Leicestershire, England, led a party of some 500 temperance enthusiasts on a railway outing from Leicester to Loughborough which he had arranged down to the last detail. This proved to be the birth of the modern tourist industry. In the course of expanding his business, Thomas Cook and his son, John, invented many of the features of organised travel which we now take for granted. Over the next 150 years the name Thomas Cook became synonymous with world travel.

Today the Thomas Cook Group employs over 13,000 people across the globe and its Worldwide Network provides services to customers at more than 3000 locations in over 100 countries. Its activities include travel retailing, tour operating and financial services – Thomas Cook is a world leader in traveller's cheques and foreign money services.

Thomas Cook believed in the value of the printed word as an accompaniment to travel. His publication *The Excursionist* was the equivalent of both a holiday brochure and a travel magazine. Today Thomas Cook Publishing continues to issue one of the world's oldest travel books, the *Thomas Cook European Timetable,* which has been in existence since 1873. Updated every month, it remains the only definitive compendium of European railway schedules.

The *Thomas Cook Touring Handbook* series, to which this volume belongs, is a range of comprehensive guides for travellers touring regions of the world by train, car and ship. Other titles include:

Touring by train
*On the Rails around France and Benelux* (Published 1995)
*On the Rails around the Alps* (Published 1996)
*On the Rails around Eastern Europe* (Published 1996)
*On the Rails around Britain and Ireland* (Second Edition Published 1998)
Touring by car
*On the Road around California* (Second Edition Published 1996)
*On the Road around Florida* (Second Edition Published 1997)
*On the Road around Normandy, Brittany and the Loire Valley* (Published 1996)
*On the Road around the Capital Region* (Published 1997)
*On the Road around the South of France* (Published 1997)
*On the Road around the Pacific Northwest* (Published 1997)
Touring by car, train and bus
*Touring Australia* (Published 1997)
*Touring Southern Africa* (Published 1997)
Touring by ship
*Greek Island Hopping* (Published annually in February)

For more details of these and other Thomas Cook publications, write to Passport Books, at the address on the back of the title page.

# ON THE RAILS AROUND

# Europe

## A Comprehensive Guide to Travel by Train

### Third Edition

Edited by Melissa Shales

**PASSPORT BOOKS**
*NTC/Contemporary Publishing Company*

A THOMAS COOK TOURING HANDBOOK

Published by Passport Books, a division of NTC/Contemporary Publishing Company 4255 West Touhy Avenue, Lincolnwood (Chicago), Illinois 60646-1975 USA.

Text:
© 1998 The Thomas Cook Group Ltd
Maps and diagrams:
© 1998 The Thomas Cook Group Ltd
London Underground map © London Regional Transport

ISBN 0-8442-4958-0
Library of Congress Catalog Card Number: 97-69672
Published by Passport Books in conjunction with The Thomas Cook Group Ltd.

Managing Editor: Stephen York
Commissioning Editor: Deborah Parker
Map Editor: Bernard Horton
Editorial Assistant: Leyla Davies

Text typeset in Bembo and Gill Sans using Quark XPress
Maps and diagrams created using GSP Designworks and Macromedia Freehand
London city centre map by ESR Ltd
Text imagesetting by Riverhead Typesetters Ltd, Grimsby
Printed in Great Britain by Fisherprint, Peterborough

This edition written and researched by
**Tim Burford**
**Ethel Davies**
**Sevil Delin**
**Jane Foster**
**Kirsty Gaston**
**Will Hardie**
**Matthew Hayes**
**Zane Katsikis**
**Dr Annie Kay**
**Mark Law**
**Susie Lunt**
**Tim Nollen**
**Marieke van Peer**
**Gillian Thomas and John Harrison**
**Ian Wisniewski**
**Wendy Wood**
**Barry Worthington**

Series and Book Editor:
**Melissa Shales**

**Photographs** The following are thanked for supplying the photographs:
*Between pp. 32 and 33:* all Ethel Davies except (i) funicular railway, Spectrum. *Between pp. 160 and 161:* all Chris Fairclough Colour Library except (i) Athens, Image Select International; Barcelona, Trip/M Feeney; (ii) Berlin and Budapest, Spectrum; (iii) Copenhagen and Hamburg, Ethel Davies; (iv) Rothenburg, Spectrum. *Between pp. 256 and 257:* all Chris Fairclough Colour Library except (i) Helsinki, Trip/M Jenkin; (ii) Bucharest, Tim Nollen; (iii) Córdoba and Cuenca, Spectrum; Cáceres, Trip/J Randall; (iv) Marseille, Trip/S Grant; Milan, Trip/M Maclaren; Biarritz, Spectrum. *Between pp. 384 and 385:* (i) Ethel Davies; (ii) Prague, Trip/T Why; Strasbourg, Spectrum; Paris, Chris Fairclough Colour Library; (iii) Calvi, Zane Katsikis; Rome, Chris Fairclough Colour Library. *Between pp. 480 and 481:* all Chris Fairclough Colour Library except (ii) Stockholm, Ethel Davies; Venice, Spectrum; (iii) Warsaw, Trip/M Jenkin; Split, Trip/M Wilson; (iv) Spectrum.

## ABOUT THE AUTHORS

**Tim Burford** is a travel writer who specialises in Eastern Europe. He has contributed to various guides covering Romania, Poland and Ukraine.

**Ethel Davies** is a freelance photographer and journalist who make her living travelling round the globe. Rail travel remains one of her favourite modes of getting around.

**Sevil Delin** read English at Oxford. She has lived in the US, Turkey, Egypt, Hong Kong and England and has visited 24 countries (6 on this assignment). Her current home is Istanbul.

**Jane Foster** entered journalism as a research assistant for the *Guardian* in Rome. She now teaches English in Split, Croatia, and continues freelance work for *Scotland on Sunday*.

**Kirsty Gaston** contributed to the second edition of this book. She studied Zoology at Oxford and has worked on the science journal *Nature*. She has travelled extensively in Brazil, India and Europe.

**Will Hardie** studied at Oxford, where he was editor of *Oxford Student*. He has travelled extensively in India, Nepal, France and Bolivia and is currently studying journalism in the United States.

**Matthew Hayes** lives in Paris. He has spent a year riding buses in India, and a year out in Champagne. He is the author of a guide to Liverpool.

**Zane Katsikis** acts as International Editor of *International Railway Traveler* so that he can assuage his need to ride the rails of Europe. He is the author of *Greece by Rail* (Bradt Publications).

**Dr Annie Kay** is a freelance travel writer and journalist. Winner of the Bulgarian Rose award for journalists, she organises special interest tours for the British–Bulgarian Friendship Society.

**Mark Law** works as a fitness instructor and freelance writer. He spent 3 years in the Netherlands and has Inter-Railed across every European country and backpacked in the USA and Mexico.

**Susie Lunt** is a freelance writer who lives in Prague. She has written a number of books and articles on Central Europe and is a Fellow of the Royal Geographical Society.

**Tim Nollen** combines two of his passions in travel writing. He lived for several years in Prague, authoring two guides to the Czech Republic and contributing to publications on Europe and Asia.

**Gillian Thomas** and **John Harrison**, who are married, both started their careers in the BBC. Now freelance travel writers, they much prefer rail to any other form of transport.

**Marieke van Peer** lived in New Zealand, Australia, Singapore and London, before she returned to her native Netherlands. She works in Foreign Exchange at Thomas Cook, Amsterdam.

**Ian Wisniewski** is a food, drink and travel writer/broadcaster, specialising in food trends and regional cuisine, spirits (particularly vodka) and Poland, where he is a frequent visitor.

**Wendy Wood** studied at Oxford and has travelled extensively in Europe, most recently exploring France, Spain, Austria and Italy. She revised the *Thomas Cook European Travel Phrasebook*.

**Barry Worthington**, a rail enthusiast, is studying for a doctorate in Baltic Studies at the University of Bradford. He researches tourism in the Baltics and is a regular visitor to that area.

## ACKNOWLEDGEMENTS

The authors and Thomas Cook Publishing would like to thank the following people for their help during the production of this book:

Ognian Avgarski, Balkania Travel, London; Ron Barrett, BritRail; Claude Bérnard, Hotel Blue Marine, Aix-en-Provence; Lynne Bobak, DER Travel Services; Sylvie Bonnafond, Lyon Tourist Office; Mikkel Clausen, Use-It, Copenhagen; Croatian NTB, London; Alison Cubie, Campus Travel; Cece Drummond, Rail Europe Inc; České dráhy; Dresden TO; John Etre, B&D France; Jela Faltányova; Slovak Tourist Board; Saro Maunula, Finnish TB; Forum Hotels; Beatrice Freiburg, German Rail, London; Nicolas Geoffroy, Provence International; Heather Goldsworthy, Holland Rail; Csaba Gyöpös; Roger Harrison, Eurostar; Nic Jagestad, Scandic Hotels; Judit Kertész, Hungarian NTO; Korčula TO; Matti Kuusela, Finnish Railways, Helsinki; Leading Hotels of the World; Britt Lightbody, Danish TB; LOT Polish Airlines; Sue Macrete-Butcher, Best Western Hotels; Robert Mackenzie, Scandinavian Seaways; Daniel Mahr, Belgian National Railways; Millbank PR; Peter Mills, Christine Lagardère and Christophe Gau, Rail Europe; Theodoros Nikoloudis, Greek NT Organization, Athens; Camilla Nordheim-Larsen, Oslo City TO/Norway TB; Russell Palmer, Switzerland Tourism, London; Agnes Padányi, Tourinform, Budapest; Charles Page and Hitesh Mehta, Rail Europe; Olenka Pierozynska, Wasteels; Polish NTO; Maria Pottle; Elsa Redfern, ICEP; Marie-France Reymond, Nice PR; Dominic Shales; Alexander Smith, Italian State TB, London; Marie-Thérése Smith, French Govt TO, London; Marion Telsnig, Austrian NTO; Leena Virtala-Pulkkinen, Helsinki City TO; Marie Vitáková, Tourism Dept, Prague; Eva Vymětalová; Jane Wilde, Swedish Tourist Board. Special thanks to the compilers of the *European Timetable* for their expertise, particularly Peter Hedderly (who updated all the rail information) and David Gunning.

5

# CONTENTS

## ROUTES AND CITIES

*In alphabetical order. Routes are listed in both directions – the reverse route is shown in italics.*
*See also the Route Map, p. 8, for a diagrammatic presentation of all the routes in the book.*
*To look up towns and other places not listed here, see the Index, p. 563.*

7

## REFERENCE SECTION

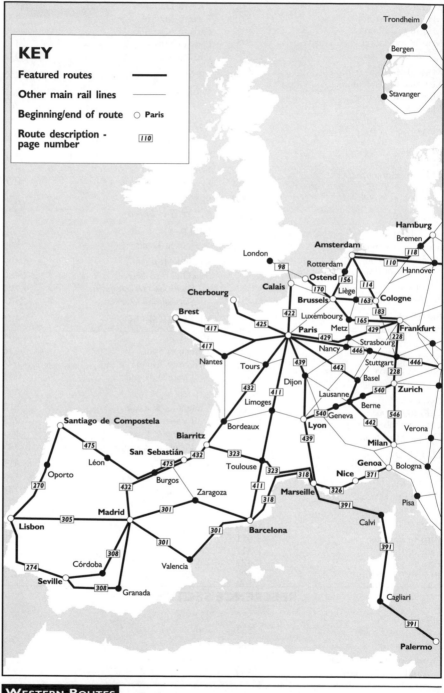

**KEY**

Featured routes

Other main rail lines

Beginning/end of route ○ Paris

Route description - page number 〔110〕

8

Trondheim
Bergen
Stavanger

Hamburg
Bremen
Amsterdam 〔118〕
London 〔98〕 Rotterdam 〔110〕 Hannover
Ostend 〔156〕 〔114〕
Cherbourg Calais 〔170〕 Liège
Brussels 〔163〕 Cologne
Brest 〔422〕 Luxembourg 〔183〕
〔417〕 〔425〕 〔165〕 〔429〕 Frankfurt
Paris Metz 〔228〕
〔417〕 〔429〕 Strasbourg 〔446〕
Nantes Nancy 〔446〕
Tours 〔439〕 〔442〕 Stuttgart 〔446〕
〔432〕 Dijon Basel 〔228〕
〔411〕 Lausanne 〔540〕 Zurich
Limoges Berne
Santiago de Compostela 〔540〕 Geneva 〔442〕 〔546〕
Bordeaux Lyon Verona
〔475〕 Biarritz Milan
Léon San Sebastián 〔439〕
Oporto 〔475〕 〔432〕 〔323〕 Toulouse Genoa Bologna
〔270〕 〔432〕 Burgos 〔323〕 Nice 〔371〕
Zaragoza 〔411〕 〔318〕 Pisa
Madrid 〔301〕 Marseille
Lisbon 〔305〕 〔318〕
〔301〕 Barcelona 〔391〕 Calvi
Córdoba 〔308〕 〔301〕
〔274〕 〔301〕 Valencia 〔391〕
Seville 〔308〕 Granada
Cagliari
〔391〕
Palermo

# INTRODUCTION

Trains are the safest, most efficient and eco-friendly system of mass transportation ever devised. They can also sometimes deliver you into the heart of the city faster than a plane. They are more comfortable than buses, as you can wander the corridors, get a choice of menu and, on overnight journeys, stretch out on a full-length bed between crisp white sheets. They don't get stuck in traffic jams. And there is the freedom of knowing that you can go almost anywhere at any time, provided you can master the timetable – which isn't such a difficult art as it might seem at first. Perhaps most importantly however, trains are also fun. There is nothing like the buzz you get from a bustling international train station with a departure board clicking away the destinations, or the fizz of excitement as the world passes by outside to the clackety-hum of the wheels. People travel by plane just to get there; many choose to travel by rail for the sheer exuberance of the journey.

In the 1960s, the first generation of bright, penniless backpackers became hooked on the Inter-Rail Pass. It was a triumphant addiction, allowing thousands to experience the joys of travel and broaden their horizons to include foreign cultures. And now Inter-Railing is no longer just the province of youngsters, as the Inter-Rail over 26 pass offers, for the very first time, the same Europe-wide coverage and value as the under 26 pass. Since the introduction of the Inter-Rail pass, there has been a proliferation of other passes such as Eurail and the Freedom Passes, designed to cater for locals and non-Europeans of all ages, for those who wish to meander across the entire continent or concentrate on one country.

*On the Rails around Europe* is designed to assist all those travelling by train in Europe. Sadly, it is impossible to cover every corner of the continent in exhaustive detail, so we have chosen routes that cover the most interesting

sights accessible by rail within the most popular countries. We simply do not have space to include Morocco, and of the troubled former Yugoslavia we cover only Slovenia and Croatia. London (p. 277) and cross-Channel connections (p. 98) are covered but other areas of Great Britain and Ireland are omitted because they are dealt with in detail in our companion book *On the Rails around Britain and Ireland* (available from all the sources listed on p. 23).

For this new edition, we have added an additional 40 pages, altered some of the journeys to reflect more practical routing, added more key cities (St Petersburg and Moscow) and transport maps, and listed the additional concessions available to rail pass holders in the Country by Country chapter. We have also added new routes: in particular, we now feature Croatia (which is welcoming travellers once again), and include a route that takes in Sardinia and Corsica.

To make your journey smoother, we recommend that you also take a copy of the latest monthly *Thomas Cook European Timetable* (the 'ETT' – see p. 23) which has much more detailed timetabling. Remember always to check the local station timetables, because there are many more short-distance trains available than even the ETT has room to show.

Finally, our researchers fanned out across Europe to try the trains, visit the destinations and update every fact. Even in stable Europe, however, anything can and does happen – governments fall, exchange rates and inflation alter prices, attractions open or close or decide to change their opening hours, railway services are cut, and so on. We apologise in advance for any errors that may creep in over the life of this edition. We need your help to keep this book up to date, so please do write in with any corrections, additions and suggestions, or simply with your experiences on the rails around Europe

# HOW TO USE THIS BOOK

## ROUTES AND CITIES

*On the Rails around Europe* is formatted to reflect the way people actually travel on rail passes: not restricting themselves to one country but crossing borders (itself very much a formality, and often completely unnoticed, at least in Western Europe) and following where the international rail lines lead them.

Therefore, the book divides Europe not into countries but into **recommended routes** – no less than 57 of them – chosen to make the most of the potential that rail offers for fast connections between cities and nations (and often for sightseeing while travelling). Each route begins and ends in a **key city**; these are the major cultural and sightseeing centres of Europe or cities with important rail connections – usually they are both. Every route and every key city has its own chapter in this book.

The routes often cross borders; some of them can be travelled in a few hours, some would require at least two days to complete without stopping. But stopping is the whole point; you can break your journey for a few hours or a few days, as you wish, at towns and cities along these routes, all of which are worth visiting in their own right. Hundreds of **smaller cities, towns, attractions and points of interest** along each route are described in the order in which you will encounter them in the direction of the route. Bear in mind that, of course, every route we have suggested can be travelled in the opposite direction to the one we have given: for instance, the Athens–Istanbul route can also be travelled in the Istanbul–Athens direction.

The order in which the routes are laid out assumes that most readers will be beginning their travel in the north-west of Europe – from London, Paris, Brussels, Amsterdam – and proceeding across the continent southwards and eastwards. Chapters on key cities are usually followed by one or more chapters describing routes beginning in those cities, unless a route

has been dealt with after the chapter of the key city at its other end; e.g. the chapter on Frankfurt is followed by routes from Frankfurt to Berlin, Munich, Vienna and Zurich, but the route from Frankfurt to Cologne comes after the Cologne chapter under the name Cologne–Frankfurt.

The routes are designed to be used as a kind of menu from which you can plan an itinerary, combining a number of them which take you to the places you most want to visit. Cross-referencing of routes throughout the book, and the planning map on pp. 8–9, make this easy.

## WITHIN EACH ROUTE

Each route chapter begins with a short introduction to the route, followed by a **route diagram** such as the one below. This summarises the route and shows the main intermediate stops, as well as intersecting routes and Side Tracks. The diagram is followed by a section on

11

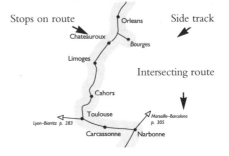

Stops on route · Orleans · Side track

Chateauroux · Bourges · Limoges · Intersecting route · Cahors · Toulouse · Marseille–Barcelona p. 305 · Lyon–Biarritz p. 283 · Carcassonne · Narbonne

**Trains**, giving a good idea of frequency of service and other rail travel advice; it is often divided as follows:

### FAST TRACK

This details the fastest rail service between the start and end cities, sometimes along a different line from the On Track.

### ON TRACK

This is the full route, which takes in the towns along the way. Each point-to-point service is described separately. Journey times and frequencies can only be approximate, and you should use the local timetables (at the station) to verify exact departure times, etc. You can pick and choose whether you visit all the suggested stops, or skip some of them.

### SIDE TRACK

This heading is frequently used after a description of a place, to highlight departures from there, off the recommended route, that lead to places of interest; these may be described in full or indicated in a paragraph or two. The extent of the Side Track (before you rejoin the main route) is shown by the grey margins and the end-sign.

## CITY DESCRIPTIONS

Whether a place is given a half-page description within a route chapter or is a key city with an entire chapter to itself, we have concentrated on practical details: local sources of **Tourist information**; **Getting around** in city centres (by public transport and on foot); **Accommodation** and **Food and drink**; post and phone **Communications**; **Entertainment** and **Shopping** opportunities; under **Sightseeing**, for reasons of space, we have often had to concentrate only on the highlights; Tourist Offices will provide you with plenty of extra information and ideas. The largest cities have all this detail; in smaller places some categories of information are less relevant and have been omitted or summarised.

Where there is a something to say which would interrupt the flow of the main description, we have placed occasional **feature boxes**.

Although we mention good independently owned hotels in many places, we always also list the hotel chains which have a property in the area, by means of code letters to save space. Many travellers prefer to stick to one or two chains with which they are familiar and which give a consistent standard of accommodation. The codes are explained on p. 559, and central booking numbers for the chains are also given there.

## MAPS

In addition to the diagram which accompanies each route, we provide maps of major cities (usually the central or historic area, or as far out as the main rail station where possible)

### Symbols used on city maps

| i | Tourist Information | 🚌 | Bus Station |
| 🖂 | Post Office | M | Metro Station |
| † | Church | ✟ | Cathedral |

## THE REST OF THE BOOK

**Travel Essentials** is an alphabetically arranged chapter of general advice for travellers in Europe. **Travel by Train** takes a more detailed look at how the rail system operates, what tickets or passes you will need, sleeping cars, and so on. **Country by Country** is designed to provide a basic run-down of facts and advice on each of the nations covered in this book. Information common to many destinations within a particular country is given here and not repeated in each city description. **Sea Crossings** summarises the many ways to reach continental Europe (both over and under the water) from London at the start of your rail trip.

At the end of the book, the final route is followed by a brief guide to **Special Trains**, that is, train journeys which are tourist attractions in their own right, whether mountain rack railways or steam trains. **Conversion Tables** provide a quick way of translating metric measures and Continental clothing sizes to their British and American equivalents. **Abbreviations** used throughout this book for brevity are explained on that page, followed by two pages of **Hotel Central Booking Numbers and Codes**, decoding the abbreviations we use throughout the book for hotel chains, and providing information for remote booking of accommodation with them. **Through Routes** supplements our network of recommended routes with details of faster long-distance rail travel.

Finally, the **Index** is the quick way to look up any place or general subject. Use it to locate places, large and small, and topics of interest. And please help us by completing and returning the **Reader Survey** at the very end end of the book. Happy travelling!

# TRAVEL ESSENTIALS

The following is a listing of helpful tips for those planning a European holiday by rail.

## ACCOMMODATION

Europe offers an excellent choice of accommodation, from five-star hotels to room only. Your main problem may lie in finding something to suit your budget. The quality of cheaper hotels in Eastern Europe may still be less than inspiring and you could do better with a private room.

City Tourist Offices are almost always your best starting point if you haven't pre-booked. If they don't handle bookings themselves (there's usually a small charge), they will re-direct you to someone who does and/or supply you with the information to do it yourself – tell them your price horizons.

If you prefer to book hotels in advance, this can usually be done by Thomas Cook or another good travel agent at the same time as you make your travel arrangements.

This book indicates which of the major international or national chains are represented in each city, by means of initials under the 'Accommodation' heading: e.g. '*BW, Hn, Hd*' means that Best Western, Hilton and Holiday Inn have branches there. Further details can be obtained from the chain's central reservations office (for phone numbers and decoded initials see pp. 559–560) or through your travel agent. Chains that operate only in a particular country or region are noted in the Country by Country section (see pp. 33–97).

### Hostelling International (HI)

For those on a tight budget, the best bet is to join **HI (Hostelling International)**. Membership of a national association will entitle you to use over 5000 HI hostels in 60 different countries and, apart from camping, they often provide the cheapest accommodation. The norm is dormitory-style, but many hostels also have single and family rooms. Many offer excellent-value dining and many have self-catering and/or laundry facilities. Membership for those over/under 18 is currently: Australia $44/16; Canada $25/12; England £9.50/3.50; Republic of Ireland £7.50/4; New Zealand $24 plus $10 joining fee; Scotland £6/2.50; South Africa R.45 (free for those under 16); USA $25/12; Wales £9.50/3.50. Buy their directory *Budget Accommodation You Can Trust* (£6.99 for the European edition), which lists hostel addresses, contact numbers, locations and facilities. Some are open 24 hours, but most have lock-out times and Reception's hours are usually very limited – so check what they are and advise them if you are arriving out of hours. It is not compulsory to reserve accommodation, but it is advisable – especially in summer, when many hostels fill well in advance and even those with space are likely to limit your stay to three nights if you just turn up. In winter (except around Christmas) bookings can be slow and it's worth asking if there are any special price deals available.

For information, to join, and to book international accommodation in advance: Australia, *tel: (02) 9261 1111*; Canada, *tel: 1 (800) 663 5777*; England (and Wales), *tel: (0171) 836 1036*; Republic of Ireland, *tel: (01) 830 1766*; New Zealand, *tel: (09) 379 4224*; Northern Ireland, *tel: (01232) 324 733;* Scotland, *tel: (0141) 332 3004*; South Africa, *tel: (021) 242 511*; USA, *tel: (0202) 783 6161*. Wherever we have given accommodation details, we have included hostels (represented by 'HI').

In places where **rooms in private houses** are an option, local Tourist Offices can usually help, by giving you a list – sometimes they will help you find space. As well as being cheaper than hotels, this form of accommodation is a good way to meet local people, but you may be expected to stay for more than one night.

### Camping

This is obviously the cheapest accommodation, if you are prepared to carry the equipment. There are campsites right across Europe, with

13

facilities ranging from basic (toilets and showers) to luxury sites with dining-rooms, swimming pools and complexes of permanent tents, aimed at tourists with children. The drawback is that they are often miles from the city centres.

There is no really good pan-European guide to campsites, but most Tourist Offices can provide a directory for their country. Either contact them before you leave home or ensure you arrive in a new town early enough to get information from the local Tourist Office.

## BICYCLES

In many European countries cycling is popular and the best way to explore locally. You can often hire a bike at one rail station and leave it at another and this can be cheaper than going to bike-hire shops. In many countries bikes can be carried on trains (for a small fee), but advance notice may be required. If you are interested, contact the relevant national Tourist Office for information before you leave.

## BORDERS

Land borders between the EU (European Union) countries are virtually non-existent and it's only if you arrive/leave by air or sea that you're likely to encounter any formalities. Checks between the EU and other West European countries are seldom more than perfunctory. Most former Eastern bloc countries, however, still go through the full routine and you should be prepared for delays when crossing between East and West.

## CHILDREN

Travelling by train with children is easier than you might think – as long as you have someone to help you haul bags and pushchairs up the steps. Most children find train travel a great novelty and thoroughly enjoy themselves. However, they can get bored on long journeys and become a menace to themselves, you and your fellow passengers, so make sure you are not short of ideas to keep them amused and have plenty of food and drink at hand.

If the children are old enough, ask them to keep a detailed travel diary. This will focus their attention on what they see and do, make them think about the whole experience (and

remember it afterwards). Collecting and displaying anything from tickets and postcards to dried flowers can become a whole new game.

Most tourist destinations in Europe are reasonably well adapted for children and babysitters are not hard to find, if you ask at the local Tourist Office or church. Many hotels offer family rooms or provide a cot in a normal double. If you can't find suitable restaurants, there is almost always a café or fast-food place with a children's menu or, at the very least, the sort of food they won't spit out. The biggest problem is keeping some sort of familiar routine going. Many sights and forms of transport accept babies for free, and children under 12 for half price.

For useful reading try: Maureen Wheeler, *Travel with Children* (Lonely Planet, £5.95/ US$10.95).

## CLIMATE

The climate in Europe is affected by three main factors: latitude (Scandinavia is colder than Spain); altitude (the Alps are colder than Belgium); and distance from the sea (the central European countries, such as the Czech Republic, can suffer surprisingly harsh winters and unexpectedly hot summers). That said, most of Europe has a relatively gentle climate. Rain is common throughout the year, except along some stretches of the Mediterranean. The summer temperature rarely exceeds 28°C (see the climate chart, which shows centigrade and fahrenheit equivalents, on the next page), except in the far south (the Mediterranean area), where it can be agonisingly hot (occasionally even 40°C) in high summer. Winter tends to be grey and wet, with temperatures hovering around -5/+5°C and relatively little snow, except in Scandinavia, the high mountains and parts of central Europe. In the far north, midsummer is the best time to travel, to take advantage of the ultra-long days. Almost everywhere else, May and September are the best months, and have the added advantage of avoiding school holiday crowds.

## CLOTHING

Most of Europe is very informal these days and you will rarely need evening clothes, or even a suit, but make sure you have some smart casual

# European Temperatures and Rainfall

This chart gives an idea of the typical ranges of temperature and rainfall you are likely to encounter at various times of the year in sample destinations across Europe. However, almost every part of Europe can experience 'unusual' conditions at any time of year, and summers are becoming warmer and drier.

|  | Berlin | Budapest | London | Madrid | Rome | Stockholm |
|---|---|---|---|---|---|---|
| January |  |  |  |  |  |  |
| Highest | 2°C/36°F | 0°C/32°F | 6°C/43°F | 8°C/46°F | 12°C/54°F | 2°C/36°F |
| Lowest | -1°C/30°F | -5°C/23°F | 1°C/34°F | 4°C/39°F | 4°C/39°F | -4°C/25°F |
| Rain days | 14 | 8 | 15 | 6 | 8 | 7 |
| April |  |  |  |  |  |  |
| Highest | 13°C/55°F | 7°C/45°F | 13°C/55°F | 18°C/64°F | 20°C/68°F | 17°C/63°F |
| Lowest | 8°C/46°F | 0°C/32°F | 4°C/39°F | 12°C/54°F | 8°C/46°F | 6°C/43°F |
| Rain days | 11 | 6 | 13 | 5 | 6 | 8 |
| July |  |  |  |  |  |  |
| Highest | 23C/73°F | 21°C/70°F | 22°C/72°F | 31°C/88°F | 31°C/88°F | 28°C/82°F |
| Lowest | 17°C/63°F | 13°C/55°F | 12°C/54°F | 21°C/70°F | 18°C/64°F | 16°C/61°F |
| Rain days | 9 | 9 | 13 | 2 | 3 | 7 |
| October |  |  |  |  |  |  |
| Highest | 13°C/55°F | 9°C/48°F | 14°C/57°F | 19°C/66°F | 23°C/73°F | 16°C/61°F |
| Lowest | 9°C/48°F | 4°C/39°F | 6°C/43°F | 14°C/57°F | 11°C/52°F | 7°C/45°F |
| Rain days | 13 | 9 | 16 | 5 | 9 | 8 |

clothes (not jeans and trainers) for evening wear. People wearing shorts or sleeveless tops may be excluded from some churches, the most traditional of which still expect women to cover their heads, so they should pack a long-sleeved shirt or blouse and a shawl or large scarf. You can encounter rain or cool weather no matter where you go, so at least one sweater or jacket and some sort of rainwear are essential.

In addition, take at least two skirts or pairs of trousers; a pair of shorts; three to four shirts or blouses and three sets of underwear and non-synthetic socks (one on, one in the wash, one spare). For women, a huge t-shirt is useful for a beach cover-up and sleeping in, as well as during the day. Shoes should be comfortable, but light, and well broken-in before you set out, and a pair of flip-flops is useful for unhygienic showers and overnight travel. Other than that, look for comfortable, easily washable clothes that pack small and do not need ironing.

For hot weather, clothes should be kept loose and made of cotton or cotton-mix. For changeable weather, it's practical to wear several layers. In midwinter, you will need a warm coat or cold-weather jacket, a scarf, hat, gloves and sensible, non-slip footwear. Pack a tube of Travel Wash (available from most chemists) and a piece of string to serve as a washing line, so you can wash clothes through as you travel and save on the expense and inconvenience of using a launderette.

## CONSULAR SERVICES

Most embassies/consulates/high commissions will lend a helping hand if their nationals have *real* problems – and charge a small fee for any services rendered. The Australian, Canadian, UK and US embassies produce (free) leaflets outlining their services.

Help should be available if: a) your passport is stolen (or a travel document that will get you home); b) if there's a death or serious accident (advice on procedures, next of kin notified – probably also sympathetic help); c) if you go to jail – don't expect sympathy, nor direct intervention, but they will explain your rights and tell you how to get a lawyer.

Should something happen to make the area dangerous (an act of God, local rebellion, etc), contact your embassy to register your presence and ask for advice.

In case of real financial trouble, embassies *may* agree to make a small loan or contact next of kin with a request for help, but they do not look kindly on people who have simply overspent. Do *not* expect them to act as surrogate travel agents, banks, interpreters, etc. That is not their function.

If your own country has no representation, contact one with which it has ties, e.g. Commonwealth citizens can try the British Embassy. They may help and you should at least get some advice about what to do next.

## CURRENCY

Most European countries place no limit on the import/export of currencies. However, almost all the former Eastern bloc countries state that the amount taken out must not exceed the amount taken in, making allowance for the amount spent while there. Some such countries check the amounts on both arrival and departure, others simply query the amount taken out if they feel it is larger than they would expect. The restrictions usually refer only to banknotes/coins – if you are carrying a large amount of cash, therefore, you should declare it on arrival in order to avoid problems when you leave the country.

That said, it is never advisable to carry more cash than necessary and it is sensible to take most of your money (but not all – some small-denomination local cash is essential) in the form of Eurocheques, travellers' cheques and credit cards – but don't rely too heavily on being able to use credit cards. Although technically illegal, many travellers in Bulgaria and Romania find it useful to carry a few small-denomination German notes and coins. There is no black market in currency in Western Europe. You may find people eager to trade in some Eastern

European countries, but you could face heavy penalties if caught. You may also be ripped off by those making the exchange, or lay yourself open to muggers working with them.

The Thomas Cook offices listed in this book will cash any type of Eurocheque/traveller's cheque and will replace Thomas Cook Travellers Cheques if yours are lost/stolen.

Always try to obtain a little local currency before you enter a new country. If you are unable to do so and arrive outside banking hours, the best bet (albeit an expensive option) is to ask the receptionist at a big hotel to change some for you. Try to ensure you always carry one or two coins of each denomination, so that you don't get caught out by not having the right ones for slot machines.

In border towns and on cross-border transport, you can almost always use either of the relevant currencies (a good way to dispose of excess coins), but you generally pay less if you choose the one in which prices are marked.

## CUSTOMS

Importing narcotics and offensive weapons is banned throughout Europe – and penalties for carrying them can be very severe; so, in your own interests, do not be tempted, and do not carry things for anyone else, especially when you are crossing borders.

Professional crooks are very good at passing themselves off as harmless and in need of help and some people are languishing in jail today because they believed a hard-luck story or did someone a 'small' favour. Pornography is also banned in many countries and, since it is notoriously difficult to define, it is better to avoid carrying anything that might offend. If you have to take a prescribed drug on a regular basis, carry something (such as a doctor's letter) that will prove it is legitimate.

There are often restrictions on the import and export of plants and fresh foodstuffs (particularly meat and meat products) and you might be asked to abandon them at borders, so be careful about stocking up just before leaving a country.

Before buying souvenirs, check which items are likely to be prohibited, such as those made of ivory or tortoiseshell.

## Customs Allowances in the EU

European Union member states (Austria, Belgium, Denmark, Finland, France, Germany, Greece, the Republic of Ireland, Italy, Luxembourg, the Netherlands, Portugal, Spain, Sweden and the UK) have set the purchase of tobacco, alcohol and perfume at the same basic allowance for each country (for the few exceptions, see the Country by Country section), and the tobacco and alcohol allowances apply to anyone aged 17 or over.

To all intents and purposes, there are no restrictions between the EU countries for goods bought in ordinary shops and including local taxes, but you may be questioned if you have excessive amounts. Allowances are:
800 cigarettes, 200 cigars, 400 cigarillos and 1 kg tobacco
+ 90 litres wine (maximum 60 litres sparkling)
+ 10 litres alcohol over 22% volume (e.g. most spirits)
+ 20 litres alcohol under 22% volume (e.g. port and sherry)
+ 110 litres beer.

The allowances for goods bought outside the EU and/or in EU duty-free shops are:
200 cigarettes or 50 cigars or 100 cigarillos or 250 g tobacco*
+ 2 litres still table wine
+ 1 litre spirits or 2 litres sparkling or fortified wine
+ 8 litres Luxembourg wine if imported via the Luxembourg frontier
+ 50 g/60 ml perfume
+ 0.5 l/250 ml toilet water.

*Some EU countries have more generous tobacco allowances for non-Europeans arriving from outside Europe, so check in the duty-free shop or with your carrier.

## Allowances for those returning home:

**Australia:** goods to the value of Aust$400 (half for those under 18) plus 250 cigarettes or 250 g tobacco and 1 litre alcohol.

**Canada:** allowances apply to anyone aged 19 or more (a year younger if you are entering AL, MN or QU). You are allowed 50 cigars and 200 cigarettes and 400 g tobacco plus 1.1 litre alcohol or 24 x 355 ml bottles/tins beer, as well as gifts not exceeding Can$60 each in value.

**New Zealand:** goods to the value of NZ$700. Anyone over 17 may also take 200 cigarettes or 250 g tobacco or 50 cigars or a combination of tobacco products not exceeding 250 g in all plus 4.5 litres of beer or wine and 1.125 litres spirits.

**South Africa:** goods to a total value of 500 Rand. Those aged 18 or more are allowed 400 cigarettes and 50 cigars and 250 g tobacco plus 2 litres wine and 1 litre spirits plus 50 ml perfume and 250 ml toilet water.

**Republic of Ireland** and **UK:** standard EU regulations apply (see foregoing notes and above).

**USA:** goods to the value of US$400 as long as you have been out of the country for at least 48 hrs and only use your allowance once every 30 days. Anyone over 21 is also allowed 1 litre alcohol plus 100 (non-Cuban) cigars and 200 cigarettes and a reasonable quantity of tobacco.

## DISABLED TRAVELLERS

Europe, in theory, provides more facilities for the disabled than many other parts of the world. In practice, however, those facilities that do exist often fall short of real needs and expectations, and there may be a shortage of helpful bystanders. Travel is feasible, but it will almost inevitably be more expensive, as it is usually only the modern trains and more upmarket hotels that cater for the disabled. You will also have to throw out any thought of spontaneity and make meticulous plans, always writing and phoning ahead to make sure you have a reservation and that there is someone on hand to help you. The amount of advance warning required for trains varies dramatically, from Austrian State Railways, who ask for three days' notice, to the ever-efficient Swiss who need only one day.

There are two main problems to face with the trains – how to get onto them, and whether there is space for you once on board. Although modern rolling-stock tends not to have wide gaps between train and platform, in many European stations the platforms are quite low and passengers have to climb steep steps to board trains. Once aboard, only the more modern carriages provide space for a wheelchair; otherwise, space will be provided in the baggage car. The new express services, such as the French TGV and the Spanish AVE, provide proper facilities for the disabled, while some Scandinavian trains have adapted hydraulic lifts, accessible toilets and spacious compartments.

Some national rail offices and Tourist Offices have leaflets about rail travel for the disabled. The Dutch also have a telephone information line *(tel: (00 31 30) 235 55 55)*. A few national networks offer discount passes for the disabled.

The best routes to travel include the main lines in Scandinavia, Switzerland, Germany, the Netherlands and France. The worst facilities are in Turkey, Spain, Hungary, Greece, Bulgaria, the Czech Republic and Slovakia.

**UK information: RADAR,** *Unit 12, City Forum, 250 City Rd, London EC1V 8AF; tel: (0171) 250 3222,* publish an annual guide called *Holidays and Travel Abroad* (£5 including postage), which contains useful addresses and gives details of facilities for the disabled in different countries, including their trains.

**US information: SATH (Society for the Advancement of Travel for the Handicapped),** *347 5th Ave, Suite 610, New York NY 10016; tel: (212) 447 7284.*

For useful reading try: Susan Abbott and Mary Ann Tyrrell's *The World Wheelchair Traveller* (AA Publishing, £3.95); and Alison Walsh's *Nothing Ventured: A Rough Guide Special* (Penguin, £7.99).

### DISCOUNTS

In many countries reductions are available on public transport and on entrance fees for senior citizens, students and the young. Some proof of your eligibility is usually required, so always carry something that will provide evidence of your status, e.g. an official document that shows your age or a student card.

If you are a student, get an International Student Identity Card (ISIC) from your student union or travel agents such as, STA and Campus Travel, as this is recognised everywhere and offers a wider range of discounts than national union cards.

Some destinations offer (for a small fee) a book of discount vouchers covering anything from museums to restaurants. Many discount passes for tourists, including some rail passes,

must be purchased before you leave home as they are not available in the country itself. Contact the relevant Tourist Offices to ask about any such deals.

### DRIVING

If you want to hire a motor vehicle while you are away, check requirements with the AA/ RAC, or your own national motoring organisation, well before you leave, so that you have time to get any necessary documentation and additional insurance cover.

To hire a vehicle (except a moped), you usually have to be over 21, with two years' driving experience. In most European countries your national licence is valid for up to six months, but you may need a translation as well and it can be easier to get an international licence. Always check that the vehicle is in good condition before you set out, with special attention to brakes, lights and tyres (including the spare).

Most road signs are standardised throughout Europe, but the quality of signposting varies dramatically, as do speed limits. Check for local peculiarities before you set out. Except in the British Isles, Europeans drive on the right.

There is a network of motor-rail services across Europe, for those who wish to take their own cars across Europe by train.

### ELECTRICITY

With a few exceptions (notably the UK, which uses 230/240V), the European countries use 220V. The shape of plugs varies and, if you are taking any sort of electrical gadget, you should take a travel adaptor. It is unlikely that you will face power cuts, but a small torch (flashlight) is a useful back-up and essential if camping.

### HEALTH

#### Before you go

Europe, as a whole, is reasonably hygienic and there are no compulsory vaccination requirements. However, it is always advisable to keep your tetanus and polio protection up to date and vaccination against typhoid and hepatitis A is also a good idea. You must be able to produce a certificate against yellow fever if you have been in a yellow fever endemic zone in the six days before entering Europe. It's always a good idea to visit your dentist for a check-up before you leave home.

If you are a UK citizen, you should fill in Form E111 before you go (available from post offices). This (free) form entitles you to treatment under the reciprocal health arrangements that exist across most of Europe, but only on the same basis as citizens of the country. This means you may have to pay up-front and reclaim the cost when you return home – and/or some of your treatment may not be free. Procedures for each country are detailed in the booklet containing the form. It's worth visiting a pharmacy before consulting a doctor: European pharmacists tend to be well trained and may well save you medical bills by pre-scribing something that solves your problem.

### Risks

Although most of Europe is temperate, there is a definite risk of sunburn in the south and in high mountain areas. Don't spend hours out-doors without using a high-factor sunblock.

Holiday romances are all very well, but don't get so carried away that you forget all about AIDS – and other unpleasant sexually-transmitted diseases. If casual sex is your scene, fine, but do take precautions – one glorious night is not worth a (short) lifetime of regret. Take your own condoms if travelling in Eastern Europe.

Rabies exists in Continental Europe and, while the risk is very small, you should be wary of stray and wild animals. Lyme disease – caught from ticks in undergrowth – is present in Central European forests. Wear long trousers and long-sleeved shirts to avoid picking up these insects. Symptoms are similar to arthritis and if they show up within 3 months of possi-ble exposure ask your doctor for a blood test; early treatment is nearly always effective.

### Food and Water

Most tap water in Western Europe is safe. If in doubt, buy tinned or bottled drinks and water and do not use ice cubes. You should boil or sterilise all tap water (including the water you use to brush your teeth) if you think there may

be cause for concern. Other common sources of infection in less-developed areas include unboiled unpasteurised milk, unwashed salads and fresh fruit (unless you can peel it yourself). In areas where the sea is polluted, be wary of fresh seafood and always avoid food which is obviously dirty or which may have been lying around for a long time. Wash your own hands before touching food.

### HITCHHIKING

The best advice is don't hitchhike. What used to be fun and a good way to meet local people is now too risky. However, in a few countries, such as Poland, there are official schemes for getting drivers and hitchers together, so that both can feel safe. Ask at the relevant Tourist Offices, either before you go or once you are in the country.

### INFORMATION

Addresses of national Tourist Offices are given in the Country by Country section. Once in a new town, look for a sign displaying a lower case **i** (often black or white on a blue or green background), which is the usual symbol for information in Europe. It may indicate merely a noticeboard (or similar), but, with luck, may point you towards a tourist information office.

Try to get hold of a street map in advance, so that you can find your way around if infor-mation offices are closed when you arrive.

### INSURANCE

Take out travel insurance that covers your health as well as your belongings. It should also give cancellation cover and include an emer-gency flight home if something goes really wrong (the hospitals in some countries are not places where you would want to linger). If you are likely to do something that might be classi-fied as risky (e.g. ski, drive a moped, dive), make sure your policy does not exclude that risk.

### LANGUAGE

Arm yourself with a copy of the *Thomas Cook European Travel Phrasebook* (£4.95/US$7.95) if you are visiting countries where language is likely to be a problem. It contains over three hundred phrases, each translated (with phonetic spellings) into: French, German, Italian, Czech, Hungarian, Polish, Bulgarian, Romanian, Portuguese, Spanish, Greek and Turkish. Phrases cover the everyday needs of a rail traveller, from arriving in a station to booking accommodation, eating out, changing money and coping in an emergency.

Before you go, learn a few basic phrases, such as: 'Hello. I'm sorry, but I don't speak ... Does anyone here speak English?' If it's a language such as Greek which uses a non-Latin alphabet, also learn the appearance of a few essential words.

Your chief asset, if you have no language in common with the people you meet, will be your willingness to use sign language. It's amazing what you can do without words, as long as you are prepared to have a go. If you want to know where the post office is, for example, showing someone an addressed envelope may get the message across. Smiles also go a long way towards breaking the ice and encouraging people to be helpful, but be careful that your friendliness is not misinterpreted.

Keep a pen and paper handy at all times, then you can ask people to write down such figures as times and prices. Similarly, if they don't understand your pronunciation, you can write down what you are trying to say and let them read it – or vice versa.

### LUGGAGE

Always travel as light as possible. The amount of space available for storing luggage on trains varies considerably. Soft-sided bags may be less secure than hard suitcases, but are lighter and easier to squeeze into cramped spaces. Backpacks are the best option if you have a lot to carry; otherwise, go for a large, zippable canvas or plastic bag, with a shoulder strap to leave your hands free.

If you're buying a backpack for the first time, shop carefully and be prepared to spend a bit more than the minimum to ensure comfort and durability (the best brands have a lifetime guarantee). Essential features are a strong internal frame, padded shoulder straps and a hip strap, to lift the bulk of the weight away from your neck. Some frames are specially adapted

for women. Don't be too ambitious about how much you can carry – 50 litres for women and 60 for men is about right.

Most stations (and other transport hubs) have baggage lockers and/or manned left-luggage offices. Many stations will forward your bags to your next destination, but check that the office there will be open when you arrive.

### OPENING HOURS

A rough guide to opening hours is given in the Country by Country section, but there are many variations and you should not assume that, for example, every bank will be open during all the banking hours listed – while some may stay open longer. Sunday is the usual closing day for shops and businesses (and public transport tends to be sparse), while many tourist attractions remain open on Sunday, but close on Monday or Tuesday. Timings are also subject to seasonal variations, with many places closing altogether in winter. The definition of summer and winter (especially in areas with a distinct seasonal difference) often changes every year and is determined by the weather in spring and autumn, so anyone travelling between the seasons should be prepared for changes to the advertised opening times.

### PASSPORTS AND VISAS

EU citizens can travel to other EU countries with a National Identity Card in lieu of a full passport, but do ensure that any identity document is valid well beyond the end of your stay. The individual requirements for West European travellers are given in the Country by Country section. As for non-European travellers, this book concentrates on requirements for citizens of Australia, Canada, New Zealand, South Africa and the USA; others should check requirements with the relevant embassies in good time to get any necessary documents. *Anyone* planning to stay more than 90 days in a single country may need a visa and should check well before travelling.

Some countries will refuse entry to anyone who does not have an onward/return ticket and visible means of support. How this is defined can vary, but in essence it means having sufficient money to cover the cost of food, accommodation and other expenses during your stay. A credit card is a practical way of avoiding precise cash requirements.

In many cases visa requirements have more to do with residence than with nationality, e.g. the visa requirements for an Indian living in India and an Indian living in the UK may be different. People who live abroad should check which regulations apply to them.

Where a country is not mentioned specifically, nationals of that country should assume that they need both a full passport and a visa. Even if you can theoretically obtain a visa at the border, it is probably easier to get it in advance. Allow plenty of time, especially if you need to get several, as it can be a long process. Bear in mind that most visa departments have short, and often eccentric, opening hours. You will also need a whole stack of passport photos and will find that many countries ask you to pay in cash or by postal order and will not accept cheques or credit cards.

## PUBLIC HOLIDAYS

These have been listed under the individual headings in the Country by Country section. Many are religious holidays, whose dates vary from year to year; these are given by name rather than date, in chronological order. The principal ones are Good Friday and Easter Monday (March/April); Ascension Day (the 6th Thursday after Easter); Whitsun/Pentecost (on Monday, 11 days after Ascension); Corpus Christi (early June) and Midsummer Day (late June). If an official holiday falls on a weekend, the following Monday or Tuesday often becomes a holiday as well. Over Christmas most things close altogether; on most other public holidays a good rule of thumb is to assume that Sunday hours/schedules will apply.

There are many local festivals (e.g. saints' days) which are celebrated only in one town but which can disrupt everything in the area. Some are noisy, colourful and great fun, others nothing more than an interruption to normal service. If time is important, check in advance to see if your visit will coincide with any sort of holiday. If it does, bear in mind that all transport services are liable to be severely restricted. Always double-check schedules locally.

## SALES TAX

Value Added Tax (known as VAT in the UK) is automatically added to most goods in Western European countries, but not, as yet, to those in the East. The level varies, but is usually 10–20% (in Spain and Switzerland it can be as low as 6% and in France as high as 23% on some items). It may, or may not, be shown separately on price tags.

In most places (except Greece), non-residents can reclaim the tax on major spending. This often applies to receipts over £30, but every country sets a different limit on how much you must spend. The refund is also intended to apply to only one article, but if you buy several things in the same shop on the same day, the authorities seldom argue.

In order to reclaim your Value Added Tax, ask the shop assistant to fill in a tax refund form for you. Show the form, the receipt and the goods to Customs on leaving the country and they will give you an official export certificate. This can sometimes be exchanged on the spot (necessary in Scandinavia, where limits are also much lower); alternatively, post the certificate back to the shop (within a month) and (in due course) they will send the refund. Many shops will send the goods directly to your home, but anything you save in paperwork at the time is likely to be offset by Customs formalities in your own country.

## SECURITY

The best way to avoid becoming a victim of theft is to give the impression that you are not worth robbing (e.g. do not flash expensive jewellery or rolls of banknotes). Use a hidden money-belt for your valuables, travel documents and spare cash. Never carry a wallet in a back pocket or leave your handbag open and use a bag with a shoulder strap slung horizontally. In public places, take precautions with anything that is obviously worth stealing – wind the strap of your camera case round the arm of your chair and place your handbag firmly between your feet under the table while you eat. Never leave luggage unattended – apart from the risk of theft, many countries are very terrorist-conscious and chances are it will create a bomb scare. Use baggage lockers if you arrive at a place one morning and intend to leave the same day. When using computerised lockers, be careful that nobody sees your re-entry code.

When you're sleeping in any sort of dormitory or on trains, the safest place for your small valuables is in the centre of your sleeping-bag. In sleeping-cars, padlock your luggage to the seat and make sure the compartment door is locked at night – if necessary, ask the attendant how to lock it. There is a tendency for backpackers to trust each other, but don't take this too far. Like other groups in society, some are the good guys and others are not. Be particularly safety-conscious in areas around travel terminals, especially in large cities.

Mugging is a problem in some areas, but not rife in European city centres, where pickpockets are usually the main threat. If you are attacked, let go of your bag (or anything else of obvious value) – you are more likely to be attacked physically if the thief meets with resistance. If you do run into trouble, report the incident to the local police without delay, even if it is only to get a copy of their report for your insurance company.

Carry half a dozen passport photos (useful for all sorts of purposes) and photocopy the important pages and any relevant visa stamps in your passport. Store these safely, together with a note of the numbers of your travellers' cheques, insurance policy and credit cards (keep this away from the documents themselves). If you are unfortunate enough to be robbed, you will at least have some identification – and replacing the documents will be much easier.

## SMOKING

Smoking is now banned in many public places and, even where it is allowed, there may be a special area for smokers. In some countries, such as France, Italy and Spain, the prohibitions are often ignored by the locals, but play safe if in doubt and ask before lighting up.

## TELEPHONES

You should have few problems finding a phone in European towns and everywhere is on direct-dial. Useful telephone numbers are provided throughout the book and in the Country by Country section you will find advice on how to make calls, together with emergency phone numbers. In the EU countries you have an extra option: *tel: 112* for all emergency services.

## THOMAS COOK

The **Thomas Cook bureaux** listed in this book cash any traveller's cheques and offer emergency assistance to holders of Thomas Cook Travellers Cheques if yours is lost or stolen. Details of **Thomas Cook Licensees** are also given in this book (look out for 'Thomas Cook Worldwide Network' signs in travel shops across Europe). These offer the benefits of the Thomas Cook Worldwide Customer Promise, available to those who have made their travel arrangements through Thomas Cook. The benefits include airline reservations and revalidation, hotel reservations, changes to travel arrangements and emergency assistance – all free of agency service charges.

## TIME

There are several time zones within Europe. The following list includes only the countries covered by this book.

The United Kingdom uses Greenwich Mean Time in winter, but is **GMT+1** hr in summer. Countries which are **GMT+1** hr in winter, **GMT+2** hrs in summer: Austria, Belgium, the Czech Republic, Denmark, France, Germany, Hungary, Italy, the Netherlands, Norway, Poland, Portugal, Slovakia, Spain, Sweden and Switzerland. Countries which are **GMT+2** hrs in winter, **GMT+3** hrs in summer: Bulgaria, Estonia, Finland, Greece, Latvia, Lithuania, Romania and Turkey.

## TOILETS

Although not a universal concept, pictures representing a male and a female are commonly used in Western Europe. The term 'WC' is also quite widespread and if you see words beginning 'toilet' or 'lava' you are probably (though not necessarily) on the right track.

In some countries you may come across places where both sexes use the same facilities, even if there are separate entrances, so don't assume automatically that you are in the wrong place. The quality varies considerably. Many

## Solo Travellers

You, and only you, decide where to go, when and for how long. The excitement and sense of adventure in this freedom inspires many to go it alone, but there are drawbacks. You have no one to help plan the trip, or share the experiences and memories. Responsibilities of finding accommodation, deciphering timetables, buying tickets and looking after bags are all yours. Naturally it's lonely at times, especially if you don't speak the local language. However, it is possible to enjoy solo travel without sacrificing companionship. It's easier to meet fellow travellers and locals than it is in a group, as they are more likely to approach you. Travellers abound in trains, ferries and youth hostels, and just asking where they have come from usually starts conversations. Locals chat, and may even invite you home for a meal, opening up whole new facets of a country. Many experienced solo travellers start alone, but keep flexible schedules, so they can spend time with people they meet en route.

Survival is harder alone, so plan carefully. Double-check that you have all the essentials when you set out – there is no one else to rely on. Nor will anyone help carry your bags, so pack lightly. You are more vulnerable to theft, so always carry valuables with you, in a money-belt or pouch. And be cautious with new acquaintances: most travellers are honest, but don't hand your bags over to someone you have just met. Keep in touch with home, in case of emergencies. It is becoming easier to make international calls from all over Europe, but you should also send postcards and, to help stave off loneliness, tell people to write to you poste restante. Finally, remember that the left-luggage office can be your best friend. Never mind sightseeing or the weight of your rucksack as you drag it round town – what will really tax your brain is what to do with your bags while you have a shower.

are modern, clean and well-equipped, others (even in Western Europe) are of the hole-in-the-ground variety and not very well maintained. So be prepared for anything. This includes always carrying some paper, as you will be very lucky if you never find it missing.

Unfortunately not all countries recognise the need for public facilities and they can be difficult to find, so make use of anything the station has to offer before you set out to explore. You can often get away with using the facilities in hotels if you look as if you might be staying there. If not, service stations or eating/drinking places are the best bet – but be prepared to buy something as, understandably, many reserve the use of their facilities for their clients.

### USEFUL READING

#### Thomas Cook Publications

The *Thomas Cook European Timetable (ETT)*, published monthly at £8.40, has up-to-date details of most rail services and many shipping services throughout Europe. It is essential both for pre-planning and for making on-the-spot decisions about independent rail travel around Europe. A useful companion to it is the *Thomas Cook New Rail Map of Europe* (£5.65). Both of these publications are obtainable from some stations, any UK branch of Thomas Cook or by phoning *(01733) 503571/2*. In North America, contact the **Forsyth Travel Library Inc.** *226 Westchester Ave, White Plains, New York 10604; tel: (800) 367 7984* (toll-free).

*Thomas Cook Travellers* (£7.99), published in the USA as *Passport's Illustrated Travel Guides* ($14.95), cover the following major European destinations: the Algarve, Amsterdam, Belgium, Berlin, Budapest, Cyprus, Florence and Tuscany, Greece (Mainland), Ireland, London, Malta, Mallorca, Munich and Bavaria, Normandy, Paris, Prague, Provence, Rome, Turkey, Venice and Vienna. If you plan on going as far as Athens and then seeing some of the Greek islands, you will find the Thomas Cook Touring Handbook *Greek Island Hopping* invaluable; as well as covering (literally) every island, it provides detailed, essential information on the complex ferry schedules. These guides and the *Thomas Cook European Travel Phrasebook*

---

## Women Travellers

Some women still feel a little apprehensive about setting off alone, but most of the hazards or hassles they may face have nothing to do with their sex. Sexual innuendo and regular chat-up lines are little more than annoying. Remember, however, that many societies are still formal and unliberated and, if you bare all in skimpy clothes, you will invite more than your fair share of hassle. To avoid irritation, dress on the conservative side, walk purposefully and confidently, and avoid direct eye contact with problematic men. Be careful whom you speak to and, while you can be perfectly friendly, keep it cool and off-limits. A short courteous answer is often more fruitful than turning your back, while a firm but polite 'no' is understood in most languages. If in doubt, invent a large boyfriend or protective father, nearby and due back soon. If you feel the need, carry a rape alarm. If you think you may want to say 'yes', make sure you have your own supply of condoms. If you don't like eating alone at night, have your main meal at lunchtime, or take a book for company.

Exercise the usual rules of caution when abroad. Don't go off with people who have been drinking or get into cars with strangers. Avoid dark alleys and lonely or red-light areas, make sure you have a clear view all round you and, if in doubt, scream first and think later. If you feel threatened, head for the nearest hotel and ask for help. If you need to go to the police, try to find a friendly witness to take with you, as many policemen are far from saintly. Most of all, remember that few of the people you meet have designs on your body. Most are nice, friendly and just want to talk or help you with heavy luggage. If you are too scared to talk to anyone, you will miss out on what could be the best parts of your holiday.

---

are available from many book shops in the UK and the USA (publisher: Passport Books) and from UK branches of Thomas Cook.

### Other useful books

The best series of guides are: *Lonely Planet* and *Rough Guides*, for budget travellers; the *Michelin Green Guides* for cultural sightseeing and the *AA Essential Guides* as excellent pocket guides for short stops. If you want to work for a while, buy *Work Your Way Around the World* (Vacation Work, £10.95). The *Travellers Handbook* is also extremely useful for pre-travel planning (WEXAS, £14.95).

### WHAT TO TAKE

A few really useful things are: water-bottles, Swiss\ Army pocket knife, torch (flashlight), sewing kit, padlock and bicycle chain (for anchoring your luggage), small first-aid kit (including insect repellent and antihistamine cream, sun-screen cream, after-sun lotion, water-sterilising tablets, something for headaches and tummy troubles, antiseptic spray or cream, medicated wet-wipes, plasters for blisters, bandages), contraceptives and tampons

(especially if visiting Eastern Europe, where they are difficult to get – try the luxury shop in the city's biggest hotel), safety matches, mug and basic cutlery, small towel, soap, toothbrush, some detergent, string (for a washing-line), travel adapter, universal plug (often missing from wash-basins), sunglasses, alarm clock, notepad and pen, pocket calculator (to convert money), a money-belt and a good book (for long journeys).

For clothing, see the clothing section on p. 14. If you wear spectacles, take a spare pair and a copy of your prescription.

If you're not sure what you're doing about accommodation, take a lightweight sleeping-bag, a sheet liner, inflatable travel pillow, earplugs and eyemask (invaluable for comfort in dormitories and on some trains, even if you look a total idiot). Strong plastic containers can come in handy and are far safer (and lighter) than glass ones. Finally, pack some plastic bags of various sizes – they weigh virtually nothing, take up very little room and are useful for all sorts of things (from storing dirty/wet clothes to keeping your lunch fresh), plus one or two elastic bands to seal them.

# TRAVELLING BY TRAIN

This chapter is packed with hints about organising an excursion around Europe by rail.

## INFORMATION AND BOOKING

### In the UK
Sources of international rail tickets, passes and information include: **International Rail Centre**, *Victoria Station, London SW1V 1JY; tel: (0990) 848848;* **Rail Europe**, *179 Piccadilly, London W1; tel: 0990 300 003;* **Wasteels Travel**, *Victoria Station, London SW1V 1JY; tel: (0171) 834 7066;* **Campus Travel** (Eurotrain), *52 Grosvenor Gardens, London SW1W 0AG; tel: (0171) 730 3402;* **Ffestiniog Travel** *Porthmadog, Gwynedd, Wales, LL49 9NF, tel: (01766) 512340.*

### In the USA
Sources of tickets, passes and information include: **Forsyth Travel Library Inc.**, *226 Westchester Ave., White Plains, New York 10604; (800) 367-7984;* **Rail Europe Inc**, *500 Mamaroneck Ave, Harrison, New York 10528,* and *2100 Central Ave, Suite 200, Boulder CO 80301; tel: (800) 4-EURAIL* (toll-free) or, for Eurostar, *tel: (800) EUROSTAR* (toll-free); **DER Tours**, *tel: (800) 782 2424.*

Several national rail networks have offices in the USA; information is listed for individual countries in the Country by Country section (see pp. 33–97).

### Elsewhere
International rail information and tickets in **Australia/Canada/New Zealand** are obtainable from Thomas Cook branches (and branches of Marlin Travel in Canada). To contact **Rail Europe** in Canada, *tel: (800) 361-RAIL (toll-free).* In **South Africa**, international rail information and tickets are available from branches of Rennies Travel (Thomas Cook licensee).

## EUROPEAN RAIL PASSES
Many countries have rail passes valid only for domestic travel. Those most likely to be of interest are detailed in the Country by Country section and can usually be purchased from any branch of the national railway and its appointed agents. Your passport is required for identification, and one or two passport-size photos may be needed.

Passes generally cover all the ordinary services of the national rail companies and can be used on most special services if you pay a supplement. However, if the pass has been purchased in North America there is no supplement to be paid. A few passes, such as Eurail, cover most supplements. Many passes also give free or discounted travel with privately owned rail companies (including steam and cog trains), buses and ferries. These are listed under 'Rail Pass Concessions' for each country in the 'Country by Country' chapter. You get details of other extras when you buy the pass.

If you are planning a long journey, consider the following international passes, which are common to most of Europe.

### Children
Although there are exceptions, the norm is for children aged 4–11 to pay approximately 50% of the adult fare and for babies under 4 to travel free – but babies are not entitled to a seat in crowded trains.

### Eurail Passes
These are available only to people living outside Europe and can be obtained from the agents listed (under 'In the USA' and 'Elsewhere') to the left. You can get the passes once you've arrived (from Rail Europe and the International Rail Centre in London, see above), but at much higher prices. Since you can buy them up to six months in advance, there is no point in waiting until the last minute.

Eurail offers unlimited travel on the national

## Inter-Rail Passes

The **Inter-Rail Pass** has launched generations of young people into the travelling life. A well-established scheme, it provides a practical and ultra-cheap way of seeing most of Europe by train. It can be bought by anyone who will be under 26 on the first day for which it is valid, if they have lived for at least six months in one of the European countries where the pass is valid (see list below), or are a national of that country and hold a valid passport. It can be purchased up to two months before travel begins. The current cost is £259 for a month and you can buy consecutive passes for longer journeys. You will not get free travel in the country where you buy the pass, but you may be eligible for some discount.

Inter-Rail provides unlimited second-class rail travel for a month on the national railways of: Austria, Belgium, Bulgaria, Croatia, the Czech Republic, Denmark, Finland, France, Germany, Greece, Hungary, the Republic of Ireland, Italy, Yugoslavia, Luxembourg, Macedonia, Morocco, the Netherlands, Norway, Poland, Portugal, Romania, Slovakia, Slovenia, Spain, Sweden, Switzerland and Turkey. It also includes a free crossing on the Hellenic Mediterranean/Adriatica di Navigazione shipping lines between Brindisi in Italy and Patras in Greece (you will have to pay port tax of approximately L.10,000 from Italy to Greece or Dr.1500 from Greece to Italy). There are free or discounted crossings on other ferries, so check.

In the UK, Inter-Rail provides a discount of 34% on rail travel and a discount on Eurostar and the rail portion of tickets between London and the Continental ports, as well as good discounts (up to 50%, depending on the company) on most ferries to Ireland and Europe, including Scandinavia.

### Zonal Inter-Rail Passes

These regional variations on the Inter-Rail Pass now apply for those over 26 as well as for those under 26. The same rules about eligibility apply. For zonal passes, Europe has been divided into eight geographical zones:

A  United Kingdom and the Republic of Ireland.
B  Sweden, Norway and Finland.
C  Denmark, Switzerland, Germany and Austria.
D  Poland, the Czech Republic, Slovakia, Hungary and Croatia,
E  France, Belgium, the Netherlands and Luxembourg.
F  Spain, Portugal and Morocco.
G  Italy, Slovenia, Greece, Turkey (including shipping lines between Brindisi and Patras).
H  Bulgaria, Romania, Yugoslavia and Macedonia.

Passes are available for 1 zone (22 days: £159); 2 zones (1 month: £209); and 3 zones (1 month: £229). If you have a definite route in mind, these can offer savings over the standard Europe-wide pass. For instance, if you bought a 2-zone pass for zones E and G, you could travel through France into Italy and on to Greece and Turkey for only £209, with a side trip through the Benelux countries on the way home.

### Inter-Rail 26+ Pass

This now offers the same benefits as Inter-Rail for those over 26. The current cost is £229 for a 1-zone pass, £279 for 2 zones, £309 for 3 zones and £349 for an all-zones pass.

railways of: Austria, Belgium, Denmark, Finland, France, Germany, Greece, Hungary, the Republic of Ireland, Italy, Luxembourg, the Netherlands, Norway, Portugal, Spain,

**26**

Sweden and Switzerland. They also cover most private railways and a few selected ferries, such as the Hellenic Mediterranean/Adriatica di Navigazione shipping lines between Brindisi in Italy and Patras in Greece (although, as with the Inter-Rail pass, you will have to pay the port tax of approximately L.10,000 from Italy to Greece or Dr.1500 from Greece to Italy. In addition to this, Eurail passholders must pay a high-season (June–Oct) supplement of L.15,000 from Italy to Greece or Dr.2500 from Greece to Italy). A complete list of bonuses is included on the complimentary map issued with your tickets.

The basic **Eurail Pass** has no age limit. It provides first-class travel on all services and even covers most of the supplements for travelling on express and de luxe trains. It also gives free or reduced travel on many lake steamers, ferries and buses. There are several versions, valid for 15 days, 21 days, 1 month, 2 months or 3 months. Current prices range from US$538 for 15 days to US$1512 for 3 months.

The **Eurail Youth Pass** is much the same, but cheaper, as it is designed for those under 26 and is based on second-class travel. There are versions valid for 15 days (US$376), 1 month (US$605) and 2 months (US$857).

The **Eurail Flexipass** is similar to the basic Eurail pass, but allows you to travel (first class) for any 10 days (US$634) or any 15 days (US$836) within a two-month period.

The **Eurail Youth Flexipass** allows second-class travel for those under 26 within a two-month period for 10 days (US$444) and 15 days (US$585).

**Eurail Saverpass** is designed for groups of 3–5 people travelling together at all times (between 1 Oct and 31 Mar two people travelling together is allowable) and offers first-class rail travel over a 15-day period for US$458, 21 days for US$594 and 1 month for US$734.

### EuroDomino Pass

This is a catch-all title for a whole series of passes allowing unlimited travel on the national railway of an individual country (but not if you are a resident of that country). Conditions of use are the same everywhere and the options available are for any 3, 5 or 10 days within a period of one month. The passes can be purchased by non-Europeans. They cover many of the fast-train supplements.

There is no age limit, but the price depends on age. Those under 26 pay less but are restricted to second-class, while those over 26 can opt for either class. The price varies according to the size of the railway network in the country chosen. The cheapest options (of the countries covered here) are for Luxembourg: from £19 (Youth) for 3 days second-class travel to £59 for 10 days first-class travel. The most expensive passes are for Italy: at £89 and £329 respectively. 1998 prices were not updated before this book went to press. However, they are not expected to differ significantly from the previous year's prices.

Passes can be purchased up to two months before travel begins. Countries currently offering them are: Austria, Belgium, Bulgaria, Croatia, the Czech Republic, Denmark, Finland, France, Germany, Greece, Hungary, the Republic of Ireland, Italy, Luxembourg, Morocco, the Netherlands, Norway, Poland, Portugal, Romania, Slovakia, Slovenia, Spain, Sweden, Switzerland, Turkey and Yugoslavia.

In the UK, holders of any EuroDomino pass can get up to 50% discount off the rail/ferry ticket from London to a Continental port. Other ferry discounts are also available.

### Europass

Available in the USA only, Europass is valid for 5 days unlimited second-class rail travel in a 2-month period. You can also purchase up to 10 additional days of rail travel. The 5-day pass costs US$326 and additional rail days cost US$42 each. The basic cost covers France, Germany, Italy, Spain and Switzerland. 'Associate Countries' can be added to extend the geographic reach of the pass. Choose from Austria and Hungary, Belgium, Netherlands and Luxembourg, Greece and/or Portugal. Prices range from US$386 for 5 days rail travel with 1 associate country to US$446 for 5 days rail travel with 4 associate countries. Two people travelling together receive a 40% companion discount.

For those under 26 the EuroYouth Pass is available for second-class travel; for details contact the agents listed (under 'In the USA') on p. 25. Various bonuses are available and listed on the map which accompanies the rail pass.

### Rail Europ Senior Card

This card is for those over 60. It offers a discount of 30% (sometimes more) off the cost of cross-border rail travel (excluding supplements) between the participating countries: Austria, Belgium, Croatia, the Czech Republic, Denmark, Finland, France, Germany, Greece, Hungary, the Republic of Ireland, Italy, Latvia, Lithuania, Luxembourg, the Netherlands, Norway, Poland, Portugal, Romania, Russia, Slovakia, Slovenia, Spain, Sweden, Switzerland, the UK and Yugoslavia.

Most countries have a rail card for their senior citizens, which is needed to buy the Rail Europ Senior Card. In the UK, the Senior Railcard is available to people over 60 (it costs £18 per annum) The Rail Europ Senior Card, available from British Rail International, costs an extra £5. It becomes valid on the day of purchase and expires on the same date as the domestic card.

### REGIONAL EUROPEAN RAIL PASSES

### Baltic Rail Explorer Pass

Available to holders of ISIC cards (see under 'Discounts' p. 18), full-time academic staff, and people of any nationality under the age of 26, this allows unlimited rail travel in Estonia, Latvia and Lithuania for 7 days (£25), 14 days (£37) or 21 days (£49). It can be purchased from Campus Travel (see p. 25).

Once you arrive in the Baltic states, there can be occasional hassles getting the pass validated (which must be done before you board trains) and it's not as cheap as individual tickets, but still preferable unless you enjoy queuing.

### Balkan Flexipass

This pass offers unlimited first-class travel in Greece, Bulgaria, Romania, Macedonia, Montenegro, Yugoslavia and Turkey for any 5 days in one month (US$152), any 10 days in one month (US$264) or any 15 days in one month (US$317).

### Scanrail Pass

This is available in both the UK and the USA and gives unlimited travel on the national rail networks of Denmark, Finland, Norway and Sweden. It is available as a consecutive pass, which offers umlimited rail travel over a 21-day period, or a flexi pass, which is valid for either 5 days travel in a 15-day period or 10 days travel within one month.

Scanrail also offers additional discounts on many ferries and boats, long-distance buses and private railways as well as good discounts at 180 Scandinavian hotels: ask for details of the **Bonus Pass**.

It is possible to get Scanrail for first-class travel, but second-class seating is almost as comfortable and second-class seats are far more likely to be available. There is a Youth version for anyone aged 25 or less and another for seniors (60 years and over).

In the **UK** Scanrail is available from **NSB Travel Bureau**, *tel: (0171) 930 6666,* and the **International Rail Centre**, *tel: 0990 848848,* for any 5 days within a 15-day period (£132; Youth £99); any 10 days within the period of 1 month (£180; Youth £135); or 21 consecutive days (£198; Youth £149).

In the **USA** Scanrail passes are available for any 5 days in a 15-day period (US$228 for first-class travel, US$182 for second class); any 10 days in a month (US$364 first class, US$292 second class); or for a full month (US$532 first class, US$426 second class). These passes, plus Scanrail passes for young people and for those aged over 55, are available from Forsyth Travel Library (see p. 25).

Scanrail also entitles you to special rates at youth hostels in Denmark, Norway and Sweden. Scanrail passes are obtainable inside Scandinavia, but the validity is different and the ones bought prior to arrival are far better value.

### Benelux Tourrail Pass

This is available in the UK and the USA, and from train stations in Belgium and Luxembourg, but not in the Netherlands. It provides unlimited rail travel throughout Belgium, Luxembourg and the Netherlands for any 5 days in a month. For those aged 26 or more, prices are £120/US$217 in first class and

£80/US$155 in second class. When two people travel together, there is a 50% companion discount.

If you are under 26, you are restricted to second class, but pay only £60/US$104.

## Central Europe Pass

This is available in the USA only and provides unlimited rail travel throughout the Czech Republic, Germany, Poland and Slovakia for any 5 days within a month. The pass is available for first-class travel only and costs US$199. There are no youth reductions.

## Czech Republic/Slovakia Explorer Pass

Available to holders of an ISIC card (see p.18), teachers and academic staff, under 26s and accompanying spouses and children of eligible persons (from Campus Travel). Covers the Czech Republic and Slovakia for seven consecutive days (or multiples thereof), in first- or second-class.

## Youth Passes

If you are under 26, there are many other discounted tickets and passes available. Some are to single destinations or for travel in single countries, others (like the examples above) to whole groups of countries. Passes come under many different names, such as Euro-Youth, Explorer Pass and BIJ (Billets International de Jeunesse).

If the Inter-Rail/Eurail passes are too general for your needs, contact an organisation that specialises in youth travel such as **Campus Travel** or **Wasteels** (see p. 25).

### TICKETS

Always buy your ticket before travelling, unless you board at an unstaffed station, or you could face heavy penalties or even criminal prosecution. Throughout Europe tickets are easily available from many travel agents as well as at stations. Eastern Europe is a little more complicated, because rail transport systems are changing as rapidly as many other aspects of life, so finding accurate information can be difficult. On the plus side, a domestic ticket bought there is often cheaper than a ticket for exactly the same route bought outside the country.

Never buy a standard ticket without asking what discounts are available, especially if you are prepared to travel outside peak periods, such as rush hour and the weekend.

Most countries have discounts for children, but there is no set definition of what constitutes a child. They are generally classed as adults at 11/12 years, but the age at which they change from infants (who travel free) to children can range from 2 to 5 years inclusive.

Quite a few countries also offer domestic rail cards which give substantial discounts to the disabled, elderly or students – although, in most cases, the international passes already mentioned are better value.

### ADVANCE RESERVATIONS

Seats on many trains cannot be booked but, when they can, it is usually worthwhile, especially in high season and around public holidays (such as Christmas and Easter), when popular routes can fill up a long way ahead and you could spend hours standing in a crowded corridor. In some cases, you may be refused permission to board at all if there are no seats available.

For a quiet journey, with a chance to sleep, choose a seat in a compartment. For a lively journey, with conversation and panoramic views all round, choose an open carriage. In both cases, window seats are less disturbed than corridor seats. Solo travellers (particularly women) should always stick with the crowds, for security.

If you are travelling during the busy summer period and have no reservation, board your train as early as possible.

Some of the major express trains (usually marked in timetables by an 'R' in a box) are restricted to passengers with reservations, and you can usually make a reservation about two months in advance. In all cases, booking is essential if you want sleeping accommodation. Bookings can usually be made by contacting the national railway representatives of the country through which you intend to travel.

In the USA, advance reservations and sleeping-cars can be booked through **Forsyth Travel Library Inc**; *tel: (800) 367 7984* (toll-free).

## SUPPLEMENTS

Rail pass holders are often exempt from the routine surcharges applied to travel on express trains, but not always. If you opt to travel by an express service, therefore, rather than a slower alternative (there almost always is one), you should ask about supplements before committing yourself.

There will certainly be a supplement for special high-speed services (such as the French *TGV,* the German *ICE,* the Swedish *X2000,* Eurostar Italia, Eurostar trains and Spanish *AVE* services), which have higher-than-normal fares for ordinary tickets.

Holders of a first-class Eurail Pass can use most of the special services without paying extra, but even they should check its validity if they want to use one of the new breed of luxury trains.

There's usually a fee for reserving seats but it is seldom large and is normally included in the supplementary payments for the faster trains. Sleeping accommodation (see p.31) always attracts charges of some kind. Sort out the extras before you start your journey – and make sure you know exactly what you are paying for. You may be able to pay the supplements on the train, but it almost always costs more than doing it in advance.

## TYPES OF TRAIN

Many of the best daytime international trains are now branded EuroCity (or **EC**). To qualify, trains have to be fast and offer a certain standard of service, such as food and drink during the journey. All have names, and the EuroCity network continues to expand, now including countries such as the Czech Republic and Poland. Eurostar trains are now in operation through the Channel Tunnel (see Sea Crossings, p. 99).

Many overnight trains carry names as well as numbers; some, such as the *Nord Express* and *Train Bleu,* having long histories. Most are just ordinary trains, but there is a new breed of high-quality night service known as EuroNight (**EN**) with air-conditioned coaches and extras such as evening drinks and breakfast, which are available even to couchette passengers.

The **IC** or InterCity label is applied by many countries to the fast long-distance trains, although there are slight variations in what they provide. The **ICE** (InterCity Express) designation also crops up in several countries, but is mostly applied to the latest high-speed trains in Germany. **IR** is the classification for inter-regional express services which make more stops than InterCity services; it is used mainly in Germany (where it stands for 'Inter-Regio') and in Italy (where it's short for 'Interregionale'). These names are all used to distinguish the faster long-distance trains from local or stopping trains. Types of train unique to a specific country are described in the Country by Country section (pp.33–97).

Most longer-distance trains in Europe offer both first- and second-class travel, but second class is the norm for local stopping services. Where overnight trains offer seating accommodation, this is usually second class only. As a rule, in Western Europe, second class is perfectly OK for all but the most ardent comfort-seeker. A few Eastern European services still leave a lot to be desired, but tickets are very cheap and it's worth paying a little more to upgrade to first class.

## FINDING YOUR TRAIN

In small stations, you are faced with a limited choice of platforms and can usually find a friendly soul to point you in the right direction. Most large stations have electronic departure boards or large paper timetables (often yellow for departures and white for arrivals) which list the routes, the times of departure, the relevant platforms and the arrival times at larger places. They are usually kept reasonably up to date, but watch out for nasty surprises, such as the seemingly ideal train which only runs on the third Sunday in August. In some stations, the platforms are also labelled with details of regular trains or the next departure and may even give the location of special carriages and the facilities on board.

If a platform is long it is possible that two trains will be leaving it at the same time, going in opposite directions, so double-check that you are boarding in the correct place: the trains often have destination boards on each carriage. It is necessary to be a little careful even when there is only one train, because quite a few split en route, with only some carriages going the full distance.

If you have a reservation, all you need do is board 'your' carriage (they are all numbered, usually on cards by the entrance). If you are not booked and the destination boards are unclear, ask an official for assistance: if officials speak no English, showing your ticket should be enough for them to put you in the right portion of the train.

First-class coaches usually have a yellow stripe along the top of the windows and large number '1's on the side of the coach, on the door or on the windows. No-smoking coaches (the majority) are distinguished by signs, usually of a cigarette with a red cross, or one red band, over it.

A sign near the compartment door often gives seat numbers and sometimes indicates which are reserved. In non-compartment trains, seats are usually numbered individually (on the back or on the luggage rack) and reserved seats may have labels attached to their head-rests (or the luggage racks). In many countries, however, reserved seats are not marked – so be prepared to move if someone who has booked boards the train.

Station announcements are often unintelligible, even if they are in your own language, but are sometimes important. If you hear one that you don't understand shortly before your train is due to leave, ask someone nearby whether the announcement concerned your train. The ideal is to find an official, but other travellers are often helpful. If a lot of people near you start to move away hurriedly, there has probably been a change of platform and, if you ask enough of them, you might actually find the new platform before the train pulls out.

## OVERNIGHT TRAINS

A night on the train, being rocked to sleep by the clatter of the wheels, is not to be missed. Sleeping-cars can cost about the same as a hotel but have the advantage of covering large distances as you rest and you won't waste precious holiday time in transit. You can also save quite a bit of money, if you are prepared to use couchettes or to curl up on the ordinary

seats. Don't do this too often without a break, however, or you will end up totally exhausted. The chatter of other passengers, the coming and going at stations and even the regular checks to make sure you still have all your bags can lead to a disturbed night. Take earplugs and an eye-mask and, as there are often no refreshment facilities, take plenty of water and a supply of biscuits with you.

If you have a rail pass and the night train is due to reach your next destination too early in the morning, consider booking to a town an hour or so further along the line; you can then get some extra sleep and backtrack to the place you actually want to visit on an early train – but don't forget to check the timetables to ensure that there is a suitable early train back!

In Eastern Europe, you may be woken for Customs and Immigration checks, which can involve a search of luggage or the compartment/berth. Within Western Europe, it's unlikely you'll notice the borders, even if you're awake, and it's highly unlikely you will be disturbed. Attendants will give you an alarm call if you tell them you are leaving the train before the final destination – specify the stop rather than the time, so you can sleep longer if the train runs late. If you want to go to sleep before other passengers have arrived, switch on their berth lights and switch off the main overhead light. Before boarding, sort out the things you will need for the night and put them somewhere easily accessible (preferably in a small separate bag), as busy compartments don't allow much room for searching through luggage.

Sleepers and couchettes can usually be reserved up to three months in advance; early booking is recommended as space is limited. If you don't have a booking, it's still worth asking the conductor once on board. Keep some local currency handy to pay him.

## SLEEPING ACCOMMODATION

Sleeping-cars have bedroom-style compartments with limited washing facilities (usually just a wash-basin) and full bedding. WCs are located at one or both ends of the coach. An attendant travels with each car, or pair of cars, and there are sometimes facilities for drinks and/or breakfast – but be prepared to pay extra.

First-class sleeping compartments usually have one or two berths and second-class compartments have two or three berths. However, there are some special sleeping-cars (described as 'T2' in schedules) which have only one berth in first class and two in second class. An exception to the norm is Spain: their T2 cars are first class and their Talgo trains have four berths in second class.

Unless your group takes up all the berths, compartments are allocated to a single sex and small unaccompanied children are placed in female compartments. In Estonia, Latvia and Lithuania berths are allocated on a first-come, first-served basis without regard to sex. You should claim your berth within 15 minutes of boarding the train or it may be reallocated.

Couchettes are more basic – and much cheaper. They consist of simple bunk beds with a sheet, blanket and pillow. They are converted from the ordinary seats at night and there are usually four berths in first class and six in second class, with washing facilities and WCs at the end of each coach. Males and females are booked into the same compartment and expected to sleep in their daytime clothes.

In a few cases (notably Italy), overnight trains have airline-style reclining seats, which are allocated automatically when you make a seat reservation. These are sometimes free if you have a rail pass.

### WASHING

Showers are still rare in European trains, but a few of the luxury-class compartments include them, such as *Gran Clase* cars on the overnight Spanish Talgos, and *Intercity Natt* cars in Sweden.

In the last few years, 'hotel' trains, with showers and toilets in some compartments, have been introduced on certain routes. These are designated *CityNightLine* or *InterCityNight* – **CNL** trains run on several routes between Germany and Austria or Switzerland, whereas **ICN** trains are found on internal routes within Germany. A few rail stations have low-cost showers for public use.

### EATING

Most long-distance trains in Europe have dining-cars serving full meals and/or buffet cars selling drinks and snacks. There is an increasing tendency for refreshments to be served aircraft-style from a trolley wheeled through the train. Dining-cars are sometimes red or indicated by a red band above the windows and doors. Quite a few services offer full meals only to first-class passengers, while others, such as some Spanish services, offer nothing but a full-scale, four-course production. Dining-cars often have set times for full meals. Buffets are usually open to both classes and serve for longer periods, but even they may not be available for the whole journey.

Always take emergency rations, including a full water-bottle and a packet of biscuits. Food and drink are usually expensive on trains so, if you need to save money, take a picnic. Long stops at East European frontiers may allow time to get out and buy food and drink. This is risky: get permission from the control officers, check that you have the right currency and make sure you have enough time.

### BAGGAGE

Lockers are invaluable if you want to look round a place without carrying heavy baggage and most stations (and other transport hubs) have them. The initial payment generally covers 24 hrs, but you are allowed to stay longer (usually up to a week, but check). The newest lockers have display panels and are automatic: you simply pay any excess when you return. With older lockers, you have to pay the excess to station staff (at the left-luggage office, if there is one). Baggage trolleys (where available) are usually free, but often supermarket-style: you need a coin to release them – which you get back when you return them to a stand.

Colour section: (i) Funicular railway from Lauterbrunnen (see p.556); Hamburg Station (p.234); inset, Linköping Station (p.198).

(ii) Brussels Station (see p.149); insets, train interiors.

(iii) Scandinavian Seaways Ferry; Copenhagen to Malmö catamaran (p.197).

(iv) Amsterdam (p.100): Amsterdam Central Station and view of a canal.

# COUNTRY BY COUNTRY

## AUSTRIA

**Capital:** Vienna *(Wien)*. **Language:** German; English is widely spoken in tourist areas. **Currency:** Schilling (ÖS); 1 Schilling = 100 Groschen.

### Passports and Visas
An EU National Identity Card is sufficient. Visas are not needed by nationals of Australia, Canada, New Zealand or the USA. Others should check.

### Customs
EU nationals may import tax and duty paid items for personal use. Non-EU residents arriving from outside Europe may bring 200 cigarettes or 50 cigars or 250g tobacco, 1 litre spirits and 2 litres wine or 3 litres beer and may bring other commodities duty free to a value of ÖS2500; ÖS1000 from the Czech or Slovak Republics or Slovenia.

### Tourist Information
There is a tourist information service of some sort in almost every small town and even village in Austria. Staff invariably speak some English. Bear in mind that opening times vary widely, and are particularly restricted at weekends in out of the way places. The green 'i' is the sign to look out for, although the official name does vary – **Fremdenverkehrsbüro** is one of the most common.

### Useful Addresses
**Australia: Embassy**, *12 Talbot St, Forrest, ACT 2603, Canberra tel: (62) 951376.* **National Tourist Office**, *1st Floor, 36 Carrington St, Sydney NSW 2000, tel: (2) 9299 3621.*
**Canada: Embassy**, *445 Wilbrod St, Ottawa, Ontario KIN 6M7; tel: 789 1444.* **National Tourist Office**, *2 Bloor St E./Suite 3330, Toronto, Ontario M4W 1A8, tel: (416) 9673381.*
**Republic of Ireland: Embassy**, *15 Ailesbury Court Appts, 93 Ailesbury Rd, Dublin 4; tel: (1) 2694577.*
**South Africa: Embassy**, *1109 Duncan St, Momentum Office Park, 0011 Brooklyn, Pretoria; tel: (12) 463361.* **National Tourist Office**, *Private Bag X18, Parklands 2121 Jo'burg; tel: (11) 4427235.*
**UK: Embassy**, *18 Belgrave Mews West, London SW1X 8HU; tel: (0171) 235 3731.* **National Tourist Office and Railways**, *PO Box 2363, London W1A 2QB; tel: (0171) 629 0461.*
**USA: Embassy**, *3524 International Court N.W., Washington DC 20008; tel: (202) 895 6700.* **National Tourist Office**, *PO Box 1142 New York NY 10108-1142; tel: (212) 944 6880, or 11601 Wilshire Blvd, Suite 2480, Los Angeles, CA 90025; tel: (310) 477 3332.*

## STAYING IN AUSTRIA

### Accommodation
The **Austrian National Tourist Office** can supply information about all types of accommodation, including camping. **Hotels** are graded on the usual five-star system, but even one-star establishments are pricey. *Gasthaus/Gasthof* indicates an **inn** and *Frühstückspension* a **Bed and Breakfast** place. The best value is usually a **private room** (look for *Zimmer frei* signs), but many require stays of several nights and some charge extra for short stays. *Jugendherberge* is the word for a **youth hostel**. In summer, some universities let rooms.

**Camping** is popular and there are lots of sites. Standards are high, with cleanliness and efficiency the keynotes; the down-side is the high prices. Many sites are open summer only. In Alpine areas there are also refuge huts – details from the local Tourist Office. For all accommodation it is advisable to book ahead for July, Aug, Christmas and Easter.

Several resorts, indicated by **GC** next to Tourist Office details, issue a guest card to visitors in higher quality accommodation. The cards entitle holders to anything from free

**33**

escorted mountain hikes to discounts for ferries or museums. The cards are generally issued by *Gasthofs* or hotels.

## Eating and Drinking

The Austrian pattern is: continental breakfast, lunch (1200–1400), coffee and cake mid-afternoon, then dinner (1800–2200). Lunch is usually more expensive in cafés than in restaurants. Drinks in bars and clubs cost more than in eating places. A filling snack, sold by most butchers, is *Wurstsemmel* – slices of sausage with a bread roll. Beer is the most popular drink, but Austrian wine is good and there are multiple *Schnapps* varieties. A service charge of 10–15% is included in restaurant bills. It is the custom to leave a further 5% if happy with the service.

## Communications

**Post offices** can be recognised by a golden trumpet symbol and are often located close to the station or main square. They all handle poste restante *(postlagernde Briefe)*. Nationwide hours are Mon–Fri 0800–1200 and 1400–1800, but offices in major towns tend to stay open during lunch and on Sat. The main post offices in cities frequently open 24 hrs. Stamps *(Briefmarke)* can also be purchased at *Tabak/Trafik* shops.

    **Telephones:** It is quite easy to use ordinary pay-phones. Most boxes have instructions in English and most international operators speak it. Even remote places have booths that take telephone cards *(Wertkarten),* slightly cheaper than cash, available from post offices, stations and some shops, or there are metered phones in post offices where payment is made afterwards. Long distance calls are approximately 35% cheaper between 1800 and 0800 and public holidays. To call abroad from Austria: *tel: 00.* To call Austria: *tel: 00 43.* To call international enquiries and operator: *tel: 08.* Note that other dialling codes are not yet uniform. Post office phone counters can give the correct ones to use locally. To call national enquiries and operator: *tel: 16 11.* **Emergencies:** Police: *133*; Fire: *122*; Ambulance: *144.*

## Opening Hours

**Banks:** in Vienna – Mon, Tues, Wed, Fri 0800–1230 and 1330–1500, Thur 0800–1230

and 1330–1730 (some stay open through the lunch hour). Elsewhere, the norm is Mon–Fri 0800–1230 and 1330–1500. **Shops:** Mon–Fri 0800–1830, Sat 0800–1300 (in larger towns many stay open until 1700 on Saturdays.) **Museums:** there is no real pattern to opening times so check locally.

## Public Holidays

1, 6 Jan; Easter Mon; 1 May; Ascension Day; Whit Mon; Corpus Christi; 15 Aug; 26 Oct; 1 Nov; 8, 25, 26 Dec. Many people take unofficial holidays on Good Fri, Easter Sun, Whit Sun, 2 Nov, 24 Dec and 31 Dec.

## Public Transport

The efficient Austrian **long-distance bus system** is run by **Bundesbus**. It is generally based by rail stations or post offices, and serves places inaccessible to trains.

    All cities have excellent **bus** and/or **tram** systems. It is possible to buy tickets on board, but cheaper to get them in advance from *Tabak/Trafik* booths. They are validated in a little machine on board, often marked with an 'E' *(Entwerter).* Major cities have cards for one or more day's travel.

    **Taxis** in larger cities charge by officially controlled meters; extra charges for luggage. In smaller towns there are fixed charges and fares for longer distances are agreed beforehand.

### RAIL TRAVEL WITHIN AUSTRIA

The national rail company is **Österreichische Bundesbahnen (ÖBB)**. Most lines are electrified and the railway system is fast and reliable, with *IC* trains every 1–2 hrs and regional trains timed to connect with *IC* services. Other fast trains are: *D* (ordinary express trains); *E* (semi-fast or local trains); *EC* and *EN (*with stops only in larger cities). Most overnight trains have sleeping-cars (up to three berths) and couchettes (four or six berths). Most overnight trains also convey seated accommodation, but often second-class only.

    Seat reservations cost ÖS20–50, depending on distance. A higher tariff is charged for travel on EC trains. The difference may be paid in advance, or on the train, where it is costs more. They can be made up to three months in advance for sleeping-cars and two months in advance for couchettes.

Almost every station offers left luggage facilities, and most hold an accommodation leaflet or town map.

### Fares and Passes

**Österreich-Puzzle** and **Österreich-Puzzle Junior** (under 26) entitle holders of this pass to unlimited travel over ÖBB and private railways within each zone – divided into West, Süd, Nord and Ost. An ID photo is necessary. They are valid for any 4 days within a 10 day period. In addition, the pass includes 50% discount on **ÖBB Bodensee Schiffen** (Lake Constance ships) and **DDSG Donau Reisen** (Danube cruises). Prices: ÖS1740 (first class) or ÖS1090 (second class), and for under-26s ÖS1060 (first class) or ÖS660 (second class).

The **Bundes-Netzkarte** is valid for a month's travel on ÖBB and private railways, including rack-railways and the Wolfgangsee lake lines. It costs ÖS4300 second class or ÖS 5900 first class. With this pass, there is no supplement to pay on EC-trains. Conditions and discounts as with Österreich Puzzle.

The **VORTEILScard** (ÖS1190) and **VORTEILScart Senior** (men over 65 and women over 60; ÖS350) are valid on the whole Austrian network (including most private railways), and entitle the holder to 50% discount on train tickets for a 1 year period. They also offer special rates for bicycle hire at Austrian Railways train stations, or with hire companies such as Arac, Avis, Hertz, Europcar. **Group excursions** (six or more persons travelling together) are entitled to a reduction of up to 30% for journeys up to 100 km, 40% from 101 km. Children get a 60% discount. Special booking procedures are necessary. Contact larger train stations in Austria for details.

### Rail Pass Concessions

| Operator, Route/Concession | Rail Pass/Discount |
|---|---|
| ÖBB St. Wolfgang Schafbergbahnhof –Schafbergspitze | IR 50% |
| ÖBB Zahnradbahn–Schneeberg | IR 10% |
| ÖBB Zahnradbahn–Schafberg | IR 10% |
| ÖBB Zahnradbahn–Wolfgangseeschiffahrt | IR 10% |
| ÖBB Zahnradbahn–Bodenseeschiffahrt | IR 10% |

| ÖBB Cycle Hire at 150 stations | IR 50% |
|---|---|
| StLB Peggau/Deutschfeistritz–Übelbach | IR 50% |
| StLB Unzmarkt–Tamsweg | IR 50% |
| DWK Linz–Passau | IR 50% |
| DDSG Melk/Krems–Vienna | IR 15% |
| Graz Köflacher Eisenbahn – und | RES 30% |
| Bergbau – Gesellschaft | RES 30% |
| Steiermärkische Landesbahnen | RES 30% |
| Montafoner Bahn | RES 30% |
| AG der Wiener Lokalbahnen | RES 30% |
| DWK Linz–Passau | EP 50% |
| DDSG Melk/Krems–Wien | EP 15% |
| Schneeberg rack railway | EP 10% |
| Schafberg rack railway | EP 10% |
| Steamer services on Wolfgang See | EP 10% |
| Steamer services on Lake Constance | EP 10% |

## BELGIUM

**Capital:** Brussels *(Bruxelles/Brussel)*. **Language:** Belgium has three official languages, in different areas: Flemish (north), French (south) and German (east). Most Belgians speak both French and Flemish. Many (especially the young) also speak reasonable English and/or German. **Currency:** Belgian Francs (BFr.).

### Passports and Visas

An EU National Identity Card is sufficient. Visas are not needed by nationals of Australia, Canada, New Zealand or the USA. South Africans do require visas.

### Customs

Standard EU regulations apply (see p.17), but there's an extra allowance of 8 litres of Luxembourg wines, if imported directly from the country.

### Tourist Information

Very useful full-colour brochures are the annual *Guide Tourist Attractions and Museums* and the less frequently updated *Belgium Historic Cities*. Both cover the whole country and are available free from Belgian Tourist Offices outside the country, as are brochures covering all types of accommodation and a map of central Brussels.

Tourist Office translates as **Office du Tourisme** in French, **Toerisme** in Flemish and **Verkehrsamt** in German, but all display the white 'i' on a green background. Most have English-speaking staff and provide free English literature on most subjects, but charge for walking itineraries and good street maps. Opening hours, especially in small places and off-season, are flexible.

## Useful Address

**Australia: Embassy**, *Arkana St, Yarralumla, Canberra, ACT 2600; tel: (06) 273 2501.*
**Canada: Embassy**, *80 Elgin St (4th Floor), Ottawa, Ontariao K1P 1B7; tel: (613) 236 7267.*
**New Zealand: Embassy**, *Willis Coroon House (2nd Floor), 1–3 Willeston St, Wellington; tel: (04) 472 9558.*
**South Africa: Embassy**, *625 Leyds St, Muckleneuk, 0002 Pretoria; tel: (012) 44 3201.*
**UK: Embassy**, *103 Eaton Sq., Victoria, London SW1W 9AB; tel: (0171) 235 5422.* **Tourist Office**, *29 Princes St, London W1R 7RG; tel: (0891) 887799* (this also gives visa information). **Belgian National Railways**, *Premier House, 10 Greycoat Pl., London SW1P 1SB; tel: (0891) 516444* – although premium-rate, this is not a recording during working hours.
**USA: Embassy**, *3330 Garfield St N.W., Washington DC 20008; tel: (202) 333-6900.* **Tourist Office**, *745 Fifth Ave, New York, NY 10151; tel: (212) 758 8130.*

### STAYING IN BELGIUM

## Accommodation

The Benelux countries (Belgium, Netherlands and Luxembourg) have a common hotel-rating system. The lowest is 'O' (accommodation only, but meeting minimum requirements of hygiene and comfort); the next is 'H' (moderately comfortable, with at least one bathroom per ten rooms). After that, you're on to the usual star system, one-star places being obliged (as a minimum) to have a wash-stand in every room and to serve breakfast.

**Hotels** tend to be pricey and you're unlikely to get anything for less than BFr.1000 (BFr.700 single). Tourist Offices don't charge for booking hotels (the deposit is deducted from your bill), and can often get reduced rates. They sometimes agree to check availability of other accommodation.

In summer, accommodation of all kinds can be hard to find and it's sensible to pre-book, especially in Bruges and on the coast. **Belgium Tourist Reservations**, *blvd Anspach 111, rte 4,*

*1000 Brussels; tel: (00) 32 2513 7484, fax: (00) 32 2513 9277,* offer a free service for hotel reservations.

A **Bed and Breakfast** guide is available from **Taxistop**, *Onderbergen 51, 9000 Gent; tel: (09) 223 23 10,* but they require stamps (6 x BFr.15) to cover postage. A leaflet covering officially-rated **campsites** should be available from your nearest Belgian Tourist Office. It lists provincial tourist authorities, from whom further information is available. Rough camping is not permitted, but some farmers may give you permission to use their land.

## Eating and Drinking

Most restaurants have good-value fixed-price menus *(plat du jour, tourist menu, dagschotel).* There's a wide variation in prices; establishments in the main squares can charge two or three times as much as similar places in nearby streets.

Try waffles *(wafels/gaufres)* and pancakes *(crêpes)* – sweet and savoury, mussels *(moules)* and freshly baked pastries. The most common snacks are *frites/frituurs/frites* (french fries with mayonnaise or other sauce) and (delicious) ice-cream. Candies are ubiquitous, notably nougat and the deservedly famous chocolates, but be warned: the ones containing cream have a very short shelf-life.

Tea comes as teabags with lemon unless you specify milk (you'll get cream), but the coffee and hot chocolate are delicious. It's easy (though not cheap) to get freshly squeezed orange and lemon. Many bottled juices are refreshingly low on sugar. Belgium produces literally hundreds of beers (both dark and light).

## Communications

Major **post offices** *(Postes/Posterijen/De Post)* open Mon–Fri 0900–1700 (some also open Fri evening and Sat morning). Stamps can be purchased at most places that sell postcards. Postboxes are smallish and bright red.

**Telephones:** Coin boxes, which are quite rare (5 or 20 BFr. coins), and phonecard booths all have English instructions. Phonecards are available at rail stations, post offices and some tobacconists. Most international calls are reduced Mon–Sat 2000–0800 and all day Sun. Numbers prefixed 077 are at premium rates.

To call abroad from Belgium; *tel: 00*. To call Belgium; *tel: 00 32*. National operator; *tel: 1307 (1207* in Flemish areas). International operator; *tel: 1304 (1204* in Flemish areas). International operators speak English. **Emergencies:** Police: *101;* Fire/Ambulance: *100*.

## Opening Hours

Many establishments close for lunch 1200–1400. **Banks:** Mon–Fri 0900–1600. **Shops:** Mon–Sat 0900/1000–1800/1900 (often later Fri/Sat). **Museums:** considerable variation, but most open six days a week: 1000–1700 (usually Tues–Sun or Wed–Mon). Small places and churches are unpredictable and can be closed at any time.

## Public Holidays

1 Jan; Easter Mon; 1 May; Ascension Day; Whit Mon; 21 July; 15 Aug; 1, 11 Nov; 25 Dec. Transport and places that open usually keep Sun times.

## Public Transport

The national bus companies are **De Lijn**, *r. Bara 107, 1070 Brussels; tel: 2526 2811,* in Flemish areas, and **Tec**, *av. Einstein 9, 1388 Louvain-la-Neuve; tel: 1048 0404,* in French areas, but there are few long-distance buses, except where the rail network is scanty. Main rail and bus stations are usually close together.

In **buses, trams** and **metros**, you generally open the doors yourself. When there are no handles, there's a button or black strip that you press. With a ticket, board at the nearest door. Without one, board at the front and buy it from the driver. Disembark by a rear door.

Each city has a **multi-ride card** *(Z-Kaart),* normally valid for ten rides, which pays its way on the seventh journey. They must be validated in each new vehicle, but nothing is deducted if your journey began less than an hour before. Multi-ride cards are available from transport and Tourist Offices. Fares depend on the length of the journey – split into fare stages. Metro station signs bear a white letter 'M' on a blue background. Tram and bus stops have red and white signs (all stops are request stops; raise your hand to indicate that the bus should stop).

**Taxis** have roof signs, but drivers seldom stop in the street, so find a rank or telephone. The rate doubles if you leave the city limits.

## RAIL TRAVEL WITHIN BELGIUM

The national railway system is **SNCB** (in the French language) or **NMBS** (in Flemish). For nationwide enquiries; *tel: (00) 32 2203 3640* (in French), or *(00) 32 2203 2880* (in Flemish), manned 0600–2230. Information offices with the rail logo ('B' in an oval) seldom give information about anything except trains.

Belgium's rail network is comprehensive and reliable, with fast services linking the cities (usually hourly). Free timetables are available at stations. Sleeping-cars/couchettes are of normal European type. Seat reservations are possible only for international journeys. Don't bank on refreshments being available. To open the doors you have to press a button (inside and out).

## Stations

Bear in mind that trains can leave simultaneously from different ends of the same platform, so check the information signs at both ends and board at the end that shows your destination.

The smallest stations have few, if any, facilities. Others have at least WCs, telephones, a left-luggage facility and snacks. Many have bike-hire facilities. There are usually two sets of timetables: one for Mon–Fri, the other for Sat, Sun and holidays. Most train information gives both French and Flemish versions of names (there's often little similarity).

## Fares and Passes

Individual tickets can be purchased up to five days in advance, but you must specify the date of travel. You can buy them on the train (provided you tell the conductor before you board), but there's a supplement if you do this. It's possible to upgrade your class of travel on board. If you have the type of pass where you nominate your own days of travel, you must fill in each date *before* you board.

For the **Benelux Tourrail Pass**, see p.28.

For those aged 12–25, **Go Pass** (BFr.1490) provides ten second-class journeys over a 6-month period, but not before 0745 on working weekdays (except July–Aug, when there are no time restrictions). The **Reductie Kaart/Carte**

**de Réduction** (BFr.600), entitles you to purchase half-price tickets for both classes, valid for one month (some restrictions apply).

**Nettreinkaart/Carte Train Réseau** allows one week's travel over the whole network for BFr.2250 (second class). Monthly, three-monthly and annual tickets are also available. A **Multi Pass** ticket is available for groups of 2–5 people travelling second class, when at least one member of the group is over 26 years old. It allows two single journeys or one return trip, and is valid for two months. The same time restrictions as Go Pass apply.

The **Weekend** ticket gives a 40% discount on a return ticket anywhere in Belgium with a maximum fare of BFr.700. A 60% reduction is available for the second to sixth travellers in a group with a maximum of BFr.480. It is valid for 4 days, for outward travel on Fridays and weekends, and return on weekends and Mondays. Validity is extended on holiday weekends.

**Benelux Weekend** ticket gives 25% reduction on returns to the Netherlands and Luxembourg for the first person and 40% to the Netherlands or Luxembourg for the second to sixth person in a group. Valid for outward travel from 1600 Thur–2400 Sun, and return travel after 0000 Sat–2400 Mon. Validity can be extended on public holidays.

## Rail Pass Concessions

| Operator, Route/Concession | Rail Pass/Discount |
|---|---|
| Transport Museum, Brussels (Nord Station) | IR free or reduced entry |
| Great Britain and N. Ireland–London–Oostende | IR 26- 34% |
| Eurostar | RES Senior rate |
| Holyman Sally Ferries Oostende–Ramsgate | RES 30% |
| Holyman Sally Ferries Ramsgate–Oostende/Dunkerque | FP 50% |
| Eurostar (Britain, France and Belgium passes only) | FP Passholder fare |
| Eurostar    EP Reduced rate on supplement to be paid | |
| Thalys high-speed trains Paris Nord–Brussels and Amsterdam | EP Reduced fare |

## BULGARIA

**Capital:** Sofia *(Sofija)*. **Language:** Bulgarian, a Slavic tongue which uses the Cyrillic alphabet. English, German, Russian and French are all spoken in larger hotels, restaurants and shops in main cities and resorts. Body language can be confusing as nodding the head up and down indicates 'no' *(ne)* and shaking it from side to side means 'yes' *(da)*. **Currency:** Leva (Lv.); 1 Leva = 100 stotinki. Local currency can be obtained only within Bulgaria and should be re-exchanged for hard currency before going through customs control. There is no restriction on the amount of foreign currency you can bring in, but amounts above $5000, or equivalent, should be declared, with exportable amounts being limited to the amount declared at import. Some goods, such as antiques or works of art, may be liable for export duty, you should check with the vendors. Receipts *(bordereaux)* will be given for every exchange transaction and when you pay for accommodation. These must be retained as they may be needed when you leave. Travellers arriving and leaving by train might find customs officials and border police over vigilant as they operate a policy of zero tolerance of even minor infringements of the rules and enforce hard currency fines. However, recent government decisions should lead to an improvement in this situation.

Major credit cards are accepted in larger hotels, restaurants and shops, and their use is spreading fast.

### Passports and Visas

A full passport is required by all visitors, with six months of validity remaining. Visa regulations were considerably relaxed in 1997, so holders of ordinary passports of EC countries no longer need visas for stays of up to 30 days. Travellers from Australia, New Zealand, Canada and South Africa need not have visas if they are on package holidays or can present Travel Agency vouchers on arrival for pre-paid accommodation and tourist services in Bulgaria. Further information can be obtained from the appropriate consulates or embassies (see below).

All visitors should register at a hotel, campsite or guesthouse within 48 hrs of arrival, using the **carte statistique**, which you obtain at the point of entry. Take care of this and make sure it is date-stamped every time you check into and out of any form of accommodation. The stamps will be checked as you leave Bulgaria.

## Customs
The allowances are: 200 cigarettes, or 50 cigars, or 250g of tobacco products, 1 litre of spirits, 2 litres of wine, and 100g of perfume.

## Useful Addresses
**Australia: Consulate–General**, *1/4 Carlotta Rd, Double Bay, Sydney NSW 2028; tel: (02) 372 7592.*
**Canada: Embassy**, *325 Stewart St, Ottawa, Ontario K1n 6K5; tel: (613) 789 3215.*
**South Africa: Embassy**, *Techno Plaza E., 305 Brooks St, Melo Park, Pretoria; tel: (012) 342 3721.*
**UK: Consular Section, Embassy of the Republic of Bulgaria**, *186/188 Queen's Gate, London SW7 5HL; tel: (0171) 584 9433.*
**British Bulgarian Society**, *Finsbury Library (Basement), 245 St John St, London EC1V 4NB; tel: (0171) 837 2304.*
**USA: Embassy**, *1621 22nd Street N.W., Washington DC 20008-1921; tel: (202) 387 7969.* **Balkan Holidays**, *Suite 508, 41 East 42nd St, New York, NY 10017; tel: (212) 573 5530.*

## STAYING IN BULGARIA

## Accommodation
In Sofia, particularly at the airport, railway station and in the city centre, various agencies offer accommodation booking, information and exchange facilities. The main hotels also have information desks which can be useful.

## Eating and Drinking
Bulgaria produces a wide variety of excellent fruits and vegetables. Soups are also popular year round, with cold ones, based on the world's finest yoghurt, available in summer. Salads are varied and good. Meat is generally pork or lamb, either cooked slowly with vegetables or grilled. Desserts include seasonal fruit, ice-creams, gateaux and sweet pastries. Vegetarians can eat salads and dishes such as stuffed peppers or aubergine dishes like *kyopolou*.

Tea is often herbal or Chinese and served without milk. Coffee is normally espresso. Bottled fruit juices are cheap and readily available, as are imported soft drinks in cans. The local beers are European lager style and excellent value. *Grozdova, slivova* and *mastika* are strong drinks, served in large measures, traditionally accompanying cold starters. Tap water is safe to drink and there are many good local mineral waters. The quality and good value of Bulgarian wine is, of course, famous.

## Communications
**Postage:** Stamps *(marki)* can be bought only from post offices *(poshta),* which are usually open Mon–Sat 0800–1730. Some may close at midday for two hours.

**Telephones:** Coin boxes are fine for local calls, but use the central telephone office (which may not necessarily be in the post office) in major towns if you want to phone further afield. To call abroad from Bulgaria dial *00* and the country code. To call Bulgaria from abroad dial *00 359.* International operator: *tel: 0123;* local operator: *tel: 121.* Directory enquiries: *991* (international), *144* (private); *145* (state and office). **Emergencies:** Police: *166;* Fire: *160;* Ambulance: *150.*

## Opening Hours
**Banks:** Mon–Fri 0900–1500. Some exchange offices are open at the weekends and for longer hours. **Shops:** Mon–Sat 0800–1900. Outside major towns, shops close between 1200–1400. **Museums:** vary widely, but often 0800–1830, with a break from 1200–1400. Many are closed on either Mon or Tues.

## Public Holidays
1 Jan; 3 Mar; Orthodox Easter Sunday and Monday, dates variable; 1, 24 May; 25 Dec.

## Public Transport
There are good rail and long-distance bus networks. **Buses** are slightly more expensive than trains, but both are very cheap for hard currency travellers. At small stops, you can only buy your bus ticket when the bus has arrived and it is clear how many spaces are available.

Local **city transport** runs frequently, but, as in most cities, is crowded during rush hour. In Sofia, buses and trams use the same tickets – each ride costs less than 10 pence. Daily and weekly cards, which make travel even cheaper, are also available.

### RAIL TRAVEL WITHIN BULGARIA

The national rail company is **Bulgarian State Railways (BDŽ)**.

The rail system is fairly comprehensive and there are three types of train: express, fast and slow. Journeys on the electrified lines between Sofia and other major cities are fast. Elsewhere, electrification is not complete and you should be prepared to travel more slowly.

Trains are very busy and seat reservations are recommended (obligatory for express trains). All medium- and long-distance trains have first- and second-class carriages and a limited buffet service. Overnight trains between Sofia and the Black Sea resorts have first- and second-class sleeping cars and second-class couchettes.

### Stations

Station indicator boards can be confusing. One platform may serve two tracks, and platforms and tracks are both numbered. Notices and signs at stations are in Cyrillic; so learn what the name of your destination looks like and ask when the train is due to arrive, so that you don't have to rely just on spotting a sign. A good route map can also be helpful.

### Fares and Passes

With the exception of Sofia Central Railway Station, which has an international ticket counter, only domestic tickets are available from stations. **Rila Travel**, with offices in all cities, handles international travel. Even for local journeys, it's better to buy your ticket in advance, as there are usually large queues at stations. You can buy tickets on the trains but that is more expensive. Rail fares are good value. A supplement has to be paid to use express trains.

## CROATIA

**Capital:** Zagreb. **Language:** Croatian, a Slavic language, written in Roman characters with five extra letters: ć, č, đ, š and ž. English, German and Italian are spoken in the tourist areas. **Currency:** Kuna (Kn); 1 Kuna = 100 Lipa. Major credit cards are widely accepted.

### Passports and Visas

All visitors require full passports. EU, American, Canadian and USA passport holders do not require visas. South African nationals must apply for a 3 month tourist visa.

### Customs

The allowances are: 200 cigarettes, or 50 cigars, or 250g tobacco products, 1 litre spirits.

### Useful Addresses

**Australia: Embassy**, *14 Jindalee Crescent, O'Malley Act 2606, Canberra; tel: (6) 286 69 88.*
**Canada: Embassy**, *130 Albert St, Suite 1700, Ottawa, Ontario, K1P 5G4; tel: (613) 230 73 51.*
**New Zealand: Consulate**, *131 Lincoln Rd, Henderson, P.O. Box, 83200 Edmonton Auckland; tel: (9) 83 65 581.*
**South Africa: Embassy**, *1160 Church St, 0083 Colbyn Pretoria, PO Box 11335, 0028 Hatfield; (12) 342 1206.*
**UK: Embassy**, *21 Conway St, London, W1P 5HL; tel: (0171) 387 1790 or 387 2022.*
**Croatian National Tourist Office**, *2 The Lanchesters, 162-164 Fulham Palace Rd, London, W6 9ER; tel: (0181) 563 79 79.*
**USA: Embassy**, *2343 Massachusetts Ave, N.W. Washington DC, 20008-2803; tel: (202) 588 5943.* **Croatian National Tourist Office**, *Parsippany, NJ 07054, 300 Lanidex Plaza; tel: (201) 428 0707.*

In countries with no Croatian National Tourist Office listed, either the Croatian Embassy or Consulate act as representative.

### STAYING IN CROATIA

### Accommodation

Massive amounts of money have already gone towards revitalising Croatian tourism, which had suffered due to the war. Many hotels are now being refurbished, and restoration projects are being carried out on buildings of historic value. Accommodation is available in class L, A, B, C and D hotels, apartment complexes, guesthouses, camping sites, youth hostels and private homes. Bookings can be made through local tourist offices.

Hotel prices vary considerably between Zagreb and the islands of South Dalmatia. For a single room in the capital expect to pay 800Kn (expensive), 500Kn (moderate), 400Kn (cheap).

On the islands, 450Kn (expensive), 380Kn (moderate), 300Kn (cheap).

## Eating and Drinking

Over the centuries Croatian food and drink have been influenced by the presence of Italian, Turkish, Hungarian and Austrian cultures.

Along the Dalmatian coast, fish and seafood predominate. Many dishes are prepared mediterranean-style, using large amounts of olive oil, garlic and parsley. Locals say that fish should swim three times: in the sea, in olive oil and in wine. Specialities include *lignje* (squid), *crni rižot* (rice in cuttlefish ink), and *škampi* (scampi). Inland, meat and dairy produce are more popular. Some of the best restaurants have gardens, and many serve *janjetina* (lamb) roasted whole on a spit. Another traditional method of preparing meat is in a *peka,* a large iron pot with a dome shaped lid, which is buried to cook under glowing embers. Cured meats, such as ham and salami, are excellent. Visit the local markets to enjoy a colourful range of seasonal fruit and vegetables, brought to town daily by farmers from the surrounding hills.

Croatians are fond of drinking. Excellent wines include the red *Dingac* (from the Pelješac peninsular) and *Zlatan Plavac* (from Hvar), and the whites *Pošip Čara* (from Korčula) and *Zlatan Otok* (also from Hvar). When staying on the coast try a herb brandy, *Travarica;* when staying inland ask for a grape brandy, *Lozovača.* Coffee *(kava)* is often served as espresso or cappuccino in bars, though most families prepare it turkish style at home. Tea *(čaj)* is normally made from rosehip *(šipak)* and served with sugar and lemon. Tap water is safe for drinking throughout the country.

## Communications

**Postage:** Postal services and telecommunications are managed by **Hrvatska Pošta i Telekomunikacije (HPT)**.

Usual post office hours are 0700–1900. Stamps *(markice)* can be bought at the post office, newspaper stand *(kiosk)* or tobacconists *(trafika)*. Letter boxes are yellow. Letters take about 5 days to reach the UK.

**Telephones:** The best place to make international calls is from a post office (HPT), where you will be allocated a numbered cabin and pay the clerk afterwards. It is also possible to make international calls from ordinary public telephone booths, though they may be few and far between. These take phone cards, which can be bought at post offices, newspaper stands and tobacconists. To call Croatia: *tel: 385.* To call from Croatia: *tel: 99.* **Emergencies**: Police: *92;* Fire: *93;* Ambulance: *94.*

## Opening Hours

**Banks:** Standard hours are Mon–Fri 0800–1900, Sat 0800–1200, but these may vary. **Shops:** There are no hard and fast rules, but most food shops open Mon–Sat 0800–2000, and close Sun. Some shops close for siesta, 1300–1700. Most open air markets open every day, mornings only. **Museums:** These vary.

## Public Holidays

Jan 1, Jan 6, Easter Mon, May 1, May 30, Jun 22, Aug 15, Nov 1 and Dec 25–26.

Some towns celebrate a local holiday for their patron saint, for example May 7 in Split.

## Public Transport

**Coaches** run to outlying areas inaccessible by train. Services are generally cheap and efficient. **Ferries** run by **Jadrolinija** link the islands to the mainland. These are cheap and efficient. An express coastal ferry leaves Rijeka every evening, and stops at various towns and islands all the way to Dubrovnik. Croatia is well connected to other countries, with Jadrolinija and **SEM** running ferries to Italy (Ancona, Pescara, Bari), and a twice-weekly Jadrolinija service to Greece (Igoumenitsa).

In summer there is also a Venice–Pula service, run by the Italian company **CF Marina**, from *Stazione Marittima San Basilio* in Venice, two ferries per week, Mon and Fri mornings.

**Buses** and **trams** are cheap, regular and efficient in all the main towns.

### RAIL TRAVEL WITHIN CROATIA

The national railway company is **Hrvatske Željeznice (HŽ)**, *tel (01) 9830.*

The main intersection for international trains is Zagreb, with direct lines to Slovenia, Italy, Austria, Germany and Hungary.

Rail services within the country are slow and the network is limited, due in part to the natural landscape, and in part to repercussions of the war. The Zagreb–Rijeka and Zagreb–Split lines are the most efficient, but other destinations may involve several changes with poor bus connections or even bus transfers. There is no rail service to Dubrovnik, but regular coaches and ferries run down the coast from Split.

The Rijeka–Ogulin track, covered by the Rijeka–Zagreb line, passes through *Gorski Kotar* and is recognised as a scenic route. The Zagreb–Split track passes through Knin, formerly a Serbian pocket which is now totally devastated, bearing witness to the recent war.

### Stations

Like the railway network itself, train stations in Croatia are rather spartan. Public amenities are minimum: left luggage and WC's. If there is no station bar, you can normally find a private kiosk nearby.

### Fares and passes

The EuroDomino pass is valid in Croatia, see p. 27. Domestic fares are cheap.

## THE CZECH REPUBLIC

**Capital:** Prague *(Praha)*. **Language:** Czech is the official language of the Czech Republic. Czech and Slovak are closely related Slavic tongues, mutually intelligible by natives of both Republics. English, German and Russian are often also understood, although Russian is less popular. **Currency:** Czech Korunas or Crowns (KcV); 1 Koruna = 100 Hellers. The Koruna is now fully convertible and there are no restrictions on foreign currencies. Credit cards are widely accepted in tourist areas.

### Passports and Visas

Full passports are required by everyone. Visas are not needed by EU or US nationals, but are needed by nationals of Canada, Australia and New Zealand. Others should check.

### Customs

The following allowances apply only to those aged 18 or over: 250 cigarettes or equivalent in tobacco, 1 litre spirits, and 2 litres wine.

### Tourist Information

**The Czech Tourism Centre**, *Národní 37, 110 15 Praha 1; tel: 2421 1458.* **Čedok Travel agency a.s.**, *Na příkopě 18, 110 00 Praha 1; tel: 2419 7350.*

### Useful Addresses

**Australia: Embassy:** *38 Culgoa Circuit, O'Malley, Canberra, ACT 2606; tel: 2901 1386.*
**Canada: Embassy:** *541 Sussex Dr., Ottawa, Ontario, KIN 6Z6; tel: (613) 562 3875.* **The Czech Tourist Authority**, *PO Box 198, Exchange Tower, 2 First Canadian Pl., 14th Floor, Toronto, Ontario M5X 1A6; tel: (416) 367 3432.*
**Republic of Ireland: Embassy:** *57 Northumberland Rd, Ballsbridge, Dublin 4; tel: (1) 668 1135 or 668 1343.*
**South Africa: Embassy:** *P.O.B. 3326, 936 Pretorius St, Arcadia, Pretoria 0083; tel: (12) 342 3477 or 433 601.*
**UK: Embassy**, *28 Kensington Palace Gardens, London W8 4QY; tel: (0171) 243 1115.* **The Czech Centre**, *95 Great Portland St, London W1N 5RA.*
**USA: Embassy**, *3900 Spring of Freedom St N.W., Washington DC 20008; tel: (202) 274 9100.* **The Czech Tourist Authority**, *Czech Center, 1109–1111 Madison Ave, New York, NY 10028; tel: (212) 288 0830.*

### STAYING IN THE CZECH REPUBLIC

### Accommodation

There is a growing choice of one–five-star hotels, private rooms and pensions, and, at a much more basic level, old-style tourist hotels, hostels and inns with a few spartan rooms. However, quality (once outside the three- to five-star range) can leave a lot to be desired. Although people are trying to upgrade as fast as possible, it can still make more sense to look at private rooms rather than cheap hotels. Credit cards are accepted in bigger hotels.

This is the most popular of the former Eastern bloc countries and the deluge of tourists has resulted in a real shortage of beds. Always book ahead. The tourist organisation, **Čedok**, runs booking offices across the country, as well as in London and New York (see Useful Addresses). There are plenty of campsites (usually

May–Oct only), most of which cater for caravans as well. Rough camping is forbidden.

### Eating and Drinking

Lunch is around 1130–1400 and dinner 1700–2200. The cuisine is rich and meat-based, but vegetarian restaurants options include fried cheese *(smažený syr)*, risotto and salads. Pork with cabbage and dumplings *(vepřo-knedlo-zelo)* is on virtually every menu, as is *guláš*, a spicy meat dish. Try goose *(husa)* and potato soup *(bramborová)*. Eating and drinking is reasonable, especially in a self-service *bufet* (where you stand while eating). *Kavárny* and *cukrárny* serve coffee (often Turkish-style) and delightful pastries. Pubs *(pivnice)* and wine bars *(vinárny)* are good places to eat. Czech beer is excellent and Moravian wine is worth a try. Beers include *pilsner, Budvar* and black beer *(černé pivo)*, spirits include herb-based *Becherovka* or *Fernet*. Drink mineral rather than tap water!

### Communications

**Postage:** There is a full postage service (including post restante), but it is slow and erratic. It is also cheap. Usual post office opening hours are 0800–1900. Stamps are also available from newsagents and tobacconists. Post boxes are orange and blue.

**Telephones:** To call abroad from the Czech Republic: *tel: 00*. To call the Czech Republic: *tel: 420*. Information: *121* (national); *0135* (international). **Emergencies:** Police: *158;* Fire: *150;* Ambulance: *155*.

### Opening Hours

**Banks:** Mon–Fri 0800–1700. **Shops:** Mon–Fri 0900–1800, Sat 0900–1200 (in Prague, shops often stay open longer on Sat and Sun). Food shops usually open earlier. Food and souvenir shops often open on Sun. **Museums:** (usually) Tues–Sun 1000–1800. Most castles close Nov–Mar.

### Public Holidays

1 Jan; Easter Mon; 1, 8 May; 5–6 July; 28 Oct; 24–26 Dec.

### Public Transport

The rail network here is good, but there is also a comprehensive long-distance bus network, run by **ČSAD** (although many parts are now privatised). Bus stations are well organised, with platforms, ticket offices and appallingly complicated schedule boards. Officially, you should book in advance, but you can buy tickets from the driver, who gives priority to those with reservations.

### RAIL TRAVEL WITHIN THE CZECH REPUBLIC

The national rail company is **České Dráhy (ČD)**. The rail network is cheap and extensive, but often crowded. Main lines are served by *EC* and *IC* trains (supplement payable), and express trains, *rychlík*. Other trains are *spešný* (semi-fast), which cost less, and *osobný* (slow) trains, which should be avoided.

All long-distance trains offer both first- and second-class travel. Some long-distance trains have dining-cars and overnight services between cities have sleeping-cars and couchette cars. Seat reservations are recommended for express and must be made at least 1 hour before departure. Bookings can be made at the counter marked 'R' at stations. Sleepers can be reserved at a limited number of stations. On international trains, air-conditioning does not work in all carriages – check with the conductor.

### Fares and Passes

See p.29 for details of the **Czech/Slovak Explorer Pass**.

**Kilometrická banka 2000** (Kč 900) is a local rail pass that allows 2000 km or six months of rail travel, with a minimum journey of 100 km and a maximum of 400 km. A bonus ticket or **Známka EC/IC** (Kč 400) used in combination with the Kilometricka banka tickets avoids the need to pay *EC/IC* supplements.

**43**

## DENMARK

**Capital:** Copenhagen *(København)*. **Language:** Danish; with three extra letters: æ, ø and å. Alphabetically, they come after z. English is almost universally spoken. '*Ikke*' translates as 'do not'. **Currency:** Danish Kroner (DKK/DKr.); 1 Krone=100 øre. Notes come in units of DKr.20, DKr.10, DKr.5, DKr.2. DKr.1, 50 ore and 25 ore.

### Passports and Visas
Full passports are not required by Norwegians or Swedes, nor do they require visas. Nationals of Australia, Canada, New Zealand and the USA do not need visas, but South Africans do.

### Customs
Standard EU regulations apply (see p. 17).

### Tourist Information
The Web Page for the Danish Tourist Board is: *http://www.turist.dt.dk*. Otherwise, all towns have a Tourist Office (look for the 'i') that distributes free maps and other information. Some also book accommodation (for a small fee) and change money.

### Useful Addresses
**Australia: Embassy**, *15 Hunter St, Yarralumla, Canberra, ACT 2600; tel: (06) 273 2195*.
**Canada: Embassy**, *47 Clarence St (Suite 450), Ottawa, Ont. K1N 9K1; tel: (613) 562 1811*.
**Danish Tourist Board**, contact *Miss Helen Bergstrom, PO/CP.636 Mississauga, Ont. L5M 2C2*.
**Republic of Ireland: Embassy**, *121 St Stephen's Green, Dublin 2; tel: (01) 475 6404*.
**New Zealand: Embassy**, *Morrison Morpeth House (18th Floor), 105–109 The Terrace, Wellington 1; tel: (04) 472 0020*.
**South Africa: Embassy**, *Sanlam Centre (8th Floor), corner Pretoria and Andries Sts, Pretoria 0001; tel: (012) 322 0595*.
**UK: Embassy**, *55 Sloane St, London SW1X 9SR; tel: (0171) 333 0200*. **Danish Tourist Board**, *55 Sloane St, London SW1X 9SY; tel: (0171) 259 5958–9*. **Danish State Railways**, for bookings only *c/o DFDS Seaways, Scandinavia House, Parkeston Quay, Harwich, Essex, CO12 4QG; tel: (01255) 240234*.
**USA: Embassy**, *3200 White Haven St N.W., Washington DC 20008-3683; tel: (202) 234 4300*. **Scandinavian Tourist Board**, *655 Third Ave (18th Floor), New York, NY 10017; tel: (212) 949 2333*.

## STAYING IN DENMARK

### Accommodation
**Hotel** standards are good and the choice is wide, but there's no official rating system. Get the (free) annual *Denmark Hotels* guide from your local tourist board. This covers hotels, pensions, inns *(kros)* and motels, together with details of various discount schemes. In Copenhagen, expect to pay a minimum of DKr.400–500 for a double, without facilities but including breakfast – elsewhere you might get this for DKr.300–400.

The tourist board produce a brochure on **hostels** (over 100 – sleeping-bags not allowed) and **camping** (about 500 fully-equipped sites and there are fines for illegal camping). Contact **Campingrådet**, *Hesseløgade 16, DK-2100 Copenhagen Ø; tel: 39 27 88 44*. Local Tourist Offices have lists of **private homes**.

### Eating and Drinking
Danish cuisine is simple, based on the excellent local produce. Lunch is normally 1200–1400 and dinner 1800–2100, but many establishments serve for longer. Look for *Dagen's Ret* (today's special), which is noticeably cheaper than à la carte. Food is quite expensive, but usually of good quality, attractively presented and with large portions.

*Smørrebrød* are open sandwiches on *rugbrød* (rye bread) or *frankskbrød* (wheat bread); try *frikadeller* (pork meat balls) and *wienerbrød (real* Danish pastries).

Tea, coffee and milk are widely available. There are many excellent local lagers (including Carlsberg and Tuborg). The local spirit is *snaps/akvavit* – potato-based and consumed in a single swallow, preferably following herring. All alcohol is expensive, although less than the rest of the Scandinavia.

### Communications
Most **post offices** in big towns open Mon–Fri 0900–1800, Sat 0900–1300. Stamps are also available from newsagents. Postboxes *(postkasse)* are red, with a yellow horn and crown.

**Telephones:** All numbers have eight digits, there are no area codes and most operators speak English. Telephone booths usually take either coins or phonecards (available from DSB kiosks, post offices and newsstands).

To call abroad from Denmark; *tel: 00*. To call Denmark; *tel: 00 45*. National directory enquiries; *tel: 118.* International operator/directory; *tel: 14.* **All emergencies:** *112.*

## Opening Hours
**Banks** in Copenhagen: Mon–Fri 0930–1600 (Thur 0930–1800). Hours vary elsewhere. Most Automatic Teller Machines will accept Visa and MasterCard (Eurocard) and some will take any card on the 'Cirrus' system. **Shops** vary, but typically: Mon–Thur 0900–1730, Fri 0900–1900/2000, Sat 0900–1300/1400. Many have longer hours. **Museums:** (mostly) every day 1000–1500 or 1100–1600. In winter, hours are shorter and museums usually close Mon.

## Public Holidays
1 Jan; Maundy Thur–Easter Mon; St Brededag Day (fourth Fri after Easter); Ascension Day; Whit Sun–Mon; the afternoon of Constitution Day (5 June); 25, 26 Dec.

## Public Transport
Long-distance travel is easiest by train, as the inter-regional bus service is fairly sparse. There are excellent regional and city **bus** services, however, many dovetailing with trains, and **ferries** link all the big islands. You can phone for **taxis**, pick them up at ranks or hail them in the street – they display a green *Fri* sign when they are available. They are metered and quite expensive, but drivers do not require tips.

Denmark is flat, with many cycle lanes, so **cycling** is an excellent option and hire costs are quite low. For information, contact **Dansk Cyklist Førbund** (Danish Cyclists' Association), *Rømersgade 7, DK-1363 Copenhagen; tel: 33 32 31 21.*

### RAIL TRAVEL WITHIN DENMARK

The state railway system is **Danske Statsbaner (DSB)**, but there are some private lines. *IC* trains are comfortable and can reach speeds of around 200 kph. *Re (Regionaltog)* trains are frequent, but slower. *IR* trains are also slower, but less frequent.

Most trains carry a refreshment kiosk. Seat reservations are recommended, but not compulsory. Special rules apply during holiday periods. Nationwide reservations: *tel: 33 14 88 80.*

## Stations
Baggage lockers are available at most stations and generally cost about DKr.20 per 24 hrs. There are usually free trolleys, but you may need a (returnable) coin.

## Fares and Passes
See p. 28 for details of the **Scanrail pass**, which allows unlimited rail travel on the national railways of Denmark (DSB), Finland, Norway and Sweden, and the **North Star Pass**.

## Rail Pass Concessions

| Operator, Route/Concession | Rail Pass/Discount |
|---|---|
| DSO Copenhagen–Malmö | IR26- 40% |
| Skagensbanen Fredrikshavn–Skagen | IR 26- 50% |
| Hjørring Privatbaner Hjørring–Hirtshals | |
| | IR 26- 50% |
| HP Hjørring–Hirtshals | IR 50% |
| SB Frederikshavn–Skagen | IR 50% |
| Transport Museum, Odense | IR 50% |
| P&O European Ferries Harwich–Esbjerg | FP 30% |
| DSO Copenhagen– Malmö (catamaran) | RES 30% |
| HP Hjørring–Hirtshals | RES 30% |
| LJ Nykøbing–Nakskov | RES 30% |

### ESTONIA
**Capital:** Tallinn. **Language:** Estonian (a member of the tiny Finno-Ugric language group, which also includes Finnish and Hungarian). Some Finnish could be useful and Russian is more widely understood in Tallinn and the north-east. It can be very difficult to communicate without a dictionary or phrasebook in the countryside. **Currency:** Kroons or Crowns (EEK); 1 Kroon = 100 Sents. There are no restrictions on the import/export of any currency, but you must change some money into Kroons when you enter Estonia. Travellers' cheques can be changed at banks (and occasionally post offices) but it's easy to get caught out, so always carry some cash. Cash machines sometimes accept Visa and other cards. Credit cards are accepted at most major hotels, shops and restaurants.

## Passports and Visas
Visitors entering the country must have valid passports. Visas are not needed by holders of full British passports, and nationals of Andorra,

Australia, Canada, Czech Republic, Denmark, Finland, Hungary, Ireland, Japan, Latvia, Lichtenstein, Lithuania, Monaco, New Zealand, Norway, Poland, Slovenia, Sweden, the USA and the Vatican City. Estonian visas are also valid for Latvia and Lithuania. As regulations are constantly changing, please check with the Estonian consulate or embassy.

## Customs
Although not a member state, Estonia applies the standard EU regulations (see p.17).

## Tourist Information
The **Eesti Express Hotline** is an information service with numbers in most Estonian cities. The Tallinn number is *6 313 222 1188*. **Info** is a new information line all over Estonia. Dial *8* and then *1188*.

## Useful Addresses
**Australia: Consulate**, *86 Louisa Rd, Birchgrove 2041, NSW 2010; tel: 61 2 818 1779, fax: 61 2 810 7468.*
**Canada: Consulate**, *958 Broadview Ave, Toronto, Ontario, M4K 2R6; tel: (416) 461 0764.*
**UK: Embassy**, *16 Hyde Park Gate, London SW7 5DG; tel: (0171) 589 3428.*
**USA: Embassy**, *2131 Massachussets Ave N.W., Washington, DC 20008; tel: (202) 588 0101.* **Consulate General and Tourist Office**, *630 Fifth Ave (Suite 2415), New York, NY 10111; tel: (212) 247 7634.*

## Accommodation
Hotels are still fairly thin on the ground. Home stays offer accommodation in farmhouses, summer cottages, homes and small boarding houses. There are three Bed and Breakfast agencies. Estonian Farmers Union produce a farm holidays brochure. Try to be back at your lodgings/hotel by 2200 (usual lock-out time), unless you've checked that it's all right to be later.

## Eating and Drinking
There are good cafés and restaurants in all large towns and new ones are opening all the time.

Ask the waiter to recommend something if you are not sure what to have. The pattern of eating is to have a large helping of *hors d'oeuvres* and modest helpings thereafter. Fish is a common ingredient. Many restaurants are open noon to midnight. Tap water is not safe to drink anywhere; buy bottled water instead. Tea and coffee are widely available. The most popular drink is beer *(olu)*, and Estonian beers (both dark and light) have a growing reputation – *Satiu, Tartu* and *Saarenma*. Vodka and brandy are better value and some bars serve mulled wine. *Vana Tallinn* is the Estonian liqueur.

## Communications
**Postage:** Stamps are sold by large hotels, post offices, news-stands, Tourist Offices, etc.
   **Telephones:** Calls to Estonia: the country code for Estonia is *372*. Dial this number, then the area code and the subscribers number. Calls from Estonia: dial *8* and wait for a long, constant tone. Then dial *00* + the country code + the area code + the subscribers number. Local calls: within Estonia telephone calls cost 1 kroon and 50 sents per minute. Dial *8* + area code + number. Pay phones accept phone cards. They can be purchased from hotels, Tourist Offices, post offices, news-stands and some shops. **Emergencies:** Police: *02;* Fire: *01;* Ambulance: *03.*

## Opening Hours
**Banks:** Mon–Fri 0930–1730. **Shops:** Mon–Fri 0900/1000–1800/1900, Sat 0900/1000– 1500/1700. In Tallinn some shops open Sun afternoons. **Museums:** The days of opening vary enormously and many open for only a few days every week, so check locally. On the days they are open, this is usually 1100–1600.

## Public Holidays
1 Jan; 24 Feb (Independence Day); Good Fri; Easter Mon (unofficial); 1 May; 23, 24 June; 25, 26 Dec.

## Public Transport
Buses travel to more destinations than trains and can be considerably quicker. Buy tickets before boarding from the ticketing windows or on the bus.

## RAIL TRAVEL WITHIN ESTONIA

**Estonian Railways (EVR)** is presently being restructured into three independent private companies, so major changes are expected. The main lines fan out from Tallinn to Narva, Tartu and Valga, with branches to Viljandi, Pärnu and Riisipere, etc. There is a suburban network of electric trains in the Tallinn area, and some local services in the south of the country.

For information about the **Baltic Express**, and services to and from Russia, see p. 536.

One company will soon be responsible for domestic services. They are presently all one class of travel, and reservations are not necessary. The loco-hauled trains to Tartu/Valga and Narva have attendants, who sell tea and coffee etc. There are no night trains. The Baltic Express is currently the only train between Tallinn and Riga. The Estonian services to Valga do not connect with Latvian services, which terminate at Lugazi in Latvia. However, the Latvian Riga–St Petersburg service calls at Valga and Vorn for Riga in the early hours of the morning, and from Riga in the late evening.

### Stations

Very little English is spoken at stations and buying tickets can be confusing. Stations now sell timetables for Estonian Railways.

### Fares and Passes

Two types of rail pass are available. The **Baltic Rail Explorer Pass** is available to students, teachers and young people – see p. 28. The **Baltic Card**, which can be bought in Scandinavia, covers 8 or 15 days second-class travel and has to be validated locally. Neither pass relieves passengers of the obligation of reserving seats or berths where necessary.

## FINLAND

**Capital:** Helsinki *(Helsingfors)*. **Language:** Finnish and, in the north, Lapp/Sámi. Finnish is complicated and defies the efforts of most foreigners. Portmanteau words are common, so look for the components. Swedish, the second language, is not widely spoken, but often appears on signs after the Finnish. Knowledge of English is scattered, but there's not much problem in Helsinki. Elsewhere, you can usually find someone able to help. The Finns are friendly and it's not unusual for a passer-by to chip in if you're obviously having problems. You can also try German, which is reasonably widespread. **Currency:** Finnmarks or Markkaa (FIM/Mk.); 1 Markka = 100 Penniä. **Forex** give the best exchange rates and have a branch at Helsinki station.

### Passports and Visas

National Identity Cards issued by EU countries, Iceland, Norway and Switzerland are sufficient. Visas are not needed by citizens of those countries, nor by nationals of Australia, Canada, New Zealand or the USA. South Africans do require visas.

### Customs

The usual EU regulations apply (see p. 17), but spirits may be purchased only by those aged 20 or over.

### Tourist Information

Tourist Offices **(Matkailutoimistot)** can be identified by the universal 'i'. Staff speak English and there's a range of literature in English, mostly free. They provide accommodation listings and/or direct you to booking centres. Most public buildings operate a numerical queue system, so look near the entrance for a machine dispensing numbers.

The optimum time to visit (and the only time for many activities) is June–Aug. In summer mosquitoes could be a real problem, particularly in the north, so take a strong repellent. Authentic Sami articles carry a round *Duodji* token.

### Useful Addresses

**Australia: Embassy**, *10 Darwin Ave, Yarralumla, Canberra, ACT 2600; tel: (62) 273 3800.* **Finnish Railways**, *c/o Bentours International, Level 11, 2 Bridge St, Sydney, NSW 2000; tel: (29) 241 1353.*

**Canada: Embassy**, *Suite 850, 55 Metcalfe St, Ottawa, Ont. K1P 6L5; tel: (613) 236 2389.* **Finnish Railways**, *c/o Forestgreen Travel Inc – Scanditours, 191 Eglinton Ave E. (Suite 202), Toronto, Ont. M4P 1K1; tel: (416) 483 0555.*

47

**Republic of Ireland: Embassy**, *Russell House, St Stephens Green, Dublin 2; tel: (01) 478 1344.*
**South Africa: Embassy**, *628 Leyds St, Muckleneuk Ext.2, Pretoria 0002; tel: (012) 343 0275.*
**UK: Embassy**, *38 Chesham Pl., London SW1X 8HW; tel: (0171) 838 6200.* **Tourist Board**, *30–35 Pall Mall, London SW1Y 5LP; tel: (0171) 839 4048.* **Norvista** (sells Finnrail), *227 Regent St, London W1R 8PD; tel: (0171) 409 7333/ 4/5.* **Scantours** (sells Scanrail), *21–24 Cockspur St, London SW1Y 5BN; tel: (0171) 839 2553.*
**USA: Embassy**, *3301 Massachusetts Ave N.W., Washington, DC 20008; tel: (202) 298 5800.* **Scandinavian Tourist Board**, *655 Third Ave, New York, NY 10017; tel: (212) 949 2333.* **Finnish Railways** (sells Finnrail and Scanrail), *c/o Rail Europe Inc., 500 Mamaroneck Ave, Harrison, New York 10528; tel: (800) 4- EURAIL or (914) 682 2999.*

### STAYING IN FINLAND

### Accommodation
Whatever your tastes, Finland can offer accommodation to suit, from luxury **hotels** to **rough camping** (allowed anywhere *suitable,* but don't intrude on residents and leave no trace of your stay). Wherever you stay will probably have a sauna: M is for men, N for women.

Ask the Finnish tourist board for the relevant (free) brochure: *Finland Hotels* (not graded, but standards are high) or *Finland Budget Accommodation* (covers all types, including camping: 350 well-equipped and graded sites, about 70 open year-round) and get details of the **Finncheque discount hotel scheme**.

About one third of the 160 **hostels** *(Retkeilymajat,* pronounced Ret-kay-loo-ma-yat) are open year-round: warn them if you will be arriving after 1800. Most of them prohibit sleeping-bags.

### Eating and Drinking
The Finns have four meals: breakfast 0700–1000; lunch 1100–1400; dinner 1600–1900; and supper 1900–midnight. There's often a fixed-price menu which represents a considerable saving. Restaurants are expensive, but you can fill up at breakfast (included in hotel prices and consisting of a substantial help-yourself buffet). You can eat reasonably at fast-food stands *(grillit),* self-service places *(kahvila)* and bars *(baari). Ravintola* is a more up-market restaurant, sometimes with dancing. For self-catering, **Alepa**, **Siwa**, **Säästäri** and **Valintatalo** are among the less expensive supermarket chains.

Finnish cuisine is very cosmopolitan. Fish is a major ingredient *(lohi* indicates salmon). Try reindeer *(poro)* and *lihapullia* (meat balls); *karjalan piirakka* (rye dough filled with rice mash topped by boiled egg); *kalakukko* (rye bread with fish and bacon) and *kiisseli* (berry mousse).

Milk, coffee, tea and hot chocolate are ubiquitous. Alcohol (including local liqueurs) is available in restaurants and bars, but only to people over 18 – and it's expensive. Beer is priced according to strength, the strongest being *olut IV.* **Alko** is the state-owned outlet for strong alcohol.

### Communications
Most **post offices** *(posti)* open at least Mon–Fri 0900–1700. The logo is a posthorn on a yellow background. Stamps can also be purchased from many shops and hotels. Postboxes are yellow.

**Telephones:** Coin boxes will always be around, but the number of card boxes that accept credit cards is increasing rapidly. If you buy a telephone card, make sure you get *Tele,* which can (at least in theory) be used nationwide – the only card that can. Tele booths have a button for English instructions. Phonecards are sold by R-kiosks (newsagents) and Tourist Offices, as well as Tele offices. Calls are cheapest at weekends and 2200–0800 Mon–Fri.

To call abroad from Finland; *tel: 990.* To call Finland; *tel: 358* – all area codes have changed; when calling long-distance within Finland, omit the first *0* of the area code. National directory; *tel: 118.* International directory; *tel: 92 090.* International operator; *tel: 020 222.* The system is being reorganised and there's a helpline; *tel: 020 202.* Most operators speak English. **All emergencies:** *112.*

### Opening Hours
**Banks:** Mon–Fri 0915–1615, with regional variations. **Shops:** Mon–Fri 0900–1800, Sat

0900–1400/1500. Stores and food shops: Mon–Sat 0900–1800/2000. **Museums:** the usual closing day is Mon, but there's no norm for opening hrs. Many close altogether in winter.

### Public Holidays

1, 6 Jan; Good Fri; Easter Sun–Mon; May Day; Ascension Day; Whitsun; Midsummer Eve and Day *(Juhannus);* All Saints' Day; 6 Dec (Independence Day), 24, 25, 26 Dec.

### Public Transport

Timetables for trains, buses and boats dovetail conveniently. *Suomen Kulkuneuvot* (published twice a year; FIM.100) covers them all in detail. Available at bus and rail stations. Rail passes and student cards provide free or discounted travel on many buses. Buses operate on 90% of public roads, reaching areas inaccessible by rail, particularly in the north. Bus-stops usually have a black bus on a yellow background for local services and a white bus on a blue background for longer-distance services. You can get tickets on board, but it's cheaper to buy them in advance (at bus stations or agents). Long-distance buses are comfortable, with reclining seats and ample leg-room. At terminals, look for the destination, rather than the bus number.

Most towns have good public transport. If you have no pass, board vehicles at the front and pay the driver for a single journey or a multi-ride ticket. Otherwise, enter by the central door and validate your ticket in the machine (usually orange). Tickets are valid for one hour and you can change within that time. Don't expect bus drivers to speak English.

**Taxis** are free when the yellow *taksi* sign is lighted. Hailing them in the street is acceptable. They are metered, with a surcharge after 1800 and at weekends.

### RAIL TRAVEL WITHIN FINLAND

The national rail company is **VR**, and comfortable trains link the major towns. The logo is a stylised *VR*: often white on blue. *Pendolinos,* which can reach 220 kph, are being introduced. Reservations are compulsory for *IC* and *EP* trains. Sleeping-cars have two or three berths per compartment. Single occupancy of a compartment costs more and a first-class travel ticket must be held. There are hand-basins in each compartment and WCs at the end of each carriage. In winter, sleeping accommodation costs less Mon–Thur than at weekends. *Presidente* is a new class of sleeper coming into service; it will have a shower at the end of the carriage and two compartments with private facilities. Long-distance trains have a buffet and/or trolley service.

### Stations

Look for *Rautatieasema* or *Järnvägsstation*. There is usually a plan showing the layout of long trains, so you can locate your carriage in advance. Many stations have no trolleys, but virtually all have baggage lockers.

### Fares and Passes

See p. 28 for details of the **Scanrail Pass**, which allows unlimited travel on national railways in Finland (VR)

The **Finnrailpass** gives unlimited second-class travel on VR for any 3 days in a month (FIM.570), any 5 days in a month (FIM.770), or any 10 days in a month (FIM.1040). There is also a first-class version: FIM.860, 1140 and 1570 respectively.

### Rail Pass Concessions

| Operator, Route/Concession | Rail Pass/Discount |
| --- | --- |
| Silja Finnet Line Helsinki–Stockholm | IR 50% |
| Silja Finnet Line Turku–Stockholm | IR 50% |
| Silja Finnet Line Helsinki–Lübeck/Travemünde | Reduced fare |
| Silja Finnet Line Vaasa–Umeå | IR26- 50% |
| Transport Museums in Hyvinkää and Jokioinen | IR Free entry |
| Silja Finnet Line Vaasa–Umeå | RES 30% |

## FRANCE

**Capital:** Paris. **Language:** French; many people can speak a little English, particularly in Paris. **Currency:** French Francs (FFr.); 1 Franc = 100 Centimes.

### Passports and Visas

An EU National Identity Card is sufficient. Visas are not needed by nationals of Canada, New Zealand or the USA. Australians and South Africans do need visas.

**49**

## Customs
Standard EU regulations apply (see p. 17).

## Tourist Information
**Syndicats d'Initiative** and **Offices de Tourisme** both give a full range of tourist information. In some major cities, Tourist Offices are called **Accueil de France** and also handle accommodation. Most Tourist Offices open Mon–Sat 0900–1200 and 1400–1800 and many also open on Sun in high season. There's a 24-hr leisure information line (in English); *tel: (1) 49 52 53 56.*

## Useful Addresses
**Australia: Embassy**, *6 Perth Ave, Yarralumla, Canberra, ACT 2600; tel: (06) 270 5111.* **Tourist Office**, *BNP House, 12 Castlereagh St, Sydney, NSW 2000; tel: (02) 231 5244.* **Rail Europe:** *c/o Thomas Cook, 175 Pitt St, Sydney, NSW 2000; tel: (02) 229 6611.*
**Canada: Embassy**, *42 Promenade Sussex, Ottawa, Ont. Q1M 2C9; tel: (613) 789 1795.* **Tourist Office**, *30 St Patrick St (Suite 700), Toronto, Ont. M5T 3A3; tel: (416) 593 6427.* **Rail Europe Inc**, *2087 Dundas East (Suite 105), Mississauga, Ont. L4X 1MZ; tel: (905) 602 4195.*
**Republic of Ireland: Embassy**, *36 Ailesbury Rd, Ballsbridge, Dublin 4; tel: (01) 260 1666.* **Tourist Office**, *35 Lower Abbey St, Dublin 1; tel: (01) 703 4046.*
**New Zealand: Embassy**, *Robert Jones House, 1–3 Willeston St, Wellington; tel: (04) 472 0200.*
**South Africa: Embassy**, *807 George Ave, Arcadia, Pretoria 0083; tel: (012) 435 564.* **Tourist Office**, *Craighall, Johannesburg 2024; tel: (011) 880 8062.* **Rail Europe:** *c/o World Travel Agency, 8th Floor Everite House, 20 De Korte Bramfontein, 2001 Johannesburg; tel: (011) 403 2606.*
**UK: Embassy**, *58 Knightsbridge, London SW1X 7JT; tel: (0171) 201 1000.* **Tourist Office: Maison de la France (MDLF)**, *178 Piccadilly, London W1V 0AL; tel: (0891) 244123.* **Rail Europe**, *179 Piccadilly, London W1V 0BA; tel: (0891) 515477* (calls cost £0.49 per min peak rate, £0.39 at other times).
**USA: Embassy**, *4101 Reservoir Rd N.W., Washington DC 20007; tel: (202) 944 6000.*

**Tourist Office**, *444 Madison Ave (16th Floor), New York, NY 10020-2452; tel: (212) 838 7800.* **Rail Europe Inc**, *500 Mamaroneck Ave, Harrison, New York 10528; tel: (914) 682 2999.*

### STAYING IN FRANCE

## Accommodation
**Accueil de France** supply free lists of most types of local accommodation, but usually charge about FFr.10 to make bookings. Advance reservations are recommended for the larger towns and resort areas in summer. You can get lists of all types of accommodation from French tourist boards before you go, but be prepared to pay. Accommodation tax (FFr.1 to FFr.6 per day) is charged, depending on the kind of accommodation.

**Hotels** have five grades: 1 (basic) to 4 (luxury). Paris is expensive: a comfortable 2-star double room in most places would average FFr.260–380; in Paris it would be FFr.450–500. Hotel prices quoted are invariably for doubles – singles often cost the same. Some places include Continental breakfast in the price. If they don't, you're usually better off going to a café.

**Relais et Châteaux** (luxury manors or châteaux with excellent cuisine), *9 av. Marceau, 75116 Paris; tel: (01) 47 23 41 42.* **Bed and Breakfast France** (excellent friendly, family-run hotels, Most offering a railway station pick-up service), their 'Le B&B' guide (£7.99 plus p&p) available from *PO Box 66, Henley-on-Thames, Oxon, RG9 1X5; tel: 01491 578803.* **Fédération National des Gîtes Ruraux** (furnished cottages), *35 r. Godot de Mauroy, 75009 Paris; tel: (01) 47 42 20 20.* Local Tourist Offices supply lists of **private homes** (chambres d'hôte).

**Youth hostels: Auberges de Jeunesse (AJ)** are sometimes HI and sometimes purely French. They are usually good quality, but no cheaper than many budget hotels.

**Camping** is popular and sites are classified. **Michelin** and **Fédération Française de Camping et Caravanning**, *78 r. de Rivoli, 75004 Paris; tel: 42 72 84 08*, produce guides. The cheapest sites with good facilities are usually *Camping Municipal*. Book early, especially for July–Aug. Alternatively, local Tourist Offices have lists of farms where camping is possible (after getting the farmer's permission) and also of **farmhouse** accommodation.

In mountain areas, a chain of refuge huts is run by **Club Alpin Français**, *24 av. de Laumière , 75019 Paris; tel: (01) 42 02 68 64.*

### Eating and Drinking

Breakfast normally consists of coffee and croissants, but other things should be available if you ask. Lunch begins 1200/1300 and dinner (the main meal) from around 1900 – after 2100 you could have problems outside tourist centres. In cafés there is a seating charge for tables: to save money, stand at the counter. In restaurants, à la carte is expensive, but the *menu du jour* can be superb value. Baguettes with a variety of fillings from cafés and stalls are cheap – as are *crêpes* (sweet and savoury pancakes), pizzas and other fast food. The home-grown fast food chain is **Quick**.

Wine is available everywhere, but in bars most people drink beer or spirits. Alcohol in bars is expensive – exorbitant in Paris.

### Communications

Most **post offices** *(PTT: Poste et Telecommunications)* open Mon–Fri 0800–1200 and 1430–1900; Sat 0800–1200, but the ones in city centres usually remain open over lunch. Look for yellow signs with *La Poste* in blue. Postboxes are mustard yellow and fixed to walls. Stamps *(timbres)* can also be purchased from any café or shop with a red *Tabac* sign.

**Telephones:** The very efficient system is run by **France Telecom** (logo: a digital dialling pad enclosed in an oval). All numbers have ten digits. Regions are as follows: *01* Paris; *02* the north west; *03* the north east; *04* the south east; *05* the south west. When dialling calls within a region, you must dial the full 10-digit number. Phone boxes are plentiful in cities and tourist areas and most have instructions in English. Many post offices have metered phones and you can pay when you have finished. Most phone booths take phonecards *(télécartes)* – available from post offices and some tobacconists; a few others accept coins or credit cards.

To call abroad from France; *tel: 00* followed by the country code. To call France; *tel: 00 33*

and knock off the zero from the area code. Operator; *tel: 13* (national), *tel: 14* (international). Directory enquiries; *tel: 12.* For all emergency services dial *112.*

### Opening Hours

**Banks:** Mon–Fri or (less common) Tues–Sat 0900–1200 and 1400–1600/1700. They usually close early on the day preceding a public holiday. **Shops:** Tues–Sat 0900–1200 and 1430–1830. A few open Mon and through the midday break, especially food shops, which also frequently open Sun morning and stay open late. **Museums:** 0900–1600 (with many variations and usually later in summer). Closed one day a week (usually Mon or Tues) and most close on public holidays. Many offer free or discounted entrance on Sun.

### Public Holidays

1 Jan; Easter Mon; 1, 8 May; Ascension Day; Whit Sun–Mon; 14 July; 15 Aug; 1, 11 Nov; 25 Dec. When they fall on Tues or Thur, many places also close Mon or Fri.

### Public Transport

Train and bus stations are usually close together, so access to the centre is easy. Bus services shown in railway timetables are run by SNCF and accept rail passes/tickets – so always ask if yours is valid. *Guide Régional des Transports* (from SNCF and bus stations: *gares routières)* is a free schedule of regional long-distance transport.

**City bus services** are good during the day, but infrequent after around 2030 and on Sun. Public transport in rural areas is sparse.

Licensed **taxis** (avoid others) are metered, with white roof-lights if they are free, orange ones if they are not: pick them up at ranks. There are surcharges for luggage, extra passengers, animals and journeys beyond the centre.

### RAIL TRAVEL WITHIN FRANCE

The national rail company is **Société Nationale des Chemins de Fer Français (SNCF)**, who operate a nationwide (premium-rate) number for information and bookings; *tel: 08 36 35 35 35.* Except in the Paris region, the network of local lines is not very extensive. French trains are fast, reliable and comfortable. The frequency of services varies according to routes and is highest on TGV lines. The French are proud of the TGV *(Train à Grande-Vitesse),* one of the fastest in the world, with speeds of up to 300 kph. Double-decker TGVs are also in service between Paris and Lyon.

Overnight trains may carry both sleeping-cars *(wagons-lits)* and tiny couchettes (six berths and mixed sexes, so don't undress). On a few routes, there are *Cabine 8* cars: second-class compartments with eight semi-reclined bunks.

Dining-cars, as such, are disappearing and in first class you usually have a meal delivered to you on a tray. On most long-distance trains there is either a buffet or a trolley service.

### Stations

**SOS Voyageurs** are available in a number of stations. They arrange can safe meeting points and will help disabled/distressed travellers.

### Fares and Passes

All tickets, except for the Inter-Rail pass, must be date-stamped before you board, by using the orange machines *(composteurs)* at the platform entrance.

For details of EuroDomino , see p.27.

France has two fare periods on most routes (more on some); blue is for quiet periods and white is for peak. SNCF issues a (free) calendar detailing the periods. Advance reservations are compulsory for sleeping-cars and the TGV. They are recommended for international travel and travel during white periods. Supplements are payable for TGVs, except *trains verts.*

Some cards entitle you to make bookings free, but the number of seats available to pass holders is limited, so book early. **Carte 12–25** is for those aged 12–25 and gives 50% discount in blue periods or 20% discount in white periods over a 12-month period.

**Carte Vermeil Quatre Temps** is for travellers over 60, providing up to 50% discount on four single (or two return) journeys beginning in a blue period. **Carte Vermeil Plein Temps** is essentially the same as Rail Europ Senior (see p.28).

**Discovery** fares are the best buy for a direct

journey across France on SNCF trains, giving up to 50% discount on main routes. Discovery fare **for two** entitles any two people travelling together on a round trip to a discount. **J8** and **J30** tickets must be bought either 8 or 30 days in advance. All discounted tickets are subject to availability.

### Rail Pass Concessions

| Operator, Route/Concession | Rail Pass/Discount |
| --- | --- |
| Hoverspeed (SeaCat) Folkstone–Boulogne Maritime | IR 50% |
| Hoverspeed Dover Hoverport–Calais Hoverport | IR 50% |
| P&O European Ferries Dover–Calais Maritime | IR 50% |
| P&O European Ferries Portsmouth–Cherbourg | IR 50% |
| Stena Line Dover–Calais (ship or Lynx catamaran) | IR 50% |
| Stena Line Newhaven–Dieppe | IR 50% |
| Irish ferries Cork/Rosslare–Cherbourg | IR 50% |
| Eurostar London–Calais–Lille–Paris | IR Passholder fare |
| Thalys high-speed trains Paris Nord–Brussels and Amsterdam | IR Reduced fare |
| Chemins de fer de la Corse rail link to Corsica | IR 50% |
| Chemins de fer de la Provence rail link Nice–Digne | IR 50% |
| Sea France Calais–Dover | IR 50% |
| Société Nationale Maritime Corse-Méditerranée: | |
| Marseille–Ajaccio (2nd class) | IR 30% |
| Marseille–Propriano | IR 30% |
| Nice–Calvi | IR 30% |
| Toulon–Bastia | IR 30% |
| Transport Museum, Mulhouse | IR Free entry |
| Waxworks: Paris, Tours, Lourdes, La Rochelle, Mont St. Michel | IR Free entry |
| Train-hotel Francisco de Goya Madrid–Paris–Madrid (Spain or France passholders only) | FP Special supplement payable |
| Train-hotel Joan Miro Barcelona–Paris–Barcelona (Spain or France passholders only) | FP Special supplement payable |
| France–Italy daytime services | FP Supplement payable |
| Irish Ferries Cork/Rosslare–Cherbourg | FP 50% |
| Irish Ferries Cork/Rosslare–Le Havre | FP 50% |
| Stena Line Dover–Calais (ship or Lynx catamaran) | FP 50% |
| Stena Line Newhaven–Dieppe (ship or Lynx catamaran) | FP 50% |
| Hoverspeed and P&O European ferries Dover–Calais | FP 50% |
| Hoverspeed Folkstone–Boulogne | FP 50% |
| P&O European Ferries Portsmouth–Cherbourg | FP 30% |
| P&O European Ferries Portsmouth–Le Havre | FP 30% |
| Chemins de fer de Provence rail link Digne–Nice | RES 30% |
| Eurostar Paris–London | EP Passholder fare |
| Thalys high-speed trains Paris Nord–Brussels and Amsterdam | EP Passholder fare |

Chemin de fer de Provence rail link Nice–Digne
EP Free
France–Italy daytime services, Pendolino, ETR 450/460/
500 and TGV internationals        EP Supplement payable

## GERMANY

**Capital**: Berlin (the functions of the capital are gradually being transferred from Bonn). **Language**: German; English and French are widely spoken in the West, especially by young people, less so in the East. In German it is customary to roll several words into one and the polysyllabic result can be daunting. You will find it less confusing if you split the words into their component parts. *Hauptbahnhof*, for example, is an amalgam of *haupt*/chief, *bahn*/railway and *hof*/yard. **Currency:** Deutsche Mark (DM). 1 Mark = 100 Pfennig.

### Passports and Visas
EU National Identity Cards are acceptable as are ID cards for citizens of the Czech and Slovak Republics, Hungary, Iceland, Liechtenstein, Malta, Monaco, Poland, and Switzerland. Visas are not needed by nationals of Australia, Canada, New Zealand or the USA. Others should check.

### Customs
Standard EU regulations apply; see p. 17. Danes must spend at least 24 hrs in Germany before taking their allowances home.

### Tourist Information
There are helpful tourist information offices in virtually every town or resort, usually within a couple of hundred metres of the station. English is widely spoken and a wide range of English-language maps and leaflets is available. Most offices offer a room-finding service.

### Useful Addresses
**UK: Embassy**, *23 Belgrave Sq., London SW1X 8PZ; tel: (0171) 235 5033.* **German National Tourist Office (DZT)**, *Nightingale House, 65 Curzon St, London W1Y 8NE; tel: (0171) 493 0080.* **German Rail Sales**, *Suite 4, The Sanctuary, 23 Oakhill Grove, Surbiton, Surrey, KT6 6DU; tel: (0181) 390 8833.*
**USA: Embassy**, *4645 Reservoir Rd N.W., Washington DC 20007-1998; tel: (202) 298*

*8140.* **Tourist Office**, *Chanin Building, 122 East 42nd St (52nd Floor), New York, NY 10168-0072; tel: (212) 308 3300.* **German Rail (DB)**, *9501 W., Devon Ave, Rosemont, Illinois 60018-4832; tel: (847) 692 4141.*

## STAYING IN GERMANY

### Accommodation
The general standard of accommodation in the West is high, but so are prices and you will be doing well if you find a room for less than DM25 in more remote areas, or DM50 in cities. Standards in the East have improved dramatically and prices have risen accordingly. All over Germany the prices vary enormously according to demand. Avoid *Messen* (trade fairs) and other special events when prices are at their highest; an events calendar is published twice yearly by the DZT. Germany is a year-round tourism and business destination, and there is no real low season for hotels. However, rates are highest between Christmas and mid March in ski resorts and July and August nationwide.

**Pensionen** or **Fremdenheime** are pensions and *Zimmer* means 'room' (generally in a private home). These are usually cheap but expect you to stay for at least two nights. Look for signs in the windows (*Zimmer frei* and *zu vermieten* indicate availability; *besetzt* means they are full) or book through the local Tourist Office. You must be prepared to pay for this type of accommodation in German cash, as credit cards and cheques are seldom accepted by small establishments.

**Jugendherberge (DJH)** are youth hostels and there are around 600 in Germany (mostly affiliated with the **HI**). In Bavaria there is an age limit of 27, elsewhere there is no limit; but preference is usually given to the young. It is necessary to book well ahead in peak season and in the East (where they are the best form of accommodation unless you can afford the top hotels). In Germany they really are youth hostels and often used by school parties, which has resulted in the introduction of a new category of accommodation, **Jugendgästehaus**, which is aimed more at young adults.

**Camping** is the cheapest form of accommodation and site facilities are generally

**53**

excellent, though few sites are conveniently close to stations. **Deutscher Camping-Club (DCC)**, *Mandlstr. 28, Munich*, publishes an annual list of 1600 sites (DM34.80). DZT publishes a free list and map showing more than 600 of the best sites nationwide. There are fewer sites in the east, but you can get a list from **Camping and Caravanverband**, *Postfach 105, Berlin*. Most sites open only May–Oct and it is advisable to book a few days in advance. A few are open all year and usually have space out of season.

## Eating and Drinking

Breakfast is any time from 0630 to 1000. Lunch is around 1200–1400 (from 1130 in rural areas) and dinner 1800–2130 (earlier in rural areas).

German cuisine is fairly rich and served in large portions, with pork and potatoes the staple ingredients, but it's easy to find lighter things, such as salads. Breakfast is often substantial (and usually included in the price of a room), consisting of a variety of bread, cheese and cold meat. Germans eat their main meal at midday, with a light supper in the evening, but restaurants and pubs also offer light lunches and cooked evening meals. The cheapest way to eat is to patronise *Imbisse:* roadside stalls serving a variety of snacks, especially *Wurst* (sausage). For lunch, the best value is the daily menu *(Tageskarte)*. There are simple restaurants *(Gaststätten* and *Gasthöfe)* which include regional dishes. A visit to a *Biergarten* or *Bierkeller* is a must.

## Communications

**Postage:** The usual post office hours are Mon–Sat 0800–1800 and the main post office in each town has a poste restante facility. Address letters to the *postlagernde*.

**Telephones:** In theory the Eastern and Western systems have been integrated, but the Eastern phone system still has some catching up to do. If you have important calls to make, make them in the West where the system is very efficient. Black telephone boxes have instructions in English and most operators speak it. **Kartentelefon** boxes take only cards, which you can buy at any post office, priced DM12 or DM50. To call abroad from Germany: *tel: 00.* There are a few exceptions, but the kiosks all

give full information. To call Germany: *00 49.* To call the international operator: *0010;* national operator: *010;* directory enquiries: *001188,* for numbers within Germany, or *00118* for numbers outside Germany.

**Emergencies**: Police: *110;* Fire: *112;* Ambulance: *112.*

## Opening Hours

These vary from place to place and are not standard even within one city. As a rule of thumb: **Banks**: Mon–Fri 0830–1300 and 1430–1600 (until 1730 Thur). **Shops**: Normally Mon–Fri 0900–1830 (until 2030 Thur) and Sat 0900–1400. Shops next to stations are permitted to sell food and drink outside these hours. **Museums**: Tues–Sun 0900–1700 (many until 2100 Thur). Some open Mon and some close for an hour or more at lunch.

## Public Holidays

1, 6 Jan; Good Fri; Easter Sun–Mon; 1 May, Ascension Day; Whit Sun–Mon; Corpus Christi\*; 15 Aug\*; 3 Oct; 1 Nov\*; Day of Prayer (third Wed in Nov); 25 Dec; 26 Dec (afternoon).

\*Catholic feasts, celebrated only in the south.

## Public Transport

All intercity travel is by train, with buses used just for travel to remote areas. Many big cities have a **U-Bahn** (U) underground railway and an **S-Bahn** (S) urban rail service. City travel passes cover both, as well as other public transport. International passes us-ually cover the S-Bahn, but not the U-Bahn. Where ferries are an integral part of the city's transport, they are often included in the city transport pass.

Local fares are expensive. A day card *(Tagesnetzkarte)* or multi-ride ticket *(Mehrfahrkarte)* usually pays its way if you take more than three rides. If there's no machine at the stop, get your ticket from the bus driver. The usual system is to get tickets from automatic machines and then validate them in little boxes in the station or on board the vehicle.

*Deutsche Bahn (DB)* is an amalgamation of the former West German *DB (Deutsche Bundesbahn)* with the East German *DR (Deutsche Reichsbahn)*. There are also some privately owned railways. Tickets should be purchased before you board, unless you are prepared to pay a small supplement.

Long-distance trains are: *ICE* (an ultra-modern service which cruises at up to 174 mph), *IC* and *IR* plus *EC* and *EN*. The *RB* and *RE* are modern, comfortable regional services linking up with the long-distance network. Local services are called *SE* or *S-Bahn*.

Most German trains offer both first and second class, but some are second class only. Overnight services often have second-class seating and sleeping accommodation (sleeping-cars with up to three berths and/or couchettes with four or six berths). Seat reservations are possible for most fast trains, but not local trains. Most long-distance trains have dining-cars as well, or a trolley or buffet service.

### Stations

German stations are efficient, clean and well staffed, with facilities that include left luggage lockers (of various sizes) and refreshments. Bicycles are available for hire at many stations.

The main station in each town is the **Hauptbahnhof** (Hbf) and any sizeable station will be able to supply a computer print-out showing the connections along the route in which you are interested.

### Fares and Passes

The **EuroDomino Pass** (only available to European citizens) covers all scheduled services, *S-Bahn* airport connections and supplements for *IC*, *EC* and *ICE* trains. Seat, couchette and sleeper reservations are extra. Available for 3, 5 and 10 days. See p. 27 for further details.

**Tramper-Monats** are summer seasonal tickets (available to anyone under 23 and to students under 27). They give second-class travel for a month on all *DB* trains (except the *ICE* – supplement payable) as well as on railway-run buses *(Bahnbusse)* and the *S-Bahn*.

**BahnCards** give half-price travel on all trains for a full year. The **DB Railcard**, obtainable in the UK and Germany, allows unlimited purchase of half-price second-class tickets in Germany. A passport photo is required.

A **Minigroup Ticket** is ideal for medium distance return journeys. The first adult pays full fare, while all the others pay half, and children a quarter of the fare. A group must be a minimum of 1 adult and 1 child, and a maximum of five adults and 1 child.

**Saver** and **Supersaver** tickets offer substantial savings on long-distance return journeys within Germany and are ideal for individual or small groups who can be flexible about their travel arrangements. Saver Tickets can be used on both regular and high-speed Inter-City express *(ICE)* services, and can be used on any day, but your stay must include a Friday night. Two passengers can save more than 50% on a second class *ICE* return from Hamburg to Munich. A SuperSaver Ticket is available on *ICE* services for travelling any day except Friday and Sunday, and staying Friday night. Both are available for up to five adults and one child.

Young people aged 12–25 can save a quarter off the regular single and return fares with a **Twen Ticket**. With a **Happy Weekend** Ticket, 1–5 passengers travelling together can get a flat fare of £16, which covers a weekend excursion on local trains and most *S Bahn, U-Bahn* and bus services. InterCity, *ICE* and fast trains are excluded.

The **Cologne Special Ticket** offers cheap travel from London–Cologne and return by rail (£89). This includes Eurostar services from London to Brussels, where you change trains for Cologne, as well as seat reservations and supplements. Travel must include a Saturday night and special conditions apply. This ticket is not available through Deutsche Bahn. *Tel: 0345 30 30 30 for information.*

### Rail Pass Concessions

| Operator, Route/Concession | Rail Pass/Discount |
| --- | --- |
| CityNightLine Dortmund–Wien (German passholders) | FP Reduced fare |
| CityNightLine Hamburg–Zurich (German passholders) | FP Reduced fare |
| CityNightLine Berlin/Dresden–Zurich (German passholders) | FP Reduced fare |
| Harwich/Newcastle–Hamburg ferry service | FP 30% |
| S-Bahn Frankfurt airport–main rail station | FP |
| S-Bahn Stuttgart airport–main rail station | FP |
| S-Bahn Düsseldorf airport–main rail station | FP |

55

| | |
|---|---|
| S-Bahn Munich airport–main rail station | FP |
| KD River Steamers; certain Rhine, main and Moselle river sections | GR Free |
| Deutsche Touring/Europabus | GR Free |
| DeutscheRheinschiffahrt KD Köln– Mainz | EP |
| DeutscheRheinschiffahrt KD Koblenz–Cochem | EP |
| TT-Line Lübeck (Travemünde)–Trelleborg (Sweden) | EP 50% |
| Regular steamer services on Lake Constance | EP 50% |
| DWK Passau–Linz | EP 50% |
| Garmisch Partenkirchen-Grainau–Zugspitze (Zugspitzplatt) and some cable cars in the summit area | EP 25% |
| Freiburg (Breisgau)–Schauinsland rack railway | EP Reduced fare |

# GREECE

**Capital:** Athens *(Athinai)*. **Language:** Greek; English is very widely spoken in tourist areas and hotels and in the islands, less widely in remote mainland areas and Athens. Many people in day-to-day contact with tourists also speak some German or Italian. Station and street signs are usually in English as well as Greek characters. You may see several different versions of the same name (for example *Sindagma, Syntagma* or *Sidagma* for Athens's central square) as there is no standard transliteration. To make things more complicated, place names are sometimes translated directly into English, so that some maps and guides may call *Plateia Syntagma* 'Constitution Square'. Greek body language can also be confusing; a backward motion of the head, very like an affirmative nod, is a negative, *nai* (pronounced nay) means yes and *ochi* (pronounced very like 'okay') means no. **Currency:** Drachmae. Coins are in denominations of 5, 10, 20, 50 and 100; notes in denominations of 100, 200, 500, 1000 and 5000.

## Passports and Visas

National identity cards issued by EU countries are sufficient for entry. Nationals of the USA, Canada, Australia and New Zealand do not require visas for stays of less than three months. Others should check. Turkish nationals are not permitted to enter Greece at all if their passports indicate that they have visited or intend to visit Turkish, occupied Cyprus.

## Customs

Normal EU regulations apply, see Travel Essentials p. 17.

## Tourist Information

The **Greek National Tourist Office** (GNTO) provides information including hotel listings, transport schedules, archaeological sites, exhibitions, festivals and other events.

## Useful Addresses

**Australia: Tourist Office**, *51–7 Pitt St, Sydney NSW 2000; tel: (2) 92 41 16 63/5, fax: (2) 92 35 21 74.*

**Canada: Tourist Office**, *1300 Bay St, Main Level, Toronto, Ontario M5R 3K8; tel: (416) 968 2220, fax: (416) 968 6533.* **Tourist Office**, *1233 Rue da la Montagne, Suite 101 Montreal, Quebec, Canada H3G 1ZZ; tel: 8711 535, fax: 8711 498.*

**Republic of Ireland:** See the UK.

**New Zealand:** See Australia.

**UK: Consulate General**, *1A Holland Park, London W11 3TP; tel (0171) 221 6467.* **Greek National Tourist Office and railway representation**, *4 Conduit St, London W1R 0DJ; tel (0171) 734 5997, fax: (0171) 287 1369.*

**USA: Embassy**, *2221 Massachusetts Ave N.W., Washington DC 20008-2873; tel: (202) 667 3169/939 5800.* **Tourist Office**, *Olympic Tower, 645 Fifth Ave (5th Floor), New York, NY 10022; tel: (212) 421 5777, fax: (212) 826 6940.* **Tourist Office**, *168 N. Michigan Ave, Suite 600, Chicago, Illinois 60601; tel: (312) 782 1084, fax: (312) 782 1091.* **Tourist Office**, *611 W. Sixth St, Suite 2198, Los Angeles, California 90017; tel: (213) 626 6696/9, fax: (213) 489 9744.*

## STAYING IN GREECE

## Accommodation

Greece is over-supplied with accommodation, from five-star hotels to pensions, village rooms, self-catering apartments, dormitories and youth hostels. You should have no problem finding a bed in Athens, Patras or Thessaloniki even in high summer (though the very cheapest Athens dorms and pensions are often very crowded in July and Aug).

Rooms are hardest to find over the Greek Easter period, so try to book ahead. Outside the Easter and July–Sept peaks, accommodation costs up to 30% less. You should also get a 10%

discount if you stay three or more nights. Cheaper places will hang onto your passport overnight unless you pay in advance.

**Youth hostels** are not good value and are being fazed out by the government. **Campsites** at major sights (including Delphi, Mistra and Olympia) can be good value, with laundries, hot showers, cafés and even swimming pools. You can get a list of sites from the GNTO.

## Eating and Drinking

Greeks rarely eat breakfast (they get up at dawn and start the day with coffee and a cigarette) but many cafés in tourist areas advertise 'English breakfast'. Traditional Greek meals are unstructured, with lots of dishes brought at once or in no particular order. Lunch is any time between 1200 and 1500, after which most restaurants close until around 1930. Greeks dine late, and you will find plenty of restaurants open until well after midnight.

The best Greek food is fresh, seasonal and simply prepared. Seafood dishes are usually the most expensive. Veal, chicken and squid are relatively cheap, and traditional salad – olives, tomatoes, onions, peppers and feta cheese drowned in oil, served with bread – is a meal in itself. Most restaurants have a bilingual Greek and English menu. In smaller places, visit the kitchen to choose what you want, or in more expensive establishments choose dishes from a display cabinet.

Coffee is easier to find than tea; iced coffee *(frappé)* is now more popular than the tiny, strong cups of old-fashioned Greek coffee. Tap water is safe but heavily chlorinated. Aniseed-flavoured *ouzo* is a favourite aperitif. *Retsina* (resinated wine) is an acquired taste; many Greeks mix it with Coke. Greek brandy is on the sweet side. Draught lager is not widely available and is neither as good nor as cheap as bottled beer; Amstel, Henninger and Heineken brewed in Greece are sold in half-litre bottles.

## Communications

**Post offices**, marked by a circular yellow sign, can be found even in quite small villages and are normally open Mon–Fri 0800–1300, Sat 0800–1200. They can change money, Euro-cheques and travellers cheques. Stamps can be bought in street kiosks and most general stores.

**Telephones:** To call Greece: *tel: 30*. To call abroad from Greece: *tel: 00*. **Emergencies**: General Emergency: *100;* Police: *100;* Fire: *199;* Ambulance *150/166;* Tourist Police (24 hr, English-speaking); *171;* Operator *100*.

**Mobile phones:** Greece has two GSM services. **Stet Hellas** *(tel: 126* for customer services) and **Panafon**.

## Opening Hours

**Banks**: (usually) Mon–Fri 0800–1400, with longer hours in busy tourist areas in peak holiday season. **Shops** set their own hours; in summer most close from around midday until early evening. **Sites and Museums:** erratic, but most should be open 0830–1500; the main Athens sites stay open until sunset in summer.

## Public Holidays

1, 6 Jan; Shrove Mon; 25 Mar; Easter; May Day; Whit Mon; 15 Aug; 28 Oct; 25, 26 Dec. Everything closes for Easter (the biggest event on the Greek calendar) but bear in mind that they use the Orthodox calendar and so the dates may not coincide with the western Easter.

## Public Transport

Most long-distance travel is by buses run by the **KTEL** consortium. All towns have well-organised bus stations with clear timetables, and buses are fast, punctual and fairly comfortable You are allocated a seat number with your ticket.

The islands are connected by a web of **ferries** and **hydrofoils**. The biggest gateway is Piraeus, the port of Athens, but there are also sailings from Thessaloniki, Kavala, Alexandroupolis and Volos in the north, from Nafplio and Githio in the south and from Patras for the western Ionian islands. Ferry schedules are listed in the Thomas Cook Guide to Greek Island Hopping, p.23.

City transport is by **bus** or (in Athens) **trolley-bus** and **metro**. Services are punctual and efficient, if crowded. On most, you buy your ticket from the driver; pre-bought tickets must be validated on boarding. In towns outside Athens, **taxis** are easy to find and good value; you can use them for long inter-city journeys too, but keep your wits about you

## RAIL TRAVEL WITHIN MAINLAND GREECE

Greek trains are run by the Greek Railway Organisation **Organismos Sidirodromon tis Ellados (OSE)** but the rail network is limited, especially north of Athens. Sleepers/couchettes are of standard European type. Reservations are essential on most express trains.

*IC* trains (supplement payable) are fast, and timekeeping is generally good, but timekeeping for other services can be erratic.

### Stations

Facilities at Greek stations are limited. Do not expect to find left luggage or English-speaking staff. All large stations, and some smaller stations, have restaurants – sometimes even open through the night.

### Fares and Passes

Many European rail passes (pp. 25–29) offer discounts on ferry services between Greece and Italy. Apart from the main Athens–Thessaloniki route where some *IC* trains operate (reservation and a hefty supplement required), most services are slow and infrequent. To make up for this, most Greek trains run through stunning scenery. If your time is limited, though, you may want to go by bus; bus fares are slightly more expensive than basic rail fares.

The **Tourism Card**, available for 10, 20 and 30 days, offers second class travel on Greek State railways for up to 5 people travelling together. **Greek Flexipass** is available in first classs only. Greek Flexipass Rail 'n Fly includes a return airline ticket, and a one-way air ticket from Athens to any Greek Island served by Olympic Airways, and is available in first and second classes.

See p. 28 for details of the Balkan Flexipass.

### Rail Pass Concessions

| Operator, Route/Concession | Rail Pass/Discount |
|---|---|
| ADN/HML Ferries Brindisi–Corfu–Patras | IR Free |
| Transport Museum, Athens | IR Free |
| HML Patras–Corfu–Igoumenitsa–Brindisi | RES 50% |
| ADN/HML Corfu–Igoumenitsa–Patras–Brindisi | |
| | EP Free (small surcharge in high season) |

## HUNGARY

**Capital:** Budapest. **Language:** Hungarian *(Magyar)*. German is widely understood, especially near the Austrian and Romanian borders and English is spoken mainly in the tourist areas. When asking about buses, make sure you pronounce it 'boos' as the English pronunciation is very similar to a rude word in Hungarian. **Currency:** Forints (Ft); 1 Forint = 100 fillérs. Due to inflation, fillérs are rarely available and pretty worthless. You can buy your currency at banks and official bureaux, but take care not to buy too much. Foreigners may import up to 300,000Ft, or unlimited amounts of foreign currency, but should have an *Értékbehozatali tanúsítvány* (export certificate) if exporting more than 50,000Ft or equivalent. Keep all your receipts. Acceptance of all major credit cards is widespread and most large hotels offer the facility. Eurocheques and travellers' cheques are accepted in small denominations. It is advisable to take Deutschmarks rather than dollars or sterling as hotel prices are very often quoted in German currency.

### Passports and Visas

All visitors require full passports. Visas are not required by EU Nationals, Canadians or citizens of the USA or South Africa. Nationals of Australia and New Zealand must obtain visas prior to travelling. All other nationalities should check with their local consulate.

### Customs

The allowances are: 250 cigarettes or 50 cigars or 250g tobacco; 2 litres wine, 5 litres beer, 1 litre spirits and 250ml cologne or perfume.

### Tourist Information

**Touriform** is the national tourist information office, with branches throughout the country and very helpful, English-speaking staff. There is an office in central Budapest, *Sütö, utca 2, H-1052 Budapest; tel: 361 117 9800, fax: 361 117 9578.*

Other offices are: **Tourism Office of Budapest**, *H-1364 Budapest; tel: 117 5694* or *266 0479,* and **Budapest Tourism Office**, *Budapest Western Railway Station, H-1062 Budapest; tel: 332 0597.*

## Useful Addresses

**Australia: Embassy**, *17 Beale Crescent, Deakin Act., 2600 Canberra; tel: 282 3226 or 285 3484.*
**Canada: Embassy**, *299 Waverley St, Ottawa, Ontario K2P 0V9; tel: (613) 230 9614.*
**Republic of Ireland: Embassy**, *2 Fitzwilliam Pl., Dublin 2; tel: (1) 661 2902 or 661 2903.*
**South Africa: Embassy**, *959 Arcadia St, Arcadia, Pretoria (PO Box 27077, Sunnyside 0132); tel: (12) 433 030 or 433 020.*
**UK: Embassy**, *Commercial Section, 46 Eaton Pl., London SW1X; tel: (0171) 235 2664.*
**Hungarian National Tourist Office**, *c/o Embassy of the Republic of Hungary, 46 Eaton Pl., London SW1X; tel (0171) 823 1032.*
**USA: Embassy**, *3910 Shoemakers St N.W., Washington DC 20008-3811; tel: (202) 362 6730.* **Hungarian National Tourist Board**, *150 E. 58th St, 33rd Floor, New York, NY 101 55-3398; tel: (212) 355 0240.*

### STAYING IN HUNGARY

## Accommodation

There is a wide range of accommodation available of reasonable to excellent quality and some superb **hotels** of international standing in the capital. Some of the 2000 castles are being turned into hotels and here the standards vary. For the medium to lower price bracket, **private rooms** are very good value as is the small **pension**.

The tourist board offer a very extensive list in all categories. Try to steer clear of the old Soviet-style tourist hotels and youth hostels as they are very basic with limited facilities. **Spas** are generally excellent and offer good weekend packages. **Campsites** are, on the whole, very good and can be found near the main resorts. Many have **cabins** to rent, but contact the authorities first in order to book. Camping 'rough' is not permitted and could net a hefty fine.

## Eating and Drinking

The Hungarians love their food and are very hospitable. The style of cuisine has been influenced to a large extent by Austria and Germany as well as by Turkey. Portions are gargantuan

and most restaurants offer a cheap fixed price menu. Lunch is the main meal of the day, and a bowl of *gulas* laced with potatoes and spiced with paprika a must. Try smoked sausages, soups (*sowcherry* soup is superb) and paprika noodles or the excellent pike-perch. Dinner is early and you should aim to begin eating well before 2100.

In order to avoid the pitfalls of phrase book ordering, try eating in an *Önkiszolgáló* or *ételbár.* These are fairly inexpensive self-service snack bars. *Csárda* are folk restaurants usually with traditional music, but menus can be limited and slightly more expensive. Still in the moderate range are the *Vendéglő,* where home cooking often features. *Étterem* are larger restaurants with a more varied menu. Check your bill carefully wherever you eat, and tip between 10 and 15%.

Hungarian wines, such as *Tokaj* and *Egrí bikavé* (Bulls Blood), and mineral water cannot be faulted, and try *pálinka,* a fire water schnapps.

## Communications

**Postage:** The postal service is fairly slow but reliable; it is undergoing improvements. Postboxes are red.

**Telephones:** The use of phonecards is becoming more widespread – they are on sale at newstands, tobacconists, post offices and supermarkets. Payphones take 10, 20 and 50 forint coins. To call abroad from Hungary: *tel: 00.* To call Hungary: *36.* **Emergencies:** Police: *107;* Fire: *105;* Ambulance: *104.*

## Opening Hours

There are no hard and fast rules, although only food and tourist shops are open Sun. Food shops and supermarkets generally open 0600/0700–1800 Mon–Fri. Other shops open around 1000–1800 (Thur –1900). Shops close for lunch and half-day closing is on Sat (1300). **Banks:** Mon–Fri 0800/1000–1800/1900 with lunch-time closing on Sat. Some also close early on Fri. **Museums:** usually Tues–Sun 1000–1800, whilst small museums are often only open during the summer. There's usually one day a week when the entry is free – find out from the Tourist Office or Hotel reception. All museums are closed on public holidays.

**59**

### Public Holidays
1 Jan; 15 Mar; Easter Mon; 1 May; Whit Mon; 20 Aug; 23 Oct; 25, 26 Dec.

### Public Transport
Budapest has three **metro** lines (a fourth is planned), and an extensive **tram** and **bus** network. Trams can also be found in Debrecen, Miskolc and Szeged, but elsewhere local services are by bus. Long-distance buses are an alternative to the rail system (**Volán busz**; *tel: 118 2122*). Try a leisurely trip on a slow ferry along the Danube or on Lake Balaton. Taxis are good value only if you bargain first and agree a price. Use a recommended taxi firm and ensure that the meter is switched on.

### RAIL TRAVEL WITHIN HUNGARY
The rail system is comprehensive and most towns are on the **Hungarian State Railways (MÁV)** network, however most trains *(személyvonat)* are very slow. The express trains *(gyorsvonat)*, *IC* InterCity trains and some *EC* EuroCity international services (reservation compulsory and supplement payable on the latter two) connect Budapest with major towns and Lake Balaton. All seats and sleepers need to be booked well in advance. Sleepers and couchettes are the standard European variety. Some express trains have a snack service but this can sell out rapidly, so it is advisable to be prepared and bring your own refreshments, and other lesser services now have primitive trolleys offering refreshments.

### Fares and Passes
The **Hungary Explorer Pass** gives unlimited first- or second-class rail travel for 7 days but must be purchased before you go. It is available to holders of an ISIC card, teachers, academic staff, under 26s and accompnaying spouses and children of eligible persons from Campus Travel outlets.

All international fares must be paid in hard currency, preferably DM. Domestic fares are very cheap, but prices are rising due to a small monthly rise in the rate of inflation; this means that for the next couple of years at least, first-class travel is a viable and comfortable option.

**EuroDomino** offers unlimited second class

rail travel in Hungary for various periods. *IC* = Intercity; *EC* = Eurocity; *EN* = Euronight (Zurich–Budapest). Air conditioning does not work in all international carriages so check first with the conductor. See also p. 27.

The **Budapest Card** offers three days unlimited travel around the city, plus free admission or discounts to many attractions.

### Rail Pass Concessions

| Operator, Route/Concession | Rail Pass/Discount |
|---|---|
| Transport Museums in Budapest and Paradfürdö | IR Free |
| GySEV private railway | RES |

### ITALY
**Capital:** Rome *(Roma)*. **Language:** Italian is the only official language, but there are strong dialectal differences. In the cities and tourist areas many people speak some English, but it's seldom spoken at all off the beaten track. **Currency:** Lira (L.).

### Passports and Visas
An EU National Identity Card is sufficient. Visas are not needed by Commonwealth citizens or nationals of the USA. Others should check.

### Customs
Standard EU regulations apply (see p. 17).

### Useful Addresses
**UK: Consulate**, *38 Eaton Pl., London SW1X 8AN; tel: (0171) 235 9371, fax: (0171) 823 1609*. **Italian State Tourist Board**, *1 Princes St, London W1R 8AY; tel: (0171) 408 1254. fax: (0171) 493 6695*. **Italian Rail Travel, Wasteels**, *adjacent to Platform 2, Victoria Station, London SW1V 1JT; tel: (0171) 834 7066, fax: (0171) 630 7628.*
**USA: Embassy**, *1601 Fuller Street N.W., Washington, DC 20009; tel: (202) 328 5500.* **Italian Government Travel Office (ENIT)**, *630 Fifth Ave (Suite 1565), Rockefeller Center, New York, NY 10111; tel: (212) 245 4822.* **Italian Rail Travel, CIT Tours Corporation**, *594 Broadway (Suite 307), New York, NY 10012; tel: (212) 697-2100.*

## Accommodation

All **hotels** are classified according to a 5-star system and inspectors set a maximum (seasonal) rate that must be displayed in each room. It does not necessarily include showers or breakfast, but extras must be listed separately, so complain (to the Tourist Office if all else fails) if your bill does not agree with the rates listed. You must, by law, obtain a receipt from all hotels.

Most establishments now term themselves hotel or **albergo**, but some are still called **pension** (one-, two-, or three-star) or **locande** (one-star). There are many **private rooms**, unofficial and otherwise. You can find the unofficial ones by looking for signs saying *affitta camere*, often in shop windows. It's worth trying to bargain, but you will usually pay about the same as for a one-star hotel. *Alberghi diurni*, near stations or in the centre, are essentially **day rooms:** you can have a wash without taking a room for the night.

There is no shortage of **youth hostels**, but relatively few belong to the **HI** and the standard varies considerably. It is often just as cheap and more convenient to stay at a one-star hotel.

**Camping** is popular and there are over 2000 sites (all Tourist Offices have information about their area), but they are often fairly expensive and/or difficult to reach without a car. There are few places where you can rough camp without asking permission.

**Touring Club Italiano (TCI)**, *Corso Italia 10, 20122 Milano; tel: (02) 85 261* or *852 6245*, publish an annual guide. Alternatively, you can get a list from **Federcampeggio**, *Casella Postale 23, 50041 Calenzano (Florence); tel: (055) 88 2391*, who can also make bookings. These two organisations produce a detailed directory of campsites, *Campeggi e Villagi Turistici in Italia*, available from bookshops in Italy (L.30,000).

**Agriturismo**, *Corso V Emanuele 101, Roma; tel: (06) 6852 342*, has information about staying in rural cottages and farmhouses. **Club Alpino Italiano**, *Via Fonseca Pimental 7, 20121 Milan; tel: (02) 26 141 378*, can supply details of mountain refuge huts.

## Eating and Drinking

Italians enjoy eating and there's a wide variety of food available everywhere, with pasta as just one of many options. A full meal will consist of antipasta (cold meats etc.), pasta, a main course, and fruit or cheese. Italian ice-cream (**gelato**) is among the world's best.

*Trattorie* are simple establishments which are cheaper than *ristoranti*. Most *osterie* are trendy and expensive. *Alimentari* stores often prepare excellent and interesting sandwiches. *Rosticerrie* sell good hot take aways, while *tavole calde* are cheap sit-down places. Smaller establishments seldom have menus: just ask for the dish of the day if you want something reasonably priced. Menus are displayed by the entrance.

Look for cover charges *(coperto)* and service *(servizio)*, both of which will be added to your bill. Prices on *Menu Turistico* include taxes and service charges.

Coffee comes in many forms, from espresso to liqueur. There are various types of Italian beer and many fine wines. Bars are good places to get a snack, such as a roll or toasted sandwich as well as to sample the local 'fire waters' such as *grappa*.

## Communications

Usual **post office** hours are Mon–Fri 0800–1330/1400, Sat 0800–1145. Some counters (such as registered mail and telegrams) may have different hours and in the main cities they may open in the afternoon. The postal service is slow and it's worth paying for anything urgent to be sent express. Stamps *(francobolli)* are available from post offices, tobacconists *(tabacchi)* and some gift shops in resorts. Poste restante *(Fermo posta)* is possible at most post offices, but you have to pay a small amount when you collect.

**Telephones:** The phone system is in a constant state of over-haul, with frequently changing numbers ranging from two to eight digits. Directories may list two numbers – try both. If they're of different lengths, the longer is likely to be the new one. Most public phones have instructions in English and take coins, phonecards *(carte telefoniche/scheda)*, or both. Cards are available from automatic machines near the phones, tobacconists and newsstands. You can make international calls by using a

**61**

phonecard, but in some small towns you must go to an office of the state phone company, **SIP**, or (occasionally) **ASST**. They often have branches in the stations; if not, you should find one near the main post office. You may also come across the old phones that take only tokens *(gettoni)*. If so, you should be able to get the tokens from whoever owns the phone, or find an automatic dispenser nearby. *Gettoni* are often accepted as small change, so don't be surprised if you are given some instead of small denomination coins.

*Scatti* phones are quite common – these are metered and you pay the operator/owner when you have finished, but they are normally in places like bars and the 'operator' may well add a service charge, so check before you commit yourself. Hotels invariably charge over the odds.

To call abroad from Italy: *tel: 00.* To call Italy: *00 39.* For English information and assistance for intercontinental calls: *170.* For English information on calling Europe and the Mediterranean area: *176.* For local operator assistance: *15.* For local directory enquiries: *12.* **Emergencies:** Fire: *115;* Police, Ambulance and other services: *113.*

### Opening Hours
**Banks:** Mon–Fri 0830/0830–1330 and 1430/1600–2200. **Shops:** (usually) Mon–Sat 0830/0900–1230 and 1530/1600–1900/1930. In July/Aug many close Mon morning or Sat afternoon. A few stay open all day, every day. **Museums:** national museums and archaeological sites usually open Tues–Sun 0930–1300/1400, some re-open 1600–1900, but there is no real pattern and smaller ones please themselves. Although Mon is the usual closing day, it is not uncommon to be a Sun or Tues, or for them to stay open all week. Most sites and museums refuse entry within an hour or two of closing time.

### Public Holidays
All over the country: 1, 6 Jan; Easter Sun and Mon; 25 Apr; 1 May; 15 Aug (virtually nothing opens); 1 Nov; 8, 25, 26 Dec.

Regional saints' days: 25 Apr in Venice; 24 June in Florence, Genoa and Turin; 29 June in Rome; 11 July in Palermo; 19 Sept in Naples;

4 Oct in Bologna; 6 Dec in Bari; 7 Dec in Milan.

### Public Transport
**Buses** are often crowded, but serve many areas inaccessible by rail and tend to be punctual. Services are drastically reduced at weekends and timetables do not always reflect this fact. Tickets for long-distance and local buses are usually obtained before boarding (some local ones are bought on board). Long-distance tickets are usually available from train stations or CIT offices, while local tickets are from machines, news-stands or tobacconists.

**Taxis** are metered, but can be expensive, with a substantial flat fare to start with and extra charges for baggage and journeys out of town, on holidays or late at night. You can hail taxis on the street, but steer clear of unofficial ones.

### RAIL TRAVEL WITHIN ITALY
The national rail company is **Ferrovie dello Stato (FS)**. High-speed express services between major cities are branded 'Eurostar Italia' and reach up to 155 mph. Reservations are necessary and there is the usual basic supplement to use the trains, plus another (usually £10–£20) before you board (which, in first class, covers such extras as hostess service, newspapers and food). Reservations are also obligatory for *IC* and *EC* services. *IR* trains are semi-fast expresses. The *espresso* are long-distance domestic trains, with both first and second class, which stop only at main stations. The *diretto* stop frequently and are very slow, while the *locale* stop almost everywhere. The rail network is extensive and the service reasonably punctual. Some long-distance trains do not carry passengers for short distances. Sleepers have single or double berths in first class, three berths (occasionally doubles) in second class; couchettes have four berths in first class, six in second class.

Most long-distance trains have refreshment facilities. Dining-cars offer a full service at meal times and snacks the rest of the day. Buffet cars are self-service, catering coaches or bar cars. Don't drink the tap water on trains. Queues at stations are often long and it's better to buy tickets and make reservations at travel agencies (look for the **FS** symbol).

## Fares and Passes

**Biglietto Chilometrico** (Kilometric Card) can be used by up to 5 people who can travel together or as a group, but the allowance is divided by the number of travellers. Valid for 2 months, it allows up to 20 journeys or 3000 km, whichever comes first. Prices: £88 (second-class); £150 (first-class). Supplements and reservations are not included and are required on all *IC, EC* and *ETR* services. The **Italy Railcard** is valid for 8, 15, 21 or 30 days unlimited travel throughout the FS rail system, although not on the 30 or so private rail operators. It is only available to travellers residing outside Italy, and a passport is required when booking. The pass includes supplements usually payable on high-speed trains (except Eurostar Italia and ETR trains), and seat reservations where these are compulsory. The ticket is also valid on FS ships, including services to Sardinia. Available from Wasteels.

## Rail Pass Concessions

| Operator, Route/Concession | Rail Pass/Discount |
| --- | --- |
| Train-Hotel Salvador Dali Milan–Barcelona–Milan | |
| | FP Special supplement payable |
| France–Italy daytime services, Pendolino, ETR 450/460/500, TGV internationals and Cisalpino | |
| | FP Supplement payable |
| Società di Navigazione 'Adriatica' Brindisi–Igoumenitsa–Corfu–Patras | RES 50% |
| FS Civitavecchia–Golfo Aranci (Olbia) | EP |
| FS Villa S. Giovanni–Messina | EP |
| ADN/HML Brindisi–Corfu–Igoumenitsa–Patras | EP |

## LATVIA

**Capital:** Riga. **Language:** Latvian is the national language, but is spoken by only about half the population. Russian is more widely understood in the capital and the east of the country, but unpopular with native Latvians. Of the three Baltic countries, Latvia has the smallest indigenous population and the language, almost wiped out by Russian (as happened in Estonia and Lithuania), is on the endangered list. Latvian is an Indo-European, non-Slavic and non-Germanic language and is similar only to Lithuanian. English and German are increasingly widely spoken. **Currency:** The new Latvian currency, the Lat, was fully introduced in Oct 1993; 1 Lat = 100 Santims.

Currency exchange outfits are numerous but changing travellers' cheques isn't so easy when the banks are closed, e.g. weekends. Credit card recognition is growing, but is far from universal. Some cash machines in Riga accept Visa and other cards.

## Passports and Visas

Full passports are required by all travellers. Visas are required universally except by nationals of Estonia, Lithuania, Hungary, UK, the Czech Republic, Slovakia, Poland, Ireland, Denmark, Iceland, Norway, the USA and Finland. They can be obtained at the airport and the sea passenger ports (but not train border crossings) by US, Australian, Canadian and most European nationals, but it is advisable to get them in advance. A Latvian visa is valid for the other Baltic countries.

However, the situation is liable to change, so check at the nearest embassy at least three weeks before travelling.

## Customs

The following allowances are for people aged 18 or over: 200 cigarettes or 200g tobacco products, and 1 litre alcohol.

## Tourist Information

**Riga Tourist Information Centre**, *Skarnu 22 , Riga LV 1053; tel: 371 722 1731.*

## Useful Addresses

**Australia: Consulate**, *PO Box 23, Kew, Victoria 3101; tel: (03) 949 96920.*
**Canada: Embassy (Consular Section)**, *112 Kont St, Place de Ville, Tower 'B', Suite 208, Ottawa, Ontario; tel: (613) 238 6868.*
**UK: Embassy**, *45 Nottingham Pl., London W1M 3FE; tel: (0171) 312 0040.*
**USA: Embassy**, *4325 17th Street N.W., Washington, DC 20011; tel: (202) 726 8213/4.*

### STAYING IN LATVIA

## Accommodation

The more sophisticated accommodation tends to cluster around Riga and the seaside resort Jurmala, once colonised by Russian holidaymakers, including Boris Yeltsin.

For **Bed and Breakfast**, **farmhouse** and **self-catering** accommodation (and fishing and mushroom-picking), contact **Lauku celotajs (Country Traveller)**, *11 Kugu St, LV 1048, Riga; tel: 371 761 7600.*

Most **camping** facilities are in the area of Jurmala and the coastline.

### Eating and Drinking

New restaurants and cafés are opening up all the time. Latvian cuisine features fish and meat, many dishes accompanied by a richly seasoned gravy. The brown granary bread and sweet pastries are excellent. There are lots of different berries in season and they are often used in delicious ice-cream sundaes.

Don't drink the tap water. Tea and coffee are both widely available. Latvian beer *(alus)* is cheap, strong and quite good – try *Aldaris, Bauskas* and *Piebalga. Kvass* is a mildly alcoholic rye drink.

You should book a table if you want to dine in a major hotel.

### Opening Hours

**Banks:** open mainly Mon–Fri 0900–1600. Some open Sat 0900–1230. **Shops:** Mon–Fri 0900/1000–1800/1900 and Sat 0900/1000–1700. Many close on Mon, as well as Sun. Food shops usually open earlier and close later. There are several 24-hour supermarkets in Riga. **Museums:** days of opening vary enormously and many open on only a few days every week, most commonly from Tues or Wed to Sun, 1100–1700.

### Communications

**Post offices** *(pasts)* are open Mon–Fri 0900–1800 and Sat 0900–1300. The Riga post ofice (on *Brivibas)* is open 24 hours. Post boxes are yellow.

**Telephones:** Look out for the new digital card phones (red, green and white). Phone cards worth 2, 5 or 10 Lats can be bought at post offices. Some coin phones are available at post offices. To call abroad from Latvia: *tel: 8, 00,* then the country code. To call Latvia: *tel: 371.* To call Directory enquiries: *079.*

**Emergencies:** Police: *02;* Fire: *01;* Ambulance: *03.*

### Public Holidays

1 Jan; Good Fri; Easter Mon (unofficial); 1 May; Mothers' Day (second Sun in May); 23, 24 June (Midsummer); 18 Nov; 25, 26, 31 Dec.

### Public Transport

Public transport is still extremely cheap for Westerners and **taxis** are usually an affordable option. Try to avoid bumped-up taxi fares by negotiating a price before you get in, although most taxis now have meters. **Buses** and **trams** are often spilling over with passengers and can be a hotbed for pickpockets.

Kiosks line the streets and station forecourts. From here buy either individual or, more sensibly, several tickets which are validated on board the buses or trams; alternatively buy from the driver. The same tickets apply for both. For longer stays a monthly transport ticket can prove convenient and, if you have student ID, an even cheaper solution. On the spot fines are charged for unauthorised travel.

The **long-distance bus network** is a popular alternative to the often slow domestic train service. Buses travel to most destinations on a relatively frequent basis.

### RAIL TRAVEL WITHIN LATVIA

The national rail company is **Latvian Railways (LVD)**. (For the Baltic Express, see p.536.) Domestic services offer two classes of travel: *servis* comes complete with an attendant and free tea and coffee in a compartment, while *tarif* comprises an open seated carriage, though refurbishments can be purchased. Trains to Liepaja, Daugaupils and Ventspils convey special carriages with six-seat compartments complete with attendants, refreshments and television. Night trains comprise two classes of travel, and it is better to book a berth in a coupé (four berths). Reservations are required on all trains, except local and suburban services. See p.47, for details of Latvian–Estonian connections.

### Fares and Passes

For the Baltic Rail Explorer Pass, see p.28.

## LITHUANIA

**Capital:** Vilnius. **Language:** Lithuanian.

64

Lithuanian and Latvian belong to the same language group and are Indo-European in origin. Russian is still common on signs around the railways and telephones. However, while Russian may be helpful, this reminder of the years of Soviet occupation would be unpopular and a phrasebook is indispensible. **Currency:** Lithuanian Litai; 1 Litas = 100 Cents. There are no restrictions on the import/export of foreign currencies. Travellers' cheques can be cashed at most banks and at major tourist hotels. Visa, Mastercard/Eurocard, Diner's Club and American Express are accepted at most banks, major hotels, shops and restaurants. Cash machines accepting Visa and other cards are appearing in Vilnius and Kaunas.

### Passports and Visas
All visitors require full passports. Visas are required for those who are not nationals of the UK, the US, Australia, Iceland, Denmark, Poland, the Czech Republic, Slovakia, Austria, Canada, Estonia, Hungary, Ireland, Italy, Japan, Latvia, South Korea or Switzerland. Visas are no longer issued at borders or airports. For most Westerners, Lithuanian visas are also valid in Latvia and Estonia, but check first.

### Customs
Allowances are constantly changing, so check just before travelling. Currently: 200 cigarettes or 50 cigars or 250 g tobacco, and 1 litre wine or 2 litres champagne or 1.5 litres beer.

### Useful Addresses
**Australia: Consulate**, *26 Jalanga Crescent, Aranda, ACT 2614; tel: (062) 53 2062.*
**Canada: Consulate**, *130 Albert St, Suite 204, Ottawa, Ontario; tel: (1613) 567 5458.*
**UK: Embassy**, *84 Gloucester Pl., London W1; tel: (0171) 486 6401.*
**USA: Lithuanian Consulate–General and National Tourist Office**, *420 Fifth Ave, New York, NY 10018; tel: (1212) 354 7849 or 354 7840.*

### STAYING IN LITHUANIA

### Accommodation
Builders are moving fast to meet the demand,

with over 45 private hotels now in Vilnius. But hotel accommodation, especially at the more comfortable end of the market, can still be hard to come by. There is a last minute booking service at the **Tourist Information and Hotel Reservation Centre**, *Vilnius Airport; tel: 26 08 75.* Prices are often listed in DM or US$, suggestive of the fact that they bear little relation to local costs. Agencies like **Litinterp Agency**, *Bernadinn 7–2; tel: 22 28 50* (for Vilnius and Lithuania), arrange accommodation with local families. If looking away from the capital, book ahead or at least have some names, addresses and phone numbers. Check out any accommodation before you part with your money.

### Eating and Drinking
Local specialities include: *cepelinai* (the national dish – meat balls in potato), *blynai* (mini pancakes) and *kotletas* (pork cutlets). Fish and dairy products are common in all dishes. Lithuanians eat their evening meal early and you should aim to order by 2000, even in places which are theoretically open much later. Service is leisurely so relax and make an evening of it. Leave no more than 1 Litas as a tip. Do not drink tap water. Tea and coffee are widely available. Vodka (the best is *Kvietine)* and very sweet liqueurs are the main spirits. Lithuanian beer *(Vtena* and other brands) is easily available. The beer bars in Vilnius are worth a visit if you want to see 'the other side' of Lithuania. They are usually large rooms where snacks and watered-down beer are sold to sometimes belligerent hard drinkers.

### Communications
**Postage:** All towns have a post office with an international telephone service.
**Telephones:** Phone cards are available from newstands. To call Lithuania: *tel: 370.* To call abroad from Lithuania: *tel: 8 10 + country code.* To call the international operator: *tel: 07* (English spoken). Directory enquiries: *09.* **Emergencies:** Police: *02;* Fire: *01;* Ambulance: *03.*

### Opening Hours
**Banks:** most banks open Mon–Fri 0900–1700, some Sat 0900–1300. **Shops:** (large shops) Mon–Fri 1000/1100–1900; many also open Sat

65

until 1600. Some close for lunch (1400–1500) and also on Sun and Mon. The local shops have their own systems and there is no pattern to this at all. **Food shops** have longer hours: Mon–Sat 0900–1400 and 1500–2000, Sun 0800–1400. Grocery stores open 0800–2000 on weekdays. **Museums:** these open on different days and at different times. Most are closed Mon and open at least Wed and Fri (entrance to many is free on Wed). Most are open at least 1100–1700, but a few open only in the morning or the afternoon, so you must check locally.

## Public Holidays

1 Jan; 16 Feb; 11 Mar; Easter Sun and Mon; 1 May; the first Sun in May (Mothers Day); 6 July; 1 Nov; 25, 26 Dec.

### RAIL TRAVEL WITHIN LITHUANIA

**Lithuanian Railways (LG)** is the national operator. There is only one class of travel on the local trains (including Vilnius–Kaunas), and reservations are unnecessary. Other trains have a first and second class seated accommodation. The Vilnius–Klaipeda 'express' service also conveys 'luxury' class new coaches, with refreshments, attendants, access to a phone etc., included in the ticket price. The night trains usually comprise of second-class coupé sleeping carriages (compartments of four berths).

For information about the Baltic Express and services to and from Russia, see p.536.

## Fares and Passes

Rail Europ Senior Card and the Baltic Rail Explorer Pass are both valid in Lithuania. See p.28 for details.

### LUXEMBOURG

**Capital:** Luxembourg City *(Ville de Luxembourg)*. **Language:** Lëtzebuergesch is the national tongue, but almost everybody also speaks fluent French and/or German and a great number speak at least some English. **Currency:** Luxembourg Francs (LFr.). Belgian and Luxembourg francs are co-rated and Belgian money is accepted everywhere. It works less easily the other way round, however, so try not to get left with Luxembourg francs when you leave.

## Passports and Visas

EU National Identity Cards are sufficient. Visas are not needed by nationals of the EU, Australia, Canada, New Zealand or the USA. South Africans do need visas. Others should check – with the nearest Belgian consulate if Luxembourg has no representation.

## Customs

Standard EU regulations apply (p.17) if you're flying. When crossing the land borders by train, you probably won't even notice them and there are no facilities for duty-free shopping.

## Tourist Information

As it is such a small country, literature covering the whole Grand-Duchy is the norm and you can get most of it from any Tourist Office in (or outside) the country. There's an annual *Calendar of Events* and *Grand-Duché de Luxembourg* is a brochure containing miscellaneous information. Most tourist literature is free and, unless you want detailed information, you can get by perfectly well without anything that isn't.

## Useful Addresses

**UK: Embassy,** *27 Wilton Crescent, London SW1X 8SD; tel: (0171) 235 6961, fax: (0171) 235 9734.* **National Tourist Office,** *122 Regent St, London W1R 5FE; tel: (0171) 434 2800, fax: (0171) 734 1205.*
**USA: Embassy,** *2200 Massachusetts Ave N.W., Washington DC 20008; tel: (202) 265 4171. fax: (202) 328 8270.* **National Tourist Office,** *17 Beekman Pl., New York, NY 10022; tel: (212) 935 8888.*

### STAYING IN LUXEMBOURG

## Accommodation

The nearest branch of Luxembourg National Tourist Office should be able to provide free brochures covering **hotels** (of all grades, plus restaurants), **holiday apartments**, **farm holidays** and **camping** in the Grand-Duchy and a **Bed and Breakfast** booklet that covers all three Benelux countries.

## Eating and Drinking

Most hotels serve breakfast until 1000. Lunch is

around 1200–1400 and dinner 1900–2200. Luxembourg cuisine is pithily described as 'French quality, German quantity', but eating out is expensive. Keep costs down by making lunch your main meal and looking for the special deals: *plat du jour* (single course) or *menu* (2–3 courses). There are takeaways, most pizzerias are good value and light meals are often available in pastry shops. Local specialities are: Ardennes ham, *treipen* (black pudding), *quenelles* (calf's liver dumplings), *thüringer* (the standard local sausage), *gromperekichelcher* (fried potato patties) and (in Sept) *quetschentaart* (a flan featuring dark-violet plums).

Luxembourg produces a variety of lagers, liqueurs and white wines. Sugar may not be added while making wine, so the Moselles are drier and fruitier than their German equivalents.

## Communications

**Post offices** *(Poste)* usually open Mon–Fri 0800–1200 and 1400–1700. Postboxes are small, bright yellow and attached to walls.

**Telephones:** Booths have instructions in the form of pictograms, usually with French and German text. Card boxes take only *télécartes*, available from post offices and some CFL offices. There are reduced rates for some international calls at weekends and in the evenings.

To call abroad from Luxembourg; *tel: 00.* To call Luxembourg; *tel: 352* – there are no area codes. Local operator: *017.* International operator; *tel: 016.* **Emergencies:** Police: *113;* All other emergency services: *112.* Emergency and international operators speak English.

## Opening Hours

Be prepared for many establishments to take a long lunch-break. **Banks:** Usually Mon–Fri 0800/0900–1600, but some stay open a little later. **Shops:** Mon 1300/1400–1800; Tues–Sat 0900–1800. **Museums:** Vary, but most open six days a week (usually Tues–Sun).

## Public Holidays

1 Jan, Feb (Carnival), Easter Mon, 1 May, Ascension, Whit Mon, 23 June (National Day), 15 Aug, 1 Nov and 25 Dec. When holidays fall on Sun, the Mon usually becomes a holiday – but only twice in one year.

## Public Transport

Apart from the capital, most towns are small and **buses** are primarily for inter-town travel. Transport terminals are never far from the centre and the major attractions are seldom too far to walk: but be prepared for a lot of hills. At bus terminals, the stops are numbered. To find the one for your bus, ignore the numbers and look for your destination. The norm is to board buses at the front and disembark further back.

**Taxis** have roof signs, but they are not allowed to pick up passengers in the street. There's usually a rank at the rail station. If not, you can probably phone for one.

### RAIL TRAVEL WITHIN LUXEMBOURG

The national rail company is **CFL**, *9 pl. de la Gare, Luxembourg; tel: 49 901.* The network is limited, but CFL run long-distance buses to fill the gaps. These are covered by multi-ride passes, as are city buses (which have no other connection with CFL). The standard of rolling-stock varies considerably, but most trains are comfortable. If doors don't open automatically and there's no handle, look for a button.

## Stations

Most stations are small and have few facilities, although you can expect WCs, timetables and a manned ticket office. The staff in small places are usually helpful.

## Fares and Passes

For details of the **Benelux Tourrail Pass**, see p. 28.

**Billet Réseau** or **Oeko–Billjee Letzeburg** is a day-card (LFr.160) valid for unlimited second-class travel on all public transport in the Duchy – CFL and bus operators AVL, TICE and RGTR (a day is considered to end at 0800 on the following day). First class travel is available on payment of a supplement. It is also possible to buy a *carnet* (block) of five one-day cards (LFr.640). Both are available from CFL offices and each ticket must be validated for the first journey of the day: on boarding buses or at rail stations. Border travel is excluded, so buy a separate ticket to cover the journey between the border and whichever station is closest. Short distance tickets are LFr.40.

67

The **Luxembourg Card** is available for 1, 2 and 3 day periods, and available at many hotels, campsites, hostels, Tourist Offices, attractions and at railway and bus stations throughout the country. It provides free transport on all trains and buses throughout the entire country, plus free entry to many tourist attractions in Luxembourg City.

## THE NETHERLANDS

**Capital:** There are two capitals: Amsterdam is administrative and The Hague *(Den Haag)* is legislative. **Language:** Dutch is the official language. However, the majority of Dutch people speak English and are happy to do so. **Currency:** Guilders; 1 Guilder = 100 cents. Guilders were once known as florins and price tags usually show 'f' or 'fl', but 'NLG' is more common in other contexts.

### Passports and Visas

EU National Identity Cards are sufficient. Visas are not needed by nationals of Australia, Canada, New Zealand or the USA. South Africans do need visas.

### Customs

Standard EU regulations apply (see p.17).

### Tourist Information

Tourist bureaux are **VVV (Vereniging voor Vreemdelingenverkeer)**: signs show a triangle with three Vs. Minimum opening times: Mon–Fri 0900–1700, Sat 1000–1200 (most open longer). The service is comprehensive, but they charge to book accommodation and for most literature: there's usually a cheap general-purpose leaflet that includes a map.

Electronic information machines are understandable if you remember that *gesloten* means 'closed' and know the days of the week *(ma t/m vr* is Mon–Fri). *Geen* and *verboden* indicate prohibitions: *Geen toegang* means 'No entry'. When queueing, stand behind the line on the floor (if one is marked).

Many attractions close Oct–Easter, while Apr–May is tulip time and the country is crowded, so (unless you want to see the tulips) June–Sept is the best time to visit.

**Museumjaarkaart** (NLG.45 from VVV and participating museums) is valid for a year and provides free entry to most museums nationwide. You can get it from the Netherlands Board of Tourism in London (see under 'Useful Addresses in the UK'), but it costs a bit more: £20. An alternative is the less comprehensive **Kortingkaart** – anyone under 26 should compare both with the **CJP (Cultureel Jongeren Paspoort)** – VVV can supply details.

### Useful Addresses

**Australia: Embassy**, *120 Empire Circuit, Yarralumla, Canberra, ACT 2600; tel: (06) 273 3111.*

**Canada: Embassy**, *Suite 2020, 350 Albert St, Ottawa, Ontario K1R 1A4; tel: (613) 237 5030.* **Tourist Office**, *Suite 710, 25 Adelaide St E., Toronto, Ontario M5C 1Y2; tel: (416) 363 1577.*

**Republic of Ireland: Embassy**, *160 Merrion Rd, Dublin 4; tel: (01) 269 3444.*

**New Zealand: Embassy**, *Investment House (10th Floor), Ballance/ Featherstone St, Wellington; tel: (04) 473 8652.*

**South Africa: Embassy**, *PO Box 117, Pretoria 0001; tel: (012) 344 3910.*

**UK: Embassy**, *38 Hyde Park Gate, London SW7 5DP; tel: (0171) 540 3200;* visa information; *tel: (0891) 171217.* **NBT (Netherlands Board of Tourism)**, *Egginton House, 25/28 Buckingham Gate, London SW1E 6NT; tel: (0891) 717777.* **Netherlands Railways**, *c/o Holland Rail, Chase House, Gilbert St, Ropley, Hampshire, SO24 0BY; tel: (01962) 773646, fax: (01962) 773625.*

**USA: Embassy**, *4200 Linnean Ave N.W., Washington, DC 20008-1848; tel: (202) 244 5304.* **Netherlands Board of Tourism**, *355 Lexington Ave (21st Floor), New York, NY 10017; tel: (212) 370 7360.*

### Embassies in the Netherlands

Unusually, these are not all in the same city. **Australia:** *Carnegielaan 4, The Hague; tel: (070) 310 8200.* **Canada:** *Parkstr. 25, The Hague; tel: (070) 364 4825.* **New Zealand:** *Carnegielaan 10, The Hague; tel: (070) 346 9324.* **Republic of Ireland:** *dr. Kuyperstr. 9, The Hague; tel: (070) 363 0993.* **South Africa:** *Wassenarseweg 40; tel: (070) 392 4501.* **UK:** *Koningslaan 44,*

*Amsterdam; tel: (020) 676 4343.* **USA:** *Museumplein 19, Amsterdam; tel: (020) 664 5661.*

## Accommodation

The Netherlands participates in the Benelux hotel-classification scheme (see Belgium, p. 36). NBT produce brochures with full-colour pictures (£1 each) for **hotels** of all grades, **holiday cottages** and official **campsites**. Standards are high; low prices reflect limited facilities rather than poor quality. Room rates start around NLG.65 for a double, but most are more. Advance booking is advisable and there's a free centralised booking service: **NRC (Netherlands Reservation Centre)**, *PO Box 404, 2260 AK Leidschendam; tel: (070) 317 54 54* (English spoken), *fax: (070) 317 032 026.* Mon–Fri 0800–2000 and Sat 0800–1400. NRC have a London branch (in NBT); *tel: (0171) 931 0801,* but they charge £7.

**Dutch Youth Hostels Association (NJHC)** are based at *Prof. Tulpplein 4, 1018 GX Amsterdam; tel: (020) 622 2859.* VVV have listings of Bed and Breakfast accommodation in their area, where it exists, or you can book nationwide through **Bed and Breakfast Holland**, *Warmondstraat 129 1e, Amsterdam; tel: (020) 615 7527.*

## Eating and Drinking

Dutch cuisine is traditionally simple and substantial. Many Indonesian restaurants offer spicy food; a good variety of international cuisine is available in cities. Most eating-places stay open all day but restaurants in small places take last orders by 2100. Look for boards saying *dagschotel* (a very economical 'special'). 'Brown cafés' (traditional pubs) also serve good-value food. *Mensas* are subsidised student canteens in university towns; very cheap and not restricted to students, but open only during term-time.

Dutch specialities include apple pie (heavy on cinnamon and sultanas), herring marinated in brine, steamed eels, *poffertjes* (tiny puff-pancakes with icing sugar) and *pannekoeken* (pancakes: try bacon with syrup). Street stalls for snacks abound, options invariably including *frites/patats* (a cross between french fries and

English chips) with mayonnaise or other sauces – in Limburg, try the regional (slightly sour) *zurvlees*. Vending machines at stations sell heated croquettes, *bami* and *nasi* being spicy.

Excellent coffee and hot chocolate are available everywhere, often topped with whipped cream – *slagroom*. Tea is hot water with a choice of teabags – ask if you want milk. Dutch beer is topped by two fingers of froth. Most local liqueurs are excellent. The main spirit is *jenever,* a strong, slightly oily gin made from juniper berries.

## Communications

The **post office** logo is *ptt post* (white on red). Most open Mon–Fri 0830–1700 and some Sat 0900–1600. Parcels can be sent only from major post offices. Stamps are sold by most people who sell postcards.

**Telephones:** Other than special *06* lines, all Dutch telephone numbers have ten digits, including the area code. Booths have a white *ptt telecom* logo and instructions in English. Cash booths are green, blue booths take only *telefoonkaarten* cards – from post offices, VVV and NS. Recorded messages in Dutch are often followed by the English version. International calls are cheapest weekday evenings and all day Sat, Sun. A few numbers prefixed *06* are free, but most are at premium rates. To call abroad from the Netherlands; *tel: 00* and pause until the dialling tone resumes. To call the Netherlands; *tel: 31.* Operator: *tel: 06 0410.* International directory; *tel: 06 0418.* National directory; *tel: 06 8008.* **All emergencies** (free): *06 11.*

## Opening Hours

**Banks:** Mon–Fri 0900–1600/1700 (later Thur). **Shops:** Mon–Fri 0900/0930–1730/1800 (until 2100 Thur or Fri), Sat 0900/0930–1600/1700. Many close Mon morning and one afternoon a week. **Museums:** vary, but usually Tues–Sun (or Mon–Sat) 1000–1700. In winter many have shorter hours.

## Public Holidays

1 Jan; Good Fri; Easter Sun–Mon; 30 Apr; 5 May (Liberation Day); Ascension Day; Whit Sun–Mon; 25, 26 Dec. You won't go far wrong by assuming that Sun hours/timetables apply.

### Public Transport

There are centralised (premium rate) numbers for all rail and bus enquiries (computerised, fast and accurate). National: *tel: 0900 9292*. International: *tel: 0900 9296*. Public transport is less frequent on Sun.

Most vehicles and carriages have yellow buttons inside and out, so you can open doors yourself if necessary.

**Taxis** have roof signs and it's customary to board at ranks or phone. You can try hailing them, but they seldom stop.

**Treintaxis** have ranks at stations and yellow roof signs. No money changes hands: you buy tickets for specific towns (a flat rate of NLG.6 for anywhere within the city limits) from any rail ticket office. They have to wait 10 mins unless there's a full load, but are good value for the outskirts (useful if you're hostelling). They are not available in Amsterdam, The Hague or Rotterdam.

**Strippenkaarten** (available from stations, city transport offices, post offices and sometimes VVV) are strip tickets valid nationwide on any city train, metro, bus or tram. The whole country is zoned and you use one section to board plus one for each zone travelled. In cities, validate them in the yellow box on buses and trams and at the entrance to metros; in smaller places, the driver stamps them. Once stamped, a section is valid for an hour, even if you change transport (so long as you don't increase the number of zones). The most common are 15 strips (NLG.11) and 45 strips (NLG.32.25). Individual tickets and short strips can be purchased from drivers, but the longer strips are much better value.

### RAIL TRAVEL WITHIN THE NETHERLANDS

The national rail company, **Nederlandse Spoorwegen (NS)**, is very efficient, providing fast and comfortable trains everywhere. Most *IC* services run every half-hour and have a trolley service. *Sneltreins* call at the principal stations and *stoptreins* serve all stations en route. Seat reservations are possible only for international journeys.

Dutch railway stations do not accept payment by credit card, so unless purchasing tickets in advance, remember to carry cash.

### Stations

Credit cards can be used to purchase international tickets, but not local tickets. Most stations have a **GWK bank** that opens long hours seven days a week and accepts credit cards. Most also have excellent cafés, snacks, WCs, baggage lockers, telephones, English newspapers and bicycle-hire offices.

### Fares and Passes

For details of the **Benelux Tourrail Pass**, see p. 28.

There are a number of Netherlands Rail Rover Tickets. The **Summer Tour Rover** is available in June, July and Aug, and allows two people 3 days unlimited travel within a 10-day period. They can be upgraded to include a public transport link. The **One Day Rover** is a popular ticket allowing unlimited travel around Holland. A **One Day Public Transport Link** can be purchased to be used in conjunction with the One-Day Rover, but cannot be purchased separately.

**Meermanskaart** is available for group travel (2–6 people), allowing unlimited travel in the Netherlands. It can be used after 0900 on weekdays, all day Sat and Sun and public holidays, except during July and Aug when it is valid before 0900 every day. Available for first and second class travel.

### Rail Pass Concessions

| Operator, Route/Concession | Rail Pass/Discount |
|---|---|
| Stena Line Hoek van Holland–Harwich (Dayrider and Twilight) | IR 30% |
| Scandinavian Seaways Harwich/Newcastle–Amsterdam | IR 50% |
| Hoek van Holland–Harwich (Dayrider and Twilight) | FP 30% |
| DFDS Newcastle–Amsterdam | FP 30% |
| Stena Line Hoek van Holland–Harwich | RES 30% |

## NORWAY

**Capital:** Oslo. **Language:** Bokmål and Nynorsk are both variants of Norwegian. Almost everyone speaks English – if not, try German. Norwegian has three additional vowels: æ, ø and å, which (in that order) follow z. **Currency:** Norwegian Kroner (NKr./NOK); 1 Krone = 100 Ore. On slot machines, *femkrone* means a NKr.5 coin and *tikrone* a NKr.10 piece.

## Passports and Visas

National Identity Cards issued by the EU, Iceland and Switzerland are sufficient. Visas are not needed by nationals of these countries: Australia, Canada, New Zealand or the USA. South Africans do need visas.

## Customs

Allowances are: European residents aged 16 or more: 200 cigarettes or 250 g tobacco and 200 cigarette papers (all doubled if you live outside Europe). Anyone aged 18 or more: 2 litres beer and 2 litres wine not exceeding 22% proof. Anyone aged 20 or more may substitute 1 litre spirits not exceeding 60% proof for 1 litre wine.

## Tourist Information

Tourist offices are **Turistinformasjon** and tourist boards **Reiselivslag**. Many things in Norway are seasonal. The definition of summer varies from year to year (affected by the weather), but always includes mid June–mid Aug). The **Midnight Sun** is visible longest at North Cape, but can be seen (early June–early July) as far south as Bodø. **Aurora Borealis (the Northern Lights)** may be visible within the Arctic Circle Nov–Feb. Film is very expensive, so take an ample supply.

## Useful Addresses

**Australia: Embassy**, *17 Hunter St, Yarralumla, Canberra ACT 2600; tel: (06) 273 3444.*
**Canada: Embassy**, *Royal Bank Center, 90 Sparks St (Suite 532), Ottawa, Ont. K1P 5B4; tel: (613) 238 6570.*
**Republic of Ireland: Embassy**, *34 Molesworth St, Dublin 2; tel: (01) 662 1800.*
**New Zealand: Embassy**, *70 Shortland St (3rd Floor), Auckland; tel: (09) 377 1944.*
**South Africa: Embassy**, *524 Church St (7th Floor), Arcadia, Pretoria 0083; tel: (012) 323 4790.*
**UK: Embassy**, *25 Belgrave Sq., London SW1X 8QD; tel: (0171) 591 5500.* **Norwegian Tourist Board (NTB)**, *Charles House, 5/11 Lower Regent St, London SW1Y 4LR; tel: (0171) 839 6255.*

**USA: Embassy**, *2720 34th St N.W., Washington, DC 20008-2799; tel: (202) 333 6000.* **Scandinavian Tourist Board**, *655 Third Ave, New York, NY 10017; tel: (212) 949 2333.*

### STAYING IN NORWAY

## Accommodation

**NTB** produce *Norway Accommodation,* a (free) brochure listing **hotels**, **cabins**, **hostels** and **hotel discount passes**. Local Tourist Offices provide lists of all accommodation in their area (including **private houses**). Most will make bookings – for a small fee. **Hotels** are expensive, but many cut rates at weekends and in summer. Many of the 90 **hostels** *(vandrerhjem)* open only in summer (the Norwegian **HI** logo is a variation: a stylised green tree and blue hut with a yellow sun).

Many of the 1500 official **campsites** (with 5-star classification) have pre-bookable log cabins for two or four people. *Norwegian Camping Guide* is available from NTB and **NAF** (Norwegian Automobile Association), *Storgt 2, 0155 Oslo; tel: 22 34 14 00.* **Rough camping** is permitted anywhere *suitable,* but don't intrude on residents or leave any trace of your stay.

**DNT: Den Norske Turistforening** (the Norwegian Mountain Touring Association), *Storgate 3, 0125 Oslo,* provide information for campers and walkers. They have branches in gateways to wilderness areas and run the mountain huts (which open at Easter and in summer). Trails are marked by their logo, a large red 'T'.

## Eating and Drinking

Eating out is very expensive and you will save a lot by self-catering. **Rema 1000** and **Netto** are supermarket chains. *Konditori* are bakeries, which often serve sandwiches and pastries relatively cheaply. Restaurants sometimes have *dagens rett* (relatively cheap full meals: NKr.60–70) and self-service *kafeterias* are also generally reasonable.

Breakfast is buffet-style, with a wide choice. Lunch is normally 1200–1500. Dinner is traditionally 1600–1900, but habits are changing and 1800–2200 is now common in towns. Fresh fish is a staple and cheaper than meat. Try *smørrebrød* (the open sandwich), *reker* (shrimps) and *kjøtkaker* (meat balls with potatoes). Street stalls dispense cheap baked potatoes with various fillings and hot dogs. Among the wide variety of ice-cream flavours is extra hot pepper!

Alcohol can raise the cost of eating from expensive to exorbitant and is served only to people over 18/20 (depending on strength), only after 1500 and never on Sun. *Gløgg* is mulled wine, popular in winter.

## Communications

**Post offices** generally open Mon–Fri 0800/0830–1600/1700, Sat 0830–1300. Postboxes have a red posthorn and crown on yellow boxes for local mail and reverse the colours for other destinations.

**Telephones: Telenor** recently revamped the telephone system and city codes no longer exist: just eight-digit numbers. *Telekorten* (phonecards) are available from **Narvesen** and post offices. Card phones are now spreading fast, some accept credit cards. It is usual to find coin and card boxes together, green marking the ones for cards. Both types have instructions in English. There's a free information service; *tel: 80 03 10 32.* Overseas calls are cheapest 2200–0800 and at weekends.

To call abroad from Norway; *tel: 00.* To call Norway; *tel: 47.* Directory enquiries; *tel: 180* for the Nordic countries and *tel: 181* for other countries. Local operator; *tel: 117.* International operator; *tel: 115.* Operators speak English. These are all premium rate calls and therefore very expensive. **Emergencies:** Police: *112;* Fire: *110;* Ambulance: *113.*

## Opening Hours

**Banks:** Mon–Fri 0815/0830–1500/1530 (Thur–1700). Some in Oslo open later, while some rural banks have shorter hours. Many have minibank machines which provide cash against credit cards. **Shops:** Mon–Fri 0900–1600/1700 (Thur 0900–1800/2000), Sat 0900–1300/1500, but many open later. **Museums:** usually Tues–Sun 1000–1500/ 1600. Some also open Mon. Some open longer in summer and/or close completely in winter.

## Public Holidays

1 Jan; Maundy Thur–Good Fri; Easter Sun–Mon; 1, 17 May (Constitution Day); Ascension Day; Whit Sun–Mon; 25, 26 Dec.

## Public Transport

Train, boat and bus schedules are linked to provide good connections. It is often worth using buses or boats to connect two dead-end lines (e.g. Bergen and Stavanger), rather than retracing your route. Railpass holders sometimes get good discounts (sometimes free travel) on linking services.

**Nor-Way Bussekspress**, *Bussterminalen, Galleriet, Schweigaardsgt 8–10, N-0185 Oslo; tel: 23 00 24 40, fax: 23 00 24 49,* has the largest bus network, routes going north as far as Kirkenes. Long-distance buses are comfortable, with reclining seats and ample leg-room. Tickets can be bought on board and booking is not necessary.

**Taxis** are metered and most easily picked up at ranks – or by phoning.

## RAIL TRAVEL WITHIN NORWAY

The Norwegian state railway is **Norges Statsbaner (NSB)**. Norwegian trains are punctual and comfortable, but do not cover the whole country: most routes converge on Oslo and the Norwegian network runs north only as far as Bodø.

Fast trains are *ICE, IC, IN* (InterNord: daytime international services) and *Et* (Expresstog). Second-class seating is comfortable and far more plentiful than first-class. Sleepers have one berth in first class and two or three in second. Couchettes have three berths. Long-distance trains carry refreshments, usually a buffet (with some hot dishes) and a trolley service.

Reservations are necessary for express and many other fast trains. Reserved seats are not marked, but your confirmation specifies carriage and seat/berth numbers. Carriage numbers are shown by the doors at the ends, berth numbers outside the compartments and seat numbers on the seat-backs or luggage racks.

## Stations

Almost all stations provide baggage lockers. Baggage trolleys are not very numerous at the smaller places. The **Narvesen** chain (branches at most stations and open long hours) sells

English-language publications and a good range of snacks. **Inter–Rail Centres** (at some city stations in the summer) work long hours and are invaluable if money is tight. They usually provide cheap showers and free baggage storage (albeit at your own risk).

### Fares and Passes

**Norway Rail Pass** is available for 7 or 14 days consecutive travel (US$195 and US$255 respectively), or 3 days travel in one month (US$135). Both passes are available in first and second classes, but first class is not worthwhile, given the small number of trains with first-class accommodation – the above prices are based on second-class travel. It cannot be bought in Britain, but is obtainable through Eurail, Rail Europe or from NSB stations in Norway. Supplements must be paid to use the scenic Flåm railway and *ICE* services. Seat reservation is compulsory on all Express, *IC* night and international trains. Children under 16 years at the start of the journey are entitled to 50% discount.

**Scanrail Pass** allows unlimited travel on the national railway of Norway (NSB). See p.28 for further details.

**Norpris** are lower priced tickets for jouneys between the major Scandinavian cities. Only available through International Rail at Victoria Station, London or Norwegian railway stations.

### Rail Pass Concessions

| Operator, Route/Concession | Rail Pass/Discount |
| --- | --- |
| Color Line Hirtshals–Kristians | IR 50% |
| HSD Express Ferries | IR 25% |
| Flaggruten Stavanger–Bergen | IR 50% |
| Fylskesbaatane i Sogn og Fjordane Express and Fjord Ferries | IR 50% |
| Larvik Line Larvik Frederikshavn | IR 50% |
| North Norway Express Narvik–Bodø/Fauske (except ferries) | IR 50% |
| North Norway Express Narvik–Tromsø/Alta/ Hammerfest/Kirkenes (except ferries) | IR 50% |
| Buses in the Møre and Romsdal regions | IR 50% |
| Buses in the Nordland, Troms and Finnmark regions | IR 50% |
| Transport Museum, Hamar | IR Free |
| Color Line Kristians–Hirtshals | RES 30% |

## POLAND

**Capital**: Warsaw *(Warszawa)*. **Language**: Polish; many older Poles speak German, while younger Poles (particularly students) are more likely to speak English in tourist areas. Russian is widely understood, but not popular. **Currency**: Złoty (Zł.). Any Polish money you have left can be re-converted when you leave. The most useful foreign currencies are British pounds, American dollars or German marks.

You are most likely to be able to change travellers' cheques or Eurocheques at large banks or certain **Kantor** exchange offices. Kantor sometimes give better rates than banks and their opening hours are longer. A branch of **Thomas Cook** will also be able to change your travellers' cheques, free of charge in the case of Thomas Cook travellers' cheques, at: *Orbis Travel, ul. Marszalkowska 142, Warsaw.*

Credit cards are widely accepted in large establishments and their use is increasing elsewhere, but they are still not universal.

### Passports and Visas

All visitors require full passports. British passport holders do not require visas (but your passport must be valid for at least six months after your planned departure date from Poland), nor do nationals of the USA or the Republic of Ireland. Nationals of Australia, Canada, New Zealand and South Africa do need visas. Others should check.

### Customs

The following allowances are for people aged 17 or over: 250 cigarettes or 50 cigars or 250g tobacco, 1 litre wine, and 1 litre any other alcoholic beverage.

### Tourist Information

**IT** tourist information centres operate within most major towns and cities, offering national as well as local information, and can usually help with accommodation. In the absence of an IT office, there will often be an **Orbis** office which can provide tourist information, arrange excursions and help with accommodation.

### Useful Addresses

**Australia: Embassy**, *7 Turrana St, Yarralumla ACT, 2600 Canberra; tel: (02) 62 73 12 11.*
**Canada: Embassy**, *443 Daly Ave, Ontario K1N 6H3, Ottawa 2; tel: (613) 789 0468.*

**Republic of Ireland: Embassy**, *5 Ailesbury Rd, Dublin 4; tel: (1) 283 08 55.*
**New Zealand: Embassy**, *17 Upland Rd, Kelburn, Wellington; tel: (4) 475 94 53.*
**South Africa: Embassy**, *14 Amos St, Colbyn, Pretoria 0083; tel: (12) 43 26 31.*
**UK: Embassy**, *47 Portland Pl., London W1N 3AG; tel: (0171) 580 4324.* **Polish National Tourist Office**, *Remo House, 310–312 Regent St, W1R 5AJ; tel: (0171) 580 8811.*
**Polish State Railways** c/o Polish National Tourist Office; *tel: (0171) 580 8811.*
**USA: Embassy**, *2640 16th Street N.W., Washington, DC 20009; tel: (202) 234 3800.* **Polish National Tourist Office**, *275 Madison Ave, Suite 1711, New York, NY 10016; tel: (212) 338 9412.*

## STAYING IN POLAND

### Accommodation

Orbis runs a chain of international and tourist standard **hotels** across the country, and some less expensive **motels**. Otherwise, your best bet will probably be a **pension** or **private room**.

In popular holiday areas, you may be able to hire a **holiday cottage** for a longer stay. In the summer season, **youth hostels** and **university rooms** are also available.

With a rapidly developing economy, a wide range of accommodation is becoming easier to find outside the major centres, and you can usually rely on Tourist Offices to help. But equally, find a good, up-to-date hotel listing and be prepared to make your own arrangements.

### Eating and Drinking

Simple meals and snacks can easily be obtained at cafés and fast food outlets, while *zajazdy,* reasonably priced roadside inns and cafés, serve typical Polish food and pastries. Restaurants in major cities are usually open between 1200–2400. Classic national dishes include beetroot soup, herrings in soured cream, potato pancakes, stuffed cabbage leaves, cabbage and sausage stew, *pierogi* (a large-scale ravioli), baked cheesecake and doughnuts. There's a heavy emphasis on soups, which can be sweet as well as savoury. Typical ingredients include fish, pork, game and soured cream. A vast range of

Polish mineral waters are drunk in preference to tap water, which is best avoided. Tea is served black and in glasses, usually with lemon, but you can specify that you would like milk. Virtually all wine is imported and expensive, while Polish beer, generally lager, has a distinctive fresh taste. The vast range of clear and flavoured vodka is excellent and inexpensive.

### Communications

**Post offices** *(Poczta)* open Mon–Sat 0700/0800–1800/2000 (main offices). Note that the word *Przerwa* on the glass windows means break and the booth is closed between the times shown. In each city, the post offices are numbered (the main office is always 1) and the number should be included in the post restante address. Post boxes are green (local mail), or red (long-distance mail).

**Telephones:** Until recently public telephones were operated exclusively by telephone tokens on sale at post offices and Ruch kiosks. Newer telephones operate on telephone cards and these are much more efficient. To call Poland: *tel: 48.* To call abroad from Poland: *tel: 901.* To call an English speaking operator: *tel: 903.* **Emergencies:** Police: *997;* Fire: *998;* Ambulance: *999.*

### Opening Hours

**Banks:** Mon–Fri 0800–1500/1800. **Shops**: Mon–Fri 0800/1100–1900, Sat 0900–1300. **Food shops:** Mon–Fri 0600–1900, Sat 0600–1300. **Museums:** these vary greatly, but are usually open Tues–Sun 1000–1600. They seldom open on public holidays and are often closed the following day as well.

### Public Holidays

1 Jan; Easter Sun–Mon; 1, 3 May; Corpus Christi; 15 Aug; 1, 11 Nov; 24, 25, 26 Dec.

### Public Transport

**PKS buses** are cheap and more practical than trains for short trips or off-beat destinations. Tickets include seat reservations (the seat number is on the back) and can be purchased in advance from the bus station. In rural areas, bus drivers will often halt away from official stops if you wave them down.

## RAIL TRAVEL WITHIN POLAND

The Polish national rail service is operated by **Polskie Koleje Panstwowe (PKP)**. The rail network is extensive, cheap and punctual, but make sure you know what type of train you're taking, as ordinary services can be very slow. Express trains link all major cities, though the network is more sparatn in Eastern Poland.

At stations, departures *(odjazdy)* are on yellow paper and arrivals *(przyjazdy)* on white. The InterCity *(IC)*, express trains *(ekspres – prefixed Ex)* and fast trains *(pospieszny)* that are almost as fast are printed in red. The black *osobowy* trains are the slowest. Trains usually have first- and second-class accommodation and Westerners generally feel first class is worth the extra cost (about 50% more, but still cheap by Western standards). Overnight trains usually have first- and second-class sleepers, as well as second-class couchettes and seats. Reservations are possible on all express and *pospieszny* (fast) services. Most long-distance trains have buffet services and the WARS (buffet) carriages can be good for a snack and a drink.

### Stations

Virtually all major stations provide left-luggage and refreshment facilities. Don't expect ticket clerks to speak English.

### Fares and Passes

The **Polrail Pass**, available from Wasteels, allows unlimited travel on the PKP network for 8, 15 or 21 days or one month, but normal fares are cheap and it's usually more economical to buy ordinary single and return tickets. Compulsory reservations are included in the price, but must be booked locally. The **Poland Explorer Pass** is available from Campus Travel to holders of ISIC cards, teachers and academic staff, plus accompanying spouses and children of eligible persons. Available for 7, 14 and 21 days travel in both first and second class. Prices start at £21 for 7 days in second class.

## PORTUGAL

**Capital:** Lisbon *(Lisboa)*. **Language:** Portuguese, which is difficult to understand when it is spoken but, if you speak any other Latin languages, you will probably understand enough

of the written form to get by. English, French and German are spoken to some extent, but mostly in tourist areas. As a rule, older people speak French as a second language, young people speak Spanish and/or English. **Currency:** Escudos (Esc.). 1 Escudo = 100 Centavos. In written form, the $ sign comes between the Escudos and the Centavos, where there would normally be a decimal point. Time zone: 1 hr behind Spain.

### Passports and Visas

EU National Identity Cards are sufficient. Visas are required by nationals of South Africa. Nationals of Canada and the USA may stay for up to two months without a visa.

### Customs

Standard EU regulations apply (see p. 17).

### Tourist Information

Portugal has a multi-lingual telephone information service for tourists, based in Lisbon, *tel: (01) 70 63 41.*

The police (dark-blue uniforms in towns and brown in rural areas) are also helpful and wear red arm bands if they are bi-lingual.

### Useful Addresses

**Australia: Embassy**, *6 Campion St, 1st Floor, Deakin ACT, 2600 Canberra; tel: (062) 85 20 84.*

**Canada: Embassy**, *645 Island Park Dr., Ottawa, Ontario, K1Y OB8; tel: (613) 729 0883.* **Tourist Office**, *60 Bloor St W., Suite 1005, Toronto, Ontario, M4W 3B8; tel: (613) 921 7376.*

**Republic of Ireland: Embassy**, *Knocksinna House, Knocksinna, Foxrock, Dublin 18; tel: (1) 289 4416.* **Tourist Office**, *54 Dawson St, Dublin 2; tel: (1) 670 9133.*

**New Zealand: Embassy**, *117 Amey Rd, Remuera, Oakland 5, Wellington 1; tel: (649) 548 266.*

**South Africa: Embassy**, *599 Leyds St, Muckleneuk, 0002 Pretoria; tel: (012) 341 2340.* **Tourist Office**, *Diamond Corner, 8th Floor, 68 Eloff St, Jo'burg 2000; tel (11) 33 74775.*

**UK: Consulate-General**, *3rd Floor, Silver City House, 62 Brompton Rd, London SW3 1BJ; tel:*

75

*(0171) 581 8722/4.* **Embassy**, *11 Belgrave Sq., SW1X 8PP; tel: (0171) 235 5331.* **Tourist Office**, *22/25A Sackville St, London W1X 1DE; tel: (0171) 494 1441.* **Portuguese Railways**, *Address as Tourist Office; tel: (0171) 839 4741.*

**USA: Embassy**, *2125 Kalorama Road N.W., Washington, DC 20008-1619; tel: (202) 328 8610.* **Tourist Office**, *590 Fifth Ave (4th Floor), New York, NY 10036-4704; tel: (212) 354 4403/4.*

## STAYING IN PORTUGAL

### Accommodation

The possibilities for accommodation in Portugal are almost endless: you name it, they've got it. You can choose anything from a five-star hotel to a campsite, from a private home to a hostel. Information about all forms of accommodation (including private homes, which range from manor houses to farms) is available from government Tourist Offices.

There are many **campsites** throughout the country. Information from the **Portuguese Camping and Caravan Association**, *Av. Coronel Eduardo Galbardo 24, 1000 Lisbon; tel: (1) 812 68 90. Pousadas* are state-run establishments in three categories. Some are converted national historic monuments, others are modern buildings in historic locations: both these types are four- to five-star standard. The third category is composed of comfortable modern inns or lodges, built in locations chosen for their wild remoteness and fabulous views: these are three- to four-star. Advance reservations are essential. For futher information or to make a reservation, contact **Enatur**, *Avda Santa Joana a Princesa 10, 1700 Lisbon; tel: (1) 848 12 21/848 90 78.* For details about youth hostels in Portugal, contact **Movijovem**, *Avda Duque d'Ávila 137, 1050 Lisbon; tel: (1) 313 88 20, fax: 352 86 21.*

### Eating and Drinking

The Portuguese pattern of eating is to have a fairly frugal breakfast and two big main meals: lunch (1200–1500) and dinner (1930–2230). Places that have evening entertainment may stay open until around midnight and, if so, tend to offer a late supper. The cafés and pastry shops usually stay open all day. There is a wide choice of eating-places. Most of the bars, restaurants and cafés serve alcohol. Eating is not expensive but, if your budget is strained, go for the meal of the day *prato do día* or *menú*. Eating is taken seriously, the cuisine flavoured with herbs rather than spices and rather heavy on olive oil. There is lots of delicious seafood and you should try some of the varieties of *caldeirada* (fish stew). Other local dishes are bacalhau (dried salted cod in various guises) and *leitão* (roasted suckling pig). The most popular pudding is a sweet egg custard.

The country is, of course, the home of port, but there are also several excellent (and often cheap) wines, such as *vinho verde*. Do not be surprised if you are charged for pre-dinner bread, olives, or other nibbles that are brought to your table unordered. If you don't want them, say so.

### Communications

**Postage:** *Correio* indicates both post-boxes and post offices. Most post offices open Mon–Fri 0900–1800, Sat 0900–1300, although the smaller ones close for lunch and are not open Sat. Most large post offices have a poste restante facility. Stamps *(selos)* can be purchased from anywhere with a sign depicting a red horse or a white circle on a green background.

**Telephones:** Kiosks that take phonecards (available from post offices and some tobacconists) are now as common as coin-operated ones. There's a surcharge (often hefty) for using phones in hotels etc. If you want to make an international call, the easiest way is to go to a post office: the clerk assigns a booth (you may have to queue) and times the call. Pay at the end. Otherwise, credit card phones are springing up in town centres. These don't always work first time (or at all), but are more convenient. The phone system is apparently permanently in a state of being upgraded and you may find some numbers have changed.

To call abroad from Portugal; *tel: 00.* To call Portugal; *tel 351.* For the operator; *tel: 118.* This is a general number for local/overseas calls and other enquiries. Ask for the service you want. **All Emergencies:** *tel: 115.*

## Opening Hours
**Banks:** Mon–Fri 0830–1445/1500. **Shops:** Mon–Fri 0900/1000–1300, 1500–1900, Sat 0900–1300. Shopping centres in cities often open daily 1000–2300 or later. **Museums:** Tues–Sun 1000–1700/1800. Some close for lunch and some are free on Sun. Palaces and castles usually close on Wed.

## Public Holidays
1 Jan; Shrove Tues; Good Fri; 25 Apr; 1 May; 10 June; Corpus Christi; 15 Aug; 5 Oct; 1 Nov; 1, 8, 25 Dec.

In addition, there are a number of local holidays for the days of the patron saints, for example, 13 June in Lisbon and 24 June in Oporto.

## Public Transport
Maps and details of the public transport system in each town are obtainable from the local Tourist Office.

Long-distance bus services are run by a variey of companies. If joining at a bus station you will normally need to purchase a ticket from the relevant office before boarding. Bus stops are marked *paragem*. You must extend your arm or the buses won't stop. **Taxis** are black with green roofs or beige and have illuminated signs. They are plentiful and cheap. Within cities they are metered but elsewhere fares are negotiable and drivers are entitled to ask you to pay for their return journey. Luggage over 30 kg adds Esc.300 to the fare and there is a 20% night surcharge (2200–0600). Tips of 10% are expected.

Lisbon and Oporto have Tourist Passes which are valid for either four or seven days and can be used on all public transport services within that city. You can buy single tickets as you board **buses** and **trams**, but you save money by buying books of tickets in advance. When you board a bus or tram, you insert one, two or three tickets in the machine behind the driver. How many you use depends on the length of the journey.

### RAIL TRAVEL WITHIN PORTUGAL

The national rail company is **Caminhos de Ferro Portugueses (CP)**. The CP network is fairly comprehensive and clean, and cheap

enough that it is hard to justify buying an inter-rail or other pass for Portugal. Punctuality is the exception rather than the norm: be prepared for (but do not rely on) your train either being an hour late, or waiting in the station for an hour. All long-distance trains have first- and second-class seating, but the local trains are usually second class only. CP has five categories of train: **Suburbano** or **Regional** (local and slow, stopping everywhere), *IR, IC* and **Serviço-Alfa** (modern and fast with few stops, mainly on the Lisbon–Oporto route; supplement payable). *IC* and Alfa trains usually have buffet-cars and many others have mini-bars. Seat reservations are recommended for long-distance travel and are compulsory on IC and Alfa trains (with supplement payable), but are not possible on regional trains.

Train timetables are available from information desks at main stations and Tourist Offices. CP also operate a general information service, based in Lisbon, *tel: (1) 888 40 25.*

## Stations
The majority have luggage lockers (Pta300–600). Larger station have railway information counters, snack bars, toilets and, possibly, a tourist information desk.

## Fares and Passes
There are very heavy fines if you board a train in Portugal without buying a ticket in advance. Tickets are available from any travel agency and most main stations. Seats must be reserved in advance on international and express trains and also certain other trains.

**Bilhetes Turísticos** allow unlimited first and second class travel on CP trains, buses and ferries. They can be bought from major stations, and are valid for 7, 14 or 21 days.

**Rail Cheque** allows a 10% reduction on tickets and other railway services. It is available in 4 different values, can be in one name or a company's name and has no time limit.

A **Cartão de Família** (Family Card) is valid for single journeys over 150 km, for a minimum of 3 people travelling together. Proof of family relationship must be shown, and the family must travel together in the same class. One full ticket must be purchased and then tickets for those over 12 are half price, and quarter-priced for those aged 4–12. **Bilhete de Grupo** (Group Ticket) allow a 20% reduction for groups of 10–25 people, and 25% for groups of 25–49. 50% is available for groups of more than 50 people. The whole group must travel together, and a minimum single journey is 75 km, return 150 km. Tickets are valid 1 month and should be applied for by the group leader at least 4 working days in advance.

**Portugal Explorer Pass** is only available from Campus Travel to holders of ISIC cards, teachers and academic staff, under 26s and spouses and children of eligible travellers. Allows 7, 14 or 21 days travel.

### Rail Pass Concessions

| Operator, Route/Concession | Rail Pass/Discount |
|---|---|
| Transport Museum, Santarém | IR Free |

## ROMANIA

**Capital:** Bucharest (Bucureşti).
**Language:** Romanian. This is a Latin-based language with strong similarities to Italian. French was traditionally the country's second language, but English is the choice of the younger generation. German is spoken, especially in Transylvania where there's also a Hungarian-speaking population.
**Currency:** Lei. It is advisable to carry most of your money as cash dollars or Deutschmarks, although a few travellers' cheques are useful as a secure reserve. Cash in particular is most easily changed at exchange kiosks rather than banks. Do not change money on the black market, although the rate is slightly better, as there's a high risk of theft. Better hotels and restaurants accept credit cards, which are essential for car rental. Most cities now have at least one *Bancomat,* an automatic cash dispenser accepting most types of Western cards; these are usually in service 24 hours and give a good rate.

### Passports and Visas

All visitors require a full passport, and unless you're a citizen of the USA, one of the formerly socialist states or a very few other countries such as Cyprus, Mexico, Tunisia or Turkey, you'll need a visa as well. This can be obtained on entry at a cost of $33; it'll cost you more from an embassy in advance.

### Customs

Adults may bring in duty-free 200 cigarettes or 300g of tobacco, 2 litres of spirits and 4 litres of wine or beer, as well as a reasonable quantity of food and medicine, one video, two cameras and other personal property. On departure you can take enough food and medicine for 24 hours only, and no more than 100,000 lei in cash.

### Useful Addresses

**UK: Embassy,** *Arundel House, 4 Palace Green, London W8 4QD; tel: (0171) 937 9667.* **Romanian National Tourist Office,** *83a Marylebone High St, London W1M 3DE; tel: (0171) 224 3692.*
**USA: Embassy:** *1607 23rd St N.W., Washington DC, 20008-2809; tel: (202) 232 4747.* **Romanian National Tourist Office,** *342 Madison Ave, Suite 210, New York NY 10173; tel: (212) 697 6971.*

### STAYING IN ROMANIA

### Accommodation

Hotels vary a great deal in quality, even within each category (one to four stars). At the bottom end they can be basic and inexpensive, while some match the highest international standards and prices. **Private rooms** may be booked at Tourist Offices in some towns, and in a few touristy places touts will meet trains at the station to offer their rooms. These may be centrally located in attractive old houses, or far out in grim suburban tower blocks, so make sure you know what you're agreeing to. **Campsites** should, with a very few exceptions, be avoided, as standards of cleanliness and hygiene can be appalling. It is wise to book in advance for hotels on the Black Sea coast in summer and in mountain ski resorts at winter weekends.

### Eating and Drinking

There are many restaurants in the main cities, offering a variety of foods, in principle. In practice you often end up with pork, with potato but without fresh vegetables. Chicken, beef and lamb are also available, and fish can be delicious, especially Danube carp *(crap)*. The traditional accompaniment is *mămăligă,* a mush of maize flour. Unsmoked frankfurters *(pariser)* and light liver sausages *(cremwurst)* equal those found in the West. Other local specialities are *sarmale,* stuffed cabbage leaves (sometimes without meat) and *mititei,* small meatballs grilled in beer gardens in summer. There's a plethora of take-away stalls, some open 24 hours, and some pizzerias which serve a very poor version of the real thing.

Fresh vegetables and fruit are delicious and easily found in markets in summertime; at other times you can buy pricey imports, notably bananas.

Tap water is perfectly safe to drink, although highly chlorinated. There are plenty of soft drinks, with CocaCola and Pepsi omnipresent. Cafés serve excellent cakes *(prăjitură),* soft drinks, beer and coffee; *turceasca* is Turkish-style ground coffee, while *Ness* is instant coffee. Wines are superb and very cheap; you should also try the plum brandy known as *tuică* (pronounced 'tswica'), or its double-distilled version *palinca.*

### Communications

Mail usually takes five days to reach Western Europe and up to two weeks to North America. Post offices can be found in every town, and usually house the telephone office as well; these allow operator-connected calls, often until 2200, although the simplest solution, especially for calls abroad, is usually to use a Direct Acess number to reach an operator at home, or to buy a telephone card (L20,000) for use in the new orange phones. These are found only in towns equipped with new digital exchanges, the number of which grows year by year. Calls can also be made through hotel operators, or from domestic phones by calling *971* (international) or *991* (long-distance). Larger telephone offices and hotels may offer fax service, but e-mail is still rare.

To call Romania, *tel: 40.* To call from Romania, *tel: 00.* **Emergencies:** Police: *955;* Fire: *981;* Ambulance: *961.*

### Opening Hours

**Shops:** most shops open between 0800 and 0900 and close between 1800 and 2000; most close for lunch (roughly 1300–1500) unless they claim to be 'non-stop'. Local food shops can open at 0600 and don't close till late. Shops are open on Saturday mornings, and an increasing number stay open on Saturday afternoons; almost nothing other than snack bars and cafés open on Sundays. Markets may be open every day or just on one day a week, depending on how important they are. **Banks:** these only open Mon–Fri 0900–1200/1300, but private exchange counters keep longer hours. **Museums:** these are usually open from 0900 to 1700 or 1000 to 1800; almost all are open at weekends and closed on Mondays (and occasionally on Tuesdays).

### Public Transport

All towns have bus services, and often trams and trolleybuses as well, while Bucharest has a metro system. Tickets need to be bought in advance from kiosks, as a rule, and cancelled on entry. Taxis are plentiful and inexpensive; if there's a meter, make sure it's in use, and if not agree a price before departure.

Trains are the best option for long-distance travel, although buses are extending their range.

### RAIL TRAVEL WITHIN ROMANIA

The Romanian rail system links all major towns; main lines are mostly electrified and reasonably speedy, although branch trains can be dreadfully slow. Service is reasonably efficient and punctual, and remarkably inexpensive. Few stations have raised platforms, which makes boarding and alighting difficult for the elderly and handicapped.

Tickets may be bought a day or two in advance from an **Agenţia de Voiaj CFR** (the **Căile Ferate Române** being the Romanian railways company), or at the station from an hour before departure. For all but local trains you must reserve a seat and pay a speed supplement in advance (tickets issued abroad include the supplement).

Avoid the *tren de persoane,* as these are very slow; an *accelerat* is a fast train that costs little more, *rapids* are faster and pricier, while fares for InterCity trains approach Western levels.

Food is rarely available other than on

**79**

InterCitys and some rapids, although drinks may be sold. Toilets on most trains should be avoided. For long-distance overnight journeys a couchette *(cuşeta)* or sleeper *(vagon de dormit)* is inexpensive.

## Rail Pass Concessions

| Operator, Route/Concession | Rail Pass/Discount |
| --- | --- |
| Transport Museum, Bucharest (Nord Station) | IR Free |

## SLOVAKIA

**Capital:** Bratislava. **Language:** Slovak is a Slavic tongue closely related to Czech. Some Russian and German, and a little English, are also understood, as are Hungarian and French. Shops where the staff are linguists tend to have signs saying so. **Currency:** Slovak Korunas or Crowns (SK.); 1 Koruna = 100 Hellers. Import and export of Crowns is not allowed, but there are no restrictions on foreign currencies. Credit cards are becoming more widely accepted in Bratislava and limited tourist areas.

## Passports and Visas

Full passports are required. Visas are not needed by nationals of the EU, South Africa or the USA. Nationals of Canada, Australia and New Zealand need visas and passports valid for at least six months. Others should check.

## Customs

The following allowances apply to people who are aged 18 or over. They are: 200 cigarettes, or 50 cigars, or equivalent in tobacco, 1 litre spirits, and 2 litres wine.

## Tourist Information

**Bratislava Information Service (BIS)**, *Nedbalova ul. 12, 814 28 Bratislava; tel: 334 059,* only has information about Bratislava. Staff can speak English and can arrange accommodation. **Satur (Slovak Tours and Travel Company)**, *Mileticova 1; 824 72 Bratislava; tel: 542 2828,* can help with accommodation as well as booking tours throughout Slovakia.

## Useful Addresses

**Australia: Embassy**, *47 Colgoa Circuit, O'Malley, Canberra ACT 2606; tel: (6) 2901 516, fax: (6) 290 1755.* This embassy also covers New Zealand. **Consulate**, *128 Exhibition St, Lev. 1, Melbourne, VIC 3000; tel: (3) 6544 755.*

**Canada: Embassy**, *50 Rideau Terrace, Ottawa, Ontario K1M 2AL; tel: (3) 749 4442, fax: (3) 749 4989.*

**Republic of Ireland: Embassy**, *107 The Sweepstakes, Ballsbridge, Dublin 4; tel/fax: (1) 660 0270.*

**South Africa: Embassy**, *930 Arcadia St, Arcadia 0083, Pretoria; tel: (12) 342 2051-2, fax: (12) 342 3688.*

**UK: Embassy**, *25 Kensington Palace Gardens, London W8 4QY; tel: (0171) 243 0803 or (0171) 727 9432.*

**USA: Embassy**, *2201 Wisconsin Ave N.W., Suite 250, Washington DC 20007; tel: (202) 965 5160-5.* **Consulate**, *1325 S. Colorado Blvd, Suite 302, Denver CO 80222; tel: (303) 692 8833 or 7034 W. Cermek Rd, Berwyn, Chicago, Illinois 60402; tel: (708) 749 2336.* **Victor International Travel Services**, *10 East 40th St, 3604 New York, NY 10016; tel: (212) 6800 730.*

## Accommodation

You should have a choice of one- to five-star **hotels**, **private rooms** and **pensions**, old-style tourist hotels, **hostels** and **inns** with a few spartan rooms or *chaty* (chalets) in the mountains. However, quality (once outside the three- five-star range), although it has improved greatly in recent years, can leave a lot to be desired. It may make more sense to look at private rooms than cheap hotels (use the local Tourist Office). Some places insist on payment in hard currency and charge high rates for foreign visitors.

Private rooms, **youth hostel** beds and hotel rooms can be booked through a variety of agencies. Local tourist information offices can also help with the search for accommodation.

Local individuals also offer rooms to arriving travellers: if the price is indicated in advance and the rooms seem acceptable on viewing, this can be the ideal solution for those travelling on a budget.

80

## Eating and Drinking

Lunch is around 1130–1400 and dinner 1800–2130. The cuisine tends to be rich and meat-based, but vegetarian dishes (such as *vy pražené syr* – fried cheese) can also be found.

*Brynzové halušky*, gnocchi with grated cheese, is typical of Slovak cuisine. Slovak food is very similar to Hungarian; pork and dumplings *(knedliky)* are on virtually every menu, as is *guláš*, a spicy meat dish served with wine.

Eating and drinking are cheap, especially in a self-service *bufet* (where you stand while eating). *Kavárny* and *cukrárny* serve coffee (often Turkish-style) and delightful pastries. Beer halls *(pivnice)* and wine bars *(vinárny)* are good places to eat. Slovak beer is good, and its wine is excellent (try *Tokaj* from South Slovakia).

## Communications

**Postage:** There is a full postal service (including post restante), which, although cheap, is slow and erratic. Usual post office opening hours are 0800–1900. Stamps are also available from newsagents and tobacconists. Letter boxes are orange.

**Telephones:** Phone connections are very poor and it may be necessary to try many times to make a connection. To call Slovakia: *tel: 421*. To call abroad from Slovakia: *tel: 00*. The code for Bratislava is *07*. Information: *120* (national); *0149* (international). **Emergencies:** Police: *158;* Fire: *150;* Ambulance: *155*.

## Public Holidays

1, 6 Jan; Good Fri; Easter Mon; 1 May; 8 May; 5 July; 29 Aug; 1, 15 Sep; 1 Nov; 24–26 Dec.

## Opening Hours

**Banks:** Mon–Fri 0800–1700. **Shops:** Mon–Fri 0900–1800, Sat 0800–1200. Food shops usually open 0800. They, and souvenir shops often open on Sun. **Museums:** (usually) Tues–Sun 1000–1700. Most castles close on national holidays and from Nov to Mar.

## Public Transport

The rail network is good, but there is also a comprehensive long-distance bus network which can often be more direct. Bus stations are fairly well-organised. Officially, you should book in advance, but you can buy tickets from the driver, who will give priority to those with reservations.

### RAIL TRAVEL WITHIN SLOVAKIA

The national rail company is **Zveleznice Slovenskej Republiky (ZvSR)**. The rail network is cheap and extensive, but the trains are often crowded. The fastest trains are *expresný*, but *rychlík* cost as much as the express. The few *spešný* (semi-fast) trains cost less. *Osobný* (slow) should be avoided. There is a supplement payable on *expresný* and *spešný* trains.

All trains offer both first- and second-class travel. Most long-distance trains have dining cars and overnight services generally have sleeping-cars and/or couchette cars, as well as seats. Sleepers/couchettes are of standard European type. Seat reservations are recommended for travel by express train, bookings can be made at the station counters marked 'R'. Sleepers and couchette reservations can be made at all major stations. The agency **MTA**, *Párièkova 29, Bratislava; tel: (07) 526 9311*, also make reservations. Night trains are not recommended unless in sleepers/couchettes. Reserve seats and sleepers or couchettes well in advance in high season.

## Fares and Passes

See p.29 for details of the **Czech/Slovakia Explorer Pass**, which covers rail travel in the Czech Republic and Slovakia.

### SLOVENIA

**Capital:** Ljubliana. **Language:** Slovenian. Although a Slavic language, it is written with Roman characters. English, German and Italian are often spoken by those involved in tourism. **Currency:** Tolar (SIT). 1 SIT = 100 stotins.

## Passports and Visas

All visitors require full passports. South African nationals need a 3 month tourist visa, and should enter the country with a return ticket.

## Customs

The allowances are: 200 cigarettes, or 50 cigars, or 250g tobacco products, 1 litre spirits.

## Tourist Information
**Slovenian Tourist Board**, *Dunajska 156, Sl-1000 Ljubljana, tel: 386 061 189 40.*

## Useful Addresses
**Australia: Embassy**, *Level 6, Advance Bank Center, 60 Marcus Clarke St, Canberra Act 2601, Po Box 284, tel: (6) 243 48 30.*
**Canada: Embassy**, *150 Metcalfe St, Suite 2101, Ottawa, Ontario, K2P 1P1, tel: (613) 565 57 81.*
**UK: Embassy**, *Suite One, Cavendish Court, 11–15 Wigmore St, London, W1H 9LA, tel: (0171) 495 77 75.* **Slovenian Tourist Office**, *2 Canfield Pl., London, NW6 3BT, tel: (0171) 372 3767.*
**USA: Embassy**, *1525 New Hampshire Ave N.W., Washington DC 20036, tel: (202) 667 53 63.* **Slovenian Tourist Office**, *345 East 12th St, New York, NY 10003, tel: (212) 358 96 86.*

### STAYING IN SLOVENIA

## Accommodation
Many **hotels** are currently being upgraded, standards are high and prices are comparable to those in EU countries. Accommodation is available in grade L (deluxe), A , B, or C hotels. Prices are higher in July and August, when accommodation may be in short supply.

Tourist Offices also have lists of **private rooms** for rent. These are categorised I and II, the former having private shower and toilet, the latter hot and cold water in the room but shared bathroom and toilet. A 30 % surcharge is sometimes made for stays of less than two or three nights.

Although there is still a shortage of Youth Hostels, during July and August it is possible to stay in **university halls of residence**. Ask at local Tourist Information Centres for details.

There are numerous, mostly small but well-equipped **campsites**, many of which have related sports facilities.

Bookings for all types of accommodation can be made through local Tourist Offices.

## Eating and Drinking
Places to eat go by many different names in Slovenia. A restaurant where you are served by a waitress is a *restauracija,* while a *gostilna* is an inn which, in general, serves, national dishes in a rustic setting. Both sometimes have a set menu *(dnevno kosilo)* at lunch, which is usually the most inexpensive option. There are also a variety of self-service places *(samopostrezna restauracija),* where you can eat standing up. People eat fast food in an *okrepcevalnica,* and they snack in a *bife* or a *kroma.*

Slovenian cuisine, like other areas of national culture, reflects historic ties with Vienna. Meat and dairy products predominate. *Weiner schnitzel* is a speciality, as is *pohana piska,* breaded fried chicken. Smoked sausages, salami and cured hams are excellent. Coffee shops offer a wide range of pastries, cakes and ice-creams. Try *zavitek,* light pastries filled with cream cheese, either sweet or savoury.

The north-eastern part of Slovenia is well known for outstanding white wines, notably *Laški* and *Renski Rizling*, while the south-western part of the country produces the red *Teran.*

The water is safe and drinkable throughout the country.

## Opening hours
**Banks:** There are no hard and fast rules in Slovenia, and every bank and every town appears to have their own rules. Most banks should be open Mon–Fri 0900–1200 and 1400–1630, Sat 0900–1100. **Shops:** These vary, but in general work Mon–Fri 0700–1900, Sat 0730–1300. **Museums:** These vary, the larger ones in the capital being open 1000–1800, the minor ones sometimes opening mornings only, 1000–1400. Some close Mon.

## Communications
**Postage:** Usual post office hours are Mon–Fri 0800–1800, Sat 0800–1200. In Ljubljana, the main post office, *Trg Osvobodilne Fronte 5,* next to the station, is open 24 hrs for letters, telegrams and telephoning. Letter boxes are yellow. The postal service is fast and efficient.

**Telephones:** The easiest way to make an international call is to go to the post office, where you can call from a cabin and pay afterwards. In Ljubljana the main Post Office, *Trg Osvobodilne Fronte 5,* next to the station, is open

82

24 hrs. Public telephones operate on phonecards, which can be bought at post offices, or tokens which can be bought at post offices or newspaper stands.

To call Slovenia, *tel: 386.* To call from Croatia prefix: *00.* **Emergencies**: Police: *113;* Ambulance and Fire: *112.*

### Public Holidays
Jan 1–2, Feb 8, Easter Sun–Mon, Apr 27, May 1–2, Jun 25, Aug 15, Oct 31, Nov 1 and Dec 25–26.

### Public transport
Some tourist destinations can be reached only by coach, such as Bohinj. Services are frequent and inexpensive. You can usually buy your ticket as you board. Coach information: *Trg Osvobodilne Fronte,* next to Ljubljana railway station, *tel: (061) 1336 136.*

On city buses there is a standard fare, to be paid with the right change into a box next to the driver. Newspaper stands and post offices sell tokens, which work out cheaper. The main cities have daily or weekly bus passes.

### RAIL TRAVEL WITHIN SLOVENIA
The national railway company is **Slovenske Železnice (SŽ)**. Train information is available from **Ljubljana Railway Station**, *Trg Osvobodilne Fronte 6; tel: (061) 1315 16,* or **Slovenijaturist**, *Slovenska 58, Ljubljana; tel: (061) 311 851.*

The Slovene railways are part of the international Eurocity system with direct lines to Italy, Austria, Hungry and Croatia. Rail travel within the country is limited, but efficient and inexpensive.

Among the scenic routes are Pivka–Ljubljana, covered by Venice–Ljubljana trains, and Jesenice–Nova Gorica, covered by **steam locomotive**. The steam locomotive trip can be arranged through **Slovenijaturist** on the Bohinj line, which runs through the Soča valley, every Thursday from mid June to mid Sept, from Jesenice through Bled and Bohinjska Bistrica to Tomlin *(Most na Soči).*

### Stations
Ljubljana Station has recently been refurbished and looks very smart. Station facilities include WC's, left luggage, bar, newspaper stands and a small Tourist Information Centre (TIC). Some of the smaller stations, however, are far more basic.

### Fares and Passes
**Slovenia Rail** is a tourist ticket available for 10, 20 or 30 days unlimited travel. Up to 5 people can travel on one ticket. Available from the 50 larger stations that deal with international traffic.

### SPAIN
**Capital:** Madrid. **Language:** Castilian Spanish is the most widely spoken language. The three other official languages are: Catalan, spoken in the east; Galego, spoken in Galicia (in the north-west), and Basque, which is common in the Basque country, Navarra, and even across the Pyrénées into France. English is fairly widely spoken by people in tourist-related industries in major cities and coastal areas. Bear in mind, when consulting dictionaries or directories, that in Spanish listings 'CH' comes at the end of the 'C' section and 'LL' at the end of the 'L' section. **Currency:** Pesetas (Pta); 1 Peseta = 100 Céntimos.

### Passports and Visas
EU National Identity Cards are sufficient, as are those issued to nationals of Andorra, Austria, Liechtenstein, Malta, Monaco and Switzerland. Visas are not needed by nationals of Canada, New Zealand or the USA for visits of up to 90 days. Others should check. Non-EU nationals must hold onward or return tickets plus a minimum of £25 (sterling) per day of their intended stay, or a minimum of Pta50,000.

### Customs
Standard EU regulations apply (see p. 17).

### Tourist Information
**Oficinas de Turismo** can provide maps and information on accommodation and sightseeing, and generally have English-speaking staff. Regional offices stock information on the whole region, municipal offices cover only that city; larger towns have both types of office.

83

## Useful Addresses

**Australia: Consulate–General**, *Level 24 St Martin's Tower, 31 Market St, Sydney NSW 2000; tel: (612) 261 24 33.*

**South Africa: Embassy**, *169 Pine St, Arcadia, Pretoria 0083; tel: (21) 22 23 26.*

**UK: Consulate–General**, *20 Draycott Pl., London SW3 2RZ; tel: (0171) 589 8989;* Visa information: *tel: 0891 600123* (24 hrs). **Spanish National Tourist Office**, *57 St James's St, London SW1A 1LD; tel: (0171) 499 0901.*

**USA: Embassy**, *2700 15th St N.W., Washington, DC 20009; tel: (202) 265 0190.* **Consulate**, *150 East 58th St (16th Floor), New York, NY 10155; tel: (212) 355 4080.* **Spanish National Tourist Office**, *665 Fifth Ave, New York, NY 10022; tel: (212) 759 8822.*

## Accommodation

Tourist Offices will give you information about accommodation, but they are not allowed to make hotel reservations. In major cities there are often hotel booking agencies at the airports and railway stations. Except when there's a fiesta, or it's peak season in tourist areas, accommodation is easy to find. Prices away from major resorts start at about Pta2500 for a double room (Pta1500 for a single). Double beds are rare (double rooms usually have twin beds) so ask for *matrimonio* if your want a double bed. The standard of rooms within any given lodging-place can vary quite a lot, so always ask to see the room before you commit yourself to that establishment. If you want en suite facilities, it's worth saying whether you prefer a shower or bath, as there's often a choice (baths are usually more expensive).

By law, places that officially provide accommodation must place a notice (updated every year) in every bedroom stating the maximum amount payable for that room. The price includes all taxes and service charges (but seldom breakfast), and you should pay no more than the stated amount (which is for the room, not per person). When paying for your room, it is a good idea to keep a copy of the quoted price or a copy of the accommodation guide

handy as, often, locals have a tendency to put the prices up for tourists.

Every type of accommodation is officially graded, which ensures that standards are usually good and, on the whole, you pay for what you get. However, there can be an overlap between different types of accommodation, e.g. the best Hostales Residencias are often better value than the low-grade (one- to two-star) hotels.

All **hotels** and **hostels** are listed in the *Guía de Hoteles,* an annual publication available from tourist offices. There are blue plaques beside doorways that state the category of accommodation: 'H' indicates Hotel, 'HS' *Hostales,* 'HR' *Hostales Residencias,* 'P' *Pensión* and 'F' *Fonda* etc. If there is also an 'R' on the plaque, do not expect a full dining service. *Paradores Nacionales* are three- to five-star state-owned establishments and can be very expensive, but usually worth it. There are around 90 in Spain and the vast majority either occupy historical buildings or are in places of outstanding natural beauty. There's a central booking service in Madrid for Paradores throughout the whole country *tel: (1) 559 00 69.* **Private homes** which offer rooms are known as *Casas Particulares.* They seldom have much in the way of facilities but are usually central and almost invariably very cheap. *Casas Rústicas* are **farmhouses** and *Refugios* are **mountain huts**. Cheap **boarding-houses/ pensions** are variously known as *Fondas, Pensiones, Posadas, Ventas* and *Casas de Huéspedes.* Slightly higher up the scale in terms of both price and facilities are Hostales and Hostales Residencias. These tend to cluster together in specific areas, often either around the station or around the main square.

There are dozens of **HI hostels** around the country and some universities offer accommodation in **student dormitories** *(Colegios Mayores)* when students are not in residence. There are over 500 **campsites** (some open all year, others just in summer) and the Tourist Office issues a list of the approved ones *(Guía de Campings),* which are classified as luxury, first, second and third class. Book locally or through the **Federación Española de Empresarios de Campings**, *General Oráa 52, Madrid; tel: (1) 562 99 94.* You can camp 'rough' in most suitable places, but not on tourist beaches.

## Eating and Drinking

In Spain, the pattern is to have a light breakfast: coffee or hot chocolate with rolls or fritters *(churros)*. The main meal is lunch (1330–1500 – nearer 1500 on Sunday). Dinner is a little lighter, but can still consist of three courses, and is eaten late, at around 2200.

Restaurants are open only for lunch and dinner, so go to *cafeterías* (usually open 0800–midnight) for breakfast and light meals/snacks. They serve tea, coffee and alcohol. Bars offer snacks *(tapas),* as well as wine and beer.

There's not a great deal of variety in Spanish cuisine and the quality is often poor, but you can eat reasonably cheaply. *Platos combinados* and *menú del día* are both good value. If you want an inexpensive light meal, ask for *raciones,* a larger portion of *tapas* (little more than nibbles, intended as aperitifs). The best-known Spanish dish is *paella,* which originated in Valencia; it is at its best when made to order – which takes about half an hour. Another famous dish is *gazpacho* (cold tomato soup), which originated in Andalusia and is found mainly in the south. An enjoyable tradition is to go *tascas*-hopping, where you move from bar to bar having *tapas* and a beer (or glass of wine) at each.

In Spain you have to choose a drinking-place according to what you want to consume. For beer, you need a bar or *cervecería,* for wine a *taberna* or *bodega.* For cider (in the north), you need a *cidrería.* The custom is to pay for all your drinks at the end of the evening, although this is changing in some resort areas. Many drinking-places have a dining-room *(comedor)* at the rear if you want a full meal, or you can go to a proper restaurant *(mesón).* It is claimed that water is safe to drink, but check for a 'potable' (drinking) notice above the tap. Mineral water is available everywhere. Coffee tends to be strong. There are some excellent wines (notably from the Rioja and Penedés regions) and Jerez is, of course, the home of sherry. *Sangría* is a very palatable drink based on wine and fruit juice. Beer is popular, but weak.

## Communications

Most **post offices** *(correos)* open 0800–1400 and 1700–1930. The larger ones offer a poste restante *(lista de correos)* facility. Stamps *(sellos)* can also be purchased from tobacconists *(estancos).* Postboxes are yellow with red stripes and over-seas mail should be put in the slot marked *extranjero.* The Spanish postal system is notoriously slow but you can pay extra for urgent *(urgente)* delivery, to speed up your over-seas mail.

**Telephones:** The state telephone company is **Telefónica** and every large town has at least one office, where you can use a booth to make a call and pay the clerk afterwards.

Public telephone booths (marked *teléfono publico* or *locutorio)* usually have instructions in English. They often accept credit cards or money as well as the *Teletarjeta* (phonecard) on sale in tobacconists, post offices and some shops. Bars also have pay telephones, but they are usually more expensive than the ordinary booths.

To call abroad from Spain: *tel: 07.* To call Spain: *tel: 00 34.* The number for the international operator depends both on where you are calling from and where you are calling to. If you are in Madrid, the number is *008* for Europe and *005* for all other continents. If you are elsewhere in Spain, the number is *9198* for Europe and *9191* for the other continents. To call the national operator: *tel: 009.* To call the local operator: *003.* **Emergencies:** Police: *091* everywhere; Fire: *080* in most towns, but can vary; Ambulance: numbers vary from place to place, so check locally.

## Opening Hours

**Banks:** Mon–Thur 0830–1630; Fri 0830–1400; Sat 0830–1300 (winter); Mon–Fri 0830–1400 (summer). **Shops:** Mon–Sat 0930/1000–1400 and 1700–2000/2030, but major stores do not close for lunch and food shops often open on Sun. **Museums:** these vary enormously, but most open 0900/1000 and close any time from 1400–2030 – the ones that stay open late usually close for siesta. Few open Mon and some also close (or open for only half a day) Sun. A long lunch break is normal, especially in the south, and you can expect to find many things closed 1300–1500 or even 1600.

## Public Holidays

1, 6 Jan; several days at Easter; 1 May; Corpus Christi; 24 June; 25 July; 15 Aug; 12 Oct; 1

Nov; 6, 8 Dec and several days at Christmas. Not all of these are official holidays, but many places close anyway. In addition to the national holidays, each region has at least four more, usually the local saints' days.

## Public Transport

There is no nationwide bus company but there are numerous regional companies *(empresas)* which, between them, provide a reasonably comprehensive (if confusing) network, so **buses** (which are cheap) can be used to fill most of the many gaps in the railway system. The city bus services are very efficient and taxis are easily available. When they are free, taxis display a green light on the roof at night and a *Libre* sign against the windscreen by day. They are metered and cheap. There are surcharges for travel on Sundays or late at night, luggage placed in the boot and travel outside the town (including to airports and stations).

## RAIL TRAVEL WITHIN SPAIN

The national rail company is **Red nacional de los Ferrocarriles Españoles (RENFE)**, operating services throughout the country. A separate company, **FEVE**, and a number of regionally-controlled railways operate lines in the coastal regions of Spain.

The two sectors of RENFE dealing with long-distance travel are **AVE** (Alta Velocidad Española: trains via the high-speed line) and **Largo Recorrido** (long distance ie. all other express services). The fastest *AVE* trains cover the 472 km between Seville and the capital in just 2¼ hrs. RENFE are so sure of the reliability of their *AVE* trains that should they cause you to arrive more than 5 mins late at your destination, you get your money back! *Talgo* (light articulated train) and InterCity expresses are among the premier Largo Recorrido services linking the principal Spanish cities. An ordinary long-distance day train is a *Diurno*, one running by night (including sleeper and/or couchette cars) is an *Estrella*. A (pricier) alternative for night travel is the *Trenhotel* (train-hotel), offering sleeping compartments with their own shower and WC.

All the above trains convey first and second classes of accommodation (called *Preferente* and

*Turista; AVE* also have a 'super-first' class known as *Club)*, and on all of them you have to reserve your place in advance. Note that fares can vary according to the type of train and time of travel.

Two other sectors of RENFE, **Regionales** and **Cercanías**, are responsible, respectively, for local stopping services and suburban trains. A new generation of more comfortable trains, usually branded *Regional Exprés* (though not expresses in the English sense of the word) is gradually being introduced. Be careful if relying on a Regional service in some of the remoter parts of the country, however. If you miss your train, the next one might be seven days later!

## Fares and Passes

For most services (but not all) RENFE accepts the European rail passes (see pp. 25–29). FEVE does not. Domestic rail fares can vary according to the date of travel and the time of departure, with higher fares for the times of peak demand. Domestic tickets are valid for two months from the date of issue and can be issued up to two months in advance.

A **Spain Explorer Pass** is sold by Campus Travel to holders of an ISIC card, teachers and academic staff, under 26s, accompanying spouses and children of eligible persons, and anyone purchasing another service to Spain (by any form of transport) from Campus Travel. It offers 5 days unlimited use on RENFE Cercanías (suburban) trains around Madrid, Barcelona and Malaga.

**Spain Flexipass** is valid for any 3 days in 2 months (US$190 first-class; US$150 second-class). Additional rail days (a maximum of 7) can be purchased for US$40 (first class) and US$32 (second class). **Spain Rail 'n Drive** provides travel for any 5 days (3 train and 2 car) within a 2-month period. Additional days can be purchased, although rail days are restricted to a maximum of two.

## Rail Pass Concessions

| Operator, Route/Concession | Rail Pass/Discount |
| --- | --- |
| Compagnie de navigation Trasmediterranea: | |
| Barcelona–Palma/Ibiza/Mahon | IR 30% |
| Valencia–Palma/Ibiza | IR 30% |
| Almeria–Mellila | IR 30% |

| | |
|---|---|
| Malaga–Mellila | IR 30% |
| Cadiz–Canaries | IR 30% |
| Algeciras–Tanger/Ceuta | IR 30% |
| Transport Museum, Madrid | IR Free |

Sevilla AVE's and TALGO's rail lines Turista, Preferente and Club train-hotel accommodation FP Reduced fares
Train-Hotel Pau Casals Zurich–Barcelona–Zurich
FP Special supplement payable
Train-Hotel Salvador Dali Milan–Barcelona–Milan
FP Special supplement payable
Train-Hotel Francisco de Goya Madrid–Paris–Madrid
FP Special supplement payable
Train-Hotel Joan Miro Barcelona–Paris–Barcelona
FP Special supplement payable

## SWEDEN

**Capital:** Stockholm. **Language:** Swedish is the official language, with three extra vowels: å, ä and ö, following z (in that order) in alphabetical listings. English is widely spoken. You may find it helpful to remember that *Daglig* is daily, *Vardagar/Vard* means Mon–Fri and *Helgdagar* covers holidays. **Currency:** Kronor or Crowns (SEK/SKr.); 1 Krona = 100 Öre. Notes come in units of SKr.10,000, SKr.1000, Skr.500, Skr.100, Skr.50 and Skr.20; coins are Skr 10, Skr.5, SKr.1 and 50ore. *Växlare* machines give change. The best exchange rate is obtained from **Forex**, which has branches at many stations. Keep receipts so that you can re-convert at no extra cost.

### Passports and Visas
National Identity Cards issued by the EU countries, Iceland, Norway and Switzerland are sufficient. Visas are not needed by citizens of these countries, Australia, Canada, New Zealand or the USA. South Africans need visas.

### Customs
The usual EU regulations apply (see p. 17), but alcohol may be imported only by those aged 20 or more.

### Tourist Information
The e-mail address for the Swedish Tourist Board is: *e-mail@swetourism.se*. Tourist Offices (**Turistbyrå**) can be identified by the 'i'. There's often a numerical queuing system in public places: get your number from a machine near the entrance. Many things in Sweden are seasonal and what constitutes summer varies from year to year (the weather can play a part),

but mid June–mid Aug is almost always included. On street signs, house numbers often follow the street name. If museums have no English information by the exhibits, ask if there's an English text you can borrow.

Anything with a *Svensk Slöjd* token is approved by the national handicrafts organisation. Authentic Sami handicrafts carry a round *Duodji* tag.

### Useful Addresses
**Australia: Embassy**, *5 Turrana St, Yarralumla, Canberra, ACT 2600; tel: (06) 273 3033.*
**Canada: Embassy**, *377 Dalhousie St, Ottawa, Ont. K1N 9N8; tel: (613) 241 8553.*
**Republic of Ireland: Embassy**, *Sun Alliance House, 13–17 Dawson St, Dublin 2; tel: (01) 671 5822.*
**New Zealand: Embassy**, see Australia. **Consulate**, *Consulate General of Sweden, Vogel Building, 13th Floor, Aitken St, Wellington; PO Box 12538; tel: (4) 499 98 95.*
**South Africa: Embassy**, *Old Mutual Building, 167 Andries St (9th Floor), Pretoria 0001; tel: (012) 211 050.*
**UK: Embassy**, *11 Montagu Pl., London W1H 2AL; tel: (0171) 917 6413.* **Swedish Travel & Tourism Council**, *11 Montagu Pl., London W1 2AL; tel: (0171) 724 5868; e-mail: sttc-info@swedish-tourism,org.u.*
**USA: Embassy**, *1501 M St N.W., Washington, DC 20005-1702; tel: (202) 467 2600.* **Swedish Travel and Tourism Council**, *655 Third Ave, New York, NY 10017-5617; tel: (212) 885 9700,* or *PO Box 4649, Grand Central Station, New York, NY 10163-4649.*

### STAYING IN SWEDEN

### Accommodation
The Swedish Travel and Tourism Council can provide a limited national list of hotels. Local Tourist Offices have listings for their area, including a range of **farmhouse** accommodation. You can also get brochures issued by individual chains, such as **Sweden Hotels**, *Sveavägen 39, Box 3377, 103 67 Stockholm; tel: (08) 789 89 00.* This purely Swedish association offers hotels with individual characters. There's

nothing impersonally mass-market about them, but they are high quality and designed to make you feel comfortable. The widespread network includes Gothenburg, Lund, Malmö, Stockholm and Uppsala. **Bed & Breakfast Service Stockholm**, *PO Box 26175, S-100 41 Stockholm; tel: (8) 660 5565,* can provide rooms and flats in the capital.

**Hotel** standards are high and the cost usually includes a sauna and breakfast. SKr.300–400 for a single/SKr.500–600 for a double is cheap, even off-peak – which is summer.

Tourist Offices charge a small fee to book accommodation. If you will be reaching any accommodation after 1800, advise them of your arrival time. Many **hostels** *(vandrarhem)* open only in summer and do not accept sleeping-bags. Room only in **private houses** is a good alternative for budget travellers. **Sveriges Campingvärdars Riksförbund (SCR)** (Swedish Camping Owners Association), *PO Box 255, S-45117 Uddevalla; tel (0522) 393 45,* lists 650 **campsites**. You can wander at will and **rough camp** for *one night* anywhere *suitable,* but you must not encroach on the residents or leave any trace of your passing.

### Eating and Drinking

Lunch is usually served around 1100–1400 and dinner 1800–2100, a bit later in cities. *Konditori* (cafés) are relatively cheap and fast-food outlets (including chains) are widespread.

Budget travellers can fill up at breakfast: a help-yourself buffet with plenty of choice. For lunch, the best value is *dagens rätt* (dish of the day): around SKr.50 – much the same as doner kebabs, burgers and pizzas (usually served with good portions of salad and/or fries). Street stalls sell cheap hotdogs and multi-flavoured ice-creams. *Husmanskost* means 'home cooking'. Traditional dishes include *Pytt i panna* (a hearty fry-up), pea soup combined with pancakes, *Smörgasbord* (usually 'eat-your-fill', including some hot dishes), *gravad lax* (marinated salmon with dill sauce) and *Jansson's temptation* (potatoes, onions and anchovies). Coffee, tea, hot chocolate and milk are usually available.

Lager comes in three strengths; the strongest (over 2.8%) is Class III/Starköl/Export. *Schnapps* is the local fire water. **Systembolaget**

(the state-owned monopoly for the sale of alcohol) sells only to people over 20, although in bars you can be 18.

### Communications

**Post offices** (look for a posthorn on yellow or a yellow posthorn) generally open Mon–Fri 0900–1800, Sat 1000–1300, but there are variations. Stamps are available at newsagents and tobacconists. Postboxes for overseas mail are yellow; blue are local: ignore the others.

**Telephones:** Public phones which take cash are decreasing in number, but most card phones accept both credit cards and **Telia** phonecards *(telefonkorten* – obtainable from most newsagents, tobacconists and **Pressbyrån** kiosks). There are English instructions and the panel displays (briefly) the cost of the call. Local calls are half-price Mon–Fri 1800–0800 and weekends. International calls are cheapest Mon–Fri 2200–0800 (North America 2200–1000) and weekends.

To call abroad from Sweden; *tel: 009.* To call Sweden: *tel: 46.* Operator: *tel: 0018.* Swedish directory: *tel: 079 75.* International directory: *tel: 079 77.* Toll-free numbers begin with *020.* **All emergencies:** *900 00.*

### Opening Hours

**Banks:** Mon–Fri 0930–1500, Thur 1600–1730. Some, especially at transport terminals, have longer hours. **Shops:** Mon–Fri 0900/0930–1700/1800, Sat 0900/0930–1300/1600. Stores and malls often open until 2000/2200 and some open Sun 1200–1600. **Museums:** vary widely. In winter, many attractions are shut on Mondays and some close altogether. re local: ignore the others.

### Public Holidays

1, 6 Jan; Good Fri; Easter Mon; Labour Day; Ascension Day; Whit Mon; Midsummer Day; All Saints' Day; 25, 26 Dec. Many places close early the previous day – or Fri if it's a long weekend.

### Public Transport

The transport system is highly efficient. For a minimal charge, you can get a *Tidtabell* (integrated timetable) at local transport offices and stations. Many regular **ferries** (even some between the Scandinavian countries) are an integral part of the system and covered (in whole or part) by rail passes and city transport cards. The biggest operator of **long-distance buses** is **Swebus**, with a nationwide network. Advance booking is required on some routes and always advisable in summer. Bus terminals are usually next to train stations.

### RAIL TRAVEL WITHIN SWEDEN

The national rail company is **Statens Järnvägar (SJ)**, but some local lines are run by regional authorities. Standards are very high. There is one central information line, charged at a local rate; *tel: (020) 75 75 75*.

The *X2000* is a luxury train (with appropriate supplements) and travels at up to 200 kph. There are smaller supplements for ordinary *IC* trains, which are fast and comfortable.

Sleeping-cars have one or two berths in first class and three berths in second class (on top of each other). Couchettes have six berths: women should specify a female-only compartment. First-class sleeping-cars (with en suite shower and WC) are available on many overnight services and second class sleeping-cars have en suite wash-basins and a (pleasant) shower and separate WC at the end of the carriage. Long-distance trains have a refreshment service, usually a buffet (with a few hot dishes) and/or a trolley service. Many trains have a family car, with a playroom for children and special facilities for the disabled. Some (to the north) even have a cinema.

Seat reservations are compulsory on *X2000* and night trains, and for journeys over 150 km on all other services. You get a carriage and seat/berth number and find your own (numbers are clearly marked). Reserved seats are not labelled and it's better to use local trains for short journeys.

### Stations

A big town's main station almost invariably shows '... C' (for Central) on the platform boards. Stations display opening times beside the entrances and the facilities are seldom accessible at other times. *Biljetter* indicates the rail ticket office. Large, detailed timetables are displayed for long-distance trains: yellow for departures, white for arrivals. *IC* services regularly use the same platforms and there's usually a diagram of the train, so you can locate your carriage and be in the right place when the train arrives. You can get English-language publications at Pressbyrån (branches at most stations), who also sell snacks and sometimes incorporate a café.

### Fares and Passes

The **Sweden Railpass** is valid for any 3 days in a one week period in first or second class, and includes *X2000* trains. The Scanrail Pass (p.28), allows unlimited travel on Swedish railways (SJ).

### Rail Pass Concessions

| Operator, Route/Concession | Rail Pass/Discount |
|---|---|
| Stena Line Göteborg–Frederkshavn (Denmark) | IR 50% |
| Silja Line Stockholm–Helsinki, Stockholm–Turku and Vaasa–Umeå | IR 50% |
| TT Line Trelleborg–Lübeck/Travemünde (Denmark) | IR 50% |
| Inlandståget AB Mora–Gällivare (summer only) | IR 50% |
| Viking Line Stockholm–Helsinki, Stockholm–Turku | IR 50% |
| Östra Södermanlands Järnväg Mariefred-Läggesta (summer only) | IR 50% |
| Transport Museum, Gävle | IR Free |
| Scandinavian Seaways Göteborg–Amsterdam, Helsingborg–Oslo | IR26+ 50% |
| Stena Sessan Line Göteborg–Frederikshavn | RES 30% |
| Silja Line Stockholm–Helsinki, Vaasa–Umeå | RES 30% |
| Viking Line Stockholm–Turku | RES 30% |
| TT Line Lübeck-Travemünde–Trelleborg | RES 30% |

## SWITZERLAND

**Capital**: Berne. **Language**: German, French, Italian and Romansch are all official languages of Switzerland. Most Swiss people are at least bilingual and knowledge of English is widespread. **Currency**: Swiss Francs (SFr.); 1 Franc = 100 Centimes.

### Passports and Visas

EU National Identity Cards are sufficient. All other travellers require a valid passport. Visas are not needed by nationals of the EU, Australia, Canada, New Zealand or the USA. Others should check.

### Customs

The following allowances are for visitors aged

17 or over: 200 cigarettes or 50 cigars or 250g tobacco, 2 litres alcohol up to 15% volume, and 1 litre over 15% volume. People who live outside Europe are entitled to twice the tobacco allowance.

## Useful Addresses

**Canada: Switzerland Tourism**, *926 The East Mall, Etobicoke, Toronto, Ont., M9B 6K1; tel: (416) 695 2090.*

**UK: Embassy**, *16/18 Montagu Pl., London W1H 2BQ; tel: (0171) 616 6000.* **Switzerland Tourism (ST) and Switzerland Travel Centre** (including trains), *Swiss Centre, Swiss Court, London W1V 8EE; tel: (0171) 734 1921.*

**USA: Embassy**, *2900 Cathedral Ave N.W., Washington, DC 20008-3499; tel: (202) 745 7900.* **Switzerland Tourism (ST)**, *Swiss Center, 608 Fifth Ave, New York, NY 10020; tel: (212) 757 5944.* **Railroad Representatives**, *Rail Europe Inc., 500 Mamaroneck Ave, Harrison, New York 10528; tel: (800) 682 2999.*

### STAYING IN SWITZERLAND

**90**

## Accommodation

Swiss **hotels** have high standards, but are expensive and you'll be very lucky to get anything for less than SFr.50 single or SFr.80 double. In rural areas it is often possible to get rooms in **private houses**, but these are few and far between in cities. Budget travellers (unless they are camping) rely heavily on **youth hostels** – so book these as far ahead as possible. Every major town and major station has a hotel-finding service, sometimes free and seldom expensive. If you want a double bed, you must ask for a 'matrimonial' or 'French' bed.

**Switzerland Tourism (ST)** can provide information on accommodation but do not make bookings. There are hundreds of **campsites** in Switzerland (most open summer only). They are graded on a one to five star system; guides are available from specialist bookshops or **Schweizer Camping und Caravanning Verband**, *Habsburgerstr. 35, 6004 Luzern; tel: (041) 23 48 22*, or **Verband Schweizer Campings**, *Seestr. 119, 3800 Interlaken; tel: (036) 23 35 23.* 'Rough' camping is not officially permitted, though it does happen.

## Eating and Drinking

There is a wide range of both food and eating-places. The cheapest are supermarket or department store cafeterias, such as those housed in the ubiquitous **Migros** outlets. Look out too for **EPA**, **Co-op**, and in Ticino, **Inova**. At lunch time (and quite often in the evenings) most restaurants have a fixed-price dish-of-the day menu *(Tagesteller, plat du jour, piatto del giorno)* that is good value. Tipping in Swiss restaurants is *not* the norm.

Swiss cheese is often an ingredient in local dishes; the classic Swiss *fondue*, for instance, is bread dipped into a pot containing melted cheese, garlic, wine and kirsch. *Raclette* is simply melted cheese, served with boiled potatoes, gherkins and silverskin onions. The ubiquitous meal accompaniment in German-speaking areas (which is most of the country) is *Rösti*, fried potatoes and onions.

## Communications

**Post office** opening times are usually Mon–Fri 0730–1200 and 1345–1830, Sat 0730–1100. In cities, however, major branches usually stay open much longer. Poste restante *(Postlagernd)* facilities are available at most post offices.

**Telephones:** The national network is **PTT** and all their offices (usually, but not always, located in post offices) sell phonecards *(taxcard)*. Phonecards are also available from most rail stations. In the PTT offices you can pay for international calls when you have finished. All telephone boxes have instructions in English and all telephone operators can speak English. The pink pages at the front of directories list local and international codes.

To call abroad from Switzerland: *tel: 00.* To call Switzerland: *tel: 00 41.* To call international enquiries and operators: *tel: 191.* To call national enquiries and operators: *tel: 111.* **Emergencies:** Police: *117;* Fire: *118;* Ambulance: *144* (most areas).

## Opening Hours

**Banks:** Mon–Fri 0800–1200 and 1400–1700. **Shops:** Mon–Fri 0800–1200 and 1330–1830, Sat 0800–1200 and 1330–1600. Many close on Mon morning. **Money change** desks are also in most railway stations and open longer hours than banks. **Museums**: the usual closing day is Mon. Opening hours vary, so check locally.

## Public Holidays

1 Jan; Good Fri; Easter Mon; Ascension Day; Whit Mon; 1 August; 25, 26 Dec. 2 Jan, 1 May and Corpus Christi are public holidays in some areas.

## Public Transport

Swiss **buses**, both long-distance and local, are famously punctual. The yellow Postbuses fill gaps in the railway network and always stop at the railway station. Free timetables are available from post offices and the Swiss Pass is valid, but there is a surcharge (SFr.5) for some scenic routes. If you don't have a Swiss Pass, it may be worth buying a regional 7-day pass (from any post office in that region). It's seldom worth buying a city transport pass as the best way to get around the centres is on foot.

## RAIL TRAVEL WITHIN SWITZERLAND

The principal rail carrier is **Swiss Federal Railways (SBB)**, known in French as **CFF** and in Italian as **FFS**; but there are many other small, private lines. The train service is fast, clean and punctual. The fastest trains are the various types of *EC, IC* and *RX* (Regional Express – limited stop services). All express trains stop only at major cities. *Regionalzüge* are slow local trains, usually following the same routes but stopping more frequently.

Some international trains have sleepers with three berths and/or couchettes for up to six people. Reservations are compulsory on special observation/sightseeing trains (e.g. the *Glacier Express*). Sleeping cars can be booked up to three months in advance, couchettes and seats up to two months ahead. If connecting by air, you can check in and book your luggage through from any station in the country.

**Rail information** is mostly centralised onto a single national number: *157 22 22* (SFr.1.19 per min charged), though many stations can still be contacted direct. Dialled from anywhere in the country (though not outside) you will be connected to an English-speaking operator, who will answer queries on timetables, fares and the like.

## Stations

Swiss railway stations are as well organised as you might expect. All main stations have railway information offices (and usually Tourist Offices) as well as shopping and eating facilities. Provincial stations display train schedules. Cycle hire is available at over 200 stations.

## Fares and Passes

European rail passes (see pp. 25–29) are valid on some private mountain railways in Switzerland or entitle the holder to a discount.

**Swiss Pass** (valid 4, 8, 15, 21 days or for 1 month) and **Flexi Pass** (valid for any 3 days in a 15-day period – up to 6 additional rail days can be purchased) cover first- and second-class rail travel, buses and regular boat services.

**Swiss Transfer Ticket** allows one day transfer from any airport or border station to any station in Switzerland and return. Valid for one month, it can only be purchased outside Switzerland from Swiss Tourism. The **Swiss Card** is the same as the Swiss Transfer Ticket, but also includes unlimited 50% discount on any day tickets. **Swiss Half Fare Card** allows an unlimited number of full fare tickets to be purchased at half price for scheduled rail services, mountain railways, post buses and lake boats. Valid for one month.

**Regional Passes** are valid for unlimited travel on trains, buses and boats (depending on the area) for any 2, 3 or 5 days out of a 7 or 15 day period. On other days within the period there is a 50% reduction. All passes (except region D) have a reduction of 50% for travel in adjoining areas. Eight areas are available. A reduced price is available to holders of Swiss Pass, Swiss Transfer Ticket and Swiss Half Fare Card. **Jungfraubahnen Pass** allows a 25% reduction on the Jungfraubahn, plus discounts on other forms of public transport.

With any of the above tickets, a free **Family Card** can be obtained from Switzerland Tourism, which entitles children aged 6–16 to travel free if accompanied by at least one parent.

## Rail Pass Concessions

| Operator, Route/Concession | Rail Pass/Discount |
| --- | --- |
| AB. Appenzellerbahn | IR 50%, FP Free, RES 30% |

| | |
|---|---|
| AL Aigle-Leysin | IR 50%, FP Free, RES 30% |
| AOMC Aigle-Ollon-Monthey-Champery | |
| | IR 50%, FP Free, RES 30% |
| ASD Aigle-Sépey-Les Diablerets | |
| | IR 50%, FP Free, RES 30% |
| BAM Biére-Apples-Morges | IR 50%, FP Free |
| BB Bürgenstockbahn | IR 50%, FP Free |
| BGF Grindelwald-First | IR 50% |
| BLM Lauterbrunnen-Mürren | IR 50%, FP Free, RES 30% |
| BOB Berner Oberland-Bahnen | IR 50%, RES 30% |
| BOB Berner Oberland-Bahnen: Interlaken Ost- | |
| Grindelwald-Lauterbrunnen | FP Free |
| BOW Oberdorf-Weissenstein | IR 50% |
| BrS Brienzersee | IR 50%, FP Free, RES 30% |
| BSG Lac de Bienne | IR 50% |
| BSG Bielersee | FP Free |
| BTI Biel-Täuffelen-Ins | IR 50%, FP Free |
| BVB Bex-Villars-Bretaye | IR 50%, FP Free, RES 30% |
| BVZ Brig-Visp-Zermatt | IR 50%, FP Free |
| CEV Chemins de fer Veveysans | IR 50% |
| CEV Chemins de fer Veveysans: Vevey-Blonay | FP Free |
| CMN Chemins de fer du Jura | |
| | IR 50%, FP Free, RES 30% |
| CMN Chemins de fer des Montagnes-Neuchâtloises | |
| | IR 50%, FP Free |
| EBT Emmental-Burgdorf-Thun | |
| | IR 50%, FP Free, RES 30% |
| FB Forchbahn | IR 50%, FP Free |
| GGB Gornergratbahn | IR 50% |
| GN Glion-Rochers-de-Naye | IR 50% |
| JB Jungfraubahn | IR 50%, FP Free |
| LAF Adliswil-Felsenegg | IR 50% |
| LAS Les Avants-Sonloup | IR 50% |
| LEB Lausanne-Echallens-Bercher | IR 50%, FP Free |
| LLB Leuk-Leukerbad | IR 50%, FP Free |
| LLPR Lenzerheide-Parpaner Rothorn | IR 50% |
| LSE Luzern-Stans-Engelberg | IR 50%, FP Free, RES 30% |
| LSE Hergiswil-Engelberg | FP Free |
| LSM Stöckalp-Melchsee-Frutt | IR 50% |
| LSMS Stechelberg-Schilthorn | IR 50%, FP Free, RES 30% |
| LSMS Stechelberg-Mürren | FP Free |
| MC Wengen-Männlichen | IR 50% |
| MC Martigny-Châtelard | FP Free |
| MO Martigny-Orsières (including bus routes) | IR 50% |
| MO Martigny-Orsières | RES 30% |
| NStCM Nyon-Saint Cergue-Morez | IR 50%, RES 30% |
| NStCM Nyon-St Cergue-Morez: Nyon La Cure | |
| (Suisse) | FP Free |
| OeBB Oensingen Balsthal | IR 50%, FP Free, RES 30% |
| Pbr Pont-Brassus | IR 50%, FP Free, RES 30% |
| RBS Regionalverkehr Bern-Solothurn | IR 50%, FP Free, RES 30% |
| RVO Regionalverkehr Oberaargau | IR 50% |
| RVT Régional du Val-de-Travers | IR 50% |
| SBN Beatenberg-Niederhorn | IR 50% |
| SGV Vierwaldstättersee | IR 50%, FP Free, RES 30% |
| SNB Solothurn-Niederbipp | IR 50% |
| STI Sensetalbahn | IR 50% |
| STI Steffisburg-Thun-Interlaken | |
| (including bus routes) | IR 50% |
| STI Automobildienst Steffisburg-Thun-Interlaken | |
| | RES 30% |
| SZU Sihltal-Zurich-Uetliberg-Bahn | IR 50%, FP Free |

| | |
|---|---|
| TB Trogenerbahn | IR 50%, FP Free |
| TBB Thunersee-Beatenberg | IR 50%, FP Free |
| Ths Thunersee | IR 50%, FP Free, RES 30% |
| Urh Untersee und Rhein | IR 50% |
| Urh (Valid only on URh boat). Untersee und Rhein | |
| | FP Free |
| VCP Vevey-Mont Pèlerin | IR 50%, FP Free |
| VHB Vereinigte Huttwil-bahnen | IR 50%, FP Free, |
| | RES 30% |
| WAB Wengernalpbahn | IR 50% |
| WAB Wengernalpbahn: Lauterbrunnen-Wengen | |
| | FP Free, RES 30% |
| YSteC Yverdon-Ste. Croix | IR 50%, FP Free, RES 30% |
| ZSG Zürichsee | IR 50% |
| CityNightLine trains Wien–Zurich, Berlin/Dresden– | |
| Zurich | FP Reduced rate |
| Train-Hotel Pau Casals Zurich–Barcelona–Zurich | |
| | FP Special supplement payable |
| BD Bremgarten-Dietikon | FP Free |
| BLS Bern-Lötschberg-Simplon | FP Free, RES 30% |
| BLT Baselland-Transport Linie 10 Dornach-Rodersdorf | |
| | FP Free |
| BN Bern-Neuchâtel | FP Free, RES 30% |
| BrB Braunwalden | FP Free, RES 30% |
| BT Bodensee-Toggenburg | FP Free, RES 30% |
| CGN Lac Léman | FP Free |
| FO Furka-Oberalp | FP Free |
| FW Frauenfeld-Wil | FP Free |
| GFM Chemins de fer fribourgeois | FP Free, RES 30% |
| IAS Les Avants-Sonloup | FP Free |
| LNM Lacs de Neuchâtel et de Morat | FP Free |
| LO Lausanne-Ouchy | FP Free |
| LRU Raron-Unterbäch | FP Free |
| LTB Ligerz-Tessenberg | FP Free |
| MOB Montreux-Oberland Bernois | FP Free, RES 30% |
| MThB Mittel-Thurgau-Bahn | FP Free, RES 30% |
| OC Orbe-Chavornay | FP Free |
| OJB Oberaargau-Jura | FP Free |
| RHB Rorsach-Heiden | FP Free, RES 30% |
| RhB Rhätische Bahn | FP Free, RES 30% |
| RhW Rheineck-Walzenhausen | FP Free |
| RVT Régional du Val-de-Travers | FP Free |
| SBB Bodensee (Lake Constance) | FP Free |
| SBB Rorschach-Romanshorn-Kreuzlingen | FP Free |
| SEZ Simmentalbahn | FP Free |
| SEZ Spiez-Erienbach-Zweisimmer | RES 30% |
| SMB Solothurn-Moutier | FP Free, RES 30% |
| SMC Sierre-Montana-Crans: Sierre/Siders-Montana- | |
| Vermala | FP Free |
| SNL Lago di Lugano | FP Free |
| SOB Südostbahn | FP Free, RES 30% |
| STB Sensetalbahn | FP Free |
| SBB Bodensee (Lake Constance) | FP Free |
| WB Waldenburgerbahn | FP Free, RES 30% |
| WM Wohlen-Meisterschwanden | FP Free |
| WSB Wynental-und Suhrentalbahn | FP Free |
| ZBB Zugerbergbahn | FP Free |
| ZSG Zürichsee | FP Free |

Bus, tram and rail travel in Asrau, Baden/Wettingen,
Basel, Bern, Biel/Bienne, La Chaux-de-Fonds, Chur,
Fribourg, Genève, Gossau (SG), Grenchen, Herisau,
Langenthal, Lausanne, Locarno, Lugano, Luzern,
Morges, Neuchâtel, Olten, St Gallen, Schaffenhausen,

| | |
|---|---|
| Solothurn, Thun, Vevey/Montreux, Winterthur, Zug and Zürich | FP Free |
| CityNightLine trains Wien–Zurich, Berlin/Dresden–Zurich | FP Reduced rate |
| ARB Arth-Rigi-Bahn | RES 30% |
| MGN Montreux-Glion-Rochers-de-Naye | RES 30% |
| PB Pilatusbahn Alpnachstad-Pilatus-Kulm | RES 30% |
| SSIF Società Subalpina di Imprese Ferroviarie | RES 30% |
| VRB/LWRK Vitznau-Rigi-Bahn-Weggis-Rigi Kaltbad | RES 30% |
| PTT Scweizerische PTT-Betriebe | RES 30% |
| AFA Automobilverkehr Frutigen-Adelboden, Frutigen-Adelboden | RES 30% |
| FART Servizio d'automobili Locarno–Brissago–Brenscino | RES 30% |
| GFM Service d'automobiles Fribourg–Bulle | RES 30% |
| MO Service d'automobiles Martigny-Gd-St-Bernhard (col or tunnel)-Aosta | RES 30% |
| SMC Sierre-Montana-Crans Orsières-Champex | RES 30% |
| Steamer services on Lake Constance Romanshorn–Frederichshafen and Rorschach–Lindau | EP 50% |
| Bürgenstock Funicular | EP 50% |
| Steamer services on Lake Constance Rorschach–Romanshorn | EP 35% |
| Funicular Alpnachstad/cable car Kriens–top of Mt Pilatus | EP 35% |
| Transport Museum, Luzern | EP 35% |
| Jungfrau region railways | EP 25% |
| Rigi Railways | EP 25% |

## TURKEY

**Capital:** Ankara. **Language**: Turkish; French, English and German are also spoken to some extent in Istanbul and coast resorts. **Currency**: Turkish Lira (TL.). No more than US$5000 worth of lira may be brought in or taken out. Do keep exchange slips.

### Passports and Visas

Citizens of Germany, Belgium, France, The Netherlands, Luxembourg, Spain, Italy, Malta, Switzerland and Greece may enter with proper identity cards in lieu of a passport. Nationals of Ireland, Italy, the UK, USA, Austria, Spain, Portugal and Israel must buy visas on arrival. They are not needed by nationals of the other EU countries, Australia, Canada, New Zealand or South Africa. Others should check.

### Customs

It is strictly forbidden to export antiques. Ownership of cellular phones must be documented in your passport. Keep a proof of purchase for new carpets. In addition to the usual prohibitions, there are restrictions on goods like photographic film, so get full details from the Turkish Tourist Office before you go.

If buying expensive or antique carpets, be prepared to pay duty for them on your return. Customs officials are seldom fooled by receipts that undervalue carpets, so don't waste your time getting them.

### Tourist Information

Most coastal resorts and some larger towns have small municipal Tourist Offices, which offer a limited range of sightseeing information but little else. Limited English is usually spoken.

### Useful Addresses

**Australia: Turkish Tourist Office**, *Suite 101, 280 George St, Sydney, NSW 2000; tel: (2) 92 23 30 55, fax: (2) 92 23 32 04; e-mail: turkish@ozemail.comau.*
**Canada: Turkish Tourist Office**, *Constitution Sq., 360 Albert St, Suite 801, Ottowa, Ontario K1R 7X7; tel: (613) 230 86 54, fax: (613) 230 36 83.*
**UK: Consulate-General**, *Rutland Lodge, Rutland Gardens, London SW7 1BW; tel: (0171) 589 0360.* **Turkish Tourist Office**, *170/173 Piccadilly (1st Floor), London W1V 9DD; tel: (0171) 629 7771, fax: (0171) 491 0773; e-mail: eb25@cityscape.co.uk.*
**USA: Embassy**, *1606 23rd St N.W., Washington, DC 20008; tel: (202) 387 3200.* **Turkish Tourist Office**, *821 UN Plaza, New York, NY 10017; tel: (212) 687 2194/5, fax: (212) 599 7568; http://www.turkey.org/turkey* and *1717 Massachusetts Ave, NW Suite 306, Washington DC 20036; tel: (202) 429 98 44, fax: (202) 429 56 49*

### STAYING IN TURKEY

### Accommodation

There are plenty of **hotels** in main towns and cities and at coastal resort areas, though much of Turkey's Aegean coast and most of the Black Sea coast remains quite untouched by tourism.

Prices and types range from luxurious and expensive to dirt-cheap and cockroach-ridden, although the quality doesn't always match the price.

The cheapest city hotels are often shabby and unappealing, with a clientele to match, but above rock bottom they are usually clean and comfortable. Always check out the room and the plumbing before you agree to take it.

In high summer, look for somewhere with air-conditioning or a fan, and always take your own plug (they are rarely provided). Eager touts often hang around bus and train stations.

### Eating and Drinking

Both eating and drinking are very cheap in Turkey, if you stick to local food – and there's really no reason not to, as the Turkish cuisine is excellent. Food tends to be based on whatever vegetables and fruit are in season, with fresh seafood, lamb and chicken (other meats are found, but less often). *Pide,* a pizza-like, meal-sized snack of unleavened bread topped with a choice of minced lamb, cheese, eggs, vegetables and herbs, is perfect if you're on a budget. Puddings are usually very sweet, many featuring semolina, honey and/or nuts.

Coffee (black and very strong) and tea (black, sweet, often vanilla-flavoured and very cheap) are both easily available. You will have to specify if you want your drink unsweetened. You may be given milk with your tea at breakfast, but seldom at any other time. There is a wide choice of local wines, some of them very good. *Raki* (anisseed-flavoured spirit drunk with water) is popular. The local beers are palatable. Most spirits are imported. Be wary of drinking tap water.

In cities, eating-places are open most of the day. In smaller places the normal eating hours are 1200–1500 and 1900–2200. In most restaurants there is a counter where you can see what's on offer, and it's customary to have a good look. If you don't speak Turkish, just point at whatever appeals to you.

### Postage

**Post offices** have yellow **PTT** signs. The main offices in Istanbul and Ankara open 24 hrs daily, smaller offices across the country open Mon–Fri 0830–1230 and 1330–1730.

**Telephones:** To call Turkey: *tel: 90.* To call abroad: *tel: 00.* Operator: 155, directory enquiries: *118.* **Emergencies**: Police: *155;* Fire:

*110;* Medical and general emergencies: *112;* Gendarme: *156.*

**Mobile phones:** Turkey has two GSM services. **Telsim**, *tel: 0800 211 4411* and **Turkcell**, *tel: 0800 211 0211.*

### Opening Hours

**Banks**: Mon–Fri 0830–1200 and 1330–1700. **Shops:** Mon–Sat 0930–1900. Shops in tourist areas often open until 2100 and also on Sun. The covered bazaar in Istanbul is open Mon–Sat 0800–1900. **Museums**: (generally) Tues–Sun 0900/0930–1630/1700. Palaces keep much the same hours, but tend to close Tues or Thur rather than Mon.

### Public Holidays

1 Jan; 23 Apr; 19 May; 30 Aug; 29 Oct. There are also two three-day Muslim festivals (at the end of Ramadan and Kurban Bayrami), but the dates for these depend on the lunar calendar and vary considerably from year to year.

### Public Transport

The rail network covers only the major cities and goes nowhere near many of the most popular tourist areas.

Outside the major cities, look to the **buses,** of which there are many, with services to absolutely everywhere. There are also luxury **long-distance coaches,** which come with lace at the windows and videos upfront. Reserve in advance to choose a good seat (well worth it, given the quality of some of the roads and driving). **Varan** and **Ulusoy** are the best coach companies, if slightly more expensive, and very safe.

For local transport, the best option is to use shared minibuses or taxis called *dolmus* (meaning 'stuffed'), which run on standard routes and leave as soon as they have a full load.

### RAIL TRAVEL WITHIN TURKEY

The national rail company is **Türkiye Cumhuryeti Devlet Demiryollari (TCDD).** Rail services in Turkey are slow and the system is limited to a handful of routes linking the major cities. The fastest express trains are the *mototren, ekspres* and *mavi tren.* Overnight services usually have sleeping-cars and couchettes, both of which should be booked in advance. You should reserve seats on the better trains. The food in dining-cars is both good and cheap.

### Stations
Services at railway stations are basic. English is not usually spoken, though staff – like most people in Turkey – often go out of their way to try to help.

### Fares and Passes
European rail passes (see pp. 25–29) are valid in European Turkey (between Edirne and Istanbul). See p.28 for details of Balkan Flexipass.

**Suburban Season Tickets** are valid on trains from the 15th of every month until the 18th night of the following month, and allow more than one journey per day. **Main Line Season Tickets** are monthly tickets available for students and adults, providing unlimited travel within that period in first- or second-class travel. **Train Tour Cards** are available to those aged under 26. They provide unlimited travel within one month on both suburban and main-line trains with 50% reduction on normal train fares. Over 55s also receive a considerable reduction on normal train fares.

Children under 8 years of age travel free of charge on main line and suburban trains provided that they travel with their families and do not request a separate seat.

## UNITED KINGDOM

**Capital:** London. **Language:** English and, in a very small way, Welsh and Gaelic. **Currency:** Pounds Sterling (£). 1 Pound = 100 Pence.

### Passports and Visas
Passports and visas are not needed by holders of EU National Identity Cards. Citizens of Australia, Canada, New Zealand, South Africa and the USA don't need visas if they visit as tourists.

### Customs
Standard EU regulations apply (see p. 18).

### Tourist Information
The **main information office** in London's **Victoria Station** covers the whole of the UK,

but you can get better information (and faster service) for Scotland, Wales and Ireland if you contact their individual tourist boards.

### Useful Addresses
**Australia: Embassy**, *Commonwealth Ave, Yarralumla, Canberra, ACT 2600; tel: (06) 270 6666.* **British Tourist Authority**, *210 Clarence St, Sydney, NSW 2000; tel: (02) 261 6034.* **Canada: Embassy**, *80 Elgin St, Ottawa, Ontario K1P 5K7; tel: (613) 237 1530.* **British Tourist Authority**, *111 Avenue Rd (Ste 450), Toronto, Ontario M5R 3J8; tel: (416) 961 8124.* **Republic of Ireland: Embassy,** *31–33 Merrion Rd, Dublin 4; tel: (01) 269 5211.* **British Tourist Authority**, *18–19 College Green, Dublin; tel: (01) 670 8000.* **Rail europe Ltd**, *123 Lower Baggot St, Dublin 2; tel: (01) 661 2866.*

**New Zealand: Embassy**, *44 Hill St, Wellington 1; tel: (04) 472 6049.* **British Tourist Authority**, *Ste 305, 3rd flr Dilworth Building, Customs/Queen St, Auckland 1; tel: (09) 303 1446.* **South Africa: Embassy**, *255 Hill St, Pretoria 0002; tel: (021) 433 3121.* **British Tourist Authority**, *Lancaster Gate, Hyde Park Lane, 2196-Johannesburg; tel: (011) 325 0343.* **USA: Embassy**, *3100 Massachusetts Ave N.W., Washington, DC 20008; tel: (202) 462 1340.* **British Tourist Authority (BTA),** *551 Fifth Ave (7th Flr), New York, NY 10176-0799 tel: (212) 986 2266.* **BritRail British Travel Shop**, *551 Fifth Ave (at 45th St), New York 10176; tel: (888) BRITRAIL.*

95

### STAYING IN THE UNITED KINGDOM

### Accommodation
There's a huge choice of upmarket establishments, from major chains to country houses. Lower down the scale are hotels in every price range, old inns, working farms, bed and breakfast places, etc. – the list goes on and on. The **BTA (British Tourist Authority), AA (Automobile Association), RAC (Royal Automobile Club)** and other organisations all publish guides that include ratings. Head for the nearest bookshop and take your pick.

### Eating and Drinking

Usual eating hours are: breakfast 0730–0900, lunch 1200–1400, afternoon tea (an institution rather than a meal) 1600–1700, dinner 1930–2130. There is a wide choice in every price bracket. Traditional British cuisine is plain, based on a diversity of excellent local produce. Try rare roast beef with Yorkshire pudding (a form of batter), fish and chips (the fish coated in batter and the potatoes thickly sliced) and 'ploughman's lunch' (bread, cheese and pickle).

The ubiquitous 'cuppa' (tea) is usually served with milk, but you can ask for black (or lemon in some places). Specify whether you want coffee black or white. The British are fond of their beer. Real ale is heavier than lager and not chilled, but cider and mead (seldom on offer) are more traditional. Any beer not designated low-alcohol is strong. There are almost as many wine bars as pubs and plenty of cocktail bars: a 'happy hour' means prices are greatly reduced.

### Communications

There's a wide network of **post offices** and sub-post offices (logo: 'post office' in yellow on a red oval background). Opening hours are usually Mon–Fri 0930–1730, Sat 0930–1300. Smaller offices may shut for lunch and on Wed afternoon. Stamps are also sold by most people who sell postcards. Postboxes are red and usually free-standing.

**Telephones:** Although the telephone system is now privatised, **BT (British Telecom**, the former monopoly), continues to operate the (plentiful) public phone booths – these were traditionally red, but the glass type have replaced them in most towns. Some take only coins, others only cards, but the newer ones take both. Most card phones take credit cards, as well as phonecards (on sale at newsagents).

There are two time zones for international calls and three for national. The most expensive time is Mon–Fri 0800–1800. The cheapest (for national calls) is all Sat and Sun. Any number beginning '0800' or '0500' is free. Any number beginning '0345' or '0645' is charged as if it were a local call. There are a number of other special numbers, listed in directories.

To call abroad from the UK; *tel: 00.* To call the UK; *tel: 44.* National operator; *tel: 100.*

International operator; *tel: 155.* National directory; *tel: 192.* International directory; *tel: 153.* **All emergencies**: *tel: 999.*

### Opening Hours

**Banks:** Mon–Fri 0930–1530. Some open Sat morning. **Shops:** Mon–Sat 0900–1730. Supermarkets have longer hours. Many open Sun (usually 1000–1600). Some have a late-closing day and many small shops habitually stay open very late. **Museums:** there are variations, but the norm is Mon–Sat 0900/1000–1730/1800 and half-day Sun (occasionally the whole day). Most sights open daily.

### Public Holidays

England and Wales: 1 Jan; Good Fri; Easter Mon; May Day (first Mon May, but this may change): Spring Bank Holiday (last Mon May); Summer Bank Holiday (last Mon Aug); 25, 26 Dec. Variations in Scotland and Ireland.

### Public Transport

The main rail network is good, but expensive unless you have a pass. The network of inter-city buses is cheaper, but slower. The biggest operator is **National Express**. Most town networks are good, but you need independent transport in the countryside as rural buses are few and far between.

### RAIL TRAVEL WITHIN THE UK

Passenger services on Britain's formerly state-owned railways have been divided up into 25 separate franchises, and their operation entrusted to more than a dozen private sector companies. The rail system, though, retains many of the characteristics of a 'national network'. There is A government-appointed 'Rail Regulator' to see that this remains so (booking office staff, for example, must advise you of the cheapest fare between any two points, even if it is not offered by the company they work for).

The country's premier trains, running between major cities, are most often referred to as *InterCity* services. They are comfortable, fast and frequent (at least hourly on all main routes), with first and standard class. There are many other long- and medium-distance regional services (usually standard class only) criss-crossing the country. Travel by these trains may be slower (because they call at more stations). It is wise to avoid all rush-hour commuter trains.

Most medium- and long-distance trains offer snacks from a trolley wheeled through the train, something more substantial from the 'buffet car', or – in the case of principal *InterCity* trains – a full waiter-service meal in the restaurant car (though the latter may be available only to those travelling first class). Sleeper trains run six nights a week between London and five Scottish destinations plus Penzance in the far south-west. Cabins are two-berth or (for a higher charge) single.

Advance reservation (essential for sleepers) is available for most long-distance services and worth asking for as on the busiest trains it is usually free, while on others the charge for a reserved seat exceeds £1.

### Fares and Passes

European rail passes (see pp.25–29) do not provide free travel in the UK, just some discounts.

However, **BritRail passes**, obtainable by non-UK residents are excellent value.

**Rover** and **Ranger** tickets offer almost unlimited travel within a defined geographical area; the **All–Line Rail Rover** covers the whole country. Rovers are valid for between 3 to 15 days; Rangers are one-day tickets, which may be restricted to use on certain trains only.

For the visitor buying a ticket on (or shortly before) the day of travel, the principal types of reduced-fare tickets are **Saver** and **SuperSaver**. Costing considerably less than ordinary, full-fare, 'open' tickets, these are valid on all trains, but there are some time restrictions. Savers are not usually valid for departures in the morning peak Mon–Fri, while SuperSavers are, in addition, not valid at any time on 'peak days', i.e. Fridays, summer Saturdays, and days on or near to public holidays.

Rail fares are an illogical maze (e.g. return tickets can be less than one-ways if you travel after 0930), so always ask if you've been quoted the cheapest available.

# SEA CROSSINGS

These pages list the main ferries operating between Britain and Ireland and the Continent at the time of going to press. Frequencies and journey times from port to port are those of the summer season.

| FROM...TO | SAILINGS | JOURNEY TIME | OPERATOR | TEL. FOR DETAILS |
|---|---|---|---|---|
| **CORK** to | | | | |
| Le Havre | 1 per fortnight | 20 hrs | Irish Ferries | (01) 855 2222 |
| Roscoff | 1 per week | 14 hrs | Brittany Ferries | (021) 277801 |
| Roscoff | 1 per week | 14 hrs | Irish Ferries | (01) 855 2222 |
| **DOVER** to | | | | |
| Calais (catamaran) | 12 per day | 55 mins | Hoverspeed | (01304) 240241 |
| Calais (hovercraft) | 9–12 per day | 35 mins | Hoverspeed | (01304) 240241 |
| Calais | 20 per day | 75 mins | P&O European Ferries | (0990) 980980 |
| Calais | 20 per day | 1 hr 30 mins | Stena Line | (0990) 707070 |
| Calais | 15 per day | 1 hr 30 mins | SeaFrance | (01304) 204204 |
| **FOLKSTONE** to | | | | |
| Boulogne (catamaran) | 5 per day | 55 mins | Hoverspeed | (01304) 240241 |
| **HARWICH** to | | | | |
| Esbjerg | 3 per week | 20 hrs | Scandinavian Seaways | (0990) 333000 |
| Gothenburg | 2 per week | 24 hrs | Scandinavian Seaways | (0990) 333000 |
| Hamburg | 3 per week | 22 hrs | Scandinavian Seaways | (0990) 333000 |
| Hook of Holland | 2 per day | 3 hrs 40 mins | Stena Line | (0990) 707070 |
| **HULL** to | | | | |
| Rotterdam Europoort | 1 per day | 13 hrs | P&O North Sea Ferries | (01482) 377177 |
| Zeebrugge | 1 per day | 13 hrs | P&O North Sea Ferries | (01482) 377177 |
| **NEWCASTLE** to | | | | |
| Amsterdam | 2–3 per week | 16 hrs | Scandinavian Seaways | (0990) 333000 |
| Bergen | 3 per week | 22 hrs | Color Line | (0191) 296 1313 |
| Gothenburg | 1 per week | 23 hrs | Scandinavian Seaways | (0990) 333000 |
| Hamburg | 2 per week | 24 hrs | Scandinavian Seaways | (0990) 333000 |
| **NEWHAVEN** to | | | | |
| Dieppe (ship) | 2 per day | 4 hrs | Stena Line | (0990) 707070 |
| Dieppe (catamaran) | 3 per day | 2 hrs 15 mins | Stena Line | (0990) 707070 |
| **PLYMOUTH** to | | | | |
| Roscoff | 1–3 per day | 6 hrs | Brittany Ferries | (0990) 360360 |
| Santander | 2 per week | 24 hrs | Brittany Ferries | (0990) 360360 |
| **POOLE** to | | | | |
| Cherbourg | 1–2 per day | 4 hrs 15 mins | Brittany Ferries Truckline | (0990) 360360 |

| From...To | Sailings | Journey Time | Operator | Tel. for details |
|---|---|---|---|---|
| **PORTSMOUTH** to | | | | |
| Bilbao | 2 per week | 32 hrs | P&O European Ferries | *(0990) 980980* |
| Cherbourg | 3–4 per day | 5 hrs | P&O European Ferries | *(0990) 980980* |
| Le Havre | 3 per day | 6 hrs | P&O European Ferries | *(0990) 980980* |
| Ouistreham | 1–2 per day | 6 hrs | Brittany Ferries | *(0990) 360360* |
| St Malo | 1–2 per day | 9 hrs | Brittany Ferries | *(0990) 360360* |
| | | | | |
| **RAMSGATE** to | | | | |
| Dunkerque (fast ferry) | 4 per day | 1 hr 30 mins | Holyman Sally Ferries | *(0990) 595522* |
| Ostend (ship) | 2 per day | 4 hrs | Holyman Sally Ferries | *(0990) 595522* |
| Ostend (fast ferry) | 5–7 per day | 1 hr 55 mins | Holyman Sally Ferries | *(0990) 595522* |
| | | | | |
| **ROSSLARE** to | | | | |
| Cherbourg | 1 per week | 17 hrs | Irish Ferries | *(01) 855 2222* |
| Le Havre | 1 per week | 21 hrs | Irish Ferries | *(01) 855 2222* |
| Roscoff | 1 per week | 23 hrs | Irish Ferries | *(01) 855 2222* |

---

## *The Channel Tunnel*

The idea of a cross-Channel tunnel was first proposed as long ago as as 1802. Early attempts were stopped for fear of invasion and the project finally got the green light in 1985. This extraordinary feat of engineering actually consists of three tunnels (two for trains, one for services and emergency use), each one 50 km long. Eurostar rail services began in late 1994 and by the end of 1997, 11 million passengers had travelled on Eurostar trains.

The advantage **Eurostar** has over ferry services, for many travellers, is that the journey is from city centre to city centre. Waterloo International is served by the London Underground and by domestic rail services (see p. 277). From Waterloo, up to 16 trains each day take 3 hrs to reach Paris Gare du Nord, whilst 10 services take just 2 hrs 40 mins to reach Brussels Midi. Some trains stop at Ashford International (for south-east England), Lille (for connections with TGV services across France) or Calais, and there are services direct to Disneyland Paris.

Waterloo International is more like an airport than a typical London rail terminus. Facilities at the modern, purpose-built terminal include shops, cafés and bars. There is an automated check-in system at all Eurostar terminals, and passengers have to check in up to 20 mins before departure. Passengers clear customs before boarding; passport and immigration checks take place during the journey.

The sleek Eurostar trains look incongruous amongst London's commuter services. Each train, a quarter-mile long, provide two classes of travel – first-class offers complimentary meals and drinks, and second-class provides an at-seat trolley service. There are also two buffet cars on each train. Discounted tickets are available to most rail pass holders.

The 20-minute trip through the Channel Tunnel seems just like travelling on any metro system. The thrill comes as you emerge in France and the train accelerates to over 180 mph across the Pas de Calais. Both Paris Gare du Nord (p. 400) and Brussels Midi (p.149) have been altered to accommodate the Eurostar trains and provide facilities for their passengers. For details and bookings, tel: *0345 30 30 30*.

**Le Shuttle**, which runs from Folkestone to Calais, is the car transporter service. Trains run up to 4 times per hour and journey time is about 35 mins. Tickets are bought at the terminal or given in exchange for vouchers. The carriages have toilet facilities, but little by way of refreshments and no seats – passengers remain in or near their car. *Tel: 0345 35 35 35*.

**99**

# AMSTERDAM

The city's name derives from a 13th-century dam on the River Amstel (the only natural waterway in the city). In the 'Golden Age' (the 17th century) Amsterdam followed only London and Paris in importance – and assumed its present shape with the building of three new canals: Herengracht, Keizersgracht and Prinsengracht. This is a delightful city in which to linger: attractive, laid-back, full of tree-lined canals and decorative architecture, with a lively street life that includes many informal performances, notably on colourful barrel-organs. Allow a couple of days just to meander, as well as plenty of time to visit the marvellously varied museums and galleries around the city.

## TOURIST INFORMATION

**Tourist Office: VVV**, *Stationsplein 10* (opposite Centraal, on the other side of the tram terminal); *tel: (06) 340 340 66*. Open daily 0900–1700. It's invariably very busy and you may queue for some time. They can produce leaflets and answer questions on most subjects, and have a computerised system for last-minute availability of rooms nationwide. There's a **booth** in Centraal (in the international area, open daily 0800–2100) and a **branch** at *Leidseplein 1* (open daily 0900–1900).

## ARRIVING AND DEPARTING

### Airport
**Amsterdam-Schiphol**, *tel: (06) 350 340 50*, is about 14 km south-west of town. The terminal is user-friendly, with several eating-places. The extensive duty-free shops have prices which really are low. The airport information desk dispenses limited tourist information. Transfers by train are the cheapest and operate every 15 mins 0500–0100 (hourly 0100–0500), the journey between Schiphol and Centraal taking 20 mins.

### Stations
**Centraal (CS)** is the terminal for all the city's trains and only 5 mins walk north of Dam. The station building is an ornate 19th-century structure and *Stationsplein* a hive of activity, so it's easy to become distracted and vulnerable to the opportunistic thieves that hang around there. Exercise caution and leave nothing unattended. There's a manned left-luggage facility, as well as lockers, but the baggage area is closed 0100–0500. If you are interested in organised excursions, the **NS Reisburo** office in the station is less crowded than VVV, but they have no general information.

Amsterdam's other stations are outside the centre and (apart from **Schiphol**) of little interest to visitors.

## GETTING AROUND

Get the free *Tourist Guide to Public Transport*, which shows all the city transport (except boats) and includes a list of the major attractions and how to reach them. Most tourist literature includes a small map of **Centrum**, the city centre, where everything of major interest is located. If you are staying more than a couple of days, however, it's worth investing in a street map – there's a good choice, so take time to select the one that best suits your needs.

The city's layout can be confusing when you first arrive, but it doesn't take long to get the hang of things. Bear in mind that *gracht* means 'canal' and that the centre follows the horseshoe shape dictated by the canals. House numbers are even on one side of a canal and odd on the other.

Centrum is large, so it's sensible to concentrate on one area at a time: get there by public transport and then explore on foot (VVV suggest walking routes).

### Tickets

VVV and **GVB** (Amsterdam's public transport company: a few doors from VVV and easily identified by the large yellow signs in the windows; open daily 0800–2230) offer a wide variety of passes for city travel, some also covering boats and/or museums, so tell them what you'd like to include. Tickets valid several days are better value than the equivalent one-day tickets.

### Metro

This is designed primarily for commuters and has few central stops.

### Trams

Trams are the most efficient method of travel in the centre; the network is extensive and services frequent and fast from early morning to midnight. The terminal is just in front of Centraal. Pressure on the lowest step keeps the door open. The circle tram no. 20 is ideal for getting to and from the various museums and shopping areas.

### Buses

Buses begin/end just across the canal in front of Centraal, but not all from the same terminal. They are less frequent than trams, but go further afield and operate limited night services: look for a black square on the bus-stop.

### Canal Journeys

The canals are an integral part of Amsterdam and provide an excellent way to appreciate the city, so take at least one boat trip: a slow, but delightful, way to travel. There are multilingual commentaries. The norm is to embark at Centraal, but you can board at any stop; there are quays in each area of interest.

**Watertaxis** are available *(Stationsplein 8; tel: 622 2181)*, but not cheap.

There are masses of **canal cruises**, operated by a number of different companies – get tickets at any quay where *Rondvaart/Rederij* boats are moored.

**Canal buses** *(Weteringschans)* run from

1000–1800 (every 20 mins or so) and issue day tickets (NLG16.50), so you can embark and disembark at will. There are six stops – with red, white and blue signs.

**Museumboats** *(Stationsplein)* leave at 30-min intervals, 1000–1700, with five intermediate stops in places convenient for museums. Get a day-ticket (NLG20, which includes a number of discounts). The boats are turquoise and the stops have turquoise signs.

For individual exploration, you can hire **canal bikes** *(Weteringschans)*. These are pedal-boats for two or four people.

There are regular (free) **ferries** across the River Ij, linking *Centrum* with northern Amsterdam: departures from *Ruyterkade* (behind Centraal).

### Taxis

The main ranks are at *Centraal, Dam, Rembrandtsplein* and *Leidseplein; tel: 677 7777*.

**STAYING IN AMSTERDAM**

### Accommodation

Although Amsterdam has accommodation of every type, it also has countless visitors and (particularly for peak season) it's sensible to book in advance, especially since VVV charge per person to make bookings. If you're stuck, consider commuting from Haarlem/Zandvoort (see p. 162).

Hotels chains include *BW, Cn, FE, Fm, GT, Hd, Hn, Ib, IC, Ma, Mc, Nv, Rn, SA, Sf, Sg, Sn, Sw* and *Tp*. **Hôtel de l'Europe**, *Nieuwe Doelenstr. 2–8; tel: 623 4836*, is a luxurious and prestigious 5-star hotel combining old style with modern facilities. Slightly less expensive, but also 5-star, with interestingly mixed décor and a choice of excellent restaurants, is **Grand Hotel Krasnapolsky**, *Dam 9; tel: 554 9111*. More famous than these is the 4-star **American Hotel**, *Leidsekade 97; tel: 624 5322*, its **Café Américain** once the haunt of artists and writers. If you fancy being afloat, try the (3-star) **Amstel Botel**, *Oosterdokskade 2–4; tel: 626 4247*, a large ship-hotel moored in the harbour. A more conventional 3-star option, offering character and comfort, is **Ambassade**, *Herengracht 341; tel: 626 2333*. Two good cheaper

(2-star) options are **Agora**, *Singel 462; tel: 627 2200*, and **Acro**, *Jan Luykenstr. 44; tel: 662 5538*, while two good budget establishments are **Bema**, *Concertgebouwplein 9; tel: 679 1396*, and **Ronnie**, *Raadhuisstr. 41B; tel: 624 2821*.

There are two **HI hostels**, both in *Centrum:* **Vondelpark**, *Zandpad 5; tel: 683 1744* (tram nos 1/2/5: *Leidseplein*); **Stadsdoelen**, *Klonveniersburgwal 97; tel: 624 6832* (tram nos 4/9 are most frequent: *Muntplein*). **Flying Pig** run two excellent private hostels in *Centrum: Vossiusstr. 46–7; tel: 400 4187*, is by Vondelpark and *Nieuwendijk 100; tel: 420 6822*, is only 500m from Centraal. If you don't mind a bit of religion, the cheapest place in town is **Eben Haezer Christian Youth Hostel**, *Bloemstr. 179; tel: 624 471* (tram nos 13/17: *Marnixstr*). **Campsite: Vliegenbos**, *Meeuwenlaan 138; tel: 636 8855* (10 mins from Centraal on bus no. 32).

Use the touts at Centraal only as a last resort. They are illegal and many of the places they represent are in the red-light district and/or unlicensed because (among other things) they do not conform with basic fire regulations.

### Eating and Drinking

Amsterdam is a good place to eat, with restaurants in every price range and a wide choice of international cuisine. Cheap food is easy to find, even in *Centrum:* the international fast-food chains are well represented and there are plenty of other takeaways, so you can get by perfectly well without ever setting foot in a restaurant. If you want a 'real' meal for a reasonable price, try one of the many traditional 'brown cafés'. Some of the city's trendiest cafés are around *Spui*, while the areas around *Nieuwmarkt, Dam* and *De Pijp* (especially along *Albert Cuyperstr.)* are the best for Eastern cuisine.

Two top-grade Dutch restaurants are **Haesje Claes**, *Spuistr. 273*, and **Die Port van Cleve**, *Nieuwe Zijds Voorburgwal 178–80*, while **De Roode Leeuw**, *Damrak 93–4*, is a brasserie that specialises in Dutch cuisine. For the best Indonesian, try **Kantjil & de Tijger**, *Nieuwe Leliestr. 140–2*, a place popular with locals and with celebrities, but **Bojo**, *Lange Leidsedwarstr. 51*, is the best value Indonesian in town – be prepared to queue. **Egg Cream**, *Sint Jacobstr.*

*19*, is an excellent and cheap vegetarian restaurant, but it closes at 2000. Amsterdam has two *mensas* (student canteens): **Atrium**, *Oude Zijds Voorburgwal 237*, open Mon–Fri 1200–1400 and 1700–1900, and **De Weesper**, *Weesperstr. 5*, open Mon–Fri 1700–1925.

### Communications

The **main post office**, *Singel 250–256*, open Mon, Tues, Wed, Fri 0900–1800, Thur 0900–2000, Sat 0900–1500, has a poste restante facility. The branch at *Oosterdokskade 3–5* is open Mon–Fri 0830–2100, Sat 0900–1200.

The telephone code for Amsterdam is *020*. At **Telehouse**, *Raadhuisstr. 48–50* (open 24 hrs a day), you pay for calls after you've finished.

### Money

**Thomas Cook foreign exchange** are at: *Dam 23–25; Leidseplein 31a;* and *Victoria Hotel, Damrak 1–5*. Outside banking hours, the **GWK** exchange at Centraal opens 24 hrs a day. Their branch at *Schiphol* opens Mon–Sat 0700–2100, Sun 0700–1800.

The English-language magazine *What's On in Amsterdam* (published every three weeks), is easily the most comprehensive guide to events and also contains pages of useful addresses. You can buy it from VVV and bookshops, but it's sometimes free from good hotels. **AUB Uit Buro**, *Leidseplein 26; tel: (06) 621 1211* (open Mon–Sat 1000–1800), also distribute information about the city's entertainments. They and VVV make bookings, but there is a charge.

### Nightlife

The nightlife is both varied and affordable. Few places have a dress policy and many stay open until 0300/0400. There are countless bars, clubs, discos and casinos. Entrance fees (where they exist) are low, but prices for drinks tend to be inflated. It is around the cafés that most crowds gather and live music is common, especially South American, rock and jazz.

**Leidseplein** (which is very touristy) and **Rembrandtsplein** (popular with locals as well as visitors) are lively, noisy centres of evening activity and there's some action in most of the

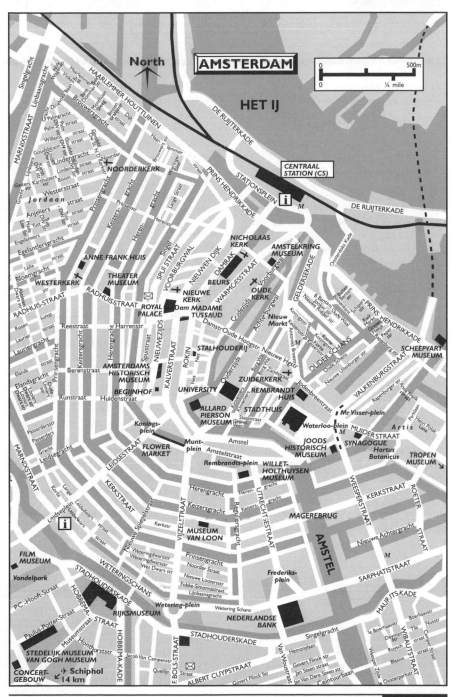

North

AMSTERDAM

HET IJ

HAARLEMMER HOUTTUINEN

DE RUIJTERKADE

CENTRAAL
STATION (CS)

STATIONSPLEIN

DE RUIJTERKADE

PRINS HENDRIKKADE

NOORDERKERK

Jordaan

Westerstraat

Anjeliers

Egelantiersgracht

ANNE FRANK HUIS

THEATER
MUSEUM

NICHOLAAS
KERK

AMSTELKRING
MUSEUM

WESTERKERK

RADHUIS-STRAAT

NIEUWE
KERK

ROYAL
PALACE

Dam MADAME
TUSSAUD

BEURS

OUDE
KERK

Nieuw
Markt

PRINS HENDRIKKADE

SCHEEPVART
MUSEUM

STALHOUDERIJ

OUDER SCHANS

AMSTERDAMS
HISTORISCH
MUSEUM

BEGIJNHOF

UNIVERSITY

ZUIDERKERK

REMBRANDT
HUIS

VALKENBURGSTRAAT

ALLARD
PIERSON
MUSEUM

STADHUIS

Mr Visser-plein

Artis

Konings-
plein

Munt-
plein

Amstel

Waterloo-plein

MUIDER STRAAT

SYNAGOGUE

JOODS
HISTORISCH
MUSEUM

Hortus
Botanicus

TROPEN
MUSEUM

FLOWER
MARKET

Rembrandts-plein

WILLET-
HOLTHUYSEN
MUSEUM

KERKSTRAAT

Leidsegracht

KERKSTRAAT

MUSEUM
VAN LOON

MAGEREBRUG

AMSTEL

FILM
MUSEUM

Vondelpark

WETERINGSCHANS

STADHOUDERSKADE

Frederiks-
plein

SARPHATISTRAAT

MAURITSKADE

PC.-Hooft-Straat

RIJKSMUSEUM

STADHOUDERSKADE

NEDERLANDSE
BANK

WIBAUTSTRAAT

STEDELIJK MUSEUM
VAN GOGH MUSEUM

CONCERT-
GEBOUW

Schiphol
14 km

ALBERT CUYPSTRAAT

0        500m

0      ¼ mile

103

other central squares. The **Jordaan** area is pleasant for an evening in a less touristy environment.

With over a hundred theatres, cinemas and concert halls, there's plenty of choice. **Stalhouderij**, *Bloemdwarsstr. 4,* stages English-language plays and there are other theatres that frequently perform works in English. Most films are shown undubbed (the exceptions state *Nederlands gesproken* on the listings) and most non-English films have English subtitles. There are several multi-screen cinemas in the area of *Leidseplein.*

Live bands (popular music) can be heard at **Paradiso**, *Weteringschans 6; tel: 626 45 21;* and **De Melkweg** (The Milky Way), *Lynbaans-gracht 234A; tel: 624 17 77.* Both often provide discos until the wee hours after a gig.

Classical and chamber music can be found at the internationally renowned **Concertge-bouw**, *Concertgebouwplein 2–6,* and ballet and opera at the very modern **Muziektheater**, *Waterlooplein 22,* where backstage tours are possible (except July). In summer, both theatres offer regular (free) lunchtime concerts. **Ijsbreker**, *Weesperzijde 23,* is a venue for international modern and experimental music. For traditional jazz, try **Bourbon St Jazz and Blues Club**, *Leidsekruisstr. 6–8,* **Café Alto**, *Korte Leidsedwarstr. 115,* and **Joseph Lam Jazzclub**, *Van Diemenstr. 242,* while **BIM-huis**, *Oude Schans 73–77,* specialises in truly improvised jazz. Organ concerts are staged in many churches, notably **Oudekerk** and **Nieuwekerk**, and regular carillon performances ring out from their towers.

South of Leidseplein is **Vondelpark** (tram nos 1/2/5), which contains **Nederlandse Filmmuseum** and the **Openluchttheater**, where alfresco performances of diverse types are staged in summer.

### The Fringe

Amsterdam is noted for its enlightened views on, among other things, marijuana and homosexuality and there is a nationwide gay and lesbian organisation based there *(tel: 623 6565; manned 1000–2200),* which will provide information about gay venues nationwide.

The city has many 'smoking' coffee-shops

where hash and pot can be purchased and smoked (usually to the accompaniment of ear-shattering music). This is not legal, but the police usually turn a blind eye. One reason for this tolerance is that it contains the problem, so do not assume it's OK to smoke elsewhere.

The red-light district is a den of thieves, so take as little with you as possible and be careful how you use your camera. Many *habitués* do not appreciate being photographed and your last sight of your camera might well be as it sinks into the nearest canal. There's no need to avoid the area, however – if you stick to the well-lit and crowded main streets, you're in little danger.

### EVENTS

Amsterdam has several water-related events and music festivals in the course of each year. The major arts event is the **Holland Festival** (June), which covers all the performing arts.

### SHOPPING

**Leidsestraat**, **Kalverstraat**, **Nieuwendijk**, **Damrak** and **Rokin** are the main shopping streets. For fun shopping, explore the small specialist shops in the alleys linking the main canals, especially in the area between **Leidsegracht** and **Raadhuisstraat**. The whole **Jordaan** area is scattered with second-hand shops and boutiques that offer the creations of up-and-coming designers. If antiques and art are your thing, look around the **Spiegelkwartier**. The Harrods of Amsterdam is the enormous **De Bijenkorf**, *Damrak.* If you go for designer labels, try along *PC Hooftstr, Beethovenstr.* and *Van Baelestr.* **Magna Plaza**, *N.Z. Voorburgwal 182,* is a shopping gallery just behind Koninklijk Paleis. Most shops in the centre of Amsterdam are open on Sunday.

The city has so many markets that VVV produce a leaflet about them, *Markstad.* The **general market**, *Albert Cuypstr.,* is the largest in the country, held Mon–Sat 0930–1700 (tram nos 4/16/24/25). The **flea market**, *Waterloo-plein* (surrounding the Muziektheater), takes place Mon–Fri 0900–1700, Sat 0830–1730.

Amsterdam has been a major **diamond** centre since the 16th century and prices are comparatively low, but it's worth shopping around.

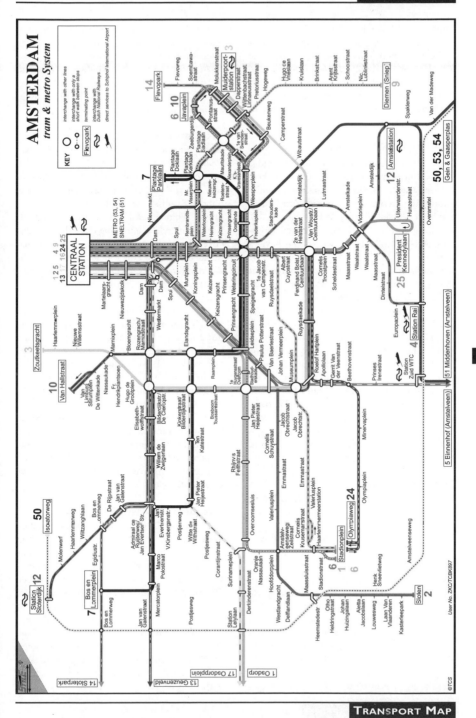

**AMSTERDAM**
*tram & metro System*

KEY
○ interchange with other lines
⇄ interchange with only a short walk between stops
terminating point
Flevopark interchange with Dutch National Railways
↗ direct services to Schiphol International Airport

105

User No. ZKC/TCBK897

©TCS

Most diamond merchants lay on free tours and hope you will buy. One of the oldest companies is **Coster Diamonds** (who re-polished the Koh-I-Noor in 1852), *Paulus Potterstr. 2–6* (tram nos 2/3/5/15: *Museumplein*). Cutting and polishing are demonstrated and you see many finished stones, with an explanation of how to assess their quality.

### SIGHTSEEING

A good brochure for information on museums, tourist attractions, shopping and dining is *Your Favourite Capital 'Amsterdam'*. This also provides information on sights to see outside Amsterdam and has a detailed city map (NLG4.50).

Amsterdam has nearly two hundred museums and art galleries. If you don't have a museum card (see Netherlands in Country by Country), consider buying the **Amsterdam Pass** (NLG33.60), which provides free or discounted admission to many attractions.

*Amsterdam City of Museums* is a free leaflet (available from VVV and some museums), which provides enough detail to enable you to decide which will interest you. If you have time to visit only a few, the ones generally regarded as unmissable are **Rijksmuseum**, the **Van Gogh museum**, the **Anne Frank house** and (less famous) the almost-addictive **Tropenmuseum**. Others (in addition to the ones below) are devoted to such diverse subjects as torture, Mondriaan, coffee and tea, chess, trams, sex, the Bible, cats and the Dutch Resistance.

### The Centre: Dam

From Centraal, *Damrak* leads directly to **Dam**, site of the original dam, with its distinctive war memorial: a favoured meeting-place for tourists. **Koninklijk Paleis** (the Royal Palace – no royalty are in residence) dominates the square. The interior reflects the glory of the Golden Age and much Empire furniture remains from the time of Louis Bonaparte (Napoleon's brother, once King of Holland).

The Gothic **Nieuwekerk** (New Church) is used for state functions and special exhibitions and regarded as an indoor extension of Dam. After a fire in 1645 the now-Protestant church was refurbished in plainer style. It contains an enormous Schonat/van Hagerbeer organ

(covered by a painted screen) and the tombs of many notables. The investiture of the Dutch rulers has taken place here since 1814.

Also in Dam is the **Madame Tussaud Scenerama**, which features waxworks, many of which are brought to life by the latest audio-animatron techniques.

### West of Dam

**Anne Frank Huis**, *Prinsengracht 263* (boat: *Prinsengracht*; tram nos 13/14/17: *Westermarkt*), is where a Jewish family hid from the Nazis for two years. They were betrayed in 1944 and only the father survived the concentration camps. Thirteen-year-old Anne recorded the family's lifestyle in a moving diary that was discovered after the war and became an international best-seller. You can see the rooms she described and other documents from the period illustrate vividly the horrors of being a Jew at that time.

For a complete change of mood, try the small **Theatermuseum**, *Herengracht 168* (tram nos 13/14/17: *Westermarkt*). It is housed in a building dating from 1638 that boasts the city's first neck gable and a notable interior. The ground floor has permanent exhibits, including a model theatre dating from 1781 and a hands-on mock-up of a backstage area.

Not far away is 17th-century **Westerkerk**, the largest Protestant church in the country, topped by the gold crown of the Austrian emperor Maximilian. The tower (Amsterdam's highest at 85m) gives one of the few bird's-eye views of the city.

### The Old City: east of Damrak

Across the canal from Centraal is **Nicholaaskerk**, with its largest dome featuring a cross donated by the prostitutes of the area. The notorious **red-light district** *(De Walletjes – Little Walls)* is (roughly) the area between *Warmoestr.* and *Gelderskade*. There are plenty of ladies in windows, showing what they have to offer; many visitors like to attend a sex show.

**Amstelkring** (Our Lord in the Attic), *Oude Zijds Voorburgwal 40* (a couple of blocks south of Nicolaaskerk), was a wealthy merchant's house, and the lower floors are furnished in 17th–18th-century style. Above them, three

106

lofts were knocked into one to provide a place of worship for Catholics during the Reformation. The lovely little chapel is intact, complete with its organ, a space saving revolving pulpit, a confessional formed from two cupboards and a superb collection of liturgical items, several jewel-encrusted.

A little further south is **Oudekerk** (Old Church), *Oudekerksplein 23,* which dates from the 14th century. It contains carved 15th-century misericordias, a great Vater Müller organ (1724), a small 17th-century organ (both restored) and stained-glass windows that include a famous 1555 Maria cycle.

## South of Dam
In **Amsterdams Historisch Museum**, *Kalverstr. 92* (boats: *Herengracht;* tram nos 1/2/4/5/9/11/14/16/24/25: *Spui*), exhibits range from the esoteric to miniature objects fashioned from silver and everyday items like decorative loaves. In the attic you can try your hand at bell-ringing. Turn right as you leave and signs lead to the **Begijnhof**, once home to pious upper-class women and still a peaceful spot, where a group of mainly 17th–18th-century gabled houses with small gardens surrounds a 15th-century church. The main entrance is off *Spui,* through a small arch.

A few blocks east, the **Allard Pierson Museum**, *Oude Turfmarkt 127* (tram nos 4/9/14/16/24/25: *Spui*), has impressive sections on Egypt, Greece, Etruria, Rome, Cyprus and Mesopotamia, including a model of an early marble quarry (with figures of the workers). The well thought-out explanations make it easy to follow developments.

The **floating flower market**, *Singel* (between *Muntplein* and *Koningsplein),* takes place Mon–Sat 0900–1700/1800. The backs of the stalls are on barges, but the fronts are firmly on terra firma and it's only by looking at the back that you realise why it's 'floating'. Nevertheless, the blooms are lovely and there's a pervasive scent of flowers.

**Herengracht** was the city's grandest canal and one stretch (between *Vijzelstr.* and *Leidsestr.)* is known as the 'Golden Bend'. This typifies the old architecture, when buildings were tall and thin (to minimise taxes based on

width) and had protruding gables (still used) to winch up furniture too big for the narrow staircases. **Willet-Holthuysen Museum**, *Herengracht 605* (tram nos 4/9), enables you to see what life inside was like in the 18th and 19th centuries. Some rooms are furnished in style, others have showcases full of *objets d'art.* Another canal house (this one 17th century) is a couple of blocks south-west: the atmospheric **Museum Van Loon**, *Keizersgracht 672* (tram nos 16/24/25). It's set up as if still inhabited and there is access to the small formal garden. The few showcases contain useful items, such as fans and parasols.

## The Museum Quarter
This district, south-west of the centre, contains museums of international status, well worth the short tram ride.

**Rijksmuseum**, *Stadhouderskade 42* (boat: *Singelgracht;* tram no. 16: *Museumplein),* ranks as one of the world's great museums. As well as an outstanding collection of Asiatic art, it contains a comprehensive selection of Dutch paintings, the 17th-century section being acknowledged as the world's best and including Rembrandt's *The Night Watch.* The superb applied arts section is extremely varied. Exhibits include four-poster beds, delicately engraved silverware, Meissen, tapestries, elaborate jewellery and tiny wooden carvings.

The **Vincent Van Gogh Museum**, *Paulus Potterstr. 7* (boats: *Museumplein;* tram nos 2/3/5/15: *Van Baerlestr.),* owns some 200 of his paintings and 500 drawings covering his whole artistic life (not all shown at the same time). Don't overlook the showcase containing many of his smaller works on the floor above the main display. Exhibits in the rest of the building vary.

At *Paulus Potterstr. 13* is the excellent **Stedelijk Museum**. This influential museum of modern art and industrial design displays mainly post-war items and although what's on show usually includes some works by Monet, Cézanne and their contemporaries, Picasso and Chagall are more typical.

## The Jewish Quarter
This lies south-east of Dam (metro: *Waterlooplein;* boats: *Muziektheater).* The Jews played a

very important part in the development of Amsterdam and formed 10% of the pre-war population, concentrated in **Jodenhoek**, but less than a quarter survived the Nazis.

**Rembrandthuis**, *Jodenbreestr. 4–6* (tram no. 9: *Visserplein*), is where the artist lived 1639–1658. It isn't very evocative, but does contain most of his engravings and a number of his drawings. Along the street is a gateway with a skull motif, leading to **Zuiderkerk** (South Church). The splendid spire is said to have inspired Christopher Wren in his rebuilding of London, and the tower can be climbed.

The nearby **Joods Historisch Museum** (Jewish History Museum), *Jonas Daniel Meijerplein 2* (tram nos 9/14: *Mr Visserplein*), is housed in converted Ashkenazi synagogues. It's been rebuilt since the war and arranged to present (primarily) the happier aspects of Judaism, with some rich religious objects and the chance to learn a great deal about Dutch Judaism. Opposite, the 17th-century **Portuguese-Israelite Synagogue** is still in use. It was once the world's largest, built by Sephardic Jews partly to snub the less powerful, but far more numerous, Ashkenazim.

### Artis

Artis, *Plantage Kerklaan 38–40* (special Artis Express boat from Centraal; tram nos 7/9/14: *Plantage Kerklaan)*, lies east of the centre. The ticket covers a **planetarium**, an **aquarium** enclosing a **zoological museum** and a **geological museum**, but the main attraction is the **zoo**: home to over six thousand animals which are in exceptionally pleasant surroundings – you feel that every effort has been made to make them as comfortable as possible. Across the street, **Hortus Botanicus** is a botanical garden with around six thousand species.

### The Docklands

Situated north of Artis, this area is home to the **Scheepvart Museum**, *Kattenburgerplein 1* (bus nos 22/28: *Kattenburgerplein)*, an exceptionally rich maritime museum housed in a 17th-century arsenal. It contains several whole (albeit smallish) vessels, in addition to hundreds of meticulous models (from a submarine to luxury liners) and a comprehensive range of nautical

paraphernalia, including such loosely connected items as plates with a whaling motif. You can go aboard an 18th-century East Indiaman, *Amsterdam,* which is moored alongside, and watch costumed personnel performing shipboard duties.

The ecology-conscious **Tropenmuseum**, *Linnaeusstr. 2* (tram no. 9: *Mauritskade),* is a place where diverse ethnological exhibits connected with everyday life today have been arranged so imaginatively that it feels as if you are visiting the Third World areas depicted – from Indian slums and Middle Eastern bazaars to South American rain-forests – all with appropriate background music. There are several hands-on items and so much to take in that you wish you had eyes in the back of your head. Time passes very quickly, so allow plenty.

### Outside Centrum

**Amsterdamse Bos**, *Amstelveenseweg 264* (bus nos 170/171/172 – or antique trams Apr–Oct), on the southern fringe of the city, is an 80-hectare park, which was inspired by Paris's Bois de Boulogne. There are facilities for swimming, rowing, canoeing, cycling and walking (200 km of tracks). **Bosmuseum**, *Koenenkade 56,* is devoted to the park, its flora and fauna.

### OUT OF TOWN

**Edam, Marken, Monnickendam** and **Volendam** can be visited in one day-trip: allow 2 hrs each for Edam and Marken, 1 hr each for the others and 2 hrs travelling. Bus nos 110/111 go to *Monnickendam*, no. 110 also serves *Volendam* and *Edam*, no. 111 goes to *Marken*. Boats link *Marken* to *Volendam* and *Edam,* but they are frequent only July–Aug.

The bus-stop in **Edam** is 5 mins walk from the centre. It's worth buying the illustrated *A Stroll Through Edam* from VVV: an attractive souvenir. Across the 'yellow bridge' is the tiny **Museum**, housed in the town's oldest brick building (c.1530), a typically narrow, gabled house with steep winding stairs and low beams. It was inhabited until 1895 and the lower floors still feel lived in.

The **cheese market** (Wed 1000–1230, July–Aug) is for the benefit of tourists, but the old weigh-house is picturesque, and Edam is well worth a visit. It's an attractive town with well preserved 17th-century architecture, featuring many decorative touches, yet it has not been swamped by tourists and retains its charm.

If you arrive in **Marken** by bus, cross the car park by the stop to reach the edge of the old village. The harbour is lined with eateries and souvenir shops, but most of Marken remains unspoiled. Cut off from the mainland by 12th-century storms, it remained an island until a 2.5-km causeway was constructed in 1957. The constant danger of floods caused stilted houses to be built and the architecture is extremely picturesque. The people are friendly and many follow the old lifestyle, so traditional dress is not unusual: the whole place is a living museum. The actual museum is tiny, but its slide-show is interesting and enhances your enjoyment of the costumes and of Marken itself.

At **Monnickendam**, VVV is in the old church near the bus-stop. The small fishing town offers an 18th-century **town hall** topped by the figure of a monk; a 16th-century **bell tower**; a **music box collection** (in the **Stuttenburgh Café**, on the waterfront); **De Waegh** (a pancake restaurant occupying the 17th-century weigh-house and full of the old apparatus); and an **eel smokehouse**, where you can often watch the work.

The main area of interest in **Volendam** is the harbour, 100m from **VVV**. The former fishing village is picturesque, but has turned to tourism in a big way, which detracts from its charm (especially after Marken). The highlight of the **Museum** is a mock street featuring a school, shops and domestic scenes. A little west of the town, and on the bus route (5-mins drive), is **Alide Hoeve**, a traditional cheese-producing farm.

**Enkhuizen** (an hour by train) was cut off from the sea when the Zuider Zee was dammed to create Lake Ijsselmeer. VVV (just outside the station) supply tickets for the unmissable **Zuiderzeemuseum** and the ferry to get there: ignore the first stop, which is just a car park. The indoor section, **Binnenmuseum**, contains such things as traditional costumes and historic fishing craft. The open-air section, **Buitenmuseum**, consists of whole streets rescued from fishing villages that were destroyed. You can enter any house with an open door and ask questions if you find someone at home. The Urk section is particularly interesting. If you have time to visit the **Flessenscheepjes Museum**, you'll see the world's largest collection of ships in bottles.

**Hoorn** (40 mins by train, en route to Enkhuizen) is renowned for the extraordinarily eclectic **Westfries Museum**, crammed with items evoking the 17th century: exhibits range from a Louis XVI dining-room to detention cells, from embroidery to an altar. Don't miss the tradesmen's loft. The traditional **Stads Bierbrouwerij** has a bar offering 100 different types of beer. Walk through the bar to reach the **Museum van de Twintigste Eeuw**, a fun museum that opened only in 1994 and contains everyday objects from the early 20th century: such as cameras, vacuum cleaners, spectacles and typewriters.

A major reason to visit the picturesque town of **Medemblik** is the steam-train journey from Hoorn's **Muzeumstoomtram**. Full details from VVV in Amsterdam.

**Alkmaar** (30 mins by train) is famous for its cheese market, Fri 1000–1200 (mid Apr–mid Sept), now about as genuine as a false tooth, but the participants enjoy themselves and the crowds are noisily appreciative. VVV is in the renovated **Waag** (weigh-house) on the edge of the market and there's a **cheese museum** above it. **St Laurenskerk**, in the heart of town, is a cruciform church with two organs. **Biermuseum de Boom** is housed in a 17th-century brewery and **Stedelijk Museum** includes a superb assemblage of 19th-century toys. There are several other small museums.

**Aalsmeer** (about 50 mins by bus no. 172) is the site of **Bloemenveiling**, the world's largest flower auction, Mon–Fri 0730–1100 (Apr–Sept). The sheer scale is impressive, but otherwise it's not very interesting to non-specialists.

The fairy-tale theme park of **Efteling** is a favourite with children (Apr–Oct). Take a train to **Hertogenbosch** (about 1 hr), then take a local bus.

**Zaanse Schans** (15 mins by train: to *Koog-Zaandijk*) is a typical (if touristy) restored 17th–18th-century village, complete with five working windmills and traditional handicrafts.

# AMSTERDAM–BERLIN

In this route across the North German Plain flat farmland predominates for much of the way and it is man's influence rather than Nature that provides the interest. Many beautiful palaces and historic buildings can be seen, particularly between Hannover and Celle. Further east, the towns of Braunschweig and Magdeburg are famous for their connection with Martin Luther.

These towns, however, are also gateways to the hilly region to the south, the Harz Mountains, which more than make up for the relative dullness of the earlier scenery and are well worth a side-trip. Goslar and Wernigerode are only two of the many picturesque small towns that decorate the Harz. The several small railways of the region are a delightful bonus for those to whom the combination of mountain views and rail nostalgia is irresistible.

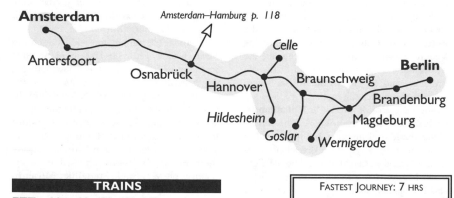

Amsterdam–Hamburg p. 118

## TRAINS

**ETT tables:** 22, 490, 492, 810.

### FAST TRACK

→ The journey between Amsterdam (Centraal) and Berlin (Zoo) takes about 7 hrs. There are 4 direct trains daily, one of which is overnight (with sleepers and couchettes).

The journey time will change dramatically when the Hannover–Berlin fast line becomes operational, and runs *ICE* high-speed services. This is likely to be some time between Sept 1998 and May 1999. The overall daytime journey between Amsterdam and Berlin can be expected to be some 5–5½ hrs.

| FASTEST JOURNEY: 7 HRS |
| --- |

### ON TRACK

**Amsterdam–(Border)–Osnabrück**
The journey between Amsterdam (Centraal) and Osnabrück can be made by any of four through trains and takes 2 hrs 45 mins. At Osnabrück this route diverges from the Amsterdam–Hamburg route (p. 118).

As with all journeys within the European Union, the border formalities are minimal.

## Osnabrück–Hannover

Trains operate alternate hours as InterRegio *(IR)* and Regional Express *(RE)* services. Journey times are about 1 hr 15 mins and 1 hr 40 mins respectively.

## Hannover–Braunschweig

There are trains every half-hour or so and the journey takes 30–40 mins.

## Braunschweig–Magdeburg–Berlin

An hourly InterCity or InterRegio service links these cities. Braunschweig to Madgeburg takes 50 mins, Magdeburg to Berlin (Zoo) takes about 1 hr 15 mins. Additional *IC* and *ICE* trains serve this route but these will be diverted to the Hannover–Berlin fast line when it opens (see note under Fast Track). Trains running over the new line will not call at Magdeburg or Brandenburg, so check your ETT carefully from Sept 1998 onwards.

## OSNABRÜCK

**Station:** 1 km south-east of the centre.
**Tourist Office:** *Markt 22/23; tel: (0541) 3232202;* (closed Sun).

Osnabrück is a mostly modern city, dominated by the **Neumarkt** shopping complex, but is worth a short stop just to stroll through the *Altstadt* and have a look at the rather lopsided **St Petrus Dom**, the pretty **Marienkirche** and the 16th-century **Rathaus** with its **Friedensaal** (Peace Hall). The **Diozesanmuseum**, open Tues–Fri 1000–1300, 1500–1700, Sat–Sun 1100–1400, is worth a brief visit.

## HANNOVER

**Station:** *tel: (0511) 19419.* This is central. Follow the red line to the information office, open Mon–Sat 0900–1800.
**Tourist Office:** *Ernst-August-Platz 2* (next to Hbf); *tel: (0511) 168 2319.* Mon–Fri 0830–1800; Sat 0830–1500.

### ACCOMMODATION

The Tourist Office can make room reservations for you at all budget levels. Chain hotels include *Dorint, Fm, HI, Ib, IC* and *Rk.* For cheap accommodation, try along *Joachimstr.* The **HI** (reservations advisable) is at *Ferdinand-*

*Wilhelm-Fricke-Weg 1; tel: (0511) 131 7674* (U-bahn: *3/7* to *Fischerhof*).

### SIGHTSEEING

The Tourist Office supplies free plans of the garden complex and the *Red Thread Guide* (DM3). The red line follows a 4200-m long path through the city centre and can be followed on foot to reach places and buildings of interest. The walk takes roughly 2 hrs.

Hannover (Hanover to the English), ancestral home of the first four King Georges of England, is a pleasantly green place that is worth visiting for its museums and gardens. The centre is a pedestrian zone. The most popular rendezvous is the famous **Kropcke Clock,** connected to *Hbf* by *Bahnhofstr.* For shopping, head for *Georgstrasse,* **Galerie Luise** and *Kröpcke-Passage.*

The high-gabled, carefully restored **Altes Rathaus** is a splendid edifice with elaborate brickwork. Alongside is **Marktkirche**, with 14th–15th-century stained glass and a bulky tower that is the city's emblem. *Kramerstrasse,* which gives a taste of the old city, leads towards the **Historical Museum,** *Pferdestr. 6, tel: 168 3052,* with such exhibits as state coaches, reconstructed farm interiors and old maps.

Across Friedrichswall, the high-domed **Neues Rathaus,** which includes models of the 17th-century city, is adjacent to the **Kestner Museum,** *Trammplate 3; tel: 168 2120,* of decorative arts. The wide-ranging **Landesmuseum,** *Am Maschseepark 5, tel: 98075,* includes natural history, a fascinating archaeological section (with Bronze Age jewellery), while the paintings include works by Holbein, Botticelli and Raphael. **Sprengel Museum,** *Kurt-Schwitters Plate; tel: 168 3875,* next door, is devoted to modern art, covering such forms as photography and graphics as well as paintings.

**Grosser Garten Herrenhausen**, 10 mins from Kropcke (U-bahn: *Herrenhausergarten; tel: 0511 168 7576)* consists of four once-royal gardens, two of which are the English-style landscaped **Georgengarten** and the formal **Grosser Garten**, the scene of spectacular fountain displays in summer. Frequent musical and theatrical performances are staged in the palace and gardens.

**111**

## ⮂ SIDE TRACKS FROM HANNOVER

The picturesque castle and town of **Celle** lie some 40 km north-east of Hannover. The medieval town is well preserved, and is overlooked by the magnificent 16th-century **Castle**, the second residence of the Electors of Hannover. Below the castle, the **Altstadt** (Old Town) is a treasury of almost 500 half-timbered houses, shops and inns dating from the 16th and 17th centuries. The prettiest, the **Hoppener Haus,** at the junction of *Poststr.* and *Rundstr.,* has an ornate carved frontage. For accommodation, try the **youth hostel,** *Weghaustr. 2, tel (01541 53208).* The **Tourist Office**, *Markt 6, tel: (051) 411 212, fax: (051) 411 2459,* handles room reservations. At the top end of the scale, the **Hotel Fürstenhof,** *Hannoversche Strasse 55/56, tel: (05141) 2010,* is one of the best hotels in Germany, with a a highly regarded haute cuisine restaurant, the **Endtenfang.**

**Hildesheim**, 50 km south-east of Hannover by rail, has one of the finest medieval market-places in Germany, and its 11th-century **Dom** and **Michaelskirche** (St Michael's Church) have been designated UNESCO World Heritage sites. Once one of Germany's most splendid Romanesque cities, Hildesheim was severely damaged during World War II, but the **Marktplatz** has been immaculately restored. The fine **Diozesanmuseum** has a magnificent collection of early medieval religious art.

There are half-hourly services between Hamburg and **Hannover**, taking about 1 hr 30 mins, which provide a connection with the Amsterdam–Berlin route (p. 110). From Hannover there are hourly trains, taking 45 mins, to **Hamelin** (Hameln). The town lives off the legend of the Pied Piper, which is illustrated everywhere and acted out every Sun in summer. It's a pleasant, if over-commercialised, old town which was little touched by the war and has plenty of historic buildings. ⬛

**Station:** *tel: (0531) 19419.* 15 mins south-east of the centre (tram no. 1 to the Rathaus).

**Tourist Office:** by the station; *tel: (0531) 79 237.* Mon–Fri 0800–1800; Sat 0900–1200.

Now a substantial industrial town, the second largest in the Lower Saxony region, Braunschweig (Brunswick) blossomed in 1166, when an influential prince, Henry the Lion, settled here. He later went on to found the city of Munich. An ancient bronze lion still guards the cobblestoned **Burgplatz**, while **Dankwarderode**, Henry's fortress, now forms part of the excellent **Herzog–Anton–Ulrich–Museum**, *tel: 0531 484 240* (the rest is on *Museumstr.).* Part of **Braunschweig Landesmuseum**, *tel: 0531 484 2625,* at Hinter Ägidien, is devoted to Jewish culture. Other buildings include the awe-inspiring 12th-century **St Blasius Dom** (where Henry is buried), with its twisted columns, candelabra and Byzantine crucifix; 11th-century **Magnikirch** and 13th–15th-century **Rathaus** (Town Hall).

## ⮂ SIDE TRACK FROM BRAUNSCHWEIG

**Goslar**, 50 km south of Braunschweig, can be reached by hourly train services, taking 1 hr. It has a finely-preserved medieval centre and has been declared a World Heritage site. It is also the centre of the **Harz**, one of Germany's most scenic mountain regions. Until reunification, these hills - the highest peak, the Brocken, is 1142m high - formed part of the border between the two Germanies and travel was restricted. The heart of the region is the **Hochharz National Park**, a 14,500 acre region of wooded slopes with some 10,000 miles of marked hiking trails. ⬛

**Station:** About 500m from the old city centre and the Elbe, which divides the city. Turn right on *Bahnhofstr.,* then left on *Danzstr.,* to reach the *Domplatz.*

**Tourist Office:** *Alter Markt 12, tel: (0391) 540 4903, fax: (0391) 540 4910.* Open Mon–Fri 1000–1800, Sat 1000–1300.

Hotel chains include *BW, Hd.* Affordable rooms in private homes can be booked through the Tourist Office.

First impressions of Magdeburg, the first major city of the former GDR that the traveller encounters on this route, are grim and grey. Now the capital of the state of Saxony Anhalt, the city suffered severe war damage and was rebuilt in dully utilitarian style. A few historic buildings survive from the city's heyday, notably the Gothic **Dom** (Cathedral), built in the 13th–16th centuries. It contains some superb religious sculpture and is the burial place of the first German Emperor, Otto the Great. From the Dom, walk along the bank of the Elbe to see the remnants of Magdeburg's once-imposing 17th-century fortifications. The **Alter Markt**, the hub of the old city, is still a bustling (if shabby) marketplace and the restored baroque **Rathaus** (Town Hall) is worth a look. Also worthy of note is the magnificent **Hegelstrasse Avenue**.

## The Harz Mountain Railways

Wernigerode is the northern terminus of Europe's most extensive narrow-gauge steam railway network. The **Harzer Schmalspurbahn** network includes 123 km of picturesque track winding through the Harz Mountains. The longest section of the network is the **Harzquerbahn**, 61 km of track between Wernigerode and Nordhausen, traversed by three trains in summer, two in winter. Some are drawn by 1950s steam locomotives, but some older engines are used for special trips.

The Harzquerbahn connects at Eisfelder Talmühle with the 46 km of the **Selketalbahn**, which runs through the scenic Selke valley. A branch line, the **Brockenbahn**, reopened in 1992 for the first time since World War II, and connects with the Harzquerbahn at Drei-Annen-Hohne, from which it ascends 19 km to the summit of Brocken mountain.

For timetables and fares, contact: **Harzer Schmalspurbahnen Gmbh,** *Forkestrasse 17, D-38855 Wernigerode; tel: (3943) 558160, fax: (3943) 32107.*

### SIDE TRACK FROM MAGDEBURG

#### WERNIGERODE

**Tourist Office: Wernigerode Tourismus**: **GM&H**, *Nicolaiplatz 1; tel: (03943) 633 035.*

In Wernigerode, try the cheap **Hotel Deutsche Eiche,** *Muhlental 36; tel: (03943) 24112;* the **Reiterhof Hasso Vaeckenstedt,** *Friederickental 1; tel: (03943) 24144;* or the more expensive but still mid-range **Gasteheim Oberbeck,** *Hillborchstrasse 4; tel: (03943) 632 662.* **Camping: Campingplate am Brocken,** *Elbingerode; tel: (039454) 42589.* **Youth accommodation: Jugendgästehause,** *Friedrichstrasse 53, tel: (03943) 632 061.*

Wernigerode's **Altstadt** is so well preserved a medieval townscape that for once the cliché 'stepping back in time' seems forgivable. The many half-timbered buildings include the **Kleinstes Haus** (Smallest House, *(Kochstr. 23),* just 10 ft wide, and the **Ältestes Haus** (Oldest House), *Hinterstr. 48,* dating back to the 14th century, but the star is probably the elaborately carved **Krummelsches Haus**, *Breite Str. 72..* The 13th-century Gothic **Rathaus** (town hall) in *Marktpl.* is considered to be one of Germany's finest.

Looming over the town is the **Schloss** — genuinely medieval, although owing much of its present appearance to 19th-century restoration. ◪

#### BRANDENBURG

**Tourist Office:** *Plauerstr. 1; tel: (0331) 237743.* Rooms in private homes are bookable through the Tourist Office; there are no chain hotels.

A centre of heavy industry, Brandenburg, 50 km east of Berlin, preserves a handful of sights worth seeing, most of them in the **Altstadt** and **Neustadt** (Old and New Towns), on separate islands in the Havel river. High points include the 14th-century **Rathaus**, and Romanesque-Gothic **Gotthardkirche** in *Altstadt,* and the 15th-century **Katharinenkirche** in *Neustadt.*

113

# AMSTERDAM–COLOGNE

The EuroCity service between Amsterdam and Cologne is fast, efficient and comfortable. The journey itself affords the opportunity to see eastern Holland, an area of hills and woodland – preserved in the Hoog Veluwe National Park. Utrecht's canals and cafés create a mini version of Amsterdam and Arnhem's museums and war cemeteries provide a moving tribute to those who fought in Operation Market Garden. The highlight of this trip, however, is crossing the Rhine and catching sight of Cologne Cathedral for the first time; it is simply magnificent.

> FASTEST JOURNEY: 2 HRS 40 MINS

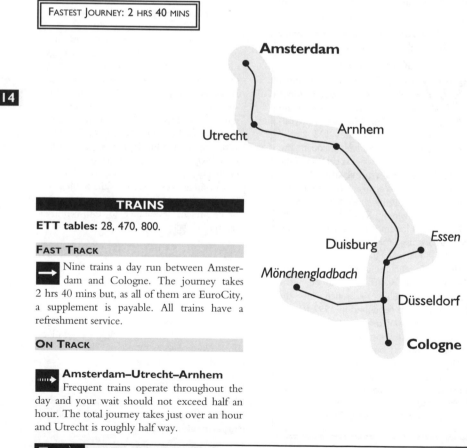

## TRAINS

**ETT tables:** 28, 470, 800.

### FAST TRACK

Nine trains a day run between Amsterdam and Cologne. The journey takes 2 hrs 40 mins but, as all of them are EuroCity, a supplement is payable. All trains have a refreshment service.

### ON TRACK

**Amsterdam–Utrecht–Arnhem**
Frequent trains operate throughout the day and your wait should not exceed half an hour. The total journey takes just over an hour and Utrecht is roughly half way.

### Arnhem–(Border)–Duisburg

There are nine EuroCity trains every day, the journey taking just over an hour. The border is at Emmerich but formalities are minimal and you don't need to leave the train.

Duisburg is a steel town of little tourist interest; only get out here if you wish to change trains to reach Essen.

### Duisburg–Düsseldorf–Cologne (Köln)

Frequent trains throughout the day link these cities. Duisburg to Düsseldorf takes about 12 mins, Düsseldorf to Cologne about 25 mins.

## UTRECHT

**Station: Centraal/CS,** to the west of the centre, separated from the old quarter by the modern Hoog Catharijne area (the country's largest indoor shopping centre). Utrecht has several outlying stations; don't get off until you reach CS, which is absolutely vast.

**Tourist Office:** *Vredenburg 90* (5-mins walk from CS; follow *Smakizelaarsveld* from the CS, which runs into *Vredenburg); tel: (0900) 414 1414.* Open Mon–Fri 0900–1800, Sat 0900–1600. There's also a booth in *CS* (open Mon–Fri 0830–1800, Sat 0930–1700), which can provide you with a free walking map to find the main (better-equipped) office.

Utrecht is large and worth a brief visit, although it's not a major tourist destination. **Domkerk,** *Domplein* (bus nos 2/22), is a late-Gothic cathedral with fine stained-glass windows. Its 112m tower (the highest church tower in the Netherlands), **Domtoren,** gives a marvellous view – if you can face 465 steps.

**Rijksmuseum het Catherijneconvent,** *Nieuwegracht 63, tel: 030 231 7296,* contains excellent medieval religious paintings and sculptures, while **Centraal Museum,** *Agnietenstr 1; tel: 030 236 2362,* exhibits items as diverse as a 9th-century Viking ship and a 17th-century doll's house.

Utrecht is the headquarters of Dutch Railways (NS). The **Nederlands Spoorweg Museum** (Rail Museum), *Maliebaanstation, Oldenbarneveltlaan 6; tel: 030 230 6206* (bus no. 3), is a must for train buffs and **Museum van Speelklok tot Pierement,** *Buurkerkhof 10; tel: 030 231 2789* (bus nos 2/22), covers mechanical musical instruments from music boxes to barrel-organs, on some of which demonstrations are given during the guided tours.

In the cellars of a medieval mansion along the wharves of the Oudegracht, an authentic steam brewery is housed – **Bierbrouwerij Oudaen,** *Oudegracht 99; tel: 030 231 1864.*

## ARNHEM

**Station:** on the north-western edge of town. **Tourist Office:** *Stationsplein 45; tel: 31 06 320 24075.* Open Mon–Fri 0900–1730, Sat 0900–1600. *Rekreatie Krant* is a free newspaper which includes listings.

### ACCOMMODATION

The only chains represented are *BW* and *RS.* The 4-star **Hotel De Bilderberg,** *Utrechtseweg 261, Osterbeek; tel: (026) 334 0843,* is a good base if you want peaceful surroundings, while the 2-star **Hotel-Pension Parkzicht,** *Apeldoornsestr 16; tel: (026) 442 0698,* is very central and walkable from the station. A good budget place is **Pension Warnsborn,** *Schelmseweg 1; tel: (026) 442 5994* (bus no. 2).

**HI:** *Diepenbrocklaan 27; tel: (026) 442 0114,* 4 km north of the station (bus no. 3 towards Alteveer: *Gemeente Ziekenhuis).* You'll see a sign with the HI logo. About 30m further on are steps leading up a forested hill to the hostel.

There are three **campsites: Camping Warnsborn,** *Bakenbergseweg 257; tel: (026) 442 3489,* open Apr–Nov (north-west of the centre, bus no. 2); **Camping Arnhem,** *Kemperbergerweg 771; tel: (026) 443 1600,* open all year (bus no. 2 towards *Schaarsbergen);* and **Kampercentrum De Hooge Veluwe,** *Koningsweg 14; tel: (026) 443 2272,* open Apr–Oct, a modest site by the Hoenderloo entrance to the park.

### SIGHTSEEING

The attractions are scattered, but there's an excellent network of buses and reaching them is not difficult. Burgers Zoo and the Openlucht are about 500m apart and there are transfers between them in the summer. It would be perfectly easy to spend an entire day at each of them, and another at De Hoge, so try to plan more than a whistle-stop.

**Burgers**, *Schelmseweg 85; tel: 026 357 6100* (bus no. 3 from the station – or from the hostel – and bus no. 13 in midsummer), is a mixed zoological complex. It includes a conventional zoo and a safari park, but pride of place goes to what is effectively a giant greenhouse in which a rain-forest and a sub-tropical desert have been created, complete with appropriate flora and fauna.

**Nederlands Openlucht**, *Schelmseweg 89,* is a very extensive open-air museum, set in delightful woodland. You can either walk around the complex or take an old tram. A one guilder ticket gives you 3 rides. There are over a hundred reconstructed buildings, mostly farms of different types (complete with appropriate livestock in many cases) and from different areas, but also houses, windmills, shops and other businesses. They have appropriate interiors and you can watch such tasks as printing and laundry being performed by traditional methods, eat typical dishes and get a good picture of Dutch rural life spanning two centuries.

The **Dutch Wine Museum**, *Velperwer 23; tel: 442 4042,* has viticulture and associated crafts. The **Airborne Museum**, *Hartenstein, Utrechtseweg 232; tel: 026 333 7710,* at Oosterbeek (8 km west of the centre – bus no. 1), is devoted to Operation Market Garden, the Allied débâcle of Sept 1944 that was immortalised in the film *A Bridge Too Far.*

To the north-west of Arnhem, the delightful 5500-hectare **De Hoge Veluwe National Park** encompasses dunes, fens, moorlands, forests and added attractions ranging from museums to free-ranging animals. There's a visitors' centre at the **Hoenderloo Gate**; *tel: (0318) 591 624* (bus nos 109/110). The other entrances are near Otterlo (bus nos 107/110 – also no. 12 in summer) and at Rijzenburg, near Schaarsbergen (bus no. 11). Once at a gate, buy a map and (unless you're a very keen walker) borrow a white bicycle (free): there's a lot of ground to cover and cycling (which takes you away from the main motor routes) is the best way to appreciate the really diverse terrain.

The **Kröller-Müller Museum** (a good 35-mins walk from the Otterlo entrance, but bus nos 12/107/110 stop there) owns one of Europe's best modern art collections, notably

278 paintings by Van Gogh (including the *Potato Eaters* and *Café Terrace at Night),* although only fifty or so are on show at any one time.

The neighbouring **Sculpture Garden** and **Sculpture Forest** make for a fascinating walk, as they contain works by Rodin, Epstein, Moore, Hepworth (and Dubuffet's extraordinary *Jardin d'Email),* along with the sort of modernistic work that resembles scrap metal. **Museonder**, by the visitors' centre, is the world's first underground museum, devoted to every form of subterranean life.

> ↱ **SIDE TRACK FROM DUISBURG**

## ESSEN

**Station: Hbf**, *tel: (0201) 19419;* central, two blocks from Munster.
**Tourist Office:** *tel: (0201) 19433.* Mon–Fri 0900–2000 and Sat 1000–1230. At south exit of Hbf – look for the Freiheit sign.

### ACCOMMODATION

Hotel chains include *Ib, Mv, Sc, Sh, Tp.*

### SIGHTSEEING

The **Essener Münster** (cathedral), founded in 852 by Altfrid, Bishop of Hildesheim, contains a superb 10th-century gold Madonna, a seven-branched candelabrum (c. AD 1000) and a **Schatzkammer** (Treasury) full of priceless items. Nearby, the small **Johanniskirche** has an interesting double-sided retable. **Alte Synagoge**, the largest synagogue in northern Europe, is a monument to Jews who perished at the hands of the Nazis.

The 19th-century mansion of the Krupp arms dynasty, **Villa Hugel**, to the south of town, is now on view. Further south, the **Folkwang Museum**, *Goethestrasse 41; tel: 0201 884 5010,* has a superb collection of 19th- and 20th-century art. In the same building is the **Ruhrland Museum.**

The Tourist Office runs guided tours of the city (Sun 1030 and Wed 1400) between the beginning of May and mid Oct. ◪

## DÜSSELDORF

**Station: Hbf**, *tel: (0211) 19419*: about 2 km from the east bank of the Rhine, where most things of interest are concentrated.
**Main Tourist Office:** *Immermannstr. 65B; tel: (0211) 35 05 05* (opposite Hbf). Mon–Sat 0800–2200 and Sun 1600–2200.

### ACCOMMODATION

The **Düsseldorf Tourist Association** *(Verkehrsverein der Stadt Düsseldorf)*, Konrad Adenauer Platz (opposite Hbf); *tel: 35 05 05*, open Mon–Sat 0800–2200, Sun 1600–2200, will book rooms and hotels. It's worth consulting the hotel booking office in *Hbf* (Mon–Sat 0800–2200 and Sun 1600–2200). Chains include *BW, Hd, Hn, IC, Rm, SA*. **HI: Jugendherberge**, *Düsseldorferstr. 1; tel: (0211) 57 40 41*, is in the Oberkassel district, just over *Rheinkniebrücke* (bus no. 835). **Campsite:** *Niederkasseler Deich 305; tel: (0211) 59 14 01* (U-Bahn: *Belsenplatz,* then bus no. 828 to *Strandbad Lorick).*

### SIGHTSEEING

Originally a centre of heavy industry, Düsseldorf is gradually throwing off this image, with fewer than one in four of the city's workforce now engaged in the iron and steel-related industries on which the city was built. Increasingly, the city is home to Germany's more creative professions. It is a hub for architects and advertising people, and six times a year hosts one of the world's major fashion shows. Düsseldorf thrives on commerce and is dominated by three modern monuments to Mammon: the **Thyssen Skyscraper, Mannemann Haus** and the **TV Tower**.

There's little of historical interest, but the museums are worth visiting and the nightlife is excellent.

The **Altstadt** (Old Town), Düsseldorf's main area of interest, is small and walkable, covering no more than one square km. Almost wholly demolished during World War II, it has been skilfully reconstructed.

**Königsallee** ('Die Kö') is an almost mandatory place for a stroll, with upmarket shops beside a tree-lined canal. Between this select shopping street and the Rhine lies *Altstadt,* marked by the **Schlossturm**, all that remains of the original 14th-century castle. A pedestrian zone that's a hive of entertainment around the clock, Altstadt has more than 200 bars crammed into its busy streets and claims to be 'the longest bar in the world'. Some pub-crawl. Düsseldorf has its own particular style of beer, *Düsseldorfer Alt,* a dark ale-like brew very different from the ubiquitous pilsener type usually associated with Germany.

**St Lambertus**, beside the river, is noted for its lopsided spire. It contains a Gothic tabernacle and a 15th-century Pietà. In *Grabbeplatz* are a wide-ranging museum of modern art, the **Kunstsammlung Nordrhein-Westfalen**, *tel: 133961 64,* with nearly 100 works by Paul Klee, and **Kunsthalle**, which hosts constantly changing exhibitions. On *Ehrenhof* are the **Kunstmuseum** (Art Museum; *tel: 899 2460* – an eclectic collection, including Rubens' *Assumption* and a superb glass section), the **Kunstpalast** (contemporary art) and the **Landesmuseum**, *tel: 446 108* (all about economics). The **Hetjens Museum**, *Schulstr., tel: 899 4201,* concentrates exclusively on ceramics. There are also museums devoted to the poets Heine and Goethe. Heinrich Heine is the city's most famous son, and his works are commemorated in the **Heinrich-Heine-Haus**, *Bilkerstr. 12–14; tel: 899 5571.*

**117**

### ⤴ SIDE TRACK FROM DÜSSELDORF

Düsseldorf's S-Bahn (suburban railway) is part of an integrated system linking the major Ruhr cities, and **Mönchengladbach** is only 20 mins away. It has a **HI**, *Brahmsstr. 156, tel: 02161 559 512,* which is an alternative if the one in Düsseldorf is full.

The 13th-century Romanesque-Gothic **Münster** has a superb central window. If you have a taste for the avant-garde in art, don't miss the **Museum Abteiberg**, renowned as one of the world's leading modern art galleries. ◢

# AMSTERDAM–HAMBURG

This route begins by accessing Friesland, the Netherlands' northernmost province. Further north, running parallel to the Dutch coastline are the Wadden Islands, unmatched for unspoilt beauty. The main route follows the same direction as the Amsterdam–Berlin route until Osnabrück. Then the way divides, the route to Hamburg taking the northern fork via the historic city of Bremen.

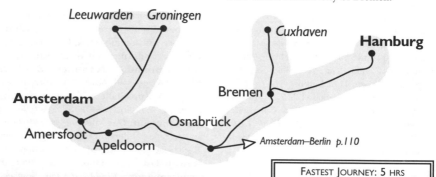

Amsterdam–Berlin p.110

| FASTEST JOURNEY: 5 HRS |
| --- |

## TRAINS

**ETT tables:** 22, 490, 492, 810, 800.

### FAST TRACK

No direct trains run between Amsterdam and Hamburg, but some international and many local services are available by changing trains at Osnabrück (about four trains during day). The journey will take about 5 hrs. Trains from Osnabrück require supplements. All have refreshment facilities.

### ON TRACK

#### Amsterdam–Amersfoort–Apeldoorn–Deventer–Osnabrück

Trains run every half-hour, taking just over 30 mins to Amersfoort (side-track here to explore Friesland) and another 30 mins to Deventer. Apeldoorn can be reached by changing trains at Amersfoort (15 mins) or Deventer (12 mins). Alternatively you can catch an hourly train directly from Amsterdam to Apeldoorn. From Amsterdam to Osnabrück, any of four daily through trains takes about 2 hrs 45 mins.

#### Osnabrück–Bremen

Trains are hourly, with occasional extra services and the journey time is about 55 mins. Supplement payable.

#### Bremen–Hamburg

Trains operate at hourly intervals and take a little under an hour. Supplement payable.

### SIDE TRACKS FROM AMERSFOORT

From Amersfoort to Groningen there are trains every 30 mins, journey time 1 hr 35–45 mins. From Groningen to Leeuwarden is another 50 mins; there are two trains an hour (only one on Sundays)

## GRONINGEN

**Station:** on the southern side of town, about 10-mins walk from VVV. Leave the station and turn right along *Stationsweg,* which becomes *Zuiderpark.* Take a left up

*Rademarkt* and the VVV is on the fifth street on the right.
**Tourist Office:** *ged. Kattendiep 6; tel: (06) 320 230 50 or 0900 202 3050, fax: 050 311 0258.* Open Mon 0930–1300 (phone only) and 1300–1800 (all services), Tues–Fri 0930–1800, Sat 1000–1700.

**Grote Markt**, the heart of the town, is dominated by the 13th-century **Martinikerk** and you can climb the ornate 97 m **Martinitoren** (June–Aug 1200–1700). Don't miss the atmospheric **Noordelijk Scheepvaart Museum**, *Brugstr 24/26; tel: 050 312 2202,* which is housed in the city's oldest building and incorporates the fascinating museum **Niemeyer Tabaksmuseum**, devoted to tobacco from 1600 to the present day. **Groningermuseum**, *Museumeiland 1; tel: 0900 821 2132,* stands on artificial islands opposite the station – you'll see the eye-catching yellow tower. Exhibits range from Chinese porcelain to modern experimental art, but the real attraction is the building itself. Opened only in 1994, its innovative architecture has really put Groningen on the map.

A unique feature of the **Hortus (Botanical Gardens)**, *Kerklaan 34, Haren* (5 km south of the city); *tel: 050 537 0053,* is the **Hidden Ming Empire**, an accurate replica of a Ming dynasty garden – even the materials used in its construction were imported from China.

Alternatively, pamper yourself at the beauty centre **Jk Maak Je Modi** (I Make You Beautiful), *Kaülsracht 13; tel: 050 318 1810,* with a hot whirlpool, massage, clay, algae and mudpacks and herbal baths.

## SCHIERMONNIKOOG

The unspoiled island is linked to Lauwersoog by ferries and Lauwersoog is linked to both Leeuwarden and Groningen by bus. The best way to view the natural attractions (including seal colonies) is to hire a bike. **VVV**, *tel: 0519 531 900.*

## LEEUWARDEN

**Station**: 5-mins walk south of the centre. Turn right on *Stationsweg*. The first left,

*Baljeestraat,* will take you to the town centre.
**Tourist Office:** at the station; *tel: (0900) 202 4060.* Open Mon–Fri 0900–1745, Sat 0900–1400.

Friesland's capital was **Mata Hari**'s home in her youth, and the recently renovated **Friesi Museum**, *tel: 058 212 3001,* has a new wing devoted to the spy's activities, both factual and as portrayed in fiction. **Museum Het Princessehof** houses the world's largest collection of 15th–17th-century Dutch tiles. It is devoted to ceramics, with a particularly rich Far Eastern section. 🔙

## APELDOORN

**Station:** on the edge of the centre, but it is not the centre that is of interest.
**Tourist Office:** VVV, *Stationstraat 72; tel: (0900) 168 1636.* Open Mon–Fri 0900–1730, Sat 0900–1300 (8 Sept–25 Apr; closed 1 Jan); Mon–Fri 0900–1800, Sat 0900–1700 (26 Apr–6 Sept).

### Sightseeing

The small town offers two major attractions, both on the outskirts (3–4 km apart) but reachable by bus from the station. In midsummer there's a bus between them.

The 17th-century **Paleis Het Loo** (bus no. 11) has been beautifully restored, contemporary records being consulted to ensure accuracy. The old stables contain royal carriages, from sledges to vintage cars, and there are extensive formal gardens.

**Apenheul** (bus nos 2/4) is primarily a monkey zoo, surrounded by a protected woodland (**Berg en Bos**). The primates live in family groups and many roam free (including ring-tailed lemurs). You are not allowed to touch them, but it's easy to come into close contact by simply sitting quietly – many of them regard this as an invitation to climb all over you. Put everything in the monkey-proof bag you will be given – their deft fingers manage to get everywhere else.

## BREMEN

**Station: Hbf**, *tel: (0421) 19419.* This is fairly central, north of the main area of interest.

**Tourist Office:** *Hillmannplatz 6; tel: (0421) 308 0038.* Close to the station. Open Mon–Thur 0930–1830, Fri 0930–2000, Sat 0930–1600, Sun 0930–1600.

### ACCOMMODATION AND FOOD

Hotels in Bremen include *BW, Ib, Ma, Mc, Nv, Pu, Sc, Sn, Sf* and *Tp.* The **HI**, *Kalkstr. 6; tel: (0421) 17 13 69,* is on the western side of *Altstadt;* bus no. 26 or tram no. 6 to *Brill.*

The **Ratskeller** (in the Rathaus) has been a bar since the early 15th century and offers 600 different wines, although it is quite pricey. Cheap eating-places can be found on and around *Ostertorsteinweg.*

### GETTING AROUND

The **Bremer Kärtchen** gives two days unlimited travel on all the city's buses and trams. With the exception of some museums, the places of interest cluster around *Marktplatz.* The **Bremen Tourist Card**, available for 2 or 3 days, offers free bus travel as well as significant discounts on the city's attractions.

### SIGHTSEEING

Like Hamburg, Bremen was a Hanseatic city and much of its 15th- and 16th- century structure survives. Together with Bremerhaven, Bremen's port at the mouth of the Weser river, Bremen is one of the *Lander* (states) which make up Germany, continuing a proud tradition of self-government which dates back to the Middle Ages.

The *Altstadt,* on the north-east bank of the river, is the main area of historical interest. *Marktplatz* is dominated by the **Rathaus**, a 15th-century structure overlaid with a Renaissance façade. It's worth joining a tour to see the splendid interior. Among the Hanseatic houses lining the square is **Schutting**, a Flemish-inspired merchants' guildhall. **Liebfrauenkirchhof** is a lovely 13th-century hall church with medieval murals and beautiful stained glass. In *Marktplatz* are two notable statues. One is a 15th-century, 10 m-high portrait of Roland (Charlemagne's nephew), which is a symbol of the town's independence. Legend has it that Bremen will remain free as long as he is standing. The other (which is modern and

much smaller) illustrates the Grimm Brothers' fairy-tale about the Four Musicians of Bremen: a donkey, a dog, a cat and a rooster.

The 11th-century twin-spired **St Petri Dom**, *Sandstr. 10–12,* is beautiful in a sombre way, with mosaic arches and elaborate figures, a 16th-century organ gallery and a 13th-century bronze font. In the **Bleikeller** (basement: open May–Oct) are some perfectly-preserved corpses, believed to be of men who fell from the roof during construction and saved from corruption by the lack of air.

To the south side of *Marktplatz* is *Bottcherstr.,* a street that is an art deco fantasy from the 1920s. It houses craft workshops, restaurants, a casino and a musical clock that chimes three times a day: at 1200, 1500 and 1800. The 16th-century **Roselius Haus** is a museum of medieval art and furniture.

The *Schnoorviertel* area (between the Dom and the river) consists of well-preserved 16th–18th-century buildings, many of which are now craft shops. Just to the east is **Kunsthalle**, *Am Wall 207* (currently closed for renovation until Spring 1998), which has an eclectic collection of works dating from the Renaissance to the present day.

The **Übersee Museum**, *Bahnhofplatz 13,* is devoted to items gathered from around the world, while the **Landes/Focke-Museum**, *Schwachhauser Heerstr. 240,* to the north-east of town, is the place to visit if you are interested in local history.

> ### ⤵ SIDE TRACK
> ### FROM BREMEN
>
> **Cuxhaven**, 110 km north of Bremen, is Germany's favourite seaside health resort, with a long sandy beach and a small offshore island, **Neuwerk**, which you can visit at low tide by horse-drawn carriage. There are frequent trains between Cuxhaven and Bremen, the journey taking just under 2 hrs.
>
> En route you pass through **Bremerhaven**, and it is worth stopping here if only to visit the fine **Deutsches Schiffahrtsmuseum** (German Ship Museum), open Tues–Sun 1000–1800, where exhibits include square-riggers and a U-boat. ⤴

# ATHENS

Modern Athens is a noisy, bustling city of more than 4 million people. The city has doubled in size in less than a generation. Many Athenians manage somehow to live a laid-back, village-style life amid the concrete apartment blocks which stretch to the horizon from the prominent landmark of the Acropolis, and hardly a corner is without a tiny café or tavern. Most visitors, though, come to see the ancient city where the seeds of modern democracy, philosophy, medicine and art were planted. Worth seeing, too, are the many Orthodox churches dating from the Byzantine era.

## TOURIST INFORMATION

The **Greek National Tourist Organization (EOT)** (HQ administration, *tel: 322 3111/9, fax: 322 4148)* maintains an information office just off *Platia Syntagma*: in the **National Bank of Greece**, *Karageorgi Servias 2; tel: 322 2545,* or *323 4130,* open Mon–Fri 0900–1830, Sat 0900–1300. The office offers sightseeing information leaflets, more practical individual fact sheets, local and regional transport schedules and up-to-date opening times of sights.

There are also EOT offices (open Mon–Fri 0900–1700, Sat 1100–1700) in the **East Terminal** of the airport, *tel: 961 2722,* and in **Piraeus Zea Marina**, *tel: 413 5730.* The tourist police in Athens *(tel: 171)* can help with lists of licensed accommodation. Their head office is *Dimitrakopoulou 77, Koukaki; tel: 922 6393.* **International Students and Youth Travel Services**, *tel: 322 1267.*

## ARRIVING AND DEPARTING

### Airports
**Athens International Airport** is 10 km south of *Platia Syntagma* in central Athens. Olympic Airways flights, both domestic and international, use the West Terminal; *tel: 926 9111.* Bus no. 19 runs to *Syntagma,* also at 30 mins intervals. All other airlines use the East Terminal; *tel: 969 4111.* For international flight information except Olympic, *tel: 939 4466/67;* for Olympic, *tel: 936 3363.* Bus no. 91 runs between the terminal and *Syntagma* every 30 mins during the day and every hour at night.

### Stations
Trains from Thessaloniki, Northern Greece, Bulgaria and Europe use **Larissa Station (Stathmos Larisis)**, *Theodorou Diligiani; tel: 524 0646* or *524 0601.* Trains from Patras and the Peloponnese use the **Peloponnese Station (Stathmos Peloponisou)**; *tel: 513 1601.* The stations are small and unimpressive; in fact, if you are looking for a prominent station worthy of a capital city you may even miss them.

The two stations are only 200 yards apart, Peloponnese being behind Larissis over the metal footbridge. They are about 2 km north-west of *Syntagma* (tram no. 1). The nearest metro stop is currently *Victoria,* about 500m to the end.

International rail tickets can be bought at Larissis station or at the **OSE offices** in Athens: *Karolou 1; tel: 524 0646/8, 6 Sina St; tel: 362 4404/6;* and *Filellinon 17; tel: 323 6747.* For domestic railway timetable information, *tel: 145;* for international services, *tel: 147.*

### Ferries
The **Piraeus Port Authority** handles services to the Greek islands, *tel: 422 6000/12.* The port itself, 8 km south-west of Athens, is served by train and metro. The Tourist Office will give you an all-island ferry timetable, which changes monthly.

If you are planning an island-hopping interlude, Thomas Cook's guidebook *Greek Island Hopping,* in the same series as this book, combines a guide to every Greek island with authoritative ferry timetable information.

## GETTING AROUND

The free map of Athens available from the Tourist Office is excellent. It indicates trolley-bus routes and metro stations and gives details of bus services. Central Athens, from *Omonia* to *Syntagma* through the *Plaka* to the Acropolis, is increasingly walkable thanks to a ban on traffic in several core blocks. Don't think about walking any further than this in July and August, when the heat and smog are unbearable.

### Metro (Subway)

There is currently only one metro line (in the process of being expanded), which runs from *Piraeus* north to the centre of town, where there are stations at *Monastiraki* (for the Acropolis and the Plaka), *Omonia* (for the Archaeological Museum) and *Victoria* (for mainline stations), then on to *Kifissia*. Tickets are available from station kiosks or self-service machines; validate them in the machines at station entrances.

A cross-town metro line, with stations at *Syntagma* and *Larissis* mainline stations, is being built. The building work is quite disruptive, although it has thrown up interesting archaeological finds, such as two Roman wells at *Syntagma*.

### Trolley-buses and Buses

Buy tickets from blue booths near bus stops or from kiosks throughout Athens. Validate tickets on board. The network is far more comprehensive than the metro; the Tourist Office map gives clear details. Most routes pass through either *Syntagma* or *Omonia*.

### Taxis

Taxis in Athens are hard to find, especially during the rush hour, around lunch-time and early afternoon. Sharing a taxi is normal – all passengers pay full fare. Some airport taxi drivers will overcharge unwary visitors; agree a fare before getting in.

## STAYING IN ATHENS

### Accommodation

The **Hellenic Chamber of Hotels** provides a booking service for hotels in Athens. They can be contacted before arrival at *Stadiou 24,*

*Athens; tel: 323 6962, fax: 322 5449/332 6962,* or after arrival in Athens at *Karageorgi Servias 2,* off *Syntagma; tel: 323 7193,* next door to the Tourist Office in the National Bank.

Hotel groups include *Ch, Hn, Ic, Ma* and *Nv.* The Tourist Office itself has a standard list of class A–C hotels. Ask for details of class D and E hotels if you are looking for cheaper options. Athens has many private hostels catering to budget travellers. Some tout for business at stations and on the trains arriving in Athens from Patras. Standards vary widely.

Hostels cluster in the *Plaka* area, which is noisy but ideally located for the main sights, or in the area between *Victoria* and the stations (where the tackiest accommodation is found). Some of the cheapest 'hostel' accommodation near the station is extremely overcrowded in high season, with tight-budget travellers sleeping on the floor and in the corridors. However, except during the height of summer you should have plenty of options. The **HI hostel**, *57 Kypselis St; tel: 822 5860,* 2 km north of *Syntagma Sq.* (trolley nos. 2/4/9), is further out than most of the private hostels. **Camping** is not a good idea; campsites are up to an hour from the centre by bus, dirty and poorly serviced, and not dramatically cheaper than hostels.

### Eating and Drinking

On a tight budget, eat on the move: *giros,* slices of veal kebab with onions, tomatoes, yoghurt and fries wrapped in flat bread, is a meal in itself and there are lots of other street snacks to choose from. Try *souvlaki* and frappé coffee. *Plaka* restaurants tend to be touristy, but those at *Plateia Filiki Eterias,* off *Kidathineon* on the edge of the *Plaka,* are a little less so. Around *Deksameni,* there are many *souvlaki* places. Try **Bakalarakia**, a basement fish restaurant at *Kidathineon 41,* for cod Athenian style; **Eden**, at *Flessa 3 (tel: 3248 858)* for vegetarian food; or **Baktairakis**, by the corner of *Mitropoleos* and *Monastiraki,* for filling traditional dishes and wine from the barrel. For even cheaper eats, head for the Pankrati suburb, north of the *National Gardens* and *Stadiou.*

### Communications

The main **post office** is at *Eolou 100; tel: 321*

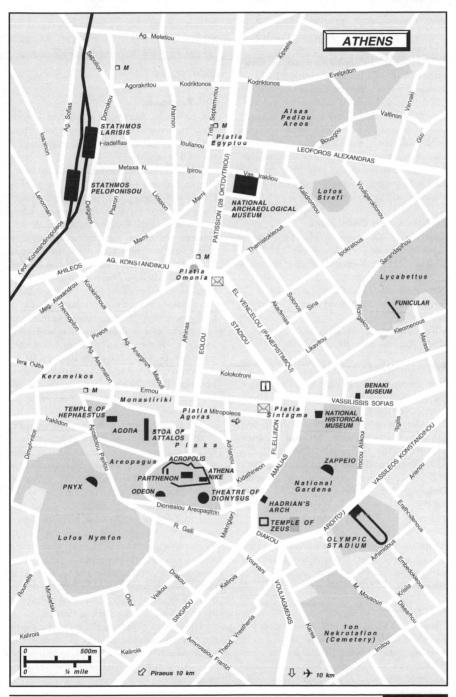

**ATHENS**

Ag. Meletiou

□ M

Agorakritou
Kodriktonos
Kodriktonos
Evelpidon
Alpetis
Valtinon
Varvaki
Gizi

STATHMOS
LARISIS

Domokou
Ag. Sofias
Ioachinon
Lenorman
Ahamon
Tritis Septemvriou
□ M
Platia
Egyptou
Alsas
Pediou
Areos
Bousgou
Kallidromiou

Filadelfias
Ioulianou

LEOFOROS ALEXANDRAS

Metaxa N.
Ipirou
Vas. Irakliou

STATHMOS
PELOPONISOU

Deligiani
Psaron
Liossion
Marni
NATIONAL
ARCHAEOLOGICAL
MUSEUM

Lofos
Strefi
Vouliagroktonou

Leof. Konstandinopoleos
Lenorman

Meg. Alexandrou
Kolokinthous

Marni
Themistokleous
Ipokratous
Sarandapihou

AHILEOS
AG. KONSTANDINOU
□ M
Platia
Omonia
EL. VENIZELOU (PANEPISTIMIOU)
Solonos
Akadimias
Sina
Lycabettus

Thermopilon
Pireos
Ag. Assumaton
Ag. Anargiron
Miaouli

STADIOU

Athinas
EOLOU
Likavitou
Ratgakou
Kleomenous
Marasli
FUNICULAR

Iera Odos
Kerameikos
□ M
Ermou
Kolokotroni
ℹ

Dimofonde
Iraklidon
TEMPLE OF
HEPHAESTUS
Monastiriki
Platia
Agoras
Mitropoleos
Platia
Sintagma
BENAKI
MUSEUM
VASSILISSIS SOFIAS

Apostolou Pavlou
AGORA
STOA OF
ATTALOS
Plaka
Adrianou
FL.ELLINON
AMALIAS
NATIONAL
HISTORICAL
MUSEUM
Sigilis
VASSILEOS KONSTANDINOU

Areopagus
ACROPOLIS
PARTHENON
ATHENA
NIKE
Kidathineon
ZAPPEIO
Irodou Attikou
Arianou

PNYX
ODEON
THEATRE OF
DIONYSUS
National
Gardens

Dionissiou Areopagitou
Makrigiani
HADRIAN'S
ARCH
Eratikolenous

Lofos Nymfon
R. Galli
DIAKOU
TEMPLE OF
ZEUS
ARDITOU
OLYMPIC
STADIUM
Embedokleous

Roumelis
Mitsfdaki
Oitof
Veikou
Drakou
Kalirois
Vourvani
Karea
Arhimidous
Krisila
Dikearhou

Kalirois
SINGROU
VOULIAGMENIS
1on
Nekrotafion
(Cemetery)
M. Mousouri
Imitou

Kalirois
Amvrossiou Frantzi
Theod. Vresthenis

0 _____ 500m
0 _____ ¼ mile

⤢ Piraeus 10 km
⇩ ✈ 10 km

**123**

*6063*, Mon–Sat 0730–2030. One branch is in *Syntagma; tel: 323 7573*, Mon–Sat 0730–2030 and Sun 0730–1330.

The **Greek Telecommunications Organisation (OTE)** has an office open 24 hrs at *Patisson 85*. The office at *Stadiou 15; tel: 322 1002*, is open Mon–Fri 0700–2400 and Sat–Sun 0800–2400. International calls can be made at both offices. You can make local calls from public coin boxes and international calls from those which bear the orange 'international' legend. You can also make calls from metered phones at 'periptero' street booths all over the city. The dialling code for Athens is *301*.

### Embassies and Consulates

**Australia:** *37 D. Soutsou St; tel: 644 7303.*
**Canada:** *Ioannou Gennadiou 4; tel: 723 9511.*
**Ireland:** *7 Vas. Konstantinou Ave; tel: 723 2771/2.*
**New Zealand:** *24 Xenias St; tel:771 0112.*
**South Africa:** *60 Kifissias Ave, Marousi; tel: 680 6645/9.*
**UK:** *Ploutarchou 1; tel: 723 6211.*
**USA:** *Vassilissis Sofias 91; tel: 721 2951.*

Most cinemas show the latest English language movies with original soundtrack and Greek subtitles; see the English-language daily *Athens News* for listings. See traditional music and dance with the **Dora Stratou Dance Theatre** in the *Philopappous Theatre; tel 324 4395*. The **Sound and Light** show on *Pnyx Hill; tel: 322 1459*, is not to be missed. **Absolut Dancing Club**, *Fillelinon 23; tel: 3237 197*, is still Athens's most popular dance venue.

During the **Athens Festival** (June–Sept), events staged in the **Odeon of Herodes Atticus** include ancient Greek drama plus classical music and ballet, performed by Greek and international companies and orchestras. For information, *tel: 322 1459.*

For gold and silver jewellery, ceramics, leather goods and fashion with a Greek slant – lots of linen and cotton knits in bright colours – try **Pandrossou Flea Market**, between *Monastiraki* and *Mitropoleos Sq..* For antiques, junk, army surplus, antique clothing and camping gear, the original **Flea Market** on *Ifestou*, on the opposite side of *Monastiraki*, is a better bet.

### The Acropolis

To many, the **Acropolis** symbolises Greece. The 'high city' served as Athens' stronghold until it was converted into a religious shrine in the 13th century BC.

Pericles built the **Parthenon** (Home of the Virgin), between 447 and 432 BC. Designed by Iktinus and Phidias, it is the finest example of Doric architecture still in existence. Close examination of the temple reveals irregularities: columns are closer together at the corners, where light can shine between them; columns are of differing widths and bulge one third of the way up; the roof line is curved. The combined effect is one of the finest optical illusions ever devised, giving the impression from afar of perfect symmetry. Today, the temple maintains its grandeur, despite the intrusions of scaffolding and cranes as part of a long-term EU-funded restoration project. Most of the dramatic friezes that adorned the Parthenon's exterior, the controversial Elgin Marbles, are in the British Museum, London, although the Acropolis Museum has some fragments.

The **Erechtheum**, to the north-west of the Parthenon, is most notable for its six *caryatids* – graceful sculptures of women. Due to the detrimental effects of air pollution, the originals have been removed and replaced by the replicas on display today. Four of the originals are on display in the Acropolis Museum.

The **Temple of Athena Nike** (Victory), with its eight small columns, stands perched on the south-west corner of the Acropolis. Built around 420 BC, during a pause in the Peloponnesian War, the temple was once the only place from where you could look out to the sea over the defensive walls; it is considered one of the finest Ionic buildings left in Greece.

The bulky **Propylaea**, the great gateway to the Acropolis, takes up most of the western end of the hill and today welcomes thousands of visitors. Arrive early if you want any peace or uninterrupted photo opportunities.

The **Acropolis Museum**, to the east of the Parthenon, contains some interesting material.

## Beyond the Acropolis

There is a fantastic view of the Acroplis and all of Attica from the **Monument of Philopappus**, though the site in itself is unimpressive and sadly defaced by graffiti.

From the Acropolis you obtain extensive panoramic views of Athens and beyond. Most of the city suburbs are anonymous concrete swathes, distinguished only by dark green awnings, but in areas close to the Acropolis you can pick out many other ancient ruins. Just below the Acropolis hill, on the south side, are two ancient theatres. The **Theatre of Dionysus**, built in the 4th century BC, was the oldest in Greece and thus can lay claim to being the first in the Western world. Only bare ruins remain, although the plan of the theatre can be identified easily, especially from above. The Roman **Odeon of Herodes Atticus** has been reconstructed and is, once again, in use. The remains of the **Temple of Olympian Zeus** are also clearly visible, east of the Acropolis. There are only a few surviving columns, but you can still absorb the grandeur of what was the largest temple in Greece. Next to it is **Hadrian's Arch**, constructed by the enthusiastic Roman builder-emperor to mark where the ancient Greek city ended and his new city began.

Across *Vassilissis Olgas,* to the north, are the **National Gardens**, which stretch up to *Syntagma Sq.* and offer a break from Athens' infamous traffic. The **Olympic Stadium**, across *Vassileos Konstandinou* from the National Gardens, stands on the site of an ancient Athenian version and was host to the first modern Olympics in 1896.

North-west of the Acropolis lie the ruins of the **Agora**, the central focus for much of ancient Athens' commercial and intellectual life. In the Agora is one of the best-preserved ancient Greek buildings, the immaculate **Temple of Hephaestus** or **Thesseion**, built in 440 BC and decorated with elaborate friezes. The **Stoa of Attalos**, built by King Attalos II in the 2nd century BC, has now been restored as a museum displaying objects found during excavations of the Agora. There are entrances

from *Adrianou, Thissio,* just off *Monastiraki,* and the path on the north side of the Acropolis. The **Areopagus**, below the entrance of the Acropolis, was the open-air meeting place for the city-state's supreme court. Across the rail lines from the Agora is **Kerameikos Cemetery**, the burial place for influential Athenians of ancient times. The **Kerameikos Museum**, *148 Ermou St,* contains discoveries from the cemetery. Round to the west of the Acropolis is **Pnyx Hill**. Here the *Ecclesia tou Demou,* or public assembly, of the Athenian State met.

## Museums and Churches

Entrance to state-run museums is free on Sun.

For an incomparable collection of relics from Athens and many other Greek sites, head to the **National Archaeological Museum**, *44 Patission; tel: 821 7717.* The line-up of exhibits is both exhaustive and exhausting: allow yourself a full day. Exhibits range through Minoan frescoes, Mycenaean gold, a phenomenal collection of over 300,000 coins, sculptures, *kouroi* and much more. Plenty of other museums offer insights into Greek life, both modern and ancient. The **Museum of Cycladic and Ancient Greek Art**, *4 Neofitou Douka St; tel: 722 8321/3,* concentrates on the simple yet powerful sculptures from Greece's most ancient civilisation, in the Cyclades Islands. The **National Gallery and Alexander Soutzos Museum**, *Vassileos Konstantinou; tel: 721 1010,* has a general but uninspired collection of mainly 19th-century Greek painting. The entertaining collection in the **Benaki Museum**, *Koumpari St* and *Vassilissis Sofias Ave; tel: 361 1617,* includes everything from ancient Greek relics through to mementoes from the War of Independence. The **Byzantine Museum**, *Varsidissis Sofia 22; tel: 723 1570,* houses icons from this later glory of Greek culture.

Several churches survive in Athens from the 10th–13th century, including **Agia Kaphikareas**, *Ermou;* **Agios Eleftherios** (or **Panagia Gorgoepikoos**), near *Mitopoleos Sq.;* and **Agia Apostoli**, near the Agora.

From **Lycabettus Hill**, the highest in Athens at 278m, the view surpasses even that from the Acropolis. Take the funicular railway up and the path down for the best round-trip.

**125**

# ATHENS–ISTANBUL

Trains can be infrequent and unreliable so make sure you check. Getting to the interesting sites, such as Delphi and the spectacular Meteora near Kalambaka, requires a bus trip. However, the train affords much better views. The cities, apart from their fantastic museums, can disappoint.

The route between Thessaloniki and Istanbul will bring you into contact with many other travellers who seem to disappear elsewhere on the journey, emerging occasionally in droves at popular sites. Arriving in Istanbul, you reach the outer limits of Europe and this guide.

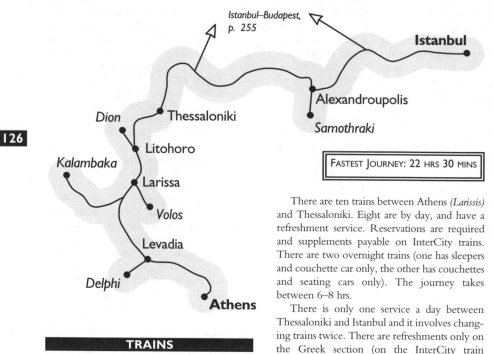

Istanbul–Budapest, p. 255

Istanbul

Alexandroupolis

Samothraki

Dion    Thessaloniki

Litohoro

Kalambaka

Larissa

Volos

Levadia

Delphi

**Athens**

**126**

FASTEST JOURNEY: 22 HRS 30 MINS

There are ten trains between Athens *(Larissis)* and Thessaloniki. Eight are by day, and have a refreshment service. Reservations are required and supplements payable on InterCity trains. There are two overnight trains (one has sleepers and couchette car only, the other has couchettes and seating cars only). The journey takes between 6–8 hrs.

There is only one service a day between Thessaloniki and Istanbul and it involves changing trains twice. There are refreshments only on the Greek section (on the InterCity train between Thessaloniki and Pithion – reservation obligatory and supplement payable). Flags painted on the bridge over the River Evros mark the frontier. The border crossing is fairly time-consuming. You have to change trains and the formalities are slow. Visas must be paid for in your own national currency, *not* in Turkish lira, and with the correct denomination note (or problems may occur).

## TRAINS

**ETT tables:** 1400, 1420, 1550.

### FAST TRACK

→ There are no through trains between Athens and Istanbul, and the most direct route involves three changes at Thessaloniki, Pithion and Uzunköprü. As the journey from Thessaloniki takes a full day you may like to break it with an overnight stop at that point.

## ON TRACK

### ▶ Athens (Athinai)–Levadia
There are eight trains a day between Athens and Levadia, but a couple of them are during the early morning hours. Two InterCity and the night (Athinai–Thessaloniki) sleeper/couchette trains also stop at Levadia. They take about 2 hrs.

### Levadia–Larissa
Ten trains a day operate between Levadia and Larissa, the journey taking about 3–4 hrs.

### Larissa–Litohoro
There are seven trains daily, but one of them runs in the middle of the night. 1–1½ hrs. Trains only call at Litohoro by request to the conductor (alighting), or handsignal to the driver (when joining).

### Litohoro–Thessaloniki
Seven trains a day, taking about 1½–2 hrs.

### Thessaloniki–Alexandroupolis
There are five trains a day between Alexandroupolis and Thessaloniki. There are two InterCity trains, reservation obligatory and supplement payable, two daytime expresses and the Evros Express overnight (with seating and couchettes). All have refreshments. *IC* trains take 5½ hrs, expresses 7 hrs.

There is one train a day between Thessaloniki and Sofia (in Bulgaria), where you can join the Istanbul–Budapest route (see p. 255). The journey takes all day.

### Alexandroupolis–(Border)–Istanbul
There is one train a day between Alexandroupolis and Istanbul (as detailed for Fast Track) and the journey takes about 7 hrs. Change of train at Pithion and again at Uzunköprü. InterCity with supplement in Greece.

## LEVADIA

**Station**: *tel: (0261) 28 046*, 3 km from the centre, but taxis are available. **Tourist Police**: *tel: (0261) 28 551*.

Levadia is a common stopping point for travellers en route to Delphi, 56 km west. The town fulfilled a similar role in ancient times. Those heading to the Oracle at Delphi could stop at Levadia's **Oracle of Zeus Trofonios** on top of Profitis Ilias, one of the two hills overlooking the town. The remains of a 14th-century **Castle** that was built over the site of the Oracle can still be seen.

## ⤴ SIDE TRACK
## FROM LEVADIA

**Tourist Office:** *Pavlou St; tel: (0265) 82 900*. Open Mon–Fri 0800–1430.

**Delphi** is synonymous with its **Oracle**, the greatest spiritual power in ancient Greece, said to be situated over the centre of the world. This belief was aided by leaking volcanic gases which induced lightheadedness and trance-like stupors. People came from far and wide to seek wisdom; questions were submitted to the Pythia (the priestess of Apollo) and her answers were interpreted by male prophets – so ambiguously that they could never be proved wrong. The most dramatic aspect of the **Temple of Apollo** (the Oracle), however, is its location, perched on the cliffs of Mt Parnassus and reached by the paved, zigzagging **Sacred Way**. Delphi is one of the largest remaining ancient sites in Greece, with a host of other ruins, notably a **Stadium** and an **Amphitheatre**. The famous bronze of a *Charioteer* is among the many beautiful artefacts on display in the outstanding **Delphi Museum**.

Thousands of visitors make the modern pilgrimage to Delphi, so come early (or out of season). Accommodation is a frequent problem here; in high season hotels and pensions are often full, many of them are closed off season. The **Stadion Hotel**: *tel: (0265) 82 251*, just up from the Tourist Office, has great views. ⤴

## LARISSA

**Station**: *tel: (041) 236 250*, 1 km from the centre of the town.
**Tourist Office**: EOT, *18 Koumoundourou St; tel: (041) 250 919*. **Tourist Police**: *86 Papanastasiou St; tel: (041) 227 900* or *222 152*.

Larissa, capital of Thessaly, is one of the few

rail junction towns in Greece and has the distinction of having recorded the hottest summer temperatures in Europe.

### ⮂ SIDE TRACKS FROM LARISSA

**Volos** was an important town in the Mycenean age and is now the main base from which to explore the beautiful, mountainous **Pelion** peninsula to the east. The city itself, from where Jason set sail in the *Argo* in search of the Golden Fleece, has little to offer except a reasonable **Archaeological Museum**. There are trains every 1–2 hrs from Larissa, taking about 1 hr. **Station**: *Odos Papadiamandis; tel: (0421) 23 712 or 25 759*. **EOT Office**: *Platia Riga Fereou; (0421) tel: 36 233, fax: (0421) 24 750*. **Tourist Police**: *217 Odos Alexandras; tel: (0421) 27 094*.

The major tourist attraction in northern Greece, **Meteora**, is reached by bus from **Kalambaka**, to which there are five trains a day from Larissa, with a change in Paleofarsalos. The journey takes about 2½ hrs. Paleofarsalos is 'On Track' between Athens and Thessaloniki, if you want to visit Meteora without going to Larissa.

**Kalambaka** has an early 14th-century **Cathedral**, which contains some 13th–14th-century paintings and a lovely marble pulpit. **Roman remains** are still visible around the cathedral. **Tourist Police**: *10 Odos Hatzipetrou; tel: (0432) 22 109*. If you can, try to stay in **Kastraki**, a much more picturesque spot and the last village before Meteora. Kalambaka is loud and crowded at night – the **Kaikis Hotel**, *Trikalon 146; tel: (0432) 75 280, fax: (0432) 75 282,* is family run and far enough out to be quiet.

The town is one gateway to the valley of the **Meteora**, 24 perpendicular rocks which soar to 600m. In the 11th century Byzantine monks began to build monasteries on the summits. Exactly how they managed this is still something of a mystery; St Barlaam, the first abbot, is said to have flown to the top mounted on an eagle. Later occupants used precarious pulley-lifts. By the 14th century there were 24 monasteries perched on the top, but the number of inhabitants decreased and now occupy only five. Nowadays their function has as much to do with showing visitors round as with religion. As in all Greek monasteries, there is a strict dress code – no shorts or bare shoulders for men or women; skirts must cover the knee. ⬑

### LITOHORO

**Station**: *tel: (0352) 81 990,* near the coast, 5 km east of town. Buses link the station to town. **Tourist Office**: *Odos Ag Nicolaou 15; tel: (0352) 81 250* (in the Town Hall). Open Mon–Sat 0900–1400, 1700–2100, Sun 0900–1400. **HI**, *2 Enipeos St; tel: (0352) 81 311 or 82 176,* has information on the various climbs. More reliable information is available from the **Greek Alpine Club (EOS)** office, *Kentriki Platia, 60200 Litohoro; tel: (0532) 81944*.

Litohoro is the access point for the 2917 m-high **Mt Olympus**, home of the ancient gods. You don't need any special equipment (other than suitable footwear) for the full ascent, but it does demand real fitness and takes two days. Book a bunk in one of the mountain refuge dormitories (hot meals and drinks available) through the EOS office. Getting to the top involves taking a taxi or hitching a lift to the car park 6 km from Litohoro, at the 1000m level; then hiking through wooded ravines to the refuge at around 2000m. It is best to spend the night here before making the demanding trek to the tops; the final 100m traverse to **Mitikas**, the highest peak, requires strong nerves.

### ⮂ SIDE TRACK FROM LITOHORO

**Dion** is one of the finest and least visited archaeological sites in Greece. There are several buses daily from Litohoro village and station to Dion village, 8 km north of Litohoro and 2 km west of the site. Highlights are the marble and mosaic floors, the **Sanctuary of Isis**, and a length of the paved road which led to Olympus. The museum, in the centre of the village, has a fine collection of finds from the site. ⬑

## THESSALONIKI

**Station**: *tel: (031) 517 517*, about 1 km west of the town centre. Bus no. 3 runs from the station to the centre, passing *Platia Aristotelous.*
**Tourist Information**: EOT Office, *34 Mitropoleos St; tel: (031) 271 888* or *222 935, fax: (031) 265 504.* Open Mon–Fri 0800–2000 and Sat 0830–1400. There is an information desk at the station which can help direct you there.
**Tourist Police**: *Odos Dodekanissou, near Platia Dimokratias; tel: 544 162.*

Thessaloniki is a large city, but many of the interesting sights are within 10–15 mins walk of the Tourist Office. Buses cover the city comprehensively. Buy tickets from the conductor, who sits at the rear.

As befits a major city, Thessaloniki has a full range of **accommodation** – ask the Tourist Office for a list. The cheaper D and E class hotels mostly cluster along *Egnatia St* – the continuation of *Monastiriou St,* east of the station. There's a fairly central **youth hostel**: *44 Al. Svolou St, tel: (031) 225 946.* A good area to eat and go out at night is *Ladadika.*

The main **post office** is at *45 Tsimiski St; tel: 264 208,* and the main **telephone office** is at *27 Karolou St (Ermou St).* **Consulates: South Africa:** *Thessabrikis 17; tel: (031) 697 594.* **UK:** *8 Venizelou St; tel: (031) 278 006.* **USA:** *59 Nikis St; tel (031) 266 121.*

### SIGHTSEEING

The second largest city in Greece was founded in 315 BC by Kassandros and named after his wife, the sister of Alexander the Great. The name means 'Victory in Thessaly'. The city became strategically vital to the Romans, straddling the Via Egnatia, their highway between Constantinople and the Adriatic, and later to the Byzantines and their Turkish conquerors. It was one of the greatest cities of the Ottoman Empire, rejoining Greece only in 1913. The old town was destroyed by fire in 1917 and Thessaloniki today is a modern, busy city, laid out along a crescent bay.

A **Museum of Byzantine Art and History** is housed in the **White Tower**, *tel: (031) 267 832,* the most prominent surviving bastion of the Byzantine-Turkish city walls. The superb **Archaeological Museum**, *tel: (031)*

*830 538,* opposite, contains the contents of Macedonian Royal Tombs discovered at Vergina in 1977. The exceptional gold-trimmed armour, weapons and gold-leaf head-dresses are eclipsed by the charred bones of the buried king, believed to be Philip II of Macedonia, father of Alexander the Great. The **Folklore Museum**, *Vassilissis Olgas 68, tel: (031) 830 591,* has a fine series of exhibits on the vanished folkways of northern Greece. The city's Roman heritage includes remains of the **Forum**, *Odos Filipou*, the **Palace of Galerius**, *Platia Navarinou*, the **Baths**, next to Agios Dimitrios church, and the **Arch of Galerius**, beside Odos Egnatia, near *Platia Sintrivaniou.* The city also has a fine collection of Byzantine churches, most notable of which are **Agios Georgios** and the restored 4th-century **Agios Dimitrios** rotunda.

Many of these are being restored and are closed with no opening date set.

## ALEXANDROUPOLIS

**Station**: *tel: 26 395* or *26 212*, by the port.

At the eastern extremity of northern Greece, this dusty, sleepy little port and railway town is little more than a stopping place for travellers heading to or from Turkey.

129

⇄ **SIDE TRACK
FROM ALEXANDROUPOLIS**

**Samothraki**, about 20 km south of Alexandroupolis, is dominated by the tree-covered slopes and bare summit of Mt Fengari, the highest mountain in the Aegean archipelago. The island's main attraction is the striking **Sanctuary of the Great Gods**, the site where the Winged Victory of Samothrace, now in the Louvre, was discovered. There are remnants of a theatre, **Temple of Hera**, and other buildings and an interesting small museum.

A daily ferry between **Alexandroupolis** and **Kamariotissa**, the island port, takes 2 hrs; in high season, hydrofoils do the trip in 1 hr. There are plenty of places to stay in Kamariotissa; the Sanctuary is just outside the hamlet of Paleopolis, 10 km from the village. ⬕

# BARCELONA

Barcelona, metropolis of the revolutionary and astute Catalan people and once home to Pablo Picasso, Joan Miró and Antoni Gaudí, is one of Europe's most enduring cities, with Roman remains, a stunning Gothic old quarter and a mass of superlative Modernist architecture.

## TOURIST INFORMATION

There are three tourist information centres: **Estació de Sants**, *tel: (93) 491 44 31,* offers information on the city, open daily 0800–2000 (summer); Mon–Fri 0800–2000, Sat, Sun and holidays 0800–1400 (winter). The other two, run by the Catalan state government *(Generalitat),* give information on Catalunya and the whole of Spain. They are located at *Gran Vía de les Corts Catalanes 658; tel: (93) 301 74 43,* open Mon–Fri 0900–1900, Sat 0900–1400, and *International terminal, Barcelona Airport; tel: (93) 315 13 13,* open Mon–Sat 0930–2000, Sun and holidays 0930–1500. For an English telephone information service run by Generalitat, dial *010.*

From June–Sept information bureaux can be found at **Estació de França**, *tel: (93) 319 57 58,* open daily 0800–2000; in *Plaça Catalunya,* near the port, and in *Plaça de la Sagrada Família* (all open daily 0900–2100). The Tourist Office also runs street information services during summer. Look for staff in red and white uniforms, with the standard 'i' symbol on their shirt sleeves.

There are two main youth information offices. **Centre d'Informació i Assessorament per a Joves**, *Calle Ferran 32; tel: (93) 402 78 00/1,* gives information and assistance on cultural, sports and leisure facilities in the city. Open weekdays 1000–1400 and 1600–2000. **Oficina de Turisme Juvenil**, *Calle Calàbria 147; tel: (93) 483 83 78,* gives advice on the best travel prices and issues IYHF cards, amongst other services. Open Mon–Fri 1000–2000, Sat 1000–1330.

**Thomas Cook Licensee:** there are several **Ultramar Express** locations around the city.

## ARRIVING AND DEPARTING

### Airport

**Aeroport del Prat** is 12 km south-west of the city. Expanded and refurbished for the 1992 Olympic Games, it now has three terminals. Airport information, *tel: (93) 478 50 00.* **RENFE trains** *(tel: (93) 490 02 02),* run every 30 mins, between about 0600 and 2230, to and from Estació de Sants (journey time: 16 mins) and Estació Plaça de Catalunya (21 mins).

The **aerobus** runs to and from *Plaça de Catalunya* every 15 mins. The service operates from the airport Mon–Fri 0600–2300, Sat and Sun 0630–2250; in the other direction, Mon–Fri 0530–2215, Sat and Sun 0600–2220. Additional stops are shown on the city map available from Tourist Offices. For information, *tel: (93) 412 00 00.*

### Stations

There are two main stations: the central **Estació de França**, *Avda Marquès de l'Argentera* (metro: *Barceloneta),* for long-distance national and direct international services, and **Estació de Sants**, *Plaça Països Catalans,* about 3.5 km from the old town; (metro: *Sants-Estació)* for suburban, regional and international trains as well as those to the airport. **RENFE information:** *tel: (93) 490 02 02.*

### Buses

**Estació de Autobuses Barcelona Nord**, *Calle Ali-Bei 80; tel: (93) 265 65 08,* is the main coach station; metro: *Arc de Triomf.*

### Ferries

From the port, virtually next door to Estació de França, ferries leave for the Balearics and Sicily. For details contact **Transmediterránea**, *tel: (93) 443 02 62* or *443 25 32.*

## GETTING AROUND

The central part of **Las Ramblas**, Barcelona's main street, is pedestrianised, while only locals would dare drive through the narrow ways of the Gothic quarter *(Barri Gòtic)*. Together, these areas form the core of the city, and are best seen on foot.

The Gothic quarter is considered by many as unsafe after dark, and the *Barri Xinès* (meaning Chinatown, although there are no Chinese: it is in fact the red-light district) on the opposite side of the *Ramblas* is definitely so.

### Metro and Suburban Trains

There are two fast and clean metro-type systems. The **Metro**, run by the city *(Ciutat)*, has five colour-coded lines. Trains are designated by the name of the last stop. The **Ferrocarrils de la Generalitat de Catalunya**, *tel: (93) 205 15 15*, run by the Catalan State, serves fewer places in the centre, but can take you out into the suburbs and beyond

The same tickets are valid on Metro and Generalitat lines and there is a flat rate for all journeys, regardless of distance or location, of Pta130. You have to pay again if you transfer between the two lines.

There are two types of card, both valid for ten journeys: T1 and T2. T1 cards are also valid on buses. Travel cards are also available which allow unlimited travel by bus and metro for 1, 3 or 5 days.

Buses run daily 0500/0630–2130/2230, with some lines continuing until 0400.

The metro runs Mon–Thur 0500–2300, Fri, Sat and the day before holidays 0500–0100, Sun 0600–midnight. Maps of the public transport system are available from *Plaça Universitat*.

### Tourist Bus

The **Bus Turístic** runs every day from 0900–2130 for most of the year, usually from late Mar to the following Jan. There is a maximum wait of 30 mins at any of the 18 stops and a full tour lasts 2 hrs 30 mins. A tourist information officer accompanies every bus, and your ticket includes discounts at several attractions.

For more information on Barcelona's public transport system, *tel: (93) 412 00 00*.

### Taxis

Yellow and black cabs can be hailed in the streets. Make sure you have change as drivers often seem not to. To order a taxi, *tel: (93) 357 77 55, 300 38 11* or *284 88 88*. For information about prices or to make a complaint, *tel: (93) 263 12 06*.

## STAYING IN BARCELONA

### Accommodation

Barcelona has as wide a range of hotels as any major European city, including the following major chains: *Hn, Md, Ml, Mp, Nv* and *Rz*. Hotels are graded in stars from one to five. Prices (excluding VAT) vary with the season from Pta43,000 (five-star) to Pta5000 (one-star) for a double room. *Pensiones* come as two- and one-star accommodation (both priced between Pta3000 and Pta5000 for a double with shared facilities). Most are located in the old part of the town, and demand is high in peak seasons.

Around the *Ramblas,* try **Pensión Noya**, *Ramblas 133; tel: (93) 301 48 31,* or **Pension Mont Thabor**, *Ramblas 86; tel: (93) 317 66 66. Plaça de Catalunya* at the top of the *Ramblas* is one of the best places to stay, but accommodation can be pricier than in the *Barri Gòtic*. **Hostal Residencia Lausanne**, *Avda Portal de l'Angel 24; tel (93) 302 11 39*, is clean and cheap with a quiet terrace at the back.

The **Eixample** is further from the action but the wide, open avenues make it pleasant and safe. **Hostal Palacios**, *Gran Vía de les Cortes Catalanes 629; tel: (93) 301 37 92*, has 30 large rooms with high ceilings and lies directly opposite the Tourist Office. More upmarket options include the one-star **Hotel Internacional**, *Ramblas 78–80; tel: (93) 302 25 66*, or the **Hotel Gravina**, *Gravina 12; tel: (93) 301 68 68*. The latter is an excellent three-star hotel with helpful, friendly staff. The rooms are comfortable and well-equipped, those at the back being slightly larger and quieter, but without balconies. For further information, try contacting the **Barcelona Hotel Association**, *Via Laietana 47; tel: (93) 301 62 40*.

Approximately 15 student halls of residence become **hostels** for young people in the summer. For details, contact a youth information centre (see Tourist Information, p.130). There are also six youth hostels, all members of **IYHF**. It is advisable to book in advance, *tel: (93) 483 83 63*. The most central are: **Kabul**, *Plaça Reial 17; tel: (93) 318 51 90,* in the Gothic quarter (metro: *Liceu/Drassanes)*; **Palau**, *Calle Palau 6; tel: (93) 412 50 80* (metro: *Liceu/Jaume)* and **Hostal de Joves**, *Passeig Pujades 29; tel: (93) 300 31 04* (metro: *Arc de Triomf)*.

Catalunya has 70% of all Spain's **campsites** and there are 12 within easy reach of Barcelona, mostly on the coast to the south of the city. **El Toro Bravo**, *Autovía de Castelldefels, Km 11, tel: (93) 637 34 62,* is one of the closest. Take bus no. 95 from *Ronda Universitat* or *Rambla Catalunya*. **Filipinas** *(tel: (93) 658 28 95)* and **La Ballena Alegre** *(tel: (93) 658 05 04)* are about a kilometre further out on the same road. For more details, call the **Associació de Campings de Barcelona**, *tel: (93) 317 44 16*.

## Eating and Drinking

Catalan cooking is known as good peasant fare, made from ingredients such as cuttlefish, serrano ham and salt cod. *Crema catalana* is a delicious local dessert, similar to *crême caramel*. Catalunya is also famous for its champenoise sparkling wine, *Cava*. It is the speciality of establishments known as *Xampanyeries*, especially around *Gràcia*.

In the evenings, many restaurants do not have a set menu, so eating out can be more expensive. The Barri Gòtic is an exception. Try along *Carrer de Avinyó* and the streets leading off it or along *Carrer de la Mercè* (be careful at night). Away from the old town, the Olympic Village is packed with bars and restaurants. As an alternative, eat a full meal at lunchtime and at night visit several bars and have a drink and some *tapas*. The *Guía del Ocio,* published weekly, has a good section on restaurants. It is available from most news-stands for Pta100.

## Communications

The main **post offices** are at *Pl. Antoni López 1* (weekdays 0800–2200, Sat 0800–1400 for most services); *Ronda Universitat 23*; and *Gran de Gràcia 118*. Telephones are available at Estació de Sants, Mon–Sat, 0800–2230, Sun 0900–2230, and at Estació de Autobuses Barcelona Nord, Mon–Fri 0800–2300. The dialling code for Barcelona is *93*.

## Embassies and Consulates

**Australia:** *Gran Vía Carlos III 98; tel: (93) 330 94 96*.
**Canada:** *Trav. de les Corts 265; tel: (93) 410 66 99*.
**Republic of Ireland:** *Gran Vía Carlos III 94; tel: (93) 491 50 21*.
**UK:** *Avinguda Diagonal 447; tel: (93) 419 90 44*.
**USA:** *Passeig de Reina Elisenda 23; tel: (93) 280 22 27*.

## ENTERTAINMENT

### Nightlife

Prepare to sleep through the next day – nightlife proper in Barcelona starts at 0100 and ends with cocktails at 0900. There is a wide range of clubs, bars and discos, catering for all musical tastes from rock to jazz; the busiest nights are Thur–Sat. Clubbing, however, is very expensive and there is often a high minimum drinks charge.

The *Guía del Ocio* has comprehensive listings of what's on in the city. The *Eixample,* particularly the streets off *Avda Diagonal* and *Plaça Reial,* is reputedly the fashionable area for bars and clubs.

### Cinemas and Music

There are about fifty **cinemas** in Barcelona, many of which show films in their original language (with subtitles) rather than dubbed. They are shown as VO *(version original)* in the listings. The **Filmoteca de la Generalitat de Catalunya**, *Avda Sarrià 33; tel: (93) 410 75 90,* shows less commercial films.

## SHOPPING

Barcelona is rapidly gaining ground as one of the great European centres of fashion and design, so clothes and leatherwork are some of the best buys, but are generally expensive. Souvenir foods, such as hams and olive oil, are also worth a look. The main shopping streets are *Passeig de Gràcia, Rambla de Catalunya* and *Avinguda Diagonal*. Wandering off these streets sometimes

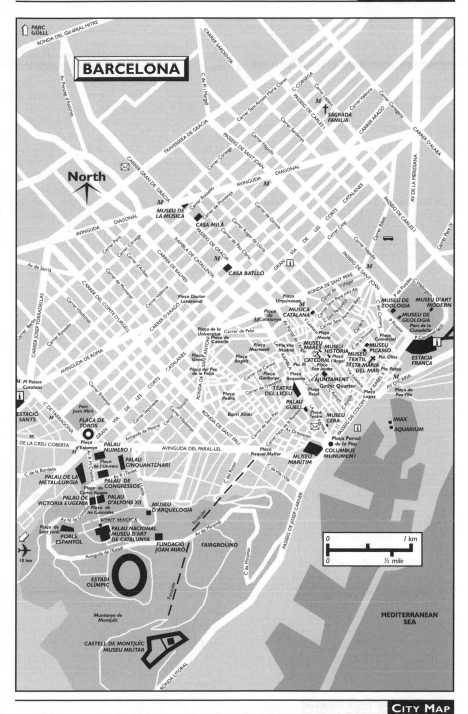

PARC GÜELL
RONDA DEL GENERAL MITRE

**BARCELONA**

Av. Princep d'Asturies

CARRER SARDENYA

Carrer Sant Antoni Maria Claret

C. CORSEGA

Carrer Lepant

PASSEIG DE CARLES I

✝ SAGRADA FAMILIA

Carrer Sardenya

Carrer València

Carrer Cartagena

CARRER ARAGO

CARRER D'ALABA

CARRER GRAN DE GRACIA

TRAVESSERA DE GRACIA

Carrer Corsega

PASSEIG DE SANT JOAN

Carrer Napols

Carrer de Girona

AVINGUDA DIAGONAL

**North**

Carrer Rosselló

MUSEU DE LA MUSICA

Carrer de Provença

CASA MILÀ

Carrer Roger de Lúria

Carrer de Pau Clarís

DE LES CORTS CATALANES

AV DE LA MERIDIANA

PASSEIG DE CARLES I

Carrer Pere IV

AVINGUDA DIAGONAL

Carrer Paris

Carrer Corsega

Carrer d'Aribau

RAMBLA DE CATALUNYA

PASSEIG DE GRACIA

CARRER DE BALMES

GRAN VIA

PASSEIG DE SANT JOAN

Carrer Casp

Carrer Napols

Carrer Ribes

Av de Sarrià

Carrer de Muntaner

CASA BATLLÓ

Plaça Doctor Letamendi

RONDA DE SANT PERE

Plaça Urquinaona

MUSEU DE ZOOLOGIA

MUSEU D'ART MODERN

CARRER DEL COMTE D'URGELL

Carrer Viladomat

Carrer València

CARRER D'ARAGO

Carrer de Pelai

Plaça de la Universitat

Plaça de Castella

MUSICA CATALANA

Plaça de Catalunya

Carrer Sant Pere més Alt

Carrer Sant Pere més Baix

MUSEU DE GEOLOGIA

Parc de la Ciutadella

CARRER JOSEP TORRADELLAS

Carrer Berlin

Carrer Rosselló

AVINGUDA DE ROMA

Plaça Martorell

Plaça Moura

Plaça Comercial

MUSEU PICASSO

Carrer Enença

DE LES CORTS CATALANES

RONDA DE SANT ANTONI

Plaça Angels

Plaça Goya

Plaça del Pes de la Palla

MUSEU MARES

MUSEU HISTORIA

MUSEU TEXTIL

STA MARIA DEL MAR

ESTACIÓ FRANÇA

M Pl Països Catalans

CATEDRAL

l'Angel

Plaça Sant Jaume

Plaça Nova

Plaça del Carme

Plaça Gardunya

Plaça Boqueria

AJUNTAMENT

Gothic Quarter

Plaça Olles

Plaça Palau

Plaça Lopez

AV D'ICÀRIA

Plaça de Pau Vila

C DE TARRAGONA

Parc Joan Miró

Carrer Sepulveda

Carrer Tamarit

RONDA DE L'Hospital

Plaça Pedro

Carrer del Carme

TEATRE DEL LICEU

Plaça Reial

PALAU GÜELL

Plaça Teatre

MUSEU CERA

ESTACIÓ SANTS

PLAÇA DE TOROS

Plaça d'Espanya

C DE LA CREU COBERTA

Barri Xinès

Carrer de Sant Pau

RONDA DE SANT PAU

Carrer Nou d Av Drassanes

PASSEIG DE COLOM

Carrer Ample

IMAX

AQUARIUM

AVINGUDA DEL PARAL·LEL

Avinguda de Mistral

Carrer Viladomat

PALAU NUMERO I

PALAU CINQUANTENARI

Plaça de l'Univers

Plaça Requel Mailer

MUSEU MARITIM

Plaça Portal de la Pau

COLUMBUS MONUMENT

PALAU DE LA METAL·LURGIA

PALAU DE CONGRESSOS

Plaça de Carles Buïgas

PALAU D'ALFONS XII

PALAU DE VICTORIA EUGENIA

Plaça de les Cascades

MUSEU D'ARQUELOGIA

C del Roser

C de Vila i Vila

PASSEIG DE JOSEP CARNER

Plaça de Sant Jordi

FONT MAGICA

POBLE ESPANYOL

PALAU NACIONAL MUSEU D'ART DE CATALUNYA

FUNDACIÓ JOAN MIRÓ

FAIRGROUND

Av de Miramar

10 km

Avinguda de l'Estadi

ESTADI OLÍMPIC

Muntanya de Montjuïc

C de Miramar

**MEDITERRANEAN SEA**

CASTELL DE MONTJUÏC MUSEU MILITAR

RONDA LITORAL

0 ———— 1 km
0 ———— ½ mile

133

pays dividends, and if you don't mind not being able to find the shop again the next day, try the streets in the Gothic quarter, near the cathedral. Barcelona's newest shopping centre, the **L'Illa Diagonal**, is in an attractive white building designed by Rafael Moreo, who won the Pritzeker Prize for architecture in 1996.

## SIGHTSEEING

Art goes hand in hand with architecture in Barcelona. In this deeply style-conscious city, there is always a brave juxtaposition of old and new.

The **Picasso Museum**, *Carrer de Montcada,* is formed from two Gothic palaces on a street just 3 m wide. The collection is largely made up of his early work, but does include *Las Meninas,* a series of paintings inspired by Velázquez's famous work.

Of the city's numerous other museums, the most unmissable are **Fundació Miró**, *Plaça Neptú, Parc de Montjuïc*; the **Fundació Tàpies**, *C. Aragó 225*; the **Museu d'Art de Catalunya**, *Palau Nacional, Parc de Montjuïc*; the **Museu Monestir de Pedralbes**, *Baixada Monestir 9*; the **Museu d'Art Modern**, *Plaça d'Armes, Parc de la Ciutadella*, and the **Museu d'Historia de la Ciutat** in the beautiful *Plaça del Rei*. They are almost all of value for the buildings alone, let alone the art they contain. Museums are closed on Mon.

The city also has an enchanting, if confusing Gothic quarter *(Barri Gòtic)*, a web of tiny dark streets radiating out from **La Seu Cathedral**, a magnificent Gothic edifice, started in 1298 but only finished in 1892. The small Romanesque **chapel of Santa Llúcia** opens off the cathedral cloister, which has a lush central garden with palm trees, ducks and magnolias. Nearby in **La Ribera** is the 14th-century **Basilica of Santa Maria del Mar**, regarded by many as one of the finest examples of Catalan Gothic architecture.

The 1992 Olympics were used as an excuse to rescue a desolate warehouse district and 4 km of seafront to create a fascinating new district of fine modern architecture.

Pride of place, however, must go to the works of the superb Modernist architect and designer, Antoni Gaudí (1852–1926). He used the city as his canvas, leaving such extraordinary, swirling masterpieces as the **Casa Milà**, *Passeig de Gràcia,* and **Temple Expiatori de la Sagrada Família**, *Plaça Sagrada Família,* to which he dedicated the last 43 years of his life. The Sagrada Família is Gaudí's 'Cathedral of the 20th century', a synthesis of all his architectural styles that incorporates complex religious symbolism and visual representations of the mysteries of faith. The result is incredible, but unfortunately unfinished. Since Gaudí's death in 1926, work has continued on the building, but progress is slow and hampered by controversy. To find out what the final structure should look like, visit the cathedral museum.

The excellent tourist pamphlet *Gaudí* details other buildings by the architect and there is a museum dedicated to him, the **Casa–Museu Gaudí**, in the **Parc Güell**, an area he designed himself as a decidedly eccentric residential garden city. Inside the park a flight of steps, guarded by a brightly coloured salamander, lead up to a large pavilion supported by over 80 columns – the original market place of the development. Above the pavilion, a colourful mosaic twists and curves its way around the perimeter of an open terrace, from which there are superb views of the city.

Another place of interest is the **Fundació Joan Miró**, which contains the spectacular *Dona i Ocell* (woman and bird) sculpture.

The best view of Barcelona is from **Montjuïc castle**, now a military museum, which is reached by cable car *(tel: (93) 318 70 74)* from *Avda Miramar* in Parc de Montjuïc. The cable car stops halfway up at the **Montjuïc amusement park**. Also near here is the **Olympic stadium**, while just across the hillside is **Poble Espanyol** (Spanish village) with replicas of famous architecture from throughout Spain.

You can also get good views of Barcelona from one of the towers at Gaudí's Sagrada Família or the **Columbus monument** at the bottom of the *Ramblas.* From the quay below the monument, *Las Golondrinas* (pleasure boats) ferry visitors around the harbour or across to the **Olympic Port**. Round trips last half an hour or two hours. If you want architecture as well as a view, try the **Torre de Collserola**, by Norman Foster.

# BERLIN

Once famous for being divided, Berlin is now just as famous for being reunited. This has entailed a vast amount of rebuilding, including the restoration of historic buildings, as well as constructing an entirely new part of the city around Potsdamer Platz. Nevertheless, Berlin offers vast amounts of greenery, notably the Tiergarten, while also having an extensive network of canals, which give the city an added perspective. Berlin is always exciting: ensured by the city's delight in dabbling with whatever is new and experimental, and as the capital of the new Germany it is all set for an inportant new era.

## TOURIST INFORMATION

The main **VTB** (tourist information office) in the *Europa Centre, Budapester Str. 10787; tel: (030) 262 60 31,* opens Mon–Sat 0800–2200, Sun 0900–2100. There are also offices at **Tegel Airport** (open daily 0530–2200) and at the south wing of the Brandenburg Gate; *tel: (030) 25 00 25,* open daily 0930–1830.

A city map (DM1) and *Berlin Magazine* (DM3.50) with tourist information are available, with the Tourist Offices also able to reserve accommodation and tickets for various events. For written enquiries contact the central administration at *Am Karlsbad 11, 0-10785 Berlin.*

## ARRIVING AND DEPARTING

### Airports

Most flights from the West are to **Berlin-Tegel Otto Lilienthal Airport**, *tel: (030) 41 011,* which is 8 km from the centre of town. Bus nos 109 and X9 connect with the U-bahn

at *Jakob-Kaiser-Platz,* and the X9 also at *Richard Wagner Platz.* Allow about an hour. Taxis are relatively inexpensive.

**Schönefeld Airport** (19 km south-west) served the East in the days of the Berlin Wall and since reunification the destinations haven't changed much. For enquiries, *tel: (030) 60 910.* The S-bahn runs to the main rail stations Haubtbahnhof (29 mins) and Zoo (48 mins), mainline trains to Lichtenberg (19 mins).

### National buses

These are run by **ZOB** (Zentraler Omnibusbahnhof), *tel: (030) 301 80 28.* The main station is at *Kaiserdamm* at *Messedamm 8* in Charlottesburg. Buses run daily to all major cities and smaller towns.

### Stations

Berlin's two major stations for long-distance main-line trains are **Berlin Zoologischer Garten** (shortened to Zoo), *Hardenbergplatz 11,* in the western part of the city and **Berlin Hauptbahnhof** (Hbf), *Am Hauptbahnhof,* in the east.

Some main-line trains also stop at **Berlin Friedrichstrasse**, *Georgenstr. 14-18,* midway between the two larger stations; and at **Berlin Lichtenburg**, *Weitlingerstr. 22,* 4 km east of Hbf. For all rail information ask at the **Bundesbahn Information Office**, within Zoo station; *tel: (030) 29749 350/1.* Open daily 24 hours.

## GETTING AROUND

Berlin's efficient public transport network combines buses, trams, underground and surface trains. Free photocopied street maps can be picked up from the Tourist Offices. A more comprehensive version costs DM5–10 from newsagents. Train maps are easy to find, but for bus maps you must go to the **BVG information centre**, within Zoo Bahnhof, *tel: (030) 256 2462.* Open daily 0800–2000. Here you can get the *Region Berlin Linienplan* (DM2) and free smaller transport maps. A public transport information office in Zoo station, *tel: (030) 297 49227*, covering the S-bahn and U-bahn, is open Mon–Fri 0600–2100, Sat–Sun 0700–2100. Taxis are plentiful, especially in the west, and relatively inexpensive; they can be flagged down on the street or from ranks at stations, airport and other key points.

## Metro

The 20 lines of the **U-bahn** (underground) and **S-bahn** (suburban surface trains) offer quick transport to most spots within the 40 km diameter of Berlin. The stations are easily recognised by the white U on a blue square or white S on a green circle and lines are colour-coded and numbered. Direction is indicated by the name of the final destination.

## Buses

These are also convenient and a good way to see the city (a good sightseeing route is no.100, which runs from Zoo station through the Tiergarten, the Brandenburg Gate and along *Unter den Linden*). Bus-stops are indicated by a green H on a yellow background.

## Boats

Various companies provide tours on the city's waterways. **BWTS**, *tel: (030) 6588 0203*, has embarcation points, including *Unter den Linden*, for a 1-hr city tour, while **Reederei Bruno Winkler**, *tel: (030) 391 7070*, starts from the Schloss bridge by Schloss Charlottenburg for a 3-hr trip. For daily boat trips along the River Spree, go to the restaurant terrace at the **Kongress Halle**, **Greenwich-Promenade** in Tegel, **Tiergarten** pier or **Wannsee** pier. For information, *tel: (030) 394 49 54 or (030) 810 0040*.

## Tickets

Tickets can be bought from automatic machines on station platforms, bus drivers or ticket offices and are validated by punching the ticket once on board or on the platform. A single allows travel on any bus, train or tram for a period of 2 hours. A 1-day bus and underground pass, valid until 0300, costs DM7.5. Available from Tourist Offices and Zoo station.

The **Berlin WelcomeCard** costs DM29 and allows you unlimited free use of public transport throughout the city and its suburbs for 72 hours; you also get free entry or reductions on city tours, museums, theatres and tourist attractions in Berlin and Potsdam. Buy WelcomeCards at stations, bus ticket offices, hotels, or the Tourist Information Offices.

## STAYING IN BERLIN

## Accommodation

Most upmarket tourist accommodation is in the west, especially in the environs of Zoo, Ku'damm and Charlottenburg, though more deluxe and tourist standard hotels are opening in the east of the city. Supply and demand make Berlin one of the most expensive German cities to stay in. The tourist information offices will make reservations for a small fee and give advice, addresses and telephone numbers. **Thomas Cook** network member **Reisebüro Helios**, *Uhlandstr. 73; tel: (030) 860 0050*, also makes hotel reservations.

There is also a wide range of top quality, international hotels, including *BW, Ch, Ex, Fm, GT, Hn, Ib, Ic, Ke, Mp, Nv, Pe, RC, Rd, Rn*. One of the most recent is the deluxe **Four Seasons**, *Charlottenstrasse 49; tel: (030) 20 338*. For a list of cheap hotels and hostels (including prices) ask for the *Accommodation for young visitors* booklet at the Tourist Office. Prices start at about DM35 for hostels, and cheap hotel rooms (pensions) start at about DM70 for a single and DM90 for a double. The most exclusive hotel is the **Schloss Hotel**, *Viehr Jahreszeiten, Brahmstr. 10; tel: (030) 895 840*, in the elegant Grünewald residential district. Designed by Karl Lagerfeld, it is set in a beautiful palace. Inexpensive options include: **Apart Hotel Hanse**; *Jenaer-str. 2, 10717 Berlin, tel: 211 50 92*; **BCA Lichtenberg**, *Rhin-str. 159, 10315 Berlin; tel: 540 01 12*; **BCA Wilhelmsberg**, *Landsberger Allee 203, 13055 Berlin; tel: 49 77 40*; **Hotel Berliner Hof**, *Tauentzien-str. 8, 10789 Berlin; tel: 25 49 50*; **Hotel Kurfürstendamm am Adenauerplatz**, *Kurfurstendamm 68, 10707 Berlin; tel: 88 46 30*; and **Hotel-Pension Wittelsbach**, *Wittelsbacherstr. 22, 10707 Berlin; tel: 873 63 45*.

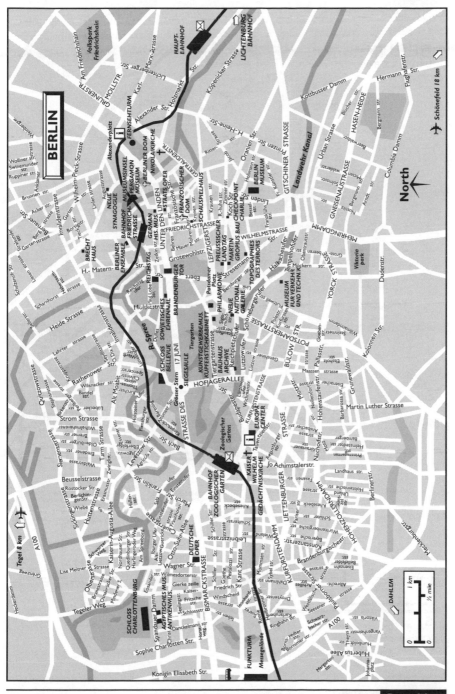

**BERLIN**
U-Bahn & S-Bahn

U7
Rathaus Spandau

Hennigsdorf S25

Stolpe Süd

Heiligensee

Schulzendorf

Tegel

S1 to Oranienburg

Waidmannslust

Wittenau (Nordbahn) U8

Wilhelmsruh

Rathaus
Reinickendorf

Eichborndamm

Karl-Bonhoeffer-
Klinik

Schönholz

Altstadt
Spandau

Zitadelle

Haselhorst

Paulsternstr.

Rohrdamm

Siemensdamm

Halemweg

Jakob-Kaiser-Platz

Alt-Tegel U6

Borsigwerke

Holzhauser Str.

Seidelstr.

Scharnweberstr.

Kurt-Schumacher-Pl.

Tegel

Lindauer Allee

Alt
Reinickendorf

Paracelsus-Bad

Residenzstraße

Afrikanische
Str.

Franz-Neumann-
Platz

Rehberge

Wollankstr.

Bornholmerstr.

Osloer
Straße
U9

Pankstr.

Gesundbrunnen

Voltastraße

U2,U12
Ruhleben

Olympia
Stadion
(Ost)

Neu-
Westend

Theodor-
Heuss-
Platz

Westend

Bismarckstr.

Kaiserdamm/
Witzleben

Sophie-
Charlotte-
Platz

Wilmersdorfer
Str.

Jungfernheide

Mierendorffplatz

Richard-
Wagner-
Platz

Turmstraße

SPREE

Deutsche Oper

Savignyplatz

Beusselstr.

Leopoldplatz

Amrumer
Str.

Birkenstraße

Seestraße

Nauener
Platz

Wedding

Westhafen

Reinickendorfer
Str.

Schwartzkopfstr.

Ernst-
Reuter-
Platz

Hansaplatz

Bellevue

Humboldthain

Nordbahnhof

Oranien-
burger
Straße

Zinnowitzer Str.

Oranienburger Tor

Lehrter
Stadtbahnhof

Friedrichstraße

Unter den
Linden

Französische
Straße

Mohr-
enstr.

S5
Charlottenburg

Uhlandstraße

Zoologischer
Garten

Kur-
fürsten-
damm

Tiergarten

Wittenberg-
platz

Nollendorf-
platz

U4

Gleisdreieck

Potsdamer
Platz

Anhalter
Bahnhof

S6,S9
Westkreuz

Grunewald

Adenauerplatz

Spichernstr.

Hohenzollernpl.

Konstanzer
Straße

U15

Augsburger
Str.

Viktoria-
Luise-Pl.

Güntzelstr.

Kurfürstenstr.

Bülowstr.

Yorckstr.
(Großgörschenstr.)

Möckern-
brücke

Yorckstr.

Halensee

Hohenzollerndamm

Fehrbelliner Pl.

Blissestr.

Berliner Str.

Bayerischer
Platz

Eisenacher
Straße

Kleistpark

Rüdesheimer Platz.

Heidelberger Platz

Bundesplatz

Rathaus
Schöneberg

Papestraße

Breitenbachplatz

Podbielskiallee

Dahlem-Dorf

Thielplatz

Oskar-Helene-Heim

Onkel Toms Hütte

Friedrich-
Wilhelm-
Platz

Walther-
Schreiber-
Platz

Innsbrucker Platz

U4

Schöneberg

Friedenau

Priesterweg

Feuerbachstraße

Südende

Attillastraße

U1
Krumme Lanke

Schloßstr.

S3 to Nikolassee
Griebnitzsee
S7 Babelsberg
Potsdam Stadt

S1 to Wannsee

©TCS Designed by R.Woods

U9 Rathaus Steglitz

Botanischer
Garten

TELTOW KANAL

Lankwitz

Lichterfelde Ost

Lichterfelde Süd.

Teltow Stadt S25

to Blankenfelde

S2

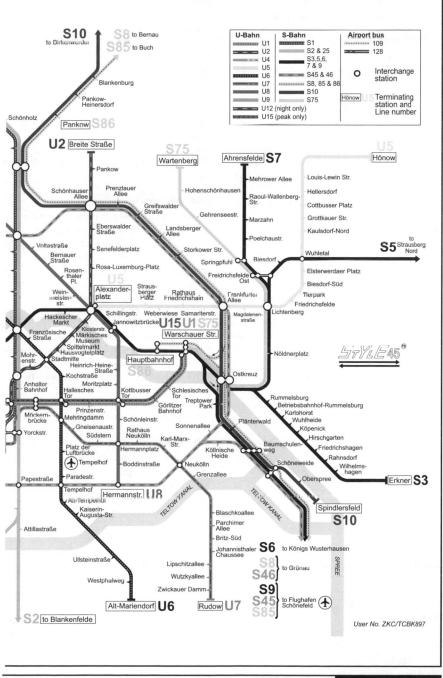

Guest rooms in private quarters can be booked through **Privatzimmervermittlung**; *tel: (030) 49 56 56.*

Most Berlin **campsites** are out of town; for a list ask at the Tourist Office. A few mins walk from **Tegel** U-bahn, an international **youth-camp** offers places for DM9 a night.

## Eating and Drinking

Berlin has a huge array of restaurants, cafés, bars and street stalls, from typically German establishments to kebab houses and pizzerias. Around Zoo station, Ku'damm and Europa Centre are plenty of fast-food snackeries and cafés.

Just off Ku'damm is *Meinehestr.*, which is much quieter and has a good selection of brasseries and German pubs, such as **Meineke X**, at no. 10; *tel: (030) 882 3158.*

In the east of the city, head for *Gendarmenmarkt*, where the adjoining streets feature smart brasseries and cafés with pavement tables. For a treat, try the cakes at coffee shops, while for cheap food and a happy evening's drinking head for the pubs *(kneipe)* around *Savigny Platz, Kreuzberg* and *Prenzlauer Berg.* **Café Kranzler**, at the Charlottenberg end of the Ku'damm; *Kurfurstendamm 18; tel (030) 882 69 11;* is a three-storey gem of wedding-cake architecture with Berlin's finest coffee and cakes; for a real Berlin meal of beer, pickles, pork hocks or meat rissoles, try **Wilhelm Hoeck's**; *Wilmersdorfer-str. 149; tel: 341 81 74.*

For a classic German beer garden experience go to **Am Neuen See**, in the Tiergarten by the Leichtenstein bridge, a good mid-town eaterie with regional and European dishes is **Merz**, *Schöneberger Ufer 65; tel: (030) 261 38 82.*

## Communications

There is a 24-hour post office at **Zoo Bahnhof**, where you can also collect mail. The post office at Tegel Airport is open Mon–Fri 0700–2100, Sat–Sun 0800–2000. Post offices are usually open Mon–Fri 0900–1800; Sat 0900–1200.

To phone Berlin, *tel: 49 (Germany) + 30 (Berlin) + number;* to phone Berlin from inside Germany, *tel: 030 + number.*

### Money

There are **Thomas Cook bureaux de change** locations throughout the city.

### Embassies and Consulates

**Australia**: *Kempinski Plaza, Uhlandstr.181–3; tel: (030) 88 00 880*
**Canada**: *IHZ Building, Friedrichstr.95; tel. (030) 261 1161*
**New Zealand**: *Bundeskanzlerplatz 2–10, Bonn; tel: (0228) 228 070*
**UK**: *Unter den Linden 32–34; tel: (030) 201 840*
**USA**: *Neustadtische Kirchstr 4; tel: (030) 238 5174.*

Berlin has a well-deserved reputation for diverse and non-stop entertainment, from opera, theatre and film to club-land and rock. There are two listings magazines: *Zitty* and *Tip*, available from newsagents for about DM4. For listings in English, *Insomnia* and *Check Point* are available from the Tourist Office.

The **Wintergarten–Das Varieté**, *Potsdamerstr 96; tel: (030) 23 08 82 30,* is a variety theatre offering entertainment of the 1920s. Classical concerts are held at **Philharmonie** and **Kammer–Musiksaal**, *Matthäikirchstr 1; tel: (030) 254 88132,* and **Kunzerthaus Berlin**, *Gendarmenmarkt 2; tel: (030) 2090 2100.* **Oranienstrasse**, in the Kreuzberg district, is the heart of a busy club and music bar scene.

Berlin is becoming much better for shopping, though prices are generally high. The West still has greater variety and includes Berlin's chief shopping boulevard **Kurfürstendamm**, 3 km of boutiques, department stores, cafés, shopping malls and the Europa Centre shopping complex. Also in ths region is *Fasanenstr.*, with designer shops, while the giant **KaDeWe** department store on *Wittenberg-platz* is the ultimate temple of Berlin's consumer society. **Friedrichstrasse** in the former east, historically the city's premier shopping street, is rapidly regaining its former status, with stores like **Galerie Lafayette** and smart shopping arcades.

Away from the centre, each of Berlin's 23 districts has its own shopping areas, such as

*Schonhauser Allee,* in Prenzlauer Berg; and *Wilmersdorfer Str.* in **Charlottenburg.**

For flea market (**Flohmarkt**) shopping, try the **Trödelmarkts** at *Str. des 17.* **Juni** (Sat, Sun; S-bahn: *Tiergarten); Charlottenburg, Ku'damm-Karree* (daily except Tues). **Winterfeld-platz** is the central food market (Wed and Sat, 0800–1400; U-Bahn: *Zoo*).

## SIGHTSEEING

Among the sightseeing tours are **Berolina,** *tel: (030) 882* 2091, with various routes departing from *Ku'damm 220/225,* and other bus stops around the city. Walking tours leave from Zoo station, led by **Berlin Walks;** *tel: (030) 301 9194.* **Velotaxis,** *tel: (030) 4435 8990* (like covered rickshaws) are another way to see the sights, and can be picked up at Brandenburg Gate, Zoo station and *Adenauerplatz.*

**Schloss Charlottenburg,** *tel: (030) 320 911* (U: *Sophie Charlotte Platz),* completed in 1790 by Frederick I for his wife Sophie Charlotte, is now a series of museums, including the **Gallery of the Romantics** within the New Wing and the **Schinkel Pavilion** (both paintings and sculpture), and the **Nering Eosander building** (18th-century furniture, paintings and porcelain). All museums are open Tues–Fri 0900–1700, Sat–Sun 0100–1700.

### Ku'damm

Running roughly westward from the Zoo intersection, 3 km-long **Kurfürstendamm** is lined with shops, restaurants, cafés and cinemas. With the fall of the wall, the Ku'damm – as Berliners call it – is gradually losing some of its importance as the western city's most prestigious street.

Opposite Zoo Bhf is the **Gedächtniskirche** (Kaiser Wilhelm Memorial Church), its war-damaged tower left unrepaired as a symbol of World War II. The church is open daily 0900–1900, with concerts on Saturdays at 1800.

Next to this is the neon-covered **Europa Centre,** a bland shopping mall. *Budapester Str.* leads past the **observation tower** in the Europa Centre to the **Zoologischer Garten** (zoo) and **Tiergarten,** with lakes and numerous themed areas, such as the English Garden.

This was the former hunting ground of the kings of Prussia.

In the middle of the Tiergarten, at Grosser Stern roundabout, stands the **Siegessäule,** a 67-m column built to celebrate 19th-century Prussian victories, worth climbing for the view. Open Mon 1300–1730, Tues–Sun 0900–1730. To the west is **Schloss Bellevue,** residence of the Federal President, and to the east the 1960s **Kongresshalle.**

### The Great Divide

All that remains of **Checkpoint Charlie,** the Berlin Wall crossing point featured in a hundred spy stories, is a swathe of rubble-strewn wasteland and the nearby **Checkpoint Charlie Museum,** *Friedrichstrasse 44; tel: (030) 251 1031.* This relates the history of the wall and numerous attempts to escape. Open daily 0900–2200. A red line is being painted on roads and pavements to mark the site of the former wall. A section can still be seen at *Niederkircher Strasse.*

The towering **Brandenburg Gate,** *Pariser Platz,* which stands between *Str. den 17 juni* and *Unter den Linden,* was built in 1788–91 as a triumphal arch for Prussia's victorious armies. The current gate is a post-war copy of architect Carl Gotthard von Langhans' building, which was itself an interpretation of the Propylaia of the Acropolis in Athens. Closed by the building of the Wall, it became a symbol of the divided Germany and was reopened in Dec 1989. An even more powerful symbol stands just to the north: the **Reichstag.** Built in 1871 to house the imperial parliament, the new German parliament met again for the first time in 1990, and will again become the seat of parliament for a reunited Germany in 2000.

### Unter den Linden

Rapidly regaining its status as Berlin's principal thoroughfare, this impressive broad boulevard features monumental public buildings, almost all of which were restored after World War II. During the Cold War it became the focal point of the Eastern sector, but at the same time a cul-de-sac ending in the Brandenburg Gate and the Wall. Since reunification, it is increasingly flanked by smart shops, restaurants and cafés, government buildings and the offices of international corporations.

Behind the **Deutsche Staatsoper** (opera house), at nos 5–7; *tel: (030) 2035 4483,* stands the **Catholic Cathedral of St. Hedwig** (founded in 1809). Further along, **Humboldt University** numbers Einstein, Marx and Engels amongst its more famous alumni.

The Baroque **Zeughaus** (Arsenal), at no. 2, now houses the **German Historical Museum**; *tel: (030) 215 020.* Since reunification, the museum's Marxist and pro-Soviet outlook has been revised yet again to reflect a new European perspective. Open daily 1000–1800 except Wed. Also look out for the **Deutsche Staatsbibliothek** (library) and the **Kronprinzen Palais**, which is opposite the **Neue Wache**, a neo-classical building that was dedicated to the victims of fascism in 1969.

Adjacent to *Unter den Linden* is the historic **Gendarmenmarkt**, with the neo-classical **Kunzerthaus Berlin**; *tel: (030) 203 090,* and the **Französischer Dom**, built in the 18th century for the Huguenots to worship in. It now houses the **Huguenot Museum**, open Tues–Sat 1200–1700, Sun 1300–1700.

## Museuminsel

'Museum Island', on the River Spree, houses four excellent museums, which together have (but do not display) some 1.2 million works of art. The most famous is the **Pergamon Museum**, one of Europe's best collections of antiquities, including Egyptian and Byzantine art. The museum's proudest possession is the 2175-year-old Pergamon altar; other treasures include the bust of Nefertiti and the astonishing Processional Way from Babylon. The **Bode Museum**, *Monbijoubrücke,* in the north-west corner, houses early Christian art, Egyptian works and 15th–18th-century paintings. The **Alle Nationalgalerie** is strong on 19th- and 20th-century art, particularly the romantics and Expressionists, including work from the *Brucke* and *Blaue Reiter* schools. The Alles Museum is used for special exhibitions. Opening hours for these museums are Tues–Sun 0900–1700; *tel: (030) 20 90 5555.*

From here take the *Rathausbrücke*, past the **Berliner Dom** in the city's Baroque cathedral, open Mon–Sat 0900–1930, Sun 1130–1930, and the **Palast der Republik** to *Rathausstr.* On the right is the restored 15th-century twin-towered **Nikolaikirche**, Berlin's oldest building. The **Rotes Rathaus** (Red Town Hall, so-called on account of its bricks), open Mon–Fri 0700–1800, leads to the base of the **Fernsehturm** (TV tower). This 365-m spike, Berlin's tallest building, includes a globe-shaped revolving restaurant and viewing gallery at 200 m, open daily 0900–2400. In the nearby *Oranienburger Strasse,* at no. 28, is the impressive **Neue Synagogue**.

### ⤴ SIDE TRACK FROM BERLIN

### POTSDAM

**Tourist Office: Touristenzentrale,** *Am Alten Markt, Freidrich-Elbert-Str. 5; tel: (0331) 21 100;* open daily 0900–2000.

**Potsdam** is a purpose-built fantasy of landscaped gardens and palaces, 30 km south-west of Berlin (easily reached by S-bahn or rail from Zoo, Hbf or *Friedrichstr.,* journey time about 20 mins). Founded in 993, the town became the seat of the Hohenzollern kings in the late 17th century, who welcomed exiled Protestants of talent from all over Europe. Its architectural treasures – most of them dating from the 18th century – have earned it World Heritage Site status.

The best feature is the 12-roomed rococo **Sanssouci Palace** (1745–47) set in the huge **Park Sanssouci**. A leisurely walk through the park reveals the **Chinese Tea House** (1754–7), the pagoda-like **Drachenhaus**, **Schloss Charlottenhof** and the **Römische Bader** (Roman Baths) (both dating from the early 19th century).

There are more delightful 17th-century buildings in the town itself and on the other side of the **Havel River**, in **Babelsberg Park**. ⤴

# BERLIN–BUDAPEST

**Berlin**

**Meissen** **Moritzburg**

**Dresden**

**Prague**

FASTEST JOURNEY: 12 HRS 30 MINS

Linking five countries, this route crosses the heart of the old Austro-Hungarian empire, including the capitals of Prague, Bratislava and Budapest. Between Dresden and Prague, trains parallel the river Elbe, winding through Saxon Switzerland and Hřensko national parks. Moravia's rolling hills and compact villages give way to the Carpathian mountains at the Slovak border. From Bratislava to Budapest, the route runs alongside the Danube Bend, passing Esztergom and Visegrád castle.

**Blansko**

*Vienna–Warsaw, p. 512*

**Brno** **Slavkov**

**Modra**

**Bratislava**

**Budapest**

## TRAINS

**ETT tables:** 60, 840, 1110, 1160, 1150, 1200, 1170.

### FAST TRACK

Two *EC* day trains, with a dining-car, take 12 hrs. An overnight train via Vienna, with sleeping cars and couchettes, takes approximately 16 hrs. From 1999, tilting trains take over daytime *EC* services with consequent reductions in journey times.

### ON TRACK

**Berlin–Dresden**
An *IC* service every 2 hrs makes the 2 hr journey.

**Dresden–Prague (Praha)**
*EC* trains about every 2½–3 hrs. A few trains

serve Hlavní (main) station; otherwise you arrive in Holešovice station.

**Prague–Brno**
Trains at least every 2 hrs, taking 3–3½ hrs.

**Brno–Bratislava**
Trains every 1–2 hrs, taking around 2 hrs.

**Bratislava–Budapest**
Ten services daily operate and there are two

different routes. *EC* trains take the Szob route, taking about 2 hrs 40 mins. Other trains take 3 hrs via Szob, or 4 hrs via Rajka.

## DRESDEN

**Stations**: **Hbf**: *tel: (0351) 471 0600*; **Neustädt**: *tel: (0351) 471 0600*. Go down *Prager Str.* for the old town.

**Tourist Offices**: *Prager Str.10; tel: (0351) 49 19 20* (near Hbf). Open Mon–Fri 0900–2000, Sat 0900–1600, Sun 1000–1400. **Neustädter Markt** *(Pedestrain tunnel); tel: (0351) 49 19 20*. Mon–Fri 0900–1800 (–1600 Sat), Sun 1100–1600. The two-day **Dresden Card** (26 DM) allows free transport, free admission to 11 museums and discounts.

**Thomas Cook licensees: Thomas Cook Urlaubreisen**, *Im Metro-Markt, Marie-Curie-str. 9; tel: (0351) 858 4356*, and **Reisebüro Helios GMBH**, *Wurzenerstr. 5; tel: (0351) 852 2324*.

Hotel groups in Dresden include *Hn, BW, Hd, Ib, IC, Ke, Me, SL* and *Tp*.

Capital of Saxony from 1547 until 1918, Dresden was one of Europe's most beautiful baroque cities until the British and American air-raids of 1945. The resultant firestorm left little standing and 35,000 dead (the death-toll was higher than that at Hiroshima). Reconstruction work has restored much of the architectural damage, particularly the baroque splendour near the Elbe. From Hbf, take *Prager Str.* to **Altmarkt**, past the **Church of the Holy Cross**, on to **Neumarkt** and the **Frauenkirche**, currently undergoing massive reconstruction.

West are the **Zwinger** (1709–1722), the **Orangery** (vast porcelain collection) and **Old Master Picture Gallery** (Tues–Sun 1000–1800). A reconstruction of the **Semper Opera House**, ruined by fire, then bombs, was unveiled in 1985. **Dresden Palace** met a similar fate, but is being reconstructed. The **Catholic Court Church**'s crypt contains the heart of Augustus the Strong.

### ⬒ SIDE TRACKS FROM DRESDEN

At **Meissen** (38 mins from Dresden Hbf) is the famous porcelain factory, which has an exhibition hall, demonstration workshop and gift shop: *Talstr. 9; tel: (03521) 541*.

**Moritzburg** (a 50-min trip from Dresden Hbf, changing at Radebeul Ost onto a steam train) boasts an immaculate moated castle, one of Europe's best.

The river steamers of **Sächsische Dampfschiffahrt** sail on the Elbe from Dresden to the Czech border: *Terrassenufer 2; tel: (0351) 437 241*. ⬒

## BRNO

**Station:** *tel: (05) 422 14 803*. For the town centre head up *Masarykova*, opposite the station (the oldest in the Czech Republic).

**Tourist Office:** Old Town Hall, *Radnická 4, 8, 10; tel: (05) 4221 1090/3267*. Try the Tourist Office for accommodation.

Hotel chains in Brno include *BW, Hd, IH*. Eating out is cheap, with plentiful portions.

Once capital of Moravia, Brno has historic buildings and marks of the 19th-century industrial boom. Chief sights (most close Mon) are within 1 km of the station. Nearby, the **Chrám sv. Petra a Pavla**, (18th–19th-century neo-Gothic Cathedral of Sts Peter and Paul), crowns **Petrov Hill**. The 13th-century **Špilberk Castle**, with baroque fortifications, was the most notorious prison in the Austro-Hungarian empire. Visit the cellar Tues–Sun 0900–1800; *tel: (05) 4221 4145*.

A little way south-west is the **Augustinian Monastery**, where in 1865 the Johann monk Gregor Mendel publicised the fundamentals of genetics, having studied the breeding of pea plants in the abbey garden. Garden and plants remain, and there is also a small museum, the **Mendelianum**, *Mendlovo nám.1; tel: 337 854*. Open Mon–Fri 0800–1700.

**Old Town Hall**, *Radnická 8*, has Gothic-, Renaissance- and baroque-style buildings. Its early parts are the oldest in Brno. In the entrance is the legendary Brno wheel and the famous 'dragon', a stuffed crocodile from 1608. In the crypt of the **Kapucínské Klášter** (the Capuchin Monastery) are 150 mummified bodies, air-dried in 1650, including that of the notorious, now headless, Baron Trenk (1711–1749), commander of Austria's pandour troops (mostly former criminals).

## SIDE TRACKS FROM BRNO

The limestone caves of **Moravský Kras** (Moravian Karst) form a series of dramatic underground rivers, stalagmites and stalactites in the middle of a forest (open daily 0800–1530). There are several trains a day to nearby Blansko (35 mins). The baroque château of **Slavkov**, 20 km east by bus, better known as **Austerlitz**, was the site of Napoleon's famous victory in 1805.

From Brno, it is possible to connect with Vienna (p. 505), from where you can join the Vienna–Warsaw route (p. 512). There are four direct trains to Vienna Südbhf daily, with more choices if you change at Břeclav. Journey time: 2–2½ hrs.

## BRATISLAVA

**Station:** Most trains serve the main station **Hlavní**, *tel: (07) 20444 84,* 1.5 km north of old town centre. Tourist Office, exchange facilities, café and left luggage. At the international ticket counter there is usually an English speaker. Trams are outside (no. 1 to old town). **Nové Město** station *(tel: (07) 60702)* is about 3 km north-east of the centre (accessible by tram).

**Tourist Office: Bratislava Information Service (BIS)**, *Panská 18; tel: (07) 333715* or *334325.* Staff speak English and maps of the town are available. **Satur**, *Jesenského 5; tel:(07) 367624,* for travel around Slovakia.

For four centuries Bratislava was a strategic part of the *Limes Romanus,* the frontier between the Roman Empire and barbarian lands to the north. In the 16th century, when much of Hungary lay under Turkish occupation, Bratislava became the Hungarian capital, a position it held for almost 250 years. Now, as capital of the Slovak Republic, the city is beginning to re-establish its international importance.

Although the city tends to suffer by comparison with Prague, Vienna and Budapest, it has a charming and relaxed, if crumbling, old centre, free from the tourist crowds of the other three.

An efficient tram, bus and trolley bus system links the old town with the suburbs. The route network is displayed inside vehicles and at major stops. There is a wide selection of tickets available, including one- and seven-day passes. **Taxis:** try **PSK**, *tel: 377 111,* and **Prof**, *tel: 302.* Charges should be 10–20SK per km.

### ACCOMMODATION

The hotel sector is responding to the increasing number of tourist arrivals, with *Fm, IC* and *IH* represented. There are no booking agencies in the station, but hawkers occasionally offer private rooms. **BIS** can book private rooms and hotels. **CKM-Slovakia**, *16 Hviezdoslavovo Nám; tel: (07) 334114* or *331607,* has a wide variety of accommodation, including university dorms in the summer and a year-round student hotel. **HI hostel:** *Bernolákova 3; tel: 497725.*

### SIGHTSEEING

Bratislava has a regional, rather than a capital, air. Even the Danube loses some of its majesty as it passes through the town, the ranks of tower blocks dominating the riverscape. However, many of the older and more distinguished buildings and squares are being refurbished, and cafés and restaurants are sprouting up. The **Castle** is the most distinctive sight in town. Its fortifications date back to at least the 9th century, but it was burnt down in 1811 during the Napoleonic wars. The present structure is 1960s vintage and displays some of the **Slovak National Museum**'s collection. During Bratislava's period as Hungarian capital, 11 kings were crowned in **St Martin's Cathedral**, across *Staromětska* from the castle. The attractive old town conservation area, largely pedestrianised, also contains **Mirbach Palace**, *Radicna St,* and the Gothic **Franciscan Church**, *Františkánské namestie,* one of Bratislava's oldest surviving structures.

145

## SIDE TRACK FROM BRATISLAVA

High above the Danube and Morava rivers, **Devín** castle is a ruined border fortress at the edge of the Little Carpathian mountains. There are frequent buses (no. 29) and boats (**Fajnorovo nábr.**; *tel: 533 5123).* **Modra** (35 mins by bus, ten daily) is a little village selling wine and ceramics, in the heart of the wine-growing region.

# BERLIN–WARSAW

This journey, starting in Germany, crosses the vast Central European Plain to link two cities that suffered greatly during World War II but are reviving dynamically. The scenery is pleasant and the route follows the Piast Trail, which links some of Poland's most historic towns.

## TRAINS

**ETT tables:** 56, 1000, 1020, 1035.

FASTEST JOURNEY: 6 HRS 30 MINS

### FAST TRACK

Four trains run daily from Berlin Hbf. Three daytime *(EC)* take about 6½ hrs (supplement payable; dining-car). The overnight train (sleeping and couchette cars only) departs from Berlin Lichtenberg and takes 8 hrs. All services require compulsory reservation. All these trains serve Warsaw Centralna station.

### ON TRACK

#### Berlin–(Border)–Poznań

Three *EC* trains and one *IC* train run daily, taking 3 hrs. The *EC* trains continue direct to Warsaw.

#### Poznań–Gniezno

There are eight fast services a day, taking 45–60 mins (40 mins on the twice-daily express train).

#### Gniezno–Toruń

Two fast trains daily, taking 1 hr 20 mins. The four local trains take about 1 hr 45 mins.

#### Toruń–Warsaw (Warszawa)

Three direct trains run daily, one during the night, taking 3 hrs. Additional journeys are possible by changing at Kutno.

## POZNAŃ

**Station:** the main station, **Poznań Główny;** *tel: (061) 852 72 21,* is a short bus ride from the centre. It has a 24-hr rail information office, *tel: (061) 866 12 12,* tourist information, *tel: (061) 866 06 67,* and currency exchange. Most international trains stop here, although some use **Staroleka Station**, 5 km south-east.

**Tourist Office:** Provincial and Central Office, *Stary Rynek 59, 61–772 Poznań; tel: (061) 852 61 56,* is very good, so pick up as much as you can. Also *ul. Kramarska 32; tel: (061) 852 98 05,* open Mon–Fri 0900–1700, Sat 1000–1400, and at the station, open Mon–Fri 0800–1600.

### ACCOMMODATION AND FOOD

There are plenty of cafés and restaurants on *Stary Rynek* (Old Market Square), as well as **Dom Turysty,** at no. 91; *tel: (061) 852 88 93,* a hotel-come-hostel, with rooms and dormitories. The city has a lot of Orbis hotels, including the centrally located **Hotel Merkury,** *ul. Roosevelta 20; tel: (061) 855 80 00.* Chains include *Nv.* Most are designed for businessmen, but there are cheaper options, particularly motels, on the edge of the city, such as

Streszynek, which also includes a **campsite** at *ul. Koszalinska 15; tel: (061) 848 31 29.*

For traditional Polish food in a classic market square setting, try the charming, antique-style **Stara Ratuszowa**, *Stary Rynek 55; tel: (061) 851 53 18,* the **Turystyczna** (within Dom Turystyezny), *Stary Rynek 91,* and **U Dylla**, *Stary Rynek 37/39; tel: (061) 852 17 76.*

### SIGHTSEEING

Poznań, provincial capital of **Wielkopolska**, was Poland's capital in the 10th century, and the first bishopric was founded here over 1000 years ago. The 17th and 18th centuries saw Swedish invasions, while the city was under Prussian rule for 125 years, finally freed at the end of the 18th century, and then falling to the Nazis in World War II. It has always been a great trade centre, lying at a geographical crossroads, resulting in a rich architectural heritage. The trading element continues: Poznań hosts international trade fairs.

Poznań's focal point is **Stary Rynek**, with its gabled burghers' houses. The 16th-century Renaissance **Town Hall**, one of Europe's finest, is best visited at midday, when two mechanical goats emerge from above the clock to lock horns. Housed here is the **Historical Museum of the City of Poznań**, *1 Stary Rynek; tel: (061) 852 613* (open Mon, Tues, Fri 1000–1600, Wed 1200–1800, Sun 1000–1500), and the **Chamber of the Renaissance**, with a beautifully painted, coffered ceiling (1555). In front of the Town Hall is a rococo fountain and a copy of the pillory used for 16th-century floggings. Also on *Stary Rynek,* at no. 45, **Muzeum Instrumentow Muziczrych** (Museum of Musical Instruments); *tel: (061) 852 08 57* (open Tues, Sat 1100–1700, Wed, Fri 1000 1600, Sun 1000–1500), is considered to be one of the finest of its kind, home to about 2000 instruments, and has a room dedicated to Chopin. The city hosts the **Henryk Wieniawski International Violin Competition** in Nov. The **Muzeum Archeologicze** (Archaeological Museum), *ul. Wodna 27; tel: (061) 852 82 51,* in the 16th-century Renaissance **Górków Palace**, has a range of exhibits from 15,000 BC–7000 BC. Open Tues–Fri 1000–1600, Sat 1000–1800, Sun 1000–1500.

In the part-reconstructed **Przemyslaw**

Castle, the **Arts and Crafts Museum**, *Góra Przemystaura; tel: (061) 852 20 35* (Wed 1200–1600, Thur, Fri, Sat 0900–1500, Sun 1000–1500), has artefacts dating from the 12th century. The **National Museum**, *ul. Marcin Kowskiego 9; tel: (061) 852 80 11* (Wed, Thur, Fri, Sat 1000–1600, Tues 1200–1800, Sun 1000–1500), has a fine art collection that includes Dutch, Spanish and Italian masters. **Muzeum Ethnograficzne** (Ethnographic Museum), *Grobla 25; tel: (061) 852 30 06,* open Tues, Wed, Fri, Sat 1000–1600, Sun 1000–1500.

Several churches form an outer ring around the market square. One of the finest is the baroque **Kóściól Farny** (Poznań Parish Church), dedicated to St Mary Magdalene. The **Jesuit Monastery**, next door, was once Napoleon's residence. It is now the venue for Chopin concerts. On the island of **Ostrów Tumski**, in the middle of the **River Warta**, stands the **Cathedral**, built in the 9th century, extended in the 14th century and heavily restored after World War II. Within the 19th-century **Golden Chapel** lie the tombs of Mieszko I and Bolesław the Brave, Poland's first two kings.

Poznań has two zoos and a vast palm house (part of Poland's largest botanical garden). For picnics, **Park Chopina** is 250m from the *Stary Rynek,* and there are more parks within 1 km. On the edge of the city is the 100 square km **Wielkopolski Park Narodowy** (Great Poland National Park), easily accessible by train.

147

### GNIEZNO

Station: *tel: (066) 26 33 44,* offers a left-luggage facility, shops and café. Within walking distance of the centre, next to the bus station. **Tourist Office**: Gniezno lacks a municipal office, but **Sol Tur**, *ul. Bolestahra, Chrobrego 39, 62–200 Gniezno; tel: (066) 26 10 12,* offers information and help with accommodation (open Mon–Fri 1000–1600, Sat 1000–1300).

Gniezno is easily manageable on foot, and the cathedral is easy to find (head west from the market square). Most newsagents sell town maps and guidebooks to the cathedral.

Ideally located by the old town market square is **Pietrak Hotel**, *ul. Chrobrego 3; tel: (066) 26 14 97.* There is one **youth hostel** at *ul. Pocztowa 11; tel: (066) 26 46 09.*

Gniezno is small but historically important, (the capital of Poland briefly in the 11th century), with settlements dating from the early Stone Age. The main attraction is the 14th-century **Cathedral**, distinguished by Romanesque bronze doors (1170) depicting the life of St Adalbertus; the interior includes the saint's red marble tomb and silver shrine. Adjacent is **Muzeum Archidieceji Gruezznieriskiej** (Archdiocese Museum), *Kulegicity 2; tel: (066) 26 37 38,* Tues–Sun 0900–1600, featuring saral and religious art. West of Lake Jelonek, **Muzeum Poczatków Panstha Polskiego** (Museum of the Origin of the Polish State), *ul. Kostrzewskrego 1; tel: (066) 264 641,* traces early Polish history. Open Tues–Sun 1000–1700.

## TORUŃ

**Station**: the main station is **Toruń Główny**, *Kujawska 1; tel: (056) 654 72 22,* which has left-luggage facilities and a restaurant. Five others share the name Toruń; nearest to the old town is **Toruń Miasto**. From the main station, bus nos. 22 or 24 will take you to the old town centre. Buy tickets in advance at Ruch kiosks. **Tourist Office**: *ul. Piekary 37/39, 87–100 Torun; tel: (056) 621 09 31.* Tues–Fri 0900–1800, Mon, Sat 0900–1600 (Sun 0900–1300 in summer). Much information available, including the free *Toruń Tourist and Business Guide.*

### ACCOMMODATION

Orbis hotels include the **Helios**, *ul. Kraszewskiego1/3; tel: (056) 250 33,* and **Kosmos**, *ul. Ks. Jerzego Popietuszki 2; tel: (056) 289 00.* **Campsite:** *ul. Kujawska 14; tel: (056) 654 71 87.*

### SIGHTSEEING

Toruń (capital of Pomerania) is second only to Kraków in terms of architectural heritage. Founded by the Order of Teutonic Knights (1233), it became part of the Hanseatic League, benefitting greatly as a trading town from its location by the Wisła *(Vistula)* River. Prospering between the 13th–15th centuries, Toruń fell first to the Swedes and then to the Prussians, only becoming part of Poland again in 1919. The city's claims to fame are excellent gingerbread (elaborately decorated with icing sugar), confectionery, and its most famous citizen,

astronomer Nicolas Copernicus, who discovered that the earth moved around the sun.

A good starting point for sightseeing is the **Rynek Staromiejski** (Market Square). Its main building, the **Ratusz** (Town Hall), was built in the 14th century, and is now home to the **Muzeum Okregowe** (Regional Museum); *tel: (056) 27038, open Tues–Sun 1000–1600,* with panoramic views from the tower, open Tues–Sun 1000–1600. Nearby is a monument to Copernicus, erected in 1853. The burgher's house at no. 35, called **Pod Gwiazdą** (literally 'under the star') was originally 15th-century, but also has ornate baroque additions. The interior features a 17th-century hanging staircase, with the building also housing the **Museum of Oriental Art**, *tel: (056) 21133.*

Near the market square at *ul. Kopernika 17,* is the **Nicholas Copernicus Museum** (the house was his family home), *tel: (056) 26748,* Tues–Sun 1000–1600. The interior has been re-created in a 15th-century manner, and has a model of old Toruń, a light and sound spectacle and various Copernicus memorabilia.

From here, head south-east to the **Ruiny Zamku Krzyżackiego** (ruins of the Teutonic Castle) on *ul. Przedzamcze,* destroyed in 1454, though still offering the best preserved remnants of the medieval city walls, and giving a good impression of how the original castle looked. Open daily 0900–1900 Apr 28–Sept 30.

Toruń has several fine churches, including the Gothic **Franciscan hall church of St Mary's**, on the old market square. The 14th-century **St James's Church**, by the attractive **Rynek Nowomiejski**, has Gothic flying buttresses, and frescos and baroque decoration within. Technically the oldest is the Gothic **St John's**, *ul. Zeglarska,* mostly dating from the mid 15th century, although the Presbytery is actually 300 years earlier. There are several other museums and delightful Gothic streets. The **Ethnographic Museum**, *Waty Gen. Sikorskiego 19; tel: (056) 28091,* is open Mon, Sat, Sun 1000–1600, Tues–Fri 0900–1600 (winter), Mon, Wed, Fri 0900–1600, Tues, Thur, Sat, Sun 1000–1800 (summer). The **Planetarium** has commentaries in English and there are boat trips along the Wisła from the landing stage on *Bulward Filadelfijski.*

# BRUSSELS
# (BRUXELLES, BRUSSEL)

Brussels is an exceptionally cosmopolitan city, the headquarters of the EU and NATO, as well as home to a sizeable number of immigrants from around the Mediterranean. This mix is reflected in the very varied lifestyle. Most sights are in a smallish area of the centre and visiting them should not take more than two or three days, but allow longer to get the feel of the ancient town and to travel a bit further afield. The city is officially bilingual and there's often little similarity between the two versions of street names (e.g. French Arts-Loi is Flemish Kunst-Wet). This chapter uses only the French ones, for convenience.

## TOURIST INFORMATION

**Tourist Offices: City:** *Hôtel de Ville, Grand-Place; tel: 513 89 40.* Open Mon–Sat 0900–1800, Sun 0900–1800 (summer), 1000–1400 (winter). If you make a hotel booking you will get a free map, but the only other thing they give away is the transport map. **National:** *r. du Marché-aux-Herbes 61; tel: 504 03 90.* Open daily 0900–1900 (summer); Mon–Sat 0900–1800, Sun 1300–1700 (winter). They dispense information about the whole country, not just Brussels, and a great deal of it (including a city map with points of interest marked) is free. Ask them about the **Brussels Tourist Passport** (BFr.220), which offers free city transport and a wide range of discounts – it's also available from museums, metro stations and hotels.

It's worth buying *Brussels Guide & Map*, easily the most comprehensive tourist leaflet – the price varies, but it's always cheaper from the Tourist Office than from bookshops.

**Info-Jeunes:** *r. du Marché-aux-Herbes 27, tel: 512 3274* (Mon–Fri 1200–1730), is a mine of information about good deals for young people.

## ARRIVING AND DEPARTING

### Airport
**Bruxelles Zaventem Airport**, *tel: 753 39 13,* is 14 km north-east of the centre. Several exchange offices and a tourist information desk, open daily 0600–2200. An express rail link operates until nearly midnight, with trains every 20 mins or so to all three main stations. The journey takes 15–30 mins and costs BFr.85. A taxi should cost around BFr.1200.

### Stations
**Midi/Zuid**, *r. de France 2* (metro nos 2/23) is the most important station and the terminals for Eurostar services, although it's in an area that is best avoided at night. The train information office (open daily 0630–2230) has a hotel booking desk (open Mon–Fri 0930–2130, Sat–Sun 1100–2030).

**Nord/Noord**, *r. de Progrés 85* (metro no. 23: change at *Rogier* from no. 2 or at *De Brouckère* from no. 1), *pl. Rogier,* on the edge of the red-light district. The terminal for many buses.

**Central/Centraal**, *carrefour de l'Evrove 2* (metro no. 1: *Centrale), blvd de l'Impératrice,* is the most convenient, only 5-mins walk from *Grand-Place.*

Midi/Zuid is to the south, Nord to the north and Central between them. Virtually all long-distance trains stop at both Midi and Nord, but many omit Central. The facilities at all three include baggage lockers, eating-places and newsagents selling English papers. Other main-line stations are of interest only for local journeys.

For all rail enquiries; *tel: 203 3640* (French) or *203 2886* (Dutch).

**149**

### GETTING AROUND

The city centre is smaller than it looks on maps and walking is the best way to get around. Away from the centre, the metro and bus network is efficiently run by **STIB**. For all city transport information, *tel: 515 20 00*. You can get free route maps from STIB kiosks, metro stations and Tourist Offices.

If stops show *sur demande*, raise your hand to the driver as the vehicle approaches. If you want to get off, ring the bell.

### Tickets

Individual tickets (BFr.50) can be purchased from drivers and multi-ride tickets from STIB kiosks, Tourist Offices, metro stations and some newsagents. Five-trip tickets (BFr.320) represent a slight saving.

There's also a tourist pass (BFr.125) that gives unlimited travel on all city transport for one calendar day.

### Metro

The terms 'tram' and 'metro' are interchangeable here. Metro stations are indicated by a square white 'M' on a blue background. *Loket/guichet* booths for tickets are in all stations and the trams run 0600–midnight. The system is comprehensive, efficient and easy to use if you know which line(s) you need, where to change (if applicable) and in which direction for each (only the terminals are indicated on signs), so study the map before setting out.

Lines are identified by number and colour (nos 1/red and 2/orange being central). Routes of the relevant line are shown on all platforms and trams and every platform has a city map with the metro system superimposed.

Doors close automatically (don't use them after the warning buzzer sounds), but you have to open them yourself: usually by exerting a little pressure on the handle and letting the hydraulics take over, sometimes by pressing a thin strip by the door. Smoking is prohibited throughout the system.

### Buses

Buses also have a comprehensive network (approximately 0600–2200), and there's a very limited night service.

### Taxis

Ranks are strategically positioned at all the stations and main squares.

### STAYING IN BRUSSELS

### Accommodation

There's a good choice of hotels in every grade, including plenty of budget establishments in the areas of *Ixelles* and *pl. Ste-Catherine*, several **hostels** (**HI** and otherwise) and a number of bed and breakfasts. Nevertheless, advance booking is recommended – essential in peak periods. Hotel chains: *BW, Cn, Fm, GT, Hd, Hn, Ib, Mc, Md, Mv, Nv, RC, Rn, SA, Sf, Sh, SL, Sn.*

If money's not a consideration and you prefer old-style charm to the modern chains, try **Royal Windsor**, *r. Duquesnoy 5; tel: 505 55 55, fax: 505 55 00*. The much cheaper (but still expensive) **Amigo**, *r. d'Amigo 1; tel: 547 47 47, fax: 513 52 77*, also has old-fashioned charm, despite the fact that it used to be a prison. **Arenberg**, *r. d'Assaut; tel: 511 07 70*, is mid-range, comfortable and central. **Arlequin**, *r. de la Fourche 17–19; tel: 514 16 15, fax: 514 22 02*, is reasonably priced and pleasant.

At the bottom of the hotel price range, but with a nice atmosphere, are **Madou**, *r. du Congrès 45; tel: 217 32 74*, and **Sabina**, *r. du Nord 78; tel: 218 26 37*. One of the cheapest places, within walking distance from North and Central stations, is **Espace du Marais**, *r. du Damier 23; tel: 02 210 0180*. **Pension Bosquet**, *r. Bosquet 70; tel: 538 52 30*, is also cheap to stay in, albeit a bit run-down.

**HI: Jacques Brel**, *r. de la Sablonnière 30; tel: 218 01 87* (metro no. 2: *Madou*, direction *Simonis*, i.e. away from the centre). A sign in the ticket hall indicates the exit: leave by the right-hand stairs and continue straight along the road to the second turning left. **Bruegel**, *Heilig Geeststraat 2; tel: 511 04 36*, is 300m from Central (behind *Notre-Dame-de-la-Chapelle*) and very modern. **Jean Nihon**, *r. de l'Eléphant 4; tel: 410 38 58*, 2 km from Central (metro: *Comte de Flandre* – 500m). **Centre Vincent Van Gogh**, *8 r. Traversiere; tel: 02 217 0158*, is the oldest youth hostel in Brussels and has the largest capacity.

The nearest official **campsite** is *75 Steenweg,*

150

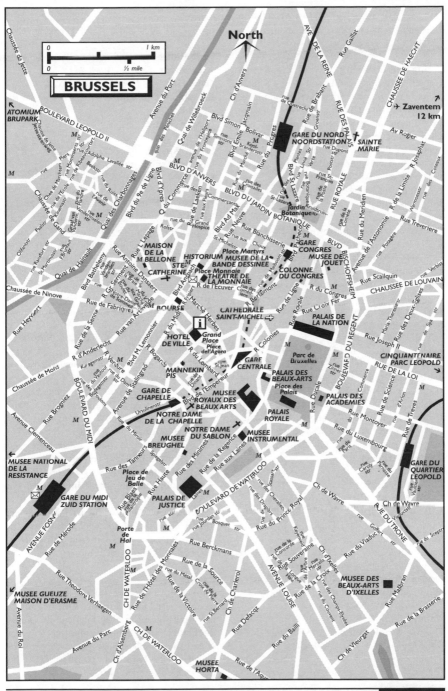

**North**

0 _____ 1 km
0 _____ ½ mile

**BRUSSELS**

← ATOMIUM
BRUPARK

↗ Zaventem
12 km

GARE DU NORD
NOORDSTATION

SAINTE
MARIE

BOULEVARD LEOPOLD II

BLVD D'ANVERS

BLVD DU JARDIN BOTANIQUE

Jardin
Botanique

MAISON
DE LA
M BELLONE

HISTORIUM MUSEE DE LA
BANDE DESSINEE

STE
CATHERINE

Place Martyrs

Place Monnaie

THEATRE DE
LA MONNAIE

BLVD
CONGRES

GARE
CONGRES

MUSEE DU
JOUET

COLONNE
DU CONGRES

BLVD
BISCHOFFSHEIM

CHAUSSEE DE LOUVAIN

BOURSE

CATHEDRALE
SAINT-MICHEL

PALAIS DE
LA NATION

HOTEL
DE VILLE

Grand
Place
Place
de l'Agora

Parc de
Bruxelles

CINQUANTENAIRE
PARC LEOPOLD

MANNEKIN
PIS

GARE
CENTRALE

GARE DE
CHAPELLE

MUSEE
ROYAUX DES
BEAUX-ARTS

PALAIS DES
BEAUX-ARTS
Place des
Palais

PALAIS DES
ACADEMIES

NOTRE DAME
DE LA CHAPELLE

PALAIS
ROYALE

NOTRE DAME
DU SABLON

MUSEE
INSTRUMENTAL

MUSEE
BREUGHEL

← MUSEE NATIONAL
DE LA
RESISTANCE

BOULEVARD DU MIDI

Place de
Jeu de
Balle

BOULEVARD DE WATERLOO

GARE DU
QUARTIER
LEOPOLD

GARE DU MIDI
ZUID STATION

PALAIS DE
JUSTICE

Porte
de
Hal

AVENUE FOSN

← MUSEE GUEUZE
MAISON D'ERASME

AVENUE LOUISE

MUSEE DES
BEAUX-ARTS
D'IXELLES

CH DE WATERLOO

MUSEE
HORTA

*Op Urrel 1650, Beersel; tel: 331 05 61,* 9 km to the south (tram no. 55: *Uccle).* Another is at *Chaussée de Wavre 205; tel: 264 41681.*

## Eating and Drinking

The Belgians enjoy eating and there's a huge choice of restaurants serving excellent food, but prices tend to be high and it's advisable to book for the more upmarket restaurants. Many bars sell food and give better value than the restaurants. In the area surrounding *Grand-Place* you can find every imaginable type of eating-place, including fast-food chains.

If you want to splash out, **Comme Chez Soi**, *23 pl. Rouppe,* offers art nouveau décor, superb cuisine and matching service. Slightly less expensive is **La Charlotte aux Pommes**, *pl. du Châtelain 40,* with excellent food and service. **Aux Armes de Bruxelles**, *r. des Bouchers 13,* is a busy place offering generous portions of Belgian food at moderate prices, and the good-value **Chez Léon**, *r. des Bouchers 18–20,* is noted for mussels and eels in green sauce. Two bars offering good Belgian cooking are **Falstaff**, *r. Henri Maus 17–23,* which has a good range and is usually crowded, and the much quieter **La Fleur en Papier Doré**, *r. des Alexiens 55,* once a hang-out of the artist Magritte. **La Dolce Vita**, *r. Middleburg 13,* is excellent value for Italian food. **Bombay Inn**, *38 r. de la Fousche,* offers good value Indian cuisine. **Wittamer**, *place du Grand-Sablon 12,* is a renowned patisserie and tea room that fully deserves its reputation.

## Communications

The **main post office** is **Centre Monnaie**, *pl. de Brouckère* (upstairs). Open Mon–Fri 0800–2000, Sat 0900–1500. There's a 24-hr post office at Midi *(av. Fonsny 48)* and other branches at Central and Nord, open Mon–Fri 0900–1700. The **telephone centre**, *r. du Lombard 30,* opens daily 1000–2200. The telephone code for Brussels is *02.*

## Money

**Thomas Cook bureaux de change** at *4 Grand-Place;* and at *19 r. des Bouchers.*

Midi station has a currency exchange, daily 0700–2200, and an automatic cash dispenser.

Currency exchange offices at Nord and Central open 0700–2000 and 0700–1900 respectively.

### Embassies

**Australia:** *r. Guimard 6; tel: 231 05 00.*
**Canada:** *av. de Tervuren 2; tel: 735 60 40.*
**Republic of Ireland:** *r. du Luxembourg 19; tel: 513 66 33.*
**New Zealand:** *blvd du Régent 47; tel: 512 10 40.*
**South Africa:** *26 r. de la Loi; tel: 230 68 45.*
**UK:** *r. Arlen 85; tel: 287 62 11.*
**USA:** *blvd du Régent 27; tel: 513 38 30.*

## ENTERTAINMENT

*The Bulletin,* a weekly English-language paper, has a comprehensive *What's On* supplement and the Tourist Office publishes a free list of musical performances. There are many clubs and discos. You can often get in free, but have to buy at least one (expensive) drink. Clustered around *Fernand Cocq* and the lower end of *ch. d'Ixelles* are lots of bars with music, many staying open until the early hours.

Operatic productions at **Opera National/ La Monnaie**, *pl. de la Monnaie; tel: 229 1211,* are of international quality. **Cirque Royal**, *r. de l'Enseignement; tel: 218 2015,* hosts touring dance and opera companies, while classical music is performed at **Palais des Beaux Arts**, *r. Ravenstein; tel: 507 8200,* and pop concerts at **Forest National**, *av. du Globe 36; tel: 340 2211.* There's a wide choice of jazz venues and many churches have free concerts on Sun.

Unless films are shown as *NV* or *VF,* they are in the original language. **Kinépolis**, *blvd Centenaire 1; tel: 474 2600* (beside Bruparck) is a 26-screen cinema that has an IMAX screen (the largest in the world), with performances in several languages. The **Cinema Museum**, *r. Baron Horta 9,* shows silent movies.

### Events

All major events centre on *Grand-Place.* These include several **jazz festivals**, **Ommegang** (a historical pageant in early July) and the **Tapis de Fleurs** (mid August biennial; even years), when the whole square is carpeted with flowers. The **National Holiday** (21 July) offers varied entertainments.

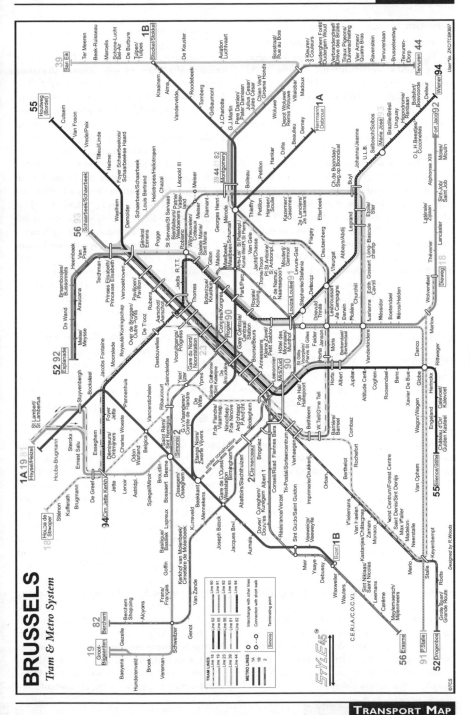

# BRUSSELS
*Tram & Metro System*

## SHOPPING

Much of the **lace** on offer is actually made in the Far East, so check that it's Belgian before buying. **Louise Verschueren**, *r. Watteau 16,* is a good place to get local lace. Of the many delicious **chocolates**, **Godiva** and **Leonidas** are most widespread. **Neuhaus** (one branch in *Galeries Royales St-Hubert*) are a little more expensive and favoured as presents. **Mary's**, *r. Royale 73,* supply the royal family.

Around *porte de Namur* and *av. Louise* (southeast of the centre) are upmarket areas for shopping. Around *r. Neuve* there are many shopping malls with a wide range of goods at affordable prices. **Galeries Royales St-Hubert** (off *r. des Bouchers),* is a vaulted arcade with lots of sculptures and a mixture of shops.

Brussels has several markets. **Midi Market** (near the station, Sun 0600–1300), resembles an African *souk* and is the place for food and clothes bargains. There's a flower market in *Grand-Place,* Tues–Sun 0800–1800.

**English-language bookshop:** W H Smith, *blvd A Max 71.*

## SIGHTSEEING

**Chatterbus**, *r. des Thuyas 12; tel: 673 18 35,* run off-beat (multilingual) trips with flexible itineraries, usually combining a walk with a bus/tram trip. June–Sept only for individuals; groups all year if booked ahead.

**Grand-Place**, with its ornate guild houses, remains the heart of the city. The most imposing building is the Gothic **Hôtel de Ville** (Town Hall), in which there are a succession of impressive rooms. The neighbouring brewers' house now contains **Maison des Brasseurs**, *tel: 511 4987* (Brewery Museum). Across the square, the neo-Gothic **Maison du Roi** houses **Musée de la Ville**, *tel: 279 4350,* covering every aspect of the city's history. The eclectic exhibits include retables, porcelain, silver and ancient documents. Don't miss the top floor: along with a selection of puppets is the extensive wardrobe of the **Manneken-Pis** (small statue of a boy peeing), the famous fountain in *r. de l'Etuve* that was designed by Jerome Duquesnoy in 1619 and has become the city's symbol. Among his more bizarre guises are Dracula, a Viking and a skin-diver.

**Centre Anspach** stretches between *blvd Anspach* and *pl. de la Monnaie*. An escalator leads up from the shopping area to **Historium**. It consists of a series of wax tableaux depicting scenes from Roman times to the present. The headphones (in English) adjust themselves to your pace. **Cathédrale St-Michel**, *pl. Ste-Gudule,* is a 13th–16th-century restored Brabantine-Gothic edifice with fine stained-glass windows, 18th-century carved-oak confessionals and some modern works in copper.

At opposite ends of **parc de Bruxelles** are the **Palais de la Nation** (Belgian Parliament) and **Palais Royale** (Royal Palace), which is open from late July for about six weeks and full of rich decorations, including Goya tapestries.

At the nearby **Musées Royaux des Beaux Arts**, *r, de la Régence 3; tel: 508 3211* (Royal Museums of Fine Arts), two separate museums (ancient and modern) are linked by an escalator. When planning which to visit first, bear in mind that they close for lunch at different times. Between them, an audio-visual show is going constantly (English earphones from the main desk). **Musée d'Art Ancien**, *r. de la Régence 3,* is light and well laid-out, containing fine examples of the Flemish school. Around a dozen works by Breughel are scattered through several rooms. Rubens, Jordaens, Cranach and Bosch are also well represented.

**Musée d'Art Moderne**, *pl. Royale 1,* is housed in an interesting modern building designed for the collection: it's underground, but with windows all the way down. Dali's *Temptation of St Anthony* is there, together with works by such artists as Ernst, Miró and Dubuffet. Walk down and take the lift back up.

**Notre-Dame-du-Sablon**, *r. de la Régence* (15th-century) once housed a statue of the Virgin said to have miraculous powers. Across the road, **place du Petit-Sablon** features a small ornamental garden, the perimeters adorned with statues of figures, each carrying objects connected with their trade, and a fountain depicting two 16th-century counts who opposed Spanish tyranny. On one corner is **Musée Instrumental**. Adolphe Saxe, inventor of the saxophone, was Belgian-born and there's a section devoted to him, as well as over a thousand instruments, some extremely ancient.

The **Notre-Dame-de-la-Chapelle**, *r. des Ursulines 4*, is Brussels' oldest church, a 13th-century structure containing the marble tomb of Breughel the Elder.

Neo-classical **Palais de Justice**, *pl. Poelaert* (metro: *pl. Louise*), is fittingly impressive. The 500-step ascent to the cupola is hard going but, on clear days, rewarded by an excellent view.

South of the centre, **Musée Victor Horta**, *r. Américain 25, Ixelles; tel: 537 1692* (tram nos 81/92), was once the home of the noted Belgian architect and the interior is typical of his flowing (art nouveau) style.

### North-west of the centre

The 102m high **Atomium**, *blvd du Centenaire; tel: 477 0977* (metro nos 1/19/81: *Heysel)*, (a gigantic model of an iron atom) was constructed in 1958 and has become another symbol of the city. Several modules are linked (escalators up, easy stairs down) to form a series of exhibits about the human body and medicine. The main attraction, however, lies in the view from the top module, to which there's a high-speed lift (keep the ticket to get into the museum). About 100 m away is **Bruparck**, *tel: 478 0505*, a leisure park where **Mini-Europe** consists of miniaturised (1:25) versions of European landmarks and **Océade** is an aquatic complex. Not far away is the **Planetarium**, *av. de Bouchout 10; tel: 478 9526*.

### East of the centre

The pleasant **parc Léopold** (metro: *Schuman*) contains **Musée d'Histoire Naturelle** (Museum of Natural History), *ch. de Wavre 260; tel: 627 4238*, where the exhibits range from dinosaurs to deadly insects.

**Parc du Cinquantenaire** (metro: *Schuman/Mérode*) surrounds the **Cinquantenaire**, a monumental arch flanked by museums. **Musée Royal de l'Armée et d'Histoire Militaire**, *tel: 734 5252* (Royal Museum of the Army and Military History) is amazingly wide-ranging. As well as an incredible array of weapons and military paraphernalia, there's a hangar full of aircraft, ranging from a hot-air balloon to passenger jets. **Autoworld**, *tel: 736 4165*, contains one of the world's best collections of vintage vehicles. **Musée Royaux d'Art et d'Histoire**

(Royal Museum of Art and History; entrance on the far side) is a vast museum with whole galleries devoted to early cultures, from Greek to South American, while other sections cover everything from the cinema to textiles.

### South-west of the centre

Beer-lovers should visit **Musée Gueuze**, *r. Gheude 56, Anderlecht* (10 mins walk from Midi), a working brewery with tours that include a sampling. Further from the centre, **Maison d'Erasme**, *r. de Chapitre 31; tel: 521 1383* (metro: *St-Guidon*) was the home of the Renaissance scholar Erasmus and has been authentically restored.

### OUT OF TOWN

There are frequent trains from Brussels to **Leuven**, the journey taking about 30 mins (board a train for 'Leuven/Louvain', not one that also mentions the university). The **Tourist Office** is in the **Stadhuis** (Town Hall), *Naamsestraat, tel: (016) 21 15 39*. Open Mon–Fri 0800–1700, Sat–Sun 1000–1700. The university was founded in 1425 and the pleasant old town itself is the main attraction, a place to wander rather than sightsee, although it does have a handful of interesting museums.

Trains from Central to **Waterloo** are hourly and take 30 mins, but it's a good 15 mins walk from the station. To get directly to the site, take **TEC** Bus W from Brussels (leaving *pl. Rouppe* every half-hour and taking 40 mins). The **Visitors Centre**, *rte du Lion 252–254; tel: (02) 385 19 12*, opens daily 0930–1830 (Apr–Oct); 1030–1600 (Nov–Mar). Ask for a combi-ticket if you intend to visit all the attractions.

Everything of interest is connected with the 1815 battle at nearby Mont St-Jean, where Wellington's Dutch-British army held out against Napoleon until the timely arrival of Blücher's Prussians. The battle is re-enacted regularly on (or close to) 18 June.

You can get a panoramic view of the battlefield if you climb 40m (226 steps), up the **Lion Mound** (only recommended for the fit). This was constructed soon after the event itself and unfortunately obliterated some of the battlefield's key features. Learn the background at the free show at the centre first.

**155**

# BRUSSELS–AMSTERDAM

Train travel in the Benelux countries is quite simply a pleasure. The trains are clean, quiet, comfortable and reliable, here connecting the capitals of Belgium and the Netherlands in just three hours. Although not a long journey, there is lots to see, including both capital cities of Holland – The Hague and Amsterdam – the vast urban sprawl of the Randstadt and the unique combination of agriculture and tourism found in the bulb growing regions around Haarlem.

> FASTEST JOURNEY: 3 HRS

## TRAINS

**ETT tables:** 18, 410, 450.

### FAST TRACK

An hourly service links Brussels with Amsterdam, taking just over 3 hrs.

### ON TRACK

#### Brussels–Mechelen–Antwerp (Antwerpen)

At least two trains an hour link Brussels Midi/Zuid, Central and Nord stations to Antwerpen Centraal. All trains call at Mechelen en route. Brussels Nord to Mechelen takes 15 mins, Mechelen to Antwerp 20 mins.

#### Antwerp–Rotterdam

The hourly Brussels to Amsterdam trains provide the link between Antwerpen Centraal and Rotterdam. and take 1 hr 10 mins.

#### Rotterdam–Delft–The Hague (Den Haag)–Leiden–Haarlem–Amsterdam

Four trains an hour run between Rotterdam and Amsterdam. Two of these call at Haarlem and Delft, all trains call at The Hague (Den Haag HS) and Leiden. Additional trains operate from Rotterdam and Delft to The Hague (Den Haag CS) and between The Hague (Den Haag CS) and Leiden. Rotterdam to Delft takes 12 mins, Delft to The Hague 7 mins, The Hague to Leiden 12 mins, Leiden to Haarlem 20 mins and Haarlem to Amsterdam 15 mins.

## MECHELEN

**Stations: Mechelen (Centraal)** and **Nekkerspoel**, *tel: (015) 41 59 11.* Most long-distance trains stop at 'Mechelen', but Nekkerspoel is just as close to the centre: about 10 mins walk either way.

**Tourist Office:** *Grote Markt* (in the modern wing of the Stadhuis); *tel: (015) 20 85 11.* Open Mon–Fri 0800–1800, Sat–Sun 0930–1700 (Apr–Sept); Mon–Fri 0800–1700, Sat 1000–1700 (Oct–Mar). A wide range of free multilingual literature, but a good town map costs BFr.20, as does a colour brochure that suggests a walking route and makes a good souvenir.

**Grote Markt** is flanked by medieval buildings, including the multi-style **Stadhuis** (Town Hall). The Brabantine-Gothic chuch of **St-Rombout** dominates the centre and provides fine views (514 steps, but in stages). The interior is largely black and white marble, with sumptuous chapels, and Van Dyck's *Crucifixion* is amongst the works of art. Two carillons (each has 49 bells) attract campanologists from all over the world and there are regular bell-ringing performances. **Museum Hof van Busleyden** is housed in a 16th-century mansion. The grotesque wooden doll by the entrance, **Op Signoorke**, is a traditional focus of rivalry between Antwerp and Mechelen. One building houses a variety of exhibits, the other is notable for a superb carillon section. The enchanting **Speelgoedmuseum** (Toy Museum) is crammed with toys of every description and is a real nostalgia trip. Your weight on the floor brings some of them to life. Another magical place is the tiny **Horlogerie en Klokkenmuseum**, crammed with antique clocks.

The church of **St Pieter-Paulus** is rich in carved oak and enormous religious paintings. The altars are largely black and white marble, but the main one is surrounded by gold ornamentation. **Sint-Janskerk** has a magnificent altar triptych by Rubens, the *Adoration of the Magi*, and many other baroque paintings.

Tapestry has been a Flemish craft for centuries and **Manufactuur Gaspard De Wit** has fine displays. There are tours of the (working) tapestry mill.

## ANTWERP (ANTWERPEN/ANVERS)

**Stations:** The main station, **Antwerpen-Centraal**; *tel: (03) 204 20 40,* is 2 km east of the centre, but linked by metro-tram. The marble and gold-decorated station is worth a visit in its own right. The bookstand stocks UK newspapers and there's an exchange office. **De Lijn's office** is in Centraal's metro-tram stop, *Diamant; tel: (03) 218 14 06,* open Mon–Fri 0810–1230, 1330–1600. You can get (free) transport maps and tickets from them. Some international trains stop at **Bechem**, 2 km to the south; local services link it to Centraal.

**Tourist Office:** *Grote Markt 15; tel: (03) 232 01 03.* Open Mon–Sat 0900–1745, Sun 0900–1645. From Centraal, take metro nos 2/15 to *Groenplaats* (direction: *Linkeroever),* then walk past the cathedral and continue along the side street facing you. It's worth buying *Antwerp Flanders Belgium* and a decent street map.

### ACCOMMODATION

The Tourist Office gets good discounts on hotels. Chains include *BW, GT, Hd, Hn, Hy, Ib, Nv, RS, Sc, Sf* and *Sn* and there are hotels in every grade, including some cheap ones near Centraal, but be wary because some rent by the hour. Bed and breakfast places are scarce. **Alfa de Keyser**, *Dekeyserlei 66–70; tel: (03) 234 01 35,* is a 4-star hotel only 100m from Centraal. **HI:** *Provincie Straat 256; tel: 230 05 22.* Located only 10 mins walk from the station. **Campsite:** *Vogelzanglaan; tel: (03) 238 57 17.*

### SIGHTSEEING

**Dierentuin Zoo**, *Kon. Astridplein 26; tel: (03) 202 45 40,* is just beside Centraal. Its attractions include a **planetarium** and a **dolphinarium**.

**Diamantmuseum**, *Lange Herentalsestr. 31–33; tel: 202 48 90* (walkable from Centraal) covers all aspects of the diamond trade, one of the cornerstones of Antwerp's fortunes.

There are (free) multilingual tours of **Onze-Lieve Vrouwekathedral**, entrance on *Handschoenmarkt*, a beautiful building that took 170 years to complete (1352–1521). The place is a veritable art gallery, highlights being four enormous masterpieces by Rubens and some recently revealed 15th-century frescos.

**Grote Markt** is home to the 19th-century **Brabo Fountain** (which depicts the legend of the city's founding), guild houses topped by golden figures and the Renaissance **Stadhuis**

**157**

(Town Hall). On 15 Aug each year Grote Markt is turned into a 17th-century market in honour of Rubens.

The unique **Plantin-Moretus Museum/ Stedelijk Prentenkabinet**, *Vrijdagmarkt 22; tel: 232 02 94*, is a well-preserved 16th-century printer's works and home. The medieval **Steen** (Castle), *Steenplein 1*, houses the **National Scheepvartmuseum**, *tel: 232 08 50* (Maritime Museum). In addition to the usual types of exhibit, there are such curiosities as a 'painting' made of stamps and a list of naval superstitions.

Not far away is the striking **Vleeshuis** (Butchers' Hall), *Vleeshouwerstr. 38/40; tel: 233 64 04*, now an applied arts museum with exhibits that include some excellent woodcarvings. On the upper storeys are superb sets of antique china and old musical instruments, lots of ticking grandfather clocks and an explanation of Egyptian hieroglyphics. A little to the north is the Dominican **Sint-Pauluskerk**, *Veemarkt; tel: 232 32 67*, a Gothic structure with a baroque tower and furnishings. Among other treasures, it contains some magnificently carved wood and three works by Rubens.

The ubiquitous Rubens was the major influence in the baroque design of the former Jesuit church of **Sint-Carolus Borromeus**, *Hendrik Conscienceplein 12; tel: 233 84 33*, and he's buried in **Sint-Jacobskerk**, *Lange Nieuwstr. 73*. This 15th-century Gothic structure has 17th-century baroque ornamentation and many art treasures. Rubens spent the last 30 years of his life in **Rubenshuis**, *Wapper 9; tel: 232 47 47* (about halfway between Centraal and *Grote Markt*; metro: *Meir*). It's an evocative place in 17th-century style, but contains only minor examples of the artist's work.

A couple of blocks west (bus nos 7/8/9) is the **Mayer Van den Bergh Museum**, *Lange Gasthuisstr.19; tel: 232 42 37*, which contains an important collection of antiques and paintings, notably those by Breughel. Antwerp's 16th-century **Begijnhof**, *Rodestr. 39* (metro: *Opera*), with its 19th-century church, is a restful area of cobbled streets and small houses.

On Sun mornings, **Vogelmarkt** (bird market), *Oude Vaartplaats*, does sell birds – plus almost everything else.

**Museum Voor Schone Kunsten** (Royal Museum of Fine Arts), *Leopold de Waelplaats; tel: 238 78 09* (bus nos 8/23), is a neo-classical building housing one of Belgium's best collections of paintings, including over twenty works by Rubens and a superb collection of 14th–17th-century Flemish art, as well as works of the Impressionist and Expressionist schools.

The **Openluchtmuseum Voor Beeldhouwkunst** (Sculpture Museum), *Middelheim Park; tel: 828 13 50* (bus nos 18/17), is dotted with sculptures, notably by Rodin and Moore.

## ROTTERDAM

**Station: Centraal/CS**, on the northern edge of the centre (blue/green metro).

**Tourist Office:** *Coolsingel 67* (5 mins walk from Centraal; follow the signs); *tel: (010) 402 3200*; Infoline, *(0900) 403 4065*. Open Mon–Thur 0900–1900, Fri 0900–2100, Sat 0900–1900; also Sun 1000–1700 (Apr–Sept). Kiosk in the station: Mon–Sat 0900–2200, Sun 1000–2200. *Inside Out* is a free monthly listing.

### GETTING AROUND

Things of interest tend to be in clusters, so take public transport between the clusters and then walk. It's worth getting a street map unless your stay is very short. **RET** *(Stationsplein* and *Zuidsplein)* and **VVV** sell good-value tickets for unlimited city travel over 1, 2 or 3 days.

Metro stations are indicated by a large squarish yellow M. The system is efficient and user-friendly, with route maps everywhere. Only two lines matter for the centre: blue/green (north–south) and red/yellow/mauve (east–west) and they intersect at only one station, where you walk from Beurs platform to Churchillplein platform (or vice versa).

Efficient trams fill the gaps in the metro and buses are more useful away from the centre.

Boat tours are operated by **Spido**, *Willemsplein; tel: (010) 413 5400* (metro: *Leuvehaven*, tram no. 5). The basic harbour tour lasts 1 hr 15 mins and tells you all you will ever need to know about **Europoort**.

### ACCOMMODATION

There are plenty of middle-range options. **VVV** can book private rooms. There are two areas with cheap hotels: about 1 km south-west of CS (try *Gravendijkwal* and *Heemraadsingel)* and just north of CS (try *Provenierssingel)*.

Hotel chains include *BW, GT, Hd, Hn, Ib, Nv, Sn* and *Tp.* **Intell**, *Leuvehaven 80; tel: (010) 413 4139*, is a modern, 4-star hotel with great harbour views and a rooftop health club. **Hotel Wilgenhof**, *Heemraadsingel 92–94; tel: (010) 476 2525* or *425 4892*, is a small 3-star establishment in a quiet, but central, location.

**HI:** *Rochussenstr. 107/109; tel: (010) 436 5763* (metro: direction *Marconiplein: Dijkzigt;* tram no. 4). Take the Nieuwbinnen exit, do a U-turn at the top of the steps and you're on *Rochussenstr.* – turn left and the hostel is about 30 m away. **Campsite: Stadscamping Rotterdam**, *Kanaalweg 84; tel: (010) 415 3440*, west of CS (bus no. 33), is open all year. There is usually cheap dormitory accommodation (mid June–mid Aug) at **Sleep-In**, *Mauritsweg 29; tel: (010) 412 1420*, 5-mins walk south of CS. This is arranged from year to year, however, so check with VVV.

**SIGHTSEEING**

As Rotterdam was virtually flattened in World War II, most of it is post-war and it's noted for imaginative modern architecture. Situated at the delta of the Rivers Rhine, Maas and Waal, it has been a major harbour since the 14th century and **Europoort** is the world's largest container port.

**Lijnbaan** is Europe's oldest shopping centre, with a very wide variety of shops. **IMAX Waterstad Theatre**, *Leuvehaven 77; tel: 404 8844*, is a gigantic audio-visual film theatre, with a screen six storeys high (closed Mon).

The exhibits at the enormous **Museum Boymans Van Beuningen**, *Museumpark 18/20; tel: 441 9400* (tram no. 5), cover historic paintings and sculpture, modern classics and contemporary art, applied art and design, and prints and drawings. **Maritiem Museum Prins Hendrik**, *Leuvehaven 1; tel: 413 2680* (metro: *Beurs/Churchillplein;* tram nos 3/6/7), is the oldest and probably the most comprehensive maritime museum in the country, containing every conceivable type of nautical paraphernalia, including whole vessels. Upstairs is a hands-on section for children, **Professor Plons**. Outside, you can board the *Buffel*, a well-restored war-

ship dating from 1863. **Maritiem Buitenmuseum**, *Leuvehaven 50/72; tel: 404 8072*, is along the waterfront. This open-air maritime museum is the place to see historic barges, port cranes and old steamships. The trio is completed by **Scheepen Uit Verre Landen** (Ships from Distant Lands), on the south side of *Wijnhaven 20a; tel: 413 8351*. This recently opened floating museum exhibits real vessels such as gondolas and papyrus craft.

**Museum voor Volkenkunde**, *Willkemskade 25; tel: 411 1055* (metro: *Leuvehaven;* tram no.5: *Willemsplein),* is an ethnological museum that hosts and displays temporary exhibitions from all over the world (closed Mon).

The 185 m **Euromast**, *Parkhaven 20; tel: 436 4811* (tram no. 6: *Euromast),* towers over the trees and the 5 mins walk is through **Central Park**. This is the highest structure in the Netherlands and a member of the exclusive World Federation of Great Towers. Even from the first platform you have panoramic views of the 37 km-long waterfront, but go right to the top on the Space Adventure, a simulated rocket flight: after blast-off you go into orbit and have breathtaking views as the capsule ascends slowly to the top, revolving as it goes.

Around **Oude Haven**, the old harbour, is where the most striking modern buildings are located, notably the complex of **Kijk Kubus** futuristic cube houses (metro: *Blaak;* tram nos 3/13/17; bus nos 32/49). One, at *Overblaak 70; tel: 414 2285*, is open to the public. It's rather disorientating, but with interesting views (the value of each house depends largely on the view). **Schielandshuis**, *Korte Hoogstr. 31; tel: 217 6767* (metro: *Beurs/Churchillplein,* tram nos 3/6), is a monumental 17th-century building that houses a museum devoted to the city's development, including a variety of historical everyday objects. At **De Dubbelde Palmboom Museum**, *Voorhaven 12; tel: 476 1533*, its sister establishment, emphasis lies on the development of Rotterdam into a world port.

**OUT OF TOWN**

**Gouda** is 25 mins from Rotterdam by train and the station is 10-mins stroll north of the centre. **VVV:** *Markt 27; tel: (0182) 513 666*. Mon–Fri 0900–1700, Sat 1000–1600. It's a quaint place

**159**

that exemplifies small-town Holland, with a ring of quiet canals around ancient buildings.

The 15th-century **Stadhuis** (Town Hall), the oldest Gothic municipal building in Holland, contains carved fireplaces and 17th-century tapestries. **Waag**, the old weigh-house, opens for trading on Thur morning (July–Aug), when suitably costumed farmers weigh cheeses by traditional methods. **Sint Janskerk** is famous for its length (123m) and 70 superb stained-glass windows. The ornate **Lazaruspoortje** (1609) once led to a hospital for lepers and is now the back entrance to the unmissable **Catharina Gasthuis**, a complex of 14th–17th-century hospital buildings which house the fascinating **Stedelijk Museum**. Among the rooms reproduced are a nursery, a torture chamber, a dispensary, rooms furnished respectively in 17th- (Louis XIV), 18th- (rococo) and 19th-century (Empire) style, and an 18th–19th-century school. The **De Moriaan Museum** (covered by the same ticket) is an 18th-century tobacco shop displaying an amazing variety of earthenware items and pipes.

## DELFT

**Station:** 5 mins walk south of the centre.
**Tourist Office**: *Markt 83/85; tel: (015) 212 6100.* Open Mon–Fri 0900–1800, Sat 0900–1730, Sun 1000–1500. Take bus no. 16 from the station to *Markt*.

Chinese **porcelain** reached Delft in the 17th century and the inspiration it provided led to the blue and white designs that made the town famous. At places still using traditional methods you can learn about the processes and watch the work. The best known are **De Porceleyne Fles**, *Rotterdamsweg 196; tel: 256 9214,* and **De Delftse Pauw**, *Delftweg 133; tel: 212 4920,* but the most central is **Atelier de Candelaer**, *Kerkstr. 14; tel: 213 1848.* **Stedelijk Museum/Het Prinsenhof** (the Prince's Court), *St Agathaplein 1; tel: 260 2358,* has a large section devoted to the struggle against the Spanish. William of Nassau/Orange, who led the fight for independence and was assassinated here in 1584 (the bullet marks are still visible). Exhibits include silverware, tapestries, paintings and Delftware. Across the road is **Nusantara Museum**, with a collection of art

from the former Dutch East Indies. **Oude Kerk** (Old Church), *Heilige Geestkerkhof,* currently closed for restoration, has an alarmingly leaning tower, a number of impressive sarcophagi and 27 stained-glass windows, mostly modern. **Nieuwekerk**, *Markt,* houses the enormous black and white marble mausoleum of Prince William, an enormous pipe organ and some rich stained glass. The 109m spire provides great views. A nice way to see the Delft is by horse-drawn tram, *Markt; tel: 256 1828* (30 Mar–12 Sept).

## THE HAGUE (DEN HAAG)

**Stations: Centraal/CS** is 5 mins walk from the centre and serves most Dutch cities, but fast services for Amsterdam and Rotterdam use **Hollandse/HS**, Holland's Spoor station (1 km south). CS and HS are linked by frequent trains and by tram nos 9/12. The Hague's other stations are suburban.

**Tourist Office:** *Kon. Julianaplein 30; tel: (06) 340 350 51,* just outside the station. Mon–Sat 0900–1730 (Jan–June and Sept–Dec); Mon–Sat 0900–1730, Sun 1000–1700 (July–Aug). *Den Haag Info* is a free monthly covering everything of interest. The free weekly *Over Uit* concentrates on films, theatres and music.

If you don't enjoy walking, buy a proper street map. The free small-scale ones are very deceptive and things that appear to be a block away can involve a long walk – unnecessarily, as there's an excellent bus and tram network.

### ACCOMMODATION

Hotel chains include *GT, IC, Mc, Mv, Nv, Sf,*

---

Colour section: (i) The Acropolis, Athens (p.124); Barcelona (p.130): view of cathedral spires and Archdeacon's House Courtyard.

(ii) Budapest (p.174): River Danube and Parliament; Bruges (p.171); Brandenburg Gate, Berlin (p.135).

(iii) Tivoli Gardens, Copenhagen (p.187); Ponte Vecchio, Florence (p.199); inset, Hamburg (p.234).

(iv) Germany: Neckar Valley (p.228); Roder Archway, Rothenburg (p.221).

*Sn* and (in Scheveningen) *Ib*. If money is a consideration, base yourself at **Scheveningen** or ask VVV about private rooms. **HI:** *Monsterseweg 4; tel: (070) 397 0011*, 10 km west of CS near Kijkduin beach: bus nos 122/123/124 from CS, then 10 mins walk: tell the driver you want the hostel. Close to it are a small cheap hotel and a campsite.

### SIGHTSEEING

The administrative capital of the Netherlands is a pleasant town, centred around **Binnenhof**, the home of the Dutch parliament (trams nos 2/3/7/8/9; bus nos 4/5/22). The 13th-century **Ridderzaal** (Knights' Hall) is of particular note and the scene of many official ceremonies.

**Mauritshuis Museum**, *Korte Vijverberg 8; tel: 302 3435* (tram nos 7/8/9/12; bus nos 4/5/10/22), is a magnificent Renaissance mansion on a lake, housing much of the royal collection: Rembrandt, Vermeer, Ruysdael, Hals, Cranach, Holbein, Breughel, van Dyck and Rubens are all represented. The rest is in **Schildergallerij Prins Willem V**, *Buitenhof 35* (tram nos 3/7/8/12; bus nos 4/5/22), which is virtually wallpapered with paintings. The neighbouring **Rijksmuseum Gevangenpoort**, *Buitenhof 33* (tram nos 3/7/8, bus nos 4/5), is in a gatehouse that was a prison for over four centuries and contains a gruesome range of instruments of torture.

**Panorama Mesdag**, *Zeestr. 65; tel: 310 6665* (tram nos 7/8, bus nos 4/5/13/22), consists of a realistic circular view of Scheveningen painted by Hendrik Mesdag, his wife and some friends in 1881 – it's well worth seeing. **Gemeentemuseum** (municipal museum), *Stadhouderslaan 41; tel: 338 1338* (tram nos 7/10; bus nos 65/88), is a higgledy-piggledy place that mixes temporary exhibitions with the permanent collection and you're sure to find something that appeals to you. **Museon**, in the same building, concentrates on popular science, from the origins of the planet to modern technology – with interactive exhibits.

The unmissable 1990s version of a panorama, at **Omniversum**, *President Kennedylaan 5; tel: 354 5454* (tram no. 10, bus nos 4/14/65/66 – or through the small garden to the rear of Gemeentemuseum), is a stunning spectacle with a wrap-around screen that makes you feel like a participant in the action. There are English earphones.

Most of the city's palaces can be viewed only from the outside. An exception is the huge **Vredespaleis** (Peace Palace), *Carnegieplein 2; tel: 302 4137* (tram nos 7/8; bus nos 4/13), which houses the **International Courts of Justice and Arbitration** and is a strange architectural mishmash, with a display of items donated by world leaders. There are tours when the Court is not in session.

A number of worthwhile small museums (with limited opening hours) include **Museum voor het Poppenspel** (Puppet Museum), **Brandweermuseum** (Fire Brigade Museum) and **Openbaar Vervoer Museum** (Public Transport Museum).

### OUT OF TOWN

**Madurodam**, *George Maduroplein 1; tel: 355 3900* (bus no. 22; tram nos 1/9), is the world's largest miniature town and includes models of the nation's landmarks. The North Sea resort of **Scheveningen**, *Sealife Centre, Strandweg 13; tel: 354 2100*, about 4 km from the city centre (tram nos 1/8/9/11), is regarded as part of it, although it has its own VVV: *Gevers Deynootweg 1134* (telephone and hours as for The Hague office). Hotels here are cheaper, but prices in the promenade eateries are inflated. The resort centres on the 19th-century **Kurhaus Hotel**, in which there's a casino. **Duinrell Theme Park** in Wassenaar has many attractions and a roller coaster; *tel: 705 155 155* (bus nos 90/43).

## LEIDEN

**Station:** 10 mins walk north-west of the centre. **Tourist Office:** *Stationsplein 210; tel: (071) 514 6846*. Open Mon–Fri 0900–1730, Sat 0900–1600.

The delightful university town of Leiden has a medieval quarter, centring on the vast **St Pieterskerk**, and some user-friendly museums. **Van Oudenheden**, *Rapenburg 28*, is an excellent archaeological museum with many objects from early Greece and Rome and an amazing array from ancient Egypt. **De Lakenhal**, *Oude Singel 32*, covers the town's history: the period-furnished rooms include a traditional kitchen and various guild rooms, while van Leyden's triptych of the *Last Judgment* is among the fine paintings. Nearby is **Molenmuseum de Valk**, *Binnenvestgracht 1,* a windmill housing a windmill museum. In the **Boerhave**, *St Agnietenstr. 10,* is an anatomical theatre, complete with skeletons and displays of early medical paraphernalia. **Voor Volkenkunde**, *Steenstr. 1,* houses temporary exhibitions from around the world and is noted for its excellent displays.

## ⬆ SIDE TRACK FROM LEIDEN

### LISSE

The **Bulb District** is an area which stretches roughly from Leiden to Haarlem and you can get a good view of the fields from trains between them – a better one from bus nos 50/51, which stop en route at the tiny town of Lisse. **VVV:** *Grachtweg 53; tel: (0252) 414 262/415 263.* Open Mon–Fri 0900–1700, Sat 0900–1600.

**Museum voor de Bloemollenstreek** is devoted to bulbs, the permanent section covering all aspects of the history and cultivation of tulips and other plants. The prime reason for visiting Lisse, however, is to see **Keukenhof Gardens** (10 mins away by local bus), a 70-acre park, with 16 km of paths, which is the showcase of the Dutch bulb industry. The gardens are open late Mar–late May and the peak is April, so it's pot luck how much there is to see in March and May. The gardens are noted for tulips, narcissi and hyacinths and there are pavilions featuring flower arrangements. Take a picnic because the cafés are invariably overcrowded. In season, special bus no. 54 goes from Leiden directly to the gardens. ⬆

### HAARLEM

**Station:** 10 mins walk north of the centre. It was built in 1908, in art deco style.
**Tourist Office**: *Stationsplein 1; tel: (0900) 616 1600* or *06 320 24043.* Open Mon–Sat 0900–1730 (Apr–Sept); Mon–Fri 0900–1730, Sat 0900–1600 (Oct–Mar). *UIT Loper* is a free listing, published every two or three weeks.

### ACCOMMODATION

Haarlem has a few upmarket hotels (including *GT*), but **Zandvoort** offers more choice in most grades.

### SIGHTSEEING

The late Gothic **St Bavo/Grote-Kerk** (1370–1520), after completion, became a popular subject for painters. Inside is the world-famous Christian Müller baroque pipe-organ, on which the young Mozart played in 1766. It is still used for regular concerts. Other features of St Bavo are the **tomb of Frans Hals** and a 16th-century rood screen and choir stalls. The town's main draw is the **Frans Hals Museum**, *Groot Heiligland 62.* Although Hals is not the only artist represented, the highlight of the collection is a group of his paintings depicting militia companies.

A once-private collection that first went on view in 1784 (making it the oldest public museum in the Netherlands) can be seen at **Teylers Museum**, *Spaarne 16.* The eclectic exhibits include old scientific instruments, fossils, gemstones, coins and drawings – some by Raphael, Michelangelo and Rembrandt. **Corrie Ten Boommuseum**, *Barteljorisstr. 19; tel: 310 324,* was founded by Willem Ten Boom in 1837 as a clock shop. Successive generations of the Ten Booms committed themselves to helping the needy and this tradition extended to the Jews in World War II. The family were betrayed in 1944 and most perished in the camps, but Corrie Ten Boom survived and the house is maintained as a monument to the family, a tribute to courage and a charity.

### OUT OF TOWN

**Zandvoort** (10 mins by train and frequent buses in summer) is the beach for Haarlem and has plenty of cheap pensions. **VVV**, *Schoolplein 1; tel: (023) 571 7947,* can supply information. Open Mon–Sat 1000–1230, 1330–1700 (Apr–Sept); Mon–Fri 1000–1230, 1330–1700, Sat 1000–1230, 1330–1530 (Oct–Mar).

It's a large resort with good facilities, including a car race-track, a dolphinarium and an ultra-modern casino. The long, sandy beaches (including one for nudists) begin 200m from the station.

# BRUSSELS–COLOGNE

Hilly, heavily wooded countryside, meandering rivers and picturesque towns and villages ensure that this is a delightful journey. Maastricht is well worth visiting; it has a charming cobbled shopping district, lively cafés and restaurants, as well as beautiful churches and centuries of history. It may also be the only Dutch city with views of hills! Its near neighbour, Aachen, also boasts a wealth of history and, although so close to Belgium and Holland, is completely German in style and character.

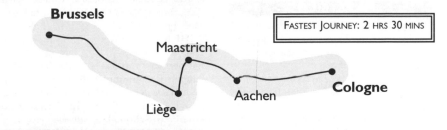

FASTEST JOURNEY: 2 HRS 30 MINS

## TRAINS

**ETT tables:** 20, 400, 402, 800, 481.

### FAST TRACK

A regular service runs every 2 hrs on the Oostende–Brussels–Cologne route (Brussels to Cologne takes 3 hrs), supplemented by new Thalys (TGV) trains (reservation obligatory and special fares), which run Paris–Brussels–Cologne every 2 hrs (Brussels–Cologne journey time 2½ hrs).

### ON TRACK

**Brussels–Liège (Luik)**

TGV service as above runs every 2 hrs to supplement the basic service of two trains every hour taking 1 hr 10–20 mins.

**Liège–Maastricht**

An hourly service throughout the day taking 30 mins.

**Maastricht–Aachen**

No through trains but many services available by changing trains at Heerlen. Journey 1½ hrs.

**Aachen–Cologne (Köln)**

Frequent trains throughout the day with journey times of around 45 mins.

## LIÈGE (LUIK/LUYK/LEUK)

**Main station: Liège-Guillemins**, *tel: 324 229 2610,* 2 km south of the centre (bus nos 1/4).
**Tourist Offices:** at the **station**; *tel: 04 252 4419.* Open Mon–Sat 0900–1730, Sun 1000–1600 (Apr–Sept); Mon–Sat 1000–1600 (Oct–Mar). **Municipal:** *Féronstrée 92; tel: (041) 21 92 21,* open Mon–Fri 0900–1800, Sat 1000–1600, Sun 1000–1400 (Apr–Oct); Mon–Fri 0900–1700 (Nov–Mar). **Provincial:** *blvd de la Sauvinière 77; tel: 04 232 6510,* open Mon–Fri 0830–1730, Sat 0900–1300 (Apr–Sept); Mon–Fri 0830–1700, Sat 0900–1300 (Oct–Mar).

Liège, a 1000-year-old city, was the ancient capital of an independent principality for eight centuries. Although now a large industrial city, it retains some noteworthy churches. Tenth-century **Cathédrale St-Paul** has a fine interior and treasury; **Eglise St-Denis** (St Denis's Church) is remarkable for its 11th–12th-century tower (once part of the city's defences) and

163

16th-century Brabant altarpiece; the octagonal **St-Jean** contains some good sculptures; **St-Jacques** features fine Renaissance windows; and **St-Barthélemy** contains a 12th-century bronze baptismal font that is one of Belgium's greatest treasures. The best museums are **Musée de la Vie Wallonne** (Museum of Walloon Life – in a former monastery, with exhibits of the agriculture and forestry of old industries and local art), **Musée d'Art Religieux et d'Art Mosan** (excellent examples of craftsmanship of the Meuse region) and **Musée de Verre** (glass items, many ancient, from around the world).

## MAASTRICHT

**Station:** 10 mins walk east of the centre. A straight route along *Stationstraat,* cross St-Servaas Bridge and then turn right into *Klein-straat* to the VVV Office.

**Tourist Office: VVV,** *Klein Straat 1; tel: (043) 325 2121.* Open Mon–Sat 0900–1800 (Sept–June); Mon–Sat 0900–1900, Sun 1100–1500 (July–Aug). Also a VVV support point in the station, Mon–Fri 0900–1900, Sat 0900–1700.

Hotel chains in Maastricht include *Bw, GT, Hd, Mc, Nv,* and there are plenty of mid-range independent choices, too. Cheaper options can be found near the station and in the Markt area. **HI: City Hostel,** *Dousberg Park, Dousbergweg 4; tel: (043) 34 66 777,* 4 km from the station. Bus nos 55/56 to *Dousberg,* the last stop, beside a swimming pool (which is free to hostellers). **Campsite: De Dousberg,** *Dousbergweg 102; tel: (043) 34 32 171,* 1 km from the hostel.

**St Servaaskerk** has a 10th-century crypt, a painted latticed ceiling and attractive stained glass. Its treasury reflects the rich patronage of earlier days. The neighbouring **St Janskerk** is a complete contrast, simplicity being the key. The most atmospheric church is the elaborately decorated Romanesque **Onze-Lieve-Vrouwe-Basiliek,** with a statue that is credited with miraculous powers. At **Museumkelder Der-lon,** *Plannstraat 21; tel: (043) 325 2121,* there are *in situ* remnants of Roman Maastricht, while medieval fortifications abound in and around the city, notably at **Fort Sint Pieter. St Petersburg Caves** are the result of centuries of excavation of marl stone. A labyrinth of over 20,000 passages remains. Two sections

are open to the public, with some interesting wall inscriptions. Daily guided tours in English from 30 June–31 Aug. The rocket-shaped **Bonnenfantenmuseum,** *av. Ceramique 250; tel: (043) 329 0190,* is a fascinating structure containing three distinct sections: archaeology, Old Masters and contemporary.

## AACHEN

**Station: Hbf** is at *Reumontstrasse 1; tel:(0241) 143 3422,* about 1 km from the city centre.

**Tourist Offices:** Opposite the **station** at *Bahnhofplatz 4, tel:(0241) 180 2965* and in the **centre** at *Atrium Eliserbrunn, Friedrich Willem Platz, tel: (0241) 180 2960.* Both are open Mon–Fri 0900-1830 and Sat 0900–1300.

**HI** is out of town at *Maria-Theresia Allee 260, tel: (0241) 71101,* bus no. 2 from Elisenbrunn to Brusseler Ring. The nearest campsite is **Camping Prall,** north of the centre at *Wintersberg, tel: (0241) 15 85 02.* Medium priced hotels include **Hotel-Restaurant Forsthaus Schontal,** *Kornelimunsterweg 1, tel: (0241) 60 83 05;* and **Hotel-Restaurant Braun,** *Lutticher Stra 517, tel: (0241) 74535.*

Now important only as a frontier town between Belgium and Germany, Aachen was a great city more than 1000 years ago, when the Emperor Charlemagne the Great enjoyed the thermal springs and made it the capital of his revived empire. His octagonal chapel is now the heart of the **Dom** (Cathedral), built on the site of the imperial palace. Some of the original structure survives and his successors added many embellishments. Charlemagne's gilded tomb is here and the imperial throne, but the latter can only be seen if you join a guided tour.

The **Schatzkammer** (Treasury) is one of Europe's richest, housing priceless objects, including a gold bust of Charlemagne and a jewel-encrusted 10th-century cross. Statues of 50 former Holy Roman Emperors adorn the façade of the 14th-century **Rathaus** (Town Hall), which incorporates two of the original palace towers. Inside are replicas of Charlemagne's crown jewels (the originals are in Vienna).

There is an excellent collection of East European art in the new **Ludwig Foprum fur Internationales Kunst,** *Julicherstr.*

# BRUSSELS–FRANKFURT

The scenery from Brussels to Luxembourg City is a wonderful example of the Ardennes landscape. This unspoilt area of thickly forested hills extends across south-eastern Belgium and Luxembourg. The Grand-Duchy offers really diverse countryside and many lovely towns. This variety is reflected in Luxembourg City, which blends the ultra-modern with a wealth of history. Just across the border is Trier, Germany's oldest city and the birthplace of Karl Marx. The onward journey to Koblenz is through the picturesque wine country of the Moselle valley.

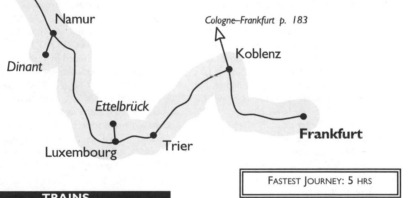

Cologne–Frankfurt p. 183

**165**

FASTEST JOURNEY: 5 HRS

Cologne–Frankfurt p. 183

**ETT tables:** 21, 430, 915, 910.

## FAST TRACK

The quickest journey is via the Brussels–Cologne route (p. 163), 2½–3 hrs. From Cologne good connections are provided by InterCity trains (with dining cars, and supplements payable) to Frankfurt. Cologne to Frankfurt takes just over 2 hrs.

## ON TRACK

### Brussels–Namur–Luxembourg
An hourly service operates between Brussels and Luxembourg with all trains calling at Namur. Brussels (Midi or Nord) to Namur takes 1 hr, Namur to Luxembourg takes 1 hr 50 mins. Extra trains run between Brussels and Namur on Mons to Fris (daily in summer).

### Luxembourg–Trier
Trains run between Luxembourg and Trier every hour with journey times of 40–50 mins.

### Trier–Koblenz
An hourly service links Trier with Koblenz with journey time of 1 hr 20 mins.

### Koblenz–Frankfurt
Hourly *IC* trains operate between Koblenz and Frankfurt taking 1 hr 20 mins.

## NAMUR

**Station:** *tel: (081) 25 21 11,* 3-mins walk north of the centre.
**Tourist Offices:** Municipal: *pl. Léopold* (about 300m from the station); *tel: (081) 24 64 49.*

Open daily 0900–1800, but often closes an hour earlier and for lunch (usually 1230–1300) out of season. They have a free brochure about the province's attractions (including Namur itself) and a worthwhile cheap street map. Provincial: *r. Notre-Dame 3; tel: (081) 22 29 98*. Open Mon–Fri 0900–1200 and 1300–1700.

### SIGHTSEEING

The town is overlooked by a medieval **Citadel**, *tel: (081) 22 68 29*, which began life as a Celtic hill fort (open daily 1 June–30 Sept; weekends and holidays 30 Mar–31 May). You can wander at will around the 15th–19th-century complex, which is on several levels, but the entrance fee covers a mini-train ride, a good video (in French) and a guided walking tour (allow 2–3 hrs for the full tour), the latter taking you through areas of the old fortifications that you could not otherwise see. It's usual to ascend by the cable car and to walk down (follow the road until you see a cannon, then take the steps which start on the right: rougher, but quicker, than following the road). The cable car (which leaves from *Pied-du-Château*) provides stunning views – better than the citadel.

**Musée Archéologique**, *r. du Pont; tel: (081) 23 16 31*, contributes to archaeological explorations in the Meuse Valley and some of the finds are among its exhibits. **Musée de Groesbeeck de Croix**, *r. Joseph Saintraint 3; tel: (081) 22 21 39*, displays mainly 18th-century *objets d'art* from the region and includes period rooms. The 18th-century **Cathédrale St-Aubin** is beautifully proportioned, with half-domes to three sides of the main one, carved wooden confessionals, lots of attractive marble and a main altar surrounded by baroque paintings. Its treasury, **Musée Diocésain**, *pl. du Chapitre; tel: (081) 22 21 64*, is alongside. Some way south of the centre is **Musée de la Forêt**, *rte Merveilleuse 9; tel: (081) 74 38 94*, which is devoted to the Ardennes flora and fauna. **Musée de la Fraise** (Strawberry Museum), *chaussée de Dinant, Wépion*, is housed in what used to be the town hall. This once central spot is now on the outskirts, about 15 mins by bus no. 4 from the current centre.

**Guy Delforge Perfume Workshop**, *Rte Merveilleuse 60, 5000 Namur; tel: (081) 22 12 19*, is unique in Northern Europe, demonstrating the different phases of perfume production.

### OUT OF TOWN

**Station:** *tel: (082) 22 28 60*. South of the river, 5-mins walk from the centre (on the north bank). The ticket office supplies a free map which includes useful information.

**Tourist Office:** *r. Grande 37; tel: (082) 22 28 70, fax: (082) 22 77 85*. Daily 0900–2000.

The tiny town of **Dinant** is very pretty, lining the banks of the River Meuse and overlooked by a towering escarpment. Trains from Namur take less than 30 mins and there are about ten a day. In summer, full-day river excursions from Namur allow you about 2 hrs in Dinant. The main attraction is **Grotte la Merveilleuse**, *tel: (082) 22 22 10*, a beautiful complex of caves full of white stalactites and waterfalls (open 1000–1800). The **Citadel**, *tel: (082) 22 36 70* (reached by cable car) houses an arms museum and a war museum, while **Park Mont-Fat**, *tel: (082) 22 27 83* (reached by chair-lift) is a pleasure ground that incorporates such natural features as a maze of underground passages, prehistoric caves (halfway up the cliff and connected to the tower by underground passages) and hanging gardens. You can obtain a **Dinant Tour** ticket, which covers all these attractions.

## LUXEMBOURG (CITY)

**Station: Gare Centrale**; *tel: 49 24 24*, is about 15-mins walk south of the centre: the 19th-century **pont Passerelle** (Passerelle Viaduct) is a direct route that provides a great view. Leave the station and turn right up *av. de la Gare*, along *Pont Passarelle*, which becomes *blvd F. D. Roosevelt*. Turn right along *r. Chimay* to the Tourist Office. The station is well equipped, even offering showers and baths. The **CFL** office opens daily 0700–2100 and sells phonecards as well as tickets for all transport (credit cards not accepted). You can get any information about trains or long-distance buses here: for city buses, consult the Tourist Office.

### TOURIST INFORMATION

**Tourist Office:** Municipal: *pl. d'Armes; tel: 22 28 09, fax: 47 48 18*, is in the old town and has information only about the city. Open Mon–Sat 0900–1900, Sun and public holidays 1000–1800. The general literature is free. Pick up a street map, a route guide for city buses and *A walk through the green heart of Europe*: two routes that cover everything of interest in the capital.

National: *in the Luxair office* (right as you leave the station); *tel: 48 11 99*, has information about the whole country and books accommodation. Open Mon–Sat 0900–1900, Sun 0900–1200 and 1400–1830 (July–mid Sept); daily 0900–1200 and 1400–1830 (mid Sept–June, except Sun Nov–Mar).

## ARRIVING AND DEPARTING

### Airport
**Luxembourg-Findel**, *tel: 48 11 99*, is 6 km to the east of town. A tourist information and hotel booking desk *(tel. 40 08 08)* opens Mon–Fri 1000–1430 and 1600–1900, Sat 1000–1345, Sun 1000–1430 and 1530–1830. The exchange office opens whenever there are flights. Bus no. 9 connects the airport and the station (about 25 mins; LFr.40). Luxair buses connect with major flights (about 20 mins; LFr.120). A taxi should cost about LFr.600, plus baggage if you have more than one case.

## STAYING IN LUXEMBOURG

### Accommodation
Hotel chains in Luxembourg City include *BW, GT, Ib, IC, Mc, Rk, RS, Sf, Sh* and *Sn*. There's quite a wide range of accommodation, most of the cheaper places being in the area of the station. At the top of the range, the superbly-located **Cravat**, *29 blvd Roosevelt; tel: 22 19 75, fax: 22 67 11*, has décor spanning several decades, retaining old-world charm in the public rooms. For good medium-price accommodation, try the fairly small **Auberge le Châtelet**, *2 blvd de la Pétrusse; tel: 40 21 01, fax: 40 36 66*, in a quiet location within easy reach of the old town. Two good budget options (ignore the seedy area) are: **Bristol**, *11 r. de Strasbourg; tel: 48 58 29* and **Carlton**, *9 r. de Strasbourg; tel: 48 48 02, fax: 48 64 80*.

**HI**: *2 r. du Fort Olisy* (3 km from the station); *tel: 22 68 89, fax: 22 33 60*. Bus no. 9:

*Vallée d'Alzette* (150m from the stop, down a steep hill). If you can't get a small room and object to showering in public, go elsewhere. **Kockelscheuer campsite**, *Rte de Bettembourg 22; tel: 47 18 15*, is south of the centre, 4 km from Centrale and 500m from the no. 2 bus stop. It's a well-equipped site, open Easter–Oct.

### Eating and Drinking
Some of the tacky eating-places in the station area are not noticeably cheaper than the much better middle-range ones in the old centre. *Pl. d'Armes* is full of eateries, with open-air entertainment on most summer evenings. There's a regular food market in *pl. Guillaume* (Wed and Sat 0800–1200).

If you want to treat yourself, **St-Michel**, *32 r. de l'Eau; tel: 22 32 15*, is very expensive, but offers superb cuisine and atmosphere. It's housed in a 16th-century building and stuffed with antiques. Far more modest, but of good standard, is the ever-popular **Club 5**, *5 rue Chimay; tel: 4617 63*. For good local food without breaking the bank, try **EMS**, *30 pl. de la Gare; tel: 48 77 99*, or **Chi Chis**, *13 pl. d'Armes; tel: 46 07 74*.

### Communications
There are two major **post offices**. The one in *pl. de la Gare 38* (in front of the station and to the left as you exit) opens daily 0600–2000, holidays 0800–2000. The one at *25 r. Aldringen (pl. Hamilius)*, opens Mon–Fri 0700–2000, Sat 0700–1900. Both offer an international telephone service.

### Money
The exchange office inside the station opens Mon–Sat 0830–2100, Sun 0900–2100. On the exterior wall of the post office in *pl. de la Gare* there's a Postomat machine (operational 24 hrs a day) which gives cash against credit cards

## SIGHTSEEING
The city of Luxembourg was founded in Roman times and is dramatically sited on a gorge cut by the rivers Alzette and Pétrusse. It falls naturally into three sections: the old centre (north of the Pétrusse gorge and home to most of the sights); the modern city and station

**167**

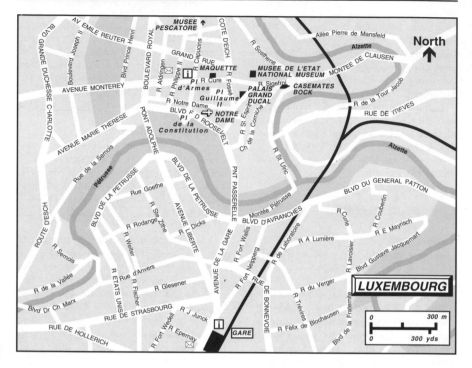

(south of the gorge); and **Grund** (the valley settlement).

As well as conventional conducted tours, you can **Walk with a Walkman** (Apr–Oct) at your own speed or take the **Pétrusse Express** (a misnomer: it's slow-moving) from *pl. de la Constitution*. Both are worthwhile for the commentary alone: a highly dramatised account mingling history and legend, with martial music, cannon fire and sketches. Or see the city by hot air balloon. Contact **Skylines International** in *Junglinster; tel: 78 90 75,* giving at least one days notice. The price includes a champagne toast and a certificate to prove that you completed your inaugural flight.

**Cathédrale Notre-Dame**, a 17th-century Jesuit church, is of mixed architectural styles. Inside the simple stone crypt is the tomb of Duke John the Blind, backed by statues of mourners. Bronze lions flank a gate through which can be seen the burial chapel of the Grand-Ducal family, with its marble floor and mosaic walls. At the other end are stained-glass windows of Christ flanked by the apostles. From

*pl. de la Constitution,* there is access to the **Pétrusse casemates**: underground passages that formed part of the city's original defences. Tours take about 45 mins and you need to be reasonably fit. If you're in any doubt, opt for the similar casemates at **Rocher du Bock**, which are less of a strain. The entrance is on *r. Sigefroi,* the site where Count Siegfried built the original fortress. It was expanded by later rulers, especially the French, who made it one of the most strongly defended cities in 17th-century Europe. There is not much to see inside, but it provides great views.

There are guided tours of the royal residence, the **Palais-Grand-Ducal**, when the Grand Duke is away (usually mid July–early Sept). **Maquette, Rathskeller**, *r. du Curé*, is a small museum showing the fortress-city at various stages of its history, while exhibits in **The National Museum of History and Art**, *Marché-aux-Poissons; tel: 479 3301,* range from the Stone Age to the 20th century (closed Mon; free). **Plateau Kirchberg**, north of the centre (across **Pont Grande-Duchesse-Charlotte,** with spectacular views), is the modern area where you will find the **European Court of Justice** and other EU offices. The **European Parliament** is in the only skyscraper in Luxembourg.

## OUT OF TOWN

About 30 mins by train north of the capital, **Ettelbrück** is the base for visiting (by bus) three of the Grand Duchy's most interesting towns. The nearby **Diekirch** offers a **15th-century church** on Roman foundations, traces of **Celtic habitation** and a museum with well-preserved Gallo-Roman floor mosaics.

Vianden is a noted beauty spot with some charming little churches and a small, but worthwhile, museum that includes dolls. It is dominated by a formidable **5th-century château**, which is far more varied than most such strongholds: the preserved sections cover several periods and these are supplemented by diverse displays. **Echternach** has several minor attractions, but the major draw is undoubtedly the 7th-century **Benedictine Abbey**, founded by St Willibrord, an English missionary monk who was famed for curing epilepsy. One wing of the basilica houses the **Musée de l'Abbaye**, which should not be missed. The major exhibits concern illuminated manuscripts (with many examples) and the techniques involved. Star of the fascinating collection is **Codex Aureus**: the gospels decorated in gold and bound in a superb 10th-century gold cover encrusted with enamel and gems – one of the greatest examples of medieval art still in existence.

## TRIER

**Station: Hbf**, *tel: (0651) 19419.* 10 mins–walk south of Porta Nigra. At least six trains run daily (far more on weekdays); the journey takes 1 hr. **Tourist Office:** behind Porta Nigra; *tel: (0651) 97 80 80, fax: (0651) 44 759.* Mon–Sat 0900–1800/1845, Sun 0800/0900–1300/1530. You can get a city map and a hotel list from machines.

## ACCOMMODATION AND FOOD

**HI:** *Am Moselufer 4; tel: (0651) 29292* (on the other side of Porta Nigra from Hbf, 30 mins walk – or bus nos 2/8 most of the way).

**Campsites:** One is in the **Schloss**, *Monaiserstr.; tel: (0651) 86210* (bus no. 40: *Zewenerstr.).* The other is on the west bank of the Moselle, *Luxembourgerstr. 81; tel: (0651) 86921.* Hotel chains with property in the area: *Rm, Sc.* Medium-priced hotels include **Hotel Haus Marianne**, *Eurener Str. 190a, tel (0651) 80 01 03;* **Pension Fritz Metzen**, *Wolkerstr. 2, tel (0651) 37575.*

## SIGHTSEEING

Trier's history dates back to 16 BC and the city houses impressive Roman and early Christian remains. The enormous, well-preserved **Porta Nigra** (Black Gate – named centuries ago for the dark patina that had already formed over the limestone façade) is the focal point of the town. To the north-east, the rococo **St Paulinus** is one of the town's finest churches. The 11th-century **Dom** (Cathedral) incorporates parts of the original 4th-century church. The **Liebfrauenkirche** (Church of Our Lady – 1235) is a pure Gothic church in the form of a Greek cross that occupies the other part of Constantine's original double-church.

The **Bischöfliches Museum**, *Wind-str.,* has medieval statuary, sacred art, models of the Roman cathedral and Roman frescos. The huge **Konstantin-Basilika**, *Konstantinpl.,* part of the Roman Emperor Constantine's palace, is the largest surviving single-hall structure of the ancient world. **Rheinisches Landesmuseum**, *Ostallee 44* (at the southern end of the pleasant and well-tended **Palastgarten**), contains a truly impressive collection of Roman remains. Close by are the **Kaiserthermen**, the fairly well-preserved Imperial Baths, and the 20,000-seat **Amphitheatre** (c. AD 100).

## OUT OF TOWN

The ride along the serpentine Mosel Valley from Trier to Koblenz is one of Germany's most attractive train journeys. The Mosel is, above all, wine country, and vineyards rise steeply on either bank of the river. Hilltops above the river are studded with castles: those most worth visiting include the **Eltz** castle near Moselkern, the imperial castle at **Cochem**, the **Marienburg** at **Zell**, and the **Landshut** castle at **Bernkastel–Kues**.

169

# BRUSSELS–OSTEND

The journey from Brussels to Ostend is rather dull – an unchanging agricultural vista broken only by various small towns. Yet it is worth taking purely to stop off at either Brugge or Ghent, which are undoubtedly the two loveliest cities in Belgium. The trains serving this route are clean, fast and modern. Each carriage has digital displays above the doors, providing useful information throughout the journey in both French and Flemish.

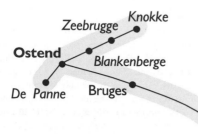

FASTEST JOURNEY: 1 HR 10 MINS

## TRAINS

**ETT tables: 400.**

### FAST TRACK

An hourly service each day, taking 1 hr 10 mins

### ON TRACK

**Brussels–Ghent (Gent)– Bruges (Brugge)**

At least two trains an hour run on this line, with journey times of 30 mins Brussels Midi/Zuid to Ghent and 20–25 mins Ghent to Bruges.

**Bruges–Ostend (Oostende)**

Two trains each hour make the 15-min run.

## GHENT (GENT)

**Station:** The main station is **Gent-St-Pieters**; *tel: (09) 222 44 44,* 2 km south of the centre (tram nos.1/10/11/12: *Korenmarkt*). **De Lijn** bus/tram information is to the left as you exit. **Tourist Offices: Municipal**, *Predikherenlei 2* (in Stadhuis crypt); *tel: (09) 225 36 41 or 226*

*52 32.* Open daily 0930–1830 (Easter–Oct); 0930–1630 (Nov–Easter). **Provincial** (East Flanders), *Woodrow Wilsonplein 3; tel: (09) 267 70 20.* Open Mon–Fri 0830–1200, 1315–1645.

Ghent is a deeply Flemish town, steeped in culture, yet very lively during the university year. For ten days in July, **Gentse Feesten** (traditionally a holiday for factory workers) dominates the town, with lots of cheap food, high beer consumption and street entertainments, as well as a variety of more formal performances.

**Sint-Baafskathedraal** contains an 18th-century marble and wood pulpit, a huge baroque organ, marble statues and ornate guild chapels. Van Eyck's masterpiece *The Adoration of the Mystic Lamb* is concealed behind a screen. The Romanesque **crypt** contains medieval tombs, Romanesque frescos and examples of local stonework. You can ascend the 90-m **belfort** by lift. The 13th-century Flemish-Gothic **St-Niklaaskerk**, *Korenmarkt,* is relatively plain, but bits of early ceiling paintings are partially visible – restoration proved too difficult. The central altar is magnificent. **Gravensteen**, *Sint-Veerleplein; tel: 225 93 06,*

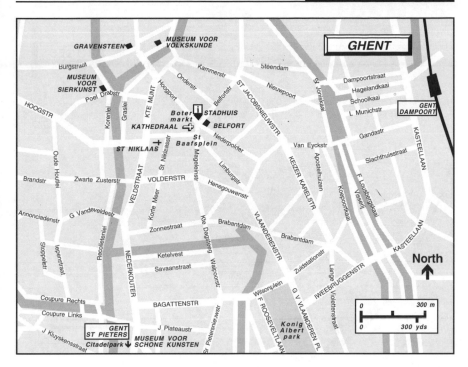

Map of GHENT showing: GRAVENSTEEN, MUSEUM VOOR VOLKSKUNDE, MUSEUM VOOR SIERKUNST, Burgstraat, Kammerstr, Steendam, Dampoortstraat, Hagelandkaai, Schoolkaai, Nieuwpoort, ST JACOBSNIEUWSTR, Onderstr, Hoogport, Belfortstr, St Jorishaai, L Munichstr, GENT DAMPOORT, HOOGSTR, Poel, Drabstr, KTE MUNT, Korenlei, Graslei, Boter markt, STADHUIS, BELFORT, KATHEDRAAL, St Baafsplein, Nederpolder, Van Eyckstr, Gandastr, KASTEELLAAN, ST NIKLAAS, St Niklaasstr, Limburgstr, Apostelhuizen, Slachthuisstraat, Oude Houtlei, Brandstr, Zwarte Zusterstr, VOLDERSTR, Magdeleinstr, Henegouwenstr, KEIZER KARELSTR, F Lousbergskaai, Visserij, Koepoortkaai, Annonciadenstr, G Vandeveldestr, Korte Meer, Kte Dagsteeg, Brabantstr, VLAANDERENSTR, Brabantdam, KASTEELLAAN, Recolletenlei, Zonnestraat, NEDERKOUTER, Iepenstraat, Stoppelstr, Ketelvest, Savaanstraat, Walpoortstr, Zuidstationstr, Lange Violetterstraat, North, Coupure Rechts, Coupure Links, BAGATTENSTR, Wilsonplein, G V VLAANDEREN, IWEEGRUGGENSTR, J Kluyskensstraat, GENT ST PIETERS, J Plateaustr, Citadelpark, MUSEUM VOOR SCHONE KUNSTEN, Pieterснieuwstr, F ROOSEVELTLAAN, Konig Albert park, 0 300 m, 0 300 yds

**171**

the 12th-century 'Castle of the Counts', has a museum that displays a selection of gruesome instruments of torture, with illustrations of how they were used. You can also walk round the ramparts and explore the castle grounds. The **Stadhuis** (Town Hall), *Botermarkt,* offers architectural styles ranging from Gothic to baroque.

In **Museum Voor Sierkunst** (decorative arts museum), *Jan Breydelstraat 5,* you can compare styles from the Gothic era to the present. Exhibits include furniture, glass, ceramics, silver and textiles, all displayed in suitable settings.

Allow plenty of time for the fascinating **Museum Voor Volkskunde** (Museum of Folklore), *Kraanlei 65; tel: 223 13 36,* which spreads through three converted almshouses. It portrays the town's lifestyle at the turn of the century and is crammed with everyday items, from toys to flat irons, hats to hurricane lanterns, as well as tableaux of various craftsmen. Situated in Citadelpark, **Museum voor Schone Kunsten** (Museum of Fine Arts), *Nicolaas de Liemaeckereplein 3; tel: 222 17 03,* contains an impressive collection of ancient and

modern art in all fields from all over Europe, although the emphasis is on Flemish paintings.

Carriage trips through the city can be made during summer holidays, weekends and public holidays, 1000–1800 (Easter–Oct). Depart from *Baafsplein.*

## BRUGES (BRUGGE)

**Station:** *tel: (050) 38 23 82,* 20 mins walk south of the centre; open 0630–2200. Buses stop in front of the station: get tickets and a free route map from the **De Lijn** kiosk (Mon–Fri 0730–1800, Sat 0900–1800, Sun 1000–1800). To the right as you leave the station is a branch of the **Tourist Office**, open Mon–Sat 1445–2100 (Mar–Oct); Mon–Sat 1345–2000 (Nov–Mar), which offers a full service.

**Tourist Office: Municipal**, *Burg 11; tel: (050) 44 86 86.* Open Mon–Fri 0930–1830, Sat–Sun 1000–1200, 1400–1830 (Apr–Sept); Mon–Fri 0930–1700, Sat 0930–1245, 1400–1700 (Oct–Mar). **Provincial (West Flanders):** *Kasteel Tillegem; tel: (050) 38 02 96,* open Mon–Fri 0830–1200, 1315-1645. *Brugge* (BFr.20), a

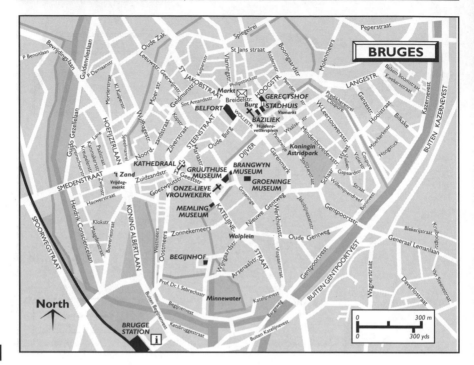

comprehensive brochure (in several languages), includes walks and a map. The monthly *Agenda Brugge* (free) details local events.

### ACCOMMODATION

Accommodation of all types is available, but book ahead. Hotel chains: *BW, GT, Hd, Ib, Nv, RS, RC, Rk, Sf, SL, Sn.* **HI: Europa**, *Assebroek, Baron Ruzettelaan 143; tel: (050) 35 26 79,* is about 1.5 km east of the station (2 km south of *Markt); bus no. 2 stops* 100m away: *Wantestraat.* A friendly place in its own grounds. For the centre (or the station), wait at the stop for bus no.2, but board no. 1. Among the private hostels is **Bauhaus**, *Langestraat 135; tel: (050) 34 10 93* (bus nos. 6/16: *Kruispoort):* good value and the bar is popular locally. **Campsite: St-Michiel**, *Tillegemstraat 55; tel: (050) 38 08 19,* 3 km south-west of the station (bus no. 7).

### SIGHTSEEING

A boat trip on the extensive canal system is a good introduction to the town, with frequent departures from quays along *Dijver.* After that,

explore on foot: most places of interest are in a small area around *Markt* and *Burg.* The Tourist Office has an English Walkman guide.

**Markt**, Bruges main square, is surrounded by guild buildings. **Belfort**, an octagonal 88-m belfry, is mainly 13th-century, but the top storey was added in the 15th century. There are 366 steps to the top, and regular concerts take place on the 47-bell carillon (including Sun 1415 all year). **Burg**, the other main square, features monumental buildings spanning several centuries. Don't miss **Baziliek van Het Heilig Bloed** (Basilica of the Holy Blood). At ground level there's an atmospheric early 12th-century stone chapel. Upstairs is a magnificent 16th-century chapel; the side chapel contains a marble altar with a silver-gilt tabernacle, behind which is kept a drop of Christ's blood. Every Ascension Day this is paraded through the streets in a magnificent 1617 shrine: a gloriously elaborate affair of jewel-encrusted gold and silver that's among the items in the treasury. Other buildings around the square include Renaissance **Civiele Griffie** (recorder's house) and the neo-classical **Gerectshof** (Court of Justice), which contains **Provinciaal Museum Het Brugse Vrije**, worth visiting for the Renaissance chimney-piece (1529). Gothic **Stadhuis** (Town Hall) has a magnificent hall with a polychrome vaulted ceiling and historic murals.

**Dijver** is the central canal; *Dijverstraat* (scene of a weekend antiques and flea market) is home to several museums. **Groeningemuseum** houses a fine collection of Flemish art from the 15th century to date, notably Primitive and Expressionist. **Gruuthusemuseum**, on the opposite side of the street, was a 16th-century palace and the décor reflects that time. **Room 17** looks into Onze-Lieve (see below): the king attended services without leaving home. The diverse exhibits include a guillotine, musical instruments and spinning wheels. **Brangwyn Museum** is noted for its collection of lace, among other items. **Onze-Lieve Vrouwekerk** (Church of Our Lady), *Mariastraat,* has Belgium's highest spire (122m). Among its treasures are a beautiful white marble *Madonna and Child* by Michelangelo, impressive royal mausoleums and humbler 13th–14th-century painted tombs. Across the road is **St-Janshospitaal**, *Mariastraat 38,* which dates back to the Middle Ages and served as a hospital until 1976. **Memling Musuem** is housed there and has six masterpieces by Hans Memling on display. Not far away, the **Kathedraal St-Salvator**, *Zuidzandst.,* contains Gobelin tapestries, a rood-loft organ, 15th-century carved stalls and a Louis XVI-style pulpit. Your visit would not be complete without a walk around the **Begijnhof** and the **Minnewater**. In the Begijnhof, the houses where the *béguines* lived are neatly arranged around a tranquil lake. The lake is home to swans, which, legend has it, Maximillian of Austria demanded the residents of Bruges look after.

### OUT OF TOWN

**Quasimodo Tours**, *Poortersstraat 47; tel: (050) 37 04 70, fax: (050) 37 49 60,* run an English-language day-trip in a minibus, which includes **Damme**, two **castles**, **Zeebrugge harbour**, sampling a waffle, a visit to **Chocolate World** and a guided tour of a brewery and beer tasting. Departs Mon, Wed and Fri. Pick-ups at various hotels or the rail station. The same company also organises a World War I battlefield tour.

## OSTEND (OOSTENDE)

**Station:** *tel: (059) 70 08 81.* The ferries and trains share a building, 10 mins walk from the Tourist Office (or bus no. 5). Baggage can be checked an hour before vessels leave.

**Tourist Office:** *Monacoplein 2; tel: (059) 70 11 99.* Open Mon–Sat 0900–1900, Sun 1000–1900 (June–Sept); Mon–Sat 1000–1800, Sun 1100–1800 (Oct–May): walk right from the station and along the sea front, then take the last turning left before the front curves. Purchase the *A–Z* brochure (BFr.10) and town map (BFr.5). The hotel brochure is free if you book from it. *Oostende Events* is a free annual listing.

The three-master **Mercator**, a training vessel in authentic style, now houses a maritime museum. **Noordzeeaquarium** (on the front) displays the flora and fauna of the North Sea. The studio where the Expressionist James Ensor worked has become a museum devoted to him: **James Ensorhuis**, *Vlaanderenstraat 27,* and many of his possessions are among the exhibits in **Museum voor Schone Kunsten** (Fine Arts Museum), *Cultuurpaleis, Wapenplein.* **PMMK (Museum voor Moderne Kunst)** (Modern Art Museum), *Romestraat 11,* contains modern paintings and sculptures.

### ⤴ SIDE TRACK FROM OSTEND

The **De Lijn Coastal Tram** can be boarded by the station. It runs the length of the coast (75 km), with Ostend in the middle of the route. Several of the (13) resorts are quiet, providing little other than watersports. Others, notably **Blankenberge** and **Knokke**, are sizeable towns. Ostend Tourist Office has a free brochure about the resorts. Every type of accommodation is available, from four-star hotels to campsites. Special tickets are available, combining visits to tourist attractions with a trip on the tram. The ticket means you don't have to queue at the attraction. A brochure is available from all 34 tram stops or from the De Lijn Office in Ostend; *tel: (059) 56 53 53.* ⤴

# BUDAPEST

Despite the damage wrought by floods, World War II and the 1956 Russian invasion, Budapest has survived as a remarkable, friendly and energetic city, split by the grey-green Danube and rich with 19th-century architecture. Historically, Budapest is not one, or even two, cities but three – the old Roman city of Óbuda (then Aquincum), the later replacement Buda established on Várhegy and the thriving commercial centre of Pest, which only formally joined the others in 1872. Today, Budapest is rightfully enjoying a renaissance. It's also an ideal location for an indulgent break, thanks to its many spas, excellent cuisine and thriving cultural life.

## TOURIST INFORMATION

The **Tourinform** tourist bureaux, located throughout Hungary, are an excellent source of information. **Tourinform**, *Sütő út 2; tel: 117 9800* (metró: *Deák tér*) are very helpful with multilingual staff (daily 0800–2000 Apr–Oct, 0800–1500 Nov–Mar). **Budapest Tourist Office** has a branch at Nyugati railway station (0800–2000; *tel: 332 0597).*

**Ibusz**, the former state-run Hungarian travel company, book accommodation and organise tours. The branch at *Vigadó út 6; tel: 118 6466,* is open Mon–Fri 0900–1700 and serves as the **Thomas Cook** office. The central office at *Petőfi tér 3; tel: 118 5707 or 118 4842* (metró: *Deák tér* or *Ferenciek tere)* is open 24 hours. In addition, there are branches at **Ferihegy Airport** (open 0700–2100), the **International Pier** (0700–2100) and at the three stations: **Nyugati**, *tel: 112 3615;* **Keleti**, *tel: 122 5429* and **Déli**, *tel: 155 2133* (0800–1800/2000).

## ARRIVING AND DEPARTING

### Airport
**Ferihegy** airport has two terminals: Terminal I, some 15 km from Budapest, and Terminal II, 21 km south-east of Budapest. Most airlines use Terminal 1 *(tel: 157 7155 or 296 7155),* whilst **Malév** (Hungarian Airlines, *tel: 267 4505)* plus a few others use Terminal 2 *(tel: 296 8000).* Airport personnel are helpful to the disabled traveller, even sending a bus with a low step to the aeroplane. For the centre, there's an extortionate taxi service or the cheap no. 93 bus (every 30 mins 0530–2100; Ft500) outside both terminal buildings for *Erzsébet tér.* Some hotels have collection services. There's also an airport minibus service which takes visitors directly to their destination; *tel: 296 8555;* Ft1000.

### Stations
There are three major stations in Budapest. **Nyugati Pályaudvar** (Western Station), *Nyugati tér; tel: 149 0115,* is a Budapest monument, designed in 1877 by the Eiffel firm from Paris (Tourist Office; **Ibusz**, *tel: 112 3615;* accommodation; exchange). **Keleti Pályaudvar** (Eastern Station), *Baross tér; tel: 113 6835,* undergoing renovation, is bustling (**Ibusz**, *tel: 122 5429; Hellas Express* car-train to Thessaloniki Tues and Fri 1 June–28 Oct; accommodation; exchange; K&H Bank Mon–Fri 0815–1800, Sat 0900–1600; left luggage: Ft3x50, 24 hrs). **Déli Pályaudvar** (Southern Station); *Krisztina körút; tel: 175 6293,* is modern and uninspiring (**Ibusz**, *tel: 155 2133;* electronic information system; post office with exchange services; accommodation; exchange).

Most international trains depart from Keleti but exceptions can occur. All three stations are fairly central, close to hotels and on the metro: Keleti and Déli on line 2, Nyugati on line 3, trams 4 and 6. International services, *tel: 342 9150,* international fares, *tel: 122 8035,* local train information, *tel: 322 7860.* Rail tickets

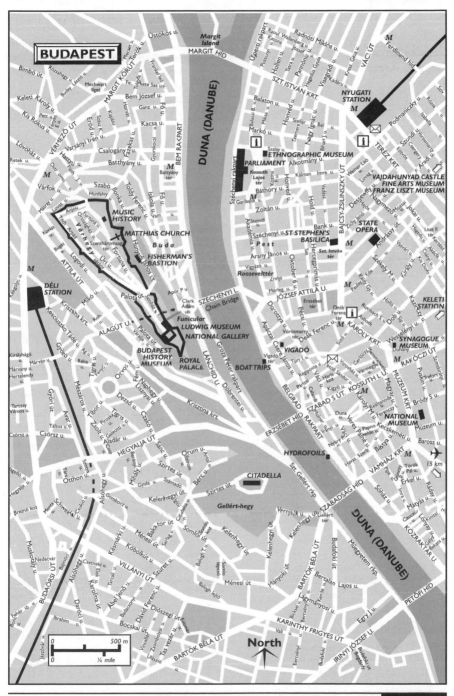

BUDAPEST

Margit Island
MARGIT HID

NYUGATI STATION

ETHNOGRAPHIC MUSEUM
PARLIAMENT
Kossuth Lajos tér

VAJDAHUNYAD CASTLE
FINE ARTS MUSEUM
FRANZ LISZT MUSEUM

STATE OPERA

MUSIC HISTORY

MATTHIAS CHURCH

*Buda*

FISHERMAN'S BASTION

*Pest*

ST STEPHEN'S BASILICA

Rooseveltter

DÉLI STATION

KELETI STATION

SZÉCHENYI L. Chain Bridge
Funicular
LUDWIG MUSEUM
NATIONAL GALLERY

VIGADÓ

BUDAPEST HISTORY MUSEUM

ROYAL PALACE

BOAT TRIPS

SYNAGOGUE MUSEUM

NATIONAL MUSEUM

CITADELLA

*Gellért-hegy*

HYDROFOILS

DUNA (DANUBE)

DUNA (DANUBE)

PETŐFI HID

0    500 m
0    ¼ mile

North

can also be bought from the **MÁV** offices, *Andrássy út 35;* Mon–Fri 0900–1700. A rail-bus service runs between the stations, *tel: 153 2722.*

### GETTING AROUND

Budapest is easy to explore if you have a street and transport guide, available from metro ticket kiosks or Tourinform. The Danube runs north to south, with the Buda hills to the west and Pest to the east. There are 22 districts indicated by Roman numerals, which appear in addresses and on maps. Buda has 6, Pest 15 and there is one on **Csepel** island in the south. Fashionable **Várhegy** (Castle Hill) is classified as district I.

Budapest rewards exploration on foot, but many sights are fairly far apart. The public transport system is first class and speedy, especially after the refurbishment of the metro tunnels. Night lines run 2300–0500 on the most popular routes. There are also 82 km of cycle lanes. The **Budapest card**, widely issued, allows free travel, admission and reductions to more than 80 sights over 3 days (Ft 2900). Public transport information, *tel: 201 9408.*

### 176

### Metro (Subway)

The metro service is fast and inexpensive and runs between 0430–2310. As there are only three lines, it is easy to use. All lines intersect at *Deák tér.* Line M1 was the first continental metro, built in 1896 and recently restored. It runs just below *Andrássy út* (the original carriages can be seen at *Deák tér* metro). **Tickets** are available from kiosks in stations or from machines requiring exact change. All tickets must be punched: on line M1 this is done on board, but on lines M2 and M3 they must be stamped in the machines at the station entrance. Tickets are non-transferable, so if you change line you need a new ticket. A one-ride fare is Ft 60 and a transfer Ft 100. One-day (Ft 500) and three-day (Ft 1000) travel passes are available, as are ten-day packs of tickets for the price of nine (Ft 540). For visitors staying longer, consider weekly (Ft 1230), 14-day (Ft 1640) and monthly passes (Ft 2460, photo required).

### Buses, Trams and Suburban Trains

For areas not on the metro, the bus, trolley bus and tram system is very useful as it covers the city extensively. A similar method for ticket stamping exists, with machines on board. Ticket inspectors wear red arm bands, ignore excuses and fine Ft 800 on the spot. The suburban network of **HÉV** trains travel several kilometres out of the city boundary as well as embracing the ruins of Aquincum and the old town of Óbuda. Maps available at the metro stations cover all suburban routes.

### Taxis

Taxis abound, so it is not difficult to find one even in high season or the pouring rain. Remember to check that the meter is running, have the address of where you are going written down and negotiate the fare before setting off. This should prevent disagreements upon arrival. Taxis are forbidden in the castle area. Reputable firms include: **City Taxi**, *tel: 211 1111,* and **Fő Taxi**, *tel: 222 2222.*

### STAYING IN BUDAPEST

### Accommodation

The city offers a wide choice of one- to five-star hotels, pensions and hostels. (In summer the heat can be extreme, so air-conditioned rooms are advisable.) Advance booking is strongly recommended, particularly in early August during the Hungarian Grand Prix. Spa hotels generally offer very competitive weekend packages.

Expensive: the **Aquincum**, *1036 Budapest III, Árpád fejedelem útja 94; tel: 250 3360,* has superb facilities, including a spa. The **Thermal Hotel Helia**, *1133 Budapest XIII, Kárpát út 62–64; tel: 270 3277,* also a spa, is luxurious. The art nouveau **Gellért**, *1111 Budapest, Gellért tér 1; tel: 185 2200,* has thermal baths, one with a wave machine. The **Danubius Hotel Margitsziget**, *Margitsziget 1138; tel: 3111 000,* is an elegant oasis on Margaret Island.

Medium: **Hotel Tanne**, *2092 Budapest, Esze Tamás utca 6; tel: 176 6144,* in the Buda Hills, is attractive and comfortable. **Buda Center**, *1027 Budapest, Csalogány u. 23; tel: 201 6333,* is basic but has air conditioning and is ideally located below Castle Hill. The immaculate **Alba**, *1011 Budapest, Apor Peter utca 3; tel: 175 9244,* is smart and efficient.

Cheap: Inside the Royal Palace, **Hotel**

**Kulturinov**, *Szentháromság tér 6; tel: 155 0122,* is spartan but inexpensive. **Hotel Citadella**, *1118 Budapest, Citadella sétány; tel: 166 5794,* is perched on Géllert Hill. The old-fashioned **Délibáb**, *1062 Budapest, Délibáb utca 35; tel: 342 9301,* is a stone's throw from City Park.

Chain hotels include *BW, Fe, Fm, Hn,Hy, Ib, Ke, Ma, Mc, Nv* and *Rd*.

**Private rooms** are less expensive than hotels. Rooms are usually a few stops away from the centre of town. These, as well as hotel and pension accommodation, are bookable at **Tourinform** and **Ibusz**. Outside the main offices and at railway stations, you may well find people offering private accommodation. It is advisable to check this out before booking, although it will usually be safe and clean as the Hungarians are excellent hosts.

**Youth hostel and student accommodation** is plentiful. Hostel organisations advertise widely at the stations and often offer free transport to hostels. **Youth Way – Hostelling International**, *Keleti station* and *Dózsa Gyorgy út 152; tel: 129 8644* or *140 8585,* daily 0700–2200, provides university dormitory accommodation. The **Hungarian Youth Hostel Federation**, *Konkoly Thege 21; tel: 156 2857,* has a list of hostels. The youth travel service **Express** is at *Szabadság tér 16.*

**Camping** is mainly limited to the Buda hills, accessible by bus (listed in tourist information leaflets). Camping at unregistered sites is forbidden.

### Eating and Drinking

Rich, spicy and meat- or fish-based, Hungarian cuisine is delicious. Cold fruit soups make wonderful starters, followed by game, goose, pike-perch or pork dishes, goulash soup or paprika chicken, washed down with sour cherry juice, palinka spirit or *Tokaji aszú* wine.

Expensive: **Gundel**, *Állatkerti út 2; tel: 122 1002,* is Budapest's top restaurant; **Kis Buda Gyöngye**, *Kenyeres utca 34; tel: 168 6402;* **Kacsa**, *Fő u. 75; tel: 201 9992,* has superb duck specialities. Medium: **Bagolyvár**, *Állatkerti körút 2; tel: 121 3550, ext. 222,* families welcome; **Kispipa vendéglő**, *Akácfa u. 38; tel: 142 2587,* closed Aug, good value set menus; **Jardin de Paris**, *Fő utca 20; tel: 201 0047,* for French cuisine. Cheap: **Govinda**, *Belgrád rakpart 18; tel: 118 1144,* for vegetarian food; **Szlovák söröző**, *Bihari János u. 17; tel: 269 3108;* **Csarnok vendéglő**, *Hold u. 11; tel: 269 2906,* for traditional fare; **Horgásztanya vendéglő**, *Fő u. 27; tel: 212 3780,* for fish.

Budapest's elegant coffee houses offer irresistible cakes, pastries and marzipans. Try **Múzeum Kávéház**, *Múzeum körút 12; tel: 138 4221;* **Angelika**, *Batthyányi tér 7; tel: 2014 847;* **Gerbeaud**, *Vörösmarty tér 7; tel: 118 1311;* **Ruszwurm cafe**, *Szentháromság utca 7;* and **New York**, *Erzsébet körút 9–11.*

### Communications

**Main telephone office:** *Petőfi Sándor út 17–19; tel: 117-5500,* Mon–Fri 0800–2000, Sat–Sun 0900–1500. The main **post office** is next door. There are 24-hr post offices near Nyugati, *Teréz körút 51,* and Keleti stations, *Baross tér 11/c.* The dialling code for Budapest is *1.*

### Embassies

**Australia:** *Királyhágó tér 8–9; tel: 214 1489.* **Canada:** *Budakeszi út 32; tel: 275 1200.* **New Zealand (Consulate):** *Teréz krt 38; tel: 131 4908.* **Republic of Ireland:** *Szabadság tér 7–9; tel: 302 9600.* **South Africa:** *Rákóczi út 1–3; tel: 267 4566.* **UK:** *Harmincad út 6; tel: 118 2888.* **USA:** *Szabadság tér 12; tel: 112 6450.*

### Money

Only change currency in official places such as banks (**Mezőbank**, *Bajcsy-Zs. út 74; tel: 131 6358*).

### SHOPPING

The main shopping streets are *Váci utca* for boutiques, including folk art and black ceramics at *Váci utca 14, Petőfi Sándor utca* and *Andrássy utca.* Best buys include records and CDs, Zsolnay and Herend porcelain *(Szentháromság u. 5),* and glass, antiques, wine, Pick and Herz salami and leather. Try the **Wine Society**, *Batthyányi u. 59* (Mon–Fri 1000–2000, Sat 1000–1800) and the **Hungarian Wine Shop**, *Régiposta utca 7–9.* Markets abound, some open air, others flea markets *(Nagykőrösi út 156).*

## ENTERTAINMENT

There is always plenty for all tastes in Budapest. Check monthly listings guides and English-language newspapers, such as the *Budapest Sun* for the latest information.

Music has always been popular in Hungary. The stunning neo-renaissance **Opera House**, *Andrássy út 22; tel 131 2550*, now 112 years old, was the first modern theatre in the world (Sat–Sun 1300–1500). **Operetta**, too, has its place, and the less ornate building at *Vigadó u. 2; tel: 117 0869*, is usually packed for patriotic programmes of light music. Seats are not reservable, so arrive in good time. **Organ recitals** are often given at **Matthias Church**, *Várhegy*, and at **St Stephen's Basilica**. The **Academy of Music**, *Liszt Ferenc tér 8; tel: 142 0179*, and the **Vigado Concert Hall**, *Vigadó tér 2; tel: 118 9903*, frequently host classical concerts.

There are many **cinemas**, often showing English-language films. **Pubs** are to be found all over the city; the **nightclubs** in the red-light area in district VII, are only for the extremely broad-minded.

## Spas

Budapest boasts ten spas, offering mixed and segregated bathing, endless treatments and often stunning architecture at affordable prices. The art nouveau **Gellért** has a much-photographed 'champagne' bath, *Kelenhegyi út 2–4; tel: 185 3555*. The **Rudas Baths**, *Döbrentei tér 9; tel: 156 1322*, the **Rác Baths**, *Hadnagy utca 8-10; tel: 156 1322*, and the **Császár Baths**, *Árpád fejedelem útja 7; tel: 212 4133*, are Turkish in origin or style.

The **Király Baths**, *Fő utca 84; tel: 202 3688*, were built in the 16th century – their green cupulas are another reminder of the Turkish occupation. The golden **Lukács Baths**, *Frankel Leó út 25; tel: 212 4133*, were constructed in the 19th century.

Hotels **Thermal**, *Margit Island; tel: 111 1000*, **Helia**, *Kárpát utca 62–4; tel: 270 3277*, and **Aquincum**, *Árpád fejedelem útja 94; tel: 250 3360*, are all modern spa hotels, whereas the charming **Széchenyi Baths**, *Állatkerti körút 11; tel: 121 0310*, are neo-baroque, within City Park. For further details, *tel: 117 8992* at Tourinform.

## SIGHTSEEING

### Buda

The Buda hills offer marvellous views of the city and the Danube. To the west lie woods and paths, circumnavigated by a cogwheel railway from *Városmajor* to *Széchenyi* hill. There is also a chair lift *(Libegő)* between *Zugliget* and János hill (0930–1700 16 May–15 Sept, 0930–1600 16 Sept–15 May), and a 12-km narrow-gauge Children's Railway (0900–1600 Apr–Sept). On **Gellért-hegy** (Gellért Hill), surveying the city and the Royal Palace, is the gigantic **Liberation Monument**, which commemorates the Soviet liberation of Budapest (bus 27 or 127). **Várhegy** (Castle Hill) was first built in the 13th century and is perhaps the most historic and important feature in Budapest; its streets have retained their medieval form. **Buda Palace** *(Budavári Palota)* was originally built as part of the fortifications of the city during the Middle Ages and remained a royal residence for 700 years. It was re-designed during the Renaissance and reconstructed during the Hapsburg era. The Nazis occupied the Palace during World War II before it was almost destroyed by the Soviets. Yet again it was rebuilt, but only the foundations and the ramparts remain. There are three museums in the palace: **Budapest History Museum**, **Museum of Contemporary History** and **Hungarian National Gallery** (Tues–Sun 1000–1800, free concerts every Tues). Walk up the hill from *Déli* or *Moskva* metro stations, or catch the *Budavári Sikló* funicular (0730–2200 daily, Ft 150) from *Clark Ádám tér* at the foot of the Chain Bridge. There is also a shuttle bus service from *Moszkva tér*. It's possible to visit the **Castle caverns** at the corner of *Dárda* and *Országház út* (open daily).

**Fisherman's Bastion** *(Halász bástya)* is neo-roman with a magnificent roof, presenting a perfect river panorama. It was here, legend has it, that the fishermen defended their city during the Middle Ages, or perhaps just sold their catch. The square is always filled with tourists, especially during public holidays, when it is awash with street entertainers and market stalls.

The statue to **St Stephen (Szent István)**, legendary King of Hungary, is overlooked by the neo-gothic **Matthias Church**, *Mátyás Templom* (0700–2000 daily), the coronation church of Hungarian kings. Here lies the tomb of King Béla III. The church was originally built in the 13th century but much-extended during the early 20th century. During Ottoman domination it was used as a mosque. The surrounding streets are cobbled, below fine baroque and Gothic buildings and façades. It's worth wandering down *Táncsics Mihály utca, Tárnok utca, Tóth Árpád sétány* and *Úri utca* to explore the district further.

Still in Buda, visit the picturesque **Margit Island** *(Margit-sziget)*. Vehicles are only allowed as far as the Thermal and Grand hotels; the miles of walks along the river are delightful. It's named after Princess Margaret, daughter of King Béla IV, who lived on the island, as had the Roman nobility before her. It's now full of rose gardens, pools and picnicking families, plus a Japanese garden, open-air theatre, cinema and two 13th-century ruins (tram 1, 4, 6 or bus 26). Up in the Buda Hills, visit some of the **hill caves**, such as **Pálvölgyi barlang** (bus 65 from *Kolosy ter,* open year-round), or **Szemlőhegyi barlang** (bus 29 from *Kolosy tér,* Wed–Mon 0900–1600). Far to the south, a new **Statue Park**, *Szoborpark, Balatoni ut* (daily 1000–sunset) is choc-full of statues and monuments from the Socialist period.

### Obuda

Further north is **Óbuda** (Old Buda). Its Roman remains recall **Aquincum**, a spa and fortified town during the 2nd and 3rd centuries AD – remnants of the forum, baths and amphitheatre are still visible. There's also a museum, *Szentendre út 139* (open daily 1000–1800). HÉV stations *Aquincum* and *Római-Fürdő.*

### Pest

This is the busy commercial sector, built in two semi-circular avenues with broad tree-lined boulevards radiating from it, and home to the elegant shopping street **Váci utca**, and the street cafés of **Vörösmarty tér**, the artists' hang-out. The imposing **Parliament**, *Kossuth Lajos tér,* has a richly ornate interior and was built in 1904. It can be visited by pre-arranged guided tour (book through the Tourist Office).

The **National Museum**, *14–18 Múzeum körút*, has what is believed to be the coronation regalia of St Stephen amongst other remains of Hungary's chequered history (open Tues–Sun 1000–1800). The 19th-century **St Stephen's Bazilica**, *Szent István tér* (Mon–Sat 0630–1900, Sun 0700–1900) is Budapest's largest church, containing the mummified right hand of its saint. The **Central Synagogue**, *Dohány utca 2–8* (Mon–Fri 1000–1500, Sun 1000–1300), built in 1867, is the second largest in the world, holding 3000 people, and forms a considerable chunk of the small Jewish quarter. Note the metal weeping-willow memorial to Hungarian Jewish martyrs. The **Jewish Museum** *(Zsidó Múzeum)* is at *Dohány utca 2* (Mon 1400–1800, Sun, Tues–Fri 1000–1300).

One thousand years of Hungarian existence are commemorated by statues of rulers and princes in the **Millenary Monument** in *Hősök tere* (Heroes' Square). This opens onto leafy **City Park** *(Városliget),* with its zoo, boating lake-cum-ice-rink and the romantic **Vajdahundyad vára** *(Vajdahunyad castle)* replicating sites from pre-Trianon Hungary and built at the end of the 19th century. Don't miss **Andrássy út**, Budapest's most famous avenue, home of the **Opera House** (tram 22). Close by is the **Liszt Museum**, *35 Vörösmarty utca* (open Mon–Fri 1000–1800, Sat 0900–1700), where the composer lived. There are also museums to the Hungarian composers, Bartók and Kodály.

### Along the Danube

**Legenda**, *Vigadó tér; tel: 117-2203* (Ft 2500), offer river cruises, including a video commentary and champagne. Boats leave Budapest for the charming town of **Szentendre** and follow the Danube bend to **Visegrád** and **Esztergom**. **Mahart tours**, *International Boat Station, Belgrád rakpart; tel: 118 1704*, run hydrofoils to **Vienna** and **Bratislava**. **Elizabeth Bridge**, named after the Empress Sisi, was rebuilt 1961–64 after the original's destruction in World War II, as was the **Liberty Bridge**. **Petőfi Bridge** has been modernised three times, latterly in 1980. The distinctive **Széchenyi Chain Bridge** was designed by Scottish engineer William Tierney and built by fellow Scot Adam Clark between 1839–49.

**179**

# COLOGNE (KÖLN)

Modern Cologne straddles the Rhine, and throughout history the city owed its prosperity to the river trade. Cologne has several claims to fame: among these, it is home to one of the world's greatest cathedrals and the place where eau de Cologne originated.

## TOURIST INFORMATION

**Tourist Office:** *Unter Fettenhennen 19; tel: (221) 221 3345, fax: (221) 33 20,* by the Dom. Mon, Tues, Thur 0830–1600, Wed 0830–1500 and Fri 0830–1200. A variety of free literature.

## ARRIVING AND DEPARTING

### Airport
**Flughafen Köln-Bonn,** south-east of the city. Information *tel: (02203) 40401/402222.* Bus no. 170 connects the airport with the Hbf in 20 mins, running every 15 mins 0700–2000 (every 30 mins earlier and later), fare DM7.70.

### Station
**Hauptbahnhof,** *tel: (0221) 19419,* is very central, just beside the cathedral (Dom). Cologne has a long railway history, and its Hbf has the distinction of being the busiest railway junction in Germany. There is an information desk and a 24-hr service point. The station closes between 0100–0400. Facilities include a coffee shop, snack bar and left luggage.

## GETTING AROUND

The city centre and the major sights are on the river's west bank. Three bridges link the centre with the east bank: from north to south, the Hohenzollernbrücke, which carries the railway line; Deutzer Brücke; and Severinsbrücke. The comprehensive public transport system includes U-Bahn (underground/subway), S-Bahn (surface suburban trains), trams and buses. A 3-day ticket costs DM20, and a 24-hr ticket DM10.

## STAYING IN COLOGNE

### Accommodation
Central rooms are almost always at a premium and the cheap hotels are very scattered. The Tourist Office may be able to help, but it's possible nothing will be available if you don't book ahead. The Tourist Office has a separate advance booking number, *tel/fax: (221) 33 20.* Hotel chains include *BW, Cn, Ex, GT, Hy, Ib, IC, Mc, Nv, Pu, Rm, Sn,* and *Tp.* Other hotels, all medium-priced, include **Hotel Esser Minotel**, *An der Malzmuhle 4-8, tel: (0221) 234141;* **Hotel Amsterdam**, *Vasulast. 4–8; tel: 1360 77791;* **Brandenburgerhof**, *Brandenburgerst. 2–4 tel: 12 28 89;* and **Gasthaus Zum Krutsche**, *Am Frankenturm 1-3, tel: (0221) 21 14 32.* The more central of the two **HI** hostels is *Siegesstr. 5A; tel: (0221) 081 47 11,* 15-mins walk from Hbf, over the Hohenzollernbrücke, a couple of blocks south of Deutz station. A second HI is at *Köln-Riehl, Ander Schanz 14, tel: (0221) 76 70 81.* The most accessible **campsite** is **Weidenweg**, *Poll; tel: (0221) 0 83 19 66,* south-east of *Altstadt* (tram 16: *Marienburg*).

### Eating and Drinking
Balanced between the beer-drinking north and the wine lands of the south, Cologne has the best of both worlds, with plenty of inns specialising in the wines of the Rhineland and the Mosel. Most are in the *Altstadt* area and all are worth a visit. There is a vast range of restaurants and bars, from an English pub (**The Tudor Pub**, *Huemarkt, Eche Galzgasse; tel: 257 78 91*) to Brazilian restaurants, such as **Viva Brazil**, *Kyffhäusserstr. 5; tel: 23 5014.* Cologne claims to have more breweries than any other city in the world (24, all producing the distinctive local beer, *kolsch*). To sample Cologne's famous beers in the right atmosphere, try **Alt Köln**, *Trankgasse; tel: 13 46 78* (near the Cathedral); **Cölner Hofbräu P.J. Fruh**, *12 Am Hof;* **Brauhaus Sion**, *5–7 Unter Taschenmacher;* **Zur Malzmuhle**, *6 Am Heumarkt; tel: 257 85 40;*

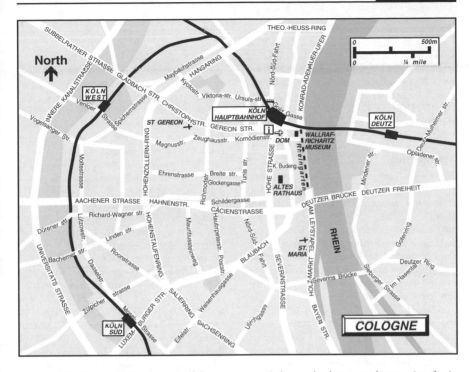

**Brauerei Paffgen**, *64 Friesenstr.*; **Gaffelhaus**, *Alter Markt*. Wine houses in the centre include **Im Stapelhauschen**, *1–3 Fischmarkt* and **Im Walfisch**, *13 Salzgasse*. **Café Reichard**, *11 Unter Fettenhennen; tel: 257 85 42* (opposite the Dom) is in a splendid neo-Gothic building.

## Communications
**Main post office:** at the Hbf, open 0700–2200 for mail and international phone calls.

## Money
**Thomas Cook foreign exchange:** *Im Metro Markt, Otto-Hahn-Str.; tel: 2236 942424; Komoedienstr. 7; tel: (0221) 202080; City-Center Chorweiler, Mailuender Passage 1; tel: (0221) 9700 300.*

### ENTERTAINMENT

Providing not only its own nightlife but also catering to Bonn – virtually a suburb of Cologne – the city is one of Germany's better after-dark places. Nightlife ranges from the latest dance clubs to cool jazz spots. The Tourist Office has a listing of what's on where.

Cologne also has a good reputation for its classical music and opera (details from Tourist Office), with hundreds of performances a year in top venues, including the **Philharmonie**, the beautiful concert close to the cathedral, and the modern **Opera House**. Cologne hosts **Karneval**, one of Europe's greatest street celebrations. This week-long festival precedes Lent and is every bit as lively (though not as crowded with foreign visitors) as Munich's Oktoberfest.

### SHOPPING

Cologne is a shopper's paradise. **Hohe Strasse**, the main pedestrian shopping street, combines souvenirs, leather goods, designer boutiques, furriers and jewellers. *Schildergasse,* the second section of the pedestrian area, stretches from the cathedral to the *Neumarkt* in a jumble of giant department stores and specialist shops. For indoor window-shopping head for the **Bazaar de Cologne**, where more than 60 shops, cafés and restaurants on three levels are covered by a huge glass dome. The centre of the art and antique world is *St Apern Strasse,* with some of the world's most expensive dealers. The area bounded by *Pfeilstr.*, *Mittelstr.* and *Ehrenstr.* is Cologne's coolest patch, with the latest fashions and music on show and lots of cafés and restaurants. If you want genuine **eau de Cologne**, look for labels saying *Echt Kölnisch Wasser* or buy '4711': **Haus 4711**, *Glockengasse,* has been the home of the perfume since 1792. Its *Glockenspiel* chimes every hour 0900–2000.

## SIGHTSEEING

Major sights are clustered around the **Dom** (cathedral), but there are sights worth seeing throughout the city. The **Cologns Bonbon** (DM26) includes a guided bus tour of the city, free museum entry, a souvenir booklet and reductions for boat trips. The **Museumscard** (DM20, single; DM36, family – 2 adults, 2 children), valid for 2 consecutive days, includes free bus and tram travel within the city zone on the first day. Contact the Tourist Office for details.

Over two thousand years old, Cologne was important in Roman times – its name, originally 'Colonia', comes from the Latin term for a military settlement. The city's Roman traces include remnants of the original, 5th-century AD city wall. By the 13th century, Cologne was a thriving metropolis of 40,000 people, protected by Europe's longest city walls – a 6 km rampart pierced by 12 massive gates. Work on the cathedral began in 1248, with the medieval city at the height of its power. After a period of decline, the 18th century saw a revival, when a supposed aphrodisiac made by distilling flower blossoms found fame as a perfume, the renowned *eau de Cologne.*

The twin spires of the Gothic **Dom**, next to Hbf, dwarf the buildings around it and dominate central Cologne. The cathedral began life as a 12th-century golden shrine housing alleged relics of the Magi, but building was interrupted in 1560 and the building remained incomplete, though in use, until the mid 19th century. In 1842, King Frederick William IV of Prussia (of which Cologne was by then part) ordered work to recommence. Some 38 years and 27 million marks later, the cathedral was completed – faithfully to the original 13th-century plan. The result justifies the wait, with stained glass covering several centuries and a magnificent chancel.

The 9th-century *Gero Crucifix* in the north chapel and the 15th-century triptych of the *Adoration of the Magi* in the south chapel, are among the world's best, although it is invidious to pinpoint any particular feature. Allow plenty of time to absorb the masterpieces in the cathedral and also those in the treasury and museum.

Within the original city wall stand a dozen Romanesque **churches**, the most important concentration of Romanesque church architecture in Germany. Substantially restored after World War II, each contains a wealth of religious art. (The Tourist Office has details.) The oldest – one of the oldest in Germany – **St Pantaleon**, *Am Pantaleonsberg 2,* dates from the 10th century. Among the more striking are **Gross St Martin**, *Gross St Martin 9,* overlooking the Rhine in the *Altstadt,* dating from 1172, and **St Aposteln**, *Neumarkt 30,* completed in 1230. **Römische-Germanisches Museum**, *Roncallipl. 4; tel: 221 23 04* or *221 45 90,* next door, was built around the *Dionysos Mosaic,* an excellently preserved work of over a million pieces that dates from around AD 200 and was discovered only in 1941. The museum contains other outstanding displays of Roman culture.

Nearby, on *Bischofsgartenstr.,* is a modern complex that includes 3 museums. **Agfa-Foto-Historama**, *tel: 221 24 11,* is a must for those interested in photography. 15th–16th-century works are the highlight of **Wallraf-Richartz-Museum**, *tel: 221 23 72,* while the **Museum Ludwig**, *tel: 221 23 82,* is home to works by 20th-century masters. The multi-style **Rathaus** (town hall) has been reconstructed and features an octagonal Gothic tower and a Renaissance façade, with a *Glockenspiel* that rings twice daily, at 1200 and 1700. Behind it, from *Kleine Budengasse,* there is access to the subterranean remains of the Roman **Praetorium**, including the grand vaulted sewer, and **Mikwe**, a 12th-century Jewish ritual bath. **Museum für Ostasiatische Kunst**, *Universitätstr.100; tel: 940 51 00* (tram nos 1/2) has a cosmopolitan collection, including a Japanese stone garden.

**City coach tours** depart daily from the Tourist Office. They include visits to Roman monuments, medieval city gates, the cathedral and shopping centres. Adults 25DM; children 8DM; obtain tickets from the driver.

# COLOGNE–FRANKFURT

Following the path of the Rhine and connecting two of Germany's most important industrial cities, this journey traverses a constantly changing landscape. The most attractive segment is that between Koblenz and Rudesheim, one highlight being the steep-sided Rhine Gorge near St Goar. The multitude of Rhine castles, rural landscape and great waterway is in stark contrast to the modern city of Frankfurt. This rather dull city is, however, probably Germany's most important finance and trading centre.

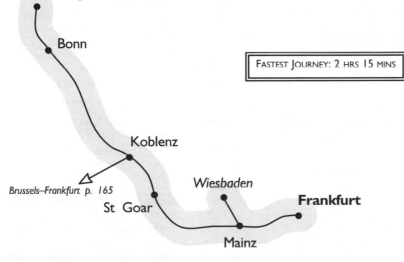

FASTEST JOURNEY: 2 HRS 15 MINS

## TRAINS

**ETT tables:** 910.

### FAST TRACK

An hourly InterCity service runs from Cologne to Frankfurt, with journey times of 2 hrs 15 mins. All trains have restaurant cars.

### ON TRACK

**Cologne–Bonn–Koblenz–Mainz–Frankfurt**

The hourly InterCity trains all call at Bonn, Koblenz and Mainz en route. Cologne to Bonn takes 20 mins, Bonn to Koblenz 32 mins, Koblenz to Mainz 50 mins, and Mainz to Frankfurt takes 32 mins. Additional expresses run between Cologne and Mainz, and frequent local trains link Cologne with Bonn and Mainz with Frankfurt, serving the smaller towns en route.

## BONN

**Station: Hbf,** *tel: (0228) 19419,* beside the bus terminal and right in the centre, on the edge of the pedestrian precinct.

**Tourist Office:** *Cassius Passage, Münsterstr. 20; tel: (0228) 194 33, fax: (0228) 77 31 00.* Open Mon–Sat 0800–2100; Sun 0930–1230. *Bonn from A to Z* has a good map and listings in English.

## Consulates

Most embassies are in Berlin, but most countries (not the UK) also have consulates in Bonn. **Australia:** *Godesburger Allee 107; tel: (0228) 81030.*
**Canada:** *Godesburger Allee 119; tel: (0228) 81 00 60.*
**New Zealand:** *Bundeskanzlerplatz; tel: (0228) 228 0725.*
**USA:** *Deichman Ave 29; tel: (0228) 339 2053.*

### GETTING AROUND

The areas of interest are quite widespread, so it's worth investing in a travel pass. There are several, some covering Cologne as well as Bonn (the transport systems are integrated), so ask the tourist office for guidance. **Bonncard** is an all-in-one entrance pass, which will get you into eleven major museums and provide unlimited travel on town buses and trains for 24 hours.

### ACCOMMODATION

There's a choice of reasonable accommodation in Bad Godesberg, which is also where the best **HI** is situated: *Horionstr. 60; tel: (0228) 31 75 16* (U 16/23: *Rheinallee*). The **campsite** is in the suburb of Mehlem, south of Bad Godesberg: *Im Frankenkeller 49; tel: (0228) 34 49 49* (U 16/23: *Rheinallee,* then bus no. 613). Both are a considerable distance from the city centre.

### SIGHTSEEING

Bonn mushroomed when it became the post-war capital of West Germany, and it is less a city than a series of linked, suburban villages.

In **Altstadt** (the old town) there are some pedestrianised streets lined with gabled 17th- and 18th-century houses. *Markt* has a much-photographed pink rococo **Rathaus**, while *Münsterplatz* is dominated by the 12th-century **Münster**, with an interior that features gold-leafed mosaics. **Beethovens Geburtshaus**, *Bonngasse 20,* is a well-arranged museum

devoted to the Bonn-born composer. On the other side of Hbf is the **Landesmuseum**, *Colmantstr. 14–16,* which exhibits a skull, discovered in 1856, near a village close to Düsseldorf. It is around 60,000 years old and a whole class of mankind has been named after the village: Neanderthal.

Heading south, the chestnut-lined *Poppels-dorfer Allee* leads to **Schloss Poppelsdorf**, now part of the university, and the **Botanical Gardens**. A few blocks west is **Robert-Schumann Haus**, *Sebastianstr. 182,* devoted to the composer. To the south is **Kreuzberg**, a 17th-century chapel with rich 18th-century embellishments.

**Bad Godesburg**, south of the city centre on the same side of the Rhine, is dominated by **Godesburg**, the most northerly of the Rhine castles. The old keep is intact and provides panoramic views. This suburb is where most of the diplomats reside; interesting if you like seeing how the other half live – mostly behind high walls and guarded, electrified gates.

Another east bank village worth visiting is **Schwarzrheindorf** (bus nos 540/550), home of **Doppelkirche**, a 12th-century church that is actually two separate chapels; one for the nobility and the other for lesser folk.

### KOBLENZ

**Station:** **Hbf**, *Bahnhofplatz 2; tel: (0261) 19419.* South-west of the centre, 25-min walk downhill (or bus no. 1) to the riverside area from which cruises *(Rheinfähre)* depart.
**Tourist Offices:** Opposite Hbf; *tel: (0261) 33134.* Open Mon–Fri 0830–1300 and 1415–1700. They provide boat schedules and a city map that includes listings. There is a **branch** by the docks, *Konrad-Adenauer-Ufer.* Open only June–Sept, Tues–Sat 1200–1825.

For **regional information:** **Rheinland-Pfalz**, *Lohrstr. 103; tel: (0261) 31079.* Open Mon–Fri 0800–1600.

### ACCOMMODATION

There are some reasonable hotels around *Hbf* and in **Ehrenbreitstein**. The **HI** is housed in the **Festung**, *tel: (0261) 73737,* and is popular, so book well ahead. The downside is that the ferry and chair lift both stop very early so, after taking a bus (nos 7/8/9/10) to *Charlottenstr.,* you end the day with a long uphill climb.

The **campsite** is at Lutzel, across the Mosel; **Campingplatz Rhein-Mosel**; *tel: (0261) 82719.* There's a ferry across during the day.

Reasonably priced hotels include **Hotel-Restaurant Schweizer**, *Aachenerstr. 66, tel (0261) 24028;* **Gastahaus-Pension Zum Rebstock**, *Poppenstr. 7, tel (0261) 42633;* **Hotel-Restaurant Burgschanke**, *Kondertal 2, tel (02606) 815.*

### SIGHTSEEING

Koblenz is at the Rhine/Mosel confluence and **Deutsches Eck** (the German Corner), the focal point of the town, is the tip of a peninsula between them. The pleasant gardens along both rivers combine to provide an attractive 8 km stroll. Another good walking area is the pedestrianised *Altstadt,* with a variety of restored buildings – several housing museums or wine cellars.

Koblenz began life under the Romans and some of their remains can be seen in the vaults beneath **Florianskirche** (c. AD 1100), which was re-modelled in Gothic style in the 14th century and further embellished in the 17th century. **Liebfrauenkirche** is a beautiful edifice which incorporates elements of several styles with some fine stained glass in a really elegant fashion, while **St Kastorkirche** contains some rare altar tombs and Gothic murals.

**Ehrenbreitstein** (across the Rhine, ferries in summer) is dominated by an enormous fortress, the **Festung**. Its earliest fortifications were built in the 12th century, but it grew to its present vast size during the 16th century. The **Sesselbahn** (cable car) operates May–Oct. As well as providing a fantastic view, the fortress contains two regional museums, albeit not particularly interesting ones. A big firework display (**Rhein in Flammen**) is staged here on the second Sat in Aug.

## MAINZ

**Station**: **Hbf**, *tel: (06131) 19419,* north-west of the centre.
**Tourist Office**: *Bahnhofstr. 15; tel: (06131) 28 62 10.* Open Mon–Fri 0900–1800, Sat 0900–1300.

---

## The Lorelei

**B**etween **St Goar** (on the west bank of the Rhine) and **St Goarshausen** (on the east bank), the river narrows and its currents become strong and dangerous to smaller vessels. Marking the spot is the **Lorelei Rock**, a 130m crag which juts from the fast-flowing river at St Goarshausen. In medieval times, this was said to be the seat of the Lorelei, whose beauty and voice lured ships onto the rocks. A ferry operates between St Goar and St Goarshausen.

Although the train gives an excellent view of the Rhine along this route, it's also fun to travel by boat. The area is very touristy in summer, so spring and autumn are more pleasant (most attractions close in winter). A comprehensive selection of Rhine trips by boat and hydrofoil is offered by **KD Line**, with departure points including St Goar, St Goarshausen and Mainz. There is an office in Koblenz, *tel: (0261) 31030,* as well as in a number of towns on the Rhine (see also Frankfurt, p. 214).

**Ferries**: **KD Line** cruises leave from the docks opposite Rathaus.

### ACCOMMODATION

There are relatively few hotels and advance booking is sensible. **HI: Otto-Brunfels-Schneise 4**; *tel: (06131) 85332,* in *Volkspark, Weisenau* (bus no. 1). **Campsite: Camping Maaraue**; *tel: (06134) 43 83,* is across the river, by Theodor-Heuss bridge (bus no. 13: *Brückenkopf-Kastel*).

### SIGHTSEEING

Distances between the places of interest are not great. Streets leading down to the Rhine have red nameplates and the streets running across them have blue nameplates. It was in Mainz, in the 1450s, that Gutenberg established the first printing press with movable type. The **Gutenberg Museum**, *Liebfrauen-pl.,* is fascinating, containing a replica of the original press and one of the few surviving vellum bibles.

*Altstadt* is a largely pedestrian zone around *Augustinerstr.* This street is touristy but others, such as the cobbled **Kirschgarten**, with its restored half-timbered houses, are charming. **Marktbrunnen**, *Markt,* is the country's oldest Renaissance fountain and is still surrounded by market stalls every Tues, Fri and Sat morning.

**Martinsdom** escaped serious bomb damage and is one of the most impressive cathedrals in Germany, a massive structure of red sandstone with six towers, surrounded by 18th-century houses. Inside the cathedral are elaborate archbishops' tombs spanning six centuries and 9th-century murals of New Testament scenes. The adjacent museum houses some superb old sculptures.

**St Ignaz**, *Gutenbergpl.,* is a rich mixture of rococo and neo-classicism, with painted cupolas and a splendid interior. In front of it is the tomb of Hans Backoffen, who designed many of the sarcophagi in the Dom as well as the 16th-century Crucifixion that marks his own tomb.

The Gothic **Stefanskirche** (to the east) has a set of deep blue stained-glass windows that were designed by Chagall to symbolise the post-war reconciliation.

North of *Altstadt* is **Landesmuseum**, *Grosse Bleiche 49–51,* which has a room of Roman remains, much better than the displays in the **Römisch-Germanisches Museum**, *Rheinstr.,* once the episcopal palace of the powerful Electors of Mainz.

### ⮎ SIDE TRÄCK FROM MAINZ

**Wiesbaden** first became a fashionable resort in the 19th century, when the gentry developed a taste for spas. Today it has 26 thermal springs (and a casino). You can have a full therapeutic treatment at the baths, or simply taste the waters in the Kochbrunnen fountain. There are frequent trains to Wiesbaden from Mainz; the journey takes about 10 mins. ⬛

186

# COPENHAGEN (KØBENHAVN)

Proud of its history, home to a 1000-year-old Kingdom and the oldest 'gågade' (pedestrian precinct) in the world, Copenhagen manages to attract young as well as old. From the traditional amusement park of Tivoli to the tranquil modern art museum of Louisiana, the city has many different things to offer the visitor.

## TOURIST INFORMATION

**Tourist office:** *Bernstorffsgade 1, tel: 33 11 13 25,* opposite the station by Tivoli's main entrance. Open daily 0900–1800 (mid Apr–May); daily 0900–2000 (June–mid Sept); Mon–Fri 0900–1700, Sat 0900–1600 (mid Sept–mid Apr). They supply information about all of Denmark. Get the map of *Wonderful Copenhagen* and a copy of *Copenhagen This Week* (published monthly), both of which are free and incorporate masses of useful information.

**USE IT**, *Rådhusstræde 13, tel: 33 15 65 18; http://www.cph96.dk/unginfo; e-mail: unginfo@ cph.96.dk,* provides youth-oriented information of all kinds. Open daily 0900–1900 (1 June–30 Sept); Mon–Fri 1000–1600 (Oct–May). While there, pick up a copy of *Playtime* magazine.

## ARRIVING AND DEPARTING

### Airport

**Copenhagen Airport**; *tel: 31 54 17 01,* is at **Kastrup**, 8 km south-east of town, and is sometimes called 'Kastrup Airport'. There is a tourist information desk and a hotel reservations desk in the arrival hall and banks in all areas. The SAS bus runs between Kastrup and København H (rail station) every 15 mins, taking 15–25 mins. Bus no. 32 (every 10 mins) takes 30–60 mins, from *Radhuspladsen*. Taxis are also available.

### Stations

The main rail station is **København Hovedbanegård (København H)**; *tel: 33 14 17 01,* with a metro station of the same name. Baggage lockers are accessible 0530–0100. There is also a bureau de change, a supermarket and a kiosk that stocks English newspapers. The **Inter-Rail Centre** in the station, daily 0700–2400 (June–Sept), provides showers and information.

### Ferries

If you want to travel directly between the Danish capital and Sweden, **Flybatarna catamarans** *(tel: 33 12 80 88),* from *Havnegade* and *Nyhavn,* provide an hourly link with **Malmö** (taking 45 mins). Another option is to take the train to Helsingør and get the 20-min ferry (which departs every 20 mins) to Helsingborg on the Swedish side. To get directly to Norway, **DFDS/Scandinavian Seaways** *(tel: 33 11 22 55),* from *Kvæsthusbroen,* operate daily between Copenhagen and **Oslo** (taking 16 hrs).

## GETTING AROUND

The **USE IT** office provides excellent guides for walking, cycling and seeing the city by bus. Bicycles are a sensible alternative to public transport: hire per day is cheaper than a 24-hr transport pass and roads are, literally, made for cycling. Try the **DSB Cykelcenter**, *Reventlowsgade 11; tel: 33 14 07 17* – this is at the station. **City Bikes** is a scheme in which the deposit of a 20 DKr coin will provide the use of one of the 1000 bicycles available from 120 racks (for the city centre only). On replacing the bike to any of the racks, the coin is returned.

### Tickets

Buses (**HT**) and trains (**S-tog, DSB** and some private lines) all form part of an integrated system in the Copenhagen area and tickets are valid on both. Fares are calculated by the number of zones travelled. There are plenty of maps, both at stations and aboard vehicles, which illustrate the zones – you can also pick up a leaflet showing them (from the station).

The cheapest ticket (DKr.10: get it on board a bus or at a metro station) covers travel in two zones for one hour. There's a sliding scale that allows extra time for extra zones: up to a maximum of six zones over a 2-hr period. A 24-hour transport pass is DKr.70 (from the Tourist Office and stations). A **klippekort** is a ten-ride ticket covering 2 or 3 zones (DKr.75 or 105). Tickets must be validated in the machines on board buses and on metro platforms.

The **Copenhagen Card** can be valid for one day (DKr.140), two days (DKr.230) or three days (DKr.295). It provides free public transport in Copenhagen (and north Zealand), gives free entrance to most attractions (including Tivoli), discounts on ferries to/from Sweden and a useful colour guide. It is on sale at the airport, DSB stations, hotels, travel agents and Tourist Offices.

## Metro and Buses

Both are frequent, running roughly 0500–0030 (starting 0600 Sun), and there's a night-bus service that runs at least hourly. The area of greater Copenhagen is best served by the **S-tog** (metro), which is also useful in the centre, between *København H* and *Østerport*. For information, *tel: 33 14 17 01.* Buses converge on *Radhuspladsen; tel: 36 45 45 45,* 0700–2130.

## STAYING IN COPENHAGEN

### Accommodation

Booking ahead is advisable if you have somewhere specific in mind, but not strictly necessary unless you're arriving in peak period (June–Aug). There are so many possibilities that it's sensible to consult the accommodation service in the Tourist Office; open daily 0900–midnight (mid Apr–mid Sept); daily 0900–2100 (late Sept); Mon–Fri 0900–1700, Sat 0900–1400 (Oct–mid Apr) – they can save you 25% on hotel prices for same-day bookings. There's a phone service; *tel: 33 12 28 80,* Mon–Fri 0900–1700 (sometimes longer).

**USE IT** don't charge for reservations and

have an external noticeboard indicating room vacancies in **hostels** and **Sleep-Ins**.

Hotel chains in Copenhagen include *BW, Cn, FE, GT, Rk, SA, Sc, Sh, Sn* and *Tp*. At the very top of the range is **Hotel d'Angleterre**, *Kongens Nytorv 34; tel: 33 12 00 95* – the place where film stars and other VIPs hang out. Not quite in the same league, but still very classy, are the **71 Nyhaven Hotel**, *Nyhavn 71; tel: 33 11 85 85* – small but select; and **Neptun**, *Skt Annæ Plads 14–20; tel: 33 13 89 00* – popular with Americans for nearly two centuries. A little cheaper, but still expensive, are **Savoy**, *Vesterbrogade 34; tel: 31 31 40 73* – beautifully designed and peaceful; and **Ascot** *Studiestræde 61; tel: 33 12 60 00* – in an old building with charm. The **Alexandra Hotel**, *HC Andersons Bl; tel: 33 14 22 00,* is a classic hotel located in the centre, across from the *Rådhus Pladsen*. Coming down to a moderate level, try **Copenhagen Admiral**, *Toldbrogade 24–28; tel: 33 11 82 82* – old and new mingle harmoniously in what used to be a granary; and **Excelsior**, *Colbjornsgade 6; tel: 33 25 22 33* – a renovated 19th-century building with a peaceful back garden.

An area in which the downmarket hotels tend to cluster is **Istedgade** (to the side of the station, away from the centre). Although it is not quite salubrious, it is still quite safe.

In the summer months, when demand is high, Copenhagen offers a good choice of hostel accommodation, but, even so, you must arrive early if you have not pre-booked. The **HI** have three hostels: **Amager**, *Vejlandsallé 200; tel: 32 52 29 08,* which is 4 km south-east of the centre, but right beside the stops for the airport bus and bus nos 46/37; **Bellahoj**, *Herbergvejen 8; tel: 31 28 97 15,* 5 km from the centre in the opposite direction: 15 mins on bus no. 2 or night-bus no. 902; and **Lynby Vandrehjem**, *Radvad 1; tel: 45 80 30 74,* about 15 km from town, S train to *Lynby St,* change to bus no. 182 or 183, direction *Hjortekjaer*. The **Sleep-In** on *Blegdamsvej 132; tel: 35 26 50 59* (open July–Aug), offers hostel-style, conveniently located accommodation.

The **YMCA/YWCA** have two **Inter Point Centres**: *Store Kannikestræde 19; tel: 33 11 30 31* (open July), and *Valdemarsgade 15; tel:*

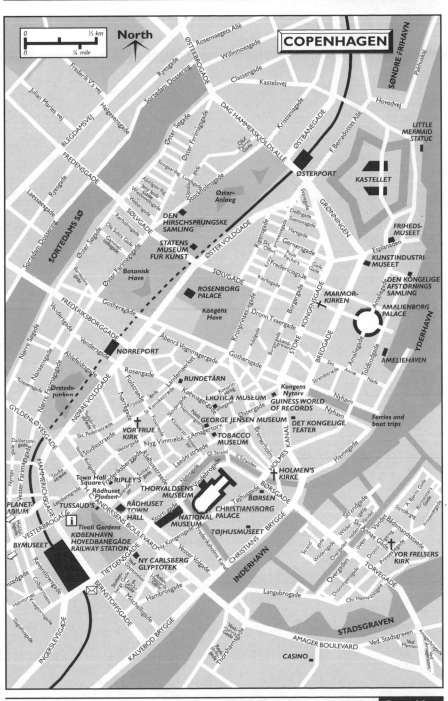

**COPENHAGEN**

North

0    ½ km
0    ¼ mile

SØNDRE FRIHAVN

Pakhusvej

Rosenvaegets Allé

Willemoesgade

ØSTERBROGADE

Ryesgade

Frederik V's vej

Julian Maries vej

Helgesensgade

BLEGDAMSVEJ

Sortedam Dossering

Classengade

Kastelsvej

Hovedvej

DAG HAMMERSKJÖLDS ALLÉ

Øster Søgade

ØSTBANEGADE

Kristianagade

LITTLE MERMAID STATUE

FREDENSGADE

Øster Farimagsgade

Stovgardvej

Lundsgade

Old Palaces Gade

ØSTERPORT

KASTELLET

Laesseesgade

Ryesgade

Abildgaardsg

Jens Juels Gade

Wiedeweltsg

Weberisgade

Stockholmsgade

Øster-Anlaeg

GRØNNINGEN

FRIHEDS-MUSEET

SORTEDAMS SØ

Sortedam Dossering

Øster Søgade

SOLVGADE

Rømholmsgade

Ole Suhrs Gade

Gammel toldbuen

DEN HIRSCHSPRUNGSKE SAMLING

STATENS MUSEUM FUR KUNST

ØSTER VOLDGADE

Delfinsgade

Suenonsgade

Haregade

Gernersgade

Rigensgade

Skt. Pauls Gade

Offers Gade

Fachers

Esplanaden

KUNSTINDUSTRI-MUSEET

Amaliegade

FREDERIKSBORGGADE

Øster Farimagsgade

Barakkevej

sade

Botanisk Have

SOLVGADE

Fredericiagade

Klerkegade

DEN KONGELIGE AFSTØRNINGS SAMLING

Vendersgade

Gyldenløvesgade

Gothersgade

ROSENBORG PALACE

Kongens Have

Dronn Tvaergade

Kronprinsessegade

Adelgade

Borgergade

STORE KONGENSGADE

Borgergade

greven

MARMOR-KIRKEN

BREDGADE

AMALIENBORG PALACE

YDERHAVN

Nørre Søgade

Vestergade

Abenrå

Vognmagergade

Gothersgade

Amaliegade

Toldbodgade

AMELIEHAVEN

NØRREPORT

Ørsteds-parken

Rosengade

Landemarket

RUNDETÅRN

Nørregade

Skt. Kaniikkestr.

Frederborggade

Krystalg

Kononh gang

Købmagergade

EROTICA MUSEUM

Kongens Nytorv

Skt. Annae

Strandstraede

Nads

**189**

NØRREVOLDGADE

Nansensgade

Ahlefeldtsgade

Tutsensgade

Studiestraede

Skt. Pederstraede

Larslejstr.

Teglgaardstr.

Slutterigade

Hemmingsen

Amagertorv.

Nørregade

VOR FRUE KIRK

GEORGE JENSEN MUSEUM

GUINESS WORLD OF RECORDS

DET KONGELIGE TEATER

Brennerholm

Nyhavn

Ferries and boat trips

Dahlerups-gade

Nyrops

Vester Farimagsgade

HAMMERICHSGADE

Studiestraede

Frederiksholtsgade

Vestergade

Rådhusstraede

Nyg Vimmelsk.

Nygade

Laederstraede

Gl. Strand

V. Strand

TOBACCO MUSEUM

GYLDENLØVESGADE

Town Hall Square

Rådhuset Pladsen

RIPLEY'S

THORVALDSENS MUSEUM

V. Voldgade

Nyhavn

HOLMES KANAL

HOLMEN'S KIRKE

A Bjorns Gade

Burmeisters gade

PLANET-ARIUM

TUSSAUD'S

RÅDHUSET TOWN HALL

H. C. ANDERSENS BOULEVARD

Stormgade

NATIONAL MUSEUM

CHRISTIANSBORG PALACE

BØRSEN

BORSGADE

Strandgade

oven

St. Anne Gade

Dronn

Prinsessegade

VESTERBROGADE

BYMUSEET

Tivoli Gardens

KØBENHAVN HOVEDBANEGÅDE RAILWAY STATION

TØJHUSMUSEET

CHRISTIANS BRYGGE

Wilders

Vander Bådsmandsstraede

Strand gade

Overgaden nede Vander

Dronn Gyldensg

Prinsesse Gade

VOR FRELSERS KIRK

Istedsgade

Reventlowsgade

NY CARLSBERG GLYPTOTEK

Ny Kongensgade

Frederiksholms Kanal

Overgaden

Dronningensgade

TORVEGADE

TIETGENSGADE

Halmtorvet

Colbjorns-gade

Gasvaerksvej

Skottens Gade

Eskils Gade

Absalons Gade

Hambrosgade

INDERHAVN

Langebrogade

Chr. Havns Voldgade

Amagerbrogade

Amagerfaeldvej

Saxogade

Mitchellsgade

Vest-lie nannede Gade

Ved Stadsgraven

Ved Mønten

STADSGRAVEN

INGERSLEVSGADE

BERNSTOFFSGADE

KALVEBOD BRYGGE

Thorshavnsgade

AMAGER BOULEVARD

CASINO

31 31 15 74 (open mid July–mid Aug) – you can join on the spot if you are not already a member. The **City Public Hostel,** *Absalonsgade 8; tel: 31 31 20 70* (open May–Aug), is another good option.

The most central **campsite** is **Bellahøj Camping,** *Hvidkildevej; tel: 31 10 11 50,* open June–Aug (bus no. 11).

### Eating and Drinking

*Copenhagen This Week* and *Playtime* have listings for all sorts of eating. Visit one of the cellar restaurants (off *Strøget).* These are a traditional part of life in Copenhagen and serve mainly Danish specialities – little has changed over the years, except that women are now welcome. Try *pølser* (sausages) from street stalls and open sandwiches: as well as being very Danish, fast-food such as this is cheap.

Another cheapish option is ethnic restaurants (particularly Chinese). The (red-light) districts **Halmtorvet** and **Istedgade** have many; **Frederiksberg** is a good area for budget eateries. The supermarket at *København H* stays open late Mon–Sat and is open all day Sun.

### Communications

The Post Office is open Mon–Fri 0900/1000–1700/1730, Sat 0900–1200. Unless some other post office is specified, poste restante mail goes to the **main post office**, *Tietgensgade 35–29; tel: 33 33 89 00;* open Mon–Fri 1000–1800, Sat 0900–1300. **Phone Home**, *Radhuset 4, tel: 33 36 86 00,* is open Mon–Fri 1000–1700, Sat 1100–1700, Sun 1300–1800.

### Money

In København H, Den Danske Bank open 0700–2100 and Forex open daily 0800–2100.

### Embassies and Consulates

**Australia:** *Kristianiagade 21; tel: (01) 35 26 22 44.*
**Canada:** *Kristen Bernikowsgade 1; tel: (01) 33 12 22 29.*
**Republic of Ireland:** *Ostbanegade 21; tel: 31 42 32 33.*
**South Africa:** *Gammel Vartovvej 8, Hellerup; tel: 31 18 01 55.*
**UK:** *Kastelsvej 40; tel: (01) 35 26 46 00.*

**USA:** *Dag Hammerskjölds Allé 24; tel: (01) 31 42 31 44.*

### ENTERTAINMENT

There are comprehensive listings in *Copenhagen This Week* and *Playtime.*

**Tivoli** amusement park is Copenhagen's playground, with everything from fairground rides to ballet – and dozens of eateries. It is best seen at night, when the fairy lights are switched on. Three nights a week (ask on arrival), fireworks are let off just before midnight.

The city's theatrical tradition is long. Amongst some 160 stages, **Det Kongelige Teater** (The Royal Theatre), *Kongens Nytorv,* reigns supreme (red lights outside mean it's sold out). **Mermaid Theatre**, *Skt Pederstræde 27,* presents English-language productions. The **Nørreport kiosk**, by *Nørreport* S-tog, sells same-day discounted theatre tickets. Films are almost invariably shown in the original language and subtitled.

The nightlife is excellent and dress is almost always informal. There is no shortage of cafés and bars with live music, notably jazz. Discos and clubs tend to get lively around midnight and stay open until 0500 (when the breakfast bars open). The admission charge is usually not very much and prices for drinks are seldom loaded – but alcohol is always expensive.

### Events

Copenhagen plays host to many events but the major annual ones are artistic: a **ballet and opera festival** in May, and an **international jazz festival** in July. Nearby **Roskilde's annual rock festival** is gaining in international stature (see Hamburg–Copenhagen p.238).

### SHOPPING

Prices are somewhat higher than other Western European capitals. Design plays an important part in Danish living and many ordinary household objects, such as kettles, candlesticks and clocks, are worth buying for that aspect alone. Streets around *Vesterbro, Norrebro* and *Studiestræde* have many trendy boutiques and shops for second-hand books, records and so forth. Nevertheless, *Strøget,* home to the two biggest department stores (**Illum,** *Ostergade 52,* and

**Magasin**, *Kongens Nytorv 13)*, is still the essential area for serious shoppers.

Some specialist places worthy of note are: **Georg Jensen**, *Amagertorv 4* (he's a famous silversmith and his designs are superb); **Royal Copenhagen**, *Amagertorv 6* (porcelain doesn't come much better than this); and **Bang & Olufsen Center**, *Østergade 3* (the ultimate in high tech). **24-hour pharmacy: Steno Apotek**, *Vesterbrogade 6c.*

## SIGHTSEEING

At the heart of the city is **Strøget** (a general name for the pedestrian-only zone), punctuated with pretty squares and invariably full of shoppers and strollers. Within the area, **Rundetårn** (Round Tower), *Kobmagergade 52,* provides an excellent view over the pitched roofs and parks.

On the far side of *Gothersgade,* the green-roofed Dutch Renaissance-style **Rosenborg Slot** (Rosenborg Palace) sits majestically in the **Rosenborg Have** (Rosenborg Garden), *Øster Voldgade,* adjacent to the **Botanisk Have** (Botanical Gardens). The palace, no longer home to the royals, is now a museum of sumptuous 17th-century interiors, with furnishings that include thrones, tapestries and chandeliers; the Crown Jewels are displayed in the basement.

From here, beaver-hatted soldiers march east to **Change the Guard** at the current royal domicile, **Amalienborg** (accompanied by a band when the Queen is in residence). This consists of a quartet of rococo palaces near the river, and framing a courtyard that's overlooked by an equestrian statue of Frederick IV. The adjacent **Ameliehaven** is a narrow strip of densely planted garden; good for picnics.

To the north, the statue of Hans Christian Andersen's **Little Mermaid (Den Lille Havfrue)** sits wistfully staring into the middle-distance: allegedly the most photographed woman in the world! Also much photographed is the small 300-year-old **Nyhavn** (new harbour), bordered by picturesque 18th-century townhouses, ships' masts and cafés. The tree-lined **Kongens Nytorv** (King's New Market), encircled by grand buildings, links the quaint harbour to one end of *Strøget.*

To the south (down Holmenskanal, over the bridge) is **Stotsholmen Island**, where politics, history and royalty converge in **Christiansborg Slot** (Christiansborg Castle). Bishop Absalon built the original castle in 1167 and the ruins are on view in the basement. Today, it is the venue for entertaining heads of state and home of the **Folketing** (Parliament), of which there are tours when it is not in session.

Museums and art galleries are usually closed on Mon. The **Ny Carlsberg Glyptotek** (New Carlsberg Picture Hall), *Dantes Plads 7,* was founded with the profits from beer sales and is probably the best gallery in Copenhagen. Especially fine are the Danish 'Golden Age' paintings, Rodin's sculptures, the Roman collection and the section of French Impressionists' work, including a room of Gaugins. Exhibits in the **Nationalmuseet**, *Ny Vestergade 10,* start with the Stone Age and lead you on a cultural tour of Denmark's history. The sculptures of Bertel Thorvaldsen (1770–1844) are scattered all over Europe, but **Thorvaldsens Museum**, *Posthusgade 2,* contains the most comprehensive round-up of his work.

The **Statens Museum for Kunst** (State Museum of Fine Arts), *Sølvgade 48–50,* is closed until summer 1998, but will reopen to house Danish art from the 17th century and works by such masters as Matisse, Picasso and Munch.

For a slightly less cultural pursuit, the **Carlsberg Brewery**, *Ny Carlsberg Vej 140, Elefantporten; tel: 33 27 13 14;* bus 6, 10 or 18, offers free tours and sampling.

## OUT OF TOWN

**Louisiana**, a museum of modern art, is one of the most popular tourist attractions in Denmark. It is located about 10-mins walk from Humlebæk station (30 mins by rail from Copenhagen). The harmonious setting, in parkland overlooking the sound, is complemented by sculptures: Henry Moore, Max Ernst and Dubuffet are all represented. Inside, most of the permanent collection is post-1945.

Similarly tranquil, **Karen Blixen Museet**, *Rungstedlund, Rungs Strandvej 111,* is set in a forested bird sanctuary where the author lived from 1931 until her death – and where she wrote *Out of Africa*. **DSB** offer special good-value packages for both, and for the more distant (over 3 hrs by train) **Legoland** (see p.193).

# COPENHAGEN– GOTHENBURG

This scenic journey takes in the dramatic 18 km Great Belt tunnel and bridge combination linking Zealand and Funen, as well as the opportunity to visit some of the lesser known yet very attractive towns of Northern Denmark. The sea crossing from Frederikshavn to Gothenberg is a convenient way to cross the border into Sweden.

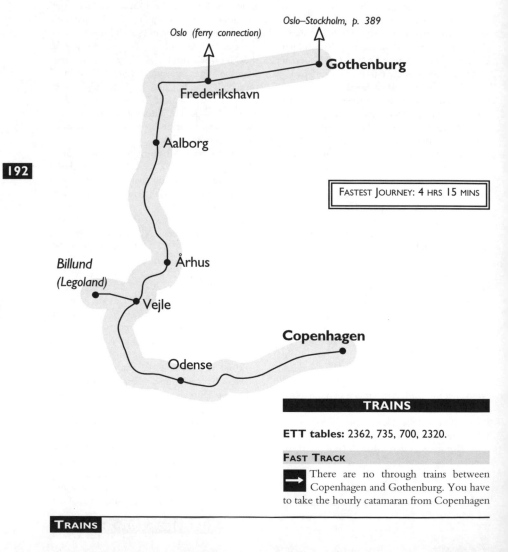

Oslo–Stockholm, p. 389

Oslo (ferry connection)

**Gothenburg**

Frederikshavn

Aalborg

FASTEST JOURNEY: 4 HRS 15 MINS

Billund
(Legoland)

Århus

Vejle

**Copenhagen**

Odense

## TRAINS

**ETT tables:** 2362, 735, 700, 2320.

### FAST TRACK

→ There are no through trains between Copenhagen and Gothenburg. You have to take the hourly catamaran from Copenhagen

Havnegard to Malmö Skeppsbron (45 mins) and continue by train to Gothenburg (3–4 hrs).

## ON TRACK

### ⇒ Copenhagen–Odense–Århus–Aalborg–Frederikshavn

InterCity trains connect Copenhagen with Odense half-hourly, and with Århus, Aalborg and Frederikshavn hourly. More options are available by changing trains en route. Copenhagen to Odense takes 1½ hrs, Odense to Århus 1 hr 40 mins, Århus to Aalborg 1½ hrs. At Korsør, the train speeds through an 8 km tunnel under the sea then emerges onto a causeway bridge, linking the Zealand 'mainland' with the island of Funen.

### Frederikshavn–Gothenburg

Stena Line operate 2–3 ferries a day in winter and up to 6 a day in summer, with journey times of 3¼ hrs, and 3 catamaran trips in winter, 5 in summer, taking 2 hrs daily. Seacat offer 3 catamarans, with a journey time of 1¾ hrs. See Country by Country for details of rail pass discounts. At Gothenburg, a connection can be made to the Oslo–Stockholm route (p.389).

## ODENSE

**Station:** *tel: 70 13 14 15.* This forms the northern boundary of the city centre. Behind it is a railway museum (**Jerbanemuseum**).
**Tourist Office:** *Rådhuset, Jernbanegade; tel: 66 12 75 20.* Open Mon–Sat 0900–1900, Sun 1100–1900 (mid June–Aug); Mon–Fri 0930–1630, Sat 1000–1300 (Sept–mid June).

An **Odense Adventure Pass** is available for 24 or 48 hrs, giving free public transport and large reductions on attraction admission fees.

Odense is the largest town on the island of **Fyn** (Funen). Hans Christian Andersen was born in the town; he turned to writing fairytales after failing in his ambitions to be an actor and playwright. **Barndomshjem**, his childhood home, has a couple of rooms crammed with his belongings, but **HC Andersen Hus**, the Andersen Museum, has more to offer.

The **Fyns Kunstmuseum** (Art Museum of Funen), offers a superb collection of Danish art. **Montergården** (the City Museum) is housed

in some well preserved 18th-century buildings. The **Museum of Photographic Art** is unique in Denmark, offering permanent and temporary exhibits. **Den Fynske Landsby** (Funen Village), 4 km south, is a splendid open-air museum with resurrected buildings from the 18th and 19th centuries furnished in period and has demonstrations of traditional crafts in summer.

## ÅRHUS

**Station:** *tel: 86 13 37 77,* is just south of the centre.
**Tourist Office:** *Rådhuset, Park Allé; tel: 86 12 35 00; e-mail: aarhconv@inet.uni-c.dk.* Open Mon–Fri 0930–1800, Sat 0930–1700, Sun 0930–1300 (23 June–14 Sept); Mon–Fri 0930–1630, Sat 1000–1300 (15 Sept–30 Apr); Mon–Fri 0930–1700, Sat 1000–1300 (1 May–22 June). An **Århus Passet** gives free bus travel and entry to all the attractions.

Denmark's second city is a large port, commercial and cultural centre. The biggest attraction is **Den Gamle By** (The Old City), Denmark's National Museum of Urban Living, a delightful open-air museum consisting of 70 houses from around Denmark, depicting 400 years of city living. Within one of the historic buildings is a museum that shows how toys were used to teach children their roles as adults. It is set in **botanical gardens**, west of the centre. **Århus Domkirke** has a 93-m nave and contains several restored, pre-Reformation frescos.

Viking remains form the core of the **Vikingemuseet**, while **Kvindemuseet** and **Besættelsesmuseet** (under the same roof) cover (respectively) the lot of modern women and Danish Resistance during World War II.

The superb **Mosegård Prehistoric Museum**, 5 km south of town, is home to the 2000-year-old **Grauballe man**, discovered in a bog in 1952.

### ↰ SIDE TRACK FROM ÅRHUS

**Legoland** in **Billund**; *tel: 75 33 13 33; (http://www.LEGO.com/world/billund),* is made from over 35 million plastic bricks. It's probably Denmark's most famous attraction, great for children and a nostalgia trip for

**193**

many adults. As well as recreations of cities and buildings from around the world, the park features a miniature version of a Danish town. Trains run hourly, with journey times of 45 mins, to reach **Vejle**, from where shuttle buses cover the 27 km to Billund. 

## AALBORG

**Station:** *tel: 98 16 16 66*, a short walk down *Boulevarden* from the town centre.
**Tourist Office:** *Østerågade 8; tel: 98 12 60 22; http://www.tourist.aal.dk; e-mail: tourist@pip.dknet.dk.* Open Mon–Fri 0900–1800, Sat 0900–1700 (15 June–end Aug); Mon–Fri 0900–1630, Sat 1000–1300 (Sept–14 June).

**Budolfi Domkirke** (St Botolph's Cathedral) is a whitewashed, mainly Gothic church with a baroque steeple. **Aalborg Historiske Museum** displays finds from Lindholm Hoje – the largest Viking burial ground in Scandinavia – a glassworks collection and period furnished rooms, while **Nordjyllands Kunstmuseum** (Museum of Modern and Contemporary Art) is home to 20th-century art and a sculpture garden. There is also a **Maritime Museum**. The **Zoo**, *Moleparkvej 63*, is one of the most up-to-date in Europe, emphasising animals in their natural environment.

## FREDERIKSHAVN

The northern terminal of the **DSB** rail line is one of the world's busiest ferry ports, but there's little of interest to detain you. The ferries use **Havnepladsen** *(tel: 98 43 11 77)*, close to the centre, and the **Stena Line** terminal *(tel: 98 20 02 00)* is about 1 km south of the rail station. For **SeaCat** bookings, *tel: 98 42 83 00.*
**Tourist Office:** *Brotorvet 1; tel: 98 42 32 66* (room booking service). Mon–Sat 0830–2030, Sun 1100–2030 (1 June–16 Aug); Mon–Fri 0900–1600, Sat 1100–1400 (17 Aug–31 May).

## GOTHENBURG (GÖTEBORG)

**Station: Göteborg C (Central)**, *tel: (031) 10 44 45.* It *is* central and is used by all *IC* trains. Open Mon–Fri 0430–0030, Sat 0530–0030, Sun 0700–0030; the rail ticket/information office opens Mon–Fri 0830–1800, Sat 0900–1600, Sun 1100–1800. Facilities include **Forex**

foreign exchange (open daily 0800–2100), **Narvesen** (a chain selling papers, snacks etc.), big and small lockers, showers (daily 0700–2100) and reasonably priced eateries. Most buses use *Nils Ericsonsplatsen;* the station yard.
**Ferries:** There are regular international ferries. For **Harwich, Newcastle, Amsterdam** and **Oslo: Scandinavian Seaways**, *tel: (031) 65 06 00,* leave from *Skandiahamnen,* south-west of the centre – 20 mins by bus. The bus meets each arriving ferry and leaves from *stop U, Nils Ericsonsplatsen,* 1½ hrs before each ferry leaves. For **Denmark (Frederikshavn)** and **Germany (Kiel): Stena Line**, *tel: (031) 85 50 00,* leave from *Masthuggs* and *Majnabbehamnen* – both in the centre.
**Main Tourist Office:** *Kungsportsplatsen 2; tel: (031) 10 07 40; http://www.gbg-co.se.* Open Mon–Fri 0900–1700, Sat 1000–1400 (Sept–Apr); Mon–Fri 0900–1800, Sat–Sun 1000–1400 (May); daily 0900–2000 (21 June–17 Aug). Pick up the free leaflet *Maps, Events and Attractions Göteborg,* which includes a map of the centre (with sights marked) and a diagram of tram routes. Also get a copy of *What's On,* a monthly guide to entertainment and museum opening hours, and *Guide,* with details of sightseeing, hotels and museums. Tickets for events are also available. **Nordstan branch:** in the centre of the huge complex opposite the station – there's a tunnel linking them. Open Mon–Fri 0930–1800, Sat 0930–1500.

**Göteborgskortet** (Gothenburg Card) is obtainable from Tourist Offices, Pressbyrån kiosks, hotels and campsites: SKr.125 for 24 hrs, SKr.225 for 48 hrs, SKr.275 for 72 hrs. It provides free public transport and free/discounted entrance to most museums and attractions, as well as a wide range of other discounts.

### GETTING AROUND

The centre's attractions are quite close together, but there's an excellent tram network if you don't feel like walking. The lines are colour-coded, so it's easy to see the stop and vehicle you need. Tram and bus stops have names and show the numbers and end destinations of lines using them. A single ticket is SKr.16, but you can save by buying a multi-ride **Magnet Kort** (SKr.100; it must be purchased in advance at

Pressbyrån), which provides ten city rides. Tickets cover all trams, buses and city boats. **Tidpunkten** supply information about routes, times and fares; *tel: (031) 80 12 35.* Main office: *Nils Ericsonsplatsen,* open Mon–Thur 0700–2200, Fri 0700–0230, Sat 0900–0230, Sun 0900–1800. Others: *Drottningtorget* (Mon–Sat 0600–2000, Sun 0700–2000) and *Brunnsparken* (Mon–Fri 0700–1900, Sat 0900–1900).

**Paddanbåtarna** (Paddan sightseeing boats), *tel: (031) 60 96 70,* depart from *Kungsportplatsen* (26 Apr–5 Oct) and their harbour cruise (multi-lingual) is recommended, but be prepared to duck low under one or two of the bridges.

### ACCOMMODATION AND FOOD

The Tourist Offices can book private rooms, as well as hotels, but charge a small fee for both. Hotel chains: *BW, FE, Nv, RC, Re, SA, Sc, Sd, Sh* and *Tp.* Also *Rk* – in the form of a cruise boat on the Göta Canal (see box opposite).

The **Sheraton Hotel and Towers**, *Södra Hamng 59–65; tel: (031) 80 60 00,* is Sweden's largest hotel and frequented by the people who matter. The **Scandic Crown Rubinen**, *Kongsportaveynyn; tel: (031) 81 08 00,* is located in the heart of the city. **Hotel Lorensberg**, *Berzeliig 15; tel: (031) 81 06 00,* is much more reasonably priced – a friendly place where imaginative use of murals depicting exterior scenes gives the interior an unusual feeling of space. For something a little different, try **M/S Seaside**, which is docked at *Packhuskajen 8; tel: (031) 10 10 35.* It offers 2–4-berth cabins and private cabins and supplies equipment for evening deck barbecues.

There are four **HI** hostels. **Torrekulla Turiststation**, *Kallered; tel: (031) 795 1495;* **Slottskogens**, *Vegagatan 21; tel: (031) 24 16 20,* and **Kärralund**, *Olbergsg; tel: (031) 84 02 00.* This last hostel is near the closest **campsite** to town: **Kärralunds Camping**, *Olbergsg; tel: (031) 84 02 00,* which has cottages as well as camping and is open all year.

There's a wide range of food on offer. The seafood is excellent, most restaurants clustering along the waterfront. For other types of cuisine, try on and around *Avenyn.* The **Nordstan** complex offers a lot of eateries, including familiar fast-food outlets and a good supermarket, **Hemköp**, which has a deli section – it's in the basement of **Åhléns City** (a big store).

### SIGHTSEEING

In summer there are English-language tours on **Lisebergslinjen** (a vintage open-air tram: July) and **Göteborgståget** (a miniature train: May–Aug). A variety of summer cruises is also available, around the harbour and further afield. Ask the Tourist Office for details of all of these.

**Göteborgs Utkiken**, *Lilla Bommen,* is a striking red and white skyscraper (one of the few in the city: 86m). Near the top are a look-out and small café that provide superb harbour views. **Lilla Bommen** itself is a delightful, charming town, which also has shops and craft workshops. Dominating the whole area, however, is the spectacular waterside **Opera House** *(tel: 31 10 80 00).* The resident company is the Göteburg Operan and performances in opera, ballet and concerts are held from Aug–May.

**Kungsportsavenyn**, usually known simply as **'Avenyn'** (The Avenue), is the hub of the city, a broad, tree-lined road with shops and eateries. Just off *Avenyn* is **Trädgårdsför-eningen**, *Nya Allén,* a park full of fragrance, flora and birdsong, dotted with works of art and other attractions, including **Rosariet** (an extensive rose garden), **Doftträdgården** (a scented garden of aromatic species) and **Palmhuset** (a palm house modelled on London's Crystal Palace). **Fjärilshuset** (a tropical butterfly house), allows you to wander among free-flying exotic butterflies and get really close, but be warned: cameras mist up in the humid atmosphere.

**Liseberg Amusement Park**, *Örgrytevägen 5* (tram no. 5: *Liseberg),* is dominated by the 150-m high **Spaceport**, which offers panoramic views. Other rides include one of Europe's longest roller coasters and a number that defy gravity: literally hair-raising.

The city's oldest secular building (1634) is **Kronhuset** (Crown Arsenal), *Postgasse 6–8.* Around it is **Kronhusbodarna**, a courtyard bounded by handicraft boutiques in 18th-century artisans' dwellings. You can watch such craftsmen as glass-blowers, goldsmiths and watch-makers – and buy their wares.

**Haga Nygata** is a renovated historical area in which the cobbled streets are lined with craft,

195

second-hand, antique, and design shops, as well as cafés and restaurants. Opposite is the **Feskekorkan**, which looks like a Victorian Church but is, in fact, a thriving fish market, open Tues–Fri 1000–1800, Sat 1000–1400.

## Museums and Galleries

Most city museums open Tues–Sun 1100–1600 (Sept–Apr); daily 1100–1600 (May–Aug), but some open earlier and close later. The leaflet, *Göteborgs Museer,* is in several languages and includes special exhibitions. The Swedish section (only) gives museum opening times.

**Göteburg's Martima Centrum** (Gothenburg Maritime Centre), *Packhuskajen,* is a museum of 14 floating ships. The star attractions are *Nordkaparen* (a dragon class submarine from 1962) and *Smaland* (a 1952 destroyer that was only decommissioned in 1979). Both are fully equipped and (provided you are agile), you can explore them thoroughly. You can board a variety of other vessels as well. The mighty **Poseidon statue** by Carl Milles stands in front of the **Konstmuseet** and **Konsthallen** (Art Museum and Gallery) at the top of *Gotaplatsen* (bus no. 40), which contains the world's best collection of Scandinavian Art, as well as works by such masters as Rubens, Rembrandt, Picasso, Van Gogh and Monet.

Don't miss the **Ethnografiska Museet** (Museum of Ethnography), *Åvägen 24* (tram no. 5: *Liseberg*). The South American collection is unique, including a stupendous collection of textiles dating from the Chilean Paracas culture of 2000 years ago. The state of preservation is almost unbelievable. It's one of the world's best collections of its kind and beautifully displayed. Borrow the comprehensive English text.

**Götesborgs Stadtmuseum** (city museum), is in *Norra Hamng,* at Ostindiska Huset (East India House), and deals with the history of Gothenburg, especially regarding its connection with the East India Company. **Röhsska Museet** (Museum of Applied Arts), *Vasag 37,* is Sweden's National Museum for Arts, Crafts and Industrial Design. **Sjöfahrtshistoriaska-museet**, *Karl Johansg 1–3* (outside the centre, near Stigbergstorget, tram nos 3/4/9), is the main museum of maritime history, easily identified by a 44m tower, with panoramic views,

---

## The Göta Canal

The idea of building a canal between Gothenburg and Stockholm, via Lake Vänern, existed for several hundred years before it became a reality. Work finally started on the Göta Canal in 1810, and by 1832 a navigable waterway linked the Kattegat and the Baltic. The canal was built to transport iron, timber and other industrial products. One of the greatest challenges facing those who constructed it was the difference in height of up to 300 ft along the projected route. To solve this, 65 locks were built along the course of the canal. Industrial cargoes have now been replaced on the 19th-century boats by tourists, as the four-day journey along the waterway has become a popular experience. Cruises between Gothenburg and Stockholm, with stops at towns and points of interest en route, are run by the **Göta Canal Steamship Company**; *tel: (46) 31 80 63 15; http://www.gotacanal.se.*

---

topped by a statue. It houses an entire fleet of models, from the Vikings onwards. Attached to it is an **aquarium**.

**Skansen Kronan** (Fort Kronan), *Skansberget,* a fortress south-west of the centre (tram no. 1), is still intact. Once menacing the Göta Älv, it's now a military museum, the best collections being of uniforms and firearms dating back to the 17th century. **Göteborgs Stadsmuseum** (city museum), *Norra Hamng,* is at *Ostindiska Huset* (East India House), an 18th-century building that is being renovated. Until work is finished, you enter by a side door and only some parts are open.

In the large nature park **Slottsskogen** (outside the city: tram nos 1/2: *Linnéplatsen),* are an **observatory**, a **children's zoo** and **Naturhistoriska Museet** (Natural History Museum).

From Gothenburg you can cut across to Stockholm (p. 482) by joining the Oslo–Stockholm route, p. 389. The journey can also be made via the Göta Canal (see box, above) if you can spare the time.

# COPENHAGEN–STOCKHOLM

This route is an excellent introduction to the beauty of the landscape of the southern portion of the country, yet still allows the opportunity to visit four impressive and historical Swedish cities en route. Sweden is known for its forests and picturesque lakes, and countless numbers of them are visible on this journey.

Copenhagen–Gothenburg, p. 192

FASTEST JOURNEY: 6 HRS

## TRAINS

**ETT tables:** 50, 702, 730, 2345, 2362.

### FAST TRACK

There is one overnight direct train from Copenhagen to Stockholm, taking 8 hrs (sleepers and couchettes only).

### ON TRACK

#### Copenhagen–(Border)–Malmö
Various companies operate fast catamarans between Copenhagen and Malmö, including one service from Copenhagen Airport; *tel: (040) 10 39 30.* Journey time: about 45 mins.

#### Malmö–Lund
A frequent local train service links Malmö with Lund, journey times are around 15 mins.

#### Lund–Linköping
Trains operate almost every two hours between

Lund and Linköping. The fastest journeys are by the X2000 high speed trains. These trains take just over 2½ hrs but require special fares and advance reservations. *IC* trains take around 3½ hrs for the journey. All trains have dining facilities.

**197**

#### Linköping–Norrköping
A 30-min journey; frequent trains all day.

#### Norrköping–Stockholm
A good service operates throughout the day with journey times of 1 hr 20 mins (on X2000) or 1 hr 50 mins (on *IC*). Most trains require advance reservations.

## MALMÖ

**Station: Malmö C**, just north of the old town. SJ information; *tel: (020) 75 75 75.* Local trains; *tel: (020) 61 61 61.*

**Ferries: Flygbåtarna catamarans**; *tel: (040) 10 39 30,* leave from *Skeppsbron* (just north of Malmö C), providing an hourly service to **Havnegåde** (near Nyhavn) that takes about 45 mins.

**Tourist Office:** *Central Station; tel: (040) 30 01 50.* Open Mon–Fri 0900–1900, Sat–Sun 1000–1400 (June–Aug); Mon–Fri 0900–1700,

Sat 1000–1400 (Sept–May). Get the very useful (free) *Malmö this Month* and details of **Malmö-kortet** (Malmö Card) – it's good value, but the cost and what it covers change every year.

## ACCOMMODATION

**City Room**, *S. Forstadg. 31; tel: (040) 795 94* (open Mon–Fri 1000–1700), supply lists of private rooms. Hotel chains include *BW, FE, GT, Re, SA, Sc, Sd, Sh* and *Tp*. **Garden Hotel**, *Baltzarsgatan 20; tel: (040) 10 40 00*, is true to its name: the very peaceful garden is on the roof. The **Scandic Hotel St Jörgen**, *Stora Nygatan 35; tel: (040) 773 00*, is located in the heart of the city, just off the main shopping street. **HI: Södergården**, *Backavägen 18; tel: (040) 822 20* (bus no. 36).

## SIGHTSEEING

Sweden's third city is a lively place. The central square, **Stortorget**, adjoins **Lilla Torg**, smaller and infinitely more charming with its medieval, sometimes lopsided, brick and timber façades, outdoor cafés and restaurants. The formidable 15th-century fortress, **Malmöhus**, open Mon–Sun 1200–1600, is now a complex with museums so diverse that there's something for everyone. The interior of **St Petri Kyrka** (St Peter's church), *Göran Olsgatan,* is whitewashed, so that the extraordinarily ornate decorations are shown to best advantage.

### ◄► Connection: Malmö to Gothenburg

X2000 trains taking 3 hrs – supplement payable – and *IR* (InterRegio) taking 4 hrs run from Malmö to **Gothenburg**, see Copenhagen–Gothenburg (p. 194).

## LUND

**Station:** *tel: (046) 15 02 20,* 5 mins walk west of the centre.
**Tourist Office:** *Stadshuset, Kyrkogatan 11; tel: (046) 35 50 40.* Open Mon–Fri 1000–1800, Sat–Sun 1000–1400 (June–Aug); Mon–Fri 1000–1700, Sat 1000–1400 (May, Sept); Mon–Fri 1000–1700 (Oct–Apr).

Lund is small, but definitely worth a visit. It was a religious centre in the 12th century and much of the medieval town is still visible.

**Domkyrkan** (the cathedral), is a magnificent structure with a fascinating crypt and an intricate astronomical clock that springs into action twice a day. **Kulturen** (Cultural-Historical Museum), *Tegnérplatsen,* open Mon, Tues, Fri, Sat and Sun 1100–1700, Thur 1100–2100, is an assemblage of buildings from as long as 300 years ago (some appropriately furnished, others empty or used for varied exhibitions: don't miss the burgher's house), with a group of rune stones outside.

## LINKÖPING

**Station:** *tel: (013) 24 23 23,* 5 mins walk east of the centre.
**Tourist Office:** *Konsistoriegatan 7; tel: (013) 20 68 35; e-mail: turistbyra@linkoping.se.* Open Mon–Fri 0900–1800 (all year) plus Sat–Sun 0900–1500 (June–Aug). Get *Next Stop Linköping*. **Hotel Ekoxen** (Tourist Spot), *Klostergatan 68; tel: (013) 14 60 70,* also supply information: Mon–Fri 1800–2200 (all year) plus Sat–Sun 1500–2200 (June–Aug).

The town's prime attraction is **Gamla Linköping**, *Malmslättsvägen* (5 mins on bus nos 203/205/207, or 20 mins walk), a museum village recreating the 19th century – it includes a small chocolate factory. Check that the individual buildings will be open, however, not just the complex.

**Linköpings Domkyrka** is one of Sweden's oldest cathedrals, with a 107m green spire that is visible for miles. The unusual interior of **St Larskyrkan** (St Lars church), *St Larsgatan,* is mainly 20th century.

## NORRKÖPING

**Station, Norrköping C:** *tel: (011) 21 22 21,* 5 mins walk north of the centre.
**Tourist Office:** *Drottninggatan 11; tel: (011) 15 15 00.* Open Mon–Fri 0900–1700, Sat 0900–1300 (longer from 21 Jun to 10 Aug).

The main reason for a stop is **Kolmården Djur & Naturpark**, *tel: (11) 24 90 00,* opening times vary. The zoo is probably Europe's largest and is in three separate sections: the **main zoo**, a **safari park** and a **dolphinarium**. A cable car offers the best view of many animals. It's 30 km north-east of town: bus no. 432 (roughly hourly) takes about 50 mins.

# FLORENCE (FIRENZE)

One of the greatest of Italy's old city–states and perhaps still the country's most beautiful city, Florence attracts so many visitors that for much of the year they vastly outnumber locals, at least in the historic centre. There is concern that tourism is beginning to damage the fabric of the medieval buildings. The city, with its extraordinary wealth of art and architecture, can be extremely crowded, and you must be prepared to wait in line to see its most famous exhibits, such as those in the Galleria Uffizi, or Michelangelo's *David* in the Galleria dell'Accademia.

## TOURIST INFORMATION

The **Azienda Promozione Turistica (APT)** has its head office at *V. Manzoni 16, tel: (055) 23320*. The **City of Florence** has tourist information offices at *Chiasso dei Baroncelli 17; tel: (055) 230 2033*, and at *Pza della Stazione* (arrival end), *tel: (055) 230 2124*. There is a combined city and province of Florence office at *V. Cavour 1r; tel: (055) 290 832/3*. All branches are open Mon–Sat 0815–1915 (except *Pza della Stazione*, which is closed Sat), Sun 0815–1345; Oct–June 0800–1400.

## ARRIVING AND DEPARTING

### Airports

**Amerigo Vespucci Airport**, 4 km north-west of the city, *tel: (055) 306 1700*, handles mainly domestic and some European services. The **airport bus** is operated by SITA, *V. Santa Caterina da Siena 157, tel: (055) 214 721*.

Pisa's **Galileo Galilei Airport** (84 km) is the main regional hub for international flights, *tel: (050) 500 707*. Hourly trains run between the airport and Florence's Santa Maria Novella rail station (1 hr). A terminal for this airport is within the station, *tel: 1478 88088 (toll-free)*.

### Stations

**Santa Maria Novella (SMN)**, *Pza della Stazione; tel: (055) 288 785*, is Florence's main rail hub. It is a short walk from the city centre; facilities include left luggage, currency exchange and an accommodation service. The main **bus station**, *tel: 1478 88088 (toll-free)*, is next door. The fast ETR 450 Milan/Florence/Rome express service stops at **Rifredi** station, 3 km north of the city centre. There is an ATM on the station platform.

## GETTING AROUND

Most sights are in the compact central zone and the best way to see them all is on foot. You can cover much of the city in two days. You can also rent bicycles from the municipal rental location at *Pza della Stazione*, next to the SMN station, and at several other outlets around the city. Town maps are available from Tourist Offices and from ATAF (see below).

### Buses

Florence's **Azienda Trasporti Autolinee Fiorentine (ATAF)** municipal buses run from 0515 to 0100. There is an ATAF information office opposite the main entrance of SMN rail station, *57 Pza del Duomo, tel: (055) 565 0222*. Buy your tickets singly from machines at main bus stops, in books of five from tobacconists or bars and cancel them in the machine on boarding. Tickets last for one hour from the time the machine stamps them, and you may change buses on the same ticket. You can also buy an all-day *turisticche* (tourist ticket) which costs less than five times the price of a single.

### Taxis

Licensed taxis are white with a yellow stripe. Prices are high (flag fall is about six times the cost of a one-hour bus ticket). Avoid un-licensed cabs, which are even more expensive.

199

## Accommodation

Europe's busiest tourism city as well as a major venue for trade fairs and for business travel, Florence has some magnificent luxury properties such as the exquisite **Villa Cora**, *V. Machiavelli 18; tel: (055) 22 98 451*, and the elegant **Excelsior**, *Pza Ognissanti; tel: (055) 264 201*. At the other end of the scale, accommodation pickings for the budget traveller are slim. Whichever rung of the accommodation ladder you plan to alight on, try to book well ahead.

The range of hotel chains in the city naturally is wide, and includes: *Ch, Ex, Hd, Nv, Pu, Sf, Sh.*

The cheapest accommodation, though not always the most appealing, is near the SMN station. Elsewhere, lodgings outside the city centre and south of the Arno are cheaper than those in the city's historic heart. The **Informazione Turistiche Alberghiere (ITA)** booth at the SMN station may be able to find you a room if you arrive without a booking; open 0830–2100 – prepare to wait in a long queue.

Florence has three **youth hostels**: advance booking is recommended at all three. They are: **Villa Camerata**, *Viale A. Righi 2/4, tel: (055) 601 451*; **Ostello Santa Monaca**, *V. Santa Monaca 6, tel: (055) 268 338*; **Villa Favard**, *V. Rocca Tedalada* (no tel., open June–Sept only, very basic space for those with sleeping bags).

There are **campsites** at: **Italiani e Stranieri**, *Viale Michelangelo 80, tel: (055) 681 1977* (Apr–Oct), and in the grounds of the Villa Camerata youth hostel (see above). A further list of **campsites** in and around Florence is available from **Centro Internazionale Prenotazione Federcampeggio**, *Casella Postale 23, 50041 Calenzano, Firenze, tel: (055) 882 391*, which also handles campsite bookings.

## Eating and Drinking

Florence has a good supply of reasonably priced eating-places. You can cut costs by opting for fixed-price *(prezzo fisso)* meals which give you a choice of first courses, a choice of main courses, and fruit or cheese. Since one of the first course choices is always pasta, this makes a filling meal.

An even cheaper option is the *tavola calda*, a buffet-style self-service restaurant where you can choose a single dish or a full meal. These are found all over town and cover and service charges are included in the price displayed for each dish.

As in other Italian towns, drinks taken standing or sitting at the bar are a great deal cheaper than those drunk at a table, and restaurants outside the main sightseeing semi-circle are usually cheaper than those catering to visitors close to the main sights. For picnic ingredients try an *alimentari* (grocery shop) – but remember that they shut for lunch.

## Communications

The main **post office** is at *V. Pelliceria 53*, open Mon–Fri 0815–1800, Sat 0815–1230. There are usually long queues. You can buy stamps from tobacconists and from stationers.

National **telephone** service at the *V. Pelliceria* post office is open 0800–2230. You can also make calls from the *V. Pietrapiana* office, open 0800–1745 daily, and at the SMN station office, open 0800–2145, closed Sun and holidays.

To phone Florence from abroad: *tel: 39 (Italy) + 55 (Florence) + number*; to phone Florence from elsewhere in Italy: *tel: (055) + number*.

## Consulates

**UK**: *Lungarno Corsini 2, tel: (055) 284 133*.
**USA**: *Lungarno Amerigo Vespucci 38, tel: (055) 239 8276*.

## Money

Eurocheques are widely accepted, but credit cards are useful only in the more expensive shops and restaurants.

Banks that change money usually display the sign Cambio (Exchange). There are also exchange kiosks at SMN station and at numerous city centre locations.

**Thomas Cook bureau de change** is located at *Ponte Vecchio, Lungarno Acciaiuoli 6R; tel: (055) 289781*. They will cash Thomas Cook travellers' cheques free of commission charge and can offer emergency assistance in the event of them being lost or stolen.

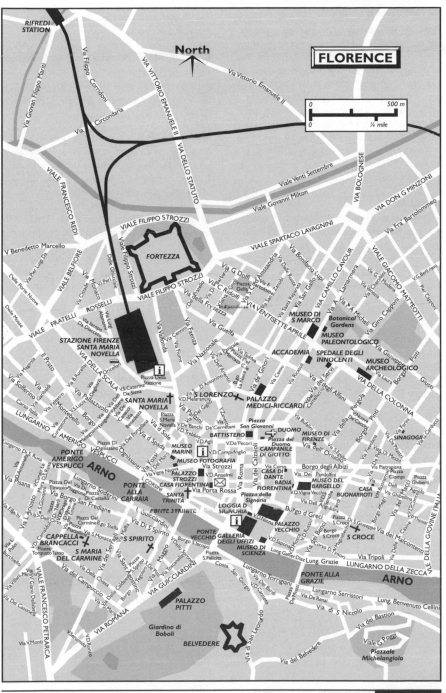

**FLORENCE**

North

0              500 m
0              ¼ mile

201

## ENTERTAINMENT

Florence offers plenty to do and see, especially out on the street. On summer evenings, street performers and fortune-tellers take over the *Pza della Signoria,* the *Pza del Duomo* and the *V. Calzaiuoli,* which connects them. At the other end of the scale, opera is as popular as anywhere in Italy, though it is an expensive way to spend an evening. The English-language listings guide *Florence: Concierge Information* can be picked up at most hotel desks. If you can read Italian, the monthly *Firenze Spettacolo* can be bought at most bookstalls.

### Nightlife
A lively, local youth culture boosted by a large, summer, floating population ensures that there are plenty of clubs and discos, though the in-place to dance changes virtually week to week. There is often an admission fee for the larger discos and drinks are usually very expensive. There are also several rock and reggae venues.

### Theatres, Cinemas and Concerts
Many recent UK and US releases come to major city-centre cinemas undubbed. There are numerous theatres, the most important of which is the **Teatro Comunale**, the venue for most opera and classical concerts. There is a big music and opera festival in May–July. At **Fiesole**, 8 km to the north-east, the July–Aug **Estate Fiesolana** is an annual festival of concerts and films.

## SHOPPING

Florence offers some of the finest quality products in the world, especially in leatherwork (particularly shoes and accessories), linen and jewellery. It also has some of the most expensive shops in the world. Cheaper buys for souvenir shoppers include hand-made paper and pottery. See where the wealthy shop on *V. Tornabuoni* and *V. della Vigna Nuova,* where, if you have to ask the price you clearly can't afford it. Then visit the *Pza Ciompi* flea-market (open daily, go early), the **Mercato Nuovo** on *V. Calimala,* the daily market in the *Pza di San Lorenzo* (for cheap clothing, silks, belts and food), or the vast Tuesday-morning market in

the *Casine* park for buys within your range. Hand-made perfumes, herbal remedies and soaps can be had from the frescoed **Farmacia di Santa Maria Novella** *(V. della Scala 16r).* Prices vary from inexpensive to outrageous. In general, olive oil, aromatic vinegars, cheese and dried mushrooms, neatly packaged, are good buys.

## SIGHTSEEING

You will pay an entrance fee for every building you visit in Florence – apart from the churches. Combined entrance tickets are available for some museums. Most museums close on Mon, and some are closed Sun as well.

The city is divided by the River Arno, with most of its glorious medieval heart on the north bank. South of the river, the *Oltrarno* district is packed with artisans' workshops; this is a traditional 'working' Florence largely untouched by the tourist circus taking place at its heart across the river. Five bridges cross the Arno. The most central, the **Ponte Vecchio**, is lined with shops specialising in jewellery. Built in 1345, it is Florence's oldest bridge and is a tourist attraction in its own right.

### North of the Arno
Most of the the important sights lie in a semi-circle north of the Arno, within a 2-km radius of the Uffizi. These include Florence's 'musts'. The **Galleria Uffizi** itself, *Pzle degli Uffizi 6,* contains works from antiquity and a vast array of others by many of the Renaissance greats such as Giotto, Cimabue, Botticelli, Michelangelo and Raphael. The **Duomo** (Cathedral) of **Santa Maria del Fiore** is topped by Brunelleschi's dome. At the base of the **Campanile** (Bell Tower), designed by Giotto in 1334, are sculpted relief panels by Andrea Pisano. The **Baptistery** (Battisterio di San Giovanni) is the oldest building in Florence, 5th–8th-century, with fine bronze doors – the 'Gates of Paradise' (East Doors, 15th-century), the North Doors (15th-century) by Ghiberti, and the South Doors by Andrea Pisano (14th-century).

The **Museo dell'Opera del Duomo**, *Pza del Duomo 9,* houses works taken from the Duomo for safe-keeping. The **Bargello**, *V. del*

*Proconsolo 4,* possesses a great collection of Renaissance sculpture, including works by Michelangelo, Donatello and Cellini. The medieval **Palazzo Vecchio**, dominating *Pza della Signoria,* is an interesting repository of frescos and sculpture and provides an insider's look at the rooms occupied by the city's rulers since the 14th century. **Orsanmichele,** *V. Calzaiuoli,* a former grain market, is now a church, the exterior of which is adorned by seminal Renaissance works of sculpture. The **New Sacristy** and **Laurentian Library**, adjacent to **San Lorenzo** *(Pza Madonna degli Aldobrandini),* were designed by Michelangelo. The **Palazzo Medici-Riccardi**, at *V. Cavour 1,* was· the home of the Medici in the 15th and 16th centuries. The 13th-century church of **Santa Croce** *(Pzza Santa Croce)* stands beside Brunelleschi's **Cappella de'Pazzi**.

Still within this semi-circle, the furnished **Palazzo Davanzati**, *V. Porta Rossa 13,* is preserved as a typical merchant residence of the 14th century; Gothic **Santa Maria Novella**, at *Pzza di Santa Maria Novella,* contains many important Renaissance works of art – including works by Massacio, Filippino Lippi, Ghirlandaio and Orcagna. The **Casa Buonarroti**, at *V. Ghibellina 70,* is a 'Michelangelo museum'. He lived here briefly, a connection fortified by a significant collection of his works.

Outside the semi-circle, 3 km north-east of the centre, lie the **Galleria Accademia** *(V. Ricasoli 60)* and the **Museo di San Marco** *(Pzza di S. Marco 1),* both essential viewing, the Accademia for Michelangelo's David and the convent of San Marco for Fra Angelico's frescos, including the *Annunciation.* Close to the Accademia (400m east), at *V. della Colonna 36,* the **Museo Archeologico** has an outstanding collection of Etruscan, Greek, Roman and Egyptian antiquities.

### South of the Arno: the Oltrarno

Cross the Arno by the Ponte Vecchio to reach the main attractions south of the river: the grandiose 15th-century **Palazzo Pitti** *(Pzza Pitti),* housing the wealth of the Medicis (it became their main residence in 1550), a fine gallery of modern art, and the huge collection of paintings from the Renaissance and the baroque in the Palatine Gallery. Nearby are Brunelleschi's fine church of **Santo Spirito**, with splendid paintings (Ghirlandaio, Filippino Lippi), which is surrounded every morning by a lively street market, and the church of **Santa Maria del Carmine**, noted for the frescos in the Brancacci Chapel by Masaccio. The **Museo Bardini** *(Pzza de'Mozzi 1)* was adorned by its 19th-century owner with salvaged sections of demolished early buildings and is a fascinating museum not only of architectural ornament, but of paintings and sculpture. Still further south, behind the Palazzo Pitti, lie the city's landscaped green lung, the **Giardino di Boboli**, a park which was laid out with vistas, avenues and fountains for the Medici in the middle of the 16th century. Beside the gardens is the 16th-century fortress, the **Forte di Belvedere.**

### Views of Florence

Despite the inevitable crowds, the view of the **old city** straddling the banks of the Arno from the **Ponte Vecchio** is still much as the Florentines' ancestors will have known it. From the top of the dome of the cathedral there is a magnificent view across the city's rooftops. A wider view of the city can be had from **San Miniato al Monte**, the church facing the city from the hill to the south, behind the Boboli Gardens. Alongside it, the wide **Piazzale Michelangelo** is a popular venue for midnight viewing of the lit city.

#### OUT OF TOWN

**Fiesole**, set on a hill 8 km north-east of the city, overlooks the valleys of the Arno and the Mugello and is a good excursion if you wish to escape the heat of summertime Florence. (Take bus no. 7 from the city centre.) It also provides excellent views of its larger neighbour.

Also founded by the Etruscans, Fiesole was once an independent city-state at war with Florence. The main sights are the **Roman Theatre** and its attendant museum (open 0900–1900, summer) and the **Monastery of San Francesco**. Both are a short walk away from the main square, *Pza Mino.*

# FLORENCE–ROME

This route meanders through the hilly heart of Tuscany and Umbria, Italy's most popular and enchanting tourist regions, visiting splendid medieval cities and picturesque hill towns, full of magnificent buildings, art treasures, and the home of St Francis. The Assisi area was hit by an earthquake in October 1997, but work started almost immediately to return the town and surrounding area to near normality. Some churches and museums may be closed as restoration work continues.

FASTEST JOURNEY: 1 HR 30 MINS

## TRAINS

**ETT tables:** 615, 620.

### FAST TRACK

There are frequent trains every day between Florence (SMN or Rifredi station) and Rome (mostly Termini station). It is worth being selective, because the journey (via Orvieto, not the On Track route) varies from 1 hr 35 mins on the high-speed tilting *Eurostar Italia* to 3½ hrs on the *IR*. Supplements are payable for the high-speed service and reservations are obligatory.

### ON TRACK

#### Florence–Arezzo
Trains are approximately hourly between Florence (SMN) and Arezzo, the journey time varying from 30 to 60 mins.

#### Arezzo–Perugia
There are six daily services direct, nine if you

change at Terontola-Cortona. The journey averages 1¾ hrs.

### Perugia–Assisi
There are 15–20 trains a day, the journey taking 20–30 mins.

### Assisi–Spoleto
Six direct trains, but if you change at Foligno (roughly 15 mins from Assisi, 20 mins from Spoleto) there are trains on both legs approximately every hour. Some connections are better than others.

### Spoleto–Rome
There are at least twelve trains a day between Spoleto and Rome (Termini). The journey takes about 1½ hrs by IC or IR trains.

## AREZZO

**Station**: *tel: (0575) 22 663* or *1478 88088 (toll-free)*. In the modern sector, west of the centre: walk up the hill to the old town.
**Tourist Office**: by the station; *tel: (0575) 377 678*. Open daily 0815–2000 Apr–Sept; Mon–Fri 0830–1800, Sat 0830–1300 Oct–Mar.
**APT**: *Pza Risorgimento 116; tel: (0575) 23 952*, post the latest information on accommodation outside, so consult that if you arrive out of office hours.

### ACCOMMODATION

Rooms are difficult to find over the first weekend of every month, but you should have few problems at other times. There are several budget options near the station. **Private Hostels: Piero della Francesca**, *V. Borgo Unto 6; tel: (0575) 354 546*, near *Pza Grande*; **Villa Severi**, *V. F Redi 13; tel: (0575) 29 047* (bus no. 4).

### SIGHTSEEING

The old town is towards the top of a hill, the modern town below it, connected by the pedestrianised *Corso Italia* and the motorised shopping street, *V. Guido Monaco*.

Arezzo was a major settlement in Etruscan, Roman and medieval times. Always a wealthy city, today its economy rests on jewellers, goldsmiths and antiques, but don't think you'll find a bargain by attending the **Fiera Antiquaria**

(Antiques Fair), in *Pza Grande* on the first Sun of every month. Hugely popular with an ever more international clientele, it's the place to buy serious antique furniture, terracotta, linen and of course jewellery.

The **Museo Archeologico**, *V. Margaritone 10*, not far east of the station, is the only major sight in the lower town. Within it is an excellent collection of Roman Aretine ware (mass-produced from 50BC to AD 60 70, this terracotta has a shiny red glaze and is adorned with bas-reliefs) and a notable collection of Etruscan bronzes and 1st-century BC vases. Nearby, is a ruined Roman amphitheatre, the **Amfiteatro Romano**.

The city's major attraction is Piero della Francesca's brilliant fresco cycle of the *Legend of the True Cross* (1452–66), on display in the 14th-century church of **San Francesco**, *V. della Madonna del Prato*, in the centre of the old town. This is one of the masterpieces of Italian Renaissance painting.

**Pieve di Santa Maria**, *Corso Italia*, is an outstanding Romanesque church with lively 13th-century carvings over the entrance, a multi-windowed square campanile and a tiered Pisan façade. It contains a notable Lorenzetti polyptych from 1320. The **Piazza Grande**, into which the apse of the Pieve protrudes, is home to several other architecturally interesting buildings, including the **Palazzetto della Fraternità dei Laici**, which has a Gothic ground floor and Renaissance upper storeys, and the pillared **Loggiata del Vasari** – which Vasari designed in 1573. On the first Sun of Sept, the square becomes the setting for a traditional joust, **Giostra del Saracino**, with four knights tilting at a wooden Saracen.

The large **Duomo** (cathedral), begun in 1278 and overlooking the north of town, has a handsome Gothic interior dominated by 16th-century stained glass. Key amongst its adornments is Piero della Francesca's fresco of *Mary Magdalene* near the organ, next to a large marble tomb possibly designed by Giotto. Behind the Duomo, the **Museo del Duomo** houses various works of art taken for safe-keeping from the Duomo itself. These include three crucifixes, the oldest of which is by Margaritone di Arezzo (1264). Not far away, the **Fortezza Medicea** (on the edge of the Parco il Prato) was built by Antonio da Sangallo the Younger for Cosimo I de' Medici (16th-century).

Just inside the western wall of the old town is the mainly 13th-century **Chiesa di San Domenico**, *Pza Fossombroni,* with a fine rose window over the door. The interior features colourful 15th–16th-century frescos, a fine *Crucifixion* by Cimabue and an *Annunciation* by Aretino. Very close (and signposted) are the **Casa di Petrarca**, *V. dell'Orto,* home of the great poet, and the **Casa di Giorgio Vasari**, *V. XX Settembre 55.* Vasari, biographer of the great Renaissance artists, was born in Arezzo and designed his own house, covering the interior with frescos. **The Galleria e Museo Medioevale e Moderno** (*V. di San Loretino 8)* contains an exceptional collection of majolica as well as sculpture dating from the 10th to the 17th centuries. **Santa Maria delle Grazie** (*V di Santa Maria)* is a particularly fine 15th-century church which contains a high altar by Andrea della Robbia.

## PERUGIA

**Station**: FS (State Railway), *tel: 1478 88088 (toll-free).* 4 km south-west of the centre (an uphill walk) or 15 mins by bus (nos 26/27/29/32/36) to *Pza Italia.* Tickets from a forecourt booth or machine by the entrance. The private *FCU* (Ferrovia Centrale Umbria) railway terminal is **Stazione Sant'Anna**, *tel: (075) 5723 947,* from which you can get a *scala mobile* (escalator) to *Pza Italia.* There is an ATM in the station.
**Tourist Office**: *Palazzo dei Priori, Pza IV Novembre; tel: (075) 572 3327* or *573 6458.* Mon–Sat 0830–1330 and 1530/1600–1830/1900, Sun 0900–1300. Get the monthly listing *Perugia What, Where, When* for detailed information.

### ACCOMMODATION

There is plenty of cheap, central accommodation, but advance booking is essential during the international jazz festival (10 days every July). **Hostel**: 2 mins from the Duomo: **HI**: *V. Bontempi 13; tel: (075) 22 880.* **Campsite**: **Paradis d'Ete**, *Colle della Trinità; tel: (075) 795*

*117,* 5 km from town (bus no. 36), or you can **rough camp** by **Lago Trasimeno**, reached by bus and train.

### SIGHTSEEING

Ignore the unattractive modern suburbs and head straight for the almost intact medieval centre, by bus or escalator. Capital of Umbria, this is a very splendid city, many of whose monuments have an undeniably martial face. Warlike and belligerent, Perugia was smitten by strife almost until the 19th century. From *Piazza Italia* the pedestrianised *Corso Vannucci,* lined with fortified palaces, cafés and shops, runs north to the city's heart in **Piazza IV Novembre**, where the Duomo is located. All the other major sights are within easy walking distance of this. The street itself is the centre of activities for a cosmopolitan crowd, almost around the clock.

The **Duomo** (cathedral), *Piazza IV Novembre,* is a large, plain medieval building, supposedly home to the Virgin Mary's wedding ring (kept inside 15 locked boxes and almost never seen). In the centre of the square, but undergoing restoration, is the 13th-century **Fontana Maggiore**, a triumph of decoration by Nicola and Giovanni Pisano.

The **Palazzo dei Priori**, *Corso Vannucci,* Perugia's civic headquarters since 1297, faces the fountain and is a somewhat forbidding structure. Dominated by crenellations, it has a great Gothic portal and long rows of windows. Fan-like steps lead up to the Sala dei Notari, which is noted for its frescos – fun rather than masterpieces. The **Galleria Nazionale dell' Umbria**, on the 4th floor, contains mainly Umbrian works (notably by Pinturicchio and Perugino). In fact this is the most important repository of Umbrian art in Italy - though it also has a few Tuscan masterpieces, including Piero della Francesca's *Madonna and Saints with Child* and a triptych by Fra Angelico.

The **Collegio della Mercanzia** is covered with magnificent 15th-century carvings, while the **Collegio del Cambio**, the Bankers' Guild, has restored frescos (among them a self-portrait) that are considered to be Perugino's finest works. It is believed he had help from the young Raphael (his greatest pupil). **Sant'Agostino**, *Corso Garibaldi*, is rather sad, with a few patches of frescos hinting at previous glories. There is still a beautiful choir and the ceiling of its Oratory is absolutely smothered in decorations. Continue along the street, to the extreme north of the centre, to reach **Sant'Angelo**, a lovely, tranquil 5th-century church dedicated to St Michael. Within, it incorporates the columns of the circular Roman temple that it replaces.

The lower section of the massive **Arco di Augusto**, *Pza Fortebraccio*, a magnificent city gate, is a rare survivor from the Etruscan era. The Romans used it as a base for their 40 BC additions, while it was added to again in the 16th century. In fact the Arco di Augusto – so-called because Emperor Augustus was involved in the Roman sections of its construction – has been worked on almost continuously for 2000 years. **San Domenico** (1305), rebuilt 1632), to the east *(Pza G Bruno)*, is an enormous church where several outstanding works of art hint at happier days. Authorship of the well-preserved 14th-century *Tomb of Pope Benedict XI* is unknown, but it's superbly crafted and clearly the work of a master sculptor. Here too is a magnificent 15th-century stained-glass window. The **Museo Archeologico Nazionale dell'Umbria**, in the monastery alongside San Domenico, includes an excellent collection of Etruscan artefacts as well as Roman sculpture.

Don't miss the 10th-century church of **San Pietro**, south-east from the centre *(Borgo XX Giugno)*. The decorations, dating from the Renaissance, are unbelievably rich, with scarcely an unadorned patch. The paintings were executed by a host of artists, including Perugino. A highlight is the magnificently carved choir.

### ↱ SIDE TRACK FROM PERUGIA

### GUBBIO

Ten buses a day run from Perugia's *Pza dei Partigiani*, by the FCU station, to Gubbio.

Apart from a few out-of-place Fascist monuments, Gubbio is a typical Umbrian hill town, largely medieval, with steep narrow streets and red-roofed pinkish houses. *Pza Grande della Signoria,* home of the turreted **Palazzo dei Consoli**, provides superb views. The **Museo Civico** contains the most complete extant record of the ancient Umbrian language, in seven bronze tablets – the Tavole Eugubine (300–100 BC). **Tourist Office:** *Pza Oderisi 6; tel: (075) 922 0693.* ↱

### ASSISI

**Station:** *tel: (075) 804 0272.* This is not in Assisi proper, but in *Santa Maria degli Angeli,* about 5 km south-west and uphill all the way. **Buses** run to the centre every half hour.
**Tourist Office**: *Pza del Comune 12; tel: (075) 812 534.* Mon–Sat 0800–1400 and 1530–1830, and Sun 0900–1300. They provide a map in English and have information about accommodation, including pilgrim hostels.

### GETTING AROUND

The centre is fairly small, full of interest and best seen on foot. If you want to go further afield, take a bus.

### ACCOMMODATION

There is plenty of accommodation of every grade, but booking is advisable – essential for Easter, the Feast of St Francis (3–4 Oct) and *Calendimaggio* (a medieval celebration of spring held in early May). **HI:** *V. Valecchi; tel: (075) 816 767,* 10-mins walk from *Pza San Pietro*. **Campsite:** *Fontemaggio; tel: (075) 813 636,* 4 km east of town and uphill. Take a taxi or follow the signs from Porta Cappuccini.

### SIGHTSEEING

**St Francis** was born in Assisi in 1182, a truly remarkable man who revolutionised medieval religious thinking, largely by practising what he preached: poverty, chastity and obedience, leading to love of God and appreciation of all living things. He founded the Franciscan order, the world's largest, and his home town became (and remains) a major pilgrimage centre. But Assisi is also famous, as a result, for a wealth of art and architecture spawned in the wake of its most famous son's life. It is still largely a medieval town, clinging to a side of Monte

Subasio way above the green and almost mythic Umbrian countryside, which, even now, is hardly different from the landscapes in the frescos of the Umbrian painters.

The **Basilica di San Francesco**, at the western end of the old town, has a collection of masterpieces that most galleries would envy. Several great artists were employed, inspiring each other into innovative forms of painting that departed from the rigid Byzantine conventions. St Francis expressed the wish to be buried simply, but the news of his death (in 1226) brought a flood of donations from all over Europe and construction of the basilica began in 1228. The basilica was badly damaged by the earthquake. It consists of **two churches:** the **lower church** (which is still open) was designed for peaceful meditation by his tomb, while the soaring upper church was intended to mollify the faction who wanted a glorious monument. Despite almost continuous Masses, dim lighting, enforced dress code (modesty is the key), ban on photography and rule of silence (largely ignored), the lower church is always packed and far from peaceful. Virtually every available inch of wall is covered by paintings and frescos of outstanding quality; the ones that attract most attention are by Cavallini, Martini and Lorenzetti. Steps by the altar lead to the **Treasury**, which contains a rich and diverse collection of items donated over the centuries, while the **crypt** contains the tomb of the saint and some of his closest companions.

The Upper Church suffered the most damage during the earthquake, and is closed while restoration takes place. In the Upper Church, are two renowned fresco cycles, one attributed to Giotto, depicting scenes from the *Life of St Francis*. The other is attributed to Pietro Cavallini. Both have suffered severe damage.

The *Pza del Comune,* in the centre of the old town, is dominated by the 1st-century AD **Tempio di Minerva** – part of its construction is incorporated into what is now the church of **Santa Maria**. The restored 13th-century **Palazzo Comunale** houses the **Pinacoteca Civica**, which contains a small but worthwhile collection of Umbrian Renaissance items, while the **Museo Civico** displays Etruscan and Roman fragments.

To the east of the centre, below the attractive **Duomo**, is the **Basilica di Santa Chiara**. St Clare was an early friend of St Francis and, with his guidance, established the Order of the Poor Clares, the female equivalent of the Franciscans. The church, memorable for its rose window, contains a Byzantine crucifix that is reputed to have started Francis on his religious career by commanding him to 'repair God's church'. He took that to mean **San Damiano** (signposted from Porta Nuova), a peaceful place that would certainly be more pleasing to St Francis than his own basilica. In the crypt of Santa Chiara is the miraculously preserved corpse of the saint herself, blackened with age.

The **Rocca Maggiore**, the old fortress, towers dramatically above the northern edge of the city, providing panoramic views of the town and surrounding countryside.

The **Basilica di Santa Maria degli Angeli**, near the station, surrounds a chapel used by St Francis and the spot where he died. Much more evocative, if you fancy a 4 km forest walk to the north-east, is **Eremo delle Carceri**, on the slopes of Monte Subasio. It was here, in caves, that the original Franciscans lived. You can see the cell later used by St Francis and the altar from where he addressed the birds.

## SIDE TRACK FROM ASSISI

### SPELLO

**Tourist Office:** *Pza Matteotti 3.* Open only in summer, *tel: (0742) 301 009.*

Spello is 10 mins by train from Assisi, the station being 200 m from the main road.

It's a typical little hill town with tiers of pink houses, cobbled alleys and churches, a picturesque place with some Roman remains. The 13th-century church of **Santa Maria Maggiore** contains a chapel full of brilliantly restored frescos by Pinturicchio and a 15th-century ceramic floor.

### SPOLETO

**Station:** *tel: (0743) 48 516* or *1478 88088 (toll-free).* In the lower town, with a long uphill walk south to the medieval town (or orange bus to *Pza Libertà* – tickets from the station bar). You can get a free city map from the station's news-stand.

**Tourist Office:** *Pza Liberta 7; tel: (0743) 220 311.* Open Mon–Fri 0900–1300 and 1400–1700, Sat–Sun 1000–1300 and 1630–1930.

### ACCOMMODATION

Book well ahead during the summer arts festival. At that time accommodation can be very pricey. At other times, look in the lower town. Alternatively, try **Foligno**, 26 km north-east and linked by trains that run until late. The **HI** is there: *Pza San Giacomo 11; tel: (0742) 52 882.*

   **Campsites:** *Camping Monteluco; tel: (0742) 220 358,* 15 mins walk south from *Pza Libertà* is very small and opens only in summer. **Il Girasole**; *tel: (0742) 51 335,* in the village of Petrognano, is larger and has a pool (hourly bus from station).

### SIGHTSEEING

The main area is fairly small, centred on *Pza del Mercato*. There are buses for travel further afield. Spoleto's fortunes have fluctuated since it was founded by Umbrians in the 6th century BC. After several centuries of power it fell into obscurity until being chosen (in 1958) to host Italy's leading performing arts festival, the **Festival dei Due Mondi**, which is well worth visiting at least once in a lifetime. When it happens, Spoleto, usually a gentle, tranquil place, is unrecognisably invigorated. The town comes alive, the medieval buildings wake from their usual slumber and prices, inevitably, soar. Still, even if you have to pay an arm and a leg for it, coffee in the sun in one of the cafés in the piazza is a memorable experience.

   **San Salvatore**, in the lower town, is located in the cemetery. Built by 5th-century monks, it has changed little since their day. The design of early religious buildings was often based on Roman temples and the church looks more pagan than Christian. Indeed, the fluted Corinthian columns inside it came from an antique temple. It's atmospheric at any time, especially so at dusk.

   About 200m south is the Romanesque **San Ponziano**, which has an interesting 10th-century crypt, but you have to ask the caretaker to let you in.

   Part of the small **Roman Amphitheatre**, *Pza Libertà* at the southern end of the old centre, has been carefully restored and is now used for festival performances. Another section is occupied by the convent of **Sant'Agata**, which houses a small collection of Roman artefacts. The **Arco di Druso** (AD 23), 100m north, leads to **Piazza del Mercato**, which was the Roman forum and is still a market and the hub of Spoleto's social life. It's a great place to linger, surrounded by attractive old streets and overlooked by the huge hulks of medieval buildings.

   Nearby, the small **Pinacoteca Comunale** is housed in the Palazzo del Municipio, a visit to which requires a guide. The décor is magnificent and some of the paintings outstanding, especially in the Umbrian section. Twelfth-century **Sant'Eufemia**, above the Duomo, is a lovely little Romanesque church remarkable for its early capitals and columns, and for the *matroneum*, the upper gallery where the women worshipped segregated from the men below.

   But the most spectacular building in Spoleto is the **Duomo** which, consecrated in 1198, is adorned on its entrance façade with eight rose windows all of differing sizes. Its campanile, propped up by a flying buttress, was constructed from various bits of Roman masonry and other un-medieval elements – and yet still manages to present itself as a perfect blend of Romanesque and Renaissance. Within, a baroque makeover rather ruined the effect, though Fra Filippo Lippi's magnificent frescos depicting the *Life of the Virgin* are timeless. Also of interest is **Cappella Erioli**, with a *Madonna and Child* by Pinturicchio, and the Cosmati marble floor.

   The **Rocca**, a huge 14th-century castle to the south-east of town, guards one of the finest engineering achievements of medieval times, the **Ponte delle Torri**: a bridge 240m long, supported by ten arches 80m high. From it there are magnificent views of the gorge it spans and there's a pleasant 2 km walk (turn right) leading to **San Pietro**, with a façade adorned by some of the region's finest Romanesque sculpture.

**209**

# FRANKFURT

Best-known as one of Europe's major financial centres and an important rail junction, Frankfurt am Main is strategically situated on the River Main at the crossroads of the historic trade routes north of the Alps. To balance its shortage of historic buildings, following severe bombing in World War II, it offers a wealth of shops to suit all pockets, a wide choice of museums and bubbly nightlife ranging from taverns serving the local apple wine to trendy discos. The skyline is dominated by a cluster of imaginatively shaped office blocks.

**210**

## TOURIST INFORMATION

**Tourismus + Congress GmbH** (Tourist Office) is at **Frankfurt Hauptbahnhof** (Hbf) station; *tel: 212 3 88 00*. Open Mon–Fri 0800–2100, Sat–Sun 0900–1800. Hotel booking service, 5DM. Also in the city centre at *Römerberg 27*. Open Mon–Fri 0900–1730, Sat–Sun 1000–1600.

### Airport

**Flughafen Frankfurt–Main** (9 km south-west of the city) is central Europe's busiest airport and one of its most modern. Information: *tel: 690 305 11*. S–Bahn suburban trains (service S8) to Frankfurt Hbf, the city's main station, leave every 10 mins from 0430 to 0030; the journey takes 11 mins and costs DM5.80. InterCity rail services to Cologne, Dortmund, Hamburg and Nuremberg stop at the airport station every hour; *tel: 19419* for information.

### Station

**Hauptbahnhof** (Hbf), Europe's busiest rail terminus, is open round-the-clock and has excellent cafés and shops. DB (German Rail)

has also opened its first airport-style lounge there with bar, armchairs and toys. Each day over 1500 trains a day depart from the 24 platforms and it is also served by 7 S–Bahn and one U–Bahn line. Announcements are usually in English as well as German. Information, *tel: 19419*. The city centre is a 15-min walk straight ahead along *Kaiserstr*.

## GETTING AROUND

Getting around is easy, with an efficient combination of S–Bahn (overground) and U–Bahn (underground) trains, trams (streetcars) and buses, all run by **RMV**, the regional transport authority. Directions to the system, in six languages including English, are on the blue automatic ticket machines at all bus stops, tram stops and stations. Transport information: *tel: 2130*.

### Tickets

Buy tickets (valid for all RMV transportation) at newspaper booths and blue auto-mat machines. A single ticket costs DM2.90 (or DM3.40 for use 0630–0830 and 1600–1830). The **Frankfurt Card**, available from Tourist Offices, gives unlimited travel on all public transport, including local and S–Bahn trains to the airport, as well as half-price admission to fifteen museums and the zoo; DM10 for one day, or DM15 for two.

### Taxis

Taxis are plentiful and metered. A short city-centre journey costs about six times as much as a single RMV ticket. To book a taxi; *tel: 23 00 01; 25 00 01; 23 00 33;* or *54 50 11*.Bikes can be hired at Hbf.

## STAYING IN FRANKFURT

### Accommodation

The range of accommodation is extensive, from a wide array catering to business travellers and conferences through to an assortment of sleazy pensions near Hbf. Between these extremes, the city offers fairly plentiful inexpensive accommodation, including Europe's biggest youth hostel. Mid-range accommodation can be in short supply during the many trade fairs. **InterCity Hotel**, *Poststr. 8; tel: 27 39 10* (which has up-to-the-minute train times on a TV screen at reception), and the small **Bauer Hotel Domicil**, *Karlstr. 14; tel: 27 11 10*, are close to Hbf. Chains include *BW, Cn, Dorint, Hd, Ib, IC, Ke, Ma, Mc, Md, Mv, Nv, Pu, Rm, Sc, Sf, Sg, Sh, Sn, Steigenberger, Tp, Travel Inn.* The Tourist Office in Hbf will book you a room. Accommodation can also be booked on arrival at the airport through **DER Deutsches Reiseburo**, *tel: 69 30 71*, 0800–2100 daily, or **Flughafen Frankfurt-Main Reiseburo**, *tel: 6 90 62 11*, 0800–2100, both in area B Arrivals. Europe's biggest **youth hostel**, **Haus der Jugend**, with 500 beds, is by the river at *Deutschherrnufer 12, 60594 Frankfurt 70, tel: 61 90 58*.

### Eating and Drinking

Given Frankfurt's less-than-exciting reputation, you are in for a pleasant surprise when it comes to food and drink. Not only does the city have a representative of virtually every national cuisine, it also has a plentiful choice of *Lokale* (taverns) serving local and regional treats like *Eisbein* (stewed pork knuckle) and *Handkäse mit Musik* (sour cheese garnished with chopped onions and caraway seeds) and *Sauerkraut*. Above all, of course, there's the original **frankfurter** – long, thin and at its tastiest eaten in a really fresh roll at a street stall. Everywhere restaurants spread their tables onto the traffic-free streets and squares from spring to autumn. You'll find a particularly good selection along *Fressgasse* and the narrow streets running north off it. For the more informal *Lokale*, head south of the river to the **Sachsenhausen** district, particularly streets like *Schweitzerstr.* or the cobbled *Gross Rittergasse* and *Kleine Rittergasse*. The city's own beverage is apple wine called *Apfelwein* (nicknamed *Stöffche*), a deceptively strong variety of cider. The *Apfelweinlokale* is a Frankfurt institution; a wreath of pine branches over the door means a freshly pressed supply is available. *Hocheimer* is wine from municipal vineyards. Queen Victoria liked it so much that its fame spread through British society as 'Hoch'.

### Communications

The Hbf post office is open 0700–2000 daily. The main city centre post office, **Hauptpostamt**, *Zeil 110, 6000 Frankfurt 1, tel: 211 10*, is open Mon–Fri 0800–1800, Sat 0800–1200. A late counter is open Mon–Fri until 2100, Sat until 1800 and Sun 1200–1600.

To phone Frankfurt from abroad the code is 49 (Germany) + 69 (Frankfurt). To phone the city from elsewhere in Germany, the code is 069.

### Consulates

**Australia**: *Gutleutstr. 85, 60329 Frankfurt, tel: 27 39 090*.
**UK**: *Bockenheimer Land-str. 42, 60323 Frankfurt, tel: 17 00 02 0*.
**USA**: *Siesmayerstr. 21, 60323 Frankfurt, tel: 75 35 0*.

### Money

**Thomas Cook bureau de change**: *Kaiserstr. 11; tel: 69 9139 7603*. Others are located at: *Am Riederbruch 10; Im Metro-Markt, Guerickestr.; Bockenheimer Landstr. 124*. City centre banks are normally open Mon–Fri 0830–1530 or 1600; suburban branches may close 1300–1430.

**211**

Frankfurt's lively and varied choice of entertainment spans everything from the latest dance craze to the best of classical concerts, opera, theatre, cinema and cabaret.

### Theatres, cinema and cabaret

The city's boasts several English-language theatres, including the **English Theatre**, *Kaiserstr. 52; tel: 24 23 16 20*. The **Alte Oper**, *Opernplatz, tel: 134 04 00*, a meticulous reconstruction (1981) of the 19th-century opera house, is a venue for musicals, jazz and rock concerts. Opera and ballet are staged at the new opera house, **Oper Frankfurt**, *Untermainanlage 11; tel: 2123 7333*. The city centre has more than 80 cinemas.

### Nightlife

Frankfurt has a lively satirical cabaret and alternative theatre scene, but you will need good German and a sharp eye for political background to make much sense of it. More accessible are the city's many music bars, invariably open late and catering to all tastes from rock and blues to jazz and piano favourites. Discos and dance clubs are also plentiful. Tickets and information on all types of events are available from the tourist information offices. The tourist board also publishes the free fortnightly *Frankfurter Woche* listing events and entertainments.

## SHOPPING

Shopping is as extensive as you would expect in a prosperous modern city of this size. The pedestrianised *Zeil*, which runs east from the *Hauptwache* U-Bahn station, has the main department stores – and the highest sales turnover in Germany. The most exclusive boutiques and haute couture are to be found in *Goethestr.*, while *Grosse Bockenheimer Str.*, the wider street parallel to it, is traditionally the location for Frankfurt's longest-established wine merchants and delicatessens, notable particularly for their dozens of different sausages. Hence its alternative name, *Fress-gasse* (feeding lane). An interesting selection of shops is also to be found across the river just beyond *Untermainbrücke*, along *Schweizer Str*. The famous **Höchst porcelain** is sold in the manufacturer's own shop, *Berlinerstr. 60*, or in the *Dalberger Haus, Bolongarostr.*, in the suburb of *Höchst* (S-Bahn nos 1/2), which also has an exhibition where modellers and painters can be seen working on designs (advance booking essential; *tel: 3009 020*).

## EVENTS

Most of the city's big fairs are for trade delegates only, but the **Main Fair** in August is definitely for everyone. Dating back to 1393, it takes over the streets, *Untermainkai* and *Mainkai,* along the north bank of the river from the **Römerberg** to *Untermainkaibrücke*. Its centre-piece is a big fun fair surrounded by beer and wine stalls and it ends with a huge firework display over the river. In April and Sept, a traditional folk fair, **Dippemess**, takes over the *Ratsweg* and *Festpl.* Open-air concerts, craft markets and a dragon boat race are part of the **Museumsuferfest** in July. **Sound of Frankfurt**, a night of dancing

with live bands, takes over the entire *Zeil* shopping street in mid July.

## SIGHTSEEING

Despite its serious side, Frankfurt is by no means just a city for business, as it offers tourists plenty to see and do. It is also pleasant for strolling around, thanks to the many traffic-free boulevards of shops, parks and the leafy banks of the **River Main**, which flows through the centre. In particular, the old **Sachsenhausen** district, reached by crossing the **Alte Brücke** (Old Bridge) or the **Eiserner Steg** footbridge, has an almost village-like atmosphere. Its little squares and cobbled alleys of half-timbered houses survived the World War II bombing more or less intact.

The *Römerberg,* a square of half-timbered and steeply gabled buildings, is at the heart of **old Frankfurt**, affectionately known as the *gut Stubb* (front parlour). Along one side is the **Römer**, the city's town hall, meticulously restored as it was in the Middle Ages. Inside, the **Kaisersaal** was the banqueting hall where the coronations of the Holy Roman Emperors were celebrated. A short walk to the east leads to **Kaiserdom**, *Domstr.*, the grand red sandstone Gothic cathedral, with a dome and lantern tower, where they were crowned. In the **Historischer Garten** beside it, excavations have revealed the foundations of Roman baths and medieval houses.

Frankfurt was the birthplace of Germany's most famous writer, Goethe. The **Goethe-Haus**, *Grosse Hirschgraben 23,* is a careful postwar reconstruction of the house where he was born in 1749. It is furnished in period style and has a museum with manuscripts and documents next to it.

The latest addition to Frankfurt's famous zoo, **Zoologischer Garten**, *Alfred-Brehmpl,* (U-Bahn 6 to Zoo), which was founded in 1858, is a nightlife house where nocturnal animals can be observed in daytime. To the north (U-Bahn 7/8 to Westend) are the extensive botanical gardens, **Palmengarten**, *Zeppelinallee,* with lily ponds and conservatories of orchids and cacti.

Daily 2½-hr **walking tours** (DM44) from the Tourist Offices at Hbf and Römerberg

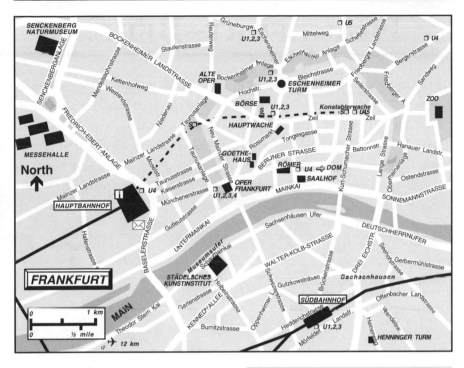

(1400 and Mar–Oct 1000) include visits to the **Goethe-Haus** and **Historisches Museum.** Circular one-hour **tram tours** (4DM) of the old town with music and *apfelwin* run Sat–Sun; information: *tel: 2132 2425.*

## Museums

Eleven of the city's forty museums are gathered on the south bank of the river along *Schaumainkai,* known as **Museumsufer** (Museum Bank). They cover a wide variety of subjects, though some (like **Museum für Post und Kommunikation** at *no.53,* about the history of Germany's post office and telephone company) are only likely to appeal to enthusiasts. Others are of more general interest, such as **Städelsches Kunstinstitut und Städtische Galerie** at *no.63,* which has one of the world's most significant collections of art from the Middle Ages to the 20th century. The exhibits in the **Historisches Museum,** *Sallgasse 19,* range from porcelain to toys. All stay open till 2000 on Wednesdays (other days 1700) and are closed Mondays.

## OUT OF TOWN

Mountain and river scenery, historic towns and villages surround Frankfurt. **Cruises** on the Main include trips to **Mainz** (37 km), where it flows into the **Rhine.** One-day and longer excursions are operated by **KD Line,** *Am Eisernen Steg, Mainkai 35, 60311 Frankfurt; tel: 28 57 28.*

**Bad Homburg** (S-Bahn 5), 12 km northwest, is famous for its casino. **Kronberg,** a 25-min ride from Hbf (S-Bahn 4) is a medieval town with a fully restored castle dating from 1230. Nearby at **Königstein** (DB train 12) are the ruins of a 10th-century castle.

Frankfurt is also the stepping off point for the 500-km '**Romantic Road**' which runs south through southern Germany's prettiest towns and scenery to **Füssen** on the Austrian border. Many places along it can be reached by train and there is also a Europabus service each day at 0800 from Hbf (Eurail and German Rail passes are accepted; Inter-Rail passholders are entitled to a 50% discount).

# FRANKFURT–BERLIN

This interesting route from Frankfurt, Germany's financial centre, to Berlin runs mostly through undulating farmland, apart from a hilly interlude and woods around Eisenach as you cross from the west into the former East Germany. It includes a string of attractive historic towns like Eisenach, associated with Luther, Wagner and Bach; Gotha, ancestral home of most of Europe's royals; Weimar, capital of the ill-fated pre-Nazi German Republic; and Leipzig with its long musical heritage. All these are now emerging from decades of neglect by both the East German regime and Western tourists.

FASTEST JOURNEY: **4 HRS 45 MINS**

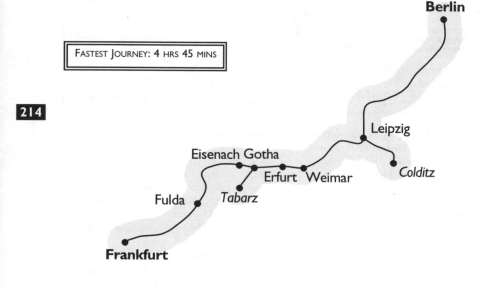

## TRAINS

**ETT tables:** 900, 810, 850.

### FAST TRACK

→ There are eight *ICE* trains hourly between Frankfurt (Hbf) and Berlin (Zoo). All have dining-cars and carry a supplement. The journey takes just under 5 hrs. There is also an overnight train, with sleepers, couchettes, first- and second-class seats, which takes 7½ hrs.

### ON TRACK

**Frankfurt–Fulda**
There is plenty of choice, with *ICE* trains hourly, *IC/EC* or *IR* trains every hour and a local service. The journey usually takes a little under an hour.

## Fulda–Eisenach
There is an hourly *IC/EC* or *IR* service throughout the day taking 50 mins *(IC/EC)* or 1 hr *(IR)*.

## Eisenach–Gotha
At least two trains every hour taking 15 mins *(IR)* or 25 mins (local train).

## Gotha–Erfurt
There are at least two trains every hour, taking about 20 mins.

## Erfurt–Weimar
Trains running from Erfurt to Weimar are frequent and take about 15 mins.

## Weimar–Leipzig
There is an *IC/EC* train every two hours, taking about 1 hr 15 mins.

## Leipzig–Berlin
There is an *IC/EC* train every two hours, the journey taking 2 hrs.

## FULDA
**Station**: Hbf, *tel: (0661) 19419*. 7 mins walk from the centre, or take a white and yellow Transity mini bus serving the centre every 10 mins; DM0.50.
**Tourist Office**: *Schloss Str. 1; tel: (0661) 10 23 45*. Open Mon–Fri 0830–1630 (Thur to 1730), Sat 0930–1400.

### ACCOMMODATION
Cheaper guesthouses near the station include **Pension Wenzel**, *Heinrichstr. 38; tel: (0661) 75335*, and **Gasthof Hodes**, *Peterstor 14, (0661) 72862*. **HI**: *Schirmannstr. 31, tel: (0661) 72276*.

### SIGHTSEEING
Fulda is an attractive town with colourful baroque façades and half-timbered buildings around small squares and along narrow alleys, all traffic-free. Its huge twin-towered **Dom** (cathedral) houses the tomb of **St Boniface** – the dagger that killed him is among the exhibits in the crypt museum on the town's 1250-year history.

The 9th-century **Michaelkirche** beside the cathedral is the oldest church in Germany and has a barrel-vaulted crypt supported by a single pillar.

In the splendid **Stadtschloss**, the private apartments of the prince-abbots who once lived there are open to visitors and an impressive array of Fulda porcelain is on show. The town's famous *Floravase*, an ornately sculptured vase nearly 7 m high, stands in its park.

## EISENACH
**Station**: Hbf, *tel: (03691) 19419*. Turn right outside for the town centre, a 5-min walk.
**Tourist Offices**: *Georgenstr. 43; tel: (03691) 79230*. Also *Markt 2; tel: (03691) 670260*. Both open Mon–Fri 0900–1230 and 1315–1800, Sat 1000–1400.

### ACCOMMODATION
The privately-owned **Hotel Kaiserhof**, *Wartburgallee 2; tel: (03691) 213513*, is very handily placed between the Hbf and town centre (expensive). **HI: Youth hostel**, *Bornstr. 7; tel: (03691) 732012*.

### SIGHTSEEING
The glory of the town is the splendid **Wartburg** on a hill on its south-west edge (12 mins by bus no. 10 from Hbf, and then 227 steps). A medieval castle with many later additions, it's an attractive complex where half-timbered buildings containing many splendid rooms surround two courtyards. Wagner used it as the setting for *Tannhäuser* and Martin Luther translated the New Testament into German there – in just 10 weeks – while being held in secret for his own protection after being excommunicated.

The 15th-century **Lutherhaus**, *Lutherplatz*, is where Luther lodged as a boy; the present half-timbered structure encloses the original house. **Bachhaus**, *Frauenplan*, once Bach's family home, is furnished in period style with documents and old musical instruments. A large statue of him stands just inside the big triple-galleried **St Georgenkirche**, *Markt*, where he was christened. Luther preached in it after making his momentuous Reformation statement at the Diet of Worms.

**215**

## GOTHA

**Station**: **Hbf**, *tel: (03621) 19419*, is at the southern end of town (tram nos. 1/2/4 to the centre; alight at *Huttenstr.*, then walk up *Erfurterstr.*)

**Tourist Office**: *Blumenbachstr. 1–3; tel: (03621) 854036.* Open Mon–Fri 0900–1800, Sat 0900–1300.

### ACCOMMODATION

The modern **Waldbahn Hotel**, *Bahnhofstr. 16; tel: (03621) 2340*, is a 1-min walk from Hbf (moderate). **HI** is at *Mozartstr. 1; tel: (03621) 854008.*

### SIGHTSEEING

This attractive little town, gateway to the **Thüringian Forest**, was the home of the Saxe-Coburg-Gotha dynasty, ancestors of the British royal family. The main market square is surrounded by colourful Renaissance and half-timbered buildings that have been beautifully restored, including the 16th-century terracotta **Rathaus**.

The plain white exterior of **Schloss Friedenstein**, on a hill overlooking the town centre, gives no hint of the ornate décor inside. Built in 1634, after the Thirty Years War, by Duke Ernst I, it now houses the municipal museum, a small baroque theatre and library of historic manuscripts.

### ↱ SIDE TRACKS FROM GOTHA

Tram no. 4 from Hbf goes to **Tabarz** in the **Thüringer Wald** (Thuringian Forest), a 1-hr ride past **Marienglashöhle**, which has lovely crystalline caves.

From **Tabarz**, a road train called *'Inselsberg Express'* goes most of the way up **Grosser Inselsberg** (916 m). It runs Apr–Nov only. ▟

## ERFURT

**Station**: **Hbf**, *tel: (0361) 19419*, a 10-min walk along *Bahnhofstr.*, or tram nos. 3/4/5.
**Tourist Offices**: *Fischmarkt 27; tel: (0361) 5626267.* Open Mon–Fri 1000–1800 and Sat 1000–1300. There is another branch at

*Krämerbrücke 3; tel: (0361) 5623436.* Open Mon–Fri 0900–1230 and 1330–1700, Sat–Sun 0900–1100.

### ACCOMMODATION

**Bauer Hotel Excelsior**, *Bahnhofstr. 35; tel: (0361) 56700*, is close to Hbf (moderate). **HI: Haus d. Jugend**, *Hagebuttenweg 47; tel: (0361) 6551532*, is a 20-min ride on tram no.6.

### SIGHTSEEING

Strolling around this small quiet town astride the gentle River Gera is a pleasure. The stylish Thuringian capital, it has a huge variety of attractive old buildings from mills to monasteries, often with poetic names.

A flight of 70 steps leads up to **Dom St Marien**, the Gothic cathedral on a hill beside the large **Domplatz**. Its beautiful stained-glass windows and carved choir stalls are real treasures, and one of the world's largest bells, the Gloriosa, cast in 1497, hangs in the middle of its three steeples. Another large church, **Severikirche**, also with three distinctive steeples, stands beside it.

An array of decorative building surround **Fischmarkt**. *Markstr.* leads off it to **Krämerbrücke**, a medieval alley lined with old houses and shops that is actually a bridge that crosses the river: you see this best from the waterside.

In the 15th century, Erfurt was noted for its altar pieces and a superb example can be seen in **Reglerkirche**, *Bahnhofstr.* To find out more on local traditions, check out the **Museum für Thüringer Volkskunde**, *140a Juri-Gagarin-Ring* (closed Mon and Tues). Exhibition gardens, planted out twice a year, are on show at the **ega-Cyriaksburg**, south-west of the town centre (tram no. 2), in the grounds of a castle with ponds and fountains – a must for gardening enthusiasts.

## WEIMAR

**Station**: **Hbf**, *tel: (03643) 19419*, is 15 mins walk north of the centre (bus nos 1/7).
**Tourist Office**: *Markt 10; tel: (03643) 24000.* Open Mon–Fri 0900–1800, Sat 0900–1600 and Sun 1000–1600 (Mar–Oct); Mon–Fri 0900–1800, Sat 0900–1300 (Nov–Feb).

### GETTING AROUND

The area of interest is concentrated in *Altstadt* and easily walkable, though horse-drawn carriages offer 45-min rides round it (Apr–Oct).

### ACCOMMODATION

**Thüringer Hotel**, *Brennerstr. 42; tel: (03643) 3675* (moderate) is by Hbf. **Flamberg Hotel Elephant**, *Markt 19; tel: (03643) 8020* (moderate) is in the heart of the Altstadt.

**HI: Germania**, *Carl-August-Allee 13; tel: (03643) 850491*, 2 mins from Hbf; and the new **Am Poseckschen**, *Humboldtstr. 17; tel: (03643) 850792*, in the centre.

### SIGHTSEEING

The entire town centre, with its wide tree-lined avenues, elegant squares and fine buildings, is officially listed as a historical monument. After decades of neglect, extensive renovation for its role as **European City of Culture** in 1999 – coinciding with the 250th anniversary of the birth of Goethe – has given it a gracious feel once more.

Smart shops, pavement cafés and a lively **Onion Fair**, which takes over the town for a weekend in October, are outward signs of Weimar's vitality. It is steeped in German culture, having been the home of two of the country's greatest writers, Goethe and Schiller, and where the ill-fated pre-Nazi Weimar Republic was founded.

The baroque mansion where Goethe lived for 50 years, **Goethehaus**, *Frauenplan 1*, displays furniture, personal belongings and a library of 5400 books. A stroll across the little River Ilm in the peaceful **Park an der Ilm** will take you to the simple **Gartenhaus**, which was his first home in the town and later became his retreat (closed Tues).

The **Liszthaus**, on the town side of the park, is the beautifully maintained residence of the Austro-Hungarian composer Franz Liszt, who moved to Weimar in 1848 to direct the local orchestra. Later he spent the last 17 summers of his life there. His piano and some scores are among the exhibits.

Schiller spent the last three years of his life at **Schillerhaus**, *Schillerstr.*, and his rooms are much as they were then, with drafts and early editions of his works. Statues of Schiller and Goethe stand in the nearby *Theaterplatz* outside the imposing **Deutsches National Theater**, where many of their plays were first perfomed.

Weimar's **Palace**, *Burgplatz 4*, houses an outstanding collection of paintings, including Dürer's *Hans and Elspeth Tucher* and several 16th-century works by Cranach. The Cranach family lived in one of the gabled buildings around the attractive *Marktplatz* and a plaque marks the house in the south corner where Bach lived during his stint as leader of the court orchestra.

The grim site of **Buchenwald** concentration camp, one of the worst horrors of the Nazi regime, is 10 km north of **Weimar** on Ettersberg hill (bus no. 6). A huge tower commemorates the 65,000 who were killed there. The site and memorial museum are closed Mon.

## LEIPZIG

**Station: Hbf**, *tel: (0341) 19419*, on the edge of the *Innenstadt* (city centre), a 7-min walk to the middle. The station, built in 1915, is one of Europe's biggest and most impressive, especially since its complete refurbishment in 1997, which included the addition of a glossy shopping mall.

**Tourist Office**: *Richard-Wagner-str. 1; tel: (0341) 710 4260*. Just inside the *Innenstadt*, a 2-min walk from Hbf. Open Mon–Fri 0900–1900, Sat 0930–1400.

### GETTING AROUND

There's a good tram network from Hbf, but most things of interest are within the pedestrianised **Innenstadt**, which is encircled by a ring road. A day card, including travel and museum discounts, costs DM9.90 (DM21 for three days).

### ACCOMMODATION

Several top-class modern hotels have been built in the city since the reunification of Germany, so accommodation is plentiful except during trade fairs, though not cheap. The new airy **Dorint**, *Stephanstr. 6; tel: (0341) 97790*, is a 10-min walk from the Innenstadt (moderate). **HI: Centrum**, *Käthe-Kollwitzstr. 64; tel:*

217

*(0341) 47 05 30,* west of the centre (tram nos. 1/2); and **Am Ausensee,** *Gustav-Eschestr. 4; tel: (0341) 461 1114,* on the north-west edge (tram nos.10/11/28), with a nearby **campsite: Am Auensee,** *Gustav-Eschestr. 5, tel: (0341) 461 1977.*

## EATING AND DRINKING

Restaurants crowd the pavements around *Kleine Fleischergasse,* such as **Zill's Tunnel,** *Barfüssgasse 9; tel: (0341) 960 2078,* a typical Saxon beerhouse serving traditional dishes. However, the most famous, because Goethe featured it in *Faust,* having dined there as a student, is the 16th-century wood-panelled **Auerbachs** cellar restaurant in the exclusive Mädler shopping arcade off *Grimmaischestr.; tel: (0341) 21600.*

## ENTERTAINMENT

Leipzig is second only to Vienna for its musical tradition, being the home of Bach, Mendelssohn and Schumann. The **Gewandhaus orchestra, Opera House** and **Thomasanerchor** (St Thomas's Church Choir), which was conducted by Bach for 27 years, have a world-wide reputation. Performances of all kinds of music take place throughout the year.

## SIGHTSEEING

Leipzig has been a cultural centre for many centuries, famous particularly for its music. **Augustus-platz,** beside the broad ring-road encircling the Innenstadt, makes a good starting point for a stroll around the pedestrianised centre, whose streets of long-neglected buildings and arcades are fast acquiring rows of smart shops and offices.

The neo-classical **Opera House** stands on one side of the vast square opposite the **Neue Gewandhaus** concert hall, home of the orchestra. The striking 34-storey sloping-top tower, **Universitätshochhaus,** a relatively new home for the 15th-century university, rises from one corner; the students call it the 'wisdom tooth'.

A plaque on an ugly university annexe nearby commemorates the 16th-century **St**

**Pauli** church, which was blown up in 1968 by order of the East German government to make way for it. In 1989, the mass demonstrations in the city were a major factor in bringing about 'the change', as the Leipzig people call it. Their candlelit vigils in **Nikolaikirche,** *Nikolaistr.,* were the focus for the city's brave peaceful revolt. The **Stasi 'Power and Banality' Museum,** *Dittrichring 24,* in the former Ministry of State Security, covers the years of communist oppression.

The central market place, **Marktplatz,** is an architectural mess, having acquired some plain modern additions. But the fine Renaissance **Altes Rathaus** has survived and now houses the **Stadtgeschictliches Museum,** covering the city's history. Beside it, the small white and gold **Alte Handelsbörse** (old trade exchange) is a 17th-century gem.

On the edge of the ring road, **Thomaskirche,** *Klostergasse,* is where Bach served as cantor from 1723 until his death in 1750. A statue of him (commissioned by Mendelssohn) stands between it and the **Bachmuseum** across the street. The new **Mendelssohnmuseum,** *Goldschmidtstr. 12,* just beyond the Ring, occupies the house where he spent his final years.

> ## ⤴ SIDE TRACKS
> ## FROM LEIPZIG
>
> **Colditz** is an attractive little town dominated by the famous 11th-century cliff-top castle. During World War II the Germans used it to imprison Allied servicemen who had won a reputation as expert escapers. 130 succeeded in getting out of it, although only 30 got all the way home. Visitors can see a French tunnel that was discovered before it could be used. Start with a visit to the **Städtisches Museum,** which contains ingenious devices made by the Prisoners of War to aid their escapes. There are regular trains from Leipzig, changing at Grossbothen. The journey takes about an hour. ⤴

# FRANKFURT–MUNICH

Vineyards stretch up the gentle slopes above the River Main as the route follows it into Bavaria, particularly through the area which produces the much respected Franconian wines. Sit on the left for the best views. As you continue south-east, the peaceful open countryside of woods and farmland is punctuated by sleepy red-roofed villages and medieval treasures like Rothenburg. Just beyond Ansbach, the route crosses Europe's watershed, the division between the rivers running north and those flowing south into the Black Sea. Finally, approaching Munich, you enter flat hop-growing country.

The section between Würzburg and Treuchtlingen is described in *Discover the Beauty of Franconia,* a railway leaflet (in English) available from the train conductor.

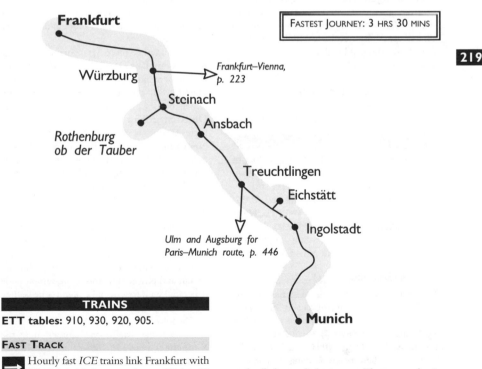

Frankfurt

Frankfurt–Vienna, p. 223

Würzburg

Steinach

Ansbach

Rothenburg ob der Tauber

Treuchtlingen

Eichstätt

Ingolstadt

Ulm and Augsburg for Paris–Munich route, p. 446

Munich

FASTEST JOURNEY: 3 HRS 30 MINS

## TRAINS

ETT tables: 910, 930, 920, 905.

### FAST TRACK

→ Hourly fast *ICE* trains link Frankfurt with Munich with journey times of 3 hrs 30 mins. Supplements are payable on these trains and all have dining cars. These travel via Stuttgart and not via the On Track route.

## ON TRACK

### ■⇢ Frankfurt–Würzburg

An hourly *IC/EC* service links Frankfurt with Würzburg. These trains have dining cars but require a supplement to be paid. The journey takes just over 1 hr. From Würzburg you can transfer onto the Frankfurt–Vienna route (p. 223) towards Nuremberg.

### Würzburg–Steinach–Rothenburg–Ansbach–Treuchtlingen

An *ICE* (supplement payable), runs every 2 hrs from Würzburg non-stop via Treuchtlingen and Augsburg to Munich (journey 2 hrs 15 mins). An hourly local service runs from Würzburg to Steinach (45 mins – side-track from here to Rothenburg), Ansbach (1 hr) and Treuchtlingen (1 hr 45 mins).

### Treuchtlingen–Eichstätt–Ingolstadt

You can go on to Munich via Ingolstadt or branch off to Nuremberg, Donauwörth and Ulm or Augsburg (see Paris–Munich, p. 446). The Treuchtlingen–Ingolstadt journey time is approximately 40 mins.

### Ingolstadt–Munich (München)

A service runs approximately hourly from Ingolstadt to Munich, taking around 1 hr.

## WÜRZBURG

**Station: Hbf,** *tel: (0931) 19419.* At the foot of vineyards on the northern edge of the town centre, a 15-min walk.
**Tourist Offices:** In front of Hbf, *tel: (0931) 373436.* Open Mon–Sat 1000–1800. **Haus Zum Falken**, *Marktplatz; tel: (0931) 373398.* Mon–Fri 1000–1800, Sat–Sun 1000–1400 (Apr–Dec), but closed Sun Nov–Dec.

## ACCOMMODATION

No shortage of hotels in all categories, including *Dorint, Maritim* and *Ring* chains. Handy for the station and moderately priced is **Pension Spehkuch**, *Rontgenring 7; tel: (0931) 54752.* **HI**: *Burkarderstr.44; tel: (0931) 42590,* on the bank of the Main, below Festung. **Campsite: Camping Canoe Club,** *Mergenheimerstr.136; tel: (0931) 72536* (tram no. 3 to *Judenbühlweg*).

## SIGHTSEEING

Two-hour guided walks around the town start from the Haus Zum Falken Tourist Office at 1400 Tues–Sun (Apr–Oct); DM13.

The domes, spires and red roofs (all seamlessly rebuilt after massive bomb damage during World War II) are seen at their best from the terrace battlements of **Festung Marienberg**, an impressive white fortress on a wooded hill above the **River Main**. It was the residence of the Prince-Bishops, converted to baroque style in the 17th century. Little remains inside, though the **Mainfränkisches Museum** displays a large collection of works by Franconian artists, including superb 16th-century wood carvings by Tilman Riemenschneider.

The Festung is best reached by bus no. 9, a 10-min ride, as otherwise it's a good 40-min walk. The walk back leads down through woods to the 12th-century **Alte Mainbrücke** footbridge, lined with statues of Prince-Bishops, and across the river to the traffic-free streets, pavement cafés and shops in the bustling town centre.

The market-place is notable for the **Marienkapelle**, a 14th-century church with Riemenschneider carvings, and the richly decorated 18th-century **Haus zum Falken**, which houses the Tourist Office. Nearby are **Dom St Kilian**, *Schönbornstr.,* which has a high baroque white chancel, and next to it the **Neumünster**, a pinkish Romanesque-baroque building, with painted ceilings, unusual green draped curtains in stucco and a pretty cloister.

The town's most important sight is the massive sandstone **Residenz**, *Residenz-pl.* Built as the new palace of the Prince-Bishops in the 18th century by Balthasar Neumann, it has been designated as a World Heritage site by UNESCO. With statues lining the roof façade, it was intended to symbolise the church's wealth and power. The rooms are sumptuously decorated with frescos and sculptures by leading artists of their day including the Venetian master Tiepolo.

Across the Main on another hill, the **Käppelle** is a graceful 18th-century pilgrimage church with twin onion-domed towers and a richly decorated interior. Its terrace also provides extensive views over the town.

## OUT OF TOWN

In summer there are river cruises – downstream to **Veitshöchheim** (which has a rococo castle and gardens) or upstream through wine-growing country to picturesque little towns like **Ochsenfurt** and **Sulzfeld**. For information, *tel: (0931) 58573.*

 **SIDE TRACK FROM STEINACH**

The train journey from Steinach to Rothenburg takes 15 mins.

### ROTHENBURG OB DER TAUBER

**Station:** Hbf; *tel: (09861) 19419,* a 10-min walk straight ahead, then follow 'Stadtmitte' signs.
**Tourist Office:** *Marktpl. 2; tel: (09861) 40492.* Open Mon–Fri 0900–1230 and 1400–1800, Sat 0900–1200, also Sat 1400–1600 (May–Oct). Accommodation reservations, 5DM and 24-hr hotel freephone. Guided tours in English at 1400 from *Marktpl.* Apr–Oct and Dec (during Christmas Market time).

### ACCOMMODATION

There is plenty of choice, including private houses, both inside and outside the old town walls. Busiest times are weekends in May, June, Sept, Oct and Dec. Opposite Hbf is the medium priced **Rotenburger Hof**, *Banhofstr.13; tel: (09861) 9730.*

HI: *Rossmühle; tel: (09861) 3177,* located in a former horse mill in the old town; not open until 1700. **Campsite: Tauber-Romantik**, *Detwang; tel: (09861) 6191,* a steep 30-min walk down the valley.

### SIGHTSEEING

This little town is 'the Jewel of the Romantic Road'. Situated on a rocky outcrop surrounded by medieval walls, its pastel-coloured steep-gabled houses – some half-timbered – are the stuff of picture-books, especially in summer, when window boxes trail with flowers.

As early as 1902, the local council, showing commendable foresight, imposed a preservation order, so it is basically the same as in the 15th century – except for its classy shops and galleries, 110 restaurants and crowds of visitors.

On *Marktpl.*, the glockenspiel on the 15th-century **Ratstrinkstube** (Councillors' Tavern), now occupied by the Tourist Office, re-enacts on the hour (1100–1500 and 2000–2200) the historic scene in 1631, during the Thirty Years War, when Mayor Nusch rose to the challenge of knocking back a gallon of wine to save the town from destruction. The annual **Meistertrunk** festivites at Whitsun commemorate his feat.

Climb the 200 steps (very steep and narrow at the top) onto **Rathaus** tower's roof for a beautiful view. Then walk down *Schmiedg.* to the **Burggarten**, shaded gardens where a castle – destroyed in an earthquake in 1356 – once stood. They provide a remarkably 15th-century view of the town and its covered walls. Another pleasant walk is along the walls which, following restoration, are intact.

Just off the market square, **St Jakobskirche**, *Klosterg.*, has two steeples and three soaring stained-glass windows dating from 1400. But it is renowned even more for its intricately-carved wood altar, the *Heiligblut-Altar*, by the famous Würzburg sulptor, Riemenschneider, which stands in the first floor West Gallery.

The **Kriminalmuseum**, *Burgg. 3–5,* displays a chilling selection of torture instruments. 🔁

### ANSBACH

**Station:** Hbf, *tel: (0981) 19419.* A 5-min walk from centre along *Karlstr.*
**Tourist Office**: *Stadthaus, Johann Sebastian Bach Platz 1; tel: (0981) 51243.* Open Mon–Fri 0900–1700 and Sat 1000–1300 (May–Oct); Mon–Fri 0900–1200 and 1400–1700 (Nov–Apr).

### ACCOMMODATION

Handy for the station is **Hotel Gasthof Augustiner**, *Karolinenstr. 30; tel: (0981) 2432,* which also has a traditional restaurant.

## SIGHTSEEING

Impressive restoration is being carried out on the half-timbered steeply-gabled baroque and rococo buildings which line the narrow streets in the old quarter of this little Franconian town, The **Markgräfliche Residenz** (Margrave's Palace), which was occupied by a long line of **Hohenzollerns**, stands on the edge. Beyond it, separated by the broad *Promenade* road, are the pretty palace gardens laid out in front of an orangerie (now a restaurant).

The **Markgrafenmuseum**, which incorporates several interesting old buildings, has displays on the margraves and the intriguing unsolved murder in 1833 of Kaspar Hauser, a young nobleman.

## EICHSTÄTT

**Station: Eichstätt Stadt**; *tel: (08421) 4409*, is served by a shuttle train from **Eichstätt Bahnhof** on the main line, a 9-min journey. The Tourist Office is a 5-min walk across the town.

**Tourist Office**: *Kardinal-Preysing-Pl.-14; tel: (08421) 7977*. Mon–Sat 0900–1830, Sun 1630–1830 (Apr–Oct); Mon–Sat 0900–1200, 1300–1700 (Nov–Mar). Information on the **Altmühl National Park**, the surrounding area, is available next door, *Notre-Dame l, tel: (08421) 6733*.

## ACCOMMODATION

**Hotel Adler**, *Marktpl. 22–24; tel: (08421) 67667*, is in a 300-year old building overlooking the bustling market square. Less expensive is the **Gasthof Ratskeller**, *Kardinal-Preysing-Pl. 8–10; tel: (08421) 1258*. **HI**; *Reichenaustr. 15; tel (08421) 4427*, 10 mins from Hbf (closed Dec–Jan).

This idyllic little town of beautifully-preserved baroque buildings nestles beside the dreamy **River Altmühl** overlooked from a wooded hillside by the **Willibaldsburg**, a splendid white palace built between the 14th and 18th centuries, which now houses the **Jura-Museum** of natural history; it is a steep but pretty 15-min climb from the station (closed Mon and lunchtimes).

The bustling **market square** of pretty gabled buildings, shops and pavement cafés

contrasts with the nearby **Residenzplatz**, a serene complex of pale green and white 18th-century mansions in a semi-circle around the imposing **Residenz**, the former bishops' residence. This is now used by the town council as offices and reception rooms (free guided tours Mon–Sat). The adjoining light and airy Gothic **Dom** (cathedral) is notable for its stained-glass windows by Hans Holbein and intricately-carved 500-year old Pappenheim altar.

## INGOLSTADT

**Station: Hbf**, *tel: (0841) 19419*. 3 km south of the centre across the **Danube**, so take bus 10 or 11; fare DM2.70.

**Tourist Office**: *Rathauspl.; tel: (0841) 305 1098*. Open Mon–Fri 0800–1200 and 1300–1700, Sat 0900–1200.

## ACCOMMODATION

One of the cheaper central hotels is **Hotel Rappensberger**, *Harderstr. 3, tel: 0841 3140*.

**HI**: *Friedhofstr 4; tel: 0841 34177*, bus no. 10 to bus station, then change to 50, 53 or 60 to *Keuztor*.

## SIGHTSEEING

Home of **Audi cars**, Ingolstadt is one of Bavaria's oldest towns. A crescent of medieval walls studded with turrets and picturesque gates surrounds the busy old quarter, where many elegant baroque houses with gables line traffic-free streets. Follow the blue arrows and you'll see the best of them (with an *Altstadrundgang* – old town circular walk – leaflet from the Tourist Office).

The town is a mixture of many styles from the 16th-century **Neues Schloss**, with its white towers and imposing battlements, which houses the **Bayerisches Armeemuseum**, *Parade-pl. 4*, a splendid collection of weapons and armour, to barracks by the Danube, now home to the **Museum für Konkrete Kunst**, *Tränktorstr. 6–8*, a remarkable modern art collection. The red brick cathedral, **Liebfrauenmünster**, commissioned by Duke Ludwig in 1425 when Ingolstadt became part of Bavaria, is impressive but the town's real gem is **Maria-de-Victoria-Kirche**, a sumptuous small rococo church in *Konviktstr.*

# FRANKFURT–VIENNA

This route from southern Germany into Austria follows the River Danube (Donau) for part of the way, accompanying it through two of Germany's most attractive old cities, Regensburg and Passau. The first half of the route is mainly through flat farmland but then, about 20 miles beyond Plattling, the river valley narrows through wooded hills. The Austrian section (beyond Passau) is through rolling green countryside, partly wooded but largely farmland dotted with tranquil villages. On the final stage, the huge ochre and cream Benedictine Abbey at Melk provides a notable landmark on the left.

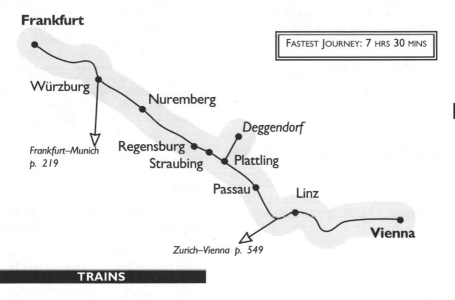

FASTEST JOURNEY: 7 HRS 30 MINS

Frankfurt

Würzburg

Nuremberg

Deggendorf

*Frankfurt–Munich p. 219*

Regensburg

Straubing

Plattling

Passau

Linz

Vienna

*Zurich–Vienna p. 549*

## TRAINS

**ETT tables:** 66, 920, 950, 888.

### FAST TRACK

➡ There are four EC trains daily (supplement payable) between Frankfurt (Hbf) and Vienna (Westbahnhof), plus one overnight EN express. The day trains have dining-cars and take about 7½ hrs. The overnight train takes 8–8½ hrs and has a dining car, sleepers and second class reclining seats. Special fares are payable.

### ON TRACK

**Frankfurt–Nuremberg (Nürnberg)–Regensburg**

There are IC/EC trains between Frankfurt (Hbf) and Regensburg every 2 hrs during the day. The journey takes nearly 3½ hrs, but there are dining-cars. If you change at either

Würzburg or Nuremberg, there are additional journeys every hour. You could also connect there with the Frankfurt–Munich route (see p.220), where Würzburg is described.

### Regensburg–Plattling–Passau

There are IC/EC trains (supplement payable) at least every 2 hrs during the day. The full journey takes 1 hr. Plattling is half-way. You can reach the Bavarian Forest (see p.226) by changing at Plattling, for Deggendorf – one of the many villages in the region.

### Passau–(Border)–Linz

Journey time varies from 1 hr 15 mins to 1 hr 40 mins, depending on whether you take an IC/EC train or an ordinary one: there are 10 trains per day, with some long gaps. Border formalities are virtually non-existent. At Linz, you can join the Zurich–Vienna route (p.549).

### Linz–Vienna (Wien)

With both ordinary trains and (more frequent) IC/EC trains, the service is at least hourly and the journey usually takes under 2 hrs. A higher fare is charged for travel in Austria by EC trains; you can pay the difference on the train.

## NUREMBERG (NÜRNBERG)

**Station: Hbf**, *tel: (0911) 19419*, on the edge of the old town centre, 5 mins to *Hauptmarkt*. **Tourist Office:** In **Hbf**, *tel: (0911) 23 36 32*, Mon–Sat 0900–1800. **Branch:** *Hauptmarkt 18, tel: (0911) 233 6135*, Mon–Sat 0900–1800; also Sun 1000–1300, 1400–1600 (May–Sept). Accommodation booking service, DM5.

### GETTING AROUND

The 4-square-km **Altstadt**, straddling the narrow **River Pegnitz**, is mostly pedestrianised, but there is a comprehensive U-Bahn, tram and bus system to go further afield.

### ACCOMMODATION

Chain hotels include *BW, FE, GT, Hd, Ib, Mc, Nv, Rk, Sc, Sn, Tp. Eilgutstr.* beside Hbf (turn left outside) has several smart hotels, including **InterCity** at *no.8; tel: (0911) 24780*. **HI** is at *Burg 2; tel: (0911) 221024*, in the castle (U-Bahn to *Plarrer*, then tram no.4). Booking

advisable. **Campsite: Dutzendteich**, *Hans Kalbstr. 56; tel: (0911) 811122;* (tram no. 12).

### SIGHTSEEING

It's hard to believe that most of the old city centre, which is surrounded by a 5-km long wall, is not original, but a faithful reconstruction after almost total destruction during World War II. The large **market square**, which is taken over by one of Germany's liveliest Christmas Markets during December, is surrounded by half-timbered buildings and overlooked by the twin-towered **St Sebalduskirche**. The terraces of the **Kaiserburg** fortifications above the north-west corner of the old town provide good views. Sights within the walls include the **Dürerhaus**, where Albrecht Dürer lived, furnished in period style, which contains several of his original woodcuts. The **Germanisches Nationalmuseum**, *Kartäusergasse 1*, founded in 1852, houses the country's largest collection of German art and culture. Outside, a striking row of 30 tall white stone columns represents the articles of the United Nations Treaty of Human Rights signed in Paris in 1948. At the foot of **Königtor** (King's tower), opposite Hbf, a small courtyard houses craft workshops in small half-timbered cottages – a good place to shop for something unusual.

Rail enthusiasts will enjoy the **Verkehrsmuseum**, *Lessingstr. 6*, just outside the wall where several old locomotives are on display, including Germany's first, which ran from Nuremburg to Fürth in 1835. 'Mad' King Ludwig's carriage is there too.

Hitler's mass rallies in the 1930s were held in the vast **Reichsparteitagsgelände**, a huge area with a vast parade ground, stadium and the shell of a massive congress hall which was never completed. One of the parts which remain, the **Zeppelin grandstand**, *Zeppelinstr.*, (S-Bahn to *Frankenstadion*, a 15-min ride) contains a moving exhibition called **Faszination und Gewalt** (Fascination and Terror). After World War II, the surviving Nazi leaders were put on trial in the city's **court**, *Furtherstr. 110*, on the western outskirts (S-Bahn 2 or tram no. 4).

## REGENSBURG

**Station: Hbf**, *tel: (0941) 19419*, is about 10

mins walk from the picturesque town centre, or take bus nos 1/2/6.

**Tourist Office: Altes Rathaus.** *Kohlenmarkt; tel: (0941) 507 4410.* Open Mon–Fri 0830–1800, Sat 0900–1600; also Sun 0930–1430 (Apr–mid Oct), located in a 14th-century building. Accommodation booking service, DM1.50.

## ACCOMMODATION

Hotel chains include *BW, Ib, Rm.* **Hotel Münchnerhof,** *Tändlergasse 9; tel: (0941) 58440* (moderate) is centrally located near the cathedral. Cheaper alternatives include **Diözesanzentrum Obermunster,** *Obermunsterpl. 7; tel: (0941) 5681 249,* and **Apollo,** *Neuprull 17; tel: (0941) 9150.*

**HI:** *Wohrdstr. 60; tel: (0941) 57402,* on an island in the Danube, 5-min walk from the centre (bus no. 5 to *Weissenburgstr.).* **Campsite: Azur,** *Am Weinweg 40, tel: (0941) 270025.*

## EATING AND DRINKING

The town claims to have the highest proportion of restaurants and bars (over 500) per head of population in Germany. Thanks to the presence of several student residences in the centre (a deliberate policy by the town council), many are reasonably-priced, like the tiny **Beim Dampfnudel-Udi,** *Watmarkt 4,* a former chapel, and **Dicker Mann,** *Krebsgasse 6.* The 850-year old **Historische Wurstküche,** *Weisselammgasse 3,* beside the Danube is Germany's oldest sausage house and sells nothing else; note the awesomely high flood marks on the walls. **Alte Linde Biergarten,** *Mullerstr. 1,* on an island in the river, is a lovely beer garden overlooking the old town.

## SIGHTSEEING

The picturesque **Altstadt,** hardly damaged in World War II and now largely pedestrianised, on the south bank of the river, has changed little in 700 years. Originally it was divided into three areas where, respectively, the princes, churchmen and merchants lived. Today, restaurants and interesting little shops occupy many of the buildings, yet it is surprisingly unspoilt by tourism.

You notice immediately that it has a distinctly Italian feel, with pretty pastel plasterwork in pinks, yellows and greens – and decorative towers on many of the former patrician houses which line the narrow streets. The town had strong trading links with Venice in the 13th century, when its merchants grew rich from the selling of silk, spices and slaves. They competed to have the biggest house (often incorporating its own chapel) in the style of an Italian fortified palace with the highest tower on top – these were never defensive, just status symbols. Originally there were 60 towers, but only 20 have survived.

The most striking is the **Baumburger Turm,** *Watmarkt.,* though the highest is the 9-storey **Goldener Turm,** *Wahlenstr.,* which now has a wine bar on the ground floor. Some of the chapels have been turned into restaurants but the tiny **Maria–Läng Kapelle,** *Pfarrgasse,* is still in use.

'Domstadt', the church area, centres on **Dom St Peter,** the magnificent Gothic cathedral which was started in the 13th century, though it was six centuries before the final touch (its twin 105m high spires) was completed. Inside, look out for amusing details like the tiny stone carvings of the devil and his grandmother just inside the main entrance – a warning to those stepping outside – and a laughing angel near the transept. It has beautiful stained-glass windows, some 14th-century, others modern, and its own interior well. The **Domschatz** (Treasury) contains some mouthwatering jewels and gold. The exterior of **Alte Kapelle,** *Alte Kommarkt,* belies the wealth of rococo decorations within, including a marble altar and superb frescos. The **Porta Praetoria** archway, *Unter den Schwibbögen,* is part of 2nd-century Roman defences.

The south-western part of town was formerly the monastic quarter and many of the old buildings survive. At the far end, the former Benedictine monastery of **St Emmeran,** was once a great centre of learning. Its 11th-century double portal survives and the crypt dates back to the 8th century.

The 12th-century 14-arch **Steinerne Brücke** over the Danube gives the best view of the medieval spires, towers and battlements along the waterfront. When it was built, it was

**225**

the only safe crossing and made Regensburg strategically important.

**Schloss Thurn und Taxis**, *Emmeramspl.*, consists of Benedictine buildings that were turned into luxurious residences in Napoleonic times. The Thurn und Taxis family pioneered Europe's postal service in the 15th century, retaining the monopoly until 1867, and now own large parts of Bavaria. The state rooms are open to the public when the family are not in residence. Its **Marstallmuseum** displays carriages of all types.

### ⤵ SIDE TRACKS
### FROM REGENSBURG

In summer, there are a variety of cruises on the Danube, departing from **Steinerne Brücke**. Destinations include **Walhalla**, where a 19th-century Greek temple modelled on the Parthenon gives a splendid view to reward the steep climb, and Straubing.

**Straubing** (which is 30 mins by train on the On Track route) is a market town dominated by a five-pointed Gothic tower and lined by the medieval façades characteristic of Bavaria's rural towns. Its **Gäubodenmuseum** contains extensive Roman artefacts discovered in the region in 1950.

The **Bayerisches Wald** (Bavarian Forest) region encompasses 6000 square km of wooded peaks, rivers, creeks and lots of tiny villages with churches, ruined castles and a traditional way of life. Within it, the **Bavarian Forest National Park** is strictly protected to safeguard the ecosystem. An hourly bus service goes round it and there are also many marked trails.

For information, contact **Tourismusverband Ostbayern**, *Luitpoldstr. 20, Ostbayern; tel: (0941) 585390.* ⤶

### PASSAU

**Station: Hbf**, *tel: (0851) 19419,* west of the centre, a 10-min walk to the right along *Bahnhofstr.* or take bus nos 7/8/9 (Mon–Fri 0630–1830).
**Tourist Offices: Main office**: *Rathauspl. 3; tel: (0851) 955980.* Open Mon–Fri 0830–1800, Sat–Sun 1000–1200, 1230–1400 (Easter–mid

Oct); Mon–Fri 0830–1700 (mid Oct–Easter). They issue a free monthly listing called *Was Wann Wo.* **Branch:** opposite Hbf: turn left and cross the road. Open Mon–Fri 0900–1700 and Sat–Sun 1000–1400 (Easter–mid Oct); Mon–Fri 0900–1200 and 1300–1700 (mid Oct–Easter).

### GETTING AROUND

With the exception of the castle, high on a hill across the Danube, everything of interest is walkable, though the 'conjunction' of the three rivers – **Danube, Inn** and **Ilz** – is 15 mins beyond the cathedral. River ferries leave from the quayside along *Fritz-Schäffer-Promenade,* in front of the Rathaus. A 45-min 'Three Rivers Round Trip' tour (Mar–Oct) is operated by **Wurm & Köch**; *tel: (0851) 929292.*

### ACCOMMODATION

Chain hotels include *Hd.* The inexpensive **Hotel Deutscher Kaiser**, *Bahnhofstr. 30: tel: (0851) 955 6615,* is opposite Hbf, but the small **Hotel Altstadt**, *Bräugasse; tel: (0851) 3370,* (moderate) is much more interestingly sited near the 'conjunction' with a pleasant terrace facing the castle across the Danube. **HI: Auf der Veste**, *Oberhaus 125; tel: (0851) 41351,* is in the castle across the Danube. Cross the bridge by the docks and be prepared for a steep climb, or take the bus from *Rathauspl.* to the door. **Campsite:** *Halserstr. 34; tel: 41457,* by the River Ilz (bus nos 1/2/3/4).

### EATING AND DRINKING

Reasonably priced restaurants spill out onto the promenades beside the Danube in summer, particularly around *Rathauspl.*

### SIGHTSEEING

Passau is a charming little town on the border with Austria. The oldest part of the town is set on a peninsula between the Danube and Inn rivers. The town's architecture is mainly baroque, rococo and neo-classical, because a major 17th-century fire destroyed most of the earlier buildings.

**Veste Oberhaus**, the former palace of the bishops and a prison for their enemies, is in a castle across the Danube on another peninsula between it and the narrower River Ils. The walk up is steep, but there are regular buses from **Hbf** and *Rathauspl*. The stronghold, which offers marvellous views, now contains the **Cultural History Museum** (54 rooms of art and artefacts spanning two millenia).

In the old town, the lofty **Stephansdom** (St Stephen's Cathedral), with its green cupolas, is a superb example of Italian baroque architecture; it has hundreds of cherubs on the ceiling and the world's largest church organ (over 17,000 pipes). Try to be there for a concert (May–Oct weekdays 1200 and Thur 1930). Behind the Dom is the cobbled **Residenzplatz**, lined with fine Renaissance buildings, including the **Domschatz** (Treasury), housed in the **Residenz**, which contains a marvellous collection of gold items and tapestries.

Also on *Residenzpl.* is the small **Spielzeugmuseum**, a collection of 19th-century toys. Next to the **Rathaus** is the **Passauer Glasmuseum**, which contains over 30,000 glass items spanning 150 years.

## LINZ

**Hbf**, *tel: (0732) 6909*. To reach the centre, take tram no. 3 to *Hauptpl.*, a 10-min ride.
**Tourist Office:** *Hauptpl. 1; tel: (0732) 7070 1777*. Open Mon–Fri 0800–1900, Sat 0900–1900, Sun 1000–1900. **Branch:** *Urfahrmarkt 1; tel: (0732) 7070 2939*. Open Mon–Fri 0800–1900, Sat–Sun 1000–1900.

The **Linz City Ticket** (ÖS399) gives unlimited travel on buses, trams, the road train and Bergbahn for 2 days and a restaurant voucher worth ÖS300.

### ACCOMMODATION AND FOOD

There is a wide range of accommodation. **Hotel Muhlviertlerhof**, *Graben 24; tel: (0732) 77 22 68* (moderate), is in an 18th-century townhouse just off *Hauptpl*. To stay near the station, try the moderate **Hotel Zur Locomotive**, *Weingartshifstr. 40, tel: (0732) 654554*. Hotel chains include *BW, Ib, Nv, Rm*. **HI: Jugendherberge Linz**, *Kapuzinerstr. 14; (0732) 78 27 20*, offers airy rooms round a courtyard.

The nearest campsite is **Campingpl. Pleschingersee**, next to the **Restaurant**

**Kolmer**; *tel: (0732) 24 78 70* (tram no. 3 from *Hbf* to *Rudolfstr.* across the river, then bus no. 32)

The pedestrian zone around *Hofgasse* is busy at night and has plenty of cheap eating places. **Klosterhof**, *Landstr. 30,* boasts the biggest beer garden in Austria. The city's traditional specialities are *Linzerschnitzel* (cutlet with a spicy coating) and *Linzer Torte* (almond pastry topped with jam).

### SIGHTSEEING

As Austria's third city, Linz's prosperity is based on its position as a Danube port. **Hauptplatz**, the 13th-century marketplace just off the river, is a large square of colourful baroque and rococo façades, with a large baroque marble monument in the middle. In 1938, Hitler stood on the balcony of *no. 1,* now the Tourist Office, to tell the Austrian people that their country had been annexed by the Nazis.

Starting from *Hauptpl.*, a yellow **road-train** provides a 25-min introduction to the central area (1000–1800 May–Sept). The 17th-century **Alter Dom**, *Domgasse,* one of the city's two cathedrals, is simple outside but tastefully baroque within; Bruckner was its organist from 1856 to 1868. The other, the huge neo-Gothic **Neuer Dom**, *Baumbachstr.,* built between 1862 and 1924, can hold 20,000 people. **Landhaus**, *Klosterstr. 7,* is where Johannes Kepler, astronomer and mathematician, developed the third law of planetary motion. A planet fountain depicts the solar system 1582-style. The **Schloss**, *Tummelpl. 10,* is a former castle used at different times as hospital, prison and barracks. Rebuilt after a fire in the last century, it now exhibits local artifacts from prehistory onwards. Nearby is **Martinskirche**, *Römerstr.,* Austria's oldest church in the country, dating back to the 700s.

Across the river, the **Pöstlingberg**, a fortress and pilgrimage church, is served by the steep **Bergbahn tram** which climbs from tram no.3's terminus at *Landgutstr.* The city's newest attraction is the **Museum of the Future** (closed Sun–Tues) in the **Ars Electronica Center**, *Hauptstr. 2.* **Boat trips** are operated from the quay, *Ernst-Koref-Promenade,* by **Wurm & Köch**; *tel: (0732) 783607.*

**227**

# FRANKFURT–ZURICH

This route between Germany and Switzerland provides an opportunity to savour superb mountain scenery as well as visiting several historic cities. It is one of Germany's most scenic routes, taking in the lovely riverside scenery of the Neckar Valley, the picturesque university town of Heidelberg and the beauty of Lake Constance.

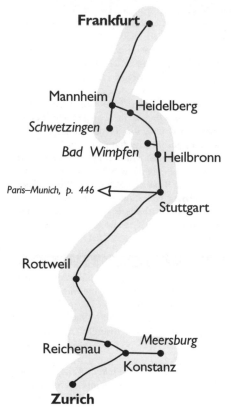

> FASTEST JOURNEY: 4 HRS

## TRAINS

**ETT tables:** 910, 930, 924, 84, 940, 946, 538, 535.

### FAST TRACK

Three direct *ICE* services run daily (supplement payable) from Frankfurt (Hbf) to Zurich (Hbf), taking about 4 hrs. These trains do not follow the On Track route but go via Karlsruhe and cross the Swiss border at Basel. With a change at Mannheim and/or Basel there is an hourly *IC/EC* service all day. All trains have restaurant cars.

### ON TRACK

**Frankfurt–Mannheim**

There are at least two trains per hour *(ICE* or *EC,* supplement payable), the journey averaging 45–50 mins.

**Mannheim–Heidelberg**

A frequent service operates, the journey taking 10–20 mins.

**Heidelberg–Heilbronn**

Two trains per hour, taking 1½–2 hrs.

**Heilbronn–Stuttgart**

Trains are irregularly spaced, but not normally more than 1 hr apart. Journey: about 45 mins.

**Stuttgart–Konstanz**

A roughly hourly service links Stuttgart with Singen, from where connecting trains run to Konstanz. The through journey takes around 3 hrs. Or at Singen you can change to the scenic line which runs north-east through the Black Forest to Offenburg (on the side-track to Freiburg on the Paris–Munich route, p. 450). The line twists and turns dramatically with long stretches high on wooded hillsides and frequent tunnels.

### Konstanz–Zurich

An hourly service links Konstanz with Zurich, with a change of train at Weinfelden. The trip takes 1½ hrs. Or as an alternative in summer, you can take a lake ferry from Konstanz to Schaffhausen (taking 4 hrs 20 mins) and then a train from Schaffhausen to Zurich (about 40 mins).

## MANNHEIM

**Station**: Hbf, *tel: (0621) 19419,* south-east of the centre, a 10-min walk straight ahead along *Kaiserring,* or tram no.3.
**Tourist Office**: *Kaiserring 10; tel: (0621) 10 10 11;* opposite Hbf. Open Mon–Fri 0900–1900, Sat 0900–1200. 2-hr city bus tours start at 1000 Fri and Sat from the Water Tower (DM19).

### ACCOMMODATION

Chains include *BW, Hd, Maritim, Nv, Rm, Sn, Tp.* The modern **Delta Park**, *Kaplerstr. 24; tel: (0621) 44510,* is a short walk from Hbf (moderate).

### SIGHTSEEING

Mannheim is essentially a busy industrial city with a large port area, built on the spit of land where the Neckar joins the Rhine. Severely damaged during World War II, the streets in its rebuilt central area, the **Planken**, are still laid out in their original 18th-century grid ('named' by numbers and letters). The city's symbol is the **Wasserturm**, *Friedrichspl.,* an impressive pink sandstone watertower, 60 m high and surrounded by gardens. The **Kunsthalle** opposite has one of Germany's finest collections of 19th- and 20th-century European art. Near Hbf, the massive baroque **Kurfürstliche Schloss**, where the Prince Electors lived, is now the university.

### SIDE TRACKS FROM MANNHEIM

**Schwetzingen** (15 mins by frequent train service) is renowned for the 18th-century **Schwetzinger Palace**. The building itself is not vastly interesting, but its extensive gardens are full of statues, follies and fountains.

## HEIDELBERG

**Station**: Hbf, *tel: (06221) 19419,* a good 20 mins walk to the edge of the **Altstadt**, or take bus no. 33 to *Kornmarkt.*
**Tourist Office**: directly in front of Hbf; *tel: (06221) 19433.* Open Mon–Sat 0900–1900; also Sun 1000–1800 (Apr–Oct). *'Heidelberg Aktuell'* is the monthly listings guide. An accommodation booking service costs DM5. The **Heildelberg Card** is valid for city travel and castle admission, DM19.80 (2 days) or DM34 (4 days). Guided walking tours in English, Mon–Fri at 1400 (Apr–Oct) from *Universitätspl.,* DM10.

### GETTING AROUND

A network of buses and trams serve the pedestrianised *Altstadt,* where a funicular ride saves the 300-step climb up to the **Schloss**.

### ACCOMMODATION

Heidelberg is a prime tourist destination so the later you book during the summer, the further away from the centre you will find yourself staying. Medium-priced central hotels include **Krokodil**, *Kleinschmidtstr. 12, tel: (06221) 24059,* which has smart rooms and friendly service (15-min walk from Hbf or two stops on tram no. 1) or the simpler **Schmitt**, *Blumentstr. 54; tel: (06221) 27296.* Chain hotels include: *BW, Hd, Ib, Rk, Rn, Tp.* **HI**: *Tiergartenstr. 5; tel: (06221) 41 20 66,* near the Zoo, 25 mins walk or bus no. 33. **Campsite**: **Camping Neckartal**, *Heidelberg-Schlierbach; tel: (06221) 80 25 06,* east of the old town (bus no. 35).

### EATING AND DRINKING

The *Altstadt* is very touristy and its restaurants lively with a student atmosphere. Many spill out onto the traffic-free streets. You are spoilt for choice along *Heiliggeistr.* and *Untere-str.* For good value, try **Im Perkeo**, *Haupstr. 75,* where you serve yourself to freshly cooked hot dishes, salads and pastries.

*Kneipen* (taverns) are an important part of Heidelberg life and in term-time they fill up with students. Try **Knosel**, *Haspelg. 20;*

**229**

Schnookeloch, *Haspelg. 8;* **Zum Roten Ochsen**, *Haupstr. 217,* or **Zum Sepp'l**, *Haupstr. 213.*

## ENTERTAINMENT

The highlight of summer is the **castle festival** throughout August, when performances (in English) of Romberg's romantic operetta *'The Student Prince'* are staged outdoors in the cobbled courtyard; for tickets, *tel: (06221) 583521.* Grand fireworks displays are held on the first Sat in June, July and Sept.

## SIGHTSEEING

Heidelberg's setting, beneath wooded hills along the banks of the **River Neckar** and overlooked by castle ruins, make it a magnet for tourists and film-makers. It has a long history and is home to Germany's oldest university (founded in 1386). Most of the buildings in the **Altstadt** date from the 18th century following wholesale destruction by Louis XIV's troops in 1693.

The city's most famous sight – star of many a film – is the part-ruined pink sandstone **castle**, high above the town. From its terraces you get a beautiful view over the red rooftops and gently flowing river. Inside you can see the **Grosses Fass**, said to be the world's largest wine vat, and the **Apothekenmuseum**, which has a 17th-century pharmacy and alchemist's laboratory.

Many fine old mansions are scattered around the old town (**Altstadt**) and one of the joys of a visit is to just wander around looking at them. The buildings around *Marktpl.* include the Renaissance **Haus zum Ritter**, and the 14th-century **Heiliggeistkirche** (Church of the Holy Spirit). **Universitätsplatz**, which has the **Löwenbrunnen** (lion fountain) in the centre, is the the location of both the 'old' and 'new' universities, **Alte Universität** (1712) and **Neue Universität** (1930), though the really modern campus is north-west of town. Until 1914, students whose high spirits had got out of hand were confined in the special **students' prison** round the corner in *Augustinerstr.* Incarceration was regarded as an honour and self-portraits are common in the graffiti on the walls.

The **Palais Morass**, *Hauptstr. 97,* is an 18th-century mansion with splendid rooms displaying works by Riemenschneider, Dürer and Van der Weyden.

Across the river, over the **Alte Brücke**, the steep **Schlagenweg** steps zig-zag up through orchards to the **Philosophenweg**. This is a scenic lane across the hillside, so-called because the views inspired philosophic meditation. Certainly it provides a beautiful panorama over the town, which looks at its best bathed in the evening sun that makes the castle's pink stones glow. The lane leads on up to **Heilingenberg**, or back down to the west end of the town (an hour's round trip on foot).

## OUT OF TOWN

**Cruises** on the **River Neckar** are run in summer by **Rhein-Neckar-Fahrgastschiffahrt**, *tel: (06221) 20181,* and **Personenschiffahrt Hornung**, *tel: (06221) 48 00 64,* departing from the quay by *Stadthalle.* Along the banks, half-timbered villages nestle in woods below old castles on rocky crags. Within a few minutes you reach **Neckargemünd** (Tourist Information: *Haupstr. 25; tel: 06223 3553)* and then **Neckarsteinach** (Tourist Information: *Hauptstr. 7; tel: 06229 92000),* which boasts four ruined castles.

## HEILBRONN

**Station**: **Hbf**, *tel: (07131) 19419,* a good 10-min walk to the centre. Frequent bus services, 1.50 DM.

**Tourist Office**: *Rathaus, Marktpl.; tel: (07131) 56 22 70.* Open Mon–Fri 0900–1730 and Sat 0900–1200.

## ACCOMMODATION

A good selection of mostly modern hotels includes the **Schlachthof**, *Frankfurter Str. 83, tel: (07131) 81413,* near Hbf. Convenient for the centre is **Rutsch**, *Deutschhofstr. 37, tel: (07131) 82862.* Both are moderate in price. **HI**: *Schirmannstr. 1, tel: (07131) 172961* (bus no. 1). **Campsite**: **Heilbronn Camping**, *tel: (07130) 8558* is at *Löwenstein,* south-east of the town by the **Breitenauer See**, one of the best and most scenic sites in Germany. Open all year.

## EVENTS

During the second week of Sept, a **Weindorf** (wine festival) takes over the town centre. The local *Swabian* wines – all 240 of them – can be sampled at stalls to the sound of 'oompah' bands.

## SIGHTSEEING

Nestling beside the **River Neckar**, Heilbronn is at the centre of one of Germany's largest wine-producing areas. The town itself is mainly modern with traffic-free streets around **Kilianskirche**, *Kilianspl.* This Gothic church, the town's symbol, has a superbly carved altar and intricate 62m belfry topped by a figure bearing Heilbronn's coat of arms. It stands over the **healing spring** after which the town is named. Don't miss the imaginative modern fountain with bronze figures in a corner of the square outside. The **Rathaus**, rebuilt in its original Renaissance style after World War II bombing, has an **astronomical clock** which performs every four hours including noon and 4 pm.

*Das Käthchen von Heilbronn*, a romantic story written by Heinrich von Kleist in 1808, put the town firmly on the map. It tells of a local girl called Kathy who becomes obsessed by a knight and marries him after being revealed as the emperor's daughter.

## ⇄ SIDE TRACKS FROM HEILBRONN

Cruises on the **River Neckar** from *Friedrich-Ebert-Brücke* near *Marktpl.* (May–Oct) go downstream to **Bad Wimpfen** and **Gundelsheim** twice a day. For information, *tel: (07131) 85430.* **Bad Wimpfen**, which can also be reached by train (20-min journey) is a picturesque old town above the river. Its cobbled streets are lined with crooked half-timbered houses. Tourist Information in the old station, *tel: (0763) 97200.* **Gundelsheim**, in the shadow of **Schloss Horneck**, is the best point from which to reach another impressive castle, **Burg Guttenberg**. This is home of a unique collection of birds of prey. ◾

## STUTTGART

**Station: Hbf**, *tel: (0711) 19419,* is only 5 mins walk from the central *Schlosspl.* along the main shopping street.

**Tourist Office**: *Konigstr.1A; tel: (0711) 222 8240,* opposite Hbf. Mon–Fri 0930–2030, Sat 0930–1800, Sun 1100–1800 (from 1300 Nov–Apr). 24-hr Fax Info-Service; *tel: (0711) 957680-4200.* Free accommodation booking service. They sell theatre tickets and the good value **City Pass**, DM27.50, for 3 days travel and museum discounts, and **Night Pass**, DM12 (free entrance to discos and bars). *Stuttgarter Monatsspiegel* is the monthly listing; the free '*Young and Fun*' covers events, discos, etc, for young people. **Youth Information**, *Rotebühlpl. 2221, tel: (0711) 2222 730.*

## ACCOMMODATION AND FOOD

Hotel prices around the station tend to be high as it is so central. **Hollis Arche**, *Bärenstr. 2, tel: (0711) 24 57 59,* is reasonably priced. **Märrlin**, *Friedrichstr. 39, tel: (0711) 29 13 15,* is a small pension four blocks away. Chain hotels include: *Bw, Ch, Hd, IC, InterCity, Mc, Mv, Nv, Rk* and *Sn.* **HI**: *Hausmannstr.27; tel: (0711) 24 15 83,* is 15-mins uphill walk from Hbf (or U15/16: *Eugenspl.*). **Campsite**: **Cannstatter Wasen**, *Mercedesstr. 40; tel: (0711) 55 66 96,* is beside the River Neckar (tram nos 1/2). Open all year.

The local wines are excellent and best sampled with traditional Swabian dishes at the many *Weinstuben* (wine bars). During the summer, open-air beer gardens spring up in the many park areas. The summer ends with a two-week **wine festival** followed in early autumn by a huge **beer festival** (across the river in *Bad Canstatt*), which is second only to Munich's **Oktoberfest**. *Calwer-str.* has a good choice of restaurants, or for more informal eating try around *Rosenstr.*, *Brennerstr.* and *Wagnerstr.*, all south-east of the Rathaus.

## ENTERTAINMENT

Stuttgart has an excellent reputation for music, particularly its opera and ballet at the **Staatstheater** in the **Schlossgarten**, *Konrad Adenauerstr.; tel: (0711) 20 20 90.* There are also numerous theatres.

231

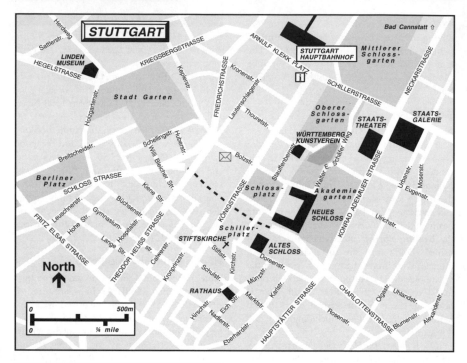

## SIGHTSEEING

The city is much better known for its vibrant cultural activities and as the home of the **Daimler-Benz** and **Porsche** motor factories than for its sights. But the traffic-free centre, radiating from the huge *Schlosspl.* with its pavement cafés, fountains and gardens, is an extremely pleasant place to stroll. Along one side is the **Neues Schloss**, the former palace of the Württemberg kings, now offices. The **Württembergisches Landesmuseum**, *Schillerpl.* occupies the **Altes Schloss** opposite, an imposing Renaissance palace. Its exhibits range from 19th-century crown jewels and Swabian sculptures to an intact Celtic grave and Renaissance clocks. The nearby **Stiftskirche**, extensively rebuilt over the centuries, has remarkable modern windows and Renaissance carvings of eleven of the rulers of Württemberg around the choir.

Round the corner, the **Market Hall** groans with delicacies on Saturdays and a **fleamarket** is held on *Karlspl.* on Thur and Sat.

The **Schlossgarten** park stretches all along the city centre as far as the **River Neckar** and then joins the **Rosensteinpark**, whose **Wilhelma** area in the north-east corner includes a natural history museum, a Moorish garden with a large lily pond and a zoo holding over 9000 animals.

The **Staatsgalerie Stuttgart**, *Konrad-Adenauer-Str.30,* which has a striking postmodern wing by James Stirling, houses one of the world's largest Picasso collections. One room is devoted to *The Legend of Perseus* by Edward Burne-Jones.

Motor enthusiasts should head for the **Daimler-Benz Museum**, *Mercedesst. 137, Bad Cannstatt* (S1 to *Gottlieb-Dailer Stadion),* where 100 historic models are on show. The smaller **Porsche-Museum**, *Porrschestr. 42,* in the northern suburb of **Zuffenhausen** (S6 to *Neuwirtshaus),* displays mostly racing-cars.

You get the best overview of the city from the memorial chapel on the **Wüttenberg hill** in *Untertürkheim,* where King Wilhelm and Queen Katarina of Württemberg are buried.

## KONSTANZ

**Station: Hbf**, *tel: (07531) 19419*, is between *Bahnhofpl.*, the eastern boundary of *Altstadt*, and **Bodensee** (Lake Constance).
**Tourist Office:** *Bahnhofpl. 13; tel: (07531) 13 13 30*. Open Mon–Fri 0900–1830, Sat 0900–1300 (May–Sept), Mon–Fri 0900–1200 and 1400–1800 (Oct–Apr). Accommodation service: DM5.

### GETTING AROUND

The quay on **Lake Constance** *(Bodensee)*, behind Hbf, offers a wide choice of boat trips and cruises on the lake and the **Rhine** (which it flows into nearby). The service is seasonal. The main operator is **Bodensee-Schiffsbetriebe**, *Hafenstr. 6; tel: (07531) 28 13 98*. DB rail passes are valid. Bicycles can be hired at **Aktiv-Reisen**, *Mainaustr. 34; tel: (07531) 98280*.

### ACCOMMODATION

There's no shortage of reasonably priced places to stay, including **Hotel Petershof**, *St Gebhardstr. 14; tel: (07531) 99 33 99*, and **Barbarossa**, *Obermarkt 8–12; tel: (07531) 22021*. Hotel chains include *Mc, Steigenberger* **HI: Otto-Moericke-Turm**, *Zur Allmannshohe 18; tel: (07531) 32260*, (bus no. 4). **Campsite: Litzelstetten-Mainau**, *Grossherzog-Friedrichstr. 43; tel: (07531) 943030*, on Mainau island, which is linked by a footbridge to the north-east corner of the town (bus no. 4 or ferry).

### SIGHTSEEING

Konstanz is an attractive little town with gardens along the water's edge and an attractive old quarter, **Niederburg**, where little alleys wind between half-timbered buildings with beautifully decorated façades. Most of it is in Germany, but the southern section spills into Switzerland.

In the bustling *Marktstätte* (Market Place), elaborate frescos on the Renaissance **Rathaus** depict the town's history. The Romanesque **Münster**, *Münsterpl.*, which dates from the 11th century, has beautifully carved choir stalls (15th-century) and a modern Hillebrand organ. Don't miss the four huge copper medallions displayed in the crypt. They look so shiny and

---

### The Neckar Valley

The route between Stuttgart and Konstanz runs through the pretty Neckar Valley. It's a journey to be taken for the scenery rather than the stops en route, though the attractive market town of **Rottweil** is worth pausing at. This is the birthplace of the world-famous Rottweiler dog. Muscular, loyal and hard-working, they are descended from Roman guard-dog stock and were bred in their present form by the region's butchers who used them to pull carts – and could presumably afford to feed them.

---

bright, it's hard to believe that they are nearly 900 years old. The 15th-century **Stefanskirche**, *St Stefanpl.*, has a fine 17th-century painted ceiling in the choir. A jolly **fountain** of 1893 stands in the market place, with bronze animals for children to play on while their parents sit at a pavement café. Another in *Untere Laube* is even more unusual. Built in 1993, it is decorated with over 30 grotesque figures intended, according to its designer, to ridicule man's modern obsession with the motor car.

**233**

### Around Lake Constance

Lake and river cruises are operated by **Bodensee-Schiffsbetriebe**, *Hafenstr. 6; tel: (07531) 28 13 98*.

On **Mainau**, a delightful 110-acre island linked by footbridge to the town, a lush colourful garden surrounds a baroque palace that was used by the Teutonic Knights for over five centuries and is still inhabited.

Ferry destinations include **Meersburg**, an atmospheric hillside town with a picturesque **Markt** and old inhabited **castle**; **Unteruhldingen**, which has an **open-air museum** (with re-creations of Stone Age dwellings) and a marvellous **basilica** that is worth the 20-min uphill walk; **Uberlingen**, a strikingly attractive town with a Gothic **Münster** and several interesting old buildings; and **Reichenau**, which has three 9th-century monasteries, each surrounded by a village.

# HAMBURG

Germany's largest seaport and the country's media capital, Hamburg is also one of the most sophisticated and cosmopolitan German cities. The historic centre, numerous parks, lakes and canals combine with a diverse range of attractions and entertainment, ensuring that Hamburg is a fascinating city to visit. It's also a gateway for onward travel by ferry to ports in the UK, Denmark, Sweden and Norway.

## TOURIST INFORMATION

The **main office** for written enquiries is *Steinstrasse 7, Hamburg 20095; tel: (040) 30 05 10.* Get the free *City map and tips from A–Z* and *Top Info* magazine, which include a map of the city rail system, full details of Hamburg travel cards and an outline guide to the city's attractions. Other Tourist Offices are at *Hauptbahnhof* (by the Kirchenallee exit); *tel: (040) 30 05 12 00,* daily 0700–2300, and at the Port, between Pier 4 and 5 on the *Landungsbrücken; tel: (040) 30 05 12 00,* daily 0900-1800 (Nov–Feb 0900–1700). A special hotline for information, hotel reservations, tickets etc. operates daily from 0800–2000; *tel: (040) 30 05 13 00.*

## ARRIVING AND DEPARTING

### Airport
**Hamburg-Fuhlsbüttel**, *tel: (040) 50750,* 11 km from town centre. A bus to the city centre takes 25 mins and costs DM8. Buses run every 20 mins between 0540 and 2300, including the Airport Express which terminates at the Kirchenallee exit of *Hauptbahnhof.* Taxi fare to the city centre is approximately DM30.

### Stations
**Hauptbahnhof (Hbf)** handles most long-distance trains. It's central and on the U-Bahn. Hbf also houses the main post office, which is

open very long hours (international phones are on the second floor). The station's main exit is on *Kirchenallee.* **Altona**, in the west of the city, is the terminal for most trains serving Schleswig-Holstein. **Dammtor**, north of the centre, is unlikely to be of interest to visitors. All rail information: *tel: (040) 19419.* Frequent S-Bahn trains link the three stations.

### Ferries
**Landungsbrücken**, *Brücke 9; tel: (040) 38 90 71 (2 km from St Pauli),* is the terminal for ferries from the UK and Scandinavia.

## GETTING AROUND

The main area of interest is small enough to be walkable. **HHV** run efficient buses, **U-Bahn** (underground) and **S-Bahn** (urban trains), as well as a limited night bus service in the central area. For all transport enquiries, call *(040) 19449,* daily from 0700–2000. A range of travel cards offer good value for money. The **Hamburg Card** includes free travel on public transport, free admission to museums, and reductions of up to 30% on sightseeing tours, lake and harbour tours. A one-day card costs DM12.50; a three-day card costs DM25.50.

The **Hummeltrain** is a 1920s style train with multi-lingual guides that covers the major sights; *tel: (040) 79 28 979.* The city is dominated by water and a boat-trip is part of the experience. **Hadag**, *tel: (040) 35 74 240,* is one of the companies that run daily English-language harbour tours Mar–Oct/Nov, departing from the *Jungfernstieg* quay; *tel: (040) 34 11 41.* Divided into the Binnen- (inner) and Aussen- (outer) alster, this 455-hectare stretch of water contributes to the city's relaxed, open-air ambience. The shortest Alster cruise takes about an hour, looping through the inner and outer lakes, but there are longer inland voyages like the all-day trip to Bergedorf or the pretty summer twilight cruise through the backwater canals. For trips around the harbour and further afield, boats depart from *Landungsbrücken* piers daily every 30 mins from 0900–1800 Apr–Oct, and hourly from 1030–1530 Nov–Mar.

## STAYING IN HAMBURG

### Accommodation

Accommodation can be booked through the Tourist Office booking service: **Tourismus-Zentrale Hamburg Gmbh**, *Postfach 10 22 49, 20015 Hamburg; tel: (040) 30 05 10*. Rooms in private homes can be booked through **Privatzimmer**, *Vermittlung-Witt u Hildebrecht, Methfesselstrasse 49, Hamburg 20257; tel: (040) 49 15 666*, and **Agentur Zimmer Frei**, *Semperstrasse 16; tel: (040) 27 87 77 77*.

As one of Europe's busiest commercial centres, Hamburg offers a wide range of hotels, including representatives of the following chains: *FE, Ma, Hd, Ic, Rm, SA*. Hamburg's most luxurious and elegant hotels are the superb **Vier Jahreszeiten**, *Neuer Jungfernsteig 9–14; tel: (040) 34940*, overlooking the Binnen Aster, and **Atlantik Hotel Kempinski**, *An der Alster 72; tel: (040) 28880*, overlooking the Aussen Alster. Both date from Hamburg's 19th-century heyday as a transatlantic liner port.

Cheaper **hotel-pensions** in the central area include **Riedinger**, *St Georgestr. 8; tel: (040) 24 74 63*; **Sarah Petersen**, *Lange Reihe 50; tel: (040) 249826*; **Schmidt**, *Holzdamm 14; tel: (040) 280 21 19*; **Zentrum**, *Bremer Reihe 23; tel: (040) 280 2528*; **Selig**, *Bremer Reihe 23; tel: (040) 24 46 89*; **Meyn**, *Hansapl. 2; tel: (040) 24 53 09*; **Kohler**, *St Georgestr. 6; tel: (040) 24 90 65*; **Kieler Hof**, *Bremer Reihe 15; tel: (040) 24 30 24*. The two **HI** hostels are at *Alfred-Wegener-Weg 5; tel: (040) 31 34 88*, central (U/S-bahn: *Landungsbrücken*) and *Rennbahnstr. 100; tel: (040) 651 1671*, in the eastern suburbs (S-bahn: *Horner Rennbahn*).

### Eating and Drinking

Hamburg's cosmopolitan nature is reflected in its restaurants, with fine dining some of the best in Germany. Seafood and fish are, of course, a speciality. Prices tend to reflect the areas in which they are located, but the places in *Rathausmarkt* are not exorbitant and it's a good place to watch the world go by. *Kirchenallee, Altona, Univiertel* and *Schanzenviertel* are cheap

eating areas. The **Ratsweinkeller**, *tel: (040) 36 41 53*, is an atmospheric basement restaurant in the Rathaus, serving regional and German cuisine, while **Friesen Keller**, *Jungfernstiegt; tel: (040) 35 76 06 20*, specialises in north German cuisine and has tables on a pontoon moored on a canal. **Kartoffelkeller**, *Deichstrasse 21; tel: (040) 36 55 85*, is in an historic merchant's house and boasts 56 different kinds of potato recipe. **Brauhaus Joh. Albrecht**, *Adolphsbrücke 7; tel: (040) 36 77 40*, is a canalside guesthouse and brewery with its own landing stage and dishes designed to go well with the beer. **Groninger Braukeller**, *Ost-West Strasse 47; tel: (040) 33 13 81*, is a typical Hamburg beercellar and restaurant with a good-value menu and brewing beer on the premises. **Bavaria Blick**, *Bernard Nocht Strasse 99; tel: (040) 31 16 31 16*, is a smart, modern restaurant with good German food and a great view of the Elbe river, being on the eighth floor.

### Money

**Thomas Cook bureau de change:** *Im Metro-Markt, Papenreye 33; Mittelweg 126; Waitzstr. 19; Wiesenhoefen 3*. There are bureaux de change at the airport and Hbf.

### Communications

**Hbf** houses the main post office, with international phones on the second floor; open 0700–0200.

### Consulates

**Canada:** *ABC Strasse 45; tel: (040) 3555 6290*. **UK:** *Harvesthuder Weg 8a; tel: (040) 44 80 320*. **USA:** *Alsterufer 27; tel: (040) 41 17 10*.

## SHOPPING

Style and flamboyance are very much the name of the game, for Hamburg is not a city to hide its prosperity. Hamburg has a superb range of department stores and boutiques, particularly for fashion, interiors, china, glass and antiques. Moreover, the city has 13 elegant shopping arcades with cafés and restaurants, between *Rathausmarkt* and *Gänsemarkt*. This is the main shopping area and can easily be covered on foot. Shops along *Neuer Wall* specialise in furniture and interiors, while the *Quartier Satin*, on

235

the *ABC-Strasse* is the place to go for designer names and antiques. *Colonnaden,* a delightful pedestrianised colonnade just off *Neur Jung-fernstieg,* has pavement cafés alongside designer shops, together with specialist tobacco, tea and coffee shops.

For an alternative shopping experience, head for **Altona Fischmarkt**, a fish and flea market held every Sunday morning from 0500 (0700 in winter). The market is home to hopeful junk-pedlars whose stock in trade seems to consist of sad piles of single taps, broken spectacles or chipped crockery. Next to them may be vendors selling pricey antiques, pet stores selling live parrots, or fish stalls selling live eels.

## ENTERTAINMENT

Local nightlife is cosmopolitan, to say the least, having evolved to fulfil the needs of hard-drinking seafaring men, as well as the city's more privileged inhabitants. In the **St Pauli** quarter, north of the Elbe riverfront, raunchy sex show clubs like the long-established **Colibri** and **Salambo** tout their delights next to casinos, discos, tattoo parlours and some of Hamburg's best restaurants. The **Reeperbahn**, St Pauli's main drag, has been going strong for generations, though there is now an element of gentrification, with a growing number of bars popular with the bohemian and media set. Theatres include the **St Pauli Theater**, *Spielbudenplatz 29; tel: (040) 31 43 44,* with musicals and international guest performances; and the **Hansa–Theater**, *Steindamm 17; tel: (040) 24 14 14,* which is Germany's oldest classical musical hall. English language productions are staged at the **English Theatre**, *Lerchenfeld 14; tel: (040) 227 70 89.* Traditional jazz can be enjoyed at the **Cotton Club**, *Alter Steinweg 10; tel: (040) 34 38 78,* and **Birdland**, *Gärtnerstr. 122; tel: (040) 40 52 77.* The **DOM Amusement Fair** is open three times a year in the *Heiligengeistfeld,* from mid Mar to mid Apr, mid July to mid Aug, and early Nov to early Dec.

## SIGHTSEEING

Hamburg is Germany's second largest city, after Berlin, and also a federal state with its own Parliament. The earliest settlements date from the 7th century, with the **Hammaburg**

**Castle**, from which the city takes its name, established in the 9th century. Its importance as a port dates from the 12th century, with Hamburg becoming a member of the Hanseatic League in 1321, making it one of the most powerful and wealthy free cities in Europe.

The oldest part of the city, which survived the great fire of 1842 and Allied carpet-bombing in World War II, is around the harbour, where two museum ships are also moored: the tall ship **Rickmer Rickmers** at *Pier 1; tel: (040) 31 95 959,* open daily 1000–1730, and the more modern **Cap San Diego** at the *Uberseebrücke; tel: (040) 36 42 09,* open daily 1000–1900 in summer, 1000–1800 in winter.

**Speicherstadt**, just east of the docks, is a district of early 20th-century red-brick gabled warehouses, between *Deichtorhallen* and *Baumwall*. The **Warehouse Complex Museum**, *St Annenufer 2 in Block R; tel: (040) 31 10 91,* is open Tues–Sun 1000–1700. **Blankenese**, reached from St Pauli by ferry, is a maze of small lanes and stairways that is more like a fishing village than an exclusive city suburb.

The neo-Renaissance **Rathaus** (Town Hall), *Marktpl.* (U: *Rathaus),* is a magnificent sandstone building constructed 1886–97. Some of its 647 rooms, which can be toured when government is not in session, are adorned with tapestries, chandeliers and paintings. Tours are conducted in English daily; for details call *(040) 36 81 24 70.* The **Rathaus Tower** is one of six towers dominating the city's skyline, the others belonging to churches: **St Petri**, *Monckebergstr.* (U: *Rathaus),* in the city centre, which dates from the 12th century; the 14th-century **St Jacobi**, *Steinstr.* (U: *Monckebergstr.);* the Gothic **St Katharinen**, *Am Zollkanal* (U: *Messberg),* which has a baroque tower; and **St Nikolai**, *Ost-West-Str.* (U: *Klosterstern),* the tallest tower, which remains in a partially ruined condition as a memorial to World War II. The most impressive church is **St Michaelis**, *Krayenkamp 4c* (U/S: *Landungsbrücken),* a 132-m high baroque structure with a crypt and a viewing level at 82m, which gives panoramic views. This is the city's symbol and a trumpet solo is played from the tower every day.

Hamburg has a good range of museums, which are usually closed on Mon, with late

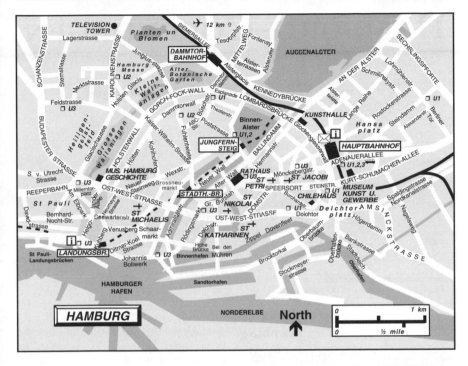

**HAMBURG**

NORDERELBE **North**

night opening on Thur. The **Kunsthalle**, *Glockengiesserwall 1; tel: (040) 24 86 26 12* (U/S: *Hbf*), has a superb art collection that dates from the Gothic period to the present day. Virtually every important artist is represented, including Canaletto, Goya and Tiepolo. The collection is complemented by the modern works in the next-door **Kunstverein**. Open Tues–Sun 1000–1800 (Thur until 2100). **Museum für Kunst und Gewerbe**, *Steintorpl. 1; tel: (040) 24 86 26 30* (U/S: *Hbf*), is the museum of arts and crafts with an excellent collection of art from ancient Egypt, Greece and Rome, along with medieval art, art nouveau and modern art, including impressive Chinese and Japanese sections. Open Tues–Sun 1000–1800 (Thur until 2100). The **Museum für Hamburgische Geschichte**, *Holstenwall 24; tel: (040) 35 04 23 60* (U: *St Pauli*) traces the city's history. The **Museum für Volkerkunde**, *Rothenbaumchaussee 64; tel: (040) 44 19 55 24* (U: *Hallerstr.*), contains a collection of ethnic and folk art. Of particular note are the Javanese shadow-puppets and pre-Columbian

jewellery. Open Tues–Sun 1000–1800 (Thur until 2100).

Among the attractions at Hamburg's tallest bulding, the 280m **TV Tower**, *Lagerstrasse 2–8* (U: *Messehallen)* are a viewing platform (open daily 1000–2300) and a revolving restaurant. Overlooked by the TV Tower is **Planten un Blomen** (U: *Stephanpl.*; S: *Dammtor),* the city's largest park, with a vast Japanese garden and illuminated fountain displays and concerts on summer nights (May–Sept). **Hagenbeck Zoo**, *tel: (040) 54 00 01 47,* in Hagenbechs Tierpark (U: *Hagenbecks Tierpark)* contains around 2500 animals (over 370 speccies) in 54 open-air enclosures surrounded by deep ditches. It was one of the first zoos to adopt this style of caging. In May and June there are Sat evening 'jungle nights' with fireworks. Open daily from 0900. **Holstenbrauerei**, *Holstenstr. 224*, offers (free) brewery tours (except Aug) that end with a sampling. For an overview of the historic centre – extensively rebuilt after the great fire of 1842 and the bombing of World War II – climb the tower of the St Michaelis Church.

# HAMBURG–COPENHAGEN

The most exciting part of this journey is the water crossing between Puttgarden, Germany and Rødby, Denmark, in which the trains follow the tracks onto ferries which sail across the border. The trains then disembark, continuing the journey on Danish tracks. The scenery is fairly uneventful, although Lübeck and Roskilde are interesting places to visit.

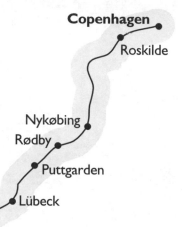

Copenhagen
Roskilde
Nykøbing
Rødby
Puttgarden
Lübeck
Hamburg

FASTEST JOURNEY: 4 HRS 30 MINS

## TRAINS

**ETT tables:** 22, 50, 825, 2375, 720.

### FAST TRACK

Seven trains a day, but two run overnight. The trip takes about 4½ hrs.

### ON TRACK

**Hamburg–Lübeck**
There are at least hourly trains throughout the day. The journey takes about 40 mins.

**Lübeck–Puttgarden–(Border)–Rødby–Nykøbing**
Five EC trains daily (supplement payable). The night trains are routed via Flensburg and use the Great Belt Tunnel. The leg between Lübeck and Puttgarden takes roughly 1 hr. Between Puttgarden and Rødby, the train is conveyed on a ferry (journey: 1 hr). The tracks on the ferry have platforms, so you can get off the train to visit the restaurant, duty-free shop and decks of the ferry. This is the main rail link between

Germany and Denmark and the cost is included in rail tickets/passes. Border formalities are minimal, sometimes non-existent. The rail leg between Rødby and Nykøbing takes about half an hour. If you're heading straight to Copenhagen, simply stay on the train (Rødby to Copenhagen takes just under 2 hrs).

**Nykøbing–Roskilde–Copenhagen (København)**
Change at Ringsted (1 hr 15 mins from Rødby) for a train to Roskilde (25 mins by local train). About 4 trains an hour run from Rinsted to Copenhagen via Roskilde daily. Journey time: about 25 mins on each leg.

### LÜBECK

**Station:** *tel: (0451) 19419.* 10 mins walk west of *Altstadt.*
**Tourist Offices:** There's a small office in the station which offers a room booking service, open Mon–Sat 0900–1300, 1500–1800. The **Central Office** is at *Breitgasse 62; tel: (0451) 122 8106/13/14,* open Mon–Fri 0930–1800, Sat–Sun 1000–1400. There is another office at *Holstentor Passage,* open Mon–Fri 1030–1830, Sat 1000–1400, Sun 1100–1300.

There are several reasonably priced hotels around Hbf. **HI**, *Am Gertrudenkirchhof 4; tel: (0451) 33433,* north east of Burgtor (bus nos. 1/3 from Hbf). The YMCA (CVJM) run a **Sleep-In**, *Grosse Burgstrasse 9–11; tel: (0451) 71920,* in the old town near Petrikirche. **Zum Goldener Anker**, *Grosse Burgstrasse 9-11, Am Burgtor,* tel *(0451) 706 0253,* is a mid-priced hotel beside the northern gate of the old city.

There's an excellent bus network, but most places of interest are in the small (and largely intact) 12th-century **Altstadt** (inner city). The town was the capital of the Hanseatic League (a 14th–16th-century trading association) and has a range of architectural styles. Twin-towered **Holstentor** is Lübeck's emblem (between Hbf and Altstadt), a 15th-century structure that was one of the four city gates. Inside is a small **Historical Museum**. Along the waterfront nearby are some lovely gabled buildings.

The Alstadt, perched on an egg-shaped island, is a World Heritage Site. The Gothic **Petrikirche**, now an art gallery, has a lift up the 50m spire: excellent for orientation. Nearby **Museum für Puppentheater**, *Kleine Petersgrube 4–6,* is devoted to theatrical puppets from all over the world. In *Grosse Petersgrube* is a music academy formed by knocking 22 handsome houses together. Both places give regular public performances.

**Markt** is dominated by the striking L-shaped 13th–16th-century **Rathaus**, typical of Lübeck's architectural style of alternating red unglazed and black glazed bricks: a style copied by the Dutch and more common in Holland. Opposite the east wing is **Niederegger Haus**, *Breitestr.,* renowned for vast displays of marzipan (the town has been producing it since the Middle Ages). Opposite the north wing is 13th-century **Marienkirche**, a brick-built Gothic church with square towers that was the model for many in the area. Later embellishments were damaged in the war and ignored in the restoration. It contains a magnificent retable and the world's largest mechanical organ (still in use).

**Heiligengeisthosspital**, *Konigstr. 9,* north of Altstadt, is very ornate inside and out. *Engelsgrubestr.* is lined by the well-preserved houses of long-ago sea captains. A block away is **Jakobikirche**, a 13th–14th-century sailors' church.

To the south of Altstadt, **St-Annen-Museum** has a first-rate collection from the 13th to the 18th-century. Nearby is the large brick-built **Dom**, which contains an allegorical triumphal arch and ornate rood screen.

<h2>ROSKILDE</h2>

**Station**: *tel: (42) 35 09 00.* Everything of interest is in the centre: about 3.5 km (downhill).
**Tourist Office**: *Gullandst 15; tel: (46) 35 27 00.* Mon–Thur 0900–1700, Fri 0900–1600, Sat 1000–1300 (Sept–Mar); Mon–Fri 0900–1700, Sat 1000–1300 (Apr–June); Mon–Fri 0900–1800, Sat 0900–1500, Sun 1000–1400 (July–Aug).

**HI**, *Horgaarden, Horhusene 61; tel: (42) 35 21 84.* Bus nos 601/604 drop you 0.8 km away.

Late June/early July sees the **Roskilde major open-air rock festival** (special campsite and a shuttle bus from the station). Many international stars are now appearing at this event.

Known as the 'Town of Viking Ships and Royal Tombs', Roskilde was Denmark's first capital and its history goes back to the 10th century. By the 12th century, however, the limitations of the harbour had become obvious and the focus of shipping shifted to Copenhagen. As the town's importance lessened, invaders ignored it and much of the old city is intact.

The twin-towered **Cathedral**, *Domkirkepladsen,* dominates the skyline. This brick edifice (c.1170–1280) replaced a 10th-century limestone one that was Denmark's first Christian church. It is the traditional burial place of Danish royalty and also contains a 500-year-old clock featuring St George and the dragon (whose dying scream marks each hour). The 400 year-old organ is one of the most important historical musical instruments in Northern Europe. In the **Viking Ship Museum**, *Strandengen,* are five 11th-century vessels that were deliberately scuttled to block the harbour entrance and protect the town from enemy fleets. The ships were brought back to the surface in 1962 and are being painstakingly restored. In summer, you can take a sailing trip on board an authentic replica.

On Wed and Sat mornings there's a fruit, vegetable and flea market in **Staendertorvet**, the town square.

239

# HELSINKI (HELSINGFORS)

Helsinki, one of the cultural capitals of Europe in 2000, is new as European cities go. Founded only in 1550, when the Swedish King Gustav Vasa decided to challenge Estonia for Baltic trade, it became the capital of Finland in 1812 (while under Russian influence). With eye-catching architecture and Eastern-influenced culture, Helsinki is a city of the sea, built on peninsulas and linked to islands by bridges.

## TOURIST INFORMATION

**City Tourist Office**, *Pohjoisesplanadi 19; tel: 169 3757* (5 blocks from the station: south on *Keskuskatu,* left on *Pohjoisesplanadi),* Mon–Fri 0930–1900, Sat–Sun 0900–1500 (May–Sept); Mon–Fri 0900–1700, Sat 0900–1500 (Oct–Apr). Most leaflets are free and include a street map. Get the very useful *Helsinki This Week.* For nationwide information, cross the road to the Finnish Tourist Board: **MEK (Matkailun edistämiskeskus)**, *Eteläesplanadi 4; tel: 4176 9211.* Mon–Fri 0830–1700, Sat 1000–1400 (June–Aug); Mon–Fri 0830–1600 (Sept–May).

The Tourist Office has information on the **Lighthouse international youth club**. Special **tourist helpers** – *Helsinki helpers* – (students wearing green and carrying green bags with an 'i') wander round the centre 0800–2000 (June–Aug) to provide general guidance.

**Helsinki Card**, from the Tourist Office, Hotellikeskus (see p.241) and travel agents, provides free public transport (including some ferries), free or discounted museum entrance and many other discounts. 24 hrs (FIM.105), 48 hrs (FIM.135) or 72 hrs (FIM.165). **Tour-Expert**, in the city Tourist Office *(tel: 622 69 90)* sells boat, bus and train and concert tickets.

**Tallink**, *Erottaja 19; tel: 2282 1277,* has the cheapest ferries and catamarans to Tallinn (see p. 532).

## ARRIVING AND DEPARTING

### Airport
**Helsinki–Vantaa**; *tel: 818 800,* 20 km north. Finnair buses depart (every 20 mins 0500–2400) from their office, *Asema-Aukio 3* (Station Yard); *tel: 818 7750.* The journey takes about 30 mins and costs FIM.25. Bus no. 615 (from the opposite side of the station) costs FIM.15, takes an hour and operates 0520–2220. Ordinary taxis cost around FIM.150, but there are special airport taxis for around FIM.50/60 if you book at least 2 hrs in advance. All hotels have details.

### Station
**Helsinki**, *tel: 010 0121* (premium-rate), open Mon–Fri 0515–0130; Sat–Sun 0515–0100. The well-equipped, award-winning art deco structure is central. English newspapers are available at *R-kioski,* a Forex office converts currency, the **VR** (Finnish Railways) information offices open 0615–2200 daily, and there are several eateries. Lockers and a lost property office are in the wing near platform 11 (open 1630–2200). The station is linked to the labyrinthine metro stop at *Rautatientori* (Railway Square) and is the terminal for many local buses, while a number of trams have stops in front of the station.

### Ferries
There are many cruises, both within Scandinavia and to Tallinn, Estonia, Germany: check whether a visa is needed for your destination. The major companies are: **Silja Line**, *Mannerheimintie 2; tel: 9800 745 52,* and **Viking Line:** *Mannerheimintie 14; tel: 123 577.*

**Long-distance buses:** *tel: 0200 4000* (premium). The main terminal is off *Mannerheimintie,* just west of the post office. Tickets can be purchased at the terminal or on board.

## GETTING AROUND

Many of the sights are in the area between the station and *Kauppatori* and trams are a quick way of reaching most of the others. A good network of buses and trams runs approximately 0600–2300 (a few continue until 0130). The public transport company is **HKL (Helsingin Kaupungin Liikennelaitos)**, with offices in *Asematunneli/Rautatientori*, **Hakaniemi** station. For information; *tel: 010 0111* (premium rate), Mon–Fri 0700–1900, Sat–Sun 0900–1700

The best way to get around is by **tram**. Tram no. 3T is frequent, 0600–0130, and has a figure-8 route, going to, or near, most of the city's main attractions. Many tram numbers are followed by a letter that denotes the direction.

The **Metro** was designed primarily for commuters. The only line serves the north and east, but it is spreading. It operates 0545–2320 (0230 at weekends) and tickets are obtained from vending machines. Single tickets for city travel cost FIM.9 and a ten-trip ticket (from R-kiosks and HKL offices) FIM.75. Tickets are valid for one hour. **City tourist tickets** (from the Tourist Office and HKL offices) give unlimited city travel for one day (FIM.25), three days (FIM.50) and five days (FIM.75).

Most local **cruises** and **ferries** leave from *Kauppatori*. Ticket kiosks on the quays indicate the time of the next departure.

**Taxi:** try **Helsinki Taxi Center** *(tel: 700 700)*, or the **station** *(tel: 651 766)*.

## STAYING IN HELSINKI

### Accommodation

**Hotellikeskus**; *tel: 171 133* (platform 11 at the station), is the hotel booking centre. Mon–Sat 0900–1900, Sun 1000–1800. There is a charge (FIM.15) for same day bookings. Hotel chains: BW, Hd, Ic, Rm, SA, Sk, Tp, but there's plenty of choice. The 4-star **Arctia Hotel Marski**, *Mannerheimintie 10; tel: 68 061,* is excellent. Five-star **Kalastajatorppa**, *Kalastajatorpantie 1; tel: 45 811*, on the coast, with an excellent restaurant, is the haunt of the rich and famous. Almost as upmarket are **Lord Hotel**, *Lönnrotinkatu 29; tel: 615 815,* and **Rivoli Jardin**, *Kasarmikatu 40; tel: 177 880*, which is cosy and central. Slightly down the scale, the small **Anna**, *Annankatu 1; tel: 616 621,* and **Arthur**, *Vuorikatu 19; tel: 173 441*, are good value.

For cheaper alternatives, try **Satakuntatalo**, *Lapinrinne 1A; tel: 695 851.* **Eurohostel** (open all year) *Linnankatu 9; tel: 622 0470*: 2 km east of the station (tram no. 4 goes within 100m, *Eurohostel*). **Stadionin retkeilymaja**, *Pohjoinen Stadionintie 3B; tel: 496 071*, on the far side of the Olympic stadium complex, is 2 km north of the station (tram no. 7A or 3T to within 500m). **Marttahotelli**, *Undenmaankatu 24; tel: 646 211*, is mid-range. **Lönnrot**, *Lönnrotinkatu 16; tel: 693 2590*, is a typical friendly low-budget choice (low by Helsinki standards at least), while **Erottajanpuisto**, *Undenmaankatu 9; tel: 642 169*, is part **HI** hostel, part cheap hotel.

**Campsite: Rastila**, *Vuosaari; tel: 316 551*, opens all year and also has cottages for two to six people. It's 14 km east (metro: *Itäkeskus* – in autumn 1998, a new metro stop will be right there called *Rastila* – then bus nos 90/90A/96).

### Eating and Drinking

The free leaflet *Helsinki This Week* gives a comprehensive listing of eating-places, categorised under such headings as 'cosy and inexpensive', 'Russian', 'gourmet' and 'seaside'. **Alexander Nevski**, *Pohjoisesplanadi 17*, is the most celebrated Russian restaurant in town: expensive, but excellent food and décor based on 19th-century St Petersburg. The **Havis Amanda**, *Unioninkatu 23*, is an excellent (and expensive) place for seafood, Finnish style. **Kuu**, *Töölönkatu 27*, is low-key yet satisfying Finnish, and **Mechelin**, *Mechelininkatu 7*, is also good for Finnish food without being at the top of the price range. **Café Strindberg**, *Pohjoisesplanadi 33*, is the place to people-watch. Try **Zetor**, *Kaivokatu 10*, an unusual pub – with a sauna and agriculturally themed décor. Students can take advantage of the exceptionally low-priced **university cafés**: *Fabianinkatu 33* and *Porthania, Hallituskatu 6*. Fried fish is available in abundance around the port, you can also pick up smoked salmon and reindeer sandwiches here, at the *Kauppahalli*; for fast food try the *Mannerheimintie* area – **Forum** offers a good choice.

### Communications

The main **post office**, *Mannerheimintie 11; tel: 02045 14400* (open Mon–Fri 0900–1700), has a poste restante section that's open daily (entrance *Asema-Aukio*) and phone and fax services. Helsinki telephone code: *9 (09* from within Finland). The area in front of the post office is being converted to a square, called *Mannerheiminaukio.* The post office will be no. 1.

## Money

**Thomas Cook licensees: Travel House Tournee Ltd,** *Siltasaarenkatu 4A; tel: (9) 7740 480;* **Tournee Elemamatkat Oy,** *Fredrikinkatu 33; tel: (9) 6801 717.*

Banks open Mon–Fri 0915–1615. **Forex** in the station (daily 0800–2100); cash exchange counter at the airport (daily 0630–2300).

## Embassies

**Canada:** *Pohjoisesplanadi 25B; tel: 171 141.*
**Republic of Ireland:** *Erottajankatu 7A; tel: 646 006.*
**South Africa:** *Rahapajankatu 1A; tel: 658 288.*
**UK:** *Itäinen Puistotie 17; tel: 2286 5100.*
**USA:** *Itäinen Puistotie 14A; tel: 171 931.*

The Tourist Office has free entertainment guides and some hotels dispense copies. *Helsinki This Week* contains monthly listings. For recorded programme information in English, *tel: 058.* Reservations for all events are handled by **Lippupalvelu,** *Mannerheimintie 5; tel: 9700 4700* (premium rate). Cultural events can also be booked with **Tiketti,** *Yrjönkatu 29C; tel: 9700 4204* (premium rate). Better yet is **Tour-Expert** (see under Tourist Information).

**Finlandia Hall,** *Karamzininkatu 4,* is the main centre for classical music. It's next door to the new **Opera House.** Films are almost invariably shown in the original language.

The evenings are lively, options ranging from discos to sophisticated nightclubs – more and more now open till 0400.

All events in the annual **Helsinki Festival** are linked by a theme. It begins late Aug and lasts two weeks, during which time the city becomes an art forum. The city Tourist Office or the Finnish Tourist Board have details.

**Mannerheimintie,** Helsinki's main artery, is home to countless shops, including the vast **Stockmann** department store (good selection

of English-language publications) and **Forum,** a complex with over 150 shops. The tree-lined **Esplanadi** is almost as busy, but the park separating the north *(Pohjoisesplanadi)* from the south *(Eteläesplanadi)* makes it more strollable. In **Tunneli** (the tunnel underneath the station), shops open until about 2200 and many open Sun. **24-hour pharmacy: Yliopiston apteekki,** *Mannerheimintie 96; tel: 415 778.*

**Kauppatori** (Market Square), by the port, has colourful waterside displays of freshly caught fish. This is where you get the best food buys. In season look for *suomuuraimet* (cloudberries), which grow under the Midnight Sun.

Helsinki is bilingual, with street names shown in Swedish as well as Finnish. As an introduction to sightseeing, there are some good boat trips from the harbour, some leave every hour.

Byzantine **Uspenski Cathedral,** *Kanavakatu 1,* is a magnificent reminder of Finland's Russian past and still serves the Orthodox community. On a hill near *Kauppatori,* the red-brick structure has green-topped towers capped by golden onion domes, each surmounted by a cross. Inside, the ceiling and upper walls are decorated and an ornate altar-screen crosses the width of the church. **Senaatintori** (Senate Square) is dominated by **Tuomiokirkko,** the domed Lutheran Cathedral designed by Engel. The interior is elegantly plain and all in curves.

The new **City Museum,** just south of *Senate Sq.,* is a high-tech survey of Helsinki's growth from a seaside village to the national capital.

The **port** is one of the most enjoyable parts of the city. From here, **Esplanadi** boulevard/park reaches inland: street musicians in summer.

**Valtion taidemuseo** (Finnish National Gallery), *Kaivokatu 2–4,* incorporates the **Ateneum** (Museum of Finnish Art), Finland's largest collection of paintings, sculptures and drawings from the 18th century to the 1960s. **Nykytaiteen museo** (Museum of Contemporary Art), under the same roof, brings it up to date – from summer 1998, this will be located next to the post office at *Mannerheimaukio.*

**Postimuseo** (Post Museum), in the post office building (entrance *Asema-Aukio),* has lots of high-tech exhibits, not just for philatelists.

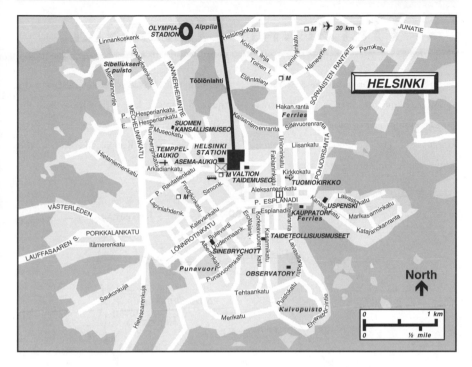

Further up *Mannerheimintie* is the **Parliament Building** on the left. **Suomen Kansallismuseo** (National Museum of Finland), *Mannerheimintie 34,* currently under renovation, has intriguing displays, including *Kalevala* paintings, that provide a guide to Finnish history and culture. The costume section is superb. The exhibition is now at *Laivurinkatu 3.* Opposite is the modern **Finlandia Hall**, whose designer, Alvar Alto, plays on his surname, which means 'wave', in the asymmetrical pattern. View the building from the other side to appreciate its effect.

**Sibeliuksen puisto** (Sibelius Park), bus no. 18, is the setting for the striking **Sibelius monument**, an attractive arrangement of steel pipes somewhat resembling an elaborate organ. The wonderful **Temppeliaukiokirkko** (Church in the Rock), *Lutherinkatu 3,* was blasted out of solid rock in 1969, to form a circular space capped by a copper-wire dome and slitted windows that make the roof resemble the sun.

The **Taideteollisuusmuseo** (Museum of Applied Arts), *Korkeavuorenkatu 23,* covers the development of applied arts and industrial design in Finland since the mid 19th century. **Sinebrychoff Ulkomaisen taiteen museo** (Sinebrychoff Museum of Foreign Art), *Bulevardi 40,* has particularly good Swedish and Russian collections. Further south, **Kaivopuisto park** forms the tip of the peninsula.

Four main **islands** hug the Helsinki peninsula, linked to Helsinki, and each other, by ferries and/or bridges. **Suomenlinna** offers a fine 18th-century fortress and a World War II U boat, *Vesikko.* **Korkeasaari** is home to **Helsinki Zoo**, which specialises in species from the Arctic. **Seurasaari** is the site of Finland's largest **open-air museum**, with 80 historic buildings. **Pihlajasaari** is a recreation centre, popular with walkers and providing the area's best beaches.

## OUT OF TOWN

At **Vantaa** is **Heureka**, the new Finnish Science Centre, *Tiedepuisto 1* (20 mins on trains H, K, P or R to *Tikkurila*). Educational for all age-groups, with fascinating interactive exhibits and a **planetarium**.

# HELSINKI–HELSINKI

Finland is known for its immense swathes of forest and thousands of lakes, and the lower portion of this route roams through flat, pretty countryside. The side track to Savonlinna brings you to Finland's greatest tourist draw, a beautiful town spread across island lakes, and a must for music lovers in July, when the world-renowned opera festival is on. The other side track to Kuopio takes you to this pretty lakeside town.

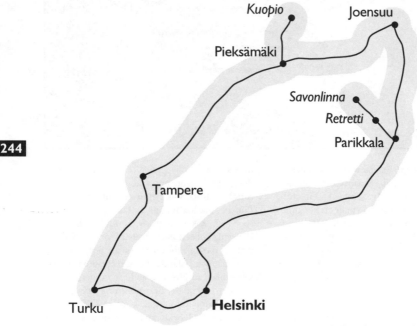

**244**

## TRAINS

**ETT tables:** 791, 792, 795.

### ON TRACK

#### Helsinki–Turku
A train every 1–2 hrs, some of which are *Pendolino* trains (supplement and reservation required). Journey time: 2 hrs. Trains that connect with the Silja Line/Viking Line ferries to Stockholm are extended to the port at Turku.

#### Turku–Tampere
Eight trains a day (all have buffets), with a 3 hr gap at most. The journey takes just under 2 hrs.

#### Tampere–Pieksämäki
Five trains, one of which arrives during the night. All have buffet cars and the journey takes 2½ hrs.

### Pieksämäki–Joensuu

Four trains, one of which travels during the night; 2 hrs 15 mins–2 hrs 30 mins.

### Joensuu–Parikkala

Four trains a day, taking just over an hour. All have a buffet.

### Parikkala–Helsinki

Four day trains, taking about 4 hrs.

## TURKU (ÅBO)

**Stations: Turku,** *tel: (02) 100 44,* is northwest of the centre, 15-min walk from the Tourist Office. Many trains continue to **Satama (Hamnen)** (the harbour). **Kupittaa** is also fairly central, but not as well equipped as Turku.
**Ferries:** At the south-west end of town. Bus no. 1 (to the main square) is more frequent than the trains.
**Tourist Offices: City Tourist Office:** *Aurakatu 4; tel: (02) 233 6366,* open Mon–Fri 0830–1800, Sat–Sun 0900–1600. The free full-colour brochure *Turku* has everything you need. **Varsinais-Suomen matkailuyhdistys (Regional):** *Läntinen Rantakatu 13; tel: (02) 251 7333,* open Mon–Fri 0900–1500, covers south-west Finland. **InterRail Centre,** *Läntiken Rantakatu 47–49; tel: (02) 253 5749,* opens Mon–Sat 0900–2100 (July–Aug).

### ACCOMMODATION

**Astro,** *Humalistonkatu 18; tel: (02) 251 7838,* between the station and the centre, has the cheapest rooms in town. **Good Morning Hotel,** *Yliopistonkatu 29; tel: (02) 232 0921,* is slightly further up the price scale. **Arctia Marina Palace,** *Linnankatu 32; tel: (02) 336 300,* is pricey but has an unbeatable riverside location. **HI** is near the Arctia at *Linnankatu 39; tel: (02) 231 6578.*

### SIGHTSEEING

**Museolinja,** a special museum bus, operates June–mid Aug.
Turku's impressive **Tuomiokirkko** (cathedral) is easily spotted by the tower's distinctive face, the result of several fires over the centuries, which has become the city's symbol.

**Turku Castle,** *Turun linna,* 2 km from the centre near the ferry terminal, is not very appealing from the outside, but the interior is a wondrous maze of passageways and halls. These fortifications were the seat of Finland's government for over 500 years – leaflets tell the rich history.
The town's newest museum is **Aboa Vetus/Ars Nova,** *Itäinen Rantakatu 4–6.* In 1992, excavations for the art museum (Ars Nova) revealed extensive remains, parts dating from the 15th century. They were left *in situ* and form the basis of 'Aboa Vetus', so history and contemporary art rub shoulders.
You can visit a trio of museum ships: **Suomen Joutsen** (a 96-m full-rigger built in 1902), **Keihässalmi** (a World War II mine carrier), both in the centre, and **Sigyn** (a 19th-century wooden 3-masted barque), near the castle.
**Sibelius-Museo** (Sibelius Museum), *Piispankatu 17,* displays over 350 musical instruments, as well as memorabilia of the composer. **Apteekkimuseo** (Pharmacy Museum), *Läntinen Rantakatu 13,* is great fun. It consists of a restored 18th-century home and a genuine old pharmacy. The latter is so complete that you feel it could open for business again at any time.
**Luostarinmäki,** *Vartiovuori Hill,* is the only area of Turku to survive a 19th-century fire and is now an **open-air museum.** In summer, students demonstrate traditional handicrafts.

## TAMPERE/TAMMERFORS

**Station:** *tel: (03) 248 2120,* 5-min walk east of the centre.
**Tourist Office:** *Verkatehtaanhatu 2; tel: (03) 212 6652/6775.* Open Mon–Fri 0830–2000, Sat 0830–1800, Sun 1100–1800 (June–Aug); Mon–Fri 0830–1700 (Sept–May). Walk up *Hämeenkatu* and turn left just before the bridge: it's on the riverside. *Tampere and its Surroundings* is a free comprehensive listing that includes a map.

### ACCOMMODATION

**Tampereen hotellivaraukset** (hotel booking centre), *Vehnämyllynkatu 6; tel: (03) 356 4800.* Open Mon–Fri 0830–1630. Hotel chains include *Arctia, BW* and *Sk.*

**245**

The four **HI** hostels include **Uimahallin Maja**, *Pirkankatu 10–12; tel: (931) 222 9460,* a hostel and hotel with reasonably priced rooms, open all year, comfortable and central (cheap). Just 1 km from the station, it's straight up *Hämeenkatu,* turn right and *Pirkankatu* is on the left. **Arctia Tampere**, right opposite the station at *Hämeen-Kata 1; tel: (03) 244 6111,* is the best mid–upper range hotel. **Camping Härmälä**; *tel: (03) 265 1355,* 5 km south of the centre (bus no. 1 to within 200m). Open mid May–Aug.

## SIGHTSEEING

Finland's second city is flanked by lakes and the rapids between them provide an eco-friendly source of energy. Tampere is also Finland's largest manufacturing centre, and the factories in town are actually quite appealing – red brick chimneys and factory buildings line the river.

**Amurin työläismuseokortteli** (Museum of Workers' Housing), *Makasiininkatu 12,* consists of 25 timber dwellings showing how workers lived during the century leading up to 1973. The buildings are *in situ* and have a genuinely lived-in feeling, aided by the deliberate untidiness of personal objects. **Hämeenmuseo** (Häme Regional Museum), *Näsin puisto park,* tells the story of ordinary people from the Stone Age to roughly where Amurin begins.

At **Tampereen Särkänniemi**, a park 20-mins walk north-west of the centre, attractions include a **children's zoo**, an **aquarium**, a **planetarium** and **Näsinneula tower** – at 168m, this is the country's tallest structure and provides a magnificent view.

A few streets to the right as you exit the station is **Tuomiokirkko** (cathedral), *Satakunnankatu,* which was built in 1907 and features some interesting works of art, while the small but ornate **Ortodoksinen Kirkko** (Orthodox Church), *Tuomiokirkonkatu 27,* dates from 1899 and is an excellent example of the neo-Byzantine style.

Don't miss the **Haiharan Nukke-ja Pukumuseo** (Haihara Doll and Costume Museum), *Hatanpää Manor, Kaukajärvi* (3 km south of the centre, 15 mins on bus no. 21). The 19th-century building is beautifully sited, in gardens on the tip of a small peninsula. It contains some 4000 dolls and puppets, the oldest being a 12th-century Incan rag doll, and a wide range of traditional Finnish costumes. The cellar concentrates on exotic exhibits, from costumed fleas and rude wooden carvings to meticulously executed Balinese-dancer dolls.

There's also a museum dedicated to **Lenin** on *Hamenpuisto,* near the end of *Hämeenkatu.* This is where Lenin met Stalin in the early 1900s – Lenin lived in Tampere after the 1905 revolution.

> ⤴ **SIDE TRACK**
> **FROM PIEKSÄMÄKI**

## KUOPIO

**Station:** *tel: (017) 211 4245,* open Mon–Fri 0800–1700. On the northern edge of town, about 500m from the central market square.

Five day trains make the journey from Pieksämäki to Kuopio, as well as the Helsinki–Oulu night train. The journey takes just under one hour.

**Tourist Office:** *Haapaniemenkatu 17; tel: (017) 182 584.* Open Mon–Fri 0900–1800, Sat 0900–1600 (June–mid Aug); Mon–Fri 0900–1700 (rest of year), by the market square. In summer, **information guides** wander round the town to provide any help tourists may need.

Hotel chains include *Arctia, BW, Cumulus, Sk.* **Hermannin Salit**, *Hermanninaukio 3A; tel: (017) 364 4961,* is 10 mins walk south of the centre and has cheap rooms and dorm beds. Moderate **Jahti**, *Snellmaninkatu 23; tel: (017) 264 4400,* is a comfortable hotel near the harbour. **Puijohoui**, *Vuorikatu 35; tel: (017) 261 4943,* is cheap and right near the station.

A provincial centre and hub for summer lake cruises, Kuopio offers several museums and good walks. The main square has an excellent market hall and fruit and vegetable stands, every day.

The main reason to stop here, however, is the outstanding **Suomen Ortodoksinen Kirkkomuseo** (Orthodox Church Museum), *Karjalankatu 1,* on top of a hill about

246

1 km north-west of the centre (bus no. 7). The Russian Orthodox religion once flourished in this area and in 1939, to safeguard them from the Germans, precious 18th-century icons and other sacred objects were gathered together from all over the country. The result is an eclectic and fascinating collection. Other sights include a pretty Lutheran cathedral, an open-air ethno museum, and a harbour with summer festivals when it's light all night. All are in the centre.

### OUT OF TOWN

The 800-year-old **Valamon luostari**, *tel: (017) 570 1504,* (Monastery of Valamo) at Heinävesi was, and is, the centre for the Russian Orthodox religion in Finland. The few artefacts that are not in the Orthodox Museum can be seen in the monastery church. You can stay on the island and guests often outnumber the monks, but shorts are not acceptable and photographs are not permitted. The Orthodox **Lintulan luostari**, *tel: (017) 563 106* (Convent of Lintula), 20 km away, also offers accommodation and is worth a visit. A full-day excursion that operates June–Aug is the easiest way to visit both briefly. If you want to stay longer, there are various options: ask the Tourist Office for details.

From Kuopio one day train and one night train continue north to **Oulu** (taking 4½–5 hrs), where it is possible to connect with the Stockholm–Narvik route, p. 486.

### JOENSUU

**Joensuu** is an interesting place to spend a few hours. It was the capital of Finnish Karelia (what was left of it after parts were ceded to the Russians in 1944) and a fair number of 19th-century wooden buildings survive. It also has a worthwhile **regional museum**, two major **churches**, **botanical gardens** and a **tropical butterfly and turtle garden**.

### PARIKKALA

Unfortunately, one of Finland's prime areas of interest is not particularly accessible, on the end of a rail spur which begins at **Parikkala**.

### SIDE TRACK FROM PARIKKALA

### SAVONLINNA

**Station:** Savonlinna-Kauppatori station is the first stop and more central than the main one. Two trains and 2–3 buses a day make the hour-long trip from Parikkala, serving Retretti (see below) en route, shortly after the crossing the Punkaharju causeway.

**Tourist Office:** *Puistokatu 1; tel: (015) 273 492.* Mon–Fri 0900–1600 (Sept–May); daily 0800–1800 (June, Aug); daily 0800–2200 (July).

**Vuorilinna**, on Vääräsaari island, just north of the rail station *(tel: 015 739 5430)* has fairly cheap rooms and a hostel.

A fashionable tsarist resort in the mid 19th century, Savonlinna has a number of attractions, but there are two which make it unmissable. **Olavinlinna**, the best-preserved medieval castle in the northern countries, was built in 1475. It's largely intact and retains a medieval character. The courtyard is the venue for an annual **international opera festival**. It's staged in July, tickets go on sale the previous Nov and it's essential to book months in advance, for accommodation as well as tickets. Contact the Tourist Office for booking information.

247

### RETRETTI

26 km away (it's on the rail spur and there are buses when the train isn't running – and the option of a cruise in summer), Retretti is a spectacular arts complex housed partly in caverns in **Punkaharju esker**, a 7-km-long Ice Age ridge of pine-crowned rocks, but also spreads into the surrounding woodlands. In addition to the many paintings and sculptures, you can attend summer concerts underground – great acoustics. The worthwhile **Lusto Suomen Metsämuseo ja Metsätietokeskus** (Lusto Finnish Forest Museum and Forest Information Centre) opened nearby in 1994. It is concerned with the inter-dependence between man and trees in the past, present and future. It's also on the rail spur (3 mins from Retretti) and there are buses at other times.

# ISTANBUL

Istanbul is unique; the gateway to Europe or to Asia, depending on which way you are travelling. To the ancient Greeks it was Byzantium. The Emperor Constantine christened it Constantinople, relocating his capital here from Rome in AD 330. Constantinople it remained until renamed by Kemal Atatürk, father of modern Turkey, in 1923. When the Roman Empire in the west collapsed in the fifth century AD, Constantinople turned eastward to rule a thousand-year empire, still known to the very end as 'Rome'. In 1453 it fell to the Ottoman Sultan Mehmet II. As the Ottoman Empire grew in strength, the city became the glittering, cosmopolitan capital of an even greater empire stretching from the Danube to the Red Sea – the city was as much Greek, Armenian, and Balkan as Turkish. This complex heritage, and its own vibrant street life, make it one of the world's most fascinating cities.

## TOURIST INFORMATION

**Main Office**: *57 Mesrutiyet Cad., Beyoglu; tel: (0212) 243 3731 or 243 2928, fax: (0212) 252 4346.* **Branches**: **Atatürk Airport**; *tel: (0212) 573 7399 or 573 4136*; **Karakoy Maritime Station**; *tel: (0212) 249 5776*; **Hilton Hotel**, *Cumhuriyet Cad., Harbiye; tel: (0212) 233 0592*; and **Sultanahmet Meydani**; *tel: (0212) 518 8754, fax: (0212) 518 1802*; **Taksim Meydani Maksem**, *tel: (0212) 245 6876*; and **Sirkeci Station**, *tel: (0212) 511 5811.* Open Mon–Sat 0900–1700, they distribute free maps and guides to Istanbul (in English) and have details on local transport.

If you have any problems, look for the special tourist police, *tel: 527 4503 or 528 5369*, who can be recognised by their beige uniforms and maroon berets.

## ARRIVING AND DEPARTING

### Airport
**Atatürk Airport** *(tel: (0212) 663 6400, fax: (0212) 663 6250)* is in Yeşilköy, 15 km west of Istanbul. Buses run every hour between Atatürk and the Marmara Hotel in *Taksim Sq.*, between 0600 and 2400.

### Stations
There are two rail terminals. **Sirkeçi Station** *(tel: (0212) 527 0050 or 520 6575)*, near the waterfront at Eminönü (express tram or 10 mins walk beside tram line to *Sultanahmet)* serves trains to Europe via Greece or Bulgaria. The bureau de change in the station will exchange only cash, but there are others immediately outside and automatic cash dispensers in the forecourt.

Rail services to Asian Turkey and beyond use **Haydarpaşa Station** *(tel: (0216) 336 0475)*, across the Bosphorus (by ferry).

Note that in Greek rail timetables, Istanbul is still referred to (in Greek script) as Constantinopolis.

## GETTING AROUND

The city is split in two by the Bosphorus straits. The Asian side is usually called *Anadolu Yakasi.* The European side is itself split by the Golden Horn *(Halic)*, an inlet of the Bosphorus. Most of the historic tourist sights are in *Sultanahmet*, south of the Golden Horn, but much of the more interesting streetlife is to be found in the *Galatasaray/Beyoglu* districts to the north, between the Golden Horn and *Taksim Square.*

There is one **express tram** line, running from Sirkeçi station west along *Divan Yolu* and *Millet Cad.*, out to the old city walls. Buy tickets from kiosks by the stops: place them in

248

the metal containers at the entrance to the platforms.

Istanbul's oldest **trams** and tramline, dating from the turn of the century, have been reprieved and refurbished and run down the 1.2-km length of *Istiklal Cad.*, the Beyoglu district's fashionable pedestrianised shopping street. They connect with the **Tünel**, a short, steep, underground railway built in 1875 to connect the hilltop avenue – then the main thoroughfare of the smart European quarter called Pera – with the warehouses and docks of the Golden Horn waterfront.

Large fleets of **buses** cover most of Istanbul, but routes can be confusing and there is no bus map, so ask for details at major stops or Tourist Offices. The major departure points are *Taksim Square, Eminönü* (near the Galata Bridge) and *Beyazit*. Tickets can be bought at kiosks or from street vendors and are surrendered into machines on board. Depending on the route taken, one or two tickets may be required.

The yellow **taxis** in Istanbul offer a simpler alternative to the buses. Fares are cheap, but ensure that the driver starts the meter when you get in. Fares double between midnight and 0600. The unique **dolmus** (communal taxis) run on set routes and cram remarkable numbers of passengers into huge, refurbished American cars or Japanese minibuses.

**Ferries** run regularly across the Bosphorus, between *Karaköy* on the European side and *Haydarpasa* and *Kadiköy;* and between *Eminönü* on the European side and *Üsküdar*. Schedules can be confusing and piers chaotic, so ask for details at the Tourist Office, or consult Thomas Cook's *Greek Island Hopping* (see Travel Essentials p. 23).

## STAYING IN ISTANBUL

### Accommodation
Chains include *Hd, Hn, Hy, Ke, Pe, Pu, Ra, Sh* and *Sw*. Most budget accommodation lies in the **Sultanahmet** district, in the back streets between *Sultanahmet Square* and the water and especially in *Yerebatan Cad.* **HI:** *6 Caferiye Sok; tel: 021 513 6150.* There is also a collection of similarly priced private hostels. Although basic and often crowded, these are cheap and

marvellously placed for Istanbul's main sights, only 2 mins walk to the Blue Mosque. There are often a few people hawking rooms to arriving rail passengers, but they are usually touting for establishments far from the centre. Make sure you know where they are and how to get there before accepting.

Most of Istanbul's top-range hotels congregate north of the Golden Horn around *Taksim* and *Harbiye,* rather characterless areas a considerable distance from the main sights. There are, however, plenty of hotels south of the Golden Horn, so it is possible to stay in this more atmospheric part of the city without having to slum it, with a particular concentration of hotels of all categories in *Beyazit, Laleli* and *Aksaray.* The Tourist Offices have a comprehensive list.

Arguably the nicest hotel in Istanbul is the **Ayasofya Pansiyonlari**, a refurbished row of traditional wooden homes, prettily painted and furnished in Ottoman style, immediately behind the Aya Sofya church. *(Soguhcesme, 34400 Sultanahmet–Istanbul, tel: (0212) 513 36 60, fax: (0212) 513 36 69).* Rooms cost around US$75 double. The Ayasofya has spawned a host of cheaper imitators in traditional wooden mansions; there are several in the streets just east of Aya Sofya and Topkapi.

A cheaper option on the other side of Sultanhamet is **Hotel Antique** *(K. Ayasofya Cad., Ogul Sok No. 17, tel: (0212) 516 49 36/516 09 97; fax: (0212) 517 63 70),* where rooms are around US$35 double.

The **Four Seasons Hotel**, *Tevfikhane Sok.1, Sultanahmet; tel: (0212) 638 8200, fax: (0212) 638 8210,* has a prime location in a former prison overlooking Aya Sofya and the Blue Mosque. Excellent quality service worth the price if you can afford it. The **Ciragan Palace Hotel Kempinski**, *Ciragan Caddesi, Besiktas; tel: (0212) 258 3377, fax: (0212) 259 6686,* directly on the Bosphorus, includes an elaborately restored Ottoman palace (although the interior décor is anything but traditional). A larger, less personal yet very high quality institution. In the moderate price range, the **Armada Hotel**, *Ahirkapi; tel: (0212) 638 1370, fax: (0212) 518 5060,* is un-touristy and tastefully traditional with all modern amenities. Near to Sultanahmet.

**249**

On **Büyük Ada**, an island in the Sea of Marmara some 40 mins away by fast catamaran, the magnificently ramshackle **Splendid Otel**, in a domed 19th-century wooden building, costs $82 for a double room.

There are four **campsites** around Istanbul, all a long way from the centre and offering no advantages to campers without vehicles.

### Eating and Drinking

Istanbul's eating options are as varied and colourful as the city itself. Surprisingly, **Sultanahmet** is a restaurant desert, with very few places to eat or drink. In the daytime, head for the **Grand Bazaar**, where there are lots of indoor and outdoor cafés, or the **Laleli** district around the university.

Istanbul, located near two seas, is naturally a great place for seafood, though it is relatively expensive. It's also a great place for vegetarians, with plenty of meat-free dishes and wonderful fresh fruit. The best place to eat is in *Çiçek Paşaji* (Flower Passage), off pedestrianised *Istiklal Cad.*, where a covered arcade and the alleys around it are packed with restaurant tables. The cheapest places are in the lane behind the arcade.

Within the Ciragan Palace, the **Tugra**, *tel: (0212) 25 33 77*, open only for dinner (1930–2330), has a fantastic view over the Bosphorus and serves expensive Ottoman cuisine. An expensive but incomparable meat grill and kebab restaurant – one of the oldest in the city – is **Beyti**, *Orman Sokak 8, Florya; tel: (0212) 663 2990*. Near the airport with garden seating in the summer (1200–2400). When you visit Topkapi Palace, stop at **Konyali**, *tel: (0212) 513 9696*, on the grounds. Lunch only – traditional fare. Two seating areas have different prices (one is self-service – no tablecloths). Breathtaking view.

Further afield, the settlements on either side of the Bosphorus are renowned for their seafood restaurants, which often afford dramatic views across the straits. These include **Ortaköy**, by the European end of the Bosphorus bridge, where, along with much eating, there is live music and dancing.

Further north, the towns of **Rumeli Kavagi** and **Anadolu Kavagi** (Asian side), are popular destinations amongst day-trippers on Bosphorus excursions. Both places seem to revolve around their copious fish restaurants.

Another good expedition is the ferry or fast catamaran trip to **Büyük Ada**, the biggest of three small islands in the Sea of Marmara. The car-free island has a harbour lined with fish and meat restaurants, and you may see dolphins on the way.

### Communications

The **main PTT office** is at *25 Yeni Postane Cad.*, near Sirkec, i Station. However, there are many branches throughout Istanbul which generally have shorter queues, both for postal services and for making telephone calls. You can make international calls at all the major PTT offices. **Pay phones** require *jetons* (tokens), which come in small, medium and large sizes and can be bought from kiosks. Few pay phones seem to function. A small *jeton* should suffice for a local call; long-distance attempts require many large ones. Card phones are more common (cards available from PTT offices). The dialling code for Istanbul is *0212* (north of the Bosphorus), or *0216* (south of the Bosphorus).

### Money

There are plenty of bureaux de change around Istanbul, especially in *Sultanahmet* and in the covered market. These *Döviz* bureaux have almost exactly the same rates. Banks usually have poor exchange rates.

Travellers' cheques are difficult to cash – some banks and post offices accept them. Due to extremely high inflation, exchange rates date rapidly, although prices stay reasonably constant in terms of Western currencies. Automatic cash dispensers are becoming more common and are convenient.

### Consulates

**Australia:** *58 Tepecik Yolu, Etiler; tel: (0212) 257 7050, fax: (0212) 257 7601.*
**Canada:** *107 Buyukdere Cad., Gayrettepe; tel: (0212) 272 5174, fax: (0212) 272 3427.*
**UK:** *34 Mesrutiyet Cad., Beyoglu; tel: (0212) 293 7540, fax: (0212) 245 4989.*
**USA:** *104–108 Mesrutiyet, Tepebasi; tel: (0212) 251 3602, fax: (0212) 251 3218.*

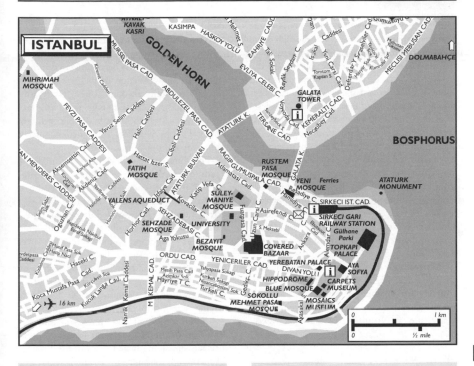

## ENTERTAINMENT

Istanbul has a thriving nightlife that caters to a range of tastes, from the urban-rich-yuppies to largely male *meyhane,* which offer a traditional experience centring on the drinking of raki. Both can be found in the side streets off *Istiklal,* in the *Beyoglu* area.

Use your discretion and be prepared to find the chicest spot in the most unlikely looking back street.

A more simple area is *Ortaköy,* which has a huge number of bars and restaurants, with the benefit of a Bosphorus view. At weekends, the streets are heaving with stalls selling jewellry, books and trinkets in a Bohemian Soho-style.

If you prefer to have a leisurely walk, try a Bosphorus walk along from Bebek to Rumeli Hisari or the ancient city walls.

## EVENTS

The **International Arts Festival** is in June and July. Its main venues are the Cemal Resit Rey Hall, Harbiye, and the Atatürk Cultural Center, Taksim.

## SHOPPING

Shopping and street life provide the best of the city's entertainment. The most famous of the markets is the **Kapali Çarşi** (Covered Bazaar), *Beyazit:* go along *Divan Yolu* from *Sultanahmet.* Not just a shopping street, but an entire district, with around 5 km of lanes, streets and alleys, the bazaar never disappoints. The pressure to buy something is strong; if you are just sight-seeing, keep moving, because the bite goes on if you so much as pause to browse. There are thousands of shops and stalls here, roughly grouped according to merchandise, with whole alleys selling gold, silver, brass or leather.

If you are going to buy anything, haggle hard; the bargaining process is a sport in itself, and is accompanied by a succession of glasses of tea brought from the nearest café (the shop-keeper pays).

Around the bazaar is a good selection of carpet shops; here too, haggling is the order of the day. There are some bargains to be had (though bear in mind that you will have to pay customs duty on your return home), but as with any work of art it takes considerable knowledge and expertise to tell the difference between first-rate and second-rate products.

The **Misir Çarşisi**, the spice bazaar near the Yeni Mosque, is equally interesting, with mounds of herbs and spices and confectioners selling dozens of different kinds of sticky Turkish delight and other colourful sweets. At weekends, the pet and pot-plant market in the square outside sells everything from geraniums to goldfish and jars of wriggling leeches. There's also a thriving street market along the waterfront by the new Galata Bridge. It mainly sells clothes, including convincing imitations of leading-brand denims; you'll also find lots of shops selling suspiciously cheap brand-name jeans on the streets leading up to Beyoglu from the Galata Bridge.

**Akmerkez**, in *Etiler*, is a huge modern shopping mall where you can find high quality clothing for reasonable prices. The chicest shopping district, where 'ladies-who-lunch' congregate, is **Nisantasi**, around *Vali Konagi St.*

## SIGHTSEEING

Its 2000-year history has left Istanbul full of monumental buildings that fight for prominence, creating a memorable skyline of domes and minarets, best seen from the Bosphorus at dawn, or the top of the **Galata Tower**, *Büyükhendek Sokak, Sishane; tel: (0212) 245 1160,* north of the Golden Horn (open daily 0800–2100). Built in 1348 by the Genoese, this now serves as a club and bar. Unlike so many other historic cities, Istanbul has been untouched by war since the Turkish conquest, so its history is more or less intact. On the other hand, the runaway development of the 1980s favoured modern unimaginative Western architecture.

Nowhere is the glut of memorable landmarks more evident than in *Sultanahmet,* where the **Aya Sofya** museum and the **Blue Mosque** sit squarely opposite one another, with the **Topkapi Palace** just a couple of hundred metres away.

### Topkapi

If you see nothing else in Istanbul, see the magnificent **Topkapi Palace** *(tel: (0212) 512 0480;* open 0930–1700, closed Tues), seat of the Ottoman Sultans from the 15th to the 19th centuries. The complex, at the tip of the old city peninsula, has now been converted into an encyclopaedic collection of the Imperial treasures, stretching through three courtyards. Allow at least a half day to take in the cream of the exhibits, which include Islamic armour, imperial robes, jewellery and precious objects, porcelain and miniatures.

The third of the palace courtyards holds the **Halls of Audience**, the **Library of Ahmet III** and, more strikingly, the glittering wealth of the **Imperial Treasury**, a staggering display of ostentation. Over-bejewelled daggers and great balls of emeralds jostle for position with gold and silver caskets and costumes stiff with silver thread and cloth of gold. Look out for the ingenious mechanical toys sent to the Sultans by European rulers eager to curry favour, and for the ruby-studded cranium of St John the Divine, seized from the monastery of Patmos.

In the centre of this inner sanctum, the **Pavilion of the Holy Mantle** houses religious artefacts, including sacred relics of the Prophet Mohammed, brought to Istanbul when the Ottoman sultans assumed the leadership of the entire Islamic world. One of the most fascinating parts of the Topkapi is the extensive **Harem** area, which housed the concubines and children of the sultans, with their attendant eunuchs. The harem can only be seen on tours, so you should go there as soon as you get to Topkapi to book for the next scheduled.

There are great views over the Bosphorus from the Palace terrace (where there is a café-restaurant), and within the Topkapi complex are several first-rate museums. Signposted off the first courtyard are the **Archaeological Museums** *(tel: (0212) 520 7740;* open 0930–1630, closed Mon), consisting of the **Archaeological Museum** itself, guardian of the Alexander Sarcophagus, the **Museum of the Ancient Orient** and **Cinili Kiosk**, the tiled pavilion, built by Mehmet the Conqueror.

The 18th-century **Ahmet III Fountain** stands at the entrance to the Topkapi. The **Church of St Irene**, the first built in Constantinople, pre-dating even Aya Sofya, is now also a museum.

## Aya Sofya

Work on **Aya Sofya** *(tel: (0212) 522 1750; open 0930–1630, closed Mon)*, formerly the Basilica of Haghia Sophia (Holy Wisdom), was started by Constantine in AD 347, but its present form is mainly due to substantial reconstruction by the Emperor Justinian in the 6th century. Aghia Sophia served as the cathedral of Constantinople until the Turkish occupation of 1453, when it was converted into a mosque.

In 1935, Atatürk turned it into a museum; a convenient non-secular label, as Aya Sofya has no conventional exhibits to offer, just the building itself. Inside, massive marble pillars support a vaulted dome 31 m in diameter and 55 m high. Aya Sofya was the the largest domed structure in the world until St Peter's in Rome was built, and its interior impresses more with its size than its decoration. Although there are some splendid mosaics around the gallery (head up the sloped flagstone walkway), the interior is an uneasy mixture; the Christian frescos which adorned the dome in Byzantine times were covered by abstract patterns while Aya Sofya was a mosque; the décor that remains is an intriguing harmony of religions.

### The Mosques and Museums

All mosques are open daily except during prayer times.

Undoubtedly the most beautiful of Istanbul's many mosques is the **Suleimaniye**, built between 1550 and 1557 for Sultan Suleyman the Magnificent by his court architect Mimar Sinan. Seen from the banks of the Golden Horn, the complex of domes and spires is the most striking sight in the old city.

Opposite Aya Sofya, the **Blue Mosque** or **Sultanahmet Mosque** was built in 1609–16 for Sultan Ahmet I in a clear attempt to outdo Justinian's Aya Sofya. Together, the two buildings form one of Istanbul's most dramatic cityscapes. The flamboyant Ahmet equipped his mosque with six minarets, a move which caused ructions with the religious authorities as it equalled the number at Mecca. Ahmet defused the situation by paying for a seventh to be built at Mecca.

The exterior of the Sultanahmet is more immediately appealing than Aya Sofya's, almost mesmeric with its sequence of nested half-domes. Thousands of turquoise *Iznik* tiles – from which the mosque gets its epithet – pick up the gentle washed light that filters in through the windows. It is certainly worth braving the touts and hustlers outside in order to view the interior. Entry is permitted outside prayer times. Be polite but firm with those who will try to convince you that it is necessary to pay ridiculously large sums for a tour, or to be let in, or to have your shoes looked after. Locals simply walk in carrying their footwear. On summer evenings a rather brash sound and light show redeems itself with some captivating floodlighting.

The **Hippodrome**, focus of Byzantine life in Istanbul, was sited in what is now the broad open space of *Sultanahmet* west of the Blue Mosque. Three columns dating from the early centuries of the Byzantine era mark the site: the 4th century **Column of Constantine**, the 6th-century **Obelisk of Theodosius**, and the bronze **Serpentine Column**. A few fragments of the Hippodrome wall can be seen nearby. Across from the Hippodrome, the **Ibrahim Paşa Palace** houses the **Museum of Turkish and Islamic Art** *(tel: (0212) 518 1906; open 1000–1700, closed Mon)*, including some priceless ancient Persian carpets.

On the other side of the Blue Mosque are the **Mosaic Museum** (open 0930–1700, closed Tues), with some Byzantine mosaics, and the quaintly named **Turkish Carpets Museum** *(tel: (0212) 518 1330)*. This latter represents the more staid end of the carpet industry in Istanbul. Open 0900–1200, 1300–1600, closed Sun and Mon.

The **Yeni Mosque** (meaning 'new', although built between 1597 and 1633) is unmissable to those arriving at *Eminönü* or crossing the Galata Bridge. There are a miserly two minarets here. Work started on the **Fatih Mosque** only ten years after the Turkish conquest. The mosque is named after Istanbul's conqueror, Fatih Sultan Mehmet, who is buried there. Istanbul's oldest mosque, however, is the **Beyazit**, next to the covered market.

The **Yerebatan Sarayi**, *tel: (0212) 522 1259*, a giant cistern beneath *Sultanahmet*, is

**253**

one of many which provided water for the city from the fourth century on. The huge cavern, its domed and vaulted roof supported by more than 300 stone pillars, was fed by water led in by aqueducts from sources outside the city. You enter the cistern from *Yerebatan Cad.* and explore it by pathways just above the surface of the water. Open 0900–1730.

Some distance west of *Sultanahmet,* the old **City Walls**, now partially restored, stretch across the landward end of the peninsula from the Sea of Marmara to the Golden Horn. Built at the command of the 5th-century Emperor Theodosius, they protected all the land approaches to the ancient city.

The **Bosphorus strait**, leading north from the Sea of Marmara to the Black Sea, is sprinkled with impressive imperial palaces and pavilions built by a succession of sultans. The best way to see them is by boat; popular excursion trips run up to *Rumeli Kavagi* and *Anadolu Kavagi* from *Eminönü,* pier 3. Three boats run each way Mon–Sat; on Sun and bank holidays there are five each way and prices are halved.

The most prominent palace en route – and the one not to miss – is the **Dolmabahce** *(Besiktas; tel: (0212) 258 5544; open 0900–1600, closed Mon, Thur),* which has a 600m water frontage. Built by Sultan Abdulmecit in the 19th century, this served as the final seat of the Ottoman sultans. It is an astonishing compromise between what the sultans thought of as modern European style and their age-old love of lavish adornment. In the enormous reception room, the weight of a four and a half ton chandelier is supported by 56 columns and glitters with 750 bulbs. Atatürk died here in 1938.

On a hill set back from the Bosphorus is the **Yildiz Palace** complex *(Besiktas; tel: (0212) 259 4570; open 0930–1600, closed Mon,*

Thur), built by Sultan Abdulhamit II at the end of the 19th century, as the absolute power of the sultans was crumbling. The palace is set in an elaborate park planted with flowering shrubs and trees from all over the world and has beautiful panoramic views of the Bosphorus. The **Sale Pavilion** (the only part currently open) reveals the dream-like luxury in which the sultans lived: small wonder that they took little notice of the world outside.

The Asian bank also has its fair share of imperial residences. Just north of the **Bosphorus Bridge**, the first to join continents, is the **Beylerbeyi Palace** *(Cayirbasi Duragi, Beylerbeyi; tel: (0212) 321 9320; open 0930–1600, closed Mon, Thur),* another 19th-century construction, this time the work of Sultan Abdul-aziz. The 19th-century sultans took turns to adorn the Bosphorus with extra palaces.

Further north the **Göksu** or **Kücüsku Palace** served as the summer residence of Abdulmecit. The second bridge across the Bosphorus, the **Fatih Sultan Mehmet Bridge**, is to the north.

## OUT OF TOWN

Take a ferry from Sirkeci or Kabatas to the **Princes' Islands**, an archipelago of nine islands, where princes were sent into exile by paranoid Ottoman sultans. **Büyükada** is the largest, and is distinctive as it has outlawed all cars. Transport is by horse carriage.

If you want a day on the beach, try **Kilyos** on the European side of the Black Sea coast. **Polonezköy**, 25 km from Istanbul, was founded in the 19th century by Polish immigrants and has retained a pastoral traditional Polish atmosphere. On the Black Sea, 70 km from Üsküdar, is **Sile**, a delightful seaside town known for its indigenous cotton cloth.

# ISTANBUL–BUDAPEST

This route winds across Bulgaria and Romania, and passing through both Sofia and Bucharest provides an insight into areas of Eastern Europe still little known by Westerners: trains are virtually devoid of backpackers. Continuing north through stunning mountains you reach Transylvania, one of the most colourful and multi-ethnic areas in Europe. Although conditions may still be primitive compared to those of the West, things are changing fast, and consumer culture (sadly accompanied by petty crime and other symptoms) is more evident than before. This part of Europe offers, by way of compensation for its lack of travel convenience, the chance to break new ground and see cultures not yet moulded by tourist expectations.

FASTEST JOURNEY: 31 HRS 30 MINS

255

## TRAINS

**ETT tables:** 61, 97, 1270, 1500, 1540, 1550 1520, 1600.

### FAST TRACK

The only direct train (the *Balkan Express*) travels via Serbia, taking about 31½ hrs. The journey via Romania (with a change in Bucharest) is probably more comfortable and takes only a few hours extra. The *Bucharest-Istanbul Express* runs overnight. Sleepers, couchettes, second-class seats and restaurant car are available. Between **Bucharest** and **Budapest** the best overnight train is the EuroNight *Ister* (sleepers, reclining seats; supplement payable), although the *Dacia* has sleepers, couchettes and second-class seats. The *Ovidius* has sleepers, first- and second-class seats.

In addition, the EuroCity *Traianus* (with a restaurant car), the *Pannonia* and *Alutus* run during the day. Reservations are required on all these trains. Customs procedures at the border can still be long and tedious, with a good chance of the carriages and baggage being searched.

## On Track

▶ **Istanbul–(Border)–Plovdiv**
The *Balkan Express* runs overnight between Istanbul and Plovdiv (10–11 hrs). The *Bucaresti Istanbul Express* also runs overnight from Istanbul to Bucharest direct, bypassing Plovdiv and Sofija. Both have sleepers, couchettes and second-class seats but no refreshments, and both cross the border early in the morning and suffer interruptions from both Turkish and Bulgarian customs and immigration officials, so don't expect a good night's sleep. There is no daytime service.

### Plovdiv–Sofia
Daytime service approx. hourly taking 2–2½ hrs. Alternatively stay on the *Balkan Express*. Some of the faster trains require reservations.

### Sofia–(Border)–Bucharest
A day train (taking 9 hrs) and an overnight train (10 hrs) run between Sofia and Bucharest. Both require reservations; there's also the *Bulgaria Express,* from Sofia and Bucharest to Moscow, but this does not (in theory) take passengers from Sofia to Bucharest.

### Bucharest–Braşov
There are twenty express trains a day between Bucharest and Braşov, all of which require reservations. Some have buffet or restaurant cars or a through-train trolley service. The fastest trains take under 2½ hrs, so overnight trains pass through in the early hours of the morning. There are also five slow trains, taking 4 hrs.

### Braşov–Sighişoara–(Border)–Budapest
Seventeen express trains per day run between Braşov and Sighişoara, including some in the early hours of the morning taking 1¾ hrs. There are also six slow trains, taking up to 3 hrs.

There are seven daily trains (three daytime) from Braşov to Budapest. Two of the overnight trains don't stop at Sighişoara. The journey takes 7–9 hrs from Sighişoara to Budapest.

## PLOVDIV

**Station:** *tel: (032) 22 27 29,* about 1 km southwest of the centre on *Hristo Botev Blvd.* There are no exchange facilities at the station so travellers arriving from Turkey must walk into town in order to obtain Bulgarian currency. The city's two bus stations are within a hundred metres of the rail station in an easterly direction. **Tourist Information: Puldin Tours** is at *34 Moskva Blvd tel: (032) 55 28 07.* **Hotel Trimontium,** *tel: (032) 23 491,* in the central square, is helpful with tourist information and sells reasonable city maps: open 0700–2200. The **Hotel Bulgaria,** *Evtimi St; tel: (032) 22 55 64,* also has maps.

## Getting Around
10–15 mins walk north-east along tree-lined *Ivan Vazov St*, diagonally across from the station, to the central square. Here you will find Hotel Trimontium and the main post office and telephone building. *Tsar Boris III Obedinitel St*, the pedestrianised main street, leads north towards the old town. Buses and trolley-buses run throughout Plovdiv, but much of the hilly Old Town is only accessible on foot.

## Accommodation
Hotel chains with properties in the city include *Nv* and *IH.* **Puldin Tours** at *34 Moskva Blvd* arrange rooms. Other commercial accommodation agencies operate along *Tsar Boris III Obedinitel St.* Plovdiv has six major hotels, but even the cheaper ones cost more than a private room. You may also find locals offering private accommodation.

## Sightseeing
Plovdiv, Philippopolis to the Macedonians and Trimontium to the Romans, was described by

---

Colour section: (i) Helsinki Cathedral (p.242); St Alexander Nevski Cathedral, Sofia (p.259); a market in Istanbul (p.248).

(ii) Bucharest Central Market (p.259); shopping in Madrid (p.293); inset, tiled walls in the Alfama district of Lisbon (p.264).

(iii) Córdoba: the Mezquita and Roman Bridge (p.313); Hanging houses in Cuenca (p.303); Cáceres by night (p.306).

(iv) Marseille (p.315); The Galleria, Milan (p.330); Biarritz Beach (p.325).

Lucian in the 2nd century AD as 'the largest and most beautiful of all cities in Thrace'. Until the late 19th century Plovdiv was more populous than Sofia and was the centre of Bulgarian cultural life. The unification of Bulgaria was announced here in 1885; Sofia became capital of the unified state and Plovdiv's influence slowly declined. Now Bulgaria's second city, Plovdiv has suburbs of industrial buildings and tower blocks which are decidedly uninspiring. However, there is still much of interest in the central Old Town, where the coarsely cobbled streets, cluttered with National Revival period houses and dotted with Roman remains, possess a charm and character not found in Sofia.

Archaeological finds date Plovdiv to around 4000 BC, and the city was occupied by Thracians and Macedonians before the Romans took over in 72 BC. Remains of Trimontium, the city of the three hills, include the partially restored 2nd-century marble **Roman Theatre**, one of Bulgaria's most notable archaeological sites. Nestling in the Old Town, the amphitheatre affords stark views over the modern suburbs to the mountains beyond.

Gladiator tournaments took place in the Philippopolis Stadium, the few surviving seats of which are opposite a cocktail bar terrace on *Ploshtad* Noemvri, in the heart of the city. The remains of the **Roman Forum**, including marble floors, can be seen in the central square near Hotel Trimontium.

The city's most important contribution to recent Bulgarian culture is the National Revival period house. This refers not to a single house, but to many, scattered around the old city. A cluster of fine examples of the style, mainly from the early 19th century, can be found towards the north end of the Old Town. The **Balabanov House** now hosts recitals and exhibits works by contemporary Bulgarian painters; the **Lamartine House** includes a museum room dedicated to the French writer and statesman, who stayed here.

The **Ethnographic Museum, Argit Koyumdjioglu House,** has exhibits on the local culture, while the **Archaeological Museum**, *1 Ploshtad Saedineni,* contains relics from Plovdiv's earliest days up to the National Revival.

### SIDE TRACK FROM PLOVDIV

Four trains a day (including one overnight service) run east to **Burgas** on the Black Sea, from where you can explore Bulgaria's increasingly popular coastal resorts. The fastest train takes less than 4 hrs and requires a reservation; others take 4–4½ hrs.

## SOFIA (SOFIJA)

**Airport:** *Sofia International, tel: (02) 88 44 33,* is 11 km from the centre. For information on international flights, *tel: (02) 72 06 72* or *tel:72 24 14* for domestic flights.

**Station:** *Central Railway Station, Knyaginya Maria Louisa Blvd; tel: (02) 31 111.* 1.5 km north of the centre. Buses, taxis, tourist information, currency exchange are all available.

**Tourist Information: Balkantourist,** *1 Vitosha Blvd; tel: (02) 88 06 55,* is a useful first stop for information. Other agencies which can help find a room or change money include: **InterBalkan,** which has offices at the airport, *tel: (02) 32 21 90,* and the station, *tel: (02) 72 01 57;* **Rila,** *5 Gurko St; tel: (02) 87 07 77,* can make international train reservations and sell tickets. Tickets are also sold by the **Travel Centre,** underneath the **National Palace of Culture,** *1 Bulgaria Square.* Expect to pay for printed information.

### GETTING AROUND

Central Sofia is fairly compact and most areas of interest can be reached on foot. Maps are clear and easy to follow, but check that they have up-to-date street names. There is a large network of trams, trolley-buses and buses; stops display the routes of each service using them. Buy tickets from kiosks or street vendors near stops. A one-day pass is good value if you are planning more than three rides, but tickets are extremely cheap. Trams (nos 1/7) run from the station along *Knyaginya Maria Louisa Blvd* and *Vitosha Blvd* through the town centre.

### STAYING IN SOFIA

#### Accommodation

In Sofia, various agencies offer accommodation booking, information and exchange facilities.

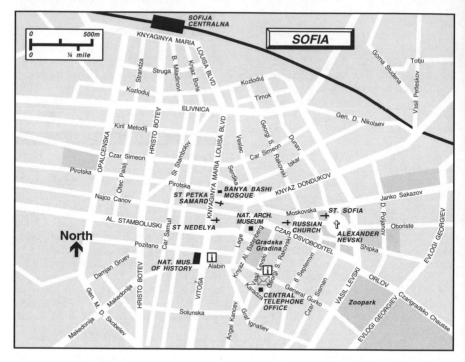

**Balkan Travel** has branches at the airport *(tel: 72 01 57)*, at the International Hotel *(tel: 68 81 08)*, and at *7 Suborna St (tel: 89 98 77)*. **Balkantourist** is at *1 Vitosha Blvd; tel: 43 331)*. Information on youth hostels and hiking is handled by **Pirintourist**, *12 Positano; tel: 87 06 87)*. Holders of **ISIC** cards can often get discounts. Ensure that whenever you book a room, the agency stamps your *carte statistique,* most will do so automatically. Private rooms are good value (£10–£15), as are the many small family-run hotels in the foothills of Vitosha at Simeonovo and Dragalevtsi. Medium range hotels include the **Rodina** and **Novotel** (£40–£50), less expensive are Serdica and Slavyanska Besseda (£20–£30). (All prices per person in a twin-bedded room). Sofia also has expensive first-class hotels for diplomatic and business visitors. Hotel chains include: *Sh, IH* and *Nv.*

### Eating and Drinking

Sofia's restaurants have increased in number and quality, but prices (for foreign visitors) remain low. Side streets off *Vitosha Blvd,* particularly to the east, have a mixture of restaurants, including western fast food outlets, Italian, Chinese and Indian restaurants. In the foothills of Vitosha Mountain, there are several traditional style taverns serving Bulgarian specialities. Some of the more popular restaurants need to be booked ahead. The **Party Club**, *Blvd Vassil Levski 3,* serves excellent Indo-Chinese food in a very stylish setting. The **Krim Restaurant**, which serves delicious Russian food, is very smart. It is situated at *ul. Slavyanska 17,* in a beautiful old house. Some of the main hotels also have good, but expensive, restaurants.

Bulgarian food is generally the best value, and good, but moderately priced, places to try it are at **The Garden Club**, *ul. Knyaz Boris 99;* **Bey Genchu**, *Blvd Dondukov;* and **Fram 1888**, near the National Palace of Culture, which specialises in fish and chicken meals. Pizza restaurants are very popular, some of which are excellent, for example **Venezia**, on *ul. Benkovski 12.* Street kiosks have excellent coffee, very cheap fast food, sandwiches, cakes and seasonal offerings like corn on the cob.

## Communications

The **Central Post Office** is at *2 Gurko St,* opposite the Rila agency. International phone calls can be dialled directly, with the minimum of fuss, from the **Central Telephone Office** on *Stefan Karadza St,* diagonally behind the post office.

## Embassies

**UK:** *65 Levski Blvd; tel: (02) 88 53 61.*
**USA:** *Unit 1335, 1 Saborna St; tel: (02) 88 48 01.*

Citizens of Canada, Australia and New Zealand should use the UK embassy.

## Money

Bureaux de change have sprouted all over central Sofia, including some open 24 hrs on *Vitosha Blvd.* There are plenty of exchange facilities in the central station. It is often possible to get a better deal at bureaux than at banks.

## ENTERTAINMENT

There are many new street cafés and bars, which are bringing lively crowds to Sofia's streets. The nightclubs tend to be aimed at the guests of the top hotels, but discos and impromptu parties can often be discovered by visiting **Sofia University** at the junction of *Vassil Levski* and *Tsar Osvoboditel Blvd.* Local clubs may just be pool tables, games machines and a bar. The best street life is on *Vitosha Blvd,* especially at the south end near the National Palace of Culture. Sofia's cinemas are inexpensive and show current films with the original sound-track, merely adding subtitles.

## SIGHTSEEING

Though Sofia is one of the oldest cities in Europe, it is still one of its least known capitals. Traces of Thracians, Romans, Byzantines, Slavs and Ottoman Turks can all be seen there. The city takes its name from the 6th-century basilica of **St Sofia**, which still stands in a central square. When Bulgaria was finally liberated from the Turks in 1878, Sofia became its capital, and many fine public buildings, squares and parks were constructed. The main sights are all nearby in a comparatively small area, easily covered on foot.

Sofia nowadays shows a more hospitable and relaxed face to the world, with its many new cafés, bars, restaurants and small family-run hotels. Its excellent museums, art galleries and concerts, and the proximity of **Mt Vitosha** (about ½ hr from the centre by public transport) make a visit worthwhile.

The **Alexander Nevski Memorial Church**, with its neo-Byzantine golden domes dominating the skyline is the most photographed image of Sofia. It was built by public subscription in gratitude to the Russian liberators. In its crypt is a superb collection of Bulgarian icons. Nearby, the tiny **Russian Church** is an exuberant, vividly decorated gem, its gold domes contrasting with its emerald green spire. The 4th-century **St George Rotunda** lies hidden in a courtyard behind the Sheraton Hotel, its interior is still being restored. The main square is now named after **St Nedelya**, a 19th-century church built on the site of many earlier ones.

The **National History Museum** has the richest collection, including fabulous Thracian gold treasures. The **Archaeological Museum**, housed in the former Great Mosque, built in 1494, has many fascinating exhibits. **Boyana Church**, with its sophisticated 13th-century frescoes, is on UNESCO's World Heritage List. It is in the foothills of Vitosha Mountains.

259

## BUCHAREST (BUCUREŞTI)

**Tourist information:** The national Tourist Office is **ONT-Carpaţi**, *Blvd Magheru 7; tel: (01) 613 07 59* or *614 51 60;* metro: *Piaţa Romană.* Open Mon–Fri 0800–2000, Sat 0800–1500, Sun 0800–1300. There's a branch at Otopeni Airport, and major hotels, such as the **Intercontinental** and **Bucureşti**, also have tourist information desks. ONT-Carpaţi will arrange tours and car hire, book hotels and private rooms, exchange money and supply maps.

Always change your money at official exchange offices or banks and keep the receipts, as the more expensive hotels may demand proof of legitimate exchange.

## ARRIVING AND DEPARTING

## Airport

**Otopeni**, *tel: (01) 212 01 38,* 16 km north of

the centre, handles almost all international flights. There is a good bus service (no. 783) to the city centre *(Piaţa Unirii)*, costing almost $1. Taxis prefer US dollars or occasionally Deutschmarks, and charge at least $25. Negotiate before you travel!

## Stations

Virtually all trains use the **Gara de Nord**, northwest of the city centre on *Calea Griviţei (tel: 952* for general information). This is chaotic and crowded, and pickpockets are busy here and nearby. It's served by the Metro, although you'll have to change trains to reach the city centre. Some services use other stations, but these are mostly local or seasonal trains. The Gara de Nord currently has the only computerised ticket office in Romania, allowing you to join any queue and buy any ticket virtually until departure time. Tickets and reservations can also be purchased between ten days and one day in advance at agencies (in Bucharest at: *Str. Domniţa Anastasia 10; tel: (01) 613 26 42;* and *Calea Griviţei 139; tel: (01) 650 72 47.*

## GETTING AROUND

A good street map is advisable, but bear in mind that many of the street names have changed, and the process is not yet over. The rather chaotic historic townplan has had a few Parisian-style boulevards superimposed, while to the south of the centre Ceauşescu demolished a huge area to build his Civic Centre and palace. This means that, other than the main north–south boulevards, there are few natural routes for public transport to follow.

## Public Transport and Taxis

The metro is efficient and fast, linking central Bucharest to the Gara de Nord and the suburbs. There are three main lines and most city maps carry a metro plan. Magnetic tickets (for a minimum of two trips) must be bought as you enter a station and passed through a turnstile.

Buses, trams and trolley-buses run throughout the city, although it can be hard to figure out their routes, as maps are rare. They are rundown, crowded and very cheap. Tickets must be bought before boarding, from grey kiosks by most stops; buy as many tickets as you'll need.

Fines for travelling without a ticket are relatively steep. Express buses, including those to the airports, require special magnetic tickets.

Taxis are plentiful and inexpensive by Western standards. State-run cabs should have and use meters, but this is unlikely with the private ones; agree on a price before travelling. These cars may also be old and in poor condition. You may prefer to phone *953* to order a cab; waiting time is usually 5–10 mins. Have a street map to hand and show the driver exactly where you want to go.

## STAYING IN BUCHAREST

### Accommodation

**ONT** can arrange both hotel and private rooms, for a hefty commission. **Private rooms** usually come with breakfast, but check first. Expect to pay US$15 (in dollars) a night for a double. Some hosts will also offer an evening meal, for about US$5. You may be offered a room by a tout at the Gara de Nord, but you should be very careful, as these will often be in outlying suburbs and of very poor standard. Hot water may only be available morning and evening, or less frequently, and even cold water may be cut off at times.

Hotels are more central and have fewer problems with water supply, and those around the Gara de Nord are barely more expensive than those in the rest of the country; this is, however, a rough guide. The cheapest of these is the **Griviţa**, at *Calea Griviţa 130; tel: (01) 650 23 27,* followed by the **Dunărea**, at *Calea Griviţa 140; tel: (01) 22 98 20,* and **Cerna**, *blvd Golescu 29; tel: 637 40 87;* the best in the area is the **Astoria**, at *Blvd Golescu 27; tel: 637 73 36.* Nearer the city centre, the best hotels in the budget price range are the **Veneţia**, *Piaţa Kogălniceanu 2; tel: 615 91 48,* and at *Strada C. Mille 18; tel: 615 37 10;* the **Hanul lui Manuc**, at *Strada Iuliu Maniu 18; tel: 613 14 15,* costs remarkably little and is one of the most attractive hotels in the country, a former *caravanserai.* Good central hotels that match Western standards include the **Ambasador**, *Blvd Magheru 10; tel: 615 90 80,* the **Capitol**, *Calea Victoriei 29; tel: 615 80 30,* and **Dorobanţi**, *Calea Dorobanţilor 1; tel: 211 54*

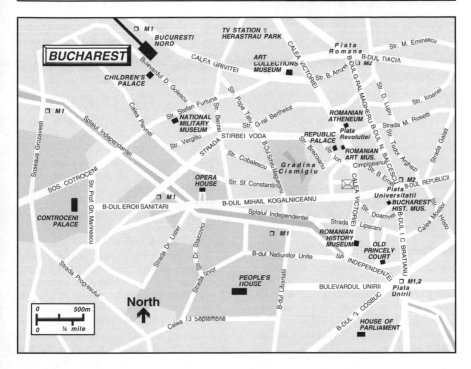

90. The top hotels reach Western standards and price levels; these include the **Inter-Continental**, *Blvd Balcescu 4; tel: 210 73 30*, the **Bucureşti**, *Calea Victoriei 63–81; tel: 312 70 70*, and the newest the **Sofitel**, *Blvd Exposiţiei 2; tel: 223 40 00*. The **Sofitel** is at the **World Trade Centre**, north of the centre towards the airport, but does have a shuttle service to town and the airport.

There are no convenient **campsites** near Bucharest; **student hostels** can be used during the summer holidays; the most convenient is at the **N. Balescu Agronomic Institute** on *Blvd Mărăşti* (bus no. 105 from the Gara de Nord, or tram 41/42 from the centre). There's also a **youth hostel**, **Villa Helga**, at *Str. Salcimilor 2; tel: 610 22 14* (bus no. 785 east from *Str. Ştefan Furtună*, near the Gara de Nord, trams 5 or 16 from the centre).

### Eating and Drinking
You can afford to eat well in Bucharest, for example at **Casă Capşa**, *Calea Victoriei 36*, the **Moldova**, *Str. Icoanei 2*, or the **Hanul lui Manuc** (see Accommodation). Less expensive are the **Bistro Atheneu**, *Str. Episcopei 3*, **Horoscop Pizzeria**, *Blvd Cantemir 2, Pasagiul Victoriei*, in the passage of the same name, **Lacto Academiei**, *Str. Academiei 29*, and **Pescarul**, *Blvd Balcescu 9*. There's a Pizza Hut in the Dorobanţi Hotel, various branches of McDonalds, and lots of good patisserie/cafés, including the **Academiei**, *Str. Academiei 3*, **Casablanca**, *Blvd Magheru 25*, **Casata**, *Blvd Magheru 28*, **Scala**, *Blvd Balcescu 36*, and, most luxurious of all, the **Bucureşti** at *Calea Victoriei 63*, in the hotel of the same name. **Panipat** is a chain of good if pricey takeaway bunshops, found all over the city.

### Communications
The **main telephone and post office**, *Calea Victoriei 37*, is around the corner from the poste restante office at *Str. Matei Millo 10*.

### Embassies
**Australia**: *c/o Liviu Buzila, Str. Dr E. Racota 16–18 #1; tel: 666 69 23*.

**Canada**: *Str. Nicolae Iorga 36; tel: 222 98 45.*
**UK**: *Str. Jules Michelet 24; tel: 312 03 03.*
**USA**: *Str. Tudor Arghezi 7; tel: 32 40 40.*

## ENTERTAINMENT

English-language newspapers and magazines, distributed free in the better hotels, list what's on. Nightlife is not great, with discos about a decade behind the times and nightclubs with tacky floorshows; in fact, one of the best ideas is a visit to the **Opera**, *Blvd Regina Elisabeta 70* (metro: *Eroilor*). Many films are shown in English, and the most interesting are shown at the **Cinematheca**, *Str. Eforie 2;* there's live jazz in the bar here at weekends, and also at the **Green Hours Bar**, *Calea Victoriei 120.*

## SIGHTSEEING

Bucharest was once known as 'The Paris of Eastern Europe', for its decadent lifestyle and for the elegant mansions lining its 19th-century boulevards. However, the city has been vandalised over the years, above all by communist planners, and, in fact, for many people the city's biggest sight is the so-called 'Ceauşescu's Palace', now officially known as the **Palace of Parliament**, a huge edifice whose construction required the demolition of a quarter of the city's historic centre. *Blvd Unirii,* lined with fountains and trees, leads from *Piaţa Unirii* (hub of the Metro system), which offers the classic view of the Palace. Tours of the interior start from the south door; these pass through a succession of grandiose public halls with chandeliers, marble and mirrors, which almost bankrupted the country.

Most other sights are along **Calea Victoriei**, the historic north–south axis, which is also lined with the city's finest boutiques. Near its mid-point is *Piaţa Revoluţiei,* scene of the most dramatic events of Ceauşescu's overthrow at Christmas 1989; here the Atheneum concert hall faces the former Royal Palace, now the **National Art Gallery** (temporary exhibitions only). To the south along *Calea Victoriei,* is the **National History Museum**, at no. 12, which houses Romania's finest archaeological collection, as well as the National Treasury and plaster casts of **Trajan's Column**, depicting the Roman Emperor Trajan's conquest of

Dacia, now Romania. To the north of *Piaţa Revoluţiei* are the **Museum of Ceramics and Glass**, at no. 107, the **Museum of Arts Collections**, at no. 111, and the **George Enescu Museum of Music**, at no. 141, all in beautiful aristocratic palaces.

Also worth seeing is the **History Museum of Bucharest** on *Piaţa Universităpii,* which forges some links with the legend of Dracula, in fact the local prince Vlad Ţepeş, Vlad the Impaler. Protests against the hijacking of the 1989 revolution by the functionaries of the communist regime were centred on **Piaţa Universităţii**, overlooked by the Intercontinental Hotel and the National Theatre; there are still interesting displays of political graffiti here, as well as memorials to those killed.

Bucharest has a large number of fine parks, many with lakes; to the north in the largest, **Herăstrău Park**, is the **Village Museum**, *Şos. Kisseleff 28,* which offers a facsinating selection of buildings, including water- and windmills from around the entire country. Elsewhere, the quintessential Bucharest experience is to be had walking through backstreets, visiting the tiny Romanian Orthodox churches, dating back as far as the 16th-century, hidden away behind modern blocks of flats.

### ↱ SIDE TRACK FROM BUCHAREST

Only 40 km from the city, lies **Snagov**, the playground of Bucharest. Magnificent villas surround the attractive lake, and on an island is a monastery which probably houses the body of Vlad Ţepeş, the original Dracula. Unfortunately, trains only come here at summer weekends, but buses and tours do operate at other times. The Romanian-Railways-owned **Complex CFR Snagov Sat**, *tel: (0179) 40460,* has rooms and camping space directly on the lake. ↰

### BRAŞOV

**Station:** *tel (068) 952,* about 2 km north of the old town. Bus no. 4 runs from the station to *Piaţa Sfatului* and *Piaţa Unirii* in the old town. **CFR Agency**, *Str. Republicii 53; tel: (068) 14 29 12.*

**Tourist Office:** *Blvd Eroilor 9,* in the lobby of the Hotel Carpaţi; *tel: (068) 14 11 96.* A few maps and leaflets are available here.

## GETTING AROUND

Buses from the station and suburbs run around the edge of the largely pedestrianised city centre.

## ACCOMMODATION

**Hotels** in the centre are expensive, and your best bet is either a **private room** (from people who meet trains at the station), or **EXO**, *Str. Postăvarului 6; tel: (068) 14 27 73,* or the **Hotel Stadion**, *Str. Cocorului 12; tel: (068) 18 74 35,* 100 m from the Autocamione bus terminal.

## SIGHTSEEING

Spectacular views of the city and surrounding mountains can be had from the summit of **Mt Timpa**, reached by a cable car and by footpaths. The central *Piaţa Sfatului* (Council Square) is dominated by the **Town Hall**, now the county **History Museum**; from its tower trumpeters sounded the warning of impending attack, by Tatars or Turks, for many centuries. Nearby, the **Black Church** overshadows the same square with its Gothic pinnacles: dating from the 14th century, this is one of the greatest monuments of Transylvania's Saxon (German) community, and displays historic prints and fine carpets brought by merchants from Turkey.

Imposing gates guard the road into the Schei quarter, southwest of the centre, where the **church of St Nicholas** stands on *Piaţa Unirii;* in its church yard is the building that housed Transylvania's first Romanian-language school, now a museum. Most of the city centre is dominated by Baroque buildings, typical of the Austro-Hungarian empire.

## ⤢ SIDE TRACK FROM BRAŞOV

The ski resorts of **Sinaia** and **Predeal** lie on the main rail line from Bucharest to Braşov, and most trains call here, making it easy for you to break your journey. One of the best hotels in Romania, although hardly expensive, is the **Palace**, *Str. Octavian Goga 4,*

*Sinaia; tel: 31 20 51,* and there are plenty of other places to stay. In any case, you should sit on the west side of the train (the left side, heading north) for spectacular mountain views.

**Bran Castle** has been associated by the tourist industry with Count Dracula and is visited by every coach tour to the area. Although there's no factual connection with Vlad the Impaler, the castle is well worth visiting. It's 26 km from Braşov, with regular buses from Livada Postei, as well as tours laid on by the Tourist Office. There is a wealth of excellent private accommodation in Bran, easily found once you're there. ⬔

## SIGHIŞOARA

**Station:** *tel: (065) 77 18 86,* about 1 km north of the centre. **CFR Agency**, *Str. 1 Decembrie 2; tel: (065) 77 18 20.*
**Tourist Office**, *Str. 1 Decembrie 10.*

## ACCOMMODATION

The state hotel, the **Steaua**, *Str. 1 Decembrie 12; tel: (065) 77 15 94,* is the only central one; new private hotels include the **Chic**, *Str. Liberăţii 44; tel: 77 59 01,* opposite the station.

**Bobby's Youth Hostel**, *Str. Tache Ionescu 18; tel: (065) 77 22 32,* operates in the summer holidays only.

## SIGHTSEEING

Sighişoara is a delightful Transylvanian town set in some of Europe's most spectacular medieval fortifications. It was one of the strongholds of the Saxon community, and also has large populations of Hungarians and Gypsies; all of their languages can still be heard here.

From the commercial centre, the old town is entered by the redoubtable **Clock Tower**, now a history museum; beyond this is an ancient house in which Vlad the Impaler was probably born, and to the right, the 15th-century **church of the Dominican monastery**, *Piaţa Muzeului 8,* is famous for its bronze baptismal fonts dating back to 1440. At the highest point of the citadel is the **Bergkirche** or Church on the Hill, *Str. Scolii 7,* built in Gothic style between 1345 and 1525, with some remarkable frescoes.

263

# LISBON (LISBOA)

Lisbon lies on seven low hills at the estuary of the River Tagus (Tejo). The city's name is said by some to derive from Alis Ubbo, the Phoenician for 'delightful little port'. Almost wiped out by a massive earthquake in 1755 (the ancient 11-mile-long aqueduct was, remarkably, left standing), Lisbon was redesigned on a grid system and rebuilt on a grand scale by the Marquês de Pombal. It's a relatively small city by European standards and charms all visitors. You need at least 2–3 days to explore the flower-bedecked old districts of narrow streets. The modern section is full of open squares and wide esplanades paved with artistically arranged mosaics.

**264**

## TOURIST INFORMATION

The main **Tourist Office** is in **Palácio Foz** *(Praça dos Restauradores); tel: 346 63 07,* open daily 0900–2000. They arrange accommodation (without taking commission), which can be scarce at Easter and midsummer.

**Municipal Office:** *Av. 5 de Outubro 293; tel: 793 46 53/65/73; fax: 793 46 28.* Open Mon–Fri 0930–1130, 1400–1700 (metro: *Campo Pequeno).*

**Thomas Cook Licensees: Star Viagens S.A.** are located at *Praca Dos Restaurados, 14; tel: (1) 346 0336; Praca Duque da Terceira, 1; tel: (1) 346 9346; Avenida Alvares Cabral, 62; Avenida Guerra Junqueira, 19B; tel: (1) 840 6715; Travessa Escola Araujo 31; tel: (1) 314 2425.*

## ARRIVING AND DEPARTING

### Airport
**Portela de Sacavém Airport** *(tel: 80 20 60)*

is 7 km north of the city, with no train link. Local bus nos 44/45/83 go to the centre or there is a special **Aero-bus** *(tel: 363 93 43)* every 20 mins that stops at various points in the city, including Cais do Sodré station, Rossio and *Restauradores.* The service operates daily 0700–2100. Tickets (Esc.430) can be bought from the driver and are valid for any journey that day on the bus, tram and funicular networks. **Taxis** are not expensive.

There is a Tourist Office at the airport; *tel: 849 36 89* or *849 43 23.*

### Stations
There are several railway stations in Lisbon. For general rail enquiries, *tel: 888 40 25.*

**Santa Apolónia Station** on the banks of the Tagus near Alfama; *tel: 888 41 81,* is the main station, handling all international trains and those to east and north Portugal. The information office in the station will help find accommodation. Bus nos 9/39/46/90 link Santa Apolónia to Rossio (which is central).

**Rossio Station** *(tel: 346 50 22)* serves the west. **Cais do Sodré Station** on *Avda Vinte e Quatro de Julho; tel: 347 01 81,* doubles as the quay for the Tagus ferries and as the station handling the local coastal services.

**Terreiro do Paço Station**, *tel: 888 22 96,* is the terminal for the ferries across the Tagus to **Barreiro**, which is the station for trains to southern Portugal. The 30-min ferry crossing costs Esc.155 (free with some rail passes and tickets) and provides a panoramic view of Lisbon. There are ferry departures whenever trains are scheduled from Barreiro.

### Buses
Express bus services to the Algarve and Porto are run by **Renex**, *tel: 887 48 71,* departing from *Cais das Cebolas* near *Terreiro do Paço.* Other express bus services are run as part of the *Rede Expressos* network and leave from the coach station at *Avenida Casal Ribeiro 18, tel: 545439* or *545775* (metro: *Saldanha).*

## GETTING AROUND

Make a point of getting a walking map of the laborinthyne Alfama district. Public transport in Lisbon is cheap, efficient and varied, consisting of buses, trams, the metro and funiculars *(elevadores)* between different levels of the city.

### Tickets

Train tickets are available from travel agencies or the Rossio and Santa Apolónia stations.

**Carris**, the Lisbon public transportation company for buses and trams, has kiosks which sell 4-day (Esc.1600) or 7-day (Esc.2265) passes that cover all Lisbon's public transport, and one or three day tickets which are relatively cheaper but only valid for the buses and trams (not the metro). Alternatively you can buy books of ten tickets.

For intensive sightseeing, buy a **Lisboa-card**, giving unrestricted metro access and free travel on most buses and trams, as well as free or discounted entry to museums and monuments. Available from *Rua Jardim do Regedor 50*, Jeronimos Monastery and the Museum of Ancient Art. Prices: 1 day, Esc.1500; 2 days, Esc.2500; 3 days, Esc.3250.

### Metro (Subway) and Trams

The **metro** *(tel: 355 84 57)* is fast and frequent, but operates only from Rossio to the north of the city. Lisbon's metro system is currently being extended. Trams are still an integral part of the city and are easy to use. **Carris** offer tram and bus tours: a slow and picturesque way to see the city. Tours leave from *Praça do Comércio* and cost Esc.2800. For information, *tel: 363 93 43* or *363 20 21;* buy tickets from the driver.

### River Journeys

In summer there are daily (and nightly) trips on the River Tagus, leaving from **Terreiro do Paço Station** at 1100 and 1500, lasting 2 hrs. For further details, contact **Transtejo**, *tel: 887 50 58.*

## STAYING IN LISBON

### Accommodation

Advance booking is strongly recommended during Expo 98 (May–Sept – see box, p.266), although the Tourist Office should be able to arrange some accommodation.

Hotel groups here include *Ex, Hd, Ib, Md, Mp, Nv, Rz, Sf, Sh* and *So.* The 4-star **Hotel Britânia**, *Rua Rodrigues Sampaio 17 (just off Av. Liberdade); tel: 315 50 16; fax: 315 50 21,* is stylish, central and friendly, if a bit pricey. The vast majority of cheap places are in the centre of town, on and around *Avda Liberdade* or the Baixa. In the latter, head for the three squares *Praça da Figueira, Praça dos Restauradores* and *Praça Dom Pedro IV.* **Pensão Ibérica**, *tel: 886 74 12,* and **Pensão Beira Minho**, *tel: 346 18 46; fax: 886 78 19,* on *Praça da Figueira 10* and *6,* both provide basic and reasonably priced accommodation. **Pensão Residencial Restauradores**, *Praça dos Restauradores 13, 4th floor; tel: 347 56 60,* offers similar deals. If these are full, try the choice on *Avda Almirante Reis* (to the east). Out of season you may be able to find something for around Esc.3000, but allow much more at Easter and in midsummer.

**HI**: *Rua Andrade Corvo 46; tel: 353 26 96* (metro: *Picoas*).

**Campsite: Parque da Câmara Municipal de Lisboa–Monsanto** *(on the road to Benfica); tel: 760 20 61; fax: 760 74 74,* has a pool (take bus no. 43 from *Rossio* to *Parque Florestal Monsanto);* **Clube de Campismo de Lisboa**, *Costa da Caparica; tel: 290 01 00,* is 5 km out of town, with a beach (bus from *Praça de Espanha*, metro: *Palhavã).*

### Eating and Drinking

Lisbon's restaurants are cheap and offer a wide choice. The **Bairro Alto** area is patronised by locals, and particularly cheap, as are the restaurants in **Alfama**. **Baixa** is aimed at tourists and more expensive, but still good value. If you're really hard-up, there are food stalls in the market behind Cais do Sodré station. Students can also use the *cantinas* on the university campus.

### Communications

The main **post office** is at *Praça do Comércio* and has a poste restante facility open Mon–Fri 0830–1830. There is branch at **Praça dos Restauradores**. International telephone calls can be made from *Praça Dom Pedro IV 68.* The telephone code for Lisbon is 01.

**265**

## Expo 98

The last World Expo of the twentieth century runs in Lisbon from May to September 1998. Timed to coincide with the 500th anniversary of Vasco da Gama's epic voyage to India, the event is billed as 'the great celebration of the Oceans'.

Expo 98's numerous exhibits will cover scientific, artistic, historic, educational, ecological and leisure aspects of the maritime world on a site which will cover seventy hectares. Over a hundred countries are taking part: they expect around 15 million visitors to visit the site, which is located in the eastern half of the city. Attractions include a Knowledge of the Seas Pavillion, an Ocean Pavillion featuring the largest oceanarium in Europe, a Pavillion of the Future and a multimedia Utopian Pavillion, as well as thirty-five restaurants, fifty fast-food outlets, circuses, street theatre, music gigs, a light show, a thirteen hundred seater auditorium and an open air amphitheatre featuring a floating stage.

A specially built station, **Esacao de Oriente**, will be linked directly to the Metro, the nearby International Airport, and bus and train services. You can also get there by boat: there's a full scale working marina. Much of the activity takes place at night along the *Coastal Way*, which borders the river.

Expo 98 runs from 22 May–30 Sept: opening hours are from 0900–0300 the next morning, although some of the thematic pavillions and offices shut up shop at 2000.

### Embassies and Consulates

**Australia**: *R. Marquês da Bandeira 8; tel: 353 07 50.*

**Canada**: *4th Floor, Avenida da Liberdade 144-156; tel: 347 48 92; fax: 347 64 66.*

**Ireland**: *R. da Imprensa à Estrella 1–4; tel: 396 15 69; fax: 397 73 63.*

**New Zealand**: New Zealand affairs are handled by the British Embassy.

**UK**: *Rua S. Bernado 33; tel: 392 40 00; fax: 392 41 85.*

**USA**: *Avenida das Forças Armadas; tel: 726 66 00; fax: 726 91 09.*

### Money

**Banks:** there is a 24-hr exchange at the airport.

### ENTERTAINMENT

There are many bars, discos and nightclubs, the streets around *Rua Diário de Notícias* (in the **Bairro Alto**) being a particularly lively area. Lisbon also has a lot of bars which feature **fado** singing and guitar playing. The best places are in the *Bairro Alto* and there may be an entrance fee or cover charge. Performances usually begin around 2200 and it's quite usual for them to stay open until 0230 or later.

The waterside *Doca St Amoro* (west of town towards Belém, under the suspension bridge) has a long row of loud and lively bars and sometimes live music – this is where trendy local youth hangs out.

Bullfights are held at the *Campo Pequeno* on most Thur evenings in summer.

There are frequent performances of operas and ballets, and many theatres and cinemas. The latter show films in their original language (with Portuguese subtitles).

Up-to-date entertainment listings are contained in the English-language magazine *What's On in Lisbon* (available from Tourist Offices, hotels etc).

### SHOPPING

The **Baixa** and **Chiado** districts are good for shopping of all kinds, while *Rua do Ouro* is a centre for jewellery. The neo-modern **Amoreiras** shopping centre on *Avenida Engeneiro Duarte Pacheco* is a huge complex with over 300 shops.

There's a dawn fish and flower market daily opposite Cais do Sodré station. Lisbon's flea market **Feira da Ladro** is held in the *Campo de Santa Clara* on Tues and Sat.

### SIGHTSEEING

Most attractions are closed on Mondays but free on Sunday morning.

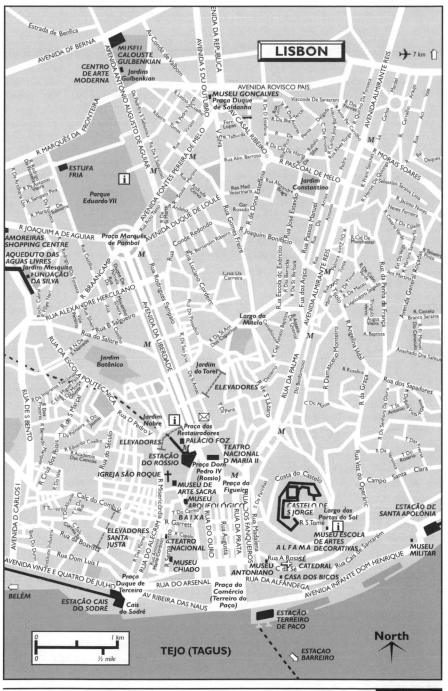

Alfama (metro: *Rossio)* is the old Moorish quarter, little changed since the 12th century, with winding cobbled streets, whitewashed houses and lots of dead ends. One of the few areas to survive the earthquake of 1755, it's a marvellous place to explore on foot.

The medieval **Castelo de São Jorge** (no. 37 bus from *Praça da Figuera)* has ten towers linked by massive battlements and stands on one of the seven hills, giving superb views over the city. A royal residence for four centuries, later it served as a prison.

The **Sé Patriarchal** (Cathedral), *Largo da Sé,* was once a fortress. It contains some notable 14th-century tombs, a magnificent Roman-esque screen and a fine collection of religious art and exquisite cloisters (Esc.100).

The **Bairro Alto** (Upper Town; Metro: *Restauradores)* is linked to *Avenida da Liberdade* by the *Elevador da Glória.* Another maze of narrow streets that survived the earthquake, it consists mainly of early 18th-century houses, some still residential and others home to much of the city's nightlife.

Adjoining the Museum de Arte Sacra is the **Church of São Roque**, with its marvellous 18th-century chapel dedicated to St John the Baptist, which was constructed in Rome, then shipped in its entirety to Lisbon.

In the **Baixa** district, the **Praça da Figueira**, **Praça dos Restauradores** and the partially arcaded **Praça do Comércio**, with its impressive triumphal arch, are all worth a visit (metro: *Rossio).*

The **Parque Eduardo VII** (metro: *Parque/ Rotunda)* is a landscaped park with a lake, a good view of lower Lisbon and some attractive tropical plants in its greenhouses.

**Belém** is a riverside suburb. The modern **Monument of the Discoveries**, on the river bank, is dedicated to the naval explorers who sailed from here, and there are various other monuments, museums and fine buildings which make it worth while spending some time in the area.

The **Belém Tower**, with its lace-like loggia, is an exquisite example of Manueline architecture. It was built during 1512–21 to protect the harbour entrance and the fifth floor has a great view across the estuary. The tower

was restored in 1845 and is furnished in period style.

The **Jerónimos Monastery**, inland from the Monument, began life as a chapel for Henry the Navigator's seamen. Vasco da Gama was royally received in the chapel when he returned from his triumphant voyages. The present building was designed by Boytac, the best of the Manueline architects, and construction began in 1502. The magnificent south door is widely acknowledged as the finest example of the style. Other features of the monastery include a series of grand tombs (including da Gama's) and a beautiful two-storey cloister. The wings of the complex are home to museums and a planetarium.

## Museums

Most museums are closed Tues morning as well as Mon.

The **Museu Nacional de Arte Antiga** on *Rua das Janelas Verdes* is home to a 15th-century polyptych which is a masterpiece of Portuguese art. Other exhibits include tapestries, ceramics, ancient sculptures and oriental rugs.

The **Calouste Gulbenkian Museum** (metro: *Palhavã)* houses the millionaire's private collection of everything from paintings and engravings to furniture and sculpture. Surrounding the museum is a delightful 17-acre park.

Next door is the **Centro de Arte Moderna Calouste Gulbenkian**, with exhibits by 20th-century Portuguese painters and sculptors.

The **National Tile Museum**, *Rua da Madre de Deus 4,* is in a 16th-century convent which was badly damaged in the earthquake, but restored in the original Manueline style. The cloister survived and the *azulejos* (decorative tiles) include a depiction of Lisbon before the earthquake.

Among the exhibits in the **Museu de Arte Sacra**, also called Museu de São Roque (metro: *Restauradores,* then take the funicular up), are some outstanding examples of the work of Italian goldsmiths.

The former riding school houses the **Museu Nacional dos Coches**: on display are some fifty richly-decorated ceremonial carriages.

## SIDE TRACKS FROM LISBON

### FÁTIMA

**Tourist Office**: *Avenida Dr José Alves Correia da Silva; tel: (049) 53 11 39.*

**Arriving and Departing:** It is easiest to get there from Lisbon by bus: there are about six per day and the journey takes 1½ hrs.

Fátima has been a pilgrimage centre since the Virgin Mary appeared there on 13 May 1917 – and again on the 13th day of the following four months. Word spread and on 13 Oct a huge crowd had gathered. Mary did not appear, but the assembled throng (some 70,000 people) witnessed the sun spinning in the sky. Ceremonies are held every year on the 13th day of all four months, but May and Oct are the biggest. The **Chapel of the Apparitions** and the **Basílica do Rosário** are the main places to visit.

### ÓBIDOS

**Tourist Office**: *Rua Direita; tel: (062) 95 92 31.*

**Arriving and Departing:** There are trains from Lisbon (Santa Apolónia or Rossio) and the journey takes about 2 hrs (ETT table: 692).

An enchanting medieval walled town, Óbidos has winding streets and small white-washed houses, their balconies brimming with flowers. It's so attractive that it has been declared a national monument.

At one time a lagoon reached almost to the town, but the waters receded and Óbidos lost its strategic importance. The many places of interest include the 12th–13th-century **Castle** (now a pousada), the 15th–18th-century **Church of the Misericórdia**, the **Renaissance Church of Santa Maria** and the 18th-century **Town Gate**.

### QUELUZ

**Tourist Office**: *Palácio Nacional de Queluz; tel: (01) 924 16 23.*

**Arriving and Departing:** Trains from Lisbon (Rossio) every 15 mins take 25 mins.

Queluz is the home of a small, pink rococo building that was inspired by Versailles and is arguably the prettiest palace in the world. It was built in the 18th century at the request of Dom Pedro III and became the summer residence of the Bragança kings. The interior of the palace is exquisitely furnished and the formal gardens have changed little since the 18th century. Admission: Esc.400; closed Tues.

### SINTRA

**Tourist Office**: *Praça da República; tel: 923 11 57.* The station is a 15-min walk from the town.

**Arriving and Departing:** The trains to Queluz continue to Sintra (the full journey taking 45 mins, ETT table: 691), so both can be visited in one day-trip.

Sintra is a beautiful town, once praised by Lord Byron as a 'glorious Eden'. The central **National Palace** is a mixture of architectural styles and has two remarkable conical chimneys. The original **Moorish Castle** (closed Wed; now in ruins) stands on a hill above the town and even higher is the Bavarian-castle-inspired **Pena Palace** (closed Mon), which is furnished in early 20th-century style and surrounded by nearly 500 acres of gardens.

### ESTORIL AND CASCAIS

These are both stylish resorts with good hotels, nightlife and diverse facilities. They are a short and scenic train ride west of Lisbon. Trains run every 20 mins from Cais do Sodré (ETT table: 691), stopping at several resorts, taking 30–35 mins for the full journey to Cascais. Estoril is a couple of stops earlier. 🏖

269

# LISBON–SANTIAGO

From the Portuguese capital, this route allows the traveller to dawdle up the coast through Oporto, centre of the port trade, and the fascinating university town of Coimbra. Sweeping golden beaches north of Viana give way to the wild Rías Bajas of Galicia, and the journey ends, fittingly, in the breathtaking pilgrimage site of Santiago.

In calculating time zones, remember that Portugal's time zone is 1 hr behind that of Spain.

> FASTEST JOURNEY: 8 HRS 45 MINS

## TRAINS

**ETT tables: 690, 695, 696, 672.**

### FAST TRACK

An express service runs Lisbon (Santa Apolónia)–Oporto (Campanhã), taking 3–3½ hrs on *Alfa* or *IC* (supplement and reservation compulsory), 4–4½ hrs on *IR* trains.

### ON TRACK

### Lisbon–Coimbra

Trains run almost every hour (with the occasional two-hour gap) from Lisbon (Santa Apolónia) to Coimbra B. The fastest trains take just over 2 hrs (*Alfa* or *IC,* reservation and supplement compulsory), about 2½ hrs on *IR* trains. Shuttle from Coimbra B (junction) connects with most trains for Coimbra (town station). Most have a buffet service.

### Coimbra–Oporto (Porto)

*Alfa, IC* and *IR* trains run every 1–2 hrs at irregular intervals during the day. Journey time 1¼–1¾ hrs. There is also an hourly local service (no refreshments), which takes 2 hrs 10 mins. For the city centre in Oporto take the train from Campanhã station for the 5-min journey to São Bento station.

### Oporto–Viana do Castelo

About ten trains a day run between Oporto (Campanhã) and Viana do Castelo, but they are unevenly spaced. Average journey time: 2 hrs, faster on IR trains; slower on stopping services.

### Viana do Castelo–Valença do Minho

There are seven trains daily from Viana do Castelo to Valença do Minho. Journey times vary from 45 mins to 1 hr 30 mins.

### Valença do Minho–(Border)–Tui

Three trains run daily. The journey takes about 10 mins and border controls are done on the train. Remember the time change: Spain is an hour ahead of Portugal.

### Tui–Redondela–Vigo

Three trains run daily, taking about 1 hr. Change at Redondela if going direct to Santiago.

### Vigo–Pontevedra

There are 18 trains a day, taking 25–30 mins. Half of these (TRD trains, every two hours) do not stop at Redondela.

### Pontevedra–Santiago de Compostela

Eighteen trains daily, taking 1–1 hr 20 mins.

## COIMBRA

**Stations: Coimbra,** *tel: (039) 246 32,* is about four blocks from the main Tourist Office. **Coimbra B,** 3 km north-west of town, handles long-distance trains, including those from Lisbon *(tel: (039) 349 98).* There are frequent trains between them, which take 5 mins.
**Tourist Office:** (Regional) *Largo da Portagem; tel: (039) 238 86* or *330 28.* (Municipal) *Praça Don Dinis, tel (039) 325 91.*

### GETTING AROUND

The main **bus station**, *Avda Fernão de Magalhães, tel: (039) 270 81,* is a 15-min walk from the centre. Major places of interest are walkable.

### ACCOMMODATION AND FOOD

There are several hotels of different grades, including *Ib* and *So.* Near the station, the slightly seedy *Rua da Sota* area is the place to look for cheap, but very basic, lodgings. **HI:** *Rua António Henriques Seco 14; tel: (039) 229 55* (bus nos 7/8/29 from *Largo da Portagem);* **Campsite:** the **Municipal Sports Complex** *tel: (039) 70 14 97* (bus no. 7 from *Largo da Portagem).*

There are cheap eating-places all over the centre: basic food is available on *Beco do Forno* and *Rua dos Gatos* (alleyways between *Largo da Portagem* and *Rua do Soto).* **Café Santa Cruz,** *Praça 8 de Maio,* in part of an old cathedral, is a great place for coffee.

### SIGHTSEEING

Coimbra was a centre of the Portuguese Renaissance and is the seat of one of the oldest universities in the world. The town overlooks the River Mondego and is a charming place with many fine old buildings, parks and gardens. It is also noted for its *fado* (melancholy Portuguese folk song).

The **University** is a baroque fantasy, with a particularly interesting library. The 12th-century **Sé Velha** (cathedral) is arguably the finest Romanesque building in Portugal, while the **Monastery of Santa Cruz** contains a 16th-century Manueline cloister and the tombs of the first two kings of Portugal. **Machado de Castro Museum** is housed in a former bishop's palace, which still retains access to the old Roman forum underneath the building. The **Convent of Santa Clara,** on the other side of the river, is gradually sinking; much of it is now underground. **Portugal dos Pequenitos** contains miniatures of Portugese monuments and houses and is fascinating for children and adults.

## OPORTO (PORTO)

**Airport: Francisco Sá Carneiro,** *tel: (02) 948 21 41/44* (bus no. 56 from *Praça de Lisboa).* There ia a tourist bureau is at the airport, *tel: (02) 941 25 34.*
**Stations: Campanhã,** *Rua da Estação; tel: (02) 56 41 41,* near the south-east edge of town, is the station for Lisbon trains. **São Bento,** near *Praça da Liberdade; tel: (02) 200 27 22,* is far more central. It handles local and regional services and is lined with beautiful *azulejos* (decorative Portuguese tiles). There are frequent connections between the stations, taking 5 mins.
**Tourist Offices:** *Praça Dom João I, 25; tel: (02) 31 75 14,* and *Rua Clube dos Fenianos 25; tel: (02) 31 27 40.*

Oporto's public transport company is **STCP**; tourist passes and day tickets can be obtained from their kiosks. Buses, trolley-buses

**271**

and one tram route serve the city. **Ribeira**, the riverside area, is the oldest part of town and the place for ferry excursions. **Endouro**, *tel: (02) 32 42 36/208 41 61; fax: (02) 31 72 60*, offers cruises.

Hotels range from one- to five-star. Major hotels include: *Ib, Md, Nv, Sh*. For cheap lodgings, try the central area around *Avda dos Aliados*. Avoid the dockside Ribeira. There's a convenient **campsite** at **Parque de Prelada**, *Rua Monte dos Burgos; tel: (02) 81 26 16* (bus no. 6 from *Praça da Liberdade*). There are also two in *Vila Nova de Gaia*: **Salgueiros**, *tel: (02) 781 05 00*, and **Marisol**, *tel: (02) 713 59 42*.

### SIGHTSEEING

The Romans built Portus and Cale at the mouth of the **River Douro**. The twin settlements prospered and gave their name to the whole country. Oporto also gave its name to the fortified wine the British called 'port', and is still home of the port trade as well as Portugal's second city. The city's main attraction is the **port lodges**, to be found in the suburb of **Vila Nova de Gaia**, linked to the city centre by the double-decker Dom Luis I Bridge. Tours of the lodges include a tasting and are often free.

In the old town, near the river, are numerous fascinating churches and museums. Among the best of the churches is the **Sé** (Cathedral), with architectural styles ranging from the 12th to the 18th centuries. The **Church of São Francisco** has a Gothic façade and an exquisite baroque interior. For superb *talha dourado* (intricate gilding), see the altar of **São Bento**. The baroque façade of the **Misericórdia Church**, designed by Nasoni, is famous.

The **Soares dos Reis Museum**, housed in the Carrancas Palace, is famed for its collection of the decorative arts, including Portuguese faïence. The **Torre dos Clérigos** is Oporto's symbol, an 18th-century granite bell-tower that affords a magnificent view. The **Palácio da Bolsa** is now the Stock Exchange, but contains an elaborate Arab Room. The **Jardim do Palácio de Cristal** is the setting for a pavilion which hosts many sporting and artistic events. To the west of the town and set amidst magnificent gardens is the **Casa de Serralves**, which boasts a fine collection of modern art.

**SIDE TRACK FROM OPORTO**

### BRAGA

**Tourist Office:** *Avda da Liberdade 1; tel: (053) 225 50.*

There are trains at least hourly to Braga (some requiring a change at Nine), including two direct *IC* trains to/from Lisbon (reservation obligatory). Buses run to Braga every half-hour. Both take about 1½ hrs.

Braga's **Cathedral** is Portugal's oldest, richly ornamented and full of priceless artefacts. From Braga you can visit the pilgrimage site of **Bom Jesus do Monte** (5 km east). The gardens are delightful and there's a funicular if you can't face the 116m climb up the ornate **Staircase of the Five Senses** to the attractive **Chapel of the Miracles**.

### VIANA DO CASTELO

**Station:** *Avda dos Combatentes; tel: (058) 82 22 96.* This is near the town centre.
**Tourist Office:** *Rua do Hospital Velho; tel: (058) 82 26 20* or *82 02 70.*

### ACCOMMODATION

Pensions are easy to find, but not necessarily cheap. Rooms in private houses are often a better bet – advertised by cards in the windows. **Campsites: Orbitur**, *tel: (058) 32 21 67,* and **Inatel**, *tel: (058) 32 20 42*. Both are by Cabedelo beach, about 2 km away. Buses leave from *Avda 25 de Abril* and the main bus station, *Central de Camionagem,* east side of the town. In season, there's a ferry from *Largo 5 de Outubro*.

### SIGHTSEEING

This old fortress town is a pleasant resort on the River Lima. On one side of the river is the beach, on the other the charming little town which is noted for Renaissance and Manueline architecture. It's also a centre of Portuguese folklore and famous for its handicrafts.

With the exception of **Santa Luzia** on the top of the **Monte de Santa Luzia** (accessible by funicular from *Avda 25 de Abril),* interesting sights are walkable. The central square, **Praça de República**, has a 16th-century fountain that has been copied all over the region. The

**Misericórdia Church** contains 17th-century *azulejos* and some impressive *talha dourado,* while the neo-Byzantine **church** of Santa Luzia is impressive in itself and affords a panoramic view of the town. The **Municipal Museum** is one of the best in Portugal, with particularly fine glazed earthenware and furniture. Viana do Castelo's **Romaria** (in Aug) is the biggest festival in the country.

There are several spectacular sandy beaches accessible by train within half an hour, on the line to Valença.

## VALENÇA DO MINHO

**Station:** *tel: (051) 82 41 55* or *55 35 36.* This is on the east side of the new town.
**Tourist Office:** *Avda de Espanha; tel: (051) 233 74/5/6.*

If you change at Valença, you may be told to buy your ticket on the train to Túy. If so, make sure you have Spanish currency handy: they won't accept Escudos.

This ancient town overlooks the Minho river and guards the border with Spain. The former stronghold consisted of two fortresses and many of the 17th–18th-century walls have survived. These, together with the narrow streets lined with white houses, impart a medieval flavour.

## TUI (TÚY)

**Station:** *tel: (986) 60 08 13.* This is central.
**Tourist Office:** *Puente Internacional (Puente Tripes) s/n; tel: (986) 60 17 89.* Summer only.

A bridge connects this tiered Spanish town to Portugal. Túy has grown around the **Cathedral of San Telmo**, the remains of which are now covered by lichen. The 13th-century cloister has twin columns and carved choir-stalls. There are also an ornate 14th-century porch and some fine Gothic sepulchres. Visit the churches of **Santo Domingo** and **San Bartolomé**, if time permits.

## VIGO

**Station:** *Plaza de la Estación; tel: (986) 43 11 14.* This is central.
**Tourist Office:** *C. Estación Marítima; tel: (986) 43 05 77.* There are also Tourist Offices near the station and the port in summer.

Vigo is a major port on a bay guarded by the Islas Cíes archipelago. The seafront is a hive of activity early in the morning and there's a lively fish market *(pescadería).* There are some attractive arcaded houses near the harbour and **Castro Castle**, the ruined fort on a hill behind the town, provides a magnificent view.

**Islas Cíes** are reached by ferry from Vigo. One of them is a bird sanctuary, but the other two can be visited. If you book ahead, *tel: (986) 43 83 58,* it is possible to camp there in summer.

## PONTEVEDRA

**Station:** *Avda Alféreces Provisionales; tel: (986) 85 13 13,* about 1 km from the centre.
**Tourist Office:** *C. del General Mola 2; tel: (986) 85 08 14.*

### ACCOMMODATION

Hotel chains include *PS.* Budget accommodation is limited. There are some *fondas* (inexpensive guesthouses) and pensiones in the streets around *C. de la Peregrina* and *Plaza de Galicia,* for example at *C. de Andrés Mellado 7* and *11.*

### SIGHTSEEING

Pontevedra, a typical old Galician town, is an attractive place. Situated on the River Pontevedra, it began life as a port, but its importance dwindled as the old harbour silted up. There's a new city, but it has grown without disturbing the old one. Parts of the original walls are visible and the old town consists of cobbled streets, arcaded squares with carved stone crosses and low houses with flower-filled balconies. Sights are in the small old city and walkable.

**La Peregrina**, an unusual chapel in the shape of a scallop shell, is situated by the partly arcaded main square, **Plaza de la Herrería**, on the boundary between the old and new areas. The Gothic façade of the **Convent of San Francisco** looks onto the Herrería. **Iglesia de Santa María la Mayor** has an impressive Plateresque façade which is flood-lit at night. The 13th-century Gothic **Convent of Santo Domingo** by the *Jardines de Vincenti* is now largely in ruins but still manages to evoke a certain splendour. The surviving wing holds part of the **Provincial Museum**, other sections of which are at Plaza de Leña.

# LISBON–SEVILLE

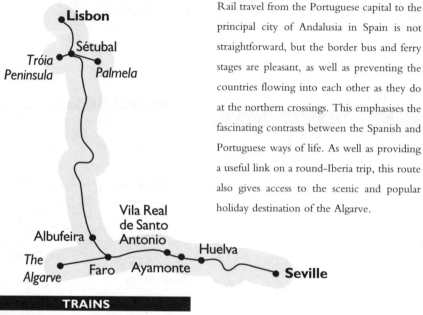

Lisbon
Sétubal
Tróia
Peninsula
Palmela

Vila Real
de Santo
Albufeira
Antonio
The
Huelva
Algarve
Faro
Ayamonte
Seville

Rail travel from the Portuguese capital to the principal city of Andalusia in Spain is not straightforward, but the border bus and ferry stages are pleasant, as well as preventing the countries flowing into each other as they do at the northern crossings. This emphasises the fascinating contrasts between the Spanish and Portuguese ways of life. As well as providing a useful link on a round-Iberia trip, this route also gives access to the scenic and popular holiday destination of the Algarve.

## TRAINS

**ETT tables: 699, 669, 665.**
With no through trains and no direct line, there is no way to cover this route quickly.

> **FASTEST JOURNEY: 10 HRS**

### ON TRACK

**Lisbon (Lisboa)–Sétubal**
There are services throughout the day (with a maximum wait of 1½ hrs) between Lisbon (Terreiro do Paço) and Sétubal. The total journey time is about 1½ hrs, including a 30-min Tagus ferry crossing, for which separate tickets are required.

**Sétubal–Albufeira**
Three trains daily, taking 3–3½ hrs. One to two IC services and an overnight train, cover Lisbon to Albufeira without stopping at Sétubal.

**Albufeira–Faro**
Over a dozen trains run between Albufeira and Faro every day, taking 30 mins–1 hr.

**Faro–Vila Real de Santo António**
There are at least 10 trains a day. The journey takes 1 hr to 1½ hrs.

**Vila Real de Santo António–(Border)–Ayamonte–Huelva**
There is no railway across the Rio Guadiana and the line from Ayamonte to Huelva closed to passenger traffic some years ago. Vila Real de Santo António Guadiana railway station is adjacent to the ferry to Ayamonte, which leaves every 30 mins on the hour and the half-hour. The crossing takes 10 mins and costs Esc.150/Pta125 (depending on direction). Ayamonte bus station is a 10-min walk from the ferry at the other end. There are six to ten buses daily between Ayamonte and Huelva (Pta550, 1 hr), and at Huelva the rail station is a 10–15-min

walk from the bus station. Alternatively, there are direct buses from Faro and Vila Real to Huelva and Seville. Time adjustment necessary – Spain is one hour ahead of Portugal.

### Huelva–Seville (Sevilla)

Three trains a day run between Huelva (Término) and Seville (Santa Justa); 1½–2 hrs.

## SÉTUBAL

**Station**: *Praça do Brasil; tel: (065) 52 68 45.* About 1 km north-east of the centre.
**Tourist Offices**: (Regional) *Travessa Frei Gaspar 10; tel: (065) 52 42 84.* (Municipal) *Largo do Corpo Santo, off Praça do Quebedo; tel: (065) 63 44 72.*

Sétubal is a large port and resort offering a range of sporting facilities, but it's somewhat short on charm. The town is a mixture of broad modern roads and old cobbled lanes lined with white houses. Make sure to sample the seafood, for which Sétubal is famous. The ramparts of the 16th-century **Castelo de São Filipe** offer a panoramic view and the harbour area is an interesting place for a stroll.

The 15th-century **Church of Jesus** was one of the earliest major structures in the Manueline style, which is perfectly illustrated by the maritime motifs, twisted pillars and the ribs supporting the vault. There's a **Municipal Museum** in the Gothic cloister, with a large collection of Portuguese Primitive paintings and 15th–18th-century *azulejos* (decorative tiles).

### ⬏ SIDE TRACKS FROM SÉTUBAL

At the tip of the Tróia Peninsula is a large tourist complex with a great range of facilities. It is accessible by ferry from Sétubal; the crossing takes 15 mins and costs Esc.120.

The peninsula is a promontory with the waters of Sado River estuary on one side and the Atlantic on the other. The estuary waters are calm and the beaches are usually crowded. The Atlantic side is quieter with good waves. The base of the promontory and part of the mainland form an area of marshland, dunes and mud flats which has been made a nature reserve for a variety of mammals and waterfowl. Dolphins and sea otters are occasionally seen in the estuary.

Situated 9 km from Sétubal (access by bus), **Palmela** is a tiered village in the foothills of the Serra da Arrábida, dominated by a 12th-century **castle**, now a luxury *pousada*. It is in a rich farming district famous for its Moscatel wine, with a colourful grape harvest festival Sept–Oct. The 18th-century **St Peter's Church** has an interior almost entirely covered with *azulejos* depicting scenes from the saint's life. **Tourist office:** *Largo do Chafariz; tel: (01) 235 00 89.* ⬏

## ALBUFEIRA

**Station**: *Estrada de Albufeira; tel: (089) 58 97 55.* About 7 km north of town, but there are good bus connections.
**Tourist Office**: *Rua 5 de Outubro; tel: (089) 58 52 79.*

Once an Arab stronghold, Albufeira is now one of the biggest holiday resorts on the Algarve coast, with high-rise hotels and apartment blocks swamping the charm of what was a quiet fishing village (but the nightlife here is good). The main beach is **Praia dos Barcos**; it's attractive and safe, but overcrowded in season. There are several other beaches nearby.

## FARO

**Station**: *Largo da Estação, just off Avda da República; tel: (089) 80 17 26.*
**Airport**: About 5 km west of Faro. Bus nos 14/16 run between the airport and town, a 20-min journey, but taxis are cheap and take about 15 mins. For information, *tel: (089) 80 08 00.*
**Tourist Offices**: (Regional) *Avda 5 de Outubro 18, 8000; tel (089) 80 04 00.* (Municipal) *Rua da Misericórdia 8–12; tel: (089) 80 36 04,* open daily 0930–1900 in summer, otherwise Mon–Fri 0930–1730.

Faro is accessible from both Lisbon and Seville in a day, and a good place to break the journey. Accommodation is plentiful and easy to find; a list is available at the Tourist Office.

Faro is the capital of, and main point of access to, the Algarve. The original city was largely destroyed by the earthquake of 1755, although a little of the old town did survive. Nowadays it is a busy industrial town and port.

275

The bizarre **Capela dos Ossos** in the **Igreja do Carmo** is lined with 1245 skulls and bones. The Cathedral (**Largo da Sé**) is mostly 17th-century. Nearby is the **Archaeological and Lapidary Museum**, with prehistoric and Roman finds including a huge Roman mosaic. The interior of the **Church of São Francisco** has panels of 18th-century *azulejos* and a chancel with *talha dourado* (gilded) decorations. Yacht cruises around the coast and big game fishing safaris can be arranged at the Tourist Office.

### SIDE TRACK
### FROM FARO

## THE ALGARVE

There are lots of cheap and convenient buses throughout the area. Occupying the south of Portugal, the Algarve is noted for picturesque villages and varied tourist facilities; from casinos and golf courses to horse-riding, handicraft shops and Roman remains. Some of its many resorts are well planned to merge with nature, others are horrendous eyesores. Inland, there are great orchards of almonds, figs and oranges, particularly attractive in Jan–early Feb.

The main area of development is the stretch from Faro to the west, which is rocky and very picturesque, with lots of small sheltered beaches. The dramatic windswept promontory of **Cape St Vincent** (near **Sagres**, at the far south-west of the country) was once thought to be on the edge of the world and the meeting place of the gods. The east (between Faro and the Spanish border) is less dramatic, featuring long stretches of sand and pine groves. It is little developed and contains the **Ria Formosa**, a peaceful nature reserve about 2 km from Olhão.

**Olhão**, about 8 km east of Faro, is a 17th-century town and an important fishing port, relatively untouched by tourism. The local style of building resulted from the 18th-century fishermen's contact with their North African counterparts with, typically, two- or three-storey square houses, called *açoteias,* whose flat roofs are used as terraces. From the pier, ferries leave for the offshore

islands of **Culatra**, **Armona** and **Farol** for a swim from a quiet beach. **Tourist office:** *Largo da Lagoa; tel: (089) 32 25 11.*

A town of Moorish origin 21 km from Olhão, **Tavira** is a charming place with pastel-coloured houses, ornate bell-towers, low bridges and twisting streets. The River Gilão runs through the town and is spanned by an attractive seven-arched bridge of Roman origin. Despite the long beaches nearby, tourism has not yet taken over and there are more churches than hotels. The 16th-century **Church of the Misericórdia** has an unusual Renaissance doorway. The market sells local produce at one end and fresh seafood at the other. **Tourist Office:** *Rua da Galeria 9; tel: (081) 225 11.*

## VILA REAL DE SANTO ANTÓNIO

**Stations**: **Vila Real de Santo António-Guadiana**, *Avda da República,* is the closest to the ferry and the centre of town. The other station is **Vila Real de Santo António**, *Rua Eça de Queiróz; tel: (059) 432 42.*

The original frontier town was destroyed by a tidal wave in the early 17th century and the Marquês de Pombal laid out the new one centred on a square with a black and white mosaic pavement radiating from a central obelisk and surrounded by orange trees; the central area took five months to build. The town is now a fishing and commercial port, with uniform architecture and grid-pattern streets.

## HUELVA

**Station:** *Avenida de Italia; tel: (959) 24 56 14.* Only 5 mins walk from the centre. Buses from Ayamonte arrive at *Avenida de Porrtugal 9; tel: (959) 25 69 00.*
**Tourist Office:** *Avenida de Alemania 14; tel: (959) 25 74 03.*

There's a good **Archaeological Museum**, which includes local finds and Romanesque sculptures, but Huelva is basically an industrial town, which swamps the few buildings of interest, such as the baroque **Cathedral** and ancient churches. The city celebrates its connection with Christopher Columbus with a festival in Aug.

# LONDON

London is one of the world's greatest cities, with something for everyone, from fine art and history to superb shopping and theatre. Its gateway airports and rail links to the Continent, now reinforced by the direct Eurostar services through the Channel Tunnel to Paris and Brussels, make it a natural starting point for overseas visitors embarking on a rail tour of Europe. Allow a minimum of 4–5 days – preferably more.

## TOURIST INFORMATION

The **main tourist information centre** is in **Victoria Station** and usually very crowded, so allow plenty of time. It's open daily 0800–1900 Apr–Oct; Mon–Sat 0800–1800, Sun 0900–1600 Nov–Mar, providing information and a hotel booking service for anywhere in the UK.

The **British Travel Centre (BTC)**, *12 Lower Regent St, London SW1* (tube: *Piccadilly Circus).* Open Mon–Fri 0900–1830, Sat–Sun 1000–1600 (Sat extended June–Sept). Services offered: local Bed and Breakfast and BABA (£5 booking fee, plus redeemable deposit of first night); booking service for guided tours and theatres; transport passes; and comprehensive multi-lingual information. Last bookings 30 mins before closing.

For information about trains to Continental Europe, contact **BR International;** *tel: 834 2345.*

(Note on phone numbers in this chapter: use the prefix *0171* if dialling from outside central London, unless another prefix is quoted in brackets.)

## ARRIVING AND DEPARTING

### Airports
**Heathrow Airport;** *tel: (0181) 759 4321,* is 24 km west of London. The Piccadilly Line underground (£3.20 one-way) and Airbuses A1/A2; *tel: (0181) 897 2688* (£6 one-way) serve all four terminals, from various pick-up points in central London. The buses run every 15–30 mins, approximately 0600–2100: allow an hour for the journey. The underground is quicker: about 40 mins from the centre. A taxi to the centre should be about £35/£40, but will be cheaper if you can share with someone in the queue. The tourist information desk at Heathrow is located by the underground station for Terminals 1, 2 and 3; open daily 0830–1800.

**Gatwick Airport;** *tel: (01293) 535353,* is 43 km south of London. Express trains (£7.50 one-way) run every 15 mins during the day, the journey to Victoria Station taking 30 mins. Other trains are slower but run around the clock. Green Line bus service, *Flightline 777,* runs every hour 0520–2300 (£7.50 one-way): allow 90 mins for the journey. There's a tourist information desk on the arrivals concourse of the South Terminal.

### Stations
There are 16 British Rail (main-line) stations (all linked by London Underground) in central London, all well-equipped with toilets, eateries, bars, newsagents and other shops. The most important are:

**Victoria;** *tel: 928 5100.* This is the terminal of the Gatwick Express and south coast towns. Victoria is also home to a number of useful information desks, such as the Rail Europe centre, a Tourist Information Centre and a hotel-booking desk.

**Waterloo;** *tel: 928 5100.* Covering the south-west region, including Portsmouth for ferry services to France and Spain. Waterloo is also the London terminal for Eurostar trains (see p. 99).

**Liverpool St;** *tel: 928 5100,* handles trains to East Anglia, including services to Harwich for ferries to the Netherlands and Scandinavia.

Other main-line stations include: **King's Cross;** *tel: 278 2477* (north-east and Scotland); **Euston;** *tel: 387 7070* (West Midlands, north-west and Scotland); **Paddington;** *tel: 262 6767* (west and Wales); and **St Pancras;** *tel: 387 7070* (Sheffield and East Midlands).

### Buses

**Victoria Coach Station**, *Buckingham Palace Rd; tel: 730 3466*, is the main London terminal for long-distance buses. **Green Line** coaches, *tel: (0181) 668 7261*, operate within a 40-mile radius of London; other areas are covered by **National Express**; *tel: (0990) 808080*.

## GETTING AROUND

The first thing you should do on arrival is arm yourself with a good street guide: try the *A–Z Map of London* (available for £2.25 from most newsagents). This covers the central area on a scale of 6 inches to the mile, highlights places of interest and has a full-colour map of the Underground, plus maps showing the West End cinemas and theatres. For more detail and a much wider area, buy (from newsagents) the full *London A–Z* or *Nicholson Street Guides*.

Free bus and Underground maps and other information about **London Transport (LT)**, including tickets, is available in most Underground stations. The main LT office on the ground level of *St James's Park Underground station; tel: 222 1234* – 24 hours a day.

Travel during rush hour (primarily Mon–Fri 0800–0945 and 1700–1830) is no fun at all, so avoid it if you can.

### Tickets

Underground fares depend on the number of zones travelled: zone 1 is the centre and may well be all you need. Single tickets are purchased in the station and allow you to change lines as often as necessary. Bus fares are determined by fare stages and not easy to define, but a single ticket (purchased when you board) is valid only for that vehicle, so you must get another ticket if you change.

**Travelcards** (available from most stations and many newsagents) are much better value. They cover all London's public transport systems (except Airbuses), giving you the freedom

to hop on and off LT buses, the Underground and some local trains. One-day passes are valid at weekends and after 0930 Mon–Fri and do not cover night buses. There are no time restrictions on the longer passes and night buses are covered, but you will need a photo. Current cost for a one-day Travelcard (covering Zones 1 and 2) is £3.50.

Passes covering only buses are also available. A one-day bus pass covering zones 1–4 is £2.70 and can be used before 0930, but not on night buses.

### London Underground

London Underground (usually simply 'the Tube'), the world's oldest and deepest metro (subway) is extensive, efficient and usually the quickest way to get around. On the down-side, it can be impossibly crowded and claustrophobic during rush hours. Most lines operate Mon–Sat from 0530 to around midnight, Sun 0700–2330. Smoking anywhere in the system is strictly forbidden.

Each line is colour-coded and has a name. There are maps throughout the system, some of the whole network and some showing only the relevant route. All stops are shown, so it's very easy to find what you need. As an additional help, boards on the platforms and the front of the trains give the final stop.

Keep your ticket handy: there are occasional inspections and it must be passed through the turnstile machine at the beginning and end of your journey.

### Buses

London's bright red double-decker buses have become a tourist attraction in their own right, but others run by private companies now vie for business on some routes and single-deckers are fairly common. The roads are often congested and travel can be slow, but some routes (e.g. no. 11/12/129) are excellent for sightseeing and the view from the top deck is always great. Most services run Mon–Sat 0600–2400, Sun 0730–2300. Restricted (often hourly) services radiate from *Trafalgar Sq.* throughout the night: night bus numbers are prefixed by 'N'.

You board and leave older buses by the open platform at the rear, take a seat and wait

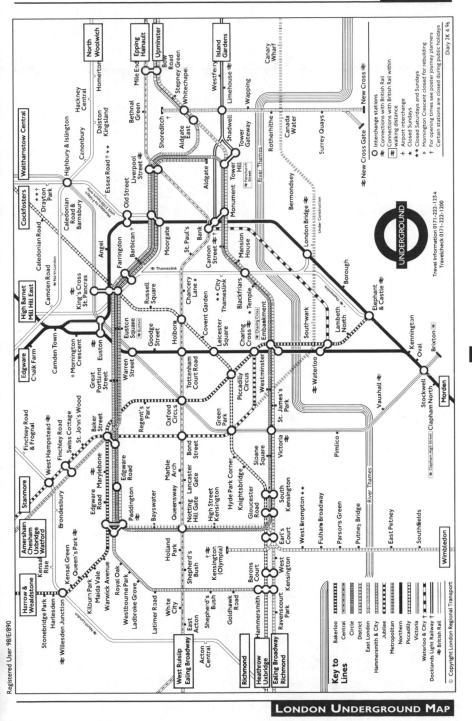

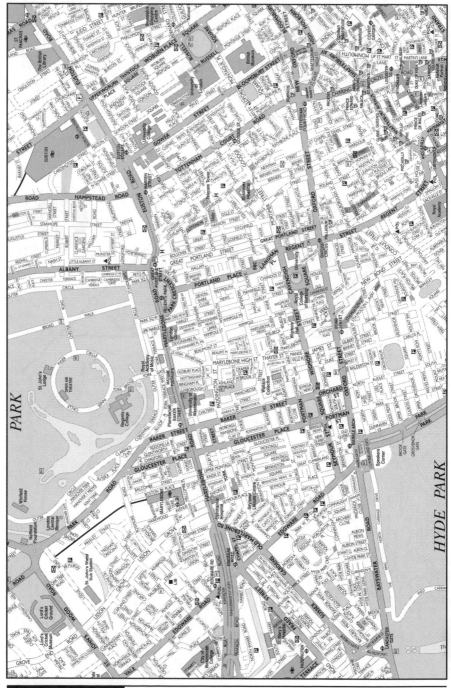

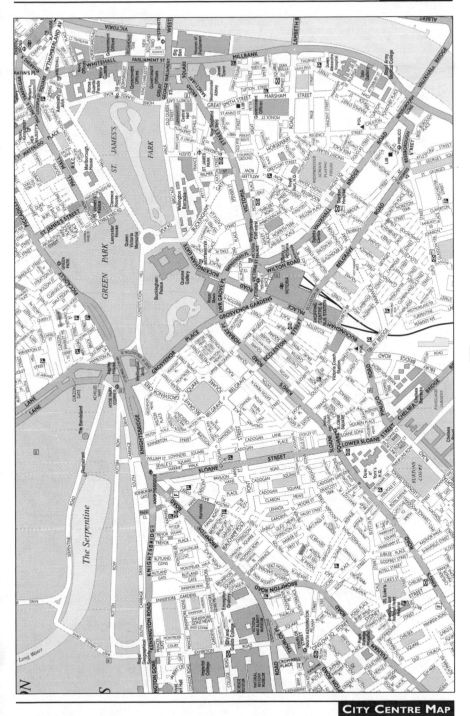

282

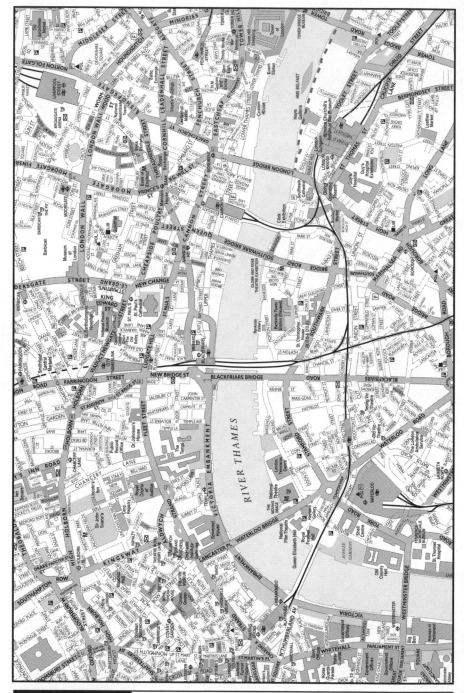

for the conductor to come round and issue your ticket/look at your pass. More modern buses have doors and you must enter at the front and pay the driver/show your pass before you take your seat – you exit by the middle door. Keep your ticket until you reach your destination as there are random checks.

Buses sometimes cover only part of the route, so check the final destination board on the front or back. There are bus-stops every few hundred metres, showing the relevant bus numbers. Many have timetables showing the full route. The red signs are request stops and the buses halt at them only if you signal: by raising your arm if you are at a stop or ringing the bell (once only) if you are on board.

### River Journeys

London grew around the River Thames and river-boats remain the best way to reach some of the attractions away from the centre (see Out of Town, p. 289). You can head east (down-river) to the **Tower of London, St Catherine's Dock** and **Greenwich**. **Catamaran Cruisers**; *tel: 839 357,* depart from *Charing Cross Pier* (Underground: *Embankment*). Most other departures are from *Westminster Pier* (Underground: *Westminster),* including **WPSA**; *tel: (0181) 940 3891,* for sailings west (up-river) to **Richmond, Hampton Court** and **Kew**. You just turn up and get a ticket on the spot.

### Taxis

London's famous 'black' cabs are often covered by advertisements, and may be painted in colours other than black, but their shape remains distinctive. Fares are not cheap, but taxis are metered and drivers have to pass a rigorous test on their knowledge of London. There are extra (metered) charges for: a lot of baggage; more than one passenger; travelling in the evening (after 2000) or at weekends.

There are taxi ranks at key positions, but you can also hail them in the street. When a taxi is free, the roof-light at the front is on. Some lights also display wheelchair signs, to indicate they are adapted for wheelchairs. Avoid the unlicensed minicabs (ordinary cars) which tout for business on the street: the reputable ones are ordered by phone.

### Accommodation

London has an enormous range of accommodation, from world-renowned hotels with mega-high prices to bed and breakfast establishments. All the major international hotel chains are represented, but, if money is no object, try one of the famous old hotels, such as the quintessentially English **Claridge's**, *Brook Street; tel: 629 8860*; the **Savoy,** *The Strand; tel: 836 4343,* built on the site of a palace and later the 'home' of Gilbert and Sullivan; **The Ritz,** *Piccadilly; tel: 493 8181,* still famed for traditional afternoon tea (book well in advance); or **Whites,** *Lancaster Gate; tel: 262 2711*, with old-style décor and views over Kensington Gardens.

Comfortable, central and a lot more affordable are **Morgan**, *24 Bloomsbury St; tel: 636 3735* (family-run and handy for the British Museum), **Bryanston Court,** *56 Gt Cumberland Pl.; tel: 262 3141* (also family-run, in converted 18th-century houses) and **Edward Lear**, *30 Seymour St; tel: 402 5401,* once the artist-poet's home.

Further down the scale, there are plenty of small hotels, ranging from dire flea-pits to clean establishments with modest facilities. Prices start at around £25 per person for something decent. The Paddington, Victoria and Earls Court areas, in particular, have a good range.

The best bet for cheap accommodation is **HI**, which has seven **youth hostels** in London. If you are not already a member, full details can be obtained from their central information office; *tel: 248 6547.*

**LIB**, *tel: 824 8844* (for bookings only), will take hotel bookings by phone up to six weeks in advance if you have MasterCard or Visa. Alternatively, for a small fee, you can book at the **Thomas Cook** hotel booking desks at Charing Cross, St Pancras, Paddington, Victoria, Euston and King's Cross stations, and at Gatwick Airport.

**Camping** in central London is not possible. The parks are locked around midnight and patrolled until they re-open. The city spreads for miles in every direction and the nearest campsites are some way out of town. **Tent**

283

**City**, *Old Oak Common Lane, Acton; tel: (0181) 743 5708* (Underground: *East Acton*), is easily the cheapest option in town (£6 per person per night). It's open June–Sept and you can either pitch your own tent or sleep dormitory-style in large tents. The price covers showers, cooking facilities, baggage storage and a personal safe.

### Eating and Drinking

London is a superb hunting ground for food, with restaurants of every conceivable type, from traditional British to those of countries you probably couldn't pin-point on a map. The cost is equally varied: from fast-food chains, where you can get something filling for about £3, to places with no prices on the menu that cost more than some would spend on food in a year.

The **Covent Garden** and **Soho** districts (there's an endless choice of Chinese places in the *Gerrard St/Wardour St* area of Soho) offer the best array of West End restaurants. Slightly away from the centre, the **Queensway**, **Victoria** and **Earls Court** areas are very lively, especially in the evenings, with innumerable cheap eateries of all types, including some of the eat-your-fill variety.

Italian, Chinese, Indian, Greek and Turkish restaurants are common and many are excellent, with a wide range of cheap dishes on offer. Many do takeaways and there are still plenty of fish and chip shops. Places with multi-lingual menus or displaying a Union Jack are designed for tourists and tend to be over-priced and of dubious quality. Food in pubs and wine bars is usually good value and often traditional. Sandwich bars, to be found in almost every street, are a good alternative for a light lunch.

If you want to try traditional English (far better than its reputation), there are a number of options. **Rules**, *35 Maiden Lane*, is noted for its excellent cuisine, but expensive – as is the **Savoy Grill**, *The Strand*, reputed to be the best in town. **Chimes**, *26 Churton St*, is an informal restaurant with moderate prices (it offers traditional cider) and **Porters**, *17 Henrietta St*, is another moderately-priced establishment offering a variety of English dishes. It's advisable to book at all of these places. At the bottom end of the scale, the **Stockpot** chain offers filling

---

> ### Thomas Cook
>
> Thomas Cook bureaux de change (and travel agencies with bureaux de change) can be found all over London. The most centrally placed are:
>
> 45 Berkeley St
> No. 1 Marble Arch
> 4 Henrietta St, Covent Garden*
> 196 Oxford St
> 431 Oxford St
> 1 Woburn Place, Russell Square
> 133 Regent St
> Piccadilly Circus Underground Station
> 89 Buckingham Palace Rd
> 43 Queensway
> 92 Kensington High St
> 15 Shaftesbury Ave
> 90 Baker St
>
> Most Thomas Cook bureaux open Mon–Sat 0930–1730; some locations have extended opening outside banking hours.

---

fare (don't expect gourmet) at rock-bottom prices. Other chains worth noting are **Bill Bentley's** and **Wheelers** (both mid-range seafood), **Café Rouge** (brasserie) and **Crank's** (cheap and good vegetarian).

If you want to self-cater, you will find shops selling foodstuffs on almost every street and there's no shortage of supermarkets: for quality at a reasonable price, **Marks & Spencer** take some beating. For food paradise, visit **Fortnum and Masons**, *Piccadilly*, and the Food Hall in **Harrods'**, *Brompton Road*.

### Pubs

There are pubs on virtually every street, including historic inns reputed to have been frequented by everyone from Ben Jonson to Charles Dickens: several books are devoted to the subject. If an organised 'pub crawl' with a well-informed leader (who tailors the evening to the tastes of the group) appeals to you, just turn up at **Temple** Underground station at 1930 any Fri evening and join the guided walk *(tel: (0181) 883 2656)*. It's £4 – plus drinks, of course. Standard pub opening times are Mon–Sat 1100–2300, Sun 1200–1500 and 1930–2230, but landlords have some leeway and many open all Sun. The minimum age for drinking alcohol in public places is 18. Children are not allowed into pubs (other than the dining area or garden – if there is one).

## Communications
The **post office** near *Trafalgar Sq. (24/28 William IV St, WC2 4DL)* is a major branch that has a poste restante facility. It is open Mon–Fri 0830–1830.

London has two **telephone** area codes. The central area is *0171* (and applies to all numbers in this chapter, unless a different code is shown) and the areas surrounding the centre are *0181*, both followed by seven digits. You need dial the area code only if you are calling from a differently coded area.

## Money
There are banks and bureaux de change on virtually every main street. Thomas Cook travellers' cheques can be cashed free of commission in the bureaux listed opposite.

## Security
Unfortunately, London is just as prone to street crime as most major cities and you should exercise caution. There are the usual number of pickpockets, bag-snatchers, con-men and so on. It is reasonably safe to walk around central London in the late evening, as most of the main streets are busy, but women on their own should avoid the King's Cross area.

## Embassies and Consulates
**Australia:** *Australia House, Strand, WC2B 4LA; tel: 379 4334.*
**Canada:** *Consular Section, 1 Grosvenor Sq., W1X 0AB; tel: 258 6600.*
**New Zealand:** *New Zealand House, 80 Haymarket, SW1Y 4TQ; tel: 930 8422.*
**Republic of Ireland:** *17 Grosvenor Pl., SW1X 7HR; tel: 235 2171.*
**South Africa:** *South Africa House, Trafalgar Sq., WC2N 5DP; tel: 451 7299.*
**USA:** *24 Grosvenor Sq., W1A 1AE; tel: 499 9000.*

There are several publications listing London's entertainments, of which the best are the weekly magazines *Time Out* and *What's On*. The daily *Evening Standard* also has comprehensive theatre and cinema listings. Keep an eye out for the equally good (and free) *TNT Magazine*. It comes out every Monday and is just left on special stands in central areas – help yourself. The same system applies to the *Traveller Magazine*, which comes out every Wednesday, but it is less comprehensive.

## Nightlife
Almost everything is on offer, including casinos, jazz clubs, discos, straight and gay clubs and pub entertainment. Most clubs offer one-night membership at the door and often have a dress code, which might be a jacket and tie or could just depend on whether you look trendy enough. Jeans and trainers are usually out. The larger rock venues are all a little way from the centre, as are many of the pubs with live entertainment.

The chief problem is that most of London shuts by midnight. Those places that do stay open late usually increase their entrance charges at around 2200 and many places charge more at weekends.

## Theatres, Cinemas and Concerts
London is one of the world's greatest centres of theatre and music. In addition to the **Royal National Theatre** (*South Bank Centre* – see next page) and the **Royal Shakespeare Company** (*Barbican Centre*), there are about 50 theatres in central London.

West End theatre tickets are expensive, but there is a **half-price ticket kiosk**, *Leicester Sq.* (the south side), for same-day performances. To book ahead, go to the theatre itself – most agents charge a hefty fee. Seats for big musicals and other hits are hard to get (unless money is no object and, even then, you should beware of forgeries), but it's always worth queuing for returns. Away from the centre, a number of reasonably-priced fringe theatres offer good-quality productions.

There's a wide range of classical music, from ultra-cheap lunchtime performances in churches to major symphonies in famous venues (for the Proms, see below).

There are dozens of **cinemas** in the West End, most offering discounts for the first showing on weekdays, but the same films can usually be found, at a lower price, a little way out of the centre.

**The South Bank Centre** (Underground *Embankment*, plus a walk over Hungerford Bridge; or *Waterloo* – slightly closer, but with a less pleasant walk) is an outstanding entertainment complex. Attractions include: **National Theatre (NT)** (three different auditoriums and some tickets are sold only on the day); **National Film Theatre (NFT)**; **Museum of the Moving Image (MOMI)** (a must for cinema buffs); **Hayward Gallery** (frequent exhibitions of contemporary art); **Royal Festival Hall** (musical performances from symphonies to jazz); and **Queen Elizabeth Hall** (solo and small group performances). Prices are slightly lower than in the West End and there are free performances on the embankment and in the lobby of the NT.

### Events

It's not difficult to see British pageantry if you time your visit to coincide with one of the many traditional annual events. These include **Trooping the Colour** (second Sat June), the **State Opening of Parliament)** (early Nov) and the **Lord Mayor's Show** (second Sat Nov). Other free spectacles include: the **London Marathon** (Apr: the world's largest and truly international); the **University Boat Race** (Sat near Easter: a traditional contest between Oxford and Cambridge Universities); the **Notting Hill Carnival** (which takes over a wide area for two days late Aug; the largest of its type in Europe, it's noisy and fun, but don't take any valuables); and the start of the **London/Brighton Veteran Car Run**, (first Sun Nov: from Hyde Park Corner). In all cases, go early to get a good view. Other major annual attractions include: **Wimbledon** (two weeks June–July: *the* tennis tournament – you can sometimes (with patient queuing) get in during the early stages) and **the Proms** (July–Aug: a series of superb concerts staged in the **Royal Albert Hall**).

The West End is full of famous shopping areas. For serious shopping, including many department stores, try **Oxford St** and **Regent St** (home to **Hamleys** toy shop). For designer clothes and upmarket window shopping, try **Bond St**, **South Molton St**, **Beauchamp Place** and **Brompton Rd** (home of **Harrods** – *Knightsbridge* is the Underground station). For books: **Charing Cross Rd**. For trendy boutiques: **Covent Garden**. For electronic goods: **Tottenham Court Rd**.

Some of London's street markets are tourist attractions in themselves. Amongst the best are **Portobello Rd** (Underground: *Ladbroke Grove* or *Notting Hill Gate*), Mon–Sat (best Sat morning) and **Camden Lock**, all week, but best on Sun (Underground: *Chalk Farm*).

**The Original London Sightseeing Tour;** *tel: (0181) 877 1722*, offers special tourist buses, some open-topped, which take in the major sights and provide a multi-lingual commentary via headphones during the journey. Departure points are *Piccadilly Circus, Marble Arch, Victoria* and *Baker St*.

You don't need to spend huge amounts of money, because many of London's attractions can be admired from the outside and some museums and galleries are free. More and more are charging, however (usually in the region of £5), and museum/gallery buffs may find it pays to purchase the **London White Card**, which covers more than a dozen of the major establishments, all of which can supply it. The current cost is £15 for three days or £20 for seven days.

Most museums and galleries open daily, year round, but check before you go. The following listing is only the briefest indication of the 'cream': unless your stay is very brief, it's worth investing in a detailed guide. Among the diverse subjects covered are: the Duke of Wellington, toys, theatre, transport, mankind and waxworks.

### Art Galleries

Of the countless art galleries, there are three which are outstanding – and admission is free, except for special exhibitions. The **National Gallery**, *Trafalgar Sq.*, displays 12th–19th-century art, with a superb cross-section of Impressionists and post Impressionists, and the neighbouring **National Portrait Gallery** offers a comprehensive display of portraits of the great and the good (Underground: *Charing Cross/Leicester Sq.*).

The **Tate Gallery** (incorporating the Clore Gallery), *Millbank* (Underground: *Westminster/Pimlico*), is home to more modern works (often controversial) and noted for its collection of Turners.

## Museums

The **British Museum**, *Great Russell St* (Underground: *Russell Sq.*), is a treasure trove of original artefacts from ancient Egypt onwards (entrance free). The fascinating **Imperial War Museum**, *Lambeth Rd* (Underground: *Lambeth North*), covers the whole history of warfare. The **Museum of London**, *London Wall* (Underground: *Barbican/St Paul's/Moorgate*), offers a beautifully displayed history of the city from 400,000 BC to the 20th century. Most visitors find the **London Transport Museum**, *Covent Garden*, and its excellent shop, fascinating.

Clustered together (Underground: *South Kensington*) are three other truly great museums. The **Science Museum**, *Exhibition Rd,* makes science understandable and interesting, with hands-on exhibits demonstrating scientific principles. Next door is the **Natural History Museum**, covering every aspect of nature, with many interactive exhibits (compare your intelligence with that of a dolphin or your weight with that of a blue whale). Among other attractions, there's a brilliant section on dinosaurs. Just across the road is the **Victoria and Albert Museum**, *Cromwell Rd*, a vast treasure house of arts and crafts, with good displays of relatively unusual things, such as wrought iron, as well as housing the national furniture, china and glass collections. You could easily spend a whole day in any of these museums.

## Sights

**Buckingham Palace**, *The Mall* (Underground: *Victoria/St James's Park*): some **State apartments** are open to the public Aug–Sept; the **Royal Mews** (horses and State coaches) can be visited year round (open Wed); the **Changing of the Guard** takes place in the forecourt (visible from the street) every morning or every second morning (depending on the season).

At the **Houses of Parliament**, *Parliament Sq.* (Underground: *Westminster*), you can hear a debate in the House of Commons, but be prepared to queue. Across the road, **Westminster Abbey** opens daily (except Sundays).

In the City of London are Sir Christopher Wren's **St Paul's Cathedral**, *Ludgate Hill* (Underground: *St Paul's*), and the **Tower of London**, *Tower Hill* (Underground: *Tower Hill*), built by William the Conqueror, once jail to traitors and now home of the **Crown Jewels** and **Beefeaters**.

### OUT OF TOWN

Just south-west of central London are the magnificent **Kew Botanical Gardens**, (Underground: *Kew Gardens);* Henry VIII's superb **Hampton Court Palace** (famous for its maze!) and **Windsor Castle** (still a royal residence, but parts of it are open). Both the latter are accessible by suburban train from Waterloo station; all three can be reached by boat (see River Journeys, p. 283).

A few miles east from the centre, **Greenwich** is home to a number of attractions, including the **Maritime Museum**, **Naval College**, **Royal Observatory**, and the refurbished **Queen's House**. All three are covered by a single ticket. Nearby, on the waterfront, is the beautifully preserved tea-clipper (sailing ship) **Cutty Sark**.

Fast train connections make day-trips to places within a much wider radius of London a practical proposition for visitors. Among the favourite excursions are **Oxford** (from Paddington station), **Cambridge** (King's Cross or Liverpool St), **Stratford-upon-Avon** (Euston), **Bath** (Paddington) and **Canterbury** (Victoria).

◄►For connections from London to Amsterdam, Brussels and Paris, see **Sea Crossings**, p. 98.

# LYON

This great metropolis at the junction of the Saône and the Rhône has been a crossroads since early Roman occupation in 43 BC. Many consider it to be the capital of gastronomy and restaurants abound. It also boasts the largest Renaissance quarter in France, museums galore, and a thriving nightlife.

## TOURIST INFORMATION

**Main Tourist Office:** *pl. Bellecour, 69000; tel: 04 72 77 69 69;* métro: *Bellecour.* Open Mon–Fri 0900–1900, Sat 0900–1800. Winter Mon–Fri 0900–1800, Sat 0900–1800. There are additional branches at *pl.-St Jean, av. Adolphe Max* (métro: *Vieux-Lyon),* open Mon–Sat 1000–1900, and at *Villeurbanne, 3 av. Aristide Briand* (métro: *Gratte-Ciel),* open Mon–Sat 0900–1700.

Youth information: **Centre Régional d'Information Jeunesse:** *9 quai des Célestins; tel: 04 72 77 00 66.* Open Mon 1200–1900, Tues–Fri 1100–1900, Sat (Sept–June) 1000–1700. For student and youth information, including jobs, accommodation, transport.

## ARRIVING AND DEPARTING

### Airport

**Aéroport Lyon-Satolas:** 32 km east of Lyon; *tel: 04 72 22 72 21.* A regular bus service runs every 20 mins between the airport and Perrache rail station (via Part-Dieu rail station), FFr.46; a 45-min journey. The buses operate 0600–2300 (Satolas-Lyon); 0500–2100 (Lyon-Satolas).

### Stations

There are two mainline stations in Lyon. Many trains stop at both. **Lyon-Perrache** is the more central. It provides left luggage facilities, 0530–2030, showers, money exchange offices, a restaurant and bar as well as **SOS Voyageurs** – an information and practical assistance service for passengers *(tel: 04 78 37 03 31),* open Mon–Fri 0800–2000, Sat 0900–1300, Sun 1530–1930. For the town centre cross *pl. Carnot,* then follow *r. Victor Hugo* to *pl. Bellecour* (15 mins). **Lyon-Part-Dieu** is on the east bank of the Rhône and serves the business district. It has similar facilities to Perrache, including **SOS Voyageurs,** open Mon–Sat 0800–2000, Sun 0900–2000; *tel: 04 72 34 12 16.*

## GETTING AROUND

Lyon is big (population 1.5 million) and divided by the rivers Saône and Rhône into thirds. On the west bank of the Saône, **Vieux Lyon** (Old Lyon) has attractive Renaissance streets. On the east bank of the Rhône is the **business centre,** the Part-Dieu rail station and high-rise offices and apartment blocks. In between, bordered by the Saône and Rhône, is the partly **pedestrianised centre** of the city, running from *pl. Bellecour* to the old silk quarter of **La Croix-Rousse.** To go further afield, take a bus, funicular or subway train (métro), run by **TCL** *(Transports en commun lyonnais); tel: 04 78 71 70 00.* Get the map *(plan de réseau)* from the Tourist Office or any TCL branch. Lyon is a relatively safe city though some care is needed around the Perrache station at night.

The **métro** is modern, clean and safe. There are four lines, A, B, C and D which criss-cross the city. It operates 0500–2400. **Funiculaires** (funicular trains) depart every 10 mins from Vieux Lyon metro station to the Roman theatre at St Just and the **Fourvière Esplanade** high above the city. **Buses** cover every corner of Lyon, generally 0500–2200, but check individual services. There are no night buses.

A one-way ticket for buses and métro costs FFr.8; a single funicular ticket FFr.12.50; a carnet of ten tickets is FFr.68; students FFr.58 or 55 off-season. A ticket *liberté,* FFr.24, gives unlimited travel on all services for one day. It is available from Tourist Offices, TCL booths or automatic vending machines.

For 24-hr **taxis,** *tel: 04 78 28 23 23.* Fare to the airport is about FFr.250.

289

## Accommodation

Lyon is a business town and filled during the week with briefcases and expense accounts. But this is a big city and you can always find a room – try around the Perrache rail station or north near *pl. des Terreaux* (métro: *Hôtel de Ville*). Chain hotels include *Ca, CF, Cn, Hd, Ib, Mc, Md, Mp, Nv, Pu, Sf*. Budget accommodation abounds – try *cours de Verdun* and *r. Victor Hugo*.

**HI**: *51 r. Roger Salengro, 69200 Vénissieux; tel: 04 78 76 39 23*. Just outside the city – take bus no. 35 (last bus at 2100) from *r. de la Charté* off *pl. Bellecour* to *George-Lévy* (30-min journey). **Centre International de Séjour**: *46 r. du Commandant Pégoud; tel: 04 78 01 23 45* or *04 78 76 14 22*. Take bus no. 53 from Perrache, direction *St-Priest* to *États-Unis Beauvisage*.

**Camping: Dardilly**; *Ecully Dardilly; tel: 04 78 35 64 55*. take bus no. 19 from the Hôtel de Ville, direction *Ecully-Dardilly* to *Parc d'Affaires*. Open year-round.

## Eating and Drinking

Lyon boasts more famous chefs than almost any other city in Europe and some of the best restaurants in France. Food is serious business, but countless small cafés exist and even on a tight budget you can eat very well.

The most traditional restaurants are the *bouchons*, travellers' inns, mainly in **Les Terreaux** and **Vieux Lyon**. They serve hearty meals based on tripe, pork and sausages, washed down with local Beaujolais wines. Lyonnais cuisine is very much meat-based, particularly pork and poultry, sausages made from intestines *(andouillettes)*, creamy sauces and potatoes. The food is undeniably rich. For good eateries in Vieux Lyon, head for *pl. Neuve St Jean, r. du Boeuf* and *pl. de la Baleine*. Away from this busy tourist area, try *r. des Marronniers* just east of *pl. Bellecour* or *r. Mercière* (métro: *Cordeliers*).

Much of the wonderful fresh produce comes from Lyon's great markets, open daily, except Mon. The largest and most animated are on *quai St Antoine* beside the Saône (métro: *Bellecour)* and along *blvd de la Croix-Rousse*, north of Les Terreaux (métro: *Croix-Rousse)*.

## Communications

**Post Office**: *pl. Antonin Poncet; tel: 0801 63 02 01*, next to *pl. Bellecour*. Facilities include poste restante, currency exchange, photocopying, and telephones. Open Mon–Fri 0800–1900, Sat 0800–1200.

## Money

There are **Thomas Cook bureaux de change** at Lyon-Part-Dieu and Lyon-Perrache stations. The bureau at Part-Dieu is open Mon–Sat 0800–1945, Sun 1000–1900 (summer), Mon–Sat 0800–1915, Sun 1300–1915 (winter). The bureau at Lyon-Perrache is open Mon–Sat 0730–1900, Sun 0930–1230, 1330–1845 (summer); Mon–Sat 0830–1230, 1330–1845, Sun 0930–1230, 1330–1845 (winter).

## Consulates

**Canada**: *21 r. Bourgelet; tel: 04 72 77 64 07*. Open Mon–Fri 0900–1200 by appointment. **UK**: *24 r. Childebert; tel: 04 72 77 81 70* (métro: *Bellecour*). Open Mon–Fri 0900–1200 and 1400–1700.

The weekly *Lyon Poche* lists the week's events (FFr.7 from news-stands). Lyon is a student city, so **clubs and discos** abound. The best areas are near the Hôtel de Ville and *quai Pierre Scize* in Vieux Lyon. Entry including first drink costs up to FFr.100 at weekends. For modern **dance**, Latin and African, as well as classical ballet: **Maison de la Danse**, *Théâtre du 8ème, 8 av. Jean Mermoz; tel: 04 72 78 18 18*. The 1200-seat **Lyon Opera House** soars up to 18 different seating levels and the company is now one of Europe's finest; *9 quai Jean Moulin*. The roof glows red as it fills up with people. Lyon was birthplace of **Guignol**, the French original of 'Mr Punch'. The **Guignol de Lyon** theatre, *2 r. Louis Carrand* in the old town, *tel: 04 78 28 92 57*, puts on shows for kids and adults alike.

Guided tours are available on Sat from the Tourist Office, *av. Adolphe Max, Vieux Lyon*, departing 1430, cost FFr.50. A general tour of the city by bus runs from Apr–Oct. Contact **Cars Philibert**, tel: *78 98 56 62*. A 3-day 'Key

**290**

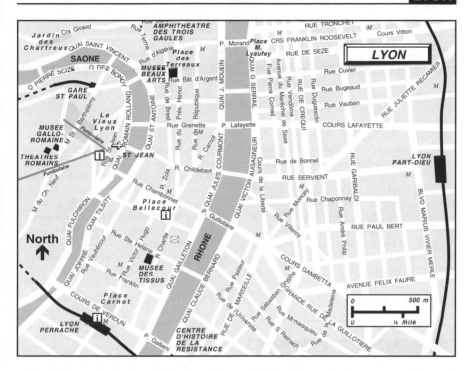

to Lyon' cheque-book is available from the Tourist Offices, FFr.90, including admission to six museums and an audio-guide package. One of the most pleasant ways to see Lyon is from the river, especially after dark when over 100 buildings are floodlit. Boat trips from Apr–Oct, from *quai des Célestins; tel: 04 78 42 96 81.* Trips last 1–1¼ hrs, FFr.42. Also lunch and dinner cruises. Lyon is famous for its *traboules* – covered passageways which link together different streets and which were once used as short-cuts by the silk traders. Mostly found in *Vieux Lyon,* the Tourist Office has a map showing the various entrances and exits.

To see Lyon on foot, start at the Tourist Office in *pl. Bellecour* and head north. *Pl. des Terreaux* has Lyon's best museum – **Musée des Beaux Arts,** *tel: 04 72 10 17 40,* France's second-largest fine arts museum. (Open 1030–1800, closed Mon, Tues, FFr.25). South of *pl. Bellecour* is a monument to Lyon's textile history, and its role as Europe's silk capital – **Musée des Tissus**; *34 r. de la Charité; tel: 04 78 37 15 05.* Open 1000–1730, closed Mon,

FFr.28. Silk made Lyon one of Europe's wealthiest cities in the 18th century. Old looms are still in use at **Maison des Canuts,** *10–12 r. d'Ivry; tel: 04 78 28 62 04.* Open Mon–Fri 0830–1200, 1400–1830, Sat 0800–1200, 1400–1800. FFr.15. Just across *Pont Galliéni* from the station is the most poignant museum in Lyon, **Le Centre d'Histoire de la Résistance et de la Déportation,** *14 av. Berthelot; tel: 04 72 73 33 54.* Open 0900–1730, closed Mon, Tues, FFr.25.

Lyon was birthplace of the cinema. The Lumière brothers invented moving pictures while working with their father, who was a local photographer. Their legacy is the **Institut Lumière,** *r. du Premier Film; tel: 04 78 78 18 95,* in *Montplaisir.* The best preserved Renaissance district in France leads back from the river in **Vieux Lyon.** The **Cathédrale St-Jean,** started in 1180, contains a unique mixture of building styles and a 14th-century astronomical clock.

Julius Caesar was responsible for developing the Roman town of **Lugdunum,** centred on the hillside of **Fourvière** above the old town.

Crowning the hill, from which there are spectacular views of the city, is the **Basilique Notre Dame de Fourvière**, built in the 19th century by the people of Lyon after they had been saved from invasion. The **Musée Gallo-Romain**, *17 r. Cléberg; tel: 04 72 38 81 90,* has an impressive collection of mosaics, coins and swords (open 0930–1200, 1400–1800, closed Mon, Tues; FFr.20), but the most interesting sight is the neighbouring **Théâtre Romain**, *8 r. de l'Antiquaille,* the oldest in France, just down the hill from the museum, with seating intact and remains of an odean and the craftsmen's district (open 0700 to dusk, free). The recently opened **Musée d'Art Contemporain**, *Cité International, 81 quai Charles de Gaulle; tel: 04 72 69 17 17,* houses an important collection of 1960s art; open daily except Mon, Tues 1200–1900; admission FFr.30.

## SIDE TRACKS FROM LYON

### PÉROUGES

There are approximately 15 trains a day (fewer at weekends) to Pérouges, taking 40 mins. The trains stop at Meximieux-Pérouges, about 2 km from the town. To reach Pérouges, turn right as you exit the station then take the first left along *r. de la Gare* to the end. The Tourist Office is on the right on *r. de Geneve* (open Tues–Sat 0930–1200, Fri–Sat 1430–1800). To reach Pérouges, turn left, take the first right after the *Gendarmerie* and then the right turn opposite the roadside Madonna (20 mins).

Pérouges is a quaint medieval hill town 35 km east of Lyon; it is described as one of the most beautiful villages in France. Its narrow cobbled streets are lined with houses dating from the 15th century. It also boasts a fortified church with walls 1.4 m thick and a short sideways tilt. In the centre of the main square is the **Tree of Liberty**, planted in 1792 to commemorate the Revolution.

### LE PUY-EN-VELAY

**Station:** about 15-mins walk to the centre; turn left, follow *av. C. Dupuy* to *sq. Coiffier,* then left on *blvd Mar. Fayolle* to *pl. du Breuil.* There is a very sparse rail service via St Etienne, taking over 2 hrs.

**Tourist Office:** *pl. du Breuil; tel: 04 71 09 38 41.* Open Mon–Sat 0830–1200, 1345–1830; Sun 0900–1200, 1400–1800 (Easter–Sept), 1000–1200 (Oct–Easter). The free *Historical Visits* outlines two interesting walking routes that pass all the historic sites.

This unusual town has a striking skyline, with a massive cathedral, a monumental statue and an ancient chapel, each dominating a volcanic peak or hill. It covers a smallish area horizontally, but the steep climbs make it hard work to explore. The peak-top attractions give stunning views. On **Rocher Corneille** (Crow Rock) is a 19th-century red statue of **Notre-Dame-de-France** (Our Lady of France), a colossal figure fashioned from cannons used during the battle of Sebastopol. The hair is 7 m long, the foot is on a serpent 17 m long, the crowned head weighs 110 tonnes and 18 people can fit inside the chest – there's an internal staircase. The 11th-century chapel of **St-Michel d'Aiguille** (St Michael on the needle) can be reached by climbing 268 steps.

**Cathédrale Notre-Dame-de-France** is best approached from *r. des Tables,* from where 134 steps lead up to the massive arched entrance. The building itself is a major attraction, a vast place notable for its stripes of black and white volcanic rock, mosaics, lovely cloister and carved grand entrance. The most famous single feature is a statue modelled from dark cedar that is known as the *Black Madonna.* Set on the high altar, this is a 19th-century copy of a figure that was reputedly brought back from the Crusades. The cathedral was a major pilgrimage stop in medieval times and the sacristy contains many ecclesiastical treasures.

Traditional lace-making is still a local industry and **Le Centre d'Enseignement de la Dentelle du Puy**, *2 r. Duguesclin,* has an exhibition and demonstration room, where the old skills are taught. Bobbin lacework from the 16th–20th centuries is among the items on display at the **Musée Crozatier**, *jardin Henri Vinay.*

# MADRID

Madrid is a large, modern city, but the area of interest to visitors is relatively small and easy to get around. Puerta del Sol, although not attractive in itself, is in the centre of the city (and of Spain, since it is the place from which all distances in the country are measured). It is an excellent spot to get your bearings.

## TOURIST INFORMATION

**Regional/provincial office**: *Mercado Puerta de Toledo, R. Onda de Toledo 1; tel: 364 18 76*, Mon–Fri 0900–1900, Sat 0930–1330. **Branch office**: *Duque de Medinaceli 2; tel: 429 49 51* or *429 44 87*, Mon–Fri 0900–1900, Sat 0900–1300. **Municipal office**: *Plaza Mayor 3; tel: 366 54 77*, Mon–Fri 1000–2000, Sat 1000–1400. **Chamartín station** (opposite Platforms 10/11), *tel: 315 99 76*, Mon–Fri 0800–2000, Sat 0800–1300. **Viajes TIVE**: *C. Fernando el Católico 88; tel: 543 02 08*. In summer there are temporary tourist stands around the city.

**Thomas Cook licensees**, **Ultramar Express**, are located around the city.

## ARRIVING AND DEPARTING

### Airport
**Madrid Barajas Airport** *(tel: 305 83 43/4)* is 16 km north-east of town. There is a Tourist Office in the International Arrivals Hall *(tel: 305 86 56)*, open Mon–Fri 0800–2000 and Sat 0900–1300. A bus operates every 10–15 mins between the airport and *Plaza de Colón* in the centre of town. The journey takes about 30 mins *(tel: 431 61 92)* and costs Pta370.

### Stations
**Chamartín Station** *(Augustín de Foxá; tel: 314 09 24)* is in the northern suburbs. It is Madrid's main station (a modern place with every conceivable facility) and handles trains to the north, north-east and north-west, including those for

France. It is also the terminal for some of the south-bound trains, but most of those stop at Atocha en route. All *cercanías* (commuter trains) stop at Chamartín.

Part of **Atocha Station** *(Avenida Ciudad de Barcelona; tel: 506 69 99)* is the main terminal for the southern, eastern and western services, and also for trains to Portugal. The older part of the station, **Puerta de Atocha** *(Glorieta Emperador Carlos V; tel: 534 05 05)*, is now the terminal for the AVE via Córdoba to Seville.

There are also two intermediate stations, **Recoletos** *(Paseo de Recoletos 4)* and **Nuevos Ministerios** (on the corner of *C. Raimundo Fernández Villaverde* and *Paseo de la Castellana)*, but no trains originate from these. **El Norte Station**, also known as **Príncipe Pío**, is to the west of town, south of *Plaza de España*. This is now only a suburban station.

All the mainline railway stations are connected to the metro. The main **RENFE office** is at *C. Alcalá 44; tel: 563 02 02*. For general **RENFE information**, *tel: 328 90 20*.

## GETTING AROUND

Excellent street maps can be picked up at the Tourist Offices or bought at news-stands.

Madrid has most of the crime problems common to any large city, but in many areas you are just as safe by night as by day since the Madrileños are sociable people and most of the streets are crowded in the evenings. Women alone should not linger around the seedier parts of *Huertas, Malasana* or *Chueca*, but can avoid problems if they head straight for their target.

### Metro
The metro (subway) *(tel: 552 59 09)* is cheap, efficient and easy to use. The lines are colour-coded and marked according to the end-destination. It operates 0600–0130 and free colour maps are available from ticket offices, Tourist Offices and most hotels. There's a flat fare (Pta130), but you save by buying *tacos* (books of ten tickets) for Pta660.

## Buses

The bus system is comprehensive, efficient and the same price as the metro, but not as easy to master. You can get a map of the whole system *(Plano de los Transportes)* from bookshops, Tourist Offices or the EMT booths on *Plaza de la Cibeles, Plaza Callao* or *Puerta del Sol.* There are also route plans on the bus stops *(paradas).* The regular city buses mostly operate 0600–midnight (there are a few night services from *Puerta del Sol* and *Plaza de la Cibeles,* with stops marked 'N', which run every 30 mins to 0200 and then every hour until 0600, but it's safer to stick to taxis if you are out late). Again you save by getting a *Bonobus* ticket (ten rides: Pta660), from tobacconists, news-stands and EMT kiosks. All long-distance buses use the brand new state-of-the-art terminal at *Méndez Alvaro* (metro: *Méndez Alvaro).* This has every conceivable facility, including hot showers.

## Taxis

Taxis can be hailed in the street and are an inexpensive way of getting around late at night; *tel: 547 82 00, 445 90 08* or *447 51 80.*

## STAYING IN MADRID

## Accommodation

Madrid offers the wide range of accommodation expected of any capital city. Among the main hotel groups are *Hd, HI, Ic, Ml, Nv, Rz* and *So.* **Brujula** is an accommodation service with offices at the airport bus station, *tel: 575 96 80,* Atocha station, *tel: 539 11 73,* Chamartín station, *tel: 315 78 94,* and on the 6th floor (above the Tourist Office) of the Torre de Madrid, *tel: 559 97 05.* It covers the whole of Spain and costs Pta300. Madrid is full of budget accommodation, which is generally well-kept, with the basic necessities, but rarely distinctive or charming. Air-conditioning is not the norm and you may have to pay extra for showers in communal bathrooms.

For a cheap place to stay around *Puerta del Sol,* try **Hostal-Residencia María del Mar** *(C. Marqués Viudo de Pontejos 7 2nd and 3rd floors; tel: 531 90 64)* or **Hostal Amaika** *(C. Esparteros 11 3rd and 4th floors; tel: 531 52 78).* Nearby, *C. Arenal* is virtually lined with

reasonably-priced accommodation. To the east of *Puerta del Sol,* good deals can be found on *Carrera de San Jerónimo* and its side streets. **Hostal Aguilar** *(Carrera de San Jerónimo 32, 2nd floor; tel: 429 59 26)* has over fifty large rooms, including proper quads for groups of travellers. There are other hostels in the same building. **Hostal Biarritz** at *C. de la Victoria 2, 2nd floor (tel: 521 92 12)* has 20 rooms, all with attractive furniture, en-suite bathrooms and air-conditioning. Although slightly more expensive it is excellent value. Other places on the same street offer similar deals.

The *Gran Vía* is a hectic and noisy thoroughfare with a not unjustified reputation for prostitution. However, together with side streets such as *C. de Fuencarral,* the area offers a surplus of accommodation to those who want it. *C. de la Montera* runs from *Gran Vía* to *Sol.* Although fairly seedy, it has a number of pleasant lodgings, including **Hostal París** *(C. de la Montera 15, 2nd and 4th floors; tel: 531 91 52)* and **Hostal-Residencia Eureka** *(C. de la Montera 7, 3rd floor; tel: 531 94 60).* There is also cheap accommodation around Atocha station, but it's not a very pleasant area at night.

**HI** hostels are located at *C. Santa Cruz de Marcenado 28; tel: 547 45 32* (metro: *Argüelles),* and at **Richard Schirrmann,** *Casa de Campo; tel: 463 56 99* (metro: *Lago).*

Madrid's **campsites** are both out of town, but compensate by having enough facilities to be self-contained. **Camping Madrid,** *tel: 302 28 35,* is 11 km from town on the N1 road to Burgos (metro to *Plaza Castilla,* then bus no. 151 to *Iglesia de los Dominicos).* **Camping Osuna,** *tel: 741 05 10* is 15.5 km from town on the Ajalvir–Vicálvaro road. Take the metro to *Canillejas,* then bus no. 105 to *Avda Logroño.*

## Eating and Drinking

The old town, south-west of *Plaza Mayor,* is full of 'typical' Spanish bars and restaurants built in cellars and stone-walled caves. However, as with the tapas bars surrounding *Plaza Mayor,* these are generally touristy and over-priced.

A better area is around *Plaza Santa Ana: Calles Echegaray, Ventura de la Vega* and *Manuel Fernández González,* all host a number of quality budget restaurants, and *Plaza Santa Ana* itself

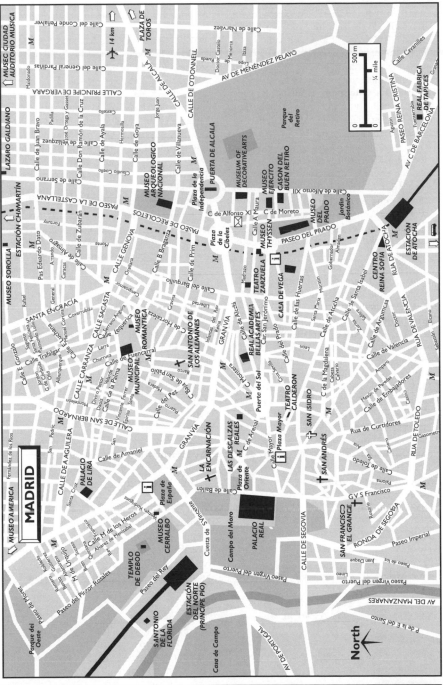

MADRID

MUSEO AMÉRICA

MUSEC CIUDAD AUDITORIO MUSICA

LAZARO GALDIANO

PLAZA DE TOROS

Calle del Conde Peñalver

14 km

Calle del General Pardiñas

CALLE PRINCIPE DE VERGARA

Maldonado

Calle de Narváez

CALLE DE ALCALÁ

CALLE DE O'DONNELL

AV DE MENÉNDEZ PELAYO

Doctor Castelo

Ibiza

Menorca

Lope

Calle Cavanilles

500 m

¼ mile

Calle de Ortega y Gasset

Calle Don Ramón de la Cruz

Castelló

Jorge Juan

Hermosilla

Calle de Goya

Calle de Ayala

Padilla

Calle de Juan Bravo

Pas Eduardo Dato

Calle de Velázquez

Claudio Coello

Calle Coello

Calle Serrano

Calle Don Ramón de la Cruz

Calle de Villanueva

PUERTA DE ALCALA

Plaza de la Independencia

MUSEO ARQUEOLÓGICO NACIONAL

Parque del Retiro

PASEO REINA CRISTINA

AV C DE BARCELONA

REAL FABRICA DETAPICES

PASEO DE LA CASTELLANA

ESTACIÓN CHAMARTÍN

PASEO DE RECOLETOS

MUSEUM OF DECORATIVE ARTS

MUSEO EJERCITO

CASON DEL BUEN RETIRO

Calle de Alfonso XII

C de Alfonso XI

C de Moreto

MUSEO DEL PRADO

Jardín Botánico

MUSEO SOROLLA

CALLE GENOVA

Fortuny

Plaza de la Cibeles

MUSEO THYSSEN

PASEO DEL PRADO

ESTACIÓN DE ATOCHA

SANTA ENGRACIA

CALLE SAGASTA

Calle de Zubarán

Monte

Calle de Prim

Calle de Barquillo

TEATRO ZARZUELA

CASA DEVEGA

RUA DE ATOCHA

CENTRO REINA SOFIA

CALLE CARRANZA

MUSEO ROMANTICO

SAN ANTONIO DE LOS ALEMANES

GRAN VIA

Calle de Alcalá

REAL ACADEMIA BELLAS ARTES

Calle del Prado

Calle de las Huertas

Calle de Santa Isabel

Calle de Atocha

Calle de Argumosa

RUA DE VALENCIA

295

MUSEO MUNICIPAL

Calle Fuencarral

Calle de San Pablo

Puerta del Sol

TEATRO CALDERON

C de la Magdalena

Calle de Valencia

CALLE DE SAN BERNARDO

GRAN VIA

LAS DESCALZAS REALES

Plaza Mayor

SAN ISIDRO

Rua de Curtidores

RUA DE TOLEDO

CALLE DE AGUILERA

PALACIO DE LIRA

LA ENCARNACIÓN

C de Arenal

SAN ANDRÉS

Calle de Toledo

Calle de Amaniel

Plaza de España

Plaza de Oriente

Calle de Bailén

SAN FRANCISCO EL GRANDE

GV S Francisco

RONDA DE SEGOVIA

Paseo Imperial

MUSEO CERRALBO

Calle M de los Heros

Campo del Moro

PALACIO REAL

CALLE DE SEGOVIA

TEMPLO DE DEBOD

Paseo del Rey

Paseo Virgen del Puerto

ESTACIÓN DEL NORTE (PRÍNCIPE PÍO)

Paseo Virgen del Puerto

AV DEL MANZANARES

Parque del Oeste

Paseo del Pintor Rosales

S ANTONIO DE LA FLORIDA

Casa de Campo

North

is great for tapas. On *C. de Echegaray*, **La Caserola** is a lively bar with a restaurant at the back and **Taberna D'a Queimada** has a homely atmosphere, in part induced by the painted jugs and dried peppers which adorn every conceivable surface. On the same street is **Taberna D'a Queimada II**, under the same ownership and just as good. **La Trucha** is a superb fish restaurant at *C. Manuel Fernández González 3*. Nearer *Puerta del Sol, Pasaje de Matheú,* which links *C. Espoz y Mina* and *C. de la Victoria,* has several restaurants, with outside tables, for example **Manacor**. **El Duero**, *C. Espoz y Mina 4,* may lack ambience and charm but serves good set meals at reasonable prices.

Pork lovers can't leave Madrid without visiting the **Museo del Jamón**. A restaurant, not a museum, its walls are covered in huge slabs of meat, and diners can feast on Iberian ham in any conceivable shape or form. There are several branches throughout the city, including *Carrera de San Jerónimo 8* (near *Puerta del Sol*).

## Communications

The main **post office** is in the **Palacio de Comunicaciones**, *Plaza de la Cibeles; tel: 537 64 94* (metro: *Banco de España*) and is worth a visit just to see the building; opening times vary according to the different services, generally Mon–Fri 0800–2130/2200 and Sat 0830–1400.

The main **Telefónica** office (for international calls) is at *Gran Vía 30*; open daily 0930–2330. There are branches at Palacio de Comunicaciones and *Paseo de Recoletos 41.*

## Embassies and Consulates

**Australia:** *Paseo Castellana 143; tel: 579 04 28.*
**Canada:** *C. Núñez de Balboa 35; tel: 431 43 00.*
**Eire:** *C. Claudio Coello 73; tel: 576 35 00.*
**New Zealand:** *Plaza Lealtad 2 (3rd Floor); tel: 523 02 26.*
**South Africa:** *C. Claudio Coello 91; tel: 435 66 88.*
**UK:** *C. Fernando el Santo 16; tel: 319 02 00.*
**USA:** *C. Serrano 75; tel: 577 40 00.*

The *Guía del Ocio* is a weekly Spanish language publication with listings of what's on in Madrid, including details of theatre, opera and clubs. It is available from news-stands for Pta125. Several monthly handouts from hotels, Tourist Offices, etc, are very useful and hold similar information, including *Enjoy Madrid, En Madrid* and *What's On in Madrid*. The free magazine, *In Madrid,* in English, gives an upbeat monthly lowdown on Madrid youth culture, including pubs, clubs and gigs, aimed at student traveller. Make sure you read one of these, at least if you want to make the most of Madrid.

### Nightlife

Madrid has excellent nightlife, centred on the numerous restaurants, bars and dance venues. Live music can be found easily. At weekends many bars stay open until 0300 and some close much later than that. Discos tend to have a cover charge, but bars with dance floors don't.

The **Malasaña** area (metro: *Bilbao/Tribunal*) is good for music and bars and popular with a wide range of age groups. It centres on *Plaza Dos de Mayo, C. de Velarde* and *C. de Ruiz.*

**Huertas** (metro: *Antón Martín*) is the area around *Plaza Santa Ana* and has a huge variety of bars that stay open until all hours.

**Paseo del Prado** (metro: *Atocha/Banco de España*) is rather more upmarket, with smart and expensive café-bars. The **Chueca** area has a lively gay scene, particularly along *C. de Pelayo.*

Internet cafés are springing up all over Madrid and seem to be all the rage at the moment. Try **La Cibertéca**, *C. General Perón 32* (metro: *Lima); tel: 556 56 03*, or **Laser**, *C. Rosario 21* (metro: *Puerta de Toledo); tel: 365 87 91.*

Madrid is not the best place in the world for shopping but, if you like to window-shop, several of the main upmarket shopping streets run off, or parallel to, *C. Serrano,* which is the Spanish equivalent of Knightsbridge or Fifth Avenue.

If you don't want to come away empty-handed, foodstuffs, such as wine or oil, is the best buy because it's fairly cheap throughout Spain. **El Rastro** (metro: *La Latina*) is a flea-market that is something of a Sunday-morning institution. It's best to go early because it can be

296

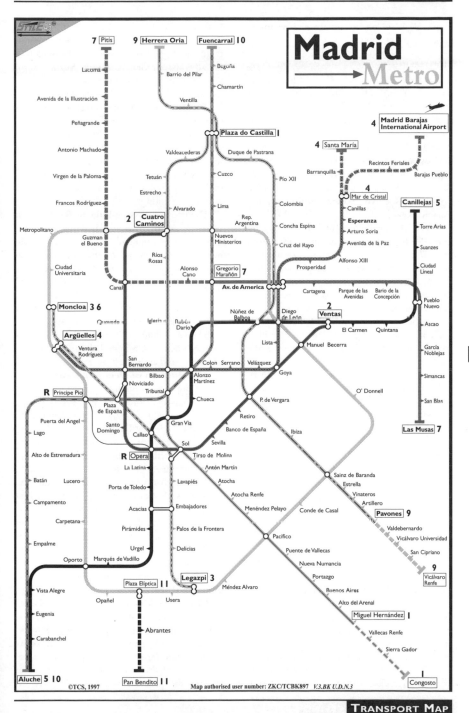

# Madrid Metro →

©TCS, 1997    Map authorised user number: ZKC/TCBK897    V.3.BK U.D.N.3

impossibly crowded by midday and begins to pack up around 1400.

SIGHTSEEING

A leaflet, *Conozcamos Madrid* (available from the municipal Tourist Office) lists walking tours for Spanish-speakers. Ask at the Tourist Office about hop-on and hop-off bus tours of the central attractions. Prices vary: expect to pay Pta750–1600 for half a day, Pta1000–2000 for a full day and Pta2000–2600 for 2-day passes. Bear in mind that practically all museums close all day on Mon, except (if there's a special event) the **Centro Reina Sofía** and the **Palacio Real**.

**Plaza Mayor** (metro: *Sol)* is a stately square surrounded by grandiose buildings dating from the 17th century, at which time it was a centre of Spanish society, where such pleasant entertainments as bullfighting and the Inquisition's *autos-da-fé* were staged. Today, the pleasures are more civilised: you can sit at a pavement café, admire the equestrian statue of King Philip III and watch the world go by. The old Hapsburg area to the south-west of Plaza Mayor is the most attractive in Madrid.

The **Retiro** (metro: *Retiro/Atocha)* is a park laid out in the 17th century, a cool place with wooded corners, formal avenues, brilliant flowers and a large boating lake. Adjoining it is the **Jardín Botánico** (metro: *Atocha),* a delightful place with three separate terraces, some of which feature vegetables as well as the more usual shrubs and flowers.

**Plaza de Oriente** (metro: *Opera)* is a small garden opposite the palace that is adorned with over 40 statues of Spanish royalty, notably a splendid equestrian statue of Philip IV. Another lovely garden is the **Campo del Marco**, behind the palace. **Plaza de la Villa** is a small square in the oldest part of Madrid, surrounded by mainly 16th- and 17th-century buildings in Renaissance, Mudejar and Baroque style.

### Galleries and Museums

**Prado** (metro: *Atocha/Banco de España)* is one of the world's greatest art galleries. Many of its paintings were collected by Spanish monarchs between the 16th and 18th centuries. Today there are individual sections devoted to Goya,

Velázquez, Murillo, Zurbarán and El Greco. The Italian and Flemish schools are also well represented. Picasso's masterpiece *Guernica* is in the art museum **Centro Reina Sofía** (metro: *Atocha),* which is also home to a fabulous collection of other 20th-century Spanish works.

The **National Archaeological Museum** (metro: *Serrano* or *Colón)* contains a major collection of articles from all over Spain, including stone-carved Iberian mother-goddesses from the 4th century BC. In the grounds is a full-scale reproduction of the **Altamira Caves**: they contain one of the world's greatest sets of early cave paintings.

The late-Renaissance **Palacio Real** (metro: *Opera)* is an 18th-century building of Italian design, with colonnaded arches. The state rooms were decorated in the 18th and 19th centuries and are full of priceless treasures: Tiepolo frescos, magnificent tapestries, glittering chandeliers, decorative clocks, silverware, gilt ornamentation and works by a variety of famous artists – which are rather swamped by their surroundings. There is also an 18th-century pharmacy, a huge hall lined by prancing horses and an interesting armoury.

The **Museum of Decorative Arts** (metro: *Retiro)* displays a stunning collection of furniture, ceramics, porcelain, glass and leather, together with a wide range of other handicrafts.

At the **Tapestry Factory** (metro: *Menéndez Pelayo)* you can watch tapestries being made by traditional methods. There's also a display of Goya cartoons.

The 16th-century **Convento de las Descalzas Reales** (metro: *Sol)* was a convent for noblewomen and handsomely endowed by their families. It still houses a closed order, but parts of it are open: it has a superb collection of 16th- and 17th-century religious art (fittingly displayed in a series of shrines) and many other treasures, including a magnificent set of tapestries with Rubens designs.

**Lázaro Galdiano** (metro: *Ruben Darío/ Avenida de América)* is a major museum with a superb collection of ivory and enamel work, jewellery and paintings. The **Thyssen-Bornemisza** museum (metro: *Banco de España)* is one of Madrid's newest attractions. After lending the city his priceless 800-piece art collection for a limited period, Baron Thyssen decided (in 1993) that it should be permanently on display to the public.

The small **Convent of the Incarnation** (metro: *Santo Domingo/Opera*) is amazing. It has a unique room that is lined with reliquaries (over 1500 of them). Some are exquisite, others grotesque.

## SIDE TRACKS
## FROM MADRID

### EL ESCORIAL

**Tourist Office**: *C. Floridablanca 10; tel: 890 15 54.*

There are plenty of trains every day (from Atocha, stopping at Chamartín, taking about 1 hr), but the Escorial rail station is about 2 km from town and it's a long uphill walk, so it's better to take a local shuttle bus to the centre. Closed Mon, but (for unclear reasons) entry on Wed is half price for Europeans only.

Taking the **Empresa Herranz** buses *(tel: 543 36 45)* from Madrid is the easier option, as they take you right to the centre. There are around 15 a day and the journey takes 1 hr from Madrid, departing from *C. Isaac Peral 10* (metro: *Moncloa).*

#### SIGHTSEEING

El Escorial is a magnificent 16th-century complex that includes a **monastery**, a **church**, a **library** with nearly 3000 5th–18th-century documents, and a **mausoleum**. Many notable works of art are on display in the complex, some forming an intrinsic part of the décor. The **palace** is of particular interest, the austere quarters of Philip II being in marked contrast to the luxurious apartments used by the Bourbons.

### ÁVILA

**Tourist Office:** *Plaza de la Catedral 4; tel: (920) 21 13 87.* The bus and train stations are about 2 km from the centre. Bus nos 1/3 run from *Avda de José Antonio* (opposite the train station) to within the city walls.

The town is easily accessible by train from Chamartín or Atocha, the journey taking approximately 2 hrs. Alternatively, you could take the bus *(tel: 530 48 00)* from *Paseo de la Florida 11* (metro: *Norte);* the journey takes 1 hr 45 mins–2 hrs.

#### SIGHTSEEING

Ávila, the highest city in Spain, is renowned for both its beautifully preserved medieval walls (the best in the country) and for its native mystic and reformer **Santa Teresa de Jesús** (now the city's patron saint).

The town's main attactions are the **Cathedral**, the **Monastery of Santo Tomás**, the **Basilica of San Vincente** and the many buildings associated with **Santa Teresa**. The Carmelite nun, canonised in 1622, spent 30 years in a convent in the city. The **Sala de Reliquias** contains a variety of relics asssociated with the saint, including her finger, the sole of her sandal and the walking stick she used in later life.

### SEGOVIA

**Tourist Office:** *Plaza Mayor 10; tel: (921) 46 03 34.* Municipal buses run from the bus and train stations to the centre.

Segovia can be reached by train or bus; the departure points are the same as for Avila, and journey times are similar. See ETT table: 671

#### SIGHTSEEING

Segovia has a remarkable number of attractions for a place its size, the most notable being the Cathedral, the Alcázar and the two-tiered aqueduct.

The **Cathedral**, which towers majestically above the rest of the town, dates from the 16th century and was the last Gothic church to be built in Spain.

Scene of the coronation of Isabelle and the marriage of Philip II to Anne of Austria, the **Alcazár** was largely destroyed by fire in 1862; much of the present structure dates from its subsequent restoration.

The two tiered granite **Roman aqueduct** was built without mortar and continued to supply the city with water until only a few years ago.

## TOLEDO

**Station**: *Paseo de la Rosa; tel: (925) 22 30 99.*
**Tourist Offices**: main office: *Puerta Nueva de Bisagra; tel: (925) 22 08 43.* There is an information booth on *Plaza de Zocodover.*

About eight trains a day run between Madrid (Atocha) and Toledo; journey time around 1¼ hrs (ETT table: 671). There are also buses every 30 mins from Méndez Alvaro bus station. The journey takes 1½ hrs and costs Pta600.

### GETTING AROUND

To get into the city centre (either the main Tourist Office or *Plaza de Zocodover)* take bus nos 5/6 from the train station and bus no. 5 from the bus station. If you prefer to walk (it's a pleasant route), it takes 20 mins.

The main sights are all within walking distance and street names are generally well marked. However, the old town is a labyrinthine place and it is easy to get lost, so get a map and refer to it regularly.

### ACCOMMODATION

Hotel chains include *PS* and *So.* The Tourist Office can provide an up-to-date list of accommodation, which can be difficult to find on summer weekends. The best cheap lodgings are in the old town: try around *C. de Juan Labrador* or *C. de Descalzos.* There is an **HI** on the outskirts of town in a medieval castle, the **Castillo San Servando***; tel: (925) 22 45 54.* The university sometimes has rooms available. **Campsites: Circo Romano***, Avenida Carlos III 19; tel: (925) 22 04 42*, not very comfortable but only a 10-min walk from *Puerta de Bisagra;* and **El Greco***, tel: (925) 22 00 90*, which has much better facilities, but is 1.5 km out of town, on *Ctra. Toledo–Puebla de Montalbán* (bus no 7 from *Plaza de Zocodover).*

### SIGHTSEEING

The main buildings in Toledo are perched on a hill and surrounded by ancient walls, with the River Tagus forming a natural moat on three sides. Christian, Muslim and Jewish cultures have mingled through the centuries to leave an array of architectural styles. It's a place with history in every street and you can easily understand how it inspired El Greco, who lived and worked here for nearly 40 years.

**Alcázar** (old fortress) has been rebuilt many times, most recently following its near-total destruction in the Spanish Civil War. It now houses a military museum. **Museo de Santa Cruz**, just east of *Plaza de Zocodover,* contains notable religious paintings and a 15th-century zodiacal tapestry.

Toledo **Cathedral** took over 250 years to complete. It's a marvellous place, with stained-glass windows, elaborate decorations and countless works of art, notably the *Transparente*: an extravagant creation of paintings and marble sculptures which catches the light in a most dramatic way. In the **Sacristy** hang paintings by El Greco, Van Dyck, Goya and Velásquez, whilst on display in the **treasury** is a huge 16th-century monstrance of gold and silver which is still paraded through the town during Corpus Christi celebrations.

In the old Jewish quarter to the south are the town's only two surviving synagogues. **El Tránsito** is a 14th-century Mudéjar edifice with a ceiling of carved cedarwood which now houses the **Museo Sefardí**, a museum about Jewish culture. The 12th-century synagogue of **Santa María la Blanca** is very different: its conversion into a Christian church did not affect the basic layout of the lovely interior, which consists of five aisles separated by horseshoe arches and supported by pillars with unusual capitals and stone carvings.

The **Iglesia de San Tomé** (church of St Thomas), dates from the 14th century and houses El Greco's famous masterpiece *The Burial of Count Orgaz.* The **Casa del Greco** is a small museum dedicated to the artist, with a number of his paintings as well as some of his personal effects.

**Iglesia de San Juan de los Reyes** (Royal Church of St John) is an elaborate mix of Gothic and Mudéjar architecture. The church was commissioned by the Catholic monarchs to celebrate their victory over the Portuguese. 🔼

# MADRID–BARCELONA

This route leads from the centre of Spain across La Mancha (home of Don Quixote) to the orange groves of València, and then follows the eastern coast into Catalonia, taking in the walled Roman city of Tarragona, and on to Barcelona. Alternatively, take the quicker route via Zaragoza: but try to stop off to admire the stunning Basílica.

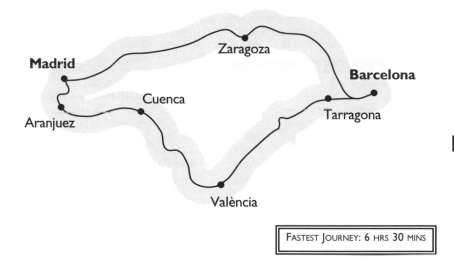

FASTEST JOURNEY: 6 HRS 30 MINS

**301**

## TRAINS

**ETT tables:** 650, 655, 659, 660.

### FAST TRACK

 The quick journey is via Zaragoza, unlike the full route below. Most trains serve Chamartín in Madrid and Sants in Barcelona. There are four day trains, taking 6½–7 hrs, and a couple of overnight trains with sleeping cars or couchettes, as well as seats. All trains have a refreshment service.

## ON TRACK

### Madrid–Aranjuez

There are suburban trains (cercanías) every half an hour between Madrid (Atocha) and Aranjuez. These take 45 mins. There are also express or regional trains approximately hourly from Atocha at irregular intervals, taking 30 mins.

### Aranjuez–Cuenca

There are four to six trains a day, the journey taking about 2 hrs.

## Cuenca–València

There are three trains a day between Cuenca and València (Nord), the journey taking about 3 hrs–3 hrs 30 mins.

## València–Tarragona

There are at least twelve trains a day between Valencia (Nord) and Tarragona. The fastest trains are the *Euromed* TGV-style trains. There are 5 per day taking 2 hrs. Special fares are payable. Expresses *(IC* or *Talgo)* takes 2 hrs 30 mins, and have buffets. Local trains also run, taking 4 hrs.

## Tarragona–Barcelona

There is a good service between Tarragona and Barcelona (mostly Sants): trains leave every half-hour or hour, taking 1 hr–1 hr 15 mins.

## ZARAGOZA

**Station: Estación del Portillo,** *Avda Clavé s/n; tel: 902 28 02 02.* 3 km north of the centre: take bus 21, or a 25 min walk. Maps of Zaragoza are available at the station.

**Tourist Office:** *Plaza del Pilar, s/n; tel: 902 20 12 00; fax: 902 20 06 35.* Open Mon–Sat 0930 –1330, Sun 1000–1400. **Regional:** *Torreon de la Zuda, Glorieta Pio XII, s/n, tel: 902 39 35 37.* Open Mon–Fri 0815–1445, 1515–2000, Sat 1000–1330, Sun 0900–1400, for a good selection of leaflets on the Aragón region.

Zaragoza is a lively city built mainly on the South bank of the River Ebro, and home to the spectacular **Basilica de Nuestro Señora del Pilar**. Although flanked by immense tower blocks and traffic-ridden *paseos,* the old town reveals graceful plazas, quaint, winding streets lined with fashionable shops and inviting bars and restaurants, and many places of historic interest.

### GETTING AROUND

Once in the old town itself, the main attractions are within easy walking distance. The Tourist Office offers guided walking tours, as well as a bus tour around the city, caught on the north (river) side of the Basilica. A cheaper alternative is to collect the free map from the Tourist Office, which has the tour marked on it, and to follow it yourself.

### ACCOMMODATION

Pick up a free accommodation guide *(Guia de Alojamientos)* from the Tourist Office. Possibly the best value is the **Hotel Las Torres**, *11 pl. del Pilar; tel: 976 39 42 50;* which affords a superb view of the Basilica. Alternatively, try the cheap **Hostal Milmarcos**, *C. Madre Sacramento 40; tel: 976 28 16 18.*

### SIGHTSEEING

The **Basilica de Nuestro Señora del Pilar** is mosque-like in its glory and displays domes of coloured tiles. It is named after the pillar within the church, where the Virgin Mary is said to have descended from heaven in a vision of the Apostle St John in 40AD. It was designed by Fr Herrera el Moza in 1679, and in the 1750s and 1760s by Ventura Rodriguez. Inside is the **Museo Pilarista**, which displays original designs for the domes by de Goya, Francisco and Ramon Bayeu and Velaquez.

The **Plaza del Pilar** was restored in the 1990s and features an interesting water monument of South America. Stand at the closest point of the pool to the Basilica, crouch down, and you will see a clear outline of the continent.

The **Museo Camón Aznar**, *C. Espoz y Mina 23, tel: 976 397328,* is open Tues–Fri 0900–1415, 1800–2100, Sat 1000–1400, Sun 1100–1400. Set in the Renaissance palace of the Pardo family, it displays most of Goya's points: Goya's birthplace was Fuendetodos, a nearby town.

The oldest site in Zaragoza is that of the **Roman Forum**, dating from 100BC to 100AD, situated in the **Plaza de la Seo**, by the cathedral. It is open 1000–1400 and 1700– 2000.

A modern attraction is the theme **Parque Zaragoza**, 1 km north from the station on Duque Alba. Open Mar–Oct, it offers ferris wheels, rollercoasters and houses of horror.

## ARANJUEZ

**Station**: *tel: (91) 891 02 02.* 1 km outside town and 10 mins walk from the palace. As you exit the station take the road to the right and then turn left at the end.

**Tourist Office**: *Plaza de San Antonio 9; tel: (91) 891 04 27.*

Situated on the south bank of the Tagus, Aranjuez has just one major attraction: a spectacular **Royal Palace**. This started life as a country house that was presented to Ferdinand and Isabella, but the present structure dates from the 18th century and is a succession of opulently-furnished rooms with marble mosaics, crystal chandeliers, ornate clocks and the like.

The Smoking Room is an exact replica of the Dos Hermanos room in the Alhambra at Granada (see Madrid–Madrid, p.309). Another room boasts a large collection of Oriental ceramic wall decorations.

In the gardens are the **Casita del Labrador** (strongly resembling the Petit Trianon at Versailles) and the **Casa de Marinos** (with royal pleasure boats).

## CUENCA

**Station**: *tel: (969) 22 07 20*. The road leads straight up to the old town, but it is a hard climb and most people prefer to take a bus (nos 1/2).

**Tourist Office**: *Glorieta González Palencia 2; tel: (969) 17 88 00*. There is also a branch at *C. de San Pedro 6; tel: (91) 23 21 19*.

The old town is a delightful place with finely carved wooden balconies, armorial bearings, impressive doorways and some breathtaking views. The main attractions are the **Casas Colgadas**: restored 13th-century tiered houses that hang over a sheer chasm.

The central **Plaza Mayor** is one of the few level parts of the old town. It is dominated on one side by the **Cathedral**, which dates from the 12th century. Do not be put off by the unfinished exterior: the inside is very fine and houses an interesting **Treasury**. The best museums are the **Diocesan Museum** and the **Museo de Arte Abstracto**. The latter is in one of the hanging houses and displays an important collection of Spanish abstract art.

## VALÈNCIA

**Stations**: The main station is **Estacio del Nord**, *tel: (96) 352 93 62*, which is centrally located. **Cabanyal**, *tel: (96) 356 21 67*, serves the ferries and is 10 mins (by rail) from Estacio del Nord. For general RENFE information *tel:*

*(96) 352 02 02*. There is also an FGV station across the river from Torres Serranos, from which a network of narrow gauge railways radiate; *tel: (96) 348 46 26*.

**Tourist Offices**: (Regional) *C. de la Paz 48; tel: (96) 394 22 22*, and at Estacio del Nord, *tel: (96) 352 85 73*. (Municipal) *Plaza Ayuntamiento 1; tel: (96) 351 04 17*, and *Avda Cataluña 1; tel: (96) 369 79 32*.

The lively modern city is a place with many lush parks and gardens, elaborate baroque façades and a sprinkling of orange trees. *Paella* (traditionally eaten for lunch, not dinner) originated here. València is also famous for **Las Fallas**, a week-long festival in mid March that centres on a competition to produce the best *ninot* (papier mâché doll). The whole town celebrates as the entries are paraded through the streets and (on the last night) ritually burned, to the accompaniment of an enormous firework display.

### GETTING AROUND

The area covered by the old town (where most sights of interest are located) is relatively small and you can easily walk between them. EMT buses operate throughout the city *(tel: (96) 352 83 99)*; most can be boarded in *Plaza Ayuntamiento*. A single trip costs Pta80, books of 10 tickets (from *tabacos* and kiosks) Pta550.

### ACCOMMODATION

Hotel chains with branches in València: *Ex, Ml* and *PS* (although the parador is in **El Saler**, 10 km south of València). Good areas for budget accommodation are around *Plaza Ayuntamiento* and *Plaza del Mercado*.

**Hostal Moratín**, *C. Moratín 15; tel: (96) 352 12 20*, is comfortable and cheap, if slightly airless. **Hostal-Residencia El Cid**, *C. Cerrajeros 13; tel: (96) 392 23 23*, gives special deals for groups and (so they say) *On the Rails* readers. **HI**: *La Paz, Avda del Puerto 69; tel: (96) 369 01 52* (bus no.19 from *Plaza Ayuntamiento*) is open July–mid Sept. The most convenient **campsite** is **El Saler**, *tel: (96) 183 00 23;* buses every half-hour from *Gran Vía Germanías*.

### SIGHTSEEING

Many historical structures were destroyed by

303

inept town planners and the Spanish Civil War put paid to most of the rest, so the town is largely modern, but two medieval gateways survive (**Torres de Serranos** and **Torres de Quart**) and there is a large old quarter with some pleasant squares and (rather run-down) baroque mansions.

**Plaza de la Reina** is dominated by two towers: the baroque spire of **Santa Catalina** and the **Miguelete**, which is the bell tower of the cathedral: climb the spiral staircase to the top for a magnificent view of the city. The **Cathedral** is the town's most interesting building: a mixture of styles ranging from the Romanesque to the baroque. A 1st-century agate chalice adorned with gold and pearls is said to be the Holy Grail and is displayed behind the altar in a side chapel.

Next door in *Plaza de la Virgen* are the **Real Basílica de Nuestra Señora de los Desamparados** and the **Palacio de la Generalidad**, a 15th-century building with gilded ceilings.

The Gothic **Lonja de la Seda** *(Plaza del Mercado),* with its exquisitely designed interior, is a reminder that Valencia was prominent in the 15th-century silk trade. Nearby is the **Mercado Central** (market), an ornate building with a stained-glass ceiling and many *azulejos.*

The **Palacio del Marqués de Dos Aguas** is a magnificent baroque monstrosity with an extraordinary alabaster doorway. It houses the **Ceramics Museum.** Across the old Turia riverbed, now a series of parks, the **Museo de Bellas Artes,** *San Pío V,* displays a fine collection of Valencian primitive paintings and works by later masters, including Velásquez's self-portrait.

**SIDE TRACKS
FROM VALÈNCIA**

**Trasmediterranea** on *Avda Manuel Soto, tel: (96) 367 10 62,* operate ferries to the **Balearic Islands** – Majorca, Minorca and Ibiza – from **Estación Marítima,** *tel: (96) 367 07 04.* (ETT Table 2510 lists the schedules).

The coastal strip from València to Castellon, named the **Costa del Azahar**

after the orange blossom that grows there, has generally suffered the consequences of mass tourism, but is still worth a visit.

**Sagunto** is an historically important city, famed for its heroic resistance to Hannibal in the 3rd century BC. Today it is notable for its 2nd-century **Roman theatre**, now much restored, and for the extensive remains of a medieval fortress which crown the nearby hill. Further north, **Peniscola** is a charming village of whitewashed houses and winding streets surrounding a spectacular 14th-century castle. ⬛

**TARRAGONA**

**Station**: *Plaza de la Pedrera s/n; tel: (977) 24 02 02.* This is centrally located.

**Tourist Office**: (Regional) *Carrer Fortuny 4; tel: (977) 23 34 15.* (Municipal) *Carrer Major 39; tel: (977) 24 19 53* (near the cathedral).

Founded in 218 BC, Tarragona prospered under the Romans and many traces of their city have survived, including the remains of temples, a theatre and the **Roman forum**. There is also a necropolis and a well-preserved aqueduct a little way out of town. The city is in two parts: the medieval walled town is on a limestone bluff overlooking the sea and the modern town is lower down, **Rambla Vella** being the dividing line. The **Passeig Arqueológic** is lined on one side by 3rd-century BC Roman walls. The **Museu Arqueológic**, *Plaça del Rei,* is crammed with Roman sculptures, bronzes and mosaics. The neighbouring **Pretori**, or Roman palace, now houses the History Museum. **La Seu** (the cathedral) should not be missed. It is a superb example of the transition from Romanesque to Gothic.

**SIDE TRACK
FROM TARRAGONA**

From Tarragona it is possible to visit **Port Aventura**, Spain's new adventure theme park. There are at least eight trains a day, the journey taking about 10 mins. For further details *tel: (977) 779900.* ⬛

# MADRID–LISBON

This route links Spain and Portugal through the harsh, desolate landscape of Estremadura, the historic homeland of the Conquistadores. Its delightful old towns owed their prosperity to the vast wealth brought back from the Americas by these adventurers

Note that Spain and Portugal are in different time zones, Portugal is in the same zone as Britain and Ireland and is thus 1 hour behind Spain, which keeps central European time. Take this into account when working out the length of a journey between the two countries: a journey from Spain to Portugal is actually 1 hour longer than the local departure and arrival times suggest, and a journey from Portugal to Spain 1 hour shorter.

## TRAINS

FASTEST JOURNEY: 9 HRS 30 MINS

ETT tables: 80, 670.

### FAST TRACK

There is only one (overnight) train between Madrid (Chamartín) and Lisbon (Santa Apolónia), departing approx 2200 hrs and arriving around 0830. Taking 9½ hrs from Lisbon and 11 hrs from Madrid (allowing for time difference), the train has sleeping cars, couchettes, second-class seats and a dining car. Special *Trenhotel* fares are payable.

### ON TRACK

#### Madrid–Talavera de la Reina

There are five trains daily between Madrid and Talavera; two are Talgos (supplement payable), however, and one of these departs from Chamartín and arrives late at night, so the three regional trains which use Atocha are the best bet: they take about 1 hr 30 mins.

#### Cáceres–(Border)–Abrantes

There are three services from Cáceres to the border at Badajoz, and two trains from there to Abrantes. Cáceres to Badajoz takes 2 hrs, Badajoz to Abrantes 3 hrs (remember time zone change). The only through train runs during the middle of the night.

#### Abrantes–Lisbon (Lisboa)

Seven trains a day run between Abrantes and Lisbon (Santa Apolónia). The journey takes 1½–2 hrs.

## TALAVERA DE LA REINA

**Station:** *tel: (925) 80 13 88.* This is about 1 km from the city centre.

Talavera is the centre of a ceramics industry and famous for the attractive blue and yellow tiles *(azulejos)* which have been produced here since the 15th century: these can be seen adorning many buildings. The **Museo Ruíz de Luna** displays 15th–19th-century pottery. The **Capilla de Nuestra Señora del Prado** is adorned with 16th–18th-century glazed tiles.

## CÁCERES

**Station**: *Avda Alemania; tel: (927) 23 51 60.* The bus and train stations are together, about 3 km from the centre. Bus no. 1 goes to *Plaza Obispo Galarza, near the Plaza Mayor.*
**Tourist Office**: *Plaza Mayor 33; tel: (927) 24 63 47.*

### GETTING AROUND

There are buses and taxis, but the way to explore the old town is on foot. The places of interest are mostly around (or just off) the *Plaza de Santa María* or the *Plaza San Mateo,* and the two plazas are not far apart.

### ACCOMMODATION

There is a good choice of hotels, including *Ml* and *PS;* the best area for both staying and eating cheaply is in the vicinity of *Plaza Mayor.*
  **Campsite**: *Ciudad de Cáceres, tel: (927) 23 04 03 or 23 01 30,* on the N-630 to Mérida

### SIGHTSEEING

Cáceres is a truly charming place crammed with so much of interest that it has been declared a World Heritage site. Yet it is relatively unknown and visitors are still almost outnumbered by the storks that have built nests on every conceivable perch. The ancient city walls surround a largely intact old town that is a marvellous place to explore. Go back after dark, just to absorb the atmosphere; you really feel that you have stepped into another century.
  The cobbled, partially arcaded **Plaza Mayor** borders the old town and is the obvious place from which to start exploring. On one side are the **Torre del Horno**, a well-preserved Moorish structure of mud-brick, and the **Torre de Bujaco**, a Moorish tower on Roman foundations. The **Arco de la Estrella** leads to the areas of interest.
  The **Plaza de Santa María** is surrounded by fine buildings, including the Gothic **Cathedral**, which contains sarcophagi and a

16th-century retable; the **Palacio de Mayoralgo**; and the 16th-century **Episcopal Palace**, decorated with engravings of the Old and New Worlds.
  The **Carvajal Palace** houses the tourism and craft council but you can visit the chapel and the first floor gallery (decorated in 19th-century style). Almost next door is the **Palacio de los Golfines de Abajo**, which has an impressive Plateresque façade and bears the coat of arms of the Catholic Monarchs. There are many other old mansions with imposing coats of arms and gargoyles. A little to the south, at the top of the hill on which the old city stands, is the 16th-century Gothic **Church of San Mateo**, which is a fascinating mixture of external styles and contains a baroque altarpiece as well as the tombs of many nobles.
  Near here is the **Casa de las Cigüeñas**, the only noble's house exempted from a royal decree and allowed to keep its fortifications. The 15th-century **Monastery of San Francisco Javier** has a fine late-Gothic church and cloister. The **Casa de las Veletas** was built on the foundations of a Moorish citadel and contains an Almohade water cistern *(aljibe)* with a vaulted ceiling supported by horseshoe arches. It houses a small provincial museum. The **Casa-Museo Yusuf Al Burch**, *Cuesta del Marqués,* is an authentic recreation of a 12th-century Arabian residence.

> ## SIDE TRACKS FROM CÁCERES

## TRUJILLO

**Tourist Office**: *Plaza Mayor s/n; tel: (927) 32 26 77.* Open Mon–Fri 0900–1400, 1700–1900.
  There is no rail link from Cáceres to Trujillo, but there are about seven buses a day from the main bus station in Cáceres. The journey takes 40 mins.
  Although a 10th-century **Moorish Castle** overlooks the town (which is 47 km east of Cáceres), Trujillo is a place built largely from the proceeds of the Peruvian conquests and known as the 'Cradle of the Conquistadores'.

306

From the bus station, it's a 15-min walk uphill to **Plaza Mayor**, at the heart of the town. The square is built on two different levels, connected by steps, and lined with once-magnificent palace-mansions, arcades and whitewashed houses. It is dominated in one corner by the **Iglesia de San Martín**, at the foot of which stands a bronze statue of Francisco Pizarro, mounted and in full regalia. The beautiful Plateresque **Palacio de la Conquista** was built by Hernando Pizarro (the elaborate window grilles and corner balcony are particularly attractive) and there are many other 16th/17th-century seigneurial mansions with lavish armorial bearings.

From *Plaza Mayor, C. de Ballesteros* leads up to the old walls in which there is a gateway to the 13th-century Romanesque-Gothic church of **Santa María la Mayor**. The church is on the site of an Arab mosque and contains Roman sarcophagi as well as the tombs of the Pizarros and other Spanish heroes. The winged retable by Fernando Gallego has over twenty panels depicting a range of religious subjects.

A short distance away is the **Casa-Museo de Pizarro**, with a reconstruction of a 15th-century *hidalgo* (nobleman's house) and an exhibition of the life and discoveries of Pizarro.

## VALENCIA DE ALCÁNTARA

**Station**: Estación RENFE; *tel: (927) 58 00 72*. About 2.5 km from the city centre.

A local bus service links Cáceres and Valencia de Alcántara. There is at least one bus a day and the journey takes approximately 30 mins. Contact Cáceres Tourist Office for further details.

The Spanish frontier town is a small, pleasant place with old walls and a ruined 13th-century Moorish castle. Within the walls are the 13th-century **Iglesia de la Encarnación**, which has a fine Gothic façade, and the 16th-century **Iglesia de Nuestra Señora del Rocamador**, with a figure of Christ, attributed to Berruguete. Some nearby dolmens testify to the presence of man in prehistoric times.

## MARVÃO

**Station**: Marvão's own station, **Beirã**, is not very near the town. Better to get off at **Castelo de Vide** station, which is itself some 13 km away and take a taxi to Marvão (there are no buses).

From Cáceres, continue on the main line until you reach Torre das Vargens. From here, there are three daily trains to Marvão, taking approximately 1 hr.

**Tourist Office**: *Rua do Dr Matos de Magalhães; tel: (045) 931 04.*

Marvão is a small, remote medieval town, perched high on a peak of the ridge which forms a natural border with Spain. The walled town is dominated by a 13th-century **Castle** on a wooded hill above the town, from which there are fine views in every direction. There are several pretty chapels with Renaissance touches. 🔼

## ABRANTES

**Station**: *Rossio ao Sul do Tejo, tel: (041) 314 06.* The station is about 4 km south of the town centre, on the other side of the River Tagus.

**Tourist Office**: *Largo da Feira; tel: (041) 225 55.* Open daily 0900–1800.

Perched high above the Tagus, Abrantes was built to defend the old Beirã province. It is a small place and retains much of its original character. Above the town, approached through a maze of flower-bedecked alleys, are the remains of a castle of uncertain, pre-12th-century, origins re-built by King Denis in the 14th century. The keep has been partially restored and is now a belvedere offering panoramic views of the town, the Tagus Valley and the mountains.

The 13th-century **Church of Santa Maria do Castelo** (in the castle grounds) was restored in the 15th century and houses a museum containing an interesting collection of Gothic works of art and *azulejos* (decorative blue and yellow tiles). The **Church of São João Baptista**, rebuilt in the 16th century, has some excellent wood carvings and a Renaissance ceiling. The 16th-century **Church of the Misericórdia** and 15th-century **Convent of São Domingos**, now a library, are also worth a visit.

# MADRID-MADRID

After a few days sightseeing in Madrid, this long trundle through Andalusia's breathtaking scenery and wealth of antiquity is a great way to unwind. The route traverses barren mountainscapes, olive groves and dazzling sunflower plantations, and offers something for everyone, from historic medieval towns to the resorts of the Costa del Sol.

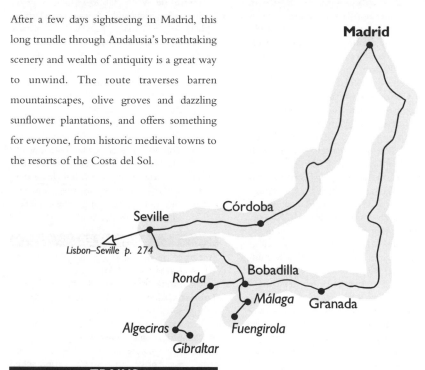

Madrid

Córdoba

Seville

Lisbon–Seville p. 274

Ronda

Bobadilla

Málaga    Granada

Algeciras    Fuengirola

Gibraltar

**308**

## TRAINS

**ETT tables: 666, 666a, 665.**

### ON TRACK

#### Madrid–Granada

A daily *Talgo* express makes the journey in 6 hrs. A supplement is charged and there is a buffet car. There is also an overnight train with sleeping cars, couchettes, second-class seats and a buffet. This takes 8½ hrs.

#### Granada–Bobadilla

Three regional trains a day classified '*Andalucía Exprés*' cut across country taking 2 hrs.

#### Bobadilla–Seville

Three to four *Andalucía Exprés* regional trains make the journey direct each day, taking 2 hrs.

Other connections are possible via Córdoba with a change of train.

#### Seville–Córdoba

*AVE* high-speed trains running almost hourly are the fastest (45 mins). Special fares are payable and Inter-Rail passes are not valid. A discount is available for Eurail and EuroDomino passholders. Trains on the parallel slower route take 1½ hrs, and the service is less frequent.

#### Córdoba–Madrid

On this line, normal tickets are refunded if your train is 5 mins late! The journey takes 1 hr 45 mins and the service is very frequent. Inter-Rail tickets are not valid but a discount is available for Eurail and EuroDomino passholders. Conventional trains are cheaper, although not as frequent and take much longer, or you can use the direct service to Barcelona.

# GRANADA

**Station**: *Avda de Andaluces; tel: (958) 27 12 72*, a 20-min walk from the centre. Buses go to the *Gran Vía* and the centre from the main road up the hill from the station.

**Airport**: 17 km from Granada on *Ctra. Málaga s/n; tel: (958) 44 70 81*.

**Tourist Offices:** (Regional) *Plaza de Mariana Pineda 10; tel: (958) 22 66 88*, open Mon–Fri 0930–1900, Sat 1000–1400. (Municipal) *Corral del Carbón, C. Mariana Pineda* (by the cathedral); *tel: (958) 22 59 90*. There is also a small Tourist Office in the Alhambra complex itself, *tel: (958) 22 04 45*, open daily 0900–1700.

**Viajes TIVE**: *C. Martínez Campo 21; tel: (958) 25 02 11*.

## GETTING AROUND

Most of the sights are within walking distance. Bus no. 2 goes to the Alhambra and there is a a a small 'train' every 20 mins. However, the walk to the Alhambra, though steep, is pleasant.

## ACCOMMODATION

There is lots of budget accommodation, especially off *Plaza Nueva, Plaza de la Trinidad, Gran Vía de Colón* and on the streets north of *Plaza Mariana Pineda. Cuesta de Gomérez* leads directly up to the Alhambra and is lined with *hostals*.

**Hostal Gomérez**, *Cuesta de Gomérex 10; tel: (958) 22 41 37*, must be one of the cheapest places in town. *Gran Vía* is a busy street, so traffic noise may be a problem, but try **Hostal Gran Vía**, *Gran Vía 17; tel: (958) 27 92 12*. Around *Plaza Mariana Pineda*, **Hostal Roma**, *Navas 1; tel: (958) 22 62 77*, has beautifully furnished rooms and spotless bathrooms. Nearby, but with less character, is **Hostal Princesa**, *San Matías 2, 1st floor; tel: (958) 22 93 81*. Near the university, **Almöhada Hospedaje**, *tel: (958) 20 74 46*, is cheap, clean and homely.

Hotel chains include *Ml, PS*. The parador is located in the former **Convent of San Francisco** within the Alhambra complex. The remains of the Catholic Monarchs were temporarily buried here before being transferred to the Capilla Real (see p.310). Also here is the small but wonderful one-star **Hotel America**, *Real de la Alhambra 53; tel: (958) 22 74 71*.

**HI**: *Camino de Ronda 171; tel: (958) 27 26 38* (bus nos 10/11 from *Acera de Darro* in the centre). **Campsite: Sierra Nevada**, *Avda de Madrid 107; tel: (958) 15 00 62*, is the nearest (bus no. 3 from *Acera de Darro*). **Granada campsite** is 4 km away at *Cerro de la Cruz, Peligros; tel: (958) 34 05 48* (bus to Peligros). Also nearby are **María Eugenia**, *Ctra. Jerez–Cartagena km 286; tel: (958) 20 06 06*, and **Los Álamos**, *Ctra. Jerez–Cartagena km 290; tel: (958) 20 84 79*.

## EATING AND DRINKING

*Plaza Nueva* and the streets around it are a good area for restaurants: this is where the locals eat. Not always cheap, but good value.

**Restaurante Torres Bermejas**, *Plaza Nueva 6*, has reasonably priced set menus and outside seating and **Restaurante Léon**, *C. Pan 1–4*, can also be recommended, while **Sevilla**, *Oficios 12*, has the best paella in town. A cup of Arabian tea in one of the bars on *Calderia Nueva* will help capture the moorish spirit.

**309**

## SIGHTSEEING

Founded, according to legend, either by Noah's or Hercules's daughter, Granada was the last of the great Moorish cities to succumb to Ferdinand and Isabella's ferocious Christian Reconquest, in 1492. The main reason for visiting the city is to see the fortress-palace, the Alhambra, resplendent on its lush hilltop.

The **Alhambra** was a citadel in the 11th century, but most of the exterior dates from rebuilding in the 13th–14th centuries and is reasonably simple, belying the wealth of decoration inside. There are three sets of buildings: the **Alcazaba** (Fortress), the **Alcázar** (Palace) and the **Generalife** (Summer Palace and Gardens). The number of visitors to some areas of the Alhambra is now being limited with timed tickets, so it is advisable to arrive in the morning.

The **Alcazaba** was predominantly used as a military outpost and is the oldest part of the present site. Its **Torre de la Vela** (watchtower), from where the Catholic flag was hoisted in 1492, commands panoramic views of Granada and the Sierra Nevada.

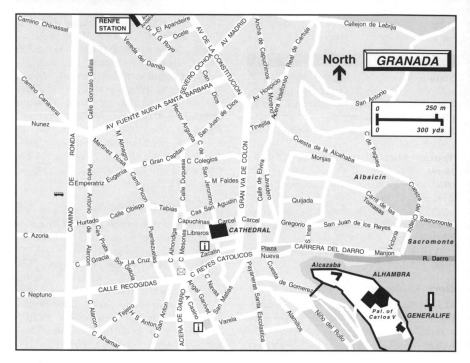

Map of Granada showing streets, the Cathedral, Albaicín, Sacromonte, Alhambra, Alcazaba, Pal. of Carlos V and Generalife. Labels include RENFE STATION, North, GRANADA, scale 250 m / 300 yds, R. Darro, and numerous street names.

The **Alcázar** was the main palace. Richly decorated and stunningly beautiful, with brilliant use of light and space, it was largely built in the 14th century. Of particular note are: the **Mexuar** (council chamber); the **Patio de los Arrayanes**; the **Sala de las Dos Hermanas**, with an incredible honeycomb cupola made up of thousands of small cells; and the **Patio de los Liones**, so-named for the famous fountain in its centre. The **Sala de Embajadores** is the largest and most sumptuous room. Its walls are covered with inscriptions from the Koran, ornamental motifs, and brilliantly glazed tiles that glint metallically in the the light. The main Christian edifice in the complex is the 16th-century **Palace of Charles V**, which houses the **Museum of Fine Arts** and the **National Museum of Hispano-Islamic Art**.

The **Generalife** is a comparatively simple building, noted primarily for its superb patios and gardens. The Moors, coming from desert areas, really appreciated water and the River Darro was diverted to supply the many pools and fountains.

In the city below the Alhambra, the **Cathedral** and the **Capilla Real** (Royal Chapel) are worth seeing. The latter contains the tombs of the Catholic Monarchs, Ferdinand and Isabella, and their daughter and her husband. Displayed in the Sacristy are some notable paintings from the private collection of Queen Isabella. Next door, the Cathedral was completed in the early 18th century, but some parts date back to the early 16th century.

The **Albaicín quarter**, on the hill opposite the Alhambra, retains some Moorish atmosphere and is a rewarding and relaxing place for a stroll out from the centre of Granada, which can be hot and hectic.

The gypsy cave-dwellings of **Sacromonte**, which are just outside the town, are also worth a visit.

## BOBADILLA

**Bobadilla–Antequera** is the main rail junction for this part of Spain. The station *(tel: 952 72 00 22)* is centrally located. Many journeys require a change here and, if time permits, the side track to picturesque Ronda and on to the British enclave of Gibraltar is very rewarding.

### ⤴ SIDE TRACKS FROM BOBADILLA

### MÁLAGA

**Airport**: 8 km from the city, *tel: (95) 204 84 84*. There is a Tourist Office in the main hall, *tel: (95) 224 00 00 ext 2098*. Trains to Málaga run every 30 mins, taking about 10 mins. There is also a bus every 20 mins (no. 19) which stops near the cathedral and takes 20–25 mins.

**Station**: RENFE, *C. Cuarteles; tel. (95) 236 02 02*, near the bus station, about 20 mins walk from the main part of town. (Bus no. 3 goes to *Alameda Principal* and *Paseo del Parque* near the centre.) Local trains for the coastal resorts leave from here as well (at a different level), and this railway is also served by another more centrally located station, **Centro Alameda**. Five trains, taking about an hour, link Bobadilla with Málaga.

**Tourist Offices**: *Pasaje de Chinitas 4; tel: (95) 221 34 45*, open Mon–Fri 0900–1900, Sat 1000–1900, Sun 1000–1400. There is a small municipal office in the bus station, *Paseo de los Tilos; tel: (95) 235 00 61 ext 260*.

### ACCOMMODATION AND FOOD

There is a good choice of hotels, including a small parador set in the gardens of the Gibralfaro castle above the town. Budget accommodation is functional but lacking in any obvious regional charm. Good areas to try for cheap lodgings are around the *Plaza de la Constitución* (north west of the cathedral) and immediately off either side of the *Alameda Principal* (although the south side is less salubrious). In high season, central Málaga is lively at night (all night); the only solution is to ask for a room away from the street, or buy earplugs. The **Pension Rosa**, *C. Martínez 10; tel (95) 221 27 16*, has reasonably sized rooms, some of which have balconies, and there are several other hostels on this street. **Hostal Andalucía**, *Alarcón Luján 12; tel: (95) 221 19 60*, has more charm than most. **Pension Juanita**, *Alarcón*

*Luján 8, 4th floor; tel: (95) 221 35 86*, has a number of small, basic rooms, all with wash-basins. South of *Alameda Principal* and slightly more expensive are **Hostal-Residencia El Ruedo**, *Trinidad Grund 3; tel: (95) 221 58 20*, and **Hostal Castilla y Hostal Guerrero**, *Córdoba 7, 2nd floor; tel: (95) 221 86 35*. **HI**: *Plaza Pío XII 6; tel: (95) 230 85 00* (bus no.18). **Campsite**: the nearest is 12 km away in Torremolinos, *Ctra. Cádiz–Barcelona km 228; tel: (95) 238 26 02*.

There are several good restaurants around the cathedral, especially along *C. Cañón*; **Cafetería El Jardín** is particularly nice. You do need to trawl through the usual tourist fare to find the really good places. *Paseo Marítimo* and the seafront in **Pedregaleje** are the best areas for bars and seafood restaurants.

### GETTING AROUND

Most sights are within walking distance, but bus route maps are posted at the stops. Bus no. 35 goes to the **Gibralfaro** from *Paseo del Parque*.

### SIGHTSEEING

The fourth largest city in Spain and a busy working port, Málaga is the communications centre for the holiday coasts on either side of it. The resolutely Spanish character of its streets, restaurants and hotels can be refreshing in the midst of the international and commercialised atmosphere of the rest of the Costa del Sol.

Málaga's historic past is most evident in the area near the port. The long, shady walks of *Paseo del Parque* are overlooked by the **Alcazaba**, a fort built by the Moors on Roman foundations. Moorish influence can be seen most strongly in its centre, where the **Museo Arqueológico**, with its collection of neolithic pottery, is located. The **Gibralfaro** castle, further up the hill, is of Phoenician origin but was later reconstructed by the Moors. Today it provides magnificent views of Málaga and the coast. Just off the *Paseo* is the **Cathedral**, set in a secluded square and built between the 16th–18th centuries. **Museo de Bellas Artes** houses a fine collection of mosaics, sculptures and paintings, including works by Murillo, Ribera and Picasso, Málaga's most famous son.

## OUT OF TOWN

A frequent train service runs west from Málaga (Centro-Alameda and RENFE stations) along the **Costa del Sol**, connecting it to the airport and the busy resorts of **Torremolinos**, **Benalmádena** and **Fuengirola**. Once a fishing village, Torremolinos is now overrun with tourists who daily migrate between the beach and the bars. Its hectic nightlife make it especially popular with the young. To the east, Fuengirola is another sun-seekers and beach-lovers paradise. It is more upmarket and slightly calmer than Torremolinos, but still a tourist hotspot.

Málaga is also at the centre of a bus network reaching out further west to many smaller resorts, and to **Marbella**, **Estepona** and as far as **Gibraltar**. Eastwards it is possible to reach **Nerja** and other assorted seaside towns all the way to Almeria. Nerja is a peaceful resort about 50 km from Málaga. Buses run approximately every hour, the journey taking 1½ hrs and costing Pta485. It is noted for its panoramic views of the coast, especially from the promenade known as the **Balcon de Europa**. Just east of the town is the **Cueva de Nerja**, a series of large caverns full of breathtaking rock formations. (**Tourist Office**: *Puerta del Mar 2; tel: (95) 252 15 31.*)

## RONDA

Four daily trains from Bobadilla take just over 1 hr to reach Ronda, and another 1¾ hrs to Algeciras. From Algeciras, an industrialised port of little interest, it is possible to visit the British colony of **Gibraltar**, or even take a ferry to **Morocco**.
**Station**: *Avda de Andalucía; tel: (95) 287 16 73,* a 15-min walk from the area of interest.
**Tourist Office**: *Plaza de España; tel: (95) 287 12 72.*

Ronda is a small town of pre-Roman origin set in the midst of the rugged **Serranía de Ronda** range. Its main claim to fame is the impressive 18th-century bridge, **Puente Nuevo**, spanning a deep gorge which divides the town in half. The view from the bridge is astonishing. It was in Ronda that Pedro Romero invented the modern style of bullfighting – on foot rather than from horseback – and the bullring is one of the oldest in Spain. Near the bullring is the **Alameda**, a public garden beside the ravine, with breathtaking views of the surrounding area. On the other side of the bridge is the old Moorish quarter, with the attractive **Casa del Rey Moro** (house of the Moorish King), an early 18th-century mansion. Ronda is at its most charming during one of the many fiestas which occur throughout the year.

## GIBRALTAR

**Tourist Office**: *Bomb House Lane 18–20; tel: 74805.*
**Thomas Cook Network Member**: **Imossi Travel**, *Imossi House, 1/5 Irish Town; tel: 73525.*

There is no direct rail connection to Gibraltar, but frequent buses run from **Algeciras**, taking about 40 mins to reach the Spanish frontier town of **La Línea**. From here you walk across the border into Gibraltar (passports needed). It is also possible to take a bus from Málaga or some of the other coastal resorts (up to 3 hrs).

The **Rock of Gibraltar** reaches a height of 430m, occupying a strategic position at the southern tip of Spain that has made it a military prize since ancient times. In 1704, Gibraltar was seized by the Royal Navy, and despite several attempts at re-conquest it has remained in British hands, becoming a Crown Colony in 1830.

The population is of mainly Genoese and Spanish descent, but the ambience tries to be as British as possible, from English-style pubs to the **Changing of the Guard** every Mon morning outside the Governor's residence *(Main St)*. To remind yourself you are nearly in North Africa, and to enjoy great views across the Straits towards the Atlas Mountains, take one of the **cable cars** that run all day from *Alameda Gardens* to the summit. They stop halfway up at the den of the famous **Barbary apes**, which live in packs on the upper reaches of the Rock.

The British military presence is low-key these days, but the **Upper Galleries**, 100m of tunnels excavated at the end of the 18th century to provide artillery positions, are evidence of Gibraltar's embattled past. 🔼

## SEVILLE

See p.478.

## CÓRDOBA

**Stations**: *Avda de América; tel: (957) 49 02 02*. This is around 1 km north of the main area of interest.

**Tourist Offices:** the **Provincial** office, *C. Torrijos 10 (Palacio de Congresos y Exposiciones); tel: (957) 47 12 35*, is open Mon–Fri 0930–1900, Sat 1000–1900 and Sun 1000–1400. The **Municipal** office, *Plaza de Judá Levi; tel: (957) 20 05 22*, is open Mon–Sat 0900–1400, 1730–1930 and Sun 0900–1400, but closing hours vary seasonally by an hour or so.

### GETTING AROUND

All the places of real interest are clustered together in a small area near the river and the best way to explore is on foot.

### ACCOMMODATION AND FOOD

Hotel chains with property in the town include *MI*, *Pr* and *So*. Cheap areas for accommodation are near the station, in and around the **Judería** (Jewish Quarter) and off *Plaza de las Tendillas*. *Plaza de la Corredera*, although cheap, is a less savoury area.

**Pension Bagdad**, *Fernández Ruano 11, tel. (957) 20 28 54*, has a beautiful central courtyard. **Hostal Luis de Gongora**, *Horno de la Trinidad 7; tel: (957) 29 53 99*, is lacking in traditional charm but is clean, quiet and comfortable. Other budget options include **Hostal Los Arcos**, *C. Romero Barros 14; tel: (957) 48 56 43*, and **Hostal Las Tendillas**, *Jesús María 1; tel: (957) 47 30 29* (although the latter can be quite noisy). There is a **Youth Hostel** at *Plaza de Juda Leví; tel: (957) 29 01 66*, and a **campsite**, **Campamento Municipal**, at *Avda del Brillante 50; tel: (957) 47 20 00* (about 2 km

north of the train station; bus nos 10/11 from *Avda de Cervantes).

There are a number of restaurants around the Judería. Cafetería-restaurante **El Rincon de Carmen**, *C. Romero 4*, has outside seating in a small and pleasant courtyard. Budget eateries can be found along *C. Doctor Fleming*.

### SIGHTSEEING

Once the capital of the Moorish caliphate and one of the greatest cities in Europe, Córdoba today is a pleasant town filled with a harmonious blend of Christian Jewish and Moorish architecture. The main attraction is undoubtedly the Mezquita, arguably the grandest and most beautiful mosque ever built in Spain.

### The Mezquita

The **Mezquita** (open winter 1000–1730, summer 1000–1900) was founded in the 8th century by Caliph Abd ar-Rahman I. It was gradually enlarged over the next 200 years and now occupies an area of around 24,000 square metres. At the foot of the bell tower (which is currently being restored), the **Puerta del Perdón** (covered with delicate carvings) leads through the massive outer walls to the **Patio de los Naranjos** (Courtyard of the Orange Trees), a classic courtyard with fountains for ritual cleansing. Inside the mosque, the fantastic **forest of 850 pillars**, joined by two-tiered Moorish arches in stripes of red brick and white stone, extends over a vast area. The overall effect is of order and unity, but the pillars are not identical: materials used in their construction included alabaster, marble, jasper, onyx, granite and wood; some are smooth, others have ribs or spirals. Most are Roman in origin and were shipped in from places as far apart as France and North Africa, then cut to size. The capitals are equally varied.

The Christian 'improvements' after the Moors departed included building a cathedral within the complex, which is incongruous but stunning, and blocking out the light that was an integral part of the design.

The **Third Mihrab** once housed the original copy of the Koran. Unlike the other two, it survived the Christian vandalism and its walls are covered in mosaics of varied colours and

**313**

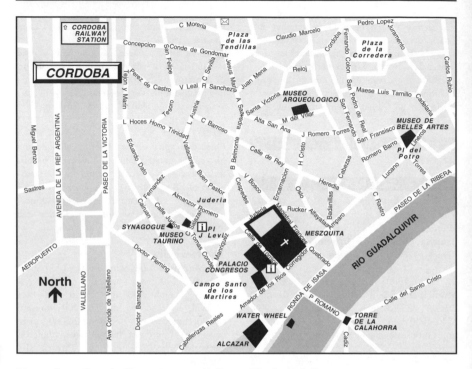

friezes of texts from the Koran. Its unusual off-centre position in the *qibla* (the south-facing holy wall) is the result of the final enlargement of the mosque in the 10th century, which because of the proximity of the river in the south and the palace in the west, had to be made on the east side.

### The Puente Romano and the Alcázar

The **Puente Romano** is a bridge of mainly Moorish construction, but the arches have Roman foundations. Downstream are the remains of an **Arab water-wheel** which originally transported water to the grounds of the Alcázar. The **Torre de la Calahorra** (on the other side of the river) is a high-tech museum with a model of the Mezquita as it was before the Christians got to work on it.

The **Alcázar de los Reyes Catolicos**, on the north bank, retains the original Moorish terraced gardens and pools. In August, these stay open until midnight, perfect for an evening stroll. Less gloriously, it was the headquarters of the Spanish Inquisition for over three centuries.

### The Jewish Quarter

The **Judería** is the old Jewish quarter, a maze of lanes surrounding a tiny **Synagogue** on *C. Judíos*. As you walk through this area, open doorways provide tantalising glimpses of chequered courtyards filled with flowers. To get a better look visit the town in May, when the **Festival de los Patios** (a type of best-kept patio competition) takes place.

### Museums

The grisly **Museo de Arte Taurino** on *Plaza de Maimónides* is devoted to bullfighting. The **Museo Arqueológico**, *Plaza de Jerónimo Páez,* is housed in a 16th-century mansion with visible Roman foundations.

The **Plaza del Potro** features an attractive stone fountain topped by a rearing colt *(potro)*, an inn, **La Posada del Potro**, where Cervantes is thought to have stayed (it gets a mention in *Don Quixote*) and the **Museo de Bellas Artes**. The museum is situated in the same building as the **Museo de Julio Romero de Torres**.

# MARSEILLE

Cosmopolitan gateway to the Mediterranean, and very different from the gritty image portrayed in films, Marseille will surprise you.

## TOURIST INFORMATION

**Main Tourist Office:** *4 La Canebière, tel: 04 91 13 89 00,* Mon–Sat 0900–2000, Sun 1000–1900 (July–Aug); Mon–Sat 0900–1900, Sun 1000–1700 (Sept–June). **Branch:** *Gare St-Charles, tel: 04 91 50 59 18.* Mon–Fri 1000–1300 and 1330–1800. Student and youth information: **Centre Information Jeunesse:** *96 r. La Canebière; tel: 04 91 24 33 50.*

## ARRIVING AND DEPARTING

**Marseille-Provence Airport:** *tel: 04 42 14 14 14* or *04 42 89 07 74.* At Marignane, 25 km north-west. Terminal 1 handles international flights; there's tourist information in the arrival area. An airport bus runs between Provence and St-Charles approximately every 20 mins 0615–2315, taking 25 mins (FFr.44). Buses run every 20 mins 0600–2150 in the other direction. Taxis to the centre cost about FFr.235 (FFr.290 Sun and at night).

**Stations: Gare St-Charles** is the main station, 15-mins walk north-east of **Vieux Port** (Old Port): head down the steps and straight along *blvd d'Athènes* and *blvd Dugommier* to *La Canebière,* then turn right, or métro: *Vieux Port – Hôtel de Ville.* Facilities include showers and *SOS Voyageurs; tel: 04 91 62 12 80;* Mon–Sat 0900–1200 and 1300–1900. **Gare Maritime** is west of the old port: follow *r. de la République.*

**Long-distance bus station:** *pl. V-Hugo; tel: 04 91 08 16 40,* next door to St-Charles (leave station and turn right).

For **ferry** information to **Corsica, Sardinia and North Africa**, contact **SNCM,** *61 blvd des Dames; tel: 04 91 56 30 10.*

## GETTING AROUND

The central (Vieux Port) area is walkable. Elsewhere, use the public transport, run by **RTM** (Réseau de Transport Marseillais). It consists of métro, buses and trams – *Plan du Réseau* (from the Tourist Office and RTM kiosks) covers the routes. The two métro lines intersect at St-Charles and Castellane. The system is easy to use, but trains stop running at 2100. Buses continue until midnight. Single tickets, available at métro stations and on board buses and trams, cover all three and are valid for 1 hr (FFr.8). Multi-ride tickets may be better value; get them from RTM kiosks or métro stations (1-day; FFr.25). Magnetic cards have recently been introduced, which are charged up using FFr.50 or FFr.100 and reduce a single trip to FFr.7.

## STAYING IN MARSEILLE

### Accommodation

There is accommodation to suit all pockets and the main Tourist Office has a free booking service: space is usually available. The most desirable (therefore most expensive) accommodation is around *Vieux Port.* For cheap, functional and tranquil hotels, try around *allées L-Gambetta* and *r. Montgrand,* but avoid streets south-west of the station (roughly the area bordered by *blvd d'Athènes, blvd Charles Nédélec, cours Belsunce* and *La Canebière):* elsewhere, the city does not live up to its shady reputation.

Hotel chains: *Ba, Ca, CF, Cn, F1, Hd, Ib, Mc, Nv* and *Sf.* Right by *Vieux Port,* **Mercure Beauvau Vieux Port,** *4 r. Beauvau; tel: 04 91 54 91 00,* is housed in a modernised coaching inn; attractive and worth the high cost. **Hôtel Lutétia,** *38 allées L-Gambetta; tel: 04 91 50 81 78,* is good value and convenient. **Hôtel Edmond-Rostand,** *31 r. Dragon; tel: 04 91 37 74 95,* combines charm with reasonable prices and is, therefore, very popular – so book ahead. The centrally located **Hôtel Pavillon,** *27 r. Pavillon; tel: 04 91 33 76 90,* is one of the better cheap places; and **Hôtel Montgrand,** *50 r. Montgrand; tel: 04 91 00 35 20,* also cheap, is within reach of the action.

**HI:** the more attractive and less expensive

**315**

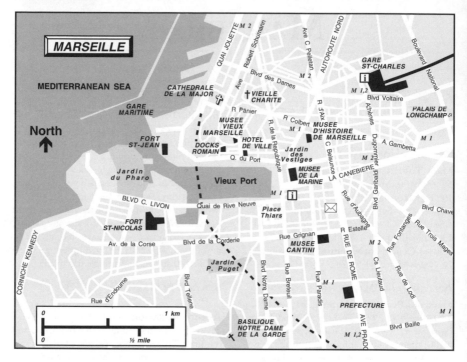

**North ↑**

hostel is **Bois-Luzy**, in the north overlooking the sea, *Château de Bois-Luzy, allée des Primevères; tel: 04 91 49 06 18*, bus no. 6: *J-Thierry/M-Richard*. You can also **camp** here in summer, if you have a tent. **Bonneveine:** *47 av. Joseph Vidal; tel: 04 91 73 21 81*, is 5 km south, in a residential district near the beach (métro: *Castellane*, then bus no. 44: *pl. Bonnefons*).

### Eating and Drinking

Marseille offers cuisine for all tastes and pockets, from street vendors to lavish belle époque restaurants. There is a staggering array of ethnic eating places and many street-corner vans that cook pizzas to order on charcoal ovens.

The famous fish-stew, *bouillabaisse*, really should be tried – the authentic version includes *rascasse*, an ugly red fish found only in the Mediterranean. The reputation of **Chez Fonfon**, *140 r. du Vallon des Auffes; tel: 04 91 52 14 38* (only open evenings), has spread around the world and (if your pockets are deep) you can sample the very best *bouillabaisse* – possibly in the company of a celebrity. More homely, and cheaper, is **Chez Madie**, *138 quai de Port; tel: 04 91 90 40 87*. Book at both places.

Oyster bars abound in the hub of Marseille's nightlife, around *pl. Thiars*, which is also a good area for traditionally ethnic and fast-food restaurants. The other culinary centre is *cours Julien/cours d'Estienne d'Orves*. More opulent restaurants are found along *corniche J-F-Kennedy*.

The bars and cafés of Vieux Port house the older crowd, the young tend to congregate around *pl. Thiars* and *cours Julien*.

### SIGHTSEEING

The Champs-Elysées aside, **La Canebière** (once 'Can o beer' to English sailors) is probably France's most famous street and leads to **Vieux Port** – a port for some 2600 years and guarded by two medieval fortresses, **St-Jean** to the north and **St-Nicholas** to the south. Remains of the original Greek harbour (**Massalia**) and 1st–3rd century BC walls can be seen in the pretty sunken garden, **Jardin des Vestiges**. Other ancient finds are on display in the neighbouring **Centre Bourse**, in **Le Musée d'Histoire de**

Marseille, while nearby **Musée de la Marine**, charts Marseille's relationship with the sea.

The oldest part of town is **Le Panier**, north of the port, and the residents consider themselves the real Marseillais. It was here, during the German Occupation, that the Resistance was based and extensive modern concrete serves as a reminder of the Nazis' vengeful destruction. Some handsome old buildings did survive, however, notably the 17th-century **Hôtel de Ville** and the 16th-century **Hôtel de Cabre** and **Maison Diamantée**, which now houses the fascinating exhibits that form the **Musée du Vieux Marseille**, *r. de la Prison*. An unexpected bonus of the German dynamite was the discovery of remains of the Roman settlement and artefacts, which can be seen *in situ* at **Musée des Docks Romains**, *pl. de Vivaux*.

**La Vieille Charité**, *2 r. de la Charité*, a 17th-century workhouse and lunatic asylum, with an attractive baroque church, now houses a science and arts centre, with regular exhibitions and two museums covering **African, Oceanic and American-Indian art** and **medieval archaeology**. South of *La Canebière*, **Le Musée Cantini**, *19 r. Grignan*, boasts an assemblage of 20th-century art in an impressively opulent 17th-century mansion – the collection is large and of variable quality.

Marseille's finest museum is the **Musée des Beaux Arts**, in **Palais Longchamp** some way east of the port (métro: *Longchamp/Cinq Avenues*), which offers an interesting mix of stoically classical works and lively impressionism.

For the best views of Marseille, visit the 19th-century neo-Byzantine **Basilique Notre Dame de la Garde**, a white church perched on a hill south of the centre (bus no. 60). From here a gold-leafed Virgin casts her benign influence over the city and the sea – sailors come here to give thanks for surviving shipwrecks. Paintings of their ordeals and models of the ships that went down are a feature of the interior.

The city's oldest church, **Abbaye St-Victor**, not far from Fort St-Nicholas, founded in the 5th century, is a fascinating mixture of church and fortress, commemorating many early martyrs – including St Victor.

**Château d'If**, the skeletal island in the bay (boats from *quai des Belges* take 15 mins) was the setting for Dumas' *The Count of Monte Cristo* and the prison is well preserved.

## ⇱ SIDE TRACK FROM MARSEILLE

### AIX-EN-PROVENCE

**Station:** 5-min walk south of the centre: take *av. V-Hugo* to *La Rotonde*. The Tourist Office is on the left.

**Tourist Office**, *2 pl. du Général de Gaulle*; *tel: 04 42 16 11 61*. Mon–Sat 0830–2200, Sun 1000–1300, 1400–2200 July–Aug; Mon–Sat 0830–2000·0830–1900 Oct–Mar, Sun 1000–1300, 1400–1800 (rest of year).

The capital of Provence, and 30–40 mins from Marseille by train, Aix is a town of culture, grace and charm. **Cours Mirabeau**, flanked by plane trees and dotted with ancient fountains, is *the* place to see and be seen. Or wander through **Vieil Aix**, the old town, of which *cours Mirabeau* is the southern boundary. This area is a maze of lively, semi-pedestrian streets and full of elegant 17th–18th-century buildings.

**Cathédrale St Sauveur** is an architectural mess, ranging from the 5th to the 17th century, but it has lovely Romanesque cloisters and contains some worthwhile medieval artefacts. The best of the museums is **Musée des Tapisseries** (Tapestry Museum), *tel: 04 42 23 09 91*, which has some excellent examples of the craft.

Aix was the birthplace of Cézanne and inspired some of his work, although he despised the town, which ridiculed him and his art. Later it came to its senses and his studio, **Atelier Cézanne**, *tel: 04 42 21 06 53*, has been lovingly preserved, exactly as it was at the time of his death and with many of his possessions. Using studs embedded in the pavement and a tourist guide you can follow a tour of the main stages of Cézanne's life. Some of his paintings are in the art collection at **Musée Granet**, *tel: 04 42 38 14 70*, which also covers local archaeological finds. Aix is renowned for its thermal springs and a **thermal centre** has recently opened; *tel: 04 42 23 81 81*. ⊿

317

# MARSEILLE–BARCELONA

Alternating between moments of clichéd yet undeniably postcard-esque beauty in the countryside of Provence and Languedoc-Roussillon and industrial nondescript towns, the view on this route becomes steadily less attractive as you near Barcelona. You'll find large numbers of backpackers – especially American high school graduates – who share the space with locals. If a reservation is advised, especially crossing the border, make sure you have one, or else conductors become irate in a variety of languages. With a huge metropolis at each end of a largely rural route, this journey allows you to experience many different types of scenery.

318

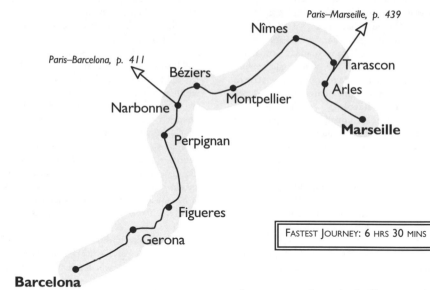

Paris–Marseille, p. 439

Nîmes

Paris–Barcelona, p. 411

Béziers

Tarascon

Arles

Narbonne

Montpellier

Marseille

Perpignan

Figueres

FASTEST JOURNEY: 6 HRS 30 MINS

Gerona

Barcelona

and some connecting trains in France require payment of a supplement.

## TRAINS

**ETT tables:** 81, 355, 656.

### FAST TRACK

Through services rely on connections into the two through Talgo trains linking Montpellier to Barcelona. The through journey will take around 6 hr 30 mins. The Talgo trains

## ON TRACK

**Marseille–Arles**
Express and local services throughout the day with journeys of around 45 mins, but frequency is erratic.

**Arles–Tarascon**
Just 10 mins apart, but services are irregular.

## Tarascon–Nîmes
Ten trains a day but there are long gaps between them, particularly mid-afternoon. Journey time: 20 mins.

## Nîmes–Montpellier–Béziers
A good service throughout the day link these cities. Nîmes to Montpellier takes 30 mins, Montpellier to Béziers 1 hr.

## Béziers–Narbonne
A good service links these two towns each day with a journey time of 15 mins.

## Narbonne–Perpignan
The 45-min journey is made by reasonably regular services throughout the day.

## Perpignan–Barcelona
Two Talgo trains (supplement payable) with restaurant cars link Perpignan and Barcelona, with journey times of around 3 hrs. Many places are accessible by changing at the frontier stations – Port Bou (travelling south) or Cerbère (if going north).

## ARLES

**Station:** a few blocks north of Les Arènes: walk down *av. Talabot* and along *r. Laclavière; tel: 04 36 35 35 35.*
**Bus Station:** opposite the rail station; *tel: 04 90 49 38 01.*
**Tourist Office:** *Esplanade Charles de Gaulle* (bus no. 4 from rail station); *tel: 04 90 18 41 20; fax: 04 90 18 41 29.* Open Mon–Sat 0900–1900, Sun 0900–1300 (Apr–Sept); Mon–Sat 0900–1800, Sun 1000–1200 (Jan–Mar and Oct–Dec). **Branch:** at the *station; tel: 04 90 49 36 90.* Open Mon–Sat 0900–1300, 1400–1800 (Apr–Sept); Mon–Sat 0900–1300, 1330–1700 (Jan–Mar, Oct–Dec). Ask about the different versions of the **Forfait** passes, which cover a variety of attractions.

### ACCOMMODATION

There's a wide choice of hotels at the lower end of the price scale, especially around *pl. du Forum* and *pl. Voltaire* (also good centres for cafés and restaurants). Chains include *Ba, BW, Ch* and *Ib.* Two elegant upmarket hotels are **Jules César**, *5 blvd des Lices; tel: 04 90 93 43 20,* in a 17th-century Carmelite convent, and **Arlatan**, *26 r. du Sauvage; tel: 04 90 93 56 66,* on the site of a 4th-century basilica (both expensive). **Hôtel Gauguin**, *5 pl. Voltaire; tel: 04 90 96 14 35,* is one of the better moderate places. **HI** (budget), *20 av. Foch; tel 04 90 96 18 25,* is 1.8 km southeast of town (bus no.8: *Fournier).*

### SIGHTSEEING

Ancient Rome meets Van Gogh and black bulls in Arles, the spiritual heart of Provence and a great place to relax and absorb history. Most major sights and museums are tucked into a tiny old town and are easily accessible on foot. In late June–early July, the **Fête de la Tradition** fills the streets with music, dance and theatre.

This is one of the best-preserved Roman towns in the world. **Les Arènes**, is a mini Colosseum, still used for bullfights (Easter–Sept), and summer theatrical productions are still staged at the **Théâtre Antique**.

After three centuries of construction, **Cathédrale St-Trophime** was almost completed by the 12th century, at which time it acquired its main door: a superb example of Provençal stone-carving that depicts the *Last Judgement.* Contents include Aubusson tapestries and the **Musée Nécropole** (Cemetery Museum), in which there's a rich selection of Roman artefacts. In the town centre, **Museon Arlaten**, *29 r. de la République,* offers wide-ranging exhibits demonstrating aspects of Provençal history and traditions, while a highlight of the modern works in **Musée Réattu**, *r. du Grand Prieuré,* is a collection of Picasso sketches. **Alyscamps** (Elysian Fields) is a beautiful cemetery which inspired paintings by Van Gogh and Gaugin. Unfortunately none of Van Gogh's works are still in the town where he cut off his ear, but the Tourist Office runs **Van Gogh tours**, which take you to some of the places that inspired his paintings.

### OUT OF TOWN

Hourly buses run between Arles and **Les-Stes-Maries-de-la-Mer**, on the coast. This is the site of an annual **gypsy pilgrimage** in late May and the main base for visiting the Camargue. The **Camargue** is now a nature reserve, an

319

area of marshland and rice fields where semi-wild white horses and black bulls roam free and the lagoons are often pink with flamingoes in summer. Countless other waterfowl, beavers and turtles also make it their home and there's a wide variety of flora. If you want to explore the area on horseback (the best way to get around), the Stes-Marie **Tourist Office** *(av. Van-Gogh; tel: 04 90 97 82 55,* open daily 0900–1300 and 1500–1900 in summer, daily 0930–1200 and 1430–1800 in winter) can supply a list of some thirty farms who have the animals for hire – by the hour, day or week. If you don't ride, the best alternative is to cycle. You can hire bikes in Arles: from the train station, *tel: 04 90 96 43 94,* **Dall'Oppio,** *10 r. Portagnel; tel: 04 90 96 46 83,* or from the Tourist Office in Arles. Alternatively, take the bus and hire a bike in Stes-Maries.

## TARASCON

**Station:** for the centre, head right; for the river and château, head left; *tel: 04 90 91 59 06.*
**Tourist Office:** *59 r. des Halles; tel: 04 90 91 03 52; fax: 04 90 91 22 96.* Open Mon–Sat 0900–1230 and 1400–1800.

Due to its location on the Rhône, the town suffered heavy bombing during World War II and is a rather drab place, but the **Château du Roi René** (a 15th-century castle on the river), is worth a visit. In the **House of Tartarin,** *55bis blvd Itam,* named after Alphonse Daudet's fictional character, you will find a model of the legendary Tarasque dragon, which lives in the Rhône and was banished to its depths by St Martha's crucifix, an event celebrated in a festival every June.

## NÎMES

**Station:** 10-mins walk south-east of the centre: head down *av. Feuchères* to *esplanade C de-Gaulle,* then along *blvd Victor Hugo; tel: 04 36 35 35 35.*
**Bus Station:** *r. Ste. Félicité* (behind the rail station); *tel: 04 66 29 52 00.*
**Tourist Office:** *6 r. Auguste; tel: 04 66 67 29 11; fax: 04 66 21 81 04.* Open Mon–Thur 0800–2000, Fri 0800–2100, Sat 0900–1900, Sun 1000–1700 (July–Aug); Mon–Fri 0800–1900, Sat 0900–1200 and 1400–1700, Sun 1000–1200

(Sept–June). **Branch:** in the *station; tel: 04 66 84 18 13,* open daily 0930-1230 and 1400–1830. There are free maps and a 24-hr information line for current events; *tel: 04 66 36 27 27.*

### ACCOMMODATION

Nîmes offers a very wide range of accommodation and space is seldom a problem, except during the major *ferias* (bullfights). For budget hotels, try *blvd des Arènes,* or around *blvd Amiral Courbet.* Hotel chains include *Ba, BW, Ch, Cn, Ct, Ib, IH, Mc, Nv* and *RS.* A 4-star option is the expensive **Impérator Concorde,** *quai de la Fontaine; tel: 04 66 21 90 30,* which has a Provençal flavour. **Hôtel La Couronne,** *4 sq. de la Couronne; tel: 04 66 67 51 73,* is cheap and close to the station. **HI,** *chemin de la cigale; tel: 04 66 23 25 04,* is 3 km from the the station (bus no. 2: *Stade).* **Campsite: Domaine de la Bastide,** *rte de Générac; tel: 04 66 38 09 21,* 5 km to the south; cheap (bus no. 4: *Générac).*

### SIGHTSEEING

A three-day pass is reasonable and allows access to all sights. The major attractions are all in the old part of town. As well as some fine medieval streets in the area around the **cathedral,** *pl. aux Herbes,* the town is full of impressive Roman sites. **Les Arènes** is a huge amphitheatre still used for *ferias,* when would-be Hemingways flock to Nîmes. The only meetings are in Feb, May and Sept. **Maison Carrée,** an outstandingly well-preserved 1st-century AD temple, now houses changing exhibitions. Next door is the futuristic **Carré d'Art,** designed by Norman Foster and containing wide-ranging displays of contemporary art forms.

To the west, the 18th-century **Jardin de la Fontaine** (Garden of the Fountain), *off av. J-Jaurès,* features a romantic **Temple of Diana.** Further north, in a park on the slopes of Mont Cavalier, rises **Tour Magne,** a mysterious 30-m tower that is one of France's oldest Roman monument and provides excellent views. The several museums are not particularly exciting.

### OUT OF TOWN

The **Pont du Gard** is a spectacular Roman aqueduct 48m above the Gard river, accessible by bus eight times a day. The site attracts two million visitors a year. Water was brought to the aqueduct from **Uzès**, a delightful medieval village centred on a formidable castle, which today has waxworks and holographic ghosts.

## MONTPELLIER

**Station:** 5-mins walk south-east of the Tourist Office: head north, along *r. Maguelone*.
**Tourist Office:** *Place de la Comédie; tel: 04 67 60 60 60; fax: 04 67 60 60 61*. Open Mon–Fri 0900–1300, 1400–1800, Sat 1000–1300, 1400–1800, Sun 1000–1300, 1400–1700 (mid Sept–mid June); Mon–Fri 0900–1300, 1400–1800, Sat 1000–1300, 1400–1800, Sun 1000–1300, 1500–1800 (mid June–mid Sept). **Branch:** at the station; *tel: 67 92 90 03*. Open Mon–Thur 0900–1300, 1400–1800, Fri 0900–1300, 1400–1700 (June–Aug).

High tech, young and trendy, Montpellier has the required selection of old houses, but the main attraction is that it's fun to visit. As a university town, with 55,000 poverty-stricken students to feed, Montpellier abounds with inexpensive, good-quality eating places, bars and hotels. The **Vieille Ville** (old town) houses many 17th- and 18th-century mansions (free guides from Tourist Office) and cobbled streets. To the west, the **Arc de Triomphe** leads to **Jardin des Plantes** (botanical gardens). **Musée Fabre**, *3961 Bonne Nouvelle,* has a fine collection of 16th–19th-century European art.

## BÉZIERS

**Station:** for the centre of town, head north along *av. Gambetta,* and *av. Alphonse Mas*.
**Tourist Office:** *Palais des Congrès 29, av Saint-Saëns; tel: 04 67 76 47 00; fax: 04 67 76 50 80*. Open daily 0900–1900 (July–Aug); Mon–Fri 0900–1200 and 1400–1830 (Mon 1400–1800 only), Sat 0900–1200, 1500–1800 (Sept–June); Sun and holidays 1000–1200 (year round). Details of local wine festivals are available here.

This is a lively town with an attractive old centre and vineyards clinging to its outskirts. The Gothic **Cathédrale de St-Nazaire**, founded in the early 13th century, replaced an earlier one that was burned down (with 20,000 people locked inside) during the Albigensian Crusade of 1209. A visit to the **Musée du Vieux Biterrois et du Vin** is recommended;

it has entertainingly diverse exhibits. Romantics should head for **Plateau des Poètes**, a lovely little park north of the station.

### OUT OF TOWN

West of town, the **Canal du Midi** leads from the Mediterranean to the Atlantic and there are day cruises through the locks and vineyards, while regular buses offer a way to reach the long, sandy beaches not far from town.

## NARBONNE

**Station:** 10-mins walk north-east of the centre: turn right along *blvd F-Mistral* to the river, and left along *r. J-Jaurès; tel: 04 67 62 50 50*.
**Tourist Office:** *pl. Salengro; tel: 04 68 49 84 86; fax: 04 68 65 59 12*. Open daily 1000–1200 and 1400–1730.

A fine Midi town, lapped by vineyards and with good beaches nearby, Narbonne is dominated by the magnificent Gothic **Cathédrale St-Juste-et-St-Sauveur**, designed to be one of the biggest churches in Christendom, but never finished because the authorities would not allow the town walls to be pulled down to build the nave. It has some lovely stained glass and the views make it worth climbing the towers. Next door is the opulent **Palais des Archevêques** (Archbishops' Palace), housing an art and archaeology museum, while **l'Horreum**, *16 r. Rouget-de-l'Isle,* is a well-preserved Roman granary, now entirely subterranean.

## PERPIGNAN

**Station:** 600 m from the centre: walk along *av. Gén-de-Gaulle* to *pl. Catatogne,* or take bus nos 2/3/12.
**Bus Station:** *av. du Gén-Leclerc; tel: 04 68 35 29 02* (north of train station, off *pl. de la Résistance*). There are regular services to the beaches (bus no. 1 or Car Inter 66).
**Tourist Offices: Municipal**, *pl. Armand-Lanoux; tel: 04 68 66 30 30; fax: 04 68 66 30 26* (30-mins walk from the station). Open Mon–Sat 0900–1900, Sun 0900–1300, 1500–1900 (June–Sept); Mon–Sat 0830–1200, 1400–1830 (Oct–May). **Regional (Pyrénées-Roussillon)**, *7 quai de Lattre de Tassigny; tel: 04 68 34 29 94*, open daily 1000–1200, 1400–1730.

Almost Spanish, the town is wealthy,

**321**

ancient – and overrun in summer. In the old town, the 15th-century fortified gatehouse, **Le Castillet**, *quai Sadi-Carnot*, houses **Casa Pairal** (a Rousillon museum). The 14th-century *pl. de Loge* is still lively, while the **Cathédrale St-Jean**, *pl. Gambetta*, is Gothically grand and the impressive **Citadelle**, to the south, protects the imposing 13th-century **Palais des Rois de Majorque** (Palace of the Kings of Majorca).

### OUT OF TOWN

**Collioure**, easily reachable by train, is a picturesque ex-fishing village overlooked by a château. Discovered by Matisse and Picasso, it still attracts artists.

## FIGUERES

**Station:** *Plaza de la Estación; tel: (972) 50 46 61.* Central.
**Tourist Offices:** *Plaza del Sol s/n; tel: (972) 50 31 55; fax: (972) 67 31 66.* There is also a branch at the bus station across the Plaza from the train station.

The **Salvador Dalì Museum**, signposted from near the station, is the only real attraction. Whether you consider Dalì a genius or a madman (or both), the surreal museum is likely to confirm your views of the man. It's a bizarre place, parts of which Dalì designed himself (including his own grave). Do not expect to see any of Dalì's well-known works.

## GERONA (GIRONA)

**Station:** *tel: (972) 20 70 93.* In the new town; 10-min walk from the river and Pont de Pedra.
**Bus Station:** *tel: (972) 21 23 19* (there is a linking door from the train station).
**Tourist Offices:** *Rambla de la Llibertat 1; tel: (972) 22 65 75; fax: (972) 22 66 12,* open Mon–Fri 0800–2000, Sat 0800–1400, 1600–2000, Sun 0900–1400. There's also a Tourist Office at the train station in summer; *tel: (972) 21 62 96,* open Mon–Fri 0900–1400.

### ACCOMMODATION

There is plenty of cheap accommodation, with all the best places in the old town – try around the cathedral and *C. Santa Clara.* Alternatively, head for the streets around *Plaça de la Constitutió.* From Oct–June it may be harder to

find rooms because lodgings are full of students. **HI:** *Cerverí de Girona, Carrer dels Ciutadans 9; tel: (972) 21 80 03; fax: (972) 21 20 23.*

### SIGHTSEEING

A 30-day pass is available (Pta800) which allows access to six museums. The medieval part of the town is on the east side of the River Onyar, and is connected by the Pont de Pedra to a prosperous new city in the west. From the bridge you can see the **Cases de l'Onyar** (picturesque houses which overhang the river). The **Gothic Cathedral**, in the heart of the old town, is approached by a 90-step 17th-century stairway. The interior has a single-naved vault with a 22m span (the largest in the world). The small altarpiece is of 14th-century silver and enamel, and in the museum is the famous 15th-century *Tapis de la Creació* (Tapestry of the Creation). The 11th-century **Banys Arabs** (Arab Baths) were rebuilt; the present ones are 13th-century Romanesque with Moorish touches. **Museu d'Art**, housed in a splendid Renaissance bishop's palace, has a wealth of beautifully displayed paintings and carvings from the Romanesque period to the 20th century. In the narrow streets of the *El Call* (old Jewish quarter) is the **Bonastruc ça Porta Centre** *(Centre Isaac el Cec),* soon to become a **Museum of Jewish Culture**, but worth a visit for its magnificent building and temporary exhibitions. The 11th–12th-century Benedictine Monastery **Sant Pere de Galligants** now houses the archaeological museum. The **Palau des Agullana** is a fine town palace from the 14th–17th centuries which, together with **Sanxt Marti Sacosta Church**, forms an attractive baroque area.

> ### ↴ SIDE TRACKS
> ### FROM GERONA
> Gerona is the transportation hub for the **Costa Brava**, with scores of buses daily to the coastal resorts. You can also get there by bus from Figueres. This once-beautiful, rugged coast is now little more than a succession of tourist developments, especially in the south, but in many places the roads are forced to zigzag inland to get from one resort to the next, leaving the more inaccessible stretches of coastline unspoiled. ↴

# MARSEILLE–BIARRITZ

Taking in a vast, variable swathe of France, this route has something for everyone: the plains dominated by Carcassonne; the bustle of Toulouse; surreal ceremony in Lourdes; the sight of the snow-capped Pyrenees from majestic Pau, and on to Biarritz with its surfers and somewhat faded elegance.

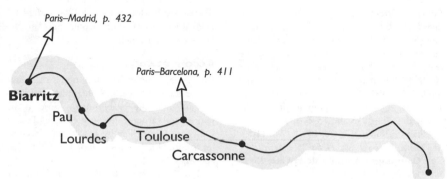

*Paris–Madrid, p. 432*

*Paris–Barcelona, p. 411*

**Biarritz**
Pau
Lourdes
Toulouse
Carcassonne

**Marseille**

---

## TRAINS

**ETT tables:** 355, 321, 325.

> FASTEST JOURNEY: 11 HRS

### FAST TRACK

A through service by day takes 8½–9½ hrs, the overnight train with couchettes and seats 9–11 hrs. Day train has a buffet between Marseille and Toulouse only.

### ON TRACK

**Marseille–Carcassonne**
Five through trains during the day, all with buffet cars, take 3–3¾ hrs. A few trains also go through during the night.

**Carcassonne–Toulouse**
A reasonable service during the day, taking approximately 45 mins at up to 3 hr intervals.

**Toulouse–Lourdes**
Trains run at irregular intervals, every 2–3 hrs. Most have no catering and journey takes just under 2 hrs.

**Lourdes–Pau**
A reasonable service all day, with approximately 1 hr interval between trains. Journey time: 30 mins.

**Pau–Biarritz**
Four or five services each day, taking 1½ hrs.

---

## CARCASSONNE

**Station:** in the Ville Basse, on the north bank of the Canal du Midi. It's a long walk to La Cité – about 30 mins and the last part uphill; cross the bridge and head straight on *r. G. Clemenceau*. Turn left onto *r. de la Liberté* and then right along *blvd Jean Jaurés*. At *Sq. Gambetta*, take *r. du Port-Vieux* and cross the old bridge, from where La Cité is signposted. Bus no. 4 goes from the station to *Sq. Gambetta*. Bus no. 2 from *Sq. Gambetta* to just outside the walls of La Cité.

**Tourist Offices:** In the Ville Basse: *15 blvd Camille-Pelletan; tel: 04 68 10 24 30*. Open Mon–Sat 0900–1900 (June–mid Sept); Mon–Sat 0900–1200 and 1400–1800 (rest of the year). In La Cité: *Tours Narbonnaises; tel: 04 68 10 24 36*. Open daily 0900–1900 (June–mid Sept); daily 0900–1200 and 1400–1900 (rest of the year). Off-season opening times may change to 0900–1215 and 1345–1830.

Chains include *BW, Ca, F1, Ib, Mc*. **HI:** *r. du Vicomte Trencavel; tel: 04 68 25 23 16*, in La Cité. **Camping: Camping de la Cité**, *Rte de Saint Hilaire; tel: 04 68 25 11 77*, close to La Cité.

### SIGHTSEEING

There are two distinct towns: the seemingly modern (in fact dating back to the 13th century), grid-like **Ville Basse** (Lower Town), on one side of the River Aude, and **La Cité** – perched on a crag on the other. The fortified Cité can be traced back to the 1st century, when the Romans conquered the region; however, most of it now dates from the 19th century, when the town was extensively restored and 'improved' by the architect Viollet-le-Duc. There are two gates: **Porte d'Aude** and **Porte Narbonnaise** (the main 13th-century entrance). Allow plenty of time to walk the streets and ramparts of the town. If you are walking up from Ville Basse, look for the footpath beside **St-Gimer**, which leads to the 12th-century **Château Comtal** (Counts' Castle) that dominates the centre – if you want to see inside, you must join a tour. Beside the château is the beautiful **Basilique Saint Nazaire**, with an 11th-century nave and 14th–16th-century stained glass.

## TOULOUSE

See Paris–Barcelona, p.414.

## LOURDES

**Station:** 10-mins walk north-east of the centre. Bus no. 1 goes to the centre and the Grotto. To reach the Tourist Office, turn right out of the station down *av. de la Gare*, and then left at the end along *Chaussée Maransin* to *pl. Peyramale*.

**Tourist Office:** *pl. Peyramale; tel: 05 62 42 77 40*. Opens daily 0900–1900, Sun 1000–1800 (Easter–Sept); Mon–Sat 0900–1200 and 1400–1800 (Oct–Easter). From Easter–end Apr, the office closes for lunch.

### ACCOMMODATION

Paris aside, Lourdes has more hotels than anywhere else in France, including plenty of budget and moderate establishments close to the station and around the castle. The Tourist Office has an excellent list of all types of accommodation. Hotel chains include *Cn, Ex, Ib, Mc*, and *Mp*.

Hostel accommodation (non-HI) can be found at **Accueil International**, *r. de l'Arrouza; tel: 05 62 94 34 54*. There are 13 **campsites**, including two along the *rte de la Forêt*: **Camping du Loup**, *tel: 05 62 94 23 60*, and **Camping de la Fôret**, *tel: 05 62 94 04 38*. **Camping de la Poste**, *r. de Langelle, tel: 05 62 94 40 35*, is 8-mins walk from the station on the street directly opposite the Tourist Office.

### SIGHTSEEING

In a mountainous riverside setting, Lourdes is surrounded by natural beauty, but it is overwhelmed by its status as a pilgrimage centre. The place swarms with visitors (over six million a year), especially in summer, and every other building is a shop overflowing with appallingly kitsch religious souvenirs.

It all began when (in 1858) the 14-year-old Bernadette Soubirous claimed to have seen the Virgin Mary in a local grotto. There were seventeen further appearances and a spring appeared by the grotto. Once word spread that its waters had effected miraculous cures, there was no looking back. The spring still flows and its water supplies local baths and drinking fountains. The 19 **baths** (rebuilt in 1955) are open to sick and healthy alike and hundreds of people plunge into them daily. To discover more about Bernadette and her life, you can visit various key locations in the centre of town, including **Boly Mill**, where she was born, and the *cachot,* where she lived during the time of the apparitions.

The **grotto area** is huge, but you can get a free map at the **Forum information centre**, *St Joseph's Gate,* off *pl. Mgr Laurence.* The buildings include the **Basilique du Rosaire et l'Immaculée Conception** (Basilica of the Rosary and the Immaculate Conception), the **crypt** (which was the first chapel) and the **upper basilica**.

The underground **Basilique St-Pius-X** holds up to 30,000 pilgrims and nightly torchlight processions take place on the esplanade.

The **Visa Lourdes** pass (FFr 139) covers seven minor attractions – good value if you want to visit all of them. The main non-religious draws are: **Château-Fort**, a medieval castle containing the very worthwhile **Musée Pyrénéen**, covering all aspects of local life; a guided tour on a little train from *av. Mgr Sempé;* and the **funicular** (from *av. F. Lagardère),* which includes a visit to some caverns.

## OUT OF TOWN

There are many regular bus excursions in and around the surrounding area, including **Parc National des Pyrénées**, which follows the Franco-Spanish border for 100 km, providing magnificent views; the **Basque country**; and the **Grottes de Betharram**, vast underground caverns full of limestone formations.

## PAU

**Station:** on the southern edge of town. It's 15-mins tough uphill walk to the centre, but the funicular railway opposite the station will take you to *pl. Royale* for free. It operates Mon–Sat 0645–1230, 1255–1930 and 1955–2140; Sun 1330–1930 and 1955–2100.
**Tourist Office:** *pl. Royale; tel: 05 59 27 27 08.* Open Mon–Sat 0900–1800, Sun 1000–1700 (July–Aug); Mon–Sat 0900–1230 and 1330–1800 (Sept–June).

Pau's attractions are easily walkable and a free map is available from the Tourist Office. This elegant town is perched on a cliff, providing panoramic views of the snow-capped Pyrénées. Its impressive château can be reached via *r. Henri IV* from the *pl. Royale*. The château was the birthplace of the charismatic French monarch, Henri IV, and contains tapestries, royal furniture and some of his personal possessions. *Son et Lumière* productions about his court are staged in July. Guided tours of the château are in French, but there are English notes. In the château is **Musée Béarnais** (the provincial museum), with eclectic exhibits relating to life in the area.

Other museums worth a visit are: **Musée Bernadotte**, *5 r. Tran,* the birthplace of one of Napoleon's marshals, whose descendants are today's Swedish royal family; and the **Musée des Beaux Arts**, *r. Matthieu Lalanne,* which has a rich collection of paintings from all round Europe.

There were many British settlers in the 19th century, after the Napleonic wars, and their heritage is reflected in the landscaped **Parc Beaumont**, where the old winter palace now houses the **Casino Municipal**.

## BIARRITZ

**Station: Gare de Biarritz-La Négresse**, 3 km from the centre, along a winding road: about 40-mins walk. Left luggage facilities open daily 0900–1200 and 1415–1800. Take bus no. 2 for a 15-mins ride to the town hall – bus no. 9 also goes there, but via a longer route.
**Main Tourist Office:** *1 sq. d'Ixelles; tel: 05 59 22 37 00.* Open daily 0800–2000 (July–Aug); 0900–1845 (Sept–June). You can get free maps and information on the whole Basque region. **Branches:** at the station open 0700–1330 and 1700–2100 (July–Aug); at *pl. Clémenceau* open daily 1000–1300 and 1600–2100 (July–Aug).

The smart set have been coming to Biarritz since the splendid beaches and mild climate were 'discovered' in the mid 19th century and, although rather less grand than it was, it is still essentially a fairly upmarket coastal resort with a string of good beaches, excellent surf and a casino.

# MARSEILLE–NICE

Leaving the universal urban atmosphere of Marseille, this train ride takes you further away from the grim and grimy realities of existence into the eternally sparkling summer of the Cote d'Azur. On the way, you pass through Aubagne, made famous by Marcel Pagnol in the tragic stories of *Jean de Florette* and *Manon des Sources*. The route swerves inland between Toulon and Frejus, affording views of Provençal farmland, before continuing along the coast, often cutting into the cliffs (sit on the right-hand side for the best views going into Nice). Approaching Nice, the glittering gold beaches and blistering sun provide the ideal setting for many wearers of Chanel – from earrings to flip-flops.

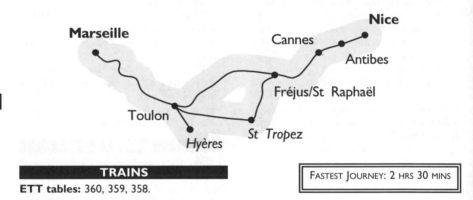

## TRAINS

**ETT tables:** 360, 359, 358.

FASTEST JOURNEY: 2 HRS 30 MINS

### FAST TRACK

Many express trains make this journey, however, there are gaps in the service, especially mid-morning. Journey time: 2½ hrs; most trains have buffets.

### ON TRACK

**Marseille–Toulon**

A frequent local service augments the express trains. Journeys take 40 to 60 mins.

**Toulon–St-Raphaël–Cannes**

Through expresses link Toulon and Cannes, all call at St-Raphaël. Toulon to St-Raphaël takes 50–60 mins, St-Raphaël to Cannes 30 mins.

**Cannes–Antibes–Nice**

The through express trains are supplemented by a good local service. Cannes to Antibes takes 15 mins, Antibes to Nice 15–20 mins.

## TOULON

**Station:** north of the centre: cross *pl. Albert 1er*, and head south down *av. Vauban*. The old town and seafront are south of *av. Mar. Leclerc*.
**Bus station: Sodetrav**, next to the rail station; *tel: 04 94 18 93 43.*
**Tourist Offices:** *Pl. Raimu; tel: 04 94 18 53 00; fax: 04 94 18 53 09.* Open Mon–Sat 0900–1900, Sun 0900–1200 (July–Aug); Mon–Sat 0900–1800, Sun 1000–1200 (Sept–June).

## ACCOMMODATION

Toulon is a cheap place to stay, but quality is not high. Hotel chains include *Ba, Ct, Hd, Ib* and *Nv*. A good bet for cheapness is **Hôtel des Allées**, *18 allées Amiral-Courbet; tel: 04 94 91 10 02*, and there's a (non-HI) hostel: **Foyer de la Jeunesse**, *12 pl. d'Armes; tel: 04 94 22 62 00*, 10 mins walk from the station, to the west of the old town.

## SIGHTSEEING

Toulon's naval past survives in the great docks, the fading extravagant architecture and the great ethnic diversity of its inhabitants. The huge ship-building yards of La Seyne are under constant threat of closure, but Toulon itself has seen something of a regeneration in recent years – although there is not too much to see. The **Musée Naval**, *pl. Monsenergue,* traces Toulon's marine development. Other museums cover the **town's history** *(69 cours Lafayette)* and **art and natural history** *(113 blvd Mar. Leclerc)*.

Toulon is best viewed from **Mont Faron**, 500 m above the Mediterranean, where there is a **zoo**, and from the **Musée Mémorial du Débarquement**, which recalls the Allied invasion of Provence in 1944 (bus no. 40 from the station to a *téléphérique* that winches you up to the summit).

## ➦ SIDE TRACKS FROM TOULON

### HYÈRES

**Station: Gare SNCF**. An infrequent rail service runs from Toulon, taking 20 mins.
**Tourist Office:** *rotonde Jean Salusse, av. de Belgique; tel: 04 94 65 18 55.*

This charming old resort first attracted winter visitors in the late 19th century; Tolstoy, Queen Victoria and Robert Louis Stevenson enjoyed its mild climate. Today, the main attraction is the beach, 5 km from the Old Town, 4 km from the station.

From Hyères you can catch a ferry to offshore islands – **Île de Porquerolles**, **Île de Port-Cros** and **Île du Levant** – which offer some of the most beautiful beaches in the Mediterranean, the remains of

16th-century forts and unspoiled nature. Take a bus from the town to the port at **La Tour Fondue** for the ferry to Île de Porquerolles (ferry information: *tel: 04 94 58 21 81)*, **Port d'Hyères** for Port-Cros and Île du Levant, *tel: 04 94 57 44 07* (ferries depart hourly in summer).

### ST-TROPEZ

**Bus Station:** close to the port; *tel: 04 94 97 88 51.*
**Tourist Office:** *Place Blanqui; tel: 04 94 97 45 21; fax: 04 94 97 82 66.*

Accessible by Sodetrav bus (eight a day in summer, taking 2 hrs) from Toulon (or from St-Raphaël), 'St-Trop' ('Saint Too Much') can be a disappointment. The best way to get around the area (more rewarding than the town) is to cycle and you can hire bikes locally – or mopeds if you don't fancy the exercise. The pretty inland villages of **Ramatuelle** and **Gassin** are worth visiting and there are 20 km of reachable beaches.

Strolling is what Tropeziens do best. But find time for **Musée de l'Annonciade** (Museum of the Annunciation), *quai H. Bouchard,* the region's finest art museum. Housed in a converted chapel on the west side of the port, it boasts a dazzling array of Impressionists – from Cézanne and Matisse to Dufy.

A walk up to the **Citadelle** offers good views – and a confrontation with the town's haughty peacocks. There are two small beaches in town. From the base of the Citadelle and the seaside cemetery, continue along the path to **Plage des Graniers**, the closest real beach. The main ones are some way from town: **Tahiti-Plage** is the jet-set hang-out and is at one end of **Pampelonne**, a 5-km stretch of sand that draws most of the crowds and is credited with starting the fashion for topless bathing. ▲

### FRÉJUS AND ST-RAPHAËL

**Station: Gare de St-Raphaël** is central: for the sea, exit the station and head right for 200 m; *tel: 04 36 35 35 35.*
**St-Raphaël bus station:** behind the rail station; *tel: 04 94 95 24 82.*

**327**

**Tourist Offices: St-Raphaël**, *r. W-Rousseau; tel: 04 94 19 52 52; fax: 04 94 83 85 40,* opposite the station. Open daily 0830–1900 (July–Aug); 0830–1200 and 1400–1830 (Sept–June). **Fréjus-Ville**, *325 r. J-Jaurès; tel: 04 94 51 83 83.* Open daily 0900–1200 and 1400–1830, they dispense a guide to the (widespread) Roman sites.

## ACCOMMODATION

**HI:** at *chemin de Counillier; tel: 04 94 53 18 75,* in a large park 2 km from Fréjus town along the RN7 road towards Cannes. **Campsites: St-Aygulf**, *tel: 04 94 17 62 49,* is 4 km from Fréjus station; bus no. 9 from St-Raphaël bus station to *St-Aygulf*. **Holiday Green**, *tel: 04 94 40 88 20, rte de Bagnols Bagnols.*

## SIGHTSEEING

The two communities almost merge and, although each has its own station and Tourist Office, they are effectively one place with three areas. **St-Raphaël** is the upmarket end and the main transport hub. **Fréjus-Plage** is a strip of tacky bars and restaurants that lies between the sea and **Fréjus town**, the historic area.

Fréjus was a Roman port, created by Julius Caesar in 49 BC and there are quite a few **Roman remains** scattered around the town. The smallish amphitheatre, **Arènes**, *r. Henri-Vadon,* is still used for bullfights and rock concerts, while occasional productions are still staged in the **theatre**.

**Fréjus Cathedral**, *pl. Formigé,* was the first Gothic church in Provence, built around the time the Romans lost power – though little building from that time survives. Don't miss the cloisters.

## CANNES

**Station:** 250 m from the sea and the Palais de Festivals: head straight (south) down *r. des Serbes; tel: 04 36 35 35 35.*
**Tourist Offices:** *Palais de Festivals, esplanade Georges Pompidou; tel: 04 93 39 24 53.* Open daily 0900–2000 (July–Aug); Mon–Sat 0900–1830 (Sept–June). At the station, *1 r. J-Jaurès; tel: 04 93 99 19 77.* Open Mon–Sat 0830–1300, 1400–1900 (July–Aug); Mon–Sat 0900–1215, 1400–1845 (Sept–June).

## GETTING AROUND

Orientation is easy: the town stretches around the Baie de Lérins, the promenade being called **La Croisette**, and the Mediterranean is a constant reference point. Everything is within walking distance and virtually all the cultural activities (including the film festival) centre on the hideous concrete **Palais des Festivals**. This is a town where the main activity is to stroll and soak up glamour – especially during the festival.

## ACCOMMODATION

At the top end of the market, Cannes' hotels are amongst the most luxurious in the world. Made famous by celebrities attending the film festival, these seaside palaces survive mainly on a diet of conferences for the rest of the year. Inexpensive hotels do exist, however, away from the sea. Try *r. Maréchal Joffre, r. Fortville* and the surrounding streets. Throughout the summer the town is crowded and reservations are imperative. If you want to be there for the film festival, you must book hotel rooms a year in advance.

Chain hotels include *Ba, BW, Ch, Cn, Ct, Hn, Ib, IC, IH, Mc, Nv, Sf* and *Tp*.

The most famous of the famous is **The Carlton**, *58 La Croisette; tel: 04 93 68 91 68,* a white extravaganza with two black cupolas – said to be modelled on the breasts of a notorious flamenco dancer who became a 'friend' to royalty. If you prefer ultra-modern, head for **Gray d'Albion**, *38 r. des Serbes; tel: 04 92 99 79 79.* At the opposite end of the price spectrum, try the adequate **Hôtel Bourgogne**, *13 r. de 24-août; tel: 04 93 38 36 73.*

There's no **HI** hostel in town, nor a really convenient **campsite**.

## ENTERTAINMENT

Cannes proudly upholds the Riviera's reputation as an overpriced, overcrowded fleshpot. Entertainment here consists of looking good, spending money and sleeping little. The bars and clubs are expensive, while the casinos attract some of Europe's most upmarket gamblers. Entry to the casinos is free, but there's a strictly enforced dress code.

Cannes' nightlife can be fun. Those with

328

less money and more sense will head to *r. Macé* and *r. F-Faure,* where bars are reasonably priced. Otherwise, promenade along *La Croisette* and spend wisely on drinks at the most happening café.

With towns all along the coast competing for custom, Cannes keeps ahead of the game by organising an ever-increasing number of special events and barely a week goes by without some kind of conference or festival – concerts of classical music, jazz and blues galas, even chess tournaments.

*The* event, of course, is the prestigious **Cannes Film Festival**, which begins during the second week in May. Public tickets for films outside the main competition are sold daily from a special office next to the Tourist Office.

### SIGHTSEEING

Glitzy Cannes, twinned with Beverley Hills, is surprisingly welcoming to those without MGM contracts or family jewels, especially if they take the trouble to wander away from *La Croisette* to the small winding streets and hidden squares a little inland.

Cannes specialises in second-hand glamour – promenades along the *Croisette* are the favourite pastime. Begin at the **Palais des Festivals**, built in 1982 and christened 'the bunker'. It is here that the red carpets are unrolled and the Rollers glide up, disgorging world-famous faces (and many that seem vaguely or not-at-all familiar), while the world of cinema pats itself on the back. Glimpses of stars are frequent (practise climbing lampposts) and, when it's all over, you may find your favourite's handprint cast in the concrete around the festival hall.

There are few other specific sights, but try climbing *r. St-Antoine* to the hill of **Le Suquet**, the oldest quarter. The **Musée de la Castre**, housed in the old citadel here, displays antiquities from around the world and gives a history of the town.

### OUT OF TOWN

Off Cannes, the **Îles de Lérins** are an antidote to chic. **Île de Ste-Marguerite** is the larger of the two, and with the better beaches. At the north end, **Fort Royal** is an impressively stark fortress built by Vauban in 1712 – and the legendary home of the Man in the Iron Mask (whose identity is debated to this day). The smaller **Île de St-Honorat** houses a small working monastery. There are daily departures from the quay next to the Palais des Festivals casino.

### ANTIBES

**Station:** for the centre, head down *av. Robert Soleau* to *pl. de Gaulle.* From here *blvd Albert 1er* leads to the sea.

**Local coastal buses** run from *pl. Gén-de-Gaulle,* others from the **bus station**, *r. de la République.*

**Tourist Office:** *11 pl. du Gén-de-Gaulle; tel: 04 92 90 53 00; fax: 04 92 90 53 01.* Open Mon–Sat 0900–2000, Sun 1000–1200 (July–Aug); Mon–Fri 1000–1200 and 1400–1800, Sat 1000–1200 (Sept–June).

Mixing chic and tackiness, Antibes is still home to the obscenely rich, but the town has a relaxed atmosphere. Take a walk along the port; the biggest boats in the northern Med moor here. Do not miss the **Musée Picasso**, looking over the sea from its home in the **Château Grimaldi**, *pl. Marijol.* Picasso worked here in 1946 and this excellent museum displays some of his most entertaining creations from that period.

The **Musée d'Histoire et d'Archéologie**, *bastion St-André* (at the southern end of the sea wall), contains traces of Antibes' Etruscan, Greek and Roman past.

### OUT OF TOWN

**Juan-les-Pins**, the playground of the coast, is where the **Côte d'Azur** originated one summer in 1921; it has beaches (many are private, but there is still some public space), bars, discos and a **jazz festival** (in July). Accessible by bus from Antibes *(pl. Gén-de-Gaulle).*

Just inland, to the west of Antibes and also reachable by bus, **Vallauris** is pottery capital of the Riviera, famous for ceramics since 1500. Picasso came here in 1946 (to make pots) and was commissioned to paint a huge fresco, *War and Peace,* in a chapel which has become the small **Musée National Picasso**, *pl. de la Libération.*

# MILAN (MILANO)

Milan is the commercial hub of Italy, a city packed with banks and financial institutions, which boasts a standard of living high even for the wealthy north of Italy. It, and its industrial and commercial acumen, were chiefly responsible for the strength of the Italian post-war miracle. Today it is deeply style-conscious, as befits one of Europe's top fashion centres. Be prepared for inflated prices.

A Celtic and Roman settlement, Milan gained importance during the Middle Ages, under the authority of a series of influential bishops, and, even then, was known for its money changers. The Visconti and Sforza families ruled Milan during most of the 13th to 16th centuries. The Viscontis started construction on the Duomo, while the Sforzas built the castle and brought to Milan many of the top artists and thinkers of the time, including Leonardo da Vinci.

Modern Milan is one of Italy's great cities. Undervisited by dawdling tourists, partly because at first glance it is not as becoming as Florence, Rome or Venice, it is nonetheless hugely cosmopolitan, a shopper's paradise and is filled with treasures.

## TOURIST INFORMATION

**Main APT office:** *Palazzo del Turismo, 1 Via Marconi; tel: (02) 809 662,* to the right of the Duomo. Free maps and guides to Milan in English. Open Mon–Sat 0800–2000, Sun 0900–1200, 1330–1700. **Branch: Stazione Centrale;** *tel: (02) 669 0532.*

**Thomas Cook Licensee: CIT Viaggi,** *Galleria Vittorio Emanuele; tel: (02) 863701.*

## ARRIVING AND DEPARTING

### Airports

**Malpensa,** about 50 km north-west of Milan, handles intercontinental and charter flights. **Linate,** 7 km from Milan, handles domestic and European flights. Buses to and from both airports depart from the **bus terminal:** *Piazza Luigi di Savoia; tel: (02) 6698 4509,* beside Stazione Centrale. For information on flights from either airport, *tel: (02) 7485 2200.*

### Stations

The vast majority of trains serve the monumental and fully equipped **Stazione Centrale,** *Piazza Duca d'Aosta; tel: 6707 0958* (metro lines 2/3). Some trains stop instead at **Stazione Porta Garibaldi,** *tel: (02) 655 2078* or **Stazione Lambrate,** *tel: (02) 675 001,* both served by metro line 2. Milan's prime position in the heart of northern Italy always helped its trade; now the city acts as the key node in Italy's railway system. For national rail information, *tel: 1478 88088.*

## GETTING AROUND

### Metro, Buses and Trams

The same tickets are used for all public transport. Single tickets (L.1500) are good for one journey on the metro or 1¼ hrs travel on buses. Tickets are available from machines in metro stations or from *tabacchi* (tobacconists) and newspaper kiosks. A day (L.3800) or 2-day pass (L.6600) are available from underground stations.

The metro, **Metropolitana Milano (MM),** is clean, efficient and easy to use. There are three colour-coded lines. Stamp tickets in the gates at station entrances.

The **bus** and **tram** systems are more com-

330

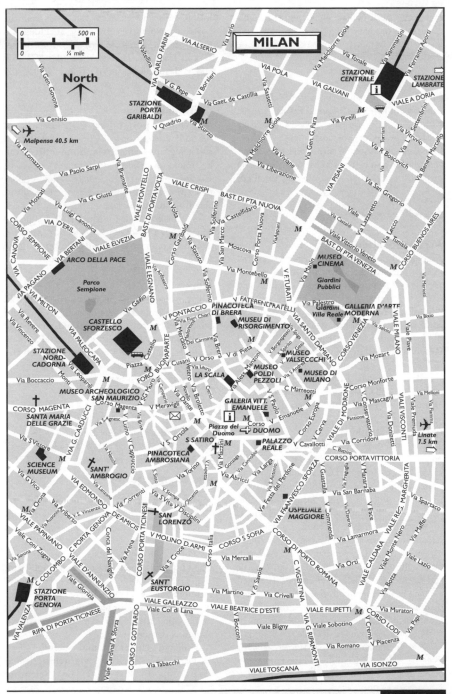

MILAN

0   500 m
0   ¼ mile

**North**

Via Gen. Govone

Via Cenisio

🛬 Malpensa 40.5 km
Via P Lomazzo

VIA ALSERIO
VIA CARLO FARINI
V G. Pepe
V Bottieri
Via Gaet. de Castillia
V Quadrio
V Sturzo

**STAZIONE PORTA GARIBALDI**

Via Lario
Via Pola
Viale Melchiorre Gioia
Via Tonale
Via Summartini
Via Ferrante Aporti

**STAZIONE CENTRALE** ℹ
🚆
VIALE A DORIA

**STAZIONE LAMBRATE** ➡

VIA GALVANI
Via Pirelli
Via Torriani
Via R Boscovich
Via Settembrini
Via Vitruvio
Via Bened. Marcello

Via Sassetti
Viale Melchiorre Gioia
Via Viviane
Via Liberazione

Via Gen. G. Fara
Via San Gregorio
Via Lecco
Via Tunisia
CORSO BUENOS AIRES
Via Lazzaretto
Via Castaldi

Via Moscati
Via Paolo Sarpi
Via G. Giusti
Via Luigi Canonica
Via Bramante
VIA D'ERIL

VIALE CRISPI
BAST. DI PTA NUOVA
Via Solferino
Via Castelfidaro
Corso Porta Nuova
Via Appani

Via San Marco
Moscova
Corso Porta Nuova

WPisani
Viale Vittorio Veneto
Viale Tunisia

**ARCO DELLA PACE**

CORSO SEMPIONE
VIA CANOVA
VIA MILTON
VIA PAGANO
VIA BERTANI
VIALE ELVEZIA

*Parco Sempione*

**CASTELLO SFORZESCO**

**STAZIONE NORD-CADORNA**

Via Boccaccio

VIALE MONTELLO
BAST. DI PORTA VOLTA
Via Volta
VIALE LEGNANO
Via Gallo
Via Antese

Corso Garibaldi
V PONTACCIO
Via Fiori Chiari
Via del Carmine
V di Pietrasanta

Via Montebello
V FTURATI
V FATEBENEFRATELLI

**PINACOTECA DI BRERA**
**MUSEU DI RISORGIMENTO**

BAST. DI PTA VENEZIA
**MUSEO CINEMA**

*Giardini Pubblici*

Via Palestro
*Giardini Villa Reale*

**GALLERIA D'ARTE MODERNA**

VIA SANTO DAMIANO
CORSO VENEZIA
Viale Milano
Viale Piave
Via Bixio
Via Mercanti
Via Salvini

Via Mozart

**MUSEO ARCHEOLOGICO SAN MAURIZIO**

**SANTA MARIA DELLE GRAZIE**
CORSO MAGENTA
Corso Magenta

**SCIENCE MUSEUM**

VIA CARDUCCI
VIA G. CARDUCCI
V S. Agnese
V S. Vittore
Via G Vico

**SANT' AMBROGIO**
VIA EDMONDO
VIA LANZONE

FORO BUONAPARTE
V SC Mario S. Carmenino
V Meravigli
V Dante

**LA SCALA**
**MUSEO POLDI PEZZOLI**
**MUSEO VALSECCCHI**

Via Borgospesso
Via Spiga
Via Gesu
Via S Andrea

**MUSEO DI MILANO**

C Matteotti
Corso Monforte
Corso Europa
V Conservatorio
V Passione

**GALERIA VITT. EMANUELE**
ℹ
*Piazza del Duomo*
Corso
**DUOMO**

V Mazzini
**PINACOTECA AMBROSIANA**
**S SATIRO**
V Torino

Via Abricci
V Larga
V Cavallotti
C Battisti

**PALAZZO REALE**

VIALE PREMUDA
VIALE VISCONTI
Via Melloni
Via Fiamma
Via Mascagni
Via Donizetti

**Linate 7.5 km** ➡

Via Corridoni

**CORSO PORTA VITTORIA**
Via San Barnaba
Giustalla
Via San Pietro all'Orto

**USPEDALE MAGGIORE**

V Festa del Perdone
V FRANCESCO SFORZA
VIA RICE. MARGHERITA
Via Lamarmora
VIALE CALDARA

V S Vincenzo
V S Disciplini
**SAN LORENZO**
V MOLINO D. ARMI
CORSO PORTA TICINESE
V S Croce
CORSO DI PORTO ROMANA
C. VIGENTINA

**SANT' EUSTORGIO**
VIALE GALEAZZO
Viale Col di Lana

**STAZIONE PORTA GENOVA**
C COLOMBO
VIA VALENZA
RIPA DI PORTA TICINESE
VIALE D'ANNUNZIO
CORSO S GOTTARDO
CORSO S SOFIA
Via Mercalli
Via Martino
V di Savoia
Via Crivelli

VIALE BEATRICE D'ESTE
Viale Bligny
Viale Bocconi

VIALE FILIPETTI
CORSO LODI
V Crema
V Papi
Via Muratori
Via Botta
Viale Monte Nero

Via Toscana

VIALE TOSCANA
VIA ISONZO
Via Isonzo

331

prehensive and consequently more complicated, but stops have details of each route serving them. Buy tickets in advance and validate them in the machines on board.

## Taxis

Milan's taxis are yellow or white and can be expensive. There's a substantial flat fare to start with and extra charges are applied for baggage and travel on holidays or late at night. There are large ranks at Stazione Centrale and *Pza Duomo* and cabs can also be booked by phone or hailed on the street. Avoid touts offering unofficial taxis.

## STAYING IN MILAN

## Accommodation

Accommodation in Milan does not escape the inflated prices of the rest of the city, but there are plenty of pensions around the station and the town centre. Major hotel groups are well represented and include *Ch, Ex, HI, Hn, Ib, Nv* and *Rm*. The tourist office will provide a full list of accommodation. Alternatively, the **Hotel Reservation Milan** service, *24 V. Palestro; tel: (02) 805 4242*, can help find a room.

**HI**: *2 V. Martino Bassi; tel: (02) 3926 7095,* (metro line 1 to QT8 station). **Camping**: *V. G Airaghi; tel: (02) 4820 0134.* Open all year.

## Eating and Drinking

The Milanese take their food seriously and are prepared to pay substantial sums for their meals, so restaurants are generally expensive. Better value eateries include the lunch spots catering for office workers, with many reasonable self-service restaurants around the town centre.

Away from the city centre, as with any Italian city, there are family-run *trattorie* and a variety of other inexpensive places. At lunch time, customers often eat standing up. *Pizzerie* and Chinese restaurants offer reasonably priced evening meals. Bars tend to serve more coffee than alcohol, along with *panini* – rolls with a multitude of fillings.

Regional specialities include *cotoletta alla milanese*, an Italian version of *Wiener schnitzel, risotto alla milanese* (rice dish) and the filling vegetable and pork soup *minestrone*. Despite being

inland, Milan has excellent fish, fresh from the coast. Inexpensive pizzerias include: **La Cucuma**, *V. Pacini 26; tel: (02) 2952 6098;* **Grand'Italia**, *V. Palermo 5; tel: (02) 877 759;* and **Malastrana**, *Ripa Porta Ticinese 65; tel: (02) 83 78 984.*

## Communications

The **central post office**, *4 V. Cordusio; tel: (02) 869 2069*, is open 24 hrs for telexes, faxes and telegrams. Public **telephone offices** can be found at *Galleria V Emanuele II, 4 V. Cordusio*, and *Stazione Centrale*. Public phones take either coins or phonecards, the latter available from automatic cash dispensers and kiosks.

The dialling code for Milan is 02. To phone Milan from abroad: *tel: 39 (Italy) + 2 (Milan) + number;* to phone Milan from elsewhere in Italy: *tel: 02 + number.*

## Money

There is no shortage of bureaux de change in Milan; sometimes it seems as if every third building is a bank. At weekends, exchange facilities are available in *Pza Duomo* and *Stazione Centrale* and in both airports. Automatic machines that convert cash are located in the town centre and in Stazione Centrale.

## Consulates

**Australia** *2 V. Borgogna; tel: (02) 7601 3330.* **Canada** *19 V. Vittor Pisani; tel: (02) 669 7451.* **UK** *7 V. S. Paolo; tel: (02) 869 3442.* **USA** *2 V. Principe Amadeo; tel: (02) 290 351.*

## ENTERTAINMENT

Milan's daily newspapers, *La Repubblica* and *Corriere della Sera* produce weekly supplements detailing Milan's entertainment, events and nightlife.

The city's most famous institution is the grand **La Scala** opera house. Donizetti, Puccini and Verdi all staged operas here. Tickets are extremely elusive, but you may be able to get them on Mondays, for performances of classical music rather than opera. The **Conservatorio** also hosts concerts.

Cinemas cluster around *Corso Vittorio Emanuele*, near *Pza Duomo*. **Nightclubs** tend to close around 0200–0300. **Le Scimmie**

(Monkeys) is one of the most famous. Two of the more trendy areas of town are **Porta Ticinese** and **Brera**. The *Porta Ticinese* and the *Navigli* (canals) district is home to a high concentration of bars and venues (the actual *Porta Ticinese* is a remnant of the 14th-century city ramparts). Cafés and bars also dot the small streets around *Brera*.

*V. Brera* is the showcase of Milan's fashion industry. The Milanese care about their clothes and smart dress is the norm for almost all nightlife throughout the city, even informal promenading.

### Events

A **festival** commemorates St Ambrose, the patron saint of Milan, on 7 Dec. It includes a street fair which takes place near the Basilica di Sant'Ambrogio (see Sightseeing).

### SHOPPING

Milan is the place to buy clothes, accessories, modern furniture and jewellery – not all of which is a practical proposition for the train traveller, whatever your budget.

Governing the façade the Milanese present to the outside world is the concept of *bella figura* ('looking good'). The 'drop-dead' chic shop in *V. della Spiga*, *V. S. Andrea*, *V. Montenapoleone* and *V. Borgospesso*. Those with smaller bank accounts shop in *V. Torino* and the department stores **La Rinascente** and **Coin**.

If you want to window-shop Milanese style in furniture, **Artemide**, *Corso Monforte 19*, in the centre of town, is one of the best. A good general shopping street is *Corso Buenos Aires*. You can buy almost anything here. Otherwise, the *Vle Papiano* **market** (Sats) in the Navigli district is good for cheap clothes and other bargains. In the Brera district there is a Mon market at the *Pza Mirabello*, while *Naviglio Grande* is the scene of the monthly **Antiques Fair** (last Sun of each month).

### SIGHTSEEING

If a city can have such a thing as a 'signature building', then Milan's is undoubtedly the **Duomo** (Cathedral), *Pza Duomo* (metro: *Duomo*). Work started in 1386, at the behest of Gian Galeazzo Visconti. Wanting a son, and finding his prayers granted, he built this remarkable edifice as a tribute to the Virgin Mary. However, it was not until 1958 that the last pinnacles were finished. The Duomo is a magical and extravagant Gothic structure, both longer and wider than St Paul's in London, overflowing with belfries, statues and pinnacles in white marble. It shimmers in the sunlight and glows in the winter fog. The comparatively stark interior contains fine stained glass and works of art dating back to before the cathedral's construction. Stairs lead up to, over and around the extensive roof system, from which there are fine views out over the city. It also provides the opportunity to examine close-up some of the adornments to the cathedral's exterior. The **Cathedral Museum** (in the Royal Palace just by the Duomo) houses sculptures, carvings and glass.

On the north side of *Pza Duomo* is the **Galleria Vittorio Emanuele II**, a monumental 19th-century iron and glass shopping arcade known as the **Salon de Milan**. Here there are elegant cafés in which to shelter from the city's interminable winter drizzle.

The Galleria leads through to *Pza Scala*, home of **La Scala** (more properly the Teatro alla Scala), probably the most famous opera house in the world. the opera season starts on 7 Dec. Book well in advance for a good seat; bookings *tel: (02) 809120*. In summer the repertoire extends to ballet and concerts as well. **La Scala Theatre Museum**, in the building, exhibits a huge array of opera memorabilia. It also provides the opportunity to see into the opera house itself.

The **Pinacoteca del Brera**, *28 Via Brera*, is Milan's finest art gallery. Founded by Napoleon and opened in 1809, the collection concentrates on Italian artists of the 14th–19th centuries, although foreign schools of the 17th–18th centuries are also represented. There are some outstanding works here – notable among them are Raphael's *Marriage of the Virgin*, Mantegna's *Dead Christ* and works by Bramante, Carpaccio, Bellini and Veronese. The gallery is housed in part of the **Palazzo di Brera**; in the courtyard stands a statue of **Napoleon I** which dates from 1809, four years after he was crowned King of Italy in the Duomo.

Further priceless art works are displayed in the **Ambriosiana Gallery,** 2 Piazza Pio XI (metro: Duomo or Cordusio). Works by **Leonardo da Vinci** include the portrait of the musician Caffurio. Caravaggio's Basket of Fruit and Raphael's cartoons for the Vatican are other star attractions. An eccentric collection of artefacts includes the glove Napoleon wore at Waterloo.

The gallery takes up part of the **Biblioteca Ambrosiana**, a library founded in the early 17th century by Cardinal Federico Borromeo. One of the greatest libraries in 17th-century Italy, it still houses a Virgil manuscript, early editions of Dante's Divine Comedy and a host of drawings by da Vinci.

Milan's single most famous painting, Leonardo da Vinci's **Last Supper** (1495–1497), now hangs in the old Dominican monastery refectory next to **Santa Maria Delle Grazie** (metro: Cadorna). The Last Supper, depicting Jesus saying 'One of you will betray me', attracts large crowds and a hefty entrance fee. Heavily restored after years of deterioration – practically since the artist finished working on it - and following drastic wartime bomb damage, nonetheless it survives and can be seen. It is one of the great paintings of the Renaissance. The church itself, a Renaissance building designed by Solari, is also worth a look.

The **Basilica di Sant'Ambrogio** (metro: Sant'Ambrogio) was built in the late 4th century by St Ambrose, patron saint of the city and former Bishop of Milan. So eloquent and smooth in speech was St Ambrose that his name was given to honey liqueur. Most of what is standing today dates from the 12th century, although the smaller campanile, 300 years older, is one of the most ancient in the region. The complex, and the basilica in particular, was the prototype for Lombardy's Romanesque basilicas. The saint's remains now lie in the crypt.

The **Basilica of San Lorenzo**, 39 Corso di Porta Ticinese, has a similar history to Sant'Ambrogio, having been built around AD 500 and reconstructed some 700 years later. A notable portico of 16 columns from a Roman temple stands in front.

**334**

### Castello Sforzesco

**Sforza Castle**, Piazza Castello, at the end of V. Dante (metro: Cairoli), is a distinctive, heavy fortress, with walls nearly 4m thick. Built by Francesco Sforza, Duke of Milan in the 15th century, on top of an earlier Visconti fortress, the castle now houses an encyclopaedic collection of galleries and museums, displaying everything from arms to furniture, from Egyptian art to musical instruments. The pick of the bunch is probably the art gallery, the **Museum of Antique Art**, with some valuable works by Michelangelo. It also houses the **Museum of Musical Instruments,** which contains a spinet on which Mozart played.

Behind the castle is **Sempione Park**, the largest green space in central Milan. At the far end is the **Arco Della Pace** (Arch of Peace), which has seen many wars in its 150-year lifetime.

The **Poldi-Pezzoli Museum**, 12 Via Manzoni (metro: Montenapoleone), was originally assembled by Gian Giacomo Poldi-Pezzoli, a well-to-do Milanese collector. It is yet another of the city's great collections and well deserves a visit. The museum includes fine Botticelli and Mantegna paintings.

Twentieth-century Italian art is displayed at the **Contemporary Art Museum**, 9 Palazzo Reale, Piazza Duomo. It has an excellent collection of works by a range of Italian artists of the this century – including De Chirico and Modigliani. The **Civic Gallery of Modern Art**, on the edge of the Public Gardens (metro: Palestro) contains works by a variety of French Impressionists and their Italian contemporaries.

The **Leonardo da Vinci National Museum of Science and Industry,** 21 Via San Vittore (metro: Sant'Ambrogio), is not just an attempt to capitalise on the great man's name. In addition to exhibits on the evolution of science, the museum has displays of Leonardo's own ideas, including a model of his famous air-screw, the precursor of the helicopter.

In the Western suburbs stands a modern structure as distinctive and monumental as either the Duomo or Sforza Castle. The **San Siro Stadium,** a futuristic construction of steel lattices and huge concrete cylinders, is visible for miles in all directions.

# MILAN–ATHENS

A long and potentially exhausting trip if you don't take your time. Bologna is a surprisingly lovely and evocative medieval university city. Ravenna and Rimini offer opposite experiences of Italy: the former glorifies and preserves its past, the latter is insistently and incessantly modern. The further south you go, the poorer the country gets. The crossing from Brindisi to Patras is longer and colder than you imagine. Unless you have a sleeping bag and soft mat, do not attempt a deck passage. While the early part of the journey is largely devoid of tourists, they reappear in great numbers on the ferry.

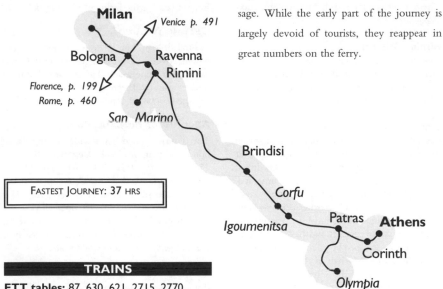

FASTEST JOURNEY: 37 HRS

335

## TRAINS

**ETT tables:** 87, 630, 621, 2715, 2770, 2785, 1450, 1455.

### FAST TRACK

➡ This involves changes and a ferry journey (see On Track) and so is not a truly fast route. In July–Aug the whole journey takes about 37 hrs. At other times, poor connections add to its length.

Between **Milan** (Centrale) and **Brindisi** (Centrale) there are two *IC* services, with dining cars, during the day, and more trains overnight, most with couchettes or sleepers. The journey takes about 10 hrs by day, 12 by night. To avoid a long wait, plan your trip around the ferry journey. You may wish to consider the longer sailing from Ancona to Patras, which has more comfortable ferries. Thomas Cook's annual guide *Greek Island Hopping,* by Frewin Poffley, describes all the Adriatic ferry routes in detail.

Eight trains run daily between **Patras** and **Athens**, approximately every 2 hrs, with one during the night. Some are *IC* and require reservations (inclusive of supplement), but the last evening service from Patras does not. The journey takes 3 hrs 30 mins–4 hrs 30 mins. Not all trains have refreshment services.

## ON TRACK

### ▶ Milan (Milano)–Bologna

Two to three trains run every hour, throughout the day. *Eurostar Italia* (reservation with supplement compulsory) are the fastest at 1¾ hrs; *IC* trains (supplement) take 2 hrs, with slower, stopping trains taking about 2½ hrs.

### Bologna–Ravenna

Nine trains run daily, taking about 1¼ hrs.

### Ravenna–Rimini

There are eleven trains daily (nine on Sun), taking about 1 hr.

### Rimini–Brindisi

Two *IC* trains, with dining-cars, run daily (supplement payable); the journey takes about 6½ hrs. There are several overnight services (taking 9 hrs), mostly with couchettes or sleepers.

### Brindisi–(Border)–Patras

Ferries run at least twice a day in high season (reservations recommended), once daily at other times. Journey time is about 16 hrs direct, or about 20 hrs via Corfu and Igoumenitsa. Dining facilities and duty-free shops are available, but there are no berths (seats recline). Border formalities are minimal. In Brindisi you must show your passport and have your ferry boarding-pass stamped by police in the building above **Stazione Marittima**. In Patras, police and customs are in the Customs House, on *Iroon Polytechniou St.*

**Hellenic Mediterranean Lines**, *8 Corso Garibaldi; tel: (0831) 528 531, fax: (0831) 526 782,* and **Adriatica Navigazione**, *85–87 Corso Garibaldi; tel: (0831) 523 825, fax: (0831) 568 332,* offer free passage to InterRail and Eurail passholders between Brindisi and Patras, although a L.10,000 port tax must be paid. Additionally, June–Oct, passholders must pay L.15,000 high-season supplement.

### Patras–Corinth (Korinthos)

Eight trains run daily, taking 1½ hrs–2½ hrs.

### Corinth–Athens (Athinai)

There are 14 trains a day, taking 1½–2 hrs.

## BOLOGNA

**Station: Stazione Centrale**, *tel: (147) 88 80 88,* 1 km north of *Piazza Maggiore;* walk along *Via del'Indipendenza* (bus nos 25/30). A memorial to casualties of the 1980 station bombing stands by the renovated station entrance.

**Tourist Offices:** railway station, *tel: (051) 246 541, fax: (051) 25 19 47,* Mon–Sat 0900–1230 and 1430–1900; airport, *tel/fax: (051) 647 2036,* Mon–Sat 0800–2000; and *6 Piazza Maggiore; tel: (051) 239 660, fax: (051) 231 454,* Mon–Sat 0900–1900 and Sun 0900–1300. All branches have free maps and guides in English (ask for the listing *A Guest in Bologna*).

### GETTING AROUND

Central Bologna can be seen on foot. The bus system covers the suburbs (the Tourist Office can issue a route map). Tickets, available from tobacconists' kiosks, are good for one hour once validated on board. An 8-trip pass is available.

### ACCOMMODATION AND FOOD

The Tourist Office has a wide-ranging list of hotels and pensions in all categories. **HI**: *5 Via Viadagola; tel: (051) 501 810;* and *14 Via Viadagola; tel: (051) 519 202,* 6 km from the centre. **Camping**: *Città di Bologna; tel: (051) 325 016, fax: (051) 325 318,* open all year.

For good cheaper restaurants (trattoria, pizzeria), try around the small streets near *Piazza Verdi,* the hub of student life.

### SIGHTSEEING

Bologna's university, founded in the 11th century, is the oldest in Europe and its buildings are scattered through the city. The medieval town itself, crammed with churches, towers, palaces and porticoes, is one of the best preserved in Italy and provides a catalogue of architectural gems. Despite its antiquity, Bologna is not stuck in the past; interwoven with the array of monuments is a vibrant, commercial city. It is also reputed to have the best cuisine in Italy.

The 16th-century **Palazzo dell' Archiginnasio**, *Via dell'Archiginnasio,* was the university's first permanent home; today that honour goes to **Palazzo Poggi**, *Via Zamboni.* The university maintains 21 museums created from work and research by its scholars. A booklet (from the Tourist Office) locates and describes important university buildings and museums.

The central square, **Piazza Maggiore**, is a good place from which to start absorbing Bologna's architectural treasures. On the four sides of the 13th-century square lie the **Palazzo Comunale** (the town hall, which now houses Bologna's modern art collection), the 15th-century **Palazzo del Podestà**, the **Palazzo dei Banchi** and the **Basilica of San Petronio**. The **Fountain of Neptune**, built in 1564, spouts in the north-west corner. At **Piazza San Stefano**, the **Churches of San Stefano** (**Crocifisso, Santo Sepolcro, Trinità, San Vitale** and **Sant'Agricola**) make up a complex, replete with cloisters and courtyards, that has retained its ancient atmosphere through the centuries.

The Bolognese architectural portfolio is also notable for its towers and porticoes. Towers, highly fashionable in the 13th century, were built as a sign of wealth, but sometimes served as upward fire-escapes from the lower wooden buildings. The two most distinctive still standing are the 98 m **Asinelli** and its inferior partner the **Garisenda**, by *Piazza di Porta Ravegnana*. Bologna's porticoes stretch throughout the city in a variety of styles, ranging from medieval through Renaissance to modern.

 **Connections: Venice, Florence and Rome**

From Bologna it is possible to travel north-east to Venice (see p. 491) or south-west to Florence (see p. 199) and Rome (see p. 460).

## RAVENNA

**Station:** *tel: (0544) 36 450*, about 500 m east of town; walk down *Viale Farini* and *V. Diaz*.
**Tourist Office:** *8 V. Salaria; tel: (0544) 35 404;* in the centre of town.

### SIGHTSEEING

Ravenna is compact and its centre pedestrianised. Its quiet air today belies its former pre-eminence, both as a capital of the Roman empire in the 5th century AD, and as the centre of Byzantine rulers in Italy during the 6th and 7th centuries AD. Remnants of these periods include a fine collection of vivid mosaics.

The major sights cluster in the north-west corner of the old town. The 6th-century octagonal **Basilica of San Vitale** features depictions of the Byzantine Emperor Justinian and Empress Theodora. **Sant'Apollinare Nuovo** dates from the same period; its walls are lined with mosaics showing processions of saints (on the men's side of the church) and virgins (on the women's side). The **Mausoleum of Galla Placidia**, lined with old mosaics in rich colours, and the **National Museum** are in the grounds.

In the south-west of town, the **Archiepiscopal Museum** has more relics from Ravenna's rich history. The 6th-century **Arian Baptistery**, *V. Ariani*, is one of the few original Arian buildings still standing, a relic from the reign of Theodoric the Goth.

## RIMINI

**Station:** *tel: (0541) 53 512;* between Rimini old town and the sea.
**Tourist Offices:** *V. Dante 86; tel: (0541) 51 331, fax: (0541) 27 927,* outside the station, and *3 Piazza Fellini; tel: (0541) 56 902, fax: (0541) 56 598,* on the waterfront. Many nearby beach resorts have seasonal offices. *Instantaneo* (ask at Tourist Offices), has comprehensive practical information.

### GETTING AROUND

Frequent buses run along the coast and around Rimini. The Tourist Office and bus information booth outside the train station have details.

### ACCOMMODATION

Almost every building close to the beach offers accommodation. The huge list at the Tourist Office, coupled with the clusters of signs advertising rooms, can be bewildering; try the booking service in the station. **HI:** *Via Flaminia 300; tel: (0541) 373 216,* near the airport, is 10-mins walk from the seafront at Miramare.

### SIGHTSEEING

Rimini, heart of the Adriatic Riviera and little more than one long beach, stretches from **Viserbella** in the north through **Viserba, Rivabella, Marina Centro** and **Bellariva** to **Miramare**. It is totally dependent on tourism and unashamedly supplies what its visitors want.

337

Regimented sunloungers, parasols and beach paraphernalia are lined up for miles on end, backed by an unbroken chain of amusement arcades, gift shops and restaurants.

### ⤵ SIDE TRACK FROM RIMINI

Most people visit **San Marino**, a 1700-year-old independent republic covering just 23 square miles, purely for its novelty value. However, there are fine views of the coast and the Apennines from the main ridge. Several buses (taking 45 mins) run daily from Rimini. ⬈

### BRINDISI

**Stations**: major trains stop at **Centrale**, *tel: (0831) 521 975;* two per day call at **Marittima**, by the port (from Centrale, walk straight down *Corso Umberto* and *Corso Garibaldi*).
**Ferries**: *Via R Margherita* (for ferries to Greece).
**Tourist Office: Head office**, *88 V. Cristoforo Colombo; tel: (0831) 562 126* (normal office hours). In high season there is also a branch at the port: *Via R Margherita; tel: (0831) 521 944.*

Brindisi's existence has always been reliant on its natural port, which was prized by the Romans as a haven for their fleet. The poet Virgil, who described it in *The Aeneid,* later died here. In the 19th century the town was an important stop on the London–India mail route; today it sees thousands of backpackers en route to the Greek ferries. Brindisi's few interesting remains include **Roman columns**, parts of the city gates at **Porta Lecce** and **Porta Mesagne**, and the **Cathedral** (built 1098–1132) containing ancient mosaics.

### ⤵ SIDE TRACKS FROM BRINDISI

About half of the ferries between Brindisi and Patras stop at Corfu and Igoumenitsa. The Ionian island of **Corfu** is popular primarily for its beaches and resorts, but the town does have some distinguished Venetian architecture. **Igoumenitsa** is a good base for exploring the rugged mountainous interior of northern Greece. ⬊

### PATRAS

**Station**: *tel: (061) 273 694.*
**Ferries**: *Iroon Polytechniou St* (for **Italy** and the **Ionian Islands**). Port tax: Dr.1500, high-season supplement to Brindisi: Dr.2500. **Port Authority**: *Othonos Amalias St; tel: (061) 341 002* (many ferry agencies are on the coast road). **Tourist Office**: *110 Iroon Polytechneiou; tel: (061) 420 303/5,* in the *Customs House.* **Tourist Police**, *53 Patreos St; tel: (061) 273 452/3.*

**Agios Andreas** is one of the largest churches in Greece, with a 43-m high dome surrounded by a dozen lower-domed bell-towers (representing Jesus and the 12 apostles). The ruined **Venetian Castle** offers a view making the climb worthwhile. There is also a reconstructed **Roman Theatre** and an **Archaeological Museum**.

### ⤵ SIDE TRACKS FROM PATRAS

From Patras trains run south through the western Peloponnese, taking 1½–2½ hrs to reach **Pirghos**, from where it's 30 mins (by train) to **Olympia**, site of the Olympic Games of ancient Greece. ⬈

### CORINTH (KORINTHOS)

**Station**: *tel: (0741) 22 520,* 500 m from the centre.
**Tourist Police**: *51 Ermou St; tel: (0741) 24 554.*

**New Corinth**, near the dramatically sheer gorge of the Corinth Canal, is linked by bus to its ancient namesake. It is unremittingly modern, but lively; in the evening artists display their wares down by the waterfront. **Old Corinth** (7 km away) is set between mountains and sea and dominated by the surviving columns of the 6th-century BC **Temple of Apollo**. Remnants of the central **forum** are flanked by the occasional row of crumbling ancient shop buildings. The **Fountain of Peirene** was built during the Roman occupation and still functions, just: it is possible to hear faint dripping from the spring deep in the arches. On the mountain top above Old Corinth are **Acrocorinth** and a **Venetian Fortress**.

# MILAN–FLORENCE

This Italian route moves between Lombardy and Tuscany via Liguria, providing a chance to enjoy some of Italy's best coastline, especially around Portofino and Rapallo. It is the best route for viewing the scenery, vineyards and fascinating medieval towns of Tuscany. In particular, do not miss the opportunity to see Siena and Lucca.

At the major seaport of Genoa the route meets the Nice–Genoa route (p. 371), which is where the city is described. By combining routes you can enjoy an itinerary that takes in the French Riviera, the Italian Riviera and Florence, with a continuation to Paris or Rome.

Milan
Pavia
Nice Genoa, p. 371
Santa Margherita Ligure
Genoa
Rapallo
Portofino
Levanto
La Spezia
Lucca
Florence
Pisa
Empoli
San Gimignano
Volterra
Siena

339

FASTEST JOURNEY: 2 HRS 40 MINS

## TRAINS

**ETT tables:** 610, 614.

### FAST TRACK

An hourly Eurostar Italia service (reservation obligatory plus supplement) runs from Milan (Centrale) to Florence (SMN), taking 2 hrs 40 mins; there are also IC trains every two hours (supplement payable) taking 3 hrs.

## ON TRACK

**Milan (Milano)–Pavia**
Trains from Milan (Centrale) are frequent; the journey takes about 25 mins.

**Pavia–Genoa (Genova)**
Trains to Genoa (Piazza Principe) are frequent, but there are long gaps between some; the fastest trains take just over 1 hr.

**Genoa–Santa Margherita Ligure**
Trains from Genoa (Piazza Principe) are

frequent but irregular (long intervals between some); the journey takes about 30 mins.

## Santa Margherita Ligure–Rapallo

Trains are plentiful but irregular (long intervals between some). The journey takes 10 mins.

## Rapallo–Levanto

At least sixteen trains run daily; the journey averages 35 mins.

## Levanto–La Spezia

Around sixteen trains run daily, taking about 20 mins.

## La Spezia–Pisa

Plenty of trains run, but depart at irregular intervals. The journey time is around 50 mins.

## Pisa–Empoli

At least one train an hour runs between Pisa (Centrale) and Empoli, the journey taking 30–40 mins.

## Empoli–Florence (Firenze)

Trains depart at least hourly for Florence (SMN), taking about 30 mins.

## PAVIA

**Station:** *tel: (0382) 23 000.* West, in modern town: 10-min walk from centre (bus nos 3/6). **Tourist Office:** *V. Fabio Filzi 2; tel: (0382) 22 156* (near station). Open Mon–Sat 0930–1230 and 1430–1800.

### ACCOMMODATION

There's a shortage of budget accommodation. Try the **Splendide,** *V. XX Settembre 11; tel: (0382) 24 703.*

Camping (May–Sept), **Ticino,** *V. Mascherpa 10; tel: (0382) 525 362* (bus no. 4).

### SIGHTSEEING

The old town itself is the main attraction, known for its medieval towers, attractive churches and peaceful squares. The **Duomo** (cathedral) (begun 1488) was completed only in the 1930s and is an architectural mess, not helped by the collapse of a tower in 1989. Far nicer is the 12th-century Romanesque church

of **San Michele**, **Via Cavallotti**, with its yellow sandstone façade and friezes depicting mythical creatures and symbolising the struggle between good and evil. It contains 14th-century bas-reliefs and a 7th-century silver cross.

The huge 14th-century **Castello Visconteo** (Castle of the Visconti), *Strada Nuova,* houses the **Museo Civico**, which contains an interesting archaeological section and some reasonable Venetian paintings (including works by Bellini). Behind the castle, the Lombard-Romanesque church of **San Pietro in Ciel d'Oro** (built 1132), *V. Griziotti,* contains the **reliquary of St Augustine** – see the Gothic marble ark on the high altar. His bones were rescued from Carthage in the 8th century.

The highlight of the area is the magnificent **Certosa di Pavia**, a Carthusian monastery, 8 km north of town with an incredible façade, including Carrara marble transported from 250 km away. Napoleon closed it down but in the 1960s it was reoccupied and the Cistercian monks now living there maintain a vow of silence. The mass of exterior ornamentation creates an amazingly harmonious whole, reflecting the major styles of three centuries. The interior of the church is Gothic, filled with paintings, statues and tombs and as elaborately decorated as the flamboyant exterior. The rest of the monastery can be seen by joining a guided tour. Buses are frequent (from *Pza Piave*), then there's a 1.5 km walk to the entrance.

## SANTA MARGHERITA LIGURE

**Station:** *tel: (0185) 286 630,* at the top of *V. Roma,* which leads to *V. XXV Aprile.*
**Tourist Office:** *V. XXV Aprile 26; tel: (0185) 287 485.* Daily 0900–1230, 1530–1900 summer; Mon–Sat 0800–1145, 1515–1745 winter.

This attractive little resort with some cheap, pleasant hotels is a good base for visiting other coastal towns. The richly decorated interior of the **Basilica di Santa Margherita** is well worth seeing.

### ↴ SIDE TRACK FROM SANTA MARGHERITA LIGURE

**Portofino**, a beautifully sited up-market resort, makes an interesting day-trip by bus.

Besides the obvious attractions, the town is famous for antique lace and the museum has a section devoted to the subject. **Monte Portofino**, just outside the town, is a 610m-long headland that is a nature reserve, with over 700 species of wildflowers and shrubs. Here there are excellent opportunities for walking - and swimming. **Tigullio**, *V. Palestro 8; tel: (0185) 284 670*, operate both buses and ferries from Santa Margherita to Portofino (and other resorts), leaving from *Pza Martiri della Libertà* and the adjoining quay. 🚶

## RAPALLO

**Station**: *tel: (0185) 50 347*.
**Tourist Office**: *V. Diaz 9; tel: (0185) 51 282*. Open daily 0930–1230 and 1600–1900.

A once-beautiful resort haunted by writers, Rapallo is now hectic and expensive, with a large marina, but there is an attractive old area with cobbled streets. Here, as anywhere along this coast, meals of fresh fish are practically unmissable. Keen walkers can enjoy the scenery while following footpaths up to the hill village of **Montallegro**, with its 16th-century **Santuario**. The less energetic can get a cable-car up from *V. Castegneto*.

## LEVANTO

**Station**: La Spezia (see below) handles enquiries concerning Levanto.
**Tourist Office**: *Pza Colombo 12; tel: (0187) 808 125*. They have details about **Cinque Terre** (see below).

A quiet little town with a long beach, good Wednesday market and plenty of cheap hotels. The real point of stopping here is to use it as a good base for exploring the Cinque Terre.

### ↗ SIDE TRACKS FROM LEVANTO

The **Cinque Terre** consists of five isolated fishing villages (**Monterosso, Vernazza, Corniglia, Manarola** and **Riomaggiore**), sheltered by cliffs and virtually unknown until the railway reached them. Each has a distinctive character and it's worth going to all five. The hourly trains take only a few minutes between each village. You can also walk, enjoying dramatic coastal scenery, but check what is involved first because the maps can be deceptive. Steer clear of these places in the height of summer. 🚶

## LA SPEZIA

**Station**: *tel: (0187) 35 373*. Turn left on *V. Siffredi* for the centre.
**Tourist Office**: *V. Mazzini 47; tel: (0187) 36 000*, by the seafront. Open Mon–Thur 0800–1400, 1430–1730; Fri–Sat 0800–1300.

Most of the old town was destroyed by Allied bombers, but La Spezia lies on a wonderful natural harbour and the surrounding hills are studded with old Genoese castles. The church of **Santa Maria** has survived, a 14th-century structure rebuilt in the 17th–18th centuries. **The Museo Navale** contains maritime objects from the 16th century onwards and the **Museo Civico** houses a collection of ancient Ligurian artefacts.

### ⟷ Connection to Corsica

From La Spezia you can reach **Corsica** (journey time: 5 hrs). In summer there are daily ferries (to Bastia), operated by **Corsica Ferries**, *Molo Italia; tel: (0187) 21 282*, and **Moby Lines**, *V. Tolone 14; tel: (0187) 21 844*.

## PISA

**Station: Centrale**, *tel: (050) 41 385* or national free-call number: *1478 88088*, south of the River Arno and 20-mins walk from the Leaning Tower, or CPT bus no.1; *tel: 505511* for further information; L.1300 one-way and L.2600 return.
**Buses: APT**, *Pza Sant'Antonio; tel: (050) 23 384*, and **Lazzi**, *Pza Vittorio Emanuele; tel: (050) 46 288*, between them cover all Tuscany.
**Tourist Offices**: *Pza della Stazione 11; tel: (050) 42 291*, Mon–Sun 0930–1900. *Campo dei Miracoli; tel: (050) 560 464*, Mon–Sun 0830–1930.

### ACCOMMODATION

There are several good budget hotels around *Campo dei Miracoli*, but they are popular and in term-time students fill the best. **Campsite: Campeggio Torre Pendente**, *Vle Cascine*

*86; tel: (050) 560 665*, 1 km west of the Leaning Tower, signposted from *Pza Manin*.

### SIGHTSEEING

Pisa was a major Mediterranean maritime power around the 12th century. Rich and influential, early on it rivalled Florence, sacked its greatest rival in the Mediterranean, Amalfi (1135), and was finally defeated in battle by that other maritime-mercantile superpower, Genoa. The innovative architecture of the Middle Ages, characterised by distinctive stripes of marble and blind arcades, became known as Pisan-Romanesque. It illustrates a fairly decorative tendency which is thought to emanate from the Pisans' contact with the Moslems of North Africa and Spain. Some of Italy's finest medieval sculptures are here, many by Nicola and Giovanni Pisano (father and son) and other Pisanos (unrelated). The main centre of interest is the **Campo dei Miracoli** (Field of Miracles) in which are situated the triumvirate of Pisa's most famous buildings: **Duomo**, **Leaning Tower** and **Baptistry**.

The 11th-century four-tiered **Duomo**, one of Italy's finest cathedrals, was the first Tuscan building to use marble in horizontal stripes (a Moorish idea). The original bronze entrance, **Portale di San Ranieri**, was cast around 1180 and is by Bonanno, one of the designers of the Leaning Tower itself. A 16th-century fire destroyed much of the interior but some of Cosmati's lovely floor survived, as did the 14th-century mosaic of Christ Pantocrator by Cimabue, in the apse, and a magnificent sculpted pulpit by Giovanni Pisano (c.1300). This, with its unwieldy mixture of classical and Christian elements, is regarded as one of the masterpieces of early Renaissance art. Some lovely ivory carvings, also by him, are in the new **Museo dell' Opera del Duomo**, which also contains an enormous selection of Roman sarcophagi and medieval works of art. Construction of the circular **Baptistry** was interrupted by a lack of funds. The three lower storeys consist of Romanesque arcades. The top half, in Gothic style, with pinnacles and a dome, was added later (again by the prolific Pisanos in the 1260s). It has a pulpit superbly carved by Nicola Pisano (c.1260), whose design spawned

a whole series of similar pulpits during this period.

The **Leaning Tower (Torre Pendente)** began life in 1173, as a campanile for the Duomo. When it was 10 m high it began to tilt and the architect fled. Construction continued, however, with successive architects trying unsuccessfully to restore the balance. It is now 5 m off true, visitors can no longer go inside and the architects continue to spend their days arguing about how to prop it up. Collapse of the campanile at Pavia has prompted serious concern about its future.

The north of the square is bounded by the white marble wall of what has been called the world's most beautiful cemetery, the **Camposanto**. A legend says that the soil in it was brought back to Pisa from the Holy Land during the Crusades. Allied bombing destroyed most of the famed frescos, but some fragments survived. Don't miss the macabre (anonymous) 14th-century cycle *Triumph of Death*.

*Pza dei Cavalieri* was laid out by Vasari around 1560 and **Palazzo dei Cavalieri** became the headquarters of the Knights of St Stephen – the last ever crusading order of knights. Their adjoining church, **Santo Stefano**, also by Vasari, has a lovely wooden ceiling and houses banners captured from the Turks during the battle of Lepanto (1571). Across the square is the architecturally interesting **Palazzo dell'Orologio** – an oddity built around the so-called 'Hunger Tower' made famous by Dante's *Inferno*.

Not far from **Ponte di Mezzo**, on the north bank of the Arno, is the **Museo Nazionale di San Michele**, *Lungarno Mediceo*, where many important artistic works (including some by the Pisani) from Pisa's old churches have been collected together for safekeeping. On the south bank, west of the bridge, is the tiny and exquisite **Santa Maria della Spina**, *Lungarno Gambacorti*, a lovely example of Gothic art, enlarged in 1323. The exterior of the church has many delicate ornamental touches; it may have been worked on by the Pisani. It takes its name from a thorn from Christ's crown of thorns, 'brought' back as a relic from the Crusades.

**Certosa di Pisa** (12 km to the east and

served by regular APT buses) is an enormous 14th-century Carthusian monastery with a frescoed church where all eleven chapels are painted in pastel colours. Each three-room cell has its own little patch of garden.

## ⇄ SIDE TRACK FROM PISA

**Station**: *tel: 1478 88088* (national rail information, free-call). Just outside the city walls, an easy walk to the centre. There are frequent trains from Pisa, Viareggio or Florence, taking about 30 mins.

**Tourist Offices:** *Pza Verdi* (just inside western city walls); *tel: (0583) 419689.* Open 0900–1900. *V. Vittorio Veneto 40; tel: (0583) 493 639 (central).* Mon–Sat 0900–1230 and 1500–1900.

### ACCOMMODATION

Finding space is always a problem, so book ahead. An accommodation service is provided by **CIV-EX**, *V. Veneto 28; tel: (0583) 56 741.* Non-bookers may have to stay overnight in Pisa or Viareggio.

**HI:** *V. del Brennero 673; tel: (0583) 341 811.* Open Mar–Oct. **Camping** is possible behind the hostel.

### SIGHTSEEING

The old town is one of the most picturesque in Tuscany. The streets, in which people go about on bicycles, are dotted with palaces, towers and handsome early churches, most of them dating from Lucca's heyday (11th–14th centuries). Start with a stroll around part of the 4 km of ancient walls that enclose the old city and are themselves encircled by a green belt, a buffer between the medieval and modern towns. Some bastions have been restored and you can get a good idea of the town's original layout.

The Romanesque **Duomo di San Martino**, in the south of the centre, has an oddly harmonious asymmetrical façade, with individually designed columns and loggias. Many of the exterior bas-reliefs are by Nicola Pisano. The Gothic interior houses several works by Civitali, notably the *Tempietto*, a gilt and marble octagon constructed to honour the *Volto Santo* (Holy Face), a painted wooden crucifix believed to be a true likeness of Christ. Legend says it was carved by Nicodemus – the man who witnessed the Crucifixion. This relic has been in Lucca since 782; indeed it was for centuries a point of call for pilgrims making their way to Rome on the ancient pilgrimage route, the Via Francigena, which passed through Lucca. There are many other excellent carvings and paintings in the Duomo. The most memorable, and certainly the most famous, is the exquisite early 15th-century *Tomb of Ilaria del Carretto* (a delicate masterpiece by Jacopo della Quercia) which, some experts believe, has been tragically over-cleaned. Also inside the Duomo is Tintoretto's *Last Supper*.

The central church of **San Michele in Foro,** which takes its name from its position in the midst of what was once the ancient Roman forum, has a remarkable façade, a multi-tiered affair of striped marble loggias with a diversity of supporting pillars either inlaid with mosaic or carved and twisted, all topped by a huge bronze of Archangel Michael. Funds ran out before the interior could be completed. Almost opposite, the **Casa di Puccini**, *V. di Poggio 30*, is now a small museum devoted to the composer, with his music as a background to most tours.

Near the western city wall is the **Pinacoteca Nazionale**, housed in *Palazzo Mansi, V. Galli Tassi 43*. The 17th-century palace is of rather more interest than the pictures it displays, the over-decorated interior including a particularly spectacular gilded bridal suite. **Torre delle Ore**, a 15th-century clock tower, adjoins the church of **San Frediano** (just inside middle of northern town wall). A fairly plain structure, it's topped by a magnificent 13th-century polychromatic mosaic of the Ascension. The interior is subtly attractive, featuring many fairly plain (but varied) columns and subdued lighting. Artistic treasures include

*Fonta Lustrale*, a 12th-century font on which three different craftsmen worked, pavement tombs, 16th-century frescos and a lace-clad mummy. Just south-east is the **Piazza del Anfiteatro**, an area of medieval buildings incorporating several arches and columns of the original Roman amphitheatre, from which the oval shape derives.

Further south-east is **Palazzo Guinigi**, *V. Sant'Andrea*, a rambling complex of interconnected medieval buildings. A climb of 230 steps leads up a turreted tower with an oak sprouting from the top.

The city's main museum, **Museo Nazionale Guinigi**, east of the centre on *V. della Quarquonia*, contains a huge and varied collection of local Romanesque and Renaissance art. 

### EMPOLI

**Station:** *tel: (0571) 74 297.*

If you have to wait here for a connection, it's worth having a look at the 5th-century green and white **Collegiata**, *Pza Farinata degli Uberti*, and the adjacent **Pinacoteca San Andrea,** containing worthwhile sculptures and paintings.

### SIDE TRACKS FROM EMPOLI

### SIENA

**Station:** *tel: 1478 88088* (national rail information, free-call). 2 km north-east (in valley below town). It is a 45-min walk to the centre, but there are regular shuttle buses (tickets from machine by entrance). Siena is about 1 hr from Empoli by train.
**Buses**: Long-distance buses (covering all Tuscany), run by **Lazzi** and **Train**, leave from *Pza San Domenico* bus station *(tel: (0577) 221 221).*
**Tourist Office:** *Pza del Campo 56; tel: (0577) 280 551.* Mon–Sat 0830–1930 (summer); Mon–Fri 0830–1300 and 1530–1830, Sat 0830–1300 (winter). This office has good maps and the useful booklet *Tourist Information*. There are also booths in the train and bus stations.

### GETTING AROUND

**Il Campo** is the central square and focal point of Siena. The surrounding area is mostly pedestrianised – most of the main sites in Siena are easily accessible on foot anyway.

### ACCOMMODATION

Private rooms are best value, but you often have to stay at least a week and they can be full of students in termtime. There are relatively few hotels, which are often full. For the Palio (early July and mid-Aug), either book well ahead or stay up all night (many do). At other times, if the Tourist Office can't help, try the **Cooperativa Siena Hotels Promotion** booth opposite San Domenico, *V. Curtatone; tel: (0577) 228 084.* Mon–Sat 0830–1900 in winter (–2000 in summer). **HI:** *V. Florentina 89; tel: (0577) 52 212,* 2 km north-west of centre (bus nos 4/15). A more central **hostel** is: *Casa del Pellegrino, V. Camporegio; tel: (0577) 44 177,* behind San Domenico. **Campsite:** *Campeggio Colleverde, Strada di Scacciapensieri 47; tel: (0577) 280 044,* 2 km north (bus no. 8).

### SIGHTSEEING

Siena, a major European power in the 12th and 13th centuries, never recovered from an outbreak of the plague in 1348. This meant that it was bypassed for several centuries and has thus changed little since medieval times. It was Florence's most tireless enemy for much of the Middle Ages, competing with it for supremacy politically, economically and artistically. It is a beautiful city, built on low hills and filled with robust terracotta-coloured buildings.

In the past, the city was divided into 60 *contrade* (wards named after animals), of which 17 remain, each with its own church, museum and central square with a fountain featuring the relevant animal. Rivalry between wards is strong, reaching a head in the twice-yearly **Palio**, the frantic, no-holds-barred horse race around the Campo. This event draws in the crowds; a somewhat dangerous race – horses running in it frequently end up dead – but that only increases the fervour in which the Palio is anticipated. It's also one of the best-known events in Tuscany. Only 10 horses can participate, so lots are drawn to decide which wards will be represented and the whole event is regarded as a matter of honour by the locals, with rehearsals for days beforehand and excitement mounting to fever-pitch. Races last only 70 seconds or so, but are preceded by a two-hour procession. Get there early if you want to watch – standing in the centre is free, if crowded.

The asymmetrical **Campo** dates from 1347. Marking the spot where several *contrade* converge, it is regarded as neutral territory and is the focus of the city's life. The arcaded and turreted **Palazzo Pubblico**, on the south side, still performs its traditional role as the town hall and its bell-tower, the 102m **Torre del Mangia**, soars above the town. The views from the top are magnificent. Part of the Palazzo Pubblico houses the excellent **Museo Civico**. Give priority to the Sala dei Pace and Sala del Mappamondo, containing the greatest treasures: Lorenzetti's *Allegories of Good and Bad Government* and Martini's *Maestà* and *Portrait of Guidoriccio da Fogliano*.

The **Duomo** (Cathedral), a few blocks west of Campo, is one of the finest of its type. The exterior includes marble of several colours as well as some works of sculpture by notable Renaissance masters, and the interior is dazzling, with not an inch left unadorned. Particularly striking is the use made of stripes of different coloured marble. The façade was redesigned in 1284, a rose window added in the 14th century and some mosaics date from the 19th century. Inside, the floor comprises 56 separate sections, on which over 40 artists worked for nearly two centuries. The elaborate 1265 pulpit is one of Nicola Pisano's best and there's a notable Donatello bronze.

The **Biblioteca Piccolomini** has some superb frescos by Pinturicchio. **The Baptistery** (beneath the Duomo) easily rivals Florence's. Here you can see relief panels by Donatelo, Ghiberti and Jacopo

della Quercia – all of them key figures in the development of the Renaissance artistic tradition. The **Museo dell' Opera del Duomo** contains many other Sienese masterpieces of painting and sculpture – as well as surviving fragments from the earliest construction of the Duomo.

**Terzo di Città** (south-west of Campo), has some of the city's finest private palaces, such as the **Palazzo Chigi-Saracini**, *V. di Citta 82*. **The Pinacoteca Nazionale**, *V. San Pietro 29*, in a 14th-century palace, has a wide-ranging, chronologically arranged selection of Sienese art.

In **Terzo di San Martino**, south-east of the Campo, is **Santa Maria dei Servi**, a massive monastic church with two frescos of the *Massacre of the Innocents:* a Gothic one by Lorenzetti and a Renaissance one by Giovani (both in the chapels) and some fine altarpieces. **Terzo di Camollia**, north of the Campo, houses two monastic churches. **San Domenico**, to the west, was founded in 1125 and houses the reliquary containing St Catherine of Siena's head and some dramatic frescos by Il Sodoma. The enormous **San Francesco**, to the east, contains Lorenzetti frescos and the adjacent **Oratorio di San Bernadino** has an interior positively glowing with frescos.

## SAN GIMIGNANO

San Gimignano (32 km north-west, half-hourly buses from Siena, via Poggibonsi) is a typical medieval hill town (even the hordes of tourists can't spoil the atmosphere), which was noted for its 70 towers, partly defensive and partly status symbols, of which 14 survive, giving the town the appearance from a distance of a mini-Manhattan. Around *Pza del Duomo* (central) are some superb medieval buildings. The **tourist office** is on the main square.

**Volterra** (regular Lazzi buses from Siena) is an Etruscan hill town noted for the alabaster that has been mined there since time immemorial. It is home to the country's best Etruscan museum.

# MOSCOW (MOSKVA)

There's no city in the world quite like Moscow. It's a tough uncompromising place, not given to turning on the charm for visitors. Spend at least two or three days seeing the sights and soaking up the atmosphere.

## TOURIST INFORMATION

There is as yet no city information office in Moscow. The **Intourist** or service desk in any major hotel will help with tours, restaurant bookings, theatre tickets and travel, but only to a limited extent with accommodation. Its head-quarters at *Mokhavaya ulitsa 13; tel: 292 1278*, is really only able to deal with tours. The large hotels also sell maps and provide some of the English-language listings publications free of charge. These include *Moscow Times* (daily), *Time Out in Moscow* (weekly), and *Where in Moscow* (very good and comprehensive).

## ARRIVING AND DEPARTING

### Airport

**Sheremetevo:** for flight information *tel: 578 7518*. Moscow's international airport is located 30 km north-west of the city. Facilities (rather run-down) include currency exchange and car rental. As the entry and departure formalities are bureaucratic, allow plenty of time for delays. If at all possible pre-book your transfer from airport to hotel. The alternative is a two-stage bus and metro journey starting from outside the terminal. One bus leaves for *Rechnoi Vokzal* metro station (every 30 mins, last bus 2030), the other for the Central Airport Station, near *Dinamo* metro station (every 90 mins, last bus 2200). You'll be pestered with offers for taxi rides: the cost is exorbitant, so negotiate a price.

### By Train

**Services to Moscow:** Helsinki, Tallinn, Riga, and Vilnius each have a night sleeping-car train to Moscow. Tables 94a–94d of the ETT show the through sleeping-car services from Prague, Vienna, and Budapest via Warsaw to Moscow, which take over 24 hrs. Berlin and Cologne both have daily through sleeping-car trains via Warsaw, taking over 24 hrs (ETT table 56). Warsaw is probably the best access point, with up to five trains daily, taking less than 24 hrs (table 94a). These journeys involve transit through Belarus, but your Russian visa (which must be obtained in advance) allows for this.

**Stations: Leningradsky Vokzal** (alternative name **Oktyabrskaya**), *Komsomolskaya ploshchad 3; tel: 262 4281*. For trains to St Petersburg, Helsinki and Tallinn. Nearest metro *Komsomolskaya*. **Rizhsky Vokzal**, *Rizhskaya ploshchad; tel: 266 1372*. For trains to Riga. Nearest metro *Rizhskaya*. **Belorussky Vokzal** (alternative name **Smolenskaya**), *Tverskaya Zastava ploshchad 1; tel: 973 8191*, for trains to Berlin, Warsaw, Vilnius. Nearest metro *Belorusskaya*.

The facilities in all terminals are primitive! There is no information in English apart from the **Intourist** office at Leningradsky Vokzal, which can sell rail tickets. Keep an eye on your bags at all times. Mainline/international tickets must be paid for in hard currency, and you have to show your passport. Apply to your hotel or the **Intourtrans** office, *Ulitsa Petrovka 15/13; tel: 929 8855*, metro *Turgenevskaya*.

## GETTING AROUND

Moscow is a vast city which, the Kremlin, Red Square and one or two other sights apart, cannot be negotiated on foot. Fortunately the public transport system is second to none. All transport runs 0600–0100. There is no authorised transport map, but most city maps include bus and tram routes and a metro plan.

Tickets for all forms of local transport are sold at metro stations and kiosks. Buy *yedinye bilyeti* and you'll be able to ride on any form of transport for a month. All tickets are either punched on board the vehicle or in the booking hall of the station. To travel on the metro you can also buy tokens *(talony)*, R2000 per single journey, which should be dropped into the turnstiles at the top of the escalator.

**346**

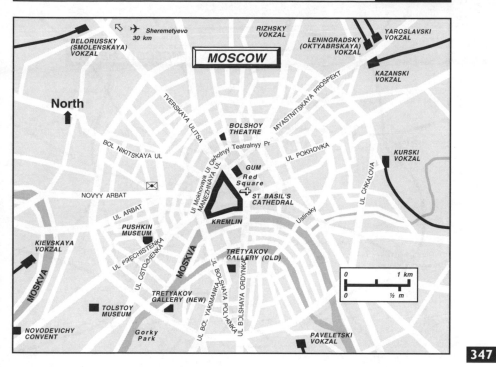

Built as a showpiece of Socialism in the 1930s and 40s, the Moscow **metro** is comprehensive, cheap, extremely reliable and a work of art in its own right. Lavishly decorated with marble, mosaics, gold and glass, each of the station interiors is intended to highlight a revolutionary or proletarian theme. The most impressive station interiors include *Ploshchad Revolyutsii, Komsomolskaya, Mayakovskaya, Kievskaya* and *Park Kultury*. A basic knowledge of the Cyrillic alphabet is all but essential for negotiating the metro. Each station has its own name, even two stations on the same site but on different lines. Stations are indicated by a large red M. Indicator boards give exit and transfer information. Check you're on the right line and heading in the right direction by studying the route map on the tunnel wall. If you're changing lines, look for a sign with the word *perekhod* and the name of the station you want. To get back to street level, follow the signs *vykhod*.

There are relatively few **trams** in Moscow. Look for the signs (T) hanging on wires above the street and adjacent to the stop. For **buses** the sign is (A) and for **trolley-buses** (m). All these vehicles are extremely crowded and there is a considerable amount of re-routing, often with no notice. Expect to be pushed and shoved throughout any journey; if you can't move near enough to the exit, shout *pazhalsta*!

There is no shortage of **taxis** in Moscow, but not all vehicles are authorised or roadworthy. To avoid being overcharged order a cab in advance from the hotel (allow at least 1 hr). If you hail a taxi on the street, look for the official cabs — yellow with a chequered band on the door. Never take a private taxi without being clear about the price in advance and never get into a cab where there is already another passenger. To call for a taxi, *tel: 927 0000*.

## STAYING IN MOSCOW

### Accommodation
Moscow is fast making up the historic shortfall of accommodation for foreigners, but there is still some way to go. There is a heavy bias towards the luxury end of the market. Hotel

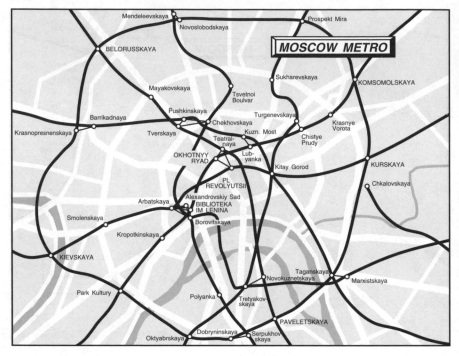

**MOSCOW METRO**

chains in Moscow include *IC, Ke, Nv, Pe, Pu* and *Rd*. There are several famous luxury hotels, dating back to the pre-revolutionary period, such as the **National**, *Mokhovaya Ul. 15/1; tel: 258 7000*, and the equally splendid **Metropol**, *Teatralny proezd 1/4; tel: 927 6000*.

Several medium-priced hotels have central locations. The **Ukraina**, *Kutuzovsky prospekt 2/1; tel: 291 6014*, is a wedding-cake sky-scraper overlooking the Moskva river. The **Intourist Hotel**, *Tverskaya ulitsa 3; tel: 956 8400*, is a soulless tower block within striking distance of Red Square. Although Moscow has a number of lower-priced hotels they can't be recommended simply because the facilities don't come up to western standards. You might try the **Belgrad Hotel**, *Smolenskaya ploshchad 5; tel: 248 7930*, which at least is clean and safe.

### Eating and Drinking
Eating out in Moscow is expensive. If you're out sightseeing and feel the need for a bite to eat, head for *Tverskaya ulitsa*, the **Arbat** or any major hotel or shopping mall. European,

American and ethnic cuisines are now widely available. Vegetarians are not catered for. The major fast-food chains are now well established. Moscow also has a number of western-style delicatessens. GUM is a good source, so is **Sadko Arcade**, *Krasnogvardeysky proezd 1*. On no account buy food from street vendors.

**Café Kranzler**, in the Hotel Baltschug Kempinski Moskau, *1 Ul. Balchug; tel: 230 6500*, is Moscow's most fashionable café. **St Petersburg**, *15/1 Mokhovaya Ulitsa; tel: 258 7094*, has live lobsters and fish every day. **Tsar's Hunt**, *186a Village Zhukovka, Rublyovo-Uspenskoye Shosse; tel: 418 7983*, serves genuine home-style Russian cuisine.

### Communications
**Central Post Office: Glavny Pochtamt**, *Myasnitskaya ulitsa 26/2; tel: 928 6311*; open Mon–Fri 0800–2000, Sat 0800–1900, Sun 0900–1900. The most convenient poste restante is the Central Telegraph Office, **Tsentralny telegraf**, *Tverskaya ulitsa 7; tel: 924 9004*. **Telephones:** the local area code is

095. For local calls you'll need to buy *zhetony* (tokens) at the metro.

## Consulates

**Australia:** *Kropotkinsky pereulok 13; tel: 956 6070,* metro: *Park Kultury.*
**Canada:** *Starokonyushenny pereulok 23; tel: 956 6666,* metro: *Kropotkinskaya.*
**New Zealand:** *Povarskaya ulitsa 44; tel: 290 1277,* metro: *Barrikadnaya.*
**Republic of Ireland:** *Grokholsky pereulok 5; tel: 288 4101,* metro: *Prospekt Mira.*
**South Africa:** *Bolshoy Strochenovsky pereulok 22/5; tel: 230 7854,* metro: *Serpukhovskaya.*
**UK:** *Sofiyskaya naberezhnaya 14; tel: 956 7200,* metro: *Biblioteka imeni Lenina.*
**USA:** *Novinsky bulvar 19/23; tel: 252 2451,* metro: *Barrikadnaya.*

## ENTERTAINMENT AND EVENTS

For tickets to major events and venues enquire at the service desk at your hotel; or try **IPS Theatre Box Office** in the Hotel Metropol. You'll pay western rates in hard currency.

Russia is famous for its high culture. The **Bolshoy** opera and ballet companies perform at the theatre of the same name, *Teatralnaya ploshchad 1, tel: 292 3119,* or sometimes at the **Palace of Congresses** in the Kremlin, *tel: 929 7901.* The Bolshoy Theatre is due for a major renovation, when the ballet will either be on tour or perform at other venues. The main venues for concerts are **Tchaikovsky Concert Hall**, *Triumfalnaya ploshchad 4/31; tel: 299 3957;* metro: *Mayakovskaya,* and **Moscow Conservatory**, *Bolshaya Nikitskaya ulitsa 13; tel: 229 8183 or 7795;* metro: *Okhotnyy Ryad.*

There are two venues of the **Moscow State Circus**: *Tsvetnoy bulvar 13; tel: 200 6889* and *Prospekt Vernadskogo 7; tel: 930 2815.*

For a uniquely Russian experience, visit the famous 19th-century **Sandunovskaya banya** (baths), *Neglinnaya ulitsa 14; tel: 925 4631.*

The most impressive celebrations take place during **Christmas** and **New Year**. Concerts and folk events take place during the **Russian Winter Festival** (25 Dec–5 Jan). The traditional Soviet **anniversaries** (1 May, 7 Nov) are still marked by small-scale demonstrations, while **Victory Day** (9 May) is commemorated

by marches. **Russian Independence Day** (12 June) – head for Red Square or the parks to see what's going on.

## SHOPPING

Moscow's main shopping street is *Tverskaya ulitsa.* Of several malls, the most famous is **GUM**, *Krasnaya ploshchad 3,* now stocked mainly with western goods. Souvenirs include the painted Palekh lacquer boxes, matryoshka nest dolls, blue and white Gzhel pottery, carved wooden toys, balalaikas and miniature samovars and the traditional fur hat. Apart from the malls, the best place for souvenirs is the **Izmailovsky Park street market** at weekends.

## SIGHTSEEING

Coach tours and excursions are organised by **Intourist**, *Mokhovaya ulitsa 13; tel: 292 2037* (payment in hard currency) and other travel companies. In summer, about the best and cheapest way of seeing Moscow is to take a boat trip on the Moskva river. Numerous embarkation points include the Ustinsky Bolshoy bridge, near the Rossiya Hotel, and the pier behind the Kievskaya railway station.

### The Kremlin

Metro: *Alexandrovskiy Sad.* Open Fri–Wed 1000–1630, but closed on other occasions at short notice, so check before setting out. The main entrance is through the **Kutafaya Tower** on *Manezhnaya ulitsa,* where tickets are sold to all sights open to the public. Moscow's first kremlin (*kreml* means 'fortress') was founded in 1156 but the present complex dates from the late 15th century. The **Cathedrals** are among the greatest artistic monuments in Russia and were the scene of all the great ceremonies of state until the demise of the monarchy in 1917. **Uspensky Sobor**, the Cathedral of the Assumption, is the work of a Bolognese architect, Aristotele Fioravanti. The interior walls and pillars are covered with 17th-century paintings of breathtaking beauty. Russian architects from Pskov built **Blagoveshchensky Sobor**, the Cathedral of the Annunciation, in just five years (1484–89). Used as a private chapel by the Tsar and his family, it is decorated with frescos by the medieval master Theodosius. The

349

exuberantly decorated exterior of **Arkhangelsky Sobor**, the Cathedral of the Archangel, is a clue to the Venetian origins of the architect, Aleviz Novy. It is the burial place of Russia's earliest rulers, Ivan the Terrible among them.

The **Patriarch's Palace**, including the **Church of the Twelve Apostles**, is now the **Museum of 17th-Century Life and Applied Arts**. The exhibitions here include two rooms furnished in the style of a wealthy boyar's residence. Some of the displays are borrowed from the **Oruzheynaya Palata** (Kremlin Armoury). This vast and stunning collection comprises priceless objects made for the Tsar and his court, including some of the famous Fabergé eggs and royal coaches.

From the famous 'Red' (or ceremonial) Staircase outside the **Granovitaya Dvorets** (Palace of Facets), Tsars progressed to their coronation – the stairs were destroyed by Stalin, but rebuilt in 1994. Also in the Kremlin are the 81-m **Ivan the Great Bell Tower**, the **Tsar's Bell and Cannon**, the **Arsenal**, **the** former **Senate** (where the President still has an office) and the modern **Palace of Congresses**.

### Red Square

Running parallel to the eastern side of the Kremlin wall is **Red Square** (Krasnaya Ploshchad): metro *Ploshchad Revolyutsii*. The most familiar sight here is **St Basil's Cathedral**, built by Ivan the Terrible. Now a museum (open Wed–Mon, 1000–1600 summer; 1100–1600 winter; closed first Mon every month), the interior is a dark, mysterious maze of corridors, vestibules and twisting staircases.

In front of the Kremlin wall is the **Lenin Mausoleum**, where the Soviet leader has been interred since his death in 1924 (open Tues–Thur, Sat–Sun 1000–1300; long queues).

Two monuments demolished in the Stalin era have recently been restored. The **Kazan Cathedral** originally dates from 1636 and is now a functioning church. The **Iberian Gate** near the red-brick **Historical Museum** takes its name from a tiny chapel dedicated to the Iberian Virgin.

The **Vorobyovy Hills Observation Platform** is the highest point in Moscow and offers a superb panorama of Moscow city. Although

well worth the trip in good weather, don't bother going if the weather is bad.

### Other Sights

Presiding over *Teatralnaya ploshchad* (Theatre Square) is the stunning neo-classical façade of the **Bolshoy**, home to the world-famous opera and ballet companies.

A beautiful artificial stream of illuminated waterfalls with ornate mosaic tiling run along **Alexandrovsky Gardens** near Red Square parallel to *Ul. Manezhnaya*. Visit at night for an even better view.

The most outstanding of all Moscow's fortified monasteries is the **Novodevichy Convent**, *Novodevichy proezd,* metro: *Sportivnaya* (open Wed–Mon 1000–1800 summer; 1000–1700 winter; closed last day of each month). This majestic ensemble contains the 17th-century **Church of the Assumption**, where some of the best choral singing in Russia takes place on Sun. Much of old Moscow was destroyed by Stalin's planners in the 1920s and 30s. One fragment to survive is the **Arbat** (metro: *Arbatskaya),* a charming 19th-century residential quarter now the haunt of buskers.

**Gorky Park** has views across the Moskva River as well as amusements, a theatre and ice rink (metro: *Park Kultury,* trolley-buses: 4, 7, 62). **Izmailovsky Park** contains the hunting lodge where Peter the Great grew up; it's also famous for its weekend art and souvenir markets (metro: *Izmailovsky Park).*

The **Tretyakov Gallery** houses the largest collection of Russian art in the world, some 50,000 paintings in all. Main gallery: *Lavrushinsky pereulok 2,* metro: *Tretyakovskaya.* Exhibition hall: *Krymsky Val ulitsa 10/14,* metro: *Oktyabrskaya* (both open Tues–Sun 1000–1830). **Pushkin Fine Arts Museum** has a collection of old masters and Impressionist and post-Impressionist art. *Ulitsa Volkhonka 12,* metro: *Kropotkinskaya* (open Tues–Fri 1000–1600, Sat–Sun 1200–1800). The **Lev Tolstoy Estate-Museum** is where the author spent the winters of 1882–1901. All 16 rooms have been meticulously preserved, offering a fascinating view of upper-class life of the period. *Ulitsa Lva Tolstova 21,* metro: *Kropotkinskaya* (open Tues–Sun, 1000–1700; closed last day of month).

# MUNICH (MÜNCHEN)

Munich, capital of Bavaria, may be best known for its beers and sausages, but it also has many imposing buildings (faithfully restored after the devastation of World War II bombing), spacious parks and a year round music calendar. The visitor soon gets caught up in its laid-back approach to life, noticeable particularly among the crowds of all ages out enjoying themselves in its many beer halls and gardens.

## TOURIST INFORMATION

Fremdenverkehrsamt München, *80331 München; tel: 233 0300,* is the administrative office. **Main tourist Office**: *Hauptbahnhofpl.,* outside the main railway station; *tel: 233 30256,* is open Mon–Sat 1000–2000, Sun 1000–1400. It offers a free accommodation service, hotel listing (DM1), city map (50 pfennigs) and theatre bookings. Publications include monthly listings and *Infopool* (Young People's Guide) in English. **Other branches:** information at the **airport**: *Central Building; tel: 9759 2815.* Open Mon–Fri 1000–2100 and Sat–Sun 1100–2000; and in the **city centre** in the *Rathaus, Marienpl.* Open Mon–Fri 1000–2000, Sat 1000–1600.

The Tourist Offices sell the **Münchner Schlüssel** (Key to Munich), a book of coupons which allows reduced entrance charges to museums, theatres and special attractions, together with a hotel booking, city transport ticket and suggestions to help you plan your visit. Price DM63–DM240 per night depending on hotel chosen.

Useful publications include *In München,* a free fortnightly listings magazine, and the useful *Munich English Information* leaflet containing answers to the 21 questions most frequently asked by visitors.

## Airport

Munich's ultra-modern **Franz Josef Strauss Airport** is Germany's second international hub (after Frankfurt). Flight information: *tel: 975 21313.* S-Bahn line S8 runs every 20 mins from **Hbf** via the **Ostbahnhof** and **city centre** to the airport between 0320 and 0055. For the city centre, get off at *Marienpl.* Journey time is 36 mins; single ticket DM13.60. **Buses** also run every 20 mins from 0650 to 1950 between the airport and Hbf; journey time about 45 mins.

## Stations

**Hauptbahnhof München (Hbf)**, *Bahnhofpl.* (about 15 min walk straight ahead to *Marienpl.*) is Munich's main railway station, and southern Germany's most important rail junction, with connections into southern, central and southeast Europe. Timetable information: *tel: 19419;* fare information: *tel: 55414;* reservations: *tel: 1308 2333.*

## GETTING AROUND

The **city centre**, pedestrianised apart from trams and cyclists, is easy to explore on foot, being only a 20-min walk across. Indeed Munich rewards **walkers** more than most German cities, thanks to its wide boulevards, gracious neo-classical buildings and neatly laid out parks. For trips further afield, use the excellent public transport system of buses, trams and trains. S-Bahn (overground) and U-Bahn (underground). Nowhere is more than half a block's walk away from a stop or station; all transport runs 0430–0200. Further information from **MVV** (city transport authority), *Thierschstr. 2; tel: 2191 3322.*

Information on S-Bahn routes, tickets and timetables from **Deutsche Bahn** (German Railways); *tel: 557 575.* The city also has an impressive 11,000 km of cycle-paths. Bicycle hire at *Radius Radverleih* at Hbf (platforms 30–36); *tel: 596 113.* Daily walking tours (in English) start from Hbf at 1000 (DM15).

**351**

## Tickets

City transport tickets can be used on trains, buses or trams but must be validated in the blue box as you board, or you are liable to be fined DM60 on the spot. Buy them at stations, newsagents, hotel desks and campsites. Singles cost DM8 (inner zone only) or DM16 and are valid 0900–0200. A **Streifenkarte** is the best value (DM15 for a strip of 10 tickets). A **Tageskarte** (day trip ticket offering unlimited use of the system) costs DM8 for inner Munich. A ticket for the length of your stay is sold as part of the **Münchner Schlüssel** discount scheme (see Tourist Information).

## Taxis

Official **taxis** are cream-coloured, plentiful and reliable; *tel: 21610.*

## Accommodation

Finding accommodation is rarely a problem except during the city's biggest tourist attractions, the annual **Oktoberfest** (Beer Festival) and **Fasching**, the Bacchanalian carnival which precedes Ash Wednesday. For a taste of real luxury, try the modern but stately **Hotel Rafael**, *Neuturmstr. 1; tel: 290 980,* which occupies a former art gallery. Its roof garden, with swimming pool, offers a spectacular all-round view of the city skyline. International chains with properties in the city include *Ch, BW, Hd, Hn, Ib, InterCity, Ke, Ma, Maritim, Mc, Nv, Rm, Sh.*

The biggest choice of hotels is around Hbf in streets like *Schillertstr.* and *Senefelderstr.* Mid-range ones there include **Hotel Haberstock**, *Schillerstr. 4; tel: 557 855,* and **Hotel Senefelder**, *Senefelderstr. 4; tel: 551 540.* Other moderately priced hotels include **Hotel Andi**, *Landwehrstr. 33; tel: 552 5560,* **Hotel Arosa**, *Hotterstr. 24; tel: 267 087,* **Hotel Brunnenhof**, *Schillerstr. 36; tel: 545 100,* and **Hotel Herzog**, *Haberlstr. 9; tel: 530 495.*

There is a good supply of budget accommodation in Munich. **HI: Jugendherberge München**, *Wendl-Dietrich-Str. 20, tel: 13 11 56,* with 380 beds (U-Bahn 1 to *Rotkreuzpl.).* Hostel accommodation is also available in

**DJH-Jugendgästehaus**, *Miesingstr. 4; tel: 723 65 60;* a last resort in summer is the **Jugendlager Kapuzinerhölzl** ('The Tent'), *In den Kirschen 30; tel: 1401 226,* a marquee in the *Botanischer Garten,* where DM10 gets you floor space. Facilities include washing machines, lockers, bicycle rental and an open-air cinema.

Munich's warm summers encourage camping; the city's biggest **campsite** is **München Thalkirchen**, *Zentrallandstr. 49; tel: 723 17 07,* open Mar–Oct (U-Bahn 3 to *Thalkirchen).*

## Eating and Drinking

Munich enjoys its food and drink at any time, but particularly during the annual **Oktoberfest** and the pre-Lent **Fasching** carnival. Good eating areas include **Schwabing**, **Gärtnerpl.** and, across the *River Isar,* **Haidhausen**. An entertaining place for cheap snacks is the open-air **Viktualienmarkt** (food market), where a score of traditional taverns sell beer, schnapps, sausage and soup. However you soon realise that the Bavarian idea of a light snack is more like a substantial meal. The city's favourite snack, particularly popular for mid-morning second breakfast washed down with beer, is the *Weisswurst,* a boiled white sausage flavoured with herbs and spices.

Munich is famous too for its many kinds of bread, but even more for its **beers**, produced by six major breweries. The main varieties are *Helles* (normal), *Dunkeles* (dark) and the cloudy orange-coloured *Weissbier* made from wheat instead of hops. There are **beer halls** and **gardens** all over the city, some more touristy than others, seating anything from 400 to 5000, often with hearty food and 'oompah' bands. Snacks include salted mackerel, giant pretzels (crisp salt-flavoured knotted biscuits), radish spirals and cheese. Waiters and waitresses in peasant costume rush around, often carrying ten *Steins* (big stone tankards) at a time. In traditional beer gardens you can bring your own food. The city's largest beer garden, beside the **Chinesischer Turm** (Pagoda) in the *Englischer Garten,* is 'the' place to meet. Each brewery has its own beer hall, including the world-famous **Hofbräuhaus**, *Platzl 9; tel: 221 676,* and the **Augustiner Gaststätten**, *Neuhauserstr. 16; tel: 2318 3257,* home of Munich's oldest brewery.

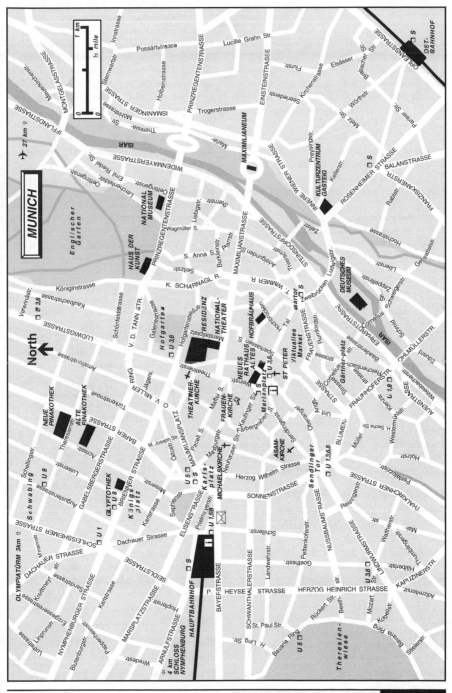

As in most German cities, the **Ratskeller** (Town Hall cellar), *Marienpl. 8; tel: 220 313,* is a traditional restaurant. Other affordable restaurants include **Donisl**, *Weinstr. 1; tel: 22 01 84,* a centuries old beer hall where locals come for their daily dose of beer and sausage. **Berni's Nudelbrett**, *Peterspl. 8; tel: 264 469,* specialises in pasta, steak and seafood with a cheap three-course menu. **Dimitri's**, *Hohenzollernstr. 13;* tel: 333 837, is a cheap and cheerful Greek restaurant. Inexpensive vegetarian restaurants include **Prinz Myshkin**, *Hackenstr. 2; tel: 26 55 96,* and **'buxs'**, *Fraunenstr. 9; tel: 29 36 84,* a self-service restaurant serving excellent salads.

## Communications

The main **post office** is at **Hbf**; *tel: 54 59 78 20.* Open Mon–Fri 0700–2000, Sat 0800–1600, Sun 0900–1500. **Poste Restante** is at *Arnulfstr. 32.* Open Mon–Fri 0800–2000, Sat 0800–1200.

To phone Munich from abroad the code is 49 (Germany) + 89 (Munich) + number. To phone Munich from elsewhere in Germany the code is 089 + number .

## Consulates

**Canada**: *Tal 29; tel: 219 9570.*
**UK**: *Bürkleinstr. 10; tel: 21 10 90.*
**USA**: *Königenstr. 5; tel: 288 80.*

## Money

**Thomas Cook bureau de change** is at *Petersplatz 10; tel: 2350 920.* Other Thomas Cook licensees are located around the city.

### ENTERTAINMENT

Munich offers a full gamut of high and low culture, from its summer **Opera Festival** to the brass band rhythms of the two-week **Oktoberfest** (late Sept in the *Theresienwiese* park) and other popular occasions. The many rock, jazz and blues bars provide a venue for home-grown and visiting bands.

The monthly *Monatsprogramm* lists all kinds of events, from live music to art exhibitions. An English-language magazine, *Munich Found,* published monthly (DM4) for expatriates living in Munich, contains up-to-date news on entertainment, restaurants, etc.

The **Bavarian State Opera** performs at the **Nationaltheater**, *Max-Joseph-pl. 2; tel: 21 85 19 19.* Opera, ballet and classical concerts are staged in the **Staatstheater**, *Gärtnerpl. 3; tel: 201 67 67,* and the ultra-modern **Gasteig Kulturzentrum**, *Rosenheim-str. 5; tel: 480 980,* three concert halls high on the right bank of the Isar. Students give free lunchtime concerts there. Several **cinemas** show English-language films which are subtitled into German rather than dubbed; these are advertised in newspapers as *OmU* films.

### Nightlife

The city's liveliest area, with pavement stalls and street performers after dark, is **Schwabing**, north of the university, which was traditionally the city's bohemian quarter. Streets there like *Leopoldstr.*, *Amalienstr.* and *Türkenstr.* are famous for their many bars, cafés and jazz cellars. Plenty of discos can also be found around **Gärtnerpl.**, which is also the city's gay area. A newer 'in' area, particularly for young revellers, is the **Kunstpark Ost**, near *Ostbahnhof,* where old dumplings warehouses have been converted into bars and nightclubs like **Babylon**, **Incognito** and the **Nachtkantine**.

### SHOPPING

The main shopping area is the wide traffic-free roadway from **Karlspl.** to **Marienpl.**, a mixture of department stores, supermarkets and fashion shops but the city's most elegant designer boutiques are along *Theatinerstr.* and *Maximilianstr.* There are expensive antique stops in *Westenriederstr.* near the **Viktualienmarkt**, and cheaper ones along *Türkenstr.* in **Schwabing**, a good place to look for off-beat items.

A busy flea market is held in *Arnulfstr.* on Fridays and Saturdays. From late Nov to Christmas Eve the **Christkindlmarkt** (Christ Child Market) is held on *Marienpl.* Candlelit stalls sell mulled wine, snacks and gifts. Best buys include traditional Bavarian Christmas decorations.

### SIGHTSEEING

Munich's main sights include the 15th-century **Frauenkirche** (cathedral), *Frauenpl.,* notable for its twin onion domes and huge tomb of Emperor Ludwig IV, the **Altes Rathaus** (Old Town Hall) dating from the Middle Ages and now housing a small **Toy Museum**, and the much larger 19th-century **Neues Rathaus**, both on the *Marienpl.*, the city's central square. Try to be there at 1100, 1200 or 1700 when the mechanical jousting knights on the **Glocken-spiel**, the ornate musical clock on the Neues Rathaus, lumber into action to mark the hour. Facing them is another of the city's landmarks, **Alter Peter** (Old St Peter's church), whose tower offers a particularly good view of the Glockenspiel. In a city with many fine rococo churches, the **Asamkirche**, *Sendlinger Str.61/ 2*, is probably the masterpiece.

*Ludwigstr.* boasts some of the city's finest 18th and 19th-century buildings. The **Resid-enz**, *Max-Joseph-Pl. 3*, the baroque palace of Bavaria's Wittelsbach rulers, has many splen-didly decorated rooms around its seven inner courtyards. The **Porzellankammer** is filled with Asian and 19th-century European china, while the **Schatzkammer** (Treasury) contains a dazzling collection of jewellery, gold and sil-ver amassed by the Wittelsbachs, including their crown jewels. The spectacular apartments of Ludwig I and the sumptuous rococo **Altes Residenztheater**, still in use for opera perfor-mances, are on show too. Beside it are the man-icured lawns and flowerbeds of the **Hofgarten** park. Just to the north-east, the **Englischer Garten** (named because of its informal land-scaping) is Europe's biggest city park, popular for the beer garden at its **Chinesischer Turm** (Pagoda) and the nudist meadow beside the River Isar.

In the *Theresienwiese*, a bronze statue of **Bavaria**, modelled on an ancient Germanic woman, and a lion towers over the park where the **Oktoberfest** is held (U-Bahn 4/5 to *Theresienwiese*).

**Schloss Nymphenburg**, summer palace of the Wittelsbachs, is worth visiting for its frescos, portrait gallery and extensive parkland with lakes and varied gardens (tram no. 17 to *Amalienburg*).

For an unparalleled view over the city, its surroundings and the River Isar flowing through its east side, go up the 290-m high **Olympiaturm** (Olympic Tower) in the Olympic park, built for the 1972 Olympics, north of the city centre. It has three viewing platforms and a revolving restaurant at the 190-m level. Open 0900–midnight; last ascent 2330. (U-Bahn 3 to *Olympiazentrum.*)

## Museums

The collection of paintings in Munich's leading **museum,** the **Alte Pinakothek**, *Barer-str. 27*, reopening in 1998 after extensive refurbish-ment, is reckoned to be among the six greatest in the world. They include 65 by **Rubens**, a small but priceless collection of **Italian** works and an unrivalled collection of great **German** masters. The collection was begun by **Duke Wilhelm IV** of Bavaria (1508–1550), who commissioned a cycle of heroic paintings from antiquity. The building itself, commissioned by **King Ludwig I**, was formally opened in 1836. Also not to be missed is the **Neue Pinakothek**, *Barer-str. 29*, which has a fine col-lection of 19th-century European artists. 20th-century art is to be found in **Haus der Kunst**, *Prinzregententstr. 1*.

The **Deutsches Museum**, *Museumsinsel 1*, on a small island in the River Isar just south-east of the city centre, is a lively celebration of German science, technology and industry with intriguing hands-on exhibits. It also has a new branch, **Flugwerft Schleissheim**, *Effnerstr. 18*, which displays all types of aircraft in Germany's oldest hangar (S-Bahn to *Oberschleissheim*; then 15 min walk). The **BMW Museum**, *Petuelring 130*, is a haven for motoring enthusiasts.

355

### ↱ SIDE TRACK FROM MUNICH

14 miles north-west of the city, on the edge of the town of **Dachau**, the Nazis' first **concentration camp** has been turned into a memorial to the 35,000 inmates, mostly Jews, who died there between 1933 and 1945. Its former administration block is now a museum. (S-Bahn 2 from Hbf to *Dachau*; then bus 724 or 726 to the *Memorial.*) ↰

# MUNICH–VENICE

This route takes you through some of Europe's finest Alpine scenery, but sit on the right for the best views. A stop in the Tyrolean capital of Innsbruck allows a change of direction eastwards, further into Austria, or west into Switzerland, by joining the Zurich–Vienna route (see p. 549 - Innsbruck is described in full in that chapter). Staying on this route, you continue south through the beautiful Dolomite mountains into Italy and to the historic cities of the Veneto.

```
FASTEST JOURNEY: 7 HRS
```

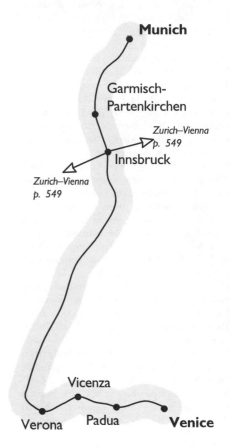

## TRAINS

**ETT tables:** 70, 890, 895, 595, 600.

### FAST TRACK

Two trains daily run from Munich (Hbf) to Venice (Santa Lucia). The day train (dining-car; supplement charged) takes 7 hrs. The overnight train (no supplement) takes 8½–9 hrs (couchettes and second-class seats). Borders are crossed at Kufstein and Brennero (minimal formalities). All trains call at Venice (Mestre) en route.

### ON TRACK

#### Munich (München)–Garmisch–Partenkirchen

The service is hourly for most of the day and the journey time averages 1 hr 20 mins.

#### Garmisch-Partenkirchen–(Border)–Innsbruck

Hourly trains, taking about 1½ hrs. The border is at Scharnitz (minimal formalities).

**Innsbruck–(Border)–Verona**

Five EC trains daily (dining-cars; supplement) taking about 3 hrs 45 mins. The border is at Brennero (minimal formalities).

**Verona–Vicenza–Padua (Padova)**

Trains are at least hourly. Verona–Vicenza takes about 35 mins, Vicenza–Padua about 20 mins.

**Padua–Venice (Venezia)**

The service to Venice (Santa Lucia) is at least hourly, the journey taking about 30 mins.

## GARMISCH-PARTENKIRCHEN

**Station: Hbf**, *tel: (08821) 19419,* centrally located between the two original villages.
**Tourist Office**: *Richard-Strauss-Pl., tel: (08821) 1806.* Open Mon–Sat 0800–1800, Sun 1000–1200. Accommodation booking service, DM8.

### ACCOMMODATION

As a popular ski resort, Garmisch-Partenkirchen has plenty of pensions and private rooms as well as hotels. Chains include *Dorint, Ra.* Two of the oldest hotels, both extravagantly decorated inside and outside but moderately priced, are the 15th-century **Posthotel Partenkirchen**, *Ludwigstr. 49; tel: (08821) 51067*; and the 16th-century **Clausings Romantik Posthotel**, *Marienpl. 12; tel: (08221) 7090.* Cheaper options include **Hotel Schell**, *Partnachauerstr, tel: (08821) 95750,* and **Buchwiesr**, *Olympiastr 17, tel: (08821) 95200.* The Partenkirchen side of town has plenty of typically **Bavarian** bar-restaurants. **HI**: *Jochstr.10; tel: (08821) 2980,* 4 km from town, in *Burgrain* (bus nos 3/4). **Campsite: Zugspitze**, *tel: (08821) 31 80,* west, near **Grainau** village; it has its own blue and white bus from Hbf.

### SIGHTSEEING

Once two quiet Bavarian villages at the foot of the 2966m **Zugspitze**, Germany's highest mountain, **Garmisch** and **Partenkirchen** were officially united to host the 1936 Winter Olympics. Though now separated only by the railway line, they retain individual personalities. Garmisch, which has the pedestrianised town centre and its famous **Casino**, *Am Kurpark,* is more expensive and upmarket, while

Partenkirchen is more traditionally Bavarian. The local history museum, **Heimatmuseum**, *Luwigstr. 47.,* displays everything from carnival masks to historic mountaineering photographs.

The town is Germany's most popular ski resort and has 52 lifts (12 open in summer) serving its 109 km of ski runs and 149 of cross-country trails. In summer it's a centre for mountain walking and climbing. The **Olympic Ice Stadium**, *Olympiastr.,* built in 1936, stays open year-round.

The **Zugspitzbahn** cog railway goes from beside Hbf to near the top of the **Zugspitze**, a 75-min journey. On the way, it stops at **Eibsee**, a mountain lake, where you can transfer to the **Eibseebahn** cable car to reach the summit. If you stay on the train, it continues up through a winding 4.5 km tunnel to **Sonnalpin** (2600m), from where the **Gletscherbahn** cable car goes the final stage to the summit. The views are fantastic. Other local peaks accessible by cable car include **Osterfelderkopf** (2050m), **Wank** (1780m), **Kreuzeck** (1650m), **Eckbauer** (1238m) and **Hausberg** (1330m), which is the base for exploring the spectacular **Partnachklamm Gorge**.

**357**

## INNSBRUCK

See the Zurich–Vienna route (p.549).

## VERONA

**Station**: *tel: (045) 888 088,* 15–20 min walk south of the centre (bus nos 11/12/13/14 from stop 'A').
**Tourist Office**: *V. Leoncino 61; tel: (045) 592 828.* Open Mon–Sat 0830–1730 and Sun 0900–1300 (Apr–Sept), Mon–Sat 0900–1800 (Oct–Mar). Also at the station. Open Mon–Sat 0800–1930; *tel: (045) 800 861.*

### ACCOMMODATION AND FOOD

There is plenty of cheap hotel and student accommodation (booking essential for the opera season, July–Aug). Hotel chains: *Hn.* **HI: Della Gioventu**, *Salita Fontana del Ferro 15; tel: (045) 590 360,* 3 km from the station, across *Ponte Nuovo* (bus nos 2/20/32/59), permits camping in the grounds. **Campsite**: *Castel San Pietro 2; tel: (045) 592 037,* open mid June–mid Sept, is walkable from the centre (bus no. 3).

For reasonably priced restaurants, look around *Pza delle Erbe*. Places to see and be seen, as well as eat, are lined along **Liston**.

## SIGHTSEEING

Walking is the best way to explore the compact city centre, or hire a bike at the station. Mostly pedestrianised, it lies in an S-bend of the **River Adige**.

Although this beautiful city of pastel pink marble thrives on the story of **Romeo and Juliet**, the real attractions are its elegant medieval squares, fine Gothic churches and massive Roman amphitheatre, the **Arena**, which comes alive during the annual opera festival in July and August. Dominating the large *Pza Bra*, it has 44 pink marble tiers which can accommodate 20,000 people. Ticket office: *tel: 045 800 5151* (hire a cushion for comfort); or contact **Liaisons Abroad** in London: *tel: 0171 384 1122*. **Via Mazzini**, which leads off it, is one of Italy's smartest shopping streets. This leads to *Pza delle Erbe,* which is surrounded by Renaissance palaces, though their burnt-orange façades are now rather worn. Originally the Roman forum, the square is now covered each day by market stalls under giant white umbrellas. An archway leads to a much serener square, *Pza dei Signori*, centre of medieval civic life. Among its treasures is the graceful 15th-century **Loggia del Consiglio** and the **Palazzo del Capitano**, which has a crenellated tower. Be sure to pause too for coffee at the **Dante** café, the most celebrated in town.

The ornate Gothic tombs of the Scaligeri family are in the grounds of the small Romanesque church of **Santa Maria Antica**. They ruled Verona when the city was at its peak in the 13th century and commissioned many of its finest buildings. An equestrian statue that once topped one of them stands outside their castle beside the river, now the **Castelvecchio Museum**, which displays weapons, jewellery and religious paintings. Beyond it, **San Zeno Maggiore**, a superb Romanesque church, has a notable Madonna altarpiece by Mantegna and magnificent 11th–12th century bronze doors.

Verona's striped red and white marble cathedral, **Pza Duomo**, is a blend of Romanesque

and Gothic styles. Among its treasures is Titian's *'Assumption'*. Across the river, there are good views from the terraces of another Roman theatre on a wooded hillside.

As for the **Romeo and Juliet** story, a delicate bronze statue of her stands in the small cobbled courtyard beneath the famous balcony of her supposed house, *Via Capuleti 27*. This restored 13th-century building was once an inn but the balcony was not added until 1935. Romeo is said to have lived around the corner at *Via Arche Scaligere 4* and Juliet's tomb to be in the crypt of a pretty Romanesque cloister, now the **Museo degli Affreschi'**, off *V. del Pontiere,* a 10-min walk south.

**Station**: *tel: (0444) 325 045,* 10-min walk south of the centre (bus nos 1/7).

**Tourist Office**: *Pza Matteotti 12; tel: (0444) 320 854.* Open Mon–Sat 0900–1230 and 1400–1730; Sun 0900–1230.

## ACCOMMODATION AND FOOD

The cheapest hotels are away from the centre or in noisy locations, so it's worth considering two-star places like **Hotel Vicenza**, *Pza del Signori; tel: (0444) 321 5121*. Book ahead for summer and autumn. **Campsite: Campeggio Vicenza**, *Strada Pelosa 241; tel: (0444) 582 311,* 20 mins by bus (no. 1) from the station. For eating out, look around *Pza dei Signori*. **Malvasia**, *Contrà delle Morette 5; tel: (0444) 543 704,* specialises in local dishes.

## SIGHTSEEING

Most places of interest in this prosperous city are in the well-preserved medieval centre, which is easily walkable though there is also a good bus network.

The city was largely rebuilt in the 16th century to designs by Andrea di Pietro della Gondola, better known as **Palladio**, who had moved there from Padua at the age of 16 to become an apprentice stone mason. He gave his name to the Palladian style of architecture which applied elegant Romanesque concepts to classical forms. His first public commission was the imposing **Basilica**, on *Pza dei Signori,* hub of the city. This medieval palace was in danger of collapsing but he shored it up brilliantly with Ionic and Doric columns.

*Corso Palladio*, the long straight main street, is lined with palaces. The **Teatro Olimpico** at the eastern end was Palladio's last work. Based on the design of ancient Roman theatres and opened in 1585, it is the oldest indoor theatre in Europe and still in use during the summer months. The acoustics are superb. **Palazzo Chiericati**, *Pza Matteotti,* houses the well-stocked **Museo Civico** which contains paintings by such masters as Tintoretto and Memling.

Palladio's most famous villa, **La Rotonda**, is on a hillside about 1.5 km south-east of the centre (bus nos 8/13). It has a round interior under a dome set in a cube of classical porticoes, a design often copied. Nearby is the **Villa Valmarana**, an 18th-century country house notable for its Tiepolo frescos and dwarfs on the garden wall.

## PADUA (PADOVA)

**Station: Stazione Ferroviaria**; *tel: (049) 875 2077,* is at the northern edge of town, 15-min walk to centre or bus nos 3/8/12/18.
**Tourist Office: APT** in the station; *tel: (049) 27767.* Open Mon–Sat 0915–1745 and Sun 0900–1200. *Padova Today* is a monthly mini-guide to what's on.

### ACCOMMODATION AND FOOD

There is a wide choice of places to stay (try around *Pza del Santo),* though booking is advisable. Two-star **Hotel Al Cason**, *V. Fra Paolo Scarpi 40; tel (049) 662 636,* is handy for the station. Or pay a little more at **Leon Bianco**, *P'tta Pedrocchi 12; tel: (049) 875 0814,* to be in the town centre. **HI: Centro Ospitalita citta di Padova**, *V. Aleardi 30; tel: (049) 875 2219* (bus nos 3/12/18). **Campsite: Montegrotto Terme**, *Strada Romana Apponese; tel: (049) 793 400* (15 mins by train, then 1 km walk). It has a pool and thermal baths.

For eating out, you should soon find a reasonably priced trattoria around *Pza del Santo,* where the local specialities include *piperata* (mutton in wine sauce). And don't miss **Caffe Pedrocchi**, *Pza Cavour,* one of Italy's most famous cafés, where writers and artists used to meet during the last century when it stayed open all night. A grand staircase leads to a series of fabulous rooms for sipping your cappuccino.

### SIGHTSEEING

Home of one of Europe's oldest universities, Padua is a busy down-to-earth town with plenty of shops and several large daily markets. Many artistic treasures lurk in its churches and museums. Though the northern parts are modern, following World War II destruction, the old town has attractive arcaded streets and squares, now traffic-free. South of the centre is *Prato della Valle,* the largest square in Italy. A market is held there on Saturdays.

In the **University**, *V. VIII Febbraio,* founded in 1222, you can see the wooden desk used by Galileo, who taught physics there, and visit the old anatomical theatre.

One work of art alone is reason enough to visit Padua – the glorious depiction of the lives of Mary and Jesus in the **Cappella degli Scrovegni** (Scrovegni Chapel), *Corso Garibaldi.* This Giotto masterpiece, which took three years to complete, has 36 panels in three tiers and is in virtually perfect condition.

Padua's other major attraction is 'Il Santo' – the **Basilica di Sant' Antonio**, *Pza del Santo,* which is visited by about five million pilgrims a year, St Anthony being one of Italy's best loved saints. The building is a mixture of styles (with a distinctly oriental flavour). The chapel contains 16th-century panels about his life, but more notable are Donatello's bronze sculptures on the high altar and marble reliefs by Lombardo. Donatello's superb monument to Gattamelata, a famous medieval *condottiere* or mercenary leader, is the central point of the square, the first major bronze of the Renaissance.

The **Oratorio di San Giorgio** is home to some fine frescos, while the works in the nearby 15th-century **Scuola del Santo** include early Titians. Just to the south is the **Orto Botanico** (Botanic Garden). Established in 1545, it was originally the university's herb garden and has changed little since.

There are some attractive 15th–16th century buildings on **Pza dei Signori**. Just south, a not very exciting cathedral is adjacent to the Romanesque **Baptistery**, lined with lovely 14th-century frescos.

**359**

# NAPLES (NAPOLI)

Naples is the unruly, raucous capital of the South. It might have a bad reputation as the city of crime but its ebullience, history, cuisine and sheer range of treasures mean that it is an essential halt on a southern Italian journey.

## TOURIST INFORMATION

**Tourist Office:** The **City Tourist Board** is at *Palazzo Reale, Pza Plebiscito; tel: (081) 418 744,* with branches in *Pza del Gesù; tel: (081) 552 3328,* Mon–Sat 0900–1900 and Sun 0900–1500 (however, it may be closed in the afternoon despite the official opening hours), and at *V. Partenope,* by Castel dell'Ovo; *tel: (081) 764 5688.* Pick up a town map and a copy of the monthly listing *Qui Napoli.* **Ente Provinciale per il Turismo** (EPT) maintains a spartan but helpful office in the Stazione Centrale; *tel: (081) 268 779.* They also have an office in Stazione di Mergellina; *tel: (081) 761 2102.* **Youth information:** *V. Mezzocannone 25; tel: (081) 552 7960.* Open Mon–Fri 0930–1330, 1500–1830, Sat 0930–1230. There is a special **Hello Napoli** freecall number for tourists, *167 251 396.*

## ARRIVING AND DEPARTING

### Airport
**Capodichino,** to the north, is reasonably close to the centre, so taxi fares are not exorbitant. There is a daily bus service to Stazione Centrale. For airport information, *tel: (081) 709 2815.*

### Stations
Most long-distance trains use **Stazione Centrale,** *tel: (081) 553 4188. Stazione Pza Garibaldi* is the metro station directly beneath Centrale. **Mergellina** and **Campi Flegrei,** also terminals for some trains, are further west.

The metro links all three stations. **Stazione Circumvesuviana,** *tel: (081) 779 2444,* handles trains to Pompeii (see p. 362) and Sorrento. It is adjacent to Centrale and is well

signposted. National rail information: *1478 88088 (toll free).*

## GETTING AROUND

The **metro** runs west to *Pozzuoli* and *Solfatara.* Trains can be infrequent and stations quiet out of peak hours. Buy tickets at kiosks and cancel them in the machines by the entrances. **Buses** are more frequent and more extensive. Buy tickets from street kiosks. Day passes are available. Frequent **hydrofoils** and **ferries** ply across the bay and out to the islands. Most leave from Molo Beverello (by *Castel Nuovo*) but some go from Mergellina. Three **funicular railways** link the old city with the cooler Vomero Hill. All three (Funicolare Montesamo, Centrale and Chaia) have recently been rebuilt and the 19th-century stations have been beautifully renovated. A local transit ticket valid for 90 mins, and good for one bus, one funicular and one metro ride, costs L1500.

## STAYING IN NAPLES

### Accommodation
The Tourist Office has a list of hotels and can occasionally help in finding a place to stay, but confirm prices with the hotel before committing yourself. Hotel chains include *Ex* and *Hn.*

Cheap hotels cluster in and around the noisy, and not particularly salubrious, *Pza Garibaldi.* Better areas to look are near the waterfront in *Mergellina* and *Santa Lucia,* where there are some cheapish options, and around *Pza Dante* in the centre. The **HI,** *23 Salita della Grotta a Piedigrotta; tel: (081) 761 2346,* is located close to Stazione Mergellina. **Campsites** are mainly in *Pozzuoli* (on the metro), west of Naples. **Volcana Solfatara,** *16 V. Solfatara; tel: (081) 526 7413,* is the nearest.

### Eating and Drinking
Naples is the birthplace of the pizza, the city's main contribution to the culinary world – authentically served with a fresh tomato sauce.

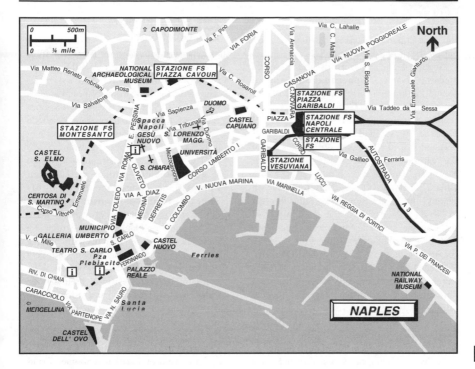

The city's food is among Italy's best, healthiest and cheapest. Pasta is the staple ingredient, as are deep-fried vegetables and seafood. There are plenty of inexpensive places to eat – try just to the west of *V. Toledo* or the many open-air food stalls around the station and *Pza Mercato*.

## ENTERTAINMENT

The best entertainments in Naples are culinary, operatic, or just strolling the streets. If you like opera at all, the **Teatro San Carlo** is well worth the ticket price. For this and other cultural pursuits, enquire at the Tourist Office. Out on the streets, you can wander for hours in the city's various districts, such as the Sanita, and be entertained by the ebullience of daily life. Behind the *Pza del Plebiscito* is the ironically named *V. Solitaria,* a long, busy, local street.

## SHOPPING

Shopping in Naples is rather specialised. Crib figures and accessories are available in the streets around the church of S. Gregorio Armeno, while **Capodimonte** figures and mimiature

tableaux are available citywide, particularly in the centre. Shopping for unfamiliar herb-infused oils and vinegars, salamis and other easily portable foodstuffs in the markets and delicatessens is a must. The shopping mall **Galleria Umberto I**, a real showcase, was built in 1887.

## SIGHTSEEING

Modern Naples is hectic, crowded and noisy. Petty crime is rife, notably pickpocketing and bag-snatching, so be very careful, especially after dark. Originally the Greek colony of Neapolis, Naples became a desirable winter resort for wealthy Romans. Of the many families that later ruled Naples, the Anjou and Aragon dynasties of the 13th–16th centuries were among the most influential and many remains from that era dot the city.

Do not miss the world-class **National Archaeological Museum**, *Pza Museo* (metro: *Pza Cavour)*, which contains an unparalleled collection from Pompeii and Herculaneum: bronzes, sculptures, mosaics, glass and, most interesting of all, mundane everyday objects.

Here too is a huge, intricate model of Pompeii and some important Roman sculpture – most notably the so-called *Farnese Bull*.

South of the museum is the heart of medieval Naples, **Spaccanapoli**, centred around *V. Benedetto Croce* and *Pza Gesù Nuovo*, where you'll find the **Gesù Nuovo**, a 16th-century church whose façade, originally part of a palace, is studded with peculiar basalt diamond-shaped extrusions. Within, it is one of the extreme expressions of the ebullient Neapolitan baroque style. Not far away, **Santa Chiara**, *V. Benedetto Croce,* dates from the 14th century. In it are some exceptionally fine medieval tombs. Attached to it, the **Cloister of the Clarisse** is notable for its walks lined with decorative terracotta tiles dating from the 18th century. Further east, the cavernous **Duomo** (Cathedral), *V. Duomo,* is dedicated to Naples's patron saint, San Gennaro. Housed here is a phial of his blood which allegedly liquefies miraculously twice every year.

Down by the waterfront, the new **Museo Ferroviario Nationale** (National Railway Museum), *Corso Giovanni/Teduccio,* is located in old railway facilities and is a real treat for rail fans. The massive **Castel Nuovo** (or **Maschio Angioino**) guards the port. The castle, begun in 1279, is chiefly recognisable for its massive round towers. The nearby **Palazzo Reale** was the seat of the Neapolitan royalty. Vast and handsome, within it are acres of 18th- and 19th-century rooms. The adjacent **Teatro di San Carlo**, begun in 1737, ranks second only to La Scala (Milan) in the Italian opera league.

**Santa Lucia**, the waterfront district to the south, is where **Castel dell'Ovo**, built by Frederick II, sticks out into the bay. The third major castle in Naples, **Castel Sant'Elmo** occupies a peak high above the city – alongside the **Certosa di San Martino**. Inside the latter, whose courtyard is one of the masterpieces of the local baroque style, is **Museo Nazionale di San Martino** which contains an important collection of Neapolitan paintings and Christmas cribs, the *presepi*. The **Museo Principe di Aragona Pignatelli**, *Riviera di Chiaia*, contains salons decorated entirely in local ceramics. This gallery houses one of the greatest of European art collections.

## ⇄ SIDE TRACKS FROM NAPLES

In some ways, the glorious **Bay of Naples** offers more than the city itself and **Sorrento** is one of the finest resorts. There are regular train services daily from Napoli Circumvesuviana to Sorrento, taking 55 65 mins. Alternatively, catch a ferry from Beverello (or Mergellina). There are about 8 sailings daily, journey time is about 25 mins.

The Circumvesuviana railway has stops at **Herculaneum** (station: *Ercolano)* and **Pompeii**, the Roman cities buried in AD 79 by the eruption of Vesuvius. Most of the objects discovered during excavations are in the museum in Naples, but the ruins are mesmeric and eerie. Herculaneum is only partially excavated, uncrowded and very well preserved. The larger Pompeii is far more impressive. **Vesuvius** itself can be scaled by chair-lift or by car and foot. From the top you can look inwards to the crater or outwards, for probably the best view of the bay area. There is also a nightly ship to **Palermo** and a weekly ship to **Cagliari**.

The island of **Capri** is renowned for its wonderful setting, mild climate, Greek and Roman remains and incomparable Blue Grotto. **Ischia**, less well known than Capri, also has a remarkable setting. There are about nine sailings daily to Capri and Ischia departing from Molo Beverello (40 mins to Capri, 80 mins Ischia). Hydrofoils depart hourly from Mergellina (journey time 35 mins for both islands).

## ↔ Connection: Naples to Athens

From Naples you can take the train via Foggia to **Brindisi**, to connect with the Milan–Athens route (p. 335). A change of train is needed in **Caserta** or **Bari** unless the overnight service is used. Journey time 5 hrs 40 mins–8 hrs 35 mins. An alternative (and extremely attractive) route goes via Battipaglia to **Taranto**. Despite the heavy industry when approaching Taranto, there is an archaeological museum, **Museo Nazionale**, which is beginning to rival Naples with its excellent collection of ancient Greek artefacts. From Taranto, continue on to Bari or Brindisi.

# NAPLES–PALERMO

This route meanders down through the southern provinces of Campania, Lucano and Calabria into the 'toe' of Italy, to Villa San Giovanni, where the trains board the ferry across the Straits of Messina and continue on to Sicily. For the adventurous traveller, there is the possibility of completing a France–Italy loop by ferry from Palermo to Corsica and then back to a French Mediterranean port.

FASTEST JOURNEY: 9 HRS

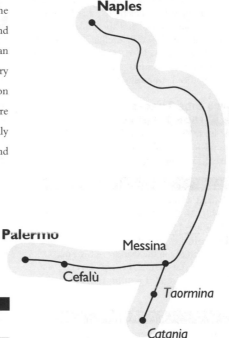

363

## TRAINS

**ETT tables:** 640.

### FAST TRACK

→ Two Inter City trains a day run between Napoli Centrale and Palermo. Both trains have buffet cars and take about 9 hrs. Supplements are payable, and take care to join the correct portion of the train, as cars for other destinations are also carried. There are also two overnight trains, one with sleeping-cars and couchettes and one with seats. These night trains take 10 hr. All trains are conveyed on a train ferry from Villa San Giovanni to Messina.

### ON TRACK

**Naples–Messina**
The Fast Track trains also call at Messina Centrale. Journey time is 6 hours.

**Messina–Palermo**
About ten trains a day run between Messina

and Palermo, with some long gaps between services. All call at Cefalù en route. Messina to Cefalù takes 2¾ hrs, Cefalù to Palermo 1 hr.

## MESSINA

**Station**: Trains from the mainland arrive on **FS** ferries at **Stazione Marittima**, a short walk to the city's **Stazione Centrale** in *Pza della Repubblica, tel (090) 675 234* – departure point for city and long-distance buses. National toll-free information number: *1478 88088*.

**Tourist Information**: *Pza della Repubblica, tel: (090) 674 236,* Mon–Sat 0900–1900.

There is limited accommodation here, and the only **youth hostel** is at *Ali* (25km) – *Pza Spirito Santo,* open May–Oct. The nearest **campsite**, **Dello Stretto**, is remotely situated on the city's northern edge at *Punto del Faro.*

Throughout its history Messina has been victim of many calamities. Earthquakes and World War II bombs have shortened the list of sites worth seeing. The **Duomo** (Cathedral), *Pza del Duomo,* is a modern reconstruction of the medieval original. Of chief interest is the ornate central entrance portal and the mosaics in the three apses. Well worth seeing, the **Museo Regionale**, *V. della Libertà 456,* contains some of the island's treasure, including works by Caravaggio and Antonello da Messina.

↪ **SIDE TRACKS FROM MESSINA**

At least 10 trains each day run to Catania from Messina, calling at Taormina en route, taking 1½–2 hrs.

## TAORMINA

**Tourist Office**: *Pza Vittorio Emanuele, tel: (0942) 23 243,* Mon–Sat 0800–1900 and Sun 0900–1300. A famous Italian fleshpot, **Taormina** is draped over the cliffs above the Ionian Sea in the shadow of Mt Etna. Of chief interest is the **Teatro Greco**, the Greek Theatre (3rd century BC, rebuilt 1st century AD).

## CATANIA

**Stations:** The station on *Corso Italia* is the departure point for the Circumetna (Ferrovia Circumetna/FCE), rather than the main **Catania Centrale**. Rail information: *tel: 1478 88088 (toll-free).*
**Tourist Office:** *Stazione Centrale, Pza Giovanni XXIII, tel: (095) 531 802,* June–Sept daily 0700–2130, otherwise Mon–Fri 0900–1300, 1600–1900.

Beyond Taormina lies **Catania**, victim for centuries of erupting Mt Etna. The best views of the volcano are from the **Circumetna** rail service (see above). The Roman theatre, **Teatro Romano**, is in *V. Vittorio Emanuele,* while the remains of the lava-built **Anfiteatro Romano**, the 3rd-century AD Roman amphitheatre, are in *Pza Stesicoro.* Catania contains important examples of the Sicilian Baroque architectural style: see the 11th-century **Duomo** *(Pza del Duomo)* with its Baroque façade,

huge **San Nicolo** and the vast ornamented **monastery** behind it – both in *Pza Dante* – and **San Giuliano** in *V. Crociferi.* The **Museo Belliniano**, *V. Crociferi,* contains relics of the composer Bellini. ↪

## CEFALÙ

**Station**: *V. Moro,* 10-min walk from *Corso Ruggero.*
**Tourist Office**: *Corso Ruggero 77, tel (0921) 21 050,* Mon–Fri 0800–1400 and 1630–1930, Sat 0800–1400 (Oct–May); Mon–Sat 0800–2030 (June–Sept); Mon–Sat 0800–2030, Sun 0800–1400 (July–Aug).

### ACCOMMODATION

There is a variety of hotel accommodation here in all categories. **Campsites**: **Costa Ponente**, *tel (0921) 20 085* and, beside it, **San Filippo**, *tel (0921) 21 184* – both about 3km west of town.

### SIGHTSEEING

Cefalù is an attractive little beach resort with plenty of restaurants, walks and views, and a variety of interesting buildings, particularly in *Corso Ruggero.*

Of greatest interest is the **Duomo,** in *Pza Duomo,* a twin-towered, fortified medieval structure that dominates the town from its position just beneath the **Rocca,** the rock which protects it. It contains some of Sicily's best preserved – and earliest (1148) – mosaics. Dating from the time of the Norman kings, these are the work of Byzantine craftsmen. See the Christ Pantocrator in the main apse: it's one of the great works of medieval Sicily.

The **Museo Mandralisca**, *V. Mandralisca 13,* contains, along with a variety of artifacts including some Greek ceramics, an important painting by Antonello da Messina, *Portrait of an Unknown Man* (c1460). Above the town, on the **Rocca** – ascend from *Pza Garibaldi* – a ruined medieval fortification provides magnificent views out over Cefalù and the coast.

## PALERMO

**Station**: **Stazione Centrale**, in *Pza Giulio Cesare,* is at the southern end of the city – *tel (091) 616 1806;* rail information: *1478 88088*

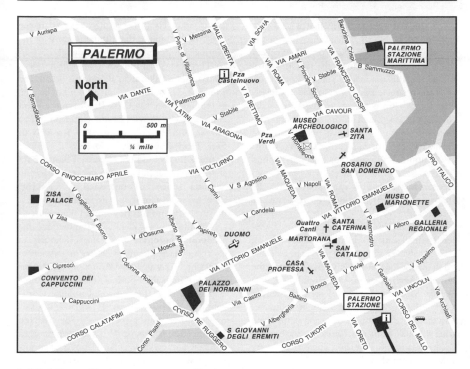

**PALERMO**

North ↑

*(toll-free).* Located in the same square, and in the streets around it, are some of the termini of local, provincial and long-distance bus services. **Stazione Marittima** (*V. Francesco Crispi, tel: (091) 602 1111*) in the east, by the port, is the focus of ferry services from Naples, Cagliari (Sardinia), Genoa, Ustica and occasional hydrofoil connections to the Aeolian Islands. There is an ATM in the station.

**Tourist Information:** handily situated in Stazione Centrale, *tel (091) 616 5914* – Mon–Fri 0800–2000, Sat 0800–1400. The main office is at *Pza Castelnuovo 34, tel (091) 583 847* or *605 8351* – Mon–Fri 0800–2000, Sat 0800–1400. Ask for *Un Mese a Palermo,* the local monthly entertainment guide. Otherwise look at the daily newspaper, *L'Ora,* for listings.

## GETTING AROUND

A good way to get around Palermo is by bus. The **Palermo City Pass** costs L1500 for an hour or L4500 for a day pass. For information, *tel: 167 018 378 (toll-free),* although only broken English is spoken.

## ACCOMMODATION

Cheap accommodation in easy to find, much of it tacky. The mid-range is well catered for. International hotel chains include: *FE, Sn.* Away from the city, at Sferracavallo near the sea, are **Baia del Corallo youth hostel** (*V. Plauto, tel: (091) 530 122)* and two **campsites** – **Camping Trinacria**, *V. Barcarello, tel: (091) 530 590,* and **Camping dell'Ulivo**, *V. Pegaso, tel: (091) 533 021.*

## SIGHTSEEING

Much undervisited, Palermo has an enormous amount to offer. A sea arrival provides its best profile: with huge **Monte Pellegrino** to the north and an arc of mountains behind the city to the west, Palermo faces the sea cradled in what is known as the Conca d'Oro, the Golden Shell. Wartime bombing, severe neglect and a bad criminal record have left their mark on Palermo. And yet it is still incomparable – as Goethe called it. Its ancient core is principally medieval – a labyrinth of narrow alleys and streets, hidden squares and ancient *souk*-like markets. More North African than Italian, the **Vucciria** in *V. Maccheronai,* or the excellent **Ballaro** in *Pza Ballaro* (near the station), signal Palermo's status as a meeting of two continents.

A main street, the *Corso Vittorio Emanuele,* running west from the sea to the Palazzo dei Normanni, was joined in the 17th century by the north–south *V. Maqueda,* which bisected the old city core, opening it up. **Quatro Canti** are an unusual series of four buildings around the corners of the intersection of these two streets. They were built in 1611 to demarcate the Baroque city. Behind this, the medieval city remains to be seen.

Of the ancient Greeks there is little evidence; they settled principally in the east of Sicily. However, their rich legacy can be studied in one of southern Italy's best museums, the **Museo Archeologico Regionale**, at *Pza Olivella.* Most important of all are the panels of relief sculpture from the temples at Selinunte, and there are ceramics, bronzes, statues and other artifacts from the Greeks as well as the Carthaginians and Romans. There is also very little architectural evidence of the Arabic period – although theirs was a very rich era culturally. However, the Normans cleverly assimilated the best of their predecessors' culture – see the hybrid Norman-Arabic style of **San Giovanni degli Eremiti** (*V. dei Benedettini*), **San Cataldo** *(Pza Bellini)*, the **Zisa** palace *(Pza Guglielmo il Buono)*, and the rich interior of the **Cappella Reale**.

The **Cappella Reale** was the private chapel of Norman King Roger II. Deep inside the **Palazzo dei Normanni**, it is lavishly ornamented within and it is chiefly renowned for its mosaics completed by Arab and Byzantine craftsmen (1150). Its ceiling is the finest surviving example of Fatimid architecture anywhere. Other mosaics in the city can be seen in the **Martorana** in *Pza Bellini* – 12th century.

The **Duomo**, in *Corso Vittorio Emanuele*, is another important building in this context, though only the exterior of its main apse has survived in its original form. See the Norman-style blind arcading richly ornamented, as if built by Arab stonemasons. The interior is less interesting; it was altered in the 18th century

and is rather bland. Of greatest interest are the royal tombs, among them those of some of the Norman kings and Emperor Frederick II.

The other great milestone of Sicilian style is the Baroque: Palermitan Baroque is ornate and ebullient. The richest examples of it can be seen in the interior of the **Casa Professa**, the Jesuit church in *V. Ponticello*, **Santa Caterina** in *Pza Pretoria*, and the little oratories of **Rosario di San Domenico** at *V. Bambinai 2*, and of **Santa Zita**, behind the church of **Santa Zita** at *V. Valverde 3*. In both, the *stuccatore* Giacomo Serpotta (1656–1732) unleashed the full throttle of his exuberant style. His remarkably realistic stucco figures run riot around the walls.

Of the city's galleries and museums, the **Galleria Regionale** at *V. Alloro 4* houses an excellent medieval art collection in addition to works by Caravaggio and Antonello da Messina and a remarkable portrait bust of Eleanora d'Aragona by Francesco Laurana (15th-century). **Palazzo Mirto**, *V. Merlo 2,* is a former private palace-museum. The **Museo Etnografico Pitre**, at *V. Duca degli Abruzzi,* contains a remarkable collection of Sicilian folk items, while **Museo delle Marionette**, *V. Butera 1,* houses a collection of traditional Sicilian puppets. More gruesomely, the catacombs in **Convento dei Cappuccini**, *V. Pitre,* house 8000 former citizens at whose corpses, fully clothed in period dress, you can gaze.

Further afield, behind Monte Pellegrino, is **Mondello** (about 10 km), Palermo's beach resort, while **Monreale** (about 8 km to the south-west), is the focus of a splendid medieval cathedral containing a great series of Byzantine-style mosaics. At **Segesta** (about 65 km), to the north west, a near-complete Greek temple survives, while at **Bagheria** (about 14km), in the south-east, the quirky Baroque **Villa Palagonia** is an oddity in an area once renowned for the holiday homes of the 17th- and 18th-century nobility. All of these are accessible by bus.

From Palermo one ferry per week runs to the port of **Cagliari** (see Palermo–Marseille chapter, pp.391–399), capital of the island of **Sardinia**. From Palermo, ferries run regularly to the Aeolian Islands.

# NICE

Nice has been Queen of the Riviera ever since Russian princes and British royalty began to grace its opulent hotels in the middle of the last century. Today it is as vibrant as ever, attracting 3 million visitors a year. But it is also a large city with a thriving life of its own.

## TOURIST INFORMATION

Tourist offices can be found at *av. Thiers, 06000 Nice* (on the left just outside the station); *tel: 04 93 87 07 07, fax: 04 93 16 85 16*, 0800–1900 in winter, 0730–2000 in summer; at *5 Promenade des Anglais; tel: 04 92 14 48 00, fax: 04 92 14 48 03*, Mon–Sat 0800–2000, Sun 0900–1800 (July–Aug); Mon–Sat 0900–1800 (Sept–June); at the airport, Terminal 1; *tel: 04 93 21 44 11, fax: 04 93 21 44 50*, Mon–Sun 0800–2200; at *Ferber*, near the airport; *tel 04 93 83 32 64, fax: 04 93 72 08 27*, Mon–Sat 0800–2000, Sun 0900–1800 (summer); Mon–Sat 0800–1900 (winter). Free hotel reservations.

## ARRIVING AND DEPARTING

### Airport

**Nice Côte d'Azur**: *Promenade des Anglais*, 7 km west of the city. Information: *tel: 04 93 21 30 12, fax: 04 93 21 31 81*. Terminal 1 handles international flights, Air Littoral and TAT; Terminal 2 handles domestic flights. Taxis to the centre cost about FFr.150, but airport buses run along *Promenade des Anglais* to the Gare Routière (bus station) every 20 mins, and the 20-min journey costs only FFr.21. Bus no. 23 to the rail station (marked 'Gare SNCF') takes 20 mins and costs FFr.20.

### Station

**Nice-Ville**, *av. Thiers; tel: 04 36 35 35 35*. Information office open Mon–Sat 0830–1830, Sun 0830–1115, 1400–1700. Frequent services to all resorts along the Cote d'Azur. Station

closed 0130–0530. Left luggage 0630–2330; baths and showers 0800–1900 in the basement. For the town centre, turn left from station to *av. Jean Médecin*, the main thoroughfare, right down to *pl. Masséna* (300m), right again to the sea, a 15-min walk. Bus to the airport from outside the station, every 30 mins (FFr.20).

### Buses

**Gare Routière** (bus station): *promenade du Paillon; tel: 04 93 85 61 81*. At *pl. Masséna* head north 300m up *blvd Jean Jaurès*.

### Ferries

**SNCM**, *quai du Commerce* (on the east side of the port); *tel: 04 93 13 66 99*. Regular crossings to Corsica (from FFr. 229 one way, students from FFr.181).

## GETTING AROUND

Nice is a big sprawling city. Broad avenues stretch back from the sea, which is lined by the 5 km *Promenade des Anglais* and shorter *quai des États-Unis*. The Old Town quarter is manageable on foot, but to get between the various museums and sights requires transport. Bus services are good. Most **bus** services radiate from *pl. Masséna*. Buy tickets on the bus; FFr.8. A carnet of 5 tickets costs FFr.32.50, and one-, five- and seven-day passes are available. Information: *10 r. Félix Faure; tel: 04 93 16 52 10*.

Renting a car or motor bike is a popular option, but the traffic is hectic and parking difficult. Rent motorbikes from **Nicea**, *9 av. Thiers*, near the station; *tel: 04 93 82 42 71*.

**Taxis** are expensive; expect to pay FFr.50 for even the shortest trip *(tel: 04 93 13 78 78)*.

## STAYING IN NICE

### Accommodation

As Nice is one of Europe's most popular destinations, a wide range of accommodation is on offer. Hotel chains include *Ca, Ho, Ib, Md, Mc, Nv* and *Sf*. One of the best-placed medium-price hotels is the **Mercure**, *2 r.Halévy* (on the corner of *Promenade des Anglais*, near *pl. Masséna; tel: 04 93 82 30 88, fax: 04 93 82 18 20*). One of the world's most prestigious hotels is the **Negresco**, *37 Promenade des Anglais; tel: 04 93 16 64 00, fax: 04 93 88 35 68*, a white and pink palace built for a former Romanian gypsy violinist, Henri Negresc by the architect of the Moulin Rouge and Folies Bergères in Paris. If you cannot afford a room (around FFr.2050 per night), at least see the Salon Royal, adorned with a Baccarat chandelier made for a Tsar.

For the budget conscious, good-value accommodation is available near the station – *r. de Suisse, av. Durante, r.d'Alsace-Lorraine* – and in Old Nice, around *pl. St François*. Nice has three **youth hostels**, all far from the centre. **Mt-Alban**: *rte de Mont-Alban; tel: 04 93 89 23 64*, 4 km out of town, uphill! (Bus no. 5 from the station to *blvd Jean Jaurès*, then no. 14 to hostel.) No reservations; open from 1000. Good view over the city. **Clairvallon Youth Hostel**: *av. Scudéri; tel: 93 81 27 63*, is up in **Cimiez**, north of the centre (bus nos 15 or 22, stop at *Scudéri*). Located in a park with a pool. **Les Collinettes**, *3 av Robert Schuman; tel: 04 93 89 23 64, fax: 04 92 04 03 10*, is open July–Aug only. The nearest **campsites** are at **Cagnes-sur-Mer** to the west, 15 mins by train. Sleeping on the beach is not allowed. Those who try can expect a hosing down in the early hours.

## Eating and Drinking

A culinary paradise, Nice is influenced by its neighbour, Italy, and the Mediterranean. The city has many specialities. *Pissaladière* is a Niçois onion tart, garnished with anchovies and olives; *socca,* a traditional lunchtime snack of flat bread made from crushed chick peas, served piping hot; and of course *salade niçoise* – the genuine article contains hard-boiled eggs, tomatoes, anchovies, cucumber, spring onions, broad beans and artichoke. *Pan bagnat* is a large bun stuffed with salad niçoise and doused in olive oil.

**Vieux Nice** (the old town) best for eating – particularly *cours Saleya,* which is covered with open-air tables in summer, *r. Ste Répararte* and the other narrow side-streets around the cathedral. North of the old town, *pl. Garibaldi* boasts the best shellfish, notably at the inexpensive **Café de Turin**, and good *socca*. **Caffè Puccini**, *Place Rossetti; tel: 04 93 13 92 73*, is cheap with a great view and atmosphere. Moderate **Le Quai**, *13 cours Saleya; tel: 04 93 92 45 95*, offers traditional cuisine. **Le Chantecler**, *Hôtel Négresco; tel: 04 93 16 64 00*, has two Michelin stars and is very expensive. The *Zone Piétonne*, around *Jean Médecin*, is good for pizzas.

## Communications

**Post Office**: *23 av. Thiers; tel: 04 93 82 65 00*. It has poste restante, money transfer and fax. Open 0800–1900, 0800–1200 Sat.

## Money

There are **Thomas Cook bureaux de change** next to and opposite the station: *12 av. Thiers, tel: 04 93 82 13 00*; and *13 av. Thiers, tel 04 93 88 59 99*. There is another at *2 pl. Magenta, tel: 04 93 88 49 88*.

Nice is the cultural and social capital of the South of France, offering a choice of opera, concerts and plays. **FNAC** (Fédération Nationale d'Achats des Cadres) in the **Nice Etoile** shopping mall, *av. Jean Médecin*, supplies tickets; *tel: 04 93 92 09 09*.

**Nice Opéra**, *4 r. St-François-de-Paule; tel: 04 92 17 40 40*, is one of the best in France, staging opera and concerts. Chamber and sacred music concerts are staged at **Cathédrale Ste-Réparate**, *pl. Rossetti*. **CEDAC de Cimiez**, *49 av. de la Marne; tel: 04 93 53 85 95*, is a major jazz venue. In summer, **Théâtre de Verdure**, *Jardin Albert I; tel: 04 93 82 38 68*, stages rock, jazz and other concerts in a marquee. **Théâtre de Nice**, *Promenade des Arts; tel: 04 93 80 52 60*, in the huge Acropolis, part of the Palais des Congrès, stages opera, ballet and concerts. **Théâtre de l'Alphabet**, *10 blvd Carabacel; tel: 04 93 13 08 88*, features more classical drama.

In summer, Nice grinds on long after midnight, thanks to its many piano bars and nightclubs, though the younger generation gravitate to the beach. Gamblers head for **Casino Ruhl**, *1 Promenade des Anglais; tel: 04 93 87 95 87*. For many it is entertainment enough simply to stroll along the *Promenade des*

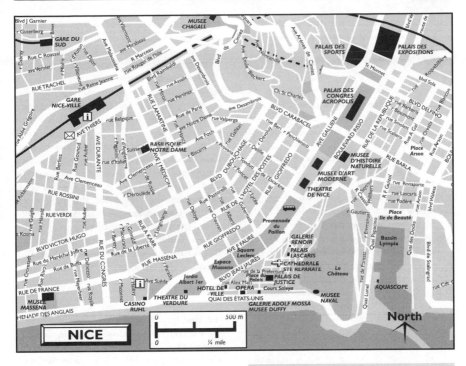

NICE

0    500 m

0    ¼ mile

North

*Anglais* or sit on the *cours Saleya* and watch the world go by.

## Events

In Feb the **Nice Carnival** and **Battles of the Flowers** involve parades throughout the day and night with a firework display and the burning of the Carnival King. In July, international stars perform in the **Nice Jazz Festival** in the Roman amphitheatre and gardens at Cimiez (tickets from FNAC and Tourist Offices).

## SHOPPING

The old town is one of the the best places to shop, for art, cheap clothes and glorious food at the outdoor markets and little shops. In *cours Saleya,* the food and flower market (0600–1730 except Sun afternoon and Mon) is replaced by a flea market on Mon (0800–1700). Craft stalls arrive on summer evenings.

For clothes and gift shops, head for the pedestrian area behind *pl.Masséna*. The **Galeries Lafayette** store and **Nice Etoile** shopping mall are in *av. Jean Médecin*.

## SIGHTSEEING

A **Tourist Train** visits the flower market, old town and castle hill during summer, from 1000–1900, in a tour lasting 40 mins. There are also guided tours of the Vieux Nice area from *5 Promenade des Anglais;* tours run Sat morning from 0900 July–Aug, and last 2½ hrs.

**Vieux Nice** seems more Italian than French (which it was until 1860). Wander the narrow streets to **Palais Lascaris**, *15 r. Droite; tel: 04 93 62 05 54,* a 17th-century palace/museum (1000–1200, 1400–1800, closed Mon and Nov). Beyond, steps lead up to the château – though little remains of it – and a colourful park, small naval museum and breathtaking views.

At the far west end of the *Promenade,* Nice's newest attractions are the tropical conservatories of the **Parc Floral Phoenix**, *405 promenade des Anglais; tel: 04 93 18 03 33.*

A museum pass costing FF120, with concessions FF60, allows 15 visits to any municipal museums. Nice boasts some of the best museums in France – and many are free. Most are easily accessible by local bus. Best of the bunch is the newly refurbished **Musée Matisse**; *164 av. des Arènes de Cimiez; tel: 04 93 81 08 08*, in a 17th-century villa amongst the Roman ruins of Cimiez – Matisse's personal collection of paintings in a beautiful setting (bus nos 15, 17, 20, 22 from *pl. Masséna*; open daily 1000–1800 Apr–Sept; daily except Tues 1000–1700 Oct–Mar). Next door **Musée Archéologique**, *160 av. des Arènes de Cimiez; tel: 04 93 81 59 57*, exhibits the copious finds dug up while excavating the Roman arenas at Cimiez (bus nos 15/17/20/22 to *Arènes*; 1000–1200, 1400–1800 (1700 in winter), closed Mon). Matisse and fellow artist Raoul Dufy are buried in the neighbouring **Couvent des Frères Mineurs**, which offers a fine view across Nice to the sea.

Also in Cimiez, the **Musée Marc Chagall**, *av. du Dr. Ménard; tel: 04 93 53 87 20*, is a graceful temple to Chagall's genius – beautifully lit to display his huge biblical canvases (bus no. 15, open 1000–1800 July–Aug; 1000–1700, Sept–June, closed Tues).

In the centre of town, the **Musée d'Art Moderne et d'Art Contemporain**; *Promenade des Arts; tel: 04 93 62 61 62*, is unmistakable: a white marble cliff rising above the street, and filled with striking pop art. Open 1100–1800, 1100–2200 Fri, closed Tues. The **Musée d'Art et d'Histoire** in *Palais Masséna, 65 r. de France, tel: 04 93 88 11 34*, is in a splendid old Italianate villa adorned with antiques and decorated with paintings by Renoir and local artists. Open 1000–1200, 1400–1800 summer, closed Mon. East of the port, **Musée Terra Amata**, *25 blvd Carnot; tel: 04 93 55 59 93*, has displays of the prehistoric inhabitants of Nice from 400,000 years ago (bus nos 1, 2, 7, 9, 10, 20; open 1000–1200, 1400–1800, closed Mon).

### Churches

In Vieux Nice, **Cathédrale de Ste-Réparate**; *pl. Rossetti*, is a dimly lit but impressive Catholic masterpiece built with Italian money in the 17th century. To the west of the station, the **Cathédrale Orthodoxe Russe St-Nicolas**, *17 blvd du Tzarévitch*, is a mighty five-domed Russian Orthodox church built on the site of a villa where the young Tsarevich Nicholas died. It was completed just five years before the Russian

Revolution with imperial roubles and remains to this day a symbol of the aristocratic opulence that characterises the Riviera (open 0900–1200, 1430–1800 summer, closed Sun morning).

The **beaches** of Nice are pebbly – there is no sand to the east of Antibes as far as the Italian border. This does not deter sun-worshippers from crowding onto the Baie des Anges beaches below the *Promenade des Anglais* all summer long. Whilst private beach clubs cover some of the central section, charging around FFr.90 for a day's hire of lounger and umbrella, most of the long beach is free. For less hectic sun-worshipping, seek out the long beach between **Cagnes-sur-Mer** and **Antibes** to the west. However, the prettiest beaches are to the east, at **Villefranche** (young, lively crowd), **Beaulieu** (old, sedate crowd) and **St-Jean Cap Ferrat** (well-heeled, laid-back crowd).

### OUT OF TOWN

Renoir spent the last years of his life in **Cagnes sur Mer**, buying an isolated house overlooking the sea. Today this is **Musée Renoir**, *chemin les Colettes; tel: 04 93 20 61 07* (1000–1200, 1400–1700, closed Tues; FFr.20), a tour of the artist's life, with rooms as he kept them 80 years ago (from the rail station, take the bus to *Beal-Les Colettes*). Above the town, its medieval citadel is now a museum; **Montée de la Bourgade**; *Haut-de-Cagnes, entrance Pl. Grimaldi; tel: 04 93 20 85 57*, open 1000–1200 and 1430–1700 (summer until 1800), closed Tues; FFr.20.

There are hourly buses from Nice to **St Paul-de-Vence**, one of the coast's most picturesque *villages perchés*. One of the most interesting modern art museums in France is here, the **Fondation Maeght**, built by the Maeght family, who were friends of Matisse; *tel: 04 93 32 81 63*, open 1000–1230, 1430–1800 winter, 1000–1900 July, Aug; FFr.25. The garden is a quirky sculpture park, designed by Miró.

**Vence**, 3 km further up the valley, is another delightful little town. Here Matisse was nursed by local nuns and repaid them by designing a simple yet breathtakingly beautiful chapel – **La Chapelle du Rosaire**, *av. Henri Matisse; tel 04 93 58 03 26*; open Tues and Thur, 1000–1130, 1430–1700. Matisse considered it his masterpiece.

# NICE–GENOA

This route takes you through both the French and the Italian Rivieras, via Monaco, ending up in the comparatively charmless Genoa. Each town on the way has a peculiar atmosphere conducive to relaxation. As you travel along, prices gradually fall, but come prepared to pay for the luxury of doing nothing to a point of exhaustion as you ponder the mansion-dotted cliffs plunging into the sea.

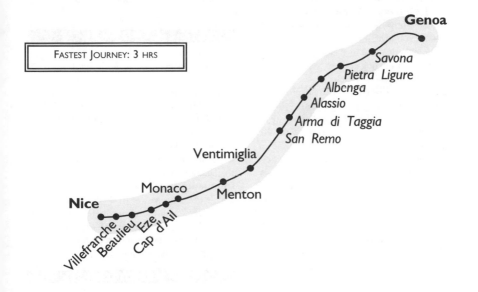

FASTEST JOURNEY: 3 HRS

Genoa

Savona
Pietra Ligure
Albenga
Alassio
Arma di Taggia
San Remo

Ventimiglia

Monaco    Menton
Nice
Villefranche
Beaulieu
Cap d'Ail
Eze

371

## TRAINS

**ETT tables:** 90, 360, 580.

### FAST TRACK

➡ Only four through trains (taking 3–4 hrs) run between Nice and Genoa, but by changing at Ventimiglia you can get a reasonable service throughout the day consisting of two day trains (with supplement) and two

overnight bound for Rome and Venice. One day train has an observation car in first class.

### ON TRACK

➡ **Nice–Villefranche–Beaulieu– Eze–Cap d'Ail–Monaco–Menton– Ventimiglia**

A frequent service operates along the coast linking all of the towns. Nice to Villefranche takes

8 mins, Villefranche to Beaulieu 4 mins, Beaulieu to Eze 3 mins, Eze to Cap d'Ail 4 mins, Cap d'Ail to Monaco 3 mins, Monaco to Menton 12 mins and Menton to Ventimiglia 13 mins.

### Ventimiglia–Genoa

Five InterCity trains supplement the roughly hourly ordinary service along the coast. The InterCity trains have buffets and take around 2 hrs. The ordinary trains call at many more stations and take 2 hrs 30 mins.

## VILLEFRANCHE-SUR-MER

**Station:** north of the centre.
**Tourist Office:** *Jardins François Binon; tel: 04 93 01 73 68; fax: 04 93 76 63 65.* Open daily 0830–2000 (July–Sept); Mon–Sat 0830–1200 and 1400–1900 (Oct–June).

Villefranche has one of the deepest ports on the coast, so it's a major stop for cruise ships and also has the liveliest beach in the region. **Chapelle de St-Pierre**, at the town end of the quay, was decorated by Jean Cocteau.

From Villefranche beach you can walk up to **St-Jean Cap-Ferrat**, a peninsula with the prettiest beaches in the region – and some of the world's most expensive properties: Elizabeth Taylor, Joan Collins and Mick Jagger are among those reputed to have second homes here. The port is lined with restaurants, tranquil even in high season and surprisingly inexpensive. If you make it to St-Jean Cap-Ferrat, don't miss the **Villa Rothschild**. Once owned by Beatrice de Rothschild, the house is a visual delight, but the gardens are stunning – an eclectic masterpiece of exotic plants, with views down to Villefranche and Beaulieu. Open 1000–1900 summer, 1400–1800 winter, 1000–1800 weekends; *tel: 93 01 33 90.*

## BEAULIEU-SUR-MER

**Station:** north of the centre.
**Tourist Office:** *pl. G-Clémenceau; tel: 04 93 01 02 21; fax: 04 93 01 44 04.* Open Mon–Sat 0900–1230 and 1400–1900, Sun 0900–1230 (July–Aug); Mon–Sat 0900–1215 and 1430–1800 (Sept–June).

'Beautiful place' (the name was bestowed by Napoleon) is a tranquil spot with a mild climate that is full of affluent retired people. Don't miss the **Villa Kérylos** – built by an archaeologist at the turn of the century, this is a faithful replication of a 5th-century BC Athenian home, complete with furnishings.

## EZE

**Station:** In Eze-sur-Mer.
**Tourist Office:** *pl. du Gal-de-Gaulle, Eze-sur-Mer; tel: 04 93 41 26 00.* Open 0900–1900 (summer); 0900–1800 (winter).

The village of Eze (as opposed to the sea-level Eze-sur-Mer) is a stiff climb, rewarded by arguably the best views on the Riviera and **botanical gardens** – but it is crammed with the less-desirable trimmings of such tourist-traps.

## CAP D'AIL

**Station:** central.
**Tourist Office:** *104 av. du 3-Septembre; tel: 04 93 78 02 33, fax: 04 92 10 74 36.* Open Mon–Fri 0915–1200 and 1430–1900, Sat–Sun 0900–1700 (July–Aug); Mon–Fri 0915–1200 and 1430–1900, Sat 0915–1645 (Sept–June).

Cap d'Ail ('peninsula of garlic') offers shingly beaches that provide excellent swimming. It's unsurprisingly lively, as it has one of the coast's best youth hostels: the **Relais International de Jeunesse**, *blvd de la Mer; tel: 93 78 18 58,* has a lovely location and an extremely friendly atmosphere among the guests, but the management is somewhat draconian. It features single-sex dormitoies, and a midnight curfew for girls.

## MONACO

**Station:** *tel: 04 36 35 35 35* or *(377) 93 10 60 15*: head straight down past *pl. d'Armes* to the port (with the palace off to the right), then turn left for the Tourist Office and casino (500m) – or take bus no. 4.
**Tourist Office:** *2A blvd des Moulins; tel: (377) 92 16 61 66, fax: (377) 92 16 60 00,* open Mon–Sat 0900–1900, Sun 1000–1200 (all year). The exceptionally helpful Tourist Office in London *(3–18 Chelsea Garden Market; tel (0171) 352 9962, fax: (0171) 352 2103)* provides free leaflets that cover absolutely everything, including a map showing the (free) lifts

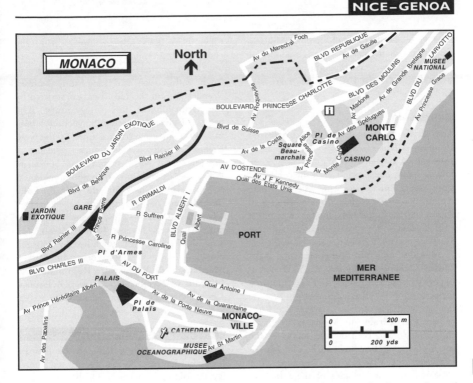

and escalators between different levels of the very hilly principality.

## ACCOMMODATION AND FOOD

Budget accommodation is scarce, *r. de la Turbie* (near the station) being the best place to look for it – otherwise, make Nice your base. The **Hôtel de Paris**, *pl. du Casino; tel: (377) 92 16 30 00,* is the hang-out of celebrities; the last word in luxury and old-style elegance. Just round the corner, on *sq. Beaumarchais,* is its belle époque rival, **Hôtel Hermitage**, *tel: (377) 92 16 40 00* – it's worth wandering through the public rooms just to look at the décor. **Hôtel de France**, *6 r.de la Turbie; tel: (377) 93 30 24 64,* is a 2-star establishment that is relatively cheap.

The **Centre de la Jeunesse Princesse-Stéphanie**, *24 av. Prince-Pierre; tel: (377) 93 50 83 20* (100 m from the station) is a godsend for 16–31 year olds – but register by 0900 or you won't get a bed.

Monaco's restaurants range from the most luxurious in Europe to simple Italian eateries. If you win big at the casino, head across the road to **Restaurant Louis XV**, in the **Hôtel de Paris**. Here, one of the world's top chefs (Alain Ducasse) masterminds menus fit for princesses. Eating with the famous is not exclusively the preserve of the wealthy, however. At **Le Texan**, *4 r. Suffren Reymond,* a Tex-Mex with the cheapest beers in the principality and good food, you could easily be brushing shoulders with Boris Becker or royalty.

## ENTERTAINMENT

Monaco is synonymous with gambling and there are several casinos, but you must be over 21 (they check). Granddaddy of them all is the most famous casino in the world, the **Casino de Paris**, *pl. du Casino,* which is worth a look for the interior gilt alone. You can play the slot machines at the entrance, but to get any further costs FFr.50, just for the pleasure of walking into the hallowed gaming rooms – and smart dress is required. The adjoining **Café de Paris** has no entrance fee, but it's definitely less classy.

The **Monte-Carlo Rally** (Jan) includes

exciting stages in the hills behind Monaco, while the second week in May is a good time to avoid the town unless you are interested in watching the **Grand Prix** – which takes over the city streets.

## SIGHTSEEING

The **Musée National des Automates et Poupées d'Autrefois** (National Museum of Automatons and Dolls of Yesteryear), *17 av. Princesse Grace,* contains just what the name suggests. In summer you can visit the State Apartments in the **Palais du Prince** (Royal Palace) and watch the changing of the guard (at 1155 precisely). There's a delightful **Japanese Garden**, *av. Princesse Grace,* just next to the sea.

Monaco's most stimulating attraction is the **Musée Océanographique**, *av. St-Martin.* In the basement is one of the world's great **aquariums**, developed by Jacques Cousteau. Wander the narrow streets of the old town. The 19th-century **Cathédrale de Monaco**, *4 r. Col-Bellando-de-Castro,* contains the tombs of the royals, including Princess Grace. The **Musée Historial des Princes de Monaco**, *27 r. Basse,* offers waxen effigies of the Grimaldis from the 13th-century to today.

Above the skyscrapers, Monaco's botanical garden, **Jardin Exotique**, offers a vast range of cacti and succulents. The ticket covers nearby **limestone caves**, where the formations are floodlit, and an adjacent **museum of prehistoric anthropology**.

## OUT OF TOWN

**La Turbie** is accessible by bus (six times a day, but doesn't run Sun) – or a steep bicycle ride. The culminating point of the Roman road *Via Aurelia,* La Turbie is renowned for the huge 6th-century BC **Trophée des Alpes** – the only other Roman monument of its kind is in Romania. There's a breathtaking view from the terrace.

## MENTON

**Station:** west of the centre. For the sea (about 300m), head down *av. Edouard VII.*
**Tourist Office:** *Palais de l'Europe, 8 av. Boyer; tel: 04 93 57 57 00, fax: 04 93 57 51 00* (left from the station for about 100m, then right).

Open 0830–1830 (July–mid Sept); 0830–1230 and 1330–1830 (mid Sept–June).

Almost in Italy, Menton is a retirement town with charm and long stony beaches. Wander around the old town, constructed by the Grimaldis in the 15th-century. The baroque **Église St-Michel** (St Michael's), built in 1640, is an attractive structure. To the west, **Palais Carnolès** was the summer residence of the princes of Monaco and now houses an interesting art collection (mainly impressionists and modern). In the **Hôtel de Ville**, the **Salle des Mariages** was lavishly decorated by Jean Cocteau and can be visited when weddings are not in progress. **Musée Jean-Cocteau**, *111 quai Napoléon-III,* was established by him and contains many of his works. In **Musée Municipale de Préhistoire Régionale** (City Museum of Regional Prehistory), *r. Lorédan-Larchey,* there are human remains some 80,000 years old.

## VENTIMIGLIA

**Ventimiglia**, which is right on the French/Italian border, has a Roman theatre and a noteworthy old town, parts of which date back to the 12th century. There is also an excellent beach here.

### ⤵ SIDE TRACKS FROM VENTIMIGLIA

The beaches along the **Riviera di Ponente** (the coastal strip from Ventimiglia to Genoa) attract many visitors, but the locals remain more interested in their thriving olive oil industry.

A little further on from Ventimiglia, you come to **San Remo**, the largest resort on the Italian Riviera, stretched out around an 8 km bay. The old town, with its narrow streets, steep steps and arches, and bits of the new town (such as the palm-lined *Corso dell' Imperatrice)* will be of interest. A short bus ride away is the small coastal resort of **Arma di Taggia**. Further along the coast, there are several other popular resorts, including **Alanio**, famed for its splendid gardens and a main street dating back to the 16th century and **Albenga** and **Pietra Ligure**, both smaller towns with fine, old centres. **Savona**, best known for a fine cathedral and its ship-breaking industry, marks the end of the best beaches as you head towards the industrial outer reaches of Genoa. 🛏️

## GENOA (GENOVA)

**Stations**: **Stazione Principe**, *tel: (10) 284 081,* handles trains to the west. Take bus no. 40 from here to get to the city centre. **Stazione Brignole**, *tel: (10) 274 30 48,* is further east and handles trains to the south and east, take bus no. 41 from here to get to the city centre. Trains to the north use both stations; use bus no. 37 to transfer between them.

**Tourist Offices**: **City centre**: *Porto Antico-Palazzina S. Maria; tel: (10) 24 871, fax: (10) 246 76 58,* open daily 0800–1830. There are also offices at *Stazione FS Principe-Piazza Acquaverde; tel: (10) 246 26 33,* open 0800–2000, at *Aeropuerto C. Colombo-Sestri Ponente; tel: (10) 601 52 47,* and at *Stazione Marittima-Terminal Goclere; tel: (10) 246 36 85* (Apr–Sept only).

### GETTING AROUND

The old part of town centres on the docks and is easily explored on foot (during the day; it's not safe at night). Elsewhere, there's a good bus service and automatic kiosks sell tourist tickets providing unlimited travel for one day (price L. 5000). There is also a funicular from *Pza del Portello* to *Sant'Anna,* high on the hill on which the town is built. There's a great view from the top and the journey is worthwhile in itself.

### ACCOMMODATION AND FOOD

Cheap accommodation is easy to find, but some of it is very tacky. Try the roads on the outskirts of the old town and (near Brignole) *V. XX Settembre* and *Pza Colombo.* There is one **Youth Hostel** *V. Costanzi; tel: (10) 242 24 57* (bus no. 40 from Brignole). The cheapest eating places for lunch are in the dock area, but most close in the evening. Street stalls all over the city sell fried seafood and chickpea pancakes.

### SIGHTSEEING

Genoa, *La Superba,* was once, like Venice, a proud maritime republic ruled by a Doge or elected ruler. Today the city's grandeur has faded, but there is an interesting old town, with a maze of tiny alleys and many old palaces and mansions. It is centred on the port, to the south and south-west of the modern city.

The **Palazzo Ducale**, *Pza Matteotti,* was once the seat of the Doge. Across the street is the church of the **Gesù**, which contains two Rubens and a Guido Reni. The nearby **Cattedrale di San Lorenzo** has some unusual artefacts: the reliquary of John the Baptist on which his severed head is reputed to have rested and a dish said to have been used at the Last Supper.

The **Museo d'Arte Orientale** is housed in the Villetta di Negro, off *Pza Corvetto.* The mosaic spire of **Sant'Agostino** points to the **Museo dell'Architettura e Scultura Ligure**, built around the cloister of a 13th-century monastery and containing ancient maps of Genoa, as well as wood-carvings and many artefacts from different periods, as far back as Roman times.

**Piazza Caricamento** is on the waterfront, and always a hive of activity with market stalls and many cafés. On one side is the **Palazzo San Giorgio**, which has housed various government departments for several centuries and has two rooms that are open to the public. **Piazza Banchi** was the heart of the old city and is now the commercial centre. From it, *V. San Luca* leads to the **Galleria Nazionale di Palazzo Spinola**, *Pza Superiore di Pellicceria 1,* which displays some excellent paintings.

To the north is *V. Garibaldi,* home to several Renaissance palaces. Two of these, **Palazzo Bianco** (no. 11) and **Palazzo Rosso** (no. 18) are now galleries with excellent collections, including Flemish and Dutch masterpieces. Both palaces are worth a visit to see the incredible décor.

If you fancy a swim, the suburb of **Albaro** (take bus no. 41 from *Principe)* has a beach with showers and other washing facilities.

Genoa's **Aquarium**, *Porto Antico,* is the largest in Europe and truly mesmerising – the harbour seals are absolutely the definition of adorable. **Nervi**, a few stops from Brignole station, has a beautiful promenade on a dramatic coast.

# OSLO

The Viking capital, hemmed in by water, mountains and trees, became a province of Denmark in the 15th century and, during reconstruction after a terrible fire in 1624, was renamed Christiania after the Danish King, regaining the name Oslo only in 1925. Today it is laid-back and sprawling, with many attractions spread over islands in Oslofjord. Allow a day for the water-oriented museums at Bygdøy, as well as a couple to enjoy the city.

## TOURIST INFORMATION

**Main Tourist Office:** *Vestbaneplassen 1 (west of Rådhus, near the harbour); tel: 22 83 00 50.* Open Mon–Fri 0900–1600 (Dec–Jan); Mon–Sat 0900–1600 (Feb–Apr, Oct–Nov); Mon–Sat 0900–1800 (May, Sept); Mon–Sat 0900–1800, Sun 0900–1800 (June); daily 0900–2000 (July–Aug). Get *The Official Guide for Oslo, What's On* and a map, all free. A small information office in **Oslo S** station opens daily 0800–2000 in winter.

If money is tight, consult **USE IT**, *Møllergt 3; tel: 22 41 51 32,* open mid June–mid Aug. Hikers should visit **DNT**, *Storgate 3; tel: 22 82 28 00,* open Mon–Fri 1000–1600 (Thur 1000–1800), Sat 1000–1400. The widely available **Oslo Card**, valid for 24 hours (NKr.130), 48 hours (NKr.200) or 72 hours (NKr.240), provides free city transport, free admission to most attractions and various discounts. The **Oslo Package** provides hotel room and breakfast and the **Oslo Card** at NKr.350 per person in a double room – free for children under 16 in their parents room. Excellent value, it's valid mid June–mid Aug and weekends year-round.

## ARRIVING AND DEPARTING

### Airport
The main airport is **Oslo Fornebu** (7 km west,

20 mins by bus). **Flybussen** (**SAS** airport buses; NKr.40) pick up from Oslo S every 10–15 mins 0600–2145 (less frequently from other points). Another option is half-hourly bus no. 31 (NKr.20). A taxi to the centre costs around NKr.120.

A new airport will open in Oct 1998 at *Gardermoen,* 50 km north. There will be a direct train from Oslo S every 10 mins, taking 20 mins. There will still be buses as now, likely to be cheaper than the train.

### Stations
The main rail station is the very central **Oslo Sentralstasjon** (known as **Oslo S** and open daily 0430–0130), *tel: 22 36 80 00 (22 36 81 11* for international enquiries). All long-distance trains stop here, as well as some local services. It's crammed with facilities of every kind. The long-distance ticket office opens daily 0630–2300. The T-bane (metro) is to the right as you leave the station. **Nasjonalteatret** station, also in the centre, handles a few long-distance trains, but is mainly for suburban services.

### Ferries
There are daily sailings by **Color Line** (*tel: 22 94 44 70*) to **Kiel** (Germany) and **Hirtshals** (Denmark – six per week in winter), **DFDS Scandinavian Seaways** (*tel: 22 41 90 90*) to **Copenhagen** (Denmark) and **Stena Line** (*tel: 22 33 50 00*) to **Fredrikshavn** (Denmark – less frequent in winter).

### Buses
Long-distance buses use **Bussterminalen**, *Schweigaardsgt 10; tel: 22 17 01 66,* which is linked to Oslo S by overhead walkway.

## GETTING AROUND
The centre's small and it's easy to reach outlying attractions on the excellent public transport.

**Trafikanten** (the tower-like construction outside Oslo S), *Jernbanetorget; tel: 22 17 70 30,* Mon–Fri 0700–2000, Sat–Sun 0800–1800. It handles transport queries, timetables and tickets. Get the (free) public transport map, *Sporveiskart for Oslo*. Single tickets, valid for 1 hr, cost NKr.18. Multi-ride tickets include day-cards *(Dagskort;* ·NKr.40) and 7-day cards *(Syv-Dagerskort;* NKr. 130).

**T-lines (Metro)** converge at *Stortinget.* There are maps on the platforms and trains have a destination board. Most **trams** converge at Oslo S and most city buses at Oslo M (on *Vaterland,* by Oslo S). Most westbound **buses** (including those to Bygdøy and Vigelandsparken) stop at the south side of Nasjonalteatret.

**Ferries** to **Bygdøy** leave (Apr–Sept) from *Rådhusbrygge 3,* near the Tourist Office, as do sightseeing boats. Ferries to **Hovedøya, Langøyene** and other islands in Oslofjord, leave from *Vippetangen* (bus no. 29). **Taxis;** *tel: 22 38 80 90,* or use the strategically positioned ranks.

### STAYING IN OSLO

### Accommodation

The Tourist Office at Oslo S supplies a list of pensions and will book accommodation, including rooms in private houses (fee NKr.20 per person).

Chains include *BW, Ch, FE, GT, Re, SA, Sc* and *Tp.* **Scandic KNA Oslo**, *Parkveien 68; tel: 22 44 69 70,* is new, comfortable and handy for the Stranden waterfront and all major sights. **Grand Hotel**, *Karl Johansgt 31; tel: 22 42 93 90,* was built in the 1870s and is hard to beat for period character. **Hotel Continental**, *Stortingsgt 24–26; tel: 22 41 90 60,* is also popular with people who can afford to choose. **City Hotel**, *Skippergt 19; tel: 22 41 36 10,* is more reasonably priced and central (two blocks from Oslo S), with comfortable old-style furniture and décor. **Norrøna Hotell and Kafe A/S**, *Grensen 19; tel: 22 42 64 00,* is mission-run: good facilities at below-average prices.

The more central of the two **HI hostels**, **Haraldsheim**, *Haraldsheimvn 4, Grensen; tel: 22 22 29 65,* is 5 km from Oslo S: tram nos 10/11 to *Sinsenkrysset Kjelsås,* or no. 17 to *Sinsen.*

**Bogstad Camping**, *Ankervn 117; tel: 22 50 76 80,* open all year (bus no. 41: *Bogstad,* taking 30 mins). **Ekeberg Camping**, *Ekebergvn 65; tel: 22 19 85 68,* is closer (about 3 km: 10 mins

on tram no. 19: *Ekeberg),* but open only June–Aug. You can camp in the forest north of town if you avoid public areas (head into the trees for about 1 km). Camping is also free on **Langøyene** island, which has good beaches, but ferries operate only 1015–1930 (June–Aug).

### Eating and Drinking

Eating out in Oslo is expensive and many places close Sun. For restaurant listings, see *The Official Guide for Oslo.*

There are a number of (expensive) options for good Norwegian food: **Restaurant Blom**, *Karl Johansgt 41B,* is something of an institution and has been frequented by many famous figures; **Theatercafeen**, *Hotel Continental, Stortingt 24–26,* is another hangout of the rich and famous; **Frognerseteren**, *Holmenkollvn 200,* and **Holmenkollen Restaurant**, *Holmenkollvn 119,* are close to the famous ski jump and offer breathtaking views; the slightly more affordable **Gamle Rådhus**, *Nedre Slottsgt 1,* is Oslo's oldest restaurant, specialising in fresh shrimps and mussels. **Kaffistova**, *Bondeheimen Hotel, Rosenkrantzgt 8,* serves country-style dishes at the lowest prices for this sort of food.

Budget areas are **Aker Brygge** and **Oslo City**, complexes with a variety of fast-food outlets. **Rema 1000**, *Holmesgt 7,* contains an excellent deli and harbourside stalls sell *ferskereker* (freshly boiled, unshelled shrimps).

### Communications

**Oslo Sentrum Postkontor** (the main post office), *Dronningensgt/Prinsensgt,* open Mon–Fri 0800–1800, Sat 1000–1500. Telephone services are also available here. The one in Oslo S opens Mon–Fri 0700–1800, Sat 0900–1500.

### Money

Post offices (most open Mon–Fri 0800–1700, Sat 0900–1300) take least commission. The bank in Oslo S opens Mon–Fri 0800–1930, Sat 1000–1700. The airport bank opens Mon–Fri 0630–2000, Sat 0700–1700, Sun 0700–2000.

### Embassies

**Canada:** *Oscarsgt 20; tel: 22 46 69 55.* **South Africa:** *Drammenvn 88C; tel: 22 44 79 10.*

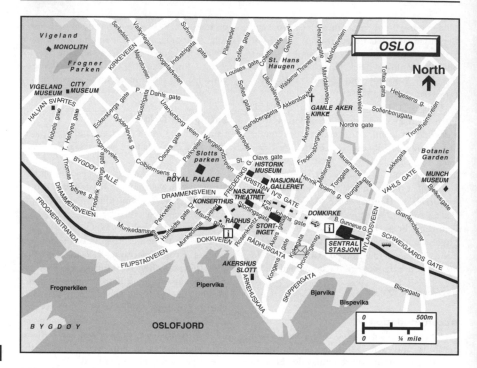

UK: *Thomas Heftyesgt 8; tel: 22 55 24 00.*
USA: *Drammensvn 18; tel: 22 44 85 50.*

## ENTERTAINMENT

See *The Official Guide for Oslo* and *What's on* for listings. Well-known operas are performed at **Den Norske Opera**, *Storgt 23C,* while the **Konserthus**, *Munkedamsvn 14,* stages folklore events in midsummer. Most films are shown undubbed. On a fine summer evening, a stroll along the lively **Stranden** boardwalk takes a lot of beating. Many boats moored there are restaurants with live entertainment.

## SHOPPING

The most attractive buys are those reflecting Norwegian craftsmanship, such as crystal, leather goods, silver and knitwear, but nothing is cheap. **Karl Johans gate** is the city's main street – part pedestrian and loaded with shops, restaurants, bars and street performers. **Basarhallene** (behind the cathedral) is an art and handicraft boutique centre, while the **Aker Brygge** complex stays open late and is a good

place to browse. Other major complexes are **Paléet**, *Karl Johansgt 37–43,* and **Oslo City**, across from the station. **24-hour pharmacy: Jernbanetorgets Apotek**, *Jernbanetorget 4B.*

## SIGHTSEEING

**Domkirke**, *Stortorget 1,* dates from 1697, but only the baroque carved altarpiece and pulpit survive from the original cathedral. The stained-glass windows are by Vigeland, but the most striking feature is the vast ceiling painting. **Nasjonalgalleriet** (National Gallery), *Universitetsgt 13* (metro: *Nasjonalteatret),* houses a huge collection of Norwegian art and includes a room dedicated to Edvard Munch. Such luminaries as Gauguin, Monet and Picasso are also represented (closed Tues). A block away, **Historisk Museum** (Historical Museum), *Frederiksgt 2,* has a comprehensive section about the Sami culture, their beliefs and lifestyle. Upstairs is an ethnographic section with a marvellous collection of masks and other Far Eastern items. The American and African sections are less spectacular, but still worthwhile.

The fortress-palace complex of **Akershus** dominates the east of the harbour; entry from *Akersgt* or over a drawbridge from *Kirkegt*. Several museums are in the extensive grounds, notably **Hjemmefrontmuseet**, a fascinating place devoted to the history of the Norwegian Resistance, many of whom were imprisoned in the castle before being executed by the Nazis. The huge **Forsvarsmuseet** (Defence Museum) goes back as far as the Vikings, the diverse exhibits including such things as bivouac tents, horse-drawn ambulances, a full-size biplane and guns from modern warships.

**Rådhus** (City Hall), **Aker Brygge** (bus/tram: *Rådhuset),* has some exterior reliefs depicting Norwegian mythology, while huge murals inside show a variety of real-life scenes. There's an accurate astronomical clock in the inner courtyard. **Kunstindustrimuseet** (Museum of Applied Art), *St Olavsgt 1* (metro: *Stortinget),* was founded in the 19th century. It covers applied arts (Norwegian and otherwise) from the 7th century to date. Notable are the *Baldisholteppet* (Baldishal tapestry), a gallery of Norwegian costumes and the Far Eastern section.

**Vigelandsparken/Frognerparken**, in north-west Oslo (main entrance from *Kirkevn)* – bus no. 20; tram no. 12: *Frognerparken* – is a lush city park and sculpture garden. Some two hundred of Gustav Vigeland's life-size statues line the central avenue, culminating in the phallic 15-m column of writhing bodies that form the *monolith of life.* For the nearby **Vigelandsmuseet** (Vigeland Museum), *Nobelsgt 32,* head south, past **Oslo Bymuseum** (Oslo City Museum), *Frognervn 67.* **Slottet** (the Royal Palace) is a grandiose work standing at the end of *Karl Johans gate,* but closed to the public.

**Munchmuseet** (Munch Museum), *Tøyengt 53* (metro: *Tøyen/Munchmuseet),* is east of the centre. The display almost always includes *The Scream.* The museum adjoins the extensive **Botanisk Hage** (botanical gardens). Other museums cover such diverse subjects as **Henrik Ibsen**, **skating** and **children's art**.

In the hills overlooking Oslo is the 62-m **Holmenkollbakken ski jump** (metro: *Holmenkollen,* then 10-mins walk), which draws the world's top ski jumpers to a festival each March. **Skimuseet** (Ski Museum), carved into the rock below the jump, has exhibits including 7th-century sleds and skis. **Tryvannstarnet observation tower** (588m), 20-mins walk north (or metro: *Frognerseteren),* is visible for miles and offers unparalleled views.

### Bygdøy

The **Bygdøy** (pronounced big-duh) **peninsula** offers beaches, picnic spots and two groups of museums (bus no. 30 runs all year to both groups). In summer (Apr–Sept), ferry no. 91 takes about 10 mins: it's about 10-mins walk from the quay to the first group, but the second quay is almost outside Framhuset.

**Norsk Folkemuseum** (Norwegian Folk Museum), consists of around 150 buildings of all types, from the Middle Ages to the 19th century. The centre-piece is a **stave church** built around 1200 in Gol. The outdoor section is complemented by two indoor museums, one covering the Sami culture and the other with particularly good sections on Norwegian handicrafts and folk costumes. Just along the road, **Vikingskiphuset** (Viking Ship Museum) houses three 9th-century ships resurrected from Oslofjord. They were bound for Valhalla, so loaded with treasures and then scuttled. The valuables were looted, but many of the ornate wood and leather items have survived.

It's a pleasant 20-min walk to the other group of attractions. In **Kon-Tiki Museum**, *Bygdøynesvn 3,* the pride of place goes to Thor Heyerdahl's balsa raft, *Kon-Tiki,* but his later (papyrus) craft, *Ra II,* is also there, with sketches of his routes, explanations of his theories and such things as replicas of Easter Island statues and an underwater tableau. The neighbouring, triangular **Framhuset** is home to *Fram,* used by both Nansen and Amundsen for their polar expeditions. Exhibits around the vessel relate to the explorations and the polar regions. Making up the trio of museums is **Norsk Sjøfartsmuseum**, a more routine maritime museum.

### OUT OF TOWN

**Viking Landet**, *Norges Parken, Vinterbro* (20-mins south by shuttle bus from the centre), is a theme park that recreates every aspect of daily life in a Viking Community.

# OSLO–NARVIK

The real attraction to this route is the scenery itself. The countryside evolves gradually from gentle and bucolic in the area north of Oslo to dramatic to outright breathtaking in the northern reaches. It also covers a lot of ground: Norway is a big country and sections of this run take up to 10 hours. Wonderful side tracks allow you to get right into the Nordic outdoors. The train from Dombås to Åndalsnes is a journey in itself, plunging through tunnels,

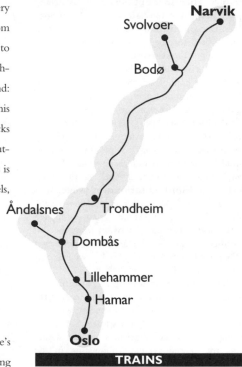

FASTEST JOURNEY: 24 HRS

380

over bridges, and past waterfalls and Europe's highest vertical canyon. The fabulous setting means heavy tourism. An equally thrilling trip, and with far fewer package-tour distractions, is the four-hour ferry (not covered by rail passes but quite cheap) from Bodø to Moskenes, in the Lofoten islands, where jagged peaks and homely fishing villages await.

Bodø is the northern terminus of the rail line (north of the Arctic Circle); alight at Fauske, the previous stop, to catch the bus to Narvik (half-price for all railpass holders except Eurail), from where you can continue by rail on the impressive Ofoten line into Sweden.

## TRAINS

**ETT tables: 785, 786.**

### FAST TRACK

No through service. Trains run between Oslo and Trondheim and Trondheim and Fauske, and buses between Fauske and Narvik. The full journey takes 24 hrs.

### ON TRACK

Reservations are required on some of the following trains. It is advisable to make an advance booking anyway as many trains get full.

**Oslo–Hamar**
Frequent daily, taking 2 hrs.

**Hamar–Lillehammer**
About ten trains a day make the 1 hr trip.

## Lillehammer–Dombås
Five trains a day, taking around 2 hrs.

## Dombås–Trondheim
Three trains run, taking about 2 hrs 30 mins.

## Trondheim–Bodø
One day and one overnight train make the 10-hr journey. The night train has sleeping cars, second-class seats and a buffet, the day train a restaurant car. Reservations obligatory.

## Bodø–Narvik
Two Norway *Bussekspress* buses run daily between Bodø and Narvik in 6½ hrs. Book through the state railway booking system.

### HAMAR
**Station:** *tel: 62 51 30 32,* on the southern edge of the centre.
**Tourist Office:** *Parkgata 2; tel: 62 52 12 17.* Open Mon–Fri 0800–2000, Sat–Sun 1000–1800 (mid June–mid Aug); Mon–Fri 0800–1530 (mid Aug–mid June). It's just west of the station and all the attractions are further west.

HI is connected with **Vikingskipet Motell** – so-named for its location near the upturned Viking ship indoor stadium used in the 1994 Winter Olympics. Located 2 km along the lake. *Tel: 62 52 60 60;* both have cheap doubles. **Seiersted Pensjonat,** *Holsetgate 69; tel: 62 52 12 44;* cheap–moderate. Chains include *Sc*.

NSB-run **Jernbanemuseet** (railway museum) is an open-air complex and offers rides on a miniature steam train. The **Domkirkeodden** peninsula (a 2-km lakeside walk) is home to **Hedmarksmuseet**, a regional museum, with an indoor section including medieval ruins and an outdoor section of fifty old buildings. The **herb garden** recreates a medieval monastery garden and there's an art centre where you can watch traditional skills. Neighbouring **Interferens Holografi museum** is devoted to holograms. A 19th-century boat, *m/s Skibladner,* travels along **Lake Mjøsa** – stops en route include **Lillehammer**.

### LILLEHAMMER
**Station:** *tel: 61 25 30 46,* west of the centre.
**Tourist Offices: Turistkontor:** *Elvegate 19;*

walk straight out of the station to *Storgata* and turn left; *tel: 61 25 92 99,* Mon–Sat 0900–1900, Sun 1100–1800 (mid June–mid Aug); Mon–Fri 1000–1700, Sat 1000–1400 (mid Aug–mid June). **Skysstasjon**, in the station, *tel: 61 26 41 99,* Mon–Fri 0730–1630, Sat 1000–1400. The free guide has an unhelpful map – a decent one costs NOK.60. *Lillehammer This Month* lists events and accurate opening times.

Hotel chains: *Co, QI.* **Inter Nor Lillehammer,** *Turisthotellveien 6; tel: 61 28 60 00,* is luxurious. **GjesteBa,** *Gamleveien 110; tel: 61 25 43 21,* is central and comfortable. **Gjestehuset Ersgaard,** *Nordseterveien 201; tel: 61 25 06 84,* another pension-type. **HI,** *Jernbanetorget 2; tel: 61 26 25 66,* the dearest in Norway.

Lillehammer hosted the 1994 Winter Olympics and many of the facilities can be visited – and in some cases used. In winter, the downhill and cross-country ski trails, skating rinks and bobsleigh runs are open. Many are open in summer too – including chair lifts and summer ski-jumping! The Tourist Office has details.

### OUT OF TOWN
At **Hunderfossen**, a theme park based on Norwegian myths, you can simulate hanging under a helicopter over a glacier. It's 13 km north (10 mins by train), near a **bobsleigh and luge track**, where you can experience a run (on wheels in summer).

### DOMBÅS
The branch line to Åndalsnes diverges here.

> ↴ **SIDE TRACK
> FROM DOMBÅS**

### ÅNDALSNES
**Station:** *tel: 71 22 10 50,* a few mins walk from the centre.
**Tourist Office:** *in the station; tel: 71 22 16 22.* Mon–Sat 0930–1830, Sun 1230–1830 (mid June–Aug); Mon–Fri 0800–1530 (Sept–mid June).

The journey itself is one reason for a visit. Another is **Geirangerfjord**, arguably the most stunning of all the fjords. The greenblue water winds for 16 km between cliffs (up to 1500m) and past cascading waterfalls. Get a bus from Åndalsnes to Hellesylt or Geiranger (at opposite ends of the fjord) and take the ferry between them (70 mins), then bus back to Åndalsnes – or on to **Ålesund**, offering a mix of architectural styles. 🛏

## TRONDHEIM

**Station:** *tel: 773 53 00 10,* north of the centre, 15-min walk to the Tourist Office: cross the bridge, after three blocks turn right on to *Olav Tryggvasonsgata* and left down *Munkegata.* There's a tourist information desk at the station. **Ferries: Hurtigruten** and other ferries leave from quays north of the station.
**Tourist Office:** *Munkegata 19; tel: 73 92 94 00/06* (entrance from Torvet). Open Mon–Fri 0830–2000, Sat 0830–1800, Sun 1000–1800 (mid May–Aug); Mon–Fri 0900–1600 (Sept–mid May). A switchboard; *tel: 73 92 93 94,* is manned 0800–1600.

### ACCOMMODATION

Hotel chains include *BW, Ch, Re, SA, Sc* and *Tp.* **HI: Rosenborg**, *Weidemannsvei 41; tel: 73 53 04 90,* 2 km east (bus no. 63; infrequent Sat–Sun). **Pensjonat Jarlen**, *Kongens gate 40; tel: 73 51 32 18,* is the cheapest pension in town. **Munken Hotel**, *Kongens gate 44; tel: 73 53 45 40,* is comfortable and cheap (for Norway). **Rainbow Gildevangen**, *Sondre gate 22b,* is classy, but not too outrageous.

### SIGHTSEEING

Norway's first capital, Trondheim was founded in 997 by the Viking king, Olav Tryggvason. **Nidaros Domkirke** (Cathedral), *Bispegata,* is cavernous and gloomy, the prime attractions being the decorative stonework, stained-glass windows and the Crown Jewels. Adjacent **Erkebispegarden** (Archbishop's Palace) contains many old weapons. **Trondhjems Kunstforening** (Trondheim Art Gallery), *Bispegata 7,* exhibits some of Norway's greatest art, while the **Nordenfjeldske Kunstindustrimuseum** (Museum of Applied Art), *Munkegata 5,* has a collection of contemporary arts and crafts. Other sights include the **Old Town Bridge**, *Gamle Bybro,* from the last century, with views of the wharf, and **Munkholmen**, an island

which used to be a prison, a monastery, and is now a preserved fortress with good beaches.

### OUT OF TOWN

Don't miss **Ringve Museum**, *Lade Allé 60,* 2 km east of town: bus no. 4: *Fagerheim* (from *Munkegata* towards Lade). The couple who donated their farm as a music museum began the extraordinary collection. You must join a tour, but it's thoroughly enjoyable. Some rooms are dedicated to composers, furnished in period and containing everything from letters to death masks; the guides play short samples of their music on antique instruments. Buildings at **Trondelag Folkemuseum**, *Sverresborg,* include turf huts and a small stave church (buses from Dronningsgata (D1): no. 8 towards *Stavset* or no. 9 towards *Heimdal / Sjetnemarka:* 10 mins).

## BODØ

**Station:** *tel: 75 52 25 53,* 300m further east of town than the Tourist Office.
**Tourist Office:** *Sjogata 21; tel: 75 52 60 00,* is called **Destinasjon Bodø**. Mon–Fri 0900–2030, Sat 1000–1600, 1800–2000, Sun 1200–1600, 1800–2000 (June–mid Aug); Mon–Fri 0900–1600 (mid Aug–May). Get *Bodø Guide,* maps and information about bus and boat trips. **Ferries: Hurtigruten** and ferries to the islands leave from quays on the road beside the station. **Long-distance bus station,** *tel: 75 52 50 25,* is 300 m further along *Sjogata.* Mon–Fri 0700–1700, Sat 0900–1400, but there's access to the lockers from the café, which stays open until 2300 (and Sun 1400–2100).

### ACCOMMODATION

Hotel chains include *BW, SA* and *Tp.* For budget accommodation that is central and a home from home, try **Opsahl Gjestegard**, *Prinsensgata 131; tel: 75 52 07 04.* **Norrøna Hotel**, *Storgate 4B; tel: 75 52 55 50,* is pleasant and central; moderate. **HI:** *Sjøgata 55* (at the station); *tel: 75 52 11 22,* is actually the top floor of the station. Open mid June–mid Aug. **Camping:** 3 km south-east of town.

### SIGHTSEEING

This is a largely post-war town. **Bodø Domkirke** (Cathedral), with a spire apart from the

## The Hurtigruten

The **Hurtigruten** is a unique combination of ferry and cruise line which sails up the coast of Norway, from Bergen in the south to Kirkenes in the Arctic Circle and back, year round. En route the ships call at 34 ports. The passing views of fjords and coastline are spectacular. A full voyage one way is 11 days; part-voyage options are available. For more information, contact your travel agent or, in the UK, **Norwegian Coastal Voyage**, 15a Berghem Mews, Blythe Road, London W14 0HN; tel: (0171) 371 4011.

main building, is a stunning construction containing rich modern tapestries. Across the road, the small **Nordlandmuseum** (Nordland County Museum), *Prinsensgata 116,* includes sections on the Samis, regional history, Arctic birds and the German occupation.

### ↴ SIDE TRACK FROM BODØ

Bodø is the best place from which to take a ferry to the spectacular **Lofoten Islands**, a chain of jagged glacier-carved mountains sheltering fishing villages, farms, sheep and thousands of birds (including puffins). The main town is **Svolvoer**, on **Austvågøy**. **Tourist Office:** *tel: 76 07 30 00,* by the harbour. Open until 2200 every night in summer. (Svolvoer is actually much better reached from **Skutvik**, which is midway between Narvik and Bodø.)

From Bodø, there are five daily ferries in summer to **Moskenes**, and one or two to **Røst** and **Værøy**, at the southern end of the island chain. **Moskenes Tourist Office**, *tel: 76 09 15 99,* daily 1000–1900 (mid June–mid Aug), 1000–1700 (early June, late Aug). There's a picturesque fishing village called **Å**, 5 km south of Moskenes, with cottages and a hostel *(tel: 76 09 11 21)* and a campsite. Fishing, caving and hiking trips can all be arranged here. Røst and Værøy are tiny and support colonies of puffins.

Both have hostels. This is really Norwegian outdoors at its best – amazing scenery and far less crowded than Geirangerfjord. ▲

## NARVIK

**Station, Narvik:** *tel: 76 92 31 21,* a few mins walk east of the Tourist Office: turn right and walk 100 m uphill, then bear left.

**Bus station:** A new bus station is being built near the boat quay – until then it is at the train station; *tel: 76 92 35 00.* Open Mon–Fri 0900–1600 (all year).

**Tourist Office:** *Kongensgata 66; tel: 76 94 33 09.* Open Mon–Sat 0900–1900, Sat 1000–1600, Sun 1400–1800 (mid June–mid Aug); Mon–Fri 0900–1600 (mid Aug–mid June).

### ACCOMMODATION

**Breidablikk Gjestehus,** *Tore Hundsgate 41; tel: 76 94 14 18,* up the hill from the main road, is an inexpensive pension. **Norlandia Narvik**, *Skistuaveien 8; tel: 76 94 75 00,* is upmarket, but cheaper than others and has great views. **HI: Nordkalotten:** *Havnegata 3; tel: 76 94 25 98.* Open Mar–Nov. 15-min walk from Tourist Office: turn left and go down the hill (bus 15 stops outside, but is infrequent Sat–Sun).

### SIGHTSEEING

The town is small and hilly, but this ensures you have attractive views while you walk. It played a vital part early in World War II and the first section of **Nordland Rode Kors Krigsminnemuseum** (Red Cross War Museum), commemorates the time (1940) when the Germans invaded to stop the '. . . greatest warmonger of this century, Mr Churchill . . .' from turning Scandinavia into a war zone! Other sections cover the rest of the Scandinavian war. For panoramic views, take the *gondolbaner* (cable car) up **Fagernesfjellet** – or walk, but allow at least 2 hrs. Some people hang-glide down.

The **Ofoten Museum** covers the history of Narvik, focussing on shipping and the building of the great Ofoten rail line, which carries ore from Sweden, and hence makes Narvik rich. There is a guided tour of the dock (the port sprawls right across the centre of town) every day at 1300 from the Tourist Office. There's also an evening walking tour of the town.

# OSLO–OSLO

Probably one of the most scenic train trips in Europe, this return circuit actually encompasses two journeys, one within another, and a catamaran voyage. The diversion at Myrdal, more than halfway along the already spectacular route between Oslo and Bergen, presents 'Norway in a Nutshell', a train/boat combination that gives a glimpse into one of the countries prettiest fjords. After visiting the city of Bergen, the 4 hour catamaran journey between the islands and skerries of South Western Norway is one of the most enjoyable ways to get to Stavanger. Even the last leg back to Oslo doesn't disappoint, passing by some magnificent rivers and mountains, and still allowing visits to some interesting cities.

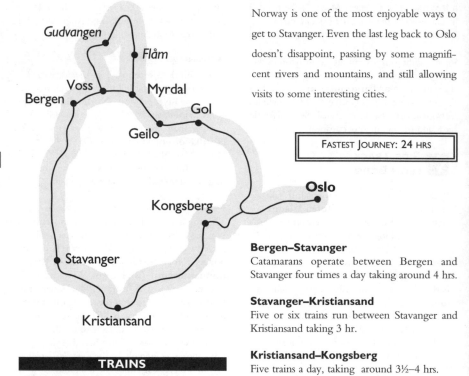

FASTEST JOURNEY: 24 HRS

## Bergen–Stavanger
Catamarans operate between Bergen and Stavanger four times a day taking around 4 hrs.

## Stavanger–Kristiansand
Five or six trains run between Stavanger and Kristiansand taking 3 hr.

## Kristiansand–Kongsberg
Five trains a day, taking around 3½–4 hrs.

Colour section: (i) Bergen; inset, a photo stop on the Flåm Railway (see p.381).
(ii) St Vitus Cathedral, Prague (p.453); insets: Strasbourg (p.448); Paris (p.400).
(iii) Corsica: Calvi (p.399); inset, St Peter's in Rome (p.460).
(iv) Advertisement.

## TRAINS
**ETT tables:** 780, 2270, 775, 781.

### ON TRACK

**Oslo–Bergen**
Four day trains take roughly 7 hrs, with restaurant or buffet cars. One overnight train takes 8 hrs and has second–class sleeping cars and seats. Reservations obligatory.

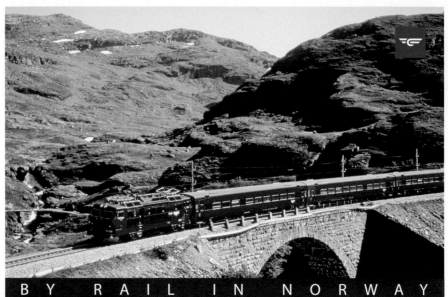

# BY RAIL IN NORWAY

### Enjoy the scenic lines !
Rail travel in Norway is an experience itself: you travel through the country's varied landscape across high mountain plateaus at up to 1200 metres, and you will pass the tall rockfaces, dense forests, breathtaking waterfalls, rivers and fjords.

Most lines are scenic, but do not miss the Flåm-line and the Rauma-line.

### A ticket to suit you...
- Eurailpass and Eurail Flexipass
  (for non-European residents only)
- Inter Rail for youth and for adults
  (for European residents)
- Scanrail for youth, adults and seniors
- Norway Rail Pass
- Euro Domino – Norway

All these railpasses are good for travel by train in Norway.

## Go as you please !

## Kongsberg–Oslo

At least 8 trains make the 1½ hr journey every day, with more running on weekdays.

### THE OSLO–BERGEN LINE

This 490 km 7-hour rail journey is one of the most strikingly beautiful in Europe. Leaving Oslo, the train climbs gently to **Gol** (207 m), after which the real ascent begins. **Geilo** (794 m) has many hotels and chair lifts. It's a centre for both downhill and cross-country skiing, with slopes suitable for beginners and intermediate skiers, and offers facilities for many wilderness activities all year round.

The train continues its climb to the holiday centre of **Ustaoset** (990 m), then crosses a bleak but magnificent mountainscape of icy lakes and rocky, snow-capped ridges. **Finse**, near **Hardangerjøkulen glacier**, is a tiny mountain village used by explorers during their Polar training. At 1222 m, it is the highest station on the line and offers year-round skiing as well as summer hiking. Shortly after leaving Finse, the train enters a 10 km tunnel, to emerge near **Hallingskeid**. The next stop is **Myrdal** and almost 1 hr later you reach the lakeside town of **Voss**, 56 m above sea level and surrounded by mountains. This is an Alpine sports centre with good facilities and a lively après-ski atmosphere. The cable car, **Hangursbanen**, runs up to 1100 m, covering a height difference of about 570 m in 4 mins. On the last leg (just over 1 hr) to Bergen, the scenery's a little less wild, although still impressive.

### ⇄ SIDE TRACK FROM MYRDAL: 'NORWAY IN A NUTSHELL'

This is a popular circuit that uses the main rail line to Myrdal and rejoins it at Voss, combining a train, bus and ferry to link them: details from the railway stations or Tourist Offices in Oslo or Bergen. It's normally a day excursion (although accommodation is available en route), but not a tour: you simply buy a ticket and follow the relevant timetable. The train, ferry and bus journeys are not covered by rail passes, except for Eurail, but it's worth paying the extra Nkr.250 for this experience.

At **Myrdal**, you board a local train for a breathtaking journey down the branch to Flåm, taking about an hour. The descent covers 866 m in 20 km (at a gradient of 1:18), with superb views of towering cliffs, chasms and cascades. There are several tunnels on the route, including one 'turnaround', in which the line makes a 180° turn completely within the mountain. The train stops at the particularly spectacular **Kjosfossen waterfall** for photographers to descend, and there are other photographic opportunities if you're quick.

The railway ends at **Flåm**, a tiny village at the head of **Aurlandsfjord**, a branch of, and the only settlement accessible by rail on the **Sognefjord**. There are at least a couple of hours to relax (there are hotels here), lunch, shop and enjoy the surroundings before boarding a 2-hr ferry journey (refreshments available) along **Aurlandsfjord** and **Nærøyfjord**. There is also an option of taking a 5-hr boat trip from here through the **Sognefjord** directly to Bergen.

Disembarking at **Gudvangen** (accommodation available here also), the bus back to Voss follows an incredibly steep and breathtakingly dramatic road out of the fjord. There's a brief photo stop at the top, then a scenic drive to rejoin the main line. ◣

### BERGEN

If in the area, dial *177* for all sorts of transport information, including trains, boats and buses.

**Station:** *Strømgt; tel: 55 96 69 00*, 10-mins walk east of the centre.

**Ferries:** The Tourist Office has details of international and local ferries, most of which leave from Vågen, the inner harbour. International sailings use *Skoltegrunnskaien*, on the east side. **Flaggruten** catamarans to **Stavanger** leave from *Strandkaien*, on the west side. Their office in *Strandkeiterminalen, tel: 55 23 87 80*, opens 0730–1730/1800. Pick up a boarding-pass 30 mins before departure. **Hurtigruten** (see p.383) uses a separate harbour at *Frieleneskaien*, west of the centre.

**Tourist Office:** *Bryggen 7; tel: 55 32 14 80*, opens Mon–Sat 0830–2100, Sun 1000–1900

(May, Sept); Mon–Sun 0830–2100 (June–Aug); Mon–Sat 0900–1600 (Oct–Apr). There's a mass of free English-language literature. Get the *Bergen Guide,* which includes maps and lists of just about everything. The **Bergen Card** (NOK.120 for 24 hrs, NOK.190 for 48 hrs, children NKr 55 and NKr 80 from Tourist Offices, hotels and campsites) offers free local transport and free or discounted admission to most of the attractions.

If you want to wander further afield on foot, or even on skis, **Bergen Turlag** (Bergen Touring Association), in DNT office, *Tverrgt 4–6; tel: 55 32 22 30,* open Mon–Fri 1000–1600 (Thur to 1800), can provide walking maps for the surrounding mountains.

### ACCOMMODATION

There's a wide range of accommodation, including private rooms. Hotel chains include *BW, FE, GT, Re, Rk, SA, Sc* and *Tp.* **HI: Montana,** *Johan Blydtsvei 30; tel: 55 29 29 00,* is on Mt Ulriken (bus no.4: *Lægdene);* open May–Sept. The **YMCA,** *4 Nedre Korskirke alm; tel: 55 31 73 732,* is very conveniently located. The most central **campsite** (open 2 July–end Aug) is **Bergenshallen,** *Vilh. Bjerknesvei 24, Landås; tel: 55 27 01 80,* 10 mins on bus no.3.

### SIGHTSEEING

An old Hanseatic port, Norway's second city is the gateway to the fjords and extremely picturesque: situated on a peninsula, surrounded by mountains and with many meandering cobbled streets of weatherboard houses with gabled roofs. It centres on the waterfront **Fisketorget,** open Mon–Fri 0800–1600, Sat 0800–1500, a working fish (and various other things) market, as well as the main tourist draw of the city. You can get almost everywhere on foot, but take the **Fløibanen** (funicular) from the centre up **Mt Fløyen** (320m), for a panoramic view. At the top are pleasant woods, excellent for picnics and walking. Facilities for the disabled are available.

At the centre of the old quarter, **Bryggen** contains a charming row of medieval houses (World Heritage listed). The atmospheric **Hanseatisk Museum** (Hanseatic Museum) is housed in one of the best-preserved timber buildings with 18th-century furnishings to provide an insight into the life of a wealthy merchant. Tiny **Theta Museum,** *Enhjørningsgården Bryggen,* was the clandestine one-room centre for Resistance operations in World War II, until it was discovered by the Nazis in 1942. When the **Bryggens Museum** was being constructed, the remains of the original (1050–1500) city were discovered and incorporated. Showcases contain everyday objects from those times, including shoes, combs, jewellery and games, and you can listen to medieval music on headphones. Upstairs, a variety of exhibits demonstrate different stages of the town's development. Close by is **Mariakirken** (St Mary's Church), *Dreggsallmenningen,* which dates from the 1100s and has been in continuous use ever since. It contains frescos (some 15th-century) and a splendid baroque pulpit.

The 16th-century **Rosenkrantztårnet** (Rosenkrantz Tower) incorporated part of the 13th-century **Bergenhus** (fortress). To understand the architectural features, get the English-language guide (free) and follow the route.

Further along the harbour is **Norges Fiskerimuseum** (a fishing museum), *Bontelabo 2.* The exhibits are mildly interesting and there's a (literally) wonderful 16th-century map, depicting imaginative sea beasts.

**Rasmus Meyers Samlinger** (Rasmus Meyer's Collection), *Rasmus Meyer's allé 7,* has an excellent collection of Norwegian art, including many works by Munch. The neighbouring **Bergens Kunstmuseum** (Bergen Art Museum) and **Stenersens Samlinger** (Stenersen's Collection), offer international fare, along with more Norwegian works, while the nearby **Vestlandske Kunstindustrimuseum** (West Norway Museum of Applied Art), *Nordahl Brunsgt 9,* has a fine display of European and Chinese decorative arts, including superb local silverwork (from the 17th–18th centuries).

The **university,** *Christiesgt,* runs the **botanical gardens** and several museums, covering natural history, maritime affairs and cultural history. A couple of blocks south is **Bergens Teatermuseum** (Theatre Museum), *Villavei 5.* The macabre **Lepramuseet** (Leprosy Museum), *Kong Oscarsgt 59,* documents the history of the disease.

West of Vågen, a peninsula stretches north,

to end in the green **Nordnesparken**. At the end of the peninsula (25-mins walk or bus no.4) is the exceptionally well arranged **Akvariet** (aquarium), which is educational – if you take time to read the explanations – and interesting: highlights include graceful rays and elegant seahorses. Try to catch feeding time at the big (outdoor) seal and penguin tanks.

**OUT OF TOWN**

**Gamle Bergen** (Old Bergen) is a picturesque collection of some three dozen 18th- and 19th-century wooden houses and shops, many furnished in period style. You can wander round for nothing, but have to join a tour if you want to see the interiors. Yellow bus nos.9, 20, 22, 70 and 80 take 10 mins: from the east side of Vågen, direction *Lønborg*.

Three fjords south of Bergen are among the deepest and most popular in the country: **Hardangerfjord** is a major target for tourists, alternating verdant lowlands and precipitous cliffs scattered with waterfalls; **Nordfjord** twists over 100 km to the foot of **Briksdal glacier**; **Sognefjord** is the longest (205 km) and deepest (1300m) in Norway; in some places the shoreline is gentle, in others it soars straight up to 1000m. Two of its most spectacular arms are **Nærøyfjord** and **Aurlandsfjord** (see 'Norway in a Nutshell'). Several boat tours, including day trips, are available from Bergen.

## STAVANGER

**Station:** *Jernbanevn; tel: 51 56 96 00,* about 10-mins walk south from the harbour: straight through the centre.

**Ferries: Color Line** international sailings leave from *Strandkaien; tel: 51 52 45 45:* to Newcastle, England, and Hirtshals, northern Denmark. **Flaggruten** *(tel: 51 89 50 90)* catamarans for Bergen use the *Hurtigbåt Express Terminal,* on the west side of the centre.

**Tourist Office:** *Roskildetorget 1; tel: 51 85 92 00; http://www.destinasjon-stavanger.no; e-mail: info@destinasjon-stavanger.no.* Mon–Fri 0900–1700, Sat 0900–1400 (1 Sept–31 May), daily 0900–2000 (1 June–31 Aug). It has maps, a city guide, regional booklets and ferry information.

The centre is small and easily walkable, with an excellent pedestrianised cobbled shopping

area. **Breiavatnet** (the central lake) is a good guide to the scale (not very large, but about half the size of the centre) and there's a good bus network to reach outlying attractions. The **Stavanger card** (pick one up from wherever you're staying; NOK.110 for 24 hrs, NOK.190 for 48 hrs, NOK.240 for 72 hrs) provides free bus travel and free admission to the town's museums/mansions and 50% discounts on other attractions. If you pay (NOK.30) to enter a museum, the ticket covers any others you visit the same day (except the Archaeological Museum and Iron Age farm).

**Gamle Stavanger** (the old town) is the area on the west side of the harbour. It's a picturesque place for a stroll, with cobbled walkways and rows of early 18th-century wooden houses at odd angles. The impressive stone **Domkirke** (St Swithun's), was established in 1125 and is the only church in Norway to have kept its original medieval atmosphere.

Museums include **Stavanger Museum**, *Muségt 16,* with taxidermy and period furniture. A little beyond it is the excellent and very modern **Archaeological Museum**, while **Sjøfartsmuséet** (Maritime Museum), occupies a restored warehouse at *Nedre Strandgt 17–19.* At **Hermetikkmuséet** (Canning Museum), *Øvre Srandgt 88A,* is a reconstructed sardine factory that was in regular use 1890–1920. Brisling sardines are still smoked here and you can sample them Tues and Thur in summer, the first Sun of the month for the rest of the year.

Other museums include the **Norwegian Printing Museum**, **Telecom Museum**, **Leedal**, an occasional Royal Residence, and **Breidablick**, a 19th-century ship owner's house. **Valbergtårnet**, a 19th-century watchtower perched on top of a hill in the centre, provides an excellent view of the harbour.

**OUT OF TOWN**

5 km west of town, at **Ullandhaug**, the **Jernadergarden** is an Iron Age farm (c.350–550 AD), discovered during archaeological digs and reconstructed as accurately as possible from historical records. Bus no.71 takes 10–15 mins (bus stop no.11 *Handelens Hus,* near the cathedral, or nos.7 and 79 from the *Sparkassen,* opposite the cathedral). From the bus stop, cross the

road and climb over the stile; the main entrance and farm buildings are over the grassy hill. Three of the original four buildings can be seen: they are wooden structures with stone walls added around the outside as an extra layer for insulation. Time your visit so that you can go inside (daily 1200–1700 15 June–15 Aug), to see how the family (about a dozen people) would have lived.

Take to the hills or water for superb views of **Ryfylke fjords** – in particular, from the extraordinarily geometric **Pulpit Rock (Preikestolen)**: a squared-off flat-topped monster with a sheer drop of 600 m to the water. To get there, take a ferry to **Tau**, then a bus to the base of the rock. It takes two hours to get to the top, so allow plenty of time. If that's not your scene, you can admire it from the bottom by taking the sightseeing boat *Clipper* for a 3-hr cruise into the steep-walled **Lysefjord** and to the base of the pulpit. You can just turn up – the **(Rødne)** office is opposite the quay. Other boat trips are available from the same location.

## KRISTIANSAND

**Station:** *tel: 38 07 75 00.* On the west side of the centre, a few blocks from the Tourist Office, along *Vestre Strandgt.*
**Tourist Office:** *Dronningensgt 2; tel: 38 12 13 14.* Open Mon–Fri 0800–1930, Sat 1000–1930, Sun 1200–1930 (June–Aug); Mon–Fri 0800–1600 (Sept–May).

Norway's fifth largest town is situated at the southern tip of the country. Protection was needed for the original settlement and the 17th-century **Christiansholm Festning**, *Strandpromenaden,* was built to guard the eastern approach to the harbour. The circular fortress is now the major sight and there are panoramic views from the walls. The old quarter, **Posebyen**, forms the north-eastern section of the centre and is typified by its well preserved little wooden houses, while the enormous neo-Gothic **Domkirke** (cathedral), *Kirkegt,* dates from 1885. The **fishmarket** on the quay is a good place to pick up some smoked salmon or prawns for a picnic lunch.

**Ravnedalen Natural Park** (15-min walk north of the centre) has a lovely collection of exotic plants and flowers in a natural valley

setting. **Dyreparken** (15 mins from the centre via bus no.1) is a virtually cageless zoo and one of Norway's most popular attractions. There is also an amusement park with a special children's area (Cinnamon Town).

## KONGSBERG

**Station:** *tel: 32 73 11 78,* on the west side of the river, next to the Tourist Office.
**Tourist Office:** *Storgt 35; tel: 32 73 50 00.* Open Mon–Fri 0900–1900, Sat–Sun 1000–1700 (26 June–16 Aug); Mon–Fri 0900–1630, Sat 1000–1400 (rest of the year).

Kongsberg is a silver town, founded in 1624 when exceptionally pure deposits were discovered in the nearby mountains. Mining remained the town's *raison d'être* for three centuries, but most of the mines *(sølvgruvene)* closed early in the 19th century, the last one in 1957. In the town centre, **Kongsbergkirke** is an enormous and beautiful baroque church, built during the silver boom, reflecting the prosperity of those days. Striking features are the all-in-one altar, pulpit and organ and the seating (according to rank). Close to **Nybrufoss waterfall** is **Norsk Bergverksmuseum** (Norwegian Mining Museum), housed in an old smelting works. Exhibits include some local finds; gold and gemstones, as well as silver. **Den Kongelige Mynts Museum** (Mint Museum) is an offshoot: coin production moved to Kongsberg in 1686 (the National Mint is still here). **Skimuseum**, in the same complex, covers the development of the sport, believed to have originated in Norway. The 32 buildings that form **Lågdalsmuseet** (folk museum, 10-mins walk south of the centre) date mainly from the 18th and 19th centuries and include Norway's only remaining turret-barn. The indoor section has traditional arts and crafts.

### OUT OF TOWN

The disused **silver mines at Saggrenda** (8 km south, bus no.11 towards *Notodden)* can be visited mid May–end Sept. Tours include a train ride into the heart of the mountain. The shafts go 560m below sea-level and it's definitely chilly at 6°C. **Heddal**, 5 km west of **Notodden** (the closest rail stop) boasts Norway's largest stave church, c.1242.

# OSLO–STOCKHOLM

The best way to get between the two capitals is by rail. This is an exceptionally pretty route through the Swedish Lake District. The stops en route allow for visits to some lesser known but, nevertheless, important fortress towns, reminders of a time when the neighbouring countries were at war with each other. This route passes through Gothenburg (see p.194), but the quicker alternative via Karlstad, on the banks of Lake Vänern, provides water vistas for virtually the entire journey.

Copenhagen–Gothenburg p. 192

## FASTEST JOURNEY: 6 HRS

## TRAINS

**ETT tables:** 770, 740, 750.

### FAST TRACK

Two day services take the direct route between Oslo and Stockholm with journey times of 6 hrs. One is a through train with buffet car, the other involves a change at Karlstd onto a Swedish X2000 high-speed train – the connection is good. Both require reservations.

### ON TRACK

#### Oslo–Fredrikstad–Halden

A reasonable *IC* service links Oslo and Halden, all trains calling at Fredrikstad en route. Oslo to Fredrikstad takes 1 hr 10 mins, Fredrikstad to Halden takes 30 mins.

#### Halden–Border–Gothenburg (Göteborg)

Three trains a day cross the border at Kornsjø for Gothenburg. Journey time: 2 hrs 30 mins.

#### Gothenburg–Örebro

There are no through trains between Gothenburg and Örebro, but journeys are available by changing trains at Hallsberg (about every 2 hrs).

#### Örebro–Västerås

Trains every 2 hrs taking 1 hr.

#### Västerås–Stockholm

A train every 2 hrs service links Västerås with Stockholm Central. Journey 1 hr 15 mins.

## FREDRIKSTAD

**Station:** *tel: 69 31 26 03*, 5-mins walk southeast of the centre.
**Tourist Office:** *Østre Brohoude; tel: 69 32 03 30.* Mon–Fri 0800–1600, Sat 1000–1600, Sun 1200–1600 (summer); Mon–Fri 0900–1600 (winter).

**Domkirke** (Cathedral), half-a-dozen blocks from the station, was decorated by Vigeland, but the main attraction is the old **fortress-town** east of the centre. Three sides are still bordered by the fortified walls and it's the best preserved fortress town in Scandinavia. Stroll round the walls, see the drawbridge (from 1567) and explore the cobbled alleys that are lined by still inhabited 17th-century buildings. The smaller **Kongsten fort**, perched on a bluff overlooking the old town, is a pleasant 15–20-min stroll.

## HALDEN

**Station:** *tel: 69 18 11 23*, on the south bank of the river.

**Tourist Office:** *Marina (Gjesthavn),* south of the station; *tel: 69 18 14 78,* daily 0800–2000 (1 June–17 Aug), Sat–Sun only 0800–1400 (May); *Langbrygge 3,* north of the train station in the main town (over the bridge); *tel: 69 17 48 40,* Mon–Fri 0900–1600 (rest of the year).

Halden is another old border post, on the lovely **Iddefjord** and overlooked by **Fredriksten Fort**, an imposing 17th-century castle just south-east of the town. It covers two separate ridges and is a veritable town in its own right, so allow plenty of time to explore. Among the many interesting historical features is the **Frederikshalds Theater** (with a fully restored baroque stage and old scenery) and **Rød Herregard**, a well furnished 18th-century manor house with a collection of weapons. For tour information (in summer), contact the **Halden Historical Society,** *tel: 69 18 54 11.* The **Marina** (Gjesthavn) is probably the friendliest and has the best facilities in Southern Norway, and offers day trips to Sweden.

## ÖREBRO

**Station:** *tel: (019) 17 22 08.* 5–10-mins walk from the centre.

**Tourist Office:** *Slottet; tel: (019) 21 21 21,* Mon–Fri 0900–2000, Sat–Sun 1000–1700 (June–Aug), Mon–Fri 0900–1700 (Sept–May).

**Örebro Slott,** a castle on a small island in the Svartån (Black) River, dominates the largely residential lakeside town. Flanked by four round towers, parts of it date from the 13th century and, despite frequent restorations, it's extraordinarily photogenic. In the summer, the

Castle hosts an important art festival of internationally famous Swedish arts. The charming **Wadköping Museum Village** (free entry) is reached by a pleasant riverside walk, past a series of secluded summerhouses tucked among the trees. It offers a collection of old well preserved weatherboard houses, with some used as craftsmen's workshops, and one as a café. **Svampen** (the Mushroom) is a 59m water tower (with a lift) that dominates the north of town and provides a panoramic view (also free).

## VÄSTERÅS

**Station:** *tel: (021) 10 21 43,* 5-mins walk south of the centre.

**Tourist Office: Utflyktsbutiken,** *Stora Gatan 40; tel: (021) 10 37 00.* Open Mon–Fri 0900–1900, Sat–Sun 1000–1500 (mid June–mid Aug); Mon–Fri 0930–1800; Sat 1000–1400 (mid Aug–mid June).

Västerås was a Viking trading centre and is now a centre of modern technology. Parts of the rather plain palace, **Västerås slott,** have survived from the 13th-century and it contains the **Västmanlands Länsmuseum** (regional museum). The archaeological section includes a 4th-century boat-grave and a full-scale period room. The neighbouring 19th-century turbine house, **Turbinhuset,** has been lovingly restored. The centre is dominated by the **Domkirka** (Cathedral), the oldest parts of which date from the 13th century. Among its treasures are a 16th-century reredos, two triptychs and a king's sarcophagus. **Kyrkbacken** (Church Hill), behind the cathedral, is the oldest surviving part of town, which retains an 18th-century atmosphere. The art museum, **Konstmuseum,** *Fiskartorget,* hosts many exhibitions of contemporary work. A 47-bell carillon rings out regularly from the modern **City Hall**.

The **Valby Open Air Museum** (10 mins from the centre by bus no.12) is a museum with 40 historic buildings taken from the area. It is located in attractive parkland and has crafts workshops as well as a farm with animals.

Situated 15 km from the centre (20 mins by bus no. 46) is **Skultuna Messingbruk,** the oldest continuously operational brassworks in Europe. Open Mon–Fri 1000–1800, Sat–Sun 1000–1600. It has a shop and museum.

# PALERMO–MARSEILLE

This is a route for the adventurous, the sybaritic and all those who seek exotic holiday lands off the beaten path. It involves travel by ferry, bus and railways of different gauges. History and archaeology buffs will find their count here on islands that played significant though ancillary roles during many important eras of Western civilisation. Sardinia is the second largest and Corsica the fourth largest islands in the Mediterranean Sea.

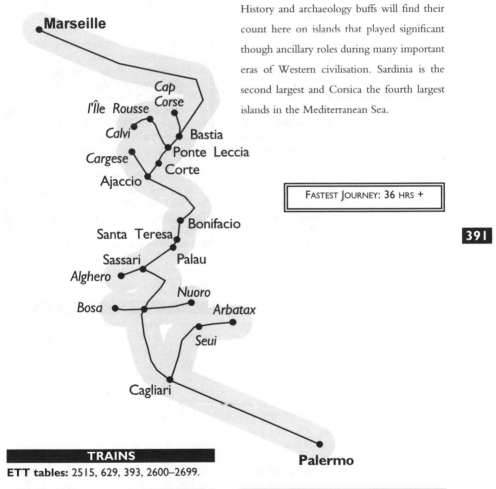

FASTEST JOURNEY: 36 HRS +

## TRAINS

**ETT tables:** 2515, 629, 393, 2600–2699.

### FAST TRACK

There is no direct ferry route from Palermo to Marseille. However, there are numerous ferry service crossings via Sardinia and Corsica to the Mediterranean coast of France. See the International Shipping section of the ETT.

### ON TRACK

**Sicily to Cagliari**

By overnight ship. Two weekly (12 hr passage) to Cagliari: one from Palermo and one from Trapani (both operated by Tirrenia Lines).

Other ferries operate to Cagliari from Naples, Civitavecchia, Genoa.

### Cagliari–Sassari

There are several daily mainline trains to Sassari (many other possibilities by changing at Ozieri-Chilivani); journey time 3–6 hrs.

### Sassari–Palau–Santa Teresa di Gallura

Sassari then FdS narrow gauge train to Palau (2 daily, taking 3 hrs 40 mins), then ARST bus from Palau to Santa Teresa di Gallura (2 daily, 45-min journey).

### Santa Teresa–Bonifacio

Four daily sailings in the winter (taking 90 mins) and up to 10 June–Sept. Schedules can be disrupted by bad weather. Contact **Moby Lines**, *tel: (0789) 755 260,* or **Saremar**, *tel: (0789) 754 788* for details.

### Bonifacio–Ajaccio

There are 4 scheduled bus services per day, and 2 on Sunday, taking 4 hrs. Buses are operated by **Eurocorse Voyage**, *tel: 04 95 70 13 83,* and the long, slow bus journey presents an ideal opportunity to discover the vineyards, mountains and valleys of southern Corsica.

### Ajaccio–Corte–Ponte Leccia–Bastia

By narrow-gauge train via Corte and Ponte Leccia; 4 trains daily taking 3 hrs 35 mins–4 hrs.

### Bastia–Marseille

Large ferries (of SNCM – Societe nationale Corse Mediterranee and CMN – Compagnie meridionale de Navigation) sail infrequently (not daily) from Bastia to Marseille. There are many other sailings to Nice (see p. 367) and Toulon (p. 326) from most Corsican ports, including Ajaccio, Calvi and l'Île Rousse. Large hydrofoils operate multi-daily frequencies from most Corsican ports to most mainland ports, but check locally for exact details. Reservation should be made well in advance for the large ferries during July/Aug and French school holiday periods.

Additional ferries (Corsica Ferries, Moby Lines) sail daily from Corsica to the mainland and hydrofoils operate multi-daily frequencies

---

## *Sardinia*

Situated almost in the precise centre of the western Mediterranean, Sardinia is an isolated mountainous island. Only the plains of the Campidani near Oristano and that of Cagliari, calm the granitic massifs that predominate and pre-date the Alps and the Appennines.

There are two rail systems: Italian State Railways **(FS)** mainline standard gauge network and Ferrovie della Sardegna **(FdS)** narrow-gauge railway and connecting buses. FS accepts all rail passes, FdS accepts no rail passes. Both systems are mainly single track and both are being extensively renovated – the FS system is being electrified, while the FdS is being rebuilt to modern standards. FS information, *tel: 1478 88088* (toll free) FdS information from ESIT (Ente Sardo Industrie Turistiche): *167 013153* (toll free). All intercity buses are operated by **ARST** (Azienda Regionale Sarda Trasporti); *tel: 1678 65042* (toll free).

to Leghorn, Genoa and other Italian ports from Bastia and l'Île Rousse.

### CAGLIARI

**Tourist Office:** Most immediate Cagliari **AAST** (Azienda Autonoma di Soggiorno e Tourismo) office is on the *V. Roma* side of the *Pza Matteotti* near the maritime, FS rail and bus stations; *tel: (070) 669 255.* Free maps and brochures in English. Open Mon–Sat 0830–1945 July–Sept; Winter 0800–1400, closed Sun.

**Main AAST office:** *97 V. Mameli; tel: (070) 664 185,* open daily 0800–1930. Five blocks up *V. Sassari* then right along *V. Goffredo Mameli* two blocks. It has a more complete selection of material. **Airport branch:** *(070) 240 200,* Mon–Fri 0900–1300 and 1600–1900. Sardinia-wide **ESIT** office is situated next door to main AAST with a complete selection of maps and brochures and FdS schedules.

**Stations: Maritime Station.** For all ships; *Pza Matteotti.* Tirennia bookings at *1 V. Campidano c/o Agenave; tel: (070) 666 065.* FS stately 19th-century marble **station** is served by mainline trains to Sassari and the northern ports of Porto Torres and Olbia, is on *Pza Matteotti, V. Sassari* side. The Cagliari FS station has a bank (Mon–Fri 0830–1330, 1430–1530) with ATM inside the main information/ticketing lobby. FdS tiny corner station is 3 km away at the *Pa Repubblica* on *V. Dante* side. Information through ESIT or at the station, *tel: 070 580 076*. Local rail schedules will be shortened as massive rail work begins.

**Buses:** ARST intercity and Cagliari city transit buses use the newish station on *Pza Matteotti*.

## GETTING AROUND

Cagliari is a compact city with all main urban sights within a 20-min walk, but some steep hills could be an incentive to taking a city bus. Local buses terminate at bus station on *Pza Matteotti* (L1200 for a single trip). Urban buses are necessary for beaches (bus P to Poetto).

## STAYING IN CAGLIARI

A wide range of accommodation possibilities exist but prices tend to climb in July and Aug. Budget hotels and **pensione** cluster on the *V. Roma* between the *Pza Matteotti* and the *Palazzo Consiglio Regionale*, but similar and much quieter places line the *V. Sardegna* paralleling *V. Roma* one block behind it. Hotel chains include: *FE*. Near the Poetto beach try the **Calamosca Sul Mare**, *tel: (070) 371 628, fax: (070) 370 346*. **Camping:** 45 mins east on the Costa Rei at Villasimius is **Spiaggia Del Riso** (Apr–Oct and Christmas Holidays), *tel: (070) 791 052, fax: (070) 797 150*. 1 hr to the west on the Costa del Sud at Teulada is the **Porto Tramutza**, *tel/fax: (070) 927 1022*. Contact ESIT for many other possibilities.

As the capital of Sardinia, Cagliari offers the greatest opportunity to sample the fine cuisine and wines specific to the island. Excellent and inexpensive seafood restaurants are located on the *V. Sardegna* and *V. Cavour* just off the port. Try the *Pza Yenne* for relaxed cafés and snack-bars serving a variety of paninis and foccaccia.

The central **post office** is on the *Pza del Carmine* up *V. Sassari* from the transport stations around *Pza Matteotti*. Open Mon–Sat 0800–1900. A 24-hour Telecom office is nearby at *V. GM Angioj*. Public phones taking coins or cards are scattered throughout the city. Cards can be purchased at newsagents or automatic dispensers.

Banks with bureau de change can be found throughout the central city area and at the airport. ATM are almost as ubiquitous. .

## ENTERTAINMENT AND EVENTS

The free, bilingual monthly *By Night* magazine (available at most Tourist Offices) provides listings for cinemas, concerts and cultural events.

The annual **Festival of Sant'Efisio** from 1 May, honoring the Saint martyred under the Emperor Diocletian, features a solemn procession with horseborne participants attired in traditional red costumes.

## SIGHTSEEING

Cagliari is the largest city on the island, and most likely of Phoenician origin. The compact old city, inside the imposing 13th-century Pisan walls, presents the most interest. Here are the majority of sites and the warren of brick paved lanes and alleys leading to the many tree-lined Piazzas that give Cagliari its charm.

The **National Archaeology Museum** in the *Pza Arsenale* contains an expansive and well documented collection of Nuraghi artefacts. The Romanesque **Duomo**, built by Pisa, is inside the massive walls. Nearby is the Roman amphitheatre. The 5th-century Byzantine **church of San Saturno** is just off the busy *Vle Cimitero*. Stroll the medieval quarter around the Bastione de Saint-Remy and the Porte di Leoni. Visit the beach at Poette and don't forget the Sella del Diavolo **stone formation** in the bay or the salt marshes beyond the dunes, for observing the cranes and pink flamingos.

The new **FdS Railway Museum** (at Monserrato in the northern suburbs) should interest railway enthusiasts, while the important **Botanical gardens**, *V. Ignazio*, is for those looking for a cool spot on summer days. The **Municipal Art Gallery**, *Vle Regine Elena*, has paintings and sculptures by local artists, and the **Museum of Mineralogy**, *V. Trentino 51*, and **Anthropology and Ethnography museum**, *V. Porcell 2*, offer an introduction into Sardinian geology and traditional village life.

393

## SIDE TRACKS FROM CAGLIARI

The FdS narrow-gauge train runs once daily to Arbatax. It allows access to the following towns, as well as spectacular mountain views from both sides of train.

**Seui** gives access to Barbagia and some of Sardinia's highest and wildest peaks through the Gennargentu mountain range. Accommodation (**Hotel Moderno**, *tel: (0782) 54 621*) and tourist services are available in the compact little mountain town.

**Arbatax** has bright red (porphyry) cliffs and many isolated coves with sandy beaches. Tourist information is available through the FdS office; *tel: (0782 ) 667 285*.

This tortuous rail line includes a unique 360-degree full circle as it descends from the Barbagia through tunnels and stone viaducts into the plateau town of **Tortoli**. Note the many large prickly pear cactus along the rail line after Tortoli. Their fruit are cherished as delicacies by locals. From Tortoli, an ARST bus runs to Nuoro (see below), to make a very scenic link (check connections) back to the mainline.

## MACOMER

**Stations:** The FdS Station *(tel: (0785) 70 001)* is 200 m across the railway square from the FS station, but many FdS rail cars shuttle around the square to meet FS trains.

Macomer is the mainline junction with FdS lines for Nuoro and the Barbagia to the east and Bosa and its coast to the west. Occasional FdS steam excursions operate from Macomer towards the sea at Tresnuraghes.

## SIDE TRACKS FROM MACOMER

The recently rebuilt FdS line to Nuoro (up to seven trains daily, taking 1 hr 20 mins) passes many groves of cork trees with their trunks characteristically stripped of bark. Cork has proven to be a valuable export for Sardinia.

## BOSA

Coastal **Bosa** serves a long, mostly unvisited and isolated coast. **Tourist Office:** *59 Corso Vittorio Emanuela* (Mon–Sat 1000–1300 and 1400–1900) can help with accommodation, though many visitors prefer to stay at Bosa Marina.

## NUORO

**Tourist Office:** *Pza Italia 19; tel: (0784) 30 083* or *32 307, fax: 33 432*.

This small town on the slopes of Mt Ortobene is a pleasant, sleepy starting point for the exploration of the villages and rough country in the Barbagia. All bus lines fan out from the concrete bunker-like FdS railway station *(tel: (0784) 30 115)* on *V. Marmora*. A compact, attractive old quarter radiates out from the pedestrianised *Corso Garibaldi*. Traditional Barbagia costumes and masks are on display in the **Regional Ethnographic Museum**, *V. Antonio Mereu 56*. 3000 or so of the costumes on display see action during the 29 Aug **Festival del Redontore**.

## SASSARI

**Tourist Office:** *Vle Caprera 36; tel: (079) 299 544* or *299 579*. Sardinia's second city, founded in the 12th century, Sassari is the capital of the province of the same name and an extremely busy modern commercial, administrative and university town.
**Station:** The combined, monumental FS/FdS *(tel: (079) 243 587)* rail station is on *V. XXV Aprile,* about 15 mins from the old city around the *Pza Castello*.

Near the station are the 13th-century **Duomo** on *Pza de Duomo* and the 1872 built, integrated *Pza Italia* with its monumental statue of Vittorio Emanuele II and **Palazzo Giordano** and **Palazzo del Governo**.

The genoese **Rosello Fountain** near the Rosello Bridge in the northern part of the centre is the symbol of the city while the ethnographic collection at the **Museo Sanna** on *V. Roma 64* is a good introduction to the several colourful traditional festivals that mark Sassari's calendar. The **Cavalcata** on Ascencion Day and the 14th of August **I Candelieri** are two occasions where participants dress in traditional costumes to commemorate important local events.

## SIDE TRACKS FROM SASSARI

FdS narrow gauge train for Alghero (up to 12 daily) takes 35 mins.

### ALGHERO

**Tourist Office:** *Pza Porta Terra 9, 07041 Alghero (Sassari); tel: (079) 979 054, fax: 974 881.* Open Mon–Sat 0800–2000 May–Sept, Sun 0800–1200 July–Aug; Mon–Sat 0800–1400, Sun 0800–1200 Oct–Apr.

The FdS *(tel: (079) 950 785)* railway station is in the Lido area 3 km from the centre, but ARST buses call in at the city park on *V. Catalogna.* Many banks with bureau de change and ATM can be found throughout the town, outside the walls.

Accommodation of all types available. The most appealing within the city is the restored convent of **San Francesco**, *V. Machin 2; tel: (079) 980 330.* **Camping: La Mariposa**, *tel: (079) 950 360,* is 2 km away and **Giuliani Youth Hostel**, *tel: (079) 930 353,* is 6 km away. Both open Apr–Oct.

Though walking along the narrow, cobblestone paved streets around the three bastions or in the centre is the best way to soak up the ambience, bicycles can be rented through **Cicloexpress**, *V. Lamarmora 39,* in the port, *tel: (079) 980 238.*

Alghero is a compact seaside resort reputedly founded in 1102 by the Genoese Doria family, but much older. Much of the present city (as well as the local dialect) within the sturdy Genoese walls dates to the Catalan era: the **Duomo** (1552) in *Pza Duomo,* the **churches of San Francesco** (late 14th-century) in the *V. Carlo Alberto,* **Misericordia** (1662), *V. Misericordia* and **San Michele** (1612), *V. Carlo Alberto,* and the entire **Piazza Civica** contain striking Catalan influences. An active fishing fleet based near the **Porta a Mare** and several local markets – one directly in the *Pza Civica* attest to the living city and assure a constant supply of fresh seafood.

### PALAU

**Palau** is the port for the small islands of **Capprera** where the hero of Italian unification,

Guiseppe Garibaldi, lived out his life, and **Maddalena**, the resort (**Tourist Office**, *tel: (0789) 736 321)* and naval base island. There are occasional ferries to Genoa, check with the local travel agency on *V. Nazionale 97; tel: (0789) 709 570.*

### SANTA TERESA DI GALLURA

**Tourist Office:** *Pza Vittorio Emanuele 24; tel: (0789) 754 127,* helpful office in the main square which will respond to written queries in English addressed to it for a free booklet on accommodation at: *07028 Santa Teresa Gallura.* A pleasant town, cited by the Romans and still called Portolongone by locals, projects out on a rocky promontory. It is a discreet summer tourism resort with all facilities expected (ATM, bureau de change, hotels and pensions) and a wide variety of isolated beaches accessible by foot or the phalanxes of small motor boats anchored in the harbour. The small town's limited hotels tend to fill in July–Aug.

### BONIFACIO

**Tourist Office:** at the port is rudimentary, but main office *(tel: 04 95 73 11 88; fax: 04 95 73 14 97)* in upper town at *place de l'Europe* is very helpful. Open daily 0900–2000 June–Sept, Mon Fri 0900 1200 and 1400–1800 (Oct–May). Online: *http://www.planetepc.fr/bonifacio.* **Ferries: Moby Lines**, *tel: (0789) 755 260,* and **Saremar**, *tel: (0789) 754 788.*

The hardy can save time climbing to the old city by using the covered stairway inside the Genoese walls on the right after leaving the port. Inter-island buses depart from the end of the bay, about a ten minute walk along the quay from the port past innumerable restaurants and cafés lining the anchorage.

Hotels of all categories abound and five campsites are located in the brush beyond the parking lot bounding the bay: **Araguina**, *tel: 04 95 73 02 96; fax 04 95 73 01 92,* is the closest to the bay and **Des Îles**, *tel: 04 95 73 11 89; fax: 04 95 72 18 77,* is closest to the beach.

The upper town is a warren of narrow streets and alleys containing intriguing buildings and churches as well as a seemingly endless number of restaurants. Sights include the **Place du Marché**, the 12th-century Pisan **Eglise Sainte**

## Corsica

Often characterised as being a mountain emerging from the sea, this unspoiled, rugged island's long history is filled by successive invasions.

France gained control in the 18th century and the future Emperor of France, Napoleon Bonaparte, hailed from Corsica. Local pundits like to claim that when France acquired Corsica, Corsica conquered France. Banditry and piracy contribute to the legendary past, but the present is a paradise for mountain trekking, undersea diving and all those who prefer the rugged outdoor life. Epicurians will find their pleasure in the fine seafoods, wines, cheeses and other culinary specialities that mark the island.

Railways are owned by the Collectivites de Corse under the name of Chemins de Fer de la Corse (CFC), but operated under contract by the French National Railways (SNCF). No rail passes honoured other than those issued locally.

Marie Majeure with its 14th-century white stone clock tower – the intricate buttresses along both sides contain an ingenious system of rain water canalisation. The 187-step **Staircase of the King of Aragon** is carved into the stone down to the water and is said to have been built one agited night in 1421. The massive 16th-century **Genoese Gate** with its drawbridge and moat open on to the medieval **Rue Longue**, equally called **Rue des 2 Empereurs**, where the family house of Napoleon Bonaparte faces that of Charles Quint.

## AJACCIO

**Tourist Office: Main Municipal office:** next to City Hall (Mairie), *Pl. du Mar. Foch, tel: 04 95 21 40 87;* open daily 0800–2100 June–Sept; Mon–Fri 0830–1800, Sat 0830–1400 rest of year. A complete tourist desk is in the bus station, open from just before the first to just after the last sailing of the day. Main **Corsica Tourism** office, *17 Blvd Roi Jerome; tel: 04 95 21 56 56,* opens daily 0900–1900 June–Sept;

Mon–Fri 0900–1300, 1430–1730 Oct–May. **Parc Naturel Regional de la Corse** has its main information centre at *2 r. Major Lambroschini; tel: 04 95 51 79 10.*
**Stations: Maritime/Bus Station**. New, purpose built structure on the Quai l'Herminier; *tel: 04 95 29 66 88;* also houses kiosks for inter-island buses, *tel: 04 95 21 28 01.* Open daily 0630 until departure of last ferry usually 2000). **Rail station**, *tel: 04 95 23 11 03.* About 500 m north of the Maritime station along the *Blvd Sampiero,* which is an extension of the Quai l'Herminier.

### STAYING IN AJACCIO

A plethora of lodging of all categories is available. In the centre between the bus/maritime stations and the rail station are many smaller hotels, while slightly further away are the more upmarket **Hotel Imperial** *(tel: 04 95 21 50 62, fax: 04 95 21 15 20)* and the **Hotel Fesch** *(tel: 04 95 21 50 52, fax: 04 95 21 83 36).* **Camping Les Mimosas** *(tel: 04 95 20 99 85),* 3 km east of the city, is well equipped. The **Relais regional des gites ruraux** *(tel: 04 95 20 51 34, fax: 04 95 20 28 96)* provides information and brochures on rural gites and isolated bed and breakfasts in the area.

The full range of Corsican and French cuisine is available and, given the large concentration of Foreign Legion bases in the area, there is a number of Chinese and other Asian restaurants and fast-food establishments. Fish and seafoods are a speciality around the coasts and hearty mountain sausages and strong goat and sheep's cheeses are a local treat. Corsica is home to a variety of white, rose and red wines produced from local grape varieties and bearing the respected French Appellation of Origin designation for their respective areas of production.

The main **post office** *(tel: 04 95 51 84 65)* is on the *Cours Napoleon* (open 0900–1700) and sub-agencies can be found throughout the city.

Public telephones accepting prepaid cards can be found throughout the city, but those accepting coins are becoming scarce. Telecards are available at most newsagents, tobacconists and major transport terminals. ATM and bureau de changes are located throughout the city. Beware of excessive charges levied on travellers cheques and low denomination bank notes – ask about these costs before changing money. Banks are open 0845–1645, closed weekends.

## EVENTS

The birth of local-boy-made-good (or is it bad?) **Napoleon** is commemorated from 13–15 Aug with parades, dances and pageants. A newer event is the **Rencontres europeenes de plongee sous-marine** *(tel: 04 95 25 12 58)*, which gathers deep-sea divers and afficionados to Ajaccio for films, conferences and special diving expeditions. This is normally held at the end of Sept.

## SHOPPING

French taxation laws favour Corsica with lower VAT and other taxes than on the continent, so all luxury goods are cheaper here than in mainland France. All ships have duty-free shops as well. Flavourful, though rather tangy, locally produced Corsican wines and cheeses should also be considered.

## SIGHTSEEING

Like most Corsican cities, Ajaccio is compact and all points are easily accessible by foot or by bus from the port side bus station. Bicycles and motorcycles can be rented from **Moto Corse Evasion** *(tel: 04 95 20 52 05)*.

Several sights related to native son Napoleon Bonaparte are of interest, including **La Maison Bonaparte** *(tel: 04 95 21 43 89;* open daily May–Sept 0900–1200 and 1400–1800, Oct–Apr 1000–1200 and 1400–1700, but closed Sun 1200 to Mon 1400) on the r. Saint Charles at the *Pl. Letizia*. The monumental **Statue of Napoleon** in the *Pl. d'Austerlitz* also provides fine views over the city and the Gulf. The **Fesch Museum** *(tel: 04 95 21 48 17;* open 0930–1200 15 Sept–15 June and 1430–1800 July–Aug, Fri from 2130–midnight; closed Sun and Mon in winter) is Corsica's major art museum with works by Raphael, Titien and Botticelli making it the best collection of Italian Primitive art outside Paris. The 1868 **Public Library** is a wing of the Fesch Museum and has one of the most exciting interiors – all in teak – of any library anywhere.

The private **Bandera Museum** *(tel: 04 95 51 07 34, fax: 04 95 51 39 60);* open Mon–Sat 1000–1200, 1500–1900 (June–Sept) and Mon–Fri 0900–1200, 1400–1800 (Oct–May) gives a Corsican perspective to different aspects of Corsica. A good introduction to the island and its sociology.

> ### ◥ SIDE TRACK
> ### TO CARGESE
>
> North along the coast from Ajaccio by bus (SAIB, *tel: 04 95 22 41 99)* on an isolated bay is an intriguing little town populated by Greek immigrants who fled Ottoman persecution during the later part of the 17th century. The **Tourist Office** *(tel: 04 95 26 41 31);* open daily 0900–1200, 1600–1900 June–Sept, Mon–Fri 1500–1700 Oct–May, has complete information on lodgings and restaurants as well as the history of the prospering village. A must is the Orthodox Chapel, facing the Catholic Church. Inside the Chapel are four icons that came from Greece, including a 12th-century Byzantine icon of the **Virgin Infant**. ◢

### CORTE

**Tourist Office: Syndicat d'Initiative**, *Pl. de la Fontaine des Quatre Canons; tel: 04 95 46 26 70* June–Sept, and *tel: 04 95 46 24 20* Oct–May. The modern rail station, *tel: 04 95 46 00 97,* has left luggage facilities.

For 14 years the Capital of Corsica, Corte has hotels, auberges, banks, ATM, shops and restaurants, making it a good centre for hikers and campers to the regional natural park, *tel: 04 95 46 27 44.* The **Museum of Corsica** contains the 15th-century citadel at the town's highest point.

### PONTE LECCIA

This is the junction for services to l'Île Rousse and Calvi. Direct narrow-gauge services run, two daily, calling at l'Île Rousse, journey taking 2 hrs. Between l'Île Rousse and Calvi, 9 additional services operate July–Sept. This exotic rail route takes a curving, mountainous passage through mostly deserted countryside to l'Île Rousse, and then hugs the seashore to Calvi.

**SIDE TRACKS
FROM PONTE LECCIA**

## L'ÎLE ROUSSE

**Tourist Office:** *Pl. Paoli, tel: 04 95 60 04 35; fax: 04 95 60 24 74.* Open 0930–1200, 1500–1800 (Apr–Oct) 0900–1300, 1430–1930 (July–Aug). Rail information: *tel: 04 85 60 00 50;* maritime information for SNCM, *tel: 04 95 60 09 56,* and for Corsica Ferries, *tel: 04 95 60 44 11.*

A handsome, compact town with fine sandy beaches, a lively centre and some of the hottest August temperatures in Corsica, this is a good base to explore the exotic mountain backcountry.

The narrower than narrow, cobbled streets of the old town between **la Place Paoli** and the rail line are worth rambling through. The **Oceanographic Museum** is worth a few hours of your time to discover the marvels of the extensive, undersea life of the Mediterranean.

## CALVI

**Tourist Office:** *tel: 04 95 65 16 67; fax: 04 95 65 14 09,* open daily 0900–1930 (June–Sept), Mon–Sat: 0900–1200, Mon–Fri 1400–1800 (rest of year). Across the street from the station, on pedestrian promenade lining the Port de Plaisance.

**Rail Information:** *tel: 04 95 65 00 61.*
**Ferries: Corsica Ferries**, *tel: 04 95 65 15 02,* or **Agence Tramar**, *tel: 04 95 65 01 38* (open 2 hrs before ship departure for ticket sales).

Hotels, pensions, restaurants and cafés abound around the lower town and the port in large numbers. But the Balagne region beyond the coast is largely devoid of services. Calvi provides the best of several worlds – lively summer beach and the potential to discover the untouched hinterland. Treks and camping tours of this region can be organised through the Tourist Office.

Little known today, Calvi played a major role in the history of Corsica. Many believe that the Genoese adventurer Christopher Columbus was born in the citadel. Though proof of this is scarce, Lord Nelson lost an

eye while bombarding the **citadel** during the Napoleonic wars. Guided tours are available through the citadel Tourist Office *(tel: 04 95 65 36 74).*

## BASTIA

**Tourist Office:** *Pl. St. Nicolas, tel: 04 95 31 00 89.* Open daily from 0800–1900, July–Aug 0700–2200. **Corsica Loisirs Aventure** *(tel: 04 95 32 54 34, fax: 04 95 32 57 58)* at *3, rue Notre-Dame-de-Lourdes,* is an association that can assist campers and trekkers in organising their exploration of backcountry Corsica.

**Stations: Rail:** *tel: 04 95 32 80 61,* contains luggage storage facility and is close to centre and port. **Maritime:** in the new port area near the *Pl. St Nicolas.* Ferry companies: **SNCM**, *tel: 04 95 54 66 88;* **Corsica Ferries**, *tel: 04 95 32 95 95;* **Moby Lines**, *tel: 04 95 31 46 29.*

Buses for many island points not served by the railway and for the north-eastern **Cap Corse** peninsula leave from various destinations. Check with the municipal Tourist Office for schedules and departure points.

**Airport: Bastia-Poretta**, *tel: 04 95 54 54 54,* is 20 km south of the city in the eastern plain. Dedicated blue and beige buses taking 40 mins leave at least 7 times daily from the *RondPoint LeClerc* near the rail station. *Tel: 04 95 31 06 65* for exact schedules.

### GETTING AROUND

Small and compact, Bastia can be covered on foot though a somewhat unreliable municipal bus system does exist. Taxis are metered and often do not respond to hailing. All companies have stands around the *Pl. St. Nicolas.*

### STAYING IN BASTIA

A variety of accommodation can be found around the old city between the railway station and the maritime port along the *Ave Marechal Sebastiani.* **Camping Les Bois de San Damiano** *(tel: 04 95 33 68 02, fax: 04 95 30 84 10;* open Apr–Oct) is 5 km south on the long Marana beach.

The Old Port area contains a large number of restaurants ranging from Corsican seafood speciality to pizzerias to tex-mex establishments. Otherwise, the daily market in the square around the City Hall behind the St Jean Baptiste Church offers a delectable array of fresh, local produce.

The main **post office** is on the *r. Cesar Campinchi* between the railway station and the *Pl. St. Nicolas*. Card operated telephones are to be found throughout the city; coin operated phones are rare. ATM and bureaux de change are found throughout the city.

## ENTERTAINMENT AND EVENTS

The evening promenade and an early evening coffee in the large and lively *Pl. St. Nicolas* seems to be the summer activity of many locals.

The annual 13th of July celebration of the changing of island rulers called **La releve des gouverneurs** is celebrated with pomp and circumstance along with archers and musket bearing locals dressed in 18th-century costumes.

The Oct music festival, **Les Musicales de Bastia** *(tel: 04 95 31 25 14)* features classical, Jazz, traditional and choral music.

## SHOPPING

A must in Bastia is the century old **Cap Corse Mattei** shop at *15 Blvd du General de Gaulle* on the *Pl. St. Nicolas*. On sale are locally produced beverages made from Quinine, oranges, peaches and even grapes. Mon–Sat, 0930–1230, 1430–2200, (–1900 Oct–Mar).

## SIGHTSEEING

Considered more Corsican than Ajaccio, at first glance, Bastia can be a bit glum, sombre and all too serious. It has little of the frivolity of Bonifacio or the relaxed atmosphere of l'Île Rousse or Calvi, but it has its charm; especially around the old port and on the citadel dominating the rocky 900m corniche overlooking the site. Bastia is the gateway to the untrammelled **Cap Corse** peninsula that stretches north-east and contains some of the most traditional Corsican settlements to be found on the island.

Besides the already mentioned *Pl.St. Nicolas* and the *r. Napoleon* that connects it with the Old Port, visitors should peak in the 1611 **Chapel of the Immaculate Conception** and its sumptuous interior. The Anglo-Corsican parliament met here for the four years England ruled the island in the 19th century. The 17th-century **Church of Saint-Jean-Baptiste** links the newer part of Bastia with the old port. The horseshoe shaped old port is as animated as the *Pl. St. Nicolas* but with much more charm as wooden fishing boats creak at anchor while the lively bars around the port seem to draw every character for miles around.

Beyond the old Port in a neighbourhood called **Terra Nova** is the **Governor's Palace** which contains the **Museum of Corsican Ethnography**. Excellent museum (open daily June–Sept 0900–1830 and to 2000 July–Aug, Oct–Apr 0900–1200 and 1400–1800) giving a geological and geographical background to the island as well as exhibiting local oil paintings from the 16th to the 19th centuries.

The 17th-century **Cathedral of Saint Mary** contains a 19th century statue in silver of the Virgin Mary said to weigh one ton. Fifty metres beyond the Cathedral is the **Baroque Oratory of the Saint Cross** containing the much venerated **Black Christ of Miracles** found in 1428 and since become the patron of local fishermen.

**399**

## ⤴ SIDE TRACKS FROM BASTIA

By bus – several per week – through the rural area of **Luri** to the protected harbor of **Macinaggio** at the northern edge of **Cap Corse**. The 17 hamlets making up Luri County are extremely traditional without much tourist infrastructure.

The main village '**A Piazza**' has some simple rooms for rent and it is the site of the annual **Corsican Wine Festival** held during the first weekend in July. Macinaggio has a small but efficient Tourism Office *(tel: 04 95 35 40 34)* on the quays of the port, which offers solid information on the village and the region.

Beyond Macinaggio, the village of **Rogliano** perches picturesquely on the flank of the mountain, while beyond is the northernmost point on the island **Barcaggio**, with its small port and large sandy beach accessible only by foot after a 20 min-walk from Barcaggio. ⤴

# PARIS

With one of the most romantic images in the world, Paris is an enchanting city, a place of elegance and gaiety, chic and shock, but it is also a busy, pragmatic capital. There is an enormous amount to see and do, so allow at least three days – far more if you're into museums and galleries.

## TOURIST INFORMATION

**Office du Tourisme et des Congrès de Paris** (Paris Convention and Visitors Bureau), *127 av. des Champs-Elysées; tel: 49 52 53 54* (métro: *Étoile/George V*). Open daily 0900–2000. Vast amounts of useful information on everything in Paris and the surrounding Île de France, a booking service for excursions, a France-wide hotel reservation desk, booking and information desks for SNCF and Disneyland Paris. Further offices at: **Gare du Nord**; *tel: 45 26 94 82*, open Mon–Sat 0800–2100 (May–Oct); Mon–Sat 0800–2000 (Nov–Apr). **Eiffel Tower**; *tel: 45 51 22 15*, daily 1100–1800 (May–Sept). There's also a 24-hr information number (in English); *tel: 49 52 53 56*.

## ARRIVING AND DEPARTING

### Airports

**Roissy-Charles de Gaulle** is 23 km northeast of the city and has a 24-hr service for flight times; *tel: 48 62 22 80*. There are three main terminals, bureaux de change (0615–2330), cashpoints, tourist information and hotel booking desk, *tel: 48 62 27 29* (0700–2300). Links to the city all operate roughly 0600–2300. **Roissyrail** trains run to *Gare du Nord* and on to *Châtelet* every 15 mins, taking 35 mins (RER B3; FFr.37) and **Roissybus** *(tel: 04 41 56 78 00)* to *Opéra-Garnier* 0540–2300 every 15 mins, taking 45 mins (FFr.55). **Air France coaches** *(tel: 43 23 97 10)* from *Gare de Lyon* and *Gare Montparnasse* to *pl. Charles de Gaulle/Étoile* and

*Porte Maillot,* operate from 0700–2100 every 15–20 mins, taking about 40 mins (FFr.65). Regular buses are slower but cost less – no. 350 serves *Gare du Nord* and *Gare de l'Est,* and no. 351 serves *pl. de la Nation.* A taxi to the centre should cost around FFr.220.

**Orly** is 14 km south and has its own information service (0600–2300); *tel: 49 75 15 15.* There are two terminals (Sud and Ouest), each with a tourist information booth (0600–2345) and bureau de change (0630–2300). All the transport options operate approximately 0600–midnight and take about 30 mins. **Orlyrail** (RER C2) runs to *Gare d'Austerlitz* every 15 mins (FFr.28) and there's a shuttle service, **OrlyVal**, to *Gare Antony* every few mins and on to *Châtelet-les-Halles* or *Denfert-Rochereau* (FFr.50). RATP Orlybus to *Denfert-Rochereau* métro station goes every 15 mins (FFr.25). Air France coaches *(tel: 01 41 56 78 00)* to *Gare Montparnasse* and *Gare des Invalides* are every 12 mins or so from 0550–2300 daily (FFr.40). A taxi to the centre should cost around FFr.160.

### Stations

If continuing on a TGV train from the north of France to the south or elsewhere, it may no longer be obligatory to pass through Paris; there is also a very handsome new TGV terminal at Charles de Gaulle airport.

There are six main rail stations in Paris, all with a wide range of services, from tourist information and left-luggage offices to bookstalls, news-stands and cafés. Each has its own métro stop and is also served by RER. SNCF enquiries for the whole country are handled centrally: *tel: 36 35 35 35.*

Trains from **Paris-Nord** reach Scandinavia, Belgium, the Netherlands and the UK (via Boulogne and Calais ferries and Eurostar Channel Tunnel services). **Paris-Est** is for north-east France, Luxembourg, Germany, Austria and Switzerland. **Paris-St-Lazare** covers Normandy and the UK (via Dieppe). **Paris-Montparnasse** serves Brittany, Versailles,

Chartres and the south-west coast, while **Paris-Austerlitz** serves the Loire Valley, south and south-west France, Spain and Portugal. Services from **Paris-Gare de Lyon** spread over eastern and south-eastern France, the Auvergne, Provence, the Alps, Italy and Greece.

## GETTING AROUND

Although it is possible to see Paris on foot, it's worth taking advantage of the efficient and well co-ordinated public transport, made up of the métro (subway) and buses of **RATP** *(Régie autonome des Transport Parisiens)* and **RER** *(Réseau Express Régional)* trains. During 1998, the RATP will be extending its network with the opening of the showcase *Meteor* line and a new East–West suburban Line E. Free maps of the networks are available from métro and bus stations (even from many hotels and big stores). *Le Petit Plan de Paris* is excellent for the centre; the *Grand Plan de Paris* is more extensive. Both are free. Street maps of Paris are available from stationers and kiosks, as well as from **Thomas Cook** bureaux de change (p. 406).

### Tickets

The same tickets are used in the metro, bus and RER systems. The network itself is divided into five zones. Green tickets are used in the two central zones, Paris proper. Others, usually yellow, are used as you get further out. Outside the central zone, you should buy a ticket from an automatic machine or the *guichet*. Bus tickets are now valid for the whole journey in the central zone. Passes can be bought at the airports, stations, Tourist Offices and some *tabacs*.

The best value for a short stay is probably the ten-ride **carnet**, currently FFr.48 (individual tickets are FFr.6.50). **Formule 1** cards give one day of unlimited city travel. You can cover zones 1–3 (FFr.38) or opt for extra zones. The **Paris Visite** pass for zones 1–3 is valid for three (FFr.95) or five (FFr.150) consecutive days and can be extended to cover other zones. You can also get a **Carte Orange** (weekly or monthly pass). The weekly *(coupon hebdomadaire/jaune)* is valid Mon–Sun (FFr.59–142, depending on the number of zones you require). The monthly *(coupon mensuel)* is valid from the first day of the month (FFr.208–526).

### Métro

The impressive métro system runs every few mins 0530–0100. Lines are coded by colour and number and named for their final destination. Maps of the whole system are at all stations and signs on platforms indicate connecting lines *(correspondances)*. To reach the platform, slot your ticket into an automatic barrier, then retrieve it.

### RER

This system consists of four rail lines (A, B, C, D – plus the new 'E' in 1998), which are basically express services between the city and the suburbs. They form a cross through Paris and have a few central stops. The numbers following the letters (usually in the suburbs) indicate a branch from the main line. There are computerised route-finders at the RER stations. These give you alternative ways to reach your destination – on foot, as well as by public transport.

### Buses

**RATP**, *53bis quai des Grands-Augustins; tel: 01 44 68 20 20,* have a separate information line, manned 0600–2100; *tel: 43 46 14 14.* Bus-stops show the numbers of the routes using them and display a map of those routes. There are onboard announcements of the next stop. Tickets must be validated when you board, but passes are just shown to the driver. Most buses run 0630–2030/2100, but some lines continue until 0030. Sun services and bank holidays *(jours feriés)* are infrequent. Night buses *(Noctambus)* are hourly 0100–0500 and have ten suburban routes fanning out from *pl. du Châtelet.*

### River Journeys

The Seine, its islands and quays together create one of the world's most beautiful stretches of urban river. Most of the boat companies operate half-hourly departures, with multilingual commentaries, throughout the day (about FFr.45) and some offer evening dinner cruises.

The glass-topped **Bateaux-Mouches** have frequent departures from *Pont de l'Alma; tel: 40 76 99 99.* For bookings; *tel: 42 25 96 10.* Other companies include **Vedettes de Paris**; *tel: 47 05 71 29,* from *port de Suffren, sq. de Vert Galant, Île de la Cité* and *Pont d'Iéna,* and **Bateaux Parisiens**; *tel: 44 11 33 33,* from *port de la*

401

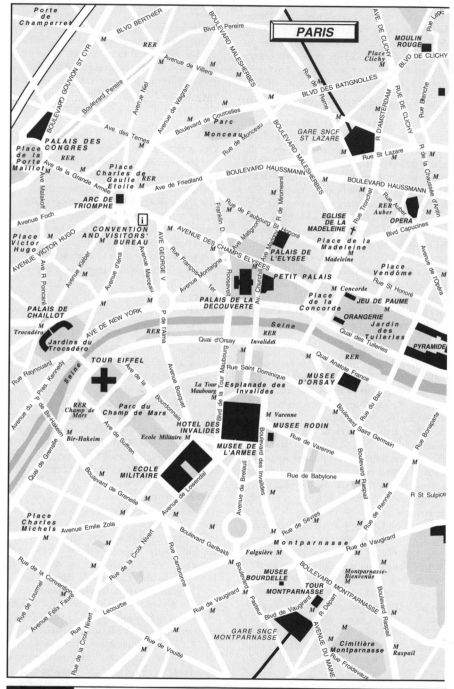

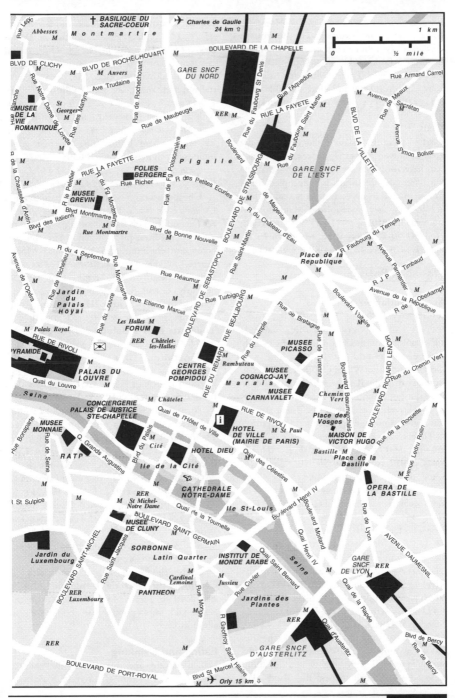

† **BASILIQUE DU SACRE-COEUR**

✈ Charles de Gaulle 24 km ⇧

M o n t m a r t r e

Rue Lepic

Abbesses
M

BLVD DE CLICHY

BLVD DE ROCHECHOUART

Ave Trudaine

M Anvers

Rue de Rochechouart

GARE SNCF
DU NORD

BOULEVARD DE LA CHAPELLE

Rue du Faubourg St Denis

Rue l'Aqueduc

RER M

RUE LA FAYETE

Rue du Faubourg Saint Martin

Avenue de Meaux

Rue de Secrétan

Rue Armand Carrel

Avenue Simon Bolivar

St
Georges
M

Rue des Martyrs

**MUSEE
DE LA
VIE
ROMANTIQUE**

Rue Notre Dame de Lorette

Rue de Maubeuge

Boulevard

RUE LA FAYETTE

**FOLIES
BERGERE**

Rue Richer

P i g a l l e

Rue de Fg Poissonnière

R des Petites Ecuries

BOULEVARD DE STRASBOURG

R du Château d'Eau

de Magenta

**GARE SNCF
DE L'EST**

BLVD DE LA VILLETTE

Avenue

Rue le Peletier

Rue du Fg Montmartre

**MUSEE
GREVIN**

Blvd Montmartre

Rue Montmartre

Blvd des Italiens

Rue Montmartre

Blvd de Bonne Nouvelle

Rue Saint-Martin

R Faubourg du Temple

Avenue Parmentier

Timbaud

de la Chaussée d'Antin

R du 4 Septembre

Rue de Richelieu

Rue Réaumur

Rue Montmartre

Rue Etienne Marcel

BOULEVARD DE SEBASTOPOL

Rue Turbigo

Rue Saint-Martin

**Place de la
Republique**

R J P

Avenue de la République

R de Oberkampf

R de

Avenue de l'Opéra

**J a r d i n
d u
P a l a i s
Royal**

Rue du Louvre

Les Halles M
**FORUM**

Châtelet-
les-Halles

RER

RUE DU RENARD

RUE DE BEAUBOURG

Rue du Temple

Rue de Bretagne

Boulevard

Rue de Turenne

**MUSEE
PICASSO**

Boulevard Beaumarchais

BOULEVARD RICHARD LENOIR

Rue du Chemin Vert

M Palais Royal

RUE DE RIVOLI

**PYRAMIDE**

**PALAIS DU
LOUVRE**

✉

Quai du Louvre

Seine

**CENTRE
GEORGES
POMPIDOU**

Rambuteau

M a r a i s

**MUSEE
COGNACQ-JAY**

**MUSEE
CARNAVALET**

Chemin
Vert

**Place des
Vosges**

Rue de la Roquette

**CONCIERGERIE
PALAIS DE JUSTICE
STE-CHAPELLE**

M Châtelet

Quai de l'Hôtel de Ville

RUE DE RIVOLI

**MAISON DE
VICTOR HUGO**

Avenue Ledru Rollin

**MUSEE
MONNAIE**

Rue Bonaparte

Rue de Seine

Q. Grands Augustins

Blvd du Palais

Cité

**Ile de la Cité**

**HOTEL DIEU**

i

**HOTEL
DE VILLE
(MAIRIE DE PARIS)**

M St Paul

Quai des Célestins

Bastille M

**Place de la
Bastille**

**RATP**

**CATHEDRALE
NOTRE-DAME**

Quai de la Tournelle

**Ile St-Louis**

Boulevard Henri IV

Boulevard Morland

**OPERA DE
LA BASTILLE**

AVENUE DAUMESNIL

St Sulpice

RER
St Michel-
Notre Dame

**MUSEE
DE CLUNY**

BOULEVARD SAINT GERMAIN

**SORBONNE**

Latin Quarter

**INSTITUT DE
MONDE ARABE**

Quai Saint Bernard

Seine

Quai Henri IV

Quai de la Rapée

**GARE
SNCF
DE LYON**

RER

Rue de Lyon

**Jardin du
Luxembourg**

BOULEVARD SAINT-MICHEL

Rue Saint Jacques

Cardinal
Lemoine

M
Jussieu

Rue Cuvier

**PANTHEON**

Rue Morge

**Jardins des
Plantes**

R Geoffroy Saint Hilaire

Quai d'Austerlitz

Blvd de Bercy

RER
Luxembourg

RER

**GARE SNCF
D'AUSTERLITZ**

Rue de Bercy

BOULEVARD DE PORT-ROYAL

Blvd St Marcel

✈ Orly 15 km ⇩

**403**

Bourdonnais, Pont d'Iéna and quai de Montebello. Buy a ticket before boarding. The **Batobus** is a water-bus (without a commentary) that operates every 36 mins 1000–1900 (Apr–Oct). The stops are the Eiffel Tower, Musée d'Orsay, the Louvre, Notre-Dame and Hôtel de Ville. You can pay (FFr.15) per stop or get a day-ticket.

## Taxis

Taxis are plentiful. Flagging them down in the street is allowed, but rarely successful. Licensed taxis have roof lights; white indicates that the taxi is free, orange means it is occupied. Fares are determined by three time zones and a host of extras, but they are regulated. Major companies include: **Alpha**, tel: 45 85 85 85; **Artaxi**, tel: 42 41 50 50; **Taxi Bleu**, tel: 49 36 10 10; and **G7**, tel: 47 39 47 39. Avoid unofficial taxis.

**STAYING IN PARIS**

## Accommodation

Whatever your price range (except rock-bottom), a lot of options are available, and finding suitable accommodation is a problem only in the busiest months (usually May, June, Sept and Oct – see also World Cup feature, p.4xx). **Bureaux d'Accueil** at the main Tourist Office and main-line stations offer a room-finding service for hostels as well as hotels. There are also automated room-finding machines at airports.

Hotel chains include: Ba, BW, Ch, Cn, Ct, Ev, FE, GH, GT, Hd, Hn, Hy, Ib, IC, IH, Mc, Md, Nv, RC, RS, Sf, Sg, Sh, SL, Sn and Tp. Some of the most expensive hotels have become attractions in their own right. The most famous is probably still **George V**, 31 av. George V, 8e; tel: 47 23 54 00, but the place now is **Le Crillon**, 10 pl. de la Concorde, 8e; tel: 01 44 71 15 00, housed in an 18th-century palace, with an opulent, marble-lined restaurant called Les Ambassadeurs. Just as luxurious are the **Ritz**, 15 pl. Vendôme, 1e; tel: 42 60 38 30, which provides up-to-date facilities in a splendid Louis XV setting, and the **Bristol**, 112 r. du Faubourg St-Honoré, 8e; tel: 01 58 43 43 00, which boasts a collection of Gobelin tapestries and is a favourite with UK politicians. If, without rising to such dizzy heights, you can afford to spend, it's difficult to beat the islands. Try

**Jeu de Paume**, 54 r. St-Louis-en-l'Île, 4e; tel: 43 26 14 18 (discreetly luxurious), or **Deux Îles**, 59 r. St-Louis-en-l'Île, 4e; tel: 43 26 13 35 (a tastefully converted 17th-century mansion).

Further down the price scale, but very central and fairly quiet, are: **Le Pavillon**, 54 r. St-Dominique, 7e; tel: 45 51 42 87 (former convent with a peaceful courtyard), and **Thoumieux**, 79 r. St-Dominique, 7e; tel: 47 05 49 75, which has an excellent bistro. The cheapest good options for hotels include **Henri IV**, 25 pl. Dauphine, Île de la Cité, 1e; tel: 43 54 44 53, and **Castex**, 5 r. Castex, 4e; tel: 42 72 31 52.

Cheaper accommodation is not hard to find. Quartier Latin (Latin Quarter) and St-Germain-des-Près, on the Left Bank, have a good range of low- to medium-price hotels. Many budget hotels are clustered round Faubourg Montmartre, in the 9th arrondissement. The area around the Gare du Nord is also cheap, but can be fairly sleazy. Self-catering apartments are arranged by **Paris Séjour Réservation**, 90 av. des Champs Elysées; tel: 01 53 89 10 50. **Tourisme chez l'Habitant**, 27 r. Rambuteau; tel: 01 34 25 44 44, covers bed and breakfast.

**Fédération Unie des Auberges de Jeunesse**, 27 r. Pajol; tel: 46 47 00 01, has a list of youth hostels in France. **AJF (Accueil des Jeunes de France)**, 119 r. St-Martin; tel: 42 77 87 80, and 139 blvd St-Michel; tel: 43 54 95 86, find beds (often cheap ones) for people aged 18–30. **HI**: **Le d'Artagnan**, 80 r. Vitruve; tel: 01 40 32 34 56 (métro: Porte-de-Bagnolet); **Cité des Sciences**, 1 r. Jean-Baptiste Clement, le Pré St-Gervais; tel: 48 43 24 11 (métro: Hoche, Porte de Pantin); **Jules–Ferry**, 8 blvd Jules Ferry; tel: 57 55 60 (métro: République); **Clichy**, 107 r. Maitre, 921100 Clichy; tel: 01 41 27 26 90. The **Woodstock Hostel**, 48 r. Rodier, 75009; tel: 01 48 78 87 76, has young, friendly staff. 10 mins walk from Gare du Nord.

Easily the most central **campsite** is **Camping du Bois de Boulogne**, Allée du Bord-de-l'Eau, 16e; tel: 45 24 30 00. Next to the Seine and very popular, so book well in advance.

### Eating and Drinking

French cuisine, and thus one of the essential tenets of Gallic culture, is currently in a state of

**404**

deep crisis. Innovation, panache and style have all leapt out of the pan and into a painful fire; even their own chefs say so. Despite the fact that Sydney, San Francisco and, *horreur* of horrors, London are sharing the gourmet limelight, Paris is still a great place to eat, with many fabulous restaurants at relatively cheap prices.

Paris is a vast *cassoulet* of culinary cultures, so to get ahead you should follow a few rules of thumb, especially if you are on a tight budget. *Cafés* and *bars* are the cheapest, and *brasseries* and *salons de thé* are more expensive. The closer to the bar you stand, the less you pay. Self-service restaurants are usually fine, if a little institutional, and a snack at a *crêperie* will usually keep hunger at bay. A trip to the supermarket and an hour's picnic in the Tuileries gardens of the Palais Royal is also a lovely way to lunch.

For evening meals, study the set menus outside most restaurants; these often provide a reasonable choice at affordable prices. The Latin Quarter, Marais, Montmartre and Montparnasse are good areas for cheap eating and multi-ethnic cuisine, especially Greek, North African, East European and Vietnamese. For kosher food, try *r. des Rosiers* and *r. Xavier Privas*. The weekly listings magazine, *Pariscope,* provides a guide to Paris restaurants.

If you can afford to dig really deep, go to **La Tour d'Argent**, *15–17 quai de la Tournelle* – they've been in business for over four centuries and French food just doesn't come any better – but you must book well ahead. Another place really worth the steep prices is **Jules Verne**, on the second stage of the Eiffel Tower: the food and service are as superb as the views. If it's beyond your pocket, descend to the first stage and eat at **La Belle France**, more café-style and much more reasonably priced, but still high enough for great views. For kosher, **Jo Goldenberg**, *7 r. des Rosiers*, is the best. Vegetarian is difficult to find, but **Country Life**, *6 r. Daunou*, is both good and cheap. A budget place for good French food is **Chartier**, *r. du Faubourg-Montmartre*, which has amazing décor. **Au Pied du Cochon**, *6 r. Coquillière*, is something of an institution, open 24 hrs and famous for its breakfast of onion soup, pigs' trotters and its real pig in a pen.

If you fancy eating alfresco, make an early evening visit to *r. Mouffetard* (métro: *Monge/ Censier Daubeton*) or *r. de Buci* (métro: *St-Germain-des-Prés/Mabillon),* where a range of mouth-watering delicacies is on offer; or try the organic products market, *blvd Raspail,* on Sun morning (métro: *Rennes*). At *La Chapelle* on Sat morning, there is a huge exotic food market.

### Communications

The main **post office**, *52 r. du Louvre,* is open 24 hrs a day for telephones and poste restante. Other services close at 1900.

The telephone code for Paris from elsewhere in France is *01,* just *1* from outside France. See also Country by Country, p. xx.

### Money

It's not difficult to obtain cash outside banking hours. The exchange office at *Gare de Lyon* stays open until 2330, there are plenty of late-opening private bureaux de change and also lots of automatic machines (which take credit cards) in strategic positions, such as transport terminals.

**Thomas Cook bureaux de change** can be found all over the centre of Paris, including most main rail stations (see p. 406). They offer money-changing facilities and a range of other services, such as phonecards and reservations.

### Embassies and Consulates

**Australia:** *4 r. Jean Rey; tel: 01 40 59 33 00.*
**Canada:** *35 av. Montaigne; tel: 01 44 43 29 00.*
**Republic of Ireland:** *4 r. Rude; tel: 01 44 17 67 00.*
**New Zealand:** *7ter r. L-da-Vinci; tel: 01 45 00 24 11.*
**South Africa:** *59 quai d'Orsay; tel: 01 53 59 23 23.*
**UK:** *16 r. d'Anjou; tel: 01 44 51 31 00.*
**USA:** *2 r. St-Florentin; tel: 01 43 12 23 47.*

### ENTERTAINMENT AND EVENTS

The monthly *Paris Sélection* and annual *Saisons de Paris* listings are available (free) from Tourist Offices. There's also a 24-hr information line; tel: *49 52 53 56.* Two inexpensive weekly listings are *l'Officiel des Spectacles* and *Pariscope,* which has an 8-page English language section *(Time Out),* both on sale at newsagents. Half-price theatre tickets can be purchased for same-

**405**

## Thomas Cook

Thomas Cook bureaux de change in Paris are open seven days a week and have extended opening hours. As well as encashing Thomas Cook Travellers' Cheques free of commission charges, and providing emergency assistance in the case of lost or stolen Thomas Cook Travellers' Cheques and to holders of MasterCards, they offer foreign exchange facilities. In addition, most sell maps and Thomas Cook publications.

Thomas Cook bureaux can be found at the following locations in Paris:

194 r. de Rivoli
25 blvd des Capucines
36–42 r. Rambuteau
4 blvd St-Michel
Port de la Bourdonnais
Tour Eiffel Champs de Mars
52 av. des Champs Elysées
73 av. des Champs Elysées
125 av. des Champs Elysées
Gare St-Lazare
8 pl. de l'Opera
Gare du Nord
Gare de l'Est
Gare d'Austerlitz
Gare Montparnasse
84 blvd de Clichy
8–10 r. de Steinkerque

classical plays by such writers as Molière and Racine. There are several other good theatres for those fluent in French.

There are regular seasons of both ballet and opera at **Opéra–Bastille**, *120 r. de Lyon*, **Opéra–Garnier**, *8 r. Scribe* (which sells cheap stand-by tickets on the day of the performance), and **Opéra–Comique**, *Salle Favard 5, 5 r. Favard*. There are also numerous concerts, held everywhere from purpose-built auditoria to museums, with a variety of free performances in several churches (including Notre Dame, every Sun evening). **Jazz** is so popular that it has a special information service: **Centre d'Information du Jazz**, *21bis r. de Paradis; tel: 44 83 10 30*. Other live music (especially rock) is also easy to find and there's no shortage of discos and other places to dance.

At **cinemas**, there are often discounts on Wed. *VO (Version Originale)* means the film is in the original language, while *VF (Version Française)* means it's been dubbed.

The most famous annual celebration is **Bastille Day** (13–14 July), when fireworks and parades mark the anniversary of the storming of the city prison in 1789.

Other major events include **Mardi Gras** (Feb); **May Day** workers' marches (1 May); the **French Tennis Open Championships** (late May–early June); **Fête de la Musique** (June); the final of the **Tour de France** along the *Champs Elysées* (last Sun July); and **Festival de Jazz** (late Oct).

### SHOPPING

People cross the world to shop in Paris – if they are rich enough. You can get everything here, but don't expect bargains. To admire designer styles, head for *r. de Faubourg St-Honoré, av. Montaigne* and *r. de Rivoli*. More reasonable prices can be tracked down at *Les Halles, St-Germain-des-Près* and the *rues de Commerce at Rennes*. The most famous department stores are **Galeries Lafayette**, *40 blvd Haussmann*, **Printemps**, *64 blvd Haussmann*, and, on the Left Bank, **Au Bon Marché**, *38 r. de Sèvres*.

**24-hr pharmacy: Dhéry**, *Galerie des Champs, 84 av. des Champs-Elysées.*

**Markets** (specialist and otherwise) are big business in Paris (both covered and open-air),

day performances from the kiosks at *15 pl. de la Madeleine* and *RER Châtelet-Les Halles* station. Both open Tues–Sat 1230–2000, and the kiosk at *pl. de la Madeleine* also opens Sun 1230–1600, but they don't accept credit cards.

Paris is famous for the huge revues staged (mainly) in Montmartre, notably **Bal du Moulin Rouge**, *83 blvd de Clichy, pl. Blanche*; **Folies-Bergère**, *32 r. Richer*; **Lido de Paris**, *116bis av. des Champs-Elysées*; and **Crazy Horse Saloon**, *12 av. George V;* but be warned – these shows are exorbitantly expensive.

The repertoire at the **Comédie Française** *(pl. de la Comédie Française)* consists largely of so the Tourist Office produces a free list. The best-known flea-market is **St Ouen** (métro: *St Ouen/Clignancourt*), held Sat–Mon 0730–1900, which consists of 16 separate markets, including **Jules-Valles** (curios, lace, and postcards), **Marché Paul-Bert** (second-hand goods), **Marché Serpette** (1900–1930 products) and **Marché Malik** (second-hand clothes and records). It is so famous, however, that bargains are hard to find. You might do better at **porte de Montreuil** (métro: *porte de Montreuil*), held Sat–Mon (0700–1930).

## SIGHTSEEING

Almost everything in Paris has an entrance fee, and this can be quite steep. Some places give you up to 50% discount if you are under 25 and have an ISIC card. **Paris Visite** gives discounts on some major attractions. The much more comprehensive **La Carte Musée** (Museums and Monuments Card) offers entrance and reductions to some museums: FFr.70 for 1 day, FFr.140 for 2 days or FFr.200 for 3 days.

There's a choice of conventional coach tours, but you get more freedom with **Paribus**, *3–5 r. Talma; tel: 01 42 88 92 88.* They offer English commentary tours and nine stops, so you can get off and on at will over the course of two days. **Caisse Nationale des Monuments Historiques et des Sites**, *Hôtel de Sully, 62 r. St-Antoine; tel: 44 61 21 50*, operate daily walking tours with specific themes. **Paris by Cycle**, *2 r. de la Jonquière, tel: 42 63 36 63*, and **Mountain Bike Trip**, *6 pl. Etienne Pernet; tel: 48 42 57 87*, offer cycling tours of Paris.

The Parisian sights tend to cluster in groups. Most monuments are on the Right Bank, while the islands in the middle of the River Seine are where the city began and offer some of the best architecture. The Left Bank is more laid-back, traditionally popular with artists and the Bohemian crowd. The following is only a small selection of the best and/or most famous attractions.

### The Islands (Les Îles)

Take time out just to wander round the largely 17th-century **Île St-Louis**, as well as the major sights on **Île de la Cité**, which is linked to it by a footbridge (métro: *Cité*). The great twin-towered **cathedral of Notre Dame**, built

between 1163 and 1345, is one of the world's finest Gothic buildings. The tiny **Ste-Chapelle** (in the courtyard of the **Palais de Justice**) has acres of stunningly beautiful stained glass – on a sunny day, it's like standing in a kaleidoscope. The **Conciergerie**, once a prison for those awaiting the guillotine, is also worth a look.

### The Right Bank (La Rive Droite)

Just over the bridge from the islands, the Hôtel de Ville marks the start of the **Marais**, a district filled with charming small streets and squares (make a point of seeing the exceptionally beautiful Renaissance *pl. des Vosges*), as well as several fine museums. The cream are probably **Musée Carnavalet**, *23 r. de Sevigne*, dedicated to the history of Paris, and **Musée Picasso**, *5 r. de Thorigny; tel: 01 42 71 25 21* (0930–1800 May–Oct, 0930–1730 winter; closed Tues), which has an excellent selection of the artist's work (métro for both: *St-Paul/Chemin Vert*).

Just outside the area is the unmissable **Centre Georges Pompidou** (also known as **Beaubourg**), *19 r. Beaubourg; tel: 01 44 78 12 33* (métro: *Châtelet-Les-Halles*), a controversial modernistic building, filled with a wonderfully cross-section of works from the great masters of 20th-century art. The centre is open 1000–2200, the gallery 1000–1800. Closed Tues.

Back beside the river, the **Louvre** (métro: *Palais-Royal*; enter via métro *Palais Ryal/Louvre* to avoid long queues) is one of the greatest art galleries in the world. Housed in what was a palace, it's a sightseeing marathon, with miles of corridors. Its most famous exhibits, the *Mona Lisa* ('La Joconde' in French) and the *Venus de Milo*, are always surrounded by vast crowds; yet other equally stunning exhibits have half the number of visitors. I M Pei's glass pyramid has formed the startling entrance since 1989. Closed Tues. From here, the formal **Jardins des Tuileries** lead along the river to the *pl. de la Concorde*. At the far end are two small but enchanting galleries; **Jeu de Paume**, *20 r. Royale; tel: 01 47 03 12 50* (métro: *Concorde/Tuileries*) hosts changing exhibitions of modern art; and the **Orangerie**, *pl. Carrousel; tel: 01 42 97 48 16*, is devoted to the Impressionists and post-Impressionists, notably Renoir, Matisse and Picasso. It was created largely as a show-

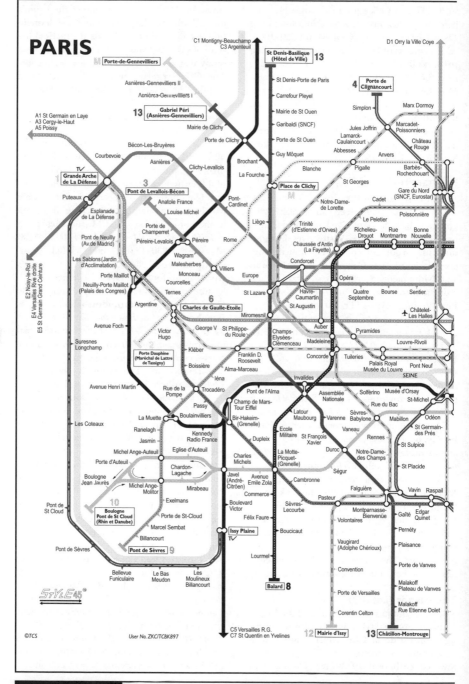

# PARIS

Porte-de-Gennevilliers

C1 Montigny-Beauchamp
C3 Argenteuil

St Denis-Basilique
(Hôtel de Ville) **13**

D1 Orry la Ville Coye

Asnières-Gennevilliers II
Asnières-Gennevilliers I

St Denis-Porte de Paris

**4** Porte de Clignancourt

A1 St Germain en Laye
A3 Cergy-le-Haut
A5 Poissy

**13** Gabriel Péri
(Asnières-Gennevilliers)

Carrefour Pleyel
Mairie de St Ouen
Garibaldi (SNCF)
Porte de St Ouen
Guy Môquet

Simplon

Marx Dormoy

Jules Joffrin
Lamarck-
Caulaincourt
Abbesses

Marcadet-
Poissonniers
Château
Rouge

Mairie de Clichy
Porte de Clichy

Bécon-Les-Bruyères

Courbevoie

Asnières

Clichy-Levallois

Brochant
La Fourche

Blanche

Anvers

Pigalle

Barbès-
Rochechouart

Grande Arche
de La Défense

TV

Puteaux

Pont de Levallois-Bécon

**3**

Place de Clichy

St Georges

M

Gare du Nord
(SNCF, Eurostar)

Esplanade
de La Défense

Anatole France
Louise Michel

Pont-
Cardinet

Notre-Dame-
de Lorette

Cadet

Poissonnière

Pont de Neuilly
(Av. de Madrid)

Porte de
Champerret

Liège

Le Peletier

Trinité
(d'Estienne d'Orves)

Richelieu-
Drouot

Rue
Montmartre

Bonne
Nouvelle

Les Sablons (Jardin
d'Acclimatation)

Péreire-Levallois

Péreire

Rome

Chaussée d'Antin
(La Fayette)

E2 Noisy-le-Roi
E4 Versailles Rive droite
E5 St Germain Grand Ceinture

Porte Maillot

Wagram
Malesherbes
Monceau
Courcelles
Ternes

Villiers

Europe

Condorcet

Opéra

Quatre
Septembre

Bourse

Sentier

Neuilly-Porte Maillot
(Palais des Congres)

St Lazare

Havre-
Caumartin
St Augustin

Argentine

Charles de Gaulle-Etoile

Miromesnil

Auber

Pyramides

Châtelet-
Les Halles

Avenue Foch

**6**

Victor
Hugo

George V

Champs-
Elysées-
Clémenceau

Madeleine

Concorde

Tuileries

Louvre-Rivoli

Suresnes
Longchamp

**2**

Porte Dauphine
(Maréchal de Lattre
de Tassigny)

Kléber

St Philippe-
du Roule

Franklin D.
Roosevelt

Palais Royal
Musée du Louvre

Pont Neuf

Boissière

Alma-Marceau

Concorde

SEINE

Avenue Henri Martin

Rue de la
Pompe

Iéna

Trocadéro

Pont de l'Alma

Invalides

Assemblée
Nationale

Solférino

Musée d'Orsay

St-Michel

Passy

Champ de Mars-
Tour Eiffel

Varenne

Rue du Bac

La Muette

Boulainvilliers

Bir-Hakeim-
(Grenelle)

Latour
Maubourg

Sèvres-
Babylone

Mabillon

Odéon

Les Coteaux

Ranelagh

Kennedy
Radio France

Dupleix

Ecole
Militaire

St François
Xavier

Vaneau

Rennes

St Germain-
des Prés

Jasmin

Eglise d'Auteuil

La Motte-
Picquet-
(Grenelle)

Duroc

Notre-Dame-
des Champs

St Sulpice

Michel Ange-Auteuil

Charles
Michels

Ségur

St Placide

Porte d'Auteuil

Chardon-
Lagache

Javel
(André-
Citröen)

Avenue
Emile Zola

Cambronne

Falguière

Vavin

Raspail

Boulogne
Jean Jaurès

Michel Ange-
Molitor

Mirabeau

Commerce

Pasteur

Montparnasse-
Bienvenüe

Gaîté

Edgar
Quinet

Pont de
St Cloud

**10**

Exelmans

Boulevard
Victor

Sèvres-
Lecourbe

Volontaires

Pernéty

Boulogne
Pont de St Cloud
(Rhin et Danube)

Porte de St-Cloud

Félix Faure

Vaugirard
(Adolphe Chérioux)

Plaisance

Marcel Sembat

Issy Plaine
TV

Boucicaut

Porte de Vanves

Billancourt

Convention

Malakoff
Plateau de Vanves

Pont de Sèvres

Pont de Sèvres **9**

Lourmel

Porte de Versailles

Malakoff
Rue Etienne Dolet

Bellevue
Funiculaire

Le Bas
Meudon

Les
Moulineux
Billancourt

Balard **8**

Corentin Celton

StYLE45

©TCS

User No. ZKC/TCBK897

C5 Versailles R.G.
C7 St Quentin en Yvelines

**12** Mairie d'Issy

**13** Châtillon-Montrouge

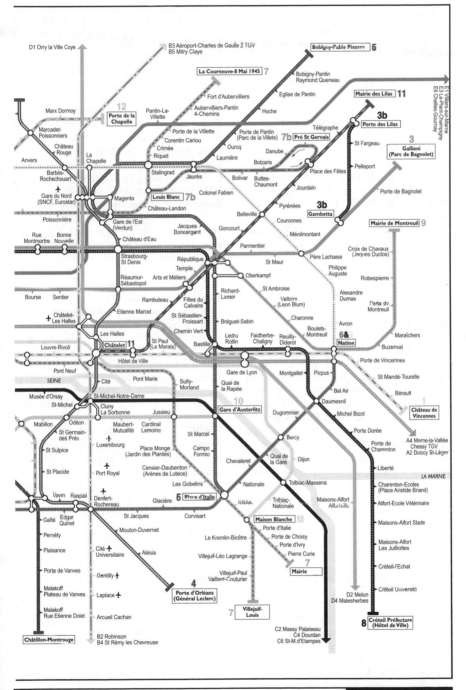

409

place for eight of Monet's large waterlily paintings, which have two superb oval rooms to themselves. From *pl. de la Concorde,* the *av. des Champs-Elysées* leads up towards the **Arc de Triomphe**, *pl. Charles-de-Gaulle Étoile;* open 0930–2300 in summer (Mon, Sun 0930–1830); 1000–2230 in winter (Mon, Sun 1000 1800).

### The Left Bank (La Rive Gauche)

Having visited the **Eiffel Tower**, *tel: 01 44 11 23 11* (métro: *Champs-de-Mars;* open 0900–2400), head towards the magnificent 17th-century **Les Invalides**, *av. de Tourville* (métro: *Latour-Maubourg/Varenne),* to see **Napoleon's tomb** and the **Musée de l'Armée** (Army Museum), with its many Napoleonic exhibits. Behind this is **Musée Rodin**, *77 r. de Varenne; tel: 01 44 18 61 10* (métro: *Varenne),* a magnificent house and garden crammed with the sculptor's works. 0930–1730; closed Sun, Tues.

Continuing along the river, the **Musée d'Orsay**, *1 rue de Bellechasse* (métro: *Solférino),* is a converted railway station that now houses a truly spectacular collection of 19th- and early 20th-century art, including works by Monet and Manet, Van Gogh and Delacroix. Not to be missed. Beyond this are the narrow medieval streets of the **Latin Quarter**, home of the **Sorbonne** University and two great parks: **Jardin de Luxembourg**, *blvd St-Michel* (métro: *Luxembourg),* and **Jardin des Plantes**, *quai St-Bernard* (métro: *Austerlitz).* Between them is the **Panthéon**, *pl. du Panthéon,* France's hall of fame, full of the remains of and memorials to the great and the glorious. **Musée National du Moyen-Age**, *6 pl. Paul-Painlevé; tel: 01 53 73 78 00* (métro: *Cluny-La Sorbonne/St Michel/ Odeon),* in a 16th-century monastery, contains a vast number of wonderful medieval tapestries and other works of art. Open 0915–1745.

### Further Out

North of the river, **Montmartre**, once the haunt of artists, climbs to a lookout point that offers the most accessible views of the city. Topping the hill are the overblown white cupolas of the basilica of **Sacré-Coeur**, built at the turn of the century and now besieged by tourists and touts. **Musée de Montmartre**, *12 r. Cortot* (métro: *Lamarck-Caulaincourt/Anvers,*

---

## The World Cup 1998

**B**etween 10th June and 12th July 1998, France will play host to the sixteenth World Cup football competition. Ten French cities are hosting matches, and Paris, in particular, is playing a large role. Visitors to France during this time can expect accommodation to be in short supply, especially in Paris, and should plan their visit accordingly. The host cities are Bordeaux, Lens, St. Denis (Paris), Nantes, Lyon, St. Etienne, Toulouse, Marseilles, Montpellier and Paris.

---

plus funicular railway) traces the history of the quarter, while second-rate artists still add colour to the teeming *pl. du Tertre.*

On the north-eastern edge of the city, **Parc de la Villette** (metro: *Porte de la Villette)* offers a range of attractions. The main one, is the vast **Cité des Sciences et de l'Industrie**, a state-of-the-art science museum, both in its architecture and in its contents; a fascinating place with countless interactive exhibits. **Parc de la Villette** can be reached by canal each Sun from *Bastille;* boats leave *Bassin del'Arsenal* in front of the Bastille column and take a leisurely 2 hrs through tunnels and up the Canal St Martin.

### OUT OF TOWN

Allow time for trips into the suburbs and a little way out of town. Sights include the châteaux of **Versailles** (RER line C to *Versailles Rive-Gauche)* and **Fontainebleau** (frequent suburban trains from Gare de Lyon to *Fontainebleau-Avon),* plus the theme parks **Disneyland Paris**, *tel: 01 60 30 60 30* (RER line A to *Chessy Marne-la-Vallée)* and **Parc Astérix** (RER line B3 to *Roissy-Charles de Gaulle).*

From Paris you can connect with **Brussels** and join the routes radiating from there: Brussels–Amsterdam (p.156), Brussels–Cologne (p.163), Brussels–Frankfurt (p.165) and Brussels–Ostend (p.170).

Frequent trains run daily from Paris (Nord) to Brussels (Midi/Nord). Journey time: 2½–3 hrs, depending on the type of train.

# PARIS–BARCELONA

Linking the French capital to Spain's chief coastal city, this route bisects France. The main stop is Toulouse, but the line is scattered with smaller places of great interest. Orléans is still dominated by its favourite daughter, Joan of Arc; Limoges is the capital of porcelain and enamel; Bourges offers a relatively unspoiled medieval hill town and Barcelona exudes energy and vibrance. There is a side track to the tiny but dramatic principality of Andorra, and another side track to Villefranche.

Paris
Orleans
Châteauroux
Bourges
Limoges
Cahors
Marseille–Biarritz
p. 323
Toulouse
L'Hospitalet
Villefranche
La Tour de Carol
Marseille–Barcelona
p. 318
Barcelona

FASTEST JOURNEY: 12 HRS

## TRAINS

**ETT tables:** 47, 310, 312, 313, 314, 315, 653, 653b .

### FAST TRACK

The only convenient way to do this route in one journey is by night. One overnight train runs from Paris Austerlitz to Barcelona Franca. It takes 12 hrs, has a restaurant car, but is restricted to sleeping-car passengers only and is not cheap. Couchettes are available on the train from Paris Austerlitz to Port Bou (the Spanish border), giving a connection to a local Spanish train to Barcelona.

### ON TRACK

#### Paris–Orléans

Services operate from Paris Austerlitz to Orleans every 1–2 hrs. Whilst some trains run into Orléans station, most trains operate to Les Aubrais, where a shuttle service connects with Orléans station. The journey takes around 1 hr.

#### Orleans–Châteauroux

Five daytime trains run from Les Aubrais station (just outside Orleans, connection by frequent shuttle train) to Châteauroux. The journey takes around 1 hr 20 min.

411

### Châteauroux–Limoges

Eight trains a day link Châteauroux with Limoges. The journey takes 1hr–1 hr 30 min.

### Limoges–Cahors

Five trains a day, 2 hr 15 min journey. Most of the trains have buffets.

### Cahors–Toulouse

A half-a-dozen trains with journey times of around 1 hr 20 min.

### Toulouse–L'Hospitalet

Four trains a day, irregular services. The trains take 2 hrs 15 mins.

### L'Hospitalet–La Tour de Carol

Four trains a day, taking 30 mins.

### La Tour de Carol–Barcelona

Four trains a day, irregularly spaced. The journey takes around 3 hrs 20 mins, and passes through breathtaking Alpine scenery.

## ORLÉANS

**Stations: Gare Orléans** is on the northern edge of the centre, by the Jeanne d'Arc shopping complex; *r. de la République* runs straight ahead to *pl. du Martroi*, in the heart of town. Gare Orléans is actually on a short spur, just off the main rail line and through-services stop only at nearby **Les Aubrais**, but a shuttle service (*navette*) links the two stations.
**Bus Station:** *r. M-Proust; tel: 02 38 53 94 75*, a block from Gare Orléans.
**Tourist Office:** in the Jeanne d'Arc centre, *pl. Albert 1er, tel: 02 38 53 05 05*. Open Mon–Sat 0900–1830, Sun 0930–1230, 1500–1830 (Oct–Mar); Mon–Sat 0900–1830, Sun 1000–1200 (Apr–Sept). **Youth information**: **Centre Régional d'Information Jeunesse**, *5 blvd de Verdun; tel: 38 54 37 70*. Open Mon–Sat 1000/1400–1800/1900.

### ACCOMMODATION

Orléans has a good selection of hotels in all grades, but it's a popular base and advance booking is recommended. For reasonably priced places, try around *r. du Fg-Bannier* and *pl. Gambetta*. Hotel chains include *Ba, BW, Ch,*

*Ct, Hd, Ib, IH, Mc, Nv* and *RS*. If you want a 3-star place near the station, there are two on *r. de la République*: **Hôtel d'Arc**, *no.37; tel: 02 38 53 10 94; fax: 02 38 81 77 47*, and **Hôtel Le Terminus**, *no.40; tel: 02 38 53 24 64*. The 2-star **Hôtel Le St-Aignan**, *3 pl. Gambetta; tel: 38 53 15 35*, is a good-value establishment with a nice atmosphere. Out of town, the expensive but pleasant **Château Les Orgeaux**, in Vitry-aux-Loges, provides a quiet refuge. Book through B&B France.
**Youth hostel** (non-HI): *14 r. du Fg-Madeleine; tel: 02 38 62 45 75*, west of the centre (bus B). Nearest **campsite: St-Jean-de-la-Ruelle**, *r. de la Roche; tel: 38 88 39 39*, 3 km west (bus D: *Roche aux Fées*), open Apr–Sept.

### SIGHTSEEING

Occupying a strategic site and occasionally France's capital, Orleans has been attacked from Roman times to World War II, yet much of the historic centre has survived. Nothing is commemorated more than the raising of the English siege of 1429 by Jeanne d'Arc (Joan of Arc). A statue of Jeanne takes pride of place in the spacious *pl. du Martroi*, the nearby **Maison de Jeanne d'Arc**, *pl. du Gén.de Gaulle*, is a reconstruction of the house where she stayed, and there is a museum that uses models to illustrate the story of the siege. The annual **Fête de Jeanne d'Arc** (May 7–8) features a 'real' Jeanne riding through the streets.
The city's most impressive monument is **Cathédrale Ste-Croix** (Holy Cross Cathedral), with its mighty twin towers and spire. Visit the crypt, which reveals a fascinating excavation beneath the church that found Roman and Gothic foundations. Across the square, the **Musée des Beaux Arts** has a wide-ranging collection, including 18th-century pastels and 20th-century art, and nearby are some handsome Renaissance mansions, the **Hôtel Groslot** and **Pavillons d'Escures**. Another restored Renaissance house, the **Hôtel Cabu**, entrance from *sq. Abbé Desnoyers*, is now home to a **historical and archaeological museum**.

### OUT OF TOWN

SNCF bus services make it possible to explore many towns and châteaux in the Beauce region. (Rail tickets often valid) To the west, **Châteaudun** has a mighty **fortress** which towers high above the plains of the Beauce.

There's a remarkable **Romanesque basilica** at **St-Benoît** and the small town of **Sully-sur-Loire** has a magnificent **moated château**, once home to the duc de Sully and to Voltaire.

At **Meung-sur-Loire**, a tour of the 13th-century **château** includes the dungeons, while **Beaugency** has a particularly impressive medieval quarter. The 15th-century **Château Dunois** houses the regional museum.

### SIDE TRACK FROM ORLEANS

### BOURGES

**Station:** about 1 km north of the centre: walk up a*v. H-Laudier* and *av. J-Jaurès*, then bear left to *r. du Commerce* and *r. Moyenne* – the **tourist office** and **cathedral** are at the far end on the left hand-side. Five trains run each day (1 hr journey) from Les Aubrais to Bourges; some involve a change at Vierzon **Tourist Office:** *21 r. V-Hugo; tel: 02 48 24 75 33; fax: 02 48 69 11 87.* Open Mon–Sat 0900–1900, Sun 1000–1900 (Apr–Sept); Mon–Sat 0900–1800, Sun 1000–1230 (Oct–Mar). It offers 'car-train' tours of the town, departing outside the Tourist Office.

The town is the capital of the historic Berry region and the inhabitants like to be called *Berruyers*, not *Bourgeois*. It's a relatively little-visited place and this has helped to preserve the medieval hill town, centred on the 12th-century **Cathédrale de St-Etienne** (St Stephen's). The western exterior of this Gothic masterpiece has exceptionally detailed and absorbing carvings, while the soaring interior features superb 13th-century stained-glass windows. The crypt and tower (covered by one ticket) are also worthwhile.

There are quite a few attractive old buildings in the old quarter of the town, so spare time for a stroll along *r. Bourbonnoux* to *pl. Gordaine* (and the general area). **Hôtel Lallement**, *r. Bourbonnoux*, is a lovely mansion combining both Gothic and Renaissance architecture, now housing the

**Musée des Arts Décoratifs** (Museum of Decorative Arts). **Palais de Jacques-Coeur**, *pl. J-Coeur*, the 15th-century home of a local financier who became the treasurer of France, is open for inspection. Although the furnishings are sparse, the building itself has some unusual features. Also hidden in the quaint medieval streets is the pretty church of Notre Dame, just off *av. Jean-Jaurès*. 

### CHÂTEAUROUX

**Station:** central, beside the Tourist Office.
**Tourist Office:** *pl. de la Gare; tel: 02 54 34 10 74.* Open Mon–Sat 0930–1230 and 1400–1900, Sun 0930–1200 and 1330–1700 (June–Sept); Mon–Sat 0900–1230 and 1400–1800 (Oct–May).

Although it's mainly a rather dull industrial town, there is a small core of old houses. The 15th-century **Château Raoul**, after which the city was named, is now the Préfecture. Nearby, the 15th-century **Porte St-Martin** began life as a city gate but later became the local jail. **Musée Bertrand** (in the 18th-century mansion of Maréchal Bertrand, a leading Napoleonic general), is devoted to fine arts, Napoleonic history and the Berry region.

### LIMOGES

**Station: Gare des Bénédictins**, *tel: 05 55 11 12 00,* 500 m north-east of the old town: straight along *av. du Gén. de Gaulle*, across *pl. Jourdan* and into *blvd de Fleurus* – or bus nos. 8/10 to *pl. Jourdan*.
**Tourist Offices:** *blvd de Fleurus; tel: 05 55 34 46 87; fax: 05 55 34 19 12,* open Mon–Sat 0900–1200, 1400–1830, Sun 1000–1400.
**Regional (Haut-Vienne):** *4 pl. D-Dussoubs; tel: 05 55 79 04 04,* open Mon–Fri 0900–1200 and 1330–1730.

Capital of the Limousin region, Limoges is a large industrial city, renowned for producing magnificent porcelain and enamel, but it has a delightful centre, **Haut-Cité**.

On the eastern edge of the old town, surrounded by well-maintained botanical gardens and overlooking the River Vienne, is the Gothic **Cathédrale de St-Etienne** (St Stephen's). Built from the 13th century

413

onwards, it has suffered from ugly repairs and reinforcements, but make a point of visiting the neighbouring **Musée Municipale de l'Evêché** (18th-century Episcopal Palace). This contains a fascinating collection of Limoges enamel, some dating back to the 12th century, as well as artefacts from Egypt and Rome.

The famous **Musée Adrien-Dubouché**, *pl. Winston-Churchill*, is home to the national collection of porcelain and faïence. There are over 12,000 pieces from around the world, including whole services featuring such celebrities as Napoleon and the British royals, as well as an interesting video on production.

The centre of the old town is a web of dark, narrow streets, filled with half-timbered houses, small boutiques, antique and china shops. On *r. de la Boucherie* is the tiny **Chapelle de St-Aurélien**, built by the butchers' guild in the 15th century. On *r. St-Martial*, the **Crypte-St-Martial** is all that remains of a once-powerful abbey and some vestiges of the 4th century are visible.

Outside Limoges is the beautiful **Château de Vauguerige**, a Bed and Breakfast with spacious rooms, friendly atmosphere and station pick-up service. Moderate–expensive.

## CAHORS

**Station:** 10 mins walk west of the centre: leave *pl. Gambetta* by *av. J-Jaurès* (to the right) and turn left on *r. du Prés-Wilson*. At *blvd Gambetta*, turn right for the Tourist Office.

**Tourist Office:** *blvd Gambetta/pl. A-Briand; tel: 05 65 35 09 56; fax: 05 65 23 98 66*. Open Mon–Sat, 1000–1200 and 1400–1800, (–1830 May–Aug), Sun 1000–1200, 1500–1700 (May–Aug only).

Important in the Roman and medieval periods, Cahors became famous for wine that, for a while, was considered to be finer than that of Bordeaux. Its major monument is the 14th-century **Pont Valentré**, west of the centre – a continuation of *r. du Prés-Wilson* – a six-arched fortified bridge with three towers, the central one housing a historical display.

**Cathédrale St-Etienne** (St Stephen's) was built in the late 11th and early 12th centuries, although the heavily-fortified façade was only added in the 14th century and the cloisters are

16th century. It features fine sculptures on the west front, a remarkable nave roof and some beautiful 14th-century wall paintings. In this area are many quiet streets with attractive old buildings and there's a similar area on the other side of town, surrounding the 16th-century **Eglise St-Bartélemy** (St Bartholomew's), *r. Château-du-Roi*. **La Barbacane** (barbican), not far away, is a remnant of the 14th-century defensive walls.

## TOULOUSE

**Station: Toulouse–Gare Matabiau**, to the north-east of the city; 15–20 min walk from *pl. du Capitole* – or take the métro (the station stop is *Marengo*). Facilities at the railway station include baths and showers.

**Main Tourist Office:** *Donjon du Capitole, pl. C-d-Gaulle; tel: 05 61 11 02 22; fax: 05 61 22 03 63*. Open Mon–Sat 0900–1900, Sun 0900–1300 and 1400-1730 (May–Sept); Mon–Fri 0900–1800, Sat 0900–1230 and 1400–1800, Sun 1000–1230 and 1400–1700 (Oct–Apr). **Branch:** at the *station; tel: 61 62 50 50*, open Mon–Sat 0930–2000, Sun 1000–2000. **Regional (Haute-Garonne):** *14 r. de Bayard; tel: 61 99 44 00*, open Mon–Fri 0900–1700.

### GETTING AROUND

The centre is walkable, but the less energetic can use the efficient bus service, run by **SEM-VAT** (*7 pl. Esquirol; tel: 61 41 70 70*) and the modern métro. Tickets cover both and maps of the network are available from the tourist offices and ticket booths. Fares are zoned and the best value is a *carnet* (strip) of ten.

### ACCOMMODATION

A wide range of hotels is available and finding space is seldom a problem. Get the (free) *Hotels Restaurants* booklet from the Tourist Office.

For budget places, look in the centre, around *pl. Wilson* (*r. St-Antoine*) and *pl. de Capitole* (*r. du Tour* and *r. P-Romiguières*). Alternatively, try *r. de Bayard* – convenient for the station, but a less pleasant area. Hotel chains include *Cn, Ct, Hd, Ib, IH, Mc, Nv,* and *Sf*.

Right in the heart of town, the 4-star **Grand Hôtel de l'Opéra**, *1 pl. du Capitole;*

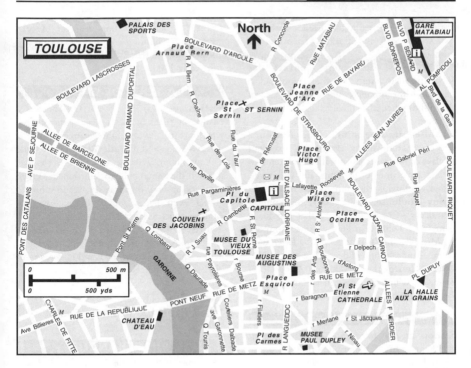

*tel: 05 61 23 41 04*, combines comfort and convenience, while the more modest **Hôtel Albert 1er**, *8 r. Rivals; tel: 61 21 17 91*, also in the centre, is excellent value. **Hôtel Grand Balcon**, *8 r. Romiguières; tel: 05 61 21 59 98* (which closes for most of Aug), is a reasonably priced place noted for its period décor and charm.

    **HI: Villa des Rosiers**, *125 av. Jean Rieux; tel: 61 80 49 93*, 3 km from the station (bus no.22: *Armand Leygues*). The municipal **campsite** is north of town and rather inaccessible without your own transport.

### SIGHTSEEING

The capital of the Midi region began life as a minor Roman settlement, then became a Visigothic and Frankish capital. It was the centre of an important county from the 10th century onwards and the site of two Huguenot massacres in the mid-16th century. Many of the grandiose town houses are built of a pinky-red brick, earning the city the epithet of *Ville Rose*. Nowadays it is a lively university town and a

great cultural and artistic centre. One of the most recent attractions is **La Cité de l'Espace**, east of Toulouse, which can be reached by bus no. 19. Situated in a large park, it features exhibitions on all space themes, with some simulations, and the rocket Ariane 5, which stands proudly in its own purpose-built garden. Open daily except Mon 0930–1900 (June–Sept), 0930–1800 (Sept–June).

    Many of the main attractions are in the old town, which centres on *pl. du Capitole*, dominated by the 18th-century **Le Capitole** (the town hall).

    The superb **Basilique St-Sernin** is all that remains of an 11th-century Benedictine monastery that was established to assist pilgrims en route to Santiago de Compostela. It is dedicated to (and holds the remains of) the first local bishop, who was martyred in AD 257. One of the largest Romanesque churches ever built, it has a five-tier tower and an extra-long nave, built to allow pilgrims room to sleep, eat and worship in the church. The 14th-century **Notre-Dame-du-Taur**, *r. du Taur*, which features some original murals inside, marks the spot where St Sernin is said to have met his grisly end.

The lovely 13th-century **Couvert des Jacobins** (Monastery of the Jacobins), *r. Lakanal*, is the strikingly simple burial place of the philosopher and theologian, St Thomas Aquinas.

**Musée des Augustins**, *21 r. de Metz*, in a former Augustinian monastery, has excellent displays of Romanesque and medieval items, as well as collections of paintings and sculptures. Other worthwhile museums are **Le Musée du Vieux-Toulouse**, *7 r. du May*, containing a miscellany of ordinary objects that provide a glimpse of Toulousian life over the centuries; **Le Musée Paul Dupuy**, *13 r. de la Pleau*, with an excellent selection of decorative arts; and **Le Musée George Labit**, *43 r. des Martyrs de la Libération*, which contains a marvellous array of Far Eastern objects.

## L'HOSPITALET

**Station**: *tel: (05) 36 35 35 35*. This tiny station is little more than a transit point on the journey to Andorra: buses leave from the station 2–3 times a day, and the journey takes 1 hr 40 mins. There are a couple of hotels outside the station car park but the place is largely uninspiring.

### SIDE TRACKS
### FROM L'HOSPITALET

## ANDORRA

Andorra is a political anomaly: it is a self-contained principality with its own government but has an area of just 470 sq. km and a population of about 65000. In a snug in the Pyrénées, it has mountainous scenery and a duty-free policy, which makes its main road traffic-laden with French and Spanish visitors stocking up on alcohol, petrol, ski-wear and electrical goods. Both the peseta and the franc are used as currency.

Andorra la Vella is the capital. **National Tourist Office:** just off *Plaça Poble; tel: (376) 82 02 14.* Stroll down the *Avinguda Princep* to the **Barri Antic** (Historic Quarter), where there are narrow stone

streets: a left turn opposite the **Hotel Pyrénées** will bring you to the **Casa de la Vall**, Andorra's house of Parliament since the early 1700's.

## LA TOUR DE CAROL

**Station**: *tel: (05) 36 35 35 35.* There is a change of trains at this isolated little station, which boasts railways of three gauges. Take the narrow-gauge SNCF **Petit Train Jaune** (little Yellow Train), which twists and turns its way through the mountains, to Villefranche. Open carriages are used on some services in summer, giving even better views. Buses leave for Andorra twice a day, taking 1½ hrs.

**Tourist Office**: (across the road); *tel: (05) 68 04 83 58.* A small office, but it has lots of information on the valley of the Carol River, a popular spot with hikers.

### SIDE TRACK
### FROM LA TOUR DE CAROL

## VILLEFRANCHE

**Station: Villefranche-Vernet-les-Bains:** *tel: (05) 68 96 34 74 11.*
**Tourist Office:** *pl. de l'Eglise; tel: 05 68 96 22 96.* Open daily 1000–1800.

Villefranche-de-Conflent is the actual town at the station. The station name, however, also refers to a town very close by, **Vernet-les-Bains**. On a hill-top overlooking the station is the enormous stone-built **Fort Liberia**, built by the military engineer Sebastien Vauban in 1681.

The narrow streets of Villefranche seem transported from the Middle Ages. To get to the fort, there is a minibus from the gate, **Porte de France**, or, leading from *r. St-Pierre,* there is a path upwards or an underground staircase with 750 steps. The fort, *tel: (05) 68 96 34 01,* is open daily 0900–1900 (Apr–Oct), 1000–1800 (Nov–Mar).

If you stay in the area, consider a trip by jeep to **Canigou**, the most majestic of the Pyrénée peaks, at 2784m. Contact Jean-Paul Bouzan, *17 blvd des Pyrénées, 66820 Vernet-les-Bains; tel: (05) 68 05 62 28.*

# PARIS–BREST

This route loops through Brittany and the Loire valley, exploring an area dotted with tiny port villages, fine beaches and lavish châteaux. If you don't want to do it all, take the TGV straight to Brest and meander back along just one arm of the route.

Major stops are Chartres, for its incomparable cathedral, and Nantes, for its Renaissance château. However, much of the pleasure of this circuit is to take side tracks to places inaccessible by rail, such as the fairy-tale Mont St-Michel, the curious megalithic island of Gavrinis, and the hidden castles that formed the Kings' playground of the Loire Valley.

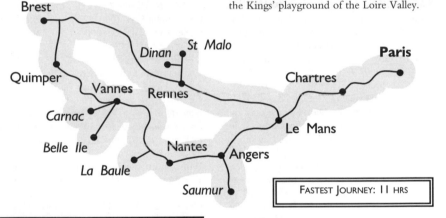

417

FASTEST JOURNEY: 11 HRS

## TRAINS

**ETT tables:** 276, 280, 281, 286, 285, 289, 335, 283.
This route is a circular exploration of Brittany. Fast TGV services from Paris serve all of the major cities concerned.

### ON TRACK

 **Paris–Chartres**
Services run approximately hourly at irregular intervals from Paris Montparnasse to Chartres, taking around 1 hr.

### Chartres–Le Mans
Seven or eight trains link Chartres with Le Mans most days, but the service is much reduced on Sun. Journey time is 1½ hrs.

### Le Mans–Rennes
TGV trains (reservation plus supplement), provide a fast service approximately every 2 hrs; journey times are around 1 hr 15 mins.

### Rennes–Brest
Four TGVs, taking just over 2 hrs. Local trains take 2½ hrs. There are some long gaps, however, so check the timetables closely.

### Brest–Quimper
Around half a dozen services link Brest with Quimper each day. Journeys take 1 hr 20 mins.

### Quimper–Vannes
Nine or ten trains a day run between Quimper and Vannes, most of these are TGVs. Average journey time is 1 hr 20 mins.

## Vannes–Nantes

Three trains a day make the run, but many other journeys are possible by changing trains at Redon. Journeys take around 1 hr 45 mins.

## Nantes–Angers

A frequent service links Nantes to Angers St Laud each day, some are TGVs. Journey times are around 40 mins.

## Angers–Paris

Five daily and many more non-daily TGVs runs between Angers St Laud and Paris Montparnasse, taking about 1 hr 35 mins.

## CHARTRES

**Station:** *pl. Pierre Sernard*. Walk up *av. J-de-Beauce* to the centre. The restaurants along this walk are better value than in the centre.
**Tourist Office:** *pl. de la Cathédrale; tel: 02 37 21 50 00; fax: 02 37 21 51 91*. Mon–Fri 0930–1830, Sat 1000–1700 (0930–1800 May–Oct), Sun 1030–1300 (also 1430–1730 May–Oct).

**Cathédrale Notre-Dame** is arguably the world's greatest example of the Gothic style. The original building was destroyed by fire in 1194; the replacement was erected within 25 years and much of it still exists today. The dazzling stained-glass windows are mostly 12th- or 13th-century and the building is covered by magnificent stone sculptures. Housed in the former bishop's palace is the **Musée des Beaux Arts**, with a permanent collection that includes some fine wooden sculptures from the Middle Ages. The signposted *circuit touristique* leads to the pleasant riverside area and old town.

## LE MANS

**Station:** south of town centre, 20 mins walk from the old quarter via *pl. de la République* and *av. du Gén. Leclerc* (bus nos 3/5/16 run this far).
**Tourist Office: Hotel des Ursulines**, *r. de l'Étoile; tel: 02 43 28 17 22*. Open daily Mon–Fri 0900–1800, Sat 0900–1200, 1400–1800, Sun 1000–1230, 1430–1700.

The famous **24-hr motor race** occurs in mid June, just south of the town. The rest of the year, true race enthusiasts can try the expensive **Musée de l'Automobile**, at the end of the motor circuit.

The winding streets of the Old Town are surrounded by a Gallo-Roman wall, and are characterised by timber-framed Renaissance houses. The **Cathédral St-Julien**, where Henry II of England was baptised, is a magnificent sight; and standing in its shadow is the much-photographed **Maison de la Tourelle**, with its Renaissance turret. Also worth seeing is the **Musée Tessé**, displaying a colourful collection of fine arts from the 14th–19th century.

## RENNES

**Station:** about 15 mins walk south-east of the centre (bus nos 1/20/21/22).
**Tourist Office:** *pont de Nemours; tel: 02 99 79 01 98; fax: 02 99 79 31 38*. Open Mon–Sat 0900–1900, Sun 1000–1200 and 1500–1700 (June–Sept); Tues–Sat 0900–1230, 1400–1830.

### ACCOMMODATION

The best place to find hotels is in the area of the station. Hotel chains include *Ba, BW, Ca, Ch, Ct, Ib, IH, Mc* and *Nv*. The only 4-star establishment in town is **Hôtel Lecoq-Gadby**, *156 r. d'Antrain; tel: 02 99 38 05 55*. **Central**, *6 r. Lanjuinais; tel: 02 99 79 12 36*, is pleasant and moderately priced, occupying a renovated 19th-century building. **Hôtel d'Angleterre**, *19 r. Maréchal; tel: 02 99 79 38 61*, is cheap and close to the station. **HI:** *10–12 Canal St-Martin; tel: 02 99 33 22 33*, 3 km out of town (bus nos 20/22: *St-Malo* – no. 2 at weekends: *Coëtlogon*). **Campsite:** *r. du Professeur M-Audin; tel: 99 36 91 22* (bus no.3), open Apr–Sept.

### SIGHTSEEING

Rennes first became important in the 10th century, but the largely wooden town was virtually destroyed by a fire in 1720 and it was rebuilt mostly in reddish granite. In the first week of July, the town is taken over by the **Festival des Tombées de la Nuit** (Festival of Nightfall), with theatre, music and people dressed in medieval costume to celebrate Breton culture.

The 17th-century **Palais de Justice** was one of the few structures to survive the first fire, but was less lucky when another fire broke out in Feb 1994 and is currently being restored. The nearby 18th-century **Hôtel de Ville** (Town Hall), *pl. de la Mairie,* contains some fine

Flemish tapestries. The **Musée de Bretagne**, *20 quai Emile-Zola,* contains various well-presented exhibits about the region, while the **Musée des Beaux Arts** (above it) houses a collection of French art from the 14th century onwards. Two of the prettiest streets in Rennes, *St Georges* and *r. St Michel,* are packed with attractive restaurants of a wide variety of cultures. Try the **Palais Gourmand**, which offers open-fire cooking at a reasonable price.

↱ **SIDE TRACKS FROM RENNES**

There are regular buses linking Rennes to many other Breton towns. The new long-distance bus station is at *blvd Solférino* (east of the station); *tel: 02 99 30 87 80.* Trains run from Rennes to St-Malo (every 1–2 hrs, journey time 1 hr) and then on to Dol, where you should change for Dinan.

The romantically named **Côte d'Emeraude** (Emerald Coast) and **Côte de Granit Rose** (Coast of Pink Granite) are lined by wild and rugged cliffs, interspersed with sheltered fishing ports, many of which are now resorts.

**St-Malo**, which has a fine white sand beach, has been carefully restored since its destruction during the war and is a good base from which to visit this coastline, as well as Mont St-Michel, by bus. The fortified monastery of **Le Mont St-Michel** (St Michael's Mount), an astonishing and unmissable sight, is perched on a craggy island that is joined to the mainland by a causeway at low tide. Visits to the abbey are only possible by guided tour (some are in English during the summer). The nearest rail station is at **Pontorson**, 9 km away, from which several buses a day run to the Mount.

A little way inland, **Dol-de-Bretagne** was built mainly in the 13th century and, although now little more than a village, it has a fine cathedral and streets lined by medieval timber-framed houses. At **Champ-dolent** stands one of the finest *menhirs* (prehistoric standing stones) on the north coast. Not far away is **Dinan**, with a feudal castle,

Romanesque church and cobbled streets of well-preserved 15th-century houses. ↱

**BREST**

**Station:** turn right and follow *av. Clémenceau* to the Tourist Office.
**Tourist Office:** *pl. de la Liberté; tel: 02 98 44 24 96; fax: 02 98 44 53 73.* Open Mon–Sat 1000–1230, 1400–1800, Sun 1000–1200, 1400–1600 (June–Sept only).

Brest was entirely destroyed in World War II and was rebuilt hastily; nowadays it is the home of **Océanopolis**, which houses a large aquarium. It is 4 km away from town, but there are buses from the station. The true pleasures here lie in exploring the surrounding country-side and coast: self-guided tours in English are available from the Tourist Office; try the light-house walk. A friendly and comfortable base can be found at **La Chatargnerie**, a chambre d'hôte bookable through B&B France, situated just outside Brest, 15 mins walk from the beach and with a private swimming pool.

**QUIMPER**

**Station:** east of town, 15 mins walk to the cathedral (on the north bank): turn right along *av. de la Gare,* then left to follow the River Odet. The Tourist Office is a bit further along and on the south bank.
**Tourist Office:** *pl. de la Résistance; tel: 02 98 53 04 05; fax: 02 98 53 31 33.* Open Mon–Sat 0900–1200, 1330–1800 (0830–2000 July–Aug); Sun 0930–1230 (mid June–mid Sept), 0930–1230, 1500–1800.

Brittany's oldest town makes a very attractive base for exploring southern Finistère. The beautiful Gothic **Cathédrale St-Corentin** features a strangely off-centre nave. Close by are the well-presented collections of **Musée Breton** and the outstanding **Musée des Beaux-Arts**, which captures the spirit of Brittany on canvas and includes many examples of Quimper's most famous product – faience porcelain. Tours of the faience factories are possible.

**OUT OF TOWN**

**Douarnenez** (45 mins north-west by SNCF bus) is a working port and home to **Le Port-Musée**, where you can explore a variety of

**419**

vessels and watch demonstrations of such nautical skills as boat-building and rope-making.

The **Crozon peninsula**, further north, is also reachable by bus. At the tip of the peninsula (forming part of the **Parc Naturel Régional d'Armorique**), **Camaret** is a small resort where a long sea wall, lined with the wooden skeletons of old boats, leads to a tower built by Vauban.

Boat trips downriver lead to **Benodet**, a popular small resort from where you can continue by boat to the **Îles Glénan** – or to **Concarneau**, a busy fishing port with a medieval closed town.

## VANNES

**Station:** a good 25 mins walk north of the centre: turn right on *av. Favrel* and left along *av. Victor Hugo.* Bear right for the Tourist Office, or ahead (on *r. Billault)* for the centre.

**Tourist Office:** *1 r. Thiers; tel: 02 97 47 24 34; fax: 02 97 47 29 49.* Open Mon–Sat 0900–1200 and 1400–1800 (Sept–June); Mon–Sat 0900–1900, Sun 1000–1200 (June–Sept).

Situated at the top of the island-strewn **Gulf of Morbihan**, Vannes makes a superb base for exploring south-eastern Brittany. At the heart of town, near **Cathédrale de St-Pierre**, the ancient market of **La Cohue** has been restored to form the excellent **Musée de Vannes**, with the old courthouse upstairs converted to combine art galleries with exhibits about the gulf. Behind the cathedral, at **Porte Prison**, you can climb a short stretch of the old ramparts.

### OUT OF TOWN

**Carnac** (south-west of Vannes and reachable by bus) is a major resort, with numerous campsites and caravan parks and a long beach that is packed in summer. In the area are some 5000 menhirs. The most famous formation is the *Alignements du Ménec*, probably dating from the 3rd century BC and consisting of over 1000 megaliths stretching for more than 1 km. If you have the money, take a **helicopter trip** over them: they are now fenced off, because of the number of visitors.

Several companies offer boat tours around the coast and islands, but to explore properly it's better to use the regular ferries – you can reach the various departure points by bus. **Belle-Île** is the largest of the islands and offers everything from fortifications and a citadel to wonderful scenery and beaches, good walking and picturesque villages. To visit **Île de Gavrinis**, take a tour from *Larmor-Baden* (south-west of Vannes). The island consists largely of megalithic remains, which are definitely linked to the standing stones at the nearby village of **Locmariaquer**, on the south-west tip of the gulf.

## NANTES

**Station:** about 1 km east of *pl. du Commerce.* The best way to get around is to use the excellent modern tram, which links station to the main sights in town.

**Tourist Office:** *pl. du Commerce; tel: 02 40 47 04 51; fax: 02 40 89 11 99.* Mon–Fri 0900–1800, Sat–Sun 1000–1800 (daily–1900 July–Aug). **Branch:** *1 r. de la Châteu; tel: 02 40 12 60 60.* Wed–Sun 1000–1300, 1330–1800.

### ACCOMMODATION

Hotel chains include *Ba, BW, Ch, Ct, Hd, Ib, IH, Mc* and *Nv.* The best in town is the 3-star **Adagio Central**, *4 r. du Couedic; tel: 02 51 82 10 00.* A good 2-star place very close to the station is **Hôtel Terminus**, *3 allée du Commandant-Charcot; tel: 40 74 24 51.* Simple, cheap and central is **Hôtel St-Daniel**, *4 r. du Bouffay; tel: 02 40 47 41 25.*

There are three **HI** hostels, of which the most accessible is **Place de la Manu**, *2 pl. de la Manufacture; tel: 02 40 20 57 25,* 400m from the station (bus no. 1: *Manufacture),* but open only mid June–mid Sept); **Porte Neuve**, *1 pl. Ste-Elisabeth; tel: 02 40 20 00 80,* is 1.5 km from the station (bus nos 40/41: *Viarme).* **Campsite: Camping du Val de Cens**, *21 blvd du Petit Port; tel: 02 40 74 47 94,* 3 km from town (bus nos 51/53: *Marhonnière).*

### SIGHTSEEING

The imposing **Château des Ducs** was home to the Dukes of Brittany, who ruled this part of the world semi-independently in the Middle Ages, and has had countless famous residents over the centuries, including such legendary figures as Bonnie Prince Charlie and the original Bluebeard (executed here). It is largely

15th-century, but traces of a 13th-century structure remain. Within the grounds are the **Musée Regionale des Arts Populaires** devoted to Breton folklore and history, and featuring murals, costumes, handicrafts and furniture.

The **Cathédrale St-Pierre-et-St-Paul** is renowned for the clever Renaissance tomb of Francois II and his second wife: both are depicted in a single statue.

The **Musée des Beaux Arts**, *r. G-Clémenceau,* has 13th–20th-century paintings, including two large works by Rubens, and there's an excellent art collection in **Palais Dobrée**, while **Musée Jules Verne**, *3 r. de l'Hermitage,* re-creates the author's fictional worlds. **Cité Radieuse** is a must for fans of Le Corbusier (no. 31 bus).

## OUT OF TOWN

There are frequent trains (1 hr trip) to **La Baule** (very popular and very expensive), which claims to have Europe's most beautiful beach.

## ANGERS

**Station:** near the Mairie, about 10 mins walk south-east of the centre (past the Jardin des Plantes) – or bus no. 22.
**Tourist Office:** *pl. du Prés-Kennedy; tel: 02 41 23 51 11; fax: 02 41 23 51 10.* Open Mon–Sat 0900–1900, Sun 1030–1300 and 1400–1800 (mid June–mid Sept); Mon–Sat 0930–1830, Sun 1000–1300 (mid Sept–mid June).

Once capital of the Counts of Anjou (the Plantagenet ancestors of the British royal family), this attractive town is dominated by the massive stone walls of the 13th-century **Château d'Angers**, but the 17 towers are actually only half of their original height and the moat has been converted into formal gardens. Inside are fantastic medieval tapestries, including the wonderful 14th-century *Apocalypse,* based on the Book of Revelations – do not miss this.

Across the river, **Hôpital St-Jean**, contains another spectacular tapestry, the 20th-century *Chant du Monde.* **Cathédrale de St-Maurice** has a medieval façade and Gothic vaulting over an unusually wide nave, lighted by stained glass dating from several different eras.

## OUT OF TOWN

If you wish to do some serious sampling of the renowned **white wine** of Anjou, visit **Maison du Vin de l'Anjou**, *5 bis pl. Kennedy,* in Angers for details of *caves* open to visitors, before heading off to the villages of **Savennières** and **La Poissonière**, where some of the best is produced. Both are accessible by local train from Angers to Nantes. Providing the perfect location for exploration of Angers, the moderate **Malvoisine**, bookable through B&B France, is an elegantly converted stable block, with comfortable rooms and gourmet cuisine. Nearby bike hire and station pick-up service.

## ⟲ SIDE TRACKS FROM ANGERS

## SAUMUR

**Tourist Office:** open Mon–Fri 0915–1900, Sun 1030–1230, 1530–1830.

Infrequent trains run from Angers (taking 20–25 mins) to the delightful town of Saumur, with its famous riding school and a château containing the town museums. The castle has a fascinating history: it housed the dungeons of the Plantagenets, was a fortress for Louis VIII, and then a country residence for the Dukes of Anjou. There are 3 or 4 English guided tours each day. The town is surrounded by vineyards and mushroom caves.

Like Saumur, the châteaux of the 225-mile long **Loire Valley** were mostly medieval fortresses converted into luxurious country residences by 16th-century nobles. Trains run along the valley at irregular intervals and connecting buses go to many of the châteaux, but a hired car (or bicycle) is a more satisfactory way to explore in depth.

The most accessible are along the Saumur–Tours line. **Villandry** is famous for its magnificent terraced gardens, which decoratively mix vegetables and flowers in formal box-hedged beds. The fortress-like **Langeais** and the more graceful **Montsoreau** and **Montreuil-Bellay** can be reached by SNCF bus from Saumur. ⬛

# PARIS–CALAIS

This route links Paris with the Channel ports of Boulogne and Calais, and is much used by travellers to and from Britain. The route runs through areas of northern France under-explored by travellers heading rapidly from/to the capital. It includes Amiens, capital of Picardy and home to the largest cathedral in France, and a side track to the picturesque town of Arras.

---

FASTEST JOURNEY: 1 HR 40 MINS

---

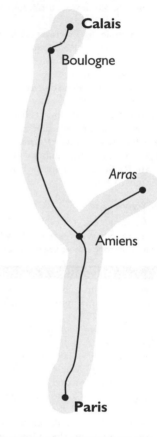

## TRAINS

**ETT tables:** 260, 265.

### FAST TRACK

One TGV (daily except Sun) runs from Paris Nord to Calais Ville; journey time 1 hr 40 mins. Three or four Eurostars and another TGV serve Calais Fréthun (1½ hrs), although this station is remote and access to town is awkward. Four or five conventional trains operate via Amiens, each taking 3–3½ hrs.

### ON TRACK

#### Paris–Amiens
At least ten trains per day make the journey of 1 hr–1 hr 50 mins.

#### Amiens–Boulogne
Five or six trains link the towns each day; journey time about 1 hr 20 mins.

#### Boulogne–Calais
Irregular services with a journey time of around 40 mins.

## AMIENS

**Station: Amiens-Nord** is the main station, about 500 m south-east of the cathedral. The grim concrete **Tour Perret** provides an easy to see marker when you return to the station.
**Tourist Office:** *12 r. du Chapeau-de-Violettes; tel: 03 22 91 79 28; fax: 03 22 92 50 58.* Open Mon–Sat 0900–1230, 1400–1830 (1900 Apr–Oct). **Branch:** at the rail station; *tel: 22 92 65 04,* open Mon–Sat 0800–1820, Sun 0930–1820. In midsummer, there's also a **kiosk** in front of the Cathedral, open daily 1000–1900.

To reach the cathedral from the station, turn

right on *blvd d'Alsace Lorraine* and then second left on *r. Gloriette*. Buses are allowed into the pedestrianised centre, but it is usually much faster to walk – and certainly the best way to explore.

The **Cathédrale de Notre-Dame** is the largest in France and arguably the purest example of Gothic architecture in the country. The relative quickness of its construction – 50 years in the 13th century – resulted in a coherence of style seldom found in such mammoth buildings. The west doorway, a 'book in stone', features the famous **Beau Dieu** portal. Bookings for the *Son et Lumière,* held Tues–Sat Apr–Oct, can be made by ringing the cathedral office; *tel: 03 22 91 83 83.* The **Picardy Museum**, *48 r. de la République; tel: 03 22 91 36 44,* contains artefacts from the cathedral, in addition to other local archaeological exhibits and a substantial collection of medieval art.

The **St-Leu** district, straddling the Somme just north of the cathedral, dates from the Middle Ages. Most of the houses on the winding streets have been restored, but there are pockets that maintain the original medieval character.

Beyond Parc St-Pierre are **Les Hortillonnages**, reclaimed marshlands that have provided food for Amiens since the Middle Ages.

Jules Verne wrote some of his pioneering science fiction works while living at *2 r. Charles Dubois,* which is now the **Jules Verne Information Centre**; *tel: 03 22 45 37 84,* an attraction more for the serious fan than for the merely curious.

### SIDE TRACK FROM AMIENS

### ARRAS

**Station:** *pl. Maréchal Foch,* 500 m south-east of the town centre.
**Tourist Office:** *Hôtel de Ville, pl. des Héros; tel: 21 51 26 95.* Open Mon–Sat 0900–1800, Sun 1000–1830.

There are around eight trains a day from Amiens to Arras, and the journey takes 45 mins–1 hr. Arras boasts fine examples of Flemish buildings along *Grande pl.* and *pl. des*

*Héros,* which have been comprehensively reconstructed following damage during both world wars. It was also famous for its tapestries, some of which can be seen in the **Musée des Beaux-Arts**, inside the **Abbaye St-Vaast**. Visit **Les Boves**, a vast tunnelling complex under the town that was a place of refuge during the numerous wars that Arras has seen.

Bookable through B&B France, the charming **Château de Grand Rullecourt**, 25 km from Arras, is a good base for exploration of the area. It has moderately priced rooms in a scenic location, and even features a bed slept in by Marie Antoinette. Station pick-up service. 🛏

### BOULOGNE

**Station: Boulogne-Ville**, 1 km south of the centre, is linked to it by all the buses that stop at the station.
**Ferries:** The **Hoverspeed** SeaCat services linking Boulogne and Folkstone use **Gare Maritime** and there are free shuttle buses between the dock and the centre of town.
**Tourist Office:** *Quai de la Poste; tel: 21 31 68 38.* Open Mon–Thur 0900–2000, Fri–Sat 0900–2200, Sun 1000–2000 (July–Aug); Mon–Sat 0900–1900, Sun 1000–1300, 1400–1700 (Sept–June). The accommodation booking service is free. From the station, turn right on *blvd Voltaire* and then left on *blvd Daunou.*

**423**

#### ACCOMMODATION

Boulogne has a slightly less touristy feel to it than Calais, and the accommodation scene is more favourable, with good value hotels to be found right in the heart of town. Hotel chains include *Ba, Ch* and *Ib.* Try the reasonably priced 3-star **Hôtel Métropole**, *51 r. Thiers; tel: 03 21 31 54 30:* convenient, pleasant, good breakfast (no other meals) and with a garden. If budget is your prime consideration, a good bet is the 1-star **Le Castel**, *51 r. Nationale; tel: 03 21 31 52 88.* **HI:** *56 pl. Rouget de Lisle; tel: 03 21 80 14 50; fax: 03 21 80 45 62.*

#### SIGHTSEEING

The **Vieille Ville** (Old Town) sits above the largely unremarkable modern city. The walk

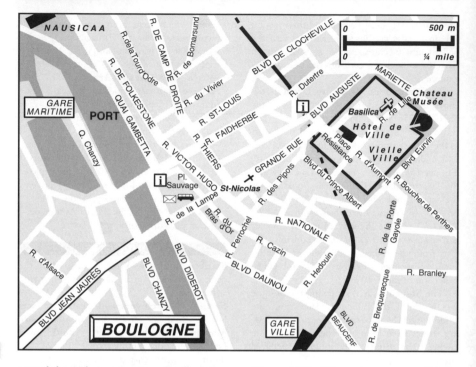

around the 13th-century city walls affords fine views of the town and harbour.

Within the ramparts, the 19th-century **Basilique Notre-Dame** draws together elements from St Paul's in London and St Peter's in Rome. Some interesting crypts from the 12th century survive below the more modern structure. At the south end of *r. de Lille* is **Le Beffroi** (The Belfry) – access is through the Hôtel de Ville.

At the eastern corner of the walled town is **Château-Musée**, *r. de Bernet*, which contains an eclectic collection of artefacts, from Aleutian masks to Greek amphorae.

The premier modern addition to Boulogne's tourist attractions is **Nausicaa**, on the seafront at *blvd Ste-Beuve*, one of the largest aquariums in France. It is equipped with underwater observation tanks for excellent views of sharks and other marine creatures.

## CALAIS

**Station: Calais-Ville** is the main station and almost opposite the picturesque **Hôtel de Ville**

(Town Hall). The other station, **Calais-Fréthun**, is near the mouth of the Channel Tunnel and likely to be of interest only as a transit point.

**Ferries:** All the companies run free shuttles between Calais-Ville station and the docks to connect with sailings. Stena, P&O and Sea-France sail from Calais Port; Hoverspeed departs from Calais Hoverport (2–3 km from main port). **Sea France**; *tel: 03 21 34 55 00*; **P&O**; *tel: 03 21 46 04 40*; **Stena**; *tel: 0232 14 67 868*; and **Hoverspeed**; *tel: 03 21 46 14 14*.

The superb Rodin statue of the **Six Burghers of Calais**, which stands in front of the Town Hall commemorates the English capture of the town in 1347. Opposite, in the Parc St-Pierre, is the **Musée de la Guerre**, devoted to a more recent conflict – World War II – and was originally used as a bunker by German forces. Also worth visiting are the **Musée des Beaux-Arts et de la Dentelle**, *25 r. Richelieu* (local lace-making exhibits), and the **Église de Notre-Dame**, the only English Tudor-style church in continental Europe.

# PARIS–CHERBOURG

The prime stop on this very scenic route is Rouen, with its famous medieval cathedral. At one end (between Paris and Rouen) is the Seine Valley, at the other is the rolling countryside of Basse-Normandie – homeland of William the Conqueror, whose exploits are recorded in the Bayeux tapestry. In addition there are many fascinating side tracks, notably to the succession of D-Day landing beaches (and the related museums scattered along the coast) and the cheese- and cider-producing towns for which the region is famous.

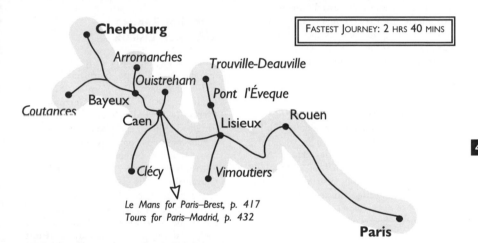

FASTEST JOURNEY: 2 HRS 40 MINS

Le Mans for Paris–Brest, p. 417
Tours for Paris–Madrid, p. 432

425

Le Mans for Paris–Brest, p. 417
Tours for Paris–Madrid, p. 432

## TRAINS

**ETT tables:** 269, 270, 272.

### FAST TRACK

An irregular service, approximately every 2 hrs (fewer on Sun), links Paris St Lazare with Cherbourg. Most trains take about 3 hrs.

### ON TRACK

**Paris–Rouen**
Trains every 1–2 hrs (fewer on Sun), taking 1 hr 10 min–1½ hrs.

**Rouen–Lisieux**
Three or four trains link Rouen Rive-Droite with Lisieux. The journey takes 1 hr 15 min.

**Lisieux–Caen**
An irregular service with journey times of 30 mins.

**Caen–Bayeux–Cherbourg**
Trains operate between Caen and Cherbourg at roughly two-hourly intervals, although service is irregular with some long gaps. All trains call at Bayeux. Caen to Bayeux takes 18 mins, Bayeux to Cherbourg 1 hr.

## ROUEN

**Station: Rive-Droite (RD)**, 1 km north of the centre, but linked by buses. While at the station, you can get a day-pass providing unlimited travel on the city buses and the new métro. **Tourist Office:** 25 pl. de la Cathédrale; tel: 02

*32 08 32 40; fax: 02 32 08 32 44.* Open Mon–
Sat 0900–1900, Sun 0930–1230 and 1430–
1800 (May–Sept); Mon–Sat 0900–1230 and
1400–1830, Sun 1000–1300 (Oct–Apr).

#### ACCOMMODATION

There are many affordable hotels in town, so
finding something to suit your budget is no
problem. Hotel chains include *BW, Ib, IH, Mc*
and *Nv*. **Hôtel de la Cathédrale**, *12 r. St-
Romain; tel: 02 35 71 57 95,* holds a superb
position overlooking the famous building. The
(3-star) **Hôtel de Dieppe**, *pl. B-Tissot; tel: 02
35 71 96 00* (opposite the station), is a moderately priced family-run establishment. Try
**Hostellerie du Vieux Logis**, *5 r. de Joyeuse;
tel: 02 35 71 55 30,* for a cheaper alternative.
**HI:** *118 blvd de l'Europe; tel: 02 35 72 06 45,* 4
km from the station (bus no. 12: *Diderot).*

#### SIGHTSEEING

The main attraction is still indisputably the
lovely **Cathédrale Notre-Dame**, one of
Monet's favourite subjects. An example of his
work showing the west front can be seen at the
attractively restored **Musée des Beaux Arts**,
*pl. Verdrel.* The Gothic church of **St-Maclou**,
*pl. Barthélemy,* was virtually destroyed in World
War II. The nearby cloisters, **Aître St-
Maclou**, *186 r. Martainville,* were once a storage area for the bodies of plague victims and are
surrounded by morbid carvings.

A 20-m high memorial marks the spot
where **Joan of Arc** was burned at the stake.
This is in *pl. du Vieux Marché,* which is also
home to a modern church dedicated to her and
a museum about her featuring waxwork figures.

The museums in Rouen cover a diversity of
subjects, including ceramics, antiquities, fine
arts, Flaubert and medicine – even wrought iron
(**Musée le Secq Tournelles**, *r. Jacques Villon).*

### LISIEUX

**Station:** for the Tourist Office, follow *r. de la
Gare* and cross *pl. Fournet.*
**Tourist Office:** *11 r. d'Alençon; tel: 02 31 62
08 41; fax: 02 31 62 35 22.* Open Mon–Sat
0830–1230, 1330–1900, Sun 0900–1230,
1400–1800 (June–Sept); Mon–Sat 0830–1200
and 1330–1800 (Oct–May).

The white **Basilique de Ste-Thérèse**,
built in the 1950s, overlooks the town; an
enormous structure that is one of the world's
biggest 20th-century churches. It commemorates a young Carmelite nun who died here at
the end of the 19th century. Thérèse Martin
had her first vision of the Virgin Mary when she
was only a child and she was canonised in 1925,
after a series of miracles. Her basilica has
become a magnet for pilgrims and the main
annual **pilgrimages** are 15 Aug and the last
Sun in Sept. In the centre of town are the elegant 12th-century Gothic **Cathédrale St-
Pierre** and the **bishop's palace**.

> ### SIDE TRACKS
> ### FROM LISIEUX
>
> Lisieux is the starting point for expeditions
> into the **Pays d'Auge**, Normandy's cheese
> and cider country. Bus Verts no. 53 heads
> south via the village of **St-Germain de
> Livret** (with a delightful chequerboard-
> patterned château) and **Livarot** (famous for
> a pungent round, orange-crusted cheese –
> you can visit a working cheese factory) to
> **Vimoutiers**, which is home to **Musée du
> Camembert**. The cheese dates from 1791
> and is credited to a farmer's wife from a
> nearby village of that name, who was given
> the recipe by a priest to whom she gave
> shelter during the Revolution. **Pont
> l'Évêque**, easily reached by train, is home
> to an eponymous creamy cheese, a calvados
> distillery and the **Musée du Calvados**.
>
> A branch line diverges for **Trouville-
> Deauville**, the Parisians' favourite two-in-
> one summer resort: famous for *planches*
> (boardwalks), the Deauville film festival
> (early Sept) and horse racing (May–Oct)
>
> Set 12 km outside Lisieux, the farm **Aux
> Pommiers de Livaye** offers pretty rooms
> at a moderate price. Station pick-up service;
> book through B&B France. ⬕

### CAEN

**Station:** 1.5 km south of the centre, but the
**Bus Verts station** is next door *(tel: 03 31 44
77 44)* and there are plenty of buses into town.
**Tourist Office:** *pl. St-Pierre; tel: 03 31 27 14*

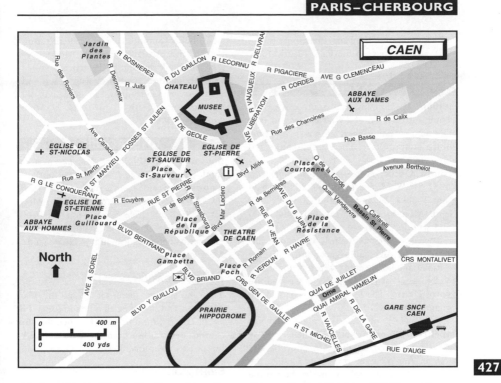

CAEN

*Jardin des Plantes*
R BOSNIERES
Rue des Rosiers
Rue des Rosiers
R Desmoueux
R Juifs
R DU GAILLON
R LECORNU
R DELIVRAN
R PIGACIERE
AVE G CLEMENCEAU
R CORDES
CHATEAU
MUSEE
R DE GEOLE
ST JULIEN
AVE LIBER VAUGUEUX
AVE LIBERATION
Rue des Chanoines
ABBAYE AUX DAMES
R de Calix
Rue Basse
EGLISE DE ST-NICOLAS
Ave Canada
FOSSES ST JULIEN
R ST MANVIEU
EGLISE DE ST-SAUVEUR
EGLISE DE ST-PIERRE
Blvd Alliés
Place Courtonne
Q de la Londe
Avenue Berthelot
Rue St Martin
R G LE CONQUERANT
Place St-Sauveur
R Ecuyère
RUE ST PIERRE
R de Brasile
Blvd Mar Leclerc
Strasbourg
R de Bernières
AVE DU 6 JUIN
RUE ST JEAN
Quai Vendeuvre
Bassin St Pierre
Q Caffarelli
EGLISE DE ST-ETIENNE
ABBAYE AUX HOMMES
Place Guillouard
BLVD BERTRAND
Place de la République
THEATRE DE CAEN
Place de la Résistance
North
AVE A SOREL
Place Gambetta
BLVD BRIAND
BLVD Y GUILLOU
Place Foch
R Romain
R VERDUN
R HAVRE
CRS GEN DE GAULLE
QUAI DE JUILLET
Orne
QUAI AMIRAL HAMELIN
R DE LA GARE
R ST MICHEL
R ST VAUCELLES
CRS MONTALIVET
GARE SNCF CAEN
RUE D'AUGE
PRAIRIE HIPPODROME

0    400 m
0    400 yds

**427**

*14; fax: 03 31 27 14 13.* Open Mon–Sat 0900–1900, Sun 1000–1230 and 1500–1800 (June–Sept); Mon–Sat 0900/1000–1200 and 1400–1830, Sun 1000–1230 (Oct–May). **Regional (Calvados):** *pl. du Canada; tel: 03 31 86 53 30.*

**Ferries: Brittany Ferries,** *tel: 31 36 36 00,* sail between Portsmouth and **Ouistreham** (Sword Beach), 15 km north of Caen: bus no. 1 makes the 30-min trip to connect with ferry sailings.

Despite extensive post-war rebuilding, there are still traces of the town ruled by William the Conqueror and the still-imposing walls of his castle now protect two museums: the **Musée de Normandie** (in the old governors' palace) is a fascinating place about the region's history, crafts and costumes, while the **Musée des Beaux-Arts** has a wide selection of Flemish, Italian and French works of art.

Churches of interest include the Romanesque **St-Nicholas** and the Gothic **St-Sauveur**, but more impressive are two abbeys, built by William the Conqueror and his wife. Queen Mathilda is buried at the **Abbaye aux**

**Dames** (Ladies' Abbey) and William at the vast **Abbaye aux Hommes** (Men's Abbey).

The high-tech **Mémorial** is a 'museum for peace'. Located on a windy plain north of town (bus no. 12), it charts world history from 1918 to the present.

### SIDE TRACKS FROM CAEN

To see the D-day beaches without a car is not easy. Infrequent buses run from Caen to two of them: **Ouistreham** and **Courseulles**. South from Caen are the deep, wooded gorges of **Suisse Normande** (Norman Switzerland), a region for outdoor activities. You need a car to explore fully, but can reach the area by bus no. 34. Possible bases are **Thury-Harcourt** or **Clécy**.

### Connections

From Caen, you can connect to two other routes in this book. Trains to Le Mans will take you onto the Paris–Brest route (see p. 417), and to Tours to the Paris–Madrid route (p. 432).

## BAYEUX

**Station:** 10–15 mins walk south-east of the centre; turn left on *blvd Sadi Carnot* and bear right onto *r. Larcher*. Turn left onto *r. St-Martin* for the Tourist Office. There are also buses into the centre.

**Tourist Office:** *Pont St-Jean/r. St-Martin; tel: 02 31 51 28 28; fax: 02 31 51 28 29.* Open daily 1000–1230 and 1500–1830 (July–mid Sept); Mon–Sat 0900–1200 and 1400–1800 (mid Sept–June).

Bayeux was one of the first towns to be liberated by the Allies and escaped much damage to its fine medieval centre, which is dominated by the spires of the magnificent **Cathédrale Notre-Dame**. The lovely crypt is part of the original structure (1077).

Save plenty of energy for the **Bayeux tapestry**: 70m of embroidered linen – probably commissioned by the Bishop of Bayeux from an Anglo-Saxon workshop. Despite the passage of time, the colours are bright and the design is amazingly detailed – it justifies its position as the world's most famous tapestry. Before looking at the real thing, spend some time at the **exhibition centre**, which will help you to interpret what you see.

The **Musée Mémoriale de la Bataille de Normandie 44**, *blvd Fabian Ware,* includes the preparations for D-Day, as well as the action, and is probably the best of several museums in the area which are devoted to the World War II Normandy landings.

### ⮎ SIDE TRACKS FROM BAYEUX

The whole Normandy coast is a succession of **D-Day beaches**, but there is little to see, except at **Arromanches** (about 10 km from Bayeux, take bus no. 74), where (at low tide) the remains of a **Mulberry Harbour** are visible – one of the floating landing-stages which crossed the Channel transporting troops and vehicles. Exploration of the region is possible from **Le Vallon**, a quiet

farmhouse outside Bayeux that also runs yoga and massage courses. Moderately priced, book through B&B France.

About three trains run daily Caen and Bayeux to **Coutances**, an attractive old town noteworthy for its Gothic cathedral. ⮎

## CHERBOURG

**Station: Gare SNCF**, *pl. Jean Jaurès,* at the south end of *Bassin du Commerce* (harbour).

**Tourist Office:** *2 quai Alexandre III; tel: 02 33 93 52 02; fax: 02 33 53 66 97.* Open Mon–Sat 0900–1830 (June–Sept), Mon–Fri 0900–1200, 1330–1800. On the far side of *Bassin du Commerce,* between the lifting bridge and *r. Maréchal Foch.*

### ACCOMMODATION

There is a large three-star *Mc* at the Gare Maritime, and several small hotels in town. **HI:** *av. L. Lumière; tel: 33 44 26 31,* open mid Apr to mid Oct, 1.5 km from the Gare SNCF by bus no. 5 to stop *Jean Moulin.*

### SIGHTSEEING

Ever since the construction of its huge break-waters Cherbourg has been an important commercial and military port. It was liberated by American troops three weeks after the landings on Utah beach – 17 days later than planned – to give the Allies a deep-water port for bringing in heavy vehicles. South-east of the Gare SNCF the **Fort du Roule** overlooks the town and port. Inside, the **Museum of War and Liberation** commemorates the Allied landings and the liberation of Cherbourg and the Cotentin peninsula. Open 0930–1730 Apr–Sept; admission FFr.15, FFr.7 for students.

### ⮎ SIDE TRACKS FROM CHERBOURG

A bus service heads down the Cotentin peninsula to **Coutances** (see above), via the villages of **Martinvast**, which has a 19th-century château, and **Bricquebec**, whose much older fortress has a mighty keep and a museum of local life. ⮎

# PARIS–FRANKFURT

This route between France and Germany crosses the border just before Saarbrücken. It takes you through the Champagne, Alsace and Moselle regions, all famous for their wines. Reims Cathedral is one of the many architectural highlights.

The first part of the route follows the same track as the Paris–Munich route (see pp. 446–452).

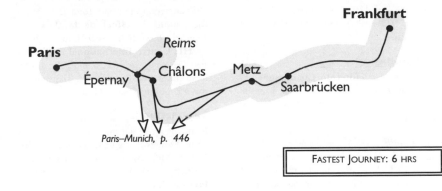

Paris–Munich, p. 446

FASTEST JOURNEY: 6 HRS

## TRAINS

**ETT tables:** 30, 390, 392, 386, 919.

### FAST TRACK

Four trains a day leave Paris Est for Frankfurt. Three of these are EuroCity expresses, taking 6 hrs for the journey. There is also one overnight train with sleeping cars (not Sat night), couchettes and second-class seats.

### ON TRACK

#### Paris–Épernay

An irregular service throughout the day links Paris Est with Épernay, and some trains continue to Reims. Paris to Épernay takes 1 hr 15 mins, Paris to Reims about 1 hr 40 mins.

#### Épernay–Châlons-sur-Marne

Six or seven trains a day run between Épernay and Châlons, but there are long periods when no trains run, so take care to check the timetable.

#### Châlons-sur-Marne–Metz

Four trains a day make the journey between Châlons-sur-Marne and Metz, as well as one overnight service. One of the day trains is a local service and takes just over 3 hrs, the others are express trains and take approximately 1 hr 30 mins, as does the night train.

#### Metz–Saarbrücken

Ten a trains a day cross this border between France and Germany. Three are EuroCity expresses with dining cars and supplements. The journey takes just under 1 hr.

### Saarbrücken–Frankfurt

A regular two-hourly InterCity service links Saarbrücken with Frankfurt, all trains have dining cars and a supplement to be paid. The journey takes 2 hr 10 mins.

## ÉPERNAY

**Station:** *pl. de la Gare,* 300m north-east of the town centre; *tel: 08 36 35 35 35.*
**Tourist Office:** *7 av. de Champagne; tel: 03 26 53 33 00.* Open Mon–Sat 0930–1230 and 1330–1900, Sun 1100–1600 (Easter–mid Oct); Mon–Sat 0930–1230 and 1330–1730 (mid Oct–Easter).

### ACCOMMODATION

The aptly-named **Hôtel de Champagne**, *30 r. Eugène Mercier; tel: 03 26 53 10 60,* is in the heart of the champagne-producing quarter (moderate).

### SIGHTSEEING

**430**

**Champagne** is definitely the reason to visit Épernay, which is surrounded by vineyards. Some of the world's greatest *'maisons'* line *av. de Champagne.* Tours through the chalk cellars of **Moët et Chandon** (no. 20), where about 100 million bottles are stored, last about 45 mins. Jean-Rémy Moët was an exact contemporary of Napoleon, who took a glass before every battle – except Waterloo. **Mercier** (no. 70) offers a high-tech tour with a jazzy slide display and a laser-guided train takes visitors through the cellars. Others are **Demoiselle** (no. 42) and **De Castellane**, *57 r. de Verdun.*

 **SIDE TRACK FROM ÉPERNAY**

## REIMS

**Station:** *blvd Joffre; tel: 08 36 35 35 35,* about 10 mins walk to the cathedral: head down *r. Thiers* and turn right on *cours J-B-Langlet.* Ten trains a day (less on Sun) run from Épernay to Reims, taking up to 45 mins.

**Tourist Office:** *2 r. G-de-Machault; tel: 03 26 77 45 25,* next to the cathedral. Open Mon–Sat 0900–2000, Sun 0930–1900 (July–Aug); Mon–Sat 0900–1930, Sun 0930–1830 (Easter–June, Sept); Mon–Sat 0900–1830 Sun 0930–1730 (Oct–Easter).

### ACCOMMODATION

Finding somewhere to stay is seldom a problem, except at the height of the tourist season. Hotel chains: *Ba, BW, Ch, Ct, Hd, Ib, IH, Mc, Nv.* If you can afford it, **Boyer Les Crayères**, *64 blvd Henry Vasnier; tel: 03 26 82 80 80,* is a sumptuous 19th-century château serving gourmet food. To be near the station, try **Hôtel de la Paix**, *9 r. Buirette; tel: 03 26 40 04 08* (moderate).

**HI: Centre International de Séjour**, *Parc L-Lagrange; tel: 03 26 40 52 60,* 1.5 km from the station (bus H from *Théâtre* in the town centre to *Pont de-Gaulle).*

### SIGHTSEEING

Reims is a major centre of the champagne trade. Houses that give tours of their cellars include **Mumm** *(34 r. du Champs de Mars),* **Taittinger** *(9 pl. St-Nicaise)* and **Piper-Heidsieck** *(51 blvd Henry Vasnier).*

The awesome **Cathédrale Notre-Dame**, started in 1211, is a masterpiece of Gothic architecture. Over twenty French kings were crowned there. The interior is mesmeric, highlighted by superb stained-glass windows, including some by Chagall, but many of the sculptures and tapestries are now housed in the **Palais du Tau**, next door. The 11th-century Romanesque **Basilique St-Rémi**, *r. Simon,* is about 1 km south-east of the cathedral.

## CHÂLONS-SUR-MARNE/ CHÂLONS-EN-CHAMPAGNE

**Station:** *av. de la Gare; tel: 03 26 66 21 46,* 1 km west of the centre; bus to centre-ville.
**Tourist Office**: *3 quai des Arts; tel: 03 26 65 17 89.* Mon–Thur 0900–1200 and 1330–1900, Fri–Sat 0900–1800, Sun 0930–1230 and 1500–1800 (mid June–mid Sept); Mon–Fri 0930–1200 and 1330–1800, Sat 0900–1200 and 1330–1830 (mid Sept–mid June).

## ACCOMMODATION

For a comfortable central hotel, try **Saint-Régis**, *22 blvd de la République; tel: 03 85 48 07 28* (moderate). **HI**: *r. Kullermann; tel: 03 26 68 13 56,* 15 mins walk from station or bus (direction *centre-ville*) to *Mgr. Tissier.*

## SIGHTSEEING

The town of Châlons-sur-Marne has officially been renamed as **Châlons-en-Champagne**, although the railway station is still signed as Châlons-sur-Marne.

Châlons-sur-Marne is the third of the **champagne-producing** towns, but the least visited. Yet parts of it are charming, with restored half-timbered houses set amongst old canals. The **Cathédrale St-Étienne** (St Stephen's) has some fine 13th-century stained-glass. Impressive windows can also be seen in the early Gothic **Église de Notre-Dame-en-Vaux**, *pl. Mgr. Tissier,* whose ruined medieval cloister has been partially rebuilt from the original stones.

## NANCY

See the Paris–Munich route, p.446.

## METZ

**Station:** *pl. Gen de Gaulle; tel 08 36 35 35 35,* 20 mins walk from the centre, or frequent minibus service.

**Tourist Office:** *pl. d'Armes; tel: 03 87 55 53 76.* Open Mon–Sat 0900–1900 (to 2100 July–Aug), Sun 1000–1300 and 1500–1700. Ask for the listing *Calendrier des Manifestations.*

## ACCOMMODATION

**Hotel du Nord**, *175 route de Thionville; tel: 03 87 32 53 29,* is comfortable and moderately priced.

## SIGHTSEEING

Metz, where the Moselle and Seille rivers meet, has an old quarter of narrow winding streets around the Gothic **Cathédrale St-Étienne** (St Stephen's), *pl. d'Armes,* which began life as two churches sharing a vault. The unified building, enhanced over the centuries, gives an overall impression of harmony. It has a vast area of stained-glass from different periods, including modern windows by Chagall. The light streaming through them gives the high vaulted interior a glow that has been called the 'Lantern of God'. The 14th-century *pl. St-Louis* is surrounded by Italian-influenced medieval mansions and arcades. The **Musée d'Art et d'Histoire**, *2 r. du Haut-Poirier,* has excellent historical displays. On the edge of town, the massive **Porte des Allemands** is a 13th- to 16th-century fortified bridge, looking more like a castle, over the Seille.

## SAARBRÜCKEN

**Station:** Hbf, *tel: (0681) 19419,* 10-min walk from the centre.

**Tourist Office**: Hbf, *tel: (0681) 36515.* Open Mon–Fri 0900–1800 and Sat 0900–1500. Also at *Grossherzogstr-Friedrich-Str. 1; tel: (0681) 36901.* Open Mon–Fri 0800–1700.

## ACCOMMODATION

There are plenty of hotels around Hbf, such as **Weinstube Jochem**, *Grülingsstr. 101-103; tel: (0681) 948500* (moderate). The restaurant area is around *St Johanner Markt.*

**HI: Jugendherberge**, *Meerwiesertalweg 31; tel: (0681) 33040.* 15 mins by bus nos 11/19 (direction *University*). **Campsite**: *Am Spichere Berg; tel (0681) 51780.* 20 mins by bus 19 (direction *Metzerstr.*)

## SIGHTSEEING

Though now just in Germany, the town has many French features, having changed between the two many times. **Ludwigskirche** and **Ludwigsplatz**, the square beside it, are among Germany's best examples of baroque architecture. The cobbled *St Johanner Markt,* (marketplace), also baroque, has a raised fountain in the centre. The **Altes Rathaus** houses the **Abenteuer Museum**, which is a rather bizarre collection about 'primitive' peoples visited by Abenteuer during his globe-trotting. The **Modern Gallerie** has a good collection of 19th- and 20th-century art, including works by Dufy, Monet and Rodin. The same ticket gets you into **Alte Sammlung**, which covers the Middle Ages to the 19th century.

**431**

# PARIS–MADRID

This route leads you through France to Spain, and affords splendid scenery contrasts, from the fairy-tale châteaux of the Loire Valley to the striking Belle Époque coastal resorts of Biarritz and Donóstia.

FASTEST JOURNEY: 13 HRS

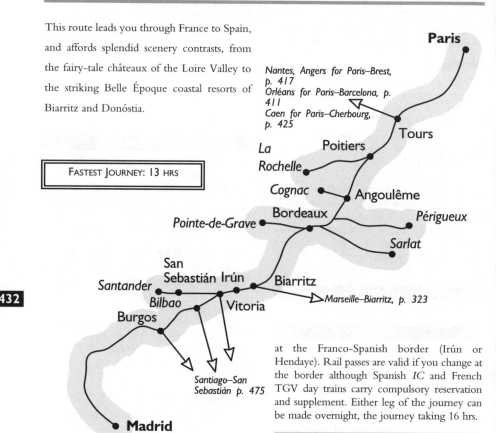

Nantes, Angers for Paris–Brest, p. 417
Orléans for Paris–Barcelona, p. 411
Caen for Paris–Cherbourg, p. 425

Paris

Tours

Poitiers

La Rochelle

Cognac

Angoulême

Bordeaux

Périgueux

Pointe-de-Grave

Sarlat

San Sebastián Irún

Biarritz

Marseille–Biarritz, p. 323

Santander

Bilbao

Vitoria

Burgos

Santiago–San Sebastián p. 475

Madrid

432

at the Franco-Spanish border (Irún or Hendaye). Rail passes are valid if you change at the border although Spanish *IC* and French TGV day trains carry compulsory reservation and supplement. Either leg of the journey can be made overnight, the journey taking 16 hrs.

## ON TRACK

**Paris–Tours**
Over a dozen TGV services run daily from Paris (Montparnasse). Four go to Tours, the others require a change of train at St-Pierre-des-Corps. The journey takes a little over an hour. The indirect journey changing at Orléans doubles the time, but allows stops at the château towns of Blois and Amboise and a changeover onto the Paris–Barcelona route (p. 411).

**Tours–Poitiers**
A dozen trains run every day between Tours and Poitiers. They actually depart from and

## TRAINS

**ETT tables: 46, 295, 300, 302, 680.**

### FAST TRACK

There are two overnight trains, which depart in the early evening each day, between Paris (Austerlitz) and Madrid (Chamartín): the *Francisco de Goya* takes about 13 hrs. It has first- and second-class sleeping-cars and a restaurant car. Rail passes are not valid on this train, fares are high and there are no seats or couchettes. Other journeys change arrive at St-Pierre-des-Corps, 3 km away, but there are efficient shuttle trains running to Tours. The TGV trains take about 55 mins, the fastest local trains generally take a little over an hour. If you are not interested in seeing Tours, there are several non-stop trains every day from Paris (Montparnasse) to Poitiers and on to Bordeaux.

### Poitiers–Angoulême

There is a train approximately every hour and most are TGVs, taking about 45 mins. The ordinary trains take about an hour.

### Angoulême–Bordeaux

There are trains (TGV and ordinary) at intervals of an hour or two throughout the day. The TGV services take an hour, while the ordinary trains take about 1 hr 20 mins.

### Bordeaux–Biarritz

Services operate at intervals of about 2 hrs from very early morning to late evening. The journey takes anything from 1 hr 45 mins by TGV to 2½ hrs by other trains. Biarritz is described in the Marseille–Biarritz route, p. 325.

### Biarritz–(Border)–Irún

There are approximately eight trains between Biarritz and Irún throughout the day, but the intervals between them are irregular. The journey takes 30 mins.

### Irún–San Sebastián (Donostia)

The journey usually takes only 15–30 mins and there are over a dozen direct trains every day, but at irregular intervals. There is also a local service operated by the private railway FV (Ferrocarriles Vascos).

### San Sebastián–Vitoria (Gasteiz)

The journey takes 1½–2 hrs. Many of the RENFE trains between Irún and San Sebastián continue to Vitoria.

### Vitoria–Burgos

There are six express trains a day between Vitoria and Burgos, not counting night trains at inconvenient hours. The journey time is 1 hr 20 mins.

### Burgos–Madrid

Between Burgos and Madrid (Chamartín) there are at least four fast trains each day. The number of stops varies, as does the journey time – approximately 3–4 hrs.

## TOURS

**Station**: *tel: 02 47 20 50 50*. Near the Mairie in the city centre.
**Tourist Office**: *78–82 Bernard Palissy Rd* (opposite the train station); *tel: 02 47 70 37 37; fax: 02 47 61 14 22*.

### ACCOMMODATION

Many people like to stay in the small villages and towns around Tours, rather than in the city itself. However, you can find a reasonable range of cheap hotels in the area around the station and the old town, near the river. Hotel chains include *BW*: **The Grand Hotel**, opposite the station; *tel: 02 47 05 35 31,* has large, clean, moderate–expensive rooms. There is a **Youth Hostel** at *Parc de Grandmont; tel: 02 47 25 14 45*, 4 km from the station.

### SIGHTSEEING

433

Founded by the Romans on the banks of the Loire River, Tours was at the centre of five major trade routes. By the 8th century, it had become an important cultural centre and place of pilgrimage. Home to one of the oldest and most influential universities in France, the city also thrived during the 15th and 16th centuries when the French court and nobility streamed into the region. Today, it is the largest city along the Loire, with widespread suburbs hiding a golden heart, much of which has been sensitively restored after serious damage during World War II.

The city's two main sights stand next to each other, just off *r. Jules Simon*. The elaborately ornate **Cathédrale de St Gatien** was built between the 12th and 16th centuries and contains fine examples of almost every sort of medieval architecture, from the Romanesque through Gothic to the Renaissance. There are some wonderful 13th-century stained-glass windows, while the **Cloître de la Psalette** to one side has some beautiful 15th- and 16th-century frescos.

Next door, in the 18th-century Episcopal Palace, is the **Musée des Beaux-Arts**, *tel: 02 47 05 68 73,* with a wide and fascinating art collection, including works by Rembrandt, Delacroix and Degas, as well as several carefully reconstructed 18th-century rooms.

The heart of the **old town**, around the *pl. Plumereau,* which offers an excellent selection of cheap–moderate restaurants, and *pl. Floire-le-Roi* on the south bank, is a maze of narrow streets, mostly pedestrianised, and half-timbered houses, many of which have been carefully restored and turned into trendy boutiques.

The 13th-century **Église de Saint-Julien**, *r. Nationale,* has some fine 20th-century stained glass, and houses the museum of **Touraine** wine. Next door, the unique **Musée de Compagnonnage**, housed in the old monks' dormitory has a fascinating collection of memorabilia from the old guild trades, while the nearby Renaissance **Hôtel Gouin**, *r. de Commerce,* is home to a small archaeology museum.

### ⇄ SIDE TRACKS FROM TOURS

Right in the centre of the most château-laden part of France, Tours is an excellent place from which to explore the adjoining valleys of the **Loire**, Loir, Cher and Indre, all strewn with such famous castles as **Amboise**, **Azay-le-Rideau**, **Chambord**, **Chenonceaux**, **Chinon**, **Langeais**, **Loches** and **Villandry**. Most are some distance apart, as well as from the city, so you will need transport – car, moped or bicycle – and a regional map (available from the Tourist Office) unless you stick to coach tours. ◣

### ↔ Connections

From Tours, there are connecting train services to **Nantes** and **Angers** on the Paris–Brest route (p. 417), to **Orléans** on the Paris–Barcelona route (p. 411) and **Caen** (Paris–Cherbourg route, p. 425).

### POITIERS

**Station**: *tel: 05 49 58 50 50.* About 15 mins walk from the centre: up a hill and a flight of stairs.

**Tourist Offices:** *8 r. Grandes Écoles; tel: 05 49 41 21 24,* and *15 r. Carnot; tel: 49 41 58 22.*

### SIGHTSEEING

Poitiers is one of the earliest Christian centres of France, with the result that today, as well as several beautiful secular buildings, it boasts an impressive array of wonderful churches. The oldest, first built in 356, is the **Baptistère de Saint-Jean**, *r. Jean-Jaurès.* Almost next door is the 12th–13th-century **Cathédrale de Saint-Pierre**, *r. de la Cathédrale.* Squat from the outside, once inside the nave soars high, crowned by some lovely 13th-century stained glass and choir stalls. Behind the cathedral is the **Église de Ste-Radegonde**, *r. de la Mauvinière,* first built in the 6th century with fine Romanesque and Gothic additions and alterations.

Some distance away, the flamboyantly decorated **Église de Notre-Dame-la-Grande**, *r. de Regatterie,* is a triumph of Romanesque art, while on the western edge of the old city is possibly the best of them all, the **Église de Saint-Hilaire-le-Grand**, an elegant, domed and arcaded Romanesque church, built mainly in the 11th century and still containing several frescos from that period. A further 10-min walk brings you to the Gothic Clunisian church of **Montierneuf**, *pl. Montierneuf.*

### ⇄ SIDE TRACKS FROM POITIERS

Clearly signposted from the autoroute, 7 km north of the city, is the massive, exciting **Futuroscope** museum and theme park. Dedicated to the photographic image, from early history to experimental cinema, it has something for everyone including a vast dome showing virtually spherical films, Imax screens, a 3D cinema and simulator.

Every Sat, Apr–Oct, and every evening, July–end Aug, the spectacular sound and light show, the *Water Symphony,* has water jets synchronised with music, images projected onto walls of water, laser and fireworks. Free to daytime visitors.

There are reduced-rate taxis just outside

Poiters station, or buses from the town centre. In the forest of hotels nearby are several offering ultra-cheap rates.

Poitiers also has a train service to the famous historic port of **La Rochelle**.

## ANGOULÊME

**Station**: *tel: 05 45 69 61 45*. This is north of the centre, on the road to Limoges, but there are a number of buses into town.

**Tourist Office**: *pl. St-Pierre; tel: 05 45 95 16 84*. Closed Mon.

Angoulême has an attractive old district, but it pales beside the other great historic centres on this route. The main reason for stopping here is so that you can head off into the depths of the surrounding countryside.

## BORDEAUX

**Airport**: *Bordeaux-Mérignac, 12 km from the city, tel: 05 56 34 50 50*.

**Stations**: *St Jean, tel: 05 36 35 35 35*. About 2 km from the south of the centre; you can walk it in about 30 mins, or there are numerous buses. Two other stations, the **Gare St Louis** and the **Gare d' Orléans**, serve local trains.

**Tourist Office**: *12 cours du 30 Juillet; tel: 05 56 00 66 00; fax: 05 56 00 66 01; e-mail: otb@mairie-bordeauxfrance*.

**Thomas Cook bureau de change**: *Gare St Jean, Parvis Louis Armand*.

### GETTING AROUND

Most of the greatest sights of interest are within a 1-square-km block in the city centre, so you should be able to get around on foot. There is a good bus network, however, and you can buy a one- or three-day pass, the **Carte Bordeaux Découverte**, from the station or Tourist Office.

### ACCOMMODATION

The city has a wide range of accommodation, suitable for all pockets. Major hotel groups represented in the city include *Me, Nv, Pu* and *Sf*.

As this is a port, many of the cheapest hotels, scattered around the grimy docks and the red-light district around the railway station, can be rather basic. However, cheap and functional accommodation can be found in a safer area of

the city in *r. Huguerie*, near the *pl. de Tourny*. There is a **Youth Hostel** (the **Foyer des Jeunes**) at *22 cours Barbey; tel: 56 91 59 51*, just under 1 km from the St Jean station.

### SIGHTSEEING

Set on the Garonne River just before it joins the Dordogne and Gironde to travel out to sea, Bordeaux is the sixth largest port in France, a busy, working city with an 18th-century centre surrounded by large amounts of industrial gloom.

Most of all, however, the city is the commercial centre of one of the world's greatest wine-growing areas, surrounded by the vineyards of Graves, Médoc, Sauternes and other great names. The area's vintners were also responsible in part for creating a tradition of great wine in those other increasingly famous areas – the Spanish Rioja and California.

To see the best of the city's historic buildings, walk from the *Esplanade* down the *cours du 30 Juillet* to the *pl. de la Comédie*, on which stands the wonderful neo-classical **Grand Théâtre**, stopping off en route at the **Maison de Vin**, *1 cours du 30 Juillet; tel: 05 56 52 82 82*, to arrange a wine tour and tasting. Take a boat tour on the Embarcadère Vedettes, which leave frequently from the *Esplanade de Quinconces*.

From the *pl. de la Comédie*, the beautiful **cours du Chapeau Rouge** leads to the *pl. de la Bourse*, a pleasant square on which stand the **Musée Maritime**, housed in the 18th-century Customs House, and the elegant **Hôtel de la Bourse**. Just to the south of this begins the **quartier Saint-Pierre**, the bustling old town filled with small boutiques and cafés.

About 1 km from here, along *r. des Trois-Canils*, you come to the city's richest gathering of fine buildings and museums, including, amongst others, the 11th–15th century **Cathédrale de St-André** and the superb 18th-century **Hôtel de Ville**, (both on *pl. Rohan*), the **Musée des Beaux-Arts**, *r. Montbazon*, and the **Musée des Arts Decoratifs**, *r. Bouffard*.

Other museums worth a visit include the archaeological **Musée d'Aquitaine**, *cours Victor Hugo/cours Pasteur*, and the **Musée d'Histoire Naturelle**, tucked into the south-west corner of the grand **Jardin Public**, *r. Duplessey*.

435

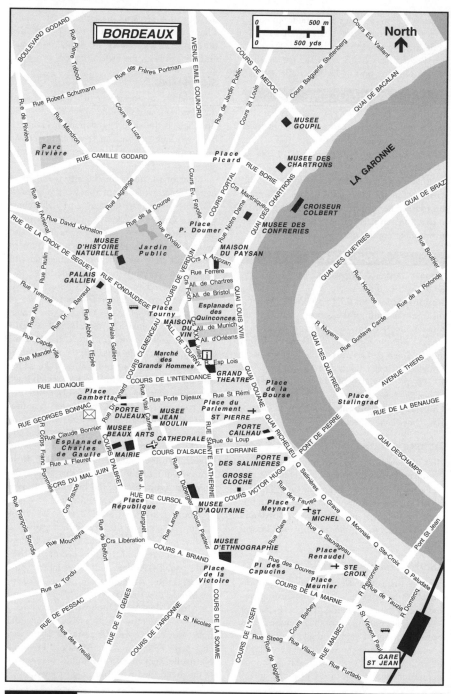

BORDEAUX

0 500 m
0 500 yds

North

BOULEVARD GODARD
Rue Pierre Trébod
Rue des Frères Portman
AVENUE EMILE COUNORD
COURS DE MEDOC
Cours Balguerie Stuttenberg
Cours Ed. Vaillant
QUAI DE BACALAN

Rue Robert Schumann
Cours de Luze
Rue de Jardin Public
Cours à1 Louis
MUSEE GOUPIL
LA GARONNE

Rue de Rivière
Rue Mandron
RUE CAMILLE GODARD
Place Picard
RUE BORIE
MUSEE DES CHARTRONS
QUAI DE BRAZ

Parc Rivière
Rue Lagrange
Cours Ev. Fayolle
COURS PORTAL
Crs Martinique
Crs Notre Dame
QUAI DES CHARTRONS
CROISEUR COLBERT
QUAI DE QUEYRIES

Rue de l'Arsenal
Rue David Johnston
Rue de la Course
Place P. Doumer
Rue d'Aviau
MUSEE DES CONFRERIES
Rue Bouthier

RUE DE LA CROIX DE SEGUEY
MUSEE D'HISTOIRE NATURELLE
Jardin Public
Crs X Arnozan
MAISON DU PAYSAN
Rue Hortense
Rue de la Rotonde

Rue Paulin
PALAIS GALLIEN
RUE FONDAUDEGE
Crs Foch
Rue Ferrère
All. de Chartres
QUAI LOUIS XVIII
R Nuyens
Rue Gustave Carde

Rue Turenne
Rue Dr. A. Barraud
Rue du Palais Gallien
All. de Bristol
QUAI DES QUEYRIES

Rue Allo
Rue Abbé de l'Epée
Place Tourny
Esplanade des Quinconces
All. de Munich
AVENUE THIERS

Rue Capde
MAISON DU VIN
All. d'Orléans
Place Stalingrad
RUE DE LA BENAUGE

Rue Mandel Ville
Marché des Grands Hommes
ALL. DE TOURNY
R Esp Lois

COURS CLEMENCEAU
COURS DE L'INTENDANCE
GRAND THEATRE
Place de la Bourse

RUE JUDAIQUE
Place Gambetta
Rue St Rémi
Place du Parlement
ST PIERRE
QUAI RICHELIEU
PONT DE PIERRE
QUAI DESCHAMPS

RUE GEORGES BONNAC
PORTE DIJEAUX
Rue Porte Dijeaux
MUSEE JEAN MOULIN
PORTE CAILHAU

Rue Claude Bonnier
MUSEE BEAUX ARTS
CATHEDRALE
Rue du Loup
PORTE DES SALINIERES
Q Salinières

Esplanade Charles de Gaulle
MAIRIE
COURS D'ALSACE ET LORRAINE
Q Grave

Rue J. Fleuret
GROSSE CLOCHE
Q Monnaie
Q Ste-Croix

CRS DU MAL JUIN
HUE DE CURSOL
COURS VICTOR HUGO
Rue des Faures
Place Meynard
ST MICHEL

Rue François Sourdis
Place République
MUSEE D'AQUITAINE
Rue Clare
Q Paludate

Rue du Tondu
Crs Libération
MUSEE D'ETHNOGRAPHIE
Pl des Capucins
Place Renaudel
STE CROIX

Rue des Treuils
COURS A. BRIAND
Place de la Victoire
Place Meunier
COURS DE LA MARNE

RUE DE PESSAC
RUE DE ST GENES
R St Nicolas
COURS DE LA SOMME
COURS DE L'YSER
Rue Steeg
RUE MALBEC
GARE ST JEAN

Rue Furtado

436

## SIDE TRACKS FROM BORDEAUX

Probably the main reason for coming to Bordeaux is to visit the great wineries spread out through the surrounding countryside. There are bus tours (ask at the Tourist Office), but also a local rail line to **Pointe-de-Grave** (ETT table 293), whose stations include such redolent names as **Château Margaux** and **Pauillac** (for **Château Mouton-Rothschild** and **Château Lafitte**). This is also the best place from which to visit **Périgueux** and the southern Dordogne, with such dramatic sights as the prehistoric cave paintings of **Les Eyzies** and the superbly preserved medieval towns of **Sarlat** and **Rocamadour**. Again, public transport is limited. ⬆

## SAN SEBASTIÁN (DONOSTIA)

**Stations: (RENFE)** *Estación del Norte, Paseo de Francia; tel: (943) 28 30 89.* Cross the ornate Maria-Cristina bridge, turn right, and it is a few minutes walk through the 19th-century area to the Old Town. **(FV) Estación Amara**, *Plaza de Easo; tel: (943) 47 08 15.* About 15-min walk from the old town.
**Tourist Offices: Regional**: *Paseo de los Fueros 1, 20004; tel: (943) 42 62 82.* Outside each of the Tourist Offices are excellent touch-screen kiosks which give print-outs of town information. **Municipal**: *Calle de la Reina Regente s/n; tel: (943) 48 11 66.*

### ACCOMMODATION AND FOOD

For budget accommodation head for the old town: hidden amongst the narrow streets are many pensiones. Try **Pensión Amaiur**, *c. 31 de Agosto,* which offers spotless, comfortable rooms and a friendly welcome. At the other end of the scale, the superb **Hotel Maria Cristina**, *Republica Argentian,* affords superb views of the Río Urumea Ibaia. Rooms can be difficult to find during July and August.

**HI**, *Paseo de Igueldo 25; tel: (943) 31 02 68.* There is a **campsite**, **Camping Igueldo** on the fringes of the city at *Peublo de Igueldo; tel: (943) 21 45 02* (bus no. 16 from *Alameda del Boulevard*).

For the best small restaurants, try the old town and the fishing harbour at the north end of Playa de la Concha.

### SIGHTSEEING

The main attractions are easily walkable, but there is a good main road bus service.

Known as San Sebastián to the Spanish and as Donostia to the Basques, this is one of the largest cities in the individualist Basque province, with a language and culture very different from that of Castilian Spain. Once a confined old town, dedicated to whaling, deep-sea fishing and the tourist trade developed by the pilgrim route to Santiago de Compostela (see p. 472), San Sebastián really came into its own in the mid 19th century, when someone recommended sea-bathing as a cure for Queen Isabella II's herpes! She arrived, along with a great retinue, and San Sebastián became the fashionable place to be.

Take time to wander the streets of the 'old' town, or *parte vieja,* nestled at the foot of Monte Urgull. It is mainly 19th century, but was rebuilt along the old lines, with a maze of small streets, tiny darkened shops and bars, arcaded plazas like the **Plaza de la Constitución**, which used to serve as a bull ring, and churches such as the beautiful baroque **Basilica of Santa María del Coro**. Also found here is the **Museum of San Telmo**, situated in a former Dominican monastery. The monastery's picturesque cloister now houses some archaeological exhibits, while the church is the setting for temporary exhibitions. At the far end of the quay are the **Naval Museum** and the **Aquarium**. You should also climb **Monte Urgull** itself, both to see the much-rebuilt fort (the **Castillo de la Mota**) and for the superb views. Standing proudly near the top of the hill is the statue of the **Sagrado Corazón de Jesús**, which watches over the city.

## SIDE TRACKS FROM SAN SEBASTIÁN

From San Sebastián, the narrow-gauge coastal railways lead west, through a series of charming, if increasingly touristy, villages, to **Bilbao** and **Santander**. Both cities are seen primarily as ports, but they are well worth a

437

visit, Bilbao for its old centre and superb art museum, Santander as an attractive resort town with a good beach. 🏊

## VITORIA (GASTEIZ)

**Station: (RENFE);** *tel: (945) 23 02 02*. Off the *Calle Eduardo Dato,* about two blocks from the cathedral and Tourist Office.

**Tourist Office: Regional**: *Parque de la Florida, s/n; tel: (945) 13 13 21*. **Municipal**: *Avda Gasteiz s/n, Esquina c. Chile; tel: (945) 16 15 98/9*.

### SIGHTSEEING

Known by the Spanish as Vitoria and by the Basques as Gasteiz, this is probably the least visited city in the Basque region, despite the fact that it is its capital. Known for making playing cards and chocolate truffles, it is also a charming and beautiful city with a skilful mix of old and new. The almost perfectly preserved medieval hill town is surrounded by elegant arcaded plazas and gardens, dating from the 17th, 18th and 19th centuries. The *casco viejo,* or old town, is a tangled web of narrow dark streets, filled with cheap restaurants and bars as well as several fine churches. Look out for the **Church of San Miguel**, beside the steps at the top of the large and open **Plaza de la Virgen Blanca**, and the old **Cathedral of Santa María**. The huge neo-Gothic **Cathedral of María Immaculada** is surrounded by parkland in the flat new town, and from here a tree-lined promenade, housing the **Military Museum** and the **Museum of Fine Art**, with its collection of antique playing cards, runs for 3 km to the village of **Armentia**.

## BURGOS

**Station**: *Plaza de la Estación; tel: (947) 20 35 60*. About 1 km south-west of the cathedral on the far side of the Arlanzon River.

**Tourist Office**: *Plaza de Alonso Martínez 7, 09003 Burgos; tel: (947) 20 31 25; fax: (947) 27 65 29*.

### SIGHTSEEING

Burgos is a large and busy modern city with an attractive old town, centred around its castle. The main attractions and hotels are within easy walking distance. The bars and restaurants here offer traditional local cuisine for excellent value.

For over 500 years Burgos was a trading crossroads. In the 11th century it became the capital of Christian Spain and the home of Rodrigo Diaz de Vivar, better known as El Cid. During the Civil War in the 1930s, it again rose to fame as the Nationalist headquarters. It was here that Franco formed his Falangist government and (18 months later) declared a ceasefire that ended the war.

The **Cathedral**, the biggest attraction, was consecrated in 1260 but work continued until the 18th century and it is now the third largest cathedral in Spain (after Toledo and Seville) and possibly also the richest. Amidst the splendour of the 19 chapels and 38 altars, all dripping in gold leaf, is El Cid's unobtrusive tomb and a grotesquely real-looking crucifix, made in the 13th century with human hair, finger nails and a body of buffalo hide. Other sights worth seeing include the statue of **El Cid** and the **Arch of Santa Maria**, a fortified 14th-century gateway, altered and decorated in 1536 to pacify Charles V. It depicts his figure and those of the founder (Diego Porcelos) and El Cid.

The annual festival in Burgos, celebrating **San Pedro**, is held on the last Sun in June. The old town is transformed with glorious floral displays, there is a procession with marching bands and street entertainment and fireworks in the evening. Watch out for ladies in traditional dress who tell you your fortune as you are walking along the street – and then try to remove it from you in reward for their efforts!

Outside the old town, the 16th-century **Casa de Miranda** houses one of Spain's best archaeological museums. On the outskirts of the city are some sights worthy of a trek: including **Cartuja de Miraflores**, a Carthusian monastery that became the royal pantheon.

> ↶ **SIDE TRACKS FROM BURGOS**
>
> Just to the east is the **Rioja wine district**, while a short way south is the wonderful Benedictine monastery of **Santo Domingo de los Silos**. 🏊

# PARIS–MARSEILLE

As the main north–south rail route between Paris and the French Riviera, the trains are, not surprisingly, often busy. The passengers are as varied as the landscape through which you travel – from sculpted farmland around Dijon to scented pines and proud poplars near Avignon and on to the craggy coastline of Marseille. Enticing glimpses of hill towns beside the languid Rhône conjure up the centuries of history along the route; the lines of vines eager to provide the wine to wash it down.

> FASTEST JOURNEY: 4 HRS 30 MINS

## TRAINS

**ETT tables:** 350, 370, 373.

### FAST TRACK

Ten fast TGV trains run daily between Paris Gare de Lyon and Marseille taking around 4½ hrs. All have buffets, but require advance reservations and a supplement. Two overnight trains, one with sleeping cars and couchettes, the other with couchettes and second class seats, take nearer 8½ hrs.

### ON TRACK

**Paris–Dijon**
TGVs operate throughout the day every 1–2 hrs, many with dining facilities in first class. The trains take 1 hr 40 mins.

**Dijon–Beaune–Mâcon–Lyon**
Trains run between Dijon and Lyon (Perrache or Part-Dieu) approximately hourly (less on Sun), most call at Beaune and Mâcon Ville en

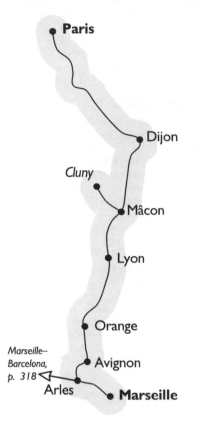

route. Dijon to Beaune takes 20 mins, Beaune to Mâcon 1 hr, Mâcon to Lyon 50 mins.

**Lyon–Orange**
Seven to ten trains a day link Lyon Part-Dieu and Orange. The journey takes around 2 hrs.

**Orange–Avignon**
Trains from Lyon continue on to Avignon, taking just 15 mins.

**Avignon–Arles–Marseille**
Trains run approximately hourly from Avignon to Marseille daily, some call at Arles. Avignon to Arles is 20 mins, Arles to Marseille 50 mins.

439

On map:
Paris
Dijon
*Cluny*
Mâcon
Lyon
Orange
*Marseille–Barcelona, p. 318*
Avignon
Arles
**Marseille**

## DIJON

**Station: Ville**, 5 mins west of the centre. The station is at the end of *av. Maréchal-Foch*, which leads to *pl. Darcy* and the start of the old town. **Tourist Offices:** *pl. Darcy; tel: 80 44 11 44.* Daily 0900–2100 (May–mid Oct); 0900–1300, 1400–1900 rest of the year. At *34 r. des Forges; tel: 80 44 11 44,* Mon–Sat 0900–1200, 1300–1800, closed Sat off-season. For FFr.15, the Tourist Office helps find accommodation.

### ACCOMMODATION

The lowest-priced hotels (mainly 2-star) tend to be in the old town; try *r. Monge.* Hotel chains include *BW, Ca, CF, F1, Hd, Ib, IH, Mc, Nv* and *Sf.* The 4-star **Hostellerie du Chapeau Rouge**, *5 r. Michelet; tel: 80 30 28 10,* has old-style graciousness. Moderately priced **Hostellerie 'Le Sauvage'**, *64 r. Monge; tel: 80 41 31 21,* was once a staging inn. **Hôtel Le Chambellan**, *92 r. Vannerie; tel: 80 67 12 67,* and **Hôtel Le Jacquemart**, *32 r. Verrerie; tel: 80 73 39 74,* are reasonable 2-star options near the ducal palace. **HI: Centre de Rencontres Internationales**, *1 blvd Champollion; tel: 80 72 95 20,* 4 km from the centre (bus no. 5: *Epirey,* or night bus A). Students could try **Foyer International des Etudiants**, *4–6 r. Maréchal Leclerc; tel: 80 71 70 00* (bus no. 4: *Billardon*). **Campsite: Camping du Lac**, *3 blvd Kir; tel: 80 43 54 72.* By a lake about 1 km from Ville (bus nos 12/18; no.12 stops closest to the site).

### SIGHTSEEING

All the sights are within easy walking distance. The Tourist Office has a suggested 2-hr walking tour of the city.

The east wing of the **Palais des Ducs de Bourgogne** (Palace of the Dukes of Burgundy) is open and fascinating, notably the marvellously carved, gold-encrusted tombs in the **Salle des Gardes** (guardsroom). But the main attraction is the **Musée des Beaux Arts**, which has one of the most wide-ranging collections in France, including paintings, sculptures, tapestries, furniture and silver.

The palace faces *pl. de la Libération,* a crescent of *hotel particuliers* (elegant 17th-century mansions) and behind the palace is an area full of these carefully restored houses, notably *r. des*

*Forges.* In parallel *r. de la Chouette,* the **Eglise de Notre-Dame** has numerous gargoyles, 13th-century stained-glass windows and a stone owl which you should touch for luck. High overhead, life-size figures on the 14th-century **Horloge de Jacquemard** (Jacquemard's clock) chime every quarter-hour. **Eglise de St-Michel**, begun at the end of the 15th century, has a Renaissance façade and a Gothic interior, and **Cathédrale de St-Bénigne**, *r. Docteur Maret,* has a patterned roof of glazed tiles (characteristic of Burgundy), and a circular crypt containing a 2nd-century sarcophagus presumed to be that of Saint Bénigne. Neighbouring **Musée Archéologique** covers the Côte d'Or, while **Musée de la Vie Bourguignonne**, *17 r. Ste-Ann,* focuses on 19th-century Burgundian life.

## BEAUNE

**Station:** east of town, just outside the old walls. Left luggage (FFr.15). For the Tourist Office, follow *av. du 8 Septembre/r. du Château,* take the first left onto *Rempart St Jean/Rempart Madelaine* and right onto *r. de l'Hôtel-Dieu* (15 mins). **Tourist Office:** *r. de l'Hôtel-Dieu; tel: 80 26 21 30.* Open Mon–Sat 0900–2000, Sun 0900–1900 (May–Sept); Sun–Thur 0900–1800, Fri-Sat 0900–1900 (Oct–Apr).

Beaune is a charming old town of cobbled streets and fine mansions. The magnificent **Hôtel-Dieu**, *r. de l'Hôtel-Dieu,* was originally built in the 15th-century as a hospital for the sick and needy. Don't miss its multi-coloured glazed roofs or the 15th-century Polyptych of the Last Judgement. This is also the centre of the **Côtes de Beaune vineyards**, some of the finest in Burgundy; the Tourist Office lists local caves that offer tastings *(dégustations).* The old ducal palace houses a museum dedicated to the subject; **Musée du Vin**, *r. d'Enfer.*

## MÂCON

**Stations: Ville** handles all ordinary trains, but TGV services use **Mâcon-Loché**, some 6 km from town, leaving you to get a taxi (FFr.100) to the centre (no buses). To reach the Tourist Office from Ville, turn left out of the station, cross *r. Victor Hugo* and follow *r. Gambetta* to *pl. Gérard Geneves; r. Carnot* is on the left (5 mins). **Tourist Office:** *187 r. Carnot; tel: 85 39 71*

37. Mon–Sat 1000–1900, Sun 1400–1800 (June–Sept), closed Sun, and lunch off-season.

The old town is a pleasant place for a stroll, with some impressive Renaissance architecture, although there are no real sights.

## OUT OF TOWN

Accessible by bus from Mâcon, the pretty little town of **Cluny** was home to a 10th-century **abbey** that became the most influential church in the world until the construction of St Peter's in Rome. What little remains of the past gives a hint of former magnificence and treasures collected by the monks are displayed in the **Museé Ochier**, in what was the episcopal palace.

The main attraction of the region surrounding Mâcon is the myriad of small wine-growing villages. The Tourist Office can provide details.

## ORANGE

**Station:** 1.5 km east of the centre: head along *av. F-Mistral/r. de la République* and turn into *r. St-Martin* after *pl. de la République* (15 mins).
**Tourist Office:** *5 cours Aristide Briand; tel: 04 90 34 70 88.* Open Mon–Sat 0900–1900, Sun 1000–1800 (Apr–Sept); Mon–Sat 0900–1800 (Oct–Mar).

Blessed with an impressive **Roman theatre** and little else, Orange is the northern gateway to Provence. Dating from the 1st century AD, the theatre has the best preserved back wall in the Roman Empire, and still hosts a summer drama and opera festival. The **Arc de Triomphe** inspired Napoleon to do better in Paris.

## AVIGNON

**Station:** to the south, just outside the city walls: head through *porte de la République* and straight along *cours Jean Jaurès*.
**Tourist Office:** *41 cours J-Jaurès; tel: 04 90 82 65 11.* Open Mon–Fri 0900–1300, 1400–1800, Sat 0900–1300, 1400–1700 (all year). In summer the office stays open for lunch. At *Pont d'Avignon*, open daily 0900–1830 (summer); 0900–1300 and 1400–1700 (winter).

## ACCOMMODATION

Try *r. Joseph Vernet* and *r. Agricol Perdiguier* (both off *J-Jaurès*) for reasonably priced hotels. Hotel chains include *Ba, BW, Ch, CI, Ib, Mc* and *Nv*.

To tread in the footsteps of the famous, visit **Hôtel d'Europe**, *12 pl. Crillon; tel: 04 90 14 76 76*, where Napoleon was the first of many – still the height of comfort and atmosphere. **Hôtel de la Mirande**, *pl. de l'Amirande; tel: 04 90 85 93 93*, is a modern, but elegant, small 4-star hotel. For something a bit out of the ordinary, try **Hôtel de Mons**, *5 r. de Mons; tel: 04 90 82 57 16*, where the odd-shaped rooms reflect its origins as a 13th-century chapel. The Logis de France 2-star **Hôtel d'Angleterre**, *29 blvd Raspail; tel: 04 90 86 34 31*, offers a wide price range. There is a (non-HI) **youth hostel** on an island in the Rhône: **Bagatelle**, *Ile de la Barthelasse; tel: 04 90 86 30 39* (bus no. 20). There are also a number of **campsites**, such as **Bagatelle**, *tel: 04 90 85 78 45*. Bus no. 20 takes you all the way there. Alternatively, take no. 10 or 11 and get off after the bridge.

## SIGHTSEEING

In 1303, troubles in Rome caused the Pope to move his power base to Avignon. Wealth flowed into the town – and remained after the papacy moved back to Rome 70 years later.

The **city walls**, built to protect the papal assets, still surround the city. Jutting from the north-eastern section is **Pont St-Bénézet**, the bridge famed in song. The most photographed sight in the city is the huge **Palais des Papes** (Papal Palace), boasting a 45 m-long banqueting hall, where cardinals would meet to elect a new pope. The adjacent Romanesque cathedral, **Notre Dame des Doms**, dates from the 12th century and contains the tombs of Pope John XXII and Pope Benedict XII. The garden of **Le Rocher des Doms**, accessible from steps by the cathedral, provides good views of the bridge and the nearby town of Villeneuve-lès-Avignon. At the end of *pl. du Palais* is the **Musée du Petit Palais**, a lesser palace which now contains Avignon's very impressive collection of Renaissance art. In the middle of the Rhône lies **Île de Barthelasse**, a favourite picnic spot, with its own summer swimming pool.

## OUT OF TOWN

To the east are the rolling hills of the **Lubéron**, made famous by Peter Mayle's *A Year in Provence*. Regular buses serve the area.

# PARIS–MILAN

Escaping the endless rolling plains of Champagne, this route rolls on into Alsace. Leaving Mulhouse and France behind, moun- tains rise tantalisingly to the South and the train enters Switzerland. Rising gently through Swiss vineyards, the train passes the first of the great Swiss lakes and on to Lausanne. With its dramatic mountain backdrop, Lausanne pre- pares the traveller for the final run to Milan, through some of the most dramatic and moun- tainous scenery in Europe. After skirting the shores of Lake Maggiore, the train arrives in Milan, which must have the most pompous and splendid railway staion in the world.

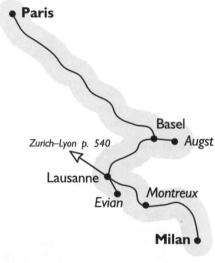

442

FASTEST JOURNEY: 7 HRS

## TRAINS

**ETT tables:** 44, 380.

### FAST TRACK

➡ Through trains from Paris (Gare de Lyon) to Milan (Centrale) avoid Switzerland. There are two TGVs (reservation compulsory with special fares payable) taking 7 hrs and an *EN* train overnight, with sleepers, couchettes and second-class seats, which takes 11 hrs.

### ON TRACK

#### Paris–(Border)–Basel (Bâle)
At least six trains run daily (more on weekdays) with some long gaps between them. Most have a buffet car and take 5–5½ hrs, although the overnight train, with sleepers, couchettes, first- and second-class seats takes 6 hrs. Border formalities take place at Basel station.

### Basel–Lausanne
Fast trains (2½ hrs) operate hourly, although every other hour you must change – across the platform at Biel.

### Lausanne–(Border)–Milan (Milano)
Six trains daily run from Lausanne to Milan (Centrale); more journeys are possible by changing at Brig. Conventional *IC/EC* trains are being replaced by *CIS* Pendolino high-speed trains, which cut the journey from 4½ to 3½ hrs. Supplements are payable on all trains and most require a reservation. Border formali- ties at Domodossola are barely noticeable.

## BASEL (BÂLE)

**Stations:** Basel occupies a corner between France and Germany and is a frontier town for both. The main station, **Bahnhof SBB**, *tel: 157 22 22,* is a 15-min walk south of the city centre (5 mins on tram nos 1/8 from the terminus in front of the station) and handles Swiss and principal German services. Facilities include left luggage (SFr.5 per day), bike rental (SFr.20 per day), showers and a post office. The French part of the station, **Bahnhof SNCF**, *tel: 36 35 35 35,* handles French services. **Badischer Bahnhof DB**, *tel: (061) 690 11 11* (in Kleinbasel, but linked to SBB by rail) handles German local services.

**Tourist Office:** *Schifflände; tel: (061) 261 50 50* or *268 68 68,* near the Mittlere Brücke. Mon–Fri 0830–1800, Sat 0830–1300. At the SBB station; *tel: (061) 271 36 84,* Mon–Fri 0830–1800, Sat 1830–1230 (longer in summer).

## GETTING AROUND

Most of the old centre is pedestrianised. Elsewhere a frequent tram service is supplemented by buses. Information and tickets (SFr. 1.20) are available from machines at every stop.

## ACCOMMODATION

Chains: *BW, GT, Hn, Mz, RC, Sh, SL, Sw, Tp, WS* **HI: Auberge de Jeunesse Bâle**, *St Alban-Kirchrain 10; tel: (061) 272 05 72,* 15-min walk from SBB station or tram no.2, then 5-min walk. A moderate hotel in the old town is **Stadthof**, *Gerbergasse 84; tel: (061) 261 87 11.*

## SIGHTSEEING

Discreet, calm and industrious, Basel has long been a crossroads for European culture. The wealth of its museums are testament to this. In no way retrospective, it is also a showcase for modern European art and design. With its hilly streets and peaceful squares, Basel is an excellent place to rest and gently imbibe the best of its illustrious residents past and future work.

Of the six bridges across the River Rhine, **Mittlere Brücke** offers the best views. The medieval centre is on the south bank, in *Grossbasel*. *Kleinbasel* is the small modern area on the north bank. Basel has been sponsoring artists since the mid 17th century and now has 27 major museums and galleries, containing Switzerland's best collection of art treasures. Most museums accept **La Carte Musées Bâle**: a 3-day pass costs SFr.23 for adults, SFr.16 with concessions and SFr.46 for families. Admission to most museums costs, on average, SFr.6/7.

Just south of the Rhine, **Münsterplatz** is dominated by the 12th-century red sandstone **Münster**, which has decorative twin towers, a Romanesque portal surrounded by elegant carvings, and a rose window featuring the wheel of fortune. Inside are the sarcophagi of nobles and the simple marble tomb of Erasmus, who spent the last years of his life here. The **Historisches Museum**, *tel: 271 05 05* (closed Tues), is housed in the Gothic **Barfüsserkirche**, *Barfüsserpl.*, where 13th–16th-century *objets d'art* include Luther's chalice, local tapestries and furniture. The 18th–19th-century sections of the collection are on display in the 18th-century **Haus zum Kirschgarten**, *Elisabethenstr. 27,* about 300m north of SBB. **Antikenmuseum** (Museum of Ancient Art), *St-Alban-Graben 5; tel: 271 22 02* (closed Mon), has a comprehensive collection of ancient Greek artefacts.

The world-class **Kunstmuseum** (Fine Arts Museum), *St-Alban-Graben 16; tel: 271 08 28* (tram no. 2), is in a building that was constructed 1932–36 to house the art treasures the town had been accumulating since the 17th century, including important works by Witz and the world's largest collection of works by the Holbein family, featuring Holbein the Younger's *Portrait of Erasmus*. Modern contributors include Van Gogh *(Daubigney's Garden)* Picasso, Braque and Dalí. Closed Mon.

The permanent collection of **Museum für Gegenwartskunst** (Museum of Contemporary Art), *St-Alban-Rheinweg 60; tel: 272 81 83,* includes pieces by Stella, Warhol and Beuys. **Basler Papiermühle**, *St-Alban-Tal 35–37; tel: 272 96 52,* is a restored medieval papermill on the waterfront, which offers a history of paper-making. Both are closed Mon.

At *Augustinergasse 2* are two museums: the **Naturhistorisches Museum**, *tel: 266 50 00* (closed Mon), which displays natural history exhibits ranging from dinosaur skeletons to minerals; and the **Museum für Völkerkunde**, an excellent global ethnographical collection.

The recently restored 16th-century **Rathaus** (Town Hall), has an ornate and very picturesque red façade that includes an enormous clock. It towers over **Marktplatz**, the historic and modern heart of Basel. Take the steep steps on *Totengasslein*, off *Marktpl.*, to the 13th-century **Peterskirche** (St Peter's Church), containing late medieval frescos. Of the two main surviving

443

medieval city gates, **St-Alban-Tor**, *St-Alban-Graben*, takes second place to the splendid 14th-century **Spalentor**, *Spalengraben*. Near here, on *Spalenvorstadt*, is the pick of the town's older fountains, the **Holbeinbrunnen**, based partly on a Holbein drawing and a Dürer engraving. By contrast, **Fasnacht-Brunnen/Tinguely-Brunnen**, *Theaterpl.*, is an extraordinary fountain (built in 1977) that resembles a watery scrapyard. A museum dedicated to **Tinguely**, *tel: 681 93 20*, celebrates the life and work of the artist who grew up in Bâle (closed Mon, Tues). **Zoologischer Garten**, *Binningerstr. 40*, west of SBB, has gained a reputation for breeding armoured rhinos, but is also known for its collections of pygmy hippos, gorillas and penguins. The Basel **Fasnacht** is the country's most riotous carnival, taking over the town at 0400 on the Mon after Ash Wednesday and lasting for three days of noisy colourful fancy dress fun.

## ↗ SIDE TRACK FROM BASEL

**444**

**Augst** is 20 mins by train (plus a 10-min walk) from SBB, but if you have time take the ferry from the dock at *Schifflände* (summer only, 1½ hrs). The extensive ruins of an old Roman settlement, **Augusta Raurica** (1000–1200, 1330–1800; closed Mon morning), have been rebuilt; the site takes some time to explore fully. Its magnificent and varied collection of mostly 4th-century objects can be seen in the **Römermuseum**, a reconstruction of a Roman home. 🏛

## LAUSANNE

**Station:** *tel: (021) 320 80 71*, between the centre and Ouchy, connected by the Metro. The Tourist Office here is limited. Left luggage and bike rental available.

**Main Tourist Office:** *ave de Rhodanie 2, Ouchy; tel: (021) 613 73 73*. Open Mon–Sat 0800–1900, Sun 0900–1300, 1400–1800 (Apr–Sept); Mon–Fri 0800–1800, Sat 0900–1300, 1400–1800 (mid Oct–Mar). Pick up a free copy of *Lausanne Useful Information*.

A walking tour (not always in English) of the old town leaves from the Town Hall at 1000 Mon–Sat.

### GETTING AROUND

The old town is perched 130 m above the lake. Walking between them is hard work, so take the **Metro** (actually a funicular). It takes less than 5 mins between the old town, the station (below it) and Ouchy (the waterfront). The old town is small and, despite the hills, best explored on foot (much of it is pedestrianised). There is also a good bus and tram network.

### ACCOMMODATION

Hotel chains: *BW, Ib, IE, Mz, MO, Mv, Nv, RC, Rd, Tp, WS*. There's plenty of budget accommodation. The new **Jeunotel**, *chemin du Bois-de-Vaux 36; tel: (021) 626 02 26*, on the lakeside just west of Ouchy, offers simple modern rooms and dormitories. **HI**: *chemin de Muguet 1; tel: (021) 616 57 82*, near Ouchy, by the lakeside. **Campsite: Camping de Vidy**, *chemin du Camping 3; tel: (021) 624 20 31*.

### SIGHTSEEING

Half Alpine and half Riviera, Lausanne is a town with a split personality. Business-like and efficient, it proudly displays all the trappings of Swiss affluence; however, throughout the city, a leisurely atmosphere pervades. With its beautiful, dramatic setting, with **Lake Geneva (Lac Léman)** to the south, and its clear, fresh Alpine air, Lausanne has a verve and dynamism which is difficult to escape. It has been a cultural centre for centuries and the medieval town surrounding the cathedral has been carefully restored. Picturesque lakeside Ouchy is excellent for watersports, boat rentals and cruises.

The upper Metro terminal is at 'Sainfe', *pl. St-François*, just south of the main area of interest and dominated by the 15th-century steeple of the 13th–14th-century **Église St-François** (St Francis' Church). Magnificent **Cathédrale de Notre-Dame**, a 10-min walk up into the town, was consecrated in 1215. Italian, Flemish and French craftsmen all had a hand in its construction and it is accepted as a perfect example of Burgundian-Gothic. Unfortunately, most of the interior decorations were destroyed during the Reformation in 1536, but the basic structure was unchanged and there are glorious rose windows, intricately carved choir stalls and some frescos. Following a tradition that has died out elsewhere, the watch is still called from the steeple every hour from 2000 to 0200.

The **Musée Historique de Lausanne**, *pl. de la Cathédrale 4* (closed Mon), is housed in the **Ancien-Evêché**, which was the bishops' palace until the early 15th century. Among the exhibits is a remarkable large-scale model of 17th-century Lausanne. Also by the cathedral is another fortified bishops' residence (15th–16th centuries), the **Château St-Maire**, now the seat of the cantonal government (part open to the public). **Escaliers-du-Marché**, a wooden-roofed medieval staircase, links the cathedral square to *pl. de la Palud,* an ancient square surrounded by old houses. It features the 18th-century **Fontaine de la Justice** and a clock with moving figures that spring to life every hour. There are also the arcades of the restored 15th–17th-century **Hôtel de Ville** (town hall).

West of the cathedral, Florentine-style **Palais de Rumine**, *pl. de la Riponne; tel: 320 67 90* (open daily), was built by a Russian family at the turn of the century. It now houses the modern university, as well as several museums, including: **Musée de Zoologie**, with a complete mammoth skeleton and a colony of (living) ants; and, currently being renovated, **Musée cantonal des Beaux-Arts**, a permanent display of 18th–20th-century French-Swiss art, plus temporary exhibits, and **Musée d'Archéologie et d'Histoire**, with relics from ancient times, most notably a gold bust of Marcus Aurelius. Take a 10-minute walk north-west (or bus no. 2) to the fascinating **Collection de l'Art Brut**, *av. des Bergières 11,* housed in the Château de Beaulieu. This compelling post-war gallery was founded by a local collector who sought the works of anyone who was not a trained or formal painter, from amateur dabblers to the criminally insane.

North of the centre is the **Fondation de l'Hermitage**, *route du Signal 2,* an early 19th-century villa full of period fixtures and fittings, which hosts top-quality touring exhibitions of contemporary art. The view from the villa gardens, over the city and the lake to the Alps, is magnificent. For more great lake views take bus no.16 to the **Forêt de Sauvabelin**, 150m above the city centre. This 140-acre beech forest offers a choice of walking paths and encompasses a deer reserve around a small lake (a natural skating rink in winter). Paths lead to the **Vivarium**, *chemin de Boissonnet,* a reptile zoo.

The **quai de Belgique** is a shady, flower-lined, waterside promenade, with great views of the Savoy Alps. The 13th-century keep of **Château d'Ouchy** is now a hotel. Baron Pierre de Coubertin, founder of the modern Olympics in 1915, chose Lausanne as the headquarters of the International Olympic Committee. The unique **Musée Olympique**, *quai d'Ouchy 1; tel: 617 73 21,* is a large modern complex, cleverly designed to retain the natural beauty of its surrounding park. It covers the history of the Olympic movement and exhibits a fascinating collection of equipment and memorabilia used by famous athletes. Audio-visual displays and interactive machines allow you to focus on 'your' sport or chosen year. Boats can be hired near the 'cruise' pier. Open all year, except Christmas Day and New Year.

### SIDE TRACKS FROM LAUSANNE

Frequent trains link the waterfront towns. **Compagnie Générale de Navigation (CGN)**, *ave de Rhodanie 17; tel: (021) 617 06 66,* operate ferries from Ouchy (and paddle-steamers in summer) to **Geneva** (western end of the lake), **Evian** (in France, southern shore), Montreux and St Gingolph.

**Montreux** (eastern end of the lake; 1½ hrs by ferry), became popular when a casino was opened in 1883. **Tourist Office:** *r. du Theatre 5, Montreux; tel: (021) 962 84 84.* The famous **Jazz Festival** occupies two and a half weeks in mid July (book well ahead). The town has a 10-km long waterside promenade bursting with blooms, while mountain railways climb the surrounding peaks. The major sight is the remarkably well-preserved 13th-century **Château de Chillon** (3 km south). Below the finely decorated 16th-century rooms is a prison where the Reformation preacher, Bonivard, was chained to a pillar for four years. Lord Byron (who carved his name on the pillar) wrote of this in his poem *The Prisoner of Chillon,* and so made the castle world famous.

# PARIS–MUNICH

This route from France to Germany takes in an unusually varied selection of towns, from Lunéville with its lovely château to the smart spa of Baden-Baden. The countryside too varies greatly, crossing the flat farmland of eastern France and later the gently wooded hillsides of Bavaria.

The first part covers the same ground as the Paris-Frankfurt route (see pp. 429–431).

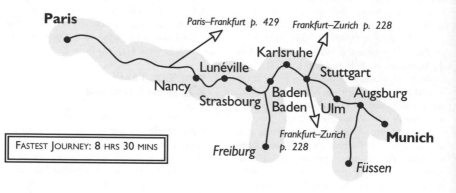

**Paris**

Paris–Frankfurt p. 429   Frankfurt–Zurich p. 228

Karlsruhe

Lunéville     Stuttgart

Nancy     Baden     Augsburg

Strasbourg     Baden     Ulm

Frankfurt–Zurich p. 228     **Munich**

Freiburg

Füssen

446

FASTEST JOURNEY: 8 HRS 30 MINS

---

## TRAINS

**ETT tables:** 32, 390, 945, 930, 936, 927.

### FAST TRACK

Two day *EC* trains link Paris with Munich. These trains have dining cars but require supplements and take 8 hr 30 mins. There is also an overnight train with sleeping cars, couchettes and second-class seats.

### ON TRACK

#### Paris–Nancy

Around a dozen trains each day. The best are the three *EC* trains, with dining cars, taking 2 hrs 45 mins. Other trains take over 3 hrs.

#### Nancy–Lunéville–Strasbourg

Half of the twelve Paris to Strasbourg trains call at Lunéville. Nancy to Lunéville takes 20 mins, Lunéville to Strasbourg just over 1 hr.

#### Strasbourg–Baden-Baden

Seven trains, including two EC trains, run from Strasbourg to Baden-Baden in Germany, taking 35–50 mins.

#### Baden-Baden–Karlsruhe

Frequent trains, including IC and InterRegio, link Baden-Baden and Karlsruhe throughout the day. Journeys take 16–20 mins.

### Karlsruhe–Stuttgart

A roughly hourly service, with trains taking around 1 hr.

### Stuttgart–Ulm–Augsburg–Munich

At least two trains each hour run between Stuttgart and Munich, calling at Ulm and Augsburg en route. Trains range from the latest ICE trains (dining cars, supplements), through EC and IC trains (dining cars, lesser supplements) to InterRegio's (buffets). Stuttgart to Ulm takes around 1 hr, Ulm to Augsburg 40–55 mins, Augsburg to Munich 30–35 mins.

## NANCY

**Station:** *pl. Thiers; tel: 08 36 35 35 35,* is a 10-min walk from the town centre along *r. Stanislas.*

**Tourist Office:** *14 pl. Stanislas; tel: 03 83 35 22 41.* Open Mon–Sat 0900–1900, Sun 1000–1700 (June–Sept); Mon–Sat 0900–1800, Sun 1000–1300 (Oct–May). Ask for the *'Art Nouveau Itinerary'* walking leaflet which gives details of the main sights.

### ACCOMMODATION

Hotel chains include *Ba, Ch, Cn, Ct, Ib, IH, Mc, Nv.* If you fancy staying in an official historic monument, **Grand Hôtel de la Reine**, *2 pl. Stanislas; tel: 03 83 35 03 01,* fits the bill, but **Le Piroux**, *12 r. R-Poincaré; tel: 03 83 32 01 10,* a Logi de France, is far more affordable. The nearest (non-HI) hostel is **Centre d'Accueil de Remicourt**, *149 r. de Vandoeuvre, Villers; tel: 03 83 27 73 67,* 4 km west of town (bus no. 26 to *Pôle Technologique).* **Campsite: Camping de Brabois**; *tel: 03 83 27 18 28,* close to it (open Apr–Oct).

### EATING AND DRINKING

One side of *Pl. Stanislas* is lined with upmarket cafés full of people people-watching. A block north, *r. des Maréchaux,* is almost exclusively devoted to restaurants with reasonable fixed-price menus. And try some *macarons* (almond biscuits), the town's speciality.

### SIGHTSEEING

Nancy is one of the most stylish towns in eastern France, though surprisingly little known for its architectural treasures. It centres around the 18th-century **pl. Stanislas**, constructed by ex-King Stanislas Leszcynski of Poland and now one of the town's three **World Heritage Sites**. Its cream stone buildings, arches and ornate black and gold gateways combine to form a near-perfect whole. The entire south side is taken up by the **Hôtel de Ville**. North of *pl. Stanislas,* through the **Arc de Triomphe**, the 15th-century **pl. de la Carrière** is another monumental square – also a World Heritage Site. The third, **pl. d'Alliance**, tucked away behind the Grand Hôtel, is a quiet shaded oasis.

The **Saint-Epvre** basilica, *pl. Joseph Malval,* in the old quarter has an impressive array of stained-glass, which makes it more remarkable than the vast **cathedral**, *Monseigneur Ruch.*

In the early 1900s, Nancy was the birthplace of art nouveau. **Musée de l'École de Nancy**, *36 r. du Sergent Blandan* (bus nos 6/16/26 to *Painlevé)* displays local examples from the early 1900s, including furniture arranged as if it were in a house. **Musée Historique Lorrain**, *Palais Ducal, 64 Grand' Rue,* housed in the former ducal palace, and **Musée des Arts et Traditions Populaires**, *66 r. Grand' Rue,* are also well worth visiting.

447

## LUNÉVILLE

**Station:** *tel: 08 36 35 35 35;* a 15-min walk from the centre.

**Tourist Office:** *Château de Lunéville; tel: 03 83 74 06 55.* Open daily 1000–1200 and 1400–1800.

### ACCOMMODATION AND FOOD

*R. d'Alsace* is a good place to look for moderately priced hotels like **Hotel du Commerce** at *no. 93; tel: 03 83 73 04 17.* Or try **Hôtel de l'Europe**, at *no. 53; tel: 03 83 74 12 34.*

### SIGHTSEEING

Lunéville has an imposing 18th-century **château**, inspired by Versailles and surrounded by magnificent gardens. Its museum has a notable collection of ancient ceramics. **Musée de la Motor et du Vélo**, opposite the château, is a private motorcycle museum with over 200 different types. The rococo church of **St-Jacques**, *pl. St-Rémy,* has a striking façade

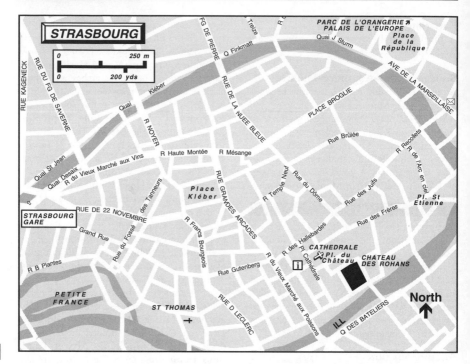

with a huge clock between two towers; also a unique baroque organ with no visible pipes.

## STRASBOURG

**Station:** *pl. de la Gare*: 10-min walk to the centre (which is on an island in the River Ill) straight along *r. du Maire Kuss* or by tram (direction *Illkirch*). **Information:** *tel: 08 36 35 35 35.* **Tourist Office:** *17 pl. de la Cathédrale; tel: 03 88 52 28 22.* **Branch:** *pl. de la Gare; tel: 03 88 32 51 49.* Both open daily Mon–Sat 0900–1900 (June–Sept); Mon–Sat 0900–1230 and 1345–1800 (Oct–May). Hotel reservations service, FFr.10. The Tourist Offices sell a 3-day **Strasbourg Pass** (FFr.56), which covers admission to a museum, the cathedral tower, a cathedral concert, boat trip and some half-price tours.

### ACCOMMODATION

There's a good choice of hotels in every grade, including ten in the wide semi-circle of buildings around *pl. de la Gare* opposite the station. **Monopole-Metropole**, *16 r. Kuhn; tel: 03 88*

*14 39 14* (moderate) is also handy for it. Or you can stay close to the cathedral, notably at **Hôtel Cathédrale**, *pl. de la Cathédrale; tel: 03 88 22 12 12* (moderate), which faces its ornate west facade; rooms at the back are cheaper. Hotel chains include *Ba, BW, Ch, Cn, Ct, Hd, Hn, Ib, IH, Mc, Nv, Sf.*

**HI: René Cassin**, *9 r. de l'Auberge de Jeunesse, Montagne Verte; tel: 03 88 30 26 46,* 2 km from the station (bus nos 3/23: *Auberge de Jeunesse*). A budget choice is **Ciarus**, *7 r. Finkmatt; tel: 03 88 15 27 88,* a 15-min walk from the station (bus nos 10/20: *pl. Pierre).*

### EATING AND DRINKING

For eating, there are plenty of cheerful moderately priced restaurants along *r. du Maroquin* (near the cathedral), *r. des Tonneliers* and in the **Petit France** quarter.

### SIGHTSEEING

The old capital of Alsace, which began life as a Celtic fishing village, has grown into one of Europe's most attractive cities, successfully combining old with new, business with tourism. The centre, on an island in the **River Ill**, has many half-timbered buldings, largely traffic-free streets (thanks to a glossy new tram network) and waterside footpaths. The **Petite-France** quarter, where 16th- and 17th-century houses surround small squares or overlook the river, is very picturesque. Three **Ponts Couverts**, covered bridges with square towers, are remnants of 14th-century fortifications.

The magnificent **Cathédrale de Notre-Dame** (colourfully floodlit July–Aug), which took three centuries to build, is an outstanding example of Gothic architecture. It has a delicate 142m spire and magnificent west façade covered in carvings. Inside there is a 13th-century **Pilier des Anges** (Angels' Pillar) and an enormously complex 19th-century **Horloge Astronomique** (Astronomical clock), which strikes noon at 1231 each day (but begins to swing into action at 1215). The tower, a 330-step climb, provides a good view all over the city.

*Pl. du Château* is named after the 18th-century bishops' residence, **Palais Rohan**, which now houses museums covering archaeology, fine arts and decorative arts. **Musée de l'Oeuvre Notre-Dame**, a huge collection of local art, notably medieval and Renaissance, is also on the square.

**Musée d'Art Moderne**, *Rue St Marguerite,* has a comprehensive collection of 20th-century art including graphics. **Musée Alsacien** (Alsatian Museum), *23 quai St-Nicolas,* covers the popular arts and traditions of rural Alsace and includes rooms furnished in period style.

Boat trips circling the island are operated by **Strasbourg Fluvial**; *tel: 03 88 84 13 13.*

The European Parliament is housed in **Palais de l'Europe**, an imposing modern building some way north of the city centre.

## BADEN-BADEN

**Station: Hbf**, *tel: (07221) 19419.* This is at **Oos**, 12 km north-west of town, but there is a bus (no. 201) every 10 mins 0500–0100; fare DM3 (4 journeys: DM9).
**Tourist Office: Haus des Kurgastes,** *Augustapl. 8; tel: (07221) 21 27 50.* Open 0930–1800.

### ACCOMMODATION AND FOOD

As the baths and casino attract many wealthy visitors, most hotels are glossy and expensive. A cheaper option, 15 mins walk from the centre, is **Hotel Deutscherkaiser,** *Lichtendaler Hauptstr. 35; tel: (07221) 72152* (bus 201 to *Eckerlestr.* from Hbf or town centre). **HI: Jugenherberger**, *Hardbergstr. 34; tel: (07221) 52223* (bus 201 to *Grosse Dollenstr.).*

For eating inexpensively in the centre, **Le Bistro**, *Sophienboulevard 4; tel: (07221) 32311,* is a small bar-restaurant whose tables spill onto the pavement in summer.

### EVENTS

Apr–Sept: **International Festival** in the new **Festspielhaus**, *Langestr.,* built onto the town's disused central railway station. Information office (in Stuttgart): *tel: (0711) 790 4166.*

### SIGHTSEEING

Very fashionable in the 19th century for gambling, particularly among Russian aristocrats, Baden-Baden soon became a **major spa resort**, thanks to its health-promoting hot mineral springs. Now following cutbacks in Germany's health insurance payments, it is developing into a major festival centre, though remains a very relaxing place with extensive parks.

Remnants of the first thermal baths, built by the Romans, can still be seen under **Römerplatz**, where the **Friedrichsbad** occupies a beautifully renovated Renaissance building opened in 1877. Adorned with marble columns, stucco and frescos, it is called the **Roman-Irish baths** because it combines bathing in thermal spring water with exposing the body to warm dry air, as in Northern Europe. A visit (allow 3 hours) costs DM36 (DM32 if booked at your hotel) and includes whirlpools, saunas, steam rooms and hot and cold baths; scrubs and massages extra. Nudity is mandatory. Open 1000–2200, 1400–2200 on Sun.

The ultra-modern **Caracalla-Therme**, *Römerpl. 11,* is an exotic indoor/outdoor pool complex with currents, whirlpools and hot and cold grottos. Upstairs (nudity mandatory) it has saunas, steam rooms and suntan areas. Two hours cost DM19. Open 0800–2200. Take your own towel.

The pump room, **Trinkhalle**, *Kaiserallee 3,* where you can drink the warm mineral water (an acquired taste!), has murals depicting the town's history as a spa.

The **Casino** in the **Kurhaus**, *Kaiserallee 1,* is Germany's oldest and biggest. Redecorated in French style in 1853, it is justifiably promoted as the world's most beautiful casino. Guests no longer have to wear formal attire, but jackets and ties are required (available for hire); no jeans or trainers. Entrance DM5; minimum stake DM5 (DM10 Fri–Sun); maximum stake DM50,000.

> ⤴ **SIDE TRACK**
> **FROM BADEN-BADEN**

**Freiburg**, 55 mins from Baden-Baden by train, is the best base for visiting the southern part of the Black Forest.

## FREIBURG IM BREISGAU

**Station: Hbf**, *tel: (0761) 19419,* is 10 mins walk west of the centre. The **Tourist Office**, *Rotteckring 14; tel: (0761) 388 1880,* is two blocks down *Eisenbahnstr.* opposite Hbf. Open Mon–Fri 0930–2000 (to 1800 Oct–May), Sat 0930–1700 (to 1400 Oct–May), Sun 1000–1200. Accommodation booking service DM5.

### ACCOMMODATION

Hotel chains include *Dorint, Mc, Nv.* **Zum Roten Bären**; *Oberlinden 12; tel: (0761) 387870,* is the oldest inn in Germany, dating back to 1120, but there are plenty of cheaper places to stay – and restaurants – around the *Altstadt.*

**HI: Jugendherberge**, *Kartauserstr. 151; tel: (0761) 67656,* at the extreme east of town (tram no. 1 to *Hasemann-str.*). **Campsites: Hirzberg**, *Kartauserstr. 99; tel: (0761) 35054,* near HI.

### EVENTS

**Late June: Zelt Music Festival** for three weeks under canvas in the *Mundenhof* park; *tel: (0761) 504030.*

### SIGHTSEEING

Freiburg, at the southern end of the Black Forest, is spread around its Gothic cathedral. Most sights are in **Altstadt** and walkable. Some of its streets have **narrow gulleys** running along them, so watch your step! These were part of the old drainage system *(Bächle)* and used for watering livestock.

The red sandstone cathedral, the **Münster**, *Münsterpl.,* is a superb example of Gothic architecture, topped by a 116m spire. The mixed Romanesque-Gothic interior is illuminated by 13th- to 16th-century stained-glass, many sections depicting the guilds who paid for them. The exterior sculptures portray biblical characters. From the tower, 331 steps up, you get a splendid all-round view.

On *Munsterpl.,* the **Historisches Kaufhaus**, an arcaded merchants' hall with statues and spires on the façade, is flanked by two handsome baroque palaces, **Erzbischofliches Palais** and **Wenzingerhaus**. The latter contains a rococo staircase and frescoed ceiling. A short stroll away, *Rathauspl.* is notable for the **Neues Rathaus**, two Renaissance mansions linked by a bridge. They face the Gothic monastery-church of **Martinskirche** and the red and gold **Haus zum Walfisch**, a recreation of the elegant house (bombed in World War II) where Erasmus lived for two years. The **Augustiner**, *Salzstr.,* the town's best museum, contains religious and folkloric art from the Upper Rhine area, as well as old masters. ⤴

## KARLSRUHE

**Station: Hbf**, *tel: (0721) 19419,* a 25-min walk south of the centre (tram nos 3/4). **Tourist Office:** *Bahnhofplatz 6; tel: (0721) 35530,* opposite Hbf. Open Mon–Fri 0900–1800 (to 1300 Sat). Free room-booking service. The local listing is *Karlsruhe Programme* (monthly).

### GETTING AROUND

There are good bus and tram services. Rhine cruises operate Easter–Nov from the western edge of town.

Hotel chains include *Rn, SC.* **HI:** *Moltkestr. 2b; tel: (0721) 28248,* west of Schlossgarten (tram nos 3/4 to *Europapl.*).

**Campsite: Turmbergblick,** *Tiengererstr. 40; tel: (0721) 496236,* 5 km east of the centre, by the **River Pfinz** in *Durlach* (train from Hbf to Durlach, then bus no.30).

### SIGHTSEEING

A major industrial and university city, Karlsruhe is not particularly interesting to tourists except for its huge **Schloss**, home of the Grand Dukes of Baden until 1918. Built in 1715 by Margrave Karl Wilhelm to get away from his wife (hence Karlsruhe, 'Karl's rest'), it's an enormous neo-classical building with extensive formal gardens. From the tower, you see clearly how he designed the city to spread out from it like a fan, with 32 streets.

Inside the Schloss, the **Landesmuseum** covers prehistory to the present day. The **Orangerie,** *Hans-Thoma-Str. 6,* has a fine selection of 19th- and 20th-century European art, while the **Kunsthalle,** *Hans-Thoma-Str. 2,* has a wide-ranging 15th- to 19th-century collection ranging from German primitives to Impressionists.

**Marktplatz,** the enormous central square near the Schloss, is dominated by a pyramid of red sandstone, under which Karl Wilhelm is buried. The pink **Rathaus** is on the western side and the Corinthian-columned **Stadtkirche** on the east.

## STUTTGART

For details, see the Frankfurt–Zurich route, pp.231–232.

## ULM

**Station: Hbf,** *tel: (0731) 19419.* 5 mins to centre through pedestrian zone.
**Tourist Office:** *Stadthaus, Münsterpl. 50; tel: (0731) 161 2830.* Open Mon–Fri 0900–1800, Sat 0900–1230. There is a free accommodation booking service.

### GETTING AROUND

Most things of interest are on the north bank of the Danube and the main attractions are easily walkable.

### ACCOMMODATION AND FOOD

There are several reasonably-priced central hotels, including **Roter Löwe,** *Ulmer Gasse 8; tel: (0731) 62031,* which is in the pedestrian zone and has a swimming pool, and **Münster-Hotel,** *Münsterpl. 14; tel: (0731) 64162,* opposite the cathedral. **HI:** *Grimmelfingerweg 45; tel: (0731) 38 44 55,* 4 km south-west of the centre (bus no. 9 from Hbf or no. 4 from *Rathaus,* both to *Schulzentrum).*

The old fishermen's quarter near the Danube has a selection of restaurants in picturesque spots. The wood-panelled **Allgäuer Hof,** *Fischerg. 12; tel: (0731) 67408,* features traditional pancakes on large platters with a choice of 42 different toppings.

### SIGHTSEEING

Ulm is an endearing old town on the **Danube** with a quaint quarter of half-timbered houses beside the **Blau,** a rushing stream which flows into it. The splendid Gothic minster, **Münster,** *Münsterpl.,* dominates a huge traffic-free square surrounded by shops. Topped by the world's tallest spire (161m), it has 15th-century carved choir stalls, a huge fresco of the Last Judgment on the rood screen and beautiful stained-glass windows, some modern. Climb the tower to see, on a clear day, from the Black Forest to the Alps.

Fortunately the **Münster** escaped most of the World War II bombs which severely damaged the town centre. Many of the buildings have been carefully restored, including the 16th-century **Rathaus,** *Rathauspl.,* which has an an intricate astronomical clock. Its exterior is covered by a series of colourful frescos. **Ulmer Museum,** *Marktpl. 9,* also a fine Renaissance building, is notable for its early Ulm paintings and an outstanding 20th-century collection.

Towards the Danube, the **Metzgeturm** (Butchers' Tower), formerly a prison, is known as the leaning tower of Ulm (36m high) as it's about 2m off the vertical. Paths lead from it to a pleasant riverside walk dotted with sculptures or up onto a stretch of the old city walls. A short way along you can drop down again into the picturesque **Fischer-und-Gerberviertel,** the old fishing and tanning quarter of half-timbered houses beside the **Blau.**

451

In an old salt warehouse, the **Deutsches Brotmuseum** (Bread Museum), *Salzstadelg. 10,* explains the history of breadmaking, complete with a full-scale model of a 1900 bakehouse.

Ulm was the birthplace of **Einstein**, marked by a memorial opposite Hbf, and also the place where **Albrecht Ludwig Berblinger**, the 'Tailor of Ulm', made man's first attempt to fly. In 1811, he took off from the *Adlerbastei* (town wall) but didn't make it across the Danube.

## AUGSBURG

**Station: Hbf**, *tel: (0821) 19419,* 10 mins west of the city centre.
**Tourist Offices:** *Bahnhofstr.* 7, 5 mins from Hbf. Open Mon–Fri 0900–1800. Also *Rathauspl.* Open Mon–Fri 0900–1800, Sat 1000–1600, Sun 1000–1300. *Tel* (for both): *(0821) 502070.*

### ACCOMMODATION AND FOOD

Hotel chains include *BW, Ib, InterCity, Ring, Rk, Rm.*
  **Ulrich Alstadthotel HG**, *Kapuzinerg. 6; tel: (0821) 33077* (moderate) is in the centre. **HI**: *Beim Pfaffenkeller 3, tel: (0821) 33909* (tram no. 2 to *Stadtwerke*). **Campsite: Campingplatz Augusta**, *tel: (0821) 707575,* 7 km from city centre (buses 301/302/305 to *Autobahnsee*). There's no shortage of places to eat in the old town centre, mostly offering hearty local *Swabian* or Bavarian dishes. Plenty of jolly beer cellars too.

### SIGHTSEEING

This busy industrial city was originally fashioned in the 16th century by two wealthy trading and banking families, the Welsers and Fuggers. The main sights are within walking distance of the central pedestrianised *Rathauspl.* Its onion-domed **Rathaus** (painstakingly rebuilt after World War II) includes a sumptuous banqueting hall whose ceiling is heavily adorned with gold leaf. There's a great view from the adjoining **Perlachturm** (70m), the tower of the **Peterskirche**, beside it.

A short stroll east down narrow alleys and over three small canals leads to the **Fuggerei**, a pioneering 'village' of social housing which the Fugger brothers built in 1516. One small house is now a museum with period furniture.

On the hilly north side of the city centre, Augusburg's lofty Gothic cathedral, **Hoher Dom**, is notable for its 12th-century stained-glass, the earliest in Germany, and paintings by Hans Holbein the Elder.

Just west of the centre, the **Annaskirche**, *Annastr.,* a delightful little Renaissance church, is where the Fuggers are buried. Across the street, the **Maximilianmuseum** is in the 16th-century mansion of the Welsers; among its exhibits is a remarkable set of furniture in solid silver. To the south, the **Schaezler Palace**, *Maximilianstr.,* an 18th-century rococo palace with a sumptuous ballroom, is now the state art gallery.

### ⮒ SIDE TRACKS FROM AUGSBURG

From **Hbf**, Europabus services (on which train tickets are valid) run to the little spa of **Schwangau** on the Romantic Road (see p.221), a convenient base for visiting Bavaria's three eccentric royal castles. **Tourist Office**: *Rathaus; tel: (08362) 81980*; open Mon–Fri 0730–1230 and 1330–1700; also Sat 0900–1200 (May–Oct) and Sun 1000–1200 (May–Sept).

The Tudor-style **Hohenschwangau castle**, built in the early 19th century by Maximilian II, was an attempt to recreate the romantic past. His son, 'mad' King Ludwig II, surpassed his father by building the fairy-tale neo-Gothic **Neuschwanstein** castle on a rocky outcrop above it. (To reach Neuschwanstein castle, take the train from Augsburg to Füssen – a 2-hr journey, with trains running at least every 2 hrs – from where frequent local buses run to the castle, which is 2 km away). The third castle, **Linderhof**, 20 km east, is a small French-style château. Among its oddities is the king's dining table, engineered to be lowered to the kitchens and then raised again for him to dine entirely alone. ⮒

# PRAGUE (PRAHA)

Prague has become one of Europe's most popular tourist destinations. A beautiful city, with an exceptionally well-preserved historic centre, it is justly famed for its superb architecture that includes Romanesque, baroque, art nouveau and Cubist styles, among many others. It has acquired a laid-back reputation that goes hand in hand with a traditionally elegant style and the creative energy of a city that is booming. Prague has a fascinating history, a lively music scene, a vast number of museums, galleries and churches, friendly bars, good restaurants and a wealth of open green spaces. Allow yourself several days at least to do it justice.

## TOURIST INFORMATION

The main office of the **Pražská informační služba** (Prague Information Service, known as **PIS**) is at *Na příkopě 20; tel: (02) 54 44 44 127.* Open Mon–Fri 0800–1900, weekends 0800–1530 (later in summer). PIS offices are also in the Old Town Hall, *Staroměstské náměstí 1,* at the Main Railway Station *(Hlavní Nádraží),* and, in the summer months, in the Malá Strana Bridge Tower *(Malostranská mosteeká věž).*

## ARRIVING AND DEPARTING

### Airport

**Ruzyně Airport**, halfway through major refurbishments, is 20 km west of the city centre (flight enquiries, *tel: (02) 2011 1111).* There are 24-hr currency exchange booths, accommodation bureaux, post and telephone facilities. Prague city bus no. 119 connects the airport every 10 mins with the *Dejvicka* Metro stop for 12Kč; **Czech Airlines** (ČSA) run a bus service every 30 mins 0530–2400 to *Dejvická* metro

and to their terminal in *Staré Město* (Hotel Penta, near Masarykovo railway station). **Cedaz**'s excellent **mini-bus** service runs door-to-door (0600–2200) and to *Náměstí Republiky,* but costs more. Fixed price taxis should charge 450 Kč to the centre, but often demand more.

### Station

**Praha Hlavní Nádraží** (Main Railway Station), *Wilsonova 2; tel: (02) 26 49 30,* is the city's main station, although some long-distance and international services also operate into **Nádraží Praha–Holešovice**; *tel: (02) 80 75 05,* in the 7th district (a little way out). Both stations are on Metro Line C, which connects to the centre. Facilities at both include exchange bureaux, left luggage, accommodation services, travel agencies, refreshments and telephones. Rail reservations can be made at the main station (open 0800–1800, English spoken; beware the long queues). Taxis from the stations are not recommended as they charge extortionate rates. At night, the main railway station park operates as a red light district and sleeping rough here is dangerous. For local and international enquiries, call the central railway information service, *tel: (02) 24 22 42 00* or *24 61 40 30.* **Masarykovo** *(Hybernská Pragnel)* and **Smíchov** *(Nádraží, Prague 5)* stations cover many local trains. Rail tickets can only be purchased in Czech currency at the station; credit card and cheque purchases must be made at Czech Railways travel agencies at the stations.

### Buses

For long-distance services, the **Central Bus Station** is at *Křižíkova 4; tel: (02) 24 21 10 60* (metro: *Florenc).*

## GETTING AROUND

Visiting the main attractions is easy, as they are mostly confined to small areas, particularly in the centre. Nevertheless, you will need to use some public transport. PIS offices issue free street plans, with public transport routes.

453

## Tickets

A 12Kč single ticket *(jízdena)* allows you up to 1½ hrs on all forms of public transport within the city; a 6Kč single ticket up to 15 mins, no transfers. A better buy are the inexpensive 1, 3, 7 or 15-day (50Kč, 130Kč, 190Kč or 220Kč) **tourist tickets** *(denní jízdenka)*, which are valid on all forms of public transport. Tickets are on sale at *tabák* or *trafika* shops (tobacconists/newsagents) or from metro station ticket desks and slot machines. Punch your ticket at the metro station entrances or inside trams and buses. Plain-clothes inspectors often flash their badge and ID pass – fines are 200Kč. Children aged up to 5 travel free; those aged 6–15 for half price. All public transport runs from about 0500 to 2400; there are also some night services, at approx. 40-min intervals. Alternatively, a **Prague card,** available from **Čedok** travel agency, *Na příkopě 18,* or **Thomas Cook** (see under Money below) combines a 3-day transport ticket with free entry to major sights.

## Metro, Trams and Buses

A wonderfully efficient and modern **metro** (3 lines; red, yellow and green) covers most areas you are likely to visit. There is also a good network of **trams** running on main arteries and across the river. Be careful, as pickpockets are rife on popular tourist routes (e.g. no. 22). The infrequent **night trams** all stop at *Lazarská,* just off *Vodičkova.* You will rarely need to use **buses** unless you are staying out in the suburbs. A funicular runs up Petřín hill between 0915 and 2045 daily (trams 9, 12, 22).

## Taxis

Avoid taxis, if at all possible – over-charging of foreigners is endemic. Always agree a fare before getting in. Reputable services include **AAA,** *tel: 1080* (English-speaking).

## STAYING IN PRAGUE

## Accommodation

Although Prague has dramatically expanded the range and quality of its hotels, many are overpriced for what they offer. If you prefer to stick to a well-known chain, the following have hotels in Prague: *BW, Fm, Hd, Hn, IC, IH, Pe.*

**Accommodation Bureaux:** *Hlavní nádraží* (**AVE**); *tel: (02) 24 22 35 21* or *26 14 27.* Open daily 0600–2300. **Čedok,** *Na příkopě 18, tel: 2419 7632; Pařížská 6, tel: (02) 23 14 302,* or *Rytířská 16, tel: (02) 26 27 14* (Mon–Fri 0900–1800, weekends 0830–1630) can make a computer check on hotels with vacant rooms. For **youth-orientated information,** try CKM, *Jindřišská 28; tel: (02) 26 05 32/26 85 07,* (daily 0900–1800), or the **Junior Hotel** (Youth Hostel) reservation office, *Žitná 12; tel: (02) 29 29 84,* (open 24 hrs). In July, Aug and Sept, CKM also lets cheap rooms in **student hostels**. You can call the **Student Hostel Booking Office;** *tel: (02) 53 99 51/59.* Accommodation **hawkers** offering private apartments/rooms wait for visitors arriving by train. Agree a price first; arrangements are generally safe.

**Dům" U Krále Jiřího",** *Lilová 10, Prahal-Staré Město; tel/fax: 242 219 83,* is a cheap 14th-century hotel in the old town. The moderate **U Zlatého Stromu,** *Karlova 6, Praha 1; tel: 242 213 85,* is ideally located and bustling. The moderate **Hotel Alta,** *Ortenovo náměstí 22, Praha 7; tel: 800 252-9,* is further out, but clean and friendly. Expensive **Hotel U tří Pštrosu,** *Dražického náměstí 12, Praha 1; tel: 573 205 65,* rewards every booking. Try **Casa Marcello,** *Řásnovka 1, Praha 1; tel: 231 1230,* for Italian style and a medieval atmosphere (expensive).

There are several **campsites** within the city boundary (camping rough is forbidden). For central information, contact **UAMK,** *Mánesova 20; tel: (02) 74 74 00* or *24 22 16 35* (closed weekends).

## Eating and Drinking

There are three main categories of eating house: *restaurace* (restaurant), *vinárna* (wine-bar/restaurant) and *pivnice* (pub). Prices range from expensive in fashionable old town locations to great value pubs serving locally brewed beer.

Although touristy, the classic and pricey **U Flekú** beer garden and cellar, *Křemencova 11; tel: (02) 2491 5119,* is worth a visit for its home-brewed black ale and beer cheese. If you want to chat in English over a Czech beer, try **U Malého Glena,** *Karmelitská 23, Prague 1; tel: 535 8115.* There are several Irish pubs, such as **Molly Malones,** *U obecníhodvora 4, Prague 1.*

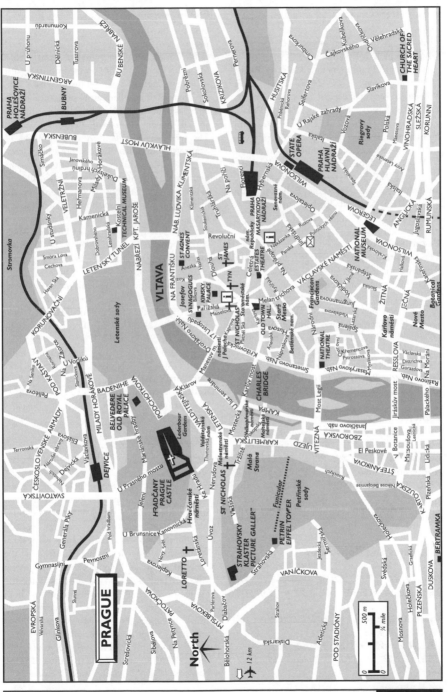

Try typical Czech pubs such as **Novoměstsky pivovar**, *Vodičkova 20 (off Wenceslas Sq.)* or **U Pinkasů**, *Jungmannovo náměstí 15,* serving Pilsner Urqnell or Budweiser.

Cafés worth testing include **Café de Paris**, *U Obecního domu 1; tel: 24 22 2151;* **Café Milena**, *Staroměstské náměstí 22; tel: 26 08 43,* and **Café Savoy**, *Vítězná 5.* **Palffy Palác**, *Valdštejnská 14; tel: 573 205 70,* and **Nebozizek**, *Petřínské sady 411; tel: 53 79 02,* are elegant restaurants in stunning locations.

Vegetarian food is available at **Radost**, *Bělehradská 120,* and **Góvinda**, *Soukenická 27;* top-notch pizza at **Pizzeria Felicita**, *Říční 5;tel: 53 35 55,* and Kosher specialities at **Metzada**, *Michalská 16; tel: 24 21 34 18.*

## Communications

The **Central Post Office** and **Poste Restante** are at *Jindřišská 14; tel: (02) 24 22 88 58* (24-hr service for stamps, parcels, telegrams and telephones). Stamps and phone-cards can be purchased here or from a *tabák* or newsagents. The older, coin-operated telephones are seldom reliable (local calls cost 3Kč), but modern phone booths accept phone cards and have instructions in English. For an English-speaking operator, *tel: (02) 0135;* to make collect calls, *tel: (02) 0132.* The Prague area code is *02.*

## Money

Banking hours are usually Mon–Fri 0900–1700. For fair dealing, go to **Živnostenská Banka**, *Na příkopě 20; tel: 2412 1111,* or **Komerční banka**, *Na příkopě 33; tel: 2402 1111.* There are plenty of automatic cash-dispensers. Exchange kiosks give poor rates. Travellers cheques and Eurocheques are widely accepted, as are credit cards.

## Embassies and Consulates

**Canada:** *Mickiewiczova 6, 160 00 Praha 6; tel: 2431 1108.*
**Republic of Ireland:** *Tržiště 13; tel: 530 902 or 530 911.*
**South Africa:** *Ruská 65; tel: 100 00 Praha 10; tel: 6731 1114.*
**UK:** *Thunovská 14, Praha 1; tel: 5732 0355.*
**USA:** *Tržiště 15, 110 00 Praha 1; tel: 5732 0663.*

## ENTERTAINMENT

Consult the English-language newspaper *The Prague Post* for weekly event listings. Czech publications, *Program* (weekly), and *Přehled* (monthly) and *Kultura v Praze* (monthly, also issued in English) give details of what's on.

There is an excellent array of classical music, opera and theatre (in Czech). The three theatres are all opulent: **Národní divadlo** (National Theatre), *Národní třída 2; tel: (02) 24 91 34 37,* **Stavovské divadlo** (Estates Theatre), *Ovocný trh 1; tel: 2421 4339,* where *Don Giovanni* was premièred, and **Statní Opera** (State Opera), *Wilsonová 4; tel: 2422 7693.* There are also many puppet and mime shows, such as those at **Image Black Light Theatre**, *Pařížská 4; tel: (02) 23 29 191;* and the famed **Laterna Magika**, *Národní třída 4; tel: 2491 4129.* **Rudolfinum**, *Jana Palacha 1; tel: 2489 3111,* is the premier amongst many concert halls.

The rock and disco scene includes venues such as the **Rock Café**, *Národní 20; tel: (02) 24 91 44 16,* and the 'experimental' **Roxy**, *Dlouhá 33; tel: (02) 24 81 09 51.* Try the dance club **Radost FX**, *Bělehradská 120.*

For good jazz, Czech or international, traditional or modern, try places like **Agharta Jazz Centrum**, *Krakovská 5; tel: (02) 22 21 12 75;* **Reduta**, *Národní 20; tel: (02) 24 91 22 46;* or **Malostranská Beseda**, *Malostranské náměstí 21; tel: 539 024.*

## SHOPPING

The Czech speciality is beautiful crystal glass. **Moser**, *Na příkopě 12; tel: (02) 24 21 12 93,* and *Malé nám 11,* offers a mailing service. In the narrow streets and *pasáže* (passages) of *Malá Strana, Nové Město* and *Staré Město* are small souvenir shops, selling glass, ceramics, wooden toys and puppets; try **Česka lidová remesla** at *Melantrichivá,* for local handicrafts, or the museum shops at Prague Castle, the Jewish Museum and the Decorative Arts Museum. These streets boast numerous luxurious shops and boutiques, many selling unique items by Czech designers. For household goods, food and other essentials, try one of the four main department stores: **Kotva**, *Náměstí republiky 8;* **Bílá labut'**, *Na Poříčí 23;* **Julius Meinl**, *Václavské náměstí 21;* and **Tesco**, *Národní 26.*

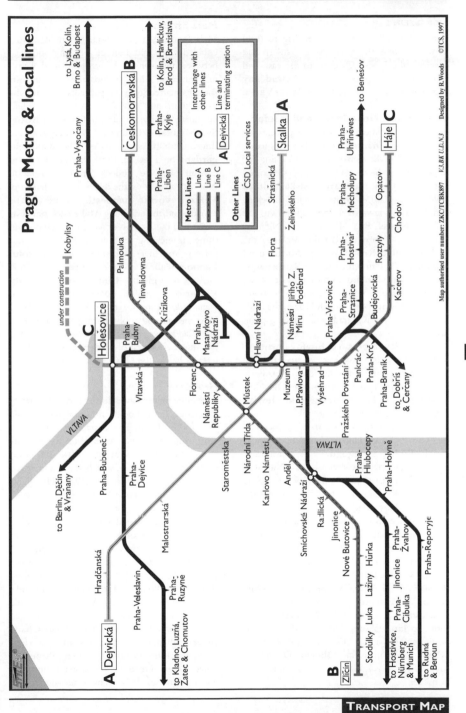

# Prague Metro & local lines

Metro Lines
— Line A
— Line B
— Line C

Other Lines
⊤ ČSD Local services

○ Interchange with other lines

A Dejvická Line and terminating station

457

Map authorised user number: ZKC/TCBK897    V3.BK U.I.N.3    Designed by R.Woods    ©TCS, 1997

Old Prague is divided into **Staré Město** (Old Town), **Nové Město** (New Town) and **Josefov** (the Jewish Quarter) to the east, and **Malá Strana** (Lesser Quarter) and **Hradčany** (Castle District) to the west of the River Vltava.

### Staré Město, Nové Město and Josefov

At the heart of **Staré Město** is the picturesque **Staroměstské náměstí** (Old Town Square), (tram nos. 17/18; metro: *Staroměstská,* line A), ringed by medieval and baroque structures. Find time to visit the **Staroměstská radnice** (Old Town Hall), with its astronomical clock and fabulous views over the Old Town, the baroque **Kostel Sv. Mikuláše** (St Nicholas Church), the baroque **Kinsky Palace**, the ancient Gothic **Kostel panny Marie před Týnem** (Týn Church), and the Romanesque **Dům U kamenného zvonu** (House of the Stone Bell), where you can visit art exhibitions. The 1915 **Monument to Jan Hus** in the middle of the square is a traditional rallying point for Czechs.

The old Jewish ghetto of **Josefov** (metro A/ tram no. 17: *Staroměstská)* was cleared in 1893, leaving behind the only functioning medieval synagogue in Central Europe (the Old-New Synagogue) and a haunting **Old Jewish Cemetery**. The surrounding buildings (which include the **Jewish Museum** at *Jachýmová 3,* the Rococo **Town Hall**, with a Hebraic **clock**, and the **Pinkas Synagogue**, with a Holocaust memorial, among others) constitute a **National Jewish Museum** (one timed ticket for all sights; 200 Kč; Sun–Fri 0900–1800 Apr–Oct, 0900–1630 Nov–Mar).

**Nové Město** is a sprawling area with fewer sights, but all visitors to Prague will spend some time in the lively **Václavské náměstí** (Wenceslas Square) (metro: *Můstek or Muzeum),* which witnessed the climax of the 'Velvet Revolution' in 1989. At the top end is the **National Museum** (see p.459), in front of which stands a statue of **St Wenceslas** and a shrine to **Jan Palach**, who burned himself to death on 16 January 1969 in protest at the Warsaw Pact invasion. **Obecní Dům**, on *náměstí Republiky 5,* is a stunning example of art nouveau.

### Malá Strana

Malá Strana is a picturesque town of narrow cobbled streets and diminutive squares squeezed between the river and the wedge-shaped plateau of Hradčany. Here, **Malostranské náměstí** (Lesser Quarter Square) is particularly worth visiting (tram nos. 12/22: *Malostranské náměstí),* dominated by the Dientzenhofers' other **Kostel Sv. Mikuláše** (Church of St Nicholas), and ringed with baroque palaces. The **Waldštejn gardens** on *Letenská,* north-east of the square contain exquisite gardens (open 1000–1800). Not far away are the even more delightful **Velkopřevorské náměstí** (Grand Prior's Square) and the adjoining **Maltézské náměstí** (Square of the Knights of Malta), which contain some interesting churches, embassies and palaces, together with the celebrated **John Lennon Wall**, a pop-art folly (tram nos. 12/22: *Hellichova).* Visit the **Church of our Lady Victorious** (Panna Marie Vítězná) on *Karmelitská 9,* to see the wax effigy of Baby Jesus, still an object of pilgrimage. Further east, off *Valdřtejuské náměstí* (Waldstein Sq.), the baroque **Ledeburské gardens** zig zag up the terraces below the Castle (daily 1000–1800).

### Hradčany

This huge hilltop castle district is the focal point of Prague (tram no. 22: *Malostranské náměstí/ Pražský hrad;* metro: *Hradčanská,* line A). Dominating the whole complex is the magnificent **Katedrála Svatého Víta** (St Vitus Cathedral), the core of which was commenced in 1344, but completed in 1929. Highlights include the **St. Wenceslas Chapel**, with walls studded by semi-precious stones and frescoes, the late Gothic **Royal Oratory**, the fabulous **baroque Tomb of St John Nepomuk** and the **oak panel reliefs** in the ambulatory.

Nearby, much of the **Starý Královský Palác** (Old Royal Palace) was built for King Vladislav Jagello in the 15th century. Don't miss the magnificent late Gothic **Vladislav Hall**, the so-called Riders' Stairway, the Spanish Hall, built by Rudolf II, and the **Bohemian Chancellery**, where the most famous of Prague's four defenestrations occurred, when Protestant nobles threw Frederick II's ambassadors from the window in 1618. The castle underwent controversial modernisation by Josip Plečnik after World War I. It's now the seat of the President of the Republic.

To the north-east are **Klášter sv. Jiří** (St George's Convent), a gallery of Czech art, and the Romanesque **Bazilika sv. Jiří** (St George's Basilica). **Zlatá Ulička** (Golden Lane) is lined by diminutive Renaissance cottages. **Franz Kafka** lived at no. 22, between 1916 and 1917. For further information on the castle district, *tel: 2437 3368.* You can buy a 100 Kč, 3-day ticket covering the entire district.

Beyond the Castle area lies an imposing district beginning with **Hradčanské náměstí** (Hradčany Square). Note the sgraffitoed **Schwarzenberg Palace** (no. 2) on the south side, the **Toscana Palace** (no. 5) to the west and the noble **Archbishop's Palace** (no. 16) to the north. If you walk up *Loretánská,* you come to the imposing **Černín Palace** (no. 5), from whose window Foreign Minister Jan Masaryk plunged to his death in 1948. Nearby is the **Loretto church of the Nativity** *(Loretánská 7),* an imitation of the famous Loreto near Ancona (open Tues–Sun 0900–1215, 1300–1630). A short stroll past the Loretto is the **Strahovský Klášter** (Strahov Monastery), whose star attraction is the **Philosophical Hall** and historical library with marvellous frescos (0900–1200, 1300–1700; *tel: 538 369).* The **Belvedere** (Summer Palace), Prague's finest Renaissance building (tram no. 22: *Belveder),* houses exhibitions – don't miss the 'singing fountain' in the gardens. South of the castle, wander through **Petřín Hill** (Petřínské sady), with its lush woods, orchards, 1891 model of the Eiffel Tower (20 Kč; 0930–2000) and funicular to Malá Strana.

## Other Sights

The beautiful sandstone **Charles Bridge**, commissioned by Charles VI in 1357, is now the standard image of Prague. At each end are high towers, and the parapet is lined by 31 statues (mainly 1683–1714, with a few copies and later works).

At **Vyšehrad** (metro C: *Vyšehrad),* south of *Nové Město,* the ancient citadel where the Slavs first settled, sights include the Slavín Pantheon of leading Czechs in the **cemetery** (0900–1900

summer, 0900–1700 winter) next to the **Church of St Peter and St Paul**, *St Martin's rotunda,* and breathtaking views over the **Vltava** from the bastions.

## Galleries and Museums

The rich **National Gallery** collection is scattered round four main venues: the **Šternberský Palác** (Sternberg Palace), *Hradčanské náměstí 15,* contains a collection of European art; the **Klášter sv. Jiří na Pražském hradě** (St George's Convent), *Jiřské náměstí 33,* houses old Bohemian art; the **Klášter sv. Anežky Česke** (St Agnes' Convent), *U milosrdných 17* (tram nos 5/14/26: *Revoluční)* is devoted to 19th-century artists of the Czech national revival (Tues–Sun 1000–2100); and **Zámek Zbraslav** (Zbraslav Castle), *Zbraslav nad Vltavou* (metro: *Smíchovské nádraží,* then bus nos 129/241), has a remarkable display of 19th- and 20th-century Czech sculpture. Three other sites for temporary and permanent exhibitions are: the **Veletržní palác** (Centre for modern and contemporary art of the National Gallery), *Dukelských hrdinů 47;* metro C: *Vltavská,* Tues–Wed, Fri–Sun 1000–1800, Thur 1000–2100; the **Wallenstein riding school**, (Valdštejnská jizdarna), *Valdštejnské náměstí 3;* tram: 22; and **Kinsky palace** (palác Kinských) *Staroměstské náměstí 12.* A 1–day National Gallery pass costs 100 Kč, a 3–day pass 200 Kč. All galleries open Tues–Sun 1000–1800.

**Národní Muzeum** (National Museum), *Václavské náměstí 68* (metro: *Muzeum;* 40 Kč), is mildly interesting for its architecture and pantheon. More stimulating is the fine collection at **Uměleckoprůmyslové Muzeum** (Museum of Decorative Arts), *Ul 17. listopadu 2* (20 Kč); (Metro/tram nos. 17/18: *Staroměstská);* and **Bertramka**, *Mozartova 169* (10 mins walk from Metro B *Andel;* 0930–1800, 50 Kč), a 17th-century villa housing an exhibition of Mozart's life and work. Unless stated otherwise, all museums are open Tues–Sun 1000–1800.

Further from the centre is **Troja chateau** (Trojský Zámek), *Trója,* with a baroque complex of exhibitions and gardens (Tues–Sun 1000–1800; *tel: 689 0761).* Boat trips on the River Vltava (day and evening) run from *Rašinovo nábřeží* (by Palacký bridge; *tel: 298 309).*

# ROME (ROMA)

The 'Eternal City', filled with museums and galleries, churches and ruins, redolent of the Caesars and the creative genius of Michelangelo, Rome needs no introduction.

## TOURIST INFORMATION

Main **tourist information office, EPT** (Rome Provincial Tourist Board): *V. Parigi 5 (near V. XX Settembre); tel: (06) 488 991 or 482 4078* (metro: *Repubblica*). Open Mon–Sat 0815–1915. Hotel reservations, listings, maps and itineraries. Other tourist and hotel information desks: **Leonardo da Vinci Airport**; *tel: (06) 65 01 02 55*; **Stazione Termini**; *tel: (06) 48 71 270*. All open daily 0815–1915 June–Sept; Mon–Sat in winter.

## ARRIVING AND DEPARTING

### Airports
**Leonardo da Vinci (Fiumicino)** is 36 km south-west of Rome; *tel: (06) 65 951*. Taxis into the centre are hassle-free, but expensive (L.60,000–70,000). Less expensive is the 45-mins train service, every 20 mins, 0600–0100, to **Tiburtina** station (for further information, *tel: (06) 65 951*). At time of going to press, a new express rail link to **Termini** had just opened.

**Aeroporto Ciampino** *tel: (06) 794 941* is closer to town, 16 km to the south-east. A bus service (**ACOTRAL** or **ATAC**) runs every 10–20 mins to **Anagnina Metro Station** (services to Termini every 30 mins between 0530 and 2230). Expect to pay at least L.50,000 by metered taxi.

### Stations
There are four main railway stations: **Termini**, *Pza dei Cinquecento; tel: (06) 4775*; seat reservations: *tel: (06) 48 84 069*, is Rome's largest, handling all the main national and international lines. A wide range of services includes bureaux

de change, tourist and hotel information. It is also well served by taxis, buses and night buses, and is the focus of the metro system.

**Ostiense**, *tel: (06) 57 58 748*, serves some long distance north-south trains.

**Roma-Nord**, *tel: (06) 36 10 441*, serves Viterbo (2 hrs); Bracciano (90 mins) and other parts of northern Lazio.

**Tiburtina**, *tel: (06) 43 42 39 72*, serves some long distance north-south trains. Trains arriving after midnight stop here.

There are ATMs in the stations. The national toll-free number for rail information is: *1478 88088*.

## GETTING AROUND

The *centro storico* (historic centre) is fairly compact, traffic-free and easy to see on foot. However, many of the most important sights lie outside this area. The main arteries are well served by buses, but stick to those and you miss Rome's ebullient streetlife, medieval alleys and baroque squares. Most hotels supply a basic street map. For more detail, and bus and metro maps, ask at news-stands, tobacconists and tourist information offices. Failing that, Romans positively glow with enthusiasm when you ask for help with directions.

### Tickets
You must purchase your ticket before travelling. Tickets are on sale at all metro stops, bus termini with green ACOTRAL kiosks, and at news-stands and tobacconists displaying ATAC (bus and tram) and ACOTRAL (metro) signs. You can also get tickets from the ATAC **Information Booth**, *Pza dei Cinquecento* (metro: *Termini*).

### Metro, Buses and Trams
The **Metropolitana** has only two lines – A and B – and is not much use in the centre. Line A (red) is open 0530–2400; Line B (blue) is open 0530–2100, Mon–Fri. Tickets are for a single journey, but there are also monthly passes, a

460

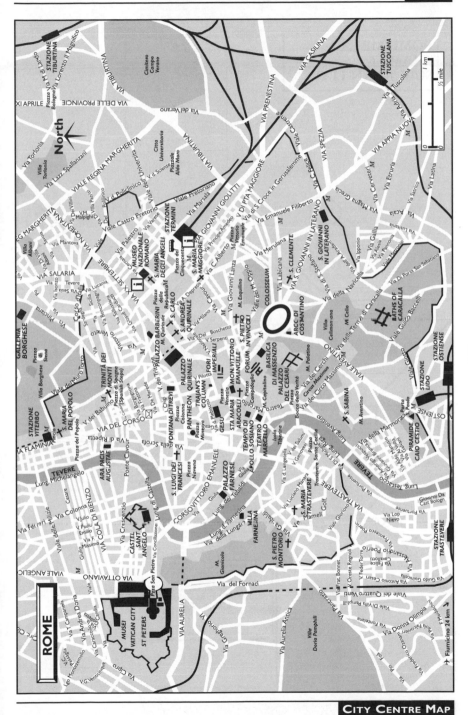

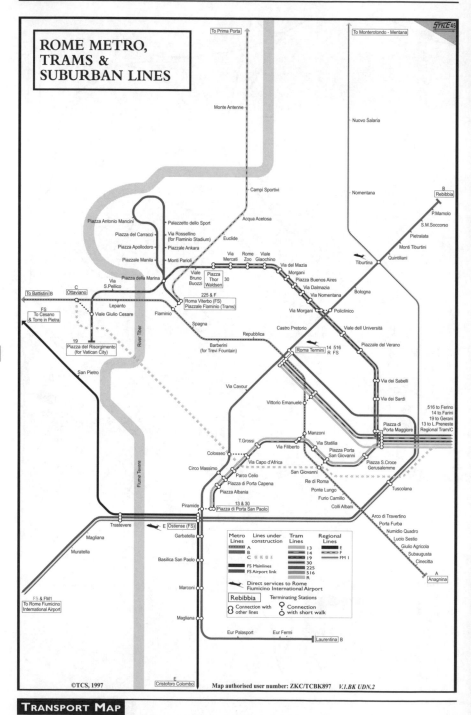

# ROME METRO, TRAMS & SUBURBAN LINES

**462**

ticket valid for 90 mins (L.800), and a 24-hr BIG ticket (L.2,000), which are valid on all forms of public transport.

Rome's excellent **bus** service is centred on *Pza dei Cinquecento*, with major stops *(fermate)* in *Pza Venezia, Largo Argentina* and *Pza del Risorgimento*. Buses are orange, the number is at the front and they generally stop without you having to flag them down. Only one (no.119, a small electric bus) is able to enter the narrow streets of the *centro storico*. Time-stamp your ticket in the machine as you enter (heavy on-the-spot fines if you are caught ticketless). The basic ticket is valid for one journey, but a block of ten (red) tickets saves money, as does a half-day ticket *(biglietto orario)*, valid from either 0600–1400 or 1400–2400. Passes include a one-day pass; an eight-day tourist pass, the *Carta Settimanale per Turisti*; and a one-month pass. For bus and tram information: *tel: (06) 46 95 44.*

**Night buses** run from 2400–0800. Buy tickets from the conductor on board. For information, look in the Tuttocittà supplement of the telephone directory.

**Sightseeing tours** are provided by **ATAC** (tickets and information from ATAC in *Pza dei Cinquecento*), **CIT,** *tel: (06) 479 11;* **American Express,** *tel: (06) 67 641;* **Green Line Tours,** *tel: (06) 482 74 80;* and **Carrani Tours,** *tel: (06) 47 42 501.* Expect to pay about L.100,000 for a full day's tour.

### Taxis
There are plenty of metered taxis, available from ranks or by phone; **Radiotaxi,** *tel: (06) 3570;* **Roma Sud,** *tel: (06) 3875;* **Capitale,** *tel: (06) 4994;* or **Cosmos,** *tel: (06) 8433.* There are surcharges for luggage, at night (2200–0700) and on Sun and holidays.

### Carriages
A ride in a *carrozzella* (open carriage) can be fun, but expensive: agree a price with the driver beforehand.

### STAYING IN ROME

### Accommodation
There are plenty of **hotels,** from the opulent,

mainly located close to the *Spanish Steps* and the *V. Veneto*, to the basic, largely clustered around the *V. Nazionale* and Termini station. Moderately priced, centrally located hotels are generally very popular, and you should book up to two months ahead in high season. For the cheaper hotels, expect to pay around L.70,000 per night, even without a private bathroom. Some do not take credit cards.

Among the major hotel groups in the city are *Ch, Ex, Fo, HI, Hn, IC, Pu* and *Sh.* Tourist Offices will provide lists of residential hotels and make bookings. **International Services**, *V. del Babuino, 79; tel: (06) 36 00 18,* has a list of **self-catering studios** and **apartments.**

If you don't mind a night-time curfew and pilgrims, several religious institutions offer cheap accommodation; try **Domus Mariae**, *tel: (06) 662 31 38;* and **Istituto Madri Pie**, *tel: (06) 63 19 67* – both near the Vatican.

**Youth hostels: Associazione Italiana Alberghi per la Gioventù (HI)**, *V. Cavour 44–47, tel: (06) 48 71 152.* Only holders of AIG or HI cards can use the **Ostello del Foro Italico**, *Vle delle Olimpiadi, 61, tel: (06) 32 36267.* The **YWCA** is at *V. C. Balbo, 4, tel: (06) 48 83 917.* The **Protezione della Giovane**, *V. Urbana 158; tel: (06) 48 81 489,* will locate accommodation for women under 25. There are **no campsites** in central Rome; although there are ten within a 45-min bus ride away.

### Eating and Drinking
Italian cafés and bars have hefty seating charges, so most Romans have their breakfast, and often lunch, standing up at the bar. You generally pay first and take your receipt to the counter. Picnics are a good alternative. Some delicatessens will fill a roll with the ingredients of your choice (try the delicatessen in the *Campo dei Fiori* vegetable market).

Restaurants are more expensive than *trattorie,* which offer substantial amounts of simple, robust Roman-style food, washed down with local wine. Some have no name, their purpose defined only by cooking smells, loud chatter and paper table cloths. Some don't even have menus, so just point to whatever seems delicious on the next table. In these, expect to pay around L.25,000 per head for three courses, bread *(coperta)* and wine. *Pizzerie* are a cheap alternative, while you can taste different wines and have delicious tiny snacks at an *enoteca*. Vegetarian restaurants are rare but most Italian menus are adaptable.

The **Campo dei Fiori** neighbourhood is best for *al fresco* (open-air) dining, while the streets off the nearby *Pza Farnese* have stylish, but reasonably cheap venues. **Trastevere** has boisterous, crowded, rough-and-ready eateries, which may involve queuing, but are worth the wait. Other popular places are around *Pza Navona* and the *Pantheon*, while the *Ghetto* and the old slaughterhouse area of **Testaccio** offer some of the best traditional Roman cooking. Read the menu in the window to gauge price.

## Communications

**Post:** the main post office, *Pza San Silvestro; tel: (06) 679 5530* (open Mon–Fri, 0800–2100; Sat 0800–1200) has 24-hr phones, fax and telex, and poste restante (address letters **c/o Palazzo delle Poste,** *Roma, Fermo Posta* – put the surname first, underlined). Stamps are available from post offices and tobacconists displaying a black-and-white **T**. Letters posted at the main post office, or anywhere within the Vatican City (use Vatican stamps in blue post boxes) arrive faster than those posted in the red pavement boxes.

**Telephones**: to phone Rome from abroad: *tel: 39 (Italy) + 6 (Rome) + number*. To phone Rome from elsewhere in Italy: *tel: 06 (Rome) + number*.

## Money

Banks (open 0830–1330; 1500–1600), hotels and bureaux de change (open 0830/0900–1300; 1530/1600–1930/2000) will change money. Major credit cards and Eurocheques are widely accepted (check before entering *trattorie* and *pensioni*).

**Thomas Cook Italia** have bureaux de change at *V. della Conciliazione 23/25, V. del Corso 53* and *Pza Barberini 21A/21D*.

## Embassies and Consulates

**Australia**: *V. Alessandra, 215; tel: (06) 854 27 21*.

**Canada**: *V. Zara 30; tel: (06) 445 981*.
**New Zealand**: *V.Zara, 28; tel: (06) 440 29 28*.
**UK:** *V. XX Settembre, 80A; tel: (06) 482 54 41*.
**USA**: *V. Veneto, 119A/121; tel: (06) 467 41*.

*Trovaroma* (published with *La Repubblica* on Thursdays) and *Metropolitan* (published fortnightly in English) are very comprehensive 'what's on' guides, available from news-stands. Rome is a busy cultural city, so also read listings sections of the daily papers like *Il Messagero, Il Manifesto* and *Paese Sera*.

**Nightlife** is limited. Most Italians like nothing better than to while away the evening in a restaurant. However, there are good venues for dancing, vibrant clubs (jazz, salsa, African, Latin) and overflowing, noisy bars. There is also a thriving gay scene.

The summer is Rome's liveliest season for **theatres** and **concerts,** with many performances set beneath the stars, or possibly within some ancient ruin or Renaissance garden. The **Teatro dell'Opera** moves out to the ruins of the **Baths of Caracalla** in July and Aug. As a rule, tickets for these events (apart from opera) cannot be booked in advance. There are also many choral concerts in the churches – watch the billboards outside for details.

Rome is a busy shopping centre, although there is nothing particularly exceptional or unusual about its wares. Best buys are from the delicatessens and grocery stores – olive oil, fragrant vinegars, dried *funghi* (mushrooms), packets of dried herbs – in and around *Via della Croce* and the *Campo dei Fiori. Via del Corso* sells cheaper versions of the designer clothing, from hats to shoes, on sale in the *Via dei Condotti* (big names like Gucci and Prada) and its parallel streets, while cheaper still are the clothes stalls of the *Porta Portese* and *Via Sannio* markets (metro: *San Giovanni*) with their astonishing arrays of second-hand hand-me-downs and ex-army tackle. Rome has a strong artisan goldsmith and silversmith tradition here (*Ghetto, Via dei Coronari, Via dell'Orso*), and is fairly well served by antique shops (*Via dei Coronari, Via Giulia, Via del Babuino).* Take-home items might include terracotta from southern Italy, kitchen equipment made by Alessi, chunks of parmesan or *peccorino* cheese, ex-reliquaries from the flea-market or bottles of heart-stopping Grappa from a liquor store.

## SIGHTSEEING

Most places charge an entrance fee; some are free on Sundays. The EPT publishes *Musei e Monumenti di Roma,* giving details of current changes and closures as well as information about exhibitions.

Rome, dominated by its seven hills (Aventine, Capitoline, Celian, Esquiline, Palatine, Quirinal and Viminal), is cut by the fast-flowing Tiber. The **Aventine**, with magnificent views over the river, is topped by ancient **Santa Sabina**, evocative of early Christian Rome, and the **Piazza dei Cavallieri di Malta,** designed in the 18th century by the architectural theorist and engraver Piranesi. At its foot are the **Circus Maximus** (begun c 326 BC), scene of ancient chariot races, and the **Temples of Hercules** and **Portinus.**

The **Capitoline** was once the sacred heart of the Roman Empire and seat of its principle temple – devoted to Jupiter. Today it is occupied by Michelangelo's **Piazza del Campidoglio,** which is dominated by Rome's town hall, the **Palazzo Senatori.** On either side of this, the magnificent **Capitoline Museums** in **Palazzo Nuovo** and, opposite it, **Palazzo dei Conservatori** (both built in the 16th century to designs by Michelangelo) constitute the world's first public museum. They house important collections of classical sculpture while, in addition, the Palazzo dei Conservatori also contains the **Pinacoteca Capitolina,** an art gallery with paintings by, amongst others, Rubens, Caravaggio and Titian. On the edge of the Capitoline, the early church of **Santa Maria in Aracoeli** occupies the site of Emperor Augustus's Altar of Heaven, the Ara Coeli. It contains important Renaissance works (Pinturicchio, Gozzoli, Arnolfo di Cambio).

The great basilica of **Santa Maria Maggiore,** *Pza di Santa Maria Maggiore,* dominates the **Esquiline** where once the cult of the mother goddess, Juno Lucina, had its temple. Nearby, **San Pietro in Vincoli,** *Pza San Pietro in Vincoli,* houses the chains with which St Peter was imprisoned, and Michelangelo's superb statue of Moses, which was intended as the main feature in the unfinished tomb of Pope Julius II. Beyond it, **Trajan's Market** (the world's first shopping mall; *V. 4 Novembre)* and **Trajan's Column** face the **Forum,** site of the temples and basilicas of Imperial Rome.

The **Celian Hill** is quiet, covered mainly by the gardens of the **Villa Celimontana,** *Pza della Navicella.* In front of it, the formal **Farnese Gardens** on the **Palatine** are filled with the ruins of Imperial Palaces. Below lies Rome's most famous landmark, the **Colosseum,** *Pza del Colosseo,* built by Emperor Vespasian in AD72. It held over 55,000 spectators and was the scene of the Roman Games and gladiatorial combats. Here, too, early Christians were fed to half-starved lions and mock sea battles and animal combats (during the reign of Titus, nearly 5000 animals were slaughtered here) were held. Beyond it are **San Giovanni in Laterano,** *Pza di San Giovanni in Laterano,* the Pope's titular seat as Bishop of Rome, and a section of the ancient **Aurelian Walls.**

At the base of the **Quirinal** is the **Fontana di Trevi,** *Pza Fontana di Trevi* – into which, to ensure your return, you must throw a coin, while on its summit sits the President of Italy's residence, the **Palazzo del Quirinale.** Also on the **Quirinal** is the **Palazzo Barberini,** *V. delle Quattro Fontane 13* which contains the **Galleria Nazionale d'Arte Antica** housing important works of the Renaissance and baroque periods. Begun in 1625 by Maderno for the powerful Barberini, it was completed with help from Borromini and Bernini. **Santa Maria della Vittoria,** *V. XX Settembre* is an important church which contains Bernini's inspired sculptural group, *The Ecstasy of St Theresa.* In the same district, Borromini's **San Carlino** *(V. delle Quattro Fontane)* and Bernini's **Sant'Andrea Quirinale,** *V. del Quirinale* provide the best examples of the Roman baroque style. Nearby, Michelangelo's **Santa Maria degli Angeli** and the **Museo Nazionale Romano** (temporarily closed) were fashioned from the ancient **Baths of Diocletian.**

465

The **Vatican City,** state within a city and home of the Pope and the Catholic Church, houses numerous treasures. **St Peter's Cathedral**, worked on by, amongst others, Bramante, Michelangelo and Bernini (whose immense colonnade precedes it), dominates the Vatican, while the vast and elaborate **Vatican Museum** *Viale Vaticano*, and the recently cleaned **Sistine Chapel** (enter from the museum), with Michelangelo's *Last Judgment*, considered his masterpiece, and his **ceiling frescos** depicting scenes from the Last Testament, draw in the crowds. Nearby is the **Castel Sant' Angelo,** built as a Roman tomb, converted into a fortress, used as a palace, and now a museum *Lungotevere Castello*.

The **Campo dei Fiori's** vegetable market adds life and colour to the district near **Palazzo Farnese,** *Pza Farnese,* and **Santa Andrea della Valle,** *Corso Vittorio Emanuele*. The **Palazzo Spada,** *V Capo di Ferro 13,* houses paintings – including those by Reni, Titian and Rubens – collected in the 17th century by Cardinal Spada. Not far away, the **Palazzo Doria** Pamphilj contains the private **Galleria Doria Pamphilj** where you can see important paintings by, amongst others, Caravaggio and Velasquez, *Pza del Collegio Romano 1A*. Another significant private art gallery is that of the Colonna family – the **Galleria Colonna** *V. della Pilotta 17,* – housed in the huge **Palazzo Colonna**. Here important works by Rubens, Tintoretto and Van Dyck are on show.

The old **Jewish Ghetto** is one of Rome's quaintest neighbourhoods. It faces the district of Trastevere – on the far side of the Tiber. On the **Janiculum**, the hill which dominates Trastevere, **San Pietro in Montorio,** *Pza San Pietro in Montorio,* is adjacent to Bramante's **Tempietto** – one of the greatest buildings of the High Renaissance. Below it are the church of **Santa Maria in Trastevere**, containing early Christian mosaics, and the riverside **Villa Farnesina,** *Via della Lungara 230*, which was decorated in part by Raphael. The **Porta Portese** is Trastevere's Sunday flea market.

The **Piazza Navona** takes its shape from the ancient Circus of Domitian, which it replaces. At its centre is Bernini's **Fountain of the Four Rivers** and, nearby, the **Piazza della Rotonda** provides the setting for the **Pantheon** – a Classical building still in use, once a temple, now a church.

The **Spanish Steps** link the *Pza di Spagna* with the **Pincio** hill and the **Villa Borghese** gardens, which contain the **Villa Giulia Etruscan Museum (Museo Nazionale Etrusco,** *Pzale di Villa Giulia 9* and the **Galleria e Museo Borghese,** *Villa Borghese* – unmissable if you like Bernini. At the base of the Pincio, **Santa Maria del Popolo** contains important Caravaggio paintings.

## ⇄ SIDE TRACKS FROM ROME

Although Rome itself would exhaust months of sightseeing, here is a selection of the best-known places just outside the city. **Via Appia Antica**, including the ancient **catacombs**, can be reached by bus. The **EUR district** (monumental architecture of the Fascist era, but also a funfair and a good Museum of Roman Civilisation) is on metro line B, as is **Ostia Antica** with the ruins of the ancient Roman port. Trains from Termini run to the **Alban Hills**, which include the wine areas of Frascati and Castelli Romani and the papal residence of **Castel Gandolfo**, as well as to **Tivoli**, site of Hadrian's Villa and the charmingly eccentric Villa d'Este, its garden flowing with fountains. The country town of **Viterbo**, with its medieval centre and magnificent Renaissance garden at Villa Lante (designed by Vignola), is well worth a visit and can be reached by train from Rome's Stazione San Pietro (110 km). 🚆

### ↔ Connection to Naples

From Rome termini there are excellent and frequent connections to **Naples** (see p. 360), either just to visit the city or to continue to Palermo (see p. 363 for details of the route) or to Greece.

# ST PETERSBURG

Russia's second city and former capital is the brainchild of one man, the westernising Tsar, Peter the Great. A place where almost every other building is a palace or architectural monument of some kind – there are more than 8000 listed for conservation – St Petersburg is still breathtakingly beautiful, despite the crumbling façades and peeling paintwork.

## TOURIST INFORMATION

There is at present no city information office in St Petersburg. The Intourist or service desk in any large hotel will help with tours, restaurant bookings, theatre tickets, train and flight reservations, etc. If you can get it, the very useful publication *St Petersburg, The Guide,* provides information on transport, accommodation, sightseeing, arts, nightlife, dining and shopping, amongst others. Available from hotels, bookstalls, airline offices, etc.

## ARRIVING AND DEPARTING

**Airport: Pulkovo**, *tel: 104 34.* St Petersburg's international airport is located 17 km south of the city centre. The limited facilities include a small gift shop, duty-free shop and two bars serving light snacks. The currency exchange office has limited opening hours and is generally unreliable. The **Route Taxi** (a 10-seater minibus) links both terminals to *Moskovskaya* metro station from 0700–2200, taking 10–15 mins. **Taxis**: **Matralen**, *Lyubotinsky proezd 5, tel: 298 364,* offers English-speaking drivers.

**Rail:** Helsinki has two day trains to St Petersburg, Tallinn, Riga, and Vilnius each have a daily overnight train. Prague (four times weekly) and Budapest (twice weekly) have direct sleeping-car services to St Petersburg via Warsaw, see ETT Tables 94a and 94c. Warsaw is probably the best point of access as it has a daily service which starts in Berlin (Table 56). These journeys involve transit through Belarus, but your Russian visa (must be obtained in advance) allows for this.

**Stations: Moskovsky Vokzal** (alternative name: Glavny), *Nevsky prospekt 85; tel: 168 4597* (metro: *Ploshchad Vosstaniya)* for trains to Moscow. **Varshavsky Vokzal**, *Obvodnovo kanala naberezhnaya 118; tel: 168 2690* (metro: *Baltiyskaya)* for trains to Poland and the Baltic States. **Finlandsky Vokzal**, *Lenina ploshchad 6; tel: 168 7024* (metro: *Ploshchad Lenina)* for trains to Helsinki. In a large glass case on platform 5 you can see Locomotive 293, which carried Lenin into hiding in Finland. The facilities in all terminals are basic, with a left luggage office, cheap snack bars and station stalls. The only information in English is at the Intourist offices. Watch your bags at all times. All tickets must be paid for in hard currency and you will have to show your passport. You can buy them either at the Intourist office or at a hotel or the Central Railway Booking Office *(Tsentralny Zheleznodorozhnye Kassy), (Griboedova) kanala naberezhnaya 24* (open Mon–Sat 0800–2000; Sun 0800–1600) at windows 100–104, 2nd floor. Metro: *Nevskiy Prospect.*

**Ferries:** Sea Terminal, **Morskoy Vokzal**, *Morskoy Slavy ploshchad 1; tel: 355 1310,* trolleybus: 10 and 12. **Parom Baltic Line** operate ferries to Ökesund (Sweden), *tel: 355 1616.*

**467**

## GETTING AROUND

While St Petersburg's majestic avenues are very fine to look at, they quickly become wearying to the tourist on foot. Fortunately, the public transport system is comprehensive and very cheap. All transport runs from 0530 to 0030, but beware during the night as bridges are lifted. There is no official transport map, but most city maps include bus and tram routes as well as a metro plan. Lost property, *tel: 278 3690.*

**Tickets** for all forms of local transport (buses, trams, trolley-buses and the metro) are sold at metro stations and kiosks. Buy *yedinye bilyeti* and you'll be able to ride on any form of transport for a month. You have to punch tickets on board the vehicle or in the booking hall of the station to validate them. To travel on the metro you can also buy tokens *(talony),* which should be dropped into one of the turnstiles at the top of the escalator.

The **metro** is cheap and fairly reliable, but far from comprehensive. All four lines are coloured coded. A basic knowledge of the Cyrillic alphabet is all but essential for negotiating the metro. Remember that each station has its own name, even two stations on the same site but on different lines. Stations are indicated by a large red M. Indicator boards in the station give exit and transfer information. Check you're on the right line and heading in the right direction by studying the route map on the tunnel wall. If you're changing lines, look for a sign with the word *perekhod* and the name of the station you want. To get back to street level, follow the signs *vykhod.*

Look for the signs (T) for **trams**, (A) for **buses**, (m) for **trolley-buses**. Most vehicles, especially on the *Nevsky Prospekt,* are extremely crowded and there is considerable amount or re-routing, often with no notice. As well as canal and river tours, there is a regular **hydrofoil** service (0900–2000 in summer, 30-min journey) to Peterhof (Petrodvorets), departing from the Neva Embankment, outside the Hermitage. This involves a highly pleasurable trip along the Neva River and is still extremely cheap. However double-check the time of the last hydrofoil back to town!

There are plenty of **taxis**, but beware of the unofficial ones: the authorised cabs have a chequered pattern and the letter T on the side. It is best to order a cab from a hotel (at least 1 hr in advance). Never take a taxi without agreeing a price in advance and never get into a cab where there is already another passenger. Official taxis: *tel: 312 0022* or *265 1313.*

### STAYING IN ST PETERSBURG

### Accommodation

Most of the newer hotels are in the luxury class and, as in Moscow, there is a distinct shortage of good-value medium-price and budget accommodation.

Hotel chains in St Petersburg include *Re.* Several major hotels have been renovated and upgraded in recent years, including two famous pre-revolutionary establishments: the **Astoria**, *Bolshaya Morskaya ulitsa 39; tel: 210 5757,* and the **Grand Hotel Europe**, *Mikhaylovskaya ulitsa 1/7; tel: 329 6000,* which made an appearance in the James Bond movie *Goldeneye.*

The **St Petersburg**, *Vyborgskaya naberezhnaya 5/2; tel: 542 9411,* metro: *Ploshchad Lenina,* has a nice location across the river from the Cruiser *Aurora.* It's about 20 mins walk from the Winter Palace and the prices are more than reasonable for the facilities on offer.

The main drawback of the **Pribaltiyskaya Hotel**, *Korablestroiteley ulitsa 14; tel: 356 0263,* metro *Primorskaya* then bus, is its remoteness from the centre. The **Mir Hotel**, *Gastello ulitsa 17; tel: 108 5165,* metro *Moskovskaya,* is competitively priced and is convenient for the metro and airport.

Some of the old Soviet hotels are still a bargain if you're prepared to put up with minor inconveniences. The best located is the **Oktyabrskaya Hotel**, *Ligovsky prospekt 10; tel: 277 6330,* metro: *Ploshchad Vosstaniya,* just across the road from the Moscow station.

The **St Petersburg International Hostel**, *3-ya Rozhdestvenskaya (Sovyetskaya) ulitsa 28; tel: 329 8018,* metro *Ploshchad Vosstaniya,* is an American venture aimed at youngsters and backpackers and will help out in a general way with information and reservations.

### Eating and Drinking

Eating out in St Petersburg is expensive. However, while private restaurants haven't proliferated to the same extent as Moscow, there is a reasonable amount of choice (though nothing specifically for vegetarians). A good starting point is the main shopping street, *Nevsky prospekt,* where you'll find eateries of all types, with the exception of most western fast-food chains – although McDonalds is now in the city. If money is no object, you're probably best advised to head for the major hotels, most of which offer Russian and international cuisines. The Brasserie in the **Grand Hotel Europe** is fairly typical in its elegant surroundings and attentive service.

For an unusual setting, try the **Austeria**, *Petropavlovskaya krepost; tel: 238 4262,* where

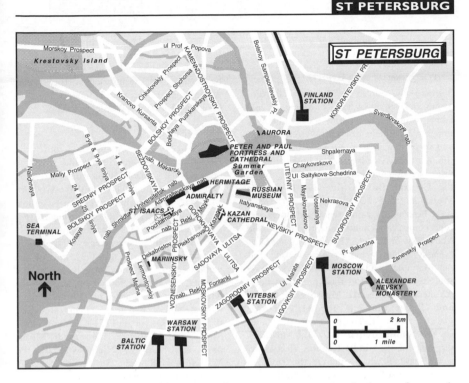

you'll be served classy Russian dishes in one of the bastions of the Peter-Paul Fortress. One of the best Georgian restaurants in St Petersburg is the **Tbilisi**, *Sytninskaya ulitsa 10; tel: 232 9391* – it's not very central but has a welcoming atmosphere, good food and fine Georgian wines. Known in the 18th century as Wulf et Béranger, the **Literaturnoe Café**, *Nevsky prospekt 18; tel: 312 6057,* is famous as the place where the poet Pushkin dined with his second before going off to be killed in a duel. The literary associations are traded on mercilessly. **Bahlsen Le Café**, *Nevsky prospekt 142*, is also expensive but has a homely atmosphere and American-style cooking. Two good lunch spots are the beautifully decorated **Nevskiy-40 Cafe**, *Nevsky prospekt 40*, and the **Beer Garden**, *Nevsky prospekt 86.*

Don't leave St Petersburg without visiting the city's famous pre-revolutionary delicatessen, still known as **Yeliseev's**, *Nevsky prospekt 52.* Even if you don't want to buy anything, the stained-glass windows, marble counters and chandeliers are definitely worth a look. There are many western-run food stores, for example **Kalinka Stockmann Supermarket**, *Finlyandsky prospekt 1,* just behind the St Petersburg Hotel.

## Communications

**Central Post Office**, *Pochtamtskaya ulitsa 9; tel: 312 83 02* (open Mon–Sat 0900–2000, Sun 1000–1800). The most convenient poste restante is **St Petersburg 1904**, *Nevsky prospekt 64.*

**Telephones**: the local area code is 812. For local calls you'll need to buy *zhetony (*tokens) from a metro station. To make an international call, go to your hotel desk or the **St Petersburg International Telephone and Telegraph Office**, *Bolshaya Morskaya ulitsa 3–5* (open daily, except 1230–1300).

## Consulates

**South Africa:** *Naberezhnaya Reki Moyki 11; tel: 553 1742,* tram no. 12.

**UK:** *Proletarskoy Diktatury ploshchad 5; tel: 119 6036,* metro: *Chernyshevskaya.*

**USA:** *Furshtadtskaya ulitsa 15; tel: 274 82 35,* metro: *Chernyshevskaya.*

## ENTERTAINMENT AND EVENTS

Theoretically you can buy tickets to all major events and venues by simply turning up and asking; however this is not usually the way things work out in practice. Western visitors end up paying in hard currency by ordering through the service bureaux of hotels, though prices are not unreasonable. An alternative is the **Central Box Office No.1**, *Nevsky Prospekt 42; tel: 311 3183.*

St Petersburg's world renowned opera and ballet company still trades under two names: the **Mariinsky** or **Kirov**, *Teatralnaya ploshchad 1.* Nijinsky, Nureyev and Pavlova all danced at the Mariinsky, and Tchaikovsky's *Nutcracker* and *Sleeping Beauty* had their premieres here. An alternative is the **MP Mussorgsky Opera and Ballet** (formerly the Maly Teatr), *Ploshchad Iskusstv 1.* The main concert venues are the **Shostakovitch B.Z.H.**, *Mikhailovskaya ulitsa 2,* the **Glinka Kapella**, *Reki Moyki naberezhnaya 20,* which continues the traditions of the Imperial Chapel Choir and the **Glinka Maly Zal**, *Nevsky prospekt 30,* the second venue of the St Petersburg Philharmonic. An all-purpose venue (rock concerts are often performed here) is the modern **Kontsertny Zal Oktyabrsky**, *Ligovsky prospekt 6.* Winter ice shows are performed at the **Yubileyni Sports Palace**, *Prospekt Dobrolyubova 18.* The **Circus**, *Ploshchad Belinskovo*, is closed July and Aug.

By far the most important festival in St Petersburg is the **Bely Nochy** (White Nights), 21 June–11 July, when the sun never sets and the city is bathed in a glowing twilight. The **Russian Orthodox Christmas** (7 Jan) and **Easter** are marked by impressive church services. Russia's newest holiday (12 June) **Independence Day**, is marked with special events.

## SHOPPING

St Petersburg's main shopping street is *Nevsky prospekt.* The beautiful shopping mall known as **Gostiny Dvor**, *Nevsky prospekt 35,* (founded in the 18th century) is still undergoing repairs – an alternative is **Passazh**, *Nevsky prospekt 48.* You can buy toiletries and other western nec-

essaries at the 24-hour supermarket near Ploshchad Vosstaniya metro.

If you want typical Russian souvenirs, begin by looking in the vicinity of **Gostiny Dvor**, where street traders usually operate. For art books, try **Iskusstvo**, *Nevsky prospekt 52.*

## SIGHTSEEING

One-hour city boat trips run from jetties by the Hermitage, Decembrist Square and Anichkov bridge on the Fontanka River from 1100–2030 every 30 mins. Book between 0900–1700, *tel: 272 4411.* River cruises leave from Riverboat Terminal, *Obukhovskoy Oborany prospect 195; tel: 262 0239.* Metro: *Proletarskaya.*

The **State Hermitage**, *Dvortsovaya naberezhnaya 32–8,* is not only one of the world's largest and most magnificent picture galleries, but also the former residence of the Russian imperial family. The **Winter Palace** was designed by the Italian architect, Bartolomeo Rastrelli, in 1754–62. A tour of the royal apartments includes the sumptuous ballroom known as the **Nicholas Hall**, the **Malachite Hall** where Alexander Kerensky's Provisional Government surrendered to Lenin's Bolshevik forces in 1917, the **throne room of Peter the Great** and the **Gallery of 1812**, with its portraits of the heroes of the Napoleonic Wars. The Hermitage catalogue is akin to a roll-call of Old Masters. All the great names are here, from Raphael and El Greco to Leonardo da Vinci. You will have to make more than one visit to walk down all 22 miles of corridors! (Open Tues–Sun 1030–1700. There are long queues to get in.)

St Petersburg's elegant main avenue, **Nevsky prospekt**, extends 5 km eastward from Palace Square to the River Neva. The imposing frontages, elaborate bridges, stunning palaces and perfectly proportioned squares combine to make it a principal sight. The avenue takes its name from the **Alexander Nevsky Monastery** at the far end of the avenue – the cemetery is the last resting place of a number of famous Russians (open daily 0800–1400).

Dating from 1703, the beautiful **Peter-Paul Fortress** was St Petersburg's first building. The present brick structure was conceived along

Renaissance lines. Inside the **Cathedral of SS Peter and Paul** are the marble tombs of Russia's imperial rulers from Peter the Great onwards.

The **Trubetskoy Bastion** was a prison almost from the word go. During the 19th century most of the revolutionary opponents of the Tsarist regime were confined here. The isolation cells are open to the public. Most of the other buildings are now interesting museums, including the **House of the Superintendent**, where political prisoners were interrogated (open Thur–Mon 1100–1700, Tues 1100–1600, closed last Tues of the month).

Moored not far from the Peter-Paul Fortress is one of Russia's most famous warships, the **Cruiser Aurora**. On the night of 7 Nov 1917 a single blank round from the bow gun was the signal for the storming of the Winter Palace (*Petrogradskaya naberezhnaya 3,* open Tues–Thur, Sat–Sun 1030–1600). There is an interesting museum inside.

A complete contrast to the Winter Palace, the **Summer Palace and Gardens** (Letny Dvorets i Letny Sad) was Peter the Great's modest summer residence. A simple, two-storey brick building in the Dutch style, the rooms contain the original furnishings as well as an intriguing collection of Peter's personal possessions (open Wed–Mon 1100–1730). The **Kazan Cathedral**, *Kazanskaya ploshchad,* open Mon–Tues, Thurs–Sat 1100–1700, has a striking colonnade modelled on St Peter's in Rome. One of the largest cathedrals in the world, **St Isaacs**, is the work of French architect Auguste de Montferrand, and took 40 years to complete. The interior was decorated with gold, bronze, precious stones, paintings and mosaics. You can climb the dome (91m) for the best panoramic view of the city (*Isaakievsky ploshchad,* open Thurs–Tues 1000–1700). The magnificent statue in the green *Senatskaya ploshchad* overlooking the river is Etienne Falconet's **Bronze Horseman**, immortalised in a poem by Pushkin; it was erected as a memorial to Peter the Great by Catherine the Great.

Housed in one of the Grand Ducal palaces, the **State Russian Museum** is a fascinating history of Russian painting from the 18th century onwards. Highlights are the canvases by artists of the Itinerant School, and works by early 20th-century artists such as Mikhail Larionov and Natalya Goncharova. *(Inzhenernaya ulitsa 4,* open Wed–Sun 1000–1700, Mon 1000–1600.)

Russia's greatest poet, **Alexander Pushkin**, lived in an apartment on the Moika Embankment from the autumn of 1836 until his death following a duel with Baron d'Anthès just a few months later. The rooms in the flat have been lovingly restored and contain many of Pushkin's personal possessions. (*Reki Moiki naberezhnaya 12,* open Wed–Mon 1100–1700, closed last Fri of every month).

No writer has closer associations with St Petersburg than the 19th century novelist, **Fyodor Dostoevsky**. Although he is most closely associated with the Haymarket, the setting for *Crime and Punishment*, it is his last home in the city that has been refurbished as a museum. *(Kuznechny pereulok 5/2,* Tues–Sun 1100–1730, closed last Wed of each month).

## OUT OF TOWN

Regular coach excursions to the environs of St Petersburg are organised by Intourist and a myriad of travel companies.

The imperial palace at **Peterhof** (sometimes called Petrodvorets), is located 29 km from St Petersburg on the southern shore of the Gulf of Finland. A hydrofoil from St Petersburg (taking 30 mins from the pier on *Dvortsovaya naberezhnay* outside the Hermitage) will take you to the **Grand Cascade**, a magnificent sequence of gilded statues and fountains. The equally splendid baroque palace is mainly the work of architect Bartolomeo Rastrelli. Open 1100–1800, closed Mon and last Tues of the month.

The main attraction at **Tsarskoe Selo (Pushkin)** is Catherine the Great's summer residence (open 1000–1700, closed Tues), a stunning baroque confection designed by the architect of the Winter Palace, Rastrelli. Twenty-two of the magnificent state rooms have been restored and opened to the public. Trains leave from the Vitebsky Vokzal for Detskoe Selo station every 20 mins (journey time 30 mins), then take bus no. 371 or 382.

# SANTIAGO DE COMPOSTELA

Santiago de Compostela has, for the last thousand years, been a magnet for millions of pilgrims. The present city was founded when the tomb of St James (Sant Iago, Spain's patron saint) was discovered in AD 813, supposedly by a shepherd who was guided to the site by a star. Destroyed in AD 997 by the Moors, the town was rebuilt during the 11th century and began its golden age. In the 12th century, the Pope declared it a Holy City: for Catholics only Jerusalem and Rome share this honour. The newer sections of the city do not have a great deal of charm, but the old town (contained within the medieval walls) is arguably the most beautiful city in Europe.

## TOURIST INFORMATION

**Regional office**: *Rúa del Villar 43; tel: (981) 58 40 81*, open Mon–Fri 1000–1400, 1600–1900 and Sat 1100–1300. **Municipal office**: *Plaza de Galicia; tel: (981) 58 44 00 or 57 39 90.*

## ARRIVING AND DEPARTING

The rail station is at *R. General Franco*, 1 km south of the old city; *tel: (981) 52 02 02.*

## GETTING AROUND

The old city is tiny and everything of interest is easily accessible on foot. A tourist 'train' tours the sights of interest, leaving *C. San Francisco* every 20 mins. Cost: Pta400.

**Estación Central de Autobuses**, *C. de San Cayetano, tel: (981) 58 77 00,* 30-min walk from the old town; bus no. 10 runs every 20 mins from *Plaza de Galicia*. There is a good local bus system and route plans are available from the Tourist Office and posted at most stops.

There are taxi ranks at the bus and train stations, *tel: (981) 58 24 50* or *59 84 88,* and at *Plaza de Galicia; tel: 56 10 28* (24 hrs).

## STAYING IN SANTIAGO

### Accommodation
There is a wide range of accommodation, from the five-star de luxe **Hotel de los Reyes Católicos**, a magnificent 16th-century pilgrim hostel built by Ferdinand and Isabella and now one of Spain's best hotels, to an array of small, relatively inexpensive guesthouses in both the old and new parts of the city. For budget accommodation in the old town, try around *Rúa del Villar* and *C. Raiña*. **Hospedaje Ramos**, *C. Raiña 18, 2nd floor, tel: (981) 58 18 59* is very central, with small, basic rooms. **Hospedaje Sofia**, *C. del Cardenal Paya 16, tel: (981) 58 51 50*, is also good value. Just outside the old town, *C. de Montero Ríos* has a number of reasonably priced hostals.

There are three large **campsites** outside the city. **As Cancelas** *(C. del 25 de Xulio 35; tel: (981) 58 02 66)* is the best option, being only 2 km from the centre (bus no. 6 from *Plaza de Galicia*). **Santiago de Compostela**, *tel: (981) 88 80 02,* is about 6 km away on the N550 road to La Coruña, while **Las Sirenas** *(Roxido–Pedro Rubia; tel: (981) 88 25 05)* is 10 km from the town. During the three weeks leading up to the feast of St James on 25 July, the town is absolutely packed and it is necessary to book accommodation well in advance.

### Eating and Drinking
There are plenty of budget restaurants around the old town, especially on the streets leading south from the cathedral. Restaurante-Bar **Los Caracoles** is a small and popular place on *C.*

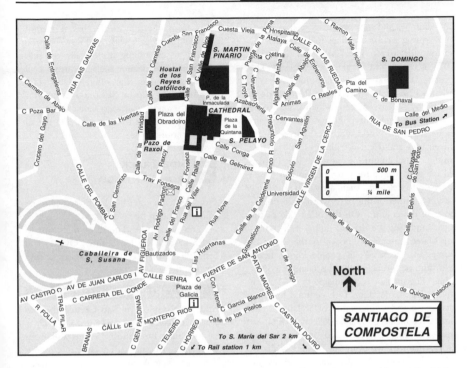

*Raíña.* **Bodecon de Xulio,** *C. del Franco 24,* has a restaurant at the back which serves reasonably-priced menús. *Campo de San Clemente,* on the edge of the old town, has two good restaurants: **La Trinidad** and **San Clemente,** both with outside seating areas.

## Communications

The main **post office** is at *Travesía de Fonseca,* tel: (981) 58 12 52, open Mon–Fri 0830–2030 and Sat 0930–1400 for most services, including poste restante *(lista de correos)* facilities.

International **telephone calls** can be made from several places in the old town, including *C. de los Bautizados 13* and *C. del Franco 48.* There are Telefónica offices at *C. de la Senra,* open daily 1000–1400, 1700–2300.

### ENTERTAINMENT AND EVENTS

*Compostelán* is a monthly guide to current events, produced in Spanish, and also in English, German and French in summer, and available from street vendors. Santiago is a lively city with a theatre, a concert hall and plenty of bars and clubs offering dancing and late-night drinking. Around the old town, free entertainment in the form of music and singing is provided by *tunas* – groups of street performers who dress in medieval clothes and busk for money.

The city's main fiesta, the **feast of St James,** takes place in the three weeks leading up to 25 July. The entertainment becomes ever more riotous until the eve of the feast itself, which begins with a massive firework display in the *Pl. del Obradoiro.* The following day the statue of St James is processed through the streets in a haze of incense, followed by *gigantes,* vast masked figures representing the Christians and Moors.

### SHOPPING

Souvenir shops abound in the old town, selling silver jewellery and memorabilia associated with Santiago, such as scallop shells and *botafumeiros* (incense burners).

### SIGHTSEEING

The old town contains an enormous number of

fine churches and monasteries as well as a host of charming secular buildings tucked down the narrow side streets. The **Cathedral** (started in 1075) is superb and should not be missed. The existing 18th-century baroque façade covers the original 12th-century façade, the **Pórtico de la Gloria** by Maestro Mateo, which is said to be the greatest single surviving work of Romanesque art in the world, with 200 exceptionally imaginative and detailed sculptures. A Jesse tree on the central column is known as the 'Pilgrim Pillar', as it is traditional for pilgrims to touch the base to celebrate their arrival in the Holy City. Centuries of this have worn deep finger-holes in the column. On the other side of the pillar and facing the altar is a figure of the sculptor Mateo, popularly known as the 'Saint of bumps on the head', as people knock heads with him in the belief that his talent is contagious. The interior is dominated by a Mexican silver altar, a dazzling 17th-century baroque altar-piece and a fine statue of St James. The museum contains a valuable collection of tapestries, including a series based on cartoons by Goya, manuscripts from the Codex Calixtus and a huge silver *botafumeiro* that is swung through the transept on special occasions.

There are four plazas surrounding the cathedral, all of them architectural gems well worth a visit. **Plaza del Obradoiro** is the largest and the site of the impressive **Hotel de los Reyes Católicos** and the former royal palace, **Pazo de Raxoi**, now a government building. Along one side of *Plaza de la Quintana* is the austere façade of the **Monasterio de San Pelayo de Antealtares**. Entrance to the church and the monastery's **Museum of Sacred Art** are via the steps at one end of the square. The 16th-century **Monastery of San Martín Pinario**, on *Plaza de la Inmaculada,* has two cloisters, one with an exquisitely designed fountain in its centre.

East of the Cathedral, the former **Monasterio do Santo Domingo** is now home to the **Museo de Pobo Galego**, devoted to Galician culture, and the **Museo Municipal**. The monastery contains a curious staircase consisting of three separate spirals, each reaching different levels, with the uppermost commanding superb views of Santiago. The 12th-century **Colegiata de Santa María del Sar**, about 2 km from the old town, has a beautiful Romanesque cloister with wild flowers sprouting from its crumbling stone walls; the pillars inside the church lean at such precarious angles that it's a wonder the building still stands. **Caballeira de Santa Susana** is a delightful park, with shady walkways, ancient oak trees and superb views of the cathedral and the surrounding countryside.

### ⇄ SIDE TRACKS FROM SANTIAGO

From Santiago you can take the coastal route south to Lisbon (see p. 264).

You can also head north on that route to San Sebastián, via La Coruña, Oviedo and Santander. You need to allow at least 2 days for this, though.

## LA CORUÑA (A CORUÑA)

**Station**: **Estación de San Cristóbal**, *Avda Joaquín Planelles s/n; tel: (981) 15 02 02,* is near the main bus station, 45 mins walk from the centre. Bus nos 1/1A go direct to the Tourist Office. Around 14 trains a day leave Santiago, the journey taking about 1¼ hrs.
**Tourist Offices**: Regional: *Dársena de la Marina s/n; tel: (981) 22 18 22.* Municipal: *Jardines de Méndez Núñez; tel: (981) 20 00 00.*

This large maritime city is famous for its association with the Spanish Armada – it was from here that it set sail for England in 1588 – and for the local heroine María Pita, who helped defend the city against the subsequent retaliations of the English navy. The town's main attractions (after its beaches) are the **Castelo de San Antón**, which now houses an Archaeology Museum, and the **Torre de Hércules**, a 2nd-century Roman lighthouse that is still in use today. The lighthouse, which was restored in the 18th century, stands at the extreme north of the peninsula, about 1.5 km from the city.

There are also a number of fine churches and gardens, including the **Church and Convent of Santo Domingo**, **Collegiate Church of Santa María del Campo** and **Jardín de San Carlos**. ⬛

# SANTIAGO–SAN SEBASTIÁN

This rail journey follows the line of the old pilgrim route (see box, p. 477). It winds across the relatively little-known north-west of Spain, joining two very different cities, the ancient pilgrimage centre of Santiago de Compostela and the chic resort of San Sebastián. It offers sights of great mountain peaks and seas of wheat and vines; tiny, perfect Romanesque chapels and magnificent cathedrals dripping in gold. At Burgos and San Sebastián, you can join the Paris–Madrid route, p. 432 (where Burgos is described), and from Santiago you can travel down the Atlantic coast to Lisbon (route p. 270).

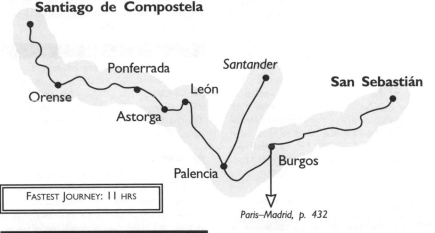

**FASTEST JOURNEY: 11 HRS**

Paris–Madrid, p. 432

Paris–Madrid, p. 432

475

## TRAINS

**ETT tables:** 672, 675, 680.

### FAST TRACK

There is no fast way to do this route, although there is a through train that takes all day. This route's whole purpose is to allow you to dawdle along the line of the pilgrim road to Santiago, a journey with magnificent scenery, and some of the finest Romanesque and medieval architecture in the world.

### ON TRACK

**Santiago–Orense (Ourense)**
There are six stopping trains a day, the journey taking about 2 hrs.

**Orense–Ponferrada**
There are six trains a day with some long intervals between trains; journey takes about 2½ hrs.

**Ponferrada–Astorga**
There are eight trains a day, but they leave at very irregular intervals and two are after midnight. The journey usually takes 1 hr 20 mins.

**Astorga–León**
The Ponferrada–Astorga trains all continue to León: allow another 45 mins for the journey.

**León–Palencia**
There are about ten trains throughout the day from around 0700 to the early hours of the next morning. The journey takes 1½ hrs.

## Palencia–Burgos

Six trains a day, some at awkward hours of the night. The journey takes about 1 hr. For the Paris–Madrid route from Burgos, see p. 432.

## Burgos–San Sebastián

About eight trains (including some during the night) make this journey, with several long gaps. The journey takes about 3–3½ hrs.

## ORENSE (OURENSE)

**Station**: *tel: (988) 21 02 02. North of the Miño River*, about 1.5 km from the city centre.
**Tourist Office**: *Curros Enríquez 1, Edificio Torre, 32003; tel: (988) 37 20 20.*

In ancient times the Romans established a settlement near three thermal springs. In the 6th–7th centuries the town became the seat of Suebian kings, but was ravaged by the Moors in AD 716 and not rebuilt until the 10th century. The modern town is a bustling commercial centre but the old section is attractive. The **Cathedral** dates from the 12th–13th centuries but was heavily renovated in the 16th–17th centuries. Its beautifully carved *Pórtico del Paraíso* is noticeably similar to the *Pórtico de la Gloria* in Santiago Cathedral (p.472). The old **Bishop's Palace** now houses the **Archaeological Museum**, while the 13th-century Romanesque **Iglesia de la Trinidad** (Trinity church) and **Puento Viejo** (old bridge) are also impressive.

## PONFERRADA

**Station**: *tel: (987) 41 00 67,* a few minutes walk from the town centre.
**Tourist Office**: *Calle de Gil y Carrasco 11; tel: (987) 42 42 36,* beside the river.

Founded in the 11th century on the site of a Roman settlement, this was a pilgrim base, named after a long-gone iron bridge across the River Sil. The largely intact old town is dominated by a huge 12th-century pentagonal **Templar Castle**, which was enlarged in the 14th century and heavily restored. The 16th-century **Basilica** and 17th-century baroque **Town Hall** are worth seeing and there are numerous attractive old buildings of humbler origin. In recent times, the town has grown into a centre of mining and heavy industry, which tends to detract from its charm.

## ASTORGA

**Station**: *Plaza de la Estación; tel: (987) 61 51 63,* about 1 km east of the town centre.
**Tourist Office**: *Plaza de España s/n; tel: (987) 61 68 38.*

Described by the Roman historian Pliny in the 1st century AD as a 'magnificent city', this is now a small country town, capital of the bleak moorland region of La Maragatería. Sections of the 6-metre **Roman walls** survive around the old town. The 15th–17th-century **Cathedral** has a bizarre mixture of styles, from late Gothic to Renaissance, baroque and Plateresque, while next door is a flamboyant **Episcopal Palace** designed by Gaudí in 1889, which now houses the **Museum of the Pilgrim Way**. Smaller buildings of interest centre on the *Plaza Mayor*.

## LEÓN

**Stations: RENFE**: *El Norte, Avda de Astorga 2; tel: (987) 27 02 02,* on the west bank of the river. **FEVE**: *Avda del Padre Isla 48; tel: (987) 27 12 10,* near the Basilica de San Isidoro.
**Tourist Office**: *Plaza de la Regla,* next to the cathedral; *tel: (987) 23 70 82.*

### ACCOMMODATION

The city has a wide range of hotels and guesthouses, ranging downwards from the ultra-luxurious **San Marcos** (see below). The Tourist Office has a list of places to stay. A good area to find budget accommodation is on and around *Avda de Roma* and *Avda de Ordoño II.*

### SIGHTSEEING

Nestling between the Bernesga and Torío rivers and surrounded by rolling *meseta* (plains), León was founded by the Romans in AD 68 as a base for the Iberian 7th Legion. Over the years, it changed hands several times and was ruled by Visigoths, Moors and Christians. In 1188 Alfonso IX summoned his first *Cortés* (parliament) here – one of the earliest democratic governments in Europe – but the court moved away permanently in the 13th century and León became little more than a trading centre until 1978, when it was made the capital of the province of León. Today it is, once again, a thriving city; an attractive place of wide streets and shady plazas. The outstanding monuments are all within easy walking distance of each other in the old city.

Of all the city's buildings, the most spectacular from the outside is the 16th-century, Plateresque **Hospital de San Marcos** (now one of Spain's finest hotels), which was founded by Ferdinand and Isabella as a pilgrim hostel. There is an **Archaeological Museum** in the church next door. What is left of the old city is still bounded by fragments of the 14th-century **city walls**, which followed the line of the original Roman (and medieval) fortifications. Thirty-one of the original 80 bastions are still standing. These are best seen around the cathedral and the Royal Basílica of San Isidoro. The **Royal Basílica of San Isidoro**, amidst the charming streets and plazas of the old town, has a not-to-be-missed pantheon, where marble pillars with superbly carved capitals support a barrel-vaulted roof covered by magnificent 12th-century frescos. The neighbouring treasury contains various reliquaries, including the finger of San Isidoro. Not far away is the Gothic **Cathedral of Santa Maria de Regla**, a graceful 13th–14th-century building with some of the finest stained glass in Europe – 125 windows, some 1800 square metres of glass, dappling the cathedral in coloured light.

### ⭢ SIDE TRACK
### FROM LEÓN

This is the best place from which to head north into the high mountains of the **Picos de Europa**, a truly stunning and relatively remote range that still shelters a few wolves and bears. Said to have been the first sign of European land seen by sailors returning from the New World, they rise almost vertically from the Bay of Biscay and offer magnificent views and walking. ⬛

### PALENCIA

**Station**: *Jardinillos s/n; tel: (979) 74 30 19,* a few minutes walk from the heart of the old city. **Tourist Office**: *Calle Mayor, 105; tel: (979) 74 00 68.*

Palencia is a long and narrow town whose prosperity comes from coal mining in the

---

## The Pilgrim's Route

Millions of pilgrims once made the arduous trek from all corners of medieval Europe to the tomb of St James the Apostle in Santiago de Compostela, bearing his badge of the scallop shell. The saint was said to have introduced Christianity to Spain, and supposedly appeared on the battlefield to fight with the Christian troops against the Moors. As churches, monasteries and hostels were built along the 'Camino de Santiago' (which is partially retraced in this rail route), it became the inspiration behind the development of Romanesque, the earliest style of medieval architecture.

---

Cantabrian Mountains to the north and grain farming on the Tierra de Campos in the south of the province. The earliest settlement was in Celtic times and Palencia was the seat of Spain's first university, founded by Alfonso VIII in the early 13th century. The main place of interest is the 14th–16th-century Gothic **Cathedral**, which has an intriguing interior, rich in both paintings and sculptures. Stone steps lead down to the Visigothic **Crypt of San Antolín**, while in the museum are some superb 16th-century tapestries and a painting of San Sebastián attributed to El Greco. Also worth a visit are the **Iglesia de Santa Clara** and the **Iglesia de San Miguel**, where an image of Christ hangs precariously from a thread above the altar.

### ⭢ SIDE TRACKS
### FROM PALENCIA

There are several fine small Romanesque churches on the pilgrim route near Palencia, most notably **San Martín de Frómista**. It is also possible to take a train north through the Picos de Europa to **Santander**, a fine coastal resort and the main ferry port to the UK. ⬛

⬌ From Palencia, the on track route goes through **Burgos**, where you can connect with the Paris–Madrid route (p. 432).

# SEVILLE (SEVILLA)

Seville, the capital of Andalusia, is a romantic, theatrical place which sparks the imagination. Its attractions include historic buildings, fictional and operatic connections (*Don Juan, Carmen* and *The Marriage of Figaro* were all set here) and fiestas, such as the April Feria and the processions of Holy Week.

## TOURIST INFORMATION

**Tourist Offices: Regional:** *Avda de la Constitución 21B; tel: (95) 422 14 04 or 421 81 57,* Mon–Sat 0900–1900, Sun 1000–1400. **Municipal:** *Paseo de las Delicias; tel: (95) 423 44 65,* Mon–Fri 0900–1315, 1630–1845. **Centro de Información de Sevilla,** *C. de Arjona s/n; tel: (95) 421 36 30.* There is also a tourist information booth at the rail station, Mon–Sat 0830–2330, Sun 0830–1400. **Viajes TIVE,** *C. Jesús de la Veracruz 27; tel: (95) 490 60 22.* There are several Tourist Information booths in strategic locations around the areas of interest, some of which give out free maps.

**Thomas Cook licensee: Ultramar Express,** *Luis de Morales 2; tel: (95) 458 2101.*

## ARRIVING AND DEPARTING

### Airport

**San Pablo Airport,** 12 km east of town, *tel: (95) 467 29 81;* tourist information desk, *tel: (95) 425 50 46.* There are no bus or train links with Seville, but taxis cost about Pta2000.

### Station

**Estación Santa Justa,** *Avda Kansas City; tel: (95) 441 41 11.* 40-min walk from the centre. Bus no. 27 goes from the station to *Plaza de la Encarnación;* no. 70 goes to *Plaza de España.* General **RENFE** enquiries, *tel: (95) 454 02 02.*

### Buses

There are two bus stations: **Prado de San Sebastián,** *C. José María Osborne 11; tel: (95) 441 71 11,* is mainly for buses to Andalucía; **Plaza de Armas, C.** *Marqués de Paradas, tel. (95) 490 80 40,* is for buses elsewhere.

## GETTING AROUND

The prime sights are in a very small area, but the secondary ones are quite widespread. Unless you are a very keen walker you'll probably want to get a few buses along the way. Most of the more interesting buildings, such as the cathedral, are east of the main street, *Avenida de la Constitución.* City tours by horse-drawn trap leave from 'ranks' next to the cathedral.

Seville is noted for its high level of petty crime and you must be on the alert for bag-snatchers and pickpockets: never leave anything of value in your hotel room or your car.

### Buses

The city bus service is efficient and route maps are often included on street maps and bus stops. C1 and C2 are circular routes around the town. Many buses pass through *Plaza de la Encarnación, Plaza Nueva* and *Avda de la Constitución.* A single ticket costs Pta120, but a **bonobus ticket** is better value (Pta550 for 10 trips), available from orange vending machines.

### Taxis

White with green lights on top, taxis in Seville are plentiful and reasonably cheap. They can be hailed in the street or ordered, *tel: (95) 458 00 00* or *462 22 22* or *496 00 00.* There is a taxi rank on *Plaza Nueva.*

## STAYING IN SEVILLE

### Accommodation

A busy tourist and business city, Seville has a wide range of hotels, including *Ml* and *Rd.* Accommodation is very difficult to obtain, unless pre-booked, during Holy Week and the April Fair. It also tends to be expensive, along with most other things in Seville.

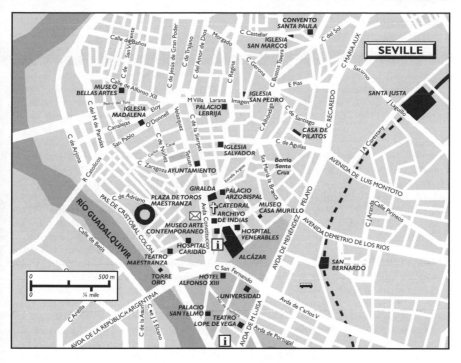

For the least expensive lodgings, try the **Barrio Santa Cruz** district: *C. Archeros*, the streets around *Plaza Nueva (C. Marqués de Paradas* or *C. Gravina)*, or the area west of *Plaza Nueva* towards the river. **Pension Fabiola**, *C. Fabiola 16 (in Santa Cruz), tel: (95) 421 83 46*, has basic rooms arranged around a central courtyard. **Hostal Aguilas**, *C. Aguilas 15; tel: (95) 421 31 77*, has a small number of clean, well-furnished rooms. **Pension Alcázar**, *C. Dean Miranda 12; tel: (95) 422 84 57*, is a pension right next to the Alcazar wall. The rooms are beautifully furnished and decorated, with ceiling fans or air-conditioning. **Hotel Simon** (1-star), *García de Vinuesa 19; tel: (95) 422 66 60*, is in a former 18th-century mansion. **HI**: *C. Isaac Peral 2; tel: (95) 461 31 54*. All three **campsites** are about 12 km out of town. The main one is **Camping Sevilla**, *Ctra. Madrid–Cádiz km 534; tel: (95) 451 43 79*, near the airport: take either the Empresa Casal bus towards *Carmona* (hourly) or the no. 70 to *Parque Alcosa* (800 m away). The other two sites are at **Dos Hermanas: Club de Campo**, *Avda de la Libertad 13; tel: (95) 472 02 50*, and **Camping Villsom**, *Ctra. Seville–Cádiz km 554.8; tel: (95) 472 08 28)* and served by buses from *Prado de San Sebastián* every 30–45 mins.

## Eating and Drinking

Seville is probably the best place to sample such typical Andalusian dishes as *gazpacho* (chilled tomato and pepper soup) and *pescaíto frito* (deep-fried fish). Eating out can be expensive, but there are a few places with excellent menus for around Pta700, such as **Café Bar El Callejon**, *C. Adriano 24*, and **Café Bar Nipal**, *Pasaje de las Delicias*. For delicious snacks try **Café Bar Guadalquivir**, *C. García de Vinuesa*. The liveliest bars and restaurants, frequented by students, are in **Barrio Santa Cruz**. For a meal with a view, try restaurants on the other side of the river by the Puente de San Telmo. The **Rio Grande** is particularly good, but expensive.

Buying your own food is a cheap option and to be recommended if you go to the **Mercado del Arenal**, *C. Arenal* and *C. Pastor*, the town's largest market.

## Communications

The main **post office** is at *Avda de la Constitución 32; tel: 421 64 76*, open Mon–Fri 0800–2100, Sat 0900–1900. The facilities for poste restante (*lista de correos*) close on Sat afternoons.

International **phone calls** can be made from *Plaza de la Gavidia 7*, open Mon–Sat 1000–1400 and 1730–2200 or *Pasaje Sierpes 11*.

## Consulates

**Australia:** *Federico Rubio 14; tel: 422 02 40.*
**Canada:** *2nd Floor, Avda de la Constitución 30; tel: (95) 422 94 13.*
**Ireland:** *P2A Sta Cruz 6; tel: 421 63 61.*
**UK**: *Plaza Nueva 8; tel: (95) 422 88 74/5.*
**USA**: *Paseo de las Delicias 7; tel: (95) 423 18 83/4/5.*

### ENTERTAINMENT

*El Giraldillo*, produced monthly, is a free guide to current events in Seville.

Seville is the home of **flamenco** and it's easy to find, but you should be selective because it is often staged specially for tourists. If you ask around, you should be able to find more genuine (and cheaper) performances. There are various clubs with flamenco evenings, but they can be quite expensive, especially during festival time in the spring. An excellent one to try is **El Gallo** in *Barrio de Santa Cruz*.

Seville is full of extremely lively bars, clubs and discos, notably in the *Los Remedios* district in the south of the city and on *C. Betis* next to the river, but little seems to happen until close to midnight. If you're looking for activity and atmosphere a little earlier in the evening, try the other side of the river, where there is a range of tapas bars, some of which have live music. **Patio de San Eloy**, *C. San Eloy 7,* is a good bet, as is **La Carbonería**, *C. Lesies* in *Barrio de Santa Cruz*. Dining out in Spain happens later than in northern Europe and North America, and nightlife doesn't get going until after dining hours. The Spanish stay up *very* late.

### SIGHTSEEING

Most places of interest are in the *Barrio de Santa Cruz*. A pleasant place for a stroll, it lives up to the idealised image of Spain; white and yellow houses with flower-bedecked balconies and attractive patios. The focal point is the **Giralda**, a minaret that has towered over the old city since the 12th century and which now serves as belfry to the cathedral. Built by the Almohad rulers 50 years before Ferdinand and Isabella's Christian Reconquest, it is in excellent condition and worth climbing (if you are reasonably fit): it was designed for horsemen to ride up and consists of a series of gentle ramps. The upper storeys provide splendid views of Seville.

The **Cathedral** is the largest Gothic structure in the world (Mon–Sat 1030–1700, Sun 1030–1330; Pta600, students Pta200). The **Capilla Mayor** has a vast gilded retable which took 82 years to complete. **Sacristía Mayor** houses the treasury and **Sacristía de los Cálices** contains Murillos and a Goya. Also of interest are the tomb of Christopher Columbus (in the southern aisle) and the **Patio de los Naranjos** (orange-tree courtyard).

The **Alcázar** was inspired by the Alhambra of Granada (see p. 309), but has been marred by later additions. Tues–Sat, 0930–1800, Sun and public holidays 1000–1300. Of particular note are the **Salon de Embajadores**, where Columbus was received by Ferdinand and Isabella on his return from the Americas, **Patio de las Muñecas**, **Salon of Charles V** and the shady, interconnected gardens separated by arched Moorish walls. The neighbouring **Casa Lonja** contains a collection of documents relating to the discovery of the Americas (Seville was the main home port of the *conquistadores*).

**Hospital de la Caridad**, *C. Temprado,* was commissioned by a reformed rake, reputed to have been the real-life inspiration for Don Juan. The church contains several works by Murillo and Valdés Leal. Ghoulish and disturbing, they are not for the faint-hearted.

---

Colour section: (i) St Petersburg (p.467); Semana Santa processions, Seville (p.478).

(ii) Stockholm at sunset (p.482); Venice (p.491).

(iii) Tomb of the Unknown Soldier, Warsaw (p.519); Tatra Mountains (p.513); inset, Split Harbour, Croatia (p.498).

(iv) Zurich (p.537): St Peter's Church; Town Hall Square, Tallinn, Estonia (p.533).

Nowadays, the 18th-century **Fábrica de Tabacos** (on *C. de San Fernando* south of the Alcázar) houses parts of the university, but it was once a tobacco factory, employing over 10,000 women (supposedly including Carmen).

South-east of the factory is **María Luisa Park**, a delightful mixture of wilderness areas and formal gardens laid out for a trade fair in 1929. It contains **Plaza de España**, which was the central pavilion, and **Plaza de América**, a peaceful place where the excellent **Archaeological Museum** (closed Mon) is situated. The Latin American countries which exhibited at the fair each built a pavilion in its own national style, most of which survive.

The **Museo de Bellas Artes** (closed Mon, free for Europeans) *Pl. del Museo* (between *Santa Cruz* and *Cartuja),* has a collection of 13th–20th-century Spanish paintings that is second only to that in the Prado. The decorative **Maestranza** (Bullring), near the river, dates from the 18th century. Fights are held every Thur Mar–Oct. A short way along the river bank is the 13th-century **Torre do Oro** (Golden Tower), named after the gold-coloured tiles that once covered its twelve sides. It now contains a small naval museum. **Cartuja Park** (across the river from the old town) was the site of Expo 92 and is due to reopen as a science and technology park with theatres and concert halls for staging cultural events.

↺ **SIDE TRACKS FROM SEVILLE**

### JEREZ DE LA FRONTERA

**Station**: *Plaza de la Estación; tel: (956) 34 23 19.* A 10-min walk from the centre of town.
**Tourist Office**: *C. Alameda Cristina 7; tel: (956) 33 11 50 or 33 11 62.*

From Seville there are several trains daily, taking about 1 hr on AVE trains and 1 hr 20 mins via any other service.

The town has given its name to its main product, sherry, and the *bodegas* are the town's main attraction. Among them you will find such familiar names as Harvey and Sandeman. Most *bodegas* offer tours that finish with a tasting for a small fee. Jerez is also known for its **Real Escuela de Andaluza de Arte Equestre** (Royal Andalusian School of Equestrian Art). The school stages a show every Thur at 1200 (on other weekdays you can watch the training sessions 1100–1300 and visit the stables). The **old town** (to the west) is an attraction in itself, with many palms and orange trees and a number of attractive old mansions. Other places of interest are: the **Centro Andaluz de Flamenco** (a centre of flamenco), the **Alcázar** and the **Plaza de la Asunción**.

### CÁDIZ

**Station**: *Plaza de Sevilla s/n; tel: (956) 25 43 01.* Centrally located, close to *Pl. de San Juan de Díos.*
**Tourist Office**: *Calderón de la Barca 1; tel: (956) 21 13 13.*

Regular services operate daily from Jerez de la Frontera to Cádiz, taking about 40 mins by Talgo and 45 mins by any other service. From Seville to Cádiz, there are around 12 services daily, the journey taking about 1½ hrs by Talgo, 2 hrs by other services.

Cádiz was founded in 1100 BC by the Phoenicians and is one of the oldest settlements in Spain. It was a vitally important port at the time of the conquest of the Americas (which was why Sir Francis Drake attacked and burnt it) and reached its height of power and prosperity in the 18th century. There is a huge carnival every Feb, which is one of the best in Spain. The **Catedral Nueva** (new cathedral) dates from the 18th century and is perfectly proportioned, with a dome of glazed yellow tiles. **Museo Histórico Municipal** contains an 18th-century ivory and mahogany scale model of Cádiz, while **Museo de Cádiz** has an eclectic display of exhibits from sarcophagi to paintings by Murillo, Van Dyck and Rubens. The chapel of the **Hospital de Mujeres** houses El Greco's *St Francis in Ecstasy* and **Oratorio de la Santa Ceuva** has, among other works, three Goya frescos.

The **Torre Tavira** offers panoramic images of Cádiz, both from the top of the tower and in the room below, via a mirror and lens on the roof. ↺

# STOCKHOLM

The Swedish capital is built on islands where the Baltic meets the fresh-water Lake Mälaren. The Stockholm archipelago consists of 24,000 islands, rocks and skerries and there's unspoiled countryside within the city limits. Cultural attractions include some imaginative museums.

## TOURIST INFORMATION

**Tourist Centre: Sverigehuset (Sweden House)**, *Hamng. 27; tel: 789 24 90;* Mon–Fri 0800–1800, Sat–Sun 0900–1700 (June–Aug); Mon–Fri 0900–1800, Sat–Sun 1000–1500 (Sept–May). From Centralstation, walk up *Klarabergsg.* to *Sergels Torg* (marked by an oddly-shaped pillar), then right on *Hamng.* There's a full information service and an **Excursion Shop** section *(tel: 789 24 15)*. Other branches: **Kaknästornet**, *Gardet; tel: 789 24 35,* daily 0900–2200 (May–Aug); daily 0900–2100 (Apr, Sept); **Stadshuset (City Hall)**, *Hantverkarg. 1; tel: 508 290 00,* daily 0900–1700 (May–Oct). Small city maps are freely available, but a larger-scale one is a good investment.

The **Stockholm Card (Stockholmskort)** (SKr.185 for 24 hrs, SKr.350 for 48 hrs and SKr.470 for 72 hrs) from Tourist Offices, stations, **Pressbyran** and most accommodation) provides free public transport, free entrance to many attractions and wide-ranging discounts.

## ARRIVING AND DEPARTING

### Airport
**Stockholm Arlanda** *(tel: 797 60 00)* is 45 km north of Stockholm. The **Flygbuss**; *tel: (08) 600 10 00* (airport bus) takes about 40 mins from Cityterminalen and runs every 10–15 mins 0425–2200; SKr.60.

### Stations
The labyrinthine **Stockholm C (Central-station)** is in the city centre (0400–midnight).

Facilities include showers (on the lower level), a bus information/ticket office and the city's longest opening hours for postal services and currency exchange. Anything you need should be in (or adjoining) the main hall. If not, try **Cityterminalen** (long-distance bus station), *Klarabergsviadukten:* across the road, but linked by tunnels. For domestic train information; *tel: (020) 75 75 75* (24 hrs); for international information; *tel: 762 28 21* (0800–2200).

### Buses
**Swebus** (Intercity), *Cityterminalen; tel: (020) 64 06 40,* open Fri 0830–1800/1900, Sat 0830–1330, Sun 1100–1800.

## GETTING AROUND

A wealth of free English-language literature includes the useful *Stockholm This Week*. *Discover Stockholm* (SKr.49) is a 150-page illustrated guide that makes an excellent souvenir.

**Storstockholms Lokaltrafik (SL)**, run the excellent bus and metro network. Main office: lower level of *Sergels Torg; tel: 600 10 00;* Mon–Thur 0830–1830, Fri 0830–1730. There's a branch in Centralstation, open Mon–Sat 0630–2330, Sun 0700–2330.

Single **tickets** (from drivers: SKr.7 to board, plus 7 per zone) are valid for 1 hr. **Rabatt-kuponger** provide 20 coupons for SKr.90 and **Turistkorten** provide unlimited travel for 24 hrs (SKr.60) or 3 days (SKr.120). There are reductions for students and seniors. Multi-ride tickets are available from **SL**, **Pressbyrån** and the **Tourist Centre**.

The metro, **Tunnelbanan (T-banan)**, has three lines (red, green and blue). Trains are fast and frequent 0500–0100. Metro stations display a blue 'T' on a white background.

**City buses** are frequent 0500–midnight and there's a night service *(nattbus)*.

**Ferries:** the main local operator is **Wax-holmsbolaget**, *Strömkajen; tel: 679 58 30.* **Båtluffarkort** allows 16 days of travel (SKr.260 from the Excursion Shop or Waxholmsbolaget

482

offices). Single tickets can be purchased when you board. **Strömma Kanalbolaget**, *Skeppsbron 22; tel: 23 33 75*, also operate summer tours. **Cinderella Boats**, *tel: (08) 20 88 25*, offer archipelago transport and guided tours.

The larger **taxi** companies, **Taxi Stockholm** *(tel: 15 00 00)*, **Taxi Kurir**, *(tel: 30 00 00)* and **Taxi 020** *(tel: (020) 85 04 00)* are usually cheapest and have fixed rates from the airport. If you take a 'Fritaxi' cab, make sure you agree the fare before setting out.

### STAYING IN STOCKHOLM

### Accommodation

**Hotellcentralen**, the official accommodation booking service, is in the main hall of Centralstation; *tel: 789 24 25*, daily 0800–1900 (May, Sept); daily 0700–2100 (June–Aug); Mon–Fri 0800–1700, Sat–Sun 0800–1400 (Oct–Apr). Advance bookings are free, but there's a fee for same-day bookings. Pick up a (free) copy of *Stockholm Hotel Guide*.

Hotel chains include *BW, FE, RC, Re, Rk, SA, Sc, Sd, Sh, Sn* and *Tp*. **Grand Hotel**, *Blasieholmskajen 8; tel: 679 35 00*, has been voted one of the best in the world. **First Hotel Reisen**, *Skeppsbron 12–14; tel: 22 32 60*, is known for its authentic maritime décor. **Hotel Stockholm**, *Normalmstorg. 1; tel: 678 13 20*, is a block from the Tourist Office and has lots of bus-stops outside (including the useful no. 47).

**HI:** try **AF Chapman**, *Skeppsholmen; tel: 679 50 15* (bus no. 65), a tall ship moored in the harbour; or **Långholmen**, *Södermalm; tel: 668 05 10*, once a prison (nearest metro: *Hornstull)*. The most central **campsite** is **Östermalm City Camping**, *Fiskartorpsvägen, Östermalm; tel: 10 29 03*, open mid June–mid Aug. **Bredäng**, *tel: 97 70 71*, 10 km southwest of the city (metro: *Bredäng)* opens all year.

### Eating and Drinking

A wide range of cuisine is available. **Den Gyllene Freden**, *Österlånggatan 51*, has been going strong since the 1720s. **Operakällaren**, *at the Opera House*, was *the* place for so long that Stockholmers often refer to it as 'the café'. It consists of several restaurants, from gourmet to **Bakfickan** (good for a cheap lunch). **Stadshus**

**Källoren**, *basement of Stadshuset*, has a great atmosphere; dishes range from a cheap lunch to the Nobel Prize banquet menu. **Kungshallen**, *Kungsgatan 44*, offers a wide choice. A kiosk on *Slussen* sells fried Baltic herring on crispbread.

### Communications

The **main post office**, *Vasagatan 28–34; tel: 781 20 55*, opens Mon–Fri 0800–1830, Sat 1000–1400. **Central Station branch** opens Mon–Fri 0700–2200, Sat–Sun 1000–1900.

**Telecenter**, *Centralstation*, open daily 0800–2100. Buy phonecards here or from vending machines in the station. The telephone code for Stockholm is *08*.

### Money

**Forex** branches include *Central Station* (ground level), daily 0800–2100; *Cityterminalen*, Mon–Fri 0800–2000, Sat 1000–1500; *Sweden House (Tourist Information Centre)*, Mon–Fri 0900–1800. **Valutaspecialisten**, *Kungsgatan 30*, opens Mon–Fri 0800–1900, Sat 0900–1600.

### Embassies and Consulates

**Australia:** *Block 5, Sergels Torg 12; tel: 613 29 00.*
**Canada:** *Tegelbacken 4; tel: 453 30 00.*
**South Africa:** *Linnégatan 76; tel: 24 39 50.*
**UK:** *Skarpögatan 6–8; tel: 671 90 00.*
**USA:** *Strandvagen 101; tel: 783 53 00.*

**483**

### ENTERTAINMENT AND EVENTS

*Stockholm This Week* carries listings. There are around seventy theatres and concert halls and, in summer, you can enjoy **free concerts** in the parks. Most films are shown in the original language. **Cosmonova Omnitheatre** (in Naturhistoriska) offers highly advanced **planetarium** performances and **Omnimax** films.

The reasonably varied nightlife concentrates around *Stureplan, Kungsträdgården, Berzelii Park* and *Birger Jarlsg.*, while **Södermalm** is the area with most pubs. Some clubs are open until 0500, and may have a minimum age limit of 25.

The major annual event is the **Stockholm Water Festival** (ten days in Aug), with varied celebrations, including many water-oriented activities. Other regular events include a **kite festival** (May), **National Day** (6 June) and an

## Skärgården Peninsula

Skärgården Peninsula (the Archipelago) is in Stockholm's back garden, an area of 24,000 islands and skerries, of which some are residential and others uninhabited. There are even one or two, such as **Grinda**, which are preserved as nature and recreational areas. A boat trip to the Archipelago gives a greater insight into the watery nature of Stockholm's existence. Regular services provide access several times a day. **Vaxholm**, a popular retreat, is an hour's journey from the centre, with other options available depending on how much time you have.

international jazz and blues festival (late June–early July). **Regattas** are held frequently in the summer. Stockholm has also been selected as Cultural Capital of Europe for 1998.

### SHOPPING

The main areas are *Hamngatan, Drottninggatan, Sergels Torg* and *Gamla Stan*. **NK**, *Hamng. 18–20*, and **Åhléns**, *Klarabergsg. 50*, are well-stocked department stores. Many shops specialise in Swedish crystal. Other specialists include: **Æter & Essencefabriken**, *Wallingatan 14* (spices) and **Stockholms Läns Hemslöjd-förening**, *Drottningg.* (Swedish handicrafts). **24-hour pharmacy: C W Scheele**, *Klarabergsg. 64; tel: 24 82 80*.

The most popular markets, a mixture of stalls and indoor food halls, are **Östermalmstorg**, **Hötorget** and **Söderhallarna**.

### SIGHTSEEING

Many museums are closed on Mon, outside summer; summaries, times and prices are given in *Stockholm This Week*.

In the 1970s, the remains of the old town wall were discovered and incorporated into **Stockholms Medeltidsmuseet** (Museum of Medieval Stockholm). On a small island accessible from Norrbro (one of the bridges linking Norrmalm and Gamla Stan, bus nos 43/62), it presents an imaginative reconstruction of

medieval life. **Medelhavsmuseet** (Museum of Mediterranean and Near Eastern Antiquities), *Fredsg. 2* (metro: *Kungsträdgården)*, has a very good Egyptian section. The nearby **National-museum** (National Swedish Museum of Fine Arts), *Blasieholmskajen*, is Sweden's largest art museum. **Historiska Museet** (Museum of National Antiquities), *Narvavägen 13–17* (metro: *Karlaplan/Östermalmstorg)*, is famous for the **Guldrummet** (Golden Room), an underground chamber that contains one of Europe's richest collections of prehistoric and medieval gold and silver jewellery.

North of the centre (metro: *Universitetet)* are three attractions: **Naturhistoriska Riks-museet** (Swedish Museum of Natural History), *Frescativägen 40*, covers animals, fossils and minerals, the basement concentrating on polar regions; **Bergianska Botaniska Trädgården** (the Botanical Gardens), *Frescati*, includes **Victoriahuset**, home of the world's largest water-lily; and at **Fjärilsa Fågelhuset** (Butterfly House), *Hagaparken*, you can see tropical butterflies and birds in a natural environment created by a 400 square-metre hothouse.

On **Kungsholmen** (immediately west of Centralstation), the 1920s **Stadshuset** (City Hall), *Hantverksgatan 1*, hosts the annual Nobel Banquet (Dec). Of particular note are the 19 million mosaics in the **Golden Room** and royal murals in the **Prince's Gallery**.

**Björkö** (an island in Lake Mälaren) is the site of the **Birka Vikingstaden** (Birka, the Viking Town), accessible by ferry from **Stadhusbron**.

### Gamla Stan (the old town)

**Stortorget**, the main square of the old town, is surrounded by medieval buildings with colourful façades and gabled roofs, while *Prästgatan St* has changed little since the 16th century. **Kunglia Slottet**, *Slottsbacken*, once the royal residence (metro: *Gamla Stan)*, offers several museums, among them the **Skattkammaren**. The old royal apartments can also be visited. **Storkyrkan** (Main Church), *Slottsbacken*, where royal marriages take place, has a fine 15th-century wooden sculpture of St George and the Dragon, while the 13th-century **Riddarholmskyrkan**, *Riddarholmen*, has been the resting-place of monarchs for six centuries

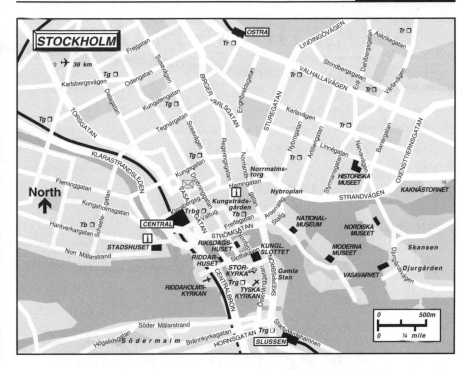

and is adorned with ornate sarcophagi and colourful coats of arms.

### Djurgården

Bus nos 44/47 stop near each of the main attractions in the city's pleasure garden. In summer there are also ferries and a private tram.

The eastern section of this large island, together with **Ladugårdsgärdet** (to the north), forms **Eko Park**, a 56 square-km nature reserve. To the north, on *Ladugårdsgärdet*, is **Kaknästornet** (TV tower), Scandinavia's tallest building, with a viewing platform at 128m.

Along the western side are various man-made attractions. Don't miss **Vasamuseet**, built to house *Vasa,* a 17th-century warship dredged up from the harbour. Explanations of her features are given and she is surrounded by exhibits. The **Nordiska Museet** (Nordic Museum) chronicles Swedish life since the 16th century. **Aquaria Vattenmuseum** (Water Museum) is a high-tech complex that enables you to spend 24 hrs in a rain-forest and get close to marine creatures (entrance fees help to save endangered rain-forest). **Gröna Lund Tivoli** offers rides and live entertainments.

**Skansen open-air museum** consists primarily of over 150 historical buildings and a large **zoo** specialising in Nordic fauna. At the **Aquarium**, walk through free-flying macaws, under a tree festooned with sloths and through a nocturnal section: the extra entrance fee is worthwhile. Skansen work with WWF and look after their animals, born in captivity.

### OUT OF TOWN

**Drottningsholms Slott** (Drottningholm Palace), home of the royal family, is 11 km west of the city (1 hr by boat; or 45 mins by metro to *Brommaplan,* then bus nos 310/323). Several rooms are on view and there are tours of the 18th-century **theatre**. **Kina Slott** (the Chinese pavilion and a World Heritage Site), at the far end of the gardens, was a summer cottage.

From Stockholm, it is possible to connect with Helsinki (p.240) via an overnight sailing.

# STOCKHOLM–NARVIK

Sweden's coastal towns north of Stockholm offer a variety of attractions, from the university setting of Uppsala to the clean refinement of Gävle (pronounced 'Yervle') and Sundsvall. A long but enjoyable bus ride connects Sundsvall with Umeå (no rail pass discounts).

The northern stretch of this route runs above the Arctic Circle, where reindeer roam and local Sami peoples retain their traditional, if modernised, ways. Travellers are well cared for by local Tourist Offices throughout, making this an easy trip.

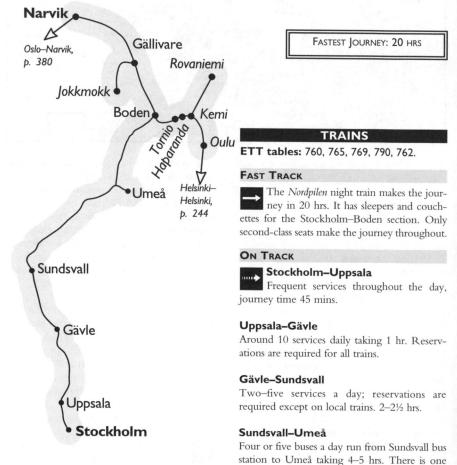

Narvik

Oslo–Narvik, p. 380

Gällivare

Rovaniemi

Jokkmokk

Boden    Kemi

Tornio Haparanda    Oulu

Umeå    Helsinki–Helsinki, p. 244

Sundsvall

Gävle

Uppsala

Stockholm

FASTEST JOURNEY: 20 HRS

## TRAINS

**ETT tables:** 760, 765, 769, 790, 762.

### FAST TRACK

The *Nordpilen* night train makes the journey in 20 hrs. It has sleepers and couchettes for the Stockholm–Boden section. Only second-class seats make the journey throughout.

### ON TRACK

**Stockholm–Uppsala**
Frequent services throughout the day, journey time 45 mins.

**Uppsala–Gävle**
Around 10 services daily taking 1 hr. Reservations are required for all trains.

**Gävle–Sundsvall**
Two–five services a day; reservations are required except on local trains. 2–2½ hrs.

**Sundsvall–Umeå**
Four or five buses a day run from Sundsvall bus station to Umeå taking 4–5 hrs. There is one overnight train from Stockholm, Uppsala and

Gävle to Umeå with sleeping-cars, couchettes and second-class seats.

## Umeå–Luleå

Four of the Sundsvall–Umeå buses continue to Luleå taking a further 4½ hrs.

## Luleå–Boden

Four trains a day make the 25-min run.

## Boden–Gällivare

Three trains a day cross the Arctic Circle (look out for the station – Polcirkeln). Journey time: 2 hrs–2 hrs 45 mins.

## Gällivare–Narvik

Three trains, taking approximately 4 hrs.

## UPPSALA

**Station:** Uppsala C, *tel: (018) 65 22 10.* East of the centre, 10-min stroll to the Tourist Office: walk straight up *Bangårdsg* to the river, turn right and cross the second bridge – the Tourist Office is halfway along the block. **Tourist Office:** *Fyris Torg 8; tel: (018) 27 48 00.* Mon–Fri 1000–1800, Sat 1000–1500, also Sun 1200–1600 (July–mid Aug). The free leaflet *Worth Seeing in Uppsala/Uppland* has tourist information and there's an adequate free map.

### ACCOMMODATION

**Room agency**; *tel: (018) 10 95 33,* Mon–Fri 0900–1700, can book private rooms. Hotel chains: BW, SC, Sd. **Hotel Svava,** *Bangårdsg 24; tel: (018) 13 00 30,* opposite the station, an easy walk from the Tourist Office. **Plantan,** *Dragarbrunnsgatan 18; tel: (018) 10 43 00,* is part hostel/part cheap hotel; turn right out of the station, 100m away. **Campus,** *Ulleråkersvägen 17; tel: (018) 711 210,* is similar. Bus nos 16/20. **Grand Hotell Hörnan,** *Bangårdsgatan 1; tel: (018) 13 93 80,* is old-style classy and more expensive. **HI:** *Sunnersta Herrgård, Sunnerstavägen 24; tel: (018) 32 42 20,* 6 km south (bus nos 4/20/50 to *Herrgårdsvägen).* **Fyris Camping,** *Idrottsg 2; tel: (018) 27 49 60,* by river, 2 km north (bus nos 4/6/25/50). Open all year.

### SIGHTSEEING

The central sights are walkable if you don't want to wait for a bus. Furthest from the station are the two Linnaeus gardens (in different directions): 30 mins at a slow pace. On summer weekends, **Lennakatten vintage railway** runs on a narrow-gauge line from Östra station (behind Uppsala C).

The twin towers of the French-Gothic **Domkyrka** dominate the skyline. It was consecrated in 1435, but there were major restorations in the 18th and 19th centuries. Virtually every inch of the side chapels is covered by tapestries or wall and ceiling paintings. The impressive sarcophagi include those of St Erik, Gustaf Vasa and Linnaeus. The **archiepiscopal museum** boasts one of Europe's finest collections of ecclesiastical textiles.

The 16th-century **Uppsala Slott** (Red Castle), overlooking the town, was built by King Gustaf Vasa, who broke ties with the Vatican and pointed his cannons directly at the archbishop's palace. Arranged in the crumbling walls are **Vasavinjetter** (Vasa vignettes: tableaux with wax figures and appropriate soundtracks), illustrating different aspects of castle life.

The **university** is Scandinavia's oldest (founded 1477). One of the buildings, **Gustavianum,** *Akademig,* contains an **anatomical theatre** where public dissections of executed convicts were a 17th-century tourist attraction (open 1100–1600 mid June–mid Sept only). Other museums in the same building cover **Egyptology** and **Nordic countries**. Millions of books, manuscripts and maps are on display in **Carolina Rediviva Universitetsbiblioteket** (library), corner *Övre Slottsg/Drottningg,* notably half of a 6th-century Silver Bible – a rare example of the extinct Gothic language, written on purple vellum.

An 18th-century professor of botany, Linnaeus (Carl von Linné), developed a system of plant and animal classification that is still in use. His former residence is now a museum, **Linnéanum,** in the small **Linnéträdgården** (Linnaeus gardens), *Svartbäcksg 27.* His **Botaniska Trädgården** (botanical gardens), *Thunbergsvägen 2–8,* are much larger.

### OUT OF TOWN

**Gamla Uppsala (Old Uppsala),** north of today's city, was the cradle of Swedish

487

civilisation and almost certainly the centre of a pre-Christian cult. Hundreds of tombs are dominated by huge grassy mounds, thought to be the resting-places of three 6th-century kings. Alongside them are the rebuilt **Uppsala Kyrka**, a church containing 15th-century frescos, and a small museum village.

## GÄVLE

**Station:** *tel: (026) 14 40 50.* At the eastern end of the city, 5-min walk from the centre.

**Tourist Office:** *Kyrkog 14, Berggrenski gården (behind Åhléns); tel: (026) 14 74 30.* Mon–Fri 0900–1800, Sat 0900–1400, Sun 1100–1600 (June–Aug); Mon–Fri 1000–1700 (Sept–May).

**Nya Järnvägshotellet**, *Centralplan 3; tel: (026) 12 09 90*, opposite the station, is cheap. Mid-range **Aveny**, *Södra Kungsgatan 31; tel: (026) 61 55 90*, is clean, near *Gamla Gefle.* **HI:** *Södra Rådmansgatan 1; tel: (026) 62 17 45*, also on the edge of *Gamla Gefle* – great location.

**Gamla Gefle** is the surviving part of the old town, with cobbled streets and pretty frame houses. At the regional **Gävleborgs Länsmuseum**, *Södra Strandg 20*, you can learn about its history. **Silvanum Skogsmuseum** (Silvanum forestry museum), *Kungsbäcksvägan 32*, a pleasant 15-mins riverside walk, covers forestry and conservation. **Heliga Trefaldighets kyrka** is a 17th-century church containing wood-carvings and an 11th-century rune stone. **Sveriges Järnvägsmuseet** (National Railway Museum), *Rälsgatan 1.* From the station, turn left down *Muréngatan* for about 1 km, passing through some pictursque former trading warehouses.

## SUNDSVALL

**Station:** *tel: (060) 183 50*, 10-mins walk from the main square.

**Tourist Office:** *ferry terminal (5-min walk east of the centre); tel: (060) 67 18 00.* Mon–Fri 0900–1900, Sat 1000–1700, Sun 1100–1700 (June–Aug); Mon–Fri 1100–1700 (Sept–May).

**Continental**, *Radhusgatan 13*, in the centre; *tel: (060) 15 00 60*, is a lovely, homely and inexpensive hotel. **Scandic** (a chain hotel), *Esplanaden 29; tel: (060) 17 16 00*, has great views from the upper floors. Moderate.

The medieval **Alnö gamla kyrka** (take bus no. 1 to Alnö) contains 16th-century frescos in

good condition. **Gustav Adolfs Kyrkan**, a red-brick edifice, has an unusual modern interior. **Norra Bergets Hantverks och Friluftsmuseum** is an open-air museum with an eclectic mix of handicrafts: to get there entails a 3-km climb up **Gaffelbyn**, but the views are great. The **Kulturmagasinet** is an interesting complex of restored warehouse buildings, now housing a small local museum and gallery.

## UMEÅ

**Station:** *tel: 15 58 70*, 5-min walk north of the centre. Basic facilities: lockers, toilets and a ticket/information office.

**Ferries: Silja Line**, *tel: (090) 71 44 00*, dock at Holmsund, 16 km out of town. A shuttle bus leaves from behind the Tourist Office one hour before ferries depart and meets incoming ferries. Journey time 20–25 mins.

**Tourist Office:** *Renmarkstorget 15; tel: (090) 16 16 16.* Mon–Fri 0800–2000, Sat 1000–1700, Sun 1100–1700 (June–Aug); Mon–Fri 1000–1800 (Sept–May).

Hotel chains: *HI, Sc.* The **Strand**, *Västra Strandgatan 11; tel: (090) 12 90 20*, is budget and has a central riverfront location. It is overshadowed, literally, by the upmarket first **Hotel Grand**, *tel: (090) 77 88 70*, and the top-market **Umeå Plaza**, *tel: (090) 17 70 00.*

Umeå is a rapidly-growing university town with a youthful population. You can shoot nearby rapids in rubber rafts (May–Sept). The main cultural attraction is **Gammlia**, a complex with seven museums, including a **Ski Museum** and an excellent **open-air museum**, but most sections open only in summer.

## BODEN

**Station: Boden C**, *tel: (0921) 772 50*, 0700–2045, 20-mins walk north-west of the centre.

**Tourist Office:** In summer there's a kiosk at the station; *tel: (0921) 624 10.* Open daily 0900–2100 (21 June–31 July). A noticeboard outside displays tourist information. If it's closed, try: *Näringslivsstiftelsen, Färgareg 10A; tel: (0921) 623 14.* Open Mon–Fri 0800–1600.

**Hotell Standard**, opposite the station; *tel: (0921) 160 55*, has mid-range rooms plus dorm beds in the basement.

Primarily a rail junction, Boden is a pleasant

488

place that's worth a look round if you have time to spare. **Överluleå Kyrka**, perched on a hillock, is a 19th-century version of the original church around which the town grew. At **Svendjefortet**, you can see impressive defences from 1901. **Garnisonsmuseet** (garrison museum), on the south-western edge of town, is full of military hardware and uniforms. The lakefront is a good place for a stroll.

### SIDE TRACKS
### FROM BODEN

### TORNIO AND HAPARANDA

**Tornio Bus station:** *Torikatu; tel: (016) 480 426,* northern edge of the centre. Up to 6 buses a day run from Boden (rail station) to Haparanda, from where local buses make the short run to Tornio.

**Tornio Tourist Office:** *Green Line; tel: (016) 432 733.* Mon–Fri 0800–2000, Sat–Sun 1000–2000 (June–mid Aug); Mon–Fri 0800–1600 (mid Aug–May); lunch break 1130–1230.

**Haparanda Bus station:** *Norra Esplanaden 4; tel: (0922) 107 75,* Mon–Fri 0745–1200 and 1330–1645. You can leave your baggage at the bus station and pick up the (free) map and *Tornio Haparanda Guide.*

**Haparanda Tourist Office:** *Köpmansgatan 7; tel: (0922) 615 85.* Mon–Sat 0900–1600.

Try **Haparanda City Hotel**, *Jorget 7; tel: (0922) 614 90,* located in a nice building on the square; good value.

Although Tornio is in Finland and Haparanda in Sweden, they are effectively one town, linked by bridges and with the major area of interest (such as it is, as this is merely the border) on an island between them: this is officially Tornio, although it is geographically closer to Haparanda. There is a border post on the bridge, but no formalities: transport and pedestrians go through without stopping. In summer (June–Aug), there are a few interesting churches and small museums (mostly in Tornio). If you want to stay, Haparanda is cheaper. Tornio is 1 hr ahead of Haparanda and schedules often ignore this time difference, so make

sure you know whether your departure time was quoted in Swedish or Finnish.

### KEMI

**Station:** *tel: (016) 221 658,* 5-min walk east of the centre: straight along *Kauppakatu.*

**Bus station:** *Asemakatu; tel: 9600 4069.* Walk round the post office building in front of the rail station and it's on the far side. It's better equipped than the rail station. Information office opens Mon–Fri 0800–1630, ticket office Mon–Fri 0730–1730. When it's closed, get tickets on board – you don't need them if you have a valid rail pass. Booking is not necessary. Finnish buses (at least 6 a day) link Tornio with Kemi rail station.

**Tourist Office: Kemin Kaupungin Matkailutoimisto**, *Valtakatu 26; tel: (016) 259 467,* 2 streets from the station. Mon–Fri 0800–1800, Sat–Sun 1000–1800 (June–Aug); Mon–Fri 0800–1600 (Sept–May).

Try **Hotel Cumulus** (part of a Finnish chain), *Hahtisaarenkatu 3; tel: (016) 22 831,* or **Hostel Turisti**, *Valtakatu 39; tel: (016) 250 876,* across from the Tourist Office – a HI member, with cheap rooms.

Spare time for a visit to **Jalokivigalleria** (gemstone gallery), at the end of *Kauppakatu* (recognisable by the crown in a glass case on the corner). The ground floor has excellent displays of gemstones. On the floor above are copies of some famous diamonds and royal regalia, as well as the genuine, but never worn, Finnish royal crown.

### ROVANIEMI

**Station:** *tel: (016) 334 6275,* south-west of the centre. The long-distance bus terminal is up the hill.

**Tourist Offices:** tourist helpers meet arriving trains Mon–Fri. It's 20 mins walk to the main **City Tourist Office:** *Koskikatu 1; tel: (016) 346 270* or *322 2279.* Mon–Fri 0800–1800, Sat–Sun 1130–1600 (June–Aug); Mon–Fri 0800–1600 (Sept–May).

Hotel chains include *Sk.* **Matka Borealis**, *Asemiaskatu 1; tel: (016) 342 0130;* cheap. **Aakenus**, *Koskikatu 47; tel: (016) 342 2051;* moderate. **HI: Tervashonka**, *Hallituskatu 16; tel: (016) 344 644.*

489

Rovaniemi is about 90 mins by train from Kemi (several a day) and the terminal for most northern trains. The capital of Finnish Lapland, 8 km south of the Arctic Circle, it acts as a gateway to the north in summer and a skiing centre in winter. It's also a jumping-off point for visiting **Santa Claus Village**. The main attraction is the **Arktikum** (Arctic Research Centre), *Pohjoisranta 4,* which covers every aspect of human and other life in the countries of the Arctic Circle and has fascinating hands-on computer programmes. 20-mins walk from the station, 10-mins from the Tourist Office.

## OULU/ULEÅBORG

**Station:** *tel: (08) 316 2111,* east of the centre. The (free) *Look at Oulu* (includes a map and useful information). From Kemi there are about 6 trains daily, taking 1 hr.
**Tourist Office: Matkailuneuvonta,** *Torikatu 10; tel: (08) 314 1295,* Mon–Fri 0900–1800, Sat 1000–1500 (June–Aug), Mon–Fri 0900–1600 (Sept–May). Take *Asemakatu* or *Hallituskatu* for six blocks, left on *Torikatu.*

Hotel chains: *Arctia, Cumulus, Sk.* **Apollo,** *Asemakatu 31–33; tel: (08) 374 344,* is cheap–moderate, right near the station. **HI,** *Kajaanintie 36; tel: (08) 311 8060,* 15 mins walk behind the train station.

**Tietomaa,** *Nahkatehtaankatu 6,* is an absorbing science and technology centre – completely non-esoteric and great fun. Virtually every section has something interactive and the whole place is expanding rapidly. **Pohjois-Pohjanmaan Museo** (North Ostrobothnia provincial museum), *Ainola park,* is also worth a visit. The harbour is lively and you can stroll across footbridges to islands in the lake. 

From Oulu, you can connect with the Helsinki–Helsinki route (p. 244) via Kuopio or Joensuu (ETT table no. 795), or Tampere (ETT table no. 790).

## GÄLLIVARE

**Station, Gällivare:** *tel: (0970) 752 00,* on the western edge of the very small town.

**Tourist Office:** *Storgatan 16; tel: (0970) 166 60.* Mon–Fri 0900–1300 and 1400–1600 (mid Aug–May); daily 0900–2000 (June–mid Aug).

For accommodation, try **Hotellet,** *Per Högströmsgatan 9; tel: (0970) 164 20,* and **Gällivare Värdshus,** *Klockljungsvägen 2; tel: (0970) 162 00;* both central and cheap–moderate. **HI,** *tel: (0970) 143 80.* Cross the bridge over the tracks in the station.

The town was once a Sami village – as recalled by the **Lappkyrkan,** *Lasarettsg,* a mid 18th-century church. There's a museum about **Sami history** and one about **sport fishing** in the Tourist Office building.

The top of the 820-m **Dundret,** the hill that looms to the south of town, is a nature reserve with panoramic views (said to cover a twelfth of Sweden). It's 7 km to the top and you should allow at least 3 hrs (many people take 6) for the full return hike, but you can get great views by going only as far as **Bornfällan** (4 km). When the **Midnight Sun** is visible, there are special bus excursions to the top of Dundret.

The town's wealth derives from copper and iron. In **Malmberget** (the site of the mines north of town) are the museum village, **Kåkstan,** and the **Mining Museum.** Tours Mon–Fri mid June–mid Aug go into the **opencast copper mine** and the **underground iron mine**.

**Vägvisaren** is a small open-air museum based on Sami culture, with traditional huts (similar to teepees) and live reindeer; 2 km from the centre, up the road to Dundret.

> ## ↰ SIDE TRACK
> ## FROM GÄLLIVARE
>
> **Jokkmokk** is a stop on the Inlandsbanan (see p. 555). Alternatively, there are daily buses from Gällivare that allow you five hours in Jokkmokk. It grew from a Sami mission into a sizeable town and its prime role today is to keep the Sami culture alive. Don't miss the **Lappkyrka** (a wooden octagonal church) or the **Ajtte,** *Kyrkog,* a museum covering the Sami culture and local flora and fauna.

# VENICE (VENEZIA)

Few places merit the description 'unique', but Venice is definitely one of them. Built on 118 tiny islands, with gondolas and boats providing the only transport and a wealth of notable buildings, it could scarcely be more romantic. Yet it is much more than simply an open-air museum, for people live and work there too. As it is very compact, the highlights can be absorbed in two or three days, though there are enough treasures to fill a lifetime of sightseeing.

## TOURIST INFORMATION

**Azienda Promozione Turistica (APT)** (Tourist administration): *Castello, 4421, 30122 Venezia; tel: 529 8711*. **Information offices:** *Pza San Marco, 2 Palazzetto Selva; tel: 522 6356*. Open 0900–1800 (July–Sept); Mon–Sat 0930–1530 (Oct–June); **Santa Lucia Station**; *tel: 529 8727;* open Mon–Sat 0800–1900, and at **Lido di Venezia**. *Viale S. M. Elisabetta; tel: 526 5721*. Open Mon–Sat 0930–1530. The free *Guest in Venice* guide lists what's on.

For **youth information**, contact **Comune di Venezia Assessorato al Gioventù**, *San Marco 1529; tel: 270 7650*. A **Rolling Venice Card**, costing L5000, allows 14–29 year olds discounted entry to museums, theatres, cinemas and cultural events, maps, cut-price shopping guide and reductions on public transport. Available from **Santa Lucia Station** (daily 0800–2000 July–Sept), or **Assessorato al Gioventù**, *San Marco, Corte Contarina 1529; tel: 274 7651* (Mon–Fri 0900–1300; also Tues and Thur 1500–1700).

## Airport

**Marco Polo International Airport** is 13 km north-east of Venice; flight information; *tel: 661 262*. Buses (ACTV no. 5 and blue ATVO) operate half-hourly (hourly in winter) between the airport and *Pzle Roma*. To continue into Venice, transfer onto a waterbus. The **San Marco ferry** service operates from the airport (daylight hours in summer) via the *Lido* to the *Pza San Marco* in the heart of Venice.

## Stations

To get to Venice itself, take a train to **Santa Lucia** station as some terminate 10 mins earlier at **Mestre** on the mainland. A frequent local service operates between Mestre and Santa Lucia. Santa Lucia has its own *vaporetto* (water-bus) stop, right outside it, at the north-east end of the **Grand Canal**. Train information; *tel: 715 555*.

## GETTING AROUND

Europe's only roadless city is a joy to explore, with its great public buildings and magnificent palaces bordering canals and narrow streets. Prepare yourself for plenty of walking – there are 400 **bridges** over 177 **canals** – and expect to get lost fairly often. However, you're never far from the **Grand Canal**, which snakes in a horseshoe through the centre.

491

## Tickets

A 24-hr *turistiche* (tourist ticket), price L15,000, enables you to use all *vaporetto* routes, and is especially useful if you plan to explore some of the city's outlying islands; 3-day tickets cost L30,000, 7-day L55,000. Tickets are sold singly or in booklets of ten from kiosks at main stops, open 0600–2100 (later at the station), and have to be validated in the machines on the piers before boarding.

## Vaporetto (Water-bus)

Other cities have the bus, train, tram or metro, but Venice has the *vaporetto*. These sturdy water-buses, operated by the ACTV transport authority, run at 10–20 min intervals in daytime and approximately hourly from midnight to 0600. Lines 1 and 82 run the length of the **Grand Canal** connecting *Santa Lucia* station to

*Pza San Marco*. Piers bear the line numbers – but make sure you go in the right direction. Line 5 is a round-the-islands service taking in *Murano* and handy if you are staying at the youth hostel on *Isola del Giudecca*, which has its own stop. Information: **ACTV**, *Pzle Roma, tel: 528 7886.*

### Water Taxi
Water taxis are sleek but expensive. L27,000 buys you a ride of up to 7 mins. **Radio Taxi**; *tel: 522 2303.*

### Gondola
The city's 400 gondolas, which can take up to 6 passengers each, provide a costly, but definitely the most romantic, means of getting around. Rates are fixed, starting at L100,000 for 45 mins in a 'procession'. If you decide to treat yourself to this once-in-a-lifetime experience, go in the evening when the canals are at their most magical. There are 'stands' on several canals.

### Traghetto (gondola ferry)
The cheapest gondola ride in Venice is on the traghetto (ferries), which cross the Grand Canal at eight points (signposted *Traghetto)* and only cost L600.

### STAYING IN VENICE

### Accommodation
Don't come to Venice looking for cheap accommodation. The city boasts some of Europe's grandest luxury hotels, like the legendary **Cipriani**, **Danieli** and **Gritti Palace**. There are slim pickings for those on a tight budget, especially in spring and autumn, when booking ahead is strongly advisable. In summer, many visitors come for the day by ferry from the **Lido**. Less expensive hotels include **Hotel Remedio**, *C. del Remedio 4412; tel: 520 6232 62*, tucked away in a 15th-century building at the back of a tiny courtyard, and **Hotel Ai Do Mori**, *C. Larga St Marco 658; tel: 520 4817.*

**AVA** (Venetian Hotel Association) has reservation desks at **Santa Lucia** station, *tel: 715 016* or *715 288*, open daily 0800–2200 (Apr–Oct) and 0800–2130 (Nov–Mar) and at

**Marco Polo International Airport**. Hotel chains include *BW, Ch, Ex, Pu, Ra.*

The main **youth hostel Albergho per la Gioventù** is on **Isola del Giudecca**; *tel: 523 8211 (vaporetto* line 82). For further hostel information, contact **Associazone Alberghi per la Gioventù**, *Palazzo della Civiltà del Lavoro, Quadrato della Concordia, 00144 Roma, tel: (06) 593 1702.*

The nearest **campsite** is on the Lido, **Camping San Nicolò**; *tel: 526 7415* (summer only).

### Eating and Drinking
Like all Italian cities, Venice takes pride in its distinctive regional cuisine which, as you would expect, leans heavily towards seafood. Rice and beans are also staple ingredients of local dishes.

Many of the restaurants around touristy areas like *Pza San Marco* and *Rialto* charge premium prices, but you only have to stroll a bridge or two away to find quieter streets and more affordable trattoria and pizzeria. Several atmospheric restaurants of varying price ranges are clustered around **La Fenice** (the opera house), like **Al Theatro**, *Campo St Fantin; tel: 522 1052* (moderate). For reasonably priced canal-side eating, try **Da Gianni**, *Zattere 918 tel: 523 7210*, which has a tasty selection of pizzas

**Bacari**, the typically Venetian **wine-bars**, are ideal for budget travellers as they sell plates of pasta or risotto as well as sandwiches. **Cafés** sell delicious slices of pizza and if you want to save money as well as time, stand at the bar where drinks cost a third as much as at a table. **Bar Foscarini**, *Rio Terra Foscari*, tucked beside the Grand Canal near the *Accademia* gallery is well-placed for people and water-watching.

The city's most atmospheric bar is **Florian**; *tel: 528 5338*, in one of the arcades around *Pza San Marco*. It occupies a series of small beautifully decorated 'drawing rooms', which are still just as they were in the 18th century when Floriano Francesconi opened it. **Lord Byron** and **Charles Dickens** were both regular customers. Expect to pay as much for a cappuccino as for a pizza elsewhere, but it's worth every lire for the surroundings and the opportunity to listen to the orchestra which strikes up in the square outside in the evenings.

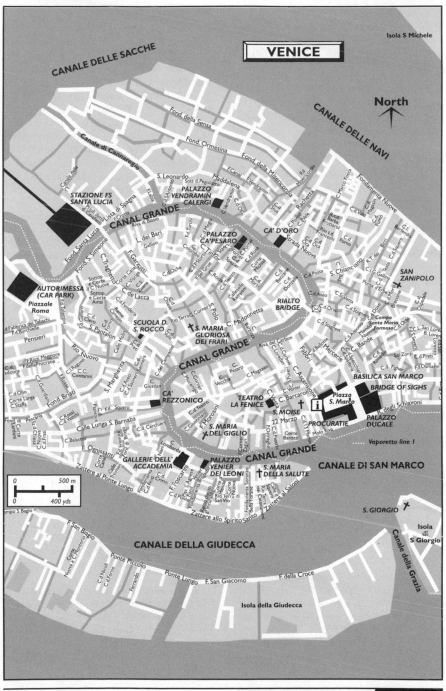

Isola S Michele

**VENICE**

**North**

CANALE DELLE SACCHE

CANALE DELLE NAVI

Fond. della Sensa

Fond. Ormesina

Fond della Misericordia

Canale di Cannaregio

Fondamenta Nuove

S. Leonardo

Maddalena

Sott. d. Pegolotto

**STAZIONE FS SANTA LUCIA**

**PALAZZO VENDRAMIN CALERGI**

**CANAL GRANDE**

**CA' D'ORO**

Strada Nuova

**PALAZZO CA'PESARO**

**SAN ZANIPOLO**

**AUTORIMESSA (CAR PARK)**

Piazzale Roma

**RIALTO BRIDGE**

Campo Santa Maria Formosa

**SCUOLA D. S. ROCCO**

Pensieri

**S. MARIA GLORIOSA DEI FRARI**

**CANAL GRANDE**

**BASILICA SAN MARCO**

Mercerie

Bande

**CA' REZZONICO**

**TEATRO LA FENICE**

Piazza S. Marco

**BRIDGE OF SIGHS**

**S. MOISE**

22 Marzo

**PROCURATIE**

**PALAZZO DUCALE**

Calle Lunga S. Barnaba

**S. MARIA DEL GIGLIO**

Corte Barozzi

Molo Riva

Ponte degli Schiavoni

*Vaporetto line 1*

**GALLERIE DELL' ACCADEMIA**

**PALAZZO VENIER DEI LEONI**

**CANAL GRANDE**

**S. MARIA DELLA SALUTE**

**CANALE DI SAN MARCO**

Zattere al Ponte Lungo

Zattere allo Spirito Santo

**S. GIORGIO**

Isola di S Giorgio

Canale della Grazia

Campo S Biagio

F. San Biagio

**CANALE DELLA GIUDECCA**

Ponte Piccolo

Ponte Lungo

F. San Giacomo

F. della Croce

**Isola della Giudecca**

| 0 | 500 m |
| 0 | 400 yds |

493

### Communications

**Main post office: Poste Centrali**, *Rialto, Fontego dei Tedeschi; tel: 522 0606.*

To phone Venice from abroad the code is 39 (Italy) + 41 (Venice); to phone Venice from elsewhere in Italy, it is *041*.

### Consulates

UK: *Campo Santa Maria della Carità 1051, Dorsoduro, tel: 522 7207.*

### Money

When changing money, always ask for a supply of small denomination bills as every shop and café always seems to be short of change.

There are **Thomas Cook bureaux de change** in *Pza San Marco 142* and *Pza Bra 2*.

The entertainment calendar is busier in summer than winter, with events like the annual 10–day **Venice Film Festival** (late Aug to early Sept). *Palazzo Grassi* is the venue for many of the exhibitions that the city stages, including its major one, the **Biennale di Venezia**, which is the largest modern art show in the world (June–Oct in even years).

The city's biggest event is **Carnival**, ten days of masked balls and street celebrations immediately before Lent. **La Vogolonga** – the long row – on Ascension Sunday is a marathon regatta around the **Lagoon** – any sort of oar-powered craft can take part. Historic **Regata Storica** (first Sun in Sept) begins with a magnificent procession of veteran boats rowed by costumed crews along the Grand Canal.

### Nightlife

The main venue for opera, **La Fenice**, now being rebuilt after a serious fire in 1996, is due to reopen in 2000. Meanwhile, performances take place in a marquee erected on the parking area of *Trettoria* island. Numerous concerts are held in the city's churches. The **Palazzo del Cinema** on the *Lido* is the venue for the annual film festival and shows international films year-round. Throughout the city, bars and clubs offer live music and late-night drinking, but the streets are safe for quiet strolls throughout the night and there is no red light area.

The Venetians' aptitude for commerce has been sharpened by more than eleven centuries of international trade and 200 years of tourism. The main shopping streets are between **Pza San Marco** and the **Rialto**, particularly *Via Merceria*. However bargains are thin on the ground, except in the **Rialto** open-air market, though many of its stalls sell little but souvenirs. Manufacturers of the city's famous **glass** include **Cenedese** and **Salviati**, which both have shops on *Pza San Marco*. More affordable, and uniquely Venetian, are the painted papier-maché **carnival masks** sold in many small stores.

Colourful **marbled paper** printed from old blocks is the most inexpensive local souvenir. Typical Venetian **jewellery** is made from thin gold chain called *la manina*, but plenty of imitations are on sale as well as the genuine article, particularly around *Pza San Marco*. Visitors to the neighbouring islands in the **Lagoon**, such as *Murano* where the glass is made, are invariably disappointed to find prices much the same as in the city centre.

The beauty of visiting Venice is that the city is a living museum – with no admission charge. Rising dreamily out of the Lagoon, it looks magnificent at any time of year and any time of day. No matter that the plasterwork has faded and the paint peeling off many of the tall **terracotta buildings** or that the **canals** can look dark and dirty. The best way to sightsee is simply to wander the narrow streets and canalsides at random, popping into churches as you pass and pausing to window-shop or sit at a pavement café whenever the whim takes you.

Most of the major sights charge a steep entrance fee, but many of the city's art treasures can be seen free, adorning church walls and altars.

A **vaporetto ride** along the **Grand Canal** – sit at the front – is probably the greatest sightseeing journey in the world. Dodging gondolas, water-taxis and delivery boats, it takes you past a succession of grand palaces and churches, and under the decorative white arch of the famous **Rialto** bridge.

## Piazza San Marco

**St Marks' Square** is the hub of the city, close to the mouth of the **Grand Canal**. Surrounded by arcades of exclusive shops and cafés, the huge square echoes with the chatter and footsteps of crowds of tourists while **pigeons** flap at their feet. Begin by taking the lift up the **Campanile di San Marco** for a panoramic view of the city and lagoon. The slender red brick tower itself is a 20th-century reconstruction of a thousand-year-old bell-tower which fell down in 1912.

Next to it, the **Museo Correr**, occupying the south side of the square, traces the history of Venice and displays 14th- to 19th-century paintings.

The **Basilica di San Marco**, consecrated in 1094, was built to house the bones of St Mark the Evangelist. It has five impressive domes, each heavily encrusted with gold mosaics, best seen from the narrow catwalks which run round an upper rim – though to appreciate them you need a good head for heights. The floor, too, is elaborately patterned in marble.

Its **museum**, in the galleries above the church, contains sculpture and carvings from all over the medieval Venetian empire. One of the highlights is the gilded bronze **Horses of St Mark**, believed to date from the 4th century and stolen from **Byzantium** by the Venetians in 1204.

Next to the Basilica along the waterfront stands the icing-white **Palazzo Ducale** (Doge's Palace), whose arches and pillars are as intricate as a wedding cake. Much of it dates from the 16th century when it was the residence of the *Doge*, the elected ruler of the city-state. Now it contains important Venetian works of art, which provide an interesting glimpse of the lifestyle of the former rulers. Stairs from it lead down to the **Ponte dei Sospiri (Bridge of Sighs)**, which crosses a narrow canal to the **Palazzo delle Prigione**, the former prison for petty offenders. Prisoners were led across it – hence the name. However, the best view of it is from another bridge, **Ponte de la Paglia**, on the busy promenade between the *Lagoon* and *St Mark's Square*.

## Canale Grande (Grand Canal): East Bank

Following the canal around from St Mark's, you pass the baroque church of **San Moise** and its neighbour **Santa Maria del Giglio** before coming to the handsome white **Ponte di Rialto** (Rialto Bridge) at the geographic heart of the city. Beyond it, the **Ca'd'Oro**, the most lavish of all Venice's aristocratic palaces, now houses **Galleria Franchetti**, a magnificent collection of paintings (including Mantegna and Guardi), Renaissance bronzes and medallions.

## Canale Grande: West Bank

Standing guard at the beginning of the canal's west bank is the domed **Santa Maria della Salute**, the greatest baroque church in Venice. Nearby the **Palazzo Venier dei Leoni**, the palace that **Peggy Guggenheim** bought specially in 1919, houses her remarkable cubist, abstract and surrealist collection. Yet another of the city's great art galleries, **Galleria dell' Accademia**, is only a short stroll away; it features Venetian artists like Bellini, Canaletto, Carpaccio, Guardi, Titian, Tintoretto and Veronese, as well as Florentine Renaissance artists such as Piero della Francesca.

A short walk west of the canal, between the *Rio della Frescada* and the *Campo di San Paolo*, the **Scuola di San Rocco** guildhall contains a magnificent collection of Tintoretto's works. Nearby, the huge red-brick Gothic church of **Santa Maria Gloriosa dei Frari** looks almost like a factory from the outside but contains paintings by Bellini, Donatello and Titian, amongst others. Both Titian and the composer Monteverdi are buried there.

## The Islands

The **Lido** is the most glamorous of Venice's islands. Here people swim, lie in the sun or go on day-trips to Venice. Made famous during the *Belle Epoque*, it still has a certain elegance. Organised sightseeing tours of the outlying **Murano** island and its neighbours, **Burano** and **Torcello**, are little more than showcase trips for the glass factories. You can visit these and other islands just as easily – and much more cheaply – on an ordinary *vaporetto no.12*.

495

# VENICE–SPLIT

This route runs from Venice through Slovenia into Croatia, taking up the Adriatic coast to finish with possible ferry connections to Italy or Greece. On the rail section from Zagreb to Split, make sure you take the route via Karlovac, avoiding Bosnia.

The theme is sea and islands. South Dalmatia offers a Mediterranean climate, emerald blue waters, and historic towns such as Split and Dubrovnik, both on the UNESCO world cultural heritage list. The islands of Korčula, Hvar and Brač are renowned for wine, hospitality and unspoilt nature.

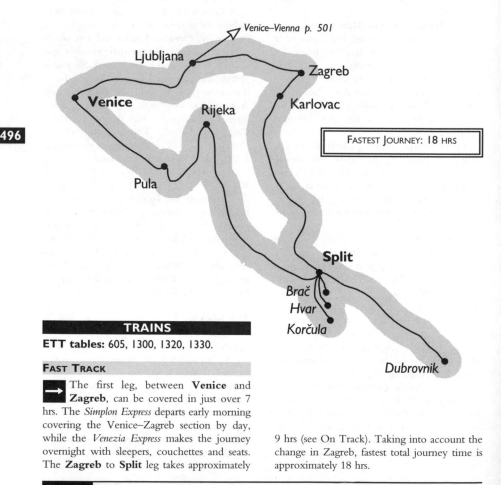

Venice–Vienna p. 501

FASTEST JOURNEY: 18 HRS

**496**

## TRAINS
**ETT tables:** 605, 1300, 1320, 1330.

### FAST TRACK

The first leg, between **Venice** and **Zagreb**, can be covered in just over 7 hrs. The *Simplon Express* departs early morning covering the Venice–Zagreb section by day, while the *Venezia Express* makes the journey overnight with sleepers, couchettes and seats. The **Zagreb** to **Split** leg takes approximately 9 hrs (see On Track). Taking into account the change in Zagreb, fastest total journey time is approximately 18 hrs.

## ON TRACK

### ➠ Venice–Ljubljana
See Venice–Vienna route, p.501.

### Ljubljana–Zagreb
Seven daytime trains and one night train connect these cities; journey time 2 hrs 20 mins. One train, the *Mimara*, is part of the EuroCity network and has a restaurant car.

### Zagreb–Split
From Zagreb there are two night trains to Split, the *Mosor* (sleepers) and the summer-only *Maestral*, seats only. The *Marijan Express* day train has first- and second-class seats and a restaurant car. All take about 9 hrs.

## ALTERNATIVE FERRY ROUTES

### Venice–Pula
From late June to early Sept, the Italian company **CF Marina** run a Venice–Pula ferry service from *Stazione Marittima San Basilio* in Venice. There are two boats a week, Mon and Fri at 0930; L.50,000.

### Pula–Rijeka
Three trains per day run from Pula to Lupoglav, with a Lupoglav–Rijeka bus connection operated by **HŽ**. Total journey time varies from 2 hrs 10 mins to 3¼ hrs.

### Rijeka–Split
**Jadrolinija**, *Riva 16, Rijeka; tel: (051) 214 483,* run an express coastal ferry service.During the summer a boat leaves Rijeka every evening, and stops at various towns and islands all the way to Split. Approximate journey time of 10 hrs.

## ZAGREB

**Station**: **Glavni Kolodvor**, *tel: (01) 9830,* in the centre of town, overlooking the first of three squares dating back to the Austro-Hungarian era, *Trg Kralja Tomislava*. The station is well equipped with toilets, left luggage, exchange offices, newspaper kiosks and a bar.
**Tourist Offices**: *Trg Bana Jelačića 11; tel: (01) 48 14 051* or *48 14 052.* Open Mon–Fri 0830–

2030, Sat 1000–1800, Sun and holidays 1000–1400. From the station walk straight across the three squares, keeping to *Praška* on the left, which leads directly to *Trg Bana Jelačića*, the main town square. As an alternative to this 10-min walk, take tram nos 6 or 13 which follow the same route. *Trg Nikole Subica Zinjskog 14; tel: (01) 4552 867.* Mon–Fri 0900–1700 only. On the third square in front of the station, responsible for guided tours.

Pick up a copy of the free monthly pamphlet, *Zagreb*, published in English, has information about events.

## ACCOMMODATION

**Hotel Esplanade**, *Mihanoviceva 1; tel: (01) 4566 666, fax: (01) 4577 907,* 200m to the left as you come out of the station, is a member of Leading Hotels of the World and undoubtedly Zagreb's most renowned hotel.

**Dom Cvjetno**, *Odranska 8; tel: (01) 530 609,* is the best of a number of student halls open mid July to end Aug as hostels. **Youth Hostel**, *Petrinjska 77; tel: (01) 434 964,* out of the station turn right off the square and take the first road to the left. Just a 100-m walk from the station, but this hostel still needs to be upgraded. 70Kn per night.

The Tourist Office, as well as various agencies, will help with all types of accommodation.

## EATING AND DRINKING
The best area for eating and drinking is **Tkalèiæeva**, a lively street leading from *Trg Bana Jelačica* up to *Gornji Grad*. The nearby **market** at **Dolac**, both open-air and underground, is the best place to shop for a picnic.

## GETTING AROUND
The city is served by a fine tram network. Single ticket 4Kn, day ticket 11Kn.

## COMMUNICATIONS
The main **post office** is next to the station.

## SIGHTSEEING
The most interesting part of Zagreb is **Gornji Grad**, the upper town. From *Trg Bana Jelačića* follow *Ilica*, to come to *Tomićeva*, where you can take the funicular up to **Strossmayer**

promenade. This is one of the best vantage points for views over the city.

**Lotrščak Tower** now houses an art gallery; if there is an exhibition in course it is possible to climb to the top. From here a cannon is fired daily at 1200. Next take *Ćirilometodska* to **St Mark's Church**, noted for its extraordinary red, white and blue tiled roof. Now follow *Kamenita* to pass through the archway, which has become a shrine, with a small altar, flowers and burning candles. Turn left up *Radićeva,* and take one of the series of steep wooden stairways to your right, which link the upper town to **Kaptol**. Visit the **Cathedral**, remarkable for the inscription of the ten commandments on the northern wall, written in 12th-century Glagolitic characters, unique to the old Slavic language. Zagreb's finest art collection is housed within the **Mimara Museum**, *Rooseveltov Trg 4; tel: (01) 448 055.* Tues–Fri 1000–1700, Sat–Sun 1000–1300; 20Kn.

Also worth seeing are **Maksimir Park** (tram nos 11/12 from the main square), and the **Mirogoj Cemetery** (frequent bus service from Kaptol in front of the Cathederal).

### OUT OF TOWN

**Medvednica** hills offer the people of Zagreb a wonderful retreat. This is an unspoilt expanse of woodland and wild flowers, within easy access of the city. Take tram no. 14 out to *Gracani* at the end of the line, change for tram no. 15, then ride the funicular (open daily 0800–2000; 5Kn), up to the highest point of **Mt Slijeme**. This can be done as a day-trip, but keen walkers may want more time to explore. A number of mountain-hut type hostels provide overnight accommodation and cheap wholesome food and drink for hikers. Try **Runolist**; *tel: (01) 45 80 318,* 40 mins from Slijeme funicular.

### PULA

**Station**: *Kolodvorska 9; tel (052) 541 733,* a 10-min walk from the centre of town. Very basic with toilets, left luggage and a bar.
**Tourist Office**: *Istarska 11; (052) 33 557.* Open Mon–Sat 0800–1930.
**Youth Hostel**: *Zaljev Valsaline 4; tel: (052) 34 211.* Take bus nos 2 or 7, 3 km out of town, then walk 200m across a field to arrive at this

clean and friendly hostel overlooking the sea, with its own outdoor bar; 70Kn a night.

Pula is renowned for its **Roman Arena**, where various cultural festivals are held during summer.

### RIJEKA

**Station**: *Krešimirova 1; tel: (051) 213 333.* Facilities include toilets, left luggage, bar and newspaper kiosks.
**Tourist Office**: *Užarska 14; tel: (051) 335 882.*

Rijeka is a friendly industrial port with cultural ties to Italy. Visit **Trsat**, a 13th-century fortification, floodlit at night, up on the hill above town. For beaches and nightlife, take a local bus to **Opatija**, a smart resort 10 km out of town.

From Rijeka you can take a Jadrolinija ferry direct to Split – see previous page.

### SPLIT

**Station:** *Obala Kneza Domagoja; tel: (021) 355 388.* The train station, coach station and ferry port are all next to each other, overlooking *Gradska Luka,* the town harbour. The historic centre is clearly visible, just 100m away.
**Tourist Offices:** *Obala Hrvatsog Narodnog Preporoda 12; tel: (021) 342 142.* Open 0730–2100, closed Sun. Information and accommodation. Situated on the seafront, better known by locals as the *Riva. Peristil 1; tel: (021) 40 685.* Open 0900–1400, 1700–2000. Guided tours on request.

#### ARRIVING AND DEPARTING

Split **airport**, *tel: (021) 551 399,* lies 20 mins away in Trogir. **Croatia Airlines** run a regular shuttle bus to and from town. The main port for passenger **ferries** is *Gradska Luka.* The chief operators are **Jadrolinija**, *tel (021) 355 399,* and **SEM**, *tel: (021) 589 433.*

#### GETTING AROUND

The historic centre, **Grad**, lies within the walls of **Diocletian's Palace**. This labyrinth of narrow paved streets, opening onto wonderful piazzas, is only accessible to pedestrians. City buses serve the new periphery, and are zoned outward to include villages such as **Trogir** and

Omiš, both of which warrant a visit. Bus tickets can be bought at newspaper stands, or directly from the driver.

## ACCOMMODATION

The Tourist Office helps with accommodation in local hotels, private rooms and self-catering units. Although Split was barely damaged during the war, there was an influx of international aid workers who used it as a base, and refugees who saw it as a safe haven. This put pressure on both space and prices, but the situation is gradually returning to normal.

## EATING AND DRINKING

Locals eat out primarily at *merenda,* a hearty fisherman's brunch served between 0900–1130. Simple eating places offer a fixed menu at budget prices. Dinner on the town is less popular. **Re di Mare**, overlooking the Špinut marina, does excellent fish at reasonable prices. Even more popular with locals is the nearby **Lučica**. For the best pizza in town visit **Galija**, *Tončićeva 12,* across the street from **Kantun Paulina**, *Matošiča 1,* serving *ćevapi,* a Bosnian speciality similar to kebabs.

For a cheap stand-up lunch with locals try *ribice,* tiny fishes deep fried and served with a glass of white wine, in a canteen style establishment opposite the fish market *(Ribarnica), Kraj Sv. Marije 8.*

Split is packed with bars, which are busy the year through. Café-life centres around **Luxor** on **Peristil**, amid a theatrical setting of Roman ruins floodlit by night.

## SIGHTSEEING

The historic centre lies within the walls of **Diocletian's Palace**, built in the 2nd-century AD by the powerful Roman Emperor from whom it takes its name. Begin a tour of the city from the seafront, taking the underground passage known as the **Podrum** to come up into **Peristil**. Here stands the **Cathederal of St Duje**, guarded by Egyptian sphinxes, incorporating an octagonal mausoleum, built for the emperor himself. Climb the tower (open 0900–1200, 1600–1900; 5Kn) for a better view of the architectural layout. Turn left off *Peristil* along the narrow paved street of *Krešmirova,* to

arrive at **Narodni Trg**, the main town square. The building styles range from Venetian to Austro-Hungarian, bearing witness to various outside powers which have dominated the city. Walk straight across the square and follow *Kraj Sv Marije* to pass the covered fishmarket, also worth a look in. Keep going straight to cross **Trg Republike**, a rather formal square, and take any one of the meandering little stepped paths up the hill to explore the old quarter of **Varoš**. You will pass several places selling *točeno vino,* local wine sold on tap. A worthwhile climb will eventually bring you out at the top onto **Marjan**, a beautiful reserve of pine forests on what is actually a peninsular, with splendid views down onto the city and out across the sea. It is possible to walk the length of the peninsular, past several pretty churches, to arrive at a recreation area known as **Bene**, with facilities for bathing and renting mountain bikes (15Kn per hr). An alternative means of reaching Bene from the town centre is to take bus no. 12 from the seafront. While staying in Split also try to visit **Pazar**, the colourful open air-market held just outside the main walls, Mon–Sat 0700–1330.

## EVENTS

The **Split Summer Festival** runs mid July to mid Aug. The programme includes concerts, opera and theatre, set against a backdrop of the city's most beautiful ancient buildings.

## ⤵ SIDE TRACKS FROM SPLIT

### BRAČ

**Ferries**: **Jadrolinija** run a regular ferry service Split–Supertar. There are 13 ferries a day in summer, taking 1 hr; 16Kn.

**Tourist Office**: in **Supertar**, *P. Jakšića 17; tel: (021) 630 551;* in **Bol**, *Uz pjacu 4; tel: (021) 635 122.*

The island of Brač is best known for the spectacular sandspit known as **Zlatni Rat**, possibly Croatia's most beautiful beach.

### HVAR

**Ferries**: **Jadrolinija** run a regular ferry

499

service Split–Stari Grad. Six ferries a day in summer take 2 hrs; 23Kn.

**Tourist Office**: in **Stari Grad**, *tel: (021) 765 763;* in the town of **Hvar**, *Trg Sv Stjepana 16; tel (021) 741 059.*

The island of Hvar is famed for its wines, lavender, pretty fishing villages and unspoilt coastline. The castle in the town of Hvar should also be seen.

## KORČULA

**Ferries:** The **Jadrolinija** coastal service Rijeka–Dubrovnik, departing from Split, calls at Korčula every day except Thur in summer. For other ferry and coach connections, ask at the Tourist Office.

**Tourist Office:** In the Loggia next door to Hotel Korčula, *Stara Riva; tel (020) 715 701;* Mon–Sat 0800–1500 and 1700–2000, Sun 0800–1200.

### ACCOMMODATION AND FOOD

The oldest, smallest and most central hotel is the B category **Hotel Korčula**, *Stara Riva; tel: (020) 711 078, fax: (020) 711 746.* Self-catering apartments and rooms in private houses are also of a high standard at reasonable prices.

Seafood and local wine predominate, and are basically good everywhere. For a friendly atmosphere in a unique setting, try the wine-cellar in the centre of the old town, **Adio Mare**, *tel: (020) 711 253.*

### SIGHTSEEING

The old town of Korčula lies on a small peninsular, which was walled for defensive purposes. The streets were laid out on a herring-bone plan, to protect against the bitter winter gales. Ask for a plan at the Tourist Office, and set out to explore the various religious, municipal and family buildings. Visit **St Mark's Cathederal**, (open 1000–1300 and 1700–1900), and the **House of Marco Polo**, who was born here. Try to see a performance of the colourful **Moreška**, a traditional sword dance, held on Thur at 2100 July–Sept.

## DUBROVNIK

**Buses**: **Coach** station: *Put Republike 19; tel (020) 23 088,* with 24 hr left luggage.

**Ferries**: **Gruž Port**, *Obala S. Radića; tel: (020) 418 000.* The Jadrolinija service (4–5 times weekly in summer and 1–2 in winter) links Split and Dubrovnik. Approximate journey time is 8–9 hrs.

**Tourist Office**: *Placa 1; tel: (020) 26 355* or *26 354,* daily 0800–2000. Pick up a copy of the free monthly city guide, *Dubrovnik,* available at the Tourist Office and hotel receptions.

### ACCOMMODATION

There are no hotels within the city walls, but a good range of all categories lie within a few minutes walk from the centre.

**Youth Hostel**, *Ulica Bana Jelačica 15–17; tel: (020) 412 592.* 100m from the coach station and 300m from the city walls. Clean and friendly; 55Kn a night.

### EATING AND DRINKING

*Prijeko,* a picturesque narrow street running parallel to the central street, *Placa,* is the main area for eating out within the city walls.

### SIGHTSEEING

The best way to begin exploring Dubrovnik is with a circuit of the **city walls**, daily 0900–1830, 10Kn. Various vantage points afford fine views over the terracotta rooftops, the baroque churches, the sea and the islands. For centuries Dubrovnik was a refined and prosperous trading port, which managed to keep its independence by paying off various would-be conquerors. The city as it stands today still bears witness to this glorious past, and is truly one of the finest examples of European urban architecture.

### EVENTS

The **Dubrovnik Summer Festival**, held mid July to mid Aug, hosts outdoor theatre and opera, classical music and jazz, attracting highly acclaimed international artists.

**500**

# VENICE–VIENNA

This itinerary runs from Venice in north-east Italy to Austria's capital, Vienna, traversing Slovenia. A dramatic alpine route, it passes through magnificent landscapes of mountains, lakes and forests. This area offers excellent opportunities for outdoor facilities. There is also a stop in Slovenia's capital, Ljubljana, an elegant but friendly university city planned around the River Ljubljanica and presided over by a fine hilltop castle.

FASTEST JOURNEY: 8 HRS

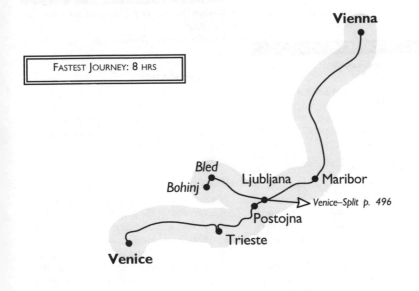

Venice–Split p. 496

501

## TRAINS

**ETT tables:** 88, 605, 1300, 1315, 980, 89a.

### FAST TRACK

The *Romulus* provides a daytime service between Venice and Vienna, the journey taking 8 hrs. It has a dining car but requires a supplement. There is also a through carriage that is transferred from one train to another at Villach, which takes over 9 hrs to reach Vienna. The overnight *San Marco* has sleeping cars, couchettes and second-class seats, and takes 10 hrs.

## ON TRACK

### Venice–Trieste

A service every 1–2 hrs links Venice (Santa Lucia) with Trieste (Centrale). Journey time: approximately 2 hrs.

### Trieste–Postojna

Three trains cross the border from Italy into Slovenia during the day. The *Venezia Express* passes through at night. They take 2 hrs to get from Trieste to Postojna. One of the trains, the *Drava*, has a restaurant car.

### Postojna–Ljubljana
Frequent services taking 1 hr.

### Ljubljana–Maribor
Frequent services, taking 2–3 hrs.

### Maribor–Graz–Vienna
Two *IC* trains, the *Emona* and the *Croatia* run from Maribor to Vienna. Alternatively, threee local trains make the journey across the border to Graz (not on Sun), where you can change trains. *IC* trains, with buffet cars, run every two hours to Vienna. The journey time from Maribor to Graz is 1 hr and from Graz to Vienna 3 hrs.

## TRIESTE
**Station: Stazione Centrale**, *Pza della Liberta 8; tel: (040) 418 612.*
**Tourist Office:** The central office is at *V. San Nicolo 20; tel: (040) 369 881,* and there is a second, smaller one in the station, *tel: (040) 420 182.* The regional information office is at *V. Rossini 6; tel: (040) 363 952.*

502

### SIGHTSEEING
Italy's easternmost city, once the chief port of the Austro-Hungarian Empire, is also the Istrian hinterland's window on the western world. Rebuilt in the 19th century, it is today a stately, solid place that relishes its role as a crossroads between east and west.

At Trieste's heart, the **Borgo Teresiano** is a stately grid of regular streets which identify this city more with its central European counterparts than with anything Italian. Here, the *Corso Cavour* straddles the **Canal Grande**, an urban waterway where the locals moor their boats. Beside it, in *Pza Ponterosso,* is the daily **market**. Trieste's civic heart lies in *Pza dell'Unita d'Italia*: see the vast **Palazzo del Comune del Governo** beside it, aglow with its mosaic ornamentation. Also in the piazza is one of Trieste's oldest cafés (1839), the **Caffè degli Specchi**. There is another, **Caffè San Marco**, on the other side of town, at *Via Cesare Battisti 18.*

The **Capitoline Hill** formed the heart of Roman and medieval Trieste, and it is here that its oldest surviving buildings are to be found.

Apart from the surviving remains of the ancient **Forum** (ancient Trieste was called Tergeste), there is the 11th-century **Cathedral of San Giusto** (beside the Forum). Still on the Capitoline, the 15th-century Venetian-built **Castello** houses the **Museo Civico** in which can be seen a collection of weaponry and armour. Still close to the cathedral, the **Museo di Storia ed Arte** houses important Roman artefacts, as does the **Orto Lapidario**. In *V. Teatro Romano* are the ruins of a Roman theatre.

## POSTOJNA
**Station:** lies east of the town, about 1 km from the centre.
**Tourist Office:** *Jamska Cesta 9; tel: (067) 62 921.*

### ACCOMMODATION
Just 150m from the caves stands the best hotel in town, **Jama**, *Jamska Cesta 28; tel: (067) 24 172, fax: (067) 24 431.* **Camping**: *Pivka*, 4 km from Postojna, has one of the area's only campsites. Ask at the Tourist Office for private rooms and other facilities.

### SIGHTSEEING
Postojna is notable for its tremendous network of caves, one of the largest in Europe, extending 27 km into the surrounding hills. About 2 million years old, the tunnels and caverns are adorned with strange rock formations, stalactites and stalagmites. When the British sculptor Henry Moore came here, he wrote in the visitors' book, 'the best exhibition of nature's sculpture I have ever seen'. A miniature railway has been provided to guide you through this magical world. The tour reveals an awesome array of chambers, with names like the Beautiful Caves, the Black Cave, the Winter Hall and the **Concert Hall**, which can accommodate around 10,000 people for musical performances. Another of the caves' attractions is the hideous amphibian **human-fish**, found nowhere else in the world. Tours hourly 0900–1800 May–Sept, less frequent out of season; SIT1800.

A few kilometres on from Postojna is **Predjama Castle**. This 16th-century construction is one of the most beautiful castles in

Slovenia. It hangs high up on a rocky cliff, and is built over an underworld cave, which can also be visited 0900–1900 in high season. Ask at the Postojna Tourist Office for information.

## LJUBLJANA

**Station**: *Trg Osvobodline Fronte (Trg OF); tel: (061) 1315 167,* a 15-min walk from the main street, *Slovenska Cesta.*
**Tourist Office:** *Mačkove 1; tel: (061) 133 01 11.* Open Mon–Fri 0800–1900, Sat 0900–1700. There is also a smaller Tourist Office in the station. For an informative guided tour of the city, organised through the Tourist Office, meet at the **Magistrat**, *Mestni Trg 1,* daily 1700 June–Sept.

### ACCOMMODATION AND FOOD

Thanks to various upgrading projects, there is now a good variety of **hotels** in all categories, the most impressive being the A category **Grand Hotel Union**, *Miklošičeva 1; tel: (061) 125 41 33, fax: (061) 21 79 10.* **Private rooms** are available for rent through the Tourist Office, but may be in short supply during the summer. Although there is no official Youth Hostel at present, rooms can be taken in **student halls of residence** during the summer break through July–Aug: **Dijaški Dom Bežigrad**, *Kardeljeva Ploščad 28, tel: 342 864,* and **Dijaški Dom Tabor**, *Vidovdanska Cesta 7; tel: (061) 321 067* – ask at the Tourist Office for further details. **Camping** is the best cheap option and Ljubljana's site is located by the Sava River: **Autocamp Ježica**, *Dunajska 270; tel: (061) 371 382.*

The riverside zone between *Stari Trg* and *Novi Trg* is the centre for bars and reasonably priced eating places.

### EVENTS

The annual **International Summer Festival** takes place in Plečnik's open air **Križanke Theatre**, attracting well known musicians, actors and dancers from all over the world, July–Aug.

### SIGHTSEEING

A part of the former Yugoslavia, and now the capital of Slovenia, an independent state which has remained distinctly aloof from the Balkan conflict, Ljubljana is a metropolis where the West meets Mittel Europa. Dominated by a hilltop fortress, it is a lively city with an important historic core.

The River Ljubljanica divides the city into two parts, joined in the city centre by a triple bridge, the **Tromostovje**. This links the city's old heart, **Stari Trg**, on the right bank, built below the hilltop castle, to **Novi Trg** on the left bank.

On the right bank, baroque **St Nikolas's Cathedral**, *Ciril-Metodov Trg,* abuts the **Bishop's Palace**. Beyond, on *Vodnikov Trg,* lies the central food **market** (open Mon–Sat 0600–1800), well worth a visit and good for picnic shopping. Going south from the cathedral, a baroque **fountain** by the Italian architect and sculptor Francesco Robba stands opposite the **Magistrat** (Town Hall) on *Mestni Trg.*

On the river's left bank, the 17th-century **Franciscan Church** dominates *Prešernov Trg.* Within, the high altar is the work of Robba, as is the one inside the 18th-century **Uršulinska Cerkev**, an important baroque edifice on *Kongresni Trg.* The left bank of the city also contains a conglomeration of museums. The **National Museum**, *Trg Herojev 1,* houses important archaeological artefacts and a natural history section whose key exhibit is a complete mammoth skeleton. The **National Gallery**, *Cankarjeva 20,* contains works from the 13th–20th centuries. The **Museum of Modern Art**, *Cankarjeva 15,* provides an interesting view of 20th-century Slovenian art. The **Architectural Museum**, *Karunova 4,* highlights the work of Jože Plečnik, one of the pioneers of modern architecture, who altered much of Ljubljana, as well as completing important works in Vienna and Prague. Antique enthusiasts may want to visit to the **flea market** at *Cankarjevo Nabrežje,* Sun 0800–1300.

503

### ⊡ SIDE TRACKS FROM LJUBLJANA

## BLED

**Station:** Lesce is the nearest station on the

main line. From here take a local bus to **Bled Jezero**, Bled Lake. Check times and connections with the Ljubljana Tourist Office. Alternatively, use the Bled Jezero rail station on the Jesenice–Nova Gorica line (ETT table 1305).

**Tourist Office:** *Cesta Svobode 15; tel: (064) 74 1122.*

## ACCOMMODATION

There are numerous hotels, the most interesting being the A category **Villa Bled**, *Cesta Svobode 26; tel: (064) 79 15, fax: 74 13 20*, which once belonged to Tito.

There is an excellent **Youth Hostel**, *Grajska Cesta 17; tel: (064) 74 52 50*, just a 5-min walk from the lake. High standard accommodation can also be arranged in private houses through the Tourist Office.

## SIGHTSEEING

The alpine lake of Bled lies on the edge of **Triglav National Park**, and the waterside town of the same name is traditionally the most popular holiday resort in Slovenia. In the middle of the lake stands an island with a 17th-century church, which can be visited by boat. On a 100m cliff, with wonderful views over the lake, stands a **Gothic Castle**, with a museum and restaurant, open daily 0800–1900; 300SIT.

In summer, Bled has facilities for bathing. Boats can be hired, 1000SIT for 3 people for 1 hr, 1000 SIT deposit. In winter the lake freezes over and is used for ice-skating. Bled is also an ideal base for skiing. There is an 18-hole golf course just 2 km out of town: **Bled Golf and Country Club**, *Cesta Svobode 13; tel: (064) 718 230.*

A trip on a **steam locomotive** along the Bohinj line, which runs through the **Soča Valley**, can be arranged through **Slovenijaturist**, *tel: (061) 131 51 67*. This operates every Thur, mid June to mid Sept, from Jesenice through Bled and Bohinjska Bistrica to Most na Soči for Tomlin.

## BOHINJ

**Station:** Bohinj Bistrice is the nearest

station. To reach Bohinj, take the train from Bled Jezero station (on the Jesenice–Nova Gorica line – see Bled; ETT table 1305). From here take a local bus to **Bohinjsko Jezero**, Bohinj Lake. Check times and connections with the Ljubljana Tourist Office.

**Tourist Office:** *Ribčev Laz 48; tel: (064) 72 33 70.*

## ACCOMMODATION

The Tourist Office will help arrange accommodation in hotels, self-catering apartments or private houses. Prices are a little more reasonable than in Bled.

## SIGHTSEEING

Bohinj Lake is less commercial than Bled Lake, so general amenities are less refined, but the serene landscape is incomparable. Despite being less accessible it undoubtedly warrants the journey. Overshadowed by the dramatic **Mt Triglav**, the symbol of Slovenia, the lake itself is magnificent. Outdoor pursuits enthusiasts and nature lovers alike cannot fail to be impressed by this territory of unspoilt alpine beauty.

For sporting activities, including mountain biking, caving, climbing, canoeing and paragliding, contact **Alpinum**, *Ribčev Laz 50; tel: (064) 723 441.*

Bohinj is also renowned for its cheese, bearing the same name. ▲

## MARIBOR

**Station**: **Železniška Postaja**, *Partizanska 50; tel: (062) 211 222.*

**Tourist Office:** *Glavni Trg 15; tel (062) 211 262.*

Maribor is Slovenia's second university town. The old town, with winding streets and rich baroque architecture, lies on the left bank of the River Drava. For centuries Maribor's existence depended on the wine trade. Down by the water's edge visit the 16th-century tower, **Vodni Stolp**, *Usnjarska 10; tel: (062) 27 743*, the oldest *vinoteka* in the country, where you can sample over 300 different Slovenian wines.

# VIENNA (WIEN)

Austria's capital is one of Europe's great cultural centres, known the world over for its music (the waltz was born here in 1820) and splendid imperial buildings. The massive Hofburg palace is the principal legacy of the 600 years when the city was capital of the Habsburg empire.

Strolling around the central area is a real pleasure thanks to its wide traffic-free streets, spacious gardens and hundreds of atmospheric places to eat and drink. Indeed nothing is more civilized than lingering in a coffee-house over a large slice of cake – undoubtedly the Viennese people's favourite pastime.

## TOURIST INFORMATION

**Main office:** *Kärntnerstr. 38; tel: 211140.* Open 0900–1900. Accommodation booking service ÖS40. There are also information and accommodation bureaux at **Westbahnhof**, open 0700–2200; **Südbahnhof**, open 0630–2200 (May–Oct), 0630–2100 (Nov–Apr); and **Schwechat Airport**, 0830–2100. **Jugend Info** (Youth Information Service) offers accommodation information in the *Bellaria underground passage, Dr Karl-Renn-Ring* (U Bahn 2/3 to *Volkstheater).* Open Mon–Sat 1200–1900; *tel: 526 1799.*

**Thomas Cook licensee: Papageno Reisen** at *Gentzg. 177; tel: (1) 478 5511,* and *Esslinger Haupstr. 81–87; tel: (1) 774 8872.*

## ARRIVING AND DEPARTING

### Airport

**Vienna International Airport** is 19 km south-east of the city at **Schwechat**. Flight information; *tel: 7007-2233.* Bus transfers (ÖS70) run to City Air Terminal, a 20-min journey; open daily 24 hours Apr–Oct, 0500–2430 Nov–Mar, and to Westbahnhof, via Südbahnhof, every hour between 0620 and 2220 (to 0330 Apr–Oct). A taxi to the airport costs around ÖS480.

### Stations

Vienna has three main stations; for information: *tel: 17 17.* **Westbahnhof,** *Mariahilferstr. / Europapl.* serves Austrian destinations to the west, and Germany, Switzerland and Hungary. **Südbahnhof,** *Wiener Gurtel/Arsenalstr.,* serves the south, including Italy, the former Yugoslavia, the Czech Republic and Hungary. **Franz-Josefs-Bahnhof,** *Julius-Tandler-Pl.,* serves the north plus Berlin and the Czech Republic. All three are 3–4 km outside the *Ringstr.* and connected to the centre by underground/subway or tram.

## GETTING AROUND

Most sights are on or inside the famous *Ringstr.,* which encircles the city centre. Now extensively traffic-free, it was enclosed by walls until the 1860s, when Emperor Franz Joseph had them knocked down to make way for this wide boulevard.

### Transport

Public transport is efficient, with U-Bahn (underground trains), trams and buses all using the same tickets. Single tickets, sold in blocks of 5, for one journey, cost ÖS17 each (under-15s travel free at weekends and school holidays). A 24-hr **Tageskarte Wien** costs ÖS50 and 72-hr **excursion ticket** ÖS130. A tourist option is the **Vienna Card** (ÖS180), available in hotels and Tourist Offices, valid for 72 hours' transport plus reduced entry to popular tourist sights and shopping discounts. Tickets must be validated on the bus or tram or at the entrance to the U-Bahn – or you face a hefty on-the-spot fine. Information; *tel: 587 3186.*

The **U-Bahn**, built in the 1960s to replace

505

many of the tram routes, has five lines, operating 0500–2400. The remaining **trams** run on 33 radial routes as well as in both directions round the *Ringstr.*, 0500–2400. The last of the day displays a blue bar at front and back. **Buses** fill gaps not covered by trams, plus some all-night services on main routes leaving *Schwedenpl.*

**Taxis** are not cheap but extremely efficient. Hail one with a 'frei' sign, or *tel: 31 300.*

**Cycling** is a pleasant way of getting around as the city is largely flat and has plenty of leafy boulevards. 500 km of **cycle paths** are marked. The Tourist Office has a free booklet, *Wien von Sattel* (Vienna from the Saddle), with route maps. Train travellers get the best hire deals at a station – Westbahnhof 0400–2400, Wien Nord 0715–2200 and Südbahnhof 0500–2400. Hire is ÖS90 per day on production of a rail ticket for the same day, otherwise ÖS150.

**Vienna Bike**, *Wasag. 28/2/5; tel: 319 12 58,* offers daily tours by bike; ÖS200 for 2–3 hrs.

A sedate 20-min tour by **Fiaker** (horse-drawn carriage) costs ÖS440, 40 mins costs ÖS880 and per hour ÖS1100. They line up on *Heldenpl.* (next to the cathedral) and outside the Hofburg and Albertina.

**Bus tours** of the city are operated by several companies, including Vienna Line; *tel: 712 46830,* whose hop-on-hop-off service stops at 13 places of interest; hourly from 0900–1700 Apr–Oct, 2-hourly Nov–Mar. A 2-day ticket costs ÖS220. 90-min **boat trips** on the **River Danube**, which is north-east of the city, and the **Danube Canal**, which passes the centre start from *Schwedenpl.* (May–Oct), operated by **DDSG-Blue Danube**; *tel: 727 50222;* fare ÖS170.

### STAYING IN VIENNA

### Accommodation

There are lots of options – and takers – so book ahead for May–Oct. Don't expect much below ÖS500 per person. Major hotel groups include *BW, GT, Hd, Hn, Ib, IC, Ma, Mc, Nv, RC, Rd, Rk, Rn, SA, Sc, Sf, Sn, Tp.*

Among the top options is **Hotel Sacher**, *Philharmonikerstr. 4; tel: 51456,* beside the **Staatsoper** (State Opera House) and main Tourist Office. The **K&K Palais Hotel**, *Rudolfspl. 11; tel: 533 13 53,* overlooking a quiet square near the canal, was the home of Katerina von Schratt, mistress of Emperor Franz Josef. **Hotel Kummer**, *Mariahilferstr. 71A; tel: 588 95,* is near the Westbahnhof. For a more moderately priced stay, guesthouses include **Pension Sacher**, *Rotenturmstr. 1; tel: 533 32 38,* on a central 7th floor next to the cathedral. The cheaper **Hotel Goldene Spinne**, *Linke Bahngasse 1A; tel: 712 44 86,* is out of the immediate centre but close to the City Air Terminal.

**HI: Jugendherberge Wien**, *Myrthengasse 7; tel: 523 6316* (U2 to *Lerchenfelder Str.,* then a short walk).

**Camping: Aktive Camping**, *Neue Donau am Kleehaüfel; tel: 220 93 10* (mid May–mid Sept) is across the Danube Canal.

### Eating and Drinking

Vienna has given the gastronomic world *Wiener Schnitzel* (a thin slice of veal in breadcrumbs), *Sachertorte* (rich chocolate cake) and *Kaiserschmarrn* (chopped pancakes with plum puree) which is almost a meal in itself. It is also the place to sample Slav food, a hangover from the days of the Austro-Hungarian empire. You'll find typically Viennese dishes in *Beisel* or *Kellern*, moderately priced wine bar/restaurants often located in atmospheric cellars. At teatime, coffee time and any other time, a *Konditorei* (cake shop/café) offers a huge array of tempting home-made cakes and pastries. Coffee also comes in many varieties. A *Kaffeehaus* serves hot dishes too.

The wide pedestrianised **Graben** near the cathedral is just one street to find plenty of cafés including **Café de l'Europe**, *Am Graben 31,* which is over 100 years old. **Café Sacher**, *Philharmonikerstr. 4,* part of **Hotel Sacher**, serves the original *Sachertorte.* **Demel's**, *Kohlmarkt 14,* has achieved legendary status for both décor and baking, offering 70 different cakes from ÖS48–85 per portion (closed evenings).

The area around the university (U-Bahn 2/4 to *Schottentor*) is a good hunting ground for cheap meals compared with some restaurants in

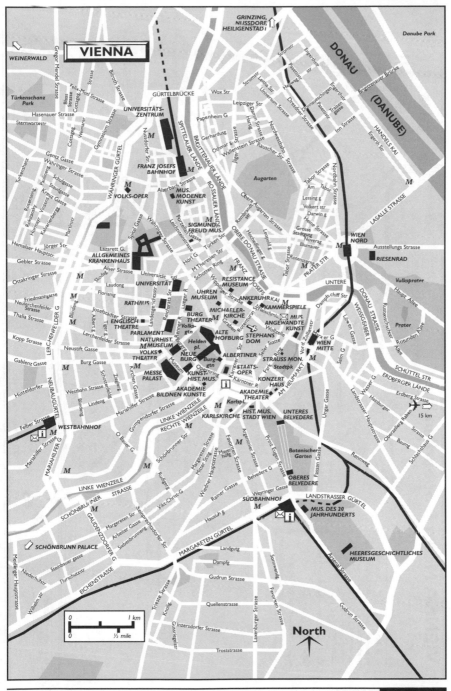

**VIENNA**

WEINERWALD

Türkenschanz Park

GRINZING, NUSSDORF HEILIGENSTADT

Danube Park

DONAU (DANUBE)

GÜRTELBRÜCKE

UNIVERSITÄTS-ZENTRUM

FRANZ JOSEFS BAHNHOF

VOLKS-OPER

MUS. MODENER KUNST

SIGMUND FREUD MUS.

Augarten

HANDELS KAI

LASALLE STRASSE

WIEN NORD

RIESENRAD

Volksprater

ALLGEMEINES KRANKENHAUS

UNIVERSITÄT

RATHAUS

RESISTANCE MUSEUM

UHREN MUSEUM

ANKERUHRKAI

KAMMERSPIELE

UNTERE

Prater

BURG THEATER

MICHAELER KIRCHE

MUS ANGEWANDTE KUNST

ENGLISCH THEATRE

PARLAMENT

NATURHIST. MUSEUM

ALTE HOFBURG

STEPHANS DOM

WIEN MITTE

SCHÜTTEL STR

15 km

VOLKS THEATER

NEUE BURG

ALBERTINER

STRAUSS MON.

MESSE PALAST

KUNST-HIST. MUS.

STAATS-OPER

KONZERT HAUS

ERDBERGER LÄNDE

AKADEMIE BILDNEN KUNSTE

AKADEMIE THEATER

WESTBAHNHOF

KARLSKIRCHE

HIST. MUS. STADT WIEN

UNTERES BELVEDERE

Botanischer Garten

SCHÖNBRUNN PALACE

OBERES BELVEDERE

SÜDBAHNHOF

LANDSTRASSER GÜRTEL

MUS. DES 20 JAHRHUNDERTS

HEERESGESCHICHTLICHES MUSEUM

MARGARETEN GÜRTEL

0       1 km

0     ½ mile

**North**

507

508

# VIENNA Metro & Suburban lines

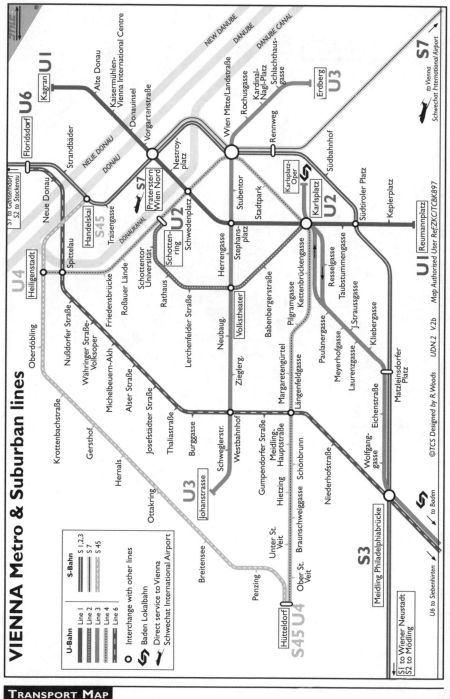

**U-Bahn**
- Line 1
- Line 2
- Line 3
- Line 4
- Line 6

**S-Bahn**
- S 1,2,3
- S 7
- S 45

○ Interchange with other lines

Baden Lokalbahn

Direct service to Vienna
Schwechat International Airport

©TCS Designed by R.Woods     UDN.2  V2b     Map Authorised User Ref:ZKC/TCBK897 the city centre, where eating out in style can cost anything from ÖS700 upwards, like **Zu Den Drei Husaren**, *Weihburgg. 4*, which offers a 7-course Viennese meal with gipsy music for ÖS1000. *Bächerstr.* is a good place to look for a moderately priced traditional meal, as at **Oswald & Kalb**, which looks rather gloomy but is full of atmosphere. **Griechenbeisl**, *Fleischmarkt 11*, a 14th-century building, looks small from the outside but is a warren of rooms within; its 3-course menu costs ÖS345. There are also plenty of *Würstelstände* (hot-dog stalls), sandwich bars like **Trzesniewski**, *Dorotheerg. 1*, and fast-food stalls at the *Naschmarkt*.

Just north-west of the city, in villages such as **Grinzing** (tram no. 38), **Heiligenstadt** (U-Bahn 4) and **Neustift am Walde** (bus no. 35A) on the edge of the rural **Wienerwald** (Vienna Woods), are the city's *Heurigen* taverns, where young local wine is served with traditional food from mid-afternoon till midnight (around ÖS250).

## Communications

The Central **Post Office**, *Fleischmarkt 19*, has poste restante facilities (open 24 hrs).

To phone Vienna from abroad: *tel: 43* (Austria) *+ 1* (Vienna) *+ number*; to phone the city from elsewhere in Austria: *tel: 01 + number*.

## Money

Banks open Mon–Fri, 0800 -1500 (to 1730 Thur in the centre); branch offices close for lunch, 1230–1330.

## Embassies and Consulates

**Australia**: *Mattiellistr. 2–4; tel: 512 85 80.*
**Republic of Ireland**: *Landstr./Hauptstr. 2; tel: 715 4246.*
**South Africa**: *Sandg. 33; tel: 326 493.*
**UK**: *Jauresg. 12: tel: 713 15 75.*
**USA**: *Botzmanng. 16; tel: 313 39.*

### ENTERTAINMENT

*Wien Magazin*, a monthly listing of all entertainment except cinemas is free from Tourist Offices. Films (including those in English) are listed in newspapers. Youth event and discount tickets are available from *Jugend-Info* (see Tourist Information).

**Nightlife** and trendies focus on the 'Bermuda Triangle', an area of lively bars, discos and pubs into which people soon disappear around *Ruprechtspl.*, particularly *Judeng. and Sterng.*

However, the city is mostly famed as one of the world's great centres of classical music. Highlights include the May and June **Vienna Festival** of plays, concerts, opera and exhibitions. The **Staatsoper** (Vienna State Opera), *Opernring 2*, one of the world's leading opera houses, stages productions Sept–June. The **Volksoper**, *Wahringerstr. 78*, offers operettas and musicals. To avoid high agency commissions, apply for tickets (ÖS50–5000)´ to **Bundestheaterverband**, *Hanuschg. 3, A-1010 Wien; tel: 513 1 513*. Standing tickets are sold an hour before the performance (be prepared to queue).

Mozart operas are performed by puppets at the **Marionette Theatre** at the Schönbrunn, though in July and Aug there are real opera performances there too. A cheaper substitute in July and Aug is the free **Film Festival** of opera, concert and ballet performances shown on a giant screen in the *Rathausplatz*.

The famous **Vienna Boys' Choir** performs in the **Hofburg** chapel, Sun 0915, Sept–Jun, ÖS60–280, standing room free. For tickets, write to **Hofmusik Kapelle**, *Hofburg, A-1010 Wien*. The choir also performs Friday 1530 at the *Konzerthaus*, ÖS390/430. For tickets contact **Reisebüro Mondial**, *Faulmanng. 4, A-1040 Wien; tel: 588 04141*.

### SHOPPING

The city's shopping hours are 0900–1800 Mon–Fri and 0900–1200 Sat.

*Kärntnerstr.* is the busiest shopping street and together with *Graben* also the place to promenade. The **Ringstrasse Galerien**, *Mahlerstr.*, just off it, is a modern mall with over 70 smart shops open until 1900 (1700 Sat). Other interesting specialist shops are to be found in the smaller streets nearby.

Department stores are in *Mariahilferstr.*, outside the ring leading to the Westbahnhof. **Augarten porcelain** is sold at the Augarten factory, *Obere Augartenstr.*, which offers factory visits (about an hour) at 0930, or *Stock im*

*Eisenpl. 3.* A good outlet for *Loden*, the traditional Austrian jacket, is **Loden Plankel**, *Michaelerpl. 6.*

## SIGHTSEEING

One of the great pleasures in Vienna is strolling around its imposing buildings, many created in the 19th century during the 68-year long reign of **Franz Joseph I**. The Tourist Office runs specialist **walking tours** (ÖS108), but finding your way around on your own is no problem as the city centre is compact and public transport easy to handle.

### The Centre

The main sights are the **cathedral** and **Hofburg** (Imperial Palace). An ornately carved spire soars over **Stephansdom** (St Stephen's Cathedral), U-Bahn 1/3 to *Stephanspl.*, Austria's most important Gothic building. Its colourful roof, tiled in jazzy stripes, is seen at its best when floodlit at night. The magnificent 14th-century **Südturm** (South tower), known to the locals as the *Steffl*, is 137 m high and the view from the top is well worth the 343-step ascent. The north tower, the **Pummerin**, which contains a giant bell, has the advantage of a lift to take you up it, but is considerably lower. Interior highlights include the **Albertine Choir**, dating from 1340, and a 500-year pulpit and organ loft by Anton Pilgrim. The fabulous Renaissance tomb of Friedrich III stands in the South Apse.

The **Hofburg,** which was the Habsburg's winter residence until 1918, *Michaelerpl. 1; tel: 533 7570,* occupies a prime position on the edge of the Ring overlooking formal gardens and lawns with plenty of shady seats. Altogether, it comprises no less than 18 wings, 54 stairways and 2600 rooms, and now houses several museums. The magnificently ornate **Imperial Apartments** have been preserved as they were in Emperor Franz Josef I's time. The crown of the Holy Roman Empire is on show in the Schatzkammer, and the richly baroque National Library contains one of the world's best collections of manuscripts.

In the **Spanish Riding School**, the famous Lippizaner horses perform on Sat and Sun (except July–Aug). Tickets (ÖS250–900) can be booked by writing to **Spanische Reitschule**, *Hofburg, A-1010 Wien; tel: 535 0186.* Or you can queue at the door of the Redoute, *Josefspl.*, to see 'morning training' without music, Tues–Sat 1000–1200, ÖS100. The **Burgkapelle** is the chapel where the Vienna Boys Choir sing on Sundays (see Entertainment).

## Galleries and Museums

Vienna's major museum, the **Kunsthistorisches Museum** (Museum of Fine Arts), *Burgring 5; tel: 525 240* (U-Bahn 2 to *Babenbergerstr.*) is based on the collection of the Habsburgs. Occupying an impressive building with ornate columns, staircases and ceilings, it boasts a comprehensive collection of Bruegels, as well as masterpieces by Dürer, Rembrandt and Titian. Other sections are devoted to classical and Egyptian antiquities.

The superb 18th-century baroque **Belvedere Palace**, *Prinz-Eugenstr. 3; tel: 795 570* (tram D), built for Prince Eugene of Savoy, has two galleries and delightful gardens. The **Österreichische Galerie** (Austrian Gallery) has important works by artists of the Biedermeier period (1814–1848), the Vienna Secession and Austrian Expressionism.

The **Baroque Museum**, at the *Rennweg* end of the park, contains works by leading baroque artists, including Georg Raphael Donner. The **Akademie der Bildenden Künste** (Academy of Fine Arts), *Schillerpl. 3; tel: 8 816 225* (U-Bahn 1/2/3 to *Karlspl.*) includes generous numbers of Flemish works by the likes of Bosch, Van Dyck and Rembrandt.

The **Museum für Angewandte Kunst** (Museum of Applied Art), *Stubenring 5; tel: 711 36 0* (tram nos 1/2), is a cornucopia of Oriental, European and Austrian artefacts. Modern art is housed in the **Museum Moderner Kunst** in the Leichtenstein Palace, *Fürsteng. 1; tel: 317 69 00* (tram D), a fine baroque building containing works by Austrian Expressionists and other leading European 20th-century artists.

The **Albertina**, *Augustinerstr.; tel: 534 83* (U-Bahn 1/2/3 to *Karlspl./Oper*), houses the world's greatest collection of drawings and prints. The delightful **Uhrenmuseum** (Clock Museum), *Schulhof 2; tel: 533 22 65* (U-Bahn 1/3 *to Schottentor)* features 900 clocks of every conceivable type. Twentieth-century design is imaginatively exhibited at **MAK** (Museum of Applied Arts), *Stubenring 5; tel: 712 8000* (U-Bahn 3 to *Stubentor).*

## Churches

Vienna abounds with intriguing churches. In the Gothic **Augustinerkirche**, *Augustinerstr. 3* (U-Bahn 1/2/3 to *Karlspl./Oper*, tram nos 1/2), the hearts of the Habsburgs are kept in silver urns.

The **Kapuzinerkirche**, *Neuer Markt* (U-Bahn 1/2/3 to *Karlspl./Oper),* is above the Capuchin crypt, where Habsburg bodies were laid to rest in impressive baroque tombs. Other examples of Viennese Gothic include the **Church of Maria am Gestade**, *Am Gestade* (tram nos 1/2), **Minoritenkirche**, *Minoritenpl. 2A,* and **Michaelerkirche**, *Michaelerpl.* (both U-Bahn 3 to *Herrengasse).*

Two superb baroque churches are the 1708 **Peterskirche**, *Peterspl.* (U-Bahn 1/3 to *Stephanspl.),* and the 1713 **Karlskirche**, *Karlspl.* (U-Bahn 1/2/3 to *Karlspl./Oper*, tram nos 1/2), the masterpiece of the baroque experts, father and son von Erlach.

he ornate 17th–18th-century **Jesuitkirche**, *Dr Ignaz Seipelpl.* (U-Bahn 1/3 to *Stephanspl.),* formerly the university church, has a spectacular interior with gold altar, pink marble columns, carved pews and a magnificent *trompe l'oeil* painted ceiling.

## Minor Sights and Musicians

Figures from Austrian history parade across the face of the curious art nouveau **Anker Clock**, *Hoher Markt 10/11* (U-Bahn 1/4 to *Schwedenpl.)* at 1200. For an idea of the architectural splendours of the late 19th-century, take tram nos 1 or 2 around the *Ring,* passing the neo-Gothic **Rathaus** (City Hall), **Burgtheater, Parliament** and **Staatsoper**.

The **Pasqualati House**, *Mölker Bastei 8*

(tram nos 1/2) is one of many lodgings used by Beethoven, who also has a museum at the **Heiligenstadt Testament Haus**, *Probusg. 6; tel: 37 54 08* (tram no. 37) in *Heiligenstadt.* Mozart's lodging, the so-called **Figaro House**, *Domg. 5; tel: 513 62 94* (U-Bahn 1/3 to *Stephanspl.)* has memorial rooms. **Schubert Museum** is at his birthplace, *Nussdorferstr. 54, tel: 317 3601* (tram nos 37/38). The **Sigmund Freud Museum**, *Bergg. 19; tel: 319 15 96*, in the house where he lived and worked from 1891 until his expulsion by the Nazis in 1938, has displays about his 'discovery' of psychoanalysis.

An architecture leaflet from the Tourist Office highlights 20th-century buildings of interest, including the anarchic-looking **Hundertwasserhaus** *(Loweng./Kegelg.)* named after the painter-architect who designed it and the small matching shopping centre. **Kunst-Haus Wien**, *Untere Weissgerberstr. 13; tel: 712 04 91* (trams N/O), was a factory but has been converted by him into an art museum in similar style.

## Further Out

The palace of **Schönbrunn**, *Schönbrunner Schlosstr. 13; tel: 811 13 238* (U-Bahn 4 to *Schönbrunn*, tram no. 58 from *Burgring),* a grand palace with fabulously rich baroque decoration, was built as the summer residence of the Habsburgs (guided tours of 40 rooms, or see 20 on your own). Mozart made his debut there aged 6. It stands in a superb park (open till sunset, free) with a Butterfly House and the world's oldest zoo.

The legendary **Prater** park (U-Bahn 1 to *Praterstern*, trams O/5/21) was originally the imperial hunting grounds, A ride on the giant ferris wheel, which has been turning there since 1897, provides a great view – but take care in the park at night.

Walking trails criss cross the rolling hills of the **Wienerwald** (Vienna Woods) on the north west edge of the city, accessible by tram no. 38.

# VIENNA–WARSAW

The route passes the vine-clad foothills of the Carpathians then fertile plains, following the River Váh before reaching endless, forested mountain ranges in northern Slovakia. Strip-farmed fields, traditionally-dressed older folk and rural villages indicate the traditions remaining in Central Europe.

FASTEST JOURNEY: **8** HRS

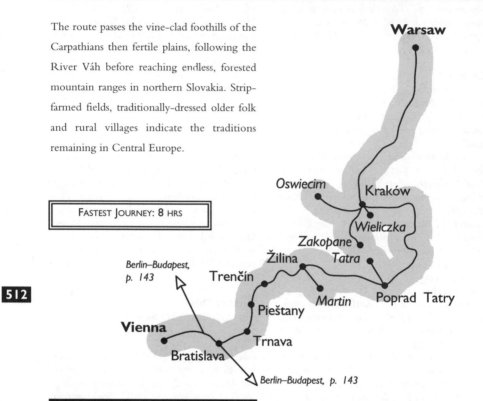

## TRAINS

**ETT tables:** 95a, 1195, 1180, 1188, 1078, 1185, 1099, 1066.

### FAST TRACK

The *Sobieski* takes 8 hrs to travel between Wien Sud and Warsaw Centralna. It has a restaurant car. The *Chopin* travels overnight and offers sleeping cars, couchettes and second-class seats; it takes 10½ hrs. Both of these trains take a much shorter route through the Czech Republic than the On Track route.

### ON TRACK

#### Vienna–Bratislava
Four trains a day, taking 1 hr 7 mins.

#### Bratislava–Trnava–Piešťany–Trenčín–Žilina
A regular service with trains every 2 hrs. Most trains have refreshment facilities but require supplements to be paid. The journey throughout takes just over 2½ hrs. There are also a couple of faster IC trains (requiring advance reservations) each day, which do not call at intermediate stations.

#### Zilina–Poprad Tatry
The 2-hourly service continues from Žilina to Poprad Tatry, with a journey time of 2 hrs.

#### Poprad Tatry–Kraków
There are no through trains from Poprad to Kraków. One connecting service is available

each day. This requires a morning departure from Poprad, a change of trains at Plaveč and gives an evening arrival in Kraków.

## Kraków–Warsaw

Fast trains operate every 2 hrs between Kraków and Warsaw Centralna. These trains require advance seat reservations, have buffets or restaurant cars, and take 2 hrs 35 mins.

## TRNAVA

**Station:** tel: (0805) 26241/24983. The centre is 10 mins walk up *Hospodárska st.*, then right down *Bernolákova brana st.*
**Tourist Office:** TINS, *Trojičné námestie 1; tel: (0805) 186 or 511 022.*

The 'Slovak Rome', Trnava is a charming university town boasting 12 churches and unspoiled, cobbled lanes.

## PIEŠTANY

**Station:** tel: (0838) 21213, is 15 mins walk west of the centre (signposted).
**Tourist Office:** Informačné stredisko Pieštany (in the Hotel Eden), *Winterova 60; tel: (0838) 27689.*

Slovakia's biggest, grandest spa, built at the turn of the century, offers cures, elegant cafés and peaceful, riverside parks.

## TRENČÍN

**Station:** tel: (0831) 419484. Walk 10 mins east through the park for the centre.
**Tourist Office:** Kultúrno-informačné centrum mesta Trenčín, *Štúrovo námestie 10; tel: (0831) 186 or 533 505.*

Trenčín, dwarfed by a towering castle on a crag, is a charming old town. It's connected by branch line to **Trenčianské Teplice spa** (with pseudo-Turkish baths).

## ŽILINA

**Station:** tel: (089) 22226, is north-east of the centre, on *Národná ulica.*
**Tourist Office:** Selinan Travel Agency, *Burianova medzierka 4; tel: (089) 620 789.*

It's worth taking a look at the Renaissance arcades in the town centre, but Žilnia is an ideal base for exploring the scenic mountain ranges nearby, or the **Kysuce Nature Reserve**.

### SIDE TRACK FROM ŽILINA

Four trains per day make the short run through from Žilina to Martin, taking 45 mins. Plenty more journeys are possible by changing at Vrútky. **Martin** is an outstanding base for walking or skiing in the Mala and Velka Fatra mountains, and for visiting the **Slovak Village Museum** (at *Jahodnicke haje*), 3 km away.

## POPRAD TATRY

**Station:** tel: (0969) 22809, is 1 km north of the town centre.
**Tourist Office:** Popradská informačná agentúra, *Nám. sv. Egídia 2950/114; tel: (092) 186 or 721 700.*

Poprad, sandwiched between the High and Low Tatra mountain ranges, is undistinguished but **Spišská Sobota** (3 km east of the station) has Renaissance houses and exquisite church carvings.

### SIDE TRACK FROM POPRAD

From Poprad, the TEZ railway climbs into the stunning alpine **High Tatra** mountains, stopping at **Starý Smokovec**, **Strbské Pleso** and **Tatranská Lomnica** for spas, hiking and skiing. Buses cover the Spiš region – unspoilt Renaissance towns amongst rolling hills, striped fields and tiny white churches: **Levoča** and **Spišský Hrad** (Spiš castle) are unmissable.

**513**

## KRAKÓW

**Station:** Kraków Głowny (main station), *tel: (012) 422 22 48 or 933* for rail information, is a short walk from the town centre and has currency exchange, information on accommodation, left-luggage facilities and a restaurant.
**Płaszów Station**, has a more frequent service to Oświęcim (Auschwitz), serves the salt mines and has some night services. It is about 30 mins from the centre by Tram no.13.
**Kraków Balice Airport**; *tel: (012) 411 19 55,* 18 km from Kraków. It offers European routes operated by LOT Polish Airlines, including direct flights to London, Paris and Rome. For

tickets and flight information there is an office at *ul. Basztowa 15; tel: 952/3.* From the airport, take a taxi, or bus B leaving every 30 mins, which takes about 20 mins to reach the centre, terminating by the Old Town.

**Tourist Office**: the useful **Central Tourist Information Office**, *ul. Pawia 8, 31–154 Kraków; tel: (012) 422 60 91,* near the station, opens Mon–Fri 0800–2100, Sat 0900–1500. Information also from **Orbis**, *Rynek Główny 41; tel: (012) 22 40 35,* open Mon–Fri 0800–1900, Sat 0800–1400, and **Dexter Travel**, *Rynek Główny 1/3; tel: (012) 421 77 06,* open Mon–Fri 0900–1800, Sat 0900–1300. The free monthly magazines *What, Where, When Kraków* and *Welcome to Kraków* contain practical details.

## GETTING AROUND

The **Stare Miasto** (Old Town), encircled by the **Planty**, a belt of greenery where the city walls once stood, is pedestrian only. Beyond this a network of buses and trams operates, with tickets on sale at Ruch kiosks. Punch both ends of the ticket on board (once only for concessions). *Kraków Plan Miasta,* the city map with a distinctive red and yellow cover, is marked with bus and tram routes, and is sold at news-stands and bookshops.

Taxis are still relatively cheap. Find them at the station or taxi stands or by phoning *919.*

## ACCOMMODATION

For those on a limited budget, finding a bed can be difficult, although **pension** style accommodation under private management is increasingly becoming available in the Old Town. The Tourist Office can make reservations and arrange **private accommodation**. It is also quite common to be approached by individuals at the station. Remember to check the location and price before agreeing. In addition to modern Orbis hotels such as **Hotel Forum**, *Marii Konopnickiej 28; tel: (012) 266 95 00,* which overlooks the Wawel Castle and is a short walk from the old town, there are period **town-house hotels** such as the Secessionist-style **Hotel Francuski**, *ul. Pijarska 13; tel: (012) 22 51 22,* built in 1912, and the antique-style **Hotel Saski**, *ul. Stawkowska 3; tel: (012) 421 42 22.* Chain hotels include *Hd.* There is a

**Dom Turisty hostel** at *Westerplatte 15; tel: (012) 422 95 00,* which is on the edge of the old town. There are three **campsites**; try **Krak**, *ul. Radzikowskiego 99; tel: (012) 637 21 22,* during the summer season, which has the highest ranking and an inexpensive motel.

## EATING AND DRINKING

*Rynek Główny* and the surrounding streets are full of inexpensive restaurants. For good traditional Polish food, try **Wierzynek**, *Rynek Główny 15; tel: (012) 422 98 96,* which is 600 years old and comes complete with suits of armour and panelling. Traditional Jewish cuisine is served at **Ariel Gallery**, *ul. Szeroka 18; tel: (012) 421 79 20.* Among the courtyard garden restaurants in the old town is **Chiniera**, *ul. Św Anny 3; tel: (012) 423 21 78,* with live music, too. There are numerous cafés around the main market square with alfresco tables, with **Kauiarnia Noworolski**, *Rynek Główny 1* (in the *Sukennice); tel: (012) 422 47 71,* an ideal choice, while the Art Nouveau café **Jama Michalika**, *ul. Florianska 45;* is renowned for pastries and cabaret.

There are plenty of cellar bars in the Old Town, like **Piwnica pod Baranami**, *Rynek Główny 26; tel: (012) 423 07 32.* For snacks, try the delicatessen-style grocers (east side of square). Planty Park is ideal for picnics.

## Communications

The **main post office** (with Poste Restante), *ul. Westerplatte 20;* opens 0730–2100, Sat 0900–1600 and Sun 0900–1100.

The telephone section is open 24 hrs (queues are common). Telephone cards, needed for international calls, and the increasingly out-moded telephone coins are on sale.

## Consulates

**USA**: *ul. Stolarska 9; tel: (012) 422 97 64.*

## Money

Central Kraków is full of *Kantors* (exchanges). Change travellers cheques and cash advances on Visa and Mastercard in bank *Pekao, Rynek Główny 31,* open Mon–Fri 0730–1900, Sat 0730–1735. Credit cards are rapidly gaining sway in restaurants and shops.

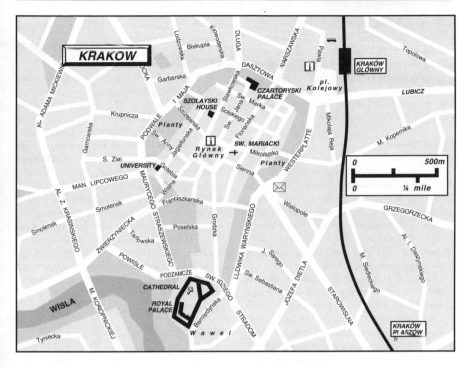

## ENTERTAINMENT

Evening activities revolve around theatres, concerts, cabaret and nightclubs. Full information and tickets can be obtained from **Centrum Informacji Kulturalnej** (Cultural Information Centre), *ul. Św Jana 2; tel: (012) 421 77 87,* open Mon–Fri 1000–1900, Sat 1100–1900. The centre also publishes a monthly listings magazine, which includes an English supplement.

Concert halls include the **Karol Szyman owski National Philharmonic**, *ul. Zwierzyniecka 1,* and **Juliusz Słowacki Theatre and Opera Stage**, *pl. Św. Ducha 3.* Jazz venues include **Kornet Jazz Club**, *ul. Krasin Skiego 19,* and **U Muniaka Jazz Club**, *ul. Floriańska 3; tel: (012) 423 12 05.*

Films are usually shown with subtitles rather than dubbed, and the 18 cinemas are a popular source of entertainment. Annual events include the **Days of Organ Music** (April) held in Kraków's churches, and the exhibition of **Christ Child's cribs** in December.

## SIGHTSEEING

Kraków became the capital of Poland in 1040, moved from Gniezno by King Casimir the Restorer. Being rebuilt after the Tartar invasion in 1241, the city entered a golden age in the 14th century, though Warsaw took over as the capital in 1596.

When Poland was partitioned at the end of the 18th century, Kraków was part of the Austro-Hungarian Empire. During the Nazi occupation, Kraków was headquarters for the General Government, being liberated by Soviet forces in 1945, when a sudden advance meant that the Nazis retreated without implementing a planned programme of complete destruction, which was undertaken in Warsaw. Thus Kraków was one of a handful of places to survive World War II, and its national and cultural significance, not to mention beauty, is immense. Poles regard it as the spiritual heart of their country; UNESCO lists it as one of the world's 12 most precious cultural sites.

Museums can have fairly erratic opening

hours, though with over 2 million works of art it's worth persevering. The best of Kraków can equally be appreciated from a walking tour, which includes designer boutiques, antique shops and antique pharmacies in the Old Town still with their original fittings. Sightseeing tours can be arranged through **InterCrac**, *Rynek Główny 14; tel: (012) 422 58 40.*

### Rynek Główny

With each side measuring 200m, this is one of the largest and most beautiful medieval market places in Europe. While Rynek Główny is never entirely swamped by the crowds, flower stalls and alfresco cafés, try visiting late at night or early in the morning for full impact. The size of the **Sukiennice** (Cloth Hall) that stands centre-stage, and the surrounding burgher's houses create a unique setting.

The Cloth Hall started as a Gothic roof over trading stalls, and was enlarged during the reign of Casimir the Great. Following a fire in 1555 it was reconstructed in the Renaissance style, and is still a thriving commercial concern, filled with stalls selling amber, silver and superior souvenirs. A branch of the **National Museum**, on the first floor, houses 18th- and 19th-century historical Polish paintings and sculptures. Open Tues–Sat 1000–1800, Sun 1000–1530.

The **Ratusz** (City Hall Tower), *Rynek Główny 1; tel: (012) 422 09 62* (open Wed 0900–1500, Thur 1100–1800, Fri–Sun 0900–1500) has a good view from top. It is all that remains of the Gothic Town Hall, destroyed in the 1820s as part of a civic rebuilding programme. Inside are some historical exhibits and a basement café. In the opposite corner of the square is the Romanesque **St Adalbert's Church**, which is the oldest and one of the smallest in Kraków. The vaults house the **Historical Museum of the City of Kraków**, including pre-Romanesque effects.

Further north, Mariacki (St Mary's Church) has an amazing wooden Gothic altar, 13m high and adorned by 200 figures, created over 12 years by Wit Stwosz, the 15th-century master carver of Nuremberg. Legend has it that a watchman was shot down from the church tower by Tartar invaders. The *hejnał,* the

melody he trumpeted to sound the alarm, is repeated hourly.

### The University district

The **University** is Central Europe's second oldest, receiving its royal charter in 1364. It was named Jagiellonian University, under the patronage of the eponymously named Polish royal family in the early 15th century. Famous alumni include the Polish astronomer Nicolaus Copernicus and Pope John Paul II. **Collegium Maius**, *ul. Jagiellonska 15; tel: (012) 422 05 49,* (open Mon–Fri 1100–1430, Sat 1100–1330) is the oldest college, and a magnificent example of Gothic architecture. Numerous artefacts on display include 35 globes, with one dating from 1510 featuring the earliest illustration of America, marked 'a newly discovered land'.

Tours of the university take in the alchemy rooms (supposedly Dr Faustus's laboratory), lecture rooms, assembly hall and professors' apartments.

### Museums

With almost 30 museums, it's as well to get a detailed guidebook from the Tourist Office. However, times can change, and museums can close unexpectedly for restoration. The **Muzeum Warodowe** (National Museum) has various branches and exhibits in the 18th-century **Czartoryski Palace**, *ul. Sw. Jana 19; tel: (012) 422 55 66* (open Tues, Wed Thur 1000–1530, Fri 1000–1800, Sat–Sun 1000–1530). Exhibits includes a large collection of ancient art, as well as works by Rembrandt and Leonardo da Vinci. **Szołayski House**, *pl. Szczepanski 9; tel: (012) 422 70 21,* (open Tues 1000–1600, Wed–Sun 1000–1530), has 14th–18th-century art and sculpture.

Modern art, from the late 19th-century, is housed at **Galleria Sztuk XXw** (Gallery of 20th-century art), *al. 3 Maja; tel: (012) 634 33 77,* which also includes military exhibits. Open Tues–Sat 1000–1800, Sun 1000–1530. The **Jan Matejko Museum**, *ul. Florianska 41; tel: (012) 422 59 26,* depicts the life of Poland's greatest historical painter. Open Tues, Thur, Sat–Sun 1000–1530, Fri 1000–1800.

The **Muzeum Historii Fotografii** is the photographic museum at *Rynek Główny 17.*

**The Ethnographic Museum**, *pl. Wolnica 1; tel: (012) 656 56 01*, is housed in the former town hall of the city of Kazimierz (now part of Kraków), which specialises in folk art. Open Mon 1000–1800, Wed–Fri 1000–1500, Sat–Sun 1000–1400.

## Wawel

The **Cathedral** and fortified **Royal Castle** (both built by King Casimir the Great) are the most important museums in Kraków, standing high on *Wawel Hill* and bordered by the Wisła (Vistula) river; *tel: (012) 422 51 55*. Open Tues 0930–1630, Wed–Thur 0930–1530, Fri 0930–1630, Sat 0930–1500, Sun 1000–1500.

The **Cathedral's** present Gothic construction dates from 1320–64, with the first church constructed here in the 11th century. Relics of the earlier building are displayed in the castle's west wing. The most famous of the 19 side chapels, built in Renaissance and baroque styles, is the golden-domed **Renaissance Zygmuntowska** (Sigismund's Chapel), built 1519–31. As the site for coronations and funerals, 41 of Poland's 45 kings are buried in the Cathedral, along with national heroes and poets. Climb the cathedral tower for a good view and see the 2½m diameter **Zygmunt Bell**, rung to celebrate church or national holidays.

Some of the **Royal Castle's** Gothic fragments, such as the **Danish Tower**, and the **Kurza Stopa** (Hen's Foot) still exist, but the majority of the Castle was rebuilt in the Renaissance style after a fire in 1502–36. The vast courtyard, with three-storey arcades, is considered one of Europe's finest examples of Renaissance architecture. Displayed in the Royal Chambers are 142 exquisite **Arras tapestries** depicting Biblical scenes, commissioned in the mid 16th century. The **Treasury** houses European and Oriental weapons, some of which were captured by King Jan III Sobieski when he defeated the Turks at Vienna in 1683. There is also a collection of royal jewels and coronation regalia.

## Kazimierz

Now part of Kraków, Kazimierz was originally a separate city when founded in 1335, and traditionally a Jewish area. Among the numerous Renaissance buildings is the oldest synagogue on *ul. Szeroka 24; tel: (012) 422 09 62*, dating from the late 15th century, and now a museum depicting Jewish history and culture in Poland. Open Wed–Thur, Sat–Sun 0900–1530, Fri 1100–1800. The Renaissance Remuh synagogue still serves its religious purpose.

## ⇄ SIDE TRACKS FROM KRAKÓW

### OŚWIĘCIM (AUSCHWITZ)

**Auschwitz**, German for Oświęcim, is synonomous with the atrocities of the **Holocaust**. In this, the largest concentration camp, between 1.5 and 2 million people from across Europe, mainly Jewish, met brutality and death at the hands of the SS.

Men, women and children were transported here in cattle trucks, often surviving for up to 10 days. They were promised jobs, some bought fictitious land. Anyone deemed unfit upon arrival was ostensibly allowed a bath and cyanide gas pouring from the shower heads poisoned up to 2000 at a time. The rest faced hard physical labour and passed daily through gates bearing the inscription *Arbeit Macht Frei* (Freedom through Work). When Soviet liberation forces arrived in May 1945 they found emaciated survivors, the machinery of death and 7000 kg of women's hair, due to be made into cloth or used to stuff mattresses. The piles of spectacle frames, shoe-polish tins, baby clothes and monogrammed suitcases are on display. Regular screenings of the liberators' films are shown in several languages.

Nearby **Birkenau** was an even more efficient Nazi death factory. Visit the **National Museum of Auschwitz-Birkenau**, *ul. Wiezniów Oświęcima 20; tel: (012) 642 40 21*. Trains (1¾ hrs) leave from Kraków, mostly from Płaszów station.

### WIELICZKA (MAGNUM SAL)

Wieliczka salt mine, *Park Kingi 1*, features, along with Kraków, on UNESCO's heritage list. Mined for 700 years, it has 350 miles of tunnelling, with 2040 chambers,

517

and used to provide 40% of the area's wealth. The mine is a dazzling feat, with 40 chapels carved entirely from salt, while larger than life size salt statues of, amongst others, **Copernicus** and **St Anthony**, can be seen in the tunnels. Most magnificent of all is the main chapel with salt chandeliers and even salt relief pictures on the walls. Open daily 0730–1830 (Apr 15–Oct 15) and 0800–1600 out of season. Guided tours are offered in English.

Trains leave from Kraków Płaszów. Contact the Tourist Board at *Danitowicza 10, 32-020 Wieliczka; tel: (012) 278 73 02.*

### ZAKOPANE

**Station: Dworzec Glowny**; *tel: (0165) 145 04,* has left-luggage facilities and currency exchange.

**Tourist Office**: *ul. Kościuszki 17, 34–500 Zakopane; tel: (0165) 12211,* open daily 0700–2100.

Zakopane (the town centre is within walking distance of the station), is renowned as a winter sports centre, being within a vast national park that comprises mountains, lakes and forests, and 300 km of marked trails for hikers. The scenery is outstanding and you can take a cable-car to the top of mountains, including **Kasprowy Wierch** and **Gubalowka**. **Zakopane** is also a centre of highland folk art with the annual **Tatran Autumn Festival** held in Sept that includes the **International Festival of Highland Folklore**, while regular exhibitions are held of paintings and artworks. **Muzeum Tatrzanskie** (Tatra Museum), *ul. Krupówki 10; tel: (0165) 15205,* open Tues–Sun 0900–1600, has many folklore exhibits. The **Zakopane** architectural style features ornate wooden houses and churches, many of which are over a century old. Museums include the **Karol Szymanowksi Museum**, *ul. Kasprasie 19; tel: (0165) 13602,* open Tues–Sun 1000–1600, which is dedicated to the composer. Trains leave from Kraków Główny, with express services taking about 3 hrs.

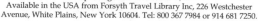

# WARSAW (WARSZAWA)

While Warsaw has its fair share of post-war concrete blocks, there are also areas of immense beauty and historic significance. Having suffered under Communism, Warsaw is now thriving under democracy; there haven't been any shortages or queues for some years. Entertainment, restaurants and shopping are coming into their own, and fast approaching the standards of major Western cities.

## TOURIST INFORMATION

The **Informator Turystyczny (IT)**, *pl. Zamkowy 1/13, 00-262 Warsaw; tel: (022) 635 18 81*, opens Mon–Fri 0900–1800, Sat 1000–1800, Sun 1100–1800. Thin on free handouts, but there is plenty to buy. **Orbis Travel**, *ul. Marszalkowska 142; tel: (022) 827 67 66*, also offers visitor services. The Tourist Office and hotels often have the free *Welcome to Warsaw* and *What, Where, When*, with a map and practical information. *The Warsaw Voice* (English-language newspaper) is also worth consulting. **Thomas Cook licensee: Pegrotours**, *47 Emili Plater Str.; tel: (22) 624 3676*.

## ARRIVING AND DEPARTING

### Airport

**Okęcie Airport**, *1A ul. Żwirki i Wigury; tel. (022) 46 17 31*, lies 10 km south of the city, with two terminals (arrivals and departures) including currency exchange, restaurant, café and washing facilities. LOT airlines now have a service direct from Manchester. Airport City Bus departs every 30 mins, stopping at major hotels and Warszawa Centralna railway station.

### Stations

**Warszawa Centralna**, (Central Railway Station), *al. Jerozolimskie 54; tel: (022) 620 50 10* (for international information); *tel: (022)* *620 45 12* (for national information); *tel: (022) 620 03 61 to 9* (for local details). Located about 30 mins walk from the old town or 10 mins by taxi, it offers currency exchange, left-luggage, café and washing facilities, but is also notorious for crime and best avoided at night.

Other large stations: **Warszawa Wschodnia**, *tel: (022) 618 34 97*, on the east bank of the Wisł (Vistula River), and the western suburban station, **Warszawa Zachodnia**, *tel: (022) 36 57 42*, 3 km west of Centralna, opposite the PKS bus station; *tel: (022) 36 55 00*.

## GETTING AROUND

The River Vistula divides Warsaw, with most sights on the west bank around the Old Town Market Square, and along the main thoroughfares (starting on *Krakowskie Przedmieście*) known as *Trakt Królewski* (Royal Route). Most tourist attractions are walkable, though public transport will probably be necessary at some stage.

### Tickets

Bus and tram tickets (daily, weekly or monthly) are sold at kiosks marked **Bilety MZK**, Ruch kiosks, sometimes by street hawkers, in restaurants and at the post office. (The newsagent at the station is handy if you've just arrived). On board, punch both ends of the ticket (once is for a concession fare). Spot checks lead to fines.

### Public Transport

The 26 tram lines and 150 bus lines operate on a grid system. Buses, which are generally crowded, run from 0430–2300 on weekdays. Night buses run every 45 mins and cost three times the normal fare. Pick up taxis at ranks, outside larger hotels, or by phone *tel: 919*.

## STAYING IN WARSAW

### Accommodation

The Tourist Office has the leaflet, *Hotels, Warsaw and the Environs*, which gives details of all accommodation, and can make reservations,

**519**

with the more expensive business hotels often charging in dollars. The **Hotel Bristol**, *Krakowskie Przedmieśie 42/44; tel: (022) 625 25 25*, is a beautifully restored art nouveau building that is one of Europe's grandest hotels. A good choice in the centre is the **Hotel Forum**, *ul. Nowogrodzka 24/26; tel: (022) 621 02 71.* Next step down are **Tourist Class Hotels**, and there are also some pensions and **budget hotels** on *Krakowskie Przedmieście* and *Nowy Świat*. For **private rooms**, try any of several accommodation bureaux near the station. There are five hostels, two belonging to **HI**, at *ul. Smolna 30; tel: (022) 827 89 52* (central) and *ul. Karolkowa 53a; tel: (022) 632 88 29* (in Wola, take tram nos 1/13/20/24 to *al. Solidarności*). There are six **campsites**, with the most central being *ul. Zwirki i Wigury 32; tel: (022) 25 43 91*. Hotel chains: *HI, Ma, Nv, IC*.

## Eating and Drinking

Privatisation has revolutionised eating out, with restaurants spanning Asian, European and South American food. Traditional Polish food has been joined by new wave Polish, featuring lighter versions of classic dishes. New wave pioneers include the **Malinowa** (within the Hotel Bristol), **Fukier**, *Rynek Starego Miasta 27; tel: (022) 831 10 13,* and **Restauracja Polska**, *ul. Nowyswiat 21; tel: (022) 826 38 77*. For traditional Polish food in an Old Town burgher's house, try **Bazyliszek**, *Rynek Starego Miasta 3/7; tel: (022) 831 18 41,* and **Swiętoszek**, *ul. Jezuicka 6/8; tel: (022) 631 56 34*. Snacks and fast food can easily be found, with plenty of al fresco cafés, particularly in the Old Town.

**Pijalnia Czekolady** (a hot chocolate café) is an antique paradise on *ul. Szpitalna 8*. **Karczma Wojtkowice Stara**, *Rynek Starego Miasta 21; tel: (022) 831 16 61,* is a recreation of an 18th-century country inn. Delicatessens, are abundant, particularly in *Nowy Świat, Krakowskie Przedmieście* and the Old Town.

## Communications

The **Main Post Office**, *ul. Swiętokrzyska, 31/33*, is open 24 hrs, for counter facilities and poste restante. Phones taking tokens are being phased out, with card-operated phones becoming the norm. To phone Warsaw: *tel: 48*

(Poland) + *22*; to phone Warsaw from elsewhere in Poland: *tel: 022.*

## Embassies
**Australia:** *ul. Estonska 3/5; tel: (022) 617 60 81.*
**Canada:** *ul. Matejki 1/5 (door on ul. Pieknej); tel: (022) 629 80 51.*
**New Zealand:** *Migolatowa 4; tel: (022) 625 14 07.*
**UK:** *Al. Róż 1; tel: (022) 628 10 01-5.*
**USA:** *Al. Ujazdowskie 29/31; tel: (022) 628 30 41-9.*

## Money
This is still very much a cash economy, and some bureaux de change *(kantor)* will not cash travellers' cheques. Try **Orbis Travel**, large hotels, or branches of **NBP**, one of which is *pl. Powstanców Warszawy*. Credit cards are accepted by many leading hotels, restaurants and shops catering for tourists. You can get cash advances on credit cards at Orbis Travel.

There is a good range of entertainment, with English and Irish pubs and plenty of discos, live music, including rock and roll, jazz, and above all, classical music. Chopin concerts are held every Sun at 1600, May–Oct by Chopin's monument in **Lazienki Park**. There are several venues for concerts and ballet, an opera house and theatres. Cinemas increasingly show American films, usually subtitled rather than dubbed. The **Pałac Kultury i Nauki** (Palace of Culture and Science), a 'present' from Stalin, houses a casino, theatres, cinemas, nightclub and one of the city's best bookshops.

Local specialities include silver, leather, crystal and amber, with **Cepelia** stores having the best selection of folk art. **Desa** is a chain of antique shops (restrictions on what can be exported). Some of the best shopping is in the **Old Town**, *Krakowskie Przedmieście, Nowy Świat* and *ul. Chmielna*, with department stores on *Marszatkowsna*. Leading hotels have boutiques and shopping arcades. Try *Wola* antique market (Sun) for clothes, furniture and books; bus B, K or no.159. Both markets are crowded by 1000.

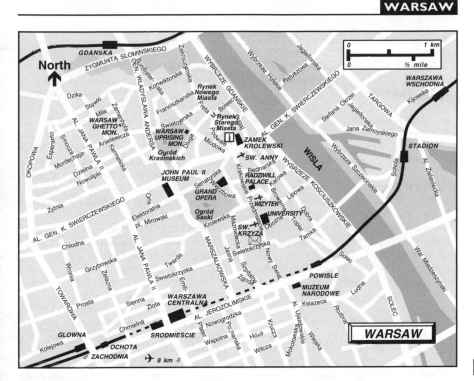

## Rynek Starego Miasta

Very much a focal point, **Rynek Starego Miasta** (the Old Town Market Square) is lined with beautiful burghers' houses, which are exact post-war reconstructions. At no. 28 is the **Muzeum Historyczne Warszawy** (Warsaw Historical Museum); *tel: (022) 635 16 25,* which chronicles the city's turbulent history. A short film, *Warsaw After All,* includes genuine footage shot by the Nazis, documenting their systematic destruction of the city. (Open Tues, Thur 1200–1900, Wed, Fri 1000–1530, Sat–Sun 1030–1630.) The **Mickiewicz Muzeum** *(nos 18/20; tel: (022) 831 40 61)* is a shrine to Polish literature, in particular the romantic poet of the same name, whose national importance is testified by his burial in Krakow Cathedral. (Open Mon, Tues, Fri 1000–1500, Wed, Thur 1100–1800, Sun 1100–1700.)

Behind the Old Town Market Square, the **Archikatedra sw. Jana**, was rebuilt in the original Gothic style. Continue along *Święto-janska* to *pl. Zamkowy,* dominated by **Zamek Krolewski** (Royal Castle); *tel: (022) 657 23 38;* Tues–Sun 1000–1630. Post-war restoration of the Castle, which includes Gothic, baroque and rococo elements, was only completed in the 1980s. Highly stylised interiors, showcase a collection of furniture, tapestries, paintings and *objets d'art.* There is also a good souvenir shop. Standing before the Castle is the **Column of King Zygmant III**, dating from 1644.

### North

The 16th-century **Barbakan** (Barbican) was once part of the city walls, but is now flanked by artists-come-entrepreneurs. Nearby is the 1855 statue of the **Warsaw Mermaid**, which has become the symbol of the city. From here *ul. Freta* leads to *Rynek Nowego Miasta* (New Market Square) past **sw. Jacka** (St. Jack's Church) and the **Marie Curie Museum** (at no.16; *tel: (022) 31 80 92;* Tues–Sat 1000–1630, Sun 1000–1430, in the house where she was born. The 18th-century New Market

Square, less flambouyant than its Old Town counterpart, accommodates the **Church of the Blessed Sacrament**, founded in 1688 by Queen Maria in memory of her husband (King Jan III Sobieski), who defeated the Turks at Vienna. From New Market Square, *ul. Długa* leads to *pl. Krasińskich,* site of a Monument and Museum to the 63-day long Warsaw Uprising, and **Kraśinski Palace** (now a library), fronting the **Kraśinski Park**.

## The Royal Route

The Royal Route starts at *Krakowskie Przedmieście* by the Stare Miasto (Old Town) and heads south, along *Nowy Świat* and *ul. Ujazdowskie,* for 10 km, all the way to **Wilanów**, the royal summer palace. This is the city's main thoroughfare. The 15th-century **Kościół Sw. Anny** (St Anne's Church), *Krakowskie Przedmieście 68*, has interiors full of baroque and rococo extravagance. The tower is open for roof-top views. Passing the **Adam Mickiewicz Monument**, you come to the **Radziwill Palace** (1643), where the Warsaw Pact was signed in May 1955. Just off *Krakowskie Przedmiescie,* in the **Ogród Saski** (Saxon Gardens), the **Tomb of the Unknown Soldier** is guarded around the clock. Dominating *Pl. Pitsudskiego* is the neo-classical **National Theatre** (1825–33). Returning to *Krakowskie Przedmiescie,* Chopin played the organ in the **Kościół Wizytek** (Church of the Visitation), while **Kościół Sw. Krzyża,** is a masterpiece of baroque, and also the resting place of Chopin's heart (in an urn on the left column by the nave).

## Museums

Pride of place amongst the many museums goes to **Muzeum Narodowe** (National Museum), *al. Jerozolimskie 3; tel: (022) 629 30 93* (open Tues, Wed, Fri, Sat, Sun 1000–1600, Thur 1000–1800), which has an impressive collection of paintings successfully hidden during the war. The **Ethnographic Museum,** *ul. Kredytowa 1; tel: (022) 827 76 41* (open Tues, Thur, Fri 0900–1600, Wed 1100–1800, Sat–Sun 1000–1700), has a collection of Polish folk art and world-wide tribal art. The new **Pope John Paul II Museum,** *pl. Bankowy 1; tel: (022) 620 27 25* (open Tues–Sun 1000–1700), has a huge collection of thematically arranged religious art, and great European works, from Titian and Tintoretto to Breughel, Rembrandt and Rodin.

**Frederic Chopin Museum,** *ul. Okólnik 1; tel: (022) 827 54 71* (Fri 1000–1700, Thur 1200–1800, Sat–Sun 1000–1400), within the **Ostrogski Palace**, has an interesting but not extensive collection of memorabilia. This is also the headquarters of the International Chopin Society. At *Krakowskie Przedmieście 5,* within the **College of Fine Art**, is the **Chopin Family Salon**; *tel: (022) 26 62 51, ext. 267;* Mon–Fri 1000–1400. This formal room, with a piano on which Chopin played, is decorated in a classical early 19th century style. Every 5 years Warsaw hosts the **Chopin Piano Competition**, next scheduled for the year 2000.

The **Lazienki Palace** (Palace-on-the-Isle), *ul. Agrykula 1; tel: (022) 625 79 44* (Tues–Sun 0930–1600), is encircled by water. It was built in Neo-Classical style at the end of the 18th century, as the summer residence of Stanislaus Augustus Poniatowski, Poland's last king. The **Lazienki Park** (daily 0930–dusk) also contains smaller palaces, pavilions, a moated amphitheatre, Egyptian temple, orangery and **Bialy Dom** (White House), renowned for its Chinoiserie interiors. The extravagantly baroque **Wilanów Palace**, *ul. Wiertricza 1; tel: (022) 42 82 01;* Mon, Wed–Sat 0930–1430, Sun 0930–1530, park open daily 0930–dusk. Located on the edge of town, it is easily reached by bus, including no. 130. Wilanów was the residence of King Jan III Sobieski, and in addition to highly stylised interiors, featuring an extensive collection of furniture and works of art, the grounds also include a baroque chapel, orangery and a museum of modern poster art.

## Jewish Warsaw

Before World War II, Warsaw had one of Europe's largest Jewish communities. During the Nazi occupation, the population fell from 380,000 to just 300. There are two great monuments: to the **Heroes of the Warsaw Ghetto**, *ul. Zamenhofa,* and the white marble **monument to Concentration Camp Victims,** *Umschlarpl.,* at the place where hundreds of thousands of Jews were herded onto trains bound for the concentration camps.

# WARSAW–HELSINKI

This intriguing route crosses no fewer than four international frontiers, chiefly those of the three newly independent Baltic Republics of Lithuania, Latvia and Estonia. The inaptly named Baltic Express (*Balti Ekspress*) allows the traveller plenty of leisure to absorb the untamed landscape: dense forests of pine and silver birch, gently undulating verdant uplands and isolated farmsteads, doubling as railway halts.

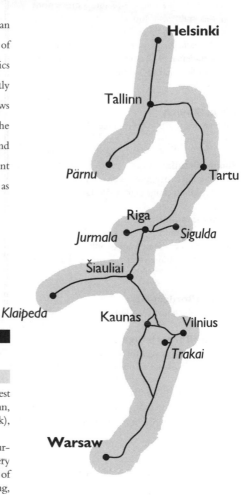

> FASTEST JOURNEY: 24 HRS

523

## TRAINS

**ETT tables:** 93, 1040, 1850, 1810, 2410.

### FAST TRACK

 There is no really fast track. The fastest possible route will be Warsaw–Tallinn, and Tallinn–Helsinki by boat (see On Track), taking over 24 hrs.

The *Balti Ekspress* makes the 21½-hr journey from Warsaw to Tallinn (one train every other day; reservation obligatory). A change of trains is necessary at Šeštokai. Before travelling, check ETT Table 93 as, at the time of writing, the *Balti Ekspress* service had been reprieved following its possible withdrawal.

For ferry information, see On Track.

### ON TRACK

**Warsaw (Warszawa)–(Border)– (Belarus)–(Border)–Vilnius**

The direct Warsaw–Vilnius train performs the journey in 12–13 hrs. This crosses Belarus, and visitors will require a transit visa. They are not issued at the frontier or on the train, and must be obtained from the visa section of the embassy in Britain, or from the consulate in Warsaw or Vilnius. Russian accommodation conditions apply to this train.

### Warsaw (Warszawa)–(Border)–Šeštokai–Kaunas–Vilnius

The *Balti Ekspress* from Warsaw to Kaunas takes 9 hrs. There are no reasonable connections with this train at Kaunas. Kaunas–Vilnius by local electric train takes 2 hrs.

If the *Balti Ekspress* is withdrawn from service, Lithuanian Railways propose a new service from Šeštokai to Vilnius, to connect with Polish services.

### Vilnius–Kaunas

Thirteen local daily trains take 2 hrs. Fastest time: 1¼ hrs.

### Vilnius–Šiauliai

There are five daytime trains taking 3–4 hrs. Two overnight trains take 5–5½ hrs.

### Kaunas–Šiauliai

Three night trains (one of which, the *Balti Ekspress,* runs alternate nights only) take 3 hrs. Local daytime trains will require a change at Kaišiadorys.

### Vilnius–(Border)–Riga

An overnight train (via Kaunas) takes 8 hrs.

### Šiauliai–(Border)–Riga

The Vilnius–Riga night train calls at Šiauliai, as does the *Balti Ekspress.* Journey time: 3 hrs.

### Riga–(Border)–Tartu

This service is now only performed by the *Balti Ekspress* in 4 hrs. See above for further information.

### Valga–Tartu

Four local trains daily, plus the *Balti Ekspress.* Journey time: approximately 2 hrs.

### Tartu–Tallinn

There are five–six trains a day. The journey takes between 3–4 hrs.

### Tallinn–Helsinki

The crossing by ferry takes about 3½ hrs, and 1½ hrs by hydrofoil. You can also sail direct to Stockholm (sailings are every other day, overnight).

**524**

---

## Rail Travel in the Baltic States

The railway administrations of Estonia, Latvia and Lithuania are making slow but perceptible improvements to stations and rolling stocks, approaching Western European standards in a number of instances. Rail travel in the Baltic States is perfectly safe, and the overnight trains are comfortable, though belongings should not be left unattended. Sleepers to and from Moscow, St Petersburg and other destinations in Russia and the CIS utilise ex-Soviet carriages and correspond to Russian practice. Travellers are advised to take a berth in a second class coupé (a compartment of four berths). Some trains, particularly the Moscow ones, convey a superior class of coupé with two berths. Reservations are compulsory, and proof of an entry visa may be required of Western visitors when booking. It is said that fares to Russian and CIS destinations are cheaper in Tallinn.

The Tallinn **ferry terminal** comprises the following separate terminal areas: Terminal A – Tallink and T. H. Ferries (Helsinki); Teminal B – Eestin Linjat (Helsinki); Terminal C – Tallink Express (catamaran; Helsinki); Terminal D – Silja Line (Helsinki) and Estline (Helsinki). The Tallinn Line Express (hydrofoil) for Helsinki uses a quay alongside Tallinn Linnehall.

### VILNIUS

**Station**: the **Stotis** (station), *tel: 63 0088,* is currently undergoing piecemeal restoration. Facilities include left luggage and exchange. Avoid the use of taxis if possible.

Rail tickets can be purchased at branches of **Baltic Travel Service**, using Visa or Mastercard.

**Buses**: the **main bus station**, *tel: 26 24 82,* is next door to the station.

**Tourist Office**: **Vilnius Tourist Information Centre** opens late 1997 at *Pilies St 42;*

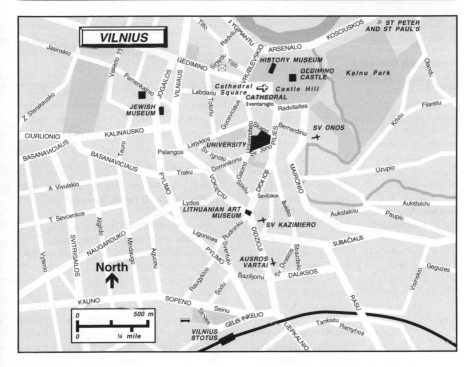

*tel: 62 07 62.* Open Mon–Fri 1000–1900, Sat 1200–1600. They will book accommodation and organise excursions. You should also pick up the candid and essential *Vilnius in your Pocket (VIYP),* on sale in the station and all over town. A joint venture by Lithuanian, Belgian and American writers, it gives hotel, restaurant and bar reviews and some sightseeing information in a lively style. **Lithuanian Student and Youth Travel,** *tel: 65 0145,* offers bargain fares for students on planes, trains and buses.

## GETTING AROUND

The most attractive part of the city is the old town. Public transport isn't essential if you have well-located accommodation – which is just as well as buses can become unbearably crowded. There are 50 bus lines and some 20 trolleybus routes. For the only public transport map see *VIYP.*

Purchase different tickets for buses and trolleybuses. Both are 60 centas each at kiosks and post offices. You pay 75 centas if you purchase the ticket on the bus. Tickets must be validated

on the bus. Buses and trolleybuses run 0500–0030.

## STAYING IN VILNIUS

### Accommodation

Vilnius now has quite a varied range of **hotels**. Most upmarket tourists end up in the **Lietuva** or the neighbouring **Turistas**, but better value is the secluded **Hotel Šarunas**, *Raitininku 4; tel: 35 3888.* Owned by a Lithuanian basketball star, it caters specifically for Western tourists and you can dine in the comfort of the 'Rooney Bar'. Just next door is a supermarket which opens late.

*VIYP* lists details of hotels, pensions and hostels in all price categories. **Lithuanian Tours,** *18 Šeimyniškiu st, tel: 72 4163,* will help with hotels, transport and sightseeing. **Litinterp** agency offers **bed and breakfast** from 50 litas, *Bernardinu 7-2; tel: 22 3850.*

The **youth hostel** headquarters is now at the **Filavetai Hostel** (the only one in Vilnius) at *Filaretu 17; tel: 69 66 27.*

To **camp**, you will have to go to **Trakai**, 25 km out of town.

## Eating and Drinking

The cheapest food is from street stalls selling sausage rolls, bananas and small pizzas, near the Palanga restaurant. There is a colourful food market on *Bazilijonu* not far from the station.

Vilnius has a remarkable selection of good restaurants (mostly non-smoking), which are increasingly out of the price range of locals. Prices can (but rarely do) reach parity with Western restaurants but the quality is then correspondingly better. They can close early. **Stikliai Alude,** *Gaono 7; tel: 22 2109,* is a good, old-fashioned hostelry with a distinctive middle-European flavour and a downstairs bar. There are generous helpings of traditional Lithuanian food and a lively folk band as an accompaniment. Open 1200–2400; expensive. The cheaper **Ritos Smuklé,** *Zirmûnu 68; tel: 77 07 86,* also serves traditional Lithuanian food.

The café **Kavine Alumnatos,** *Universiteo gatve 4,* is a favourite with students. If you want a quick snack try **Kavine Medininkai,** *Aus* ᵛ *tros Vartu; tel: 61 40 19,* an inexpensive café and restaurant. For watered-down beer and atmosphere on tap, visit Vilnius's beer bars (see *VTYP* for details). There are now several fast food establishments.

## Communications

The **central post office,** *Gedimino pr 7; tel: 61 6759,* opens Mon–Fri 0800–2000, and Sat and Sun 1100–1900. Phone and telegram, *tel: 23 03 98.* Phone cards are now in use.

## Embassies

**Canada:** *Gedimino 64; tel: 22 08 98.*
**UK:** *2 Antakalnio Gatve; tel: 22 2070.*
**US:** *Akemnu 6; tel: 22 30 31.*

The main shopping streets in Vilnius are *Gedimino* and *Pilies.* Western commercialism still has some way to go but there is an increasing range of choice.

There is a branch of Lithuania's first supermarket chain, **IKI,** on *Jasinskio 16.* **Vuezapas**

supermarket chain sells Western groceries and products.

Gift shops selling handicrafts and amber proliferate behind doors in the old town.

Streets empty at about 2000 and are not generally well-lit. Areas to avoid on your own at night are *Uzupio* and *Kalvariju* and the station late at night.

Guided tours of the city are available from **Vilnius State Travel Bureau** (the new Tourist Office).

Meandering Vilnius is serene, green and many parts are undergoing restoration. There are generous helpings of baroque architecture, especially ecclesiastical, with churches on almost every street corner. But there is also a bucolic quality to the town – many of the crumbling houses and grassy courtyards have a distinctly pastoral air. Museums close on Mon or Tues.

**Castle Hill**, overlooking the city, is a good place to get your bearings, but for an even better view climb the sole surviving tower of **Gedimino Castle**, built in the 14th century and 48m high. The Lithuanian tricolour was hoisted here in October 1988, a deeply symbolic act of independence. Archaeological finds from the castle are on display in the small tower museum **Vilniaus pilies muziejus**. At **Lower Castle Museum**, *Cathedral Sq. 3,* there is a large archeological excavation under way. Tours available, *tel: 62 99 88.*

**Katedos aikste** (Cathedral Square) is the focal point of the town and was the site of anti-Soviet mass-demonstrations in the run-up to independence. The **Arkikatedra Bazilika** (Cathedral), was originally dedicated to the god of thunder. Reconstructed 11 times, the most recent being in the classical style of 1777–1801, it was an art gallery in the Soviet era. The baroque Kazimieras Chapel inside is the burial place of several members of the royal family and worth a visit. Behind the Cathedral, the popular **Kalnu Park** is a shady, streamside sanctuary, which leads to the church of **Sts Peter and Paul**.

## Churches

**Sv. Petro ir Povilo Baznycias** (Sts Peter and Paul), *Antakalnio 1,* is the supreme example of baroque church architecture in Lithuania. The interior is decorated with over 2000 lively stucco figures by Italian sculptors. **Sv. Onos** (St Anne's), *Maironio 8,* is an equally eminent example of Gothic church architecture, with an intricate and delicate façade using 33 different types of brick. **Sv. Kazimiero** (St Casimir's), *Didžioji 34,* was founded by the Jesuits in 1604 and takes its name from Lithuania's patron saint. It was designated a Museum of Atheism under the Soviets.

The **Aušros Vartai** (Gates of Dawn), *Aušros Vartu 12,* were originally part of the town fortifications. The chapel in the gatehouse was built in 1671 to house an image of the virgin and has been a place of pilgrimage ever since. The **Orthodox Church of the Holy Spirit**, *Ausros Vartu 10,* contains the miraculously preserved bodies of three saints in a glass case in the crypt.

## Museums

The **Lietuvos nacionalinis muziejus** (Museum of National Culture and History), *Arsenalo 1,* traces Lithuania's fascinating story from the Stone Age to the inter-war period of independence. A new gallery is devoted to modern Lithuanian history. **Lietuvos valstybinis žydu muziejus**, *Pamenkalnio 12* and *Pylimo 4,* (the State Jewish Museum).

Pre-war Vilnius was one of Europe's greatest centres of Jewry (in 1914 nearly 50% of the population was Jewish) with a strong publishing and intellectual tradition. During World War II, 95% of Vilnius's Jewish population was killed and 96 synagogues were destroyed. A reminder of Soviet occupation, the **KGB museum**, *Gedimino 40, entrance at Auku 4,* is in the prison cells of the secret police headquarters. Some of the guides are former inmates of the prison.

There are two museums displaying Lithuanian art, **Lietuvos dailes muziejus** (the Lithuanian Art Museum), *Didžioji 31,* and the folk art **National Gallery**, *Studentu 8.*

The **university** is one of Vilnius's most elegant classical complexes. Its history begins in the 17th century but it was closed for more than 80 years (1832–1919) by order of the Tsarist regime. St John's Courtyard is dominated by the church, with its organ-like multipillared façade. In an adjoining courtyard, look out for the observatory tower (1569).

### ↗ SIDE TRACKS FROM VILNIUS

One hundred thousand people, 70% of them Jews, were murdered by the Nazis at **Paneriai**, 10 km from Vilnius. This is now the site of the **Paneriu muziejus** (Museum of Genocide), *Agrastu 15.* Closed Tues, Sun. Set in the forest, the grassed-over death pits serve as a chilling reminder.

27 km from Vilnius, Lithuania's former capital, **Trakai**, is distinguished by its restored red-brick 14th-century fortress, which stands on an island surrounded by five lakes. Castle open daily 1000–1900. Tours in English, *tel: 51 527.* Trakai is the home of the Karaites, a heretical Jewish sect descended from the bodyguard of the Lithuanian Dukes. There is an interesting museum and *Kinessa* (prayer house).

**Tourist Office:** *Vytanto 90; tel: 51 934.* Local trains run to Trakai from Vilnius.

**Klaipeda** and **Palanga** make an excellent longer excursion, and could be combined with a visit to Šiauliai. There is an 'express service' from Vilnius during the day composed of first, second and 'luxury' class coaches. A return by the evening train would allow a stay of nearly six hours. There are overnight services in both directions, comprising second class coupés of four berths. The sleeper service runs via Kaunas, but not the day service. All trains stop at Šiauliai. Klaipeda is a port city with an old quarter. Take the ferry to Smiltyné for the **Maritime Museum**, **Aquarium** and **Dolphinarium**, or explore the spectacular **Curonian Spit** with its sandhills. Frequent taxi-buses from Klaipeda to Palanga, Lithuania's seaside resort, where a visit to the world famous **Amber Museum**, is a must. **Tourist Office:** *Klaipeda-Tomo 2* and *Palanga-Vytauto 106.*

527

Klaipeda is the starting point for ferries to and from Mukran (18 hrs), Travemünde (28 hrs) and Kiel. There is also an infrequent service to Copenhagen in Denmark. 🛳

## KAUNAS

**Station**: *tel: 22 10 93,* is about 20 mins walk from the old town, but is worth it as it includes *Laisvès Aleja,* a pedestrianised boulevard that the citizens are justly proud of. Left luggage facilities (closes around 2000). The station is open 24 hours, and is regularly patrolled by the police. **Buses: Bus station,** *Vytayto 24; tel: 20 1655.* **Tourist Office:** There is no office, but useful publications are *Kaunas in Your Pocket (KIYP),* and *Kaunas this Week,* available at kiosks, bookshops and hotels.

### GETTING AROUND

Kaunas has two distinct centres of gravity: **Senamiestis** (the old town), a peninsula bordered by the converging Neris and Nemunas Rivers; and **Naujamiestis** (the new town). Trolleybuses and buses are plentiful but aren't strictly necessary – the distance across town is only 3–4 km. Buy tickets from kiosks and validate them on board.

### ACCOMMODATION AND FOOD

The choice of accommodation is still very limited. There are several low-budget out-of-town hotels (see *KIYP)* but you'll have to book well in advance. **Litinterp,** *Kumeliu 15/4; tel: 22 8718,* can arrange single rooms from 60 litas. The **Youth Hostel** on *Prancuzu 59; tel: 74 8972,* has 51 rooms from 40 litas with IYHA cards.

Restaurants bars and cafés are on the increase: check *KIYP* for listings and reviews.

### SIGHTSEEING

Lithuania's second largest city and the interim capital under Polish Occupation (1920–40), Kaunas is described as more typically Lithuanian than Vilnius.

It has also succumbed relatively little to the ravages of a war-riddled history. All museums are free on Wed.

From the remains of the 14th-century **Castle**, wander down to the much better pre-

served **Rotušes aikšte** (Town Hall Square). Over 25% of the 16th-century houses bordering the square, of which **Gildija** (no. 3) is the oldest, have been restored. The 53-m high, white-tiered baroque spire in the middle of the square, marks the **Town Hall**. On the south side is **St Francis Church** and **Jesuit monastery,** used as a school under the Soviets, but now returned to believers. On the banks of the River Nemunas, stands **St Vytautas Church**, dating from the 1400s. The single-towered brick **Cathedral**, now a basilica, stands at the junction of *Vilniaus gatve,* which leads into the new town.

The central pedestrianised avenue, *Laisves aleja* (Freedom Avenue) is dominated by the beautiful blue and white Catholic church, **St Michael the Archangel** on *Independence Square.* It was designed by Russian architects at the end of the 19th century, which accounts for the neo-Byzantine design. The avenue itself is now the focal point of the town's commercial and social life. A slab in front of the Music Theatre marks the spot where the 19-year-old Romas Kalanta immolated himself in protest against the Soviet regime. The monument obliquely opposite represents Vytautas the Great slaying his enemies – Russian, Pole, Tartar and German soldiers lie vanquished beneath him.

At *64 Putvinskio gatve,* the **žmuid–zinavičius Collection** (Devils Museum), *tel: 20 35 14,* houses 1700 devil statues, including Hitler and Stalin dancing over Lithuania. Open summer 1200–1800 except Mon and the last Tues of the month. From *Unity Sq.,* take the funicular up to Aleksotas or Žaliakalnifs – very near to **Christ's Resurrection Church,** for a great view.

The **Military Museum of Vytautas the Great**, *Donelaičo 64,* displays the wreckage of a plane flown by Darius and Givenus.

On the northern perimeter of Kaunas, *žemaiču plentas 73,* a museum and powerful memorial sculptures mark the Ninth Fort, where the Nazis massacred tens of thousands. Lithuania's main open-air folk museum, **Rumšiskes**, *T. Masiulio 21; tel: 76 43 92,* lies 12 km east of town. Open 1100–1900 (Easter–Nov 1), closed Mon and Tues. Take trolleybus no. 9 or bus no. 22 to the terminus, then the boat from Kaunas Sea Dock. By rail, the station is *Pravieniškes* (5 km away).

## ŠIAULIAI

**Station**: *tel: 43 0652*, a short walk from the pedestrianised town centre.
**Buses**: bus station *tel: 436 3864.*
**Tourist Office**: the **Apeja** at *Varpo 22A*; *tel: 42 3741* can help with accommodation, guides and maps. Open Mon–Fri 0900–1800.

### SIGHTSEEING

Founded in 1236, Šiauliai is Lithuania's fourth-largest town, named after the battle of Saule, where Lithuanians defeated the German Livonian Knights.

Most visitors to Šiauliai come to see the extraordinary **Hill of Crosses,** some 10 km north of the town. The Pope's visit caused much publicity but the importance of these 80,000 crosses lies more in the symbolism of resistance, hope and suffering, than in the overt sign of Catholic worship. The origins are obscure although the highly decorative crosses show Pagan influence. But it is the Soviet failure to extinguish this spiritual torch that is most remarkable. Each time the crosses were bulldozed, they would slowly reappear again, planted mostly under the cover of darkness. The authorities took note of visiting cars and surrounded the hill with polluted water, but these, and other measures were equally ineffective. What is equally staggering, considering the number of crosses, is that those standing today have all been planted since 1975.

Šiauliai itself is somewhat devoid of historical sights, although it does have a Renaissance **Church of Sts Peter and Paul,** at the junction of *Tilzes* and *Ausros Aleja,* with one of the tallest spires in Lithuania (70m). In **Sun Clock Square,** at the bottom of *S. Salkausko,* a tall column supporting a golden figure with a bow and arrow, functions as a huge sundial.

The **Photography Museum,** *Vilniaus gatve 140,* verges on the unexciting but accompanying local exhibitions might make the stop worth while.

Finally, head towards the charmingly eccentric **Cat Museum,** *Žuvininku gatve 18,* which features such humble exhibits as a tin of cat food.

## RIGA

**Station**: Riga has one main station, **Stacijas laukums,** *tel: 23 3095,* a few minutes walk from the old town. At the international booking office (across the car park), English is spoken, but purchases must be made in cash and it closes at 2000. There is a left luggage office in the basement, but the lockers in the subway near platform 4 may be more convenient. A Pavoks Banka branch is open daily 0830–2100 and cashes travellers cheques.

The station contains a 'tourist bureau', which arranges international travel. There is a 24-hr supermarket opposite the station.
**Buses**: buses are a better form of transport than trains in Latvia. The **Autoosta** (main bus station), next to the central market, *tel: 721 3611,* is a good centre for both long-distance and city buses. Turn left as you leave the railway station.
**Tourist Office: Riga Tourist Information Office** (guesthouse upstairs), *Skarnu 22; tel: 722 1731.* This will help with tourist information, maps and guides, sightseeing, bicycle rental and some accommodation.

Don't be misled by the blue signs with a white letter 'i' (for information) at the station and around town. These will lead you to a travel agent.

Other sources of information include the **Hotel Riga** and **Hotel de Rome,** on *Aspazijas Bulv. Riga In Your Pocket,* published in English and updated every two months, is invaluable for listings and all sorts of insider information.

### GETTING AROUND

The very crowded buses, trams and trolleybuses operate 0530–1100. Tickets are purchased on buses, trams and trolleybuses. There is a flat fare of 14 sentimes. Most vehicles now have conductors. There are many taxi ranks, but those outside the big hotels tend to be more expensive. Most taxis now have meters. Journeys after 2200 are 50% more expensive.

### ACCOMMODATION

Riga is becoming increasingly well served with

hotels of all categories. Most are cheaper than in the West, but some still cost more than US$100 a night.

Good value within the low budget range is the pre-war **Hotel Viktorija**, *Čaka 55, tel: 27 2305*. It is conveniently located and all the rooms are being upgraded.

Owned by British Latvians, **Rovdi un Draugi**, *Màrstala 1; tel: 722 0372*, has single romms from £26. The cheapest option is **The Avéna**, *Palasta 5*, used by the circus Oct–April. Basic but clean.

For cheaper options, try the private accommodation agency, **Patricia**, *Elizabetes 22-4a; tel: 728 4868*, which offers centrally located rooms in guesthouses from $15 a night without breakfast.

**HI:** There are two **youth hostels** in Riga. The **Placis**, *Laimdotas iela 2A; tel: 755 1824*, is recommended. Take trolleybus 4 to *Teika* stop.

## EATING AND DRINKING

For local colour and authenticity, the 1930s **Central Market**, *Negu iela 7* (behind the station), located in ex-World War I airship hangars, is unmissable. Breathe in the heady mix of cheeses and smoked meats. The buffet bars in the meat market sell cheap, hot food. As elsewhere in the Baltics, avoid expensive imported produce.

Most internationally recognised chocolate bars are on sale, as are things like fruit juices. Riga's *Black Balsam* is a mix of cognac, ginger and oak bark, drunk with vodka or coffee, which can be purchased from a specialist shop opposite the station. Another local speciality is a particular brown bread called *Rupjmaize*, sometimes used with cream to make soup.

There are plenty of green open spaces in Riga, so picnicking is a real possibility. Try the area around the Freedom Monument, or the Kronvalda Parks and Esplanade. New restaurants and bars are opening weekly. The area around St Mary's Cathedral is a good place to look both for these and for the numerous cafés dotted all over the old town. The latest 'in' place is the *Konvonthof* shopping, café, leisure complex.

If you're tired of the local cuisine try the pizzas at **Lulu Pica**, *Gertrudes 27*. **Andaluzijas**

**Suns,** *Elizabetes al. 83/85*, has excellent food and is in great demand so be sure to book.

## Communications

The **main Post Office,** *Brivibas bulv. 19; tel: 701 8738*, near the Freedom Monument, is open 24 hrs and has plenty of telephone cabins (pay after the call). To use other public phones, buy phonecards from shops, newstands, etc.

## Embassies

**Canada:** *Doma laukums 4; tel: 78 30141.*
**UK:** *Alunana 5; tel: 73 38126.*
**USA:** *Raina bulv. 7; tel: 21 0005.*

## SIGHTSEEING

**TAS Agency** run daily walking tours of old Riga ($40 for up to 7 people). **RigaCity Tours,** *tel: 951 4308*, run coach tours four times daily. You could also try **Latvia Tours** coach trip.

A silhouette of spires rising above the Daugava River, gabled roofs, a recently renovated Old Town, and Europe's largest collection of art nouveau buildings – Riga is the most cosmopolitan of the Baltic capitals, suggesting a wealth that eludes the people of today, as they struggle with the fall-out of independence.

A wander through the old streets in central Riga takes in most of the city's architectural beauties. Museums are often closed on Mondays and sometimes Tuesdays.

The **Vecriga** (old town) lies sandwiched between the old moat and the Pilsetas canals. For a view over the rooftops head for **Peterbaznica** (St Peter's Church), *Skarnu iela 19*, named after Riga's patron saint. Although first built here in 1209, the prototype of its elegant steeple was only completed in 1694. It has since been twice destroyed and rebuilt, in the wake of lightning (in the 18th century) and by German bombs (in 1941). The 120m steeple (there is a lift to a viewing platform) is crowned by a weather rooster the size of a pig.

The **Occupation Museum Fund**, *Strēlnieku Laukans 1; tel: 721 2715*, covers Soviet and Nazi occupation of Latvia from 1940–1982. Open 1100–1700, closed Sat and Mon.

The medieval **House of the Blackheads** (destroyed in World War II) is being rebuilt

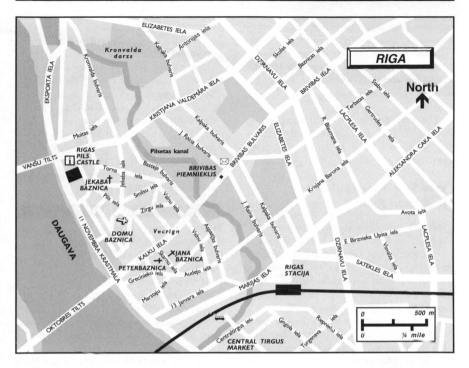

next to this museum. It is intended to be complete for the anniversary of Riga's founding in 2001. The progress can be viewed from behind a fence.

The striking skyline is dominated by the **Domu Baznica** (St Mary's Cathedral), *Doma laukums 1* (admission charge), on the city's central square, and the green spire of **Jekaba Baznica** (St Jacob's Church). The organ (1883) and the stained glass are St Mary's most impressive features, best enjoyed while listening to one of the many organ concerts. The cathedral is flanked by the light brown Latvia Radio House and the Stock Exchange. It was to the Cathedral Square that Latvians came to protest for freedom in 1990.

Immured in the walls of **Jana Baznica** (the Church of St John), *24 Skamu iela,* are the bodies of two 13th-century monks, buried alive to fulfill a local superstition and ensure the church would stand forever. From the churchyard you can see part of the city wall.

The **'Three Brothers'**, *17, 19*, and *21 M Pils iela* are the most famous of Riga's old houses. The earliest, with the small windows, is from the 15th century. The **Museum of Riga's History and Navigation** is at *Palasta 4.* Open 1100–1700, closed Mon and Tues. The **Open Air Ethnographic Museum**, *Brivibas 440; tel: 799 4510,* is open daily 1000–1700. Take bus no. 1 to *Balo wida.*

The rather run-down **Riga Castle**, *Pils laukums 3,* is worth visiting mainly for its **Museums of Latvian History**, **Foreign Art** and **Latvian Literature**. The building is currently being converted into the presidential palace.

The **Pulvertornis** (Gun Powder Tower), *Torna iela,* was initially part of the city wall. It earned its name in the 16th century, when it was used to store huge quantities of the lethal powder, turning it into a potentially monumental bomb. Today it is incorporated in the **Latvian War Museum**.

The **Brivibas Piemnieklis** (Freedom Monument), *Brivibas Bulv.,* is a highly symbolic, 42m obelisk, commissioned in 1922 during a brief gasp of freedom. (Latvia has lived for centuries in an almost perpetual state of occupation by Germans, Swedes and more recently Nazis and Russians.) During the years of Soviet occupation the area was closed off, but the monument itself was, surprisingly, never dismantled. A mounted guard is changed every hour.

The remains of the town wall incorporating the Swedish Gate, opposite Jacob's Barracks, is now a restored range of buildings housing shops, houses and offices.

### SIDE TRACKS FROM RIGA

**Jurmala**, Latvia's seaside resort, 20 km west of Riga, has been a popular holiday destination since the early 19th century. The name, meaning seashore, applies to a string of towns and resorts that hug the beaches, sand dunes and pine woods (all 30 km of them) along the Baltic shore. Following a five-year clean-up programme, the main beaches are now safe for swimming. However, many of the resorts are still decayed. The best places to visit are **Majori** and its vicinity.

There are shops, cafés and a new tourist information office on *Jomas iela* (Majori) which will book accomodation if you want to stay. Jurmala is reached by train (half hourly) to Majori or Dubulti, or by boat along the Lielupe and Daugava Rivers. A new service is planned which will make it possible to make a day trip from Riga by rail.

**Sigulda** is an equally popular antithesis to city life. Thick with greenery, and dotted with caves and castles, Sigulda overlooks the Gauja River valley and is known as the Latvian Switzerland. In winter people come here to ski and in summer for walking and boating.

**Sigulda Castle** (1207) stands in tatters. Behind it, the 19th-century **New Castle** is now a restaurant. From the town, a bridge and cable-cars, 40m above the river, cross to the north bank. A short walk east from here are **Krimulda Castle**, **Turaida Castle** (whose red-brick tower offers an excellent view), and **Gutmanis Cave**, daubed with 300-year-old graffitti. Place a flower on the grave of the Rose of Turaida, and ask someone to tell you the story. Bob-sleighing and skiing are also available. Horses and horse-drawn carriages can be hired. Take the Cesis or Valmiera train and alight at Sigulda.

If you want to visit **Rundale Palace** (the Baltic Versailles) contact travel agents, such as TAS and Latvian Tours, who operate coach trips that include a guided tour – usually in English or German – of the palace. The palace is not accessible by public transport. ⬆

## TARTU

**Station**: *tel: 439 2220,* a short walk from Toomemagi Hill. Special booking office for international travel, and left luggage available.
**Bus Station**: *Turu 2; tel: 477 227.*
**Post Office**: *Vanemuise 7.*
**Tourist Office**: *Raekoja Plats 14; tel: 432 141.* Open Mon–Fri 1000–1800, Sat 1000–1500. Stocks pocket guides to the town, literature, dictionaries, glossy Western magazines and the essential *Tartu This Week*.

The TIC can book accommodation, which costs 700–800EEK in the centre. and 100–200EEK on the outskirts.

### SIGHTSEEING

Estonia's second-largest town is surprisingly small, but richly packed with a cultural heritage that, for some, makes it the real capital. There is a walking tour in English at 1500, which can be booked at TIC. The town's fame stems largely from its university, first founded by the Swedes in 1632. It was closed by the Russians between 1700 and 1832 but today 8000 students attend its courses. The colonnaded yellow and white university building, **Ulikooli**, *Ulikooli 18,* is considered Estonia's best neo-Classical piece.

Round the corner, sloping, cobbled *Raekoja Plats* (Town Hall Square) is presided over by the pink and white Dutch-style **Town Hall** (1782–89) and flanked by low, brightly coloured classical houses. A major restoration project is the reconstruction of **St John's Church** (Vanni Kirik), which was partly destroyed in the war.

Overlooking the square, spacious **Toomemagi Park** covers an area larger than the old town. Statues of famous Estonians, monuments and the shell of the red brick Gothic cathedral punctuate the English-style park. **Inglisild** (Angel's bridge) and **Kuradisild** (Devil's Bridge) earn their names from linguistic confusion. The word 'Angel' was confused with 'English' and 'Devil's Bridge' is the unfortunate translation of the name of the man who pioneered the use of rubber gloves in surgery.

For some local history visit **Local History Museum**, *2 Oru St,* or the **Museum of the University** in the former choir of the Cathedral. The **Estonian National Museum** is in the process of reorganisation. A superb folklore and costume gallery is now open at *Kuperjanou 9.*

---

 ### SIDE TRACK
### FROM TARTU

A visit to **Polux** with its lake, and **Taevaskoda** with its sandstone caves and picnic areas can be made by train from Tartu. 🛤

---

### TALLINN

**Station**: *Balti-jaam, tel: 640 1651.* Left luggage, exchange offices (although none will cash travellers cheques), good station buffet .

The old town is but a few minutes walk away. Cross the road by the subway and walk up *Nunne,* opposite the station, to *Pikk.* Then walk through *Voorimehe* passage to the Town Hall Square. Trams 1/2 link the station to *Viru Valjak.* For the passenger terminal at the harbour, alight at *Fat Margaret Gate* (Suur Rannavävau) and walk along *Sadama,* passing the Linnahall. See p.524 for ferry information.
**Buses**: there is a good network of local and long-distance buses in Estonia, often faster than the train but more expensive. The main **bus station**, **Autobussijaam**, is at *Lastekodu 46; tel: 642 2549.*
**Tourist Office**: there is a helpful **City Tourist Office** adjacent to *10 Raekoja Plats; tel: 631 3940* (the postal address is *Mündi 2, Tallinn*). Open Mon–Fri 0900–1700, and Sat and Sun 1000–1500 (often 1 hr later in

summer). Here you can get maps, books, guides, travel information and a free fact sheet listing cheap accommodation.

### GETTING AROUND

Getting around on foot is no problem, although the climb through the cobbled streets of the old town can be quite steep. Buses, trams and trolleybuses skirt around the old town. Tickets can be bought in advance from kiosks or from the driver and should be punched on board. Single tickets are valid for one journey, on one form of transport. A standard ticket is 4EEK per journey. Available passes are monthly or 10-day, with a student discount on production of an ISIC Card.

There are **ferries** to Helsinki and Stockholm from the **Tallinna Reisisadam** (harbour), a 15-min walk from the city centre (also accessible by tram nos 1/2 or transfer buses from the city centre). Ferry information; *tel: 631 8975.* For ferries to Helsinki, contact **Tallink**, *tel: 640 9800;* **Eestin Linjat**, *tel: 631 8606;* **Sitja Line**, *tel: 631 8331.* For the **hydrofoil** to Helsinki, departures are from Tallinn Linnahall (Tallinn Line). See also p.524.

### ACCOMMODATION

The suitably named **Palace Hotel** is certainly not typical of what's currently on offer, although there is a building boom underway and most hotels are in the process of making much needed renovations.

For the moment, those seeking modest accommodation will find more choice, and it is always advisable to book ahead. Check you have hot water and that your room is satisfactory before moving in. The further out of town you go, the cheaper it gets.

Excellent value for its three stars and far superior to the rival **Viru** is the **Hotel Olümpia**, *Liivalaia 33, tel: 63 15315,* a skyscraper just outside the old town containing a sauna with superb views of old Tallinn.

Mid range hotels include **Central Hotel**, *Narva Mnt. 7; tel: 633 9800,* and **Rataskaevu**, *Rataskaevu 7; tel: 441 939,* in the old town. At the cheaper end of the market is **Eeslitall**, *Duntiri 4–6; tel: 631 3755,* above the restaurant, in the old town.

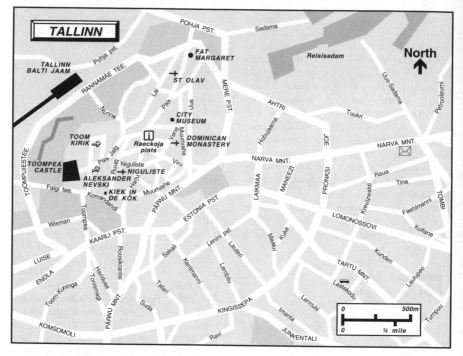

**Bed and Breakfast** agencies: *Sadama 11; tel: 602 091; Mere puistee 6; tel: 441 187;* **CDS Reisid Agency (superior)**, *Raekoja Plats*.

The only **Youth Hostel** in Tallinn is currently **Mereurik**, *Sopruse 182; tel: 529 604.* Trolleybus no. 4 from the station. Basic but clean. 100EEK per night. Try the **Estonian Youth Hostel Association**, *Tatari 39; tel: 646 1457.*

## EATING AND DRINKING

The old town, especially around *Raekoja plats,* is full of cafés, restaurants and cellar bars and the best thing to do is browse until one takes your fancy. The cellar restaurant, **Vanaema Juures,** *Rataskaevu 10/12, tel: 44 8504* is already proving popular so you'll need to book. There are homely Estonian dishes on the menu, including Baltic herring and meatballs. Tea-time could well be the best part of the day if you go to **Maiasmokk,** *16 Pikk.* An inexpensive option is **Kloostiri Ait,** *Vene 14,* a café/bar that serves meals sometimes accompanied with live music. If you're in need of an early breakfast, there's

**McDonalds** on *Viru 24;* open daily 0800–2400, but very little else outside the hotels.

## Communications

The **central post office,** *Narva maantee 1; tel: 641 1333,* is open Mon–Fri 0800–1900 and Sat 0900–1700. You can also get stamps at big hotels and the tourist office.

Pay phones now accept phonecards – purchased from hotels, TIC's, post offices and newstands. International calls may be dialled direct.

## Embassies

**Australia:** *Gonsiori 21, EE0001 Tallinn; tel: 646 6090.*
**Canada:** *13 Toom-Kooli, Tompea; tel: 631 3570.*
**UK:** *20 Kentmanni; tel: 631 3462.*
**USA:** *20 Kentmanni; tel: 631 2021.*

## ENTERTAINMENT

For art exhibitions and concert performances, see the listings in *Tallinn This Week.* The old town is full of bars and outdoor cafés in the summer. Two good hangouts for young people are **Nimeta Bar** (Pub with no name) on *Suur-Karja 4*, and **Tehas nr. 43** (Factory no. 43) on *Pikk 43*. Alternatively, try a sauna, an integral part of Estonian culture. Look out for the numerous music festivals over the summer. Folk and rock music usually feature.

The more expensive hotels usually have one (the Olympia has large windows and a fantastic view). Public saunas are probably cheaper and a good way to meet and mix with the locals. Ask at the tourist office.

## SIGHTSEEING

A walking tour leaves daily at 1400 from **CDS Reisid**, or enquire at TIC, both *Raekoja Plats*.

Independent since August 1991, Estonia stands face to face with Finland, and of all the Baltic capitals, the gallop towards capitalism seems most obvious in Tallinn. (Nowhere else will you find a guidebook to shopping.) Though it has suffered in the interim, with only 22 years of independence in nearly seven centuries, Tallinn prospered as a Hanseatic trading town from the 13th century. Today, its well-preserved medieval remains make it the most beautiful of the Baltic capitals.

You could rush around in a day, but try to spend longer. *Tallinn, A Travel Guide*, is a useful, illustrated, 70-page booklet with good background on the sights. *Tallinn This Week* has an adequate if much briefer run-down.

## Toompea (The Upper Town)

Toompea, the fortified hill-top, was traditionally home of the rulers, gentry and ecclesiastics and was once an independent community. Whoever had most recently conquered Tallinn (Estonia has variously been part of the Danish, Livonian (German), Swedish and Russian orbits) would hoist their flag on **Pikk Herman** (Tall Herman), at 50 m the tallest of the castle's three remaining round towers. From **Castle Hill**, the view of the lower town is of yellows and reds, roof tiles, and slender church steeples.

At *Toom kooli 6*, **Toom kirik** (The Dome Church or St Mary's Cathedral) is the oldest church in Tallinn (first mentioned in 1233 but reconstructed after a fire in 1684). The interior is resplendent with sarcophagi, tombs and coats of arms. Further south on *Lossi plats* is the **Aleksander Nevski** (Russian Orthodox Cathedral), attractive in its way but wholly at odds with its architectural surroundings. (The interior mosaics are worth seeing.) Peter the Great stayed in the post office opposite on a visit to Tallinn in 1711. The baroque **Toompea Castle** is now the home of Estonia's parliament.

The round cannon tower below *Lossi plats* on *1 Komandandi* is **Kiek in de Kök** (literally 'peep in the kitchen'). From here the watchmen could supposedly see into the homes below, hence the name. There is a branch of the **City Museum** inside, which includes regular photographic displays.

## Vanalinn (The Lower Town)

*Pikk jalg* leads into the lower town, the heart of which is **Raekoja plats** (Town Hall Square). Whippings and market stalls once animated this spacious square dominated by Europe's oldest town hall (1371–1404). Arcaded, with narrow Gothic windows and crowned by a slender 17th-century steeple, the weather vane is of **Vana Toomas** (Old Thomas), the patron saint of Tallinn.

It's worth climbing the tower for excellent views of old Tallinn. The **Raeapteek pharmacy** at no. 11 was in the hands of the Burchart family for over 350 years and the adjacent passageway **Saia kang** (White-bread passage) was once home to a cluster of bakeries.

The lower town's glory comes from the ornate 15th- and 16th-century merchants' houses that line the streets: *Pikk jalg* has some of the best. **Ajaloomuuseum** (the State History Museum) is at no. 17 (once the Great Guild House). No. 24, also a guild house, belonged to the Brotherhood of Blackheads, the unmarried merchants named after their patron saint, the African St Mauritius.

Further down *Pikk jalg*, **Oleviste kirik** (St Olaf's Church) has two patrons: the Norwegian king, Olaf, and Olev the builder, who braved contemporary superstition to construct the steeple and fell to his death when doing so. As prophesied, a snake and a frog were seen emerging from the mouth of the fallen Olev.

535

Tallinn is still equipped with a surprising number of the bastions which fortified its town wall (there were as many as 60 in the late 16th century. **Paks Margareeta** (Fat Margaret), *70 Pikk,* is a stout, pock-marked tower 24 m in diameter, with walls nearly 5 m thick enclosing a maritime museum.

Parallel to *Pikk jalg, Lai jalg* is home to the **Tarbekunstimuuseum** (the Applied Arts Museum), at no.17, while the group of burghers' houses at nos 38–40 are nicknamed 'The Three Brothers' on account of their masculine appearance. The **Tallinna linnamuuseum** (City Museum), *Vene 17,* houses an exhibition of 18th–19th-century Tallinn and 14th–18th-century crafts, in a 15th-century merchant's house.

Amongst Tallinn's best churches are the ruins of the 13th-century **Dominiiklaste Klooster** (Dominican Monastery), *Vene 16,* housing a remarkable collection of stone carvings; the essentially 15th-century **Niguliste kirik** (Church of St. Nicholas), *Niguliste 13,* with sacred art exhibits; and the **Puhavaimu kirik** (Holy Ghost Church) at *Puhavaimu 2.* This 14th-century Gothic church was later taken over by the Lutherans. The well-preserved interior, with its unusual twin aisles, has several outstanding features, most notably a double-winged folding altarpiece dating from 1483.

*Katarriina Käik* is a picturesque alley wth craft shops and cafés off *Vene.* There is a market selling knitwear and traditional souvenirs in *Müürivahe,* near the Viru gate.

## OUT OF TOWN

A short bus ride from Tallinn (bus nos 1/8/34), at Pirita, is the ruined convent of **St Birgitta**. Dating from the 14th century and finally destroyed by Russian forces in 1577, it's a massive complex of cloisters, guest rooms, cellars and medieval parlours, dominated by the surviving walls and façade of the main church. Visit **Maarjamäe Palace**, *Piritatee 56,* en route. There is an interesting museum of recent history.

Ask at the kiosk for a key to the tower for views across Tallinn Bay. Just across the road is a modern self-service restaurant and there's also a yachting marina. A local bus runs to nearby **Forest Cemetery**, where the Estonian famous are buried.

**Kadriorg,** 2 km from Tallinn, was the royal seaside summer residence built by the Russian Tsar Peter the Great for his Estonian wife Catherine. The palace, a mixture of French and Italian influences, set in **Kadriorg Park**, is still closed for renovation, but the house where Peter stayed, in the grounds, can be visited.

**Rocca-al-Mare** is a large open-air folk museum. There are weekend folk performances, where traditional Estonian fare and beer are served in a country tavern. Bus 21 from the railway station or 45 from the post office. Open 1000–1800.

If you are interested in the Soviet past, a visit to **Paldista** is a must, to see the remains of the submarine school, barracks and security installations, together with what is left of the Orthodox and Lutheran churches. The cemetery is full of the casualties of the place – Soviet seamen and toddlers who may have lived too close to the reactors (now removed). Frequent electric trains run from Tallinn. Some travel agents organise tours. Enquire at the Tallinn TIC.

---

### ↗ SIDE TRACKS FROM TALLINN

**Viljandi** is an unspoilt typical Estonian town, with a ruined castle overlooking a lake in a wooded setting. It is a venue for folk events. **Pärnu** is Estonia's premier seaside resort. It has a historic old town with an attractive beach and gardens/parkland. A wide range of accommodation is on offer. Pärnu is a base for boat trips to the islands of **Kihnu** and (for the more adventurous) **Ruhnu**, where folk costume is still sometimes worn. Bed and Breakfast is available on the islands – enquire at the Atlas or Reisau agencies in the town. A trip is also possible to the railway museum at Lovasaare. **Tourist Office:** *Munga 2; tel: 372 44 40639.* Pärnu is the venue for a variety of music and arts festivals. ↘

# ZURICH

Zurich, Switzerland's largest city, comes as a surprise. Despite its stern reputation as one of the world's major financial centres, it has all the attributes needed to charm visitors – a picturesque setting on the River Limmat beside Lake Zurich, mountains around, smart shops and lively restaurants. Indeed one of its greatest assets is that it seems so untouristy.

## TOURIST INFORMATION

The efficient well-stocked **Tourist Office** is on the station concourse, *Bahnhofpl. 15; tel: 211 40 00.* Open 0830–2030 (to 2130 May–Sept). They sell a street map (SFr.1, or SFr.3 with index), provide a free accommodation service and issue the fortnightly listing, *Zurich News*, and monthly *Zurich Guide*, both free.

## ARRIVING AND DEPARTING

### Airport
**Zurich–Kloten Airport** is 12 km north-east of the city centre; information; *tel: 258 34 34.* Trains run every 10–15 mins from the Hauptbahnhof; journey time 12 mins.

### Station
**Zurich Hauptbahnhof (HB)**; *tel: 157 22 22,* is on the west side of River Limmat and leads out onto *Bahnhofstr.* the main shopping street.

## GETTING AROUND

The centre of Zurich is comparatively small and easy to explore on foot. All buses and trams, run by **VBZ Züri-Line**, leave the terminal outside the HB every 12 mins (6 mins in peak time) 0530–2400. Buy your ticket from machines at stops before boarding; 1-hr costs SFr.2.10, 24 hrs SFr.7.20 or 3 days SFr.20. Various daily city **coach tours** and **guided walks** are organised by the Tourist Office, departing from HB.

**Taxis:** *tel: 222 22 22,* or hail one in the street. **Bikes** can be hired at HB.

**Boats:** Glass-roofed cruisers offer circular 1-hr trips along the **Limmat** from outside HB by the Swiss National Museum. Lake cruises by **Zürichsee-Schiffahrtsgesellschaft**, *tel: 482 10 33,* leave from *Bürklipl.* at the tip of the lake.

## STAYING IN ZURICH

### Accommodation
There is a wide choice of hotels. Chains include: *BW, Ch, EG, FE, Hn, IE, MO, Mv, Nv, RC, Rn, RS, Sf, Sh, SL, Sn, Ss, Sw, Tp, WS.* Just across *Bahnhofbrücke* from HB, **Hotel Limmatol**, *Limmatquai 142, tel: 261 4220* (moderate) occupies a turn-of-the-century art deco building. The only hotel on the riverside is **Zum Storchen**, *Am Weinpl. 2; tel: 211 5110* (expensive). At the other end of the price range, **Hotel Biber**, *Niederdorfstr. 5; tel: 251 90 15,* has dormitories and private rooms. **HI:** *Mutschellenstr. 114; tel: 482 35 44,* south of the city in Wollishofen (tram nos 7/10 to *Morgental,* then 15-min walk). **Campsite:** *Seestr. 559, Wollishofen; tel: 482 16 12* (bus nos 61/65 from *Bürklipl.*).

### Eating and drinking
The Tourist Office issue a restaurant guide, *Gastro Zürich-City,* which includes many affordable places among the 196 listed. Local specialities include *Kalbgeschnetzeltes* (veal in cream sauce) and the less expensive pork version, *Shweingeschnetzeltes.* There are numerous fast-food and conventional restaurants around the huge station complex. **Walliser Kanne**, *Linthescherg.  21; tel: 211 31 33,* a 2-min walk away, serves fondue, raclette and dishes from the Valias area, in a dark wood-panelled setting. The largest selection of eating places is on or just off *Niederdorfstr.,* the main nightlife area which stretches for about 1 km on the east side of the river, a block back from it. Fierce competition keeps prices at a reasonable level,

537

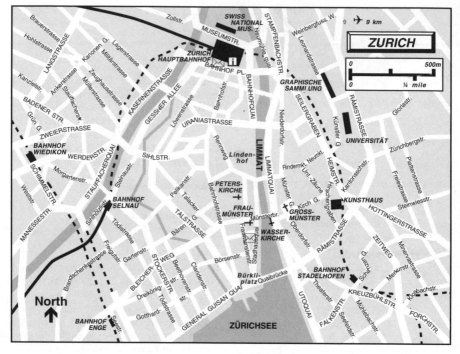

even in the smarter roads and squares that lead off it to the east. One of its best value establishments for hearty local food is the 100-year-old **Rheinfelder Bierhalle**, at *no. 76; tel: 251 54 64*. The more stylish **Adler's Swiss Chuchi**, part of Hotel Adler, *Roseng. 10; tel: 266 96 96*, serves local dishes (moderate). The acclaimed **Le Dézaley**, *Römerg. 7; tel: 251 61 29*, is slightly more expensive but excellent for fondues. The best vegetarian food in town is claimed by **Hiltl Vegi**, *Sihlstr. 28; tel: 221 38 70*, which opened in 1898, though it's certainly not cheap. For a novel experience which combines sightseeing and dining, board the **ChuChi Chäschtli** tram, which serves typical Swiss dishes on the move. It runs May–Oct and covers a loop around both banks of the Limmat starting at *Bellevuepl.*, which is where you should board if you wish to dine.

## Communications

To phone Zurich from abroad: *tel: 41 (Switzerland) + 1 (Zurich)*; to phone Zurich from elsewhere in Switzerland: *tel: 01*.

## Consulates

**UK:** *Dufourstr. 24; tel: 261 15 20.*
**USA:** *Dufourstr. 101; tel: 422 25 66.*

## ENTERTAINMENT AND EVENTS

There's no shortage of bars, clubs and street performers on and around *Niederdorfstr.*, a lively – and safe – area for tourists despite its reputation as the city's red light district. Zurich's acclaimed opera company performs at the **Opernhaus Zürich**, *Falkenstr. 1; tel: 262 09 09*. Concerts are given at the **Tonhalle**, *Gothardstr; tel: 206 34 34*, which was inaugurated by Brahms in 1895.

In mid April is the **Sechseläuten**, the city's spring festival, when its guild members celebrate the end of winter by parading in historic costumes before burning *Böögg*, a huge snowman, on an enormous bonfire. July sees the **Zurich Festspiele**, a 3-week music festival inaugurated in 1997; box office; *tel: 215 40 82*. In Aug, there is a **Street Parade** of young people and deafening music to celebrate love, peace and tolerance.

## SHOPPING

The main shopping street is *Bahnhofstr.* Look out particularly for **Franz Karl Weber** at *no. 62,* which sells toys of all sorts, including a big selection of model trains, and cuckoo clocks. **Augustingasse,** off it, has several very smart boutiques. Shopping hours are Mon–Fri 0900–1830, Sat 0800–1600, though a few stay open until 2100 on Sat. Shops in the HB open daily 0800–2000.

## SIGHTSEEING

Lake and mountain scenery, open-air cafés, chic shopping and ancient squares all help to make Zurich a place to enjoy the good things of life. The best view of the lake and city is from **Quaibrücke,** which crosses the **Limmat** where the lake flows into it.

On the west bank of the Limmat, the **Swiss National Museum,** *Bürklipl.,* housed in a 19th-century mock castle, is devoted to Swiss history. Reconstructed rooms depict different periods and there is an impressive display of old weapons. A stroll away, the city's highest spot, **Lindenhof,** is a wide terrace of lime trees overlooking the river. It's a favourite with local people who come to grapple with chess – three sets of giant pieces are there for anyone to use. The nearby 13th-century **Peterskirche** is remarkable for its 16th-century clock tower; each of the four faces, the largest in Europe, is 8.7 m wide. Near **Münsterbrücke,** the 13th-century **Fraumünster** has five outstanding stained-glass windows by Marc Chagall.

Across the bridge, the twin towers of the Romanesque **Grossmünster** (cathedral), offer great views from the top, daily 1330–1700. It has stained glass by Giacometti and a statue of Charlemagne in the crypt. Nearby, **Wasserkirche** (Water Church), on *Limmatquai,* is attached to the 18th-century **Helmhaus,** cloth market hall, where contemporary art exhibitions are staged. Other old **Zunfthäuser** (guild halls) also line *Limmatquai,* some now converted to restaurants. **Kunsthaus** (Fine Arts Museum), *Heimpl.,* has a collection ranging from late Gothic to contemporary, including Giacometti sculptures. Take a stroll along *Spiegelg.,* a quiet narrow road off *Niederdorfstr.,* to see the house where Lenin once lived *(no.14).*

The famous **Lindt chocolate factory** at *Kilchberg,* just south of the city (bus no. 165 from *Bürklipl.),* has a small museum – where visitors get free samples – but it is only open Wed–Fri 1000–1200, 1300–1700. **Museum Rietberg,** *Gablerstr. 15,* (tram nos 6/7) is in the **Villa Wesendonck,** where the composer Wagner lived. It contains one of Europe's most important collections of Asian and African art.

The **Uetliberg Railway** (S-Bahn no. 10) goes up from HB to just below Uto-Kulm (871 m), where you get a memorable view of the city, lake and – in the distance – the Alps. This is a good starting point for mountain walks: a panoramic 90-min to 2-hr promenade takes you to **Felsenegg,** where you can take the cable car down to **Adliswil,** then S-Bahn no. 4 back to the city.

### ⮂ SIDE TRACK FROM ZURICH

The **Principality of Liechtenstein,** independent since 1719, is 80 km south-east of Zurich, on the Austrian border. The full train journey takes 1½–2 hrs. Liechtenstein is a green and mountainous country covering only 158 square km, though 99 per cent of its visitors (mostly day-trippers who come by bus) only see the capital **Vaduz.** Trains don't call there, so get off at Sargans or Buchs and take a bus over the border (there are no formalities on the frontier). It's a small two-street town where, to judge from queues in the **Tourist Office** *(Städtle 37; tel: (041) 75 232 1443;* Mon–Fri 0800–1200 and 1330–1700), the main attraction is having your passport stamped (SFr.2). The **State Art Collection,** in the same buildng, features some excellent works from the private collection of the Prince who lives, with his family, in a handsome hillside castle, **Schloss Vaduz** (not open to the public).

As Liechtenstein produces its own stamps, it attracts philatelists from all over the world. The small **Postage Stamp Museum,** in the same block as the Tourist Office, displays some of its rare stamps.

Swiss Passes are valid on the Principality's comprehensive bus system. ⬣

**539**

# ZURICH–LYON

This route is concentrated on Switzerland's two most cosmopolitan cities: the picturesque small-town capital Berne; and pacific Geneva, home of the International Red Cross, the World Health Organisation, the European section of the United Nations and, of course, the Geneva Convention. The main line is fast, with pleasant sections, but take the opportunity to side-track to the country's two most spectacular mountain excursions – the Jungfrau and the Matterhorn – for the really stunning Alpine scenery (sit on the left as you head towards Lyon for the best views). Between Lausanne and Genève (after Nyon), if the weather is clear, there is an excellent view of Mont Blanc across the still waters of Lac Léman.

Paris–Milan, p. 442

Berne

Zurich

Interlaken

Lausanne

Zermatt

Geneva Paris–Milan, p. 442

Lyon

540

FASTEST JOURNEY: 5 HRS 20 MINS

## TRAINS

**ETT tables:** 505, 372, 560, 576, 564.

### FAST TRACK

➡ There are no direct services between Zurich and Lyon, but fast trains run hourly between Zurich (Hbf) and Geneva (Cornavin), taking 3 hrs, and some have good connections with those for Lyon (Part-Dieu), which take about 1 hr 50 mins from Geneva.

### ON TRACK

▥ **Zurich (Zürich)–Berne (Bern)**
Day trains run 2 or 3 times per hour between Zurich (Hbf) and Berne (Hbf), taking 1 hr 10 mins–1 hr 40 mins.

### Berne–Geneva (Genève)

Trains run hourly (with an extra service every second hour) by day from Berne (Hbf) to Geneva (Cornavin), taking 1¾–2 hrs, calling at Lausanne (roughly halfway), where you can connect with the Paris–Milan route (see p. 442).

### Geneva–(Border)–Lyon

Nine trains run daily between Geneva (Cornavin) and Lyon (Part-Dieu), taking about 1 hr 50 mins. Most also serve Lyon Perrache, which lengthens the journey by about 10 mins. Border controls are at Cornavin and must be completed before access to the platforms is allowed.

## BERNE (BERN)

**Station: Hbf,** *tel: (031) 21 11 11,* is at the western end of the old centre.

**Tourist Office: Verkehrsbüro**, in the station complex; *tel: (031) 311 66 11*. Open daily June–Sept 0900–2030; Mon–Sat 0900–1830 and Sun 1000–1700 Oct–May.

## GETTING AROUND

Berne's main thoroughfare runs east–west through the town centre linking Hbf and Nydeggbrücke and changes name four times: *Spitalgasse, Marktgasse, Kramgasse, Gerechtigkeits-gasse*. Other than the museums, almost everything of interest is on or just off this street. There's an excellent tram and bus network. Buses 9A and 15 and trolleybus 12 cover this street, including the *Bärengraben*. Departures from track 1 in the *Vorpl*. outside the station.

## ACCOMMODATION

Cheap accommodation is not plentiful in Berne but at least most of it is quite central. **Hotel** chainsinclude: *BW, Mv, RC, Sh, WS*. There are four reasonably priced 2-star hotels inside the old town: **Hospiz zur Heimat**, *Gerechtigs-keitgasse 50; tel: (031) 311 04 36* (bus no. 12 to *Rathaus*); **Nydeck**, *Gerechtigskeitg. 1; tel: (031) 311 86 86* (bus no. 12 to *Nydegg*); **Goldener Schlüssel**, *Rathausg. 72; (031) 311 02 16* (tram 9 to *Zytglogge*). Another good 2-star hotel, **The National**, *Hirschengraben 24; (031) 381 19 88*, is just a short walk from Hbf, while the friendly one-star **Marthahaus-Garni**, *Wyttenbachstr. 22a; tel: (031) 332 41 35*, is a short bus ride (no. 20) north to *Gewerbeschule*.

**HI**: *Weiherg. 4; tel: (031) 311 63 16*, 10-min walk from Hbf, just below *Bundeshaus*. **Campsites**: **Fichholz**, *Strandweg 49; tel: (031) 961 26 02*, 3.5 km south-east of centre (tram no. 9 to *Wabern*), also **bungalows**; **Eymatt**, *Hinterkappelen; tel: (031) 901 10 07*, 5 km north-west of the centre (Postbus from Hbf).

## EATING AND DRINKING

The area around *Spitalg., Bärenpl.* and *Zeughausg.* is good for menu browsing. The best value lunch is at the pleasant self-service restaurant of the EPA department store which straddles *Zeughausg.* and *Marktg.* Two characterful establishments are to be found on *Gerechtigs-keitg.* At no. 62 is the **Klötzlikeller**, Berne's oldest wine cellar (dating from 1635) serving snacks and full meals; *tel: (031) 311 74 56*. At no. 18, **Belle Epoque** is a popular small daytime café serving pastries and snacks in period surroundings; *tel: (031) 311 43 36*. At no. 51 is **Arlequin**, offering national and local dishes at reasonable prices; *tel: (031) 311 39 46*. Vegetarians should try **Menuetto**, *Herrengasse 22; tel: (031) 311 14 48*. For a picnic with a view, cross the Nydeggbrücke and walk to the lovely **Rose Garden**, or cross the Lorrainebrücke to the **Botanical Gardens**.

## SIGHTSEEING

Berne was founded in 1191 by Berchtold V, Duke of Zähringen. who (supposedly) declared he would name his new city after the first creature he killed while hunting. The poor victim, a bear, thus became the town's ubiquitous mascot. A fire in 1405 virtually destroyed the original wooden settlement and subsequent building was in sandstone. The reconstruction was unusually harmonious, with 6 km of arcades and a deliberately non-uniform roof-scape. The overall impression is strikingly medieval and the old town was listed as a UNESCO World Landmark in 1983.

From the Hbf direction, the first of the many monumental fountains is the **Pfeifer-brunnen**, on *Spitalgasse*, a flamboyant 16th-century creation with technicolour carvings and flowers around the base. Continuing on to *Bärenpl.*, the 13th-century **Kafigturm** marks what was then the western boundary of the town. The **Bundeshaus** (parliament building) to the right, is open to visitors. A lookout point around the back, provides fine views over the river and, on clear days, you can see the Alps.

Straight ahead is the city's famous clock tower, **Zytgloggeturm**, which was the original western gate, first built in the 12th century. (To the left is the city's most famous fountain, the **Kindlifresserbrunnen**, depicting a child-eating ogre). In the 16th century, an astronomical clock was added to the Zytgloggeturm on its *Kramg.* face. At exactly 4 mins to each hour, a mechanical jester summons a lion, a rooster and a procession of bears.

To the right is *Münsterpl.*, home of the Gothic **Münster**. Construction started in 1421, continuing through the Reformation. Although many decorative touches were removed, it retains a magnificent depiction of the Last Judgment above the main entrance, elaborate carvings on the pews and choir stalls and superb 15th-century stained glass. The 100m steeple (Switzerland's highest) was topped off in 1893.

Back on the main street (by now *Gerechtig-keitsgasse),* you pass **Gerechtigkeitsbrunnen**, where the blindfolded Goddess of Justice stands over the severed heads of historical figures. Cross the river by the 15th-century **Nydegg-brücke** and climb the hill facing you to look back on the picture-postcard view of the city.

Just across the Nydeggbrücke, to the right, are the 500-year-old **Bärengraben** (bear pits), the forlorn-looking home of Berne's mascots. The plump brown beasts are generally eager to accept food (on sale there) and may even perform tricks. At least they breed happily in their concrete bunker and the cubs usually make their first public appearance at Easter.

The **Kunstmuseum** (Fine Art Museum), *Hodlerstr. 8–12* (near Lorrainebrücke, north of Hbf), is worth a detour. It has a fine display of works by Ferdinand Hodler and the world's largest collection of Paul Klee paintings. Look too for exhibits by such diverse artists as Fra Angelico, Matisse, Kandinsky, Cézanne and Picasso. The other major museums are around *Helvetiapl.,* south of the River Aare, across the *Kirchenfeldbrücke* (tram nos. 3/5). **Kunsthalle**, *Helvetiapl. 1,* hosts temporary exhibitions of contemporary art. Opposite, **Schweizerisches Alpines Museum** contains an interesting assemblage of items connected with the history of mountaineering. **Bernisches Historisches Museum**, on the south side of *Helvetiapl.,* is a large and varied historical collection including superb Flemish tapestries and church treasures.

The **Schweizerisches Schützenmuseum**, *Bernastr. 5,* is devoted to firearms and the country's shooting tradition, which goes back to the days of William Tell. Close by, the **Natur-historisches Museum** (no. 15) features African animals, the inevitable bears and Barry, the St Bernard dog who rescued over 40 people. Philatelists should not miss one of the world's largest collections of postage stamps, in the nearby **Schweizerisches PTT Museum**, *Helvetiastr. 16.*

### Embassies

**Australia:** *Alpenstr. 29; tel: (031) 351 01 43.*
**Canada:** *Kirchenfeldstr. 88; tel: (031) 352 63 81*
**Consulate:** *Belpstr. 11; tel: (031) 311 22 61.*
**UK:** *Thunstr. 50; tel: (031) 352 50 21.*
**USA:** *Jubiläumsstr. 93; tel: (031) 357 70 11.*

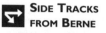

## SIDE TRACKS FROM BERNE

### ZERMATT

The rail journey to Zermatt takes 3½ hrs and involves a change in Brig. The Zermatt train is outside in the street – Swiss railways recommend at least 7 mins for connections. **Tourist Office:** by the station, *tel: (028) 66 11 81.* Although only a small place, Zermatt is a major ski resort and a car-free centre for mountain walking. Its popularity largely rests on its proximity to the 4477m **Matter-horn**, which is best appreciated by walking a little out of town. The town is madly touristy, but nothing (except the frequent clouds) can detract from the glory of its magnificent jagged peak. The **Gornergrat mountain railway** and a network of cable cars provide superb views of the whole area.

### INTERLAKEN

**Stations: Ostbahnhof**, *tel: (036) 22 27 92,* is on Lake Brienz, a 10–15-min walk from the centre. **Westbahnhof**, *tel: (036) 26 47 50,* by Lake Thun, is central. The two stations are 15 mins apart on foot, 5 mins by rail. It is the Ostbahnhof that connects with the railway to Jungfraujoch. From Berne, Westbahnhof is the first stop and the journey, by hourly trains, averages 50 mins – sit on the left as you head south.
**Tourist Office:** *Höheweg 37; tel: (036) 22 21 21.* Mon–Fri 0800–1200, 1400–1800, Sat 0800–1200 Sept–June. Mon–Fri 0800–1830, Sat 0800–1700, Sun 1700–1900 July–Aug.

### GETTING AROUND

You don't need transport for getting around town, but hiring a bike to explore the adjacent lakesides can be fun. Horse-drawn carriages (at a price) are available for hire outside both stations.

## ACCOMMODATION AND FOOD

There's no shortage of **hotels**, many catering largely for tour operators, but private rooms are better value. Register early in the height of the summer and winter seasons. Hotel chains include: *BW, Sn* and *WS*.

Three-star **Hotel Weisses Kreuz**, *am Höheweg; tel: (036) 22 59 51*, is central and offers comfortable simple rooms at competitive rates. There's an excellent private **hostel: Balmer's Herberge**, *Hauptstr. 23; tel: (036) 22 19 61*, 15-mins walk from both stations, in the suburb of Matten (bus nos 5/15). **HI:** *Aareweg 21; tel: (036) 22 43 53*, 20 mins walk east from Ostbahnhof, in the village of Böningen on Lake Brienz (bus no. 1). Seven **campsites** are close by, so ask the Tourist Office for details.

Interlaken doesn't offer a wide choice of interesting cheap eats. **Bernerhof**, *Bahnhofstr. tel: (036) 23 16 10*, is conveniently central and relaxed with a fairly extensive menu, while vegetarians should try **Vegetaris** downstairs in the Hotel Weisses Kreuz (see above).

## SIGHTSEEING

Interlaken began life in 1130, as a village surrounding an Augustinian monastery. That has long gone but the 35-acre meadow south of *Höheweg* (the main street, which runs between the stations) was once part of the monastic grounds and has been deliberately left undeveloped so that the view of **Jungfrau** (4158m) and other peaks looming magnificently beyond, is undisturbed.

The town's main attraction these days is as a base for exploring these spectacular mountains. On the other side of *Höheweg* is the distinctive 19th-century **Kursaal** (Casino), which in addition to gambling (high rollers should note that the ceiling for bets is only SFr.5) stages concerts and folklore evenings. Just off *Höheweg* you can watch cheese being made at **Chäs-Dörfli**, *Centralstr. 3* (Wed, Thur mid May–Sept). Across the River Aare is the old part of

town known as **Unterseen**, with the oldest buildings in the region. Cross the bridge and walk along the river to **Marktplatz**, with its 17th-century town hall and palace, 14th-century church and **Touristik Museum**.

Interlaken's most popular excursion is the 2½ hr journey to **Jungfraujoch**, the highest railway station in Europe (3454m). The narrow-gauge railway rack is operated by the **Berner Oberland Bahn (BOB)** consortium. Services are hourly, and changes of train are necessary in Lauterbrunnen or Grindelwald *and* Kleine Scheidegg. The earlier you start the better to increase the chance of clear views. Ostbahnhof has weather reports. This trip is undeniably breathtaking, but also very expensive (currently SFr.153), although you can save about a quarter by taking the (very early) first train. There are much cheaper funicular rides up **Harder Kulm** (1320m) and **Heimwehfluh** (669m); both close to town.

A boat or bus ride will take you to the **Beatushöhlen** – dramatic cliff caves along the Thunersee. For the best views of Interlaken and the lakes of Thun and Brienz, from which the towns take their names, catch a train to Wilderswil for the rack railway to **Schynige Platte**. There's an excellent Alpine garden at the summit. Beyond Lauterbrunnen, a bus ride to **Trummelbach waterfalls** (actually inside the mountain face) is a good afternoon's trip. The cliff steps are not for the infirm, though. 🔼

**543**

## GENEVA (GENÈVE)

**Stations: Gare de Cornavin**, *tel: (022) 731 64 50*, is the main terminal, 10-mins walk north of the centre (bus nos 5/6/9). **Gare Genève Eaux-Vives**, *tel: (022) 736 16 20*, on the eastern edge of the city, is the terminal for SNCF trains from Annecy and St Gervais (30-min walk from Cornavin station or bus no.12). **Tourist Office:** In **Gare de Cornavin**; *tel: (022) 738 52 00*. Mon–Fri 0800–2000, Sat–Sun 0800–1800 mid June–mid Sept; Mon–Sat 0900–1800 mid Sept–mid June. A smaller central office is at *pl. du Moulard 4; tel: (022) 311 99 70*. *Genève Agenda* is the city entertainment guide.

### GETTING AROUND

Geneva's sights are fairly scattered and a bit of route-planning is worthwhile. There is a good network of buses and one tram route. From May to Sept, **Compagnie Générale de Navigation de Lac Léman (CGN)** operate regular lake ferries from *quai du Mont-Blanc* and *Jardin Anglais,* 10 mins walk straight ahead out of the station subway down *Rue des Alpes; tel: (022) 311 25 21.*

### ACCOMMODATION

Most **hotels** are expensive, but there are plenty of **hostels** and **private rooms**. Ask at the Tourist Office for a copy of *Info-Jeunes,* which lists useful information. There are at least a dozen hotels listed here which are within walking distance of the centre, offering a room with shower for SFr.30–50. Just as cheap are the many **university** and **religious institutions lodgings** on offer. Those with the most attractive and central location are the **Logements Universitaires**, *r. de Candolle 4; tel: (022) 705 77 20,* in the beautiful *Parc des Bastions,* adjacent to the old town. Hotel chains include: *BW, Ch, Ex, Hd, Hn, Fm, IC, Mv, Pe, Pu, Rd, Tp, WS.* **HI:** *r. Rothschild 30; tel: (022) 732 62 60,* 15 mins from Cornavin (bus no.1). **Campsites: Camping Sylvabelle**, *chemin de Conches 10; tel: (022) 347 06 03,* 3 km south east (bus nos.8/88) also **bungalows**; **Camping de l'Abarc**, *rte. de Vernier 151; tel: (022) 796 21 01,* 6 km west (bus no.6); **Camping Pointe-à-la-Bise**, *Vésenaz; tel: (022) 752 12 96,* 7 km north-east, close to Lac Léman (bus E).

### EATING AND DRINKING

Because of its French influence and cosmopolitan nature, Geneva claims to be the culinary centre of Switzerland. The majority of places, however, cater for international business people. Good places to look for reasonably priced restaurants are on the *r. de Lausanne* (turn left out of Gare de Cornavin) and around *place du Cirque (blvd Georges-Favon).* On the latter, try the **Cave Valaisanne et Chalet Suisse** for all things Swiss; *tel: (022) 328 12 36,* while close by the simple café-style **Grappe Dorée**, *blvd Georges-Favon 14; tel: (022) 29 77 98,* offers several local cheese specialities. Consult *Info-*

*Jeunes* (see Accommodation) for a list of University restaurants (the most central is the **Cafétéria UNI-Bastion** at *Place de l'Université* by the Parc des Bastions) and for other cheap eats. Parc des Bastions is also great for picnics.

### SIGHTSEEING

Geneva is at the western tip of **Lake Geneva (Lac Léman)**, and is split by the River Rhône into two distinct sections. The international area is on the **Rive Droite** (right bank, to the north) and the old town on the **Rive Gauche** (left bank, to the south).

On Rive Droite (bus nos 5/8/14/F/Z) is *pl. des Nations,* near which most of the international organisations are grouped. **Musée International de la Croix-Rouge**, *av. de la Paix 17,* is a stern building with high-tech exhibits tracing the history of the Red Cross and its Islamic offshoot, the Red Crescent. Profoundly moving, it covers man's inhumanity to man and natural disasters. **Palais des Nations**, *av. de la Paix 14,* was built 1929–37 to house the League of Nations, which was dissolved in 1940 and replaced by the UN in 1945, when Geneva was chosen as the European headquarters. There are guided tours. **Musée Ariana**, *av. de la Paix 10,* next to the UN building, now houses some 18,000 objects covering seven centuries of international glassware and ceramics. Between here and the lake is the lovely **Jardin Botanique**, a perfect place for a quiet stroll (once away from the main road). It includes a deer and llama park and an aviary.

On Rive Gauche, south of the centre, the **Jardin Anglais**, on the waterfront, is famous for its **Horloge Fleurie** (floral clock), while the city's trade mark, the 140m high fountain known as **Jet d'Eau**, spouts from a nearby pier.

The unofficial centre of the **old town** *(la vieille ville)* is the lively **Place du Bourg-de-Four**, Geneva's oldest square. Take *r. de l'Hôtel de Ville* to the 15th-century **Hôtel de Ville** (town hall), where the first Geneva Convention was signed in 1864. Adjacent is the old arsenal and the 12th-century **Maison Tavel**, now an excellent museum, with several period rooms and exhibits covering the 14th–19th centuries.

The original 12th–13th-century Gothic

544

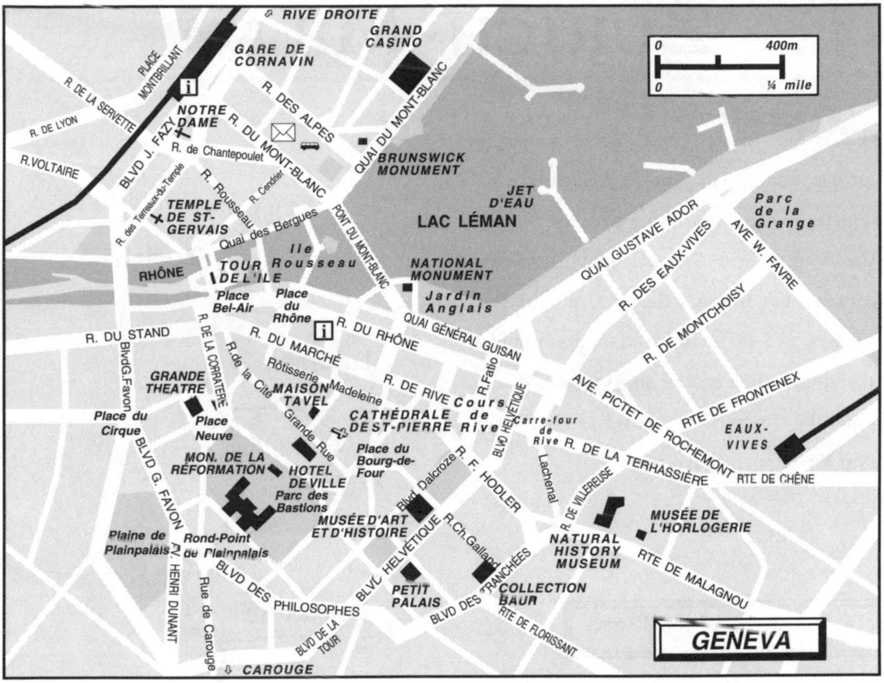
RIVE DROITE
GRAND CASINO
GARE DE CORNAVIN
PLACE MONTBRILLANT
R. DE LA SERVETTE
R. DE LYON
R.VOLTAIRE
NOTRE DAME
R. DES ALPES
QUAI DU MONT-BLANC
R. DU MONT-BLANC
R. de Chantepoulet
BLVD J. FAZY
BRUNSWICK MONUMENT
R. des Terreaux-du-Temple
R. Rousseau
R. Cendrier
TEMPLE DE ST-GERVAIS
Quai des Bergues
PONT DU MONT-BLANC
JET D'EAU
LAC LÉMAN
Parc de la Grange
Ile Rousseau
TOUR DE L'ILE
RHÔNE
NATIONAL MONUMENT
Jardin Anglais
QUAI GUSTAVE ADOR
R. DES EAUX-VIVES
AVE W. FAVRE
Place Bel-Air
Place du Rhône
R. DU RHÔNE
QUAI GÉNÉRAL GUISAN
R. DE MONTCHOISY
R. DU STAND
R. DE LA CORRATERIE
R. DU MARCHÉ
Rôtisserie
R.de la Cité
BlvdG.Favon
GRANDE THEATRE
MAISON TAVEL
Madeleine
R. DE RIVE
Cours de Rive
R.Fatio
BLVD HELVÉTIQUE
AVE. PICTET DE ROCHEMONT
RTE DE FRONTENEX
Place du Cirque
Place Neuve
Grande Rue
CATHÉDRALE DE ST-PIERRE
Carre-four de Rive
EAUX-VIVES
Place du Bourg-de-Four
R. DE LA TERRASSIÈRE
RTE DE CHÊNE
MON. DE LA RÉFORMATION
HOTEL DE VILLE
Parc des Bastions
Blvd Dalcroze
R. F. HODLER
Lachenal
R. DE VILLEREUSE
BLVD G. FAVON
MUSÉE D'ART ET D'HISTOIRE
R.Ch.Galland
MUSÉE DE L'HORLOGERIE
Plaine de Plainpalais
Rond-Point de Plainpalais
NATURAL HISTORY MUSEUM
AV. HENRI DUNANT
BLVD DES PHILOSOPHES
BLVD HELVÉTIQUE
PETIT PALAIS
BLVD DES TRANCHÉES
COLLECTION BAUR
RTE DE MALAGNOU
Rue de Carouge
BLVD DE LA TOUR
RTE DE FLORISSANT
CAROUGE
0 400m
0 ¼ mile
GENEVA

545

façade of the **Cathédrale de St-Pierre** has incongruous 18th-century additions. Most interior decorations were stripped out in the Reformation, but there are some fine frescos in the neo-Gothic **Chapelle des Maccabées**. Calvin preached here and his chair has been saved for posterity. The north tower, reached by a 157-step spiral staircase, offers a great view of the old town. Beneath the cathedral is the **Site Archéologique**, where catwalks allow you to see the result of extensive excavations, including a 4th-century baptistery and a 5th-century mosaic floor. Two blocks south, the vast marble **Musée d'Art et d'Histoire**, *r. Charles-Galland 2,* has several rooms in period style, Hodler landscapes and the famous painting *The Fishing Miracle,* by Witz, which portrays Christ walking on the water – of Lake Geneva. There are also large sections on subjects such as arms and porcelain.

The 19th-century **Petit Palais**, *terrasse St-Victor 2,* has an impressive array of modern art and includes works by Cézanne, Renoir and the Surrealists. Nearby, the **Collection Baur**, *r. Munier-Romilly 8,* contains some lovely Japanese and Chinese objets d'art, ranging from Samurai swords to jade and delicate porcelain.

Don't miss the amazing assortment of timepieces in the **Musée de l'Horlogerie et de l'Emaillerie**, *rte de Malagnou 15.* It's an experience to be there when they sound the hour. West of the cathedral, **Parc des Bastions** houses the university (founded by Calvin in 1599) and the vast **Monument de la Réformation** (erected in 1917), a 90m-long wall featuring four central characters – Farel, Calvin, Bèze and Knox – each over 4.5m high. **Carouge**, south of the River Arve (20 mins by tram no.12), is a baroque suburb with fine 18th-century architecture.

Centred on the plane tree-shaded *pl. du Marché* is a picturesque bohemian area of Italian-style arcaded buildings, many restored and now home to small shops and a thriving community of craftsmen. Try to visit on Wed or Sat morning when the market is on.

# ZURICH–MILAN

This is one of the most scenic routes in Europe, taking you on a wriggling tour though the rugged snow-capped heart of the Alps. Starting from Switzerland's largest city, it leads south through the St Gotthard Pass and past two of Switzerland's most popular lakeside resorts, Lucerne and Lugano. Then, near Lake Como, it crosses into Italy for the short final stretch to Milan.

> FASTEST JOURNEY: 3 HRS 40 MINS

546

## TRAINS

**ETT tables:** 84, 550, 555, 552, 551, 548, 549.

### FAST TRACK

There are through trains every 2 hrs. Changing at Arth-Goldau gives a departure every hour. Most journeys take 4½ hrs, but a few *Cisalpino* high-speed trains (reservation, including supplement, obligatory) do the journey in 3 hrs 40 mins. Most trains have a dining-car or buffet service. Border formalities are minimal.

### ON TRACK

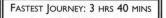 **Zurich–Lucerne (Luzern)**
The service is hourly, taking 50 mins.

**Lucerne–Lugano**
There is an hourly train, and on alternate hours

Lugano can be reached quicker by changing at Arth-Goldau. Faster trains (no supplement to pay until Italy) take about 2 hrs 45 mins.

**Lugano–(Border)–Milan (Milano)**
Hourly *EC/IC* trains (supplement) take 1½ hrs, while the few *Cisalpino* high-speed trains take 1 hr (reservation, including supplement, obligatory). The border is crossed at Chiasso, but formalities are minimal.

## LUCERNE (LUZERN)

**Station:** On the south bank of the River Reuss, where it meets Lake Lucerne ~ (041) 157 22 22,

**Tourist Office:** *Frankenstr. 1; tel: (041) 410 71 71* (by station). Open Mon–Fri 0830–1800, Sat 0900–1700 (Apr–Oct); Sun 0900–1300 (mid May–Oct); Mon–Fri 0830–1200 and 1400–1800, Sat 0900–1300 (Nov–Mar). Also in the **station basement**: open 1100–1800 mid Mar–mid Oct. Accommodation booking service free.

### ACCOMMODATION AND FOOD

Lucerne is a popular tourist destination so advance booking is advisable for its limited range of cheap options, especially in summer. Hotel chains include: *AC, BW, IE, MO, Rk, SL, Tp.*

For a one-star room with a view in a picturesque central location on the River Reuss, try the **Pickwick**, *Rathausquai 6; tel: (041) 410 59 27.* The much grander **Hotel des Balances**, *Weinmarkt; tel: (041) 410 30 10,* once the town hall, is decorated with *trompe l'oeil* paintings on the front and has a riverside terrace at the back (expensive). **Backpackers Lucerne**, *Alpengasse 42; tel: (041) 360 0420,* offers student-style accommodation by the south shore of the lake (10-min walk from the station). **HI: Jugendherberge**, *Sedelstr. 12, Am Rotsee; tel: (041) 420 88 00,* by the lake north-west of town (bus no. 18 to Gopplismoos; after 1930, tram no. 1 to *Schlossberg* plus 15-min walk). **Campsite: Lido**, *Lidostr. 8; tel: (041) 370 21 46* (bus no. 2 to *Verkehrshaus),* on the north shore of the lake.

There are reasonably priced restaurants and cafés all round Lucerne's many squares and waterside promenades. The town's speciality is *Kügelipasteti,* a large meat and mushroom vol-au-vent covered in rich sauce.

### SIGHTSEEING

The busy centre, on either side of **River Reuss** at the end of **Lake Lucerne**, is small and includes most of the town's attractions. Its picturesque setting makes it a honeypot for tourists, particularly the 14th-century **Kapellbrücke**, a wooden-roofed footbridge that straggles crookedly over the river. As you cross it, you pass under a succession of 111 triangular-shaped paintings depicting local and national history. Thirty date back to the 17th century, but the remainder are reproductions following a disastrous fire which destroyed most of the bridge in 1993. Halfway across, the bridge goes through a sturdy 13th-century octagonal **Water Tower**, which has undergone several changes of function over the centuries, including use as a gaol. A short distance further down the river, another medieval roofed bridge, the **Spreuerbrücke**, is also lined with 17th-century paintings, in this case depicting the macabre *Dance of Death.*

Near the south end of Kapellbrücke, the **Jesuit Church** looks plain from the outside but has a gorgeous pink-and-white baroque interior dating from 1677. **Nolliturm**, on the riverbank near the north end of Spreuerbrücke, is a fortified gate that marks one end of a well-preserved stretch of **Musegg Wall**, the old fortifications. You can follow this all the way (and climb three of its nine surviving towers) as it curves eastwards to end just off *Löwenpl.*

The graceful twin-spired **Hofkirche** (Cathedral), off *Schweizerhofquai,* near the lake has an organ with 4950 pipes and a 10-ton bell. The city's mascot, the **Löwendenkmal** (Lion Memorial), *Löwenstr.,* a massive but very touching portrayal of a dying lion, carved out of the cliff-side, commemorates the Swiss Guards massacred at the Tuileries in Paris during the French Revolution. Nearby is the **Gletschergarten** (Glacier Garden), *Denkmalstr. 4,* a bed of smooth rocks pitted with holes, created millions of years ago by the Reuss glacier. There's an ingenious mirror-maze here too.

The **Picasso Museum**, *Furreng. 21,* just off the old **Kornmarkt** square, contains a small collection of his later paintings and also photographs of him. The **Richard Wagner Museum**, *Wagnerweg 27,* by the lake 1.5 km south-east of the centre (bus nos 6/8 or walk east along the lake from the station), occupies the house where he lived during the time he composed *Siegfried* and the *Meistersinger.*

The **Verkehrshaus** (Swiss Transport Museum), *Lidostr. 5,* 2 km east of town (near the campsite), reached by a pleasant lakeside walk (or bus no. 2), is one of the country's leading museums with exhibits from pennyfarthings to space rockets, a 360-degree cinema and plenty of 'hands-on' exhibits.

Other museums are: **Historiches Museum** (History Museum); **Natur-Museum** (Natural History Museum) and the **Kunstmuseum** (Museum of Fine Arts).

## ↰ SIDE TRACKS FROM LUCERNE

Many of the small settlements around Lake Lucerne, which covers 114 square km, are serviced by regular local boat services as well as excursion cruises in summer (bookable at the Tourist Office). Visit **Altdorf** (where William Tell shot the apple from his son's head), **Vitznau** to go on Europe's oldest rack railway (or by cable car) up **Mt Rigi** (1800m), or **Alpnachstad** to take the world's steepest rack railway (doesn't run in snow) up **Mt Pilatus** (2132m), which is also accessible by cable car from **Kriens**. At **Engelberg**, 16 km south of the lake, the huge Rotair, the world's first rotating cable-car, gives an unparalleled view of the permanently snow-capped **Mt Titlis** (3239m). ⬛

548

## LUGANO

**Station:** *tel: (091) 923 75 01,* at the top of the town. From it a funicular descends to the middle (otherwise a 6-min walk), half-way down to the lake.

**Tourist Office:** *Palazzo Civico; tel: (091) 921 46 64,* on the lakeside opposite the central landing stage. Open Mon–Fri 0900–1830, Sat 0900–1230 and 1330–1700, Sun 0930–1300. Accommodation booking service: SFr.4.

### ACCOMMODATION AND FOOD

**Hotel Federale**, *V. Regazzoni 8; tel: (091) 922 05 51* (moderate) is opposite the station. Others and a big choice of restaurants are around the lake. **HI: Lugano-Savosa**, *V. Cantonale 13; tel: (091) 966 2728* (bus no. 5 from station to *Crocifisso*.

### SIGHTSEEING

Lugano, the largest town in the Italian-speaking canton of **Ticino**, is a handsome resort of Lombardic arcades and piazzas beside **Lake Lugano**. It climbs the hillside around a horse-shoe bay surrounded by verdant mountains, so

is an ideal base for walking as well as watersports. There are fountains in the lake (June–Oct) and the lakeside promenade becomes a popular place to stroll or roller-blade after 2000 in July and Aug when vehicles are banned from it.

**Funiculars** climb the two mountains guarding the bay: up **Monte Brè** (930m) from *Cassarate* and up **San Salvatore** (912m) from *Paradiso,* both 20-min walks from the centre or take bus no. 1. The former provides magnificent views over the town, while the latter offers a panoramic sweep into Italy.

The 16th-century **Cattedrale San Lorenzo** is on the hillside immediately below the station. The other notable church is the lakeside **Santa Maria Degli Angioli**, which has a marvellous Renaissance mural of the Passion and Crucifixion.

**Thyssen-Bornemisza**, an outstanding collection of 19th and 20th-century paintings and watercolours is housed in the **Villa Favorita**, *Riviera 14* (only open Fri–Sun Easter–Oct). The **Cantonal Art Museum**, *Via Canova 10,* also has many interesting 20th-century works.

**Navigazione Lugano**; *tel: (091) 971 52 23,* operate a wide choice of boat trips from the central landing stage to picturesque villages on the lake such as **Gandria** near the Italian border, or **Melide** where you can visit **Swissminiatur**, a model version of Switzerland. Or you can hire a pedalo there.

## ↰ SIDE TRACKS FROM LUGANO

**Locarno** on **Lake Maggiore** is an hour by train from Lugano (changing at Bellinzona). From it the scenic **Centovalli** ('100 Valleys') route crosses the border to **Domodossola** in Italy. The 53 km line clings to dramatic hillsides, soars across dozens of steep valleys (hence its name) and around **Santa Maria Maggiore**. Afterwards, to continue exploring Switzerland, the major rail junction at **Brig** is 42 km north of Domodossola through the **Simplon Tunnel**.

There are frequent trains from Lugano to **Como** on **Lake Como**, another of Italy's beautiful lakes (taking about 50 mins). ⬛

# ZURICH–VIENNA

Soon leaving Switzerland, this route goes right across Austria. It runs along valleys and the spectacular Alpine scenery of the Arlberg pass, taking in some of the prettiest towns in Europe, including Salzburg, a must for classical music lovers. At Innsbruck, it crosses the Munich–Venice route (see p. 356) which offers a change of direction, either north into Germany or south into Italy.

**549**

FASTEST JOURNEY: 9 HRS

## TRAINS

**ETT tables: 86, 520, 950, 960.**

### FAST TRACK

Two day trains and one overnight train link these two cities. The day *EC* trains take 9 hrs. The night-time *Wiener Walzer* is one of the latest Hotel Trains and is to a very high standard. It takes just over 10 hrs and has sleeping cars, couchettes and reclining chairs.

### ON TRACK

#### Zurich–Innsbruck

Two through trains and a couple of connecting services operate on this route. The journey takes 3 hrs 45 mins.

#### Innsbruck–Kitzbühel–Salzburg

EC trains every 2 hrs link Innsbruck and Salzburg. *IC* trains every 2 hrs take 1 hr from Innsbruck to Kitzbühel, 2½ hrs from Kitzbühel to Salzburg.

#### Salzburg–Linz–Vienna

An hourly service calling at Linz. Salzburg to Linz takes 1 hr 20 mins, Linz to Vienna 2 hrs. Refreshments are available on most trains.

## INNSBRUCK

**Station: Hbf**, tel: *(0512) 17 17*. Several tram and bus routes connect with the *Altstadt,* or a 10-min walk down *Salurnerstr.* and then right into *Maria-Theresiastr.*

**Airport:** tel: *(0512) 22 5 25*, is 5 km west reached by bus F from the *Hbf* in 15 mins, or 10 mins by taxi from *Maria Theresiastr.* (ÖS120).

**Tourist Office:** Innsbruck Information: *Burggraben 3; tel: (0512) 53 56*, on the edge of *Altstadt,* open 0800–1900, Sun 0900–1800.

**Hbf:** *tel: (0512) 58 37 66,* open 0900–2100, July–Sept until 2200. Accommodation booking service, ÖS40 deposit. They sell concert tickets, ski/cable car passes and public transport tickets.

## GETTING AROUND

Innsbruck is a compact city and most sights are easily walkable from the central *Altstadt,* old town area, which is pedestrianised. However, bus tours (ÖS160) can be booked at the Tourist Office. A 24-hr ticket for the excellent tram, bus and trolley bus system costs ÖS45 (single ÖS21). An **All Inclusive Card**, covering local transport (including cable cars) and entrance to 18 museums and attractions, is good value; 24-hr card ÖS200, 48-hr ÖS280, 72-hr ÖS350, from Tourist Offices and museums. Bikes can be hired from the station, ÖS90 per day.

## ACCOMMODATION

Budget rooms are scarce in June, when only three hostels are open, but 'summer hotels' usually open in **university accommodation** July and Aug. The family-run **Sailer**, *Adamgasse 6–10; tel: (0512) 5363,* notable for its Tyrolean restaurant and décor, is handy for the station (moderate). In the old town, the **Goldener Adler**, *Herzog-Friedrichstr. 6; tel: (0512) 58 63 34,* (expensive) has welcomed guests from Goethe to Duke Albert of Bavaria. The **Schwarzer Adler**, *Kaiserjägerstr. 2; tel: (0512) 58 71 09* (expensive), an inn since the 17th century, has expanded into part of the adjoining monastery. Hotel chains include *BW, Rk, Sc, Sn.* **Pension Paula**, *Weiherburgg. 15; tel: (0512) 29 22 62,* (cheap) is below the *Alpenzoo* (transport as youth hostels). **HI**: Relatively central hostels are **Glockenhaus**, *Weiherburgg. 3; tel: (0512) 28 65 15,* and **St Nikolaus**, *Innstr. 95; tel: (0512) 28 65 15,* both on the opposite side of the river from the *Altstadt* (bus K from *Hbf* to *St Nikolaus,* then walk up hill). **Campsite: Camping Innsbruck Kranebitten**, *Kranebitter Allee 214; tel: (0512) 28 41 80,* is west of town (bus O).

## EATING AND DRINKING

The **Altstadt** area is generally expensive, though **Restaurant Ottoburg**, *Herzog-Friedrichstr. 1; tel: (0512) 57 46 52,* is a pleasant

traditional *Weinkeller* and restaurant. Moderately priced alternatives include the **Sailer** and **Schwarzer Adler** (see Accommodation), which serve traditional meals like venison with ham and dumplings, or the **Stieglbrau Restaurant**, *W. Greilstr. 25; tel: (0512) 58 43 38.* For a snack, try **Hortnagel Pronto**, *Maria-Theresiastr. 5; tel: (0512) 59 729,* part of the smart deli next door. **Central Café**, *Gilmstr. 5; tel: (0512) 59 20 65,* is a typical coffee house.

## ENTERTAINMENT AND ACTIVITIES

Tyrolean brass bands play in front of the **Golden Roof** at 1100 Sat mid May to Sept, and in the *Hofgarten* at 1100 Sun mid May–June, 2030 Tues late-June–mid Aug and 2030 Sat July–late Aug. Concerts are staged in the **Provincial Theatre**, *Rennweg 2; tel: (0512) 52 074,* and **Congress Hall**, *Rennweg 3; tel: (0512) 5936.* An **Early Music Festival** is staged in July and Aug; *tel: (0512) 56 15 61.* Try the **Treibhaus**, *Angerzellg. 8, tel: (0512) 58 68 74,* for live groups, or **Utopia**, *Tschamlerstr. 3; tel: (0512) 58 85 87,* for jazz and rock.

Innsbruck is an ideal base for walking in the Alps. Miles of marked trails are on offer, including several starting from the **Nordkette** above the *Zoo*. Free guided hikes in the mountains start daily June–Sept from Congress Hall, *Rennweg 3;* also free 'Lantern' hikes to a mountain hut in **Igls** on Tues evenings. Other outdoor pursuits include mountain biking (the Nordkette has three approved routes), rafting, paragliding, and, of course, skiing – 53 lifts giving access to 112 km of runs. Skiing is possible even in summer on the **Stubai glacier**, to which the Tourist Office organises day-excursions including lift pass and ski hire, ÖS599.

## SHOPPING

**Heimatwerk**, *Meranerstr. 24,* offers good Tyrolean clothing at reasonable prices. The city is also a good place to buy sports gear. Try **Sporthaus Witting**, *Maria-Theresiastr. 39.* The local crystal manufacturer, **Swarovski**, has a shop in *Herzog-Friedrichstr.* **Brakmayer**, *Leopoldstr.,* offers a vast range of traditional and modern pewter. Delightful handmade silver filigree jewellery is sold at **W. & B. Bliem**, *Herzog-Friedrich-Str. 15.*

## SIGHTSEEING

Innsbruck, the 800-year old **Tyrolean capital** on the River Inn, is a bustling city overlooked by the **Karwendel** mountains to the north and the **Patscherkofel** mountains to the south. The *Altstadt* area is dotted with splendid 15th- and 16th-century buildings, many with elaborate stucco decorations and traditional convex windows to catch extra light on the narrow streets. Its most famous sight is the 15th-century **Goldenes Dachl**, *Herzog-Friedrichstr. 1,* a golden roof of 2657 gilded copper tiles over the balcony which Emperor Maximilian I added in 1500 to the Neuhof, the residence of the Tyrolean princes. The **Maximilianeum** inside is a glittering exhibition on Maximilian, who was the Habsburg Emperor in the early 1500s. The **Stadtturm** (city tower) opposite the balcony offers excellent views across the rooftops to the mountains. Nearby, **Dom zu St Jakob**, the striking baroque cathedral, has an amazing ceiling (depicting St James) painted by C. D. Asam and a golden altar featuring Cranach's famous Madonna.

The **Hofburg** (Imperial Palace), *Rennweg,* has a sumptuous ballroom lined with portraits of Empress Maria Theresia's family, who also feature in 28 larger than life bronze statues on Emperor Maximilian's grand tomb in the 16th-century **Hofkirche**, the court church. The neighbouring **Tiroler Volkskunst Museum**, *Universitätsstr. 2,* concentrates on Tyrolean culure, displaying traditional costumes and wood-panelled rooms in period styles. The **Ferdinandeum**, *Museumstr. 15,* is more diverse, with beautiful old stained-glass, medieval altars and works by Cranach and Rembrandt.

A short walk due south of the centre is the Tyrol's most beautiful rococo church, **Basilika Wilten**, *Leopoldstr.* A cream and white-grey building, it is strikingly light and airy inside thanks to its many windows. By contrast, the baroque **Stiftskirche Wilten** across the road is decorated in heavy black and gold.

On the hillside north of the Inn river, the **Alpenzoo**, *Weiherburgg. 37; tel: (0512) 29 23 23,* the highest zoo in Europe, is home to 140 species of animals, all native to the Alps. 20 mins on foot or by bus or tram (a special bus Z runs hourly from *Maria-Theresienstr.* May–Sept) and then on the **Hungerburg funicular** (free with zoo ticket).

The funicular continues on up to the **Hungerburg** plateau, where it links with the Nordkette cable car which goes up to **Seegrube** (1905m) and then the Nordkette II to **Hafelekar** (2334m). From there the views stretch over the Alps. In winter, the area is one of the most challenging in the Tirol for skiers.

South-east of the town centre (tram nos. 3/6), **Schloss Ambras**, *Schlossstr. 20,* is a splendid medieval castle containing Hapsburg portraits and weapons belonging to Archduke Ferdinand.

## SIDE TRACKS FROM INNSBRUCK

**Igls** is a pretty Alpine village (900m) in the mountains 5 km south-east of the city (bus J or tram no. 6) offering tennis, golf, mountain biking and children's clubs in summer and skiing in winter. **Tourist Office**: *Hilber Str., tel: (0512) 377101.* Open Mon–Fri 0830–1800; also Sat 0900–1200 Dec–Mar and mid May–mid Sept.

**Fulpmes**, another small village, 16 km south of the city, is worth a visit if only for the pleasure of the ride to it on *Stubaitalbahn.* This rattling tram (from Hbf) has been trundling up the Stubai valley since 1904. The route passes a few small villages but is mainly through green fields and forest. **Tourist Office:** *Gemeindezentrum; tel: (05225) 622 35.* Open Mon–Fri 0800–1800 Sat 0800–1200.

In **Wattens**, (frequent buses from Hbf; 40 min journey), **Swarovski Kristallwelten** (Crystal Worlds), *Kristallweltenstr. 1; tel:(05224) 51080,* is a multimedia extravaganza on the theme of crystals. The famous glass made in the factory there is on sale.

## KITZBÜHEL

**Station: Hbf**, *Bahnhofspl.; tel: (05356) 4055 1385.* A 10-min walk to town centre; turn left outside Hbf, then right across River Ache and along *Hornweg.* Bike hire at station: ÖS100 per day (ÖS50 with rail ticket).

**Tourist Office:** *Hinterstadt 18; tel: (05356) 621 550.* in the pedestrianised central area. Open Mon–Sat 0830–1830, Sun 1000–1200 and 1600–1800 (July–Sept, Christmas–New Year and Feb–mid Mar); Mon–Fri 0830–1200 and 1430–1800, Sat 0830–1200 (rest of year). Free accommodation booking service and free street and hiking trail maps.

## ACCOMMODATION AND FOOD

Hotel chains include *BW, RC* and *Rk*. The traditionally-Austrian **Hotel Resch**, *Alfons-Petzold-Weg 2; tel: (05356) 2294*, has been run by the same family for four generations. **Gasthof Eggerwirt**, *Gänsbachgasse 12; tel: (05356) 2151*, is country baroque in style. Both are moderate and very near the town centre. Cheaper are **Frühstuck pensionen** (bed and breakfast) such as **Hörl**, *Josef-Pirchl-Str. 60; tel: (05356) 3144*. **HI: Skiheim Rote Teufel**, *Ehrenbachgasse 48; tel: (05356) 5669*, 10-min walk south from centre. **Campsite: Camping Schwarzsee**, *Reitherstr. 24; tel: (05356) 2806*, is near Schwarzsee station, or a 35-min walk from the town centre.

The mountain air and plenty of healthy exercise – walking in summer and skiing in winter – give most visitors a hearty appetite, so it is no surprise that there is an excellent choice of good value restaurants serving ample portions. Most are part of hotels, like the **Goldener Grief**, *Hinterstadt 24; tel: (0536) 4311* (moderate). For a special occasion, the one in **Romantikhotel Tennerhof**, *Griesenauweg 26; tel: (0536) 3181*, has an excellent reputation (expensive). During the ski season, restaurants up on the ski slopes are open too.

## ENTERTAINMENT AND ACTIVITIES

The ski elite arrive in Jan for the **Hahnenkamm Ski Competition**, a World Cup leg down one of the world's trickiest ski runs. Spectator tickets are available at the gate. In July and Aug there are free **open air concerts** near the *Rathaus*. End July sees the **Austrian Men's Tennis Open**.

In summertime, hikers can buy a lift pass valid for any 3 days in seven (ÖS340) and the nearby **Schwarzsee** lake warms up to a suitable temperature. From Christmas to Easter, the town swarms with skiers attracted by its 60 lifts, 30 km of cross-country trails and lively après-ski nightlife.

## SIGHTSEEING

This small medieval town is a picturesque sight with its tree-lined streets, steeply-gabled pastel-coloured buildings and mountains rising steeply on either side of the valley. The **Heimatmuseum**, *Hinterstadt 34*, occupies the town's oldest house, dating back to the 13th century. Its three floors cover, respectively, prehistoric European mining, the work of the Tyrolean painter **Alfons Walde** and winter sports.

At the top of the **Hahnenkamm** lift, the small **Bergbahn Museum** tells the history of skiing in Kitzbühel since its start in 1893 and also the development of its lift system. Near the top of the **Hornbahn** lift, around 200 Alpine flowers and grasses bloom in their natural environment in the **Alpine Flower Garden**, 1880m high.

## SALZBURG

**Station: Hbf**, *tel: (0662) 17 17*, on the northern edge of the new town, 20 mins walk from the old centre (bus nos 1/5/6/51 to *Staatsbrücke*, the main bridge).

**Airport:** 4 km west of the city, serves European destinations. Bus no. 77 every 15 mins (30 mins late evenings, Sat afternoon and Sun) 0600–2300 connects *Hbf* with airport; journey time about 15 mins. A taxi to the city centre is around ÖS140, *tel: (0662) 8111*. For **airport information**, *tel: (0662) 85 12 23*.

**Tourist Offices:** City centre: *Mozartpl. 5; tel: (0662) 889 87 330.* Open 0900–1900 June–Sept (to 2000 Jul–Aug); Mon–Sat 0900–1800 Oct–May; **Hbf**, *platform 2a, tel: (0662) 889 87 340.* Open 0845–2030 May–June, Sept, 0800–2130 July–Aug, 0845–1945 Oct–May 0800–2130. Accommodation booking service, ÖS30.

## GETTING AROUND

Most of the centre is pedestrianised and within walking distance, though the bus and trolley bus network is excellent. Tickets cost ÖS18 from automatic vending machines. Day passes are ÖS38. **Fiaker** (horse-drawn carriage) rides are available in *Residenzpl.*

## ACCOMMODATION

During festivals, it pays to book early as accommodation often becomes scarce. If you fancy staying in style in the *Altstadt*, the **Goldener Hirsch**, *Getreideg. 37; tel: (0662) 84 85 11*, originally four medieval townhouses, is the top hotel but very expensive. The nearby **Hotel Elefant**, *Sigmund-Haffnerg. 4; tel: (0662) 84 13 17*, is in a 700-year-old building (expensive). For a cheaper alternative, just opposite Hbf, try **Hotel Sandwirt**, *Lastenstr. 6a; tel: (0662) 87 43 51*. Hotel chains include: *BW, Hd, Mc, Nv, RC, Rd, Rk, Rm, Sh, SL, Sn, Tp*.

**HI: Jugendherberge**, *Haunspergstr. 27, tel: (0662) 87 50 30*, open July–Aug, and **Youth Hotel Obermair**, *Paracelsusstr. 9; tel: (0662) 87 96 49*, open all year. Both are about 5 mins walk from Hbf. **Campsites** include **Nord Sam**, *Samstr. 22, tel: (0662) 66 04 94*, (bus no. 33). Open Apr–Oct.

## EATING AND DRINKING

Serious gastronomes should try **Gasthof Auerhahn**, *Bahnhofstr. 15; tel: (0662) 451 052*, with a garden and much-lauded proprietor cook. More moderately priced is **s'Herzl**, *Getreideg. 37; tel: (0662) 848 511 889*, or **Mundenhamer**, *Rainerstr. 2; tel: (0662) 875 693*, near the *Hbf.* Traditional Salzburg fayre is served in the **Zum Mohren**, *Judengasse 9; tel: (0662) 84 23 87*, where the Mozart family liked to eat. Less expensive is **Der Wilde Mann**, *Getreideg. 20; tel: (0662) 841 787*, which serves a mighty *Wiener Schnitzel*. **Café Tomaselli**, *Alter Markt 9; tel: (0662) 844 488*, is where the elegant have taken coffee for the last two centuries. Also worth trying are **beer gardens**, especially the **Augustiner Brau**, *Augustinerg. 4*; tel: (0662) 431 246, where beer is brewed by the monastery and served in giant steins from traditional wooden kegs, and the **K&K Stieglkeller**, *Festungsg.*

## ENTERTAINMENT

The big event is **Salzburger Festspiele**, late July–end Aug. For major performances, tickets have to be booked months ahead from **Kartenbüro der Salzburger Festspiele**, *A-5010 Salzburg, Postfach 140; fax: (0662) 84 66 82*. Operas cost ÖS400–4200, and concerts cost ÖS400–2000 though modern concerts drop to ÖS100. Last minute standing tickets may be available in the *Kleine Festspielhaus*. Events connected to the festival include an opening *Fackeltanz* (torch-dance) in the *Residenzpl.* and performances of *'Jedermann'* ('Everyman'); standing tickets only sold at the *Dompl.* door one hour before. Other events include **Mozart Week** in late Jan (advance tickets: **Internationale Stiftung Mozarteum**, *A-5024 Salzburg; tel: (0662) 87 31 54)*, and an **Easter Music Festival**. In addition, there is always a concert somewhere in the city every day of the year. The **Marionetten Theater**, *Schwarzstr. 24; tel: (0662) 88 21 41*, presents operas 'performed' very convincingly by puppets which 'sing' to recordings.

## SIGHTSEEING

Salzburg's wealth grew originally from its salt industry. After Vienna, it is Austria's biggest tourist draw, and with good reason. As well as music – with both Mozart and *'The Sound of Music'* connections – its Prince Archbishop rulers bequeathed it a fine castle, palaces, churches and squares. Much of the city's appearance dates from the 17th century, when most of the old buildings were pulled down to make way for Italian-style squares with spectacular fountains. In 1997, the **Altstadt**, nestled at the foot of **three steep hills** beside the River Salzach, was designated a World Heritage Site.

On **Mönchsberg** (Monk's mountain), high above the Altstadt, looms the formidable **Festung Hohensalzburg**, *Mönchsberg 34*, once the stronghold of the Archbishops of Salzburg. Construction of the castle began in 1077 and continued until the 17th century. The complex, which has extensive views, is almost perfectly preserved and has everything from medieval torture chambers to impressive early Gothic state rooms (seen only on guided tours) plus Austria's only barrel organ, a 200-pipe affair that booms out after the 7th-century 35-bell carillon of the **Glockenspiel**, *Mozartpl.*, has pealed (at 0700, 1100 and 1800). The castle can be reached on foot from *Festungsg.* behind the Dom, or the *Festungsbahn* (lift).

Alternatively, the Mönchsberglift operates from *Gstätteng.* (by *Museumpl.*) and takes you to

**553**

the **Café Winkler**, where paths lead across to the castle.

Narrow *Getreideg.*, always thronged with tourists, is bordered by 17th- and 18th-century houses whose ground floors are now occupied by shops with decorative wrought iron signs. **Mozarts Geburtshaus**, *no.9,* is where the composer was born in 1756 and spent most of his first 17 years. It's now a museum containing stage sets for his operas and a tiny violin he used as a child. The family subsequently lived in the **Mozart-Wohnhaus**, *Makart-pl.,* across the river, recently rebuilt in its original style following World War II destruction. The rooms are furnished in period style, including a small ballroom where concerts are held.

The elegant *Residenzpl.*, which has a large ornate fountain in the centre, is dominated by the **Residenz**, the former Prince-Archbishop's palace, built after the need for fortification had passed. Mozart conducted in its grand rooms. Tours are hourly.

Across the river is **Schloss Mirabell**, *Mirabellpl.,* built in the 17th century for Prince-Archbishop Dietrich's mistress, who managed to bear him 15 or 16 children. Rebuilt in the early 18th century and further reconstructed after a fire in the 19th century, it now houses public offices and the **Marmor Saal**, an ornate white and gold venue for chamber music concerts. The style spills out on to the incredible **Angel Staircase**, with its marble cherubs, visible to passers-by.

### Churches

The **Dom**, in the adjacent *Dompl.*, is considered to be the finest early baroque church north of the Alps. A magnificent light-filled building, it has four domes and space inside for 10,000 people. Mozart worked there as *Konzertmeister* and court organist. The connecting **Dommuseum** has an odd selection of items treasured by the Renaissance rulers, such as conch shells and a whale's tooth.

The **Franziskanerkirche**, *Hofstallgasse,* is a mishmash of architectural styles combining baroque with remnants of early frescos. More successful is **Kollegienkirche**, *Universitätspl.,* which remains cool and collected within the baroque ethic. **St Peterstift**, *St Peter Bezirk,* on the other hand, rivals wedding cakes in its baroque pastel mouldings. There is also an ancient and, when uncrowded, atmospheric cemetery and catacombs *(Katakomben)* dating back to 250AD.

### The Sound of Music

For those who want to relive *The Sound of Music* (filmed around the city in 1964), there's a choice of English-language tours (about ÖS330) lasting 3–4 hrs. Or you can do your own. **Nonnberg Abbey**, near the *Festung,* is where Maria Von Trapp was a teacher. The grounds of **Schloss Hellbrunn** (see below) was the venue for Liesl and Rolf's first kiss. **Schloss Leopoldskron**, behind the Mönchberg, played parts of the Von Trapp house, the **Petersfriedhof Cemetery** is where the family hid and the **Festspielhaus** was the venue for their last performance. **Mondsee** (hourly buses from *Hbf )* was substituted in the film for Nonnberg Abbey, where the von Trapp wedding actually took place.

### Museums

**Baroque Museum**, *Mirabellgarten Orangerie,* covers 17th- and 18th-century painting and sculpture. **Museum Carolino Augusteum**; *Museumpl. 6,* ranges from Iron Age relics to reconstructions of period rooms. **Residenzgalerie**, *Residenzpl. 1,* has a selection of international Old Masters of the 16th–19th centuries.

### SIDE TRACKS FROM SALZBURG

Just south of town (5 km) is the ornate 17th-century **Schloss Hellbrunn** (bus from *Hbf* or *Mirabellpl.).* The gardens of this Italian-designed pleasure-palace are noted particularly for their sculptures and fountains, especially those that could shoot up unexpectedly from stone stools to surprise drunken guests.

The big **Fuschlsee** lake (25 km east) is where Salzburgers go to swim or enjoy the beach, but midweek is calm, even in the height of summer. Buses to **Fuschl am See** leave from *Hbf* and *Mirabellpl.* approximately hourly. ◢

# SPECIAL TRAINS

## STEAM TRAINS AND LITTLE RAILWAYS

The following is a selection of minor lines, sometimes operated by steam train, which head off the beaten track into areas of spectacular scenery. There are many more such lines in Europe, and specialist operators, and enthusiasts' clubs and literature can suggest other worthwhile trips.

### AUSTRIA

Sixty km west of Vienna lies **St Pölten**, from where a narrow-gauge line turns south for **Mariazell**, a religious pilgrimage centre. After about 45 mins en route, the scenery changes from farming country to the spectacular gorge of the River Pielach between Kirchberg and Laubenbachmühle. The journey then makes a steep, half-spiral climb to Winterbach, which offers stunning views. The hotel by the station has similarly impressive views. The station at Mariazell is 2 km below the town, but some bus services run between town and station. Rail passes are valid on this service.

Branching off the main line from Vienna to Venice is the **Unzmarkt–Tamsweg** railway, which winds for 90 mins up the valley of the River Mur, into the Tauern mountain range via the busy but pretty town of Murau. In summer, midweek steam trains run from **Murau** to **Tamsweg**.

### FRANCE

The narrow-gauge line from **La Tour de Carol** to **Villefranche** (rail passes valid) provides one of the highlights of train travel in France, with excellent mountain views and a rustic charm of its own. In summer there are special bright yellow open carriages. Connecting trains run from Villefranche to the coast at **Perpignan** (p. 321).

The **Nice** to **Digne** railway in southern France was closed for several months due to flooding, but this beautiful little line through the mountains of Provence is now back in full operation.

### GERMANY

The Harz Mountains National Park is traversed by several railways, the best known of which are the **Wernigerode–Nordhausen** line, running through small, unspoilt villages like Sorge and Elend, and the **Wernigerode–Brocken** line. The Brocken line climbs into the mountain which, until the fall of communism, was off limits to westerners because of the Russian military installations at its peak. Some trains are pulled by steam locomotives. The **Gernrode** to **Harzgerode** and **Hasselfelde** system nearby, operated by the same company, is less busy but equally charming.

### NORWAY

The spectacular **Flåm** railway, with 20 tunnels in as many kilometres, leaves the Oslo–Bergen line (see p. 384) at **Myrdal**. Connection can be made at Flåm with catamarans that sail along the fjord. Passholders pay a supplement.

### POLAND

Steam trains still operate some services on the **Poznań** to **Wolsztyn** line, although these could finish at any time. The line passes through typical Polish countryside where old farming methods are still much in evidence. From May to mid July, look out for the storks' nests that sit atop tall structures. Rail passes valid.

### PORTUGAL

Take a train along the Douro Valley from **Oporto** to **Pocinho**, just for the ride. Services are limited and the journey takes about 4 hrs, so a round trip in a day necessitates an early start. Accommodation is available in Régua and Pinhão, both en route.

The branch line from **Tua** to **Mirandela** is also scenic and highly recommended.

Rail passes are valid on both lines.

555

### SPAIN

The coastal line from **San Sebastián** to **Ferrol** has varied scenery, including mountains, rivers, and the coast, along its length. Allow several days for the journey, for there are not many trains and connections between them are rather haphazard.

### SWEDEN

The privately operated **Inlandsbanan** runs slowly through the centre of Sweden late June to early Aug. A daily railbus runs on each of the two sections of the line, and there are steam trips at weekends during July.

### SWITZERLAND/ITALY

A lesser-known line is the **Centovalli** (100 valleys) route from **Domodossola** (Italy) to **Locarno** (Switzerland). There is a very steep climb from Domodossola to Santa Maria Maggiore. It affords stunning views as the line clings to impossible hillside ledges, crossing into Switzerland to reach Locarno, an upmarket resort on Lake Maggiore.

Other spectacular journeys in Switzerland, include: the **William Tell Express** from Lucerne to Lugano (incorporating a trip on a restored paddle-steamer on Lake Lucerne); the **Panoramic Expresses** from Montreux to Lenk via Gstaad, some of which are first class only; the **Bernina Express** from Chur to Tirano through the dramatic Albula Pass and over the very top of the Bernina Pass, the latter without a long tunnel; and the well known **Glacier Express**, a 6-hr delight from Zermatt to St Moritz traversing the very heart of the Swiss Alps. A funicular railway runs steeply up from Lautersbrunnen (near Interlaken) to Grütschalp, with a connection for Murren. The views are breathtaking and you can take a cable car back down the valley from Murren.

## CRUISE AND LUXURY TRAINS

These aristocrats of the railway world provide a taste of luxury and 1920s and 1930s atmosphere. They are expensive, of course (check with agents for full price details), but they are the nearest equivalent on land to the world of the cruise liner. For full details consult the main agent shown.

### AL ANDALUS EXPRESS (SPAIN)

Seven days of luxury, cruising around Andalucía in 1920s vintage carriages carefully restored for maximum comfort. Departs from Seville for Córdoba, Granada, Ronda and Jerez de la Frontera. A Barcelona–Santiago de Compostela service by the same train runs July and August.
**Information:** Spanish National Tourist Offices.
**Booking (UK): Cox & King**, *4th Floor, Gordon House, 10 Greencoat Pl., London SW1P 1PH; tel: 0171-873 5002*. **Mundicolor**, *276 Vauxhall Bridge Road, London SW1V 1BE; tel: 0171-828 6021*.

### CANTABRIAN EXPRESS (SPAIN)

This is a very comfortable week-long, 1000 km sightseeing journey leaving every Sat from either Santiago de Compostela or San Sebastián along the northern Spanish coast and through the foothills of the Picos de Europa.
**Information and booking:** Emilia Gonzalez, Transcantábrico-Feve, *Avda Santander s/n, 33001 Oviedo, Asturias, Spain; tel: (Spain +) 985 529 0104*.

### VENICE-SIMPLON-ORIENT EXPRESS

The original Istanbul-Orient Express commenced in 1883. Running from London to Istanbul, it achieved an almost legendary status. Now, however, the re-invented Venice Simplon-Orient Express runs over part of the route. It is a privately run cruise train that has become a byword for opulence. All the carefully restored carriages, in both the British and the continental sections, were used on the original train in the 1920s and 30s.

The journey is from London Victoria, the Folkestone-Boulogne SeaCat, Paris, Basel, (linking here with a Düsseldorf, Frankfurt section) and continuing through Zürich, Innsbruck and Verona to Venice. Services also run to Vienna and Budapest. The train runs weekly, leaving London on Thurs and Venice on Wed. Numerous travel packages are available, with return flights and accommodation.
**Information/booking (UK):** Venice Simplon-Orient Express, *Sea Containers House, 20 Upper Ground, London SE1 9PF; tel: 0171-928 6000*.

556

# CONVERSION TABLES

## DISTANCES (approx. conversions)
1 kilometre (km) = 1000 metres (m)  1 metre = 100 centimetres (cm)

| Metric | Imperial/US | Metric | Imperial/US | Metric | Imperial/US |
|--------|-------------|--------|-------------|--------|-------------|
| 1 cm | 3/8ths in. | 10 m | 33 ft (11 yd) | 3 km | 2 miles |
| 50 cm | 20 in. | 20 m | 66 ft (22 yd) | 4 km | 2½ miles |
| 1 m | 3 ft 3 in. | 50 m | 164 ft (54 yd) | 5 km | 3 miles |
| 2 m | 6 ft 6 in. | 100 m | 330 ft (110 yd) | 10 km | 6 miles |
| 3 m | 10 ft | 200 m | 660 ft (220 yd) | 20 km | 12½ miles |
| 4 m | 13 ft | 250 m | 820 ft (275 yd) | 25 km | 15½ miles |
| 5 m | 16 ft 6 in. | 300 m | 984 ft (330 yd) | 30 km | 18½ miles |
| 6 m | 19 ft 6 in. | 500 m | 1640 ft (550 yd) | 40 km | 25 miles |
| 7 m | 23 ft | 750 m | ½ mile | 50 km | 31 miles |
| 8 m | 26 ft | 1 km | 5/8ths mile | 75 km | 46 miles |
| 9 m | 29 ft (10 yd) | 2 km | 1½ miles | 100 km | 62 miles |

## 24-HOUR CLOCK
(examples)

| | | |
|---|---|---|
| 0000 = Midnight | 1200 = Noon | 1800 = 6 p.m. |
| 0600 = 6 a.m. | 1300 = 1 p.m. | 2000 = 8 p.m. |
| 0715 = 7.15 a.m. | 1415 = 2.15 p.m. | 2110 = 9.10 p.m. |
| 0930 = 9.30 a.m. | 1645 = 4.45 p.m. | 2345 = 11.45 p.m. |

## TEMPERATURE
Conversion Formula: $°C × 9 ÷ 5 + 32 = °F$

| °C | °F | °C | °F | °C | °F | °C | °F |
|-----|-----|-----|-----|-----|-----|-----|-----|
| -20 | -4 | -5 | 23 | 10 | 50 | 25 | 77 |
| -15 | 5 | 0 | 32 | 15 | 59 | 30 | 86 |
| -10 | 14 | 5 | 41 | 20 | 68 | 35 | 95 |

## WEIGHT
1kg = 1000g  100 g = 3½ oz

| Kg | Pounds | Kg | Pounds | Kg | Pounds |
|----|--------|----|--------|----|--------|
| 1 | 2¼ | 5 | 11 | 25 | 55 |
| 2 | 4½ | 10 | 22 | 50 | 110 |
| 3 | 6½ | 15 | 33 | 75 | 165 |
| 4 | 9 | 20 | 45 | 100 | 220 |

## FLUID MEASURES
1 litre(l) = 0.88 Imperial quarts = 1.06 US quarts

| Litres | Imp.gal. | US gal. | Litres | Imp.gal. | US gal. |
|--------|----------|---------|--------|----------|---------|
| 5 | 1.1 | 1.3 | 30 | 6.6 | 7.8 |
| 10 | 2.2 | 2.6 | 35 | 7.7 | 9.1 |
| 15 | 3.3 | 3.9 | 40 | 8.8 | 10.4 |
| 20 | 4.4 | 5.2 | 45 | 9.9 | 11.7 |
| 25 | 5.5 | 6.5 | 50 | 11.0 | 13.0 |

## MEN'S CLOTHES

| UK | Europe | US |
|----|--------|-----|
| 36 | 46 | 36 |
| 38 | 48 | 38 |
| 40 | 50 | 40 |
| 42 | 52 | 42 |
| 44 | 54 | 44 |
| 46 | 56 | 46 |

## MENS' SHOES

| UK | Europe | US |
|----|--------|-----|
| 6 | 40 | 7 |
| 7 | 41 | 8 |
| 8 | 42 | 9 |
| 9 | 43 | 10 |
| 10 | 44 | 11 |
| 11 | 45 | 12 |

## LADIES' CLOTHES

| UK | France | Italy | Rest of Europe | US |
|----|--------|-------|----------------|-----|
| 10 | 36 | 38 | 34 | 8 |
| 12 | 38 | 40 | 36 | 10 |
| 14 | 40 | 42 | 38 | 12 |
| 16 | 42 | 44 | 40 | 14 |
| 18 | 44 | 46 | 42 | 16 |
| 20 | 46 | 48 | 44 | 18 |

## MEN'S SHIRTS

| UK | Europe | US |
|-----|--------|------|
| 14 | 36 | 14 |
| 15 | 38 | 15 |
| 15½ | 39 | 15½ |
| 16 | 41 | 16 |
| 16½ | 42 | 16½ |
| 17 | 43 | 17 |

## LADIES' SHOES

| UK | Europe | US |
|----|--------|-----|
| 3 | 36 | 4½ |
| 4 | 37 | 5½ |
| 5 | 38 | 6½ |
| 6 | 39 | 7½ |
| 7 | 40 | 8½ |
| 8 | 41 | 9½ |

## AREAS
1 hectare = 2.471 acres

1 hectare = 10,000 sq meters

1 acre = 0.4 hectares

# ABBREVIATIONS

To save space the following abbreviations have often been used in the text. Abbreviations for hotel chains are explained on pp. 559–560.

## Currency Units

| | | | | | |
|---|---|---|---|---|---|
| **BFr.** | Belgian Franc | **Kč** | Czech Koruna | **ÖS** | Austrian Schilling |
| **DKr.** | Danish Krone | **Kn** | Croatian Kuna | **Pta** | Spanish Peseta |
| **DM** | Deutsche Mark | **L.** | Italian Lira | **SFr.** | Swiss Franc |
| **Dr.** | Greek Drachma | **Lat** | Latvian Lat | **SK** | Slovak Koruna |
| **EEK** | Estonian Kroon | **Lei** | Romanian Lei | **SKr.** | Swedish Krone |
| **Esc.** | Portuguese Escudo | **LFr.** | Luxembourg Franc | **SlT** | Slovenian Tolar |
| **FFr.** | French Franc | **Lv.** | Bulgarian Leva | **TL** | Turkish Lira |
| **FIM** | Finnish Markka | **NKr.** | Norwegian Krone | **Zl** | Polish Zloty |
| **Ft** | Hungarian Forint | **NLG** | Netherlands Guilder | | |

## Rail Passes

These are used under 'Rail Pass Concessions' in the 'Country by Country' chapter.

| | | | |
|---|---|---|---|
| **EP** | Eurail Pass | **IR** | Inter-Rail Pass |
| **FP** | EuroDomino/Freedom Pass | **RES** | Rail Europ Senior Card |

## Addresses and Places

**558**

As well as the abbreviations, with their full versions and the English meanings, we also give the English equivalents of some words often found in place names and street signs.

**Altstadt** (Germany) Old Town
**av.** (France) Avenue
**Avda** (Spain, Portugal) Avenida, (Catalonia region of Spain) Avinguda; i.e. Avenue
**Bhf** (Germany) Bahnhof; i.e. Rail Station
**blvd** (France) boulevard, (Romania) bulevardul; i.e. Boulevard
**C.** (Spain) Calle, (Catalonia region of Spain) Carrer; i.e. Street
**Centre Ville** (France) Town Centre
**Château** (France) Castle, Palace
**Ctra** (Spain) Carretera, i.e. Main road
**Dom** (Germany, Scandinavia) Cathedral
**Duomo** (Italy) Cathedral
**Église** (France) Church
**-g. (German)** -gasse i.e. Avenue
**-gade** (Denmark) Street
**Gamla By** (Denmark) Old Town
**Gare** (France) Station
**-gata(n)** (Sweden) Street
**-gate(n)** (Norway) Street
**Hbf** (Germany) Hauptbahnhof; i.e. Main Rail Station

**-kerk** (Netherlands) Church
**-kirche** (Germany) Church
**Landstr.** (Germany) Landstrasse; i.e. Road
**pl.** (France) place, (Germany) -platz; i.e. Square
**Pza** (Italy) piazza; i.e. Square
**Plaza** (Spain) Square
**-plein** (Netherlands) Square
**r.** (France) rue, i.e Street
**R.** (Portugal, NW Spain) Rua; i.e. Street
**Rådhus** (Scandinavia) Town Hall
**Rathaus** (Germany) Town Hall
**Schloss** (Germany) Castle, Palace
**Stathmos** (Greece) Station
**-str.** (Germany/Austria/Switzerland) -strasse, (Netherlands) -straat; i.e. Street
**tér** (Hungary) Square
**ul.** (Poland) ulica, (Czech) ulice; i.e. Road
**út** (Hungary) Street
**V.** (Italy) Via; i.e. Street
**-vägen** (Sweden) Street
**-veien** (Norway) Street
**-vej** (Denmark) Street
**Zentrum** (Germany) Town Centre

# HOTEL CODES
## AND CENTRAL BOOKING NUMBERS

The following abbreviations have been used throughout the book to show which chains are represented in a particular town. Most chains have a centralised worldwide-reservations system in every country where they have hotels (occasionally these do not cover hotels within the country itself). Most telephone calls are either completely free (usually incorporating 800) or charged at the rate for a local call (e.g. 0345 in the UK). (Aus=Australia, Can=Canada, Ire=Ireland, NZ=New Zealand, SA =South Africa, UK=United Kingdom, USA=United States of America.)

**Arctia**
Sweden *46 8 610 5050*
See also Scandic *(Sc)*
**Accor**
This is a group name that encompasses Ibis, Mercure, Novotel and Sofitel, with central reservation nos (handled by Resinter worldwide) that cover them all
Aus *(1 800) 642 244*
Can *(1 800) 221 45 42*
UK *(0171) 724 1000*
USA *(1 800) MERCURE*

Ba **Balladins**
France *(1) 64 46 49 00*
UK   *(0171) 287 3171*

BW **Best Western**
Aus *(1 800) 222 422*
Can *(800) 528 1234*
Ire *(1 800) 709 101*
NZ *(0800) 800 567*
SA *(0800) 120 886*
UK *(0800) 393130*
USA *(800) 528 1234*

Ca **Campanile**
UK *(0181) 569 6969*
France *(1) 64 62 46 46*

Ch **Choice**
Aus *(008) 090 600*
Ire *(1 800) 500 600*
NZ *(0800) 86 86 88*
UK *(0800) 444444*
USA/CAN:
*(800) 228 5150* (Comfort)
*(800) 228 5151* (Quality)
*(800) CLARION* (Clarion)
*(800) 228 3323* (hearing impaired, TTY phone)

Cn **Concorde**
Can *(800) 888 4747*
UK *(0800) 181591*

USA *(800) 888 4747*
(See also Supranational)

Ct **Climat de France**
Can *(514) 845 1236*
France *(05) 11 22 11*
UK *(0171) 287 3181*
USA *(800) 332 5332*

Ev **Exclusive**
See Forte *(FE)*

Ex **Excelsior**
UK *(0345) 40 40 40*

Fl **Formule 1**
contact individual hotels

FE **Forte**
(Also covers Exclusive and Méridien)
Aus *(800) 622 240*
Can *(800) 225 5843*
Ire *(800) 409040*
NZ *(800) 454040*
SA *(011) 442 9201*
UK *(0345) 404040*
USA *(800) 225 5843*

Fm **Forum**
See Inter-Continental *(IC)*

GT **Golden Tulip**
Netherlands *(06) 02 27711*
Aus *(800) 221 176*
Can/USA *(800) 344 1212*
Ire *(01) 872 3300*
NZ *(0800) 656 666*
SA *(021) 419 2965*
UK *(0800) 951 000*

Hd **Holiday Inn**
Aus *(800) 221 066*
Can *(800) 465 4329*
Ire *(1 800) 553 155*
NZ *(0800) 442 222*
SA *(0800) 11 7711*
UK *(0800) 897121*
USA *(800) 465 4329*

Hl **Hostelling International**
UK *(0171) 248 6547*

Hn **Hilton**
Aus *(1 800) 222 255*
Can *(800) 445 8667*
NZ *(0800) 448 002*
SA *(011) 880 3108*
UK *(0345) 581595*
USA *(800) 445 8667*

Hy **Hyatt**
Aus *(1 800) 131 234*
Can/USA *(800) 233 1234*
Ire *(1 800) 535 500*
NZ *(0800) 441 234*
SA *(0800) 991 029*
UK *(0345) 581 666*

Ib **Ibis**
See Accor

IC **Inter-Continental**
(Also covers Forum)
Aus *(008) 221 335*
Can/USA *(800) 327 0200*
NZ *(0800) 654 343*
SA *(011) 331 7422*
UK *(0345) 581237*

IH **Inter Hotel**
France *(1) 42 06 46 46*
UK *(0171) 287 3231*

Ke **Kempinski**
Can *(800) 426 3135*
UK *(0800) 868588*
USA *(800) 426 3135*
(Also bookable through Lufthansa)

Ma **Marriott**
Aus *(1 800) 251 259*
Can *(800) 228 9290*
NZ *(0800) 441 035*
UK *(0800) 221222*
USA *(800) 228 9290*

Mc **Mercure**
Aus *(1 800) 64 22 44*
Can *(1 800) MERCURE*
UK *(0181) 741 3100*
USA *(1 800) MERCURE*
(Also see Accor)

**559**

| | | | | | |
|---|---|---|---|---|---|
| Md | **Méridien** | Rn | **Renaissance** | | Can *(800) 843 3311* |

*Md* **Méridien**
Aus *(800) 622 240*
Can *(800) 543 4300*
NZ *(800) 45 4040*
UK *(0800) 40 40 40*
USA *(800) 543 4300*
(Also bookable through
Forte and Air France)

*Ml* **Melia**
See Sol *(So)*

*Mv* **Mövenpick**
Switzerland *(01) 712 22 22*
UK *(0800) 898317*
USA *(800) 344 6835*

*Nv* **Novotel**
Can *(800) NOVOTEL*
UK *(0181) 748 3433*
USA *(800) NOVOTEL*
(See also Accor)

*Pe* **Penta**
UK *(0990) 300200*

*Pr* **Primevere**
See Choice *(Ch)*

*PS* **Paradors of Spain**
Spain *(03) 488 08 01*
or *(01) 542 51 03*
UK *(0171) 402 8182*
USA *(212) 686 9213*

*Pu* **Pullman Hotels**
see Accor

*RC* **Relais & Chateaux**
France *(1) 45 72 90 00*
Aus *(02) 9957 4511*
UK *(0171) 287 0987*
USA *(212) 856 0115*

*Rd* **Radisson**
See SAS

*Re* **Reso**
See Supranational

*Rk* **Romantik**
Germany *(06188) 95020*
Aus *(02) 968 1783* or
*(02) 957 0538*
Can *(416) 695 1449*
Ire *(01) 661 9466*
NZ *(09) 799 716*
UK *(0181) 392 1589* or
*(0171) 408 0111*
USA – bookable through
all AAA travel agencies

*Rm* **Ramada**
Aus *(1 800) 222 431*
Can *(800) 854 7854*
Ire *(1 800) 252 627*
NZ *(0800) 441 111*
UK *(0800) 181 737*
USA *(800) 854 7854*

*Rn* **Renaissance**
As Ramada, except:
Can/USA*(1 800) HOTELS 1*

*RS* **Relais du Silence**
France *(1) 44 49 90 00*

*Rz* **Ritz Carlton**
Aus *(1 800) 252 888*
NZ *(800) 443 030*
UK *(0800) 234000*

*SA* **SAS**
(Also covers Radisson)
Aus *(1 800) 333 333*
Can *(800) 333 3333*
Ire *(1 800) 557 474*
NZ *(0800) 443 333*
UK *(0800) 191991*
USA *(800) 333 3333*

*Sc* **Scandic**
Finland *358 9 69 69 01*
UK See Holiday Inn *(Hd)*

*Sd* **Sweden Hotels**
Sweden *(08) 789 89 00*

*Sf* **Sofitel**
Can *(800) SOFITEL*
UK *(0181) 741 9699*
USA *(800) SOFITEL*
(See also Accor)

*Sg* **Sterling**
Aus *(1 800) 655 147*
Can *(800) 637 7200*
Ire *(1 800) 626 466*
NZ *(09) 309 1016*
UK *(0800) 220761*
USA *(800) 637 7200*

*Sh* **Sheraton**
Aus *(800) 07 3535*
Can *(800) 325 3535* or
*(800) 325 1717* (hearing
impaired)
Ire *(1 800) 535 353*
NZ *(0800) 443 535*
UK *(0800) 353535*
USA *(800) 325 3535* or
*(800) 325 1717* (hearing
impaired)

*Sk* **Sokos**
Finland *(90) 131 001*
(See also Supranational)

*SL* **Small Luxury**
Aus *(008) 251 958*
Can *(800) 525 4800*
NZ *(0800) 441 098*
SA *(011) 331 2911*
UK *(0800) 282124*
USA *(800) 525 4800*

*Sn* **Supranational**
(Also covers Concorde,
Reso, Sokos and
Welcome Swiss)

Can *(800) 843 3311*
UK *(0500) 303030*
Ire *(01) 660 5000*
SA *(0800) 119 000*
USA *(800) 843 3311*

*So* **Sol**
(Also covers Melia)
Spain *(901) 14 44 44*
UK *(0800) 962720*
USA *(800) 33 MELIA*

*Sw* **Swissôtel**
Switz *(0800) 55 1011*
Can *(800) 637 9477*
UK *(0800) 614145*
USA *(800) 637 9477*
(Also bookable through
Swissair)

*Tp* **Top**
Germany *(0211) 57 80 75*
Aus *(008) 221 176*
Ire *(01) 872 3953*
NZ *(09) 303 4526*
SA *(011) 312 672*
UK *(0171) 402 8182* or
*(0181) 446 0126* or
*(0990) 300 200*
USA *(800) 223 6764* or
*(800) 44 UTELL*
(Also bookable through
Lufthansa)

*WS* **Welcome Swiss**
See Supranational

---

### Swiss Chains

The following abbreviations refer to hotel chains in Switzerland. The telephone numbers given are local, so include the dialling code for Switzerland if calling from outside that country.

*AC* Alpine Classics
*(01) 482 19 81*

*EG* E&G Hotels Schweiz
*(036) 53 44 88*

*IE* Inter-Europe-Hotels
*(041) 40 22 44*

*MZ* Manz Privacy Hotels
*(01) 211 55 00*

*MO* MinOtel Suisse
*(021) 320 46 38*

*Ss* Swiss Leading Hotels
*(01) 383 96 96*

# THROUGH ROUTES

Some travellers wish to make their way as quickly as possible to a chosen city to begin their more leisurely travel from that point. This will more often mean going through two or more consecutive routes in this book without stopping. The following table shows a selection of possible longer through routes, as an aid to journey planning, with approximate summer frequencies. All these through routes may also be taken in the reverse direction to that shown but the number of trains per day may differ. Some of the trains require payment of supplements and many involve overnight travel. Not all services are daily.

Always consult the international section in the latest issue of the *Thomas Cook European Timetable* (ETT), which gives up-to-date schedules for these and many other international long-distance trains. Services shown from London include travel through the Channel Tunnel.

| Through Route | ETT table no. | Approx journey time | Trains per day | Notes |
|---|---|---|---|---|
| Amsterdam–Venice | 73 | 16 hrs | 1 | Change at Basel and Milan |
| Amsterdam–Milan | 73 | 13 hrs | 1 | Change at Basel |
| Amsterdam–Rome | 73 | 21 hrs | 1 | Change at Cologne and Basel |
| Amsterdam–Vienna | 28 | 13 hrs | 2 | Change at Cologne |
| Barcelona–Lyon | 81 | 8 hrs | 2 | Change at Montpellier (day) and Cerbère (night) |
| Brussels–Milan | 43 | 12 hrs | 2 | Direct |
| Brussels–Naples | 43 | 19 hrs | 1 | Change at Milan |
| Brussels–Rome | 43 | 17–18 hrs | 3 | Direct or change at Milan |
| Brussels–Zurich | 40 | 8 hrs | 4 | Direct or change at Basel |
| Cologne–Milan | 73 | 10–11 hrs | 6 | Direct or change at Basel |
| Cologne–Rome | 73 | 15–16 hrs | 4 | Change at Basel and/or Milan |
| Frankfurt–Warsaw | 55 | 16–17 hrs | 2 | Direct or change at Dresen |
| London–Berlin | 20 | 12–14 hrs | 4 | Change at Brussels and Cologne |
| London–Cologne | 20 | 6 hrs | 6 | Change at Brussels |
| London–Copenhagen | 20 | 15–17 hrs | 3 | Change at Brussels, Cologne and Hamburg (day), Brussels and Cologne (night); alternative route, ferry Harwich–Esbjerg, 27 hrs |
| London–Hamburg | 20 | 10–12 hrs | 6 | Change at Brussels and Cologne (day), Brussels and Liège (night); alternative route, ferry Harwich–Hamburg, 24 hrs |
| London–Rome | 43 | 23 hrs | 1 | Change at Brussels and Milan |
| London–Warsaw | 24 | 20 hrs | 1 | Change at Brussels and Cologne |
| London–Zurich | 40 | 12 hrs | 3 | Change at Brussels |
| Paris–Berlin | 20 | 10–12 hrs | 5 | Direct or change at Cologne |
| Paris–Prague | 30 | 15–16 hrs | 3 | Direct or change at Frankfurt |
| Paris–Vienna | 32 | 13–16 hrs | 4 | Direct or change at Munich |
| Paris–Zurich | 41 | 6–8 hrs | 8 | Direct or change at Basel |
| Stockholm–Berlin | 50 | 14 hrs | 2 | Change at Malmö |

Available in North America only

# ORDER FORM
## European Rail Passes
### Prices are U.S.$ Effective from Jan. 1, 1998

### EURAIL PASS (17 Countries) 1st Class
| 15 Days | ❏ $538 | 2 Months | ❏ $1224 |
| 21 Days | ❏ $698 | 3 Months | ❏ $1512 |
| 1 Month | ❏ $864 | | |

### EURAIL FLEXIPASS – 1st Class
10 Days in 2 Months ❏ $634
15 Days in 2 Months ❏ $836

### EURAIL SAVERPASS – 1st Class
| 15 Days | ❏ $458 | 1 Month | ❏ $734 |
| 21 Days | ❏ $594 | | |

*Price is per person / 3 people must travel together at all times. (Two people may travel together between Oct. 1st and March 31st). Children 4–11 half fare. Children under 4 free.*

### EURAIL YOUTHPASS* – 2nd Class
| 15 Days | ❏ $376 | 2 Months | ❏ $857 |
| 1 Month | ❏ $605 | | |

### EURAIL YOUTH FLEXIPASS* – 2nd Class
10 Days in 2 Months ❏ $444
15 Days in 2 Months ❏ $585
*\*Pass holder must be under age 26
on first day of use.*

### EURAIL DRIVE PASS
There is an excllent Rail/Drive Program that combines a Eurail Pass with Hertz or Avis Rent-a-Car. Call us for a brochure and prices.

### EUROPASS (5 Countries)
#### France/Germany/Italy/Switz./Spain
SPECIAL OFFER: The 2nd Adult traveler purchasing a EuroPass of any duration pays only half of the base pass price. Both travelers must travel together at all times. Prices include companion discount.

### 5 COUNTRIES EUROPASS – 1st Class
| 5 Days in 2 Months | ❏ $261 |
| 5 Days with 1 associate country | ❏ $309 |
| 5 Days with 2 associate countries | ❏ $333 |

### 5 COUNTRIES EUROPASS – Youth Class
| 5 Days in 2 Months | ❏ $216 |
| 5 Days with 1 associate country | ❏ $261 |
| 5 Days with 2 associate countries | ❏ $286 |

*EuroYouth Pass available for ages up to 26 in 2nd Class at substantial discounts. Call us for prices.*

### BRITRAIL PASS – Unlimited travel every day
| Validity period | Adult | |
| | First | Standard |
| --- | --- | --- |
| 8 Days | ❏ $375 | ❏ $259 |
| 15 Days | ❏ $575 | ❏ $395 |
| 22 Days | ❏ $740 | ❏ $510 |
| 1 Month | ❏ $860 | ❏ $590 |

*BritRail Passes offer unlimited travel in England, Scotland and Wales.*

562

## For Travelers from North America
CALL TOLL FREE 1-800-367-7984. ASK FOR DEPT. OE8
(Major credit cards accepted)

FORSYTH TRAVEL LIBRARY

### FORSYTH TRAVEL LIBRARY, INC.
#### 226 Westchester Avenue, White Plains, New York 10604
*Forsyth Travel Library, Inc., is the leading agent in North America for the European and British Railroads and distributor of the famous Thomas Cook European Timetable. We are international rail travel specialists. Free catalogs upon request listing all rail passes, timetables, accessories and maps. All prices shown are in US Dollars. Prices subject to change.*

# INDEX

# READER SURVEY

If you enjoyed using this book, or even if you didn't, please help us improve future editions by taking part in our reader survey. Every returned form will be acknowledged, and to show our appreciation we will give you £1 off your next purchase of a Thomas Cook guidebook. Just take a few minutes to complete and return this form to us.

When did you buy this book? _____

Where did you buy it? (Please give town/city and if possible name of retailer)

When did you/do you intend to travel in Europe?

For how long (approx.)? _____
How many people in your party? _____

Which cities and other locations did you/do you intend mainly to visit?

Did you/will you:
- ☐ Make all your travel arrangements independently?
- ☐ Travel on an Inter-Rail pass? ☐ Travel on a Eurail Pass?
- ☐ Use other passes or tickets, please give brief details: _____

Did you/do you intend to use this book:
- ☐ For planning your trip?
- ☐ During the trip itself?
- ☐ Both?

Did you/do you intend also to purchase any of the following travel publications for your trip?
Thomas Cook European Timetable
Thomas Cook New Rail Map of Europe
Thomas Cook European Travel Phrase Book
Other guidebooks or maps, please specify

Have you used any other Thomas Cook guidebooks in the past? If so, which?

Please rate the following features of On the Rails around Europe for their value to you (Circle VU for 'very useful', U for 'useful', NU for 'little or no use'):

| | | | |
|---|---|---|---|
| The 'Travel Essentials' section on pages 13–24 | VU | U | NU |
| The 'Travelling by Train' section on pages 25–32 | VU | U | NU |
| The 'Country by Country' section on pages 33–97 | VU | U | NU |
| The recommended routes throughout the book | VU | U | NU |
| Information on towns and cities | VU | U | NU |
| The maps of towns and cities | VU | U | NU |
| The 'Special Trains' section on pages 555–556 | VU | U | NU |

Please use this space to tell us about any features that in your opinion could be changed, improved, or added in future editions of the book, or any other comments you would like to make concerning the book:

Your age category: ☐ under 21 ☐ 21-30 ☐ 31-40 ☐ 41–50 ☐ over 50

Your name: Mr/Mrs/Miss/Ms
(First name or initials)
(Last name)

Your full address: (Please include postal or zip code)

Your daytime telephone number:

**Please detach this page and send it to: The Project Editor, On the Rails around Europe, Thomas Cook Publishing, PO Box 227, Peterborough PE3 6PU, United Kingdom.**

We will be pleased to send you details of how to claim your discount upon receipt of this questionnaire.